P9-BJR-796

Twentieth-Century Literary Criticism

Guide to Gale Literary Criticism Series

When you need to review criticism of literary works, these are the Gale series to use:

If the author's death date is:

You should turn to:

After Dec. 31, 1959
(or author is still living)

CONTEMPORARY LITERARY CRITICISM

for example: Jorge Luis Borges, Anthony Burgess,
William Faulkner, Mary Gordon,
Ernest Hemingway, Iris Murdoch

1900 through 1959

TWENTIETH-CENTURY LITERARY CRITICISM

for example: Willa Cather, F. Scott Fitzgerald,
Henry James, Mark Twain, Virginia Woolf

1800 through 1899

NINETEENTH-CENTURY LITERATURE CRITICISM

for example: Fedor Dostoevski, Nathaniel Hawthorne,
George Sand, William Wordsworth

1400 through 1799

LITERATURE CRITICISM FROM 1400 TO 1800
(excluding Shakespeare)

for example: Anne Bradstreet, Daniel Defoe,
Alexander Pope, François Rabelais,
Jonathan Swift, Phillis Wheatley

SHAKESPEAREAN CRITICISM

Shakespeare's plays and poetry

Antiquity through 1399

CLASSICAL AND MEDIEVAL LITERATURE CRITICISM

for example: Dante, Homer, Plato, Sophocles, Vergil,
the Beowulf poet

(Volume 1 forthcoming)

Gale also publishes related criticism series:

CHILDREN'S LITERATURE REVIEW

This ongoing series covers authors of all eras. Presents criticism on
authors and author/illustrators who write for the preschool
through high school audience.

CONTEMPORARY ISSUES CRITICISM

This two volume set presents criticism on contemporary authors
writing on current issues. Topics covered include the social sciences,
philosophy, economics, natural science, law, and related areas.

ISSN 0276-8178

R

Volume 22

Twentieth-Century Literary Criticism

**Excerpts from Criticism of the
Works of Novelists, Poets, Playwrights,
Short Story Writers, and Other Creative Writers
Who Died between 1900 and 1960,
from the First Published Critical Appraisals
to Current Evaluations**

**Dennis Poupard
Editor**

**Marie Lazzari
Thomas Ligotti
Associate Editors**

**Gale Research Company
Book Tower
Detroit, Michigan 48226**

STAFF

Dennis Poupard, *Editor*

Marie Lazzari, Thomas Ligotti, *Associate Editors*

Paula Kepos, Serita Lanette Lockard, *Senior Assistant Editors*

Sandra Liddell, Joann Prosyniuk, Keith E. Schooley,
Laurie A. Sherman, *Assistant Editors*

Sharon R. Gunton, *Contributing Editor*
Melissa Reiff Hug, *Contributing Assistant Editor*

Lizbeth A. Purdy, *Production Supervisor*
Denise Michlewicz Broderick, *Production Coordinator*
Eric Berger, *Assistant Production Coordinator*
Kathleen M. Cook, Maureen Duffy, Sheila J. Nasea, *Editorial Assistants*

Victoria B. Cariappa, *Research Coordinator*
Maureen R. Richards, *Assistant Research Coordinator*
Daniel Kurt Gilbert, Kent Graham, Michele R. O'Connell, Filomena Sgambati,
Vincenza G. Tranchida, Mary D. Wise, *Research Assistants*

Linda M. Pugliese, *Manuscript Coordinator*
Donna Craft, *Assistant Manuscript Coordinator*
Jennifer E. Gale, Maureen A. Puhl, Rosetta Irene Simms, *Manuscript Assistants*

Jeanne A. Gough, *Permissions Supervisor*
Janice M. Mach, *Permissions Coordinator, Text*
Patricia A. Seefelt, *Permissions Coordinator, Illustrations*
Susan D. Battista, Margaret A. Chamberlain, *Assistant Permissions Coordinators*
Sandra C. Davis, Kathy Grell, Josephine M. Keene,
Mary M. Matuz, *Senior Permissions Assistants*
H. Diane Cooper, Colleen M. Crane, Mabel C. Gurney, *Permissions Assistants*
Eileen Baehr, Margaret Carson, Anita Williams, *Permissions Clerks*

Frederick G. Ruffner, *Publisher*
Dedria Bryfonski, *Editorial Director*
Ellen T. Crowley, *Associate Editorial Director*
Christine Nasso, *Director, Literature Division*
Laurie Lanzen Harris, *Senior Editor, Literary Criticism Series*
Dennis Poupard, *Managing Editor, Literary Criticism Series*

Library of Congress Catalog Card Number 76-46132
ISBN 0-8103-2404-0
ISSN 0276-8178

Computerized photocomposition by
Typographics, Incorporated
Kansas City, Missouri

Printed in the United States

Contents

Preface

It is impossible to overvalue the importance of literature in the intellectual, emotional, and spiritual evolution of humanity. Literature is that which both lifts us out of everyday life and helps us to better understand it. Through the fictive lives of such characters as Anna Karenina, Jay Gatsby, or Leopold Bloom, our perceptions of the human condition are enlarged, and we are enriched.

Literary criticism can also give us insight into the human condition, as well as into the specific moral and intellectual atmosphere of an era, for the criteria by which a work of art is judged reflects contemporary philosophical and social attitudes. Literary criticism takes many forms: the traditional essay, the book or play review, even the parodic poem. Criticism can also be of several types: normative, descriptive, interpretive, textual, appreciative, generic. Collectively, the range of critical response helps us to understand a work of art, an author, an era.

Scope of the Series

Twentieth-Century Literary Criticism (TCLC) is designed to serve as an introduction for the student of twentieth-century literature to the authors of the period 1900 to 1960 and to the most significant commentators on these authors. The great poets, novelists, short story writers, playwrights, and philosophers of this period are by far the most popular writers for study in high school and college literature courses. Since a vast amount of relevant critical material confronts the student, *TCLC* presents significant passages from the most important published criticism to aid students in the location and selection of commentaries on authors who died between 1900 and 1960.

The need for *TCLC* was suggested by the usefulness of the Gale series *Contemporary Literary Criticism (CLC),* which excerpts criticism on current writing. Because of the difference in time span under consideration *(CLC* considers authors who were still living after 1959), there is no duplication of material between *CLC* and *TCLC.* For further information about *CLC* and Gale's other criticism series, users should consult the Guide to Gale Literary Criticism Series preceding the title page in this volume.

Each volume of *TCLC* is carefully compiled to include authors who represent a variety of genres and nationalities and who are currently regarded as the most important writers of this era. In addition to major authors, *TCLC* also presents criticism on lesser-known writers whose significant contributions to literary history are important to the study of twentieth-century literature.

Each author entry in *TCLC* is intended to provide an overview of major criticism on an author. Therefore, the editors include fifteen to twenty authors in each 600-page volume (compared with approximately fifty authors in a *CLC* volume of similar size) so that more attention may be given to an author. Each author entry represents a historical survey of the critical response to that author's work: some early criticism is presented to indicate initial reactions, later criticism is selected to represent any rise or decline in the author's reputation, and current retrospective analyses provide students with a modern view. The length of an author entry is intended to reflect the amount of critical attention the author has received from critics writing in English, and from foreign criticism in translation. Critical articles and books that have not been translated into English are excluded. Every attempt has been made to identify and include excerpts from the seminal essays on each author's work.

An author may appear more than once in the series because of the great quantity of critical material available, or because of a resurgence of criticism generated by events such as an author's centennial or anniversary celebration, the republication or posthumous publication of an author's works, or the publication of a newly translated work. Generally, a few author entries in each volume of *TCLC* feature criticism on single works by major authors who have appeared previously in the series. Only those individual works that have been the subjects of vast amounts of criticism and are widely studied in literature classes are selected for this in-depth treatment.

Organization of the Book

An author entry consists of the following elements: author heading, biographical and critical introduction, principal works, excerpts of criticism (each followed by a bibliographical citation), and an additional bibliography for further reading.

- The *author heading* consists of the author's full name, followed by birth and death dates. The unbracketed portion of the name denotes the form under which the author most commonly wrote. If an author wrote consistently under a pseudonym, the pseudonym will be listed in the author heading and the real name given in parentheses on the first line of the biographical and critical introduction. Also located at the beginning of the introduction to the author entry are any name variations under which an author wrote, including transliterated forms for authors whose languages use nonroman alphabets. Uncertainty as to a birth or death date is indicated by a question mark.

- The *biographical and critical introduction* contains background information designed to introduce the reader to an author and to the critical debate surrounding his or her work. Parenthetical material following many of the introductions provides references to biographical and critical reference series published by Gale, including *Children's Literature Review, Contemporary Authors, Dictionary of Literary Biography, Something about the Author*, and past volumes of *TCLC*.

- Most *TCLC* entries include *portraits* of the author. Many entries also contain illustrations of materials pertinent to an author's career, including holographs of manuscript pages, title pages, dust jackets, letters, or representations of important people, places, and events in an author's life.

- The *list of principal works* is chronological by date of first book publication and identifies the genre of each work. In the case of foreign authors where there are both foreign language publications and English translations, the title and date of the first English-language edition are given in brackets. Unless otherwise indicated, dramas are dated by first performance, not first publication.

- *Criticism* is arranged chronologically in each author entry to provide a useful perspective on changes in critical evaluation over the years. All titles by the author featured in the critical entry are printed in boldface type to enable the user to ascertain without difficulty the works being discussed. Also for purposes of easier identification, the critic's name and the publication date of the essay are given at the beginning of each piece of criticism. Unsigned criticism is preceded by the title of the journal in which it appeared. When an anonymous essay is later attributed to a critic, the critic's name appears in brackets at the beginning of the excerpt and in the bibliographical citation. Many critical entries in *TCLC* also contain translated material to aid users. Unless otherwise noted, translations within brackets are by the editors; translations within parentheses are by the author of the excerpt.

- Critical essays are prefaced by *explanatory notes* as an additional aid to students using *TCLC*. The explanatory notes provide several types of useful information, including: the reputation of a critic; the importance of a work of criticism; the specific type of criticism (biographical, psychoanalytic, structuralist, etc.); a synopsis of the criticism; and the growth of critical controversy or changes in critical trends regarding an author's work. In many cases, these notes cross-reference the work of critics who agree or disagree with each other. Dates in parentheses within the explanatory notes refer to a book publication date when they follow a book title and to an essay date when they follow a critic's name.

- A complete *bibliographical citation* designed to facilitate location of the original essay or book by the interested reader follows each piece of criticism.

- The *additional bibliography* appearing at the end of each author entry suggests further reading on the author. In some cases it includes essays for which the editors could not obtain reprint rights.

An appendix lists the sources from which material in each volume has been reprinted. It does not, however, list every book or periodical consulted in the preparation of the volume.

Cumulative Indexes

Each volume of *TCLC* includes a cumulative index to authors listing all the authors who have appeared in *Contemporary Literary Criticism, Twentieth-Century Literary Criticism, Nineteenth-Century Literature Criticism*, and *Literature Criticism from 1400 to 1800*, along with cross-references to the Gale series *Children's Literature Review, Authors in the News, Contemporary Authors, Contemporary Authors Autobiography Series, Dictionary of Literary Biography, Something about the Author, Something about the Author Autobiography Series*, and *Yesterday's Authors of Books for Children*. Users will welcome this cumulated author index as a useful tool for locating an author within the various series. The index, which lists birth and death dates when available, will be particularly valuable for those authors who are identified with a certain period but whose death date causes them to be placed in another, or for those authors whose careers span two periods. For example, F. Scott Fitzgerald is found in *TCLC*, yet a writer often associated with him, Ernest Hemingway, is found in *CLC*.

Each volume of *TCLC* also includes a cumulative nationality index. Author names are arranged alphabetically under their respective nationalities and followed by the volume numbers in which they appear.

A cumulative index to critics is another useful feature in *TCLC*. Under each critic's name are listed the authors on whom the critic has written and the volume and page where the criticism may be found.

Acknowledgments

No work of this scope can be accomplished without the cooperation of many people. The editors especially wish to thank the copyright holders of the excerpted criticism included in this volume, the permissions managers of many book and magazine publishing companies for assisting us in securing reprint rights, and Anthony Bogucki for assistance with copyright research. We are also grateful to the staffs of the Detroit Public Library, the Library of Congress, University of Detroit Library, University of Michigan Library, and Wayne State University Library for making their resources available to us.

Suggestions Are Welcome

In response to various suggestions, several features have been added to *TCLC* since the series began, including: explanatory notes to excerpted criticism that provide important information regarding critics and their work; a cumulative author index listing authors in all Gale literary criticism series; entries devoted to criticism on a single work by a major author; and more extensive illustrations.

Readers who wish to suggest authors to appear in future volumes, or who have other suggestions, are cordially invited to write the editors.

Authors to Be Featured in *TCLC*, Volumes 23 and 24

Sherwood Anderson (American short story writer and novelist)—Among the most original and influential writers in early twentieth-century American literature, Anderson is the author of brooding, introspective works that explore the effects of the unconscious upon human life. Anderson's "hunger to see beneath the surface of lives" was best expressed in the short stories comprising *Winesburg, Ohio: A Group of Tales of Ohio Small Town Life. TCLC* will devote an entire entry to critical discussion of this work.

Max Beerbohm (English critic and caricaturist)—Among the most prominent figures of the fin de siecle period in English literature, Beerbohm was the author of fiction, dramas, and criticism characterized by witty sophistication and mannered elegance. "Entertaining" in the most complimentary sense of the word, Beerbohm's criticism for the *Saturday Review*—where he was a longtime drama critic—exhibits his scrupulously developed taste and unpretentious, fair-minded responses to literature.

Henri Bergson (French philosopher)—One of the most influential philosophers of the twentieth century, Bergson is renowned for his opposition to the dominant materialist thought of his time and for his creation of theories that emphasize the supremacy and independence of suprarational consciousness.

Edgar Rice Burroughs (American novelist)—Burroughs was a science fiction writer who is best known as the creator of Tarzan. His *Tarzan of the Apes* and its numerous sequels have sold over thirty-five million copies in fifty-six languages, making Burroughs one of the most popular authors in the world.

Joseph Conrad (Polish-born English novelist)—Considered an innovator of novel structure as well as one of the finest stylists of modern English literature, Conrad is the author of complex novels that examine the ambiguity of good and evil. *TCLC* will devote an entry to critical discussion of his *Nostromo,* a novel exploring Conrad's conviction that failure is a fact of human existence and that every ideal contains the possibilities for its own corruption.

Euclides da Cunha (Brazilian historian)—Cunha is the author of *Os sertoes (Rebellion in the Backlands),* considered by many critics to be one of the greatest works in Brazilian literature. A factual account of the Canudos rebellion in Brazil in 1896 and 1897, the work exhibits a deep concern with Brazilian national identity and has exerted a strong influence on twentieth-century Brazilian fiction.

John Davidson (Scottish poet)—Davidson is remembered primarily as the author of poems that reflect the changing social and philosophical attitudes of the late Victorian era, and his works have been recognized as instrumental in effecting the transition from nineteenth- to twentieth-century themes in English poetry.

Grazia Deledda (Italian novelist and short story writer)—Deledda was the second woman to win a Nobel Prize in literature, which she was awarded in 1926 for her naturalistic novels of passion and tragedy set in her native Sardinia.

Joseph Furphy (Australian novelist)—Furphy's most famous work, *Such Is Life,* is a complex comic novel combining sketches, tales, literary parody, and philosophical speculation in the guise of a realistic chronicle by its fictional narrator, Tom Collins.

George Gissing (English novelist)—Gissing was the author of novels portraying in meticulous detail the lives of the English lower classes. His works combine Victorian melodrama with concern for the individual's alienation from society and are considered notable examples of the literature of transition between the Victorian and modern novel.

Edmund Gosse (English novelist and critic)—A prolific man of letters in late nineteenth-century England, Gosse is of primary importance for his autobiographical novel *Father and Son,* which is considered a seminal work for gaining insight into the major issues of the Victorian age, especially the conflict between science and religion inspired by Darwin's *Origin of the Species.* Gosse is also important for his introduction of Henrik Ibsen's "new drama" to English audiences and for his numerous critical studies of English and foreign authors.

Frank Harris (Welsh editor, critic, and biographer)—Prominent in English literary circles at the turn of the century, Harris was a flamboyant man of letters described by one critic as "seemingly offensive on principle." His greatest accomplishments—which were achieved as editor of the *Fortnightly Review,* the *Evening News,* and the *Saturday Review*—have been overshadowed by his scandalous life, his sensational biographical portraits of such contemporaries as Oscar Wilde and Bernard Shaw, and his massive autobiography, which portrays Edwardian life primarily as a background for Harris's near-Olympian sexual adventures.

Muhammad Iqbal (Indian poet and philosopher)—Considered one of the leading Muslim intellectual figures of the twentieth century, Iqbal was a political activist and the author of poetry calling for social and religious reform.

Henry James (American novelist)—James is considered one of the most important novelists of the English language and his work is universally acclaimed for its stylistic distinction, complex psychological portraits, and originality of theme and technique. *TCLC* will devote an entire entry to critical discussion of his novella *The Turn of the Screw,* which is considered one of the most interesting and complex short novels in world literature.

Jerome K. Jerome (English novelist and dramatist)—Jerome was the author of humorous fiction and some of the most popular plays of the Edwardian era.

Alfred Kubin (Austrian novelist)—Known primarily as a graphic artist, Kubin is also the author of *The Other Side,* a fantastic novel that has been cited as an influence on Franz Kafka's *The Castle* and on the literary movements of Surrealism, Expressionism, and the Theater of the Absurd.

Sinclair Lewis (American novelist)—A prominent American novelist of the 1920s, Lewis is considered the author of some of the most effective satires in American literature. In his most important novels, which include *Main Street, Babbitt,* and *Arrowsmith,* he attacked the dullness, smug provincialism, and socially enforced conformity of the American middle class. *TCLC* will devote an entire entry to critical discussion of *Main Street.*

Dmitri Merezhkovsky (Russian novelist, philosopher, poet, and critic)—Although his poetry and criticism are credited with initiating the Symbolist movement in Russian literature, Merezhkovsky is best known as a religious philosopher who sought in numerous essays and historical novels to reconcile the values of pagan religions with the teachings of Christ.

Charles Nordhoff and James Norman Hall (American novelists, historians, and essayists)—Nordhoff and Hall collaborated on the novels *Mutiny on the Bounty, Men against the Sea,* and *Pitcairn's Island,* a trilogy comprising one of the most compelling and widely read maritime narratives in popular fiction.

Frank Norris (American novelist)—Norris is recognized as one of the first important Naturalist writers in American literature. His most important novel, *The Octopus,* was the first volume in an unfinished trilogy concerning the production and distribution of wheat that Norris envisioned as an American counterpart to Emile Zola's *Germinal,* an epic portrayal of the effects of deterministic forces on laborers.

Boris Pilnyak (Russian novelist and short story writer)—Pilnyak's *Naked Year* was the first important novel to depict the effect of the Bolshevik Revolution on Russian society. His energetic, episodic, and stylistically heterogeneous narratives were widely imitated by postrevolutionary writers, making Pilnyak one of the most influential Soviet literary figures of the 1920s.

Kenneth Roberts (American novelist)—Roberts's works, many of which are set in New England during the American Revolution, are considered among the best historical novels in American literature.

Romain Rolland (French novelist, biographer, and dramatist)—Rolland was a prominent man of letters and noted pacifist who is best known for his novel *Jean-Christophe,* a ten-volume life of a musical genius in which the author propounded his antinationalist and antimaterialist views. A distinguished musicologist and critic, Rolland also wrote many dramas that demonstrate his theory of a "theater of the people" devoted to the inspirationally heroic and to social change.

Oswald Spengler (German philosopher)—Spengler rose to international celebrity in the 1920s on the basis of *The Decline of the West,* a controversial examination of the cyclical nature of history. Although frequently deprecated by professional historians, *The Decline of the West* became one of the most influential philosophical works of the twentieth century.

Leslie Stephen (English biographer and critic)—A distinguished man of letters, Stephen is ranked among the most important literary critics of the late nineteenth century.

Simone Weil (French philosopher and essayist)—Weil was a social activist and mystic whose writings explore the nature of God, the individual, and human society.

Oscar Wilde (Anglo-Irish dramatist, novelist, and poet)—A crusader for aestheticism, Wilde was one of the most prominent members of the nineteenth-century "art for art's sake" movement. *TCLC* will devote an entire entry to his play *The Importance of Being Earnest,* which is considered his best and most characteristic work as well as the apogee of drawing-room farce.

Additional Authors to Appear
in Future Volumes

Abbey, Henry 1842-1911
Abercrombie, Lascelles 1881-1938
Adamic, Louis 1898-1951
Ade, George 1866-1944
Agustini, Delmira 1886-1914
Akers, Elizabeth Chase 1832-1911
Akiko, Yosano 1878-1942
Aldanov, Mark 1886-1957
Aldrich, Thomas Bailey 1836-1907
Aliyu, Dan Sidi 1902-1920
Allen, Hervey 1889-1949
Archer, William 1856-1924
Arlen, Michael 1895-1956
Austin, Alfred 1835-1913
Austin, Mary Hunter 1868-1934
Bacovia, George 1881-1957
Bahr, Hermann 1863-1934
Bailey, Philip James 1816-1902
Barbour, Ralph Henry 1870-1944
Barreto, Lima 1881-1922
Benét, William Rose 1886-1950
Benjamin, Walter 1892-1940
Bennett, James Gordon, Jr. 1841-1918
Benson, E(dward) F(rederic) 1867-1940
Berdyaev, Nikolai Aleksandrovich
    1874-1948
Beresford, J(ohn) D(avys) 1873-1947
Bialik, Chaim 1873-1934
Binyon, Laurence 1869-1943
Bishop, John Peale 1892-1944
Blackmore, R(ichard) D(oddridge)
    1825-1900
Blake, Lillie Devereux 1835-1913
Blum, Leon 1872-1950
Bodenheim, Maxwell 1892-1954
Bowen, Marjorie 1886-1952
Byrne, Donn 1889-1928
Caine, Hall 1853-1931
Cannan, Gilbert 1884-1955
Carswell, Catherine 1879-1946
Casely-Hayford, E. 1866-1930
Churchill, Winston 1871-1947
Coppée, Francois 1842-1908
Corelli, Marie 1855-1924
Croce, Benedetto 1866-1952
Crofts, Freeman Wills 1879-1957
Cruze, James (Jens Cruz Bosen) 1884-
    1942
Cummings, Bruce 1889-1919
Curros, Enriquez Manuel 1851-1908
Dall, Caroline Wells (Healy) 1822-1912
Daudet, Leon 1867-1942
Davis, Richard Harding 1864-1916
Day, Clarence 1874-1935

Delafield, E.M. (Edme Elizabeth Monica
    de la Pasture) 1890-1943
Deneson, Jacob 1836-1919
Devkota, Laxmiprasad 1909-1959
DeVoto, Bernard 1897-1955
Douglas, (George) Norman 1868-1952
Douglas, Lloyd C(assel) 1877-1951
Dovzhenko, Alexander 1894-1956
Drinkwater, John 1882-1937
Drummond, W.H. 1854-1907
Durkheim, Emile 1858-1917
Duun, Olav 1876-1939
Eaton, Walter Prichard 1878-1957
Eggleston, Edward 1837-1902
Erskine, John 1879-1951
Faik, Sait 1906-1954
Fadeyev, Alexander 1901-1956
Ferland, Albert 1872-1943
Field, Rachel 1894-1924
Flecker, James Elroy 1884-1915
Fletcher, John Gould 1886-1950
Fogazzaro, Antonio 1842-1911
Francos, Karl Emil 1848-1904
Frank, Bruno 1886-1945
Frazer, (Sir) George 1854-1941
Freud, Sigmund 1853-1939
Froding, Gustaf 1860-1911
Fuller, Henry Blake 1857-1929
Futabatei, Shimei 1864-1909
Gladkov, Fydor Vasilyevich 1883-1958
Glaspell, Susan 1876-1948
Glyn, Elinor 1864-1943
Golding, Louis 1895-1958
Gould, Gerald 1885-1936
Guest, Edgar 1881-1959
Gumilyov, Nikolay 1886-1921
Gyulai, Pal 1826-1909
Hale, Edward Everett 1822-1909
Hawthorne, Julian 1846-1934
Heijermans, Herman 1864-1924
Hernandez, Miguel 1910-1942
Hewlett, Maurice 1861-1923
Heyward, DuBose 1885-1940
Hope, Anthony 1863-1933
Hostos, Eugenio Maria de 1839-1903
Hudson, W(illiam) H(enry) 1841-1922
Huidobro, Vincente 1893-1948
Hviezdoslav (Pavol Orszagh) 1849-1921
Ilyas, Abu Shabaka 1903-1947
Imbs, Bravig 1904-1946
Ivanov, Vyacheslav Ivanovich 1866-
    1949
James, Will 1892-1942
Jammes, Francis 1868-1938

Johnson, Fenton 1888-1958
Johnston, Mary 1870-1936
Jorgensen, Johannes 1866-1956
King, Grace 1851-1932
Kirby, William 1817-1906
Kline, Otis Albert 1891-1946
Kohut, Adolph 1848-1916
Kuzmin, Mikhail Alexseyevich 1875-
    1936
Lamm, Martin 1880-1950
Lawson, Henry 1867-1922
Ledwidge, Francis 1887-1917
Leino, Eino 1878-1926
Leipoldt, C. Louis 1880-1947
Lima, Jorge De 1895-1953
Locke, Alain 1886-1954
Long, Frank Belknap 1903-1959
Lopez Portillo y Rojas, Jose 1850-1903
Louys, Pierre 1870-1925
Lucas, E(dward) V(errall) 1868-1938
Lyall, Edna 1857-1903
Maghar, Josef Suatopluk 1864-1945
Manning, Frederic 1887-1935
Maragall, Joan 1860-1911
Marais, Eugene 1871-1936
Martin du Gard, Roger 1881-1958
Masaryk, Tomas 1850-1939
Mayor, Flora Macdonald 1872-1932
McClellan, George Marion 1860-1934
McCoy, Horace 1897-1955
Mirbeau, Octave 1850-1917
Mistral, Frederic 1830-1914
Monro, Harold 1879-1932
Moore, Thomas Sturge 1870-1944
Morley, Christopher 1890-1957
Morley, S. Griswold 1883-1948
Mqhayi, S.E.K. 1875-1945
Murray, (George) Gilbert 1866-1957
Nansen, Peter 1861-1918
Nobre, Antonio 1867-1900
Obstfelder, Sigbjorn 1866-1900
O'Dowd, Bernard 1866-1959
Ophuls, Max 1902-1957
Orczy, Baroness 1865-1947
Owen, Seaman 1861-1936
Page, Thomas Nelson 1853-1922
Parrington, Vernon L. 1871-1929
Peck, George W. 1840-1916
Phillips, Ulrich B. 1877-1934
Pinero, Arthur Wing 1855-1934
Pontoppidan, Henrik 1857-1943
Powys, T. F. 1875-1953
Prévost, Marcel 1862-1941
Quiller-Couch, Arthur 1863-1944

Randall, James G. 1881-1953
Rappoport, Solomon 1863-1944
Read, Opie 1852-1939
Redcam, Tom 1870-1933
Reisen (Reizen), Abraham 1875-1953
Remington, Frederic 1861-1909
Riley, James Whitcomb 1849-1916
Rinehart, Mary Roberts 1876-1958
Ring, Max 1817-1901
Rohmer, Sax 1883-1959
Rozanov, Vasily Vasilyevich 1856-1919
Saar, Ferdinand von 1833-1906
Sabatini, Rafael 1875-1950
Saintsbury, George 1845-1933
Sakutaro, Hagiwara 1886-1942
Sanborn, Franklin Benjamin 1831-1917
Santayana, George 1863-1952
Sardou, Victorien 1831-1908
Schickele, René 1885-1940
Seabrook, William 1886-1945
Seton, Ernest Thompson 1860-1946

Shestov, Lev 1866-1938
Shiels, George 1886-1949
Skram, Bertha Amalie 1847-1905
Smith, Pauline 1883-1959
Sodergran, Edith Irene 1892-1923
Solovyov, Vladimir 1853-1900
Sorel, Georges 1847-1922
Spector, Mordechai 1859-1922
Squire, J(ohn) C(ollings) 1884-1958
Stavenhagen, Fritz 1876-1906
Stockton, Frank R. 1834-1902
Su, Hsuan-ying 1884-1919
Subrahmanya Bharati, C. 1882-1921
Sully-Prudhomme, Rene 1839-1907
Sylva, Carmen 1843-1916
Thoma, Ludwig 1867-1927
Tomlinson, Henry Major 1873-1958
Tuchmann, Jules 1830-1901
Turner, W(alter) J(ames) R(edfern)
   1889-1946
Upward, Allen 1863-1926

Vachell, Horace Annesley 1861-1955
Van Dine, S. S. (William H. Wright)
   1888-1939
Van Dyke, Henry 1852-1933
Vazov, Ivan Minchov 1850-1921
Veblen, Thorstein 1857-1929
Villaespesa, Francisco 1877-1936
Wallace, Edgar 1874-1932
Wallace, Lewis 1827-1905
Walsh, Ernest 1895-1926
Webb, Mary 1881-1927
Webster, Jean 1876-1916
Whitlock, Brand 1869-1927
Wilson, Harry Leon 1867-1939
Wolf, Emma 1865-1932
Wood, Clement 1888-1950
Wren, P(ercival) C(hristopher) 1885-
   1941
Yonge, Charlotte Mary 1823-1901
Zecca, Ferdinand 1864-1947
Zeromski, Stefan 1864-1925

Readers are cordially invited to suggest additional authors to the editors.

Chairil Anwar

1922-1949

Indonesian poet and essayist.

Considered Indonesia's greatest modern poet, Anwar was the first to use the Indonesian language to create succinct and emotionally powerful Modernist poetry. Although his total output was extremely limited, consisting of only about seventy-five poems, his impact upon the development of his nation's literature was enormous, a fact which is reflected in the common appellation for postwar Indonesian poets—"Chairil's Generation."

Anwar was born on the island of Sumatra, which was at that time under Dutch colonial rule. Although little is known about his early years, critics surmise that he had a comfortable childhood from the fact that he attended an expensive Dutch school at a time when most native children received no formal education at all. In 1940, however, Anwar and his mother moved to Djakarta, Java, when his father reportedly married a second wife. Thus cut off from his father's support, Anwar was unable to continue his education, and he spent his time writing poetry, reading the works of Federico García Lorca and Rainer Maria Rilke, and seeking poetic inspiration in the cafes, streets, and brothels of Djakarta. The quality of Anwar's poetry was immediately recognized by the critics and writers to whom it was shown, but the poet was prevented from publishing by the Japanese invasion of 1942 and the subsequent suppression of all potentially inflammatory writings. It was not until late 1949, when Indonesia's social and political situation had finally become stabilized, that his work appeared in print. Anwar, however, did not live to see the publication of his works; he had died of cirrhosis, syphilis, and typhus early in 1949, at the age of twenty-six.

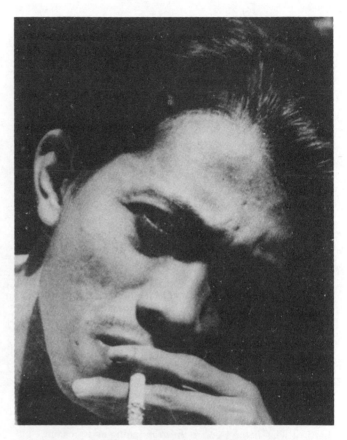

Anwar's poetry represents a conscious and dramatic rejection of both the Dutch-influenced literature of his country's long colonial period and the poetry of the *Pudjangga Baru* movement which immediately preceded Anwar's era and which looked to nineteenth-century Western poetry for its models. Although the *Pudjangga Baru* writers did use Indonesia's native language, bahasa Indonesia, it is generally agreed that their intent was simply to mimic European Romantic style and that Anwar was the first to explore the creative possibilities of bahasa Indonesia. Acutely aware of the emotional impact of words, Anwar manipulated his language to create the strong rhythms, alliterations, and repetitions that are the characteristic features of his style. His diction has been called economical, a consequence of his scrupulous avoidance of stylistic ornamentation in order to achieve a powerful sense of intimacy and immediacy. While the organic unity and simplicity of Anwar's work gives the illusion of a spontaneous confession, each poem was in fact revised and polished extensively to create the desired emotional effect.

The idea of unity was of central importance to Anwar, who believed not only in the Modernist concept of the integration of form and content in works of art, but also in Eastern metaphysical monism, which inspired his goal "to reach an absolute accounting with everything around me." As a result, his primary subjects—love, sexuality, anguish, pain, and death—are both acutely personal and essentially universal. Seeking to convey the absolute truth about his subject matter, Anwar advocated ruthless honesty and total disregard for literary and social conventions: "The young would-be writer must first be a careful inspector, a scratching, probing critic down to the very essence. Everything, everything as far as the hand and the probing, insistent, shining dissecting knife can go. Everything! Including the sacred banyan trees, till now unapproachable. But the future writer—real writer!—must climb on, must chop off all the leafy, superfluous branches." This iconoclastic spirit informs all of Anwar's work and is the primary feature of his poetry.

Critical response to Anwar's poetry has been universally favorable. Many of his poems are considered masterpieces, while relatively few are judged unsuccessful. For this poetic achievement, he is credited with both the modernization of Indonesian poetry and the general reawakening of that country's literary artists.

PRINCIPAL WORKS

Deru tjampur debu (poetry) 1949
Kerikil tadjam dan jang terampas dan jang putus (poetry) 1949
[*Sharp Gravel*, 1960]

Tiga menguak takdir [with Rivai Apin and Asrul Sani]
    (poetry) 1950
Selected Poems (poetry) 1963
The Complete Poetry and Prose of Chairil Anwar (poetry,
    essays, lectures, and letters) 1970
The Complete Poems of Chairil Anwar (poetry) 1974

CHAIRIL ANWAR (letter date 1943)

[*In the following excerpt from a letter written to his friend H. B.
Jassin, Anwar emphatically states his position on the subject of
poetic creation.*]

Often, in going about with artists I know, I'm startled.
Dumbfounded! Because suddenly I find some of them not at
all what I imagined (and hoped), with very different ways,
talking differently—they prove that they're really clerks, *clerks,*
sometimes expert businessmen!

And it's not just I who say this. After studying what these
people have produced . . . . . . what a crime, they're all neither
this nor that, and slapdash to boot. Aren't they fed up with
this sort of thing? If not, when, when . . . . . . ?! I've felt like
getting drunk . . . . . . !!!

They're horribly influenced by—let me give it a name—"the
law of inspiration." I'll mention two whom I know personally:
S[am Amir] and A[zhar]. Pushing at creation suddenly gets
you there, just all of a sudden, they say. A real discovery! An
inspiration.

But they go further: we must hold onto faith and belief in these
times, we must go on putting things onto paper. And . . . . . .
that's it, done! But I won't swallow this! If they're right, the
ideas, the principles of art or philosophy drop down to us out
of the sky, like sunlight, warming us up and ripening just like
that! And the result? Of course, neither this nor that! And isn't
that just what always comes from moaning and groaning. Till
now our art has been thin, superficial. No more of the old
windbags. No more gentle gas of *that* sort! Much less their
oozing . . . . . . !! The artist . . . must deal sharply, boldly in
considering things—and in discarding them. And someone who
just follows along won't be able to do this. Because he has no
principles of his own; he's still a long way from knowing what
he's about. He's powerless.

Listen!

When Beethoven died, they found books full of notes. The
preparatory work for those clear, sweet melodies was marvellously thorough. This great musician prepared himself for years,
and only then did a single ripe fruit—ripe on the inside and
the outside—get plucked. His *Missa Solemnis* was the work
of more than five solid years. (pp. 171-72)

We have to think, balance, choose, analyze, criticize, and
sometimes just throw it all out. To tie things together!

If our work is neither this nor that, only half-baked, maybe
we'll turn into improvisers in the end. Oh, really big improvisers! But improvised art is nothing compared to art produced
by creative power, by thought, by concentration. To me this
is life and death itself!

Don't, don't think I'm exaggerating! You know that's not my
way.

This is how my ideas are running: If our confidence is firmly
rooted in the creation of art, all our life will be centered on
that alone!

One more thing . . . ! What I've set out here is not a "recipe"
to keep our writing from having its own stages, its own internal
phases. No. Here is its purpose: evil and ugliness, moderation,
beauty—they all *exist*. We can't ever change that by our writing. So it's up to us. Only as *real* artists can we give our
utmost, everything, as nearly as possible!

When we read foreign writing, when we listen quietly to Beethoven, we'll feel in them an awareness, an excitement of both
body and soul, slanted neither to the left nor to the right. . . .
Thought, ideas, count for a great deal in the best works of art.
Thinking: that is, balancing, weighing, and discarding with
careful good sense.

Again! I reject simply following along—I'm fed up with timid
middle-of-the-roadism. I can't work that way.

Nor am I like court dancing girls, reciting old pantuns while
they whirl around, their heads thrown back—ah, but I don't
want to defile the idea of inspiration; what am I saying?—just
see what figures they have, the women who oppose dancing . . . . . . !!! (pp. 173-74)

> *Chairil Anwar, in his* The Complete Poetry and Prose
> of Chairil Anwar, *edited and translated by Burton
> Raffel, State University of New York Press, 1970,
> 208 p.*

JAMES S HOLMES (essay date 1962)

[*In the following excerpt, Holmes discusses the development of
Anwar's poetry and suggests some possible influences.*]

No doubt Chairil Anwar had written verse of some kind before,
but the first poems that have survived date from late in 1942.
The six months from February through July, 1943, the very
heart of the War, were his most fruitful period: twenty-eight
poems out of an extant total of some seventy-five.

These poems were something entirely new in Indonesian writing. As T. S. Eliot has pointed out, there are some poets who
can show us "what great poetry can do without—how *bare* it
can be." This is undeniably what Chairil Anwar did for his
Indonesian contemporaries. In place of the *Pudjangga Baru*
sonnet, with its exact rhymes (a *tour-de-force* in Indonesian),
its strict metrics (alien to the Indonesian linguistic pattern) and
its padded lines (alien to good poetry anywhere), he offered a
tense, dynamic verse in which each word and rhyme was tested
for its effect within the totality of the poem, and every form
was an organic structuralization. In place of the poetic diction,
the romantic tone and the derivative imagery prevailing in the
verse of the thirties, he wrote in a direct, almost crude language
that was stripped bare of ornament and affectation.

"WILLINGNESS" (**"Penerimaan"**)

If you like I'll take you back
With all my heart.

I'm still alone.

I know you're not what you were,
Like a flower pulled into parts.

Don't crawl! Stare at me bravely.

> If you like I'll take you back
> For myself, but
>
> I won't share even with a mirror.

It is clear that while he was making this sharp break with the generation before him, Anwar, too, looked to Dutch writers. One major influence was Hendrik Marsman, who just after the First World War wrote expressionist poems very similar in tone and structure, and at times in phrasing, to those Chairil Anwar was to write twenty years later. The use of organic rather than traditional forms was no doubt the most important thing Anwar could learn from Marsman, but certain attitudes and images probably also derived from him, notably the key image of the mirror, which runs through a number of Anwar's poems: "the mouldy black mirror," "shiny mirrors," "one by one / Mirrors drip off you. . . ."

A second Dutch influence was not a contemporary, and hardly a poet. This was Eduard Douwes Dekker, or Multatuli, an eccentric breaker-of-images who was the one exciting writer in the doldrums of the Dutch nineteenth century. Multatuli's *Ideeën* ("Ideas") are a long series of jottings, ruminations, aphorisms and anecdotes addressed to an imaginary Fancy. Chairil Anwar found he could adapt this technique to his purposes: in a talk he gave to a circle of young artists in July, 1943, he addressed himself in charged, staccato Multatulian prose to an imaginary Ida (the name is as clearly related to *Ideeën* as the function is to Fancy), and several of his poems of the period are also directed to her. Too much the *honnête homme* to make use of masks or objective correlatives, he thus nevertheless found a method of objectifying his emotions.

But if Anwar borrowed from Marsman and Multatuli, it was only tools and techniques he borrowed; the poems were clearly his own. They were the poems of a new kind of Indonesian. The *Pudjangga Baru* writers, breaking loose from the shackles of Indonesian tradition had been quick to turn to new, Western traditions with clear-cut standards and norms, just as their more politically minded contemporaries had rejected aristocratic and colonial principles in favor of the ideal of freedom, *merdeka*. Chairil Anwar was the first to cast off all the prescribed values and virtues, old or new, and stare frankly and unashamedly into the soul he himself exposed to view. There are poems in which he tries to come to terms with God and religion.

> I don't reach out for the bright day anymore
> Let the honeyed words melt
> If He comes to collect them.

There are others in which he attempts to analyze and define his libidinous sexuality.

> She winks. She laughs.
> And the dry grass blazes up.
> She speaks. Her voice is loud.
> My blood stops running.
>
> When the orchestra begins the "Ave Maria"
> I drag her over there. . . .

The "broken" images and the repeated references to "blood" and "wounds" in many of the poems may stem partly from the troubled times, but surely they are also expressions of the torn personality of the new Asian.

> I stare into the mirror.
> This face is covered with wounds.
> Whose is it?

For Anwar the only certainty would seem to have been that, though he had no possibility of knowing quite where he was going, he had to search back and forth, like a rat in a trap, until he found a way of getting there.

None of Anwar's poems were published during the Japanese occupation: they were felt to be too subversive of the "positive ideals" of the Greater East Asia Co-Prosperity Sphere to get by the censor. But typed copies were passed from hand to hand, and by the end of the war Anwar had achieved a certain fame among younger Indonesian writers.

August, 1945, brought the capitulation of the Japanese and the proclamation of the Indonesian Republic, and soon afterward came something of a cultural explosion in the archipelago. No longer burdened by censorship, either Dutch or Japanese, literary magazines sprang out of the ground, and there was poetry everywhere. Anwar's wartime verse found its way into various of the new reviews, and for other emerging poets such as Rivai Apin and Asrul Sani it was the one major influence. As several of them have admitted, it was only after reading his poems that they came to understand the literary possibilities of the Indonesian language.

Chairil Anwar became the acknowledged model of the younger writers, who called themselves the Generation of '45. He was the model but not the leader, for he possessed practically none of the qualities of the literary organization man. He could poke his finger through the hollowness of earlier Indonesian writing and launch an appeal to "make everything completely new," but his life was too disorganized for the arranging of meetings and the editing of reviews. He was too apt to disappear suddenly in the midst of the planning, deserting all the literary ado for the sailors of the harbor area, the prostitutes of downtown Djakarta or the soldiers fighting the Dutch in the mountains. And yet, throughout the Indonesian Revolution, he more than anyone else represented all that was new in Indonesian writing.

And somehow, in his disordered life, he continued to turn out poetry. Even before the end of the Japanese occupation he had written to a friend, the critic H. B. Jassin: "What I'm sending you—what I call 'poems'—these are nothing but experiments for later stages. It's not mature work yet! I still have to go through several phases before I'll write any really mature poems." A few weeks later, in another note, he added: "In my prose, and in my poetry, too, I'll dig down and root out every word until I've gone deep enough to find the germinal word, the germinal image."

Even so, there does not seem to be any really pronounced development in the later poems. The opening of the British and American information services in Djakarta helped Anwar to broaden his acquaintance with Western poetry, and from the critical comments he made and the poems he translated we know that he now read Eliot, Auden and a number of other poets. A friend tells of riding with him in a bouncing, creaking bus while he declaimed from memory one verse of Emily Dickinson's after another. Perhaps it was because of this contact with Anglo-Saxon poets that he began to show more interest in formal structure, but it may simply have been the result of a more conscious approach to the problem of poetic creation, the natural result of growing older. Among the Dutch poets his attention would seem to have shifted somewhat from Marsman to Marsman's contemporary, J. J. Slauerhoff—a lonely, querulous *poète maudit* who sailed from port to port as a ship's doctor without feeling at home anywhere except, as he said, in his poems. (Compare Anwar's "My house is built of heaped-up poems.'') Slauerhoff's poetry has a surface bite that is close to Anwar's own tone, early and late. It is also permeated by the sea, and in Anwar's later verse there is greater emphasis than before on ships, seas and ports.

The impetus for this development need not be attributed to Slauerhoff alone. In the postwar period Anwar wrote less, and less easily than in his first years as a poet, and he cast about consciously for sources of inspiration. One source he hoped to tap was Indonesian folk traditions, many of which are naturally of the sea. A result is the incantatory **"Tjerita buat Dien Tamaela"** (**"A Tale for Dien Tamaela"**) which is based on a legend from Miss Tamaela's native Spice Islands in the east of Indonesia.

> I am Pattiradjawane
> Whom the Gods watch over
> I alone.
> I am Pattiradjawane
> Foam of the sea.

He also sometimes found a stimulus towards poetry in the verse of others. Later, during the fifties, the Indonesian critics waged a heated debate on whether or not Anwar was guilty of plagiarism. **"Tjatetan th. 1946"** (**"Notes for 1946"**), for instance, is based on a verse by Donald Bain that Anwar found in an anthology of British war poetry, while **"Orang Berdua"** (**"Together"**) derives from Marsman's ''De Gescheidenen'' (''The Separated''). Yet both are genuine Indonesian poems that no one but Chairil Anwar could have written.

In his later years, at any rate, Anwar took his poetry, like his life, where he found it: in anthologies or on the waterfront made little difference. And to the very last he was overflowing with schemes and projects. In April, 1949, he told a friend that he wanted to go to Macassar, across the Java Sea on the island of Celebes, to note down sea chanties from the Buginese sailors. He had plans to translate García Lorca. And he was thinking about the possibility of a trip to India and Europe. (pp. 10-16)

Late that same year of 1949, the Dutch recognized Indonesian independence, and so did the world at large. The *élan* of the revolutionary years gave way to a slower, more orderly process of consolidation and development, in poetry as in politics. It is hard to say how Anwar would have adjusted to this new phase in Indonesian history. Surely, though, he would have disavowed the revived demand for a more ''positive'' poetry, whether ''modern,'' Marxist or Moslem; surely he would have repeated once more: ''We must be honest again, Ida.''

It was this blurting, anguished honesty that stood out more than anything else in Chairil Anwar's poetry when it was brought together, the year of his death, in two thin volumes, *Deru Tjampur Debu (Thunder Mixed with Dust)* and *Kerikil Tadjam dan Jang Terampas dan jang Putus (Sharp Gravel and What Was Plundered and Broken)*. It is an honesty that has since set a signal example for poets in Indonesia. Indeed, in a world where word manipulators are busy on all sides piously turning war into peace and peace into war, it is a virtue that poets everywhere might do well to cultivate. (p. 16)

> *James S Holmes, in an introduction to* Selected Poems
> *by Chairil Anwar, translated by Burton Raffel and*
> *Nurdin Salam, New Directions, 1963, pp. 7-16.*

BURTON RAFFEL (essay date 1967)

[*An American poet, novelist, and critic, Raffel is well known for his studies and translations of Indonesian literature. In the fol-*]

[*lowing excerpt, he discusses Anwar's major themes and stylistic techniques.*]

Anwar wrote only seventy-odd poems (not counting assorted others, some assembled in collections, that have all disappeared without a trace), but his was a complete revolution of language, of form, and of outlook; the effect was irrevocably to transform *bahasa Indonesia* as a literary tongue.

"A GRAVESTONE" ("Nisan")

For Grandmother

> Bukan kematian benar menusuk kalbu
> Keridlaanmu menerima segala tiba
> Tak kutahu setinggi itu atas debu
> dan duka maha tuan bertachta.
>
> It is not really death that stabs at my heart
> But your willingness to take whatever may come:
> I do not know how high above dust
> and sorrow you have been enthroned.

This little rhyming quatrain, written in October 1942, was the beginning. (The close dating of Anwar's poetry follows Jassin's pioneering research.) Its direct, somewhat exalted tone suggests but does not yet embody the driving intensity of his greatest work. The directness, however, is the key: at 20 Anwar was prepared and able to express *himself*, saying what *he* felt, and employing the words and forms that seemed to *him* right and proper. The bars were down all over Indonesia:

> The future writer—real writer!—must climb on, must chop off all the leafy, superfluous branches. . . . An immense, roaring voice whistles and shouts in his ear: Stop! Stop! Hey, Destroyer, Peace-Breaker! But I've got guts enough to barge right into the house of holiness, right into the parlor itself! I'm not stopping outside in the yard. I'm going straight on . . . straight on, understand?!!!

And directness also meant for him, as for many avant-garde writers in Western countries, a virtual identity between art and the artist: the poet must live his poetry, be his poetry.

> Everything, everything . . . *must* be experienced, endured (in his spirit, his aspirations, his emotions, his thoughts, his own knowledge of life) by the poet himself, must become a part of him, his gladness and sadness, *his* possessions, belonging to his spirit.

(pp. 81-2)

Anwar did not write easily, facilely, but wrote and rewrote, sometimes could not write at all, sometimes wrote a single line in a day's intense labor. The second poem in what was to become a small but magnificent corpus was not finished until two months after the first, in December 1942.

"LIFE" ("Penghidupan")

> Lautan maha dalam
> mukul dentur selama
> ngudji tenaga pematang kita
>
> mukul dentur selama
> hingga hantjur remuk redam
> Kurnia Bahgia
> ketjil setempuk
> sia-sia dilindung, sia-sia dipupuk.

The bottomless ocean
is always banging
testing the strength of our dikes

always banging
until it smashes to bits
the Blessing of Happiness
a little heap
pointlessly watched over, cultivated in vain.

The form has become more irregular, the rhyming pattern is his own invention: A B C B A C D D. The number of words per line had been unorthodox in the October 1942 quatrain, with only one line there employing the traditional four words; but that irregularity too has become more pronounced, two months later. The second poem is also longer—more significant a fact than it might seem, because Anwar was intent on the greatest compression he could manage. Only two poems in his principal collection (all the collections of his verse are post-humous), *Deru Tjampur Debu (Noise Mixed with Dust),* have more than twenty lines.

In February of 1943 there was an explosive breakthrough: Anwar wrote no fewer than seven poems, among them several of his best and at least one that attains greatness. (And 1943 continued to be his most prolific year: six poems in March, three in April, only one in May, but then five in June and six, possibly seven, in July. Roughly 40 per cent of his entire poetic output appeared in the space of half a year. It should also be noted that he was still several days short of his twenty-first birthday when he completed this creative spurt.) The third of his poems, **"Dipo Negoro"** (about a nineteenth-century nationalist hero), is a patriotic piece of great enthusiasm and energy but little poetic merit; it does however handle the language with singular freedom, breaking into the text proper with repeated capital-letter exclamations (*MADJU*, "FORWARD") and ending with four lines, each of which consists of a single word: "Forward. / Attack. / Charge. / Strike." Anwar's next, his fourth poem was, as it turned out, the second half of a two-part poem not finished until November of 1945, and ultimately entitled **"Whistling Song" ("Lagu Siul").** It is bitter love verse, in an irregular, freely rhymed form. But it was in the fifth poem, **"In Vain" ("Sia-Sia"),** that everything suddenly fell into place:

Penghabisan kali itu kau datang
Membawa kembang berkarang
Mawar merah dan melati putih
Darah dan Sutji
Kau tebarkan depanku
Serta pandang jang memastikan: untukmu.

Lalu kita sama termanggu
Saling bertanja: apakah ini?
Tjinta? Kita berdua tak mengerti

Sehari kita bersama. Tak hampir-menghampiri

Ah! Hatiku jang tak ma memberi
Mampus kau dikojak-kojak sepi.

The last time you came
You brought bright flowers,
Red roses, white jasmine,
Blood and holiness,
And spread them in front of me
With a decisive look: for you.

We were stunned
And asked each other: what's this?
Love? Neither of us understood.

That day we were together.
We did not touch.

But my heart will not give itself to you,
And does not care
that you are ripped by desolation.

Here, the blunt directness is sharp and hard, perceptive, intense, beautiful. The technical sophistication is immense: Lorca, and certain contemporary Greek poets, Cavafy among them, come immediately to mind. Anwar's language is stripped, bare of metaphor and simile alike. It only talks, it only describes, yet in words of such perfect balance, in rhythms so utterly expressive, that the taut poignancy of the last strophe (one can hardly call these stanzas, at least in the sense that "stanza" has been used so far) surges out powerfully. There is nothing left of traditional Malay poetry, here: "Everything completely new" was both the idea and the reality. "Apart from the stripped clarity of utterance, what is most striking is the willingness to engage any experience.... This is poetry entirely alien to slogans and attitudes; primarily it is poetry of personal concern, but its eloquence touches and occupies a larger world." (pp. 82-5)

Written in March 1943 (as was **"Me" ("Aku"),** perhaps his most famous work), [**"An Ordinary Song" ("Lago Biasa")**] seems to me the incarnation of libidinous sexuality. Not abstract sexuality, but Anwar's own: if the incident described in **"An Ordinary Song"** ... did not in fact take place, others like it did. This *was* an "ordinary song" for him. The jagged, broken rhythms are the rhythms by which he lived:

Ia mengerling. Ia ketawa.
Dan rumput kering terus menjala
Ia berkata. Suaranja njaring tinggi
Darahku terhenti berlari

She winks. She laughs.
And the dry grass blazes up.
She speaks. Her voice is loud
My blood stops running.

The quatrain rhymes (most of Anwar's poetry rhymes, though it is rarely *rime riche*); the halting, lurching motion of the lines, however, is as unlike anything that had ever been written in *bahasa Indonesia,* before Anwar, as the music of Stravinsky was unlike even the advanced harmonic experiments of Debussy. Much of Stravinsky's work, early and late, is indeed "motor music," basically rhythmic and perpetually in motion; Anwar too makes insistent use of pulsing metrical variations. In an article printed shortly after his death, in 1949, Anwar makes this rhythmic concern entirely explicit:

The tools and devices with which the poet can express himself are the materials of language, which he uses *intuitively.* By "manipulating" the lofty and the low he can achieve a pattern, an organization, and then he can create variations within the pattern—using rhythm as a unifying element. The melody of words can help establish a poet's form, as language becomes now heavy and slow, now light and quick. Further, the poet can choose extraordinary words, weighed and considered with great care, or words which solidify and unify his poetic intent....

It was in part the disorganization of the time that made Anwar's personal disorganization possible, even encouraged it, while it also made him representative of his time. Anwar exaggerated his life's disorganization, in person and in his poetry:

> Because he lived so restlessly, he could not endure working in an office, chained to a desk every day. When he was asked what he worked at, he answered: ''I'm a Poet.'' His residence was not fixed, he moved from one place to another, from one friend's house to another, from one hotel to another. A typical remark: ''When I die I don't want it to be in a bed. I want to die in the middle of the street.''

It was the patient, laborious organization of his personal disorganization that made his poetry revolutionary:

> Ketika orkes memulai ''Ave Maria''
> Kuseret ia kesana . . . . . .
>
> When the orchestra begins the ''Ave Maria''
> I drag her over there . . . . . .

The honesty is appalling, and because of the art with which it is presented to us, extraordinarily effective. Anwar holds nothing back: the restraints under which Yamin, Sanusi Pané, and Rustam Effendi labored, restraints that were dissolving in the work of the *Pudjangga Baru* poets, have vanished, and with them other restraints, social, moral, even political. A ''patriotic'' poem addressed to Indonesian President Sukarno is scarcely in the approved tone for communicating with the chief of state. It is, however, unmistakably Chairil Anwar's tone:

''AN AGREEMENT WITH FRIEND SUKARNO''

(''Persetudjuan Dengan Bung Karno'')

Ajo! Bung Karno kasi tangan mari kita bikin djandji
Aku sudah tjukup lama dengan bitjaramu, dipanggang
    atas apimu, digarami oleh lautmu

Dari mula tgl. 17 Agustus 1945
Aku melangkah kedepan berada rapat disisimu
Aku sekarang api aku sekarang laut

Bung Karno! Kau dan aku satu zat satu urat
Dizatmu dizatku kapal-kapal kita berlajar
Diuratmu diuratku kapal-kapal kita berlajar
Diuratmu diuratku kapal-kapal kita bertolak & berlabuh

Hey! Friend Sukarno, give me your hand and let's set
    everything shipshape
I've heard enough of your speeches, been roasted by
    your eloquence, salted by the sea-flood of your voice

From the day this country set itself free
I've marched along next to you
Now I'm on fire, now I'm flooding over

Friend Sukarno! You and me, we're made out of the
    same stuff, we've got the same veins
Our ships sail in what you're made of and I'm made of
Our ships pull up and drop anchor in your veins and in
    mine too.

This does not rhyme; its long-limbed phrases are delicately tuned to the great sweeping phrases of all political oratory, and President Sukarno's not least of all. (The poem was written, incidentally, in 1948, but Anwar's tone, style, and subject matter did not essentially change from beginning to end.) (pp. 87-9)

The discipline of the Word (''let the Word be our one fundamental Principle!!'' he wrote in 1945) remained the only pattern his life had. Fiercely romantic as he was, in art as in life, there was nothing romantic or irrational about either the theory or the practice of his ''fundamental Principle.'' His contempt for the fuzzy mysticism he saw in the *Pudjangga Baru* school was exceeded only by his scorn for those contemporaries whom he called ''inspirationalists,'' those who believed in some sort of *deus ex machina* as the source of art, those who sought art in trances or in waiting, or in writing, as furiously as they could, the first words that came into their heads and every word that came into their heads. ''What do you get that way?'' he snorted, in the 1943 speech from which I have already quoted. ''Warm chicken shit!! . . . Till now our art has been thin, superficial. No more of the old farts. No more gentle breezes of *that* kind!'' He knew that ''wisdom and insight aren't enough, you've got to work up energy and enthusiasm.'' He knew that vitality was ''the fire of life.'' But he was desperately clearheaded about the difference between mere vitality and beauty. One was a precondition, the other a final result; ''vitality is all of a piece, from top to bottom,'' but ''there's no sameness about beauty . . . beauty is a balancing, a synthesizing of life's vibrations.'' (pp. 90-1)

Before briefly surveying the remainder of Anwar's poetic output, one further example from that first great spurt, in early 1943, should be set out. It demonstrates a side of his work that can easily be overlooked:

''OUR GARDEN'' (''TAMAN'')

Our garden
doesn't spread out very far, it's a little affair
in which we won't lose each other.
For you and me it's enough.
The flowers in our garden don't riot in color
The grass isn't like a carpet
soft and smooth to walk on.
For us it doesn't matter
Because
in our garden
You're the flower, I'm the bee,
I'm the bee, you're the flower.
It's small, it's full of sunlight, this garden of ours,
a place where we draw away from the world and from people.

Anwar did not often feel, or allow himself to feel, that sort of tenderness. The original text has some incidental rhyming; essentially it has the same easy free-verse flow as the translation. The language is kept carefully simple, conversational (*manusia,* ''people,'' the last word in both original and translation, is used in its colloquial form '*nusia*). The rhythms move lightly, without the jolting effects we have seen in other poems. It is ''soft'' without being sentimental; the risky flower and bee image is given a quiet twist, to purge it of conventional overtones:

> Kau kembang, aku kumbang
> aku kumbang, kau kembang
>
> You're the flower, I'm the bee,
> I'm the bee, you're the flower.

The sound-play created, in *bahasa Indonesia,* cannot be re-created in English: *kau,* ''you,'' and *aku,* ''I, me,'' form one sound variation; *kembang,* ''flower,'' and *kumbang,* ''bee,'' form a second sound variation; these and the insistent but somehow not strident *k* alliteration, playing across every word in these two lines, all keep off any sickly sweet odor. (There are two further initial *k* sounds in the next line, one placed at the very front of the line, one cleverly, delicately, at the very end, a gentle reminder, a masterful stroke.)

One of Anwar's most famous experiments, though not I think one of his best poems, seems to have been written at the very end of, or not long after the end of, this February-July 1943 burst of activity. Titled simply **"1943,"** it breaks violently with every prior canon of poetic form:

> Ratjun berada direguk pertama
> Membusuk rabu terasa didada
> Tenggelam darah dalam nanah
> Malam kelam-membelam
> Djalan kaku-lurus. Putus
> Tjandu.
> Tumbang
> Tanganku menadah patah
> Luluh
> Terbenam
> Hilang
> Lumpuh.
> Lahir
> Tegak
> Berderak
> Rubuh
> Runtuh
> Mengaum. Mengguruh
> Menentang. Menjerang
> Kuning
> Merah
> Hitam
> Kering
> Tandas
> Rata
> Rata
> Rata
> Dunia
> Kau
> Aku
> Terpaku.

> There's poison in the first swallow
> It feels as though one's lungs are rotting
> Blood melting into pus
> The evening pitch-black
> The roads stiff-straight. The opium
> Used up.
> Collapsing
> My hands catch brokenly
> Smashed
> Drowned
> Lost
> Paralyzed.
> I wake
> Stand
> Rattle
> Fall
> In a heap
> Roaring. Thundering
> Challenging. Attacking
> Yellow
> Red
> Black
> Barren
> Empty

> Flat
> Flat
> Flat
> Is the world
> You
> And me
> Nailed down.

Anwar wrote this, notes Anthony Johns, after seeing a small baby, knowing it was healthy but already infected by life, by the necessity to breathe, to grow, to live. The one-word line, used here almost as a form, has both its attractions and its advantages, especially when used as a contrasting device. Anwar used it elsewhere, as we have already seen; it had also been used, on occasion, by such an unexperimental poet as Amir Hamzah and by another *Pudjangga Baru* writer, J. E. Tatengkeng, whose "Flowers," *Kuntjup*, printed in his 1934 collection, consists of twenty-four lines, half of them lines of but a single word. Neither Hamzah nor Tatengkeng, however, had used the device in as slashing a way as Anwar's. It is in my opinion a short-circuiting of the creative process, used as it is here. The poet convinces himself that when he has written *Kuning/Merah/Hitam*, "Yellow/Red/Black," he has composed a stark picture. It is indeed stark; it is not, however, a picture, it does not contain any composition. This is not the abstractionism of, say, Jackson Pollock, but the undigested raw material from which an abstraction could be composed. (It is, in Anwar's own terms, mere "vitality.") There is an enormous difference between the three uncontrolled lines just cited, and those which follow:

> Kering
> Tandas
> Rata
> Rata
> Rata
> Dunia
> Kau
> Aku
> Terpaku.

> Barren
> Empty
> Flat
> Flat
> Flat
> Is the world
> You
> And me
> Nailed down.

These lines are still somewhat excessive, but they have an organization, a progression, a point to make; they are composed, and therefore, whatever their quality, they are poetry. To hurl "Yellow/Red/Black" onto the page is like placing three blobs of primary pigment on a canvas, one under the other. The entire poem has, from a technical point of view, a sense of uneasiness, of strain; there is a vast difference between a raid on the inexpressible and a wild sortie into "somewhere." In July of 1943 Anwar had broached the same theme—life infecting life—in a brief poem whose title is (literally) a question mark. In eight simple lines (none of them of only one word, and all of them rhyming) he in fact did invade the inexpressible:

> Let's not stop here
> The beer is stale, and scarce at that
> And we want barrels and barrels
> Go on, let's go on . . . . . .!!

Off to a place where the bottles stand in rows
And it's girls who bring it to us.
Oh red lips, the first of death's sewers
O life, are you still laughing?

The contrast between "Oh red lips, the first of death's sewers /
O life, are you still laughing?" and the approach taken in the
poem **"1943"** is the difference between an idea embodied,
given poetic flesh and blood, and an idea only stated, left
undeveloped. Embodiment and elaboration were far more usual
for Anwar; it is the way of "beauty," rather than the path of
unelaborated "vitality." He knew the difference between energy and poetry, even if his critics sometimes do not. (pp.
96-100)

1946 was the second most prolific year for Anwar. He wrote,
in all, fourteen poems, and fully half of them are among his
greatest, with not a really poor one among the remainder. Two
of the poems are sonnets; he used the form only once more,
in 1947, for one of his most perfect poems, **"Tuti's Ice Cream"**
("Tuti Artic"), which I shall quote shortly. One of the two
1946 sonnets, **"To the Painter Affandi"** **("Kepada Plukis Af-**
fandi"), inverts the form, starting rather than concluding with
the sestet. The more orthodox sonnet—with one exception it
is rhymed orthodoxly—is **"News from the Sea"** **("Kabar Dari**
Laut"):

I was really a fool that time,
wanting to sleep with you;
forgetting how quickly a sailor can find himself alone
   on a sad sea,
returning with his blue destination.

Now there's a wound on my body,
widening, spilling out blood,
where you kissed me, then, with a wild lust
and I was too weak and surrendered.

Life goes on between the stern and the rudder.
A boundary only strengthens memory.
And crazy laughter is reflected in the quiet whiskey.

And you? Is your job worship and praise,
Or is there something washed up between them,
A bird that by morning is dead beside its cage?

The poem catches fire, I think, only in the sestet—which has
some of the cutting edge of good *pantun* imagery, though it is
not at all in either *pantun* rhythm or *pantun* language.

The turning toward the sea is new in Anwar's poetry: it seems
to dominate the entire year, perhaps because he was thinking
of seeing more of his own country, perhaps because he longed
to travel abroad, perhaps, too, because in the middle of fame
and importance he was growing restless and felt pressured,
even harried. **"For D. S.'s Album"** **("Buat Album D. S."),**
first describes a lonely girl waiting for her sailor sweetheart,
singing as she waits. Happiness is predicted, a cheerful ending
for all concerned. And then the poem concludes:

A marvellous song!—but do you understand,
my sadly sobbing little sister,
That a deserter will always be deserted,
That even in that far country the sun never goes
   backward?

(Again, "little sister" = *adik*.) The singing girl in her white
dress is 'like something in a dream," but Anwar was a poet
of this sour but real world, not a poet of dreams. The sea
compulsion is clear in **"My Love's on a Faraway Island"**

("Tjintaku Djauh Dipulau"), a bitingly ironic love song; it is
equally obvious in **"Twilight at a Little Harbor"** **("Sendja di**
Pelabuhan Ketjil"):

This time no one's looking for love
between the sheds, the old houses, in the make-believe
of poles and ropes. A boat, a *prau* without water
puffs and blows, thinking there's something it can
   catch.

The drizzle comes harder and darkens. There's an eagle
   flapping,
pushing sulkily off, and the day swimming silkily
to meet temptations yet to come. Nothing moves.
And now the sand and the sea are asleep, the waves are
   gone.

There's no one else. I'm alone. Walking,
combing the cape, still drowning the hope
of just once getting to the end of it and saying goodbye
   to everything
from the fourth beach, where the last sob could be
   hugged tightly to me.

Knowing how personal Anwar's poems are likely to be, and
knowing something of the drift of the poems written all during
this year of 1946, it is not hard to see what this poem probably
meant to him. As he walked along the beaches he too was "a
prau without water," puffing and blowing, "thinking there's
something [he] can catch." The eagle soars, but "sulkily";
the future, inexorable, "swimming silkily" to meet him (and
all of us), is only "temptations yet to come." Alone, he continues to walk, physically on the shore but "still drowning the
hope / of just once getting to the end of it." The suicidal final
lines speak, I think, for themselves. Earlier in the year he had
written, in **"Notes for 1946"** **("Tjatetan Th. 1946"):**

These hands will drop wearily,
As a game of light in the water loses its shape in mist.
. . . I chisel a gravestone, and pick at it.

He had there worked through to what was, for him, a more
basic resolution:

So don't blink: stare, sharpen your pen,
Write because the page is empty, because dry throats
   will receive drops of moisture.

And there is a similar confrontation, though again a different
resolution, in **"Nocturno,"** described by Anwar as a fragment
(the original manuscript of what was probably intended to be
a fair copy of the poem is rather heavily corrected—but then,
Anwar would also make corrections on galleys):

I shouted—but no voice answered,
The sound congealed in the frozen air.
In my body desires stretched,
Dead too.
The last dream asked for power,
The axe was broken, swung in vain,
And my heart was strangled.

Stranded . . . . . . I tasted ashes and dust
From a left-over song.
A memory of the ghostly emptiness
And the fever that will stiffen us.

. . . .

Pen and poet, both dead,
Turning!

The penultimate line first read, before it was crossed out in the manuscript (I think accurately decipherable even in a poor photostatic reproduction), "Pen and poet, both dead, betrayed." Anwar then substituted the penultimate line as it now stands; wrote a final line that I can only partially decipher (there is the word "desire," and the first three words may read "it's not a guide (pilot, navigator) I want"; the line seems to trail off and was perhaps unfinished even before its rejection by the poet); and at last cut through to what was his final solution, the single word "turning." In English these two final lines, incidentally, are quite literal, although the translation as a whole does not show that until these final lines the poem is closely rhymed. However they read, the rejected lines, and the entire poem as finally written, show once again how buffeted and weary Anwar felt. There had been poems of that nature before; there were to be others; but the concentration was unusually intense in this second most fertile year of his poetic existence. His basic response continued to be defiance of "emptiness" and "the final treachery": "Once more, friend, one line more," he calls out at the end of **"To a Friend"** (**"Kepada Kawan"**) "Shove your sword to the hilt / Into those who've diluted the pureness of honey!!!" (pp. 101-04)

Anwar wrote only four poems in 1947, two of them magnificent, all of them extremely good. There is still some concern for the sea, in **"Heaven," "Sorga,"** a wryly beautiful commentary on religious faith, but it is as though seen, now, from a distance: "there's a contemplative voice inside me, / stubbornly mocking: Can you ever / get dry after a soaking in the blue sea, / after the sly temptations waiting in every port?"

Like my mother, and my grandmother too,
Plus seven generations before them,
I also seek admission to heaven,
Which the Moslem Party and the Mohammedan Party
    say has rivers of milk
And thousands of houris all over.

But there's a contemplative voice inside me,
Stubbornly mocking: Can you ever
Get dry after a soaking in the blue sea,
After the sly temptations waiting in every port?
Anyway, who can say for sure
That there really are houris there
With voices as rich and husky as Nina's, with eyes that
    flirt like Jati's?

The same imperturbable wit glitters through **"Poems for Basuki Resobowo"** (**"Sadjak buat Basuki Resobowo"**), a dialogue between a persistent, timid questioner and a sophisticated, knowledgeable respondent who perpetually twits and teases.

Is this much of a journey?
Only a step!—Maybe *you* can go further!
But how?
Ask the fallen leaves for yourself,
Ask the dying tune that becomes a song!

What stays behind to be remembered?
See the hens who no longer look up
Or the dull wind, the falling star!

How long a journey?
Maybe a century . . . no, no, just a second!
But *why* this journey?
Ask the house, that was born dumb!
Ask my children's children, freezing in there!

Is something reaching out?
Is something letting go?
Ah, find your own answers!—I'm just killing time.

The third poem, **"Evening in the Mountain"** (**"Malam di Pegunungan"**), is almost more good-humored than wry: I quote it entire.

I think: is this the moon that freezes everything,
Whitens the houses and stiffens the trees?
This time I'm really eager to get an answer;
Eh, there are little boys running about, chasing each
    other's shadows!

And then there is his glowing sonnet, **"Tuti's Ice Cream"** (**"Tuti Artic"**); the Indonesian original is so tightly compact, and *bahasa Indonesia* is so terse a tongue, that the translation runs to twenty lines rather than fourteen. (Would it have occurred to anyone before Anwar, incidentally, to rhyme *ternganga*, "yawns, gapes," with *Coca-Cola*?)

Between present and future happiness
The abyss gapes.
My girl is licking at her ice cream:
This afternoon you're my love,
I adorn you with cake and Coca-Cola
Oh wife in training.
We have stopped the clocks' ticking.

You kissed skilfully, indelibly.
—When we cycled I took you home
—Your blood was hot, soon you were a woman,
And the stiff old man dreamed dreams
That leaped over the moon.

Every day's beau invited you on,
Every day's beau was different.
Tomorrow we'll meet and not know each other:
Heaven is this minute's game.

I am like you, everything ran by,
Me and Tuti and Greet and Amoi . . . . . .
Dilapidated hearts.
Love's a danger that quickly fades.

Even here, where "the abyss gapes," the tone is wry but not bitter, sorrowful but resigned. At 25 Anwar is a "stiff old man," a "dilapidated heart"; he knows quite well that time cannot be stopped, youth cannot be recaptured, love cannot be reapproached once it has been abandoned. It is perhaps a sad poem; it is certainly not an anguished one, as were so many of those written in 1946. As Anwar puts it in one of the weaker poems he wrote in 1948, **"A Sentry at Night"** (**"Perdjurit Djaga Malam"**): "Time goes on, I don't know where it's going . . . . . ."

There were seven poems, that next year. One of them, **"An Agreement with Friend Sukarno"** (**"Persetudjuan Dengan Bung Karno"**), is quoted . . . above. Of the other six written in 1948, two are weak, three good, one great—the latter being **"At a Mountain Resort"** (**"Puntjak"**) a love poem haunted by "the old question still growing, blooming, the old, old question, the question." So too in a brief untitled poem Anwar declares: "I don't know when or why anymore / And don't ask who'll dig the last grave." In **"For Miss Gadis Rasid"** (**"Buat Gadis Rasid"**) he cries out, at the end:

Let's run off, free our searching souls to be like doves
Flying
learning the ways of the desert, not ever meeting, not
    ever touching the ground
—*the only possible nonstop flight*
In vain.

The penultimate line is in English in the original. Doubt, and fear, are again "growing, blooming." Whatever the precise content of the "old, old question," it is the need to escape, to survive, which comes to the fore once more. **"Ina Mia,"** a distinctly tender poem about a prostitute, "touches, groping, / only the rind of hope"; Anwar there evokes "The mist of an old love, a lost love . . . felt trembling for a moment / among the leaves gone gray as dust," then brings reality back with a swift, devastating stroke, as a soldier comes "hurrying around the corner." But in the untitled poem that ends his output for 1948, the haunting question returns. After a long backward glance the poem ends, nobly:

See the yellow-gold love fade:
And for me who have chosen
the sight blurs, the leaves around are falling
the house disappears into tall leafy fir trees
no shadows go floating across the window pane.
The marbles, the top, the hobbyhorse, the toy boats,
See the yellow-gold love fade:
When the wonderful storm comes
rolling the marbles, spinning the top,
spurring on the hobbyhorse, blowing the little boats
I'll be long since stiffened.

He already knew (and of course did not know, too) that he had very little longer to live. His final notebooks, the poems he copied out, the poems he translated, the poems he was working at on his own, all show a preoccupation with death. It had never been a theme very far from his heart; it was terribly close, now. One of the unrevised fragments of original poetry, from those final notebooks, helps show that the nobility of the passage just quoted was no accident, the maturity and perception of his last poems no freak of temporary understanding:

Let's
Leave here
Just as we planned, just
As we agreed
Once

And one by one
Give up everything
In this most progressive of worlds

Before we go
Let's strip the waving trees
Let's shave off women's long, waving hair

But don't cut down desire

Anwar died at 2:30 in the afternoon, on April 28, 1949; he had been in the hospital, often delirious with fever, since April 22. Seven poems were written in that truncated final year, among them one of his best. **"The Captured and the Freed"** (**"Jang Terampas dan Jang Luput"**) was published also under two divergent titles:

Darkness and a passing wind rake me.
I shiver, and so does the great room where the one I
    want is lying.
The night sinks in, the trees are as dead as columns of
    stone.

At Karet, at Karet (where I go next), the cold wind
    blows just as noisily.

I'm tidying my room, and my heart, in case you come
And I can set free a new story for you;
But now it's only my hands that move fiercely.

My body is quiet and alone, the tale and the time go
    stiffly, icily by.

One of the divergent titles of this poem is **"For Mirat"** (**"Buat Mirat"**), that being the name of his quondam fiancée; I have assumed that she was by now his wife. I do not know exactly when or where this poem was written (it was published posthumously), but it was at Karet, on April 29, 1949, that he was buried. (pp. 105-10)

Burton Raffel, "Chairil Anwar," in his *The Development of Modern Indonesian Poetry, State University of New York Press, 1967, pp. 80-110.*

A. TEEUW   (essay date 1967)

[*In the following excerpt, Teeuw discusses Anwar's poetry and its significance in the development of modern Indonesian verse.*]

It is not easy to name a single characteristic which could sum up the poetry of Chairil Anwar; in any case it is impossible to name as such a general characteristic a dominant mood, or a central subject or a well-rounded philosophy. There is something provisional about his poetry, reflecting a personality in the making. Indeed this may be the most characteristic feature of it. The only thing these poems have in common is their intensity, their radical preoccupation with life in all its forms and facets, and therefore with death—for no one who takes life seriously escapes confrontation with death. In this respect also, Chairil Anwar is decidedly very much akin to the Dutch vitalist, Marsman. But life was everywhere—the struggle against death and for life took place on all fronts, and was total. Wherever Chairil recognised that intensity in a fellow poet, he was open to what is called "influence". Although the greatest influence on the form of his poetry, especially perhaps the earliest poems, was Marsman, in fact it is immaterial whether this influence was that of a Rilke, a Slauerhoff, a Conrad Aiken or a Hsu Chih-Mo.

On the other hand, everyone can find in Chairil something to his liking—even the Japanese censor in the poem **"Diponegoro,"** which does allow itself to be read as a war poem against the white colonial oppressor. The political leader of the struggle for independence readily and approvingly quotes the great poem **"Krawang-Bekasi,"** in which Chairil Anwar seems to identify himself completely with the revolutionary struggle. For Christians there are the poems **"Doa"** (**"Prayer"**) and **"Isa"** (**"Jesus"**) as clear "evidence" of Chairil Anwar's positive confrontation with Christianity. And for the Moslem the poem **"Dimesjid"** (**"At the Mosque"**) is equally clear evidence that Chairil Anwar met Allah in the mosque and contended with him. Besides that, in **"Tjerita Buat Dien Tamaela"** (**"Story for D. T."**) one can find scarcely less convincing evidence of an inner link between Chairil Anwar and the life of the primitive people, a kind of natural primaeval paganism. Beside the writer of the romantic love poem **"Taman"** (**"Garden"**), stands the lonely sceptic of **"Kesabaran"** (**"Patience"**) written in the same month, and the writer, almost choked with loneliness and fear, of **"Hampa"** (**"Empty"**) written a month later.

So there is in the work of Chairil Anwar a diversity, typical of a personality "in the making," who assails life, full of ecstasy, *prenant son bien où il le trouve* ["taking his material from wherever he finds it"], open to everything that life offers, intense, human, sometimes cheerful, sometimes (though rarely) even happy; but more often, just as with Marsman, his work seems to be dominated by the sombre, by death and terror of it, by tragic loneliness, by lack of real communication; even if this mood is expressed in many different ways, sometimes gloomy and heavy, then again ironical, sceptical or sadly reconciled. For this reason it is so difficult, or even impossible, to represent the "real Chairil" by quoting a few fragments. Against any one poem there is always another which can be quoted to demonstrate the opposite. The lines which are often quoted to characterise him are from the poem which is called **"Aku"** (**"I"**) in one collection, and **"Semangat"** (**"Spirit"**) in another. In these lines he compares himself to a solitary wild animal.

> Aku ini binatang djalang
> Dari kumpulannja terbuang

> I am a solitary animal / Cut off from its herd.

a poem expressing, on the one hand, the poignant pain of loneliness, but on the other hand, the irrepressible passion for life:

> Aku mau hidup seribu tahun lagi.

> I want to live a thousand years more.

>   (pp. 149-50)

[What] is distinctive in [Chairil's] poetry is less what he says than how he says it. Where his poetry is unique and where it breaks new ground is in its characteristic intensity rather than in the themes or the contents:

> hidup hanja menunda kekalahan

> Life is but an attempt to defer defeat.

is as a line of verse just as startling and effective as the lines quoted from **"Aku."** It is pure poetry, and bears witness to a consummate craftsmanship.

I use this last word deliberately and in my opinion in agreement with Chairil Anwar's own ideas on the writing of poetry and the responsibility of the poet. Already early on he was aware that writing poetry was a difficult and laborious business, which perhaps began with inspiration, but certainly did not end with it:

> There are two kinds of inspiration. Not everything which can strike a chord in the mind is a true inspiration.

> We must be able to evaluate, to choose, to analyse and sometimes to discard entirely. And after that we can begin to organise . . . .

> I state categorically: it is thinking which has a great influence on the product of art which is of a high calibre. Thinking which includes weighing and deciding soundly and accurately. . . .

Elsewhere, also in 1943, he indicates that the poet cannot lag behind modern technique and scholarship:

> Knowledge and technique are in this period already advanced . . . We are already capable

of taking, not only ordinary photos, but X-rays as well, right to the marrow of the bones. . . . Let us be clear, then, Ida. We are living now at a thousand kilometres per hour. Clear and short do not necessarily mean empty, not at all. In a short sentence such as: *sekali berarti, sudah itu mati* "to be relevant but once, then die," we can embody all the aims of our life. So it is clear, not empty.

Chairil's verses show that he was aware of this responsibility as a poet, it had become flesh and blood to him. As R. Nieuwenhuys, discussing the notorious sloppiness of many aspects of his existence, once strikingly formulated it: "Chairil Anwar must have preserved his last inner reserve for his poetry." And the wonder of his poetry was that with one blow he brought to maturity the immature, newly evolved *Bahasa Indonesia*— X-raying it with his verses. At the beginning of the official recognition of *Bahasa Indonesia,* he proved that this language was entirely adequate, not only as an instrument of communication at the level of everyday life and of politics and government, but also for understanding at the highest level between men, that is, for poetry; and that the greatest vitality and intensity of living were communicable through this language, as well as any other. He was clearly conscious of that responsibility, he realised that nothing less than this was at stake. . . . (pp. 151-52)

Chairil Anwar in his poetry, at least in a number of his verses, gained mastery over the power of words and determined their usage. That is the magic of poetry which lends power to the ordinary word; Chairil possessed that mysterious power which is so difficult to explain. He used words in such a way that they became new and he so combined them that they illuminated each other. He made use of a symbolism, shocking in its novelty, which however was incidental rather than systematic. James Holmes has pointed out the symbolic function of the mirror [see excerpt dated 1962]; and the repeated use of the pen and the word as the ultimum refugium of the poet speaks for itself (**"Nocturno, Tjatetan Th. 1946,"** **"Notes of 1946"**); the sea is also a dominant motif in his poems, the sea upon which the poet is the *kelasi bersendiri* (the solitary sailor), whose life is enacted *antara buritan dan kemudi* (between stern and rudder) and where the beloved dwells far away on an island, unattainable. (*Tjintaku djauh dipulau*). Colours play an important role in his poetry, but on the other hand he does not eschew in his verses the traditional Indonesian image; for example, the symbolising of a relationship between lovers in terms of the flower and the bee

> dalam taman punja berdua
> kau kembang, aku kumbang.

> in our common garden / You are the flower, I am the bee.

Neither has Chairil Anwar in any sense avoided the formal, more traditional poetical devices. On the contrary, he knew that a magical effect could be produced by means of ordinary language devices, by merely deepening, enriching and extending their potential, a not inconsiderable potential which is so seldom apparent in ordinary usage. In doing so he did not restrict himself to words. Morphologically he has exploited the potentialities of Indonesian, as can be demonstrated from the poem . . . **"Kepada Pelukis Affandi."** For example the derivative *meninggi*, from *tinggi*, "high," turning the static adjective into a dynamic verb: the artist doesn't just stand on a high tower, he raises himself onto it. The combination of *ketjemasan derita, ketjemasan mimpi* in the same strophe is also effective. Here also we have a process not unknown in Indonesian, the verbal *ke-an* form combined with a subject-complement (of the type *kedatangan musuh*, ''attacked by the enemy''). But because the basic word *tjemas* here is really an adjective—with which such a complement cannot normally be used—he stretches the language at this point to a clearly expressive effect.

In this way Chairil continually occupies himself with language, active, inventive, intense. Obviously the most remarkable outcome of this is his use of words. After all, it was especially in its vocabulary that Indonesian was in need of broadening and supplementing. Since Chairil Anwar the Indonesian language has developed in the pattern set by him; in his work the old and the new, the foreign and the indigenous appear indiscriminately and plentifully. Sometimes by design and sometimes by chance he explores the possibilities for extending the narrow Malay vocabulary, the possibilities available in regional languages, the Djakarta dialect, Dutch and English. The first line of his poem **"Persetudjuan dengan Bung Karno"** (**"Agreement with Bung Karno"**) symbolises by its colloquial words the bond with the *rakjat:*

Ajo! Bung Karno *kasi* tangan mari kita *bikin* djandii.

Come on, Bung Karno, let's shake hands and let's
    make an agreement.

And besides this, there occur repeatedly such words as *iseng, punja* and *bisa,* which were scarcely acceptable at the time when he was writing his poems. As with his use of *beta* immediately at the beginning of his **"Tjerita Buat Dien Tamaela,"** he at once conjures up the East Indonesian scene. And elsewhere he does not avoid Dutch or English words:

Hilang *sonder* pusaka, *sonder* kerabat

Living without heirloom, without family ties.

or:

Adikku jang lagi keenakan mendjilat *es artic;*
Sore ini kau tjintaku, kuhiasi dengan sus + *coca cola.*

My darling who just loves licking her ice-cream, / This
    afternoon my love,
I will adorn you with cake and coca-cola.

Chairil Anwar knew too that the poet had a powerful means of strengthening the force of the words through sound itself. And he knew, consciously or unconsciously, that in this respect Indonesian had its own possibilities, different from those in Dutch, but not less effective. With regard to this, his poetry can be likened to that of Amir Hamzah—I would dare to postulate an essential agreement, because there existed between the two of them an essential similarity in poetical ability. Chairil also did not avoid the use of traditional rhyme; many of his poems rhyme, as can be ascertained from the verses quoted here. But Chairil Anwar, like Amir Hamzah, knew that because of the structure of the language, end rhyme could lack effect in Indonesian, and that much more effective was the emphasis on individual words through all kinds of sound effects from word to word rather than from line to line, using for example internal rhyme and assonance. He was revolutionary enough to realise that the ordinary traditional poetical means, provided they are used individually and creatively, could be used to heighten the effect, and indeed it would be harmful to dispense with them. Chairil's poems abound in sound effect, and it is precisely these sound effects which play such an important role in the work of Amir Hamzah. One can compare lines such as

Ini m*uka* penuh l*uka*
Siapa p*unja*

This face / full of wounds / Whose is it?

or:

Segala men*ebal,* segala meng*ental*
Segala tak kuk*enal*
Selamat ting*gal* . . . !!

Everything thickens / Everything congeals / Everything
    is strange to me / Goodbye . . . !!

or here again:

Darahku meng*ental-*p*ekat.* Aku tump*at-*p*edat,*

My blood congeals, I am dense, compact.

where not only the consonant rhyme, and the *e-a* vowel sequence three times in succession are highly suggestive, but also the accumulation of ''stops'' greatly underline the despair and the breakdown of life as expressed by the words. (pp. 152-55)

As we have said before, Chairil remained in people's minds partly because he continued to be so controversial. In this connection, attention must be drawn to two points. The first point is Chairil's plagiarism. . . . From the material we have available, it cannot be denied that, in a few cases, Chairil has been guilty of what is ordinarily called plagiarism—he rewrote and published the poems of others without mentioning his sources. At least in one case, this apparently was for a very commonplace, but none the less real reason; he could afford to pay for the injection he needed with the money he received for an original poem, but not with the money he received for a translation. In other cases the question is more complicated, and above all it is far from being clear to what extent Chairil himself was aware of the fact that he more or less rewrote other poems in Indonesian. With his personality, the processes of digesting others' material and creating his own were very much akin, if not interchangeable. Moreover, the circumstances of his own life and the chaotic state of Indonesia during the years he was writing poetry, could be regarded as giving him good excuse if he did not in fact succeed in keeping these processes apart. The greatness of his poetry, then, is scarcely diminished by those cases of apparent or real plagiarism which have so far come to light.

The controversy over the appraisal of Chairil Anwar after his death is of much greater interest, because here we see something of the development of Indonesian culture, and of the conflicting trends and ideologies. On the one hand, the admiration and even veneration which Chairil Anwar already enjoyed during his lifetime and which persisted after his death were unstinted and restrained. For many years the day of his death has been more or less officially commemorated, both on a national scale and in smaller local circles and groups, and often became the occasion for recitals of his poetry and for high sounding eulogies. One does rather get the impression, though, that acquaintance with his work was far from always being commensurate with the praise accorded to him. But it is precisely the manysidedness of the themes in his verses and the variety of his moods and motifs which result in the fact that the nation and the individual could identify with him in one respect or another. Everyone could find something to admire in him, could recognise something of himself in him.

On the other hand, reservations were expressed, criticisms were levelled at him and even doubt was cast on the significance of his poetry. That critical note was sounded especially by the artists of the political left, who had early on pronounced the whole of the *Angkatan 45* ["Generation of '45"] dead, and directed their criticism particularly at Chairil's poetry. They saw his Western individualism as decadent and in conflict with the real ideals of the revolution, which was the struggle for the *rakjat*.

For example, Klara Akustia criticised Chairil Anwar's poetry as early as 1951. He recognised the significance of Chairil as an innovator as far as form was concerned.

> Improvement of the form of literary works began with Chairil Anwar. But Chairil Anwar also launched individualism and anarchy into our literature. This was Chairil's unhealthy aspect.

> We can draw the conclusion about Chairil Anwar that the new literary form he devised is acceptable, but his outlook on life is not.

This criticism of Chairil Anwar as an individualist and anarchist and as such, making no contribution to the Indonesian revolution (as interpreted by the Marxists), or indeed, being in conflict with this revolution, grew louder as the *Lekra* artists secured a stronger hold on Indonesian cultural life. This was especially marked after 1959, and the defenders of Chairil Anwar and the universal humanism of the *Angkatan 45* found things increasingly difficult after that year. This was clearly demonstrated by a very cautious attempt by Jassin and others to salvage something of the ideals of the forty-fivers and to reestablish the position of Chairil in the framework of the revolution and the *Pantja Sila,* the five basic principles of the Indonesian revolution. They did this through the *Manifes Kebudajaan,* issue on 17th August 1963. This Cultural Manifesto (*Manikebu*) led to fierce reactions, prosecution almost of the *Manikebuis* who were pilloried by the Communists as the betrayers of the revolution. In that period the denigration of Chairil Anwar became fiercer than ever. It is all the more remarkable then, that on the 1st May, 1965, Chairil Anwar was again officially commemorated in an address by no less a personage than the *Ketua Pembina Djiwa Revolusi,* (Senior Builder of the Revolutionary Spirit), the minister Ruslan Abdulgani. The latter dwelt upon the worthy aspects of his work and life within the framework of the Indonesian revolution, naturally making a very one-sided selection from his total oeuvre.

And now, most recently, the *Angkatan 66* ["Generation of '66"] have re-established Chairil Anwar in his old glory; they have accepted him as the leader and inspirer of their cultural revolution; as Jassin has put it in his picture of the rise of this new generation:

> The verses of Chairil Anwar again filled the pages of pamphlets and newspapers, they filled the air via *Radio Ampera,* and in devotional meetings they gave a new spirit to the fighting students.

So Chairil Anwar remains a living and present force in the development of Indonesia. Through his personality and his poetry he contributed to the formation of that new Indonesia, and helped to give it direction. In particular he vindicated, once and for all, the great idea of one *Bahasa Indonesia* as a total and complete means of communication, of one Indonesian nation, in the most profound form of communication, verse. Because of this, he will never lose the position he occupies in the opening stages of the history of the new Indonesia. (pp. 157-59)

> *A. Teeuw, "Chairil Anwar," in his* Modern Indonesian Literature, *Martinus Nijhoff, 1967, pp. 145-59.*

ADDITIONAL BIBLIOGRAPHY

Johns, Anthony J. "Genesis of a Modern Literature." In *Indonesia,* edited by Ruth T. McVey, pp. 410-37. New Haven: Yale University, 1963.
    Discussion of Anwar's poetry in the context of postwar Indonesian literature.

Oemarjati, Boen S. *Chairil Anwar: The Poet and His Language.* The Hague: Martinus Nijhoff, 1972, 159 p.
    Textual and linguistic analysis of several of Anwar's poems, focusing in particular on his creative use of bahasa Indonesia.

Léon Bloy

1846-1917

French novelist, short story writer, diarist, and essayist.

Bloy was a central figure in the Catholic Literary Revival, a movement which arose in reaction to the trend toward secularism in nineteenth-century French and English literature. His best known works are his two autobiographical novels, *Le désespéré* and *La femme pauvre (The Woman Who Was Poor)*, and the eight volumes of his journal, which recount the events of his personal and intellectual life in great detail. Possessed of a religious faith that was both devout and obsessive, Bloy felt compelled to write "only for God," and his works reflect this aim in their distinctly evangelical tone. He was also markedly intolerant of all that did not conform with his own beliefs, and his writings are rife with denunciations of his contemporaries. Bloy's popularity was severely limited during his lifetime by the often scatalogical quality of his prose, which offended many readers, but those who were not repelled by Bloy's invective found him to be a genuinely illuminating Christian writer, and he is often credited with the creation of the Catholic novel.

Born in Périgueux, in southwestern France, Bloy was the son of a civil servant and his wife, who was of Spanish descent. Bloy's father was an agnostic and left the religious training of his seven sons to their mother, who instructed them in the strict Catholic faith of her ancestors. Mystically inclined since early childhood, Bloy interpreted the fact that two children reported seeing an apparition of the Virgin Mary at La Salette only a few months after his birth as a divine indication that his life would be somehow linked to the mother of Christ in a special way. His childhood, however, showed no evidence of this link, being entirely prosaic and distinguished only by his rather unruly nature. Bloy left home at the age of seventeen, having completed only a few years of school, and traveled to Paris, where he hoped to study art. Instead, he spent several unhappy years working at various clerical jobs for which he was temperamentally unsuited and which provided insufficient income for tuition at the expensive Parisian art schools.

In 1869, a chance meeting with Jules Barbey d'Aurevilly, a prominent but somewhat disreputable Catholic novelist, changed Bloy's circumstances considerably. Barbey offered Bloy a position as his personal secretary and soon realized that the young man was a talented writer. Following Barbey's example, Bloy began to compose essays which dealt with questions of theology, but his doctrinal intransigence and unpleasant imagery made these unsuitable for the Catholic intellectual journals of the day, and they were routinely rejected. Although he attempted to intervene with editors on Bloy's behalf, Barbey's reputation as an author of scandalous works severely limited his influence. Throughout his career, Bloy earned very little money from his work, and while many critics believe that he consistently exaggerated accounts of his adversities in order to appear more pious, it is clear that he did indeed rely heavily on charity. Frequently, Bloy would demand contributions from friends and acquaintances only to repay their kindness with bitter recriminations, proudly calling himself "the ungrateful beggar." This aspect of Bloy's character has been the object of much attention: sympathetic critics have felt the need to

justify such apparently un-Christian behavior in a devout man, while detractors have treated it as a glaring fault.

Two events which occurred in 1877 proved crucial to Bloy's work. First, Bloy became acquainted with Abbé Tardif de Moidrey, whose biblical exegesis provided the basis for Bloy's own interpretation of the scriptures. Then, Bloy became emotionally involved with an impoverished young prostitute, Anne-Marie Roulé, and the bizarre events of their relationship inspired the writing of his first novel, *Le désespéré*. After Bloy persuaded Roulé to convert to Catholicism, she began to experience what they both believed to be visions in which the Second Coming was predicted. However, as Roulé became increasingly distracted by these episodes the conclusion that she had degenerated into psychosis was unavoidable, and she was institutionalized. Nevertheless, Bloy continued to believe that Roulé's visions had been divine revelations, often alluding in his writings to a great secret which had been entrusted to his keeping through the medium of Roulé.

In 1890 Bloy married the daughter of a Danish poet, and although the marriage was a happy one, the couple was perpetually in debt and both of their sons died in infancy. During this period Bloy's works, devoted to the glorification of God's name, went virtually unread. As he grew older, Bloy became convinced that God had ordained for him much suffering and possibly martyrdom. After the publication of *The Woman Who Was Poor*, a fictionalized account of the events of his marriage, Bloy abandoned the novel form altogether and confined his efforts to the clarification of his exegetical theories. He thus gained some repute as a theologian and attracted a small following of young Christian writers and thinkers. Two of these, Jacques and Raissa Maritain, became his constant companions, remaining with him long after his bitterness and ingratitude had alienated his other friends. Although Bloy was comforted by the presence of the Maritains, the fact that God had remained ostensibly callous to his suffering distressed him greatly to the end of his life.

Critics agree that an understanding of Bloy's unique theological views is essential to the correct interpretation of both his fiction and nonfiction works. From Abbé Tardif, Bloy learned to consider the scriptures not simply as religious teachings but as a paradigm which explained through symbols the operation of the will of God in all human events. Bloy took this supposition one step further. Assuming that the Bible itself could be considered a series of symbolic parables about the nature of the Holy Trinity, he maintained that all of human existence could thus be explained in terms of the interaction of the three figures described in Catholic doctrine as the Father, Son, and Holy Spirit. This heterodoxy forms the theoretical basis of Bloy's discussions of history and provides a major thematic element of his novels. In his long essay *La chevalière de la mort,* for example, Bloy considers Marie Antoinette a martyr and as such a manifestation of Christ. Similarly, in *Le sang du pauvre* Bloy equates the suffering of the poor with the suffering of the crucified Savior. While Bloy wrote many such essays, critics note that nowhere is his theory of history systematically or comprehensively applied, since he perceived his work as a matter of divine inspiration rather than as a scientific endeavor.

Bloy's novels are generally considered to be his best works. *Le désespéré,* however, is thought to be marred by the intense bitterness Bloy felt at the time of its composition, at least partially the result of Roulé's disagreeable fate. The novel contains many long passages devoted to the vilification of persons with whom Bloy had had some personal or professional difference, often awkwardly interposed into the narrative. Nevertheless, critics find this account of a man's extreme adversity compelling and admit that it occasionally attains the level of genius, though they find this genius more fully developed in Bloy's second novel, *The Woman Who Was Poor.* Depicting the existence of a woman who retains her faith and goodness despite astonishing trials, this novel has been called the "true expression of Bloy's inner voice." Bloy believed that the church had lost the power to instruct its members and that the duty had thus fallen to artists. *The Woman Who Was Poor,* then, presents a portrait of true Christian behavior to be taken as a model. Most critics, however, consider the real merit of this novel to be its powerful, elegant prose style and its sensitive portrayal of human anguish.

Critical opinion of Bloy's work is remarkably diverse. Many of the young writers who became his religious and literary disciples considered him a most pious Christian and the greatest of novelists. In addition, critics sympathetic to his religious views tend to esteem his work more highly than do those with other ontological approaches. Stanislas Fumet, an early biographer and devotee, called Bloy "the most astonishing writer of his time," and lamented that his critical reputation did not reflect his true greatness. Other critics, however, have been more moderate in their praise. Rayner Heppenstall acknowl-

edges the evocative power of Bloy's prose, but considers his theological opinions "intellectual chains" which prevented him from realizing his full potential as a writer. Nevertheless, critics agree that Bloy's novels display great talent and sensitivity despite their flaws, and they maintain that whether or not he actually influenced the work of later Catholic writers such as Paul Claudel and Charles Péguy, his creation of a body of work derived entirely from his deep religious convictions did indeed prepare the way for them.

PRINCIPAL WORKS

*Le révélateur du globe: Christophe Colomb et sa
    béatification future* (essays) 1884
Le désespéré (novel) 1886
La chevalière de la mort (history) 1891
Le salut par les Juifs (essays) 1892
Sueur de sang (short stories) 1893
Histoires désobligeantes (short stories) 1894
La femme pauvre (novel) 1897
    [*The Woman Who Was Poor,* 1939]
Le mendiant ingrat (journal) 1898
Exégèse des lieux communs (essays) 1902
Mon journal (journal) 1904
Quatre ans de captivité à Cochons-sur-Marne (journal)
    1905
Celle qui pleure (essays) 1908
    [*She Who Weeps,* 1956]
L'invendable (journal) 1909
Le sang du pauvre (essays) 1909
Le vieux de la montagne (journal) 1911
Le pèlerin de l'absolu (journal) 1914
Au seuil de l'Apocalypse (journal) 1916
La porte des humbles (journal) 1920
Lettres à sa fiancée (letters) 1922
    [*Letters to His Fiancee,* 1937]
Lettres à Véronique (letters) 1933
Léon Bloy: Pilgrim of the Absolute (letters, essays, journal
    entries, short story, and novel excerpts) 1947
Oeuvres complètes. 20 vols. (letters, essays, journals,
    short stories, and novels) 1947-49

ERNEST DIMNET (essay date 1924)

[Dimnet was a French Catholic priest and educator and a well-known literary critic. In the following excerpt, he discusses several aspects of Bloy's literary reputation.]

Léon Bloy, the so-called "last Catholic writer," certainly realized Catholicism as few people can do. He had a mystic soul, like Carlyle, whose intellectual disciple he was, and, like Carlyle again, he constantly interpreted history, especially the history of our own times, by moral or religious canons. He was less a believer than a seer, thinking of Christ and the saints as if he were actually living with them, and his spiritual life meant so little of an effort that it was irrepressible. Poverty and obscurity were no conditions of his peculiar saintliness, as they are frequently supposed to be. He did not relish them, and, like Barbey, would rather have talked as if he were a millionaire choosing to live in the humblest of lodgings up at Montmartre because his faith was his own and was as much his pride as his genius.

There was no display of humility in Léon Bloy, as there is none in Hilaire Belloc—who, however, sometimes reveals the true Christian's self-depreciation in touching, childlike traits. If you look at his pictures, two of which are by himself, and one is painted in highly romanticist and symbolical shark-oil, you will see at once that the man is in revolt against possible misapprehension, and has brought his superior intelligence to the realization of himself as well as of everything else. Nobody can withstand this capacity when it reaches a certain degree. We do not resist it in Léon Daudet, whose conceit is only saved from being called conceit by his talent. How could we resist it in a man like Léon Bloy, who was conscious of the mysterious uplifting of his inward revelation besides? This the visitors who constantly sought Léon Bloy in his two rooms felt in the very atmosphere of his ever disappointed, but never for one instant depressed, existence; and we his mere readers feel it in his books. Only four or five of them make a pretence of being objective, and their very titles—*Le Désespéré, La Femme Pauvre, Un Brelan d'Excommuniés*—belie the intention; the rest consist of Diaries—eight or nine volumes—and of letters in which Bloy endlessly talks of himself or abuses his enemies. Analyse the strange power of that oldest of old-fashioned novels, *Evelina,* and you will find that interest of the author in herself which lends immortal life to what would otherwise be poor literature.

Add to this another irrepressible realization, the realization of human inferiority which, at nineteen, drove Léon Bloy to a monastery—where he only stayed a week—as it has driven others to suicide. Bloy was a Catholic but he would not be blind. His great eyes were wide open on the shortcomings at which most religious people wink. No anti-religious writer has indulged in such bitter sarcasms at the expense of priests or of the Roman congregations. Even Zola could not have written the four untranslatable pages on the surgcon Esculape Nuptial—in **"L'Exégèse des Lieux Communs"**—but if he had he would have been regarded as an insulter of religion. Yet, analyse that story, constantly on the verge of grossness and more than once plunging into it, you will see nothing but hatred of that stupidity which engenders sin. Bloy was no Saint Francis; he was a Montmartre Dante so sure of his faith that he was never afraid of injuring it by descriptions which are a scandal to the weak and a delight to Homais the apothecary.

Conviction and imagination of such intensity inevitably produce literature. Bloy, the master of invective, the merciless painter of lowness, but the sincere Christian, the sight of whom ravished those who saw him in a church, was, in the multitudinous charm of his conversation, another Mallarmé. In his books he was, to say the least, another Huysmans, violent and gaudy, but irresistible. It is by this side that he appeals to the new school of writers—no matter how remote from any religious tendency—who call Anatole France "jujube," and want reality to be so nude that it will appear flayed. How long the tendency will last we cannot tell, but that it fills the literature of today is visible even in Salmon's "La Négresse du Sacré Coeur," and accounts for what would otherwise be incomprehensible: the glorification of a writer who was certainly not of the first order.

Ernest Dimnet, "The Work of Léon Bloy," in The Saturday Review, *London, Vol. 138, No. 3602, November 8, 1924, p. 468.*

FRANK HARRIS (essay date 1927)

[*Harris was a highly controversial English editor, critic, and biographer who is best known as the author of a maliciously* inaccurate biography of Oscar Wilde, a dubious life of Bernard Shaw, and a massive autobiography which portrays Edwardian life primarily as a background for Harris's near-Olympian sexual adventures. A man frequently referred to in colorfully insulting terms, he was by most accounts a remarkable liar and braggart, traits which deeply color the quality of his works and their critical reception. His greatest accomplishments were achieved as editor of the* Fortnightly Review *and the* Saturday Review of London. *As editor of the* Saturday Review *he helped launch the careers of Shaw and H. G. Wells, hiring them as drama critic and literary critic respectively, during the mid-1890s. Shaw later wrote that Harris "had no quality of editorship except the supreme one of knowing good work from bad, and not being afraid of it." Harris's fame as a critic rests primarily upon his five-volume* Contemporary Portraits (1915-30), *which contain essays marked by the author's characteristically vigorous style and patronizing tone. In the following excerpt from one of the portraits, Harris describes the bitterness manifested in Bloy's works.*]

How many people in France will remember Léon Bloy I wonder, though he died less than a decade ago? Yet he was a Parisian figure of the day and worthy of something more than a passing notice. He was certainly the most ill-conditioned and venomous writer of our time—perhaps, indeed, of any time; a man the very current of whose blood appeared to have been turned with the bile of envy, contempt and all uncharitableness.

Bloy had never a good word for any one and there were simply dozens of people whom he loathed and wrote about with a passion of disgust and disdain. His hatred ignored all differences of race and rank: now it was the Pope he turned upon and again his poor inoffensive maidservant; in one chapter he would curse his coal-merchant and his concierge, Madame Lebaudy, for the good she did, and M. François Coppée for the verses he wrote. Neither the rich nor the poor; neither good writers nor bad; neither politicians nor policemen could avoid his venom. Whatever son of Adam he met he hated and you could never tell whom he loathed most, Paul Bourget or his own Confessor.

For years Bourget was his pet target: he confessed willingly that he had gone to Bourget to borrow money and Bourget, a hard-working and not over rich man of letters, gave him a hundred francs or twenty dollars. That was enough for Bloy: in his next book he pilloried Bourget, tore his writings to pieces and his pretences to be considered a dandy and man of the world: "thirty-six pairs of boots he has," cried Bloy, "and fifty pairs of cunningly creased trousers, and not an original idea in his head, nor a good impulse in his dried-up liver." Then he went to work and showed that Bourget's "Essays on Psychology" were for the best part borrowed from his forerunners and that his novels were one and all jejune trite essays enlivened by scraps of amorous personal experience. Some of Bloy's analyses were fiendishly clever; many of his winged words stuck and burned like the barbed *banderilleras* of the bull-ring. For with all his bitterness and envy, Bloy was a real writer. His books were for the most part a sort of journal and not even the Goncourts could write a more interesting or effective diary.

"I fell today upon a new Confessor," he writes, "a painful and grotesque experience. Like every one else I've often met bad Confessors; but this one was execrable. Never have I been snapped up and tossed aside with such speed; I felt like a rat in a terrier's jaws. *In momento, in ictu oculi* he can break you the back of a sinner."

Like most of those who have learned Latin late in life, Bloy loved to quote it and particularly the Latin of the Roman Church.

"I was created," he writes somewhere, "for strife and suffering"; and the words painted him. Verily his hand was against every man and every man's hand against him.

All his life he suffered from dire poverty. In vain he wrote book after book: after he had twenty to his credit or discredit he could not count two thousand readers, and two thousand readers hardly pay for the bare cost of printing and binding an ordinary volume. So he had either to starve or to beg and men don't usually give much to a beggar even when he is a man of talent.

In spite of Bloy's bitterness, his life-story is of surpassing interest and makes one ask how long will it be before the State comes to the help of talent unappreciated by the general public? Bloy's biography can be given in his own words:

"I have lived without shame or fear," he writes, "in a solitude peopled only by hatreds, by the loathing and savage desire to tear and rend which the contempt of my contemporaries has engendered in me."

Bloy was a devout Catholic and so after venting his rage on all his fellows he turned upon God Himself: "Remember, O Lord," he cried once, "that I have had to pity you."

On another day we have this brief note: "No news yet from God." It would be laughable were it not sincere and therefore pitiable. He has prayed to God for help and has had no answer and so he writes:

"It is dishonour to promise and not keep one's word. The dishonour of God. Why, why should I be so whipped and scorned that I can't silence such evil thoughts?"

And finally the great painting phrase: "I pray like a beggar asking alms at the door of a farmhouse that he longs to set ablazing."

Twenty volumes filled with cries of suffering and hate and the tide of bitterness never ebbs; indeed, rises, rises steadily till it submerges the throne-room of the man's adoration. In one volume he tells how he goes to the sacristy to borrow five francs (a dollar) from the clergyman; the poor curate denies him. Forthwith Bloy writes down the bitter jibe: "Who lives by charity, has none." The seamstress he has ordered arrives late: Bloy puts down his injury to be published in his next book: "She sews and shall not reap." The proprietor of his room wants his rent, long overdue: Bloy pictures him to the life in a vitriolic page. His maid-of-all-work loses her temper and answers him back. Bloy sketches her—face and figure, mind and rags—for his readers' contempt. We thus learn, day by day, what he sees and says, reads and writes. And whatever he sees, irritates him, and whatever he says, he says with fury; what he reads is with disgust, and what he writes is to give pain. (pp. 216-19)

Frank Harris, "Hatred in Art: Léon Bloy," in his Latest Contemporary Portraits, *The Macaulay Company, 1927, pp. 215-20.*

JUSTIN O'BRIEN   (essay date 1939)

[*O'Brien is an American critic who has written extensively on modern French literature and has translated important works by André Gide, Albert Camus, and Paul Valéry. In the following excerpt, O'Brien praises* The Woman Who Was Poor.]

One of the most powerful Roman Catholic novels of our time is now first published in America some forty years after its appearance in France and twenty years after its remarkable author's death. Novel is hardly the proper term [for **The Woman Who Was Poor**] if one uses that word as a substantive; Léon Bloy himself calls it "a long digression on the evil of living" and insists that it should appeal only to those "who are insubordinate to the accepted canons, and claim rights of pasturage outside the fields marked out by the legislators of Fiction."

But there is a story here. Clotilde Maréchal's miraculous escape from poverty and surroundings of spiritual filth to idyllic happiness with her kindly benefactor Gacougnol and later with her husband, the fiery miniaturist Léopold, only to slip again into unspeakable torments which she bears in fortitude, thanks to her inner light, forms a stirring narrative. Though the characters are for the most part modeled on the author's friends, they remain abstractions, since Bloy, in his reaction against naturalism, was not interested in simulating life. Nevertheless, his pages abound in realistic descriptions whose violence and scatological imagery would honor Céline, such as the vituperation of the French national holiday's hysterical madness, the noisome description of the hovel in which Clotilde's only child dies, or the final thrust in the description of Clotilde's mother, whose bankrupt lover "would not at all have minded marketing his loving partner, but could not see his way to offering her services now, except as a mop for cleaning mortuary slabs in a leper hospital." Or take that definitive ticking-off of the man Poulot, former sheriff's officer:

> This good man was phlegmatic and heavy, with about as much joviality as a tapeworm in a chemist's shop. Still, when he had drunk a few glasses of absinthe, with his wife, as they soon learned, his high-boned cheeks would glow like a couple of lighthouses on a stormy sea. And then, from the center of a face whose tint oddly reminded one of a Tartar camel in the molting season, there jutted out a bugle of a nose whose tip, usually veined with purplish streaks, would at times display a sudden rosy hue and glow like an altar lamp.
>
> Beneath it there shrank from sight a weak, flaccid mouth, shaded with one of those bristly mustaches favored by certain bailiff's men, to give an air of military ferocity to the professional cowardice of their calling.
>
> There is little to be said about his eyes; at the best, their expression might be compared to that in the eyes of a sated seal, when it has gorged its fill and is giving itself up to the raptures of digestion.
>
> The whole man gave an impression of pusillanimous humility, accustomed to tremble before his wife, and so acclimatized to the background that he seemed to be casting his own shadow on himself.

But this is better than Céline, for Bloy's vitriolic violence of language has more point to it. In fact, only one French writer of today even approaches Léon Bloy in this respect, and he, too, is a Catholic—that is, Georges Bernanos, whose *Diary of My Times* recently appeared in English.

This "wrecker," as he called himself, also gave himself the title of "Pilgrim of the Absolute." From the depths of his own unspeakable poverty, Bloy often wrote like a madman to record his search for God. His disgust for lukewarmness of any kind, which he often found in his fellow-Catholics, was but the reflection of his thirst for the absolute and his constant passion for justice. "My wrath," he wrote, "is only the effervescence of my pity." Few men have felt a similar need to believe in both heaven and hell. Though never ceasing to assert that he wrote only for God, he deeply influenced many men, until he became known as a great converter. Among others, the philosopher Jacques Maritain and his wife and sister-in-law owe their conversions to Léon Bloy. Young intellectuals made pilgrimages to his cottage on the heights of Montmartre as they were later to address fervent letters to Paul Claudel in his oriental outposts.

The Woman Who Was Poor, which, with the tract entitled **"Salvation Through the Jews,"** is Bloy's masterpiece, cannot but have an invigorating effect upon its readers. Regardless of its qualities as a novel, its value as a spiritual essay, formed of numerous digressions, is very great. To apply to Bloy his dedication to the unworthy Octave Mirbeau of his violent indictment of Zola, one meets in these pages the vigorous personality of "the famous despiser of false art, false greatness and false goodness."

> *Justin O'Brien, "Escape from Evil," in* The New York Times Book Review, *June 4, 1939, p. 7.*

GRAHAM GREENE   (essay date 1939)

[*Greene, an English man of letters, is generally considered the most important contemporary Catholic novelist. In his major works, he explores the problems of spiritually and socially alienated individuals living in the corrupt and corrupting societies of the twentieth century. Formerly a book reviewer at the* Spectator, *Greene is also deemed an excellent film critic, a respected biographer, and a shrewd literary critic with a taste for the works of undeservedly neglected authors. In the following excerpt, Greene objects to the intense negativity of Bloy's prose.*]

It is a waste of time criticising Léon Bloy as a novelist: he hadn't the creative instinct—he was busy all the time being created himself, created by his own angers and hatreds and humiliations. Those who meet him first in this grotesque and ill-made novel [*The Woman Who Was Poor*] need go no further than the dedication to Brigand-Kaire, Ocean Captain, to feel the angry quality of his mind. "God keep you safe from fire and steel and contemporary literature and the malevolence of the evil dead." He was a religious man but without humility, a social reformer without disinterestedness, he hated the world as a saint might have done, but only because of what it did to him and not because of what it did to others. He never made the mistake by worldly standards of treating his enemies with tolerance—and in that he resembled the members of the literary cliques he most despised. Unlike his contemporary Péguy, he would never have risked damnation himself in order to save another soul, and though again and again we are surprised by sentences in his work of nobility or penetration, they are contradicted by the savage and selfish core of his intelligence. "I must stop now, my beloved," he wrote to his fiancée, "to go and suffer for another day"; he had prayed for suffering, and yet he never ceased to complain that he had been granted more of it than most men; it made him at the same time boastful and bitter.

He wrote in another letter:

> I am forty-three years old, and I have published some literary works of considerable importance. Even my enemies can see that I am a great artist. Also, I have suffered much for the truth, whereas I could have prostituted my pen, like so many others, and lived on the fat of the land. I have had plenty of opportunities, but I have not chosen to betray justice and I have preferred misery, obscurity and indescribable agony. It is obvious that these things ought to merit respect.

It is obvious too that these things would have been better claimed for him by others. It is the self-pity of this attitude, the luxurious bitterness that prevents Bloy from being more than an interesting eccentric of the Roman Catholic religion. He reminds us—in our own literature—a little of Patmore, and sometimes of Corvo. He is near Patmore in his brand of pious and uxorious sexuality which makes him describe the character of Clotilde, the heroine of this novel, as "chaste as a Visitationist Sister's rosary," and near Corvo in the furious zest with which he takes sides against his characters: "She bellowed, if the comparison may be permitted, like a cow that has been forgotten in a railway truck." Indeed the hatred he feels for the characters he has himself created (surely in itself a mark of limited imagination) leads him to pile on the violence to a comic extent—"a scandalous roar of cachinnation . . . like a bellowing of cattle from some goitred valley colonised by murderers."

No, one reads Bloy not for his characters, who are painted only deformity-deep, nor for his story—an unlikely tale of horrible suffering endured by a poor and saintly girl—but for the occasional flashes of his poetic sense, for images like: "upright souls are reserved for rectilinear torments"; for pas-

Bloy at 19.

sages with a nervous nightmare vision which reminds us of Rilke:

> A little middleclass township, with a pretension
> to the possession of gardens, such as are to be
> found in the quarters colonised by eccentrics,
> where murderous landlords hold out the bait of
> horticulture to trap those condemned to die.

We read him with pleasure to just the extent that we share the hatred of life which prevented him from being a novelist or a mystic of the first order (he might have taken as his motto Gauguin's great phrase—''Life being what it is, one dreams of revenge'') and because of a certain indestructible honesty and self-knowledge which in the long run always enabled him to turn his fury on himself, as when in one of his letters he recognises the presence of ''that bitch literature'' penetrating ''even the most *naïf* stirrings of my heart.''

> *Graham Greene, ''Man Made Angry,'' in* The Spectator, *Vol. 162, No. 5790, June 16, 1939, p. 1060.*

F. J. SHEED (essay date 1940)

[*An English author and critic, Sheed is best known as the founder of the publishing house of Sheed and Ward, which specialized in the dissemination of the works of such Catholic Revival authors as G. K. Chesterton and Hillaire Belloc. In the following excerpt, Sheed discusses* The Woman Who Was Poor *from a Christian point of view.*]

In the ordinary novel we read about people as mediocre and anaemic as ourselves: in fact any given character might be oneself crawling across the page. After such reading, Léon Bloy's novel **The Woman Who Was Poor** crashes in our ears like an explosion: we seem to be watching not men but monsters. But the ghastly thing is that here too the people are ourselves—as Bloy sees us.

The truth is that Bloy sees life life-size. We habitually do not. As we look at the surface of human action, or an inch or two below, our vices and other people's look commonplace enough, merely a ruffling of the surface. Lust, for instance, has a pretty wide range: superficially it means no more than a nice little man getting nice little thrills or a nasty little man getting nasty little thrills. But there's nothing ''little'' about what is really happening in the bottom of the soul—the continuing strife between nothingness and Omnipotence. So Bloy sees it. His people are like planets and comets and dead suns and this is no exaggeration since an immortal soul dowered with knowledge and will is immeasurably more magnificent in itself and more catastrophic in its ruin than any planet. We are prepared to concede this as a fact but think no more about it. Bloy could never stop seeing it, or see it tranquilly.

Therefore his villains particularly seem monstrous. He makes us see the very maggots writhing in them—Poulot and his mistress, Isidore Chapuis and his—she looked like ''a mop for cleaning mortuary slabs in a leper hospital.'' But what he calls ''respectable people'' are even more horrifying—perhaps because their resemblance to ourselves is more easily seen. Gacougnol's heir, and the agent who passed Leopold and Clotilde's premises as sanitary, and the daily-Mass-going landlady grinding her tenants—all these would probably have looked normal enough to us if we had met them in the flesh. But here we meet them in the spirit and for the moment we understand the ''delicious sensation'' Bloy felt that day in 1897 when so many rich Catholics were burnt to death in the fire that broke out at a charity bazaar.

But with that we touch our finger on his one great weakness. He did not quite see that even mediocre people, even utterly depraved people—even Isidore Chapuis—are loved by God. Chapuis and Ballot and the rest do not repent: one almost feels that Bloy would have been disappointed if they had. ''I should be ashamed to treat a mangy dog as God treats me,'' Bloy once cried. And that is exactly how he treats Chapuis. Yet if the one sorrow is not to be a saint (as Clotilde says at the end), then Chapuis is the most sorrowful thing in the book—far more so than Clotilde herself.

But this is a reflection that comes afterwards. While we are reading the most moving story of Clotilde Maréchal, we live in Bloy's world and judge with his judgments. To have read the book is ''a revelation, like coming out of the void.'' For good or ill, Bloy had to write **The Woman Who Was Poor**. A critic has said that Bloy's words were like lava, and nobody blames a volcano for hurling its lava off its own racked chest. So Bloy wrote his novel: and it is a marvel to us that he ever slept quietly with all that monstrous life inside him; and indeed there is no reason to think that he ever did sleep very quietly either before or after writing it.

In Europe **The Woman Who Was Poor** has had a most profound influence on all writing throughout this century. In England and the United States the book started more quietly—after all it was different, and that is an awful handicap: if novels aren't all exactly alike, where are we? But if it started quietly it will not die quickly. I think religious novels in the English language will begin to show some effect of Bloy. (pp. 61-3)

> *F. J. Sheed, ''Léon Bloy,'' in his* Sidelights on the Catholic Revival, *Sheed & Ward, 1940, pp. 61-3.*

ALBERT BÉGUIN (essay date 1944)

[*In the following excerpt from an essay originally published in France in 1944, Béguin discusses how Bloy's literary intentions are exemplified in his statement that the true value of art is its function as a ''confession of faith, prayer, and truth.''*]

A mind directed towards the Absolute and piercing all its veils, a soul living in the expectation of Divine Justice and yearning for it even more than for Mercy, such was the vocation peculiar to Léon Bloy. And that is the source of the mystery which shrouds his being.

What he himself said of **Le Salut par les Juifs** could be applied to his work as a whole: rather than a book, it is ''the outline of a book.'' Bloy *was unable* to say everything, for, in lighting up the depths, he recovered a view of things which human thought had lost for centuries. After the Fathers of the Church, and the simple believers at the full tide of the Middle Ages, there was no one who still had the secret of grasping reality without splitting it up into compartments; no one with the type of understanding that sees things only in relation to the whole of what is, was and will be. The modern mind, since the Renaissance, and even since the last phase of the Middle Ages, has turned away from that contemplation which, while embracing a whole system, is organised round a single centre—the only possible centre being the Redemption. Bloy goes back to a universe comparable to that of early Christendom, and this is what makes him obscure to us, who are only the first generation of his readers. We may take it that he is inaugurating a perfect and salutary renewal of our powers of vision, and the process will hardly be completed without the compulsion of events, when the bankruptcy of our errant civilisation at last becomes so glaring that our eyes are violently opened. Such a spiritual revolution could only be roughed out by the painful labours of the Pilgrim of the Absolute. It will probably take his successors centuries to finish off the cure begun by this oculist of the soul, whose purpose was nothing less than to make it natural for us to see the invisible world.

"I have always said the same thing," he wrote at the end of his life. In this single thing, repeated under a great variety of figures and images, lies the essential clue to the strangely anachronistic sayings of this man who was "dazzled by the Face of God." Pascal—for whom Bloy had no love, but to whom it is permissible to compare him in spiritual stature— said that "every writer has a meaning to which all the conflicting passages of his work ultimately go back." In Bloy's case we are on the track of this meaning as soon as we realise how he harped upon the overwhelming discovery with which he was favoured in early maturity; that, having entered upon the contemplative life through suffering, he loved it and asked for it, not through a romantic cult of sorrow but because he saw in human torments an echo of the agony of Jesus Christ, "crucified until the end of the world" and tortured by the delays to which man's obstinate refusal subjects the coming of the Kingdom of God; and that, for this reason, every increase of horror meant for him that God was at hand, that this was the beginning of the great tribulation which should precede the final kindling of souls by the Holy Ghost, and the fulfilment of time. Bloy lived like the Church herself—*expectans expectavi*—waiting for that to happen which should put an end to all happenings. And he was unable to curb his great anger against everything which, by postponing the hour of his hopes, prolonged the sufferings inflicted by men upon their Redeemer. "The angers which burst from me are but the very faint echoes of a Curse from on high, which I have the surprising misfortune to reverberate," he wrote one day. And in a letter dated 1905 he added this profound definition of himself:

> You think that in me religious feeling is a special form of rebellion. It is just the opposite. Mad as this may seem to you, I am by nature obedient and tender-hearted. That is why I write ruthlessly, having to defend Truth and bear witness to the God of the poor. That's all. My most vehement pages were written by love, often with tears of love, in hours of unutterable peace.

This prophet was a poet. But a poet who, more than most, was conscious of the inadequacy of earthly beauty. "In our fallen state, Beauty is a monster," he writes. He knew that human words are inadequate and only serve to note the existence of the ineffable. This comment of his with reference to the Scriptures may also be applied to poetic language: words, in their diversity, all have the same substance, which defies human expression; they are "iridescent veils before the same tabernacle." Hence his exertion as a writer painfully conscious of the insurmountable gap between what he expressed and what he wished to express, namely "the sight of God"; he knew well enough that man has lost it, and yet he could not do otherwise than strain after it with all his heart. This accounts for the difficulties of his toil, and the disappointment which he often admitted, as, for instance, in a letter dated 14th April 1886 to Louis Montchal:

I never manage to put my soul into what I write, and I have an ideal of love, of life and of eloquence which only serves to reduce me to despair, since it is inaccessible.... I am condemned to this stupid trade of writing, which is certainly not my true vocation. I was born a warrior, a crusader if you like, in an age when war is dishonoured and crusades are impossible.... If by some miracle I became rich, I should drop literature and make myself the servant of the poor. I should find it much more beautiful and useful to have a leper, whose sores I was clumsily dressing, spit in my face, than to devote my time to the inept pursuit of adjectives and participles....

Nevertheless, great writer that he was, with his inexhaustible vocabulary, the cadence of his sentences, the patristic Latinity of his eloquence, and the profoundness of his imagery, Bloy had to find a justification for his art: "It is indispensable that Truth should appear in Glory. Splendour of style is not a luxury, it is a necessity." His great longing called down the Glory of God upon earth, and his need for verbal invention matches his need to detect the presence of mystery, not in order to say what it is but to say where it dwells—which is everywhere. His studies in symbolical exegesis (as a follower of Abbé Tardif de Moidrey and a forerunner of the great commentaries of Claudel) had taught him the multiple significance of words and the allusive value of symbols. Looking below the surface, he set out to discover what each thing typified and what place it occupied in the plan of God; to fit it into the endless succession of analogies which forms the secret fabric of the created world and extends mysteriously into the invisible.

Thus, painfully tracing through a thousand forms "the history of the Three Persons of the Trinity"; continually recounting the Passion; eternally impatient for the final Descent from the Cross, which, in the temporal world, will dispel the desolation of man and set a term to the unfathomable "conflicts of Mercy with Justice"; Bloy, at whose every step mysteries increase and multiply, opens for our contemplation *abysses*—his favourite word—not of darkness but of dazzling light. They can be reached only by ceaselessly dispersing the false brightness of a superficial understanding. Where everything seemed simple, Bloy makes us aware that everything is incomprehensible and forces us to marvel.

Thus nothing could be further from the truth than to suspect that a personal lack of balance lay at the root of this continual "disarticulation" of appearances, which was Bloy's way of arousing stupefaction and bringing out the hidden lineaments of the real. There was never a mind more sturdily balanced than this vigorous intellect which turned the disruption of accepted stabilities into a method of thought and a demand for attention. (pp. 7-11)

> *Albert Béguin, in an introduction to his* Léon Bloy: A Study in Impatience, *translated by Edith M. Riley, Sheed & Ward, 1947, pp. 1-12.*

SISTER MARY ROSALIE BRADY   (essay date 1945)

[In the following excerpt, Brady examines Bloy's themes and style.]

Léon Bloy [is] considered by many as an outstanding representative of the period preceding the modern Catholic literary revival. Although standing on the horizon of a new era, Bloy showed certain characteristics which mark him as a figure in the waning literary period known as Naturalism. Despite the "Catholic flavor" pervading his ideas, there is an ever present naturalistic constituent. No serious writer can avoid reflecting in some manner the peculiarities of thought which characterize an epoch; therefore it was impossible for Bloy to have escaped such influences. Besides by his detailed definition of naturalism he indorsed the idea that an author has the duty to spare no means that will render things more "real" in the most naïve sense of the word.

Moreover, Bloy's temperament provided a background suitable for the acceptance of naturalistic principles. An early developed hatred of society, a melancholy bordering on despair, an unbridled sensuality which did not hinder his apostolic zeal, but certainly affected, at least in a negative sense, his mystical aspirations, are factors extremely enlightening to the understanding of his complex personality.

While stressing sanctity as the only possible goal for a Christian, he did not underestimate one of God's most gracious gifts to man, freedom of will. God does not compel a man to become a saint but He manifests His desire of man's sanctification by bestowing indirect means that will further this end. Sorrow and suffering, if willingly accepted in union with Christ, have this tremendous sanctifying power. Bloy however would have them precipitate the soul into an abyss of perfect love without even the intermediate state of penitence. Suffering, conceived not as a selfish concern, but one to be gratuitously shared with others by making an oblation of it in their behalf, compelled Bloy, in a sense, to become a victim soul without the necessary spiritual maturity. Theoretically, he well understood the problem of suffering. He could not sanction the attempt to abolish suffering as a solution to all problems. In Bloy's estimation such a step would but reduce civilization to a society of swine. But his eulogy of suffering at times becomes unbearable as for example when he even regrets the lack of suffering in Paradise. A generally morbid outlook causes him to hover between saintliness and pathology as is evidenced in his inability to participate in the liturgical joy of the Church in the celebration of her feasts.

Bloy showed how poverty, a specific form of suffering, is to be borne. Never tolerating half measures he thought one must be miserably poor to be numbered among the elect. Begging in imitation of the saints, and of God Himself, was the degree of poverty he recommended and tried to live. Yet his mendicancy evolves into a kind of beggar radicalism which seems unaware not only of the Church's position in discrediting even the zeal of religious orders that depended solely on alms, but also of the most elementary condition of life in an economically organized world. His annoyance at the formality of expressing gratitude and his constant appeal for relief from others caused him to be known as an "ungrateful beggar," a title his diary records prove at times correct. His interpretation of the role of money as synonymous with Christ's Blood and as an absolute proof of friendship led him to some analogies that are manifestly fantastic. Emphasizing poverty as a hallowed condition, he could not consistently tolerate the rich, who by the very fact of their wealth cause the suffering of others. As a nation, Americans were especially hated because of the capitalistic economy of their country which favors the accumulation of wealth by individuals. His "holy hatred" divorces itself from charity when he gloats over the sinking of a vessel and the burning of a theater, simply because wealthy proprietors were among the victims. Yet when his vehemence was challenged as implying an exclusion from salvation of all except the miserably poor, he responded magnanimously and in a truly Catholic spirit that such a stand was impossible since Christ came not for any particular class of society but for souls.

Besides the universal advantages for sanctity afforded by suffering and poverty, each man by his specific vocation is appointed to accomplish a certain mission that will further his personal salvation. In this sense, Bloy felt he had an extraordinary talent for writing, in spite of the accusation of pride that would be alleged against him for his constant preoccupation with his own gifts. Having adopted the most rigid principle of justice, he set out as an author with an apostolic mission, to right wrongs, but encountered difficulties as a layman. Religious life had been considered as a vocation best suited to further his ends. Because of the penetrating character analysis of a retreat master, his own discomfort, at cloistral confinement and the tedium of peace experienced there, he had to abandon the plan.

To let an injustice pass by without striking out boldly against it was sheer cowardice in his opinion. Since most of his own suffering was caused by the "conspiracy of silence" that he thought maliciously planned to crush his attempt at writing, it was not silence which he meted out to his contemporaries. Those responsible for his misfortune and the injustice of discrediting his charismatic claims, the Catholic laity and clergy, were not spared his biting denunciation. But besides a defensive attitude he assumed the position of coadjutor in the spreading of Catholicism since so many converts were gained to the Church by the reading of his books. Yet Bloy remains an enigma because of his antithetical pride-humility complex and the shrouding of his task in mystery. If Bloy may claim any genius it is in the realm of faith. His own sincerity was so convincing that converts were willing to go the whole way with this "pilgrim of the absolute," as he preferred to name himself. It must be acknowledged that few writers have exercised the same influence on the intelligentsia in search for truth. The ability to transform his readers, to impose on them new habits of thought and to recreate their moral and intellectual life gives him a definite place in Catholic culture and literature in general.

Bloy's greatest "bête noire" was the bourgeois class which symbolized mediocrity, by its standard of living. Their use of hackneyed expressions attributed in part to intellectual poverty but more especially to cowardice prompted them to reject the more rigorous teachings of the gospel. Mediocrity which condoned a spirit of compromise was worse than sin to his eyes. The most appalling thing about this insidious vice was that it claimed among its advocates Catholic laity and clergy alike. Their yielding to the line of least resistance and their more lenient interpretation of the Bible were attitudes incompatible to his ideal of sanctity which called for an ever ready enthusiasm and heroism.

In defending the decree of Pius X on the benefits of daily and of children's Communion, Bloy is magnificent and of the advance guard. However in presenting only opposition on the part of the clergy, he fails to mention the stand of thousands of others, who, like himself, welcomed the decree enthusiastically. Bloy's assaults on society, in general, arise from the fact that, his vision dazzled as it is by medieval splendor, can not but be blind to the good of his own age. One great stumbling block is that Bloy the visionary speaks too often in historical terms without sufficient historical foundation. His conception of the complete sinfulness of the present is no less distorted than his fulsome praise of everything medieval. Old France represented chivalry and Catholicism and embraced epochs in which the bourgeois had not as yet assumed an attitude of equality. Beyond cultural aims Bloy argues that his condemnation of the class is occasioned by its absorption in material prosperity which of itself precludes heroism, the basis of sanctity. The excuse, that a merciful God is "not so demanding with His creatures," a typical bourgeois retort, aroused his anger to white hot heat and occasioned a volley of denunciatory remarks.

Interest in historic study fired his ambitious project of writing a universal history. The design being too gigantic, he was forced to transfer his interest to a less extravagant endeavor. As Bloy lived for heroes and hero worship, he was better equipped to study a century through a representative personage of the epoch. His philosophy of history rested on a Providential basis. Just as each individual had his special mission so did each nation play a certain role in the profound Providence of God's plan. As a Frenchman, Bloy was so concerned especially with his own country, that he emphatically declared, "necessary to God," despite her religious infidelities. Quite consistently then, every nation had a lesser role in comparison with that of France and necessarily shared in his "sacred hatred," since they jeopardized her progress. But for all his historical theories, he can not be taken seriously because of his rejection of documentation. His view is rather that of a Romantic, for his political and national bias prevents the utterance of any poised judgment.

Parallel to his definite views on Providence, interpreted arbitrarily, is his intense Marial piety. Our Lady of La Salette, a Mother in tears, was his almost exclusive concept of the Virgin. Since the apparition had made so definite an impression on his intellectual as well as on his religious life, it is easily understood why he stresses only the sorrowful aspects of Mary's life. Yet his own morbid seeking of unhappiness and suffering leaves suspect his otherwise devotional attitude regarding Mary. Envy, so to speak, at the popularity of Our Lady of Lourdes, in contrast to the inattention to the message of Our Lady of La Salette, led him to see ecclesiastical politics as the root of the trouble. Chaotic conditions in the world were moreover traceable to the inattention accorded to the message of La Salette and to the anti-Semitic current prevalent at the time. In spite of his premise, that the Jews were God's chosen people with an inherent claim to sanctity, he offers only an enigmatic interpretation of the Jewish question.

Bloy's devotion to the saints, their relics, the reception of the sacraments, for the most part, is expressed in sound Catholic terminology. His blunders stem from his habit of indulging in philosophical and theological speculations for which he was untrained. But the genuineness of his love for things Catholic cannot be denied regardless of the naturalistic language which he justifies as perfectly admissible for expressing spiritual concepts and experiences.

Bloy's ideas on sanctity, suffering, genius, poverty, mediocrity and Providence took more artistic form in his two novels by the leitmotifs he employed. As he expressed himself in the literary style of so many of his contemporaries, it is through the mouthpiece of his characters that we are made aware of his naturalistic Catholicism. But just because his autobiographical novels alone would overstress Bloy's naturalism, those studies which approach novelistic treatment have been included so that his noble and heroic qualities might not be obscured. The naturalistic literary motifs of a psychological nature prove

to be neurotic possessions of an emotionally unbalanced personality. His preoccupation with reminiscences and confidences of an almost sacramental nature shows that these devices were often employed for their autotherapeutical value. How justifiable he imagined his naturalistic approach to Catholic problems is indicated by the theoretical admission of a poor literary principle that a book is only immoral if it fails to treat religious subjects.

As a result of such a close combination of the spiritual and the carnal it is easy to see how this type of thinking is necessarily reflected in the language. The staggering Catholic vocabulary, unintelligible to non-Catholics and inadmissible to Catholics because of its lack of spiritual refinement, is balanced by an inexhaustible fund of naturalistic terms used literally and figuratively according to his need, a need arising from a dependence on a natural coarseness to give full vigor to his thoughts. While one must reject such vulgarity either from a cultural or aesthetic point of view, such a condition still seems less reprehensible than Catholic terminology for the most materialistic objects and vice versa the most disgusting realistic terms to describe spiritual experiences and Catholic conceptions. Furthermore, almost by language alone, is it proved that Bloy's Catholicism, radical and ready to sacrifice, apostolic and zealous, has nevertheless the still vulgar quality of feeling at home in a common naturalistic sentiment and speech as well as in a popular "miraculous" atmosphere.

Bloy disclosed his particular alliance with the literary movement of his day by the impressionistic side of his style. In his novels, a "genre" for which he displayed no native genius, certain characteristics of this particular literary style are pronounced. A decided fondness for the periodic sentence, the relegating of the verb to an unimportant position, the preponderance of nominal elements, abstracts in preference to adjectival forms, the unconventional position of the adjective, nuances obtained by a tentative gradation of increasingly exact words: these are the features of a conscious striving to impress his readers. Absorbed as he was with his own experiences and impressions, he was incapable of producing anything more than an autobiography. With a very sound instinct for style, he set himself almost at the outset of his career to describe intimately and faithfully the crudest things of life, the most remote one would expect from his own taste so avowedly Catholic, but which at the time were esteemed "real" and "natural." Besides the impetus of the moment there was as well in Bloy, probably as a result of his past experiences, a highly developed affinity for groveling in vulgarity. His style, ingenious, complicated, full of shades and of research, borrows from all vocabularies, takes colors from all palettes and notes from all keyboards, but particularly from the plebeian and pathological one. A struggle to render what is most inexpressible in thought, what is vague and most elusive in the outline of form, and a striving to translate the subtle confidence of neurosis, the dying confessions of passions grown depraved from the strange hallucinations of the obsession, cause his naturalistic style to be necessarily impressionistic. In other words Bloy was intensely preoccupied with expressing those visible aspects of things which the art of design can express but which before 1860 were prohibited to the art of speech. Therefore the sometimes tortured elaboration of his style is chiefly due to his perpetual effort to squeeze tones and colors from this foreign medium. A reader of Bloy is conscious of his general hyperaesthesia, or his general alertness to the onrush of sensations which might justly be termed morbid if they were not so completely intellectualized. Not only is the sense of vision marked in Bloy but his hearing also is acute. One is puzzled as to whether the poet or the painter predominates. His deliberate attempts with odors reflect another especially naturalistic leaning. Bloy is at once the ultra-modern child of a decadent civilization and the victim of nostalgia for ascetic medievalism. Therefore, his originality springs from the fact that to him such counter tendencies are not opposed, but on the contrary harmonious, as they were in many similar Catholic types of the Baroque Age. In descriptions of persons there is a pronounced flair for the voluptuous notwithstanding the unctuous oil of the spiritual that flows from time to time, for the purpose of calming the waves of sensuality.

A nature as powerful and passionate as that of the Tertullian-like Bloy could not submit entirely to the formalities of any accepted style regardless of the taste of the period. Although it proves beyond doubt that he had availed himself of the same literary devices as his fellow writers, he was not a type who could long be fettered by restraints. Rather did he discard any ornaments which cramped his true style, that of the pamphleteer. One feels immediately the power of his ''speech style''— a style which is animated, sanguine and magnetic. Ever concerned with style and with himself, Bloy analyzed his own stylistic qualities. His analysis, penetrating and at least in this instance indisputable, discovered his writing to have the following constituents: barbaric strokes, violence of color, whirling insistence, obstinate revolutions on cruel similes. Nor is it surprising that a man with unrestrained vulgarity and at the same time militant Catholic ideas should employ a vigorous style. Constantly at war with the present world and its institutions, simply because he failed to sympathize with men and society, Bloy necessarily resorted to bitterness in delivering his message. While at times he is an original thinker, the truth or beauty of the thought is tortured by an irresponsible, inflexible, self-opinionated firmness maintained to the point of sheer obstinacy; logic is pressed to the point of fallacy, imagination and ardor border sometimes on rapture, but more often on madness.

Every critic acknowledges his mastery in irony. By the sarcastic aping of Catholic language, paradoxical insistence, hammering repetitions and permutations, anaphora and word echoes, positive tone adverbs, superlatives, amassing of nouns and adjectives, his principles were forcefully voiced. Yet for all his vehemence, when he reduces his insistence and exaggeration to a consciously controlled degree, he brings to the fore also rhythmical and euphonic tendencies. There is at times such a poetic quality to his style that some readers are captivated to the extent of forgetting that this self-controlled style, in proportion to the whole, is as rare in Bloy as are his normal Catholic ideas uttered in a subdued and poised tone. Emotional and doctrinal exaggeration expressed with naturalistic roughness, and a sentimental vocabulary and imagery, far outweigh his passages of a ''remembering in tranquillity'' composure. (pp. 220-28)

> *Sister Mary Rosalie Brady, in her* Thought and Style in the Works of Léon Bloy, *1945. Reprint by AMS Press, 1969, 242 p.*

RAYNER HEPPENSTALL   (essay date 1947)

[*Heppenstall was an English novelist, critic, and autobiographer who wrote extensively of his experiences with such literary figures as George Orwell and Dylan Thomas. As a literary theorist, he is closely allied with the philosophy of the nouveau roman (New Novel). Heppenstall's later novels demonstrate his allegiance to this school, and he has written perceptively on New Novelists Alain Robbe-Grillet, Michel Butor, and Nathalie Sarraute. Heppenstall has been widely praised for the philosophical and theoretical complexity of his literary criticism. In the following excerpt, he discusses Bloy's novels and examines the relationship of Bloy's religious beliefs to orthodox Christian tenets.*]

The French Catholic novel of to-day was initiated single-handed by Léon Bloy. This will of itself perhaps explain Bloy's own rather exiguous and frequently confused achievement in the form. For he wrote but two novels, and as a novel neither of them is fully satisfying. Yet it is as a novelist that he should be regarded, because of the trend of his influence and because his writing outside the form of the novel also has a narrative and dramatic rather than an ideological movement. (p. 15)

Le Désespéré . . . has at least one of the technical virtues of a good novel. Its themes are unambiguously present on the first page. There is no prolonged clearing of the throat. The novel opens with the hero, Caïn Marchenoir (Bloy himself), writing a letter to Alexis Dulaurier (Bourget? Huysmans?) to ask for money with which to bury his father who is just about to die of horror at his son's violent and improvident ways. "I am writing to you," says Marchenoir, "because a soul given over to its own nothingness is without other recourse than to the futile literary gymnastic feat of formulating that nothingness." What did Marchenoir *père* represent? Mediocrity. Is Dulaurier the constant friend of Marchenoir's misery? No. Marchenoir despises him. His reason for writing to Dulaurier is that Dulaurier has a lot of money which he does not deserve. Marchenoir-Bloy characterised himself elsewhere (it is the title of one of his eight diaries) as "the ungrateful beggar." Part One of *Le Désespéré* proceeds to the narration of Dulaurier's successful but unedifying literary career and his condescending ill-treatment of Marchenoir. Follows a retrospective account of Marchenoir's early life, his sudden conversion . . . , his struggles to gain a footing in the post-war literary world, a series of extremely unattractive love-affairs and the discovery of Véronique. Marchenoir *père* dies and is buried at Périgueux. His son receives money from a devoted friend, an engraver, Leverdier, and goes to the Grande Chartreuse to make a retreat.

This narrative follows Bloy's own life-story closely. Born in 1846 and a pauper for the greater part of his life, Bloy was in fact the recipient of some form of mystical illumination in the night watches during the war of 1870. (p. 16)

The Véronique of real life was called Anne-Marie Roulet. Like the Véronique of the novel (though with less domestic and financial excuse), she was a prostitute. Under the influence of Bloy, she began to exhibit symptoms of sanctity and illumination and recounted to Bloy visions and prophecies which underlie a great deal of his work. In the end, she went mad. She was Bloy's mistress for a time. The most heroic moral feat of Bloy's life was the breaking of sexual relationship with Anne-Marie Roulet while maintaining the closest religious and spiritual (or psychological) intimacy with her. In the novel, Marchenoir contrives to redeem Véronique without sleeping with her. It is too easy. Véronique falls in love with Marchenoir. He converts by denying her. This is reminiscent of the cut-and-dried psychology of Paul Bourget, of which Bloy was frequently contemptuous. The truth was in this case more interesting. In Part One of *Le Désespéré,* there is no sufficient conflict.

Part Two covers the period of a religious retreat at the Grande Chartreuse. Letters are exchanged between Marchenoir and Véronique which indicate that Marchenoir, having established

Barbey d'Aurevilly.

his lack of a vocation for the religious life, is falling in love with Véronique, but that the process torments him.

Upon his return to Paris, in Part Three, Marchenoir is confronted with one of the most ludicrous and shocking situations in world-fiction. Leverdier relates to his friend how Véronique, in order to prevent Marchenoir falling in love with her, has cut off her hair (which hung to her knees), has sold the hair (to a taxidermist?) and, with the proceeds, has gone to a Jew of doubtful occupation and paid him to pull out all her teeth. "*A cet énoncé inouï, Marchenoir tourna sur luimême et, s'éloignant obliquement, à la façon d'un aliéné, les deux bras croisés sur sa tête, se mit à exhaler des rauquements horribles*" ["At this extraordinary statement, Marchenoir turned inward and, drawing aside, in the manner of a madman, both arms crossed over his head, began to emit horrible, hoarse cries."] And well he might. Bloy's refusal to present his sainted harlot as she was has involved him in the most dreadful plight, coupled as it is with a serious lack of humour. Véronique in the novel is not mad (she becomes so quite unexpectedly in the last few pages), yet she does what could only not be ludicrous in a mad woman. Of the real Anne-Marie Roulet, just before she became really high, the incident of the teeth could have been recounted and would have seemed credible. In Véronique, it is presented by Bloy as a further symptom of great character, perhaps indeed as a direct result of the influx of supernatural grace (and let us remember that Bloy was forty years old when

he wrote *Le Désespéré*). But of this extraordinary silliness in Bloy, we shall find other, though less glaring, instances.

The extraction of Véronique's teeth solves none of Marchenoir's problems. It enables him to rail further at the mediocrity of priests, one of whom, Véronique's director, ticks her off severely, failing to appreciate the sublimity of her action. But in the end Marchenoir concludes that Véronique, without teeth and hair, is not less, but more, beautiful. He becomes increasingly amorous of her, and yet the two continue to inhabit the same apartment in the same odd condition of *concubinage céleste* ["divine concubinage"]. Working at his book on the divine symbolism of history one night, Marchenoir loses control of himself and staggers, with endless *grincements* and panting, to Véronique's door, only to find that she has been praying all night. This cools him off. When Véronique does in the end go mad, Marchenoir is run over on the way back from the asylum. The novel concludes, as it began, with a letter, this time to Leverdier, the constant friend, who is in the country. Marchenoir dies without priest. He dies, like his father, of mediocrity, but of other people's mediocrity and not his own. He also dies of poverty, the superlative crime.

I have tried in this summary neither to simplify facetiously nor to extenuate the naïveté and clumsiness of *Le Désespéré*. What cannot be made plain in a summary is how little the quality of the book depends upon its plot. It is the flow of metaphysical fantasy which keeps the book going. The incidents hold it up. (pp. 17-19)

The passages in *Le Désespéré* which are of unquestionable excellence are certain descriptions of the Grande Chartreuse, the account of Marchenoir's (Bloy's own) conversion and some briefer dogmatic-exegetical rhapsodies on Christ the Poor Man, the central figure in Bloy's general mythology.

The prose at its best is magnificent. In its colour and its rhetorical weight, it is un-French. In its dependence upon epithet it is wholly French. Bloy characterises his own writing in that of Marchenoir and speaks of "*la violente couleur de l'ecrivain, sa barbarie cauteleuse et alambiquée*" ["the violent opinion of the writer, his cunning and subtle barbarity"]. . . . (p. 19)

The Woman who was Poor . . . is shorter, less purely autobiographical, less unrelievedly gloomy and more skilful than *Le Désespéré*. Its digressions are more pertinent and at the same time more quotable. The first part of the book displays even a sense of humour, and a moral situation of the kind later developed by François Mauriac is clearly present. Marchenoir, who died at the end of *Le Désespéré*, reappears (and dies again) in *The Woman who was Poor,* but he is not the central figure. His place is taken by a new avatar of Anne-Marie Roulet, this time given the name of Clotilde Maréchal. Only at the beginning of the book is she placed in a setting resembling that of the real-life Anne-Marie. She does not go mad. She does not live in *concubinage céleste* with Marchenoir. On the contrary, she marries a friend of Marchenoir, a book-illustrator and man of action, Léopold (Bloy himself had begun his career as an illuminator). It is as though Bloy, himself now married to Jeanne Molbech, daughter of a Danish poet, in a sunnier phase of his own life, were reviving Anne-Marie in order to enquire how she would have fared if she had known men less bitterly uncompromising than himself and if she had had a chance of happiness. At the same time, extreme poverty is still the climate, and there is still a good deal of railing (but in a more detached and satirical vein) against the successful literary figures of the time. (pp. 20-1)

Except for a few months after committing Anne Marie Roulet to the lunatic asylum, Léon Bloy made communion every day of his adult life. Since there were periods during which he took scarcely any other food, he may be said literally to have lived upon the wafer and the wine which are regarded by Catholics as substantial body and blood of Christ. This is, I believe, regarded as a religious excess. But everything in Bloy is excess. If "exuberance is beauty" and "the road of excess leads to the palace of wisdom," Bloy should have been, in Blake's sense, a superlative artist and superlatively wise.

It would be fatally easy to regard Bloy from the standpoint of the psychologist. This has in fact been done by Ernest Seillière, who argues that Bloy's whole life and work were an enormous structure of megalomania. Seillière points to the claims made by Bloy to have received (*via* Anne-Marie) a specific revelation, known only to himself, and to have been marked out for a leading rôle in the new scheme of salvation, which involved some form of Second Coming. Bloy, according to Seillière, first sought to ally and later to identify himself with God, he and Jesus Christ constituting one embodiment of *le Pauvre*. The answer to this is very simple. It is that, despite enormous deprivations, Bloy lived to the age of seventy-one in full possession of his faculties. What looks like persecution mania and what look like delusions of grandeur are not so in the clinical sense. A streak of coprophily may be detected in Bloy's constant use of images drawn from the privy, but that it did not assume the proportions of a sexual perversion many years of happy marriage indicate.

Bloy had in fact a complete and sustained vision of the world, and it is clearly stated in the two novels which he wrote in his fortieth and fiftieth years. "Complete" is indeed the key-word. Bloy's total imaginative effort was to extend and interlock the two most perfect philosophical structures of the European mind, the horizontal Aristotelian classification of species or great chain of being and the vertical Christian doctrine of the communion of saints, which insists that not only are all living men brothers but that the living, the dead and the unborn constitute a single community, that the dead can "pray" for the living and the living for the dead or the unborn.

When a coin is given to a beggar with a bad grace, says Bloy in *Le Sang du pauvre,* this coin "pierces the poor man's hand, falls, pierces the earth, makes holes in the suns, flies across the firmament and compromises the universe." In this context, Bloy gives to such mysterious inter-relatedness of things the name of "reversibility"—"*nom philosophe du grand dogme de la communion des saints*" ["philosophical name of the great dogma of the communion of the saints"]. Clearly it is not philosophy as the academies understand it. Remy de Gourmont's verdict on Bloy was that his books appeared to be the result of a collaboration between St. Thomas Aquinas and Gargantua. At the same time, such asides are not mere rhetorical flourish. Bloy's view of money was entirely consistent. "*L'argent, c'est le sang du pauvre*" ["Money is the blood of the poor"], is the key-statement. Money flows through the universe like blood, and the rich man is a cannibal.

But all the profane functions enter into the scheme of redemption. Sex, for instance. The body of any woman is, for Bloy, the body of the Blessed Virgin, a tabernacle of Christ. The body of a woman is, moreover (not "represents" but "is"), the Garden of Eden. This being so, it is clear that prostitution is more than economic misfortune, and marriages of convenience or the social activities of an *allumeuse* ["vamp"] cosmic disasters. A sombre epithalamion in *The Woman who*

was Poor describes what happens to the universe when Léopold and Clotilde marry. In the space of a minute, a hundred persons have died and a hundred are born, "*une centaine de vagissements et une centaine de derniers soupirs*" ["a hundred babies' cries and a hundred final sighs"]. In an hour's time, there are six thousand corpses under the bed. For the joy of lovers must be paid. In order that two people may abstract themselves for a while from the suffering world, the sufferings of the rest of mankind are increased. "*Au moment même où vous bêlerez de volupté*" ["in the same moment you bleat with pleasure"] through the walls of the marriage-chamber may be heard the weeping and the gnashing of teeth of the man who had no wedding garment and was cast into outer darkness. "*L'Heure qui passe! Voyez-vous ce défilé de soixante Minutes frêles aux talons d'airain dont chacune écrase la terre*" ["That hour which passes! Do you see this procession of sixty fragile minutes with talons of bronze, each of which crushes the world"].

An equally remarkable passage in *Salut par les Juifs* describes the effect of the Crucifixion upon the animals during the period when darkness covered the earth. In *La Femme pauvre,* Marchenoir discusses the animals with Clotilde. Marchenoir insists that the animals suffer not only through but for man. Clotilde desires to know whether such a belief is concordant with divine justice, since the animals die without hope of salvation. Marchenoir's reply echoes Kant on the *Ding an sich* ["thing in itself"], though it is improbable that Bloy read Kant.

> . . . You would like to know how they are rewarded or paid off. If I knew and could tell you, I should be God, *mademoiselle,* for then I should know what the animals are *in themselves* and no longer, merely, in relation to man. Haven't you noticed we can only perceive beings and things in their relations with other beings and other things, never in their ground and in their essence? There is not a man on earth who can rightly affirm, with full assurance, that any perceptible form is indelible and bears within itself the character of eternity. We are "sleepers" . . . and the outside world figures in our dreams as "a riddle in a glass." We shall not understand this "world of lamentation" until all hidden things are revealed to us. . . . Till then, we have to accept, with the ignorance of sheep, the sight of universal immolation, telling ourselves that if grief were not shrouded in mystery, it would have neither power nor beauty to enroll martyrs and wouldn't even deserve that the animals should endure it.

At the centre of Bloy's "reversible" universe stands the figure of Christ the Poor Man, Christ the scandal of the bourgeoisie. This Christ is a suffering Christ and a Christ who has need of humanity. Such a figure verges on heresy in the West. Angelus Silesius said, "I know that without me God cannot live an instant," and his isolated cry finds numerous echoes in the East, if we are to believe M. Berdyaev. Jehovah was frequently said to be angry. In the West, enquiries into the emotional life of God are discouraged.

The intellectual content of Marchenoir-Bloy's conversion in *Le Désespéré* is uncommon. Two thousand years of the silence of God could not be endlessly protracted. "*Il conclut au conditionnel désespoir des millénaires* . . . ["it ended in the conditional despair of the millenia . . . "]. He kneaded a handful of time to make himself an eternity and manufactured his hope from the bitterest pessimism. He persuaded himself that we are dealing with a Lord God emasculate by His own Will, infertile by decree, bound, nailed, perishing in the incrustable reality of His Essence, as He had been, symbolically and visibly, in the bloody adventure of His Hypostasis. He had the intuition of a kind of Divine Impotence, contracted *provisionally* between Mercy and Justice, towards some ineffable recuperation of a Substance wasted by Love.'' It is not the business of a literary critic to assist the Holy Office in smelling out heresies. In the context of this vision and generally in the work of Bloy and his successors, we are, however, confronted with certain specifically literary problems. For all literary creation is myth-making activity, and we may therefore suppose that a practising myth-maker who happens also to owe allegiance to a fixed and embodied mythology is likely to find himself in difficulties.

The moral difficulties of a Catholic novelist have been closely examined by François Mauriac in *Le Roman* (1928) and again in *God and Mammon*. Mauriac's specific difficulties were further analysed by Charles du Bos in *François Mauriac et le problème du romancier catholique* (1933). It would be interesting to see these three essays studied by some non-Catholic critic. Here let us content ourselves with stating the moral problem of the Catholic novelist in its simplest terms. ''Dare he presume to justify himself in rooting out the most unusual sins, to which his professional interest will lead him, when their presentation in a book may scandalise and even corrupt his more simple Catholic reader?'' To a non-Christian, this problem appears a little superficial and indeed a little comic (it is possible that a communist would understand it), but one has only to read Mauriac on the problem to see that it really travails him.

Of this kind of scruple, Léon Bloy was apparently incapable. He was, however, greatly affected by a second and more fundamental difficulty, which is only hinted at by Mauriac and du Bos. In *God and Mammon*, Mauriac allows it briefly to be seen that, instead of giving coherence and direction to his work, the faith tends to distract him, to absorb his energies, to fix him in lyrical ecstasy, in the *folie de la Croix* [''madness of the cross'']. This conflict was stated already by George Herbert in the seventeenth century.

> Nothing could seem too rich to clothe the sun,
> Much less those joys which trample on his head.
>
> As flames do work and wind when they ascend,
> So did I weave myself into the sense.
> But while I bustled, I might hear a friend
> Whisper, ''How wide is all this long pretence!
> There is in love a sweetness ready penned:
> Copy out only that, and save expense.''

The truth of the matter is that the creative imagination, dealing with experience according to its own laws, makes discoveries which the praying, the believing soul does not acknowledge. There is a sense in which the creative imagination is repugnant to Christianity and to any fixed and embodied myth. It is a question of time and space, of the dramatic, the dynamic qualities of existence. (pp. 22-7)

When a new tradition of absolute faith begins, as it began in France with Bloy, may we not then expect that it will conceal a heresy? For no heretic begins by proposing to be a heretic. All heresies begin with a desire to purify and strengthen the faith.

There is Manichaeism of the ordinary kind in Bloy, the Manichaeism which condemns the natural order as evil in itself. There is also a political Manichaeism which divides the world between the poor and the bourgeoisie. The poor are represented by Christ, Who is, quite simply, *le Pauvre*. What demiurge is responsible for the bourgeoisie? Bloy, luckily, does not say. Péguy, who stood in far greater danger of excommunication, was less extreme in this matter. Péguy distinguished clearly between poverty and destitution (*pauvreté* and *misère*) and stated that, while the former is man's normal and blessed state, it is every man's duty to destroy the latter. Bloy makes of destitution-poverty not so much a vocation as a sacrament. Though he did not propose this addition with the bland cynicism which prompted Montherlant to suggest that divorce should be made a sacrament, yet he was looking for the truth in premises long vacated by the faith to which he belonged. (pp. 27-8)

> Rayner Heppenstall, ''Two Novels by Léon Bloy,'' in his The Double Image: Mutations of Christian Mythology in the Work of Four French Catholic Writers of To-day and Yesterday, Secker & Warburg, 1947, pp. 13-28.

JACQUES MARITAIN (essay date 1947)

[*A French philosopher and educator, Maritain was the foremost spokesman for the Catholic Literary Revival in France as well as a vigorous proponent of the theology of Thomas Aquinas, which affirms the validity of Aristotelian philosophy and recognizes no conflict between reason and faith. His own philosophical system, which has been described as a modified form of Thomism, emphasizes the importance of rationality in theology, thereby opposing the intense mysticism of much nineteenth-century theology. Maritain wrote a large number of essays supporting his beliefs, and his works are universally applauded for their fluid and elegant prose and their logical coherence. Both Maritain and his wife, Raïssa, became close friends of Bloy in his later years, and it was largely through Bloy's evangelical efforts that they became converted to Catholicism. In the following excerpt, originally published in Charles Peguy's* Cahiers de la Quinzaine *in 1927, Maritain defends Bloy's work as a profession of devout faith.*]

We can give nothing we have not received, being in the likeness of Him who has received everything from His Father. That is why the more one gives, the more one needs to receive, the more one is a beggar. Bloy was a fearful beggar who would not put up with mediocrity in men, and whom God was to satisfy only with the vision of His Glory. It seemed at times that in his desire for the beatific vision he voluntarily closed his eyes to ordinary lights, and preferred to grope his way toward the pure Effulgence. This mystical impatience is, to my mind, at the very source of his art.

His main concern was to ''give the idea and the impression of mystery,'' that is, of our incapacity of looking directly at the light which shines on us, and to give at the same time, by means of a most riotous flowering of images, a perceptible likeness of that truth which we do not yet know by intuition, which we know only through a mirror, in riddles. ''It is essential,'' Bloy would say, ''that Truth be in Glory. Splendor of style is not a luxury, it is a necessity.'' Basically Léon Bloy was a *pilgrim of the Holy Sepulchre*. ''If Art is part of my baggage, so much the worse for me! My only recourse is the expedient of placing at the service of Truth what has been given me by the Father of Lies. A precarious and dangerous device, for the business of Art is to fashion Gods . . .''; ''I am simply a poor man who seeks his God, sobbing and calling Him along all roads . . .''; ''The clearcut truth, which bursts forth in all my books, is that I write only for God." Bloy was the very opposite of the Anarchist who hates all "bourgeois"; he was a Christian who hated the *Bourgeois,* which—for those who understand—is one of the modern names of the old Enemy. He had a horror of disorder, lack of balance, sentimentalism, the negative and revolutionary spirit. "I write the most vehement things with great calm. Rage is powerless and suits especially those in revolt. It happens I am an *obedient* meter-out of justice." He placed above everything absolute fidelity to supernatural truth. "Too much human knowledge and too little divine knowledge," he said in speaking of Villiers de l'Isle-Adam. "I get the same impression from him as from Edgar Poe. These poets did not pray, and their contempt—while sometimes eloquent—is but the bitterness of their earthly impatience. They are full of earth, like idols."

I know it is as easy as it would be unjust to sketch of Bloy a heinous caricature, using for documents absurd bits of gossip, or lining up a certain number of texts chosen from a work that includes a great diversity of matter, part of which has vituperation as its main object. Do we reproach Juvenal for not having composed bucolics? The important thing is to put these elements in their place—time, in any case, will take care of all this—and to give our attention to what is foremost in a soul so exceptional by its prodigious lyrical gifts, its excessive sufferings, and its great love of Christ crucified.

Despite his profound affection for the Middle Ages, Bloy was a contemporary neither of Saint Bernard nor of Saint Thomas Aquinas. An anachronism even more violent and strange is that he was in fact a contemporary of Tertullian and Origen, a Christian of the second century astray in the Third Republic. How could he not have "vomited forth" his seeming contemporaries—those thankless shades in whose reality he could never believe?

To get an idea of Bloy one must put aside easy analogies. In him were confronted as in their pure state, as if outside the climate of human reason—whether it take on the clothing of philosophy or the clothing of prudence—the privileges of the Christian and those of the Poet. The theological virtues and the gifts of the Holy Ghost planted in a profound and intuitive soul famished for the divine vision, a soul whom genius oppressed; a poor human heart preyed upon by all that is super-human in the divine requirements, and by all that is inhuman in the despotism of art; the great storms, the nights, the tears of a most harsh mysticism in an atmosphere of violence and passion, above an indomitable earth, finding no other outlet than in the dazzling forms of a ferociously Spanish imagination. . . . Impatient as was Hello to see and to touch, Bloy, it would seem, never was willing to renounce completely the splendors of the tangible, in order to seek beyond, in the darkness of a purely spiritual contemplation, Him who is above all images and all thought. Perceptible and tangible signs of God—such were the objects of his never-sated hunger. Thus it is in the world of forms and images that the mystical keys have their repercussion, and there take shape the melodies of a most genuinely Christian sense of the absolute requirements of the Lord. But this likewise leads to discord and disproportion: the feeling of mystery, so pure in itself, so lofty in Bloy, sometimes translates itself by means of lightning flashes and a darkness which are too material. The true perception of what is unique and exceptional in the operation of the Holy Ghost in every docile soul (at least as far as the *manner* of doing ordinary things is concerned) was to become, with him, a taste for extraordinary deeds and romantic grandiosity which he projected in his double, Marchenoir.

But what of it! These venial deficiencies were the ransom paid for the incomparable efficacy of his work in turning toward God the hearts of men—of men who most of the time live in the senses, and who need to be led to the intelligible by means of the tangible. Imagine the three theological virtues donning the sumptuous and squalid rags of a most violent lyrical sensibility, in order to go about begging in city squares and streets. Bloy liked to repeat that he wrote not for the righteous—neither for the perfect, nor for those who are progressing, nor for those who are beginning—but for the sleeping ones who needed his suffering and his outbursts, for publicans and "for scoundrels." A category to which you certainly do not belong, "hypocritical reader, my fellow man, my brother," but to which belong, in these miserable days, a sorry multitude, redeemed, nonetheless, by the blood of the Lord. Without grace, what are we? Buried souls, muttering as in a dream; Bloy draws these souls out toward the light by very reason of the union in his work between the tangible and the spiritual. The individualistic and imaginative aspect, the esthetic splendor which the religious absolute takes on with him, somehow puts this absolute within the grasp of such souls. They hear him when he tells them: "All that happens is divine . . ."; "There is but one sadness and that is for us not to be *saints* . . ."; "You do not enter paradise tomorrow, or the day after, or in ten years, you enter it *today* when you are poor and crucified." A beggar sitting at the door of a church, showing his bleeding sores to passers-by. Thus does Bloy call these souls into the house of truth and then take them up to the altar of the living God.

"When a lover of grandeur and of the forsaken passes before a forsaken man, he will recognize grandeur, if grandeur be there." To what forsaken man does this line of Ernest Hello—which Bloy often repeated—apply better than to Bloy himself?

But I hear people asking: How do you account for Bloy's personal attacks? His violence, his injustice toward this man or that? Let the reader take note, at this point, of what is exceptional in the case of Léon Bloy. Villiers de l'Isle-Adam, in the presence of someone importunate or impudent, would look at the person with extreme and manifest effort, blink, stretch out his neck, bringing his head forward, and exclaim, discouraged, "I'm doing all I can, sir, but I can't see you." Bloy was *by nature* incapable of seeing and judging in themselves individuals and particular circumstances. He did not discern them. From this came—for anyone considering their immediate object—the immoderate excess of his fits of violence. The truth was that they were aiming at *something else.*

In these demonstrations of violence one must first of all see the consequence of a very special kind of *abstraction,* certainly not philosophic, but artistic; or, if one prefers, a very special kind of typification: every event, every gesture, every person, here and now, was instantaneously transposed, torn from all contingencies, from the concrete conditions of the human setting which explain it and make it plausible, and was transposed, in the eyes of this fearful visionary, into the pure symbol of some devouring spiritual reality.

One must also see in these fits of violence a consequence of his strange absorption in his own interior world. Bloy was among "those who are troubled by the outcries of the Disobedience, and live withdrawn into their own souls." When he was but a young child his mother often found him sitting silently, bathed in tears, weeping for hours without ascribable motive. A boundless melancholy—both natural and supernatural—weighed on him; a certain number of apperceptions of mortal acuteness, such as the mystical gifts can awaken in a soul of this kind, filled his heart. The crucifying vision of universal forgetfulness for God and His Love; the vision of hatred for the Poor, of the abjectness and cruelty peculiar to a world where the Gospel is no longer known—all this made the passion of the Lord perpetually present to him, fashioning his spiritual life upon the agony and the abhorrence of the Mount of Olives. That is what existed for him: this spiritual universe—and his faithful sorrow. The rest were but phantasms, a useless and uncertain show. And as apperceptions existed in him from the start, with their attendant aura of vigorous reality, and very early exerted pressure from all sides upon his mind, it was enough that some exterior object, passing in the shadow of his suffering, present some appearance of the vices or the tepidity he detested for Bloy to seize upon it as upon a detestable symbol, and submit it to his indignation as an "obedient meter-out of Justice." His blows might fall most deplorably wide of the mark; the victim chosen might deserve neither to be empaled nor scalped, might on the contrary deserve every laurel: through this victim—a perishable form— he reached the invisible monster, the monument of spiritual iniquity which oppressed his heart and the hearts of a great number of his brothers.

Without doubt this way of acting offered, for many, serious disadvantages. His love of God showed itself in none too charitable colors, and his zeal for Justice, which was really Léon Bloy's constant passion, seemed somewhat to neglect the moral virtue of the same name. Yet we would be quite unperspicacious if we did not discern either this love or this zeal, of which only He who will judge us has measured the intensity; and if

Caricature of Bloy as a medieval crusader.

we did not realize that the very enormity of Léon Bloy's verbal violence made it much less dangerous to his enemies than to himself. Could he be said to be an exasperated, envious, soured "pamphleteer"? No picture could be more false. (pp. 7-13)

> *Jacques Maritain, in an introduction to* Pilgrim of the Absolute *by Léon Bloy, edited by Raïssa Maritain, translated by John Coleman and Harry Lorin Binsse, Pantheon Books, 1947, pp. 7-23.*

E. T. DUBOIS (essay date 1950)

[In the following excerpt, Dubois assesses the value of Bloy's work.]

[Bloy] could never be described as an accomplished writer. He broached many subjects, covering a wide range of social, historical, moral and theological problems, and treated them all with that violence and one-sidedness which aroused so much hostility. The structure of his novels suffers from the same defects. They lack the final polish of a Flaubert. Bloy never wanted to convey a complete picture or idea. His wish was rather to kindle a fire which could burn even more fiercely than the blazing Bazar de Charité. He wanted indeed to rouse his countrymen from a century-long sleep—a sleep so profound that his thundering voice only succeeded in awakening a few here and there. Violence and exaggeration form a natural part of his work, which was concerned with restoring its original forcefulness to Christian tradition. Moreover we must not forget that in literature we often find a kind of simplification and overstress of the problems facing the writer. If he wants his reader to see poverty in all its physical, moral and spiritual wretchedness, he has to detach it, as it were, from life as a whole and paint it in strong colours to make the desired impression. Real life is more complex, more involved, and covers a much larger field. It is well to bear this in mind if we want to do Bloy justice, though it will not suffice to explain the peculiar blend of violence and charity, of arrogance and humility, of the ruthless pamphleteer and the devoted man of prayer, revealed in the work and person of Léon Bloy. The more we read and penetrate the work of this strange personality the more difficult it seems to find a clue to all its contradictions. For he appears to us under two completely different aspects. He is a man of incredible obstinacy, of almost unparalleled vanity and self-assurance. He shows no charity to those with whom he disagrees. In fact his sympathies, if any, are of an extremely narrow, entirely national range, and are withdrawn on the slightest provocation. Yet we also see him re-establishing Christian values which had grown all too thin and faint. He had rediscovered the strength and beauty, the very new and everlasting truth of Christianity; and he wished to impart it to his fellowmen. In this he is not unlike one who was almost his contemporary in this country, and who discovered that all his explanations of this strange universe had already been given before with divine authority. But unlike the author of *Orthodoxy*, Bloy completely lacked any sense of humour, nor had he Chesterton's capacity for engaging in arguments and debates with his fellow-men. Bloy concentrated on re-stating certain aspects of Christianity which were important to his time, and which more than others seemed to have lost their original forcefulness.

It will be easier for us to do him justice if we consider him in the framework of his time, remembering that French literature, and indeed European literature in general, had passed and was still passing through a phase of disbelief and irreverence. He restored poverty to its original dignity, and it seems that his work here was particularly valuable. In a world bent upon making money, poverty could no longer be regarded as anything but disgrace and failure. It is true that people were beginning to be aware of "social" problems, but it was merely from a humane, anthropocentric, economic point of view. Bloy emphasised the dignity of the poor, a dignity gained by the sanctification of poverty through Jesus, who had raised it to the divine plane. Those who judged the world by monetary values found themselves confronted by a man to whom poverty, which they treated disdainfully, seemed most precious. He recalled the world to the dignity of the human person, which is so often insulted in the poor precisely by those who claim to alleviate social evil. In our day, the dignity of the human person as the basis of a just society has been reaffirmed intellectually by philosophers like Jacques Maritain, Bloy's godson; but the application of the principle to society is indeed a slow process. At the time when Bloy wrote, Catholic Action had hardly developed, and only one of the Papal Encyclicals on social questions was written during his life-time. He did not discover any practical solution for social wrongs; but he did insist on the respect due to all human beings, and on the dignity of the poor as being those nearest to Christ. Even in Catholic circles, material success and love of money had come to take too large a place. His attitude towards poverty was, for his day, extraordinary, for he considered it neither as a social problem nor as a subject of literature, but *sub specie aeternitatis.*

Again, poverty is only one aspect of the larger problem of the corporateness of human society. At a point in history when, on the one hand, individualism had reached the height of its power, and on the other, attempts were being made to discover a new social solidarity, Bloy proclaimed that both elements existed in the harmony of the Mystical Body of Christ. He could not argue along logical lines; but in his strangely intuitive way he understood that each man was at once a unique creature and most closely linked with his fellow-creatures and with God. It has been pointed out before that he was a forerunner of Catholic Action and the Catholic social teaching of our time; but this fact can hardly be emphasised enough.

When we read, not without amazement, his strange description of *L'Heure de la Noce,* we touch on the almost mystical depth of his spirituality. He was undoubtedly akin to all victim souls; he understood the efficacy of the offering of personal suffering for others; and this understanding is certainly not a common one. He lived so intensely in the Mystical Body that his relation with his fellow men remained almost entirely on that plane. He made a truly Christian offering of his sufferings for the redemption of others, and prayed for the souls in purgatory with unusual fervour. We know from his journal that he often recited the Office of the Dead in the depth of night, when the souls called him, as he said. He had a deep personal love of Our Lord, to whom he recommended his friends and all who suffered, thus completing the offering of his life and prayers. The reader of these pages will already be familiar with his devotion to Our Lady, which was of unceasing loyalty. His reason for proclaiming the message of Our Lady of La Salette opens up yet another aspect of his spirituality. He saw that what mankind most stands in need of, now and always, is penance. When knowledge of the divine revelation becomes vague and its acceptance reluctant, then even the faithful regard penance as something too austere, and Our Lord is thought of as being too "kind" to ask us to do such violence to our nature. But to Bloy Christianity was not "kind," nor did it represent a gentle rule of life. Rather it was frightening in its harshness,

and yet it was a thing of joy and love. He puts its austere, ascetic character right to the fore, and made himself its defender. His orthodoxy acted as a brake on him; it was only by a hair's breadth that he escaped spiritual pessimism. Poverty, suffering, penance, and the redemptive power of each marked his spirituality as one of extreme austerity but one which was warmed and lightened by the grace of the sacraments regularly received.

In spite of all this Bloy remains a puzzle. The fervent Catholic whose charity stopped short at the Rhine and the Channel, and flowed very sparingly even within these narrow frontiers, leaves us with a psychological problem not easily solved. We are bound to ask ourselves again and again: how is it possible for a man who went to Mass and received Holy Communion daily, who prayed with great love, to rejoice at such a human catastrophe as the fire at the Bazar de Charité or to write as he did of his fellow-men across the Rhine? (Those across the Channel received less but hardly kinder attention.) We can only assume that his psychological make-up was of a strangely broken and unbalanced nature. His character indeed showed the power of extremes, of passionate love and hatred. His mind, too, as he admitted himself, lacked the balance of rational and logical thinking. Intuition unchecked by reason can develop into something fantastic, indeed terrifying. He seems to have received gifts of spiritual understanding of unusual richness, but at the same time his emotional and intellectual nature was not equipped to bring these gifts to their full development. This man who was steeped in the Scriptures, where he discovered vistas which had been closed to many; who prayed with such fervour and perseverance, and who took the teaching of Our Lord so literally as a rule for his life, nevertheless does not strike us as the saintly person we might expect. There are, no doubt, elements of sanctity in Bloy; but there often seems little to connect them with the man revealed in his work. It is very likely that his spirituality did not reach its fulness because (with the exception of the Abbé Tardif de Moidrey) he lacked a spiritual director almost all his life. Out of pride, no doubt, he refused to submit to any man; and yet he stands truly as the humble Pilgrim of the Holy Sepulchre before God and Our Lady. There is in him an almost Protestant reliance on private judgment which is oddly opposed to the Catholicity of his belief. Even in his ideas and conceptions of spiritual matters, as with regard to the Jews or the so-called secrets of Our Lady of La Salette, he insists without the slightest hesitation on his own interpretation, in the second case completely disregarding the opinion of almost the entire body of the French clergy.

His very language and style show this marked unbalance. One sees it in his choice of rare words and obscure references, and in the unevenness and sudden change of tone in his writing. He had no desire for objectivity, nor did he care for detail. All his work is of a definitely personal, almost wilfully individualistic character.

He could say with Faust *"Zwei Seelen wohnen ach, in meiner Brust''* ["Ah, two souls live in my breast"]; and yet the two apparently contradictory sides of his character—humility before God and self-assurance before his fellowmen: passionate love of souls and passionate hatred of pharisaism—can both be accounted for as the expression of his strong faith. But they are bound to meet with hostility and scorn from men who see his character only from one angle. He truly loved his fellowmen and with a love so great that it inspired the violence of his attacks. But his hatred of pharisaism overshadowed his love, and blinded him to the fact that while such hatred is a

Christian's duty, it is equally his duty to love the pharisee himself as his fellow-man. Bloy, however, would not discriminate between crime and the criminal, and it is this fact which causes so much misunderstanding of an otherwise deeply Christian man. There is much in him that was hidden so deeply in the intimate life of his soul that it cannot be discussed by anyone. We do not wish, however, to explain away the violence, lack of charity and inability to deal with everyday life which must have been so irritating to his contemporaries. He was unable to adjust himself to certain conditions, and seems to have carried the conviction of the rightness of his own views to such a point that he could no longer make contact with his fellow-men. In this he was like Molière's Alceste, who also practised truthfulness with such onesided obstinacy that he had to retire from society. But in spite of the exaggerated character of Bloy's work it has borne rich fruit. Its forcefulness could not remain unnoticed or without response, and perhaps therein lies the justification *a posteriori* of what must seem and indeed is unacceptable and untenable in it.

As we have already mentioned, Bloy entirely lacked any sense of humour, and regarded everything he said and wrote with a seriousness which imposes a great strain on the reader. It is impossible not to smile at times at the *bizarreries* which he pronounces with such touching naïveté, or again as one reads one feels a quite justifiable anger. The blending of so many contradictory forces in his character makes his work uneven, incoherent and bewildering. It has immense power, because he tried to incorporate everything, even his very self, in it. His was indeed an extraordinary vocation: to awaken love of God and His Church by means of—or should we say in spite of—violence and hatred, both so utterly opposed to the God of love. But perhaps his natural temperament was only the outer layer which covered a truly Christian soul.

It is possible, too, that the unevenness of his work arises from his inability to shape the greatness of his vision into form. . . . Remy de Gourmont put it aptly: "His books look as if they had been written by St. Thomas Aquinas in collaboration with Gargantua"; which is, after all, a very complimentary remark.

It may well be that Bloy's chief importance lies in the influence of his personality on a few outstanding souls who seem to have gained grace through him. His strong personality, with its deep devotion and faithful life of prayer, could not fail to have its effect. It was crowned in his godsons, who not only received the gift of faith, but carried on much of Bloy's thought, developing it and kindling in others the fire of Faith which alone brings life to men. He brought back to the Church several people who seemed in need precisely of a soul like his, so full of fire, strength and absolute conviction, to draw them out of their stagnation or despair. His faithfulness to the doctrines of the Church was a timely example in an epoch of individualism, material progress and greed for money. This faith roused a response in others, who felt themselves called to adapt the incoherent thoughts and vociferations of Bloy into a more harmonious system, and thus gave his work a wider sphere and a more effective influence. He strikes us—if the comparison may be allowed, though it is incomplete, as every comparison must be—as rather like St. John the Baptist, a forerunner, *vox clamantis in deserto* ["a voice crying out in the wilderness"], inheriting some of the character of the Old Testament, yet living in the spirit of the New. (pp. 98-106)

> *E. T. Dubois, in her* Portrait of Léon Bloy, *Sheed & Ward, 1950, 125 p.*

JORGE LUIS BORGES   (essay date 1952)

[*Borges was an Argentine short story writer, poet, and essayist whose writings are often used by critics to illustrate the modern view of literature as a highly sophisticated game. This interpretation of Borges's works is supported by his respect for stories that are artificial inventions of art rather than realistic representations of life, his use of philosophical conceptions as a means of achieving literary effects, and his frequent variations on the writings of other authors. Such characteristic stories as "The Aleph," "The Circular Ruins," and "Pierre Menard, Author of the Quixote" are demonstrations of the subjective, the infinitely various, and the ultimately indeterminate nature of life and literature. Accompanying the literary puzzles and the manipulations of variant models of reality, there is a somber, fatalistic quality in Borges's work which has led critics to locate his fictional universe in close proximity to the nightmarish world of Franz Kafka and the philosophical wasteland of Samuel Beckett. In his literary criticism, Borges is noted for his insight into the manner in which an author both represents and creates a reality with words, and the way in which those words are variously interpreted by readers. With his fiction and poetry, Borges's critical writing shares the perspective that literary creation of imaginary worlds and philosophical speculation on the world itself are parallel or identical activities. In the following excerpt from an essay published in* Otras inquisiciones *in 1952, Borges discusses the nature of Bloy's Catholicism.*]

The idea that the Sacred Scriptures have (aside from their literal value) a symbolic value is ancient and not irrational: it is found in Philo of Alexandria, in the Cabalists, in Swedenborg. Since the events related in the Scriptures are true (God is Truth, Truth cannot lie, etc.), we should admit that men, in acting out those events, blindly represent a secret drama determined and premeditated by God. Going from this to the thought that the history of the universe—and in it our lives and the most tenuous detail of our lives—has an incalculable, symbolical value, is a reasonable step. Many have taken that step; no one so astonishingly as Léon Bloy. (In the psychological fragments by Novalis and in that volume of Machen's autobiography called *The London Adventure* there is a similar hypothesis: that the outer world—forms, temperatures, the moon—is a language we humans have forgotten or which we can scarcely distinguish. . . . It is also declared by De Quincey: "Even the articulate or brutal sounds of the globe must be all so many languages and ciphers that somewhere have their corresponding keys—have their own grammar and syntax; and thus the least things in the universe must be secret mirrors to the greatest.")

A verse from St. Paul (I Corinthians, 13:12) inspired Léon Bloy. *Videmus nunc per speculum in aenigmate: tunc autem facie ad faciem. Nunc cognosco ex parte: tunc autem cognoscam sicut et cognitus sum.* Torres Amat has miserably translated: "At present we do not see God except as in a mirror and beneath dark images; but later we shall see him face to face. I only know him now imperfectly; but later I shall know him in a clear vision, in the same way that I know myself." 49 words do the work of 22; it is impossible to be more languid and verbose. Cipriano de Valera is more faithful: "Now we see in a mirror, in darkness; but later we shall see face to face. Now I know in part; but later I shall know as I am known." Torres Amat opines that the verse refers to our vision of the divinity; Cipriano de Valera (and Léon Bloy), to our general vision of things.

So far as I know, Bloy never gave his conjecture a definitive form. Throughout his fragmentary work (in which there abound, as everyone knows, lamentations and insults) there are different versions and facets. Here are a few that I have rescued from the clamorous pages of *Le mendiant ingrat, Le Vieux de la Montagne* and *L'invendable.* I do not believe I have exhausted them: I hope that some specialist in Léon Bloy (I am not one) may complete and rectify them.

The first is from June 1894. I translate it as follows: "The statement by St. Paul: *Videmus nunc per speculum in aenigmate* would be a skylight through which one might submerge himself in the true Abyss, which is the soul of man. The terrifying immensity of the firmament's abysses is an illusion, an external reflection of *our own* abysses, perceived 'in a mirror.' We should invert our eyes and practice a sublime astronomy in the infinitude of our hearts, for which God was willing to die.... If we see the Milky Way, it is because it *actually exists in our souls.*"

The second is from November of the same year. "I recall one of my oldest ideas. The Czar is the leader and spiritual father of a hundred fifty million men. An atrocious responsibility which is only apparent. Perhaps he is not responsible to God, but rather to a few human beings. If the poor of his empire are oppressed during his reign, if immense catastrophies result from that reign, who knows if the servant charged with shining his boots is not the real and sole person guilty? In the mysterious dispositions of the Profundity, who is really Czar, who is king, who can boast of being a mere servant?"

The third is from a letter written in December. "Everything is a symbol, even the most piercing pain. We are dreamers who shout in our sleep. We do not know whether the things afflicting us are the secret beginning of our ulterior happiness or not. We now see, St. Paul maintains, *per speculum in aenigmate,* literally: 'in an enigma by means of a mirror' and we shall not see in any other way until the coming of the One who is all in flames and who must teach us all things."

The fourth is from May 1904. "*Per speculum in aenigmate,* says St. Paul. We see everything backwards. When we believe we give, we receive, etc. Then (a beloved, anguished soul tells me) we are in Heaven and God suffers on earth."

The fifth is from May 1908. "A terrifying idea of Jeanne's, about the text *Per speculum.* The pleasures of this world would be the torments of Hell, seen backwards, in a mirror."

The sixth is from 1912. It is each of the pages of *L'Âme de Napoléon,* a book whose purpose is to decipher the symbol Napoleon, considered as the precursor of another hero—man and symbol as well—who is hidden in the future. It is sufficient for me to cite two passages. One: "Every man is on earth to symbolize something he is ignorant of and to realize a particle or a mountain of the invisible materials that will serve to build the City of God." The other: "There is no human being on earth capable of declaring with certitude who he is. No one knows what he has come into this world to do, what his acts correspond to, his sentiments, his ideas, or what his real name is, his enduring Name in the register of Light.... History is an immense liturgical text where the iotas and the dots are worth no less than the entire verses or chapters, but the importance of one and the other is indeterminable and profoundly hidden."

The foregoing paragraphs will perhaps seem to the reader mere gratuities by Bloy. So far as I know, he never took care to reason them out. I venture to judge them verisimilar and perhaps inevitable within the Christian doctrine. Bloy (I repeat) did no more than apply to the whole of Creation the method which the Jewish Cabalists applied to the Scriptures. They

thought that a work dictated by the Holy Spirit was an absolute text: in other words, a text in which the collaboration of chance was calculable as zero. This portentous premise of a book impenetrable to contingency, of a book which is a mechanism of infinite purposes, moved them to permute the scriptural words, add up the numerical value of the letters, consider their form, observe the small letters and capitals, seek acrostics and anagrams and perform other exegetical rigors which it is not difficult to ridicule. Their excuse is that nothing can be contingent in the work of an infinite mind. Léon Bloy postulates this hieroglyphical character—this character of a divine writing, of an angelic cryptography—at all moments and in all beings on earth. The superstitious person believes he can decipher this organic writing: thirteen guests form the symbol of death; a yellow opal, that of misfortune.

It is doubtful that the world has a meaning; it is even more doubtful that it has a double or triple meaning, the unbeliever will observe. I understand that this is so; but I understand that the hieroglyphical world postulated by Bloy is the one which best befits the dignity of the theologian's intellectual God.

No man knows who he is, affirmed Léon Bloy. No one could illustrate that intimate ignorance better than he. He believed himself a rigorous Catholic and he was a continuer of the Cabalists, a secret brother of Swedenborg and Blake: heresiarchs. (pp. 209-12)

> Jorge Luis Borges, *"The Mirror of Enigmas,"* translated by James E. Irby, in his Labyrinths: Selected Stories & Other Writings, *edited by Donald A. Yates and James E. Irby, revised edition, New Directions, 1964, pp. 209-12.*

DONAT O'DONNELL [PSEUDONYM OF CONOR CRUISE O'BRIEN] (essay date 1952)

[*An Irish politician, historian, and critic, O'Brien served as Ireland's representative to the United Nations from 1955 to 1961 and has since held positions in the Irish government and in academia. He has written numerous studies of Irish history, of the United Nations, and of modern politics, and his works are often praised for their iconoclasm as well as their insight. Although O'Brien has concentrated his attention primarily on political and historical matters, his literary opinions are also highly esteemed, and he has written important studies of Catholic writers and the influence of politics on literature. In the following excerpt, O'Brien discusses dominant themes in Bloy's work.*]

"God," said Léon Bloy, speaking of the Bible, "cannot talk about anything but Himself."

M. Sartre, if the remark were brought to his attention, would certainly point out that the same was true of Léon Bloy, and he would be right after a fashion. Bloy's two novels, *Le Désespéré* and *La Femme pauvre,* are certainly autobiographical, if the apotheosis of the author, combined with lengthy and scurrilous abuse of his rivals, may be so described; the great bulk of his other writings consists of letters, diaries, and pamphlets, revolving around the same themes: even his exegetical works cannot safely be assumed to lack a personal source and application. The whole body of the work—and it should be taken as one composite body—is the soliloquy of a historical misfit: "A contemporary of Tertullian," in Maritain's phrase, "strayed into the nineteenth century." The monstrous iterations and wildly contorted metaphors, the extravagance of verbal violence, the powerlessness to define character except in terms of white (self and temporary allies) and black (the world), all reveal a state of mind very close to the self-absorption of certain types of lunatic.

Yet the work, despite its omnipresent egotism and intermittent insanity, has its own peculiar extralogical system, and a power of implicating the reader, however complacent in his own sanity he may be, in a world whose incoherence seems in some way familiar. In that tufted fantastic forest, where appearances blend and reverse themselves with such ease, one cannot help picking up the scent of a quarry: that equivocal or "amphibological" game, Saint Hubert's stag or will-o'-the-wisp, which Bloy spent his life pursuing. He hunted on a horse that was lame in one wing: the critic must follow dubiously on foot, or swing himself perilously by the contagious poison ivy of metaphor above the swamp of pseudo-science. By any method a kill is unlikely, but the chase may not be without interest.

The place to which Bloy's pursuit persistently tends is Paradise: "The lost Eden whose recovery is the aim of all human effort." The terrestrial Paradise, *Paradisum voluptatis,* constantly recurs in his work, in different, yet related, guises. Only once does he describe it in conventional terms, as "an Annunciation meadow full of dandelions and buttercups under very humble apple-trees, looking like confessors and kissing the earth with chalice-laden branches" (*Les XII Filles d'Edmond Grasset*). This is a caption and reads like one, but with it there goes a strange warning to the young lady in the picture who sits under the tree: if she follows one of the mystic rivers from this Paradise she will reach "her real home on the calcined shore of an Orinoco of blood lit by furious stars." No doubt there may have been several immediate reasons for thus bringing hell into heaven—dislike of the work for which he was being paid, dislike of the woman in the picture, or of some other woman—but one feels a deeper motive: an utter dissatisfaction, reflected in the clumsy wording of the first part of the caption, with the conventional Paradise, and an instinctive linking of the idea of Paradise with the idea of pain. This strange connection is made more explicitly elsewhere. His own childhood, he tells us in an autobiographical part of *Le Désespéré,* was spent in "coveting a Paradise of torture": in a letter to a friend he writes of knowing "the ecstasy of the Paradise of pain"; he notes in his diary that Paradise can be reconstituted only by all the sufferings of the Gentiles and the Jews; the sufferings of Jesus were the Paradise of his Saints. Paradise is pain, or the counterpart of pain, or both: this unsolved equation was something fixed in his mind as these references, scattered over twenty-five years of his life, clearly show.

But Paradise is not only pain, it is death itself: not death as a transition, but the place of physical disintegration, the cemetery. "Paradise is the cemetery," he exclaims again and again in his diary. And in his most considerable work, that in which his idea of Paradise is most developed, *La Femme pauvre,* he elaborates this through a fable. A "formidable Pilgrim" seeks throughout the world for the lost Eden. This Pilgrim, who "sweated psalms through all his pores" and looked like "an old hymn of impatience," avoided the sun, and traveled along the bottom of rivers and the sea bed, seeking "the brazier of beatitude which the Deluge could not put out." After more than a hundred years "he stops for the first time and dies, in a lepers' cemetery in the middle of which is the Tree of Life and under it the Spirit of the Lord walking, like us, amid the tombs." One remembers that Bloy liked to speak of himself as not an artist, but a Pilgrim of the Holy Sepulchre.

Besides the images, or identities, of pain and death, there is only one other of equal, or greater, power. It is that of woman and, specifically, the female sexual organs. "The second chapter of Genesis with the description of the earthly Paradise," he wrote to his future wife in November 1889, "is, in my eyes, a symbolic figure of *Woman.*" A month later he elaborated this idea in a very remarkable letter, which he himself regarded as of such importance that he reproduced it several years later with a few amendments in *La Femme pauvre.* It is worth quoting at some length in the form preserved in *Lettres à sa fiancée.* He is describing the central idea of a novel, *La Prostituée,* which he was never to write:

> For woman—a temporarily, *conditionally* inferior creature—there are only two ways: the most august maternity ["beatitude" in *La Femme pauvre*] or the title and quality of an instrument of pleasure, pure or impure love, holiness or prostitution. Between the two there is only the *respectable woman,* that is the female of the *bourgeois,* the absolute reprobate whom no holocaust can redeem. A saint can fall in the mud and a prostitute mount to the light, but the horrible brainless gutless ruminant they call a respectable woman, who once refused the hospitality of Bethlehem to the Infant God, can never escape, either up or down, from her eternal non-existence. But all women have one point in common—the assured conviction of their dignity as dispensers of joy. *Causa nostrae laetitiae! Janua Coeli!* God alone knows in what ways these sacred formulae blend in the meditation of the purest women and what their mysterious physiology suggests to them.
>
> As for me, believing only in absolute ideas, I shall ignore all known systems of psychology and go straight to the monstrous affirmation by which I believe it possible to explain everything: Every woman, *whether she knows it or not,* is persuaded that her sexual organs ["her body" in *La Femme pauvre*] are Paradise. *Plantaverat autem Dominus Deus Paradisum voluptatis a principio* (Genesis II. 9). Therefore no prayer, no penance, no martyrdom has power enough to win that inestimable jewel and the weight of the nebulae in diamonds could not purchase it. Judge of what she gives when she gives herself, and measure her sacrilege when she sells herself. Assuredly this is all very ridiculous. But here is my quite unexpected conclusion ["taken from the Prophets" in *La Femme pauvre*]: Woman *is right* to believe all that and assert it so ridiculously. She is infinitely right since that part of her body was once the tabernacle of the living God and no one can set limits to the *solidarity* of that confounding mystery.

Pain, death, the womb, Paradise—the quadruple association requires, in itself, little commentary: we have seen the same constellation, somewhat obscured, in the work of Péguy and Claudel: here it blazes in the sky. (pp. 203-07)

Most Catholics, not possessed of the subtlety of a Maritain, would regard all this—if they read it—as "unhealthy," shot through with personal revelations, blasphemy, and a suspect excitement. Fortunately they are prepared to take Bloy, like most of the other "great Catholic writers," on trust. The bourgeois materialist would regard it as a clot of illusions, the result of burdening a hysterical brain with metaphysical rubbish: a hemorrhage of personal troubles in the form of grandiose generalities. But there is, I think, an approach that would reveal that Bloy's world is not as closed as it seems, is in fact relevant in rather an unexpected way to the external historical realities of his time.

The starting point is to regard Bloy's theory of "eucharistic money" as *a statement in mystical terms of the Labor Theory of Value. The poor* are the working class: *money* (meaning capital, prices, and wages) is their blood, i.e. is the expression of their toil. It follows that *the cross* represents the means of production, which at a given time both sustain capital and necessitate the oppression of the working class (crucifixion of *money* and *the poor*). *The Jews,* being the capitalist class, may be partly identified with the means of production (*the cross*) during the period of high capitalism (*the crucifixion*). Eventually, however, the last stage of monopoly capitalism is reached: the working class having touched its lowest depth of destitution, *la misère*—the *Holy Ghost*—makes his appearance: he has a distinct affinity to both *the Jews* and *the cross,* since he comes as the final result of capitalist operation of the means of production, which has sucked up all the produce of labor (consummated the crucifixion). Only then is the working class (*Christ, the poor*) able to take revolutionary action: the descent *from the cross* means at the same time the general strike (dissociation of the working class from the means of production) and the final break with the capitalist class (taking *the cross* as *the Jews*). This cannot be accomplished without violence

(*fire*) and in the final conflict the Church will be opposed to the working class (will persecute *Christ*). Yet, from the time of monopoly capitalism and the appearance of *la misère,* final victory is assured: only thus can we attain the classless society (*the earthly Paradise*).

Like most allegories this one should not of course be pressed too far, but the points of correspondence between Bloy's private myth and the central myth of Marxism—with which he was certainly not familiar—are surprisingly numerous. It is true that the two systems of prophecy have a certain common basis. Marx himself belonged to a Rabbinical family, steeped in Biblical exegesis; the Messianic aspect of his doctrine has been rightly stressed. There was, after all, also a common basis in objective fact: both Bloy and Marx perceived more clearly than their contemporaries the sickness of their society, the provisional nature of capitalism, and the historical importance of economic power: "Money more formidable than prayer and more conquering than fire."

But to underline the similarities is to become all the more conscious of the gulf that separates the two men: Bloy, for all his historical perceptions, utterly committed to supernatural interpretation and aloofness from the battle; Marx, for all the element of poetry and myth in his system, equally committed to a practical and revolutionary role. Christopher Caudwell, most subtle of Marxist critics, defined religion as "a reality, but a *fantastic* reality." He would certainly have claimed that Bloy was expressing in fantastic terms—and so evading—the realities with which Marx grappled scientifically. Such an an-

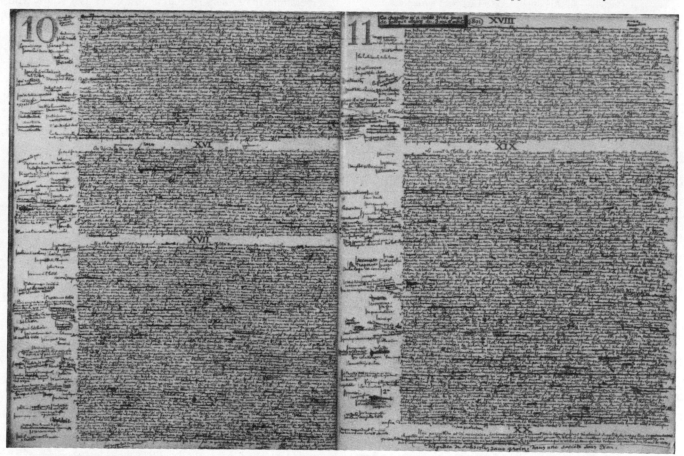

Bloy's manuscript for La femme pauvre.

tithesis would be rather too neat—it is a question, for example, whether the earthly Paradise is any more "fantastic" or less "scientific" than the classless society—but it does force us to ask what there is left out, what there is of importance in Bloy which such an analysis ignores. This more than half-crazed man, who sometimes thought he was God, who made a Paradise out of his longing for death and his mother, and then twisted all history and the Catholic religion into a high fantastic road to reach that Paradise—why should anyone read him except for clinical purposes?

The first answer and indeed the last—although it requires qualification and analysis—is that his style is unique. Of that style he himself has left us a loving description which is at the same time a magnificent example.

> His violent coloring, his cautelous and alembicated barbarism; the giratory emphasis and stubborn winding of certain cruel images constantly twisting back on themselves like convolvulus; the unheard-of audacity of the form, as numerous as a horde and as rapid, although heavily armed; the sober tumult of the vocabulary, plumed with flames and ash like Vesuvius in the last days of Pompeii, slashed with gold, encrusted, crenelated, denticulated with ancient gems like the reliquary of a martyr; but above all the prodigious enlargement which such a style conferred at once on the least ambitious thesis, the tiniest and most acclimatized hypothesis;—all this appeared to Leopold a magic mirror in which he could decipher his own soul, with a gasp of admiration.

The style here is the man in a fuller sense than usual: the baroque ebullience of the decoration is at its best when the subject is Bloy himself: "They saw his soul moving about in him as one might see some great imprisoned Infanta come and press her face at the stained-glass windows of the burning Escorial."

As the splendor of this image corresponds to the crazy splendor of Bloy's conception of himself—"they do not know who I am"—so do each of its parts refer one to an aspect of his prophetic work. *Infanta* and *Escorial* recall his Spanish mother and the intransigence of his Catholicism: the Escorial being *in flames* conveys his sense of his own martyrdom and his emphasis on pain (supported by the plan of that gridiron palace); the *fire* also suggests that apocalyptic vision of the "burning solstice of the summer of the world" which never ceased to haunt him: the fact that the soul is an *Infanta* rather than a Prince hints at the femaleness of his interior image and the *burning house* has of course a sexual connotation: the idea of an *imprisoned heiress* suggests his conception that the tribulations which were heaped on him had something to do with his being in some unrevealed way elect: the idea of an *imprisoned woman* suggests irresistibly the tragedy of Anne-Marie and this impression is heightened by the fact that we see her through stained glass ("The Church is shut up in a hospital for madwomen") in the light of flames, a frequent symbol of madness: the curious, vaguely sinister, sense of impassivity we get about the Infanta (she *presses her face against* the windows but we are not told that she makes any attempt to open them) accords with the atmosphere of insanity, but also carries those ideas of mystery and the acceptance of predestined suffering which are so essential to Bloy. Furthermore, a very strange and moving perspective in time is opened up by an

ambiguity in the French. The adjective *incendié* applied to the Escorial can mean either *burning* or *burned-out*. *Burned-out* is indeed normally the primary meaning, but here one is likely to reject it after a little consideration because of the presence of the *windows,* which would have melted in the completion of the fire, and also because of the unlikelihood of imprisoning someone in a burned-out building. Yet common sense cannot altogether expunge from the mind the half-formed vision of the great Princess moving like a ghost, imprisoned by her own will or some obscure sentence, through some abandoned gallery or chapel which the flames had partly spared in the ruined building. This survives as a shadow-meaning and deepening of the image. We feel that the Infanta goes on living in the Escorial after the fire is over: *just as Anne-Marie lives on in Bloy after the conflagration of her reason.* Bloy seems both still obsessed by the vision of Anne-Marie *in the flames* of her madness and also aware that her visions (the face at the window) still continue in what, after the disaster, remains of him (the ruined building): she *is his soul.* There is also the twist—which would be characteristic of Bloy—of the possibility that the burned-out Escorial, with its single august and enigmatic inhabitant, *is the Church:* which again brings us back to Anne-Marie, about whom the whole image turns, from whatever point you choose to contemplate it.

I do not claim of course that this rather elaborate structure was consciously worked out and intended to appear in the simile. But Bloy could not help writing with the full weight of his unique experience and prophetic intuition. The author of *L'Exégèse des lieux communs,* aware of the very remote reverberations in ordinary speech, almost never uses words with a flat literalism: his metaphors vibrate in a prophetic air. This is so even when the metaphor is apparently trivial or frivolous, like the endless zoological figures of speech which lie in wait for his personal enemies and literary rivals. A few of these might perhaps be taken at their face value: the epigram on Gautier and his impeccable verse—"Theophile Gautier? An oyster in a pearl"—needs no exegesis. But when he says that the vices of Catulle Mendès would "make a black bison go white with horror"; or that a disillusioned bourgeois would be comparable to a winged hippopotamus; or that the perpetual goings and comings in Zola's novels would make an albatross sea-sick—his hyperbolical humor has a special significance. These creatures—which teem in all Bloy's polemical work—serving as foils to the incomparable vileness of his victims, seem themselves to have the endearing innocence of beasts in a drawing by Thurber or Jean Effel. But the importance of animals, their innocence, and their sufferings are serious components of Bloy's prophecies. The beasts, suffering through man's fault, have not lost the power of seeing what is invisible to man: "a simple restoration of the earthly Paradise which, for the last six thousand years, exists only in the anxious and suffering retina of these unconscious ones." So that even in the tumult of controversy the metaphor seems to twist upwards: unnoticed, a Dutch mirror concentrates the image of that Paradise which is never out of his thought.

Similarly the monotonous torrent of scatology, which made his name a scandal to the *bien-pensants,* has its significance in the general scheme. It expresses his humiliation at his exile and his contempt for the condition of fallen man as well as for those who believe that that condition is the natural and only possible one. If he plastered his opponents with dung, covered them over with what Mr. Flann O'Brien has exquisitely described as "a thin layer of buff-coloured puke," it was because

> The Vision of Christ that thou dost see
> Is my Vision's Greatest Enemy.

The enemies are those who believe in progress, who think that the earth can again be turned, by material means, into some kind of Paradise—what he savagely calls "the shitty Paradise of the Republicans." And he feels himself befouled by them, and by having to work in this odd medium, to the point of martyrdom, the point where filth achieves a kind of apotheosis: "I shall ascend to Paradise with a Crown of Turds!"

The great feature of the work, then, is its integrity—the same sort of integrity that one finds in one of the great French cathedrals, where every detail, quaint, exuberant, or obscene, is yet conceived in the same spirit and executed with the same verve as the great motifs of the Crucifixion or the Last Judgment. By sheer passion Bloy succeeded where since the pre-Raphaelites so many wistful archaizers had failed: he wrote a medieval work about the nineteenth century. Yet integral and medieval though it is, and though it revives the symbolism of the Scriptures in the days of the symbolism of the *décadents,* the work is modern in one very important respect: it is, as well as being a *Summa,* an immense self-portrait. It is a poem in which the mystical interdependence of all life—the "reversibility of the Communion of Saints" extended—is always implied and therefore there are no absolute lines of demarcation between the personal, the historical, and the religious. Bloy's private agonies, the progress of the nineteenth century, the preparation for the Second Coming: these can be fused into one work because they are felt to be the same; *felt,* and in a very real way, for the agent of fusion is pain. Pain is the very stuff of history, religion, and consciousness itself.

"Pain," wrote Bloy in one of his first works, "is everything in life and, because it is everything, we draw from it, as from the inexhaustible bosom of God, all the types of our thought."

Because of its very anachronism, its extension in time and eternity, the work seems to accumulate a superhumanly vast charge of suffering: to be a hymn of all the inarticulate pain of Christendom, from the lazar-houses of Saint Louis to the factories of nineteenth-century England. And all this pain, for which Bloy's own sufferings are the "medium," calls with a tremendous voice for the recovery of the earthly Paradise. If Bloy was mad—and it would seem that he was at least very near madness at the time when, with Anne-Marie, he evolved the categories of thought on which his work is based—his madness was capable of picking up and re-transmitting, in a kind of code, the radiations of a collective mind, itself not so very sane. Moreover that very sensitivity, that "communion of pain," may have made him aware, as he claims to have been, of the trend of future events: the events that were already in his time being shaped by forces whose existence Marx had plotted in prose and he himself had transfigured in ecstatic poetry. He constantly spoke of impending terrible events, the coming of "the Cossacks and the Holy Ghost," and thought that humanity's sense of the nearness of doom was responsible for its aimless and insane conduct. "Could it be that we are approaching some divine solution, the prodigious proximity of which is sending the needle of the human compass spinning crazily on its axis?"

It had some cause to spin. (pp. 215-22)

Donat O'Donnell (pseudonym of Conor Cruise O'Brien), "The Paradise of Léon Bloy," in his Maria Cross: Imaginative Patterns in a Group of Modern Catholic Writers, *Oxford University Press, 1952, pp. 203-22.*

KURT F. REINHARDT (essay date 1969)

[Reinhardt was a German-born American critic who wrote several studies of Catholic theology. In the following excerpt, he describes the disillusionment with the practices of modern Christians that informs Bloy's works.]

Two main themes can be discerned in what Bloy's wife and his friends termed his "prophetic mission." The first is his anticipation of the epochal catastrophe which he envisaged as the sequel of the modern defection from Christ and Christianity. The second is the praise of poverty as the only legitimate imitation of Christ. In the novel *Le désespéré* Bloy says of himself that "as a perpetual dreamer I was never able to see things as they actually are" and that "there existed perhaps never a more helpless and inept individual whenever it was a question of seizing opportunities."

It is interesting and rewarding to consider briefly the principal concepts of Bloy's philosophy of history. Like Nietzsche, he was looking in history for the revelation of the mystery of existence. For him, however, history was above all the history of the divine will. Historical facts were for Bloy the raw material in which "the style of the divine Word" documents itself with an iron necessity. History was a mysterious and symbolic divine language which told of the ways in which man was being tried and tested by his Creator. Through "the chaotic sea of facts" he wanted to penetrate to the recognition of the "boundless solidarity of everything that has happened in different times and at different places." Bloy's many shocking accusations and condemnations of the bourgeois, the rich, the landlords, the popes, the Jews, the Freemasons, philosophers, technocrats, musicians, writers, journalists, Englishmen, Germans, and Protestants are manifestations of the disgust with which this worshipper of the Absolute looked upon all those who are satisfied with less than the Absolute—upon all those, including himself, who are not saints. His revolt grew out of a depth of resentment and existential anguish as did the similar outcries of revolt of a Kierkegaard, a Nietzsche and an Unamuno. Their common starting point is the great lament over the agony of Christianity and the apostasy of modern man. Bloy tried to persuade his contemporaries that they were living in that world-historic hour when professing "Christians" were crucifying the Holy Spirit.

In *Le désespéré* we read that the present civilization of "Christians" and "good Catholics" is "the snow-like leprosy of religious sentimentalism." Looking at modern Christendom, "we must ask ourselves whether Sodom and Gomorrah were not devout and saintly in comparison with this modern sewer of innocence." Our "good Christians dishonor God more than the most fanatical enemies of Christianity were ever able to."

Léon Bloy was, in short, an author so overpowered by his own existential anguish that he lost more and more the freedom of a personal perspective and therewith also the possibility of taking a personal, critical decisive stand with respect to his own ego. Above all, he lacked completely a redeeming sense of humor, and it was perhaps this lack which caused him to take himself and his sufferings much too seriously. His constant gesticulating and his often pompous and fuzzy prose are expressions of a discordant and split psyche which is striving for powerful self-assertion and self-assurance at any price.

What Bloy—despite basic differences—has in common with the present generation of Roman Catholic writers (for example, Mauriac, Julien Green, Waugh and Graham Greene) is the realization and conviction that the time is past when one could naively and safely call oneself a Christian and actually live the life of a pagan. Bloy was the first among European Christian novelists to point out the dangers of a provincial pharisaical denominationalism, and he was one of those few who defined religious faith in terms of risk and resolute daring in personal existential action. (pp. 76-7)

In the first volume of the *Journal* (titled **Le mendiant ingrat**) Bloy endorses exclusively the integral Roman Catholic point of view: "Everything that is not exclusively and unconditionally . . . Catholic, belongs to the gutter." . . . Or: "In my justified pride I possess the boldness of bragging about the many enmities which I have made among the professional pundits by my aggressive need for independence." . . . "I have the honor of being the most feared and therefore also the most maligned writer of my time." . . . "The unbelievers curse me because I scoff at their sophistries, and the believers detest me because I dare hurl their cowardice into their faces." . . .

Bloy reproaches the Church and certain members of the clergy for their crass materialism and for their soft, sentimental piety: "Every Christian who is not a hero is a pig." He regarded it as his divinely appointed task to be or become the "pilgrim of the Absolute." Bloy was one of the first to call attention to the weakening of religious faith in France, especially among the working class and the peasantry. And yet he again and again emphasizes his own unworthiness while at the same time asserting the total integrity of his motives: "Actually, I am one of the meek and obedient. This is why as a writer I regard it as my task to be inexorable in the defense of truth and to bear witness to the God of the poor. That is all. The most violent pages of my books were motivated by love, were often written with tears of love, in hours when I felt surrounded by an unfathomable peace." (pp. 79-80)

In **The Woman Who Was Poor** Bloy depicts that most desolate and abject poverty which surrounded him in Paris and which he himself experienced through most of the years of his life. This is why he could say: "We do not enter paradise tomorrow or the day after or ten years hence; we enter it today *if* we are poor and crucified." The novel is autobiographical, especially in its second half, in the portrayal of the tragic life and love of Clotilde and Léopold. The theme of poverty as it is presented here shows a peculiar fusion of medieval and romanticist ideas. Bloy, as has been pointed out, associates the degradation of the human person with the civilization of the nineteenth and twentieth centuries. Man has become drunk with his material success, with scientific progress, and his greed for money and pleasure has increased proportionately. As a consequence the poor are deprived of the last vestiges of their human dignity. The thesis which Bloy advances pleads for the restoration of the poor to their proper place in society as creatures formed in the image of God. Bloy hated every thought of mediocrity, and it was mediocrity that he saw embodied in the "bourgeois." Even more, if possible, he despised the "respectable woman" (*la femme honnête*). She, too, is too mediocre: neither hot nor cold, neither a saint nor a real sinner: "Woman has only two ways of living, either a life of sanctity or a life of sensual pleasure. . . . Between these two there exists only *la femme honnête*, that is to say, the female of the bourgeois—the ultimate reprobate whom no sacrifice can redeem." In this sense the reader must interpret the shocking portrayal of Mademoiselle Planude in **La femme pauvre**. She is a practicing Roman Catholic woman and as such "very respectable," but she is at the same time a landlady and thus a hardened *petite bourgeoise*. And nothing could be more despicable, nothing

more hypocritical: "Mademoiselle Planude would kneel at the Holy Table with a little bag worn next to her chaste skin, in which title deeds and IOU's were tied up jointly with religious medals and scapulars."

The novel analyzes the underlying reasons for the moral and spiritual decadence of the Catholic laity. Bloy holds the clergy responsible for this spiritual decline, particularly what he calls the "clerical confectionery of Saint Sulpice." "A saintly clergy," Bloy writes, "produces a virtuous laity, a virtuous clergy produces a respectable laity, and a respectable clergy produces a profane laity." As a matter of fact, too many priests, Bloy contends, favor their wealthy parishioners. The typical average homily distinguishes carefully and often with cautious casuistry between the *commandments* and the *counsels* of the Gospels in order not to offend the average bourgeois churchgoer. While the commandments simply state the minimum required to get by, the counsels stipulate the maximum as enunciated in the Sermon on the Mount. (pp. 81-2)

Pain was for Bloy the mysterious affinity in man which made of him the eternal companion of divine beauty. Human pain he saw enclosed and enshrined in the divine pain, in the folly of the Cross.

While the theory of art for art's sake symbolizes for Bloy the poet in his ivory tower, he saw poetry always as a result of suffering and therefore capable of contributing its weighty share to the religious work of redemption, a redemption bought with the poet's blood. Thus, for Bloy, poetry and art were linked closely with the eternal destiny of Man: *L'art pour le salut*, that is, he regarded it as the destiny of art to contribute to man's salvation.

Bloy never regarded himself primarily as a writer. His one and only aim was to serve God, and he tried to serve Him with his writing, which he regarded as his greatest gift: "I am a pilgrim of the Holy Sepulcher—I am just that and nothing else."

The main sources of Bloy's thinking and writing were quite consistently the Bible and the liturgy of the Church. He likened himself to the Old Testament Prophets, and he thought he had inherited from them the voice of one who calls his people to repentance. But he realized well enough that he was only a feeble tool used by Providence: "Rest assured that I am simply a poor and humble Christian, nothing else, nothing more. It has pleased God to bestow on me a gift for literary expression such that I was an old man before I recognized my sad soul under this disguise" (see *Le vieux de la montagne*). He quite consistently lived in a self-created world of absolutes. From that dizzy height he looked down upon the world and upon men and judged it and them. He would not tolerate contradiction and he disliked debates and discussions with other members of the literary guild.

There obviously were striking contrasts and contradictions in Bloy's character. On the one hand, he was incredibly stubborn, vain and apparently self-assured, lacking in a charity which would have made him at least respect those with whom he disagreed. On the other hand, he rediscovered the strength and the truth of an integral Christianity whose immortal values he wished to impart to his fellowmen. He did not and could not offer a palpable practical solution for the social injustices of his age, but he did insist on the inherent dignity of the human soul and especially on the human dignity of the poor as the ones who were closest to Christ. With respect to the two extremes of individualism and socialism, he proclaimed the social solidarity of all the members of the Mystical Body of Christ, in which individualism and socialism appear, as it were, harmonized in a higher synthesis. (pp. 90-1)

Kurt F. Reinhardt, "Léon Bloy: 'Pilgrim of the Absolute','' in his The Theological Novel of Modern Europe: An Analysis of Masterpieces by Eight Authors, Frederick Ungar Publishing Co., 1969, pp. 74-92.

JENNIFER BIRKETT   (essay date 1975)

[*In the following excerpt, Birkett explains the thematic unity of Bloy's novels.*]

[Bloy took] a love intrigue as the unifying theme of both his novels (*Le Désespéré* and *La Femme pauvre*) and the vehicle through which he presented his most important religious statements. My purpose here is to establish the way in which love intrigue and doctrinal statement interrelate in these works, and to show how Bloy's own experience, as well as literary influences, conditioned his choice and presentation of the theme.

The evidence of *Le Désespéré,* confirmed by Bloy's diary and early letters, is that the combined forces of poverty, timidity and religious scruples at first encouraged Bloy in an ascetic idealism which in 1869 dismissed the flesh as "ces chaînes de fange" ["these bonds of filth"] and saw spiritual life as consisting in "l'oubli absolu des sens" ["the absolute obliteration of the senses"]; the only love was the love of God. There are indications that the misogynistic pose Bloy adopted as a consequence of this theory was occasionally threatened during the following years, but his first serious (and secret) liaison with the prostitute Anne-Marie Roulé, the Véronique of *Le Désespéré,* did not begin until February-March 1877.

Bloy embarked on the affair with a sense of guilt, evident in the recasting and reinterpretation of events in his letters of this period and in *Le Désespéré* itself, but also with a conviction of its necessity. At La Trappe (22 September-2 October 1877) he tried to renounce Anne-Marie for a religious vocation; failing this, he attempted to convert her and eventually decided that marriage was the only solution. However, marriage proved financially impossible. In September 1878, Anne-Marie was converted at the Basilica and the relationship moved on to a new spiritual plane. It was at this time that her visions of the Second Coming began, probably inspired by Bloy's explanations of the doctrines of Tardif de Moidrey and Ernest Hello. She was interned in Sainte-Anne on 29 June 1882, and Bloy saw no more of her before her death on 7 May 1907.

Bloy found Berthe Dumont begging in the streets in the winter of 1883-84. This affair, pitched in a lower key than the first, was allowed to become common knowledge; the couple frequented Huysmans and Anna Meunier, and Bloy referred to Berthe as his fiancée and even his wife. They set up house at Fontenay-aux-Roses 5 March 1885. During this period of relative calm *Le Désespéré* was conceived (September 1884) and the first number of *Le Pal* appeared (4 March 1885). Then on the night of 10-11 May 1885, Berthe died of tetanus; Bloy, impoverished by his new review, was forced to borrow money for her funeral.

Letters to Louis Montchal describe Bloy's anguish at Berthe's death at the same time as they formulate the themes of *Le Désespéré,* built on a conflation of Bloy's two unhappy experiences in love. Very quickly, the loss of Anne-Marie becomes primary, and with it Bloy's overwhelming sense of the bitterness and disillusionment of love. On 31 December 1885

he tells Montchal that chapters 20 and 21 are completed, describing the death of Marchenoir's son and his meeting with the prostitute Véronique. The episode is a transposition of Bloy's own sufferings: "J'ai tout arraché de mes entrailles" ["I tore out all my entrails"]. It appears that Bloy, like Barbey, is beginning to conceive of his book as an apology for human weakness. . . . With this less rigorous morality Bloy still combined a high Romantic idealism, also encouraged by Barbey's circle: "J'ai un idéal d'amour, de vie, et d'éloquence qui ne sert qu'à me désespérer parce qu'il est inaccessible" ["I have an ideal of love, of life, and of eloquence which only makes me despair because it is unattainable"] (14 April 1886). His novel gradually became an attempt to give coherent expression to the conflict implied in these two attitudes.

Bloy was disappointed that the book's chief success on its publication in 1886 came from its polemic content (the chapters satirizing his literary contemporaries). He wrote to Montchal 19 January 1887:

> Une chose m'ennuie dans ta lettre, c'est que tu parais n'avoir été frappé que de la partie épisodique de mon livre, lequel n'est pas un pamphlet, mais un roman psychologique des plus fouillés. Je donnerais tout le festin de Beauvivier qui est pourtant, je le crois, une chose forte, pour le personnage de Véronique, les chapitres 28ᵉ, 63ᵉ, 64ᵉ, 65ᵉ et 68ᵉ, le séjour à La Chartreuse, le symbolisme et la fin de Marchenoir.

> [One thing in your letter bothers me, that you seem not to have been struck by the episodic part of my book, which is not a pamphlet but a most probing psychological novel. I would trade all the feasting of Beauvivier for the character of Véronique, chapters 28, 63, 64, 65 and 68, the sojourn at Chartreuse, the symbolism and demise of Marchenoir.]

These are all groups which relate either directly to the love affair or to the digressive passages with which it is imaginatively connected. Critics have not so far tried to connect the two; one of the most sensitive of Bloy's contemporary readers, Maurice Dullaert, complained of a structural weakness in the novel in its failure to establish any conjunction between the central narrative and the philosophical digressions. The narrative, he argued, provided only a "sketchy" framework for the "magnificent" pages on history, liberty, suffering and the failure of the Redemption which were the main source of interest. Closer analysis shows that the two are in fact formally and thematically interdependent—different perspectives on the same problem, between which Bloy deliberately moves. They are intimately linked, as Bloy's own experience in love is intimately linked with his doctrine.

In the hope of disarming accusations that this experience was responsible for his religious options, Bloy makes no mention of the love nexus until chapter 16, by which time Marchenoir's early life and conversion and the main lines of his philosophy have been set out. Only then, in this chapter, does he offer his own explanation of the relationship between carnal experience and Catholic doctrine. Marchenoir's own conduct falls far short of "[les] héroïques puretés qu'il avait rêvées" ["the heroic purity of which he dreamed"]; but he believes that his imperfections and moral struggles have brought him to a deeper understanding of Catholicism and its appropriateness to human nature than the advocates of strict purity have ever reached. His account of his conversion (''l'exacte genèse de ce catholique ballotté par d'impures vagues au-dessus d'absurdes abîmes'' [''the precise genesis of this Catholic tossed by impure waves above absurd abysses'']) shows how carnal love can be a means of understanding spiritual love. His religious and emotional sensibilities were revealed to him simultaneously, almost by an act of Providence. . . . The violence of carnal passion offers the only terms adequate to present his new and revolutionary concept of religion as an enthusiasm: ''le sentiment religieux est une passion d'amour'' [''religious feeling is a lover's passion'']. Like human love, religious emotion tears apart and inflames the personality; it is wholly instinctive, allowing no controls or rational choices. Both loves are involuntary and irrefutable. . . . Both leave the creature vulnerable. The vulnerability created by passion softens the heart in preparation for grace by imposing the humiliation, suffering and self-revulsion which mould the religious character.

Bloy goes on to claim that guilty passion has its own merit. (Here he goes further than the Barbey of *Un Prêtre marié*, whose heroine's sufferings became meritorious because of her purity and innocence.) At his father's deathbed, Marchenoir is overwhelmed by remorse at the recollection of his past affairs; through Marian imagery, the merit of his remorse is applied to relieve his father's suffering in Purgatory. But these affairs are over. It is less easy to justify suffering from an affair with Véronique which is still in progress. . . . The solution to this problem is worked out through the rest of the novel. Bloy describes the intensity of suffering experienced within the relationship and explains its meaning by working it into the cosmic theme that all suffering forms part of Christ's redemptive Passion.

He organizes his plot to show Marchenoir not entering voluntarily into the affair, but constrained to it by Fate, or Providence (chapter 22). Attracted by Marchenoir's chastity, Véronique forces herself upon him. Converted by his intransigeance, she becomes a responsibility he cannot refuse. Theirs is a relationship of two destitute creatures, the poor servant willingly submitting to a poor master. (These are the terms in which Tardif de Moidrey and the thirteenth-century mystic Angela de Foligno, whom Bloy read in Hello's translation, had described the relationship between Christ and the individual Christian or the Church.) It is only at the Charterhouse—under the aegis of the Church—that Marchenoir discovers, with the help of his confessor, an unsuspected carnal desire for Véronique. She is untouched by this; she is the ''perle évangélique'' [''evangelical pearl''] whom he has ransomed, the creature to whom, Christ-like, he has restored the purity and dignity of the flesh of the First Creation. . . . In the figure of Véronique, Bloy and Marchenoir salvage the ascetic ideal.

However, Marchenoir, like Christ, is degraded and disfigured in exact proportion to Véronique's past sins, having freely accepted responsibility for these—responsibility which could not have been laid on Véronique, creature of her environment. Linked to her in intention, if not in fact, by the sacramental bond of marriage, Marchenoir shares her expiation in the flesh. In him, all her sins are made visible. The unconscious undermining of his will to chastity is a mirror-image of her former condition; and through the ugliness of his jealousy he evokes with nightmare acuteness the shame of each incident of her past and the horror of the alienation from God which her submission to carnality implied. . . . The latent analogy here is Christ's suffering for the Church, and the disfigurement of

Marchenoir that of Christ on the Cross, the Suffering Servant. The image masks a moral evasion on Bloy's part; Marchenoir is absolved from the guilt of his own lust—for which, despite his disclaimers, he ultimately makes Véronique responsible—whilst still claiming the merit of acknowledging and regretting it.

In the act of redemption, the redeemed object must co-operate. Bloy extends his narrative into new dimensions in the digressions which show how the sufferings of the contemplative Church and those of the whole of history are necessary contributions to the redeeming Agony of Christ. He then immediately returns to the narrative to show how this pattern repeats itself, in little and intensified, in the relationship of Marchenoir and Véronique. Marchenoir appeals to his mistress for some heroic act of consolation and resolution to strengthen him in his weakening efforts against the sins he has taken on for her. He emphasizes her sacramental character of Woman and her consequent special capacity for expiatory sacrifice. . . . The reference here is to the compassionate suffering of Mary at the Foot of the Cross, as in Faber's doctrine. Véronique responds with an act of self-disfigurement which only adds an extra, spiritual, dimension to her attractions. She becomes for him the perfect image of Woman, object of lust and of spiritual desire, Magdalen and *Mater Dolorosa*—''cariatide de lupanar, transformée en un pilastre éclatant de la Tour d'Ivoire'' [''whorehouse caryatid, transformed into a shining pillar of the Ivory Tower''] . . .—and their relationship, with all its spiritual dangers, is permanently sealed.

In these conditions, Marchenoir admits that his proposal to redeem the world with the help of Véronique is a hazardous venture; but the Church again intervenes to support him. The Carthusian P. Athanase declares that the dangers of his venture will leave him relying on faith alone, and blesses the mission. From this point, the relationship becomes an increasingly explicit allegory of the redemptive compassion of humanity with Christ. The couple share a martyrdom imposed by fellow-Catholics hostile to enthusiasm, and by the atheists of the literary circles at whom Marchenoir directs his evangelism. . . . Their martyrdom is not optional, but one set in the nature of things. Marchenoir's carnal attraction towards Véronique is as inevitable as Christ's impulse to unity with Creation; and equally inevitable is the suffering both impulses involve. The violence of the novel's language intensifies to express this inevitability. Even Marchenoir's religious practices conspire to tempt him closer to the body of his mistress. . . . (pp. 65-70)

The two modes of love which Véronique inspires in Marchenoir are expressions of the two aspects of Creation—the redeemed and the fallen—whose conjunction Bloy would like to suggest is the highpoint of human experience. This is demonstrated to perfection in the episode in chapter 65 in which Marchenoir's desire to seduce Véronique, painted in strongly sensual language, is transformed into pure compassion at the sight of her suffering on his behalf. This episode, potentially the most decadent in the book, is also the one which produces the most complete identification of the lovers with one another and with Christ, being the moment of most intense anguish. Véronique turns from her crucifix to address Marchenoir, hitherto the representative of Christ, with Christ's liturgical reproach to his people from the Cross (''*Quid feci tibi* . . .'').

In this novel, then, it would appear that the Church's teaching on compassionate suffering is invoked by Bloy to ratify a relationship of whose moral status he is in doubt. In defending carnal love in the terms he chooses—especially the analogy of

Christ and the Church—he goes much further than Barbey in elaborating a case for a new moral attitude, but we must recognize at the same time that there is a latent negative note in his challenge which undercuts his claims; the carnal love he depicts is never consummated, operates always in suffering, and ends in madness and death. The spiritual dimension called upon to redeem it finally swallows up and negates it. This is conceded with a struggle in *Le Désespéré*, but in Bloy's second novel, *La Femme pauvre* . . . , accepted without question. (p. 70)

Earlier studies of *La Femme pauvre* have concentrated too much on the isolated figure of woman as object of desire, and have consequently been far too ready to find for Bloy unorthodox or even heretical analogues. Ernest Beaumont, for example, in his article "*La Femme pauvre* and feminine mythology," misses altogether the concept of the couple, who redeem the universe by their shared suffering, and ignores the fact that there are other victims in the novel beside the woman, whose sufferings do not become meritorious until a preliminary sacrifice by Man (Gacougnol and Marchenoir) which creates in her a state of responsibility. He also leaves aside the long climax of the novel in the *dual* holocaust of Léopold and Clotilde, and therefore does not fully explain the creative—redemptive—function which Bloy's conclusion tries paradoxically to argue is inherent in the possession and renunciation of earthly love. The strength of Bloy's claim is doubtful; but it seems important to see it as attached to contemporary French Catholic orthodoxy rather than minority aberrations.

This emphasis on the compassionate function of Woman is constant from Bloy's first idea for his novel. His original intention was to present this in a negative form, reminiscent of Barbey, illustrating the sacrilege involved in a woman's selling her love. In the finished novel, presumably under the influence of Jeanne, the negative aspect is concentrated into the eight opening chapters describing Clotilde's fall and her period of remorse and despair before meeting Gacougnol. Against the background of her mother's sordid marriage and the squalor of her surroundings, Bloy traces her chaste and humble progress to an inevitable seduction which she tries to pretend is real love, but which her lover's mediocrity and her mother's cupidity maintain inexorably on a mercenary and humiliating level, as a futile and gratuitous act. Her engagement as an artist's model is described as a second prostitution. The hysteria with which she approaches the proposition is more than mere prudery; it is justified psychologically by the tensions created by her previous experience, and doctrinally in the sense of the letter to Jeanne, which Bloy explains again here. Clotilde is being asked to join a conspiracy to deny the intrinsic dignity of the human body, which lies in its ability to engage all its faculties in an enthusiasm, passion or ideal incapable of temporal fulfilment. The artist sees his art as an ideal satisfying in itself; and it is to illustrate this that he proposes to buy the body and the modesty of Clotilde, who becomes a part of Creation diverted from its real redemptive purpose. . . . At this extreme of humiliation, Gacougnol intervenes. The idea of sacrilege is dropped, and the novel begins to explain the positive value of the love Clotilde has to offer. Because of their physical structure, all women are images of Mary, in her redemptive role as vehicle of the Incarnation, which she earned by the immaculate humility and submissiveness which caused God to desire her. Woman is wholly Love and object of desire. The only two modes in which she can exist are beatitude and lust, in both of which she is an impersonal channel of pleasure or grace—"dispensatrice de la Joie" ["bestower of Joy"]. Clotilde (like Véronique) combines both; her childish inno-

cence combined with tender maturity has for Gacougnol an irresistible emotional appeal which inspires a spiritual yearning: "pauvre petite chair amoureuse. . . . Il sortait de cette physionomie comme une main de douceur qui tirait l'âme de ses enveloppes et la colloquait comme dans une prison de cristal" ["poor little loving being. . . . It came from her countenance like a gentle hand which drew the soul from its envelopes and enclosed it as in a prison of crystal"]. . . . (pp. 73-5)

The desire she inspires takes immediate effect as the imposition of suffering on those associated with her. The compassion she inspires and the consolation she offers build up and sustain a nexus of mutual needs which Bloy sees as the images of the interdependent Creation God intends. In her relationship with Léopold, this is clearly illustrated. After the scandal of Gacougnol's death, Clotilde draws away, reluctant to impose on her admirer; consequently, the renewing of their relationship is both providential and an act of free choice by Léopold. It occurs under the aegis of the triumphant Virgin, whom Clotilde has been imagining receiving the homage of a repentant prodigal France—the implication is that their relationship figures this national repentance. Clotilde refers to their mutual unhappiness and her compassion for Léopold, and then betrays her own need with a request for food. The joint appeal of her beauty and her distress mediates to him a moment of magnificence which is the first stage of his conversion. . . . The moment completes the restoration of Clotilde, who then hears Léopold's confession and absolves him, clearing the way for the infusion of grace which the Church later accomplishes. The two lovers enter married life mutually purified, to encounter the sufferings which compose their union. Léopold's blindness, continual poverty, the deaths of Marchenoir, Lazare Druide, and their son André, maintain in them the awareness that there is no final earthly happiness. The high point of their terrestrial union is the fire of physical and mystical suffering which confirms their perfect identity in sacrificial love, coinciding with the separation of their physical bodies. The last chapter illustrates the dynamism inherent in the separation. With the earthly Léopold set eternally out of reach, Clotilde is left fixed in the state of frustrated longing which is the condition of perfective efforts and the highest state which can be reached on earth; accounted by Bloy earthly beatitude.

What is most interesting in Bloy's two novels is the consistency of their ideas. There is, of course, a conspicuous shift in emphasis from the angry revolt in *Le Désespéré* against the suffering Bloy found associated with love to a submissive acceptance in *La Femme pauvre,* which is due to the different nature of the two relationships presented—in the first novel, a liaison with a former prostitute which flies in the face of social convention, and in the second, a respectable marriage with a woman whose only real sin is her poverty. The doctrine chosen to justify the protagonists' unhappiness remains the same; the suffering of both couples acquires meaning by its attachment to Mary's Compassion with Christ. This is the Catholic image at the heart of Bloy's concept of suffering, and also at the heart of his contemporaries' devotions; and it is to this centre that his and their emphasis on such doctrines as vicarious suffering and solidarity within the Communion of Saints should be related. When this point of interpretation is reached we can finally see that the interest of Bloy's adaptation of doctrine to experience goes beyond the merely personal. Its purpose is not simply to justify his own sexuality but to express a desire for a restored solidarity and unity in his society—prodigal France—which links up with the desires of his contemporaries. That the unity aspired to should be expressed in this particular devotion—in the negative mode of suffering—is one of the contradictions built into the politics of the whole Catholic Revival. (pp. 75-6)

> *Jennifer Birkett, "The Theme of Love in the Work of Léon Bloy," in Nottingham French Studies, Vol. XIV, No. 2, October, 1975, pp. 65-76.*

ADDITIONAL BIBLIOGRAPHY

Beaumont, E. "*La femme pauvre* and Feminine Mythology." In *Studies in French Literature Presented to H. W. Lawton by Colleagues, Pupils, and Friends,* edited by J. C. Ireson, I. D. McFarlane, and Garnett Rees, pp. 29-49. Manchester: Manchester University Press, 1968.
  Analyzes Bloy's concept of the role of women in man's salvation.

Birkett, Jennifer. "Barbey d'Aurevilly and Léon Bloy: Love and Morality in the Catholic Novel." *Nottingham French Studies* XIV, No. 1 (May 1975): 3-10.
  Discusses Bloy's concept of the function and nature of the novel.

Boyd, Ernest. "Léon Bloy: Ungrateful Beggar." *The Saturday Review* XX, No. 7 (10 June 1939): 17.
  A review of *The Woman Who Was Poor* that is primarily concerned with a negative portrayal of Bloy's life. Regarding Bloy's work, Boyd asks: "What, then, is the importance of Léon Bloy? Is he readable? The answer is yes, if one is not bored or disgusted by his religious ravings, for which . . . a certain theological bias is necessary to induce either horror or respect." He is a writer who "all admirers of vigorous invective and brutal satire will appreciate" and *The Woman Who Was Poor* "is full of excellent talk about art, literature, and music. . . .' "

Freemantle, Anne. "In Praise of Poverty." *New York Herald Book Review* 24, No. 17 (14 December 1947): 12.
  Contends that the tone of everything that Bloy wrote "is the groaning and travailing of all creation, even of the animal, vegetable, and mineral kingdoms."

Fumet, Stanislas. "Léon Bloy: Imperfect Splendor." *Renascence* VII, No. 1 (Autumn 1954): 11-16.
  Assesses Bloy's life and literary importance. Fumet calls Bloy "a most astonishing writer in his generation. His style alone, which has been imitated widely, should have been enough to assure him of a prominent place in manuals of literature. However, he does not have a place in any of them. One thinks inevitably of those histories of painting where no mention is made of Tintoretto or of El Greco. For Bloy wrote as these men painted: a skilled page by Bloy is the equivalent of a canvas by either of these two."

Heppenstall, Rayner. *Léon Bloy.* Cambridge: Bowes and Bowes, 1953. 62 p.
  Views Bloy in the context of orthodox Catholic beliefs and discusses the effect Bloy's writings had upon Heppenstall's own thought.

Lalou, René. "The Contemporary Novel." In his *Contemporary French Literature,* pp. 287-335. New York: Alfred A. Knopf, 1924.
  Examines Bloy's philosophy through quotations from his works.

Norman, Mrs. George. "The Enigma of Léon Bloy." *The Dublin Review* 201, No. 403 (October 1937): 235-49.
  Comments on apparent contradictions in Bloy's life and thought.

O'Malley, Frank. "The Passion of Léon Bloy." *The Review of Politics* 10, No. 1 (January 1948): 100-15.
  Explanation of Bloy's theology.

Ottensmeyer, Hilary. "Léon Bloy and the Accusation of Heresy." *Renascence* XIV, No. 2 (Winter 1962): 93-101.
  Places Bloy in the context of nineteenth-century religious thought.

Pfleger, Karl. "Bloy: Pilgrim of the Absolute." In his *Wrestlers with Christ,* pp. 29-71. New York: Sheed and Ward, 1937.
  Analysis of Bloy as a religious thinker and evangelist.

Robert Desnos

1900-1945

(Also wrote under pseudonyms of Lucien Gallois, Pierre Andier, Valentin Gullois, and Cancale) French poet, novelist, short story writer, dramatist, essayist, and critic.

Desnos was one of the original members of the Surrealist movement and one of the most adept at its experimental techniques. He especially aroused admiration in other members of the group with his proficiency at automatic writing and "speaking thought" while in hypnotic sleep. Ultimately, however, Desnos rejected the methods and doctrines of Surrealism systematized by André Breton as too limiting, turning instead to more traditional and structured verse forms such as the alexandrine line and the sonnet. Nevertheless, Desnos's writings both before and after his association with Surrealism are unified by his celebration of ecstatic love.

The son of middle-class parents, Desnos grew up in Paris. He was a poor student, and at the age of fourteen left school and his family, supporting himself by a succession of jobs and serving his compulsory two years in the military. Endowed with a natural talent for writing, Desnos began publishing poetry by the age of seventeen. Soon afterward, he made friends with future Surrealists Roger Vitrac, Benjamin Péret, and André Breton. In 1922 Desnos began publishing transcriptions of his dreams in Breton's new avante-garde journal *Littérature*. He was soon excelling at the Surrealists' experiments with automatic writing and speech, amazing the rest of the group with long verbal monologues spoken while in a hypnotic dream state. Paul Eluard, the Surrealist most committed to poetry, said of Desnos that he "could speak as few poets can write." During this Surrealist period, Desnos was a sexual libertine, drank and gambled heavily, and used drugs during times of stress. With the publication of *A la mystérieuse,* Desnos began to write love poetry, inspired first by his ten-year unrequited passion for Yvonne George and, after her death, by his affection for Youki Foujita, whom he met in 1927 and married soon afterward. At the same time, Desnos was becoming uncomfortable with the Surrealist group's political activity. He also felt restricted by Breton's proscriptions on art as well as the leader's increasing domination of the group. Desnos wanted to experiment with traditional poetic meters and techniques, and he endeavored to gain wider dissemination of his work by becoming a contributor to several mainstream Paris periodicals. He slowly separated from the other Surrealists, and an attack by Breton accusing Desnos of "non-involvement" and "journalistic activities" led to a public break from the group in 1929, though Desnos retained several friends among the Surrealists and continued to call himself a Surrealist "in its most open sense" for the rest of his life. During the 1930s he wrote radio scripts, advertising, and songs, as well as much prose and poetry in traditional forms. With the advent of World War II Desnos devoted himself to writing resistance poetry, was arrested by the Gestapo in 1944, and deported to Nazi concentration camps, where he died of typhoid fever in 1945, only days after the camp had been liberated by the Allies. Nearly all the poetry he wrote while imprisoned was lost, and much of his earlier work was not published until after his death. In

1946 Breton publicly expressed regret for his and the Surrealist's estrangement from Desnos.

Although Desnos's writing underwent many changes during his lifetime, his career can be divided into two major periods separated by the year of his disassociation from Breton, 1929. The works that Desnos wrote before that date have received the greatest critical attention. Desnos's first major work, *Rrose Sélavy,* is a collection of 150 brief aphorisms constructed mechanically by taking words from the first part of a sentence and transposing their letters in the manner of a spoonerism; for example: *"L'acte des sexes est l'axe des sectes."* Desnos continued experimenting with language in *L'aumonyme* and *Langage cuit,* juxtaposing homonyms that are not logically connected and repeating key words in order to suggest various possible meanings of each word. More importantly, though, in *Langage cuit* Desnos began to use his irrational wordplay to evoke emotion, "communicating feeling as though in spite of language," as J. H. Matthews has written. It is clear that Desnos's early linguistic experimentation and practice with automatic writing freed his work from the rigors of rationality, allowing words to create meaning through their evocative power rather than through logical definition. The aim of the Surrealists was to speak directly from the subconscious of the writer to that of the reader, without intervention from the rational mind.

To this effect, Desnos wrote with a purposeful lack of logical coherence.

With the publication of the novel *Deuil pour Deuil* and the poetry collection *A la mystérieuse*, Desnos turned his attention toward the single theme of love, particularly love in the form of a mystical longing in which desire becomes its own fulfillment. In both *Deuil pour deuil* and a second novel, *La liberté ou l'amour!*, Desnos presented a protagonist who unsuccessfully pursues the woman he loves. Closely related to this theme is that of a mystical union between Desnos's narrator and an enigmatic lover who may or may not actually exist. Desnos wrote of such experiences occurring to him over a period of several months in *Journal d'une apparition*, and concluded that the "apparition," who visited him at night when he left his door open for her, was a real woman because he had perceived her through the same senses by which he perceived the rest of the world. This denial of objective reality and affirmation of the mystical was central to the Surrealist philosophy as defined by Breton.

Critics are divided in their approach to Desnos's post-Surrealist work. Though most agree that Desnos reached the peak of his creative power toward the end of his Surrealist period with *La liberté ou l'amour!* and *Les ténèbres*, many believe that he turned toward consciously artistic writing and structured verse forms purposefully, while a few, notably Mary Ann Caws, who calls Desnos's later novel *Le vin est tiré* "unreadable," contend that Desnos was unwillingly becoming more "rigid" as time progressed. Yet others point out that it is probable that by 1929 Desnos felt he had simply exhausted the possibilities of Surrealism, as did several of the other Surrealists who left Breton's group at the same time to concentrate on more conventional forms. Among Desnos's most notable later works are *Le vin est tiré*, a novel which explores and ultimately condemns the use of drugs, and his last collection of poetry, *Contrée*, which includes meditations on his Surrealist days.

Despite his abandonment of Surrealism, Desnos is still considered a major contributor to the growth and success of the movement. What Breton had envisioned in theory, Desnos achieved in fact, possibly better than any other writer. He is now studied more as a representative of this movement than as the individualist he became during the latter half of his career, and within the movement he is remembered as a prototypical Surrealist, perhaps the one who delved most deeply into the Surrealist world.

PRINCIPAL WORKS

Rrose Sélavy (aphorisms) 1922
L'aumonyme (poetry) 1923
Langage cuit (poetry) 1923
Deuil pour deuil (novel) 1924
A la mystérieuse (poetry) 1926
C'est les bottes de sept lieues cette phrase: "Je me vois" (poetry) 1926
Journal d'une apparition (journal) [written 1926-27]
La liberté ou l'amour! (novel) 1927
Les ténèbres (poetry) 1927
Corps et biens (poetry) 1930
The Night of Loveless Nights (poetry) 1930
   [*The Night of Loveless Nights*, 1973]
Les sans cou (poetry) 1934
Fortunes (poetry) 1942
Etat de veille (poetry) 1943

Le vin est tiré (novel) 1943
Le bain avec Andromède (poetry) 1944
Contrée (poetry) 1944
30 chants-fables pour les enfants sages (verse) 1944
La place de l'étoile (antipoème) (drama) [first publication] 1945
   [*La place de l'étoile (an antipoem)* published in *Modern French Theatre: An Anthology of Plays*, 1964]
Domaine public (poetry) 1953
De l'érotisme considéré dans ses manifestations écrites et de point de vue de l'esprit moderne (essay) 1953
Cinéma (scenarios and criticism) 1966
22 Poems (poetry) 1971
The Voice (poetry) 1972

*The original title of this work is in English.

Translated selections of Desnos's poetry have appeared in the following publications: Barnstone, Willis, and others, eds., *Modern European Poetry;* Benedikt, Michael, ed., *The Poetry of Surrealism;* and Fowlie, Wallace, ed., *Mid-Century French Poets.*

ANDRÉ BRETON   (essay date 1928)

[*Breton was a French poet, prose writer, and critic who is best known as the founder of Surrealism. One of the most influential artistic schools of the twentieth century, the Surrealist movement began in 1924 with Breton's* Manifeste du surréalisme. *Strongly influenced by the psychoanalytic theories of Sigmund Freud, the poetry of Arthur Rimbaud, and the post-World War I movement of Dada, Breton proposed radical changes in both the theory and methods of literature. He considered reason and logic to be repressive functions of the conscious mind and sought to draw upon the subconscious through the use of automatic writing, a literary technique closely related to the psychoanalytic technique of free association. Breton's theories, however, reached far beyond the realm of literature; he considered Surrealist art a means of liberating one's consciousness from societal, moral, and religious constraints, thereby enriching and intensifying the experience of life. While Breton's creative works are considered to be uneven, his importance as a literary theorist remains unquestioned. In the following excerpt originally published in French in 1928, Breton discusses Desnos's facility with automatic writing and speech.*]

Once again, now, I see Robert Desnos at the period those of us who knew him call the "Nap Period." He "dozes" but he writes, he talks. It is evening, in my studio over the Cabaret du Ciel. Outside, someone is shouting: "Come one, come all, come to the Chat Noir!" And Desnos continues seeing what I do not see, what I see only after he shows it to me. He borrows the personality of the most singular man alive as well as the most elusive, the most deceptive, the author of *Le Cimetière des Uniformes et Livrées*, Marcel Duchamp. Desnos has never seen him in real life. What in Duchamp seemed most inimitable through some mysterious "plays on words" (Rrose Sélavy) can be found in Desnos in all its purity and suddenly assumes an extraordinary resonance. Those who have not seen his pencil set on paper—without the slightest hesitation and with an astonishing speed—those amazing poetic equations, and have not ascertained, as I have, that they could not have been prepared a long time before, even if they are capable of appreciating their technical perfection and of judging their wonderful loftiness, cannot conceive of everything involved in their creation at the time, of the absolutely oracular value they assumed. Someone who was present at those innumerable ses-

sions would have to take the trouble to recount them dispassionately, to describe them precisely, to situate them in their
true atmosphere. A discussion of this point is actually called
for. Of all the subsequent appointments Desnos, his eyes closed,
made for me with himself, with someone else, or with myself,
there is not one I feel, even now, I have the heart to miss, not
one, at the most unlikely place and time, where I am not sure
of finding whomever he has told me about. (pp. 31-2)

> André Breton, in his Nadja, translated by Richard
> Howard, Grove Press, Inc., 1960, 160 p.

J. H. MATTHEWS (essay date 1966)

[Matthews is a Welsh critic and educator who has written extensively on the Surrealists. In the following excerpt from his Surrealism and the Novel, Matthews discusses La liberté ou l'amour!,
stressing Desnos's rejection of conventional novel form and content.]

The despair underlying [La Liberté ou l'amour!] is the characteristic mood of the period of transition from Dadaism to
surrealism, when Dada's universal rejection had not yet been
entirely replaced in the surrealists by the confidence that was
later to imbue the mature work of Breton, Éluard, and Péret
with irrepressible hope. This mood gives vitality to a denunciation of self-contented society. . . . A fitting analogy would
be Buñuel's film L'Age d'or (1930), which depicts the agonizing frustrations of love and shows how lovers can be kept
apart by an indifferent, even hostile, society. Of the deepest
significance in La Liberté ou l'amour!, certainly, are the echoes
of Sade and the presence of Jack the Ripper, whose path more
than once crosses that of the hero and heroine.

According to Rosa Buchole [in her L'Evolution poétique de
Robert Desnos (1956)], Desnos presents a tragic dilemma in
the conflict between liberty and love. She does not consider,
apparently, the hypothesis that the title of La Liberté ou l'a-
mour! may suggest less alternative choices than strictly interchangeable forms of experience. Seen thus, the novel not only
fits logically into the pattern of Desnos' work, but also conforms more closely to general surrealist attitudes. Considered
in this perspective, the "suffocating violence" Buchole very
rightly stresses . . . would not be, as she contends, the image
of "a false conflict," . . . but a total liberation which, being
necessary to ensure autonomy of action and to guarantee liberty, is the prerequisite of love and its very expression.

Desnos represents revolt in his hero, the Corsair Sanglot, and
in his heroine, Louise Lame. Through his essentially marginal
figures, unrestricted in their movements by the claims of time
and place, he proposes no moral regarding social behavior.
Indeed, protest is expressed in his novel through total indifference on the personages' part and not through frustrated opposition. The Corsair does not affirm his refusal to be bound
by convention: he demonstrates it—through sadism, for example, and through membership in the Sperm Drinkers' Club.
The Club's practices are described at some length in pages
suppressed from the original edition by order of the Tribunal
Correctional de la Seine. The Club was founded in the Restoration, we are informed, "under the double aegis of love and
liberty."

The role of eroticism in La Liberté ou l'amour! is to express
a philosophy of protest and revolt. It has the same value in
Desnos' pseudonymously published La Papesse du diable . . . ,
in which perhaps even more than in his earlier novel, eroticism

may pass at first glance for gratuitous. However, Desnos affirms in De l'érotisme, "Any philosophy which does not contain
an EROTIC is incomplete." On the same page, he explains why
this should be so, when asking, "Also, what man preoccupied
with the infinite, in time, in space, has not constructed this
"EROTIC" in the secret of his soul; what man caring about
poetry, disturbed by contingent or distant mysteries, does not
like to withdraw into that spiritual retreat in which love is at
once pure and licentious in the absolute?" In Desnos' novels
the erotic stands for the affirmation of individual values. Or
so their author implies in De l'érotisme: "The erotic is an
individual science, everyone resolves as far as he can the secondary questions and is in accord with his fellows only in noting
the insolubility of the eternal questions, the existence of which
we shall never tire of proclaiming." . . .

Desnos does not propose to caricature society through the private problems of the Corsair Sanglot and Louise Lame. . . .
The full significance he attributes to his main personages may
best be anticipated if we examine De l'érotisme, where we are
informed: "Outside psychoanalysis and less than in any other
literature there is no possible lie in erotic literature. In this
spiritual mirror the author never leaves anything but an image
of himself. One must be very vain to wish in such material to
express the souls of others." . . . Are we to conclude that
Desnos does not expect his hero's conduct to take on personal
meaning for his readers? This, certainly, is the opinion of Rosa
Buchole. While recognizing in the characterization of the Corsair the influence of Lautréamont's hero Maldoror, and something of Jack the Ripper and Fantômas, she concludes that he
"remains nevertheless an unreal being, of indefinable consistency, in one dimension only, such as could be conferred upon
him by the cinematographic film." . . . These words formulate
a criticism of Desnos' method which cannot go uncontested.

The story told in La Liberté ou l'amour! belongs to "an astonishing period" of the narrator's life, when each minute of
the night "placed a new imprint on the moquette of [his]
room." . . . After the example of Breton (who has reported in
Les Pas perdus how he would leave the door of his room open
at night in the hope of a visit from a mysterious unknown
woman), Desnos writes, "My door, then, was open to mystery." Out in the street, leaves falling from the trees take the
form of gloves. Beneath a gigantic advertising poster from
which Bébé Cadum majestically surveys the scene, we are
introduced to the Corsair Sanglot.

Desnos' hero refuses to take a place in the categorized world
of rationality. Even so, the special receptivity displayed by
Desnos permits communication between him and the Corsair.
(pp. 66-70)

[Authorial intervention] in La Liberté ou l'amour! . . . marks
Desnos' unquestioning belief in the personages he has created.
These are not puppets used to prove a point or to advance a
theory. The reflections they occasion require no more justification than the spontaneity with which the narrator's thoughts
are formulated. Just as Desnos is ready to follow Louise Lame—
"stumbling among the gloves which now were all intertwining,
my head heavy with intoxication, I pursued her, guided by her
leopard-skin coat" . . .—so we are ready to accompany him.
To be exact, either we are ready to follow all the way, or we
turn back at once.

Desnos scorns the art of persuasion. "If I had been one of the
kings, oh Jesus, you would be dead in the crib, strangled, for
having interrupted my magnificent journey so soon and broken

my liberty; then, no doubt, a mystical love would have enchained me and drawn me, a prisoner, along the routes of the globe I would have dreamed of traveling in liberty.'' . . . To the extent that Desnos abandons the three-dimensional presentation which guarantees characters of realistic novels their credibility, the figures in *La Liberté ou l'amour!* are obstinately one-dimensional. In presenting them thus the novelist risks much, but nothing more than is risked in all works genuinely inspired by the surrealist spirit. While it declines to conform to the public's preconceptions, surrealism aims to impose its own terms. (pp. 67-70)

The Corsair travels just as easily beneath the sea . . . as on land. This is evidently because he is urged on by an instinct for love which acknowledges no barriers. He can continue, then, even when plunged up to the neck in a field of sponges. Nothing surprises him, because every strange phenomenon encountered in the pursuit of love is but incidental to it. The Corsair possesses a freedom of spirit that allows him to interpret the countryside about him entirely according to his wishes. . . . And nothing detains him or impedes his progress—not even the nude body of a woman in the Invalides or Monceau district of Paris. . . .

Although the narrator mentions one ''strange adventure,'' he informs us, even before relating it, that it ''did not move him unduly.'' . . . Neither time nor space can oppose the ''ideal relationship'' produced by the ''imaginary straight line which links any being to any other.'' . . . The connection between the various episodes of *La Liberté ou l'amour!* is truly one of imagination. Hence the novelist's lack of concern for rational developments, and even for the normal sequence which the reader's curiosity would demand. Time and again, narrative continuity is broken, with such complete disregard for expectations that we must acknowledge that there is evidence of deliberate intent, in interruptions like the following: ''Let Louise Lame's hearse go to the devil then, and the body of Louise Lame and her coffin and the people who are doffing their hats and those following behind. What does this foul carcass matter to me or this carnival parade?'' . . . Desnos can afford to dispose of his heroine in this brutal fashion because, as he explains and then later confirms by resurrecting Louise, he does not believe in material death, but prefers to live in eternity: ''Louise Lame's hearse can pursue its way through Paris without accident, I shall not salute it as it passes. I have an appointment tomorrow with Louise Lame and nothing can stop me from keeping it. She will come, pale perhaps under a crown of clematis, but real and tangible and submissive to my will.'' . . . (p. 71)

Desnos writes: ''Corsair Sanglot then strayed into a great palace planted with high columns, so high indeed that the ceiling was invisible. Then his historiographer lost him from sight and from memory.'' . . . And then he feels free to recall his hero—in the very next paragraph. In *La Liberté ou l'amour!* imaginative ties keep the narrator in contact as much with Corsair as with Louise Lame. Rationality is not the basis necessary for the survival of these personages, or for their presence. They appear just when their creator requires them to do so. Meanwhile, those for whom reason is an essential ingredient in life and in people receive fair warning: ''You will read or you will not read, you will find interest here or you will find boredom, but I must express in the mold of sensuous prose love for the one I love.'' . . . And Desnos adds: ''Be absurd, then, novel in which I pretentiously wish to imprison my lusty aspirations toward love, be insufficient, be poor, be disappointing.'' . . .

Later on, the fifth chapter of *La Liberté ou l'amour!* transcribes the following exchange:

ENIGMA

''What is it that climbs higher than the sun and goes down lower than the fire, that is more liquid than the wind and harder than granite?''

Without reflection, Jeanne d'Arc-en-Ciel replies: ''A bottle.''

''Why?'' asks the sphinx.

''Because I wish it.''

''Fine, you can pass, Oedipus.'' . . .

The reply comes without reflection and relies not upon knowledge previously acquired in one manner or another, but solely upon desire. Desnos' meaning is evident, and is confirmed by his pointed reference to the ''ridiculous seraphim of logical deduction.'' . . . ''There is nothing,'' he explains, ''that cannot be proved unfounded and I really despise those who remain between the two burning poles of thought on the old equator of scepticism.'' . . . His own position is unassailable: ''I know by the way, having experienced it, what abandon is. If you desire this proud lust, that's good, you can follow me. Otherwise I ask only your indifference, if not your hostility.'' . . .

Rosa Buchole experiences some difficulty in discussing *La Liberté ou l'amour!* because she finds it ''halfway between oneirism and novel.'' . . . She is right enough to distinguish this from the conventional novel and is entitled, also, to see in its loosely knit episodic form something close to the surrealist film scenario.'' . . . But to the surrealist, formal classifications are less important than the spirit which infuses the completed work. . . . [Desnos' novel] takes from the conventional novel only what its author needs. Desnos is content to borrow, adapt, modify, even to brutalize a literary genre that for him has no merit in itself, but in which he finds certain elements suited to his purpose. The formlessness of his work is his final protest, the expression of his discontentment with a rigid universe without sympathy for man's desire. In *La Liberté ou l'amour!* one is made aware of the sense of anguish with which Desnos infects his personages and from which they draw life. We may not hope to see in them ''the whole man.'' But the novel which shows their predicament is one surrealist's answer to the psychological novel: intuitive sympathy and community of aim taking the place of psychological penetration and rational analysis. The picture is necessarily incomplete and without the sense of perspective, firmness of line, balance or harmony the reader may feel entitled to expect. But reassurance, whether through content or form, is not Desnos' intent. Characteristically, his *La Liberté ou l'amour!* closes on an incomplete sentence. (pp. 72-3)

J. H. Matthews, ''Rene Crevel and Robert Desnos,'' in his Surrealism and the Novel, *The University of Michigan Press, 1966, pp. 59-73.*

J. H. MATTHEWS (essay date 1969)

[*In the following excerpt, Matthews traces Desnos's literary development from his early work through his surrealist period.*]

Between 1922 and 1923 Desnos composed one hundred and fifty brief statements, grouping them under the title *Rrose Sélavy*. Sometimes *Rrose Sélavy* adopts an interrogatory mode: ''Amoureux voyageurs sur la carte du tendre, pourquoi nourrir vos nuits d'une tarte de cendre?'' (Amorous travelers on the chart of tenderness [the *Carte du Tendre* was a seventeenth-century allegorical map of the tender sentiments], why feed your nights on a tart of cinders?) Sometimes it is affirmatory: "Rrose Sélavy propose que la pourriture des passions devienne la nourriture des nations" (Rrose Sélavy proposes that the rottenness of passions become the nourishment of nations). In some places the tone is mocking; in others again frankly obscene. Yet in every case, the sentence before us owes its existence to the application of the same verbal technique. Nevertheless, far from producing an impression of monotony, the strictly regular manner in which Desnos applies his method results in a remarkable variety of effects.

Breton, we remember, was not to define surrealism until 1924, when he wrote in his *Manifeste du Surréalisme:*

> SURREALISM. Pure psychic automatism by which we propose to express either verbally, or in writing, or in any other manner the real functioning of thought. Dictation of thought, in the absence of all control exercised by reason, outside all aesthetic or moral preoccupation. . . .

Thus the most striking feature of *Rrose Sélavy,* lying in its mechanical nature, is that, in advance of Breton's published definition, it shows Desnos practicing a technique which, in suppressing reason's control and appealing directly and unquestioningly to chance, came close to achieving the precious state of *distraction* which Breton's first manifesto declared on its last page . . . might be sought through automatism.

In *Rrose Sélavy* the simple interchange of the initial letters of words, accompanied by syllable manipulation, produces poetic statements which remain grammatically impeccable, while escaping rational censorship. There can be no doubt, then, that Desnos was seeking consciously, through the method applied in these texts, the equivalent of the freedom attainable in the absence of conscious control during self-hypnosis. In testimony to his confidence in chance he wrote, "Les lois de nos désirs sont des dés sans loisir" (The laws of our desires are dice without leisure) asking, "Isn't Rrose Sélavy's slang the art of transforming storks into swans?"

Whereas reason recommends that we begin a sentence only when we know how it is to end, chance, introduced into *Rrose Sélavy* by the arbitrary appeal to unforeseen meaning and represented here in the substitution of the initial letter in two words reasonably related (*carte du tendre*), produces results common sense cannot foresee (*tarte de cendre*). What impresses most in *Rrose Sélavy,* consequently, is that the art of transforming swans into storks requires the poet's attention to the word as sound, not as meaning. In this way, the second half of the poetic statement can continue to be a mystery, even from the poet himself, until the first part has been modified by a strictly mechanical process.

Rrose Sélavy gave Desnos an inkling of what can be accomplished, once one ceases to be attentive to words as semantic entities and considers them as an arrangement of phonemes. Phonetic modification entails the discovery of a new meaning, uncovered when the absence of conscious intention—reason's control—is guaranteed by the application of a mechanical method. Hence the key to new significance is to be sought in audition. This is the conclusion to which *Rrose Sélavy* brought Desnos, before encouraging him in the hope that he might progress further in protest against reason's censorship of poetic language.

In writing *L'Aumonyme* . . . next, Desnos showed in what direction he felt progress could be made. Underlying *L'Aumonyme* is the aim which remained central for Desnos: "Exhausser ma pensée / Exaucer ma voix" (To heighten my thought / To give ear to my voice). Elevation of thought to a new level of communication was to be achieved by continued attention to the voice, to the sounds uttered, instead of to the thoughts expressed. The poet becomes:

$$\text{Prisonnier des} \quad \begin{smallmatrix}\text{syllabes}\\\text{mots}\end{smallmatrix} \quad \text{et non des sens}$$

Turning his attention away from the idea with which the word is associated, and concentrating upon the sounds his voice lets him hear when he listens to The Lord's Prayer, Desnos writes: "Notre paire quiète, ô yeux! / que votre «non» soit sang (t'y fier?)."

As in *Rrose Sélavy,* the role of the poet consists in noting arbitrary changes in sense, now produced by the interplay of homonyms:

> En nattant les cheveux du silence
> six lances
> percent mes pensées en attendant.

Voluntarily surrendering conscious control of his poem's development, Desnos interests himself in auditive impressions forming a bridge connecting two or more meanings. So far as there is a relationship between *silence* and *six lances,* for instance, it eludes reason while addressing to the ear alone its initial claim to recognition. (pp. 56-8)

Like the use of the arbitrary substitution of letters in *Rrose Sélavy,* the exploitation of homonyms in *L'Aumonyme* protects the poet's imagination against strain. Once again, appeal to the arbitrary permits him to approach his poetic statement, just as the reader does, without foreknowledge or preconception. He shares instead of anticipates our discovery, much as Tanguy did when, after painting a canvas, he turned it upside down. The principle of discovery by inversion remains sufficiently analagous for us to identify in poet and painter the same instinct to fend off conventional associations, habitual thought processes, and past experience.

In the early poetry of Desnos we observe the results of surrealism as *play.* The *jeu de mots* is an amusement, no doubt. At the same time, it probes beyond the limits of previously accepted poetic language, overthrowing or circumventing the barriers erected by the reasonable. From the beginning of his poetic career, Desnos' treatment of language earned him enviable freedom, as letter manipulation and homonyms supplied the key to a world of poetic perception quite inaccessible without their aid.

In *L'Aumonyme,* Desnos' method of linguistic exploration continued to yield memorable images ("tes regards chaussés de vair"). Meanwhile his verse was divesting itself of the air of rigidity to which he had committed it, intentionally, by utilizing the techniques of *Rrose Sélavy.* But, while *L'Aumonyme* had taught him that "Words are our slaves" ("P'oasis"), he still had to learn in what way words can be used, once we have enslaved them. He was now ready to write *Langage cuit.* . . .

In *Langage cuit* Desnos continued his efforts to provide poetry with a new vocabulary. "Of course," comments Pierre Berger, "he knows he is going into a blind alley, but is it not a necessary blind alley?" It is more accurate to regard the narrow constriction imposed upon language by Desnos' verbal experiments as calculated to facilitate escape from an impasse—the one created by reason's tendency to discipline poetic expression. Certainly, his experimentation does result in liberation, evidence of which is visible in *Langage cuit.*

"One will search his work in vain," remarks Berger of Desnos, "for an obscure text—excepting perhaps certain poems collected under the title *Langage cuit.*" . . . Explaining the exceptional nature of these obscure poems, Berger writes somewhat apologetically, "But there it was a matter of seeking a vocabulary, trying experiments. This was laboratory work." A glance at the texts should suffice to dispel the uneasiness engendered by Berger's remark.

In the repetitions that are a feature of the first poem of *Langage cuit* ("**Vent nocturne**") we have an invitation to reconsider the meaning of words: "Sur la mer maritimes se perdent les perdus / Les morts meurent en chassant des chasseurs" (On the maritime sea the lost are lost / The dead die hunting hunters). Desnos speaks of "Cieux célestes" ["Celestial skies"] and "terre terrestre," ["terrestrial earth"] only to highlight the question with which he closes his poem: "But where is the celestial earth?" Thus obscurity, leaving its mark upon *Langage cuit,* does not do so by means of a mysterious or exotic vocabulary, but by virtue of the confrontation, within the poem, of familiar words disengaged from their normal function, and brought into relationships for which we have no precedent: "This old man still violet or orange-tinted or pink / wears trousers of elephant trunk" ("**Langage cuit**"). (pp. 59-60)

In *Langage cuit,* Desnos faces the task of communicating feeling as though in spite of language, so indicating that emotion needs no authority from grammar or logical sense. Beneath the title "**Au Mocassin le Verbe**" he begins a poem with:

> Tu me suicides, si docilement.
> Je te mourrai pourtant un jour.
> Je connaîtrons cette femme idéale
> et lentement je neigerai sur sa bouche.
>
> You suicide me, so obediently.
> I shall die you however one day.
> I shall know that ideal woman
> and slowly I shall snow on her mouth.

Langage cuit administers a jolt to aesthetic predispositions, whether by simple inversion of a poetic commonplace ("your bucklers are breasts!") or by more complex means as in "**Coeur en Bouche**": "L'éponge dont je me lave n'est qu'un cerveau ruisselant / et des poignards me pénètrent avec l'acuité de vos regards" (The sponge with which I wash is but a streaming brain / and daggers pierce me with the sharpness of your glances). Yet Desnos' reasons for writing in this way are not founded solely in anti-aesthetic protest. The couplet just quoted shows other influences making themselves felt upon an evolution which becomes noticeable when we turn from the early verbal experiments to the maturing poetry of *A la Mystérieuse,* written in 1926.

These influences are primarily of an emotional nature. They relate to the poet's perception that love provides the focus for poetic expression. Becoming the dominant theme of his poetry, love makes him modify his attitude toward language, persuading him to adopt an approach to words less clinical, less detached, and warmed now by the necessity to communicate, while yet permanently marked by the affranchisement gained in early years.

After *Langage cuit,* a revolutionary conception of poetic language ceases to be Desnos' main concern. His apprehension that the language of poetry must be placed at the service of one all-absorbing theme, love, has the consequence of diverting his attention from linguistic experimentation. The patently gratuitous quality, making many of the texts of *Rrose Sélavy* acts of provocation and nothing more, gives place to a sense of purpose, ensuring Desnos' mature surrealist verse its unity. For so long the object of attentive scrutiny, language is reduced at last to a secondary role, supporting feeling. At no time during his association with surrealism, however, does Desnos surrender the verbal freedom won during his early years as a writer. He no longer seeks satisfaction in the creation of striking poetic word play, but in the communication of a vision, achieved in large measure because he has learned once and for all that "Words are our slaves."

In the surrealist love poetry of Desnos, words are always slaves to feeling, to be used and even abused according to the demands of emotion. It is not surprising that the tone is mesmeric. The poem frequently takes on an incantatory quality, in which Desnos' glad surrender to words is vindicated in triumph, by the vision they capture, over contingent circumstance. Transformation and metamorphosis here take possession of the universe. It is as though the explosion of the rational world of conventional relationships, brought about in *Rrose Sélavy* and *L'Aumonyme,* has earned the poet release from respect for stability. A new-found freedom is at the core of his poetic experience. He has no hesitation in writing in *C'est les Bottes de sept Lieues, Cette Phrase "Je me vois,"* . . . "The disciplines of light have never invented anything but unopaque shadows [*des ténèbres peu opaques*]."

Under the influence of love, Desnos presents reality in mutation. The mysterious person he loves in *A la Mystérieuse* changes before his eyes ("I have dreamed of you so much you lose your reality"). Meanwhile he himself feels a liberation he never has known before ("But still I pursuing myself or incessantly overtaking myself"), as he enters "Unknown countries through which I travel accompanied by creatures." Woman remains elusive, though, as she is in "**Les Espaces du Sommeil**":

> Il y a toi sans doute que je ne connais pas, que je
>   connais au contraire.
> Mais qui, présente dans mes rêves, t'obstines à t'y
>   laisser deviner sans y paraître.
> Toi qui reste insaissable dans la réalité et dans le rêve.
>
> There is you no doubt whom I do not know, whom I
>   know on the contrary.
> But who, present in my dreams, persist in allowing
>   yourself to be sensed in them without appearing.
> You who remain elusive in reality and dreams.

The familiar yet distant woman is "however present without knowing it," an "international and material mirage" created by the poet's desire. Her presence reduces the universe to submissiveness, so that he can write in *C'est les Bottes de sept Lieues, Cette Phrase "Je me vois,"* "I feel my beginning is near like the June corn" ("**Destinée arbitraire**"). Now the voice of Desnos makes itself heard with a tone characteristic of his maturity as a surrealist. The first poem of *Les Ténèbres* . . . , "**La Voix de Robert Desnos**," communicates a feeling of power great enough to dominate the universe: "belfries and poplars bend to my desire / the former give way the former collapse." Reality becomes obedient to the poet's voice when he notes, "earthquakes do not shake me but bring everything down upon my orders."

Writing later in **"Le Poème à Florence"** (dated November 4, 1929), Desnos declares, "Les verrous sont poussés au pays des merveilles" ["Bars have sprung up in the country of marvels"]. But if reason bars the door on the marvelous, Desnos believes, then the dream will unbar it. Hence a line from **"Désespoir du Soleil"** provides a fitting epigraph for *Les Ténèbres:* "Let us dream let us accept dreaming it is the poem of the new day." Continuing in *Les Ténèbres* to expand poetic discoveries made five years earlier, Desnos dreams with words, stretching to the maximum—beyond breaking point, in fact— the rational connection between the elements of his images, bidding us witness, in a dream universe, the combination of two incompatibles. "Women's nails will be strangled swans," we are assured in **"Au Petit Jour."** The promise made in verses like this one sustains the prophetic poetry which is Desnos' prerogative. So the poem **"Vie d'Ebène,"** with its confident use of future tenses, announces the inevitable replacement of conventional reality by a universe fulfilling the poet's desires:

Un calme effrayant marquera ce jour
Et l'ombre des réverbères et des avertisseurs d'incendie
        fatiguera la lumière

A terrifying calm will mark that day
And the shadows of lamp standards and fire-alarms
        will fatigue the light

Conviction that the transformation of the world will be to his advantage gives the poet's voice a self-assurance untroubled by the spectacle of change. Whereas **"Vie d'Ebène"** betrays no nostalgia for the stability of the old world, it insistently emphasizes the inevitability of the replacement of the old by something more in accord with the poet's needs. This, no doubt, is why, when reading the poems of Desnos, one is reminded of the paintings of Paul Delvaux. Poet and painter share in a sense of mystery. Both greet with calm acceptance the strange transformation of the real to which their work bears witness. In Desnos, especially, the principle of inversion which, in his early poetry, was no more than a linguistic device useful in upsetting the conventional, has become fundamental to the poetic vision, giving it a special nature. Thus in **"L'Aveugle,"** written in 1929, blindness is presented as a blessing: "She went with eyes closed in a country of mother-of-pearl / Where life took on the form of a crescent." To protect the vision his loved one owes to blindness, the poet feels obliged to put out her eyes, as soon as her sight has been restored by an operation. Meanwhile, through the special perception of the blind, from which the real world is excluded, Desnos reveals things reality hides from our eyes. In the poem **"Pour un Rêve de Jour"** he offers such typically fleeting and ever-changing insights as the following:

Un cygne se couche sur l'herbe voici le poème des
    métamorphoses Le cygne qui devient boîte
    d'allumettes et le phosphore en guise de cravate

[A swan sleeps on the grass here is the poem of
    metamorposes The swan who becomes a match
    box and the phosphorus by way of a tie]

The presence of a swan transformed into a match box, wearing phosphorus as a tie, does not mean that the deliberate suppression of intrusive reality, so dramatically represented in **"L'Aveugle,"** has released the poet once and for all from his feeling of oppression. On the contrary, while the young Aragon seems in his poetry free from the weight of time, and even Eluard is able to keep at a safe distance the depressing feelings from which love saves him, Desnos is not so fortunate. Unable

to surmount with complete satisfaction the idea of dissolution, he lets us see death, just as much as the affirmation of a fuller sense of life. In **"Avec le Coeur du Chêne,"** indeed, love appears as partly the creation of death, when the poet tells us that "Isabelle la vague [. . .] is but an image of the dream through the varnished leaves of the tree of death and love."

Preoccupation with death marks even those images in which Desnos asserts his faith in the liberating effect of love's influence. From *A la Mystérieuse* comes this comparison:

Comme une main à l'instant de la mort et du
naufrage se dresse comme les rayons du soleil
couchant, ainsi de toutes parts jaillissent tes
regards.

[Like a hand at the instant of death and of the
shipwreck rising up like the rays of the setting
sun, thus from everywhere spring your glances.]

Although we see, here, the loved one's glance likened to a hand at the moment of death and shipwreck, love does give a sense of domination, we can be sure. It is described in **"Trois Etoiles"** as "une belle dame" to whom the sea is responsive:

The seaweed obeys her and the sea itself is
transformed into a crystal dress, when she appears on the beach.

Even so, the experience of love does not always save the poet from anguish. **"La Voix de Robert Desnos"** complains that the woman he loves does not listen, hear, or reply. In **"Trois Etoiles"** Desnos finds himself

Master of all at last except the love of his fair one
Master of all he has lost and slave to what he still retains.

The consequence is not regret, however. Nor is it a sense of failure. Instead, Desnos' verse acquires a tension that gives it a distinctive mood, its triumphant note as well as its undertone of impending despair. Nowhere in surrealist literature better than in Desnos are we made conscious of an urgent necessity, a pressing need which precludes frivolity. As early as the first poem of *A la Mystérieuse,* Desnos sings quite without bitterness of the pain of love: "Oh pain of love! / How necessary you are to me and how dear." Willing retreat into dreams has nothing to do with evasion, since in the oneiric universe Desnos continues to face the problems of life and death:

I dreamed last night of demented countrysides
and of adventures dangerous as much from the
point of view of death as from the point of view
of life which are also the point of view of love.

The interdependence of life and death, of exaltation and despair, explains the surrealist poetry of Desnos, and gives it depth. Sometimes the tone is jocular, as when, in *C'est les Bottes de sept Lieues, Cette Phrase "Je me vois,"* he writes: "You will place on my grave a life belt / Because one never knows" (**"Les Grands Jours du Poète"**). Even when it is anguished, though, as in the long poem with which Desnos' association with surrealism comes to an end, *The Night of Loveless Nights* . . . , the fascination of the void is not strong enough to take the place of the affirmation of desire: *The Night of Loveless Nights* closes aggressively upon the line "O Révolte!"

Desire never ceases to take its origin in the deepest aspirations of the poet, from which all posturing and self-indulgence are excluded. The experience of love is measured by the threat of dissolution, which Desnos views without self-deception; without resignation either. When reading his poetry, one has no excuse for making the error of dissociating the destructive program surrealism has proposed and sought to implement from a constructive program implicit in its rejection of many poetic ideals surrealists have found they cannot pursue without infidelity to their fundamental aims. As Desnos puts it in **"Paroles des Rochers"** from *Les Ténèbres:*

> The profound infinite suffering desire poetry love revelation miracle revolution love the profound infinite envelops me in garrulous shadows

Consideration of the works published by Desnos during his affiliation with surrealism—both prose and verse—imposes the conclusion that, as a surrealist, Desnos never departed from the attitude which found expression in a text written during the mid-twenties, **"Journal d'une Apparition."** This text relates how, between November, 1926, and January, 1927, it seemed to Desnos that he was visited nightly by an unnamed woman, who would sit by his bed, as he lay "sleeping dreaming without being able to distinguish exactly between dream and reverie." The **"Journal"** is prefaced by a brief introduction reflecting faithfully the outlook which gives Desnos' poetry its peculiar quality.

Noting, "The marvelous still consents to lay its gloved hand on our tired forehead and to guide us into surprising labyrinths," Desnos observes, "But if the day only comes when so many marvels at last give us wings, then like Icarus we die of our good fortune, or like Daedalus we land up in a less beautiful country that, henceforth, we persist in considering the only reality." At such times, he appreciates, we hesitate to regard the labyrinth of the marvelous as anything other than "a hollow dream." Yet, rejecting the sense of failure to which doubt commits us, Desnos affirms: "I shall escape this process of decay [*déchéance*]. One day, sooner or later, I shall be able to re-enter the labyrinth I have lost." Dismissing, next, the hypothesis that, in seeing his nocturnal visitor, he has been a victim of hallucination—"An explanation of what, for the vulgar herd, is perhaps a freakish occurrence but which could not be one for me"—Desnos prefers another explanation:

> [She] really came to visit me. I have seen her, heard her, I have smelled her perfume and sometimes she even has touched me. And since eyesight, hearing, smell and touch agree in recognizing her presence, why would I doubt her reality without suspecting the other commonly accepted realities of being illusory, when they are checked out, in the last analysis, by the same senses? How will I acknowledge in the latter the power to enlighten me in certain cases, and to take advantage of me in others?

Upon his answers to these questions depends more than Desnos' own estimate of the experiences reported in **"Journal d'une Apparition."** So far as they incorporate an attitude toward life and toward the world, these answers affect, in the final analysis, our estimate of Desnos' poetry. If he were to reply that either nothing is real or that all is real, then his argument would persuade few readers that his theoretical postulations are worthy of attention. Few would be disposed to place confidence in his verse. But, as those who have read him attentively know, Desnos is too adventurous a poet to take inspiration in such equivocal premises. They are prepared to find that, replying

to his own questions, Desnos supplies the key which unlocks the originality of his surrealist poetry:

> Anyway, for me it is less a matter of making people admit the reality of things normally taken for illusory than of placing dream and reality on the same plane. I care little after all, whether everything is false or everything is true.

Desnos never argues, never resorts to blandishment. At most, he admits his readers as witnesses to his dialogue with love, allows them to see the dream that is reality, and the reality that is dream. We are not asked to choose between the imagined and the real. For in their intermingling in poetic truth lies, for Desnos, the assertion of revolt. (pp. 61-7)

J. H. Matthews, "Robert Desnos (1900-1945)," in his Surrealist Poetry in France, *Syracuse University Press, 1969, pp. 55-67.*

HERBERT S. GERSHMAN   (essay date 1969)

[Gershman was an American critic and educator who specialized in French literature of the nineteenth and twentieth centuries. In the following excerpt from his critical history The Surrealist Movement in France, *Gershman discusses Desnos's place in the Surrealist group.]*

Robert Desnos was early considered the most promising of the surrealists, "the one," according to Breton, "who has perhaps come closest to surrealist truth, the one who, in works as yet unpublished and throughout numerous experiments in which he took part, has thoroughly justified my hopes for surrealism and encourages me to expect much more of it. At the present time Desnos *speaks surrealistically* at will." Paul Eluard, of all the surrealists the one most overtly and completely committed to poetry, referred to him as "the most spontaneous, the most free, a poet always inspired and who could speak as few poets can write." What subsumed this attractive spontaneity was a verbal eroticism, a *joie de vivre* unique in the group, which was to Desnos what liberty was to Breton and fraternity to Eluard.

The determining orientation in Desnos' poetry came in 1922, with his entry into the surrealist group, and specifically with the group's enthusiasm for the puns and spoonerisms signed Rrose Sélavy. Axiomatic in form, they recall the inverted proverbs of Lautréamont's *Poésies*, especially at their most successful when they bring together wit and chance in an outrageous juxtaposition of terms disturbing in their implications and hilarious in their conclusion. Although rarely unconscious in inspiration, they cannot help but question the well-ordered world of convention:

> Rrose Sélavy demande si les Fleurs du Mal ont modifié les moeurs du phalle: qu'en pense Omphale?
> (***Domaine public*** . . .) . . .

> Rrose Sélavy propose que la pourriture des passions devienne la nourriture des nations. . . .

> L'acte des sexes est l'axe des sectes. . . .
> (pp. 62-3)

Desnos' early importance was due principally to the ease with which he was able to drop off into a hypnotic trance and, while in that state, comment in sybilline terms on questions put to him. As Breton saw it, Desnos and others similarly endowed thus became recorders of the Unconscious oracle and as such capable of dredging up uncommon truths. Whether these states were authentic is open to doubt. Blaise Cendrars, who knew Desnos after his expulsion from the surrealist camp, mentions that on the several occasions the subject was raised Desnos "merely winked and smiled knowingly." When Desnos began using his "oracular" talents in the cause of literature, that is, when he began writing rhymed, coherent verse—and seeking publication to boot—the "literary alibi" and dream-work "stereotype" so feared by the surrealists as sources of counterrevolutionary activity made their unwelcome appearance. Nothing could be more incongruous than a sometime revolutionary disbursing clichés molded in an alexandrine form, even if it were a Gothic cliché as seen by Rimbaud, or Fantomas. (p. 65)

The Desnos that came to surrealism in September 1922, shortly after the Breton-Tzara rupture, brought with him a mild interest in radical causes, a vague acquaintance with Louis de Gonzague-Frick, and a strong interest in literature. Hypnotic seances and the use of semiautomatic techniques gave his work a new orientation without in any way modifying his goals. To Breton, Desnos' ability to plunge to the depths of the unknown and surface with a treasure trove of popular phraseology, café puns, and an occasional meaningless phrase was ample proof of the validity of his theories. Even if they were a bit too pat, too clever, Desnos' revelations had an uncommonly convincing point of departure—much more so than, say, Eluard's. Regardless of its literary quality, however that be judged, *his* verse was surrealist, and as such was of inestimable value as an example of the reality that lay behind convention. (pp. 66-7)

His last poem, with its play of light and shadow, dream-thought and action, fatigue and hope—devoid of rhetorical frills and the clever search for *le mot juste*—merits a place apart.

"Le Dernier poème"
J'ai rêvé tellement fort de toi,
J'ai tellement marché, tellement parlé,
Tellement aimé ton ombre,
Qu'il ne me reste plus rien de toi.
Il me reste d'être l'ombre parmi les ombres
D'être cent fois plus ombre que l'ombre
D'être l'ombre qui viendra et reviendra
    dans ta vie ensoleillée.

*(**Domaine public** . . .)*

[The Last Poem
I dreamed so strongly of you,
I walked so, talked so,
So loved your shadow,
That nothing remains to me of you.
All that's left is for me to be
    the shadow among the shadows
To be a hundred times more shadow
    than the shadow
To be the shadow that will come
    and come again into your
    sunlit life.]

All language has its own rhetoric, its own commonplaces, but Desnos' last poem has so thoroughly integrated them that they are one with the sentiment, almost a language of soul to soul, as Rimbaud might have said, for we sense an enormous affection which the words themselves point to but do not exhaust. (p. 67)

    Herbert S. Gershman, "The Early Literature of Surrealism," in his *The Surrealist Revolution in France*, *The University of Michigan Press*, 1969, pp. 35-79.

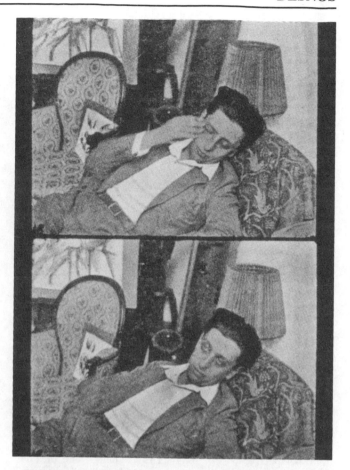

Desnos during a sleep-talking session. Photograph by Man Ray. Copyright, Juliet Man Ray, 1986.

TATIANA GREENE (essay date 1973)

[*In the following excerpt, Greene examines Desnos's film criticism, prefacing her study with a quote from his essay "La morale du cinéma": "I have always tried not to write criticism. As far as the cinema is concerned, I have confined myself to expressing desires."*]

Jean Cocteau assembled some of [Desnos's] writings under the title of *Critical Poetry (Poésie critique)*. Modifying this term, but only slightly, I shall call by the name *poetry of criticism* those texts of Robert Desnos grouped under the title of "Critique," which, together with scenarios and synopses of films, form the volume called *Cinéma*. In these texts, Desnos joins to objective description the passionate conviction and the exaltation characteristic of the major part of his work.

Rather than judging the merit of certain cinematic productions, Desnos uses them as a starting point for his declarations on love, on dream, on hope, or simply on the role that man should play in the world. It is this aspect of his criticism that is truly *poetic*. Desnos condemns criticism, in fact, since it is in his eyes only the "most mediocre expression of literature." . . . In his refusal of the merely literary, he goes so far as to regret the necessity for sub-titles, occasioned only by the fact that the spectator does not understand the language of "silent things" (to use Baudelaire's expression), which the cinema ideally is. "Literature ruins everything." . . . (p. 17)

The cinema, in Desnos' view, should play the same role that opium and hashish play for Baudelaire, multiplying the power of the mind, leading to what Baudelaire terms "orgies of the imagination," alone able to bring about a genuine "moral health," which instead should have come from "a constant elevation of desire, a tension of spiritual forces toward the heavens...." The presence on the screen of those "men and ... women luminous in the darkness" ... is magical, as it unrolls in those "ténèbres" ["shadows"] that reappear so often in the work of Desnos and are in large measure responsible for the "lumière surréele" ..., the surrealist light, in which his poetry and his criticism evolve.

The criticism of Desnos is often the equal of Baudelaire's in originality, and of an analogous character: both praise "The heroism of modern life." Both see in concrete beings what Desnos calls "the alliance in love of the spiritual and the material." Moreover, for Desnos, night, sleep, and dream are the very world of poetry. "And how could we not identify the shadows of the cinema with the nocturnal shadows, films with dreams!" ... By those statements, he places himself not only in the lineage of Baudelaire and his "Théâtre de Séraphin," with its "rêve hiéroglyphique" ["hieroglyphic dreams"], but still more in that of Nerval.

Of the latter he says in the **"Reflections on Poetry"** (his literary testament since they are dated January 1944) that he is the master we should follow, whose "mysterious domain" we should try to discover. For Nerval there is little to distinguish waking from sleeping: the sense of immortality one sees in Nerval ("That is true then, I said ... we are immortal.") is akin to Desnos' certitude of eternity ("this sense of eternity, about which I care more than anything else ..." ...; "I believe I am living, therefore I am eternal" (*La Révolution Surréaliste*, January 1925). Nerval speaks, in *Aurélia*, of "infinite perspectives," of "long series of stairs," and of a day "three times more brilliant than natural daylight"; whereas Desnos writes of the perspective of eternity and, in his text **Deuil pour deuil** ..., itself like a long surrealist scenario:

> J'ai vécu des existences infinies dans des couloirs obscurs ... sans pourvoir guider mes pas dans ces grandes étendues jaunes et ensoleillées....

> (I have lived infinite existences in obscure corridors ... without being able to direct my steps into those great yellow sunlit stretches....)

This cinematic world of dark corridors is also a world of myth, of what Pierre Albouy calls a "marvelous at once psychic and objective." And yet for Desnos the cinema is only a *pis-aller,* an approximation of the world of dreams, the most efficacious way, perhaps, of joining that world.

> There exists a cinema more marvelous than any other. Those to whom it is given to dream know that this undeniable life to which their sleep is consecrated can never be equalled in its unexpected and its tragic quality by any film. The taste for and the love of the cinema stem from the desire of dream....

For the spectators, says Desnos, the cinema should become, if possible, an "unprecedented adventure," for thus they could share in the "semi-divine" existence of the film characters. (And Baudelaire called the fourth part of the *Paradis Artificiels* "L'Homme-Dieu.") One day it will be shown that as a source for the creation myth of energy, the cinema will be "the most

magnificent instrument that men have ever invented." ... (p. 18)

The hypersensitivity that Baudelaire describes in his "Théâtre de Séraphin" and the states of ecstasy that are associated with it are analogous to this energetic interaction of dream and darkness created by the best cinematic works, transporting us to the world of the *"Merveilleux"* ... as do certain works of art: "The dream, splendor of the day and magician of life, is also the splendor of the night. When we were children, our eyelids lowered on the nocturnal theater of stars, it led us to the chimerical country of Grandville, where the comets are pretty women walking over the Milky Way, or to the deep forests of Gustave Doré...." (Is this not like a film of Méliès?)

"We were born," Desnos writes in 1927, "under the sign of L'Exposition Universelle" ..., a declaration astonishingly reminiscent of Baudelaire's essay "L'Exposition Universelle/ 1855," which begins with these lines: "Few occupations are as interesting, as appealing, as full of surprises and revelations for *a critic,* for *a dreamer....*"

A Parisian like Baudelaire, like Nerval (whose wanderings in the Paris of Saint Eustache are described in *Aurélia*) a stroller of the nocturnal Paris of Lautréamont, a "peasant of Paris" (but was he ever a "flâneur des deux rives"?) ["stroller of the two banks"], Desnos is also "un homme *très ancien*" ["a *very old* man"], from before the Commune, scarcely distant in psychological time from the epoch of crinolines. And I do not think there is any real difference, as far as certain states of their creative dreaming are concerned, between Desnos on one hand, and on the other Baudelaire, Nerval, and even Lautréamont. Desnos, a contemporary traveler ("le voyageur moderne" is a term he uses five times in an article entitled **"Cinéma frénétique et cinéma académique"**), finds in "frenetic cinema" a model for what should be this art menaced by "the man of letters," a pejorative term that reminds us of Baudelaire's scathing *"modernes professeurs-jurés d'esthétique"* ["modern professor-jurors of esthetics"]. All these poets explore great "Forêts de symboles" ["Forests of Symbols"].

Baudelaire:

The most gifted are those solitary travelers who have lived for years in the depths of woods, in the middle of vertiginous meadows.

Desnos:

Lost in a deep forest whose ground is made of moss and pine needles and whose light is filtered by the tall eucalyptus trees with their hanging bark ... the modern traveler seeks the marvelous.... He makes his way under the tall trees, in search of adventures worthy of his imagination.... (pp. 18-19)

Baudelaire, for his part, speaks of the "epic side of modern life," declaring, "Parisian life is fecund in poetic and marvelous subjects. The marvelous envelops us, nourishing like the atmosphere; but we do not see it." For Desnos as for Baudelaire—and André Breton—imagination is the "queen of the faculties," uniting moral sense to creative activity.

On the other hand, certain texts of *Cinéma* are also *chants* ["songs"], in the sense of Lautréamont's *Chants de Maldoror.* Already **"Le Fard des Argonautes"** (1920) might have reminded us of the invocation to the "vieil océan" ["old ocean"], and it is certain that the author of the Lautréamont-like recounting of *Deuil pour deuil* must have been fascinated by the *ange maudit* ["accursed angel"] whose halo, at that time, must have seemed completely new to the poet born in 1900.

Several of Desnos' articles, particularly those of the year 1927, with their feverish rhythm, their fullness and balance of phrasing, their frequent use of the first-person pronoun often followed by a verb in the negative, are exactly in the [Maldoror tradition].

> Je ne suis pas de ceux qui croient que l'amour le plus pur est un amour d'eunuque pour un mannequin de glace (**"Amour et Cinéma"** . . .).

> (I am not one of those who believe that the purest love is the love of a eunuch for a glacial mannequin.)

> Je ne suis pas de ceux dont la foi est médiocre, qui respectent les opinions des autres: si je la respectais, j'insulterais la mienne. (**"le Cuirassé Potemkine"** . . .).

> (I am not one of those whose faith is mediocre, who respect the opinions of others: if I were to respect it, I would be insulting my own.)

The article entitled **"La Morale du cinéma"** is for the most part a *chant* in the Maldoror tradition, at least by its rhythm, its animal vocabulary, and its metamorphoses.

> Ce phare à feu tournant la vie détermine dans le ciel de belles étoiles de mer. Les jours et les nuits se succèdent, comme des fauves séduisants. . . .

> (This lighthouse with the revolving light life determines in the sky beautiful starfish. The days and the nights follow upon each other, like seductive wild beasts. . . .)

The text **"Amour et cinéma"** contains long majestic sentences, apostrophes to diabolic beings: "Beautiful heroines of the screen, perfect heroes, modern succubi and incubi . . ."; insult seems near to imprecation: "In vain does the filthy shame . . . attack this fame, love will always triumph"; "The impotent . . . burn the books of Sade and conceal in their soul luxuries of mud. . . ." Desnos also evokes a violent eroticism, not without a certain spirituality, such as in the following passage when, after the future negative used twice ("Thus we shall not see naked women surging up miraculously on the screen . . ."; "Thus we shall not see the multiple and supreme harmonious gestures of love . . ."), there comes a third future negative which, as if by an unconscious *tour de force*, affirms the preeminence and the permanence of love: "but the desire of love will not be diminished by it in any way." . . . This text closes with a declamatory stanza where the future negative of "They will not prevent," used twice, settles into the description of a rapid movement over a docile medium, all the while mingling paradoxically with sounds, cries, cataclysms, and the crumbling of walls.

> They will no more prevent [love] from tormenting our hearts than they will prevent the battleship Potemkin from sailing full speed ahead over a calm sea, under a sky traversed by the flapping of sympathetic banners and the word BROTHERS!, at the sound of which the walls

> crumble, a word shouted a million times over by men of good will. . . .

However, the exaltation of Desnos is tinged with a profound disenchantment, and since we see no more on the screen than "despicable landscapes," he declares, in **"Mélancolie du cinéma,"** as if giving up the battle.

> Our lyric hearts are absent from most of our conversations. And our tongues, oh heroes of the film screen, are perhaps more silent than yours. . . .

Baudelaire, in "Le Voyage," affirmed (but to death itself), "Nos coeurs que tu connais sont remplis de rayons" (Our hearts which you know are filled with rays). The exaltation of Desnos gives way to silence; whereas Baudelaire prepares, in the company of the "old captain," for silent and "mysterious domains."

In 1923, it was "artificial commonplace life" . . . that disappointed Desnos. But the cinema, which, more powerful than opium, was supposed to multiply the powers of the mind and permit us to live marvelous adventures, has finally shown us the ridiculousness of our existence, of "the life which takes us to Florida when we are dreaming of Hedjaz and whose real daylight never offers us the ideal visage which haunted our night." . . .

The ideal is inaccessible. But Desnos pursued it in this ebullient language that the mysteries of the cinema and the dream of a new reality inspired in him. (pp. 17-21)

> *Tatiana Greene, "Robert Desnos and 'La Poésie de Critique'," in* Dada/Surrealism, *No. 3, 1973, pp. 17-22.*

I. D. McFARLANE (essay date 1973)

[*McFarlane is an English educator, biographer, and critic specializing in French language and literature. In the following excerpt, he discusses prominent symbols in Desnos's love poetry.*]

More often than not, Desnos' poetry expresses the frustrations of a love that is unable to coincide with its object. Like Chateaubriand, he experiences a generalised yearning seeking satisfaction in some real, individual vessel; but the *sylphide* either eludes him or does not exist. If and when it does, we read of lovers who meet only once, whose dream belongs to past or future, in whom *je* and *tu* cannot blend into a *nous* . . . , who undergo 'rêves parallèles' . . . , and the theme of the might-have-been persists:

> Marche nuptiale de nos reflets oubliés dans une glace quand la femme que nous devrions rencontrer et que nous ne rencontrerons jamais vient s'y mirer. . . .

> [Wedding march of our reflections forgotten in a mirror when the woman we must meet and will never meet comes to see herself there. . . .]

The mirror is associated with time that stands between possibility and realisation; but it also skirts the problems of illusion and identity, and reinforces the preoccupation with the dream which no less than reality holds the *innamorata* at a distance. . . . Desnos' conception of love is woven into a fabric of absence, dream and mirage; but the sense of illusion may spread from the relationship that cannot be fulfilled into a disconcerting attitude towards the identity of both lover and loved, an attitude that may show itself in fanciful and humorous fashion as in the more solemn register:

> Oui, je t'ai rencontrée, c'était bien toi.
> Mais quand je me suis approché et que je t'ai appelée et
>   que je t'ai parlè,
> C'est une autre femme qui m'a répondu. . . .
>
> [Yes, I met you, it was surely you.
> But when I approached and that I called you and that I
>   spoke to you,
> It was another woman who answered me. . . .]

(pp. 231-32)

The gap between dream and authentic love needs filling by poetic means; the greater the tension generated in this space, the more urgent the need to people it with a fabulous country and denizens able to give shape and substance to his yearning. For it is the world of dreams that will sustain him, even though these poetic fictions are, in proportion to their substance, a measure of his existential failure or void. (pp. 232-33)

Many features of [Desnos'] poetic geography go back to youthful memories, fairy tales, Jules Verne, though with the grimmer tones of Hans Andersen; and to these are joined aspects of Parisian, urban existence. In this kaleidoscope where space and time, as we ordinarily understand them, are often warped, we find a recurring pattern of symbols, animate or not, that might be described as elemental or archetypal. Though Desnos eschews a firm *symbolique* in favour of a more flexible symbolism, there often occurs a repeated correlation between symbol and feeling or within the imagic clusters, as he himself suggests:

> Et puis, voici les champs, les fleurs, les steppes, les
>   déserts, les plaines, les sources, les fleuves, les
>   abîmes, les montagnes
> Et tout cela peut se comparer à nos deux coeurs. . . .
>
> [And then, here are the fields, the flowers, the steppes,
>   the deserts, the plains, the springs, the rivers, the
>   chasms, the mountains
> And all of that can compare itself to our two
>   hearts. . . .]

These associations between land and sea, fairy tale and urban life, are found not only in the poems but in [*La Liberté ou l'Amour!*]. Desnos likes to bring sea and forest together, either at the level of fanciful geography or in symbolic collocation . . . ; but more commonly the two cover separate areas of meaning and emotion. (p. 233)

The sea, with its rich bunch of associations, forms a vital part of his symbolism, even though once he denied such significance, only to affirm that "la mer n'existe pas car la mer n'est qu'un rêve" . . . ["the sea does not exist since the sea is only a dream"], thereby restoring its symbolic function. It symbolises life, as does swimming ("Nous nageons, nous vivons" . . .) ["We swim, we live"]; even if the latter has depressing associations with the siren . . . , elsewhere it is mentioned in the hope that love and freedom might be reconciled. . . . At all events, the sea is immersing and enwrapping, but also purity, as the Satyr suggests. It is the symbol of love, usually attracting the idea of reflection, mirrors, iridescence, illusion and therefore solitude, sometimes even death. . . . (pp. 233-34)

Three marine themes form constants in Desnos' world. The first is sea-weed, which has its place in the Surrealist scheme of things; its symbolism often overlaps with that of the sea,

but it is related imagically to other features, in themselves important: the stars, the staircase or rocks such as granite. Then there is the shipwreck: storm and jetsam haunt the poet's mind. In the shadow of Rimbaud, Desnos may develop the theme of the outward bound voyage (towards freedom and possibility), and sometimes the cognate topic of safe return to harbour may be broached, but these pale into insignificance compared with the shipwreck. . . . The other symbol is foam, often present to suggest vitality and promise. It recurs very frequently and is one of the key images that Desnos, in accordance with his practice, uses not only to touch off a certain group of responses in the reader but as a link image that brings other images simultaneously into play.

The landscape has its own chart of symbolic reference, and Desnos' imaginative needs tend to concentrate attention on a limited number of *lieux symboliques*. To begin with, there is the desert theme, not as prominent as some, but persistent for all that: Desnos invokes the "muses du désert, ô muses exigeantes" and in [*La Liberté ou l'Amour!*] he also relates the desert to the creation of illusion. More normally we have the fairy-tale forest (perhaps with castle), denoting obstacle or barrier, though a different meaning is conferred on the trees that make up wood or forest. The symbolism of childhood stories is doubtless reinforced by the example of Apollinaire, in whose poetry the forest develops its own thematic abundance. . . . The castle or tower of legend, reminiscent of the sleeping Beauty, may be brought into the landscape:

> De longues avenues entre des frondaisons
> S'allongent vers la tour où sommeille une dame
> Dont la beauté résiste aux baisers, aux saisons,
> Comme une étoile au vent, comme un rocher aux lames . . .
>
> [Of long avenues between foliage
> Stretching toward the tower where sleeps a girl
> Whose beauty resists kisses, seasons,
> Like a star in the wind, like a billowing rock]

but more usually the castle develops as a variation on the prison or cage ("Tu revois la prison, c'est le château sans âge" . . .) ["You see again the prison, it is the ageless chateau"]. Incidentally, birds play only a modest role in Desnos' symbolism, but when they appear, it is often as prisoners in a cage. And in Desnos, the prison-motif, so dominant, denotes the denial of freedom but also adds harmonics to the theme of the criminal. Most of the buildings described by the poet are symbols of exclusion; only rarely do we see the inside of a house, and when we do, we see it from outside, not by entering this or that room. Either the door is being shut or is already locked ("La porte se ferme sur l'idole de plomb" . . .) ["The door closes itself on the idol of lead"] or the windows, behind which Desnos suggests lovers or an empty space, are viewed from the street by the solitary passer-by:

> Voici venir le temps des croisades,
> par la fenêtre fermée les oiseaux s'obstinent à parler
>   Comme les poissons d'aquarium.
> A la devanture d'une boutique
>   Une jolie femme sourit.
> Bonheur tu n'es que cire à cacheter
>   Et je passe tel un feu follet. . . .
>
> [Here comes the time of crusades,
> Through the closed window the birds
>   are resolved to speak
>   Like aquarium fish.
> In front of a shop

A pretty girl smiles.
Happiness you are only sealing wax
And so I pass a will-o'-the-wisp]

Furthermore, the house is the fabric that surrounds staircases and corridors, symbols of unfulfilled and sometimes unending aspiration which recur with impressive insistency and are related to his symbolic figures, Don Juan descending the stairs or the siren standing on the staircase of the castle. The sense of futility is sometimes made more explicit and we are given the feeling of vainly seeking a way through a maze.... (pp. 234-36)

Into this landscape Desnos introduces a number of denizens: the central figures of [*La Liberté ou l'Amour!*], Corsaire Sanglot and Louise Lame with their symbolic names and strange *avatars,* lead the column of characters who are nearly all endowed with a cluster of common traits. The men are haunted by their amorous dream, whether it looks to past or to future, and the intense feelings aroused between dream and fruition take us into a world of cruelty and sadism:

Le pirate avait eu des chagrins d'amour
C'était une espèce de chevalier au coeur de pierre
Qui violait les captives en rêvant à son amour
Versons un pleur sur le pirate....

[The pirate had had sorrows of love
He was a kind of knight with a heart of stone
Who ravished the captives while dreaming of his love
Let's shed a tear on the pirate]

The phantom appears as a wanderer along an endless road, solitary, alienated from society and often assuming the guise of a criminal. In [*La Liberté ou l'Amour!*] the lover is described as a "jeune bagnard" ["young convict"], but the association is rather with imprisonment suffered by any man in love, and Desnos adds two other harmonics: the link between love and shipwreck and that between captivity and liberty in the realm of love.... The anti-social exploration of crime, in unsatisfied love, is a constant in Desnos' sketches; significantly crime and love mingle in the dark ("L'Assassinat, fidèle amant de la nuit" ...) ["The Assassin, faithful lover of the night"], and the poet evokes "le voyageur de la nuit" ["the traveller of the night"] who makes his way on in the hope that the "ténèbres bavardes" ["talkative shadows"] might bring response to his love. He is above all a *passant* ["passer-by"]; among the variations on this basic theme, we have the deprived, the blind, and also Don Juan in Spain and the Satyr. The poles of Desnos' projection are Corsaire Sanglot and Fantomas—so beloved of the Surrealists and whose name brings together the themes of love, impishness merging into crime, solitude, metamorphosis and mirage. The female figures are all sirens in one shape or another, elusive, pitiless, and like the males are "vagabondes" ... or *passantes;* on one occasion the siren is called "la Fantomas".... Their identity may assume various forms, corresponding to Desnos' perplexity about the "visage de l'amour" ["face of love"]; but the *innamorata*'s face is never described, what fascinates the poet are the *chevelure* ["hair"], the eyes, the hands especially, but also *l'ombre* ["the shadow"]. These amorous pairs thread their way through Desnos' mythological countryside, though in [*The Night of Loveless Nights*] he also uses the persona of the first person singular to express his feelings. In this world animals play a minor part; apart from the caged birds, we find the horse, closely linked in [*Corps et Biens*] ... with the theme of love, and the various marine fauna acquire a modest symbolic value, the crab, the lobster,

above all the *hippocampe* which in "**Siramour**" is a projection of the poet himself. (pp. 236-37)

What has emerged so far, I believe, is that Desnos' poetic world contains a number of major features that tend to recur, whether they concern landscape, "character" or smaller object or category. Heterogeneous in their origins and "normal" context, they achieve a kaleidoscopic effect by the manner in which Desnos throws them together in varying patterns. He removes them from their everyday associations and he may personalise certain elements (flowers, rocks, mines). He subjects them to divers metamorphoses, as he himself has mentioned on occasion; this is intimately connected with the "protée insaisissable" ["imperceptible proteus"] that constitutes his dream of love, for movement, mirage and metamorphosis inevitably go together. He talks of the "décor mobile de mes rêves" ... ["mobile decor of my dreams"] and is well aware that his intimations of experience require unusual means of expression:

Tu viens au labyrinthe, où les ombres s'égarent,
Graver sur les parois la frise d'un passé
Où la vie et le rêve et l'oubli, espacés
Par les nuits, revivront en symboles bizarres. ...

[You come to the labyrinth, where the shadows lose
     their way,
To engrave on the walls the frieze of a dead one
Where life and dream and oblivion, separated
By nights, live again in bizarre symbols.]

However, though Desnos achieves his poetic effect in great measure by this series of imagic patterns, much depends also on his use of verbs and his exploration of counter-syntax which received stimulus from his surrealist days but correspond to the deep-seated needs of his poetic vision. Moreover, some of these disconcerting exercises reveal their links with the categories through which Desnos apprehends experience and of which the most important seem to me to be: illusion; liquidity/hardness; sound/silence; iridescence/darkness; solitude; journey and ascent/fall.... Though we have rejected the presence of too rigid a *symbolique* within his imagic framework, it does seem that for Desnos certain phenomena are more or less closely bound up with certain qualities, states of mind, values, and when he seeks to express these, his mind tends to bring together these associations which in the everyday world would hardly bear one another company. This mechanism we have seen working at the level of landscape, but it also operates in the way images and properties are associated with objects and feelings.... (pp. 239-40)

[Not] all Desnos' poetry is a meditation on disillusioned love. Even in his more despondent moments he still accepts "douleurs" ["suffering"], solitude and the closeness of despair to enthusiasm ...; and he always hoped that the ideal would become reality and that beyond the world of his dream there lay a promised land:

Je ne veux plus être qu'une voile emportée au gré des
     moussons vers des continents inconnus où je ne trouverai
     qu'une seule personne. ...

[I no longer wish to be but a runaway sail at the mercy of
     monsoons toward unknown continents where I will find
     only one person]

and significantly, the realm of pure love would be shorn of all the "accessoire poétique" ["poetic accessory"] he had constructed and exploited to preserve the existence of his dream:

> Etre aimé par elle
> Non pas une nuit de toutes les nuits
> Mais à jamais pour l'éternel présent
> Sans paysage et sans lumière. . . .

> [To be loved by she
> Not one night of all nights
> But forever for the present eternal
> Without landscape and without light]

The lineaments of Desnos' ideal love begin to take shape: removed from the orbit of time . . . , she has ceased to be the *passante*. . . . Love involves the total absorption of the lover in the beloved and its expression is reduced to an intense statement bare of imagery or oblique formulation. And yet we are still in an area of uncertainty: does the poet see dream simply as dream or does it become reality? . . . Does the *innamorata* serve as more than a peg on which the poet may hang his love? In **"Siramour,"** . . . he suggested that only *his* love and *his* memory could keep *her* alive. Does there come a moment when the lover is so immersed in the object of his love that he ceases to be aware of her objective reality? Several poems hint that the dream has acquired a measure of self-sufficiency. . . . (pp. 241-42)

What is certain is that for Desnos the immersion of the self in the dream—or reality—of one's love leads to a stripping of the "accessoire poétique," whereas love experienced as gap between dream and reality urges the poet to the creation of a more formally structured and imagically rich world; but the "voix de Robert Desnos" ["voice of Robert Desnos"] sounds at both ends of the range with unmistakable individuality and equal success. (p. 243)

I. D. McFarlane, "Love and the 'Accessoire Poétique' in the Poetry of Robert Desnos," in Order and Adventure in Post-Romantic French Poetry: Essays Presented to C. A. Hackett, E. M. Beaumont, J. M. Cocking, and J. Cruickshank, eds., Barnes & Noble Books, 1973, pp. 231-43.]

MARY ANN CAWS (essay date 1977)

[*Caws is an American critic and educator who is noted for her prolific contribution to the study of the Dada and Surrealist movements and for her translations from the works of the most significant figures of those movements. In the following excerpt, Caws offers an overview of Desnos's work during the 1920s, drawing specific attention to* La Liberté ou l'amour! *and* Les Ténèbres, *and compares this surrealist work to Desnos's later writing.*]

In his "Manifesto" of 1924, Breton said of Desnos that he was

> of all of us, perhaps the one who came the closest to surrealist truth, the one who . . . in the course of the multiple experiences to which he has lent himself, has fully justified the hope which I once placed in surrealism and who encourages me to expect a great deal of it still. Today Desnos *speaks surrealist* when he chooses to. The prodigious agility he displays in following his thought orally produces all the splendid discourse we could want, all of it lost, Desnos having better things to do than to write them down. He reads in himself like an open book and makes no effort to retain the sheets flying away in the wind of his life.
>
> (p. 8)

From 1927 to 1929, during the period when Breton and the others, having turned from anarchism to communism, were chiefly involved in the effort to reconcile surrealism and political activity, Desnos gradually separated himself from the group: he had come under attack for his "non-involvement" and the strain led to the open break in 1929 and to Desnos' own **"Third Surrealist Manifesto."** . . . (p. 9)

The situation of Robert Desnos within the surrealist movement must be taken into account before any individual assessment of his works can be undertaken, or any detailed analysis attempted. Even after Breton's attacks on him, even after his supposed formal separation from the movement, which he had "betrayed" by his writing of formal alexandrines, his occasional mockery of the sacreds of surrealism, and, finally, his journalism, Desnos never ceased to call himself a surrealist. He used the term "in its most open sense," as he explains in his own **"Troisième manifeste"** (Breton wrote prolegomena for a third manifesto, but never the manifesto itself).

The remarkable powers of Desnos in regard to automatic writing were alluded to frequently by the other members of the group, especially Breton, who was generous in his praise. Desnos' talent was first recognized in the era of "hypnotized slumbers": these experiments with sleepwriting were intended to liberate the unconscious and give it free creative rein. In *Une Vague de rêves*, Louis Aragon describes the heady exal-

Gouache *by Robert Desnos.*

tation of this period in which Desnos' particular prowess became evident:

> Their slumbers are lengthier and lengthier. . . .
> They fall alseep just from watching each other
> sleep, and then they carry on dialogues like
> persons from a blind and distant world, they
> quarrel and occasionally you have to snatch the
> knives out of their hands. Real physical rav-
> ages, difficulty on several occasions of pulling
> them out of a cataleptic sleep where a hint of
> death seems to pass. . . .

Aragon describes Desnos' particular talent thus:

> In a café, amid the sound of voices, the bright
> light, the jostlings, Robert Desnos need only
> close his eyes, and he talks, and among the
> steins, the saucers, the whole ocean collapses
> with its prophetic racket and its vapors deco-
> rated with long oriflammes. However little those
> who interrogate this amazing sleeper incite him,
> prophecy, the tone of magic, of revelation, of
> revolution, the tone of the fanatic and the apos-
> tle, immediately appear. Under other condi-
> tions, Desnos, were he to cling to this delirium,
> would become the leader of a religion, the foun-
> der of a city, the tribune of a people in revolt.

Either through some extraordinary effort of the will or through some even more extraordinary chance, Desnos demonstrated an incredible fertility of imagination, dictating, writing or drawing feverishly, answering questions with a sustained lyric power at first impressive to Breton and the others but finally discouraging to them. As Desnos points out, Breton, who bent for hours over a manuscript, was not likely to accept with good grace this spectacle of facility. Perhaps Desnos exaggerated this dramatic side of the experiments precisely to impress the leader of the group—Breton had on repeated occasions to force Desnos to awaken—but perhaps also it was in the long run exactly this drama and this facility which served to turn Breton against the poet who had been more impressive than the others.

The rift between the two men, far apart in temperament, is apparent as early as 1926-27 and Desnos' expulsion from the surrealist "chapel" in 1929 is hardly surprising. He had already left that chapel of his own volition, declaring its dogma too narrow and too "mystical," its claims to freedom unjustified, and its total rejection of traditional forms too limiting. The separation culminated in a message he sent to a meeting on the rue du Château in March, 1929: "Absolute scorn for all activity, whether it be literary or artistic or anti-literary or anti-artistic, an absolute pessimism concerning social activity." He did not at this point reject any possibility of further collaboration, but he firmly refused what seemed to him too arbitrary a discipline. In the "Second Manifesto," Breton condemned him for not choosing between "marxism and anti-marxism," and Desnos, insisting always on the absolute freedom of the poet, condemned in his turn what he called the obscurantism of Breton.

Claiming that Breton's lofty exaltations of the illogical, and diatribes against the heretical, "paved the road for God," Desnos turned to interests of a sort which seemed to him more genuinely liberating. Breton always considered *journalism* a pejorative term, indicating a concern with the lesser and the trivial at the expense of the essential and the poetic. Desnos, on the other hand, considered the *journalier* or the daily affairs of life including the most trivial, to be the possible matter of the poetic.

A comparison may be made here with Blaise Cendrars' eulogies on the poetics of advertising (in *Modernités,* 1927, the essay called "Publicité = Poésie"). It is, he says, an affirmation of optimism and pleasure, a proof of vigor and art, a triumph of lyricism. Desnos' attitude is similar. Nothing farther from the strict surrealist principles can be imagined, however, and it is not hard to see why, from that point of view, Desnos' comportment was shocking. What was to him openness was to Breton non-revolutionary and therefore non-poetic: it was commercialism.

But it is not in fact the themes of Desnos' work or its subjects which are the most revealing in the context of his separation from the surrealist group. It is true that these become more "realistic," that the images of mermaid and dream . . . make way for other images and for the eventual condemnation of dream and dream-inducing drugs in his late novel *Le Vin est tiré*. It is true that in many cases these latter images are more expected, more trite. It is true that his resistance poetry is far more simplistic than his surrealist poetry and therefore less interesting to the critic. More germane, however, to the basic split between the surrealist way of seeing and expressing and Desnos' own vision and expression is the problem of traditional and novel style. Desnos, always an experimenter, tried out a variety of styles: he wrote simple verses and much intricate prose poetry, some meditations on the dream adventure, extremely complicated in structure, and then alexandrines, and sonnets in a classical form. One of the main points of Breton's public attack on Desnos in the *Second manifeste* was the latter's fondness for quoting alexandrines and composing them (see, for example, the pseudo-Rimbaud at the beginning of *La Liberté ou l'amour!*). In the surrealist code, a liberated or novel form must bear witness to the new vision; more precisely, a traditional form, however brilliant, betrays that vision. But Desnos was not content to experiment in present and future forms, and constantly experimented in the forms of the past as well.

Some of his last poems, in *Contrée,* are in fact written in sonnet form: we might interpret this as a regression toward fixity, voluntary or involuntary ("Je me sens me roidir avec le paysage" [I feel myself growing rigid with the landscape], he says in one of these). Or again we may see them as a further experiment in openness to all forms, or as a simple statement that any form is as viable as any other to a poet of the modern consciousness. (Desnos always wanted to combine one thing with its opposite: poetry with mathematics and dream with logic, as in the postface to *Fortunes;* the delirious and the lucid **"Réflexions sur la poésie"** [*Domaine Public*]; the mind and the senses *De l'érotisme considéré dans ses manifestaions écrites*). These poems might then, in the very fixity of their form and landscape, be a deliberate contrast to an expression of freedom, just as the poems now published with *Contrée* and given a title reminiscent of mythological culture, *Calixto,* might be seen as using the traditional landscape of myth and the traditional alternations of light and dark images for a statement of what seemed to Desnos a "present" reality. (pp. 11-14)

Desnos' famous novel of 1927, *La Liberté ou l'amour!,* is above all a lyric invocation of movement, of the possible range of the adventuring spirit, and an examination of its limits. In the brief space of the book the action is governed neither by chronological nor spatial laws: the scene shifts from an unidentified desert to the Place de la Concorde, back to the desert, to an English boarding school, to the beach at Nice. The main characters, Corsair Sanglot and Louise Lame (and her double, the mermaid), in their unending wanderings from one place to another constantly encounter, or just miss encountering, an assortment of others; . . . personal encounters replace plot, being the human equivalents of the image in its marvelous juxtapositions. Paragraphs and even sentences start with one situation and end with, or remain suspended in, a completely different situation. The entire text is full of the agents, the memory, or the means of motion, such as railroad tracks still hot from the passing of a recent train, the smoke of a moving locomotive, the sirocco in the desert or the wind over the city, elevators and buses; the countless ships, boats, steamers, yachts, and galleys, are the privileged vessels of adventure. To which the author's own pen must be added, as a winged instrument of poetic risk: "Ma plume est une aile et sans cesse, soutenu par elle et pour son ombre projetée sur le papier, chaque mot se précipite vers la catastrophe ou vers l'apothéose." . . . (My pen is a wing and every word, borne by it and by its shadow on the paper, rushes either toward catastrophe or apotheosis.) Rapidity is the determining characteristic of surrealist writing in its automatic phase, a means of releasing the mind from its inhibitions. (It is interesting to note, in this connection, that Breton established a table of speeds at which the automatic texts of *Les Champs magnétiques* were written.)

For the ordinary or prudent people who care about the crops they can raise in their enclosed and protected fields, who have no knowledge of the wind's existence or of the exalted climate of dangers, as Desnos phrases it, he has nothing but scorn. His angriest outcries are directed against the persons, real or fictitious, who might prevent the free adventuring of the hero-poet. "Si j'avais été l'un rois, ô Jésus, tu serais mort au berceau, étranglé, pour avoir interrompu si tôt mon voyage magnifique et brisé ma liberté." . . . (If I had been one of the kings, you would have been strangled in your cradle, Jesus, for having interrupted my glorious voyage so soon, and for having destroyed my freedom. . . .) When Louise Lame shouts repeatedly at Corsair Sanglot that he must not leave, he shoves her aside and rushes down the stairs as she sinks to the floor, disheveled and sobbing. For the adventuring hero who is always the center of Desnos' films, novels, and poems, the idea of friendship holds the same dangers as that of love, both being fatal traps ("pièges à loup") to be avoided at the cost of any suffering, his own or that of others. Hence the ambiguous title of the book, where we may read "Liberty or Love!" either as a demand for both at once, if they are seen identical, or for one above the other, if they are seen as opposed. In fact, the entire novel turns upon this very ambiguity.

More surprising, but characteristic of Desnos' extreme dualism of attitude, even the notion of adventure itself is taken as a possible hindrance to the peculiar exaltation of the Corsair's enthusiasm, or more precisely, his reverse enthusiasm ("enthousiasme à rebours"). "Depuis qu'il avait compris et accepté la monotonie de l'Eternité, il avançait droit comme un bâton à travers les aventures, lianes glissantes, qui ne l'arrêtaient pas dans sa marche." . . . (Once having understood and accepted the monotony of Eternity, he pursued his unswerving path through all the adventures, slippery vines which did not halt his advance.) This paradoxical rejection of temporal adventures and metamorphosis for the dull freedom of eternity, as unexciting as anything else in Desnos' terms, can be seen as parallel to the author's rejection of realistic or colorful scenery for his narration, in favor of the open spaces of desert or ocean; both are refusals to narrow the field of the action, even if the result is often an abstract background. The combination of rapid

transformation and transmutation with various techniques of repetition give to the novel the hypnotic power of plainsong as well as a certain cinematographic interest, easily the equal of that provided by the scenarios.

From the opening poem through the last pages of the novel, the image of an ebony ship recurs again and again, as the promise of unrestricted adventure and as the reminder of risk. Like Breton's wish that the crow would replace the dove in Noah's ark, like the replacement of humor by black humor in the surrealist universe, the darkness of the ship's wood is one of the true images of surrealist hope, balanced only by the clarity of the other vessel which is the bottle or its crystal fragments (the instrument through which the poetic mass is celebrated, the "Dive bouteille" of Desnos).

"Navire en bois d'ébène parti pour le pôle Nord . . ." (Ebony ship under way for the North Pole . . .): beyond the typical contrasts such as the ebony darkness and the icy glare of the North Pole, this phrase reveals an element of the voyage perhaps unexpected in the light of the emphasis on *disponibilité* or mental liberty. The ship set out with a definite destination, whereas one might more easily imagine complete freedom in the image of an undetermined movement, without a specific goal. But it is clear that for Desnos, a vivid sense of the concrete and the particular is an indispensable ingredient of the marvelous, commanding both his lyricism and his parodies of lyricism. The idea of order or direction, far from being irreconcilable with a notion of liberty, is essential to it. The ship, which does not drift about aimlessly in the sea, is considered here the positive image of freedom, later to be called in question by the figures of mermaids and the theme of shipwreck.

And the pirate hero of the book is in no way a man of disorder, although at times he wanders lost. In a visit to an asylum for the insane, a passage set in the classic framework of heroic pilgrimage, lesson, and departure, he is taught the guiding role that the senses are supposed to play. To be deprived of "sens" is to be at once without feeling, without one's natural senses, and without direction. (Here it is interesting to note that Desnos intended to give the title "Sens" to a collection of poems he was putting together at the end of his life. . . .) Again the idea of freedom is seen as antithetical to the abstract wandering of the unattached hero: "Stupide évocation de la vie libre des déserts. Qu'ils soient de glace ou de porphyre, sur le navire ou dans le wagon, perdus dans la foule ou dans l'espace, cette sentimentale image du désordre universel ne me touche pas." . . . (Stupid evocation of the free desert life. Whether the deserts be made of ice or of porphyry, located on the ship or in the train, lost in the crowd or in space, this sentimental image of disorder does not move me.) That the Corsair should spend a night in one of the cells, watched over by an ebony angel whose color is also that of the ship, may not seem to befit his character, but the scene creates nevertheless a scenic parallel to the personality of his figurative double, the madman pictured here in a straitjacket. The freedom of this two-sensed "senselessness" (exactly that which Breton extols, but finally refuses in *Nadja*) is a useless freedom for the surrealist hero, who leaves at dawn, determined never to be imprisoned in ordinary traps or domestic settings, in prosaic or normal temporal limits. Here, as often in reading Desnos, we think of Mallarmé, specifically of the poem "Brise marine" with its refusal of the calm lamp on the domestic table in favor of the "songs of sailors." (Yvonne George's singing of exactly those songs at the Olympia lends to the thought a special appeal.) Mallarmé's white page, in its paralyzing purity, seems itself to be the double of this disordered desert which is also a page. As Mallarmé's page is also a frozen winter lake imprisoning the swan whose potential traces, like his wings, are captive, so Desnos' desert, to which he compares the page of his own writing, is also itself the ice floes imprisoning the ship—*La Liberté ou l'amour!* The galley slave of love is doomed to have his servitude fixed or immortalized on the page as in the ice, thus making at least a verbal mockery of his potential freedom. The question of similarity and distance between Gide's "disponibilité" ["detachment"] and the ideal liberty of "l'amour fou" or surrealist love is worth debating.

The surrealist hero grapples with these dualities in an epic scene: "L'éternité voilà le théâtre somptueux où la liberté et l'amour se heurtent pour ma possession.... Je ne saurais choisir, sinon que demeurer ici sous la coupole translucide de l'éternité".... (Eternity is the sumptuous theater where liberty and love struggle each to possess me.... I could never make any choice except that of remaining here under the translucent cupola of eternity.)

Eternity, seen as the tedium of the infinite, is the marvelous monotonous backdrop glimpsed or invisible behind the rapidly changing surface of the adventure. The sun is immobile, and a desperate and eternal cleanliness surrounds the action. At times, such movement as there is has not the slightest implication of vigor or nobility: in one of the city landscapes of ennui, the only being is "un personnage minuscule qui circulait sans but défini" ... (a minuscule person who moved about aimlessly), with exactly the "senselessness" Corsair Sanglot refused. Corsair Sanglot himself, as the embodiment of dualities, has the proportions of myth, an impassioned and immoderate love of action both physical and imaginary. The heroic qualities of his person and his adventures are seen in their true perspective in the realm of the mental. Even when lost, he is "plus perdu dans sa vaste intuition des événements éternels que dans l'étendue sablonneuse de la plaine équatoriale" ... (lost more in his own vast intuition of eternal events than in the sandy reaches of the equatorial plain). The surface phenomena seem far less real than the events taking place in spite of them: the hero and the heroine converse inside themselves, they meet each other's gaze in spite of all the apparently restrictive screens of "obstacles, maisons, monuments, arbres" (obstacles, houses, monuments, trees).

Within the constantly alternating patterns of balance and opposition to be traced in all the great surrealist prose poems, the movement of metamorphosis and journey is contradicted by a cessation of motion at once terrifying and desired. The free motion of the ship may represent the ideal form of directed openness, but the arresting of the ship's movement is a corresponding form of imprisonment. All the voyage offers in variety and epic connotation is threatened at the moment when the ebony ship is stopped in a negative landscape of absence:

> Navire en bois d'ébène parti pour le pôle Nord voici que la mort se présente sous la forme d'une baie circulaire et glaciale, sans pingouins, sans phoques, sans ours. Je sais quelle est l'agonie d'un navire pris dans la banquise....

> (Ebony boat underway for the North Pole, death now presents itself in the guise of a circular and frozen bay, without penguins, without seals, without bears. I know the agony of a ship caught in the ice floes....)

Closely linked to the image of the ship is that of love, already seen as a trap, but here identified with a more noble if equally imprisoning set of ideas: "Tu n'es pas la passante, mais celle qui demeure, la notion d'éternité est liée à mon amour pour toi.... Je me perds dans ta pensée plus sûrement que dans un désert.... Tu n'es pas la passante, mais la perpétuelle amante et que tu le veuilles ou non." ... (You are not the one who passes, but the one who remains. The idea of eternity is linked to my love for you.... I lose myself in your thought more surely than in a desert.... You are not the passerby, but the perpetual lover, whether you wish to be or not.) The real setting of this novel is the mind, and it is only in this setting that the hope of love someday reconciled with liberty can be realized, in spite of, or, from the surrealist viewpoint, because of its contradictions. Speaking of the slave galley where he will be a willing prisoner, Desnos perfectly exemplifies the constant ambiguity of perception on which its abnormal exaltation depends: "Qu'elle soit bénie, cette galère! ... qu'elle sera luxueuse la chaîne qui nous unira! qu'elle sera libre, cette galère!" ... (Blessed be that galley ship! ... what a luxurious chain will link us! how liberating that ship will seem!) (pp. 32-7)

It is in his lyric novels that Desnos writes his most characteristic and involved prose poetry: the narrative often seems secondary to the style, for which it serves as a mere prop. (p. 37)

Of course *Deuil pour deuil* and *La Liberté ou l'amour!* are also written in the form of novels, a form they undermine by the easy predominance of their images and their odd lyricism over any pretence at plot. All question about occurrences or development of situation or psychological characterization would be as pointless as a demand to know what happens next after the encounter between the sewing machine and the umbrella on Lautréamont's dissection table. The essential value of the perception is grasped instantly or not at all. Surrealism always emphasizes the moment in its constant novelty rather than traditional continuities and temporal developments. "Toujours pour la première fois" (Always for the first time), said Breton. Differing perceptions are linked to each other by the strength of a connecting wire, or a *fil conducteur,* as are distant elements of experience or imagination, but again these links do not imply any organic, logical, or chronological enchaining. Metamorphosis takes place chiefly within the observer's eye, and it is always rapid. Since instantaneous observation replaces structured unfolding, usually only the most formal architectural framework of the sentence or the poem holds the perceptions together. (It has been remarked that the "normal" linguistic patterns of surrealist prose or poetry are often radically opposed to surrealism's "freed" content or vision. We shall see that this is usually not the case with Desnos, who deliberately contradicts syntactical as well as semantic norms.)

As for the essential scenery and figuration in the Desnos novels, which are in reality long narrative poems in prose, the meetings or associations between a light blue jacket, a skeleton, and a blonde virgin, or between a white-helmeted explorer, a pirate, and a woman clothed only in a leopard-skin coat are signs of the marvelous, encounters whose importance will be magnified by all the resources of surrealist genius until they assume the proportions of myth. The background of deserted and sunny squares pervaded by ennui remind us not only of the early de Chirico, but also of Breton's meditation on ennui in "Poisson soluble" and of his "mysterious road where fear lurks at every step"; the evocation of human loneliness by the presence of ruins and deserts, of hotel rooms and vast expanses of sea, is a successful surrealist and post-symbolist technique. Furthermore, the transformation of coffee into tea, of wine first into a dove and then into a crown, and of the wineglass into an hourglass and finally into a glass eye can be taken as perfect illustrations of Breton's remarks on openness and fusion. (pp. 38-9)

In the development of Desnos' greatest poetry, there is a noticeable change from the early linguistic experiments and poetic jokes, such as *L'Aumonyme* and *Langage cuit* of 1923, to the serious and often tragic love poems of *A la mystérieuse* of 1926, where meditations on the real and the illusory, and on the presence and absence of the woman loved, are found side by side with presentations of a vague menace in the natural world or of a startling landscape.

Each of the poems in the latter volume has an unmistakable inner coherence and certain of them have an exterior brilliance, although the collection as a whole has not the accumulated intensity of *Les Ténèbres* (1927), where the themes of adventure, love, and presence, of the waking and the nocturnal dream in its relation to reality merge with the greater theme of poetic language itself. In every poem of *Les Ténèbres* one is acutely aware of the self-critical poet already seen in the poetic novels, where the cause of linguistic adventure was paradoxically treated alongside that of surrealist love, sometimes as identical with it, and then again as its irreconcilable opposite—the two senses, contrary but joined, of *La Liberté ou l'amour!* In these poems, Desnos tests his own poetry for its fidelity to his dream and to a wider acutality beyond. This time, however, the adventure of the poet's dreaming is clearly separate from that of his love, and the latter is frequently sacrificed to make way for the former; in fact, the very value of love is denied whenever the two are compared. Intensity of experience and expression seem finally to depend on the poet's isolation. (pp. 57-8)

Les Ténèbres contains some of the most complex surrealist poetry ever written. The twenty-four poems demonstrate a wide range of forms, from the several dense circular poems of ten or eleven lines in which the end joins on to the beginning, to far longer poems where the brief conclusion is occasionally set apart from the main body of the poem in a formal echo to the isolation felt within the poem itself. The length of the lines ranges from a single word (for example, "Crie") to an uninterrupted flow of a hundred words; there are prose poems with as many as six sentences included in the space of one indentation, others with shorter and evenly spaced divisions and of a repetitive form, while a few poems show an extremely various and complex texture, where for instance among sixteen short lines there suddenly appears a very long one, completely distinct in tone. Within these poems of description, of statement, of lamentation, an extensive series of questions ("Eh quoi?" [What then?]), threats ("Mort à la voile blanche" [Death to the white sail]), exclamations ("Quelle évasion!" [What an escape!]), break up the interior rhythm. Yet the latter may be balanced by an equally extensive series of appositions whose links are assured, if not made explicit, so that the surface jerkiness overlies a genuine continuity:

> L'infini profond douleur désir poésie amour
> révélation miracle révolution amour l'infini
> profond m'enveloppe de ténèbres bavardes . . .

> (The profound infinite sorrow desire poetry love
> revelation miracle revolution love the profound
> infinite surrounds me with talkative shadows)

The strength of the passage is such that the elements in apposition tend to fuse with one another, without the daylight banality of connectives which would, ironically, weaken the sense of enveloping shadows and the unmarked interior cohesion they surround.

Now Desnos, like the baroque poet he partly is, chooses images of light to play against dark, of flowering and fire to play against the depths. In particular, the star, the crystal bottle, and the sea are paralleled by and opposed to coal, anemone, abyss within the imaginative focus of his writings, which he considered to be the individual and visible parts of one long poem "elaborated from birth to death." These images and the works containing them are all closely linked, as around the central focus of a star various ideas spread partial illuminations. Now the star suggests to Desnos the starfish—that is the mermaid also, the captivating singer of sailor songs or Yvonne George—and thus the starfish of the "anti-poem" *La Place de l'étoile*, written in 1927 and revised in 1944, is at once connected with the sky and the sea: she reappears in Man Ray's film *L'Etoile de mer*, based on Desnos' poem or anti-poem. In the long poems "Sirène-Anémone" and "Siramour," the mermaid and the star are sisters and rivals, the star vies with coal too as a giver of equal light, thus the fire and the sea are joined, and opposed to the shadows, darkness, and ashes which are their doubles. Just so, desert and town, sea and sand, voyage and shipwreck, forest and road are seen as inseparable complementaries, each leading to the other, so that the notion of crossroads or conjunction remains primary in the imagination for the reader as for the poet. A theoretical and metaphoric basis for this reliance on opposites juxtaposed can be found in all the images of communicating vessels and conducting wires common to the theories of surrealism. The violence of the illumination depends often on the unexpectedness of the opposed elements, but in Desnos it depends rather on the repetitions of a small number of images in their interconnections.

Desnos makes a frequent and complex use of interpenetrations of images and of their mutual definition. In a typical poem of these years, the convergence of imagery is so marked as to make possible the suppression of one central image, all the while pointing implicitly to that image as the location of the original impulse for the poetic statement. If the image said to be suppressed in one poem appears frequently as the clearly predominant element of other texts, the initial perception of its centrality receives additional support.

Often within a particular poetic universe of great cohesiveness, constructed about a constantly recurring small number of images each of equal importance, a central poem can be found whose elements and their interrelations may serve as paradigms for all the other poems, whatever their date. Each poem of the given set may point in some way, explicitly or implicitly, to this particular key poem. Rather than discussing abstracted components of the poet's sensibility, style or his images, the reader may choose (usually through a series of experiments) the text which appears central to him, distinguish in that text the salient factors, explaining how they are marked as high points (set off from the others by the poet), and what other elements in the text justify or determine them. Then those stressed elements should be matched to those same elements stressed elsewhere in order to sketch a precise or post-text profile of the particular poetic imagination in question. Any poem and any series of poems can be read in both directions, so that an image may be justified by one following it, and vice versa. A text written before another can be retrospectively clarified by the later one; these parallel readings stress the continuity of a particular language, of the chain of obsessive imagery over the discontinuity of chronological points taken as separate texts.

It is within *Les Ténèbres* that the most significant clues to Desnos' evolution are to be found. This collection contains twenty-four connected aspects of tenebral vision, corresponding, perhaps, to the hours of the night and day seen as the temporal space of the continuing surrealist dream (as in Breton's *Vases communicants*). The alternations of night/day, language/silence, faith/doubt, or love/loneliness often perceived in the other surrealist poets are arranged in more difficult patterns than is customary in the poetry of Tzara, Eluard, Péret, or even Breton. Sometimes apparent, and sometimes hidden within the poem, are various complicated and disturbing oppositions of involvement and separation between the poet and the poem, between the poet and the language or vision, between the poet and the reader. The overall force of the poems seems to deny the power of poetic language and the marvelous vision by the disintegration of elements within the poem, while the poet seems to pursue his adventure beyond the space of the poem, thus denying us any participation in it. At least three possible interpretations can be given of this poetic attitude: first, that Desnos' experience necessarily bars any observer. This might be true, but no more so for him than for any of the other surrealists; consequently, it would not be sufficient to explain the peculiar nature of his poetry. Second, that Desnos is here predicting, implicitly, his final journey beyond the surrealist experience of the shadows to the more open poem of the day ("poème du jour") which he mentions in two of these texts. Finally, that these poems are a confirmation of Desnos' own statement that beyond all free poetry there is the free poet. . . . (pp. 88-91)

The early Desnos considered himself above all a poet of love and of a particular love, which formed the subject of all he wrote. One of the most powerful poems in *A la mystérieuse* ends with these lines where surrealist pride and personal simplicity meet:

> . . . moi qui ne suis ni Ronsard ni Baudelaire
> Moi qui suis Robert Desnos et qui pour t'avoir connue
>   et aimée,
> Les vaux bien.
> Moi qui suis Robert Desnos, pour t'aimer
> Et qui ne veux pas attacher d'autre réputation à ma
>   mémoire sur la terre méprisable. . . .
>
> (. . . I who am neither Ronsard nor Baudelaire
> I who am Robert Desnos and who, for having known
>   you and loved you,
> Am their equal.
> I who am Robert Desnos, in order to love you,
> Wanting to attach no other reputation to my memory on
>   this despicable earth.

What then is the relation between the actual text and the adventure of dream, the supposedly equivalent of poetry? Do the closed doors in the early collection *Les Ténèbres* have a necessary link with the paralyzed landscape visible in the late collection of *Contrée*? Is the admitted poetic impotence within the enforced limitations of the latter "real" landscape found after the early dream has subsided, prefigured in the laments of loneliness and emptiness at the center of the surrealist theater of shadows ("les arbres solitaires du théâtre" [the solitary trees of the theater])? To what extent did Desnos finally discover

himself to be a "free" poet, in spite of the paralyzed and frozen landscape about him?

The statements made by Desnos himself are questions rather than assertions. His style remains one of a chosen ambiguity; his earliest and strongest works seem to have no exterior conclusion and to suppose no interior closure. In that they fit our contemporary state of mind. But in the later poems, the framework is clear, and the landscape limited, while the poetry itself acquires the formal limitations of rhyme scheme and pattern which might seem the parallel of that landscape. We might think of the evolution of Paul Eluard and of Louis Aragon to a more formal and easier, more predictable, scheme of poetry after their first, difficult and surrealist verse, in the interest of the majority of readers and partly for political reasons. (But Desnos always wrote alexandrines on the side, for which he was greatly criticized by Breton.) One may see him writing, in these last poems, a pathetic and fixed end to his own early ambiguities, on which all the force of his surrealist summons seemed to depend.

In a voluntary contrast to his praise of the unknown, of the mysterious and the tenebrous, his static portraits of mythical personages such as the nymphs Calixto and Alcestes and his still pictures of a clear and petrified landscape (such as "**Le Coteau**," "**Le Cimetière**," "**La Clairière**," "**La Caverne**," "**La Sieste**," "**La Ville**," "**La Maison**" in *Contrée*) are as shocking to a surrealist-oriented sensibility as is the surrealist attitude to a non-surrealist sensibility. That the subtle critic of the cinema should forsake movement for portraiture and for still life (or more precisely, "nature morte"), is the most difficult of all desertions for the admirers of his early period.

And that he should have taken this step consciously, informing us of it, is the final stumbling block. To experience all the ambiguous potentialities of surrealism at its most mobile and most complex and then to go beyond them to a fixed form is surely as extraordinary as the choice of shipwreck which Desnos made explicitly so many times. But shipwreck is no less logical than navigation, he claims, and perhaps no less adventurous a choice. Desnos is no more trapped in his own shipwreck than his heroine the mermaid is trapped in the sea. On the other side of the poems of obvious adventure, Desnos claims to find another adventure; beyond all the surrealist poetry of freedom, he claims the possible existence of the free poet.

The eventual alienation of Desnos from his reader comes after we have weathered all the early insults and deliberate deceptions. For the farewell of the poet to the mermaid prefigures another and more final one, that of the poet to the reader, a farewell situated within the fragile, appealing, and often tragic temporality of the work:

> Adieu déjà parmi les heures de porcelaine
> (And now farewell among the porcelain hours)

But neither the poet's separation from the mermaid, nor the reader's final exclusion from the imaginative adventure place any limit upon the adventure of the text. In the last message from Desnos in the concentration camp at Theresienstadt to his wife Youki on January 7, 1945, he states with complete conviction that for him, the relation of the poet to poetry is never touched by exterior circumstances, that the faith in poetic adventure can still be completely justified, in the long run and in the smallest detail, in spite of everything else. "As for the rest, I find a shelter in poetry. It is really 'the horse running on the crests of the mountains' which Rrose Sélavy mentions in one of her poems and which I have found to be justified word for word.'' It is as if, at last, the two terms of freedom and love (*La Liberté ou l'amour!*) had found their resolution—and even, perhaps, their identification—on the summits of the surrealist imagination, where finally no distinction was to be made, between mermaid, star, and anemone, between open sea and ice floe, between the mountain, the desert, and the page or the poem.

For in spite of the self-doubting text, the adventure was always to be one of language, with those doubts a source of primary action and continuing complexity. Desnos made, in 1926, a **"Confession d'un enfant du siècle,"** which at once bears perhaps the most telling witness to that active language and makes the most fitting, because most ambiguous, answer to the question of his being remembered: ''The only tense of the verb is the present indicative.'' Of that sentence he might have said, as of his love poetry which finds its source in the same sentiment, that he wanted to be remembered by it only; like a serious gamble on presence. (pp. 131-33)

> *Mary Ann Caws, in her* The Surrealist Voice of Robert Desnos, *University of Masachusetts Press, 1977, 222 p.*

ADDITIONAL BIBLIOGRAPHY

Benedikt, Michael. Introduction to *Modern French Theatre: An Anthology of Plays,* edited by Michael Benedikt and George E. Wellwarth, pp. ix-xxxv.
    A discussion of *La place de l'étoile.* Benedikt remarks: ''Despite the subtlety of its methods, *La place de l'étoile* is as ambitious as any drama in the post-Jarry theatre: the abolition on the stage of all boundaries usually accepted for practical reasons.''

Breunig, LeRoy C. ''To Hear a Poem: Desnos' 'Sol de Compiegne.' '' *Teaching Language through Literature* XXII, No. 2 (April 1983): 3-14.
    A phonetic study of ''Sol de Compiegne.''

Caws, Mary Ann. ''Desnos' 'Le Paysage.' '' *The Explicator* XXVI, No. 9 (May, 1968): Item 71.
    Discusses Desnos's late poem ''Le Paysage'' and contrasts Desnos's Surrealist and post-Surrealist poetry.

————. ''Ode to a Surrealist Baroque: Sceve, Gongora, and Desnos.'' In her *A Metapoetics of the Passage: Architextures in Surrealism and After,* pp. 67-77. Hanover and London: University Press of New England, 1981.
    Traces the influences of Sceve and Gongora on Desnos.

Dutton, K. R. ''The Text and the Sense of Desnos' 'Ideal Maitresse.' '' *Australian Journal of French Studies* XVI, No. 2 (January-April 1979): 257-69.
    Detailed textual study of ''Ideal Maitresse.'' ''The aim of this paper is to propose a reading of the poem as a whole which takes account both of the relationships between its internal elements and of its particular significance in the collection [*Language Cuit*] in terms of the development of certain obsessive images which were to pervade much of the later work of Desnos.''

Esslin, Martin. ''The Tradition of the Absurd.'' In his *The Theatre of the Absurd,* pp. 281-349. Garden City, N.Y.: Doubleday & Co., 1969.
    Brief discussion and plot summary of *La place de l'étoile.*

Leonard, Byron, ''A Surrealist Poet at the Movies: Robert Desnos.'' *Stanford French Review,* II, No. 1 (Spring 1978), 103-13.
    Discusses Desnos's love for cinema and examines aspects of his film criticism.

Sonnenfeld, Albert. ''Desnos-Eros.'' *Dada/Surrealism,* No. 13 (1984): pp. 104-14.
    Discusses erotic and cerebral elements in Desnos' poetry, demonstrating that ''much of what passes for hallucinatory eroticism or *écriture automatique* in Desnos' poetry is fraudulent simulation of incoherence; it is nonetheless, indeed perhaps all the more, great poetry.''

Wills, David. ''Icarus in Timbuktu.'' *Australian Journal of French Studies* XIX, No. 3 (September-December 1982): 295-308.
    Semiotic study of Desnos's work.

Georges Feydeau

1862-1921

French dramatist.

An immensely popular playwright at the turn of the century, Feydeau is today considered a major figure in French comic theater. Skillfully manipulating the conventions of vaudeville and the bedroom farce, Feydeau created plays which are known for their precisely staged and wildly unlikely coincidences, misunderstandings, and mistaken identities. Critics, however, have also found in his plays an intellectual dimension not generally present in the works of other practitioners of vaudeville, and although the farce has been largely superseded by other comedic forms in modern theater, Feydeau's plays are still well received by audiences.

Born in Paris, Feydeau was the son of novelist Ernest Feydeau and a celebrated Polish beauty named Lodzia Zelewska. Although the elder Feydeau was only a minor literary figure, his wealth and position placed him in the society of such notable authors as Théophile Gautier, Gustave Flaubert, and Jules and Edmond de Goncourt, who describe young Georges in their diaries as an enchanting but lazy child. Influenced by this literary atmosphere and encouraged by his father, Feydeau began to compose plays well before his tenth birthday. After Ernest Feydeau's death in 1873, however, Zelewska married a well-known journalist, and the couple attempted to dissuade Feydeau from embarking on a career in the uncertain and, in their opinion, somewhat undignified world of the theater. Toward this end they secured for him a position in a law office. Feydeau nevertheless spent his evenings at the theater, and at social gatherings he frequently performed his comic monologues: Feydeau wrote and performed the first of these monologues, *La petite revoltée,* in 1880, and the piece was an immediate success in Parisian salon society. He quickly produced five more monologues, and these were recited by several of the most renowned comedians of the day.

Feydeau wrote his first play, *Par la fenêtre (Wooed and Viewed),* in 1881, initiating a period of theatrical successes which culminated in 1886 with the enormously popular *Tailleur pour dames (Fitting for Ladies).* There followed, however, an interval during which Feydeau wrote several poorly received plays, and he stopped writing altogether in 1890 in order to study the work of France's great vaudevillians, hoping thus to refine his own technique. Two years later, Feydeau returned to the stage with an unprecedented coup de theatre. His *Champignol malgré lui (A Close Shave)* ran for well over one thousand performances and inspired novels, songs, sequels, and an operetta. Both the play and its author became known throughout France, and Feydeau was proclaimed the King of Vaudeville. Moreover, unlike *Fitting for Ladies,* this play was followed by a long series of popular and lucrative comedies which secured for Feydeau a preeminent place in French theater.

Feydeau's personal life, however, was not characterized by the same degree of success as his professional life. In 1889, he married a wealthy and beautiful woman, Marianne Carolus-Duran, and while the early years of their marriage are reported to have been peaceful and happy, their relationship later became quite hostile. Indeed, Feydeau's son stated that the dismal

portrait of marriage presented in Feydeau's later plays is based on the author's own marital experience, with Madame Feydeau serving as the model for the irrational and relentless shrews featured in those plays. In addition, Feydeau was melancholy by nature, possibly the victim of chronic depression, and his condition worsened with age. In 1909, he left his home and moved to a hotel, where he lived alone for the next ten years. During this period he contracted a severe venereal disease, hastening his descent into madness. By 1919 he had become quite deranged, imagining himself an animal or an emperor, and his children were forced to have him institutionalized. Thereafter his condition deteriorated rapidly, and he died two years later.

Critics generally divide Feydeau's work into three phases. The first, corresponding to the plays written between 1880 and 1890, represents Feydeau's apprenticeship, during which he experimented with the themes and techniques of vaudeville comedy, which in the commercial theater included burlesque humor, stylized stock characters, and complicated plots. Although vaudeville was still the most popular theatrical genre of fin-de-siècle Paris, many, including Feydeau, believed it had become stale and ossified. Feydeau sought to revitalize vaudeville through the use of new elements. Drawing upon the recently established ideas of the Naturalists, he renovated the stock characters and contrived plots of the genre, giving them greater dimension and verisimilitude while still maintaining much of the artifice that is considered the essence of conventional farce. Feydeau also utilized the customs and morality of his own time to update the traditional conflicts of vaudeville. As a result he was able to derive humor not only from the action of his comedies, but from the realistic foibles of his characters and from social satire as well. It is, however, action which dominates Feydeau's plays, and they are renowned for their furious pace and complex plots. Indeed, critics frequently remark that it is nearly impossible to summarize a Feydeau play, since he typically intertwines several plot lines in a manner so precise as to defy separation. It is this skill that is generally recognized as Feydeau's greatest talent.

The second phase of Feydeau's career, from 1890 to 1908, saw the creation of his best and most popular works. The plays of this period are thematically similar to those of the earlier period but display Feydeau's growing stylistic finesse in their coordinated action and comic caricatures. It was also during this period that Feydeau fully developed the satiric qualities that distinguish his work from that of other vaudevillians. In his masterpiece, *La dame de chez Maxim (The Lady from Maxim's)*, for example, much humor is derived from the desire of respectable citizens to practice what they perceive as correct social behavior, no matter how ludicrous that behavior might be. Nevertheless, as in all bedroom farce, the primary focus of humor in Feydeau's comedies is male-female relationships. In Feydeau's case, the relationships are usually adulterous ones, providing a wealth of comic possibilities in botched concealments and unforeseen encounters. Feydeau explained that he used a formula in writing his comedies, creating two characters who should under no circumstances meet and then having them do so as soon as possible. Critics note that the plays of the middle period capture the gaiety and insouciance generally associated with the *belle époque* while at the same time pointing out its more ridiculous aspects. Many critics also believe that close examination of Feydeau's comedies reveals an essentially negative perspective: the consistently immoral and deceitful actions of his characters present a cynical view of human nature, while the results of their behavior often bring real pain and suffering.

This dark side of Feydeau's comic vision prevails in the one-act plays written during the final phase of his career, which lasted from 1908 to 1916. These plays, shorter, simpler, and less farcical than his earlier works, deal primarily with the subject of marriage, which is depicted as the continual struggle of two irrevocably yoked and hopelessly incompatible creatures. The mischievous women of the longer plays are replaced by malicious shrews, while the bumbling but often vindicated cuckolds have become completely subjugated husbands. Critics believe that the thematic changes evident in the late plays are due primarily to Feydeau's personal problems, but note also that Feydeau, knowing vaudeville must eventually give way to new forms of comedy, was in fact attempting to evolve a new style.

Feydeau's opinion in this matter was essentially but not entirely correct. After the death of its "king," vaudeville did enter a period of decline, along with the farce form in general, both superseded by more modern comedic forms. It was not until 1941, when the Comédie-Française added *Feu la mère de madame (Better Late)* to its repertoire, that interest in Feydeau's work was renewed. Within a few years more Feydeau plays were added to the repertoire, and English translations of his work began to appear. Many critics were appalled; some ex-

pressed contempt for the entire farce genre, while others objected only to the particularly bawdy quality of Feydeau's comedies. Some critics and most audiences, however, found Feydeau's work delightful. Still enormously popular in France, his plays have been translated into dozens of languages despite difficulties posed by his frequent use of double-entendre and innuendo, and they are regularly performed in more than seventy countries.

(See also *Contemporary Authors*, Vol. 113.)

PRINCIPAL WORKS

Par la fenêtre (drama) 1881
    [*Wooed and Viewed* published in *Four Farces*, 1970]
Amour et piano (drama) 1883
    [*Call Me Maestro* published in *Ooh! La-La!*, 1973; also
       published as *Romance in A Flat* in *Feydeau, First to
       Last*, 1982]
Gibier de potence (drama) 1884
    [*Before We Were So Rudely Interrupted* published in *Ooh!
       La-La!*, 1973; also published as *Fit to Be Tried; or,
       Stepbrothers in Crime* in *Feydeau, First to Last*, 1982]
Fiancés en herbe (drama) 1886
    [*Budding Lovers*, 1969]
Tailleur pour dames (drama) 1886
    [*A Gown for His Mistress*, 1969; also published as *Fitting
       for Ladies*, 1974]
La lycéenne (drama) 1887
Un bain de ménage (drama) 1888
L'affaire Edouard [with Maurice Desvallières] (drama)
    1889
Le mariage de Barillon [with Maurice Desvallières]
    (drama) 1890
    [*On the Marry-Go-Wrong* published in *Four Farces*,
       1970]
Champignol malgré lui [with Maurice Desvallières]
    (drama) 1892
    [*A Close Shave*, 1974]
Monsieur chasse! (drama) 1892
    [*13 Rue de l'amour*, 1972; also published as *The Happy
       Hunter*, 1973; also *The Chaser and the Chaste* in *After
       You, Mr. Feydeau!*, 1975]
Le système Ribadier [with Maurice Hennequin] (drama)
    1892
Un fil à la patte (drama) 1894
    [*Cat among the Pigeons*, 1970; also published as *Not by
       Bed Alone* in *Four Farces*, 1970; also *Get Out of My
       Hair* in *Three French Farces* (Frederick Davies, ed.),
       1973; also *On a String* in *After You, Mr. Feydeau!*,
       1975]
L'Hôtel du Libre-Echange [with Maurice Desvallières]
    (drama) 1894
    [*Hotel Paradiso*, 1957]
Le dindon (drama) 1896
    [*There Is One in Every Marriage*, 1970; also published as
       Sauce for the Goose, 1974; also *Paying the Piper* in
       After You, Mr. Feydeau!, 1975; also *The French Have
       a Word for It*, 1983]
Dormez, je le veux! (drama) 1897
    [*Caught with His Trance Down* published in *Feydeau,
       First to Last*, 1982]
La dame de chez Maxim (drama) 1899
    [*The Lady from Maxim's*, 1971; also published as *St.
       Shrimp* in *Ooh! La-La!*, 1973]

FRANK WADLEIGH CHANDLER (essay date 1920)

[*Chandler was an American critic whose primary area of interest
was modern drama. In the following excerpt, he offers a descriptive overview of Feydeau's works.*]

[Georges Feydeau], best known out of France for *La Dame de
chez Maxim* . . . , is the author of many [pieces] . . . of rol-
licking fun, more or less Rabelaisian in quality. Although his
plots, like this, are far from moral, they are so evidently capers
of the imagination removed from the actual that they bear no
ethical import. In *La Dame de chez Maxim*, for example, a
physician, having imbibed too freely one evening, awakens
next morning to find that he has brought home a fair dancer,
who must be got out of the way of his wife. The credulous
wife he sends to the obelisk in the Place de la Concorde at the
command of the Angel Gabriel, to meet one at whose words
there will be born to her a noble son. This reminiscence of
Massuccio's well-known Italian novella Feydeau combines with
the more usual confusion of an uncle who mistakes the dancer
for the wife of the physician, and insists that both shall accompany him to his château in Touraine. Here the dancer passes
to another lover, and is presently supposed by a third person
to be the wife of the uncle. So errors accumulate, and the
laughter grows, the first act alone keeping the audience convulsed for an hour.

Representative, also, of the skill of Feydeau in handling situations such as would have rejoiced the heart of Scarron, Fielding, and Smollett, is *L'Hôtel du libre-échange* . . . , written

with Maurice Desvallières. The wife of an architect, piqued at
her husband, visits with her lover a hotel, to which are brought
other couples, including the husband and a lady. The scene
shows a stairway in the center, with doors on each side, and
a scramble of the characters from room to room. Somewhat
similar in its mixups is *Les Fiancés de Loches* . . . , by the
same authors. A provincial druggist, his old-maid sister, and
a sentimental brother journey to Paris all intent upon marriage,
but, mistaking an intelligence office for the matrimonial bureau
they would visit, are sent as three servants to a physician. In
Le Ruban . . . , by Feydeau and Desvallières, the comic is less
mechanical, and the scientist who, to capture the red ribbon
for his anti-Pasteurian researches, depends upon ministerial
influence, finds that his wife can more readily procure the
fulfillment of his ambition.

Sometimes Feydeau, as in *Le Dindon* . . . , spins a plot over-
long and involved. As a rule, however, he is too volatile to
weary, even though play after play exhibit the same old deceptions of husbands and wives, and chance meetings between
those who seek to evade each other. Now we have, as in *Un
Fil à la patte* . . . , a gay youth who tries to impress his sweetheart that he is a saint, whereas she has vowed to accord her
hand only to a man of the world. Again, as in *Champignol
malgré lui* . . . , by Feydeau and Desvallières, we have the
lover of an artist's wife forced to pose before her provincial
relatives as her husband. In *Monsieur chasse* . . . , the wife
who suspects a husband's story of going hunting with a friend,
seeks revenge by meeting that friend at his rooms, only to be
disturbed by the husband and his lady of the moment. Wrong
doors are opened, women faint, and men in dishabille dash
across the stage pursued by the police.

For drollery nothing is better than *Le Système Ribadier* . . . ,
by Feydeau and Maurice Hennequin. The heroine is a widow,
who, discovering among the effects of her deceased husband
a list of 365 excuses with which to hoodwink her, resolves by
this knowledge to controvert the schemes of her second husband, whom she has married because his initials happened to
be the same as those of the first, thus obviating all need of remarking her linen. But the jovial Ribadier has devised a special
system of evasion superior to any employed by his predecessor,
putting the lady to sleep by means of magnetic passes. No
wonder his system is eagerly borrowed by other husbands!

In the vein of roaring farce are Feydeau's *On purge Bébé* . . .
and *Occupe-toi d'Amélie*. . . . The first is as absurd in depicting
the struggles of parents with their *enfant terrible*, who refuses
his dose of purgative waters, as in following the schemes of
the father, a manufacturer of pottery, who aspires to provide
every soldier with a product of his art for private use. As for
Occupe-toi d'Amélie, it is hilarious in its supposition of a sweetheart loaned by one friend to another, obliged to pass as the
latter's bride, and awaking with him in the same room but
unable to recall whether they have kept their vow to the first
that their union be only a matter of form. Here, before long,
each of the principal personages is mistaken for some other,
and grotesqueness reaches its climax when the heroine, concealed beneath a quilt, bounds across the stage, endeavoring
to escape.

Character is rarely developed by Feydeau, though the captain
of reservists in *Champignol malgré lui* is Molièresque in promising to treat his charges indulgently, and then raging in the
next breath at one who has failed to stand straight. There is a
touch of characterization, also, in the ridiculous farce *Mais
n'te promène donc pas toute nue* . . . , depicting the despair of

a deputy whose ministerial ambitions are imperiled by the naïve immodesty of his wife. Somewhat more analytic is Feydeau's treatment, in **Le Bourgeon** . . . , of the youth, who, expecting to enter the Church, is disturbed by thoughts of love, and warned by a priest to pattern after Saint Anthony, yet excused by a regimental surgeon on the ground that "Nature speaks in him." Quite improbably, Maurice's pious mother commends to him an actress whom he has chanced to save from drowning. When, after a course of lessons from the lady, Maurice would wed her, he is advised to settle down in a bourgeois match with his little cousin. But why not marry Etiennette, he asks the priest. "Did not our Lord raise up the repentant sinner?"

"Yes, but He did not marry her."

"Yet He said, 'Much will be forgiven you, because you have loved much.'"

"Exactly!" says the priest; "Etiennette has loved too much." (pp. 163-67)

Frank Wadleigh Chandler, "Makers of Mirth," in his The Contemporary Drama of France, *Little, Brown, and Company, 1920, pp. 156-89.*

MARCEL ACHARD (essay date 1948)

[*Achard was a French dramatist and screenwriter whose many light comedies have been well-received in both France and the United States. In the following excerpt, which originally appeared as the introduction to Feydeau's* Théâtre complet, *Achard praises the precision of Feydeau's comedies and discusses their development.*]

In a Feydeau play, the events are linked together with the precision of a well-oiled machine. The *qui pro quo* precedes the imbroglio. Unexpected *coups de théâtre* superabound, follow one upon the other, and frequently become entangled. That is generally why the critics give up when they attempt to recount Feydeau's plots. They begin their review in fine spirits, joyously setting down events and characters; but they soon realize that they have covered sixteen single-spaced pages and aren't even halfway through the first act. So they complete their article by saying:

"But go and see it."

Of course they are right. And, obviously, I cannot hope to succeed where they have failed. Even Francisque Sarcey, the best of them all, gave up when it came to Feydeau.

"Allow me to stop here in my analysis," he writes, in his review of **La Dame de chez Maxim.** "All farces congeal when they are transferred from the stage to a cold description of them. I merely wished to convey some idea of the author's marvelous agility and firmness of touch."

I am not more cunning than Sarcey; and not being a professional critic, I lack the ability to deal in generalities. Unfortunately, it is not enough simply to say that everything is regulated by an infallible geometry which marks the point of departure and traces the graph of the action. I still must prove it. I must try to assemble the pieces of this puzzle. And this is somewhat like being in the position of the clockmaker who has to dismantle the carillon on the Strasbourg cathedral.

It is impossible to cut anything in Feydeau's plays. The most amazing thing about them is the infallibility with which all things are regulated, explained, and justified, even in the most extravagant buffoonery. There is not a single incident, once introduced, of which we cannot say: "Yes, that's true—it could not have happened in any other way."

There is not a single detail, not one, which is not necessary to the action as a whole; there is not a single word which, at a given moment, does not have its repercussion in the comedy—and this one word, I have no idea why, buries itself in our subconscious, only to issue forth at the precise moment when it must illumine an incident we were not anticipating, but which we find entirely natural, and which delights us because it sounds improvised—and because we realize that we should have foreseen it.

As I said before, it is quite impossible to cut anything from a Feydeau play. Students in drama classes have often mentioned this to me. Those who shamelessly cut a scene of Musset, or Beaumarchais, or Marivaux, dumbfoundedly agree that Feydeau's comedies will not stand up under their sacrilegious blue-penciling; and they see the precise mechanism falling to pieces before their eyes. That is because the author of **La Main passe** brought to his choice of situations the same relentless discrimination that Paul Valéry used in selecting each word of his poems. There is a kind of Mallarmé-like strictness in Feydeau's discovery of poetry—the comic poetry of a logarithmic table. (pp. 357-58)

There are three periods in Georges Feydeau's work, and all three are ruled by the female character. When the heroine changes, the style, pace, and quality of the comedy change too.

The first period is dominated by middle-class ladies. They have not sinned—yet—but they dream about it all the time. They are charming, unstable, and a bit mad. They are despotic mistresses and rather uncommendable wives. As Feydeau says: "They breathe virtue, and are forthwith out of breath." They are more emancipated than the heroines of Labiche, but not unlike them. They say: "What a pity one cannot take a lover without deceiving one's husband!" Though they are all smiles at the idea of sin, they cannot stand being themselves deceived—their only recourse is to apply the law of retaliation. It is only in those fleeting moments when they give no thought to what they are saying that we can be sure of what is really going on in their heads. Still, they know what's what. "One may doubt the man who says, 'I love you,' but one can be sure of the man who does all he can to conceal his love."

This is the period of **Monsieur Chasse, La Main passe, Dindon, La Puce à l'oreille** and **l'Hôtel du Libre-Échange.**

The second period deals with the *cocottes,* or *dégrafées* as they were called at the time—Amélie, Bichon, *la môme Crevette.* These girls have character. They are amusing, aggressive, ridiculous. A whole cosmopolitan menagerie, a whole rich fauna of rakes, weaklings, refugees, and deadbeats follow in the wake of these ladies. Standards are rising.

And because these girls are given to all kinds of lunacy, the author can profit from them in the multiplication of his own. They are likely to say anything—but they say it so well that they are quoted by a duchess, the wife of a subprefect, twelve society ladies, and a priest. When one of their set marries and becomes the Duchesse de la Courtille, they say, quite reasonably:

"That makes one less chippy, but not necessarily one more lady."

They are trollops, but good trollops. They are as nice to their brother as they are to the *valet de chambre*.

Their chief preoccupation is jewels; but, if their lovers object, they attempt to appease them: "Look, I had that diamond he gave me set into a ring—just for you." They frolic gaily in the midst of situations that are excruciating for everybody else. Because they are pretty and have nothing to lose, they are amiably content to be the cause of all catastrophes.

They do not complain of their condition. One of them, who had been a lady's maid, is questioned by her former mistress:

> "Then, you became a—"
>
> "Cocotte, yes, madame."
>
> "But how could you?"
>
> "Ambition."

This is the era of sparkling successes—*La Dame de chez Maxim, Je ne trompe pas mon Mari,* and *Occupe-toi d'Amélie.*

The last period is the reign of the untamed shrews: it is also the period of his masterpieces, his one-act plays. Feydeau has now given up cataclysmic encounters, disguises, pistol shots, conditional threats, brawls, booby-trapped rooms, apparitions, magnetism, spiritualism, anesthetizing ecstasy. He abandons all his accessories, concentrating on nothing but his excruciating buffoonery, which he will bring to bear upon a married couple—a weak and rather stupid man in the clutches of a terrible, fascinating, and pitiless shrew.

The names of the characters change: in *Mais n'te promène donc pas toute nue,* they are Ventroux and Clarisse; in *On Purge Bébé,* Follavoine and Julie; in *Léontine est en avance,* Toudoux and Léonie; in *Feu la Mère de Madame,* Yvonne and Lucien. But only the names are changed. Feydeau planned to publish this series of comedies in a single volume, to be called *Du Mariage au Divorce.* What we find in these four plays are the irritations, the interminable wranglings, the small, horrible catastrophes in the lives of a man and woman who are united only by habit. If the author had not made these ill-mated couples pass before fun-house mirrors that warp and magnify, they would be Strindberg characters.

The language in which they express themselves has been the subject of much discussion. Obviously it is not "the elegant French of Labiche, nor the delicately shaded language, full of scintillating color, which illuminates the dialogues of Meilhac." Nor is it a revival of the solemn grandiloquence of Bossuet parodied by Georges Courteline.

It is an abrupt and chaotic language, marked by an abundance of absurd and stupefying notions. It is a conjurer's raiment: from the sleeves, the pockets, the collar, come fish, flowers, an omelet, a rabbit, soap bubbles, a cannon ball, or a display of fireworks. The speech changes with the milieu, the class, the occupation of the characters; it runs with the action, keeping up with its antics and its perilous leaps. It is the *maillot* of the acrobatic clown, the skin on the muscles.

Georges Feydeau was indeed a great master of comedy. The greatest after Molière. The miracle of Feydeau is the brilliant animation by means of which the unfortunate Pinglets and Petypons are stirred up, carried off, and swept away. Feydeau's plays have the consecutiveness, the force, and the violence of tragedies. They have the same ineluctable fatality. In tragedy, one is stifled with horror. In Feydeau, one is suffocated with laughter. We are occasionally given some respite by the heroes of Shakespeare and Racine, when they melodiously bemoan their fate in beautiful poetry. But Feydeau's heroes haven't got time to complain. It is characteristic of their destiny to make us laugh, while the small catastrophe, which barely manages to come off, paves the way for an immense vexation, which, we know, will be only the first in a whole series of new ones. Jean Cocteau believes the gods create highly perfected infernal machines for the annihilation of the human race. The god Feydeau controls his infernal machine from a practical-jokes-and-novelty shop. (pp. 361-63)

> *Marcel Achard, "Appendix: Georges Feydeau," translated by Mary Douglas Dirks, in* Let's Get a Divorce! and Other Plays, *edited by Eric Bentley, Hill and Wang, Inc., 1958, pp. 350-64.*

PETER GLENVILLE (essay date 1957)

[*Glenville is an English actor and director. In the following excerpt, he discusses* Hotel Paradiso, *which he produced, directed, and adapted in its 1956 production, as a typical example of Feydeau's farces.*]

The plays of Feydeau (there are about forty of them) are immaculately constructed. They are concerned largely with the appetites and follies of the average human being caught in a net devised by his own foolishness. The net is of course the Feydeau plot, the situation; it becomes increasingly complicated and outrageous as the farce proceeds, but every detail is logical and plausible, and is engineered, however unwittingly, by the characters themselves. Nothing happens that is purely capricious or unexplained. And yet the plot thickens with the precision of a monstrous infernal machine, inflicting calamities on the characters involved, and eventually Nemesis, hilarious, triumphs.

There is nothing sentimental about Feydeau's farces. There are no pretty young people who find true love; neither does virtue triumph—since none of his characters can boast of it. Feydeau creates his characters from the cynical premise that all men and women are naughty and predictable knaves, and they inevitably get their comeuppance. Morals and idealism don't enter into the question. He is not interested in what people should be, or even, on occasion, can aspire to be, but rather with what they almost inevitably, and amusingly, *are. Hotel Paradiso* is no exception to this rule. The characters are not individual or unique. They are universally recognizable types. They correspond to the classical humors of Ben Jonson, or to the inevitable and classic roles of the *commedia dell' arte.* The dominating wife dominates, the hen-pecked husband with a roving eye lets his eye rove. The worm turns: The pretty, impulsive woman gives way to an impulse which her prettiness provokes. The characters don't utter witticisms or felicitous phrases, but talk in the flat and exact tones of the middle class to which they belong; and what they say is funny because it is true to type. When the situation is cleverly manipulated, the cliché can be funnier than the epigram: The inevitable can make one laugh as much as the unexpected. Feydeau unfolds his monstrous plot openly before our eyes, and we hold our breath hoping that what must happen, will happen; and yes, the husband *does* go into the wrong hotel bedroom! And he *does* find. . . .

Feydeau's plays are written with an expert eye to the visual effect. When well acted, they are funny to watch, as well as funny to listen to. In fact, in many good productions of his plays the dialogue is completely lost in the laughter of the audience; but then what is happening always tells its own story, even if the words are not heard. His farces have much in common with the early silent films of Mack Sennett and the Keystone Cops. . . . Moreover Feydeau calculates exactly when the comedy is based on what is said; at this point he makes the action simple. And when the comedy arises from what is being seen and done, he is careful that his dialogue should include no line which has to be heard for the proper understanding of the goings on. I have considered the idea of producing *Hotel Paradiso* as a silent film, since so much of the humor comes from mime and action. Its situations are concerned with the complications and ludicrous calamities of everyday life, and are arranged in a pattern of such perfect precision and increasing momentum that we welcome each step toward pandemonium with the same delighted expectation with which we view the approach of a self-important character toward a banana peel.

The play does not attempt wit, nor is it profound. The laughter it provokes is from the belly rather than from the head. It appeals to the child in all of us. It is a riot which should never be allowed to degenerate into a romp. It requires great expertness from the actors. The outrageousness of the characters in the play requires the utmost sincerity in the playing. The energy, with which the persons in the story have to combat the comic horrors which beset them, has to be calculated by the actors with a delicate nicety of taste and timing. However wildly pandemonium may reign in the plot, the actors need the control and the exactitude of tumblers and tightrope dancers. They have to be *in extremis* without going to extremes. They have to be stylish but with panache; over life-size without being untrue. While the whirlpool of comic incident increases in speed and violence, the orchestration of the playing must be disciplined to a musical beat. In another of Feydeau's plays there is a frenzied scene in which about fifteen people are involved in a maelstrom of emotional misunderstandings. One of the characters, at a given moment, has the line, "Well, that's it!" The author knew that there was only one way of saying that line which would be funny and cause a giant laugh from the audience; and to make sure that it would be spoken correctly, he wrote a bar of music over the line to indicate the one and only proper inflection.

This precision is a far cry indeed from the inner probings of the actor of the Stanislavsky school; it has more in common with the art and discipline of the ballet dancer and the acrobat. It also, of course, has to be illumined by the colors and personality of the actor, but the latter has always to keep his eye on the exact requirements of the score. Rhythm, accent and timing are more important in farce than personal idiosyncrasy, no matter how diverting. When a great comedian lends his talents to these requirements, the result should be, in its own genre, a work of art. A famous French actress said to me last year in Paris, "If you can act perfectly in a Feydeau farce, you can act well in anything!"

It has often been unhappily proved that what makes people laugh in Europe does not necessarily make people laugh in America, and vice versa. Sometimes, however, comedies are equally successful on both sides of the ocean. At least it can be said of *Hotel Paradiso* that its characters and situations are not particular to any country, or indeed to any time. Wit changes its values in different countries more than does humor. The *mot* may be *juste* in one continent and meaningless in another. However, no matter where they live, men will always be bullied by their wives and brave an occasional spree. Pretty wives,

left alone, will always have tantrums and occasionally carry out threats to find consolation "elsewhere." It is from these broad universal premises that the plot of *Hotel Paradiso* develops.

One thing is certain: It is useless to watch *Hotel Paradiso* with a detached and dispassionate eye—determined to evaluate rather than to enter into the fun. You either succumb helplessly in your seat, or the play leaves you cold. (pp. 66, 86-7)

Peter Glenville, "Feydeau: Father of the Pure Farce,"
in Theatre Arts, *Vol. XLI, No. 4, April, 1957, pp. 66-7, 86-7.*

RICHARD HAYES (essay date 1957)

[*In the following excerpt, Hayes discusses the characteristics of Feydeau's theatrical world and the mechanics of his comedies as exemplified by* Hotel Paradiso.]

The world of Feydeau is alien to the ethical, romantic Anglo-Saxon, for it is a world indifferent to sentiment or morality or psychological nuance. Its characters are flat: monstrous dilations—"humours" in the Jonson sense—of a single trait: the termagant wife; the leering upstairs maid; the cringing, carnal, cornered husband. Their relation to the sharply stylized figures of the *commedia dell' arte* might also be established. The climate reeks of bourgeois immutability, and the plot is a tissue of mild salacities. Indeed, the typical Feydeau farce is a massive documentation of what Mr. W. H. Auden calls the conventional images of Paris as "the city of the Naughty Spree—Mademoiselle Fifi, bedroom mirrors and bidets, lingerie and adultery, the sniggers of school boys and grubby old men." . . . Yet Feydeau's preoccupation was not with this innocuous titillation, nor with verbal wit, nor even an ironic posture of the mind, but rather with mechanical form—what I am forced to call, mixing two genres, the mathematics of theater. The man who wrote *Hotel Paradiso* was a passionate architect—profoundly humorless, I do not doubt—obsessed with the vision of a kind of monstrous infernal machine closing in on its ludicrous victims; nothing seems to have interested him but the infinite permutations of the absurd. He forces one to realize freshly that farce is but the systematic inversion of tragedy. Desdemona's handkerchief; the carpet which Agamemnon treads; Charles Bovary's foolish cap—symbols of fatality all—become in the Feydeau world a box of cigars, a face towel, a top hat, agents of a passive but insane diabolism, operating in the service of a satanic indifference and inexorable logic which would have dazzled Sophocles.

The pleasures farce affords are intellectually inexhaustible; are those of the comic sense, however, something richer? Baudelaire makes a distinction (in *The Essence of Laughter*) between the "significantly comic"—an imitation—and the "absolutely comic, or grotesque"—a creation. He awards a proportionate superiority to the latter because "it is much closer to nature, has a *unity* which must be grasped by intuition." I take *Hotel Paradiso* to belong to this genre of the absolutely comic; it is a parody of nothing but itself; not even remotely does it suggest an ideal of the useful or the rational. It also passes Baudelaire's acid test for the grotesque by provoking immediate laughter. But the absolute as a constant climate is insupportable, and this passionate abstraction is doubtless what accounts for the fatigue one senses in the middle reaches of *Hotel Paradiso,* as of a mathematical formula extended logically into infinity. One wants the impure relief of sentiment and

Drawing of Feydeau by Leonetto Cappiello.

morality; the complex, soiled actuality of the merely comic. (p. 154)

Richard Hayes, ''The Mathematics of Farce,'' in *Commonweal, Vol. LXVI, No. 6, May 10, 1957, pp. 154-55.*

J. G. WEIGHTMAN   (essay date 1959)

[*An English journalist, translator, and educator, Weightman has written widely on French literature and history, English literature, and sociology. In the following excerpt, he explains why he considers Feydeau's works undeserving of their status as classics of modern French theater.*]

The theatre is a strange and unpredictable institution. No one at the first night of Georges Feydeau's farce, *Le Dindon,* in 1896, can have guessed that more than half a century later it would be presented as a revered part of the French cultural heritage. Imagine Zola, if he had deigned to attend, watching it through his pince-nez and contemptuously weighing its chances of immortality. It is the grossest comedy about adulterous situations among crass bourgeois whose thoughts never rise above their waists, and the climax is a scene in Act Three in which a married woman comes to offer herself to a bachelor who has been courting her, only to find that he cannot cope having just spent eleven hours in bed with a prostitute.

Is it to enjoy this sort of thing that I have worn out two copies of the *Petit Larousse Illustré* in my attempts to learn the French language?

I think not, and I say so as a great admirer of good bawdry. Feydeau is just not good enough. The two pieces of his I have seen, this one and *Occupe-toi d'Amélie,* are not plays but anthologies of farcical situations. In both a bed occupies the centre of the stage. I have rarely felt sadder than when watching Madeleine Renand crawling about under this bed in the Barrault production of *Amélie* about two years ago. My gloom was almost as great when I saw that excellent actress Danielle Darrieux wasting her talent in the film version of the same farce. Nor could I find it in my level and franchophile heart to laugh much at *Le Dindon* either, however perfectly it was acted.

It is not that these farces are simply vulgar and obscene; they are that, all right, having been deliberately written for the after-dinner entertainment of a philistine public at a definite historical period. The trouble is that they are neither strongly vulgar nor wittily or poetically obscene. They are just very clever fabrications, using sex in the easiest way not as a theme but as a pretext, and their so-called characters are as dry and brittle as insects. It is their almost complete lack of humanity, no doubt, which has kept them alive, whereas the serious bourgeois plays of the time are now hopelessly dead. Actors can use the farces as ''pure'' theatre, as exercises in speed and line and movement. It must be enormous fun to take part in one, but frankly are they not rather humiliating for the rest of us to watch? I cannot believe that Feydeau has really become a classic. If he has, there are several other boulevard classics at present in the making, Sacha Guitry is a transcendent genius, and the British Council should organise an exhibition of English comic picture postcards.

J. G. Weightman, ''What Price 'La Gloire'?'' in The *Observer, March 22, 1959, p. 23.*

NORMAN R. SHAPIRO   (essay date 1960)

[*Shapiro is an American critic and translator who has rendered numerous works of French literature into English, including two volumes of plays by Feydeau. In the following excerpt, he discusses how the suffering and punishment of characters in Feydeau's comedies indicates a harshly realistic view of human life informing the artificial and humorous events of these works.*]

For modern observers who seek philosophical overtones in the theatre, Feydeau's comedies (or at least a large number of them) do lend themselves to serious discussion. Alfred Capus, Feydeau's contemporary, once defined the essence of life as ''the struggle of the human will against chance.'' This ''struggle,'' transposed into the framework of a comedy, is the very essence of Feydeau's theatre, in which seeming chance is really a well-regulated creation of the author. The playwright, like a master puppeteer, assumes a god-like role, creating around his helpless characters a universe of seeming absurdity in which their efforts to resist their destiny are frantic but fruitless. Some, consequently, are tempted to see in such a universe an embodiment of the absurd, finding in Feydeau's merciless and often gratuitous imbroglios a foretaste of the existentialist view of the human condition. As such, Feydeau's theatre is eminently cruel. Thus the comment of Jean Cassou, in his discussion of Feydeau's mathematically perfect plot-construction: ''Cruelty goes hand in hand with his mathematics.'' And the critic perceives the reason for this cruelty: ''This logic of an artist and man of the theatre knows itself to be the same as the logic that governs the designs and actions of human society.'' In other words, Feydeau's characters are often the victims of a relentless whimsy which delights in recreating, in a comical dramatic fiction, the absurdity and inexplicability of real life.

Many are the innocents who suffer the ''slings and arrows'' of Feydeau's brand of ''outrageous fortune.'' Perhaps the prototype is the hapless Dr. Petypon in *La Dame de chez Maxim* (*The Girl from Maxim's* . . .). The sedate doctor awakes one morning to find that, after a night of unaccustomed revelry, he had unwittingly brought home the notorious entertainer, ''Môme Crevette.'' Petypon is horrified, realizing that he will never be able to convince his wife that the whole affair was a terrible mistake, and that his relations with ''La Môme'' have been wholly honorable. Consequently, he tries his best to remedy the situation before his wife can discover it. Feydeau, however, does not let him escape so easily. Complications accumulate around the poor doctor as his every effort leads only to more involvement. To be sure, at the end of the play the author pulls the right strings and charitably disentangles his marionettes, but not until Petypon has suffered a veritable martyrdom far outweighing his innocent error. (pp. 117-18)

The same near-tragic overtones dominate Feydeau's late one-act plays of domestic strife, originally intended as part of a collection to be entitled *Du Mariage au divorce* (*From Marriage to Divorce*). Throughout these five plays, among the most admirable of his repertoire, Feydeau portrays, in different situations and with ever-mounting intensity, the frustrations suffered by the innocent husband at the hands of his illogical, demanding, and often shrewish wife. Like the many characters of his theatre trapped in absurd imbroglios not of their own making, these husbands are enmeshed in the network of their wives' irrationality. Thus an innocuous Follavoine, in *On purge Bébé* (*A Laxative for Baby* . . .), finds himself faced with many a misfortune as the result of his wife's hopeless indiscretions and Feydeau's merciless imagination. Beset by one embarrassing situation after another, Follavoine, to climax his tribulations, is challenged to a duel through no fault of his own. Such undeserved suffering is compounded in Feydeau's last play, *Hortense a dit: "Je m'en fous!"* (*Hortense Said: "I Don't Give a Damn!"* . . .) The unpretentious dentist Follbraguet can take no more of his wife's maddening behavior and stalks from his office, determined never to return to the marital bedlam. So distraught is he that he never even gives a thought to the frantic patient who remains bound and gagged in the dentist's chair, left to suffer in his turn for a situation which is not even remotely his own.

In these examples—and they could be multiplied—we see a quality of Feydeau's humor which can easily, and without exaggeration, give rise to considerations of a serious nature. It is only a short step from the undeserved (though comical) sufferings of a Petypon, . . . a Follavoine *et al.*, victims of seeming circumstance and chance, to an appreciation of the far less comical torments of an innocent Humanity beyond the bounds of theatrical fantasy. Here, then, is an element of what we may call Feydeau's ''realism''; stripped of its surface humor, the problem of innocent suffering reveals a thoroughly anti-idealistic, anti-romantic vision of Man's lot, devoid of optimistic misconceptions. One does not have to look far into a typical Feydeau comedy to perceive an undercurrent of pessimism regarding the human condition.

This same ''realism'' is manifest in another aspect of Feydeau's theatre. If many of his harassed characters suffer undeservedly,

others, on the contrary, have indeed earned their fate. Often it is a ''comic flaw'' on their part which brings about, as a sort of punishment, the situations in which they find themselves. In such cases it is not the human condition in an unpredictable universe that Feydeau portrays, but rather the follies of human nature itself; for it is the affected, the over-reaching, the idealistic—in a word, the ''non-realistic''—who are made to appear ridiculous and suffer for their fault.

In some instances this ''punishment'' is little more than a momentary mortification of an over-blown ego, as in one of Feydeau's earliest plays, the one-act *Par la fenêtre* (*Through the Window* . . .). Emma has come to the home of her neighbor Hector with an unusual request:

> EMMA. Monsieur, I've come to you because you're my neighbor. I live just across the way.
>
> HECTOR. Delighted, I'm sure. . . .
>
> EMMA. (*Sitting down near the window*) And now, monsieur, would you please make love to me!
>
> HECTOR. (*Aside*) What? . . . She wants me to . . . Is she out of her mind? (*Aloud.*) I beg your pardon, did you say you want me to . . .
>
> EMMA. (*Getting up and moving toward him*) Yes, if you please. But first, monsieur, I want you to know how I feel about you.
>
> HECTOR. (*Bowing rather fatuously*) Oh, Madame! (*Aside*) What a romantic young woman! A Juliet looking for a Romeo!
>
> EMMA. (*Graciously and somewhat embarrassed*) Monsieur, I think you are ugly . . .
>
> HECTOR. What?

This magnificent ''what'' is the bursting of Hector's lyrical bubble. Far from seeing in him a dashing Romeo, Emma wants merely to use him to arouse her husband's jealousy by staging a mock love-scene before the open window.

The same ego-deflation is suffered by the Prince of Valence in *Champignol malgré lui* (*Champignol in Spite of Himself* . . .), written in collaboration with Maurice Desvallières. The prince is a representative of the decadent nobility, unsuited by his aristocratic background to meet the demands of a practical world, yet no less filled with noble pretensions. As a reservist doing his several weeks of military service, he has been put to work at a splendid reception given by his commanding officer. Needless to say, he is spared no humiliating manual labor. As if this were not punishment enough for his unrealistic self-evaluation, Feydeau intensifies his humiliation in a brief exchange with one of the domestics. Charlotte has yielded to the temptation of trying on her mistress' elegant party-dress for one glorious moment, hoping that she will not be discovered. At just that point the Prince enters, mistaking her for an aristocratic guest. His first thought is to assure her that, despite his uniform he is in reality more dignified than he appears:

> THE PRINCE. Mademoiselle! You see me in uniform, but I'm really not what you take me for.

Charlotte's reply properly stifles his pretensions:

> CHARLOTTE. Well, let me tell you something. I'm not what you take me for either!

THE PRINCE. I'm the Prince of Valence!

CHARLOTTE. Really! Well I'm the maid!

THE PRINCE. The maid!

After a series of humiliating experiences at the hands of his superior officers, the Prince's pride might have been somewhat soothed by a bit of amorous banter with one of his own class. Instead, his humiliation is only compounded. His disillusion is a punishment imposed upon him by the author for his noble expectations. (pp. 119-21)

If Hector [and] the Prince of Valence . . . are only mildly punished for their failings with a moment or two of embarrassment, other Feydeau characters fare not so well. *Le Ruban* (*The Ribbon* . . .), another product of Feydeau's collaboration with Desvallières, presents a typical example. It depicts the machinations and misfortunes of Dr. Paginet, an "anti-microbian" whose research has gained him far less fame than he would like to believe. Yet it is on the basis of these misguided scientific efforts that he seeks the coveted ribbon of the *Légion d'honneur*. Despite his lack of qualifications, Paginet's mania seems about to be satisfied, for the official government publication carries an announcement of his nomination. No sooner has the good doctor bedecked himself with an enormous ribbon, inversely proportional to his merits, than he learns that the announcement was in error, and, to add salt to his wounded pride, that his wife has been named *chevalier* for her philanthropic work. Here indeed is a punishment which "realist" Feydeau metes out to his over-ambitious hero. Through Paginet Feydeau takes pleasure in exposing the absurdity of a whole segment of society bent on gaining the esteem of their fellows with a trinket in their boutonnière. For those who did not really deserve it—and they were many—a decoration was a superficial and false ornament that bore impressive witness to human vanity. And for Feydeau such vanity is a cardinal sin worthy of punishment. Yet, of course, we are dealing with comedy, and the punishment cannot exceed its bounds. Once Paginet has suffered enough in his creator's eyes, Feydeau relents. He lets the pseudo-scientist have his ribbon (though by the purest of accidents), but not until his own attitude toward the folly of human affectation has been made perfectly obvious. (pp. 121-22)

One of the common figures that recurs throughout Feydeau's theatre is that of the outraged wife who, learning of her husband's infidelity, decides to exact the penalty of retaliation, or at least so she threatens. Such a decision betrays a firm belief in social equality and is but one element in Feydeau's ridicule of the budding feminist ideal. For him the vociferous manifestoes of the feminists were little more than a form of visionary idealism which he took several opportunities to deride. The headstrong heroines imbued with such ideals must expect to suffer for their notions in Feydeau's "realistic" universe. The most extreme example of such a heroine is Micheline Plantarède in *Je ne trompe pas mon mari* (*I Don't Cheat on My Husband* . . .), written in collaboration with René Peter. Despite the emphatic denial of the title, Micheline decides to prove her social equality by duplicating her husband's extra-marital adventures. For this she enlists the aid of a rather baffled Saint-Franquet:

MICHELINE. (*Emphatically*) My friend, six months ago you said to me: "If you're ever unfaithful to your husband, promise that it will be with me."

SAINT-FRANQUET. What?

MICHELINE. Well, my friend, the time has come. I've decided to be unfaithful, and here I am . . . My husband is cheating on me, I have proof of it. Here I am! Take me! I'm yours!

SAINT-FRANQUET. I beg your pardon!

MICHELINE. (*All in one breath*) I said: "Here I am, take me, I'm yours!"

SAINT-FRANQUET. (*Stunned, repeating her words*) "Take me, here I am, I'm yours!" (*He falls into a chair.*)

Once Micheline has carried out her plan, however, she is unprepared for the consequences. In fact, once her actions have become known, she is quite appalled by the whole affair, realizing to what extent it will result in embarrassment and danger to her reputation. In short, she is unprepared to suffer the punishment that Feydeau imposes upon her, not for immorality but rather for assuming prerogatives not naturally belonging to her sex.

Another feminist over-reacher is Léontine in *Monsieur chasse!* (*Monsieur Goes Hunting!* . . .). Unlike Micheline she stops short of accomplishing her vengeance (as do Feydeau's other vindictive heroines). Yet her determination is none the less dictated by a desire to prove her husband's equal, and her punishment is no less characteristic. In the first act Léontine has assured the family friend Moricet that nothing short of the infidelity of her husband, Duchotel, would make her yield to his persistent advances: "Oh, you'll see! Just let me find out that my husband is cheating on me, that he's having an affair, and I swear I'll come to you and say: 'Moricet, help me get my revenge!'" . . . In the next act, when her suspicions have indeed been roused, her first thought is of vengeance, and true to her word, Moricet will provide the means. In a fit of rage she apostrophizes the absent Duchotel:

LÉONTINE. Oh! Now it's my turn! I've been too easy! But you'll see, my friend, you'll see! An eye for an eye! . . . And just to start things off I'm going to write to Moricet. . . . Oh, yes! Revenge! Revenge!

Moricet is only too happy to comply. He takes the irate Léontine to his bachelor apartment, looking forward to his role as avenger. Léontine, however, thinks twice about her decision and, at the last moment, realizes that she is about to act in unwise haste. Despite Moricet's protests she would willingly leave him in the lurch. Unfortunately, before she can make her escape from his quarters a series of bizarre circumstances beset her, in typical Feydeau manner, making her regret all the more her desire for revenge. Léontine's attempted vengeance, then, leads only to a comical imbroglio, once again a punishment for her female self-assertiveness.

Although we have by no means exhausted the examples that might be brought to bear, it can be seen from those we have cited that the question of punishment and suffering plays a considerable part in Feydeau's theatre, and that it illustrates a dominant quality which we can call his "realism." For, on the one hand, Feydeau enjoys dramatizing the absurdity of the human condition, portraying his characters caught up in a network of unfathomable circumstances for which they are not responsible. Here his "realism" shows through clearly, producing a stylized interpretation of real life, exaggerated to be sure, for comic effect, but not enough to obscure the fact that real life is quite similar indeed. On the other hand, many of Feydeau's characters have no right to complain to the Heavens of their destiny. They have brought it on themselves, so to speak. By their affectation, their over-ambition, their romantic and idealistic notions they have offended their "realistic" creator who reserves for them the punishment of embarrassment, of disappointment, and most of all, of utter confusion.

As creator of a comic universe, then, Feydeau enjoys supreme authority over his creatures. If he freely punishes those whose human failings offend him, he shows also by his indiscriminate persecution of the innocent that he is bound by no moral law, and that he, as creator, is answerable to no higher authority. As such a creator Feydeau has left us a particularly "realistic" view both of the human condition in an unpredictable universe and of human nature with its many shortcomings. (pp. 124-26)

Norman R. Shapiro, "Suffering and Punishment in the Theatre of Georges Feydeau," in The Tulane Drama Review, *Vol. 5, No. 1, September, 1960, pp. 117-26.*

ROGER J. STEINER (essay date 1961)

[*Steiner is an American critic and educator. In the following excerpt, he examines techniques that contribute to the success of Feydeau's comedies and the reasons for the perennial appeal of these works.*]

A Feydeau plot could be thought of as a perfectly oiled and adjusted mechanism with swift progression, tremendous speed, and perfect timing. The interrelationship of the characters could be defined as a tightly drawn skein. This type of writing requires in all roles a kind of acting which demands extreme skill, precise timing, a tremendous finish and artistry, and a self-effacing dedication. A hundred pages of instructions for each play left nothing to chance: the position of characters on the stage, the scenery and properties, the intonation of the actors, a musical score for a certain bit of laughter, the exact number of seconds a pause should take, the exact measure of music at which the curtain should be raised, bits of stage business in minute detail. Feydeau insisted that his actors subordinate their individualities to his text. Yet paradoxically, the text itself was based upon the personalities of the actors. He worked with much the same group of actors and was intimately associated with them in rehearsals. He created roles with certain actors in mind. In fact, one night Georges Feydeau, inveterate *noctambule* that he was, walked around Paris with the actors Michel Georges Michel and Marcel Simon and dictated the entire third act of *Occupe-toi d'Amélie* improvising it as they went along. The relationship between playwright and performer so close that the very genesis and creation of the play has to do with the interaction of their personalities harks back to the *Commedia dell' arte*.

Feydeau builds an illusion of coherence by this mathematically deliberate attention to the interaction of every minute detail. Everything is explained or justified. Entrances and exits are motivated. Encounters find logic. Information is masterfully planted in the dialogue to be used at a later time. A line altered or deleted would throw this delicate mechanism out of balance like a wrench thrown between the cogs of a wheel. Barrault comments: "Son écriture est extrêmement choisie, serrée. Dès qu'il nous arrive d'en changer un mot, la phrase y perd" ["His writing is extremely precise, tight. As soon as we think of changing a word of it, we lose a whole sentence"]. An un-

fortunate director once asked Feydeau to cut a play ten minutes. Feydeau asked how many pages of text that would mean. "Twenty-one," was the reply. "Very well," said Feydeau, "then raise the curtain at page twenty-one and go from there." The play was not altered. In constructing the machinery of a play Feydeau's calculations are so accurate that there is an air of fatality and inevitability about his creations. The movement of the plot, while surprising, is never erratic—the movement is as regulated as a pendulum; it has been compared to an "horloge de Strasbourg à poupées drolatiques" ["Strasbourg clock with funny mechanical figures"]. The audience nods a hearty assent to the last line of *Le Dindon:* "C'était écrit, je suis le dindon!" ["It was fate, I am the dindon!"] (the turkeycock, the dupe, the "goat"). The play could turn out no other way. "C'était écrit," for Oedipus Rex, as well. At first glance, it would seem futile to compare Greek tragedy with the outrageous farces of Feydeau: the skirmishes in and out of beds and boudoirs, the chance encounters with scantily dressed ladies, the substitution of characters in beds wired for sound (all in a spirit very much in keeping with the tradition to which *Le Mariage de Figaro* belongs). Yet, profundity of theme apart, a farce by Feydeau has the steady, fatal movement of an Oedipus gradually realizing that he is aggressor and victim. The universe of Feydeau is an inexorable world in which there is no room for repentance or chance. It is a system "clos sur lui-même, adéquat à lui-même, parfaitement logique, mathématiquement exact: donc tout doit concourir à une crédulité universelle" ["closed on itself, adequate in itself, perfectly logical, mathematically exact: so all must converge in a universal credulity"]. The master technician who makes such a fantastic world plays the same role to the theatre that Ingres plays to painting. Anouilh, Achard, Roussin, and a host of others owe much to Georges Feydeau for instruction in technique.

Feydeau found no secret, magic formula. He did use several rules of thumb which Sophocles, Shakespeare, Molière, and other great masters used. One rule is: never let the audience feel tricked; therefore, never let it see the strings attached to the puppets; make the spectator believe in the freedom of the characters by audaciously introducing characters who must, by rights, never meet. While writing *Champignol malgré lui,* Feydeau spent a whole month solving the problem of a difficult confrontation. In *La Dame de chez Maxim* he was faced with perhaps the most difficult problem of this kind in all of his work, how to confront the real Mme Petypon with a *môme* ["urchin girl"] whom the General believes to be the real Mme Petypon. Feydeau rested a full two years before this problem, and then solved it with two words: "Ma tante!" ["my aunt!"] (spoken by the real Mme Petypon, who thinks that the *môme* is the General's wife).

Another technique is the use of foils. In *Le Dindon* Feydeau creates a number of "foils-in-reverse," a foil employed not to brighten and set off another character but rather to tone another character down to plausibility. In *Le Dindon* the mistress who insists upon adultery makes more credible the wife who threatens adultery (the *lex talionis* being a standard reflex of many Feydeau women).

A third way to hide the manipulation of plot and gain an illusion of reality is to introduce an unexpected turn of events, a *coup de théâtre,* in order to twist the course of events in the desired direction. Marcel Achard had reason to speak of Feydeau as "le Galilée d'un monde qui tourne à l'envers" ["the Galileo of a world which turns backward"].

Georges Feydeau once explained to Lucien Guitry the basic model on which his plays were constructed: "Deux personnages principaux: celui qui donne les coups de pied au derrière et celui qui les reçoit" ["Two principal characters: he who delivers the kicks in the behind and he who receives them"]. By that statement and in his work, Feydeau places himself in the vast, timeless tradition of the circus clown, the Punch-and-Judy show, the custard-pie days of the early cinema, and one of the oldest traditions, stemming from the drama of Greece and Europe and harking back to pre-history. This tradition requires as rigorous a craftsmanship as any other. In Feydeau's case, it meant putting together plays like a puzzle or a game with a "précision géométrique" (Kléber Haedens) which can be compared to the skill of a billiard player. . . . (pp. 50-2)

The libertine nature of the tradition of harvest festivals and traveling carnivals and fairs is by no means absent in these plays. If the comic theatre had its background in the fertility rites of Spring, it is certainly not to be wondered that much modern comic theatre uses satyric motifs. Feydeau makes us think of the *jalos,* the *vavassor* of the Old French lyric (poetry said by some scholars to have roots in the old fertility rites). For instance, in *Le Dindon* Pontagnac exclaims to Lucienne concerning her husband: "Laissons cet imbécile de côté" ["Let's forget about that imbecile"]. He is referring to husbands in general—he hasn't yet met Lucienne's. In Feydeau a glimpse of the satyr lurks behind the *grivoiserie* ["naughty story"] often present. Lucienne asks Pontagnac if he is married. "Un peu" ["A little"] is the answer. Armandine replies to the room clerk who wants to give her a room with twin beds: "Vous vous imaginez que j'invite des spectateurs?" ["Do you imagine I'm inviting some spectators?"]

The comic tradition in which Feydeau's work stands comprises more elements than simply the libertine. In *Le Dindon,* for instance, Feydeau's use of improperly spoken French for comic effect has a parallel in the comic use of dialects in the fifteenth-century farce, *Maistre Pierre Patelin.* Another relationship between *Le Dindon* and *Maistre Pierre Patelin* is the use of a favorite comic theme, the *trompeur trompé* ["deceiver deceived"]. Feydeau's Pontagnac is a predatory character much like the fifteenth-century Pierre. Neither of them tastes the full fruits of victory because his own tricks are turned against him.

The sanguine prediction that Feydeau's theatre will live must take into account that some of the charm of a Feydeau revival comes from the aura of "quaintness" of the 1890's. Will these plays be only period pieces to future generations to whom the 1890's have no special appeal? The plays are, to be sure, written within the framework of the social conventions of the time and they have the carefree atmosphere of *flânerie* ["leisure"] which suggests the "gay 90's." Yet there is no attempt to synthesize the *fin de siècle* in this type of theatre and one disfigures Feydeau's work by forcing it into the mold of a comedy of manners.

Feydeau's plays do not grow old because they have nothing to do with particular intellectual trends of the age, particular social attitudes or problems. There is no apparent purpose in a play by Feydeau other than entertainment. The purpose of lust is lust and the plays move like precise machines without ideas to jumble the works. There is no ax to grind, no distinctive ideological background to obtrude. In Feydeau's plays nothing is said, but everything seems to be happening. His characters have no profound depth or personality; they are puppets, the strings masterfully hidden, which move in a timeless equation, a schematic diagram of pure action, of uninterrupted move-

ment, of unrelenting rhythm. Brilliant paradoxes and outrageous juxtapositions are delineated surely and powerfully by means of a delicate mechanism which is pure action and which should delight audiences for some time to come.

Feydeau's plays remain alive because they always find an audience. The interrelationship between audience and actor was certainly uppermost in Feydeau's mind—witness the frequent "asides" of the characters at a time in the history of the French stage when other playwrights were insisting on naturalism. The frankly theatrical quality of Feydeau's plays puts them squarely in the permanent tradition of the comic and they should have a secure place in the living stage for many generations to come.

Feydeau is a specialist in constructing a perfect machine to promote laughter. Within the limits he sets for himself, he has tremendous skill. Those writers like Yves Mirande who have tried unsuccessfully to complete one of his unfinished plays, know how inimitable he is. Some of his admirers would make of him a classic like Molière. "Georges Feydeau est, après Molière, le plus grand auteur comique français" ["Georges Feydeau is, after Molière, the greatest French comic author"], said Marcel Achard [see excerpt dated 1948]. If one accepts the premises of this type of comedy—of the type of comedy whose sole purpose is to entertain—Marcel Achard's remark, *boutade* ["caprice"] that it is, has a certain relevancy. Feydeau is unquestionably the greatest writer of a certain type of comedy since Molière. Feydeau lacks the many facets of Molière, but in regard to technique, the comparison is not ridiculous. Those who would be brusque in pointing out that Georges Feydeau, after all, is not Molière might well consider the authentic qualities needed to captivate audiences for half a century. (pp. 52-4)

Roger J. Steiner, "The Perennial Georges Feydeau," in Symposium, *Vol. XV, No. 1, Spring, 1961, pp. 49-54.*

LEONARD C. PRONKO (essay date 1975)

[*A Philippine-born American critic and director, Pronko has written extensively on European and non-Western drama. In the following excerpt, he contrasts Feydeau's comedies with those of his English contemporaries and compares the French dramatist's portrayal of human life to the absurdist world view of the Existentialist philosophers.*]

Feydeau's theater blends a varied array of comic techniques with the study of manners, deft touches of truthful characterization, and an overview which can be called metaphysical. Using theatrical languages, oral, visual, and kinesthetic, he arrives at effects that many contemporary critics have called poetic. Cocteau and the surrealists saw in him the poetry of the irrational so widely explored by the latter, and the visual poetry of the theater prescribed by the former. The French drama critic Robert Kempt compared the piling up of surprises and the abundance of episodes to the irresistible lyricism of jazz percussion, while the playwright-critic Thierry Maulnier found a kind of poetry in Feydeau's bewildering inventiveness. For actor [Jean-Louis] Barrault, the dramatist endows his characters with the poetic gift of creation: through habit or distraction they make real what is only suggested, as when Amélie's father, the retired traffic policeman Pochet, transforms her apartment into a busy thoroughfare by his stern commands and admonitions.

Early achieving international popularity, Feydeau has suffered from the difficulties involved in adjusting such complex works to a foreign context. The reader or viewer who must approach

Feydeau in 1905.

his plays in English should be forewarned that what he will experience may be far from what Feydeau intended. (pp. 191-92)

Difficulties of translation are perhaps compounded by the understanding of farce among English-speaking people. Feydeau is the quintessence of French farce, as it developed traditions somewhat different from those of English farce in the nineteenth century. Like all farce, Feydeau's is highly physical, delighting in chases, disguises willful or not, quick-moving appearances and disappearances, and even the "low comedy" of kicks in the pants, collapsing chairs and other embarrassing mishaps. Like other farces, his too deal with the absurd as though it were the most normal of circumstances.

Unlike most French farce before him, however, and unlike all English farce, Feydeau's plays carry both physicality and absurdity to an incredible degree of paroxism. Changing formulas, here he stresses the chase, there the mistaken identity; here the absurd of situation, there the more grim absurd of human suffering. Compared to the masterpieces of English nineteenth-century farce, any major play of Feydeau's glows with a hard, bright light which derives from its uncompromising, if somewhat disguised, attachment to truth, and from its purposeful excess in using the techniques of the genre pushed to the nth degree.

The complications and savage humor of *Champignol malgré lui* cannot even be approximated by that pleasant and most favorite of madly English farces, *Charley's Aunt*, which was its precise contemporary, both opening during the final months of 1892. The naughty intrigues and hair-raising adventures of

Cis and Mr. Posket at the Hôtel des Princes in Sir Arthur Wing Pinero's run-about farce, *The Magistrate* (1885), pale in the company of Pinglet, Marcelle and Paillardin at the Hôtel du Libre-Echange. And W. S. Gilbert's enchantingly ironic *Tom Cobb* (1875), whose hero is subtitled (as any of Feydeau's might be) "Fortune's Toys," becomes artifice pure and simple when placed alongside any of Feydeau's major works.

The truth is that English farce blunted its edge with sentimentality and at least the suggestions of moralizing. Like melodrama and thesis plays in both countries, English farce affirmed the status quo and entrenched the public more securely in its comfortable beliefs. In this good homely entertainment there was no place for *cocottes,* adultresses or philandering husbands. When French *vaudevilles* were adapted for English audiences, which happened often, guilty couples were whitewashed by marriage, mistresses became girl friends, and *cocottes* were deodorized or expunged.

The traditions of French farce, unattenuated by Victorianism, allowed Feydeau to deal with the same areas of real life that were dealt with in serious drama. In England, it was apparently felt that wicked women and adultery were the province of serious theater where they could be appropriately punished. Accordingly, Pinero, England's outstanding farceur in his youth, relegated those tasty subjects to his dramas, reserving for his farces only situations which were capable of being resolved in such a way as to show that, after all, domestic joys are superior to more dazzling lures.

With the sharp-edged blade of truth, Feydeau cuts through these pious myths, suggesting that love, in or out of wedlock, is something of a disappointment. In the tradition of farce, all must end well—but, after the dizzying adventures of his "toys of fortune," we are rarely prepared to conclude that all is for the best. Happy endings in Feydeau are only temporary solutions.

They are temporary solutions because life lies at the center of Feydeau's plays. Rather than evasion into a misty world of wish-fulfilment, we are brought face to face with the absurdity of our predicament, incarnated in a mechanism of such perfection, speed, and violence that human struggle is useless. Here lies the fundamental seriousness of Feydeau. Expressed in the entire structure of his plays, his view of man's lot does not reaffirm our lazy pretenses, but serves, as all serious theater must, to raise doubts. It destroys our self-satisfaction and security, throws all into question, and by its very violence strikes deeper than more serious ideas expressed discursively might do. (pp. 194-97)

If it is clear from a reading (or preferably, a viewing) of Feydeau's infernal machines that men are the victims of the gods, it is equally clear that men are particularly vulnerable to divine machinations because they have certain inherent weaknesses. Like the hero of classical tragedy led by hubris to match himself against a force which is greater than he, Feydeau's weak mortals are usually responsible for their own catastrophes. Unheroically, they are unaware of pitting themselves against unbeatable odds, for they rarely suffer from lucidity. It is *we* who gain lucidity from contemplation of their woes.

Bouzin (*Un Fil à la patte*) hopes to profit from the anonymous bouquet left for Lucette, and drops his own card into it, thereby loosening on himself the fury of the gods—or at least that of the jealous Latin American general—and spends the rest of the play fleeing, not sure just why. Pontagnac (*Le Dindon*), prompted by the demon of lust (or simply habit), dares to enter an honest woman's home in pursuit of her; this insistence results in the loss of his own wife, and leaves him holding nothing but the bag. Dr. Petypon *(La Dame de chez Maxim)* spent a night on the town and finds la Môme Crevette inextricably wedged into his life. Marcel *(Occupe-toi d'Amélie)* did the same and ultimately finds himself married to the wrong woman.

Through blindness, foolishness, stupidity, weakness, selfishness, avarice, and other human foibles, Feydeau's characters set off the machinery that will trap them. The moral of the tale—if moral there is—would appear to be that we foolish mortals are not entirely innocent. Shocked and amazed, we look at the shambles of our lives, not realizing that it is we who have brought the whole structure tumbling about our ears.

And yet, modern in its ambiguity, this theater also shows us victims who are innocent: deaf old Mme Pinchard, Paillardin who only went to the Hôtel du Libre-Echange in a professional capacity; Chandebise who goes to the Hôtel du Minet Galant to warn his friends of impending danger. Foolish or smart, selfish or altruistic, guilty or innocent: all are condemned. The world of Feydeau *is* the world of the Absurd in which man is invariably pitted against forces that resist his search for happiness and meaning, and rarely allow him to attain even the more realistic goals of peace and pleasure.

This bitter lucidity which pierces the frenzied running around, and the violent energy which emerges from such a paradoxical encounter, make Feydeau excruciatingly modern. They explain in large part his immense appeal today to audiences, actors, directors and critics alike.

In a precise way, Feydeau's characters embody the definition Camus gave of absurdity. It is not man that is absurd, he claimed. Nor is it the universe. Absurdity lies precisely in the meeting of these two: men with their hopes, dreams and needs placed in a blind, silent, meaningless universe. Indeed, in Feydeau man seems so ill-fitted to his habitat that one sometimes feels the universe is quite actively inimical, pulling the carpet out from under the feet of unsuspecting mortals. This is the vision so clearly sensed by Thierry Maulnier when he witnessed the Comédie-Française revival of *Le Dindon* in 1951:

> How could one help feeling without an almost unbearable anguish the call which emanates from Feydeau's creatures, a cry of accusation against a universe where man himself, with his wish for reason and happiness, is the most irreparable absurdity?

Like some spastic Sisyphus chasing a stone uphill only to see it roll down again, Feydeau's characters—like ourselves—are caught on the treadmill of absurdity. (pp. 197-99)

> *Leonard C. Pronko, in his* Georges Feydeau, *Frederick Ungar Publishing Co., 1975, 218 p.*

STUART E. BAKER (essay date 1981)

[*In the following excerpt from his study* Georges Feydeau and the Aesthetics of Farce, *Baker describes and evaluates Feydeau's work.*]

Not all of the thirty-nine plays included in the nine volumes of Feydeau's *Théâtre complet* can properly be called farces, but the exceptions are few, and most of these contain farcical elements. The great majority of the plays are remarkably consistent in the tone, subject matter, and methods which have caused Feydeau's name to be linked so firmly to the expression

"French farce." His consistency and rarely faltering devotion to farcical laughter provide an excellent opportunity to study the nature and methods of one particular variety of farce in its pure form.

Feydeau was neither an experimenter nor an innovator; his talent lay not in originality—whether in subject matter, dramaturgy, or psychological insight—but in his ability to exploit fully the farcical possibilities inherent in the dramatic conventions which he adopted. He took standard themes, methods, and situations, and pushed them to their comic extremes. His originality lay in the wealth of his comic invention and in the comic tricks and devices with which his plays abound, but this is precisely the area in which a *vaudeville* was expected to be original. When Feydeau complained of plagiarism by others he was thinking of such gimmicks and devices. Accused of using a standard device to deceive his wife, one of Feydeau's erring husbands declares indignantly, "I'm no farce writer! I don't need other people's ideas in order to invent new plays!"

Even if this represents Feydeau's own indignation, many of his ideas were simply new twists given to previously employed comic devices. For example, the method used by the gentleman above to deceive his wife—hypnotism—may have been an original way to be unfaithful, but it had been used as the central device of at least one other *vaudeville* four years earlier. Feydeau himself was to use the same trick, with yet another twist, several years later in *Dormez, je le veux! (Sleep! I command you!)*

The course of Feydeau's career and the evolution of his style reflect his inclination (and that of his audience) toward the familiar. The same situations, character types, and problems recur again and again in different combinations and in different variations. His plays were often constructed according to standard plot formulas or patterns which allow them to be grouped into simple and logical categories. The largest and most important of these groups consists of eleven three-act plays which involve some form of deception practiced upon a husband, wife, lover, or mistress. In many ways these plays form the core of Feydeau's work. They include nearly all of his most successful and enduring full-length plays, while the plays which stray furthest from this pattern are usually those which were least successful originally and those least often revived. (pp. 25-6)

The plays cannot be neatly divided into precise chronological periods, but it is possible to detect gradual changes in his work over the thirty-six-year span of his career. It is difficult to know how much such changes were due to the evolution of the author's attitudes or to changes in society and theatrical tastes; they are probably a reflection of both. There are two major trends. The first is a movement toward greater verisimilitude in certain aspects of the plays, particularly in the initial premises, dialogue, and characters. Standard theatrical conventions which had been staples of the *vaudeville* form, such as the opening expository monologue, were gradually eliminated. The theatrical buffoons and improbable fools who inhabit the earlier plays were gradually replaced by characters much closer to reality. The language became more realistic, and comic advantage was taken of the idiosyncrasies of speech heard among the various inhabitants of Paris. Feydeau, always attentive to detail, even included lengthy footnotes admonishing his actors to use a more realistic style of acting. The second trend was toward a more intense and almost savage comic vision. Both in treatment and in his choice of targets for laughter, the comedy of his later plays often borders on—but never crosses into—bitterness and cruelty. One of the last of the many monologues he wrote, *Un Monsieur qui est condamné à mort (A Gentleman Condemned to Death)*, ends, as the title suggests, with the innocent and completely bewildered narrator sent to the guillotine. Suffering has always been a favorite subject of farce, but in his later plays Feydeau often goes well beyond the conventional cuckolds, pratfalls, and blows to focus on pains that are both more real and more extreme.

These tendencies contributed to the value of his work, not by elevating it above the level of farce, but by intensifying its farcical quality. A sense of the reality of life as it is lived—or better, as it is felt—is a vital element of farce. This is particularly true of the more unpleasant realities. Feydeau's inclination toward the familiar is not irrelevant here. The reality of farce does not consist of discoveries or truths to which the audience must be educated; it is the reality of the familiar and the commonplace, of those things which are already known or believed to be true.

Counterbalancing the unpleasant realities and the familiar pains is a sense of fantastic madness which is present in all of Feydeau's plays. In the majority of his plays he creates this madness by subjecting his characters to a world which had all the characteristics of a fun-house: well-oiled machinery propels its victims through a series of mirrored mazes, expected surprises, and absurdly frightening experiences. It ushers them past distorting mirrors and threatening apparitions, but it never abandons them and usually delivers them safely out on the other side.

To achieve this effect, Feydeau refined and developed techniques already characteristic of the nineteenth-century French *vaudeville*. This form, which has nothing in common with the American vaudeville, was a mixed genre which ranged from the sentimental to the savagely farcical. (pp. 27-8)

If we are to accept Feydeau on his own terms, we must be willing to accept his irresponsibility. Having said that, it can be acknowledged that his irresponsibility is a crucial factor in his ability to outlive so many of his more serious contemporaries. The issues and problems that Feydeau used are not that different from those dealt with in varying degrees of gravity by his contemporaries. He may be directly indebted to them for some of his basic themes. The incompatible couple in Porto-Riche's *Amoureuse* (1891), for instance, might be the prototype of a number of Feydeau husbands and wives. Other writers treated adultery, cupidity, vanity, and cynicism, but Feydeau refused to weight his plays down with the moral judgments that many others could not resist. When he once strayed from his usual practice (in *Le Bourgeon*) he produced what [Jacques] Lorcey is compelled to call a "frightful melodrama," although the play is not at all without its strong points. The plays which have survived are those in which judgment is withheld, in which the vices of the characters and the situations in which they find themselves are regarded with a good-humored but total objectivity. It would be more accurate to say that Feydeau's longevity is dependent, not on skirting the social and moral questions of his age, but on his refusal to provide them with answers.

Feydeau was careful to avoid offending or shocking the prejudices of his audience, but he also took care not to affirm them. His plays illustrate the negative viewpoint that [Bonamy] Dobrée claims is inherent in comedy. Dobrée speaks of three types of comedy: "critical" comedy, which deflates or satirizes; "free" comedy, which is irresponsible; and a third category, which deals with the "disillusion of mankind" and "comes when the positive attitude has failed, when doubt is creeping in to undermine values, and men are . . . laughing in the face of it all." Feydeau might be said to combine the last two approaches. He never quite abandons the irresponsible clowning of his earliest plays even when his work more realistically reflects the attitudes of his time. He neither criticizes nor endorses, illustrating Dobrée's assertion that "comedy gives us the courage to face life without any standpoint," and allows us to observe without committing us to judgment.

Does this mean that the value of Feydeau lies in the undercurrent of disillusionment and melancholy that many critics see beneath the gaiety and irresponsibility? It is hard to deny that the melancholy is there, for Feydeau himself underlined it in remarks about himself and his work. He told Brisson in an interview: "Do not be surprised if I am moody (*triste*). That, indeed, is my usual disposition. . . . I never laugh in the theatre. I rarely laugh in private. I am taciturn and rather unsociable." He claimed that a good *vaudeville* should be based on a "tragic" situation, and added, "Moreover, that is why the authors you call comic are always sad. They think 'sad' first." This underlying melancholy is seen by some to imply hidden depth. Shapiro, for instance, praises Feydeau by asserting that "one does not have to scratch far below the surface of a typical Feydeau comedy to find a fatalistic vision of the human condition and, along with it, an undercurrent of pessimism" [see excerpt dated 1960].

But fatalism and pessimism do not make a good playwright. Perhaps the most significant thing about Feydeau's pessimism is that it is *not* obvious in his plays; it must be sought beneath the surface. It is inferred rather than experienced directly. What is manifest is a persistent refusal to take seriously the situations on which his plays are based no matter how "tragic" or "sad" he might have perceived them to be in life. Excepting always *Le Bourgeon*, there is no attempt to mingle tears with laughter, or even a strong indication of bitterness or heavy irony in his portraits. Feydeau's disillusionment and melancholy are of the kind suggested by Dobrée; they lead him to eschew positive or even definitive standpoints and to seek refuge in laughter. He refuses to take seriously even his own pessimism. His attitude toward the world and its troubles is no more complex than that expressed by Hortense in the title of his last play [*Hortense a dit: "Je m'en fous!"*], an attitude endorsed by Follbraquet when his wife tells him of the maid's insolence:

> MARCELLE. I reprimand her, and she says, "I don't give a damn."
>
> FOLLBRAQUET. Fine! Why don't you do the same?
>
> MARCELLE. You permit it! You'll let her say "I don't give a damn" to me!
>
> FOLLBRAQUET. That proves that she's philosophical.

This is the "philosophy" expressed in Feydeau's plays: *Je-m'en-foutisme* (I-don't-give-a-damnism); a deliberate comic indifference in the face of the assorted trials of living. (pp. 108-10)

Order and clearly explained causal relationships are characteristics Feydeau shared with nearly all of his contemporaries. Like many of them, he presents a strictly defined world that reflects his urban bourgeois audience. He differs from them in his refusal to be taken seriously, in maintaining an atmosphere of frivolity even while treating subjects that others regarded with gravity. Frivolity had its uses, for it allowed him a kind of amoral objectivity that produced a more honest picture of his society than that of many more serious writers. Feydeau's observation of people is exaggerated and extreme, but the distortions are easily recognized as such. They are not the result of attempts to interpret, explain, or philosophize. Beneath the extravagance his audience would recognize characteristics they could have seen in themselves or their neighbors. Only in that atmosphere of fantasy could they see themselves so honestly portrayed without offense. This is true not merely for Feydeau's favorite themes of marriage, love, and adultery. It can be seen even in an atypical play like *Cent millions qui tombent*. Feydeau's picture of a society that values money, particularly the lavish expenditure of money, as the principal criterion of worth and respectability might almost have been drawn from Thorstein Veblen's *The Theory of the Leisure Class*. As an observation of human society, *Cent millions qui tombent* compares most favorably with Mirbeau's *Les Affaires sont les affaires* and Becque's *Les Corbeaux*, the two best known plays of the period on the subject of greed. Both of the latter plays have their virtues, but each portrays greed in traditionally moralistic and melodramatic terms, pitting a cynical and consuming passion for money against a virtuous lack of concern with material profit. Respectability, it is implied, is on the side of virtue, and the desire for money corrupts both. Feydeau comes closer to the truth when he equates money with respectability and leaves virtue entirely out of the picture. For all his frivolity, Feydeau's portrayal of his society's attitudes toward money is actually more perceptive and honest. (pp. 111-12)

Shaw, Pinter, and Ionesco, in their diverse uses of farce, demonstrate that it has greater versatility than is generally suspected of this slightly regarded form. They are serious writers, however, and in utilizing farce for their own ends, they must necessarily alter it drastically. They include farce in a larger vision that finally transcends farce. By contrast, Feydeau neither adds nor subtracts, but stays entirely within the boundaries of the farcical mode, devoting himself to developing to the fullest the possibilities contained within that circumscribed view of the world. The devotion to the narrow aims of farce gives Feydeau's work a kind of "purity" that has been noted by a number of critics. [Edwin Daniel] Yahiel, for example, feels that the essence of Feydeau's theatre is a "pure and objective idea of the comic." And [Georges] Versini writes that Feydeau's *vaudevilles* "belong to pure theatre." They operate, he says, in accordance with unchanging laws and have not aged because they are "outside of life and, because of that, outside of time." Richard Hayes made a similar comment in a review of *Hotel Paradiso*, Peter Glenville's adaptation of *L'Hôtel du Libre-Echange* [see excerpt dated 1957]. Hayes refers to the distinction Baudelaire makes "between the 'significantly comic'—an imitation—and the 'absolutely comic, or grotesque'—a creation." He places *Hotel Paradiso* with the absolutely comic, for "it is a parody of nothing but itself; not even remotely does it suggest an ideal of the useful or the rational."

The "absolute" or abstract side of Feydeau's art is only one part of his complex method, but it is one that may appear more obvious and important to us than it did to his contemporaries. The mechanical and abstract aspect of farce is but one side of a careful balancing of contrasting elements. Farce needs the constant reference to daily life, to life as it is seen and felt, in order to maintain its vitality. As the context in which they were written becomes increasingly remote, Feydeau's plays will probably appear even more dominated by their fantastic, grotesque, and mechanical side. In the process, they will lose a

significant part of their power to amuse. Except as an exercise in a certain "style," the "absolutely comic" may turn out not to be very funny.

Feydeau's observations of the society in which he lived are less obvious to us than might be the case because the end result of his theatre is not observation of reality, but its distortion. He was not offering new insights or attempting to make his audience see what they had never seen before. He showed them an image of themselves with which they were already most familiar, but he presented it through a carnival mirror. He could rely on them to recognize their image beneath the distortions, but we, less familiar with the lines and colors of the original, might be tempted to dismiss Feydeau's extravagant rendering of it as sheer fantasy, unrelated to anything in reality. Our confusion could be increased if we do not realize that even many of the distortions themselves would have been recognized by Feydeau's public, for they often parallel the fears, anxieties, and frustrations that change the way the world is perceived. While it represents no "ideal of the useful or the rational," and exists for no purpose greater than or beyond itself, Feydeau's theatre is not created purely of imagination, but is based on a rather sophisticated form of "imitation."

The evaluation of Feydeau's work must rest finally on the fact that within the context of its determined frivolity, it represents a highly developed art, which, while avoiding serious ends, is nevertheless deeply relevant to an essential part of our human nature. His excellence lies in his ability to choreograph his ordinary characters in a dance of mathematical precision, and to set emotions and motivations worthy of the naturalists into patterns that seem as delightfully artificial as a Gilbert and Sullivan patter song. He did not set out to satirize the world in which he lived, to point out its foibles, but that may have been an indirect result of his efforts. He simply took advantage of what his age provided, of the outlandish foreigners who visited Paris, of the sensational *cocottes*, and above all of a society whose obsession with appearances and sexual scandal was ideal material for his sophisticated and highly civilized farce. (pp. 113-14)

> *Stuart E. Baker, in his* Georges Feydeau and the Aesthetics of Farce, *UMI Research Press, 1981, 163 p.*

MANUEL A. ESTEBAN (essay date 1983)

[*Esteban is a Spanish-born American critic and educator. In the following excerpt from his biographical and critical study of Feydeau, he surveys Feydeau's major plays.*]

The twelve or so comedies that Feydeau produced between 1881, the date of *Par la fenêtre*, and 1890, the year of *Le Mariage de Barillon*, correspond to the period of his apprenticeship. Many of these deserve mention but only a handful merit closer study. The study of some of these early comedies, however, is justified not only because they were successful when they first appeared and continue to attract and entertain modern audiences, or because several of them have been considered worthy of translation into English in recent years, but primarily because these early plays provide useful gauges by which to measure Feydeau's later triumphs.

Along with monologues and *saynètes*, short theatrical sketches, one-act plays were favorites of salon *habitués*. No *soirée* could be considered complete unless a drawing-room theatrical presentation was given either by professionals, or, at least, by talented amateurs. Feydeau's growing reputation as the author and often performer of a series of monologues had assured him access to some of the leading social and artistic salons of the period. His first play, *Par la fenêtre,* was still another effort to ingratiate himself with these influential patrons. It was also a calculated attempt to draw attention from popular theatrical quarters. This rather juvenile but amusing comedy was received with enthusiasm and caught the interest of a very special spectator, Francisque Sarcey, who predicted a bright future for its young playwright.

The plot line of Feydeau's first theatrical effort is rather simple. Hector, a lawyer, is alone in his apartment, his wife having gone to mother in a fit of unfounded jealousy. As he is about to sit down to have the dinner he has prepared for himself, Emma, an authoritarian and excitable neighbor, comes to demand her help. To punish her husband for his excessive and unfounded jealousy, she wants Hector to court her in front of a huge window which she opens wide, though it is the dead of winter. He is also forced to serve her dinner and to place the table in front of the window so that her husband can best see them. Hector, who has already caught a cold, cannot but obey this apparently crazy woman who insults him unceremoniously and threatens to tell his wife that he has shamelessly courted her if he does not do as she commands. Furthermore, if everything goes according to plan, he can expect to be challenged to a duel to be fought, of course, as in Brazil, with hand drills. As Hector's fear turns to terror, Emma sees her husband in a tête-à-tête with an unknown woman and rushes out "to scratch his eyes out!" (pp. 76-7)

Left alone, Hector, who has been freezing all the while, sneezes. As he goes to the window to close it, he sees Emma's husband, Alcibiades, with a woman whose dress he recognizes as his wife's. Hector wants revenge now: "An eye for an eye! A tooth for a tooth! A wife for a wife! . . . And a hand drill for a hand drill!" . . . When Emma returns, he pushes her to the window, wants to crush her in his arms, smother her with kisses, and make love to her. Finally she draws out of him that his sudden change is the result of having seen his wife with Alcibiades. She explains that the woman was no other than the maid Hector's wife had fired and who was wearing a dress given her by her mistress at a happier moment, hence all the confusion. For her part she had returned to thank him for his unwillingness to oblige. All is restored to order again.

A modest little comedy light years away from the diabolically intricate plays that were to make Feydeau the undisputed master of *vaudeville, Par la fenêtre* contains in embryo several of the elements that were to mature into full-fledged characteristics of his theater. Alcibiades, the jealous Brazilian alluded to, responsible for most of the events, but not present in the action, foreshadows the *rastaquouère,* the irascible Latin whose fiery temperament and violent jealousy make him explode at the slightest provocation and seek retribution for his easily wounded pride by means of one of the abundant pseudo-heroic duels. Alcibiades represents also the first of many foreigners to be caricatured by Feydeau.

Hector's jealous wife, though not present in the action, is an obvious precursor as well, not so much of the women Feydeau created in his early and middle period but of the wives that people the plays he composed at the end of his career, those bitter domestic one-act comedies which he wanted to gather together under a common and telling title, *Du Mariage au divorce.*

In her reaction to her husband's ways, and in her attitude and behavior toward Hector, we discover in Emma still another

prototype. She is once again the first in a long line of dominating, headstrong, whimsical, petulant women determined to make their husbands pay dearly for their wayward behavior, and to avenge themselves impetuously and irrepressibly. She is also a model in that she heads the list of the many women who exasperate and frustrate husbands, lovers, or aspiring lovers, by their very personal brand of illogical logic and seemingly rational absurdity.

Although not one of Feydeau's most remarkable comedies, *Par la fenêtre* is quite humorous and entertaining. Those present at its performances must have agreed with Francisque Sarcey, the celebrated and influential drama critic, that its author showed a great deal of potential. Time was to prove their verdict correct.

In his second comedy, another one-act play, Feydeau based the whole action on a situation created by a device that he was to use repeatedly and with excellent results in his career: the *quiproquo,* a legacy from the well-made play. *Amour et piano* opens as Lucile, left alone by her mother, awaits the arrival of a famous music teacher whom she has never met and whose name she does not recall. Then Edouard Lorillot, a young provincial, arrives and thinks he is in the apartment of Mlle Dubarroy, a famous entertainer and courtesan whom he wants to court in order to be fashionable. Lucile mistakes Lorillot for the famous maestro.

The humor created by this original *quiproquo,* literally "this for that," is all the more comical because the rather innocuous series of questions and replies that compose the actual discussion of the conditions, the arrangements, the number and length of the monthly meetings, the cost per meeting, and the possibility of fringe benefits result in an abundance of misunderstandings, most of which are laden with sexual innuendo. (pp. 77-9)

Structurally, this play is simple if compared to the extremely complicated but precision-made plots of later masterpieces. Thematically, we are still leagues away from Feydeau's patented depiction of a world in which absurdity reigns, of a society composed of self-indulgent, egocentric, and egoistic individuals in a constant quest for physical pleasures, of a domestic universe where moral virtues are scarce or skirted, where adultery is a favorite pastime, where marriage gradually resembles a terrestrial hell. No hate, no vengeance, no cruelty, no frenzy, are present in *Amour et piano.* Instead, the mood that predominates is one of disarming innocence, gaiety, charm, and requited love. (p. 80)

Although Francisque Sarcey had recognized a definite talent in the young author of *Par la fenêtre,* it is quite unlikely that he or anyone else would have been so clairvoyant as to predict that, only five years later, and only after a total of four one-act plays, Feydeau was capable of producing as accomplished a comedy as *Tailleur pour dames.*

This play merits close scrutiny not because it represents Feydeau's first major triumph and financial success but rather because, although a much shorter and somewhat less complex play than his later highly acclaimed full-length comedies, it reveals an author in near-absolute control of all facets of playwriting. For the first time the creator of this play clearly announces the great master that he was to become. (p. 81)

[Much] of the laughter is elicited by a variety of misunderstandings and mistaken identities, which weave an incredibly complex crisscross pattern whose natural consequences momentarily engulf the characters and delight the audience.... Yet, in spite of the labyrinthine situations Feydeau creates, spectators have no difficulty whatsoever in following the plot line and, what is more amazing—and this is a tribute to Feydeau's instinct for the theater—the resolution comes very late in the third act and many complications which by now border on the tragic are resolved with apparent ease and verisimilitude. Certainly these were not characteristics of Feydeau's immediate predecessors who required much of the first act for the exposition and much of the third for the denouement.

Although much of the comedy is created by misunderstanding and mistaken identities, Feydeau uses many of the stock traditional devices, and some that would become patently his own, to elicit laughter. Thus, he employs asides, infelicitous liaisons, verbal humor, suggestive names, falls, slaps, personal tics. (pp. 84-5)

Either because of their regional accents, their ignorance, their insolence, or their excessive familiarity with their masters, servants are always good sources of comedy. The servant in this play, Emile, is still a rather undeveloped character but does play a significant role. As in *Amour et piano,* where Baptiste, the servant, elicits the first laughter, here it is Emile who gets the first response from the audience with one of his absurd observations. As the play opens, Emile appears and before he does any work he yawns loudly. Then with "Cartesian" profundity he states: "It is proven that it is at the precise moment that we wake up that we feel the most like sleeping. Therefore man should wait until he awakes before going to sleep!" (p. 85)

Monsieur chasse, Feydeau's favorite play, deals with one of the most common themes in his repertory: adultery. It also features common subsidiary characteristics, the potential lover trying desperately to seduce the wife of his best friend, the confident and unfaithful husband, prone to lying, "inconsiderate" enough to interrupt his friend's seduction at the least opportune moments but blind and unwittingly generous enough to facilitate and even encourage the lover's objective, and the wife who, upon discovering her husband's extramarital escapades sets out to seek immediate revenge. This is basically the situation that exists in this play. (p. 96)

[In *Monsieur chasse* Feydeau for the first time] provides very explicit, detailed, and precise stage directions and insists categorically upon having actors interpret in special ways so as to create very calculated and anticipated effects. If rhythm, tempo, movement were his forte in the last few plays of the early period, here he carries them to absolute virtuosity. Also, for the first time, though not the last in his career, he has not one but two men caught with their pants down. In order to exploit this comical finding, he has them walk dignifiedly on the stage incongruously attired in hat, coat and tie, and long underpants. This is also the first play in which the bed is given the place of honor. In Feydeau's hands, the bed is no longer the locus of nocturnal repose but a battleground where sexual squirmishes are fought. As daring as convention would allow, Feydeau's bedroom scenes are always suggestive and comical.

Though the situations in which Feydeau places his characters may be new, the methods and techniques used to place them there form part of traditional *vaudeville* and part of his welltried and successful bag of tricks. The difference between this and his earlier plays is one of degree, for in this play all complications are aggravated. (pp. 99-100)

Though one of his greatest financial successes, and though Champignol became a legendary figure, ***Champignol malgré lui*** is not one of Feydeau's best comedies. It is true that his contemporaries received it with almost hysterical laughter. It is equally true that, judging from the number of performances, only ***La Dame de chez Maxim*** surpassed it in popular acclaim. Still, revivals of this comedy have been scarce and, whatever revivals there have been, have met with moderate success. This play, exceptionally difficult to summarize, suffers from a lack of moderation, from a series of subplots not as carefully connected to the main plot as was Feydeau's usual practice, and from excessive absurd situations. These flaws, however, barely lessen the comedic impact of this play. (pp. 103-04)

Francisque Sarcey wrote that on the opening night of *L'Hôtel du Libre-Echange,* the volume of laughter had been growing so gradually that by the end of the second act it had become deafening to the point of requiring the actors to finish the act in pantomime. This initial success proved quite durable. After a rather lengthy hiatus, during which the play sank into oblivion, it was successfully revived in 1956 at the Marigny. Under the title ***Hotel Paradiso,*** this has become one of the most recognizable of Feydeau's plays in the English-speaking world. In 1965 a film version based on an adaptation by Peter Glenville made this play accessible to a much larger audience. (p. 107)

Structurally and technically, this comedy is not unlike some of the ones discussed thus far, having much in common particularly with *Monsieur chasse,* a similarity that was recognized when the play first appeared. Whereas all major characters converged on 40 rue d'Athènes in *Monsieur chasse,* the place of unwanted encounters here is the Hôtel du Libre-Echange, where, in the second act, as is often the case, the biggest concern of the characters is to avoid being seen by those people whom they least expected to see. The confined area of the stage, so marvelously exploited by Feydeau, makes their efforts all the more difficult and comical.

A most comical play, *L'Hôtel du Libre-Echange* elicits laughter by traditional means and by the devices that Feydeau developed and found effective in previous comedies. But as always, his fertile imagination permitted him to create new comical characters to be afflicted with curious speech impediments, some of which are more or less believable on a rational level, more or less essential to the fabric of the imbroglio, others quite fantastic and present for purely comical effects. (p. 110)

Feu la mère de madame was the first play to enter the repertory of the Comédie-Française, in 1941, but Feydeau's real status as a classic was not consecrated until 1951, when Jean Meyer and Pierre-Aimé Touchard revived *Le Dindon* in an attempt to boost receipts at the national theater. Their instincts served them well. This revival was a great success, as had been its premiere in 1896.

Serious questions about marriage, love, and fidelity are raised more insistently in this play than in previous ones. Still, the main lines of the plot depart little from Feydeau's established formula. (p. 113)

In this play Feydeau returns to a source of comedy he had exploited with much success in his earlier plays but had neglected in recent years: servants. Gérôme, Rédillon's old male servant, is quite a character. Related to Rédillon through the latter's father, Gérôme's foster brother, he addresses the young man in the familiar *tu* whereas Rédillon uses the more polite *vous,* a reversal of the common master-servant form of address which scandalizes even Armandine, the *cocotte.* Gérôme has

Feydeau (left) with Sarah Bernhardt at the wedding of Sacha Guitry and Yvonne Printemps in 1919. Collection Jacques Lorcey.

taken so seriously the last words of his foster brother to look after the child Rédillon, that his protective attitude borders on the ludicrous, treating the thirty-two-year-old like a child, chiding him for returning home after eleven, for not eating properly, and, above all, for his marathonic love-making sessions, after which, since he cannot stop them, he forces him to drink fortified wine to replenish his lost energy. One of the most comical exchanges occurs when Gérôme reports on the visit of an antique dealer who has a new and rare acquisition, "a chastity belt from the fourteenth." "From the fourteenth what?" queries a less than knowledgeable Armandine. "What do I know, from the fourteenth cuckold, probably," clarifies a down-to-earth Gérôme. . . . (pp. 116-17)

Feydeau also elicits a great deal of laughter out of a series of masterful double-entendres which, seemingly innocent out of context, are filled with sexual innuendo.

As said earlier, this play raises some serious issues. More and more Feydeau's emphasis seems to gravitate in the direction of comedy of character and manners studying particularly human relationships. Acts 1 and 3 provide most of the serious message with the most biting commentary in the first few scenes of the opening act. Pontagnac is, without any doubt, the most despicable seducer created by Feydeau. He is cynical, "I don't cheat on her once without feeling sorry for her," says

he of his wife, a woman who is for him "like a book I have often leafed through. . . ." He is a man without principles and quite used to buying people off as Feydeau subtly illustrates when, to stop Lucienne from telling on him, Pontagnac places a five-franc coin in her hand.

Feydeau does not let him go through life unscathed and unhurt. At the end of the play he is left alone "holding the bag," as it were. He is well aware of how severe his punishment has been and how little he has obtained in return. (pp. 118-19)

After the excesses and extravagance of *La Dame de chez Maxim* and *La Duchesse des Folies-Bergère,* Feydeau returned to a much more restrained and better brand of comedy. Following the premiere of *La Main passe,* critics congratulated him for having combined masterfully the elements of *vaudeville* with the comedy of manners, a feat, they failed to indicate, that he had accomplished earlier in *Le Ruban* and *Le Dindon,* to mention but two of the plays in which Feydeau blended successfully the coarser aspects of *vaudeville* with serious observation and critical acuity. (p. 120)

In *La Main passe* Feydeau continues to demonstrate his control over all aspects of the theatrical experience. Time and again he indicates with painstaking detail how to ensure that the whole play is performed flawlessly and as he saw it in his imagination. In one of several footnotes he meticulously explains how to achieve the most comical effect from Massenay's wearing Hubertin's pants which must look much too big at the waist and much too short. He is equally concerned about not making Hubertin's drunkenness seem vulgar. Hubertin, he notes, must not stagger, he must only sway lightly as he walks; he must trip over his own feet ever so slightly, but must regain his balance almost immediately; he must be heavy-eyed, but must speak clearly, never slurring; he must never lose his dignity.

Clearly conscious of the potential comical effects of any situation, Feydeau asks his *metteurs en scène* to make certain that as the curtain is raised in answer to the applause of the audience at the end of Act 2, Hubertin is still in the same hunter-like position he was in as the act ended, and that as soon as Francine, Massenay, and Coustouillu return to the stage to accept the applause, he must start shooting at once. They must flee as if genuinely fearing for their lives. Feydeau thus prolongs the laughter generated by the chaotic conclusion to the act, and blurs somewhat the line between fiction and reality.

The line between comedy and tragedy is also often blurred by Feydeau, though comedy, of necessity, always triumphs eventually. In Feydeau's theater the ever-present cruel fate, that capriciously victimizes so many characters, takes on a variety of shapes and forms. In this play, for instance, the recording cylinder, a recent invention that Chanal owns and displays with great satisfaction, is, as Paul-Louis Mignon intelligently pointed out, like the pride of Oedipus, the cause of his own downfall. But the general tone and circumstances of the play and the important fact that the recording phonograph can be seen as a symbol of Chanal's puerile self-satisfaction and complacency, renders comical a potentially serious situation, and makes Chanal more ridiculous than tragic. Still, beneath the surface, Feydeau reveals a world of threatening and unknown forces, a world, as Jean Cocteau acutely observed, worthy of Kafka. (pp. 123-24)

La Main passe is an unusual play. It is the only four-act play Feydeau ever wrote. It is the first in which a main female character actually commits adultery and, what is more, not just once but twice in the span of the play. It is also the first time that the illicit couple is seen in bed after the adultery has been consummated, and the first time that an illicit couple becomes a married couple, and that the lover-turned-husband divorces his mistress-turned-wife to remarry his first wife.

This play is unusual also in that Feydeau gives some new twists and variations on the typical and old theme of the love-triangle. He also probes deeper into marriage and love, licit and illicit. (pp. 125-26)

La Puce à l'oreille is by any estimate one of the two or three most comical plays Feydeau ever wrote. Sidesplitting and persistent laughter tires spectators so much that they hardly have time to realize that the objects of their hilarity are in fact victims, often innocent victims, of an infernal machine, of a capricious destiny that buffets them about at random. For Chandebise, whose only flaw, if flaw it can be called, is to have temporarily failed, through no fault of his own, in his conjugal duties, the punishment is utterly out of proportion. For this minor fault, he is driven to the brink of insanity. A good husband, faithful to a wife he adores, he is sent on a nightmarish itinerary during the course of which he is repeatedly manhandled, mistreated, and threatened with death by Homénidès; he is brutally expelled from Rugby's room, accused of alcoholism, and made to drink foul-tasting medicines, made to question his sanity; and, to top it all, he is brutalized, tormented, hu-

miliated, and insulted at every turn by the sadistic proprietor of a hotel of ill-repute. Many other characters find themselves in difficult and incomprehensible situations, but few suffer as much unwarranted punishment as Chandebise. Like a Kafka character, he is assailed by unknown forces for incomprehensible reasons. But whatever serious comments Feydeau makes here and in many other *vaudevilles,* laughter generally drowns their impact and keeps spectators from reflecting. (p. 135)

Un fil à la patte is not only one of Feydeau's undeniable masterpieces, as he fuses all aspects of his trade into perfect communion, but it is also one of the most comical plays he ever wrote. This play . . . marks an important departure from past practices in that it does not feature the tribulations of an honest married woman but introduces the *cocotte* in the leading female role and, through her, the demimonde. This change from wives to *cocottes,* however, does not spell any less trouble for those men who come into close contact with them. (pp. 138-39)

The success of this play depends largely on the characters Feydeau creates, and on the peculiar characteristics he bestows upon them. Fontanet, for instance, otherwise a charming man, is afflicted by a serious case of bad breath, an affliction which Feydeau drains of all its potential comedy. General Irrigua is, however, the single most comical character in the whole play. His personality, at once caricatural and individualistic, is the prime source of his comedic appeal. An ex-Minister of War sentenced to death in his country for having gambled away most of the money with which his government entrusted him to procure war material, he is of unequal humor, savagely frank, exceedingly passionate, excessively effusive, and inordinately jealous. He spends most of the play chasing rivals, real or imaginary, and challenging them to duels. He threatens to kill at the slightest provocation and knows no compromise. Incapable of subtlety, his social graces are as polished as his French which he tortures and mutilates at the turn of each phrase. He mixes French and Spanish continually. Colloquial expressions become unrecognizable in his mouth. Proper names are destroyed: Bois d'Enghien, for instance, becomes Bodégué. In his love scene with Lucette he constantly excuses himself to consult Antonio, his interpreter. Comically, all the words he seeks to know are almost identical in both languages. Yet he still manages to render them unrecognizable. What is most ironic and comical is that before he joined the army, this man was a professor who supplemented his meager salary by giving private lessons. He taught French! "Een my country I know how to speak French bery good. Ees when I come here, en Francia, for some reason, I no speak so good. . . ."

Feydeau's mastery of the technical and structural aspects is accompanied by a growing delicacy of touch in characterization and social commentary. To some extent the first act of this play could be termed a tableau of manners in which Feydeau first introduces us to the demimonde, the world in which *cocottes* reign supreme. He was to give us other views of this world in subsequent plays, culminating in **Cent millions qui tombent,** a play unfortunately left unfinished, but this is the first time we see a *cocotte* in her own domain. What Feydeau offers us is a vision of a demimonde whose members, though socially marginal, share the same concerns as the *bourgeoisie:* social status, money, pleasure, and marriage. (pp. 142-43)

If in *Le Dindon* Feydeau had strayed ever so slightly from his mainstream of production by requiring his audiences to think while making them laugh, in *La Dame de chez Maxim* his main objective was to amuse, to entertain, to leave out bitterness and pessimism. And the public all over the world rewarded him for giving it such pure folly, such intense entertainment. According to his own account, this comedy, one of his most popular in France, provided him with the biggest financial returns, enough to permit him to devote the next two years exclusively to painting, his real vocation.

It took Feydeau four months to complete this, the longest of his plays, and one of the most complex in its structure. The situations he created and the many intricacies of the various strands of the plot are interwoven in a labyrinthine manner. But as usual, every detail, every *quiproquo*, every inventive situation is so logically prepared, flows so naturally, is so much the unavoidable effect of an earlier cause, that though easy to follow it is paradoxically difficult to recount. (p. 144)

Much of the laughter here is elicited by traditional means: numerous and sequential slaps; several chases and the inevitable falls that result from them; elegant and stuffy women, young and old, kicking one another as each quite undignifiedly attempts to swing her leg up high over a chair as they emulate [famous Moulin Rouge singer and dancer] Crevette. . . . There are even walking and transportable human "poufs" ["upholstered tabourets"]. (pp. 148-49)

The characters are quite comical. The general, for instance, is a typical soldier, not much better than those portrayed in *Champignol malgré lui.* He is obtuse, stubborn, uncultured, longwinded, and prone to having others duel. The witnesses care much more about obeying blindly the established rituals than about the individuals involved. Compassion seems unknown to them. Indeed, they feel cheated and consider the principals frivolous when the duel does not take place. (p. 150)

In the second act Feydeau takes the opportunity to present a tableau of provincial manners. He satirizes the aspirations of provincials to behave as Parisians. Their insatiable thirst for anything Parisian renders them utterly blind and makes them behave in a ludicrous manner which borders on the pathetic. The way in which even the duchess, the general, and the abbé, of all people, imitate indiscriminatingly the unrefined, vulgar mannerisms, language, and antics of Crevette, reveals at once their insecurity, their frivolity, and their foolishness. Even the oldest women in the room pathetically and idiotically attempt to emulate the vulgar swinging of Crevette's buttocks. . . . Feydeau pokes further fun at these provincials. Instead of being scandalized by the import of the sexually suggestive song Crevette sings, their ignorance and naïveté make them find in it deep moral and religious meanings. Only their snobbism and vain desire to be fashionable could have blinded them to the point of not recognizing Crevette for what she is.

Môme Crevette is the one character who best incarnates the qualities that made this one of Feydeau's most popular comedies. This is a very demanding role since the actress playing it must be able not only to sing and dance well, but must also be able to act at a variety of registers, being successively seductive, disarmingly innocent, affectionate, caressing, rebellious, impulsive, ladylike, and vulgar, though with taste. Above all, she needs to be charismatic. Armande Cassive played this role to perfection and became Feydeau's favorite actress. She made Môme Crevette so famous that it was said that during the year 1900, hordes of visitors came to Paris for two reasons: for the Universal Exposition and to see *La Dame de chez Maxim.* Such was her success that Feydeau's next play, the extravagant *La Duchesse des Folies-Bergère,* featured, once again, the inimitable Môme Crevette with a cast of many high-class *cocottes* framed by the best of all possible locales, Maxim's.

In this play Crevette reappears as the seemingly sedate, dignified, and aristocratic wife of the Orcanian Duke Pitchenieff, whose main task is to procure women for his young king. Her outer façade, however, barely hides the irrepressible Crevette. As soon as she comes back to Paris, she returns to the site of her early joys and successes, Maxim's, where, at one point, she can be seen dancing impudently on the shoulders of an eccentric who refers to the famed restaurant and its patrons as *"le Paris de la décadence."* Her libidinous nature and her taste for riches have not abandoned her. Fidelity continues not to be one of her virtues. Still a capable actress and the possessor of unsurpassable aplomb, she not only deceives her husband with their king, for whom the duke has quite unwittingly procured his own wife, but she has the audacity, when all evidence condemns her, to forgive his suspicions and unbecoming jealousy. Even her colorful antics resurface. *La Duchesse des Folies-Bergère* closes in the same manner as *La Dame de chez Maxim,* with Crevette throwing her leg high up in the air, swinging it over a chair, and exclaiming childishly *"Et allez, c'est pas mon père!"* ["Go on, it is not my father!"] There is, however, an added dimension to her character. A married woman now, she worries about appearances and attempts to give the impression of a respectable wife. The security of marriage is overpowering for all the women in Feydeau's theater, even *cocottes.*

An acknowledged masterpiece that has the singular honor of being the first play in the first volume of Feydeau's complete works, *Occupe-toi d'Amélie* is the last completed play in which unbridled gaiety, carefree madness, and unrepentant frivolity and extravagance still reign supreme. (pp. 150-52)

A very lengthy comedy whose humor can be less readily appreciated at reading than that of many other plays, *Occupe-toi d'Amélie* is a very visual play overflowing with a certain atmosphere of insouciance and playfulness that relaxes and entertains. This is not to say that Feydeau does not depend here on his accumulated arsenal of comical devices and patented situations. He does. But there is little in this play that is totally new and original. Once again, for instance, Feydeau relies on foreigners. The prince and General Koschnadieff both speak to each other in their native but fictitious language composed of inherently comical sounds. Van Putzeboum, whose name is already quite ludicrous, has a very particular way of speaking French. (p. 155)

[In *Occupe-toi d'Amélie*] Feydeau presents several situations in which comedy of manners, social criticism, and farce are brilliantly fused. In the famous wedding scene he accomplishes just such fusion. But he does much more. He announces the Pirandellian principle of the extratheatrical reality of the theater. With the exception of the organizer and those who perform the ceremony, all participate in what they know is a make-believe wedding. All is so well done, so real, the actors of the charade are so convincing in their roles, that if they did not know any better, they would swear it is an actual wedding. Irony of ironies, reality invades fiction, the actors become characters in a real wedding, and Marcel and Amélie, while convinced that they are playacting, find themselves joined in matrimony. Appearances and lies, which are always made to pass for real life in the theater, become a theatrical reality that the participants cannot accept. This play within a play, like a double negative that has an affirmative meaning, translates into reality and, as in Pirandello's world, becomes difficult to distinguish between mimesis and life. (p. 156)

A much gayer and more carefree comedy than some of the earlier plays that contain biting social satires and a pessimistic view of people and their institutions, *Occupe-toi d'Amélie* closes the cycle of Feydeau's great full-length masterpieces but hardly announces the bitter one-act domestic comedies with which he was to cap his illustrious career.

With *Feu la mère de madame* Feydeau inaugurates a series of one-act plays devoid almost of all action but profound and probing despite their brevity. Feydeau, who had always subordinated the *moraliste* to the mirthmaker, emerges in his last cycle as an acute observer of human behavior. This is not to say that he makes a clean break with his past production. Quite the contrary. What he does is focus sharply on and magnify mercilessly certain aspects of the life he had observed. He transposes to the stage the miseries and woes of conjugal existence. (pp. 157-58)

The fact that Feydeau chose a collective title, *From Marriage to Divorce,* for these five one-act bitter comedies attests to the unity of his inspiration; the fact that, as Feydeau's own family was to recognize, Mme Feydeau was the main model for all the five leading ladies, explains why Yvonne, Julie, Clarisse, Léonie, and Marcelle resemble each other and differ much less in personality than in the salient negative traits that particularize them and in the situations and circumstances which Feydeau creates for them and to which they must react.

Their husbands too differ greatly from earlier ones. Some of them continue to be as selfish, self-centered, vain, and fatuous as their predecessors. But whereas the latter's faults often plunged them into difficult predicaments from which they emerged at the last possible moment, thanks to luck and more than average ingenuity, the former cannot be accused of seeking extramarital entertainment though they too seem to pay for some indiscretion. Their most imposing enemy is not a capricious fate; it is their wives. They are all the victims of wives who forever place obstacles in their paths, embarrassing them, humiliating them, often destroying them and their careers. These husbands can never win an argument as they are confronted with a baffling system of female reasoning that challenges rationality and logic. If they attempt to impose themselves, domestic life is but a continual nightmarish struggle; if, to find peace, they relent, they incur the wrath and scorn of wives who despise weakness. The husband is no match for his wife. He is no longer the king of his castle. Quite the contrary, he is belittled, frustrated, maligned by his wife. He has abdicated his authority and his dignity. He is totally subjugated, psychologically castrated.

The battle of the sexes continues, but on a more intense and sordid level. Sex, so much the catalyst in earlier works, is no longer a cause for discord; it is hardly a subject for discussion. Buckets filled with filthy water, chamber pots, purges and constipations, are now what pits husband against wife. The sordidness of their discussions symbolizes accurately how Feydeau came to view marriage. Gone are any signs of affection, any attempts at real communication, any willingness to compromise. What remains of marriage is a battleground in which the two sexes methodically and cruelly tear each other apart. (pp. 158-59)

The five plays that Feydeau wanted to group under *Du Mariage au divorce* offer a mosaic of domestic situations which, though hardly tragic in Aristotelian terms, do show human tragedy in a minor key, but the pains are no less felt for that. In his longer and gayer comedies there is the hint of a capricious fate that maliciously buffets about not only those guilty of impropriety but innocent ones as well. Generally, however, this same fate, which toys with the characters and pushes them repeatedly to the brink of catastrophe, magnanimously extricates them, almost in *deus ex machina* fashion, from their worst predicaments, furnishing them at least a safe return to their previous ''normal'' existence, and giving them occasionally even a chance for a better relationship with their spouses. The protagonists of Feydeau's last cycle are much less fortunate. From beginning to end they experience more anguish than their predecessors and none of the ''good'' moments. Furthermore, they are not given a chance to make amends and no promise for a better tomorrow. For Lucien, Follavoine, Ventroux, Toudoux, and Follbraguet, discontent will yield to unhappiness, torment will give way to torture; their nightmare will persist as long as they remain married. Is this the stuff of which comedies are made? (pp. 172-73)

Manuel A. Esteban, in his Georges Feydeau, *Twayne Publishers, 1983, 194 p.*

ADDITIONAL BIBLIOGRAPHY

Gilliatt, Penelope. ''Feydeau.'' In her *Unholy Fools: Wits, Comics, Disturbers of the Peace: Film & Theater,* pp. 183-87. New York: Viking Press, 1973.
    Defends Feydeau's use of stylized characters as essential to the humor of farce.

Parshall, Peter F. ''Feydeau's *A Flea in Her Ear:* The Art of Kinesthetic Restructuring.'' *Theater Journal* 33, No. 3 (October 1981): 355-64.
    In-depth analysis of the action of *A Flea in Her Ear,* which Parshall considers ''the source of much of its artistry.''

Shapiro, Norman R. Introduction to *Four Farces,* by Georges Feydeau, pp. xiii-liv. Chicago: University of Chicago Press, 1970.
    Extensive discussion of Feydeau's technique, its evolution, and its impact.

''Forms of Shock Treatment for a World Out of Plumb.'' *The Times Literary Supplement,* No. 3616 (18 June 1971): 689-90.
    Review of *Four Farces* which analyzes the nature of farce and its relation to other comedic forms.

Van Druten, John. ''A Gem from the French Crown.'' *Theatre Arts* XLII, No. 3 (March 1958): 19-21.
    Summary of *Going to Pot* in which Van Druten questions the assertion that Feydeau's comedies are second only to those of Molière.

W(illiam) W(ymark) Jacobs

1863-1943

English short story and novella writer, novelist, and dramatist.

Jacobs was one of the most popular English humorists of the early twentieth century, though he is best remembered today for his horror classic "The Monkey's Paw." The major part of Jacobs's work consists of stories about seamen on the Thames wharfs, and he is particularly noted for his quiet, unadorned style and droll humor, as well as for his vivid depiction of seaport life. Occasionally criticized for a lack of intellectual substance in his fiction, Jacobs has been more properly appreciated for his simple, unpretentious humor.

The son of a wharf manager and his wife, Jacobs grew up in the dockland area of Wapping, London. He was educated in private schools and entered the civil service as a clerk in 1879, a job that he hated. Around the age of twenty, he began to write humorous articles as a pastime, and by 1885 was publishing them in magazines for "extra pocket money." Many of these early stories were published in the *Idler* and *Today* magazines, both edited by Jerome K. Jerome, a prominent humorist of the period who was enthusiastic about Jacobs's work. Jacobs's first collection of stories, *Many Cargoes*, was published in 1896; after its second printing the following year, he was established as a popular humorist. Almost every story he subsequently wrote was first published in the *Strand Magazine*, which paid him well for his work. Cautious by nature, Jacobs did not quit his civil service job to devote himself entirely to writing until the publication of his third book, *Sea Urchins*, in 1899. He married soon after, and his unpleasant relationship with his wife may have contributed to the consistently low view of women expressed in his fiction. Jacobs's wife was a militant suffragette and socialist, while he was intensely conservative, and they quarreled constantly. Jacobs wrote prolifically at the beginning of his career, but his output abruptly diminished around 1911, and he wrote very little beyond a few adaptations of his stories for the stage during the last seventeen years of his life, a period that nevertheless marked the height of his popularity and saw the republication of many works written earlier in his career. Jacobs's works fell into obscurity after his death, although since 1969 a number of them have been reissued, reflecting continued enjoyment of his fiction.

Jacobs's fame during his lifetime rested on the particular type of humorous story he wrote rather than on any single work. His comic action usually revolves around simple surprise-ending plots; Jacobs leads his readers to expect one outcome and then produces another. The basic type of story Jacobs wrote remained unchanged throughout his career, though he was ingenious in devising new situations for his limited number of basic plots. The characters are sometimes motivated by money, sometimes by marriage or the avoidance of marriage, but nearly all the plots contain trickery or deception. One memorable character recurring throughout Jacobs's work is the Night Watchman, who relates many of the stories and provides a consistently "seaman"-like tone by narrating in the same dialect that the other characters use in dialogue. Critics observe that the use of dialect and slang for description and characterization effectively serves to involve the reader in the story.

The action of Jacobs's stories occurs primarily around London seaports, but very seldom does a story take place at sea. Like his short stories, Jacobs's novels often feature seaport settings and characters and are for the most part humorous. Most critics agree that Jacobs's sense of humor is very restrained and droll rather than ostentatiously comic, though some, notably G. K. Chesterton, consider him inordinately funny. Furthermore, his skill as a humorist elicited comparisons to such classic predecessors as Aristophanes and Charles Dickens. A strong qualification to this praise was made by Arnold Bennett, who viewed Jacobs's work as intellectually vacuous. Bennett's attack drew many defenses of Jacobs which cited the merits of his humor, though critics were nonetheless ready to admit that he was a minor writer.

In addition to his humorous fiction, Jacobs also proved himself to be a master of the horror story, notably with "The Monkey's Paw." Famous for its powerful blend of terror and pathos, "The Monkey's Paw" has been widely anthologized and adapted for performance on stage and in movies. The story, about a talisman that grants wishes in the most horrible ways imaginable, is one of what Chesterton called Jacobs's "amazing tales of tragedy . . . [that] stand alone among our modern tales of terror in that they are dignified and noble." Jacobs's horror fiction drew a mixed reaction from those who had nothing but adulation for his comedy, yet even when writing primarily about Jacobs's humor, most critics feel obligated to mention "The Monkey's Paw" at least in passing.

As an author, Jacobs knew his limits and carefully remained within them. He wrote to produce a single desired effect upon the reader—occasionally horror, but usually laughter—and that effect was built up by every line. Jacobs's humor was not intended to provide psychological insight or social awareness, but rather to give simple amusement, and critics agree that he did this with great success.

PRINCIPAL WORKS

Many Cargoes (short stories) 1896
The Skipper's Wooing. The Brown Man's Servant
      (novellas) 1897
Sea Urchins (short stories) 1898; also published as *More Cargoes*, 1898
A Master of Craft (novel) 1900
Light Freights (short stories) 1901
At Sunwich Port (novel) 1902
*The Lady of the Barge (short stories) 1902
Odd Craft (short stories) 1903
Dialstone Lane (novel) 1904
Captains All (short stories) 1905
Short Cruises (short stories) 1907
Salthaven (novel) 1908
Admiral Peters [with Horace Mills] (drama) 1909
Sailor's Knots (short stories) 1909
Beauty and the Barge [with Louis N. Parker] (drama) 1910
Ship's Company (short stories) 1911
Night Watches (short stories) 1914
The Castaways (novel) 1916
Deep Waters (short stories) 1919
Sea Whispers (short stories) 1926
The Warming Pan (drama) 1929
Master Mariners (drama) 1930
Matrimonial Openings (drama) 1931
Double Dealing (drama) 1935
Selected Short Stories (short stories) 1975

*This collection contains the short story "The Monkey's Paw."

THE CHAP-BOOK (essay date 1897)

[*In the following excerpt, the critic reviews Jacobs's first collection of stories,* Many Cargoes.]

He is a bold man who nowadays attempts to launch another craft upon the crowded estuary of sea-tales. There are so many vessels moving on its surface, from the tall merchant-man to the blustering steam-tug, that the water sometimes seems to be almost overcrowded. However, in ***Many Cargoes,*** Mr. Jacobs has really taken us aboard quite a new craft. Here are by no means the traditional tales of buccaneers and buried treasure. No strange-oathed Silvers and Long Toms; but only oily gentlemen in overalls, who smoke short pipes as they lean from dingy companion-ways, and exchange greetings across some stretch of placid water.

These stories, perhaps a score in number, with one exception, deal with the trade along the English Coast. London is their principal port of entry and Wapping apparently their shoreward limit. Mr. Jacobs makes his points with emphasis, and we are never allowed to remain in doubt as to the place toward which his shaft is directed, but after all, and best of all, the stories are distinctly humorous. The picture of the ironical mate, who, upon being told by the captain that he must occupy the biscuit and onion locker, gruffly asks if he may not, instead, take up his quarters in the butter firkin, is certainly a vivid one. The first tale in the book, **"A Change of Treatment,"** is really capital comedy when one thinks of the gullible captain, coddling the entire starboard watch upon soft toast and currant jelly, while the mate is near to bursting with rising choler at the imposition.

The stories are redolent of side-lights and marlin; they bring strong whiffs of salty air, and we may surely for the time leave buried the ancient controversy between American and English humor, as we read these most amusing yarns.

      A review of "Many Cargoes," in The Chap-Book, *Vol. VII, No. 10, October 1, 1897, p. 363.*

G. K. CHESTERTON (essay date 1906)

[*Regarded as one of England's premier men of letters during the first half of the twentieth century, Chesterton is best known today as a colorful bon vivant, a witty essayist, and the creator of the Father Brown mysteries and the fantasy* The Man Who Was Thursday (1908). *Much of Chesterton's work reveals his childlike joie de vivre and reflects his pronounced Anglican and, later, Roman Catholic beliefs. His essays are characterized by their humor, frequent use of paradox, and chatty, rambling style. In the following excerpt from an essay originally published in the* Tribune *in 1906, Chesterton asserts that Jacobs's stories return to a tradition of classical comedy earlier found in the works of Charles Dickens.*]

Mr. Jacobs is in a real sense a classic. When I say he is classical, I do not merely mean that he is eminently able; Mr. Rudyard Kipling (for example) is eminently able, but he has not the pure marmoreal classicism of Mr. Jacobs. Compared with Mr. Kipling, Mr. Jacobs is like the Parthenon.

He is strictly to be described as classical for this reason—that he is a return to the central and sane tradition of humorous literature. He is the child of Dickens, and he has wiped out the weary interregnum between himself and his father. We find ourselves again in a farce older than Aristophanes; and we realize that of all the iron elements in the eternal soul none is more fixed or more enduring than its frivolity. Man has remembered his ancient laughter. In the period between the end of Dickens and the appearance of Mr. Jacobs we have had a great number of really great wits and of really great humorists. We have had men like Whistler whose wit seemed almost inspired, and whose repartee came like a bolt from the blue. We have had humorists like Mr. Max Beerbohm whose humour was so dainty and delicate as to be a kind of topsy-turvy transcendentalism. But these great wits and great humorists had one genuine defect—they could not laugh. They could smile, they could sneer, they could in desperate cases chuckle; but laughter, which is an elemental agony, shaking the jester himself, was a thing outside their mode of life.

There is no necessary connexion between wit and mirth. A man's wit overpowers his enemies; but his mirth overpowers him. As long as a man is merely witty he can be quite dignified; in other words, as long as he is witty he can be entirely solemn. But if he is mirthful he at once abandons dignity, which is another name for solemnity, which is another name for spiritual pride. A mere humorist is merely admirable; but a man laughing is laughable. He spreads the exquisite and desirable disease by which he is himself convulsed. But our recent comedians have distrusted laughter for exactly the same reason that they have distrusted religion or romantic love. A laugh is like a love affair in that it carries a man completely off his feet; a laugh is like a creed or a church in that it asks that a man should trust himself to it.

A man must sacrifice himself to the God of Laughter, who has stricken him with a sacred madness. As a woman can make a fool of a man, so a joke makes a fool of a man. And a man must love a joke more than himself, or he will not surrender his pride for it. A man must take what is called a leap in the dark, as he does when he is married or when he dies, or when he is born, or when he does almost anything else that is important.

Now there are at least four points in which Mr. Jacobs represents the return to the great comic classics; and this is the first of them—the fact that he re-establishes humour as something violent and involuntary and outside ourselves. His best humour is outside criticism, in the sense that physical pain is outside criticism. With him as with Dickens, an absurdity is an absurdity as a blow in the face is a blow in the face. You cannot pause to call the joke a bad joke. You cannot pause to call the joke a good joke. It is simply a fact of natural history that you, having read a certain remark two minutes before, are now rolling about on the carpet and waving your legs in the air.

There can be no criticism about this comic genius, because nobody in its presence can remain in a critical frame of mind. When, let us say, Mr. Dick Swiveller is cut out by Mr. Cheggs, the market gardener, he prepares a dramatic departure, and Miss Wackles says she is very sorry. ''Sorry!'' says Mr. Swiveller, ''sorry in the possession of a Cheggs!'' Nobody reading those words for the first time could ever decide whether they were low comedy or high comedy, broad humour or fine humour, large, small, long, short, fat, or thin humour; he would merely realize that they were humorous. He would be stunned by the simple fact that the thing was funny.

So it is in the best of Mr. Jacobs' work. In one of his stories, for instance, the night-watchman expresses a contempt for the pugilistic device of the punch-ball, and recalls the exploits of a more uncorrupted pugilist who was in the habit, when he wanted practice, of putting on a soft hat like a Nonconformist minister and going into a pub and contradicting people. ''He'd 'ave no more thought of 'ittin' a pore 'armless ball than I should of thought of 'ittin' 'im.'' That kind of sentence has the same direct Dickens quality. It is an unanswerable absurdity. It is very difficult to judge it, although doubtless after some little time or in some special detachment we can judge it. But we can only judge it after we have laughed at it. In other words, we can only judge it after we have acquitted it.

The second point is this: that he re-establishes the old comic importance of the thing called plot. Many other modern humorists have written short tales that were inspirations, fancies, glimpses, ideas. He alone has written short tales that are ingenious merely as tales. Every one of Mr. Jacobs' stories is an amplified anecdote; that is to say, it is a thing with a complication and a climax, a climax which must be at once expected and unexpected. In this matter Mr. Jacobs is entirely in line with the oldest mirth of mankind. The great classic conception

of a good story is that it should have a point, and that the principal character should sit down on it. Thus, for instance, the story of Polyphemus and No-man is an enlarged anecdote. Thus the many old tales of ingenious riddles and still more ingenious answers (such as that of King John and the Abbot of Canterbury and several about Solomon and the Queen of Sheba) are all enlarged anecdotes. The fun is not merely in the characters, it is in the whole framework of the thing; it is structurally funny, architecturally funny. Here, then, we have the second of the four classical qualities of Mr. Jacobs. We have here the fact that he is greatly concerned with the argument of his epic; with the thing to be done and the outer fate that falls upon his characters. And he feels and satisfies that desire for mere funny incidents well narrated which was once satisfied in savage tents and is still satisfied in smoking-rooms.

His third agreement with the classics lies in his lucidity. His humorous style is indeed allusive; and the nature of that allusiveness I shall discuss in a moment; but it is perfectly popular and clear. Consequently he has no concern with that air of mystery in which so many able moderns have wrapped their amusement. The old jester was disappointed that men did not see the joke. The new jester is delighted that they do not see the joke. Their blank faces are a proof of his own exquisite and individualised talent; the joke is too good to be seen. Laughter has been from the beginning the one indestructible brotherhood, the one undeniably social thing. But these moderns have made even laughter a lonely thing. They are always hunting for a humour that shall be completely original. But if a thing were completely original it would be completely unintelligible. If a man made an entirely new language it would not be a language at all. Mr. Jacobs represents here again a return to the normal; to a humour that is rich but simple, to a humour that is humorous but also obvious, to a humour which is not vulgar but which is common.

But there is one point in which Mr. Jacobs touches greatness, compared with which all these others are unimportant. This is his achievement as an interpreter of a great element of the democracy. He is the artistic expression of the humour of the people; a point in which (in the phrase of the French Revolution) ''the people is supreme.'' He exaggerates that popular humour undoubtedly. But that popular humour is itself in its nature an exaggeration; and the more exaggerated his popular humour is, the more like it is to popular humour. He overstates the actual statements of navvies or sailors; but they themselves would over-state them if they could. It would be a mistake to say that he made plebeian satire an art; but the plebeians have already made it an art. It would be truer to say that Mr. Jacobs' gibes are masterpieces where the real gibes of the street are merely works of art. Mr. Jacobs' labourers say better things than most real labourers, but the same kind of things. The first bears the same relation to the second that the rustic songs of Shakespeare bear to the rustic songs of Stratford-on-Avon.

''Take your face 'ome and bury it; not under plants as you're fond of.'' That might stand as a comparatively central and typical example of the tradition of satire that can actually be heard in the streets. That has all the three essential characteristics of the wit of the populace. First, it is poetical, or, at least, close to poetry; for everything that is close to the people is close to poetry. It is poetical, I mean, in the essential sense that it is connected with the ultimate enigma of nature and with wild and beautiful images. There is all the strength of a dark and grotesque lyric of Heine in the idea of the hideousness of the buried head polluting the very process of life, and distorting the very flowers and leaves. It is like the tale of the Pot of Basil. Second, the expression typifies popular humour in the fact that it is a joke about the body, about physical ugliness; a kind of joke that is an essential of moral health. To take the body seriously is to take the first step towards all the disasters that destroyed the Pagan civilization. Of all the quaint sanities which are the secrets of Christianity perhaps the sanest is the fact that it feels the body to be something grotesque. And of all forms of taking the body seriously, not one (not even the vile thing called hygiene) is so bad as the form that takes ugliness seriously as a sacred unmentionable thing. If you make a point of delicacy out of ugliness, you make a religion out of ugliness. Our moderns think it very shocking to pour any derision upon the body: they prefer to pour it upon the soul.

But the people never are and never can be moderns. That is why I am a democrat. The men in the street laugh at a man's nose which they can see, and which is often absurd, not at his religion, which they cannot see, and which is never absurd. Mr. Jacobs is the champion of the old, healthy habit of telling people how funny they look. All his conversationalists are given to being what is called "personal." I do not know anything more reasonable than being personal when you are talking about a person. But undoubtedly for the last thirty years our discussions have been growing more impersonal. There has been more airiness, detachment, and refinement in our arguments, and in consequence much more swindling in our public service.

No one can forget the almost endless list of Mr. Jacobs' popular discussions of physiognomy. There was Mr. Bob Pretty, who told his colleague, the old game-keeper, that he "'oped his face wouldn't get knocked about like that," and when the game-keeper indignantly denied that his face had been knocked about, said, with sudden meekness, "Oh! I beg your pardon. I didn't know it was natural." There was the sarcastic bar-keeper, who met his match in the more sarcastic boy, telling the youth to take the head off his beer, or he'd "muss his moustache up." To whom the boy replied that "as long as it didn't turn 'em red he didn't mind so much." There was the meditative miller, who remarked to the farmer with inconsiderate emphasis on the mystery of where the farmer's daughter could have got her good looks from. "She's no more like you than you're like a warming-pan—not so much."

Finally, the farcical speech of Mr. Jacobs' characters is undoubtedly ingenious, and even elaborate, but in this respect more than in any other it is the real speech of the populace. The real speech of the real mob is more intricate than medieval heraldry. To anybody who has ever talked to the man in the street it must be infinitely amusing to hear the philosophers of aristocracy talking about the sort of joke the vulgar can understand. There is not one of those philosophers of aristocracy who could before an impartial tribunal hold his own for five minutes against a cabman. Mr. Jacobs is in literature the voice of the inspired cabman.

But the wit of the cabman and the populace is not merely excellent—it is even subtle. It is even too subtle. Slang is the very reverse of a coarse thing. It is, if anything, an over-complex and over-civilized thing. It has some of that systematic indirectness which makes a darkness in the late medieval philosophy and poetry. This twisted luxuriance is perfectly represented in the admirable locutions of Mr. Jacobs' angry sailors. Taking the nose, or mental capacity, or family circumstances of an enemy as a mere text or starting point, the Jacobs sailor

gets out of it a sort of jungle of tropical taunts. One thing at least Mr. Jacobs has done—he has compiled the most reliable encyclopaedia of insults that can be purchased in the market.

I repeat, then, that I find Mr. Jacobs a classic; that is, a return to the enduring style. Many who have enjoyed his books will think that I have here taken him too seriously. On that point I have one word to say in conclusion. I have had no space to deal adequately with his amazing tales of tragedy, such as **"Jerry Bundler"** or the admirable **"Monkey's Paw."** But if the reader will look at them he will notice this fact: that they stand alone among our modern tales of terror in the fact that they are dignified and noble. They rise out of terror into awe. Everyone will remember the mother who wished to see the mangled nothing that was once her son. Everyone will remember that other tale of the son who sat in darkness because of his blasted face, and its final sentiment, "Here is to the children my son saved." Everyone will remember them; but it is more important that, ghastly as they are, everyone will be glad to remember them. His humour is wild, but it is sane humour. His horror is wild, but it is a sane horror. His farce is classic farce because, however violent it is, it leaves the heart more happy. And his tragedy is classic tragedy, because however heartrending it is, it leaves the heart more strong. (pp. 28-35)

G. K. Chesterton, "W. W. Jacobs," in his A Handful of Authors: Essays on Books and Writers, *edited by Dorothy Collins, Sheed and Ward, 1953, pp. 28-35.*

ARNOLD BENNETT (essay date 1908)

[*Bennett was an Edwardian novelist who is credited with bringing techniques of European Naturalism to the English novel. His reputation rests almost exclusively on* The Old Wives' Tale *(1908) and the Clayhanger trilogy (1910-16), novels which are set in the manufacturing district of Bennett's native Staffordshire and which tell of the thwarted ambitions of those who endure a dull, provincial existence. In the following excerpt from an essay published in the* New Age, *October 24, 1908, under Bennett's pseudonym Jacob Tonson, Bennett criticizes Jacobs's lack of development as an author and his indifference to "general ideas."*]

It is a long time since I read a book of [W. W. Jacobs]. Ministries have fallen since then, and probably Mr. Jacobs' prices have risen—indeed, much has happened—but the talent of the author of *Many Cargoes* remains steadfast where it did. *Salthaven* is a funny book. Captain Trimblett, to excuse the lateness of a friend for tea, says to the landlady: "He saw a man nearly run over!" and the landlady replies: "Yes, but how long would that take him?" If you ask me whether I consider this humorous, I reply that I do. (p. 53)

Salthaven is bathed in humour.

At the same time I am dissatisfied with *Salthaven*. And I do not find it easy to explain why. I suppose the real reason is that it discloses no signs of any development whatever on the part of the author. Worse, it discloses no signs of intellectual curiosity on the part of the author. Mr. Jacobs seems to live apart from the movement of his age. Nothing, except the particular type of humanity and environment in which he specializes, seems to interest him. There is no hint of a general idea in his work. By some of his fellow-artists he is immensely admired. I have heard him called, seriously, the greatest humourist, since Aristophanes. I admire him myself, and I will not swear that he is not the greatest humourist since Aristophanes. But I will swear that no genuine humourist ever resembled Aristophanes less than Mr. Jacobs does. Aristophanes was passionately interested in everything. He would leave nothing alone. Whereas Mr. Jacobs will leave nearly everything alone. Kipling's general ideas are excessively crude, but one does feel in reading him that his curiosity is boundless, even though his taste in literature must infallibly be bad. "Q." [Sir Arthur Quiller-Couch] is not to be compared in creative power with either of these two men, but one does feel in reading him that he is interested in other manifestations of his own art, that he cares for literature. Impossible to gather from Mr. Jacobs' work that he cares for anything serious at all; impossible to differentiate his intellectual outlook from that of an average reader of the *Strand Magazine!* I do not bring this as a reproach against Mr. Jacobs, whose personality it would be difficult not to esteem and to like. He cannot alter himself. I merely record the phenomenon as worthy of notice. (pp. 54-5)

> *Arnold Bennett, "W. W. Jacobs and Aristophanes,"*
> *in his* Books and Persons: Being Comments on a Past
> Epoch, 1908-1911, *George H. Doran Company, 1917,*
> *pp. 53-6.*

ROBERT C. WHITFORD (essay date 1919)

[*In the following excerpt, Whitford discusses characteristics of Jacobs's humor.*]

Mr. William Wymark Jacobs is one of the few comic writers of our day whose writings have at all the flavor of literature. On this account his literary product may profitably be subjected to the vivisection of critical analysis, and the result of such an investigation amounts in plain words to this: he is a humorist, pure and simple, and, with all his limitations, by no means a typically English humorist. His purity and simplicity are easier to prove, however, than his cosmopolitanism. For while it is not hard to see that his humor is free from contamination and admixture and is of no great complexity, it is difficult not to see that its subject matter is exclusively British. From *Many Cargoes* to *The Castaways,* his books have been concerned chiefly with the amiably spontaneous and natural selfishness, hypocrisy, and general dishonesty of prosperous and cheerful English people of the lower classes. In a typical story he involves characters drawn from life and a plot based upon some extravagant project of deceit,—an elaborate practical joke it may be, or an equally complicated scheme for getting money by false pretenses. The crafty plans always go wrong and in the going rouse the risibilities of most male readers and of many women.

Behind the intention of Mr. Jacobs to write a comic story there is never a mixture of motives. It is quite evident that with him the joke is the thing. His comedy has rarely a bit of pathos about it, and rarely a touch of sympathy for human weakness or misfortune. Nor is there a clearly satirical note in his laughter; his mockery seems to have no reformatory purpose. Indeed he apparently has in his humorous tales no high artistic purpose of any sort beyond that of the literary fun maker. Even the direct art of story-telling is with him subordinate to the incidental joke and the comic tableau. Ludicrousness of situation is the fuel for his engine of laughter; surprise plot, comical characterization, felicitous wit of style he leaves, for the most part, to daintier artists. Perhaps he was a realist when he began to write stories; certainly his early characters were copied from life. But his later people are to some extent caricatures of the earlier, and the situations upon which his plots depend are often extravagantly unreal. He clearly subordinates other elements of his narrative to the prime matter of humorous effect.

Most significantly, he subordinates and, in fact, eliminates all high consideration of difficulties and mysteries of life. This oneness of purpose which causes Mr. Jacobs to write pure humor uncontaminated by any general ideas whatever, Mr. Arnold Bennett names "intellectual sluggishness." He finds it "impossible to gather from Mr. Jacobs' work that he cares for anything serious at all; impossible to differentiate his intellectual outlook from that of an average reader of the *Strand Magazine*" [see excerpt dated 1908]. It may be that in that sentence he has struck upon the secret of the humorist's great success. Jacobs, writing carefully and skillfully, a bit vulgarly now and then, but with never an attempt to solve a big problem, never more than a reticent mention of sex or gender, never the impropriety of a too realistically salty oath, produces just that kind of pure humor which suits the taste of Anglo-Saxon middle classes.

Purity alone, however, is not enough; to appeal to an extensive reading public, humor must also be simple. No doubt Mr. Jacobs realized that fact from the beginning of his yarn-spinning progress, for the fun of almost any one of his tales is simplicity itself. His plots, of which there are said to be but four, are neither complex nor conspicuous. His directness of purpose and admirable deftness of method, economy of means, and compactness of effect in description and characterization, qualities highly praised by Mr. H. T. Baker in *The Contemporary Short Story,*—all make for a pleasant and easy understanding of the incidental background for his humor. His technique of story-building, in some respects remarkable, is largely a matter of dexterity in smoothing away all, even the smallest, wrinkles or rough edges or complicated turnings of style, plot, or character-drawing which might confuse the most obtuse reader or distract his attention from the matter of principal importance, the excuse for laughter.

The building of Jacobs' stories, then, though not a simple process, is simple in result. In a somewhat different sense the humor itself for the sake of which the stories are told is extremely simple. Much of it is of the crudest and most primitive, the sort of thing which produces laughter at the painful discomfiture of any of our fellow animals who violate the inexorable laws of nature, particularly the law of gravitation. More of the Jacobs humor, since after all it is intended for the amusement of at least semi-civilized readers, consists in the depiction of comparatively harmless incongruities of speech or action. Here embarrassment takes the place of bruises; but the comedy, if less clownish, is no more merciful. Of the more complex humor which sympathizes while it laughs and is near to tears even when it is laughing hardest, there is but little in the cleverness of Mr. Jacobs. He is not intolerant of the weaknesses of his characters; neither does he attempt to condone the frailties which generate the fun. In his humor at its best there is scarcely one wink of satire or of pathos.

This simple, unmixed humor of his is widely popular with male readers in the United States as well as in Great Britain, and not without reason, for it is in quality hardly more English than American. The characters and setting are always British, to be sure, and the stories have not that ethical force and purpose which William Dean Howells has attributed to American humor. In several other respects, however, the comedy of Jacobs has an equal appeal for John Bull and Brother Jonathan.

In order to demonstrate the intermediate or intermediary position of Jacobs, it is necessary to mention the conventional items of differentiation between the humor of Great Britain and that of America. An English humorist, Mr. P. G. Wodehouse, declares that the difference is the difference between a puppy with a kind master and a puppy with a master who bullies it. The lucky dog is the American, of course. In general, it is common to assert that American humor is less restrained and formal than that of the Mother Country. But the elements of distinction may be stated more definitely. Professor Leacock identifies three conspicuous characteristics of American humor: the assumption of simplicity; freedom from convention, amounting sometimes to positive coarseness; and exaggeration. On the other hand, the principal characteristics of comic literature in latter-day England might be classified as follows: subtleties of wit for humorous effect; assumption of superior cleverness; extreme conventionality with especial deference to class-distinctions. Familiarity with the qualities of American humor may be taken for granted, but those of English humor as here enumerated require perhaps a few words of explanation. First, the typical English humorist has in the past presumed that he will be too witty for his readers and therefore has taken pains to explain his jokes. Secondly, he has found it desirable to confine himself to certain well defined and commonly accepted subjects for humorous comment. The truly British joke must be as stiffly dignified as a member of Parliament. Likewise it must never touch upon any matter which "the young person" might not discuss with another young person in the presence of a dowager duchess.

The typically American quality of over-statement is absent from the humorous stories of Jacobs, though there is something like it in the grotesquely absurd situations in which he places some of his characters. Possibly there is a Yankee touch in this paragraph from *Mixed Relations:*

> The mate grunted, and walking away, relieved his mind by putting his head in at the galley and bidding the cook hold up each separate utensil for his inspection. A hole in the frying pan the cook modestly attributed to elbow-grease.

In general, however, the true Columbian exaggeration is quite beyond Mr. Jacobs. But in other respects he is not a typically English humorist. Notably, he does not habitually explain his jokes. He allows his readers to take them or leave them. Though he often depends on cruder means of provoking laughter, he is not without wit, but he does not feel that he must annotate his cleverness for the benefit of witless readers. Such bright bits as the following he allows to shift for themselves:

> The brig sought her old berth at Buller's Wharf. It was occupied by a deaf sailing-barge, which, moved at last by self-interest, not unconnected with its paint, took up a less desirable position and consoled itself with adjectives.

> Another chap I knew, after waiting years and years for 'is rich aunt to die, was hung because she committed suicide.

With regard to the most important distinction between American and English humor on the basis of their relative adherence to conventionality, Jacobs is in a mean or medium place. He is sufficiently conventional to refrain from realism in the matter of sailor-language and to preserve a respectable reticence with regard to the unpleasant details of seasickness and utter drunkenness. He follows Dickens, the master humorist of England, in his choice of comic characters from the lower classes; and here he is in the true classical tradition. But upon occasion he treats the upper middle class and even the nobility with no

great respect, making them as weakly human as the rest. Much of his humor is of the crudest kind known to organized society. Two samples will prove this assertion:

> Her first husband had a wart on his left ear and a scar on his forehead where a friend of his kicked him one day.

> Mrs. Pearce came in with a pair of Alf's socks that he'd been untidy enough to leave in the middle of the floor instead of kicking them under the bed.

Not only does he make jokes which are primitively coarse. Some of his most humorous stories are in very plot and conception vulgar. One of the most laughable of the famous Nightwatchman's yarns, for example, is of his difficulties with a half-clad Zulu woman who followed him home because she was infatuated with his nephew. Even the most delicate of his funny stories has a certain lowness about it which no doubt makes it unfit for the refined eyes of the nobility and gentry and which as indubitably contributes to the eagerness with which the tales of W. W. Jacobs are read through even the most highly cultured *pince nez* and *lorgnette* on our side of the Ocean sea.

Even staid pedagogues who pose as illustrious understanders and admirers of witty subtleties read these tales and laugh loudly. Yet the fact remains that there is nothing very profound or deeply thoughtful about the humor of W. W. Jacobs. It is easy to comprehend and involves nothing to strain the weakest of adult intellects. As mental food it is much like New Orleans molasses, good in small quantities, not highly nutritious, wholesome, but not refined. And it is sufficiently different from typical English humor to be capable of being laughed at by democratic Americans. (pp. 246-51)

> *Robert C. Whitford, "The Humor of W. W. Jacobs,"*
> in South Atlantic Quarterly, *Vol. XVIII, No. 3, July,*
> *1919, pp. 246-51.*

J. B. PRIESTLEY (essay date 1923)

[*A highly prolific English man of letters, Priestley is the author of numerous popular novels that depict the world of everyday, middle-class England. In this respect, Priestley has often been likened to Charles Dickens, a critical comparison that he dislikes. His most notable critical work is* Literature and Western Man *(1960), a survey of Western literature from the invention of movable type through the mid-twentieth century. In the following excerpt from an essay published in the* London Mercury *in November 1923, Priestley disparages the criteria upon which adverse criticism of Jacobs was based and defends Jacobs's position as an artist.*]

If Mr. W. W. Jacobs' stories had been concerned with absinthe and prostitution instead of beer and matrimony; if they had first appeared in the *Pale Review* instead of the *Strand Magazine,* and had been afterwards brought out in small private editions instead of such-and-such a sevenpenny or shilling series; if, in short, they had succeeded in depressing a handful instead of amusing a multitude of readers, then the very persons who never mention Mr. Jacobs would long ago have called him a great artist. Delicate appreciations of his art would have made their appearance in our English literary journals, and superior persons in America, following their usual custom, would have produced thesis after thesis analysing his technique. Actually, Mr. Jacobs is not, of course, a great artist, but, nevertheless, he is an artist, and now that he has entertained us for so long, there is perhaps no danger in calling him one. No doubt most capable readers have long since recognized this fact, but they do not seem to have thought it a subject worth discussion, and in all probability simply because Mr. Jacobs happens to be very popular. Literary conditions are becoming so topsy-turvy that popularity is almost a short cut to critical oblivion: it is as if the critics and the railway-bookstall clerks had agreed to divide contemporary literature between them and not encroach upon each other's territory. Of this popularity there can be no question; it began with the publication of his first book, nearly thirty years ago, and it is not yet at an end. If, as Coleridge (who would modify his statement if he lived to-day) once remarked, an author can be said to have achieved fame when his books are to be found in obscure country inns, then Mr. Jacobs is indeed famous. We have found him in the remotest little inns and have blessed the kindly or forgetful traveller that left him there; we have pounced upon him in the bookshelves of spare bedrooms here, there, and everywhere; the night-watches have often found us listening to the night-watchman; Ginger Dick, Peter Russet, and old Sam Small have gone with us and "fleeted the time" on the longest railway journeys; and we have sneaked into the company of the old man at the "Cauliflower," and Bob Pretty and the rest, many a time when our reputations, bank-balances, and families demanded that we should be otherwise engaged. For my own part, I am ready to confess that I could not name more than one-third of our author's volumes and could not say which story is in which volume, and yet I must have read most of his stories over and over again at odd times, and am quite ready to read them all over again. Mr. Jacobs has no message for the age; he has not imagined any Utopias, nor even invented a new religion; he has not helped to solve any of our more urgent problems, except that of obtaining liquid refreshment at a minimum of cost; no transatlantic critic has yet written an essay on the "Something-ism of Jacobs," comparing him with Strindberg and Wedekind; and yet he need not despair. He has the satisfaction of knowing that he has only to leave one of his volumes in the same room with any normal English-speaking person, and that person, opening the book and coming across some such beginning as this:

> "Strength and good-nature"—said the night-watchman, musingly, as he felt his biceps—"strength and good-nature always go together. Sometimes you find a strong man who is not good-natured; but then, as everybody he comes in contact with is, it comes to the same thing.

> "The strongest and kindest-'earted man I ever come across was a man o' the name of Bill Burton, a shipmate of Ginger Dick's. For that matter 'e was a shipmate o' Peter Russet's and old Sam Small's too. . . ."

will be compelled to settle himself (and perhaps herself) down, neglect his business, and read and enjoy to the end. And at the end, such a reader, hurrying to take up the threads of business again, will not find the world a worse place than it appeared to him when he began; his wits will have been sharpened, and he will have been mellowed and heartened by laughter. Certainly, Mr. Jacobs, perched though he is on the dubious heights of popularity, need not despair.

The few little notices of Mr. Jacobs one has seen here and there have always pointed out that his youth was spent in the neighbourhood of the London docks, and the writers would seem to imagine that by hanging about the waterside and keep-

ing his ears open, a man can almost automatically become the author of *Many Cargoes* and *Odd Craft*. Clearly this will not do. Mr. Jacobs' knowledge of sailors and the seafaring life in general has obviously played its part in his authorship, but it does not explain him. Mr. Conrad and Mr. H. M. Tomlinson, I take it, know a great deal about the sea and the docks, but they are no more capable of writing, say, *The Skipper's Wooing* than Mr. Jacobs is of writing *Nostromo* or *London River*. One writer [C. Lewis Hind (see Additional Bibliography)], talking about the way in which he used to meet our author occasionally at literary gatherings in the late 'nineties, remarks: "Obviously the men and women that he met on these occasions were of little use to him in his stories. Not one of us understood the difference between a barque and a schooner; we knew something about Guy de Maupassant and Flaubert, but nothing about marline-spikes or capstans. Where W. W. Jacobs got his intricate nautical knowledge from I know not. He never paraded it: he never said 'Avast there' or 'Shiver my timbers'" . . . But Mr. Jacobs is not a Clark Russell with a little comedy added, and it is quite possible that in order to appreciate him to the full it is more important to know something about Maupassant than it is to know something about a marline-spike. Actually, only about one-half of his stories deal with the adventures of sailormen, and even then the adventures usually take place ashore; while the rest have nothing whatever to do with the sea, though for the most part they find their characters in classes not far removed from that of the common sailor. Among this latter group is that series, spreading from volume to volume, which is supposed to be told to successive travellers by the old man (that adept at obtaining drink and tobacco at other people's expense without any apparent loss of dignity) at the "Cauliflower Inn" at Claybury, that series which might be called the epic of Bob Pretty, most ingenious of village rascals. I would not willingly alienate any fellow-enthusiast's sympathies at the outset by a too rash assertion of my own preferences; but I am not sure that these Bob Pretty stories are not among the very best things that Mr. Jacobs has done. Who could forget, having once read, that episode of the Prize Hamper, when the great Bob not only succeeded in winning the hamper, but also managed to obtain its value in money as well from the unsuccessful competitors; or that of the poaching, when the keepers rescued nothing more than a sack of cabbages from the middle of a very cold and muddy pond; or that encounter between Bob and the unfortunate conjurer who tried to do the famous watch trick?

These frequent references to the sea are important because they tend to show that Mr. Jacobs, when he has been approached at all by criticism, has been approached from the wrong direction. He has actually been mistaken for a realist. Such writers probably imagine that captains of small coasting vessels, when they come ashore, are immediately plunged into the most astonishing and farcical intrigues involving an imaginary rich uncle from New Zealand and what not; that a pint or two of ale given to any lighterman or bargee will result in funny tales of plot and counterplot that only need a touch here and there to make them into the most delicious short stories. But not only is Mr. Jacobs not a reporter, but an artist; he is also, in his own way, a most finished, conscientious and delicate artist. He is himself such a master of craft that if you take from him nearly everything that usually goes with his work, that is, his humour, his dexterity in certain kinds of comic dialogue and narrative, his knowledge of the habits and the point of view of certain classes, if you take away all this, he will yet produce an excellent short story of quite a different kind. He has not a sufficiently poetic mind, not enough acquaintance with those borderland states of the human spirit, to write a horror story of the highest class, but, nevertheless, in **"The Monkey's Paw,"** and some other similar things, he has done very well. This incomplete but sufficiently astonishing success in work so far removed from that which we usually associate with his name must be largely set down to the credit of his technique; it is one proof of his mastery of form. And it is this, along with his very fine sense of humour, that has made him the excellent short-story writer he is, so that any reference to particularly favourable opportunities for observing and reporting will not explain him. It is worth recollecting that at the time Mr. Jacobs began writing definitely localized fiction was becoming the fashion; every new novelist had to have his own particular district; London was being cut and carved and slices of it were being served out to ambitious young writers. Mr. Zangwill was given the Jewish quarters, Mr. Morrison took the East End, Mr. Pett Ridge claimed the suburbs, and so on; thus it fell out that Mr. Jacobs, having written a few stories of seafaring men, was presented with Wapping, Rotherhithe, and the docks. This part of the world, with the addition of a few sleepy little coast towns, his Sunwich Ports, and the village of Claybury, served its purpose as a kind of map reference to the setting of his stories; but actually, like most original writers, he was soon busily engaged creating a world of his own.

Comedy demands a world of its own. The merest hint of war, famine, or pestilence would shatter, say, a story by Jane Austen, and so she took care to create a world in which the visit of somebody's niece or the engagement of the neighbouring vicar is an event of the highest importance. Mr. Jacobs presents us with a world just as small, bright, and artificial as that of Jane Austen. Knowing exactly what he wanted to do, the kind of effect he wanted to make, he took away and refashioned the slender stock of material necessary for his setting, and boldly left out all the rest, all the darker crimes, the devastating passions, the bleak tragedies that are found everywhere in this world and that would have shattered his tiny comedies into minute fragments. To leave out so much in this fashion may seem easy, but actually it is very difficult, demanding, as artificial comedy always does, a nice taste and great tact on the part of the artist. As an example of Mr. Jacobs' delicate discrimination we need only take his treatment of that mainspring of action in life and literature, love. Love, which spins the plot here in many of these stories just as it does elsewhere, is not a passion at all with Mr. Jacobs, but merely a desire for (or sense of) possession, leading to comic rivalries during courtship and comic jealousies after marriage; the merest glimmer of sentiment is sufficient; and he usually contrives to end his little comedies of courtship in some such fashion as this:

> He turned after a short distance for a last look at the house, and, with a sudden sense of elation, saw that she was standing on the step. He hesitated, and then walked slowly back.
>
> "Yes?" said Prudence.
>
> "I should like to tell your mother that I am sorry," he said in a low voice.
>
> "It is getting late," said the girl softly; "but, if you really wish to tell her, Mrs. Porter will not be here to-morrow night."

which tells us that all is well with the young couple. If we are sentimentally inclined, we may allow our imaginations to brood over them, but Mr. Jacobs has retired from the stage for the little comedy is ended. All this is as it should be; a single

sentence by Mr. D. H. Lawrence would be a monster in such surroundings and would ruin everything; Mr. Jacobs contrives with exquisite skill. It is worth remarking, however, that his treatment of love, like his treatment of other important matters, though it is primarily dictated by his limited form of art, does follow in its details the kind of life that is supposed to be treated in these stories. In other words, the comic rivalries and jealousies we get here are the kind of comic rivalries and jealousies we should expect to discover among sailors and their people about the docks. Realism does not break in, but it is allowed to enter, art having posted its guards and sentries all over the place. This is true of the general setting, and it is true of the action and the dialogue as well; they all represent a useful working compromise between realism, the representation of things as they ordinarily appear, and a deliberate, highly self-conscious art, anxious only to achieve certain effects that things as they are never seem to bring off neatly; but it is a compromise like those that married couples are often said to arrive at, one in which the lady, art, has most of her own way.

This world of Mr. Jacobs, which is not unlike a tiny part of the Dickens world all cleaned up, painted, and burnished, is a very pleasant one indeed, so pleasant as a background to our imagination that some of the pleasure we get from these stories is nothing more nor less than the poetical pleasure we always get from what is called "atmosphere." It is a little world from which all the darker shades have been banished, a world filled with sleepy little ports, tiny coasting vessels, trim cottages that usually have a rose-garden or "a small, brick-paved yard, in which trim myrtles and flowering plants stand about in freshly ochred pots" and perhaps "neatly grained shutters and white steps and polished brass knockers," happy little taverns ("an old-world bar, with its loud-ticking clock, its Windsor chairs, and its cracked jug full of roses"), pretty, saucy girls with a string of admirers, comic policemen, love-lorn intriguing third mates, henpecked sea-captains, and philosophical night-watchmen. Here, in this bright limited world, with all its properties ready to be set on the stage in a few seconds, at once false and true, and certainly very English, is a delightful setting for comedy. Into this setting Mr. Jacobs projects what we may call farces, for we must now pass from setting to plot, and Mr. Jacobs' plots, the bare action of his little stories, for the most part belong to the realm of stage farce. There is an ingenious little plan to deceive some one or other, a great many lies are told, and then in the end, as a rule, the biter himself is bitten. Very often the plan involves an imaginary wealthy uncle or a mythical long-lost son, or, if not these, then either a legacy, a fortune-teller, a pretended deed of heroism, or a comic feud with the police. And nearly always these little plots of his are fantastic, artificial, and deliberately, shall we say, standardized, so that once we are in the Jacobs world we know exactly what kind of queer action people will take. A summary of one or two of the stories will do more to show the character of the action than pages of explanation. Thus, an impudent second officer, walking ashore, spies a very pretty girl, and learns that she and her mother, a widow, live alone, and also that she had a brother who went to sea many years before and never returned. Having learned this and a few other particulars, the young man boldly marches up to the door and announces himself as the long-lost brother and son. His impudence carries him through at first, but he is asked to call again, and when he does so, a huge woman, the charwoman of the house, promptly rushes in and claims him as her long-lost husband. The women have won the day. . . . Again, there is the strong man whom the night-watchman was on the point of introducing to us above; he who was amazingly powerful, but very sociable and good-humoured. Unfortunately, when he went out with Ginger Dick and the rest, he would never touch beer, which he said had a bad effect upon him, but only such slops as lemonade. Finally, however, his friends persuaded him to drink as they did, and the unhappy sequel was that he proved to be very nasty indeed in liquor, giving them all a good hiding and creating an uproar wherever he went. The following day, Ginger Dick and the other, not relishing his companionship, tell him that a certain landlord he encountered the night before is dying from the effect of his boisterous social methods. This ruse, however, only makes a desperate man of him, and he proceeds to further his chances of escaping by tying up his friends one by one as they come into the room, and going off with their money. This is farce worked out like neat little problems in algebra.

But the plot, that is, the main lines of the action, the central situation, is not the story. If it were, we should have grown tired of Mr. Jacobs years ago. His humour seems to demand plots of this kind, but they are only the beginning. Any second or third-rate humorist could invent such situations, which are the stock-in-trade of the confirmed writer of farces and the terror of the playgoer; and if they are to be transformed into something rich, if not strange, a Jacobs is necessary. These things are artificial, as artificial as Restoration Comedy; but now there enters Mr. Jacobs, the comic realist, who pours into these common, though quaint little vessels, his own rich bubbling brew, an essence distilled from Wapping and Rotherhithe, though we may admit that it is a sublimated Wapping, a glorified Rotherhithe. The result is something that is not mere farce on the one hand, nor the mere realistic humorous "sketch" on the other, but an art that makes use of both and transcends them, a kind of midsummer night-watchman's dream. (pp. 103-14)

J. B. Priestley, "Mr. W. W. Jacobs," in his Figures in Modern Literature, *1924. Reprint by Books for Libraries Press, 1970; distributed by Arno Press, Inc., pp. 103-23.*

ALFRED C. WARD (essay date 1924)

[*In the following excerpt, Ward considers Jacobs's critical standing among his contemporaries and discusses the elements of plot, characterization, dialogue, description, and style in his fiction.*]

William Wymark Jacobs has been manifoldly blessed as a writer—not least because the arbiters of fame have never taken him seriously. His fellow-authors admire him unstintingly, as well they might, for perhaps none among them has found it possible to carry so much cargo in so small a vessel. Jacobs's little craft has done the voyage from St. Katherine's Docks to Ipswich and thereabouts times without number, and he has been quite happy as its unpretentious master. No doubt if he had cared to shout from the masthead he could have founded a bargee school in literature, and had his disciples and imitators. But as it is, he has been content to do a small thing and to do it well. The probability is that his name will not long survive his own physical surcease; that there will be little attempt to claim a place for him among the immortals: yet it is worth noting that he has been compared with Aristophanes, the greatest of Greek comic writers—even as George Eliot was compared with Sophocles and Stephen Phillips with Shakespeare! There is no need to pursue the comparison as between Jacobs and the author of the *Frogs,* although a good many modest people might prefer to have written W. W. Jacobs's stories.

Among the contemporary creative writers who have taken notice in print of the author of *Many Cargoes* is Arnold Bennett [see excerpt dated 1908], who, after registering cordial appreciation of Jacobs's steadfast talent, proceeds to quarrel with him because he "discloses no signs of intellectual curiosity." "Mr. Jacobs," we read, "seems to live apart from the movement of his age. Nothing, except the particular type of humanity and environment in which he specializes, seems to interest him. There is no hint of a general idea in his work." To take Arnold Bennett's last point first, surely there is *more* than "a hint" of a general idea in W. W. Jacobs's stories: an implicit statement, through and through, of the general idea that to provoke hearty laughter among a multitude of readers is sometimes as serviceable as to stimulate intellectual curiosity. Laughter can pall upon those who laugh continuously, perhaps; though as to that few can speak without reserve, because the gods seldom permit men to laugh without limit; but at least it can be averred that few things pall so swiftly as unmitigated intellectual curiosity. Those who concede Arnold Bennett's criticism that it is "impossible to gather from W. W. Jacobs's work that he cares for anything serious at all," might desire to add enviously: "Happy Mr. Jacobs!"

Americans have the advantage of Englishmen in being able to approach Jacobs's stories from the outside. Probably, however, there is no need to go so far as America for that experience; perhaps Scotland would be far enough—or even Manchester. Those who read *Many Cargoes* from the cockney standpoint, are unable to know to what degree its humour is a kind of private conspiracy among those who know the cockney lingo and understand what passes for humour among those who are familiar with the street gamin.

W. W. Jacobs operates in a strictly limited field of operations: the Thames waterside—Wapping and Rotherhithe. Upon occasion he steps a little distance outside, but only for a weekend, as it were; and, usually, London's riverside is only the starting-place, since his characters almost invariably embark forthwith upon some short coastal voyage on a barge or a small schooner. Yet still we remain in the company of Londoners, who mainly constitute the scanty crews of these vessels. Where Jacobs differs from other "regional" writers is in his—shall it be called laziness? or living apart from "the movement of his age"? He makes no attempt whatever to universalize his characters. Dan and Harry and Sam and the boy are like no one else than Dan and Harry and Sam and the boy. Perhaps they exist nowhere at all outside Jacobs's stories; or, at any rate, if they *are* to be met in the flesh, it is only on Thames-side or on the little ships that ply therefrom. They represent the apotheosis of the cockney: ready of tongue, resourceful of vocabulary, strong in repartee, ever prepared to turn a penny (honestly if need be) and fertile in practical jokes. They are simple souls; and in at least one respect they resemble their author—they are utterly and sublimely devoid of intellectual curiosity!

A painstaking and ingenious professor has gone to the trouble of setting down the thirty-six (or is it thirty-seven?) plots which exhaust all the possibilities open to the fiction writer. There are no new plots; no one can invent a new plot, it is said; writers can harp only upon the strings which have already been plucked a hundred thousand times. For many, this may be a most galling limitation; for Jacobs, however, it represents a range of freedom which is far beyond his most ambitious longings. Without pretending to statistical exactness, the estimate may be ventured that all Jacobs's many stories would fall well within the compass of half a dozen plot-situations. And in regard to very many of his stories, he might aptly be called a virtuoso upon a one-string fiddle.

There is an activity familiar to cockneys as "besting": it consists in striking an unfair bargain with a neighbour or stranger, or in taking what is known (also idiomatically) as "a mean advantage." In a considerable measure W. W. Jacobs's stories are studies in the art of "besting," and an example of the art is to be found in the story called **"In Borrowed Plumes."** Captain Bross, skipper of the *Sarah Jane,* had already been warned twice by the owners for not being aboard at the time the vessel was due to sail. They threatened that a third defection would lose him his berth. That third time came, and the mate of the *Sarah Jane,* anxious to get the skipper's job, was keen to start at the very moment appointed. Shortly before sailing-time, the ship's boy, who was also the skipper's nephew, received a note to say that his uncle had lost all his clothes. Tommy was implored to take a suit to the stated address, but he could find nothing save a few garments left aboard by his aunt. The captain was consequently compelled to rush back to the *Sarah Jane* in female attire, and the ensuing voyage became a battle of wits between the Captain and the mate: the one frantically endeavouring to borrow or make some clothes; the other maintaining a careful guard over the crew's wardrobe, after he had caused every needle to be thrown overboard.

The disturbing fact is evident, then, that Jacobs does not show human nature in its nobler or more amiable moods; he does not purvey moral uplift; if one of his characters can do a bad turn to another he will; and very few of his people need to be warned that hell is paved with good intentions—of such intentions they are mostly innocent. Nevertheless, it is improbable that even the most ingenious first offender would inform even the most ingenuous magistrate that he had been seduced from the paths of rectitude by reading W. W. Jacobs! These night-watchmen and longshoremen and bargees take little account of fine distinctions between *mine* and *thine,* but their roguery is of the venial kind familiar to all who have experienced the mutual process of "finding" and "losing" in army life. Withal, the atmosphere of Jacobs's stories is clean and sunny, and he is ever distant from risky situations.

In a rough-and-ready division, it may be said that literary criticism directs attention to five elements in prose fiction: (1) Plot; (2) Characterization; (3) Dialogue; (4) Description; (5) Style.

Reviewing W. W. Jacobs's stories, it is immediately evident that their interest is not evenly distributed under these heads. The careful husbanding of plot-material has already been remarked; but notwithstanding this, there remains the surprising fact that in the plots lies a considerable part of the attraction exercised by *Many Cargoes* and its companion volumes. Experience of W. W. Jacobs's methods speedily assures the reader that nothing of an extraordinarily exciting character is at all likely to happen; yet this in no way diminishes attention, inasmuch as the author has the faculty of sustaining interest throughout his story. In a word, the plot is diffused rather than drawn up to a climax; nearly every paragraph has its inherent story-interest, so that the reader is not fobbed-off with incidental matter which he feels compelled to endure in order not to miss something essential in the plot. There is climax of a kind in most of Jacobs's stories, but the culminating point does not tower above the body of the narrative. It is conceivable that an irresistibly curious reader might wish to turn to the last page, illegitimately, in order to see what happens; but he does

so with the assurance that it will be fully worth while afterwards to double back in order to savour the characteristic quality of the author's sentences—a quality which is independent of and additional to any stylistic merit.

This characteristic quality could be illustrated almost at random in any story; here, an excerpt from **"The Cook of the 'Gannet'"** will serve. Ships' cooks and their tantrums are a favourite theme with Jacobs; and this particular cook was a widow, Mrs. Blossom, who had been shipped aboard the *Gannet* by her cousin's husband, the skipper, who (as he himself expressed it) was "trying a new experiment." The lady became a mutineer almost as soon as the voyage began, defied the officers and inveigled the crew:

> The only thing which ventured to interfere with her was a stiff Atlantic roll, which they encountered upon rounding the Land's End.
>
> The first intimation Mrs. Blossom had of it was the falling of small utensils in the galley. After she had picked them up and replaced them several times, she went out to investigate, and discovered that the schooner was dipping her bows to big green waves, and rolling, with much straining and creaking, from side to side. A fine spray, which broke over the bows and flew over the vessel, drove her back into the galley, which had suddenly developed an unaccountable stuffiness; but though the crew to a man advised her to lie down and have a cup of tea, she repelled them with scorn, and with pale face and compressed lips stuck to her post.

The Night-Watchman.

That is a passage which might be withdrawn completely from the narrative without diminishing the intrinsic interest of the story. Yet it is not superfluous: it does add something material, helping to complete the picture; and in a suitably limited way it has its own independent interest. When the source of that interest is sought, a process of elimination indicates that the interest is not mainly attached to characterization, nor to description, nor to prose style, and certainly not to dialogue. The passage is, therefore, related to the plot (or as it might more explicitly be termed, the *situation*); it is a something added which demonstrates the author's fertility and resource within the bounds which he sets himself. (pp. 227-34)

[The] second point in the critical sequence [is] characterization. If the term characterization suggests serious psychological examination, or any endeavour to portray solemn consistency in behaviour, then Jacobs recks naught of such. But if to have created a human type which is inseparably associated with an author's name is to have achieved success in characterization, then W. W. Jacobs is thus distinguished. He is one of the very few writers who have been well served by an artist illustrator, for in Will Owen he found a coadjutor who has rendered as good service to him as Phiz rendered to Dickens. But is any illustrator moved to create memorable figures on the visual plane, unless the author has first powerfully created memorable figures on the imaginative plane? Perhaps Ginger Dick and Peter Russet and old Sam Small might interchange names without the most assiduous reader's recognizing any strangeness in the characters so designated; because it is not so much by their individual features and qualities that they are to be recognized, as by the tricks they play upon one another. The fame of the night-watchman has spread far and wide; but is he always the same night-watchman, or does the author apply the name indifferently to any one of a dozen night-watchmen? And do we keep him in remembrance by reason of some specially striking quality with which he is endowed by his creator, or is it only because one of his profession had not previously been prominent in fiction? He is W. W. Jacobs's substitute for the chorus which the Greeks found indispensable: like that chorus, the night-watchman fills the rôle of ideal spectator, but he doubles it with the rôle of ideal raconteur—an office appropriated to the messenger in Greek drama. We know very little about the night-watchman; little more than that he had an inexhaustible stock of yarns, that he was accustomed to stow huge pieces of tobacco in his cheek, and that he frequently had a far-away look! However much his ready tongue may be admired, it is difficult to suppress a very slight inclination to doubt his strict veracity; as, for instance, when he tells the story (in **"The Rival Beauties"**) of the sea-serpent which followed a ship for days on end, like a hungry kitten! But sea-serpent or no sea-serpent, nothing but homage and gratitude is adequate return to the night-watchman for recording the name of that ship—the *George Washington!* . . . Most likely, W. W. Jacobs has full confidence and implicit faith in his night-watchman, but he does not extend equal credence to all informants. At the beginning of **"An Elaborate Elopement"** he writes:

> I have always had a slight suspicion that the following narrative is not quite true. It was related to me by an old seaman who, among other incidents of a somewhat adventurous career, claimed to have received Napoleon's sword at the battle of Trafalgar, and a wound in the back at Waterloo.

A discipline which careful writers impose upon their pens is most stern economy in the employment of qualifying adjectives and adverbs; but the effect which can be produced for purposes of humour by judicious understatement is shown by the use of the words *slight* and *somewhat* in the foregoing passage. Note, also, that wound "in the back!"

The dialogue in Jacobs's books is their great merit. He is unexcelled in the reproduction of cockney speech; not that he does actually reproduce it—no writer could do that without intolerable prolixity and muddled repetition. He is, however, one of the few writers who are able to suggest faithful reproduction by selecting a few salient features and carefully avoiding exaggeration. Moreover, he does preserve that quite unappreciated mordant wit and ironical humour which remain with the one-time London street-arab throughout life. While fuddled Captain Bing is being rowed out to the *Smiling Jane*, he addresses the boatman severely in these words:

> "When I was a young man, I'd ha' pulled this boat across and back afore now."
>
> "When you was a young man," said the man at the oars, who had a local reputation as a wit, "there wasn't no boats; they was all Noah's arks then."

Anyone who has heard a cockney humorist in his persevering moods, will recognize the fitness of this piece of repartee in this particular situation; and even in those few words from the boatman, the authentic voice of the cockney is heard, albeit his "native wood-notes wild" are necessarily denuded of the chromatic colouring which no true cockney would deny himself.

As in his dialogue, so in his descriptions, Jacobs is a veritable Londoner. While the barge *Sir Edmund Lyons* runs under sail down the Thames estuary on a beautiful morning:

> The miniature river-waves broke against the blunt bows of the barge, and passed by her sides rippling musically. Over the flat Essex marshes a white mist was slowly dispersing before the rays of the sun, and the trees on the Kentish hills were black and drenched with moisture.

A pleasant morning scene, which your true cockney would see with his eye, but hardly take to his heart; that organ would be stimulating another physical sense—as W. W. Jacobs knows well, for he goes on at once to add:

> A little later, smoke issued from the tiny cowl over the fo'c'sle and rolled in a little pungent cloud to the Kentish shore. Then a delicious odour of frying steak rose from below, and fell like healing balm upon the susceptible nostrils of the skipper as he stood at the helm.

Enough has been said as to Jacobs's plot-material, characterization, dialogue, and description to suggest that these serve as a media for humour which rarely flags. Jacobs has, quite naturally, sown wild oats of the kind for which all humorists have a powerful affection—the terrible and uncanny. **"The Monkey's Paw"** is an effort in this kind, and a successful effort; but although the most horrible and uncanny fate that can befall any writer is, probably, to be compelled to be funny in season and out, W. W. Jacobs performs his assigned task with an air of such hearty enjoyment that there is surely little occasion for regret if his few "shockers" are regarded with a cold and unfraternal eye. (pp. 235-39)

Alfred C. Ward, "W. W. Jacobs: 'Many Cargoes'," in his Aspects of the Modern Short Story: English and American, University of London Press, Ltd., 1924, pp. 227-39.

A. ST. JOHN ADCOCK (essay date 1928)

[An English author of numerous works, many of which concern the city of London, Adcock served as editor of the London Bookman from 1923 until his death in 1930. In the following excerpt, Adcock discusses the varied qualities of humor, horror, and sentiment in Jacobs's works, praising his stylistic control and characterizations.]

In addition to a prevailing sense of humour, [Jacobs] has a subtle and potent sense of the weird, the gruesome, the terrible, and a sense of sentiment and pathos, which he employs sparingly and with a touch so light and apparently casual that a careless reader may miss the delicacy of his skill even while he is moved by the effects of it. Mostly his sentiment and humour are so artfully blended that the one is almost indistinguishable from the other. This is very neatly and charmingly done in the closing scene of "The Skipper's Wooing"; and again as neatly and as charmingly in "At Sunwich Port", where young Hardy, having put himself to infinite trouble in the service of the Nugent family in order to ingratiate himself with his irascible enemy, Captain Nugent, has at last won the freedom of the premises and is making love to Kate in the garden with a dogged determination that breaks down all her coquettishness:

> "If you would do anything to please me," she said at length, in a low voice and without turning her head, "would you promise never to see me or speak to me again, if I asked you?"

> "No," said Hardy promptly.

Miss Nugent sat silent again. She knew that a good woman should be sorry for a man in such extremity, and should endeavour to spare his feelings by softening her refusal as much as possible, little as he might deserve such consideration. But man is impatient and jumps to conclusions. Before she was half way through the first sentence he leaned forward and took her hand.

> "Oh, good-bye," she said, turning to him with a pleasant smile.

> "I'm not going," said Hardy quietly. "I am never going," he added, as he took her other hand.

(pp. 152-54)

Always [Jacobs] writes with restraint, and with a luminous economy of words, and with a genius for suggesting twice as much as he tells; nowhere is his own personality obtruded in humorous comments or facetious asides. His style is austere in its simplicity; the humour of his stories is not more in their plots than in their characters, their dialogue, and in the quietly droll, tersely, and evasively humorous turns of phrase in which the action is unfolded and the psychology of his men and women revealed. Many of the stories dispense with the love interest altogether; when they do not, the heroine is as often as not a mature widow set upon marrying again, or a young girl who is hoydenish, very pretty, very self-possessed and smart at repartee; there is a family likeness, too, between the pert, irrepressible boys in Jacobs' diverting collection, but his

elder women and old and young men are amazingly varied in character, despite the narrow range of the world to which he restricts himself. The Night Watchman is the greatest of his humorous creations, as Falstaff is Shakespeare's. Though the majority of his tales are compact of unalloyed humour, there are two or three, notably "The Monkey's Paw" and "The Brown Man's Servant", which show him as a master of eerie mystery and horror, who challenges comparison with Poe; the effect of "The Brown Man's Servant" is heightened by a wry humour which Poe had not, and the uncanny grimness of "The Monkey's Paw" by a pathos that is wrought to a pitch of almost painful intensity when the knock comes on the door at night and the heart-broken mother, after struggling desperately with the bolts, flings the door open and there is nothing there. This, like "Beauty and the Barge" and other of his stories, has been as successful on the stage as in Jacobs' books; it is the most perfect thing artistically that he has done, and so far from agreeing that "he is only wearisome when he attempts to write in other veins than the humorous," I have never ceased to wonder why he has not given us more stories in this kind, since he is as fine and as effective an artist in writing them as in writing those joyous comedies and farces that made him rich at first and keep him so. It is currently preached as a literary dogma that artistic work cannot be popular, and popular work cannot be artistic, but Jacobs has opened a door to heresy, for his books are both. (pp. 155-57)

A. St. John Adcock, "William Wymark Jacobs," in his The Glory That Was Grub Street: Impressions of Contemporary Authors, The Musson Book Company Limited, 1928, pp. 147-57.

HENRY REED (essay date 1947)

[An English poet, translator, dramatist, and critic, Reed earned acclaim with his first volume of poetry, A Map of Verona (1946), which reflects his experiences as a conscript in World War II and includes the much-anthologized poem "Naming of Parts." Subsequently he devoted himself to writing both serious and satirical plays for BBC radio. In the following excerpt from his introduction to Dialstone Lane, Reed discusses the distinguishing traits of Jacobs's writing and places Dialstone Lane among the best and most characteristic of Jacobs's novels.]

Years ago, I discovered in an old magazine a symposium of brief articles by well-known story-writers called 'How I Write.' This author and that explained his enormous gestations, the questions and difficulties that beset him, the nature and the presumed origin of his inspiration. The first idea was always something 'given'—by God, one gathered—and, exhaustingly, the writer had to labour at interpreting it. The last and shortest statement on the subject came from W. W. Jacobs. 'I first of all,' he said, 'assemble a few sheets of paper, a bottle of ink, some pens, and a blotting-pad.' He added that he would stare at this 'unresponsive material' for some time, and then, if nothing further happened, he would wearily rack his brains until he had managed to squeeze a story out of them. This was his usual method; occasionally, however, a story would suddenly step forward and seem to write itself. 'I then re-write it,' he concluded.

Hence, I think, the precision and economy and, within its limits, the perfection of his art. There is no maundering, no display, no self-indulgence; his stories are executed in a cool and practical way. A complete plot, with a reversal of fortune, a victory or a defeat in it: he is not content with less than this. His kind of story is something no longer attempted, and if he had imitators none of them have survived. Atmosphere, the characteristic of the present-day short story, he was at no pains to create; yet his name calls up at once an atmosphere wholly his own, and given off by his four or five distinct and clear-cut scenes: the sailors' lodging-houses in London; the wharves; the small neat homes of widow-women and retired sea-captains in harbour villages; the pub at Claybury. His characters and scenes do not range widely, but the variety and ingenuity of his plots are always surprising. (pp. v-vi)

Dialstone Lane is probably the best of his half-dozen long stories. The most, after all, that Jacobs could do with a novel, and yet retain his characteristic manner, was to interweave several short stories and pack them tightly and neatly inside yet another one. He does this with amazing precision and liveliness, and the shifts from one group of people to another are perfectly timed. The unostentation of his methods does something to disguise his remarkable achievement in creating fourteen characters cleanly and distinctly within the space of a short novel. He has created them all before, of course—but of what novelist can one not say that by the time he has reached his tenth book? And if you like his short stories it is delightful to be able to dwell longer with their best characters. *A Master of Craft* is a more ambitious novel than *Dialstone Lane;* it has a brilliant plot, and the inevitable widows' tea-party is of Jacobs's best. Furthermore, its light evocations of scene and its more or less serious love story are things we do not find elsewhere in Jacobs. But, like his macabre stories, they are things which his contemporaries could do equally well, and in *Dialstone Lane* there is nothing that is not Jacobs's own. In *A Master of Craft* an odd streak of realism intrudes: the fight on the road is not a pleasant one; the Wheeler family and the villainous old country couple, though accurately drawn, sophisticate the taste of the rest of the story; and Jacobs avoids such scenes in his later novels. *Dialstone Lane* preserves intact its author's special gifts: *At Sunwich Port, Salthaven* and *The Castaways* do not improve on it.

It is Jacobs at his best, and it is therefore enchantingly amusing to re-read. I have said that the characters are his stock types; but they have, so to speak, their very best clothes on. And since there are so many of them, fresh collisions are devised which produce new and larger sparks: the scenes between Selina Vickers and Captain Bowers, for example, or the astonishing introduction of Captain Brisket into the Clarks' drawing-room. The Clarks and the Scobells are, in their separate ways, lower down in conjugal disenchantment than any married couples in Jacobs before them. ("'Yes,' said Mr. Clark, in a burst of unwonted frankness, 'but it ain't quite the same thing. I've got a wife, and Mrs. Scobell has got a husband—that's the difference.'") The episode at the tea-table is a small masterpiece of dialogue; so is the later scene where the two wives lament the presumed deaths of their husbands. The Beatrice and Benedick scenes are not disproportionate to the rest. The relations between Jacobs's young men and women are always the same: they spend the whole time scoring each other off—it is the one thing in which Jacobs sometimes makes us conscious of repetition from book to book. Yet the scenes are extremely well done in themselves: the passage about the two-pound bet in chapter three is brilliant. Above all, *Dialstone Lane* shows Jacobs in complete mastery of two things which are essential if a comedy is to ripple fluently and amusingly along: he knows how to make the end of one piece of confusion slyly contain the beginnings of another; and he knows how to allot to a character a remark or an act which the reader can anticipate, and *then* how to cap it with something absolutely

Illustration by Will Owen for Dialstone Lane.

unexpected. The book has the placid mellowness of a wine which two wars have failed to disturb. (pp. vii-viii)

Henry Reed, in an introduction to Dialstone Lane *by W. W. Jacobs, Eyre & Spottiswoode, 1947, pp. v-viii.*

V. S. PRITCHETT   (essay date 1947)

[*Pritchett is a highly esteemed English novelist, short story writer, and critic. Considered one of the modern masters of the short story, he is also one of the world's most respected and well-read literary critics. Pritchett writes in the conversational tone of the familiar essay, a method by which he approaches literature from the viewpoint of a lettered but not overly scholarly reader. A twentieth-century successor to such early nineteenth-century essayist-critics as William Hazlitt and Charles Lamb, Pritchett employs much the same critical method: his own experience, judgment, and sense of literary art are emphasized, rather than a codified critical doctrine derived from a school of psychological or philosophical speculation. His criticism is often described as fair, reliable, and insightful. In the following excerpt from an essay published in the* New Statesman and Nation *on May 10, 1947, Pritchett discusses the deliberate artificiality with which Jacobs presented life.*]

Jacobs had the fortune to grasp a small, fixed world at its moment of ripeness and decline, a time always propitious to the artist. A Thames-side clerk, Jacobs knew the wharves where the small coasting ships and land-hugging barge fleets tied up on their rounds between London and the wizened, rosy little towns of the Essex estuaries. This was a fading traffic: the cement, the flour, the bricks, the road flints, were more and more being diverted to the railway; the small mills and shippers were being devoured by the larger firms; the little towns with their raucous taverns and fighting inhabitants had already quietened; and unemployable and unspeakable old men sat on the posts of the empty quays, refining upon their memories of a past, spicy in its double dealing, prone to horseplay and cheered by the marital misfortunes of others:

> "Love?" said the nightwatchman, as he watched in an abstracted fashion the efforts of a skipper to reach a brother skipper on a passing barge with a boathook. "Don't talk to me about love, because I have suffered enough through it. There ought to be teetotallers for love the same as wot there is for drink, and they ought to wear a piece of ribbon to show it, the same as teetotallers do. . . . Sailormen give way to it most; they see so little o'wimmen that they naturally have a high opinion of 'em. Wait till they become nightwatchmen, and having to be at 'ome all day, see the other side of 'em. If people only started life as nightwatchmen there wouldn't be one arf the falling in love that there is now."

To these rosy and high-tempered seaports whose lattice windows flashed with the light of the silver estuary mud, no stranger ever came, unless it was a gentleman-painter who disgusted the patriots by painting only the ruins; the yachtsmen, holidaymakers and estate agents of a later day had not yet appeared, to dissolve the nightwatchmen in free drinks and to develop in the young an even more ferocious financial cunning than their fathers had. In other words, Jacobs found a world unstained by change, its inhabitants contentedly absorbed in the eternal human problem of how to get the better of one another, a fruit mellow and ready to fall into the comic artist's hands. The coachmen of Dickens, the landowners of the Russians, the booby squires of Sheridan and Fielding had been in their time precisely at this point of ripeness. The talent of Jacobs is a small one, when he is compared with the masters, but like theirs, his types are not chosen until they are already dated; like theirs his humour is fantastic and artificial. No notions of realism or social purpose, as Mr. Henry Reed rightly says in an introduction to *Dialstone Lane* [see excerpt dated 1947], cross his mind: he writes, so to say, from the ivory fo'c'sle. He recognises that in his nightwatchmen, his decisive widows, his sailormen, he is dealing with an advanced and sophisticated culture which has become firmly barnacled on the coarse surface of common life; and that the elegance, the speed, the riposte and the intricate plotting of something like Restoration comedy, can alone do justice to his highly-developed people. Any page of his many short stories will illustrate this; indeed, only in his macabre stories, like **"The Monkey's Paw"** or, as Mr. Reed points out, in the ambitious *Master of Craft*, will one find anything like realism. I take this from *Dialstone Lane:*

> "I've got her," said Mrs. Chalk triumphantly.
>
> "Oh!" said Mr. Chalk.
>
> "She didn't want to come at first," said Mrs. Chalk. "She'd half promised to go to Mrs. Morris. Mrs. Morris had heard of her through Harris the grocer and he only knew she was out of a place by accident. He . . ."

Her words fell on deaf ears. Mr. Chalk, gazing through the window, heard, without comprehending, a long account of the capture of a housemaid which, slightly altered as to name and place, would have passed muster as an exciting contest between a skilled angler and a particularly sulky salmon.

Mrs. Chalk, noticing his inattention at last, pulled up sharply.

> "You're not listening!" she cried.
>
> "Yes, I am; go on, my dear," said Mr. Chalk.
>
> "What did I say she left her last place for, then?" demanded the lady. Mr. Chalk started. He had been conscious of his wife's voice and that was all. "You said you were not surprised at her leaving," he replied slowly, "the only wonder to you was that a decent girl should have stayed there so long."

Mrs. Chalk started and bit her lip. "Yes," she said slowly. "Go on. Anything else?"

> "You said the house wanted cleaning from top to bottom," said the painstaking Mr. Chalk.
>
> "Go on," said his wife in a smothered voice. "What else did I say?"
>
> "Said you pitied the husband," continued Mr. Chalk thoughtfully.

I have quoted only the overture to the gruelling hazards of Mr. Chalk's relations with his wife; Jacobs has something like Fielding's gift, which came from the stage, for capping situation with situation, for never letting sleeping dogs lie. Two things will strike us about that passage: first, the lack of conventional facetiousness. Facetiousness gets shriller and lighter; humour sinks deeper and deeper into its ribald and wicked boots. The other point is that the extreme elaboration of Jacobs's wit, the relentlessness of his innuendo, are applied to the traditional subjects of the English music-hall: the mother-in-law, the knowing widow, the fulminating wife and the henpecked husband, the man who can't pass a pub. Fighting, black eyes, man-handling, horseplay, stealing of people's clothes, assuming disguises, changing names, spreading lying rumours, the persecution of one man by his mates for a lark, are the common coin. A man in love is fair game. Bad language is never given verbatim, but it is never let pass. (The old jokes about swearing are given a new polish. Mr. Henry Reed quotes this jewel: "The langwidge 'e see fit to use was a'most as much as I could answer." Only Mark Twain's Mississippi boatmen could equal that.) The laziness of the working-man is another stock joke which, in spite of political pressure, has not yet died; indeed only the false teeth joke is missing. The feminine side of the mixture is conventional music-hall too. There is no sex. There is no hint of illicit love. With this goes a low opinion of married love. Young girls are pretty, tidy, heartless and always deceptively grave. They flirt. They terrorise with their caprices like any Millamant. They outwit everyone. It is their brief moment. Presently they will become mothers of ten squalling kids; and their husbands will be beating them; or they will become strong-willed monsters, the scolds of the kitchen, the touchy and jealous Grundys of the parlour.

Material of this kind dates when it is used realistically and it would be simple to show that Jacobs draws the working-class and the lower middle-class as they were before even the Nineties; and treats them as comics for reasons that are, unconsciously, political. It is certain that Polly and Kipps, for example, are greater characters than the Nightwatchman or thick-headed knockabouts like Ginger Dick, simply because Wells relates them to something larger than themselves. That is to attribute no artistic falsity to Jacobs's characters; they are merely limited and within those limits they are perfect. Jacobs's general impression of the poor is sound; the psychology of sailors, shopkeepers and so on is exact. And one important aspect of working-class character, or at any rate of male character when very ordinary men are thrown together, is strongly brought out and justifies his intricate plots from Nature; I refer to the observation that the rapid, oblique leg-pulling talk, with its lies and bland assertions which no one believes, is part of the fine male art of cutting a figure and keeping your end up. The plots in Jacobs are the breath of the fantasticating life of men. They are superior to the plots of a writer like O. Henry. They spring naturally from the wits of the characters as trickery comes naturally to cardsharpers; they seem to pour off the tongue.

The flavour and the skill of Jacobs are of course all in the handling of the talk. At first sight the talk looks like something merely funny in itself; but Jacobs had the art of adding the obstacle of character to narrative:

"Come here," said the mate sternly.

The boy came towards him.

"What were you saying about the skipper?" demanded the other.

"I said it wasn't cargo he was after," said Henry.

"Oh, a lot you know about it!" said the mate.

Henry scratched his leg but said nothing.

"A lot you know about it!" repeated the mate in rather a disappointed tone. Henry scratched the other leg.

"Don't let me hear you talking about your superior officer's affairs again," said the mate sharply. "Mind that!"

"No sir," said the boy humbly. "It ain't my business of course."

"What ain't your business?" said the mate carelessly.

"His," said Henry.

There is no doubt that Jacobs is one of the supreme craftsmen of the short story. It is extraordinary that he should have brought such pellucid economy to material that was, on the face of it, stuff for schoolboys, or the Halls; but in doing so, he transformed it. The comic spirit was perhaps his thwarted poetry. He knew his limits. The only carelessness or rather the only indifference in his work appears in his novels. Of these *A Master of Craft* suggests a partial attempt at the Mean Street realism of the period; and a desire to go beyond his range; it contains a lady-killing skipper—instead of the usual skipper-killing lady—and he is, for Jacobs, an ugly character. Jacobs shows his wounds a little in this book; but, for some reason, he slips back into his shell. I think we may be glad he decided to remain in the ivory fo'c'sle. The artificial, the almost pastoral Jacobs of *Dialstone Lane* is more satisfying. The spring

sunlight of pure malice and self-possessed sentiment gleams on this story about three gullible townsmen who dream of going to sea; and the story has two immortally awful wives in it: the oppressed and the oppressor. But it is a major error in the plot that the dream voyage actually takes place. Jacobs would never have been so slapdash in a short story. (pp. 235-41)

V. S. Pritchett, "W. W. Jacobs," in his Books in General, *Chatto & Windus, 1953, pp. 235-41.*

JOHN WAIN (essay date 1960)

[*Wain is one of the most prolific English authors of contemporary fiction and poetry. He is also recognized as a significant, if minor, twentieth-century critic. Central to his critical stance is his belief that, in order to judge the quality of a piece of literature, the critic must make a moral as well as an imaginative judgment. James Gindin has called him "an excellent literary critic, intelligent, perceptive, and able to analyze and explain what he sees clearly and cogently." In the following excerpt, Wain discusses some possible reasons for the decline of Jacobs's popularity during the years following his death in 1943.*]

The very completeness of Jacobs's disappearance is an illustration of something that bulks very large in the life of a comic writer. Fashions in humour change with bewildering speed, and the world of the comic writer is as tough as the world of the circus strong-man. Once the day comes when he cannot lift that weight, he makes way for someone who can—and there is no argument and no second chance. So perhaps it is inevitable that the comparison should be with a writer whose jokes have turned to dust. Such a comparison might help to answer the question, What makes a joke keep? And are the best jokes the ones that keep longest?

W. W. Jacobs, to begin at the beginning, was an English writer of humorous short stories whose popularity hit a peak some time before 1914 and stayed at that peak till about 1940. Some of his pieces were sentimental or morbidly horrific; one of these, **"The Monkey's Paw,"** seems to be the only fragment of his work that made any impression in America. But in England Jacobs was best known as a funny man; in fact his character 'the Night-Watchman', in whose quaint *argot* many of his stories were told, must have been one of the best-known people in English fiction. As a boy at school, I came in at the tail-end of Jacobs's popularity; my friends and I used to pass his books from hand to hand and chortle unwearyingly over the jokes. I realize, now, that we were the last generation for whom Jacobs worked. It is a taste that links us with our fathers, but will never link us with our sons. Ask any company of 21-year-olds nowadays if they have heard of Jacobs, and watch the puzzled frowns. I find it almost incredible that he has disappeared so abruptly. The formerly solid earth opened in some odd moment when one's back was turned, and Jacobs, together with his gallery of permanent characters—the Night-Watchman, Ginger Dick, Sam Small, Peter Russet, Bob Pretty and the Oldest Inhabitant—disappeared for ever.

Was this inevitable? Does humour always go out of fashion? By no means. We can make a fair distinction between durable and non-durable humour. If we look at Shakespeare, for instance, we see at once that the jokes based on character and situation are still as funny as they were; it is the purely modish humour of word-play and parody that has died. Falstaff, from the moment he enters with that magnificent opening line, 'Now Hal, what time of day is it, lad?' is the great comic figure he must always have been. (This is not to deny that there are some people, mostly women, who just don't think the Falstaff scenes are funny. Such jokes simply don't work with them. But these, you can be sure, existed in Shakespeare's day too. This is not a question of fashion, but of temperament.) Chaucer's jokes, except where they happen to be on subjects that have passed completely out of memory, are still supremely funny. So is a lot of the comedy of ancient Greece.

It is not, then, an immutable fate that puts comic writing out of date. But there is one heavy law, to which I can think of no exceptions. Changes of fashion, in every other art reversible, are in comic writing irreversible. The things we think funny to-day in older writers have been thought funny without interruption down the centuries. Once the joke is lost, it stays lost. A novelist or poet can have a period 'out', as Donne or Sterne did, and come back with a resounding bang. But a joker, once buried, is never dug up. Of course, there may be a few years here and there in which a good comic writer is buried by prudery as the Victorians buried Restoration and classical comedy. But banning a writer is a different matter from reading him with a yawn; those Victorians (and they were, whether surprisingly or not, quite numerous) who did read *The Country Wife* or *Lysistrata* didn't deny that they were funny.

Let us take the matter a little further. When a joke goes out of date it is usually because an attitude has disappeared. What a man finds funny is a sure guide to his character, and, for historical reasons, the characters of whole societies, and therefore of the people in them, can change—not, perhaps, basically, but certainly enough to drive a lot of jokes out of circulation. Jacobs went out because he wrote within the convention that the English working man is funny—I mean funny *per se*, funny before he does or says anything funny. With his strange accent, his inability to pronounce the letter 'h', his comical clothes, he has only to walk into the pages of a book and the reader gets his facial muscles ready for a smile. That, at any rate, was the convention. It sprang, of course, from middle-class complacency and middle-class bewilderment. Both the writer and his reader were genteel persons who had, owing to the rigidity of English life, very little contact with the working man, who consequently remained a puzzle; they could not think what sort of life went on in those rows of blackened little houses, or what it was really like to do that sort of work. The novel, and fiction generally, is (in Europe at any rate) essentially a bourgeois form. Neither the working class nor the aristocracy figure in it at all centrally. An aristocrat, in an English novel, is just as likely to be a comic figure—when he is not merely a focus for envious fantasies—as a labourer. So the lower-deck, below-stairs character was shown as funny because a laugh is the natural human reaction to something you don't understand. And also because it kept him in his place. And also because, not having been educated and therefore finding the world full of mysteries, he tended to mispronounce words, to hold on to quaint beliefs, to make laughable mistakes. And lastly because, as anyone can see, the English working class *are* funny, in the good sense; they have humour and gaiety, more so in many cases than the higher-ups.

Nothing in Jacobs's writing suggests that he ever questioned these conventions. Here is a specimen. (The situation: three sailormen have been asked to speak words of caution to a youngster, nephew to one of them, who is about to jump into an early marriage.)

'Twenty-one is young,' ses Ginger, shaking his head. ''Ave you known 'er long?'

'Three months,' says the nevy. 'She lives in the same street as I do. 'Ow it is she ain't been snapped up before, I can't think, but she told me that she didn't care for men till she saw me.'

'They all say that,' ses Ginger.

'If I've 'ad it said to me once, I've 'ad it said twenty times,' ses Peter, nodding.

'They do it to flatter,' ses old Sam, looking as if 'e knew all about it. 'You wait till you are my age, Joe; then you'll know; why, I should ha' been married dozens o' times if I 'adn't been careful.'

'P'r'aps it was a bit on both sides,' ses Joe, looking at 'is uncle. 'P'r'aps they was careful too. If you could only see my young lady you wouldn't talk like that. She's got the truthfullest eyes in the world. Large grey eyes like a child's, leastways sometimes they are grey and sometimes they are blue. It seems to depend on the light somehow; I 'ave seen them when they was a brown—brownish-gold. And she smiles with 'er eyes.'

'Hasn't she got a mouth?' ses Ginger, wot was getting a bit tired of it.

'You've been crossed in love,' ses the nevy, staring at 'im. 'That's wot's the matter with you. And looking at you, I don't wonder at it.'

Such passages as this are a strange mixture of genuinely good writing, polished and well timed, and inert convention which has dated badly. Jacobs has a useful gift for extracting humour out of very simple situations, without flogging them to death; on the other hand, he also expects us to be amused at the stylized lingo full of dropped h's, 'wot', and the rest of it. This kind of thing is really a form of pastoral; the characters are no more like real sailors than a Dresden figure is like a real shepherd; they are simplified figures, constructed to live in a world of utterly harmless comedy where vice is typified by one half-pint too many and trouble by a spell of nagging from the wife. It has, I surmise, gone out of fashion because no one to-day is interested in such innocence. And if they were, they would hardly people their pastoral landscape with working-class figures, for that convention has also gone out. In the 'thirties, the British left-wing conscience woke up uneasily to the fact that the working man simply did not appear in English literature; they set to work to remedy this, and the result was a flood of 'social realism' which usually showed proletarian life as an unending round of misery and humiliation; that tide has receded in its turn, but while it lasted it did a lot to wash away the Jacobs kind of humour. (pp. 530-34)

John Wain, "A Jest in Season: Notes on S. J. Perelman, with a Digression on W. W. Jacobs," in The Twentieth Century, *Vol. 167, No. 1000, June, 1960, pp. 530-44.*

JOSEPH H. HARKEY (essay date 1969)

[In the following excerpt, Harkey discusses the structure of "The Monkey's Paw."]

In the early lines of W. W. Jacobs' "The Monkey's Paw," an altogether chilling story, is embedded the germ of the entire story. Mr. White and his son Herbert were playing chess, the father,

> (1) who possessed ideas about the game involving radical changes, (2) putting his king into . . . sharp and unnecessary perils. . . .

> . . . .

> "Hark at the wind," said Mr. White, who, (3) having seen a fatal mistake after it was too late, (4) was amiably desirous of preventing his son from seeing it.

Contained in this passage are four elements that foreshadow the action of the story, although Jacobs is never heavy-handed in working out the tale as a projection of its opening paragraphs. The obvious parallel to the game of chess, is, of course, the game of life. While Mr. White's choosing a small sum (two hundred pounds) when he made his first wish on the monkey's paw might make him seem less than radical, we must remember that he snatched the paw from the fire when the old soldier tossed it there. Had White been one merely to accept life, he would have taken the soldier's advice and let the paw burn.

The second element, that of putting his king into "sharp and unnecessary peril," comes with the first wish. White had no way of knowing that he was endangering Herbert's life in requesting the £200, but the soldier's demeanor when he told of the magical powers of the paw should have warned a less radical man to let the paw burn. As it turned out, the £200 wished for came as an indemnity for Herbert, who was killed when he fell into some working machinery. While the gothic tone of the story is not such that one would expect a pun on the "sharp" peril, certainly the peril was *unnecessary*. White planned to use the £200 requested to pay off the mortgage, but there was no urgent need for it to be paid off immediately.

White's seeing a fatal mistake after it was too late was the third element. The fatal mistake here is not the death of his son, however, but something even more terrible—the resurrection of his son with his face still mangled from the machinery. When Mrs. White insisted that White make a second wish—to bring Herbert back—White feared that the wish might bring the son back mutilated. Nevertheless, his fear of his wife caused him to make the second wish. It was only much later, when they heard a noise at the door, that White sensed it was his mutilated son and frantically sought the paw to make a third wish.

This wish—that Herbert be dead again—was an acting out of the fourth element. But it is not the son he is preventing from seeing the fatal mistake this time. It is his wife, who is not aware that the second wish did not include the request that Herbert be restored whole. The third wish prevented the heart-struck mother from seeing the hideous creature outside the door.

Thus in the opening two paragraphs, Jacobs has given us a *micro*-story which contains all the elements of the *macro*-story, if one may use those terms. Still, his symbolic foreshadowing is not heavy-handed. The use of the words "amiably desirous" to describe White's efforts to prevent his son from seeing his mistake, for instance, would seem incongruous were they to describe his effort to prevent his wife from seeing their son. Indeed, despite the symbolic relationship of the chess game to the story proper, Jacobs handled it in such a sophisticated manner that the effect of the game on the reader is suggestive, hinting of the dangers implicit in Mr. White's radical ideas about the game—of life, while at the same time giving us with a few bold strokes a preliminary sketch of the central character in the story. (pp. 653-54)

> *Joseph H. Harkey, "Foreshadowing in 'The Monkey's Paw'," in* Studies in Short Fiction, *Vol. VI, No. 5, Fall, 1969, pp. 653-54.*

BENNY GREEN (essay date 1975)

[*Green is an English jazz musician, novelist, and critic. In the following excerpt, he comments on Jacobs's decline into obscurity, while affirming his craftsmanship and humor.*]

In 1944, having won a prize in the caucus race of youth club life, I was asked to nominate the book of my choice. I named an anthology of W. W. Jacobs short stories. In time the book vanished into that limbo which serves as the repository for all the unwanted artefacts in the universe. Whatever happened, I still sometimes wonder, to my suede shinpads, my monthly editions of *The Ring*, my George IV silver threepenny bit? Once they were deeply cherished, but that didn't save them. As for Jacobs, I think I must have passed him on with some disdain to a younger cousin even less literary than I was; perhaps I exchanged him at our local secondhand shop for Leacock or Ellery Queen. The point is that in 1944 Jacobs's books were still popular enough for an unintellectual adolescent to be interested in him. He had died in the previous year, so perhaps I saw an obituary somewhere which tickled my fancy. That was thirty years ago, and today Jacobs has become so remote and obscure a figure as to have joined the nostalgia trade, a relic from a vanished world. . . .

[Middle-brow] magazine fiction of the type in which Jacobs specialised has been unfashionable for too long now for any but the very hardiest spirits to survive, and Jacobs has not been one of them. It is sometimes said, usually by boobies, that this kind of literature has been usurped by the telly-drama, when the truth is that the average telly-drama, having no literary antecedents of any kind, could not possibly have usurped anything or anybody except its own asinine self. Where in TV fiction would a character open an episode by remarking, "Sail-ormen 'ave their faults, I'm not denying it. I used to 'ave myself when I was at sea"?

Structurally Jacobs derives from the old O. Henry formula where the plot is a reversal of what we are supposed to expect. Most of the cockney vernacular tales follow an identical pattern. Somebody sees an easy touch and tries to keep it from his greedy friends; they cheat and connive to diddle him out of his good fortune; the good fortune turns out to be bad news; the biter is bit. The pervading atmosphere is one of cheerfully callous amorality; there are no finer feelings in a Jacobs short story, and all his women are sadistic termagants whose intractable viciousness provides decent men with the diversion of the only really important blood sport, which is avoiding getting married. In one Jacobs story . . . , the nastiest practical joke a man can think of is to leave his friend lots of money in his will provided he weds the first woman who asks him. Notice that Jacobs takes it for granted that whoever she is, she will turn out to be a pest.

Within the narrow scope of his style, Jacobs manipulated the strings with considerable wit. Take the story '**The Money Box**', where the premise is so commonplace that the rest of us probably thought of it ourselves years ago. Two sailors decide to try to save their shore-leave money by depositing it with an old salt who will dole it out, a bit every day, and thereby make it last. The first thought to occur to us is that Jacobs will make the old salt abscond with the funds, but this he does not do. Then the two young men demand their money in one lump, and the old boy refuses. They threaten violence. So far the story has proceeded along predictably humdrum lines. But now watch what Jacobs does with the situation. He makes the two desperately thirsty young men pawn their spare clothes to raise the wind. This gives them the idea of stealing the old man's clothes and pawning those too, thereby bringing off the double ploy of raising more money and gaining revenge. After they have pawned the clothes and spent the money, the old man tells them that their money is stitched into the lining of the very coat they have pawned. So the old man takes *their* clothes and pawns them so as to redeem his own coat, which they must agree to if they want their money back. The story ends with the two sailors trapped naked in their own bedroom for three days. Perhaps that sort of thing will never win a literary prize, but it takes some working out and putting down. Jacobs apparently wrote at a snail's pace of a hundred words a day, and the proof that his travail was worth it is contained in [*Selected Short Stories*, by W. W. Jacobs], which conveys a charming illusion of casual chat flowing easily off the page into the mind's eye. I have an idea that this kind of honest craftsmanship is not to be sneezed at, and that much modern fiction is bedevilled by the deafening sound of sneezing on all sides. . . . [The] hedonistic reader could do worse than dip into the Wapping pubs and whopping lies of W. W. Jacobs's canny maritime drunks.

> Benny Green, "Wapping Lies," in The Spectator, Vol. 235, No. 7673, July 19, 1975, p. 85.

WALTER ALLEN (essay date 1981)

[*Allen is an English novelist of working-class life and a distinguished popular historian and critic of the novel form. In the following excerpt, he describes the most notable characteristics of Jacobs's stories.*]

W. W. Jacobs, who produced sixteen books, the majority of them collections of short stories, was an exquisite minor artist. Born in Wapping on London River, he set his stories mainly on the Thames; his characters are skippers and mates and sailors on coastal schooners, lightermen and watchmen of wharves, and their women, wives, daughters, and sweethearts. Realism was not his aim. He was a master of artificial comedy and of his own mannered dialogue, which was based on Thames speech.

He wrote with the utmost economy. Everything is dramatized. Farce may be present as the basic element of his stories, but it is always modulated by an extremely subtle, low-keyed humour.

Within these limits, which are admittedly very narrow, Jacobs is a master. We read his stories partly to savour the skill and freshness with which he deploys material of a kind that has entertained men and women at all levels of sophistication since the birth of language. His success is evident in the comic fairyland he created.

> Walter Allen, "Jacobs, Wells, Conrad, Bennett, Saki, de la Mare," in his The Short Story in English, Oxford at the Clarendon Press, Oxford, 1981, pp. 76-91.

ADDITIONAL BIBLIOGRAPHY

"The Little Touches." *The Academy* LIX, No. 1484 (13 October 1900): 305.
    Review of *A Master of Craft* with an overview of Jacobs's work.

Greene, Hugh, ed. Introduction to *Selected Short Stories*, by W. W. Jacobs, pp. 5-9. London: Bodley Head, 1975.
    Discusses Jacobs's life in relation to his writing.

Hind, C. Lewis. "W. W. Jacobs." In his *More Authors and I*, pp. 170-74. New York: Dodd, Mead and Co., 1922.
    Discusses Hind's personal acquaintance with Jacobs and the characteristics of his work.

Marble, Annie Russell. "Whimsicality and Humor." In her *A Study of the Modern Novel: British and American since 1900*, pp. 185-216. New York: D. Appleton and Co., 1928.
    General discussion of Jacobs's blend of comedy and sentiment.

Newte, Horace. "The Art of W. W. Jacobs." *The Bookman*, London LXXI, No. 421 (October 1926): 18-20.
    Discussion of Jacobs's humorous stories. Newte points out subtleties and insights in Jacobs's work not generally credited to the author.

Osborne, E. A. "Epitome of a Bibliography of W. W. Jacobs: Parts I, II, and III." *The Bookman*, London, LXXXVI, Nos. 512, 513, 514 (May 1934; June 1934; July 1934): 99-101, 138-42, 204-06.
    Three-part essay primarily concerned with a careful cataloguing of the early editions of Jacobs's books.

Perrin, Noel. "Banter on the Bridge, Farce on the Fo'c'sle." *Book World* XIII, No. 29 (17 July 1983): 4.
    Review of *Many Cargoes* primarily devoted to plot summary of its first two stories.

(Theodora) Sarah Orne Jewett

1849-1909

(Also wrote under pseudonyms of Alice Eliot and Sarah C. Sweet, among others) American short story writer, novelist, and poet.

Jewett is considered one of the chief figures of the New England local color movement in fiction during the late nineteenth century. As such, her works are often compared with those of Harriet Beecher Stowe, Rose Terry Cooke, and Mary E. Wilkins Freeman. In her stories and sketches Jewett depicted the deteriorating maritime communities of the Maine coastal district in which she lived, emphasizing setting and character for the purpose of illuminating life in rural New England. Critics unanimously agree that in her masterwork, *The Country of the Pointed Firs,* Jewett most successfully developed the subjects, themes, and techniques which had characterized her previous short story collections. Regarding the collection for which Jewett is best remembered, Warner Berthoff has concluded: "*The Country of the Pointed Firs* is a small work but an unimprovable one, with a secure and unrivaled place in the main line of American literary expression."

Jewett was the second of three daughters born to Caroline (Perry) and Theodore Herman Jewett, a wealthy and respected physician in rural South Berwick, Maine. Once a great port community, South Berwick had fallen into decline with the Embargo Act of 1807, and the Civil War later ended the predominance of sailing in the region. With the absence of the sailing professions, many young men abandoned the New England coast in search of wealth and adventure in the developing West, leaving behind a population that was largely female and elderly. In Jewett's childhood, however, many of the former sea captains, including her paternal grandfather, were still alive, and they often told tales of the departed era in which Berwick had prospered.

As a child Jewett suffered from arthritis, and consequently her attendance at school was irregular. Dr. Jewett, believing that the open air would improve his daughter's health, often allowed her to accompany him in his carriage as he visited his patients throughout the coastal district. In this way, Jewett was first introduced to many of the New England characters whom she would later recall in her fiction. Jewett's father also tutored her in literature and local history, and he frequently called her attention to regional animal and plant life. In 1865, Jewett graduated without distinction from Berwick Academy. She never viewed herself as a superior student, and she would always consider her father's practical instruction to be her most valuable education.

For the most part, Jewett's youth was uneventful, secure, and happy. She was encouraged by her father to read extensively but with discrimination from his comprehensive library; among the many works she read during her adolescent years was Stowe's *The Pearl of Orr's Island* (1862), a novel critics often cite as a forerunner of the local color movement in American fiction. Set along the coastline of Maine, Stowe's novel led Jewett to recognize for the first time that her own people and the countryside she knew well were worthy material for literature. She was further inspired when tourism started to flourish in the

region, and summer visitors from the cities invaded rural communities such as South Berwick. As she later explained: "When I was, perhaps, fifteen, the first 'city boarders' began to make their appearance near Berwick; and the way they misconstrued the country people and made game of their peculiarities fired me with indignation. I determined to teach the world that country people were not the awkward, ignorant set those people seemed to think. I wanted the world to know their grand, simple lives; and, so far as I had a mission, when I first began to write, I think that was it." Jewett began to write poems and short stories while she was still in her teens, but these early compositions indicate little of her later achievement. Some of these works were published in various small magazines under such pseudonyms as "Alice Eliot" and "Sarah C. Sweet." As her ambitions grew, so too did the caliber of the publications to which she submitted her work. Her first notable success came just before her twentieth birthday when William Dean Howells accepted the short story "Mr. Bruce" for the *Atlantic Monthly.* Guided by Howells's comments and suggestions, and by her own understanding of rural life in New England, Jewett subsequently produced a number of successful local color stories and sketches for the *Atlantic;* these she revised and collected in her first book, *Deephaven.* The success of this first collection gained Jewett many literary admirers and friends, and her close association with the *Atlantic Monthly* brought her frequently into the Boston home of its editor, James T. Fields, and his wife Annie, an esteemed philanthropist and literary hostess. In their Charles Street salon, eminent American writers and editors often gathered, and they welcomed Jewett into their circle.

After her father died in 1878, Jewett became more intimate with Annie Fields, and when the elder woman's husband died in 1881 the two women became constant and lifelong companions in a close friendship of the kind known as a Boston Marriage. They traveled extensively, making several trips to Europe during which Jewett became acquainted with Alfred Tennyson, Matthew Arnold, Henry James, Christina Rossetti, and Rudyard Kipling. Although she thrived on such encounters, Jewett invariably returned to South Berwick every summer to write. She believed that her travels enabled her to focus more clearly on the unique aspects of her home community, its limitations and its delights. As she once explained: "One must know the world so well before one can know the parish." In September, 1902, Jewett's spine was seriously injured when she was thrown from a carriage in South Berwick. One to whom writing was never, in her own words, "a bread and butter affair," she did not return to work after the accident. The remaining years of her life were spent in leisure—visiting and corresponding with friends. She suffered a stroke in the spring of 1909 and died in June of that year at her home in Maine.

In their setting, subjects, themes, and narrative techniques, the stories and sketches collected in *Deephaven* foreshadow Jewett's later mastery. Howells has remarked that these early stories "are all touched with a hand that holds itself far from every trick of exaggeration, and that subtly delights in the very tint and form of reality." A principal device in *Deephaven* and many of her later works is the spectator-narrator, an outsider—frequently from the city—who visits a New England country district and reports her impressions of its characters and its culture to the reader. The *Deephaven* collection is woven around the observations of a young woman who arrives from the city to spend the summer in the village house of her companion's deceased aunt. Jewett never used a male persona, and she later cautioned Willa Cather against such a practice. Commenting on an early story by the younger writer, Jewett reasoned: "The lover is as well done as he could be when a woman writes in the man's character. It must always, I believe, be something of a masquerade. I think it is safer to write about him as you did about the others, and not try to be he!" Although Jewett is generally considered unsuccessful in her characterizations of men, her rendering of women has been especially praised by critics, who particularly note her sympathetic portrayal of relationships between women. Many of her female characters are self-reliant, optimistic, and versatile; few are married. Nan Prince, in the semi-autobiographical novel *A Country Doctor*, chooses to reject marriage in favor of her vocation, medicine. In her choice she sees the opportunity to "make many homes happy instead of one," introducing a prominent subject throughout Jewett's works: the duty of the individual to be useful to society. The decaying community in which Jewett was raised is reflected in her portrayal of numerous old women, such as those in "The Dulham Ladies" and "The Queen's Twin." The first story depicts two characters who attempt to regain their lost youth by donning hairpieces which appear ridiculous to observers; in the latter story the protagonist imagines herself Victoria's twin because they share a birth date and because she once saw the monarch on a trip to London. While

these tales are recognized chiefly for their humor, critics also praise the pathos and gentleness with which Jewett relates them.

Jewett spoke of her works not as stories, but as "papers," preferring impressions and episodes to intricacies of action. As she once wrote to editor Horace Scudder: "I have no dramatic talent. It seems to me I can furnish the theater, and show you the actors and the scenery, but there is never any play." Her aim was toward naturalism, and she modelled her writing after Gustave Flaubert's exhortation "to write of ordinary life as one writes history." In writing of ordinary life in New England, Jewett was writing the history of its ordinary people—Yankee widows and spinsters, farmers, fishermen, and aging sea captains. According to Martha Hale Shackford: "There is nothing spectacular nor very tense in her presentments of life; she shows people living simple, normal, average lives, and the tissue of their existence is not external event but the slow pondering of life, and still slower exchange of comment about it." Critics agree that the influence on Jewett of this limited, deteriorating society, which was falling further and further away from the more industrial American norm, cannot be overestimated. Equally significant is the influence of nature on Jewett's work. According to many critics, her description of the natural environment never simply serves as an isolated background, but is integrated into the action and is subtly evoked by her characters, who speak in dialect of "ellum trees" and "rosbry bushes." Critics find Jewett's most important examination of the relationship between humanity and the natural world in her much-anthologized short story "A White Heron," which relates the dilemma of a young girl who must choose between love of nature and human love. As Josephine Donovan has explained: "'A White Heron' resolves the conflict between urban and rural by affirming the values of country life and rejecting the evils of the industrial city . . . , while at the same time acknowledging the limitations of the country world and recognizing the excitement and opportunity for growth the city represents."

While "A White Heron" is Jewett's most popular work, critics have agreed that *The Country of the Pointed Firs* represents her highest achievement. In this collection, which is regarded as the culmination of her local color writing, Jewett wove a consummate tapestry of New England idylls. Thematic conflicts prominent throughout her works—"the female versus the male" and "country versus city" (with their attending subthemes "tradition versus progress" and "the pastoral versus industrial")—are repeated and refined in *The Country of the Pointed Firs*. Female friendships again form the primary link between the individual and society, and it is women who continue the rural cultural traditions. The spectator-narrator once more provides the frame as a writer from the city comes to Dunnet Landing in search of a suitable place to work. She stays for the summer as the boarder of Mrs. Almira Todd, an herbalist. Setting and character are again emphasized over action, and Jewett has been enthusiastically praised by critics for her characterization of Mrs. Todd, a woman whose association and identification with the local landscape is complete. In many ways similar to Jewett's earliest collection, *Deephaven*, *The Country of the Pointed Firs* is recognized by critics as the decidedly superior collection. Olive Cross has noted of the later work: "Again the situations are simple, sometimes even trivial; but the writer has gone far beyond mere observation and description that record facts correct in detail. Here she catches the lights and shadows that play upon the people, the freshness of the air they breathe." Critics of each succeeding generation have judged *The Country of the Pointed Firs* a

masterpiece of local color fiction. As Alice Brown has concluded: "It is the acme of Miss Jewett's fine achievement,
blending the humanity of the 'Native of Winby' and the fragrance of the 'White Heron.' No such beautiful and perfect
work has been done for many years; perhaps no such beautiful
work has ever been done in America."

Although the popularity of Jewett's works has suffered as the
way of life she so vividly recorded has receded into history,
students of American literature are made familiar with at least
the quintessential Jewett in her "A White Heron," which appears in many survey textbooks. Because of her stature among
New England local colorists, she continues to be read, studied,
and criticized in conjunction with other New England writers.
While her popularity may have diminished, Jewett has never
gone unregarded by critics. The feminist critics of the 1970s,
for example, have added many fresh scholarly assessments to
the body of Jewett criticism, particularly noting the role of
women in nineteenth century American society as represented
in her works. Nevertheless, her chief contribution to American
literature is for the most part considered to reside in the vi-
brancy with which she depicted the disappearing way of life
in maritime New England. As John Eldridge Frost has recognized: "The local color sketch she brought to a degree of
perfection that has not been excelled. The quality of her style,
especially in *The Country of the Pointed Firs*, gives her high
rank among the prose writers of America."

(See also *TCLC*, Vol. 1; *Contemporary Authors*, Vol. 108;
Something about the Author, Vol. 15; and *Dictionary of Literary Biography*, Vol. 12: *American Realists and Naturalists*.)

PRINCIPAL WORKS

Deephaven (short stories) 1877
Play Days (juvenile fiction and poetry) 1878
Old Friends and New (short stories) 1879
Country By-Ways (short stories) 1881
A Country Doctor (novel) 1884
The Mate of the Daylight, and Friends Ashore (short
     stories) 1884
A Marsh Island (novel) 1885
A White Heron, and Other Stories (short stories) 1886
The Story of the Normans (juvenile nonfiction) 1887
The King of Folly Island and Other People (short stories)
     1888
Betty Leicester (juvenile fiction) 1890
Strangers and Wayfarers (short stories) 1890
A Native of Winby, and Other Tales (short stories) 1893
Betty Leicester's English Xmas (juvenile fiction) 1894;
     also published as *Betty Leicester's Christmas*, 1899
The Life of Nancy (short stories) 1895
The Country of the Pointed Firs (short stories) 1896; also
     published as *The Country of the Pointed Firs* [enlarged
     edition], 1910; and *The Country of the Pointed Firs*
     [enlarged edition], 1919
The Queen's Twin, and Other Stories (short stories) 1899
The Tory Lover (novel) 1901
Stories and Tales. 7 vols. (novel and short stories) 1910
Verses (poetry) 1916
Sarah Orne Jewett Letters (letters) 1967
The Uncollected Short Stories of Sarah Orne Jewett (short
     stories) 1971

[WILLIAM DEAN HOWELLS] (essay date 1877)

[*Howells was the chief progenitor of American realism and the
most influential American literary critic during the late nineteenth
century. The author of nearly three dozen novels, he successfully
weaned American literature away from the sentimental romanticism of its infancy, earning the popular sobriquet "the Dean of
American Letters." Through realism, a theory central to his fiction and criticism, Howells sought to disperse "the conventional
acceptations by which men live on easy terms with themselves"
that they might "examine the grounds of their social and moral
opinions." To accomplish this, according to Howells, the writer
must strive to record detailed impressions of everyday life, endowing characters with true-to-life motives and avoiding authorial
comment in the narrative. Howells was among the first to publish
Jewett's work when he accepted her short story "Mr. Bruce" for
the* Atlantic *in 1869. An admirer of Jewett's New England idylls,
Howells became her literary advisor and friend, and it was he
who encouraged her to collect her early stories in* Deephaven. *In
the following excerpt, Howells offers an appreciative review of
that collection.*]

The gentle reader of [the *Atlantic*] cannot fail to have liked,
for their very fresh and delicate quality, certain sketches of an
old New England sea-port, which have from time to time appeared here during the last four years. The first was **"Shore
House,"** and then there came **"Deephaven Cronies"** and
"Deephaven Excursions." These sketches, with many more
studies of the same sort of life, as finely and faithfully done,
are now collected into a pretty little book called ***Deephaven***,
which must, we think, find favor with all who appreciate the
simple treatment of the near-at-hand quaint and picturesque.
No doubt some particular sea-port sat for Deephaven, but the
picture is true to a whole class of old shore towns, in any one
of which you might confidently look to find the Deephaven
types. It is supposed that two young girls—whose young-girlhood
charmingly perfumes the thought and observation of the whole
book—are spending the summer at Deephaven, Miss Denis,
the narrator, being the guest of her adored ideal, Miss Kate
Lancaster, whose people have an ancestral house there; but
their sojourn is only used as a background on which to paint
the local life: the three or four aristocratic families, severally
dwindled to three or four old maiden ladies; the numbers of
ancient sea-captains cast ashore by the decaying traffic; the
queer sailor and fisher folk; the widow and old-wife gossips
of the place, and some of the people of the neighboring country.
These are all touched with a hand that holds itself far from
every trick of exaggeration, and that subtly delights in the very
tint and form of reality; we could not express too strongly the
sense of conscientious fidelity which the art of the book gives,
while over the whole is cast a light of the sweetest and gentlest
humor, and of a sympathy as tender as it is intelligent. **"Danny"**
is one of the best of the sketches; and another is **"The Circus
at Denby,"** which perhaps shows better than any other the play
of the author's observation and fancy, with its glancing lights
of fun and pathos. A sombre and touching study is that of the
sad, simple life so compassionately depicted in **"In Shadow,"**
after which the reader must turn to the brisk vigor and quaintness of **"Mrs. Bonny."** Bits of New England landscape and
characteristic marine effects scattered throughout these studies
of life vividly localize them, and the talk of the people is
rendered with a delicious fidelity.

In fact, Miss Jewett here gives proof of such powers of observation and characterization as we hope will some day be
turned to the advantage of all of us in fiction. Meanwhile we
are very glad of these studies, so refined, so simple, so ex-

quisitely imbued with a true feeling for the ideal within the real.

[William Dean Howells], in a review of "Deephaven," in The Atlantic Monthly, *Vol. XXXIX, No. CCXXXVI, June, 1877, p. 759.*

WILLIAM MORTON PAYNE (essay date 1884)

[*The longtime literary editor for several Chicago publications, Payne reviewed books for twenty-three years at the* Dial, *one of America's most influential journals of literature and opinion in the early twentieth century. In the following excerpt, Payne favorably reviews* A Country Doctor.]

A Country Doctor, by Sarah Orne Jewett, is one of the most satisfactory books of the season. The writer has not attempted to do more than lay fully within her power; and consequently has done most admirably a work for which her many studies and sketches of New England provincial life have so well fitted her. Upon its own plane and within its own limits the execution is almost perfect. Here we may find close and accurate observation, delicacy of touch, genuine discrimination, firm and sympathetic grasp of character, and instinctive refinement. The story, as we might naturally expect from the nature of the writer's previous work, is simplicity itself; but the fascination of its manner is such as to leave no desire for any greater intricacy of plot. Indeed, anything more intricate would not be in harmony either with the style or the type of life which it presents. It belongs to the class of novels with a purpose—the purpose in the present case being to serve as a plea for the adoption of the medical profession by women; and this purpose becomes just a little obtrusive towards the end of the story—a very little indeed, but enough so to slightly detract from the value of what would otherwise be a faultless piece of work. At all events, the choicest part of the book is the earlier half, in which this purpose is as yet hardly foreshadowed, and which portrays the childhood and early youth of the heroine in a way of which the full charm can only be felt upon such a careful and lingering perusal as the book well deserves.

William Morton Payne, in a review of "A Country Doctor," in The Dial, *Vol. V, No. 51, July, 1884, p. 66.*

TH. BENTZON [PSEUDONYM OF MARIE THÉRÈSE BLANC] (essay date 1885)

[*Bentzon is the pseudonym of Marie Thérèse Blanc, a French novelist and critic. Her interest in American literature and her desire to interpret American culture to French readers prompted Bentzon to translate* A Country Doctor *and several of Jewett's short stories into French. The two authors subsequently became intimate friends. In the following excerpt from an essay published in France in* Revue des Deux Mondes *in February, 1885, Bentzon analyzes* A Country Doctor, *viewing its feminist theme as a departure from Jewett's earlier, nature-oriented work.]*

Before giving here the analysis of *A Country Doctor,* we shall make known its author. The preceding works of Sarah Orne Jewett, and what they reveal of this singularly sympathetic personality, lend a good deal of weight to the crusade begun by her with as much frankness as prudence in favor of the free woman. Her patronage is among those that oblige the most recalcitrant to take up a doubtful cause. No author can be less suspected than Miss Jewett of firing bold pistol shots to as-

semble and amuse the crowd. She had limited herself up to now to exquisite pictures of nature. (p. 3)

The thread of simple and brief stories that alternates with the effects of the sun, with the promenades and the pure and simple vagabondage of familiar speech, this thread, light as that of a cobweb, would not be able to support many embroideries. The skillful worker knows how to embellish it without overburdening it. Her heroes, her heroines, are only accessory figures sketched in two strokes, expressive and good likenesses notwithstanding, just what is necessary in order to give life to the picture—landscape as in **"The Landless Farmer,"** an interior picture as in **"Good Luck,"** sea effect caused by a ray of sunshine as in **"The Mate of the Daylight,"** little scenes of clerical habits and country customs seen through a magnifying glass as in **"A New Parishioner,"** etc. The uncouthness of dialect, introduced here and there, develops without affectation the rare purity of style, as flowing as it is original.

A jewel in this modest genre is the little book which, by means of the walks and conversations of two young girls, gives us so vivid an impression of the appearance of the New England coasts and of the character of the inhabitants of an old abandoned port, *Deephaven.* One leaves this reading fortified in mind, as are physically, by the salt air, the two friends who tell us about their summer stay on this unpretentious beach. Together they establish themselves alone, while their parents travel and, from the beginning of the story, bursts forth this taste for independence that education encourages instead of suppressing in the American woman. The happy hermits of *Deephaven* are naively delighted to run their little household, to feel weighing upon them the burden of material life, to have to be occupied with provisions under penalty of famine. Notice that they are persons as cultivated as intelligent, capable of reading Emerson in their free moments. But the free moments are here much better employed in the open air. In their company we take on the tastes of children of six years; we wander in the sand looking for shells, from the height of the lighthouse we are present at innumerable sunsets; we listen attentively to the stories of old retired sea captains who form the society of the place; we discover tragedies in the inscriptions in the cemetery which recall so many shipwrecks. They row, they fish like little sailors and are not lacking in gentility for it; briefly, their society is so attractive that we also leave with regret this Deephaven where one could have easily been bored and where on the contrary one always had a good time, thanks to an imperturbable good humor, to the happy faculty of enjoying everything, to the discernment full of benevolence which makes the observer guess at a diamond in the rough, a savory fruit in its spiny or rough bark, a beautiful soul beneath the tanned skin of the roughest sea wolf.

To enjoy the slightest things, to get something out of everything, this is the secret that Miss Jewett teaches in every line without preaching; for her there is no life irremediably ruined, no misfortune that does not have its good side: "The great griefs of our youth sometimes become the charm of our mature age; we can remember them only with a smile." Those who expect too much from fate will go to her school with profit and will find it well to know the spinsters whose adorable varieties she presents to us, from the placid Miss Horatia, who preserves silently in the depths of her heart the memory of a fiancé lost at sea, happy in her widowhood because she feels the romance of her youthful years etched more and more clearly instead of fading away, as a long faithfulness ennobles her in her eyes and in the eyes of her neighbors; from that touching

Horatia who one day sees the so-called dead man for whose return she weeps, without recognizing her, in the guise of an old debauched vagabond drunkard, succored in passing with a mixture of horror and compassion, to the servant Melissa, who keeps to the end of her laborious career the resistant greenness of the cedar, her rough qualities of *freshness, toughness,* and *quaintness,* untranslatable in any language, *la fraîcheur, la solidité, la bizarerie,* which seem to represent them, only giving a feeble and incomplete idea; from Miss Catherine Spring, the model housekeeper, who, in going to fetch a penny's worth of cream, brings back a fortune in her milk jug, to Miss Sydney, who after having loved flowers with a selfish passion ends by sacrificing her loved ones to the pleasures of the little sick one in a children's hospital, to the joy of poor beings who are flowers in their own manner, flowers ready to blossom in the garden of whoever consoles them, flowers which bless you for having blessed them, which love you for having loved them, flowers which have eyes like yours, thoughts like yours, a life similar to your life.

The art of interesting us in details, even in the infinitely small details of cooking for example, in the words of Sarah Jewett, to the same point as in the works of a Van Ostade or a Gerard Dow; outside she listens to the grass growing, so to speak, and she makes us share her sensation; on the hearth, she flatters our sense of smell with the appetizing aromas of a family supper; she forces us to appreciate the savory confection of pound cake. She *is* realistic; in the sense that all that seems unbelievable, falsely exalted, repels her strangely; she has used, however, the fantastic or semi-fantastic element in two of her stories: "**A Sorrowful Guest**" and "**Lady Ferry.**" "**A Sorrowful Guest**" is a poor devil who is unceasingly obsessed by hallucinations; during the war, on the eve of a battle, he has exchanged a strange vow with his best friend: each has sworn half seriously, half jokingly, that the first to die would come back to haunt the other. Now, one of the companions disappeared, is believed killed; immediately the constant horrible illusion begins for the survivor. This phenomenon of a stricken imagination must evidently be the prelude to madness since at the end of the story it so happens that the would-be dead man, the inconvenient ghost, was only a deserter. (pp. 6-8)

There is also insanity in "**Lady Ferry,**" this ruin of the past so old, so old that one cannot count her age, and who believes herself condemned to life eternal; but for the child who is supposed to tell us about her relations with the would-be immortal mummified in all her finery of the last century, it is the very fable of the old age of Tithon transported to a sorrowful reality. The skill of the author is to make us feel the mixture of surprise, curiosity, and fearful attraction that the confident little girl experiences, of the wanderings of this fairy skeleton, to whom, in a burst of pity, she one day gives the kiss which will withdraw a last tear from those sightless eyes, impatient to close: "I pray God not to leave you lingering like me, apart from all your kindred, and your life so long that you forget you ever were a child."

This world is a school that prepares us for larger horizons; the lesson is almost interminable for Lady Ferry. We learn, however, with a sigh of relief which proves to the people most taken with life how redoubtable such a fate would be, that this arid and desolate lesson has belatedly had an end, that the immortal one is dead.

A care for the simple and the true which accompanies her ever through the caprices of fantasy, a moral conclusion ingeniously contrived, this assures Miss Jewett's books their just renown among good books. It remains to be seen if she will succeed in the novel as she has succeeded in her pastoral sketches, where philosophy and humor join the picturesque element always superabundant. Her little stories in *Old Friends and New* betray more than one awkwardness, more than one fault of arrangement. The subject that she does not know or does not wish to pursue disappears beneath digression; she systematically bypasses violent scenes. One notices it especially in "**A Lost Lover,**" where a pathetic situation turns short before the climax and, to our regret, remains suspended rather than untangled; it is even worse in the story of the woman doctor, the only work of long and exacting labor that this penetrating but non-inventive pen has produced. Passion, movement, variety—none of these must be asked of *A Country Doctor.* All the gentle seduction of talent of Miss Jewett seems to be concentrated on one goal: to obtain the grace of the strong woman, the free woman, to show what her strength and liberty cost her, how many female virtues continue to flourish beneath male faculties acquired at the price of sacrifices which compel our respect, if not our sympathy. (pp. 8-9)

It is surely curious to follow, step by step, the progress of intellectual and moral nature as it grows, as a shrub develops with its periods of rests and its sudden bursts, the acts and the works representing those signs of vitality which, as far as the plant is concerned, are called flowers and leaves, but minute observation does not suffice to give interest to a novel. The novel has nothing in common with a work of morality, education, or pure psychology. Frigidity is its greatest fault; in vain one piles on numerous secondary personages who have no solid bond with the subject; it is only one more fault. In life, many figures pass thus on our road to disappear, leaving, however, a trace of their influence. No matter! Once again poetic reality is submitted to rules which will never be grasped by the so-called novelists whose talent has scientific pretensions.

One moment, we can believe that Nan, after a few years of living at home, as she reaches the age when imagination opens its wings, when the unknown begins to tempt young girls, is going to feel a battle taking place within herself. The impetuous *moi* that she gets from her mother will no doubt battle the resolutions which example have suggested to her, as powerful in us as heredity, of which it is perhaps too often a question in this book. She dreams, she languishes, she seems to be bored, she accumulates new experiences and stops at nothing; often galloping on a farm horse, she seeks in this violent exercise a means of escaping the trouble in her mind. It is no longer a question of calling her the little doctor, for she no longer seems to bring to the books of medicine haphazardly leafed through that childish interest that formerly made her old friends smile. One notices in her more reserve; she neglects housework. The doctor is worried about this something to which his adopted child aspires, a something he is perhaps incapable of giving her. But no, unfortunately, for we should need absolutely a bit of the unforeseen, Nan will not for a single moment be distracted from the vocation which torments her and which is betrayed by these queer symptoms, inseparable from the choice of a condition. If nothing satisfies her any longer, it is because the time has come to give a real shape to her dream and she is afraid that she will not be encouraged at the moment of acting, whatever indulgences her tutor had once shown her for what he perhaps called childishness. . . .

Thus, as her tutor wished, things came from themselves, following their natural course. Nan has no illusions about the difficulties to conquer: she is ready, she has the sentiments of a reformer, of a radical facing the task that awaits her; she faces the storm, she is intoxicated by it in advance. . . .

Nan dedicates two years to prove her vocation by working with him. As ignorant as she still is, she has a diagnostic instinct, as a painter has for color, or a composer for harmony. Study and experience will develop this natural gift; but she possesses it, and their conversations during the long evenings by the fireside or the long trips from one farm to another, make her learn all that the courses in medical school do not reveal. Already she knows neither disgust nor prudery at the bedside of her patients, nor fear in the presence of death: her mind is filled with it, she has assiduously carried on the profession of a nurse at the same time that she has begun, under an enlightened teacher, the ordinary studies when the time comes for her to leave the port.

Here the author sketches many difficulties: it would be curious to see Nan in a large city, abandoned to herself; a bit of romantic emotion could be the result; but we know nothing about this period, however interesting, of the life of a woman doctor, except that all the protections that contribute to urging on a young man are refused to a girl. What does honor to the former harms the latter, rather; the mass of honest people from whom she would not wish to separate herself for anything in the world, disapproves tacitly of the efforts one would highly praise if they were justified by a bit of beard. . . .

A very nice scene is the one where, in the middle of a certain half sentimental walk, Nan finds the opportunity to reset the broken arm of a peasant, under the eyes of Gerry, who observes her with the mixture of admiration and repugnance that you can imagine. He feels himself weak, useless before her; he would have liked to fill the role of the surgeon, and this inversion of roles repulses him. At the same time, he feels a strong desire to place an obstacle in the path of what Nan calls her vocation, to win over this serious childish fantasy aroused in solitude by an old man. He gets excited about it, passion plays a role in it (at least the author affirms it, because we do not see any trace of it), a communicative passion which staggers the resolutions, so well affirmed, of the future lady doctor: "It seemed to her that the coming of Death at her life's end could not be more strange and sudden than this great barrier which had fallen between her and her girlhood, the dear old life which had kept her so unpuzzled and safe. So this was love at last, this fear, this change, this strange relation to another soul." (pp. 10-12)

She feels herself carried away by an impetuous flood and is astonished that certain conditions of life, which until then she had scarcely given any consideration, seem so necessary from this time on. She sees herself seated at a peaceful hearth, in the house where she already reigns, content with her lot, regarding from afar her unbounded projects like a vanished dream. It does not matter what she loved before, she loves George Gerry; her ambitions abandon her one by one, she values only George's love; nothing is worth the happiness that two human beings seek hand in hand; but as the shadows give way to the light of day, her duty appears clearer and clearer, this duty which must rule everything, even love; the reasons to follow a path once chosen present themselves very strongly. She finds the strength to resist this temptation and to attach herself desperately to her work, even though she must sacrifice to it everything that is the happiness of other women. Heaven has not given her powerful faculties in order to let them go down the drain. That is her conclusion. She still loves George Gerry

but she comes to hate the love that undergoes such tests. . . . (pp. 12-13)

Assuredly there remains in our imagination a lovable type of woman, intelligent and naive at the same time, who accomplishes very naturally and simply a strange destiny. To make it stand out more in contrast, Miss Jewett has placed as a pale hothouse flower, beside this superb and vigorous lily of the fields, the figure of Eunice Fraley. Brought up according to the old traditions in a provincial town, the trembling slave of an authoritative mother and of the principles she inherits from this mother, who will treat her as a child until her dying day, without independent ideas, without an existence proper for her, so to speak, poor Eunice awaits the liberator who must finally bring her to life. Among us there are many copies of this blurred pastel. We can state the justness of the touches, the exactitude of the resemblance.

If *A Country Doctor* is not a novel, it is at least a very interesting gallery of portraits and landscapes, a magic lantern with multiple pictures of singular newness, for which nothing is missing except to light it sufficiently. There where the flame of passion and the stress of plot are wanting, the accumulation of picturesque and psychological details cannot suffice, especially when they do not succeed in hiding the thesis which imposes itself antipathetically upon a great number. We should like a larger place to be made for the test of love, that the struggle be longer and more cruel in Nan's heart, that she remain bloody and wounded from it; especially we should wish Gerry to show himself, eloquent in defending the cause of marriage instead of pleading it in a manner which recalls the devil's advocate destined to be beaten in a kind of churchly conference apparently outmoded.

Orthodoxy, only, loses in the present case, the good old orthodoxy of the family. With whatever proportion and suitability the opinions of Miss Jewett are expressed, they are those of Doctor Leslie: the life of a man is elevated, fortified by domestic happiness; a woman's, on the other hand, cannot be shared; a woman is completely her lord and master's or gives herself completely to a social task. To be adequate for a double mission as man is, is beyond her forces; she must dedicate herself body and soul to household duties or to public professional duties. Let her choose then between two destinies of which one, the result of progress and the transformations which accompany it, is not superior to the other, but merely different. (pp. 13-14)

The novel lives by the shock of passions, and Miss Jewett does not seem to know it. This does not take anything away from her merit as a writer and thinker, even to break new ground discreetly in regions which would be suspect to us with any other guide. She makes us appreciate the beauties of them, the grandeur; she leads us straight to the immaculate snows, to pure ether, skillfully avoiding the precipices, sparing us the mud which so many others, under pretext of realism, apply themselves to discover right away. We do not persist any the less in believing that a happy compromise between the didactic form and the romantic form, the essay, properly speaking, is the genre which best suits her flowing pen.

This mixed genre can get along without invention; it neither demands that one imagine, nor that one concentrate; all the most serious theories are in their place, in their marvelously elastic framework beside a jest or a paradox; it suffers from the fact that the subjects are confused with one another like crazy creepers, without being studied in depth to their fullest development; it does not demand, on the other hand, the difficult art of transition. In brief, the little boat whose cruise was so well described in **"River Driftwood"** is the skiff that the author of *A Country Doctor* ought to man by preference. No passenger will complain that it is drifting, especially if he has the good fortune to glimpse, gliding capriciously along the waterway, figures as original, and as attractive at the same time, as Nan, produced fresh as a rose from the laboratories and amphitheatres where she has remained a woman while becoming a doctor. This proven miracle ought to be rare enough for one to write it down. (pp. 14-15)

> *Th. Bentzon [pseudonym of Maria Thérèse Blanc], "Le Roman de la Femme-Médecin," translated by Archille H. Biron, in* Appreciation of Sarah Orne Jewett: 29 Interpretive Essays, *edited by Richard Cary, Colby College Press, 1973, pp. 3-15.*

SARAH ORNE JEWETT (essay date 1893)

[*In the following excerpt from her preface to a later edition of* Deephaven, *Jewett recalls the personal motives and social conditions that prompted her to write a collection of stories set in a New England coastal town.*]

The short lifetime of [*Deephaven*] has seen great changes in the conditions of provincial life in New England. Twenty years ago, or a little more, the two heroines whose simple adventures are here described might well have served as types of those pioneers who were already on the eager quest for rural pleasures. Twenty years ago, our fast-growing New England cities, which had so lately been but large towns, full of green gardens and quiet neighborhoods, were just beginning to be overcrowded and uncomfortable in summer. The steady inflow of immigration, and the way in which these cities had drawn to themselves, like masses of quicksilver, much of the best life of the remotest villages, had made necessary a reflex current that set countryward in summer. This presently showed itself to be of unsuspected force and significance: it meant something more than the instinct for green fields and hills and the seashore; crowded towns and the open country were to be brought together in new association and dependence upon each other. (pp. 1-2)

The young writer of these Deephaven sketches was possessed by a dark fear that townspeople and country people would never understand one another, or learn to profit by their new relationship. She may have had the unconscious desire to make some sort of explanation to those who still expected to find the caricatured Yankee of fiction, striped trousers, bell-crowned hat, and all, driving his steady horses along the shady roads. It seemed not altogether reasonable when timid ladies mistook a selectman for a tramp, because he happened to be crossing a field in his shirt sleeves. At the same time, she was sensible of grave wrong and misunderstanding when these same timid ladies were regarded with suspicion, and their kindnesses were believed to come from pride and patronage. There is a noble saying of Plato that the best thing that can be done for the people of a state is to make them acquainted with one another. It was, happily, in the writer's childhood that Mrs. Stowe had written of those who dwelt along the wooded sea-coast and by the decaying, shipless harbors of Maine. The first chapters of "The Pearl of Orr's Island" gave the young author of *Deephaven* to see with new eyes, and to follow eagerly the old shore paths from one gray, weather-beaten house to another where Genius pointed her way.

In those days, if one had just passed her twentieth year, it was easy to be much disturbed by the sad discovery that certain phases of provincial life were first waning in New England. Small and old-fashioned towns, of which Deephaven may, by the reader's courtesy, stand as a type, were no longer almost self-subsistent, as in earlier times; and while it was impossible to estimate the value of that wider life that was flowing in from the great springs, many a mournful villager felt the anxiety that came with these years of change. Tradition and time-honored custom were to be swept away together by the irresistible current. Character and architecture seemed to lose individuality and distinction. The new riches of the country were seldom very well spent in those days; the money that the tourist or summer citizen left behind him was apt to be used to sweep away the quaint houses, the roadside thicket, the shady woodland, that had lured him first; and the well-filled purses that were scattered in our country's first great triumphal impulse of prosperity often came into the hands of people who hastened to spoil instead of to mend the best things that their village held. (pp. 3-5)

That all the individuality and quaint personal characteristics of rural New England were so easily swept away, or are even now dying out, we can refuse to believe. It appears, even, that they are better nourished and shine brighter by contrast than in former years. In rustic neighborhoods there will always be those whom George Sand had in mind when she wrote her delightful preface for *Légendes Rustiques:* Le paysan est donc, si l'on peut ainsi dire, le seul historien qui nous reste des temps antehistorique. Honneur et profit intellectuel à qui se consa-

Front cover of Jewett's first book, Deephaven.

crerait à la recherche de ses traditions merveilleuses de chaque hameau qui rassemblées ou groupées, comparées entre elles et minutieusement disséquées, jetteraient peut-être de grandes lueurs sur la nuit profonde des âges primitifs'' [''The rustic, it might be said, is the sole historian of prehistory left to us. Honor and intellectual profit to whomever devotes himself to searching each hamlet for its marvelous traditions, which—gathered, grouped, compared, and minutely dissected—perhaps might throw great flashes of illumination against the profound night of primitive ages'']. There will also exist that other class of country people who preserve the best traditions of culture and of manners, from some divine inborn instinct toward what is simplest and best and purest, who know the best because they themselves are of kin to it. It is as hard to be just to our contemporaries as it is easy to borrow enchantment in looking at the figures of the past; but while the Judges and Governors and grand ladies of old Deephaven are being lamented, we must not forget to observe that it is Miss Carew and Miss Lorimer who lament them, and who insist that there are no representatives of the ancient charm and dignity of their beloved town. Human nature is the same the world over, provincial and rustic influences must ever produce much the same effects upon character, and town life will ever have in its gift the spirit of the present, while it may take again from the quiet of hills and fields and the conservatism of country hearts a gift from the spirit of the past.

In the Preface to the first edition of *Deephaven* it was explained that Deephaven was not to be found on the map of New England under another name, and that the characters were seldom drawn from life. It was often asserted to the contrary, while the separate chapters were being published from time to time in *The Atlantic Monthly,* and made certain where the town really was, and the true names of its citizens and pew-holders. Therefore it appeared there were already many ''places in America,'' not ''few,'' that were ''touched with the hue of decay.'' Portsmouth and York and Wells, which were known to the author, Fairhaven and other seacoast towns, which were unknown, were spoken of as the originals of this fictitious village which still exists only in the mind. Strangely enough, the Atlantic Ocean always seems to lie to the west of it rather than to the east, and the landscape generally takes its own way and furnishes impossible landmarks and impressions to the one person who can see it clearly and in large. Some early knowledge of the secret found later in the delightful story of **''Peter Ibbetson''** appears to have been foreseen, but a lack of experience and a limited knowledge of the wide world outside forced the imaginer of Deephaven to build her dear town of such restricted materials as lay within her grasp. The landscape itself is always familiar to her thought, and far more real than many others which have been seen since with preoccupied or tired eyes.

The writer frankly confesses that the greater part of any value which these sketches may possess is in their youthfulness. There are sentences which make her feel as if she were the grandmother of the author of *Deephaven* and her heroines, those ''two young ladies of virtue and honour, bearing an inviolable friendship for each other,'' as two others, less fortunate, are described in the preface to *Clarissa Harlowe.* She begs her readers to smile with her over those sentences as they are found not seldom along the pages, and so the callow wings of what thought itself to be wisdom and the childish soul of sentiment will still be happy and untroubled.

In a curious personal sense the author repeats her attempt to explain the past and the present to each other. This little book will remind some of those friends who read it first of

light that lit the olden days;

but there are kind eyes, unknown then, that are very dear now, and to these the pages will be new. (pp. 5-8)

> *Sarah Orne Jewett, in a preface to her* Deephaven, *Houghton, Mifflin and Company, 1893, pp. 1-8.*

ALICE BROWN   (essay date 1897)

[*Brown was an American novelist, dramatist, biographer, and critic who is best remembered for her fiction set in New England. In the following excerpt, she offers an enthusiastic review of* The Country of the Pointed Firs.]

The Country of the Pointed Firs is the flower of a sweet, sane knowledge of life, and an art so elusive that it smiles up at you while you pull aside the petals, vainly probing its heart. The title is exacting, prophetic; a little bit of genius of which the book has to be worthy or come very ''tardy off.'' And the book is worthy. Here is the idyllic atmosphere of country life, unbroken by one jarring note; even the attendant sadness and pathos of being are resolved into that larger harmony destined to elude our fustian words. It is a book made to defy the praise ordinarily given to details; it must be regarded *au large.* For it takes hold of the very centre of things. The pointed firs have their roots in the ground of national being; they are index fingers to the stars. A new region unrolls before you like a living map, whereof The Bowden Reunion and Captain Littlepage are twin mountain heights, warm in sunshine and swept by favoring airs. The Reunion indeed bears a larger significance than its name. It stirs in us the dormant clan-spirit; we understand ancestor-worship, the continuity of being. All the delicate humor, the broidery of the day, ''like fringe upon a petticoat''— the pictorial pies, the alien guest with her pseudo-likeness to ''Cousin Pa'lina Bowden about the forehead,'' the woman who ''wouldn't get back in a day if she was as far out o' town as she was out o' tune''—this thrills you with a fine and delicate pleasure; but meanwhile your mind marches grandly with the Bowdens, you throb like them with pride of race, you acquiesce willingly in the sweet, loyal usages of domesticity. The conception has its tap-root in the solid earth; but Captain Littlepage's story of the unknown country ''up north beyond the ice'' takes hold on things remote: it breathes the awful chill and mysticism of the Ancient Mariner. Here are the powers of the air portrayed with Miltonic grandeur. Less tangible even than the denizens of the Beleaguered City, they throng and press upon the mind, making void all proven experience. It is as strange and true a page out of the unseen possibilities of being as Kipling's story of the dead sea-snake. It is not, moreover, the only hint of the inter-relations of known and unknown. Even the herbs in Mrs. Todd's garden could not all be classified. There was one that sent ''out a penetrating odor late in the evening, after the dew had fallen, and the moon was high, and the cool air came up from the sea.'' You would not know that herb for a world of science. It is mystical as moly, and so it shall remain.

Mrs. Todd and Mrs. Blackett are as real as the earth. For pure fascination, Mrs. Todd can never expect to vie with her mother; she did ''lurch about steppin' into a bo't''; it was not she who put forth the grave axiom that it was scarcely ''advisable to maintain cats just on account of their havin' bob tails.'' But she is the colossal figure of a simple woman dowered with sorrow and loss, who set her feet firmly on the ground—

To crush the snake and spare the worm.

who made personal grief no reason for bickering with the universe, whose moral life went sanely with the stars, and whose nostrils were delighted with sweet savors from the earth which had denied her. Too often are we taught that great grief and finer feeling are the concomitants of revolt; but it is the larger mind which links them to sweetness, serenity, and obedience. Here is quiet revelation of human tragedy, but none of that fierce rebellion through which individual suffering eats its own heart and the heart of the onlooking chorus. Even the self-exiled Joanna, pursued by the phantom of the unpardonable sin, cannot afflict us irremediably; for still was she surrounded, as with a sea, by faulty human love, and still, as we read, the tranquil company of the firs bids us be patient till her affliction shall be overpast.

To pluck the flowers of humor, quaint philosophy, and legend here is as hopeless as to make a Poyser anthology. You are simply bewildered by the richness and lifegiving balm of this herby garden. It is the acme of Miss Jewett's fine achievement, blending the humanity of the **"Native of Winby"** and the fragrance of the **"White Heron."** No such beautiful and perfect work has been done for many years; perhaps no such beautiful work has ever been done in America. (pp. 249-50)

Alice Brown, "Profitable Tales," in The Book Buyer, *Vol. XV, No. 3, October, 1897, pp. 248-50.*

HENRY JAMES   (letter date 1901)

[*James was an American novelist whose works are valued for their psychological acuity and complex artistic form. Throughout his career, James also wrote literary criticism in which he developed his artistic ideals and applied them to the works of others. Among the numerous conceptualizations he formed to clarify the nature of fiction, he defined the novel as "a direct impression of life." The quality of this impression—the degree of moral and intellectual development—and the author's ability to communicate this impression in an effective and artistic manner were the two principal criteria by which James estimated the worth of a literary work. In the following excerpt from a letter to Jewett, James evaluates her historical novel* The Tory Lover.]

Let me not criminally, or at all events gracelessly, delay to thank you for your charming and generous present of *The Tory Lover.* He has been but 3 or 4 days in the house, yet I have given him an earnest, a pensive, a liberal—yet, a benevolent attention, and the upshot is that I should like to write you a longer letter than I just now—(especially as it's past midnight) see my way to doing. For it would take me some time to disembroil the tangle of saying to you at once how I appreciate the charming touch, tact & taste of this ingenious exercise, & how little I am in sympathy with experiments of its general (to my sense) misguided stamp. There I am!—yet I don't do you the outrage, as a fellow craftsman & a woman of genius and courage, to suppose you not as conscious as I am myself of all that, in these questions of art & taste & sincerity, is beyond the mere twaddle of graciousness. The "historic" novel is, for me, condemned, even in cases of labour as delicate as yours, to a fatal *cheapness,* for the simple reason that the difficulty of the job is inordinate & that a mere *escamotage* ["trickery"], in the interest of each, & of the abysmal public *naïveté,* becomes inevitable. You may multiply the little facts that can be got from pictures, & documents, relics & prints, as much as you like—*the* real thing is almost impossible to do, & in its essence the whole effect is as nought. I mean the evolution, the representation of the old CONSCIOUSNESS, the soul, the sense, the horizon, the action of individuals, in

whose minds half the things that make ours, that make the modern world were non-existent. You have to think with your modern apparatus a man, a woman—or rather fifty—whose own thinking was intensely otherwise conditioned. You have to simplify back by an amazing tour de force—& even then it's all humbug. But there is a shade of the (even then) humbug that *may* amuse. The childish tricks that take the place of any such conception of the real job in the flood of Tales of the Past that seems of late to have been rolling over our devoted country— these ineptitudes have, on a few recent glances, struck me as creditable to no one concerned. You, I hasten to add, seem to me to have steered very clear of them—to have seen your work very bravely & handled it firmly; but even you court disaster by composing the whole thing so much by sequences of speeches. It is when the extinct soul talks, & the earlier consciousness airs itself, that the pitfalls multiply & the "cheap" way has to serve. I speak in general, I needn't keep insisting, & I speak grossly, summarily, by rude & provisional signs, in order to suggest my sentiment at all. I didn't mean to say so much without saying more, now I have touched you with cold water when I only meant just lightly & kindly to sprinkle you as for a new baptism—that is a *re*-dedication to altars but briefly, I trust, forsaken. Go back to the dear Country of the Pointed Firs, *come* back to the palpable present *intimate* that throbs responsive, & that wants, misses, needs you, God knows, & that suffers woefully in your absence. (pp. 263-64)

Henry James, in a letter to Sarah Orne Jewett on October 5, 1901, in American Literature, *Vol. XXVII, No. 2, May, 1955, pp. 263-64.*

[PAUL ELMER MORE]   (essay date 1910)

[*More was an American critic who, along with Irving Babbitt, formulated the doctrines of New Humanism in early twentieth-century American thought. The New Humanists were strict moralists who adhered to traditional conservative values in reaction to an age of scientific and artistic self-expression. In regard to literature, they believed a work's implicit reflection of support for the classic ethical norms to be of as much importance as its aesthetic qualities. More was particularly opposed to Naturalism, which he believed accentuated the animal nature of humans, and to any literature, such as Romanticism, that broke with established classical tradition. His importance as a critic derives from the rigid coherence of his ideology, which polarized American critics into hostile opponents (Van Wyck Brooks, Edmund Wilson, H. L. Mencken) or devoted supporters (Norman Foerster, Stuart Sherman, and, to a lesser degree, T. S. Eliot). He is especially esteemed for the philosophical and literary erudition of his multi-volume* Shelburne Essays *(1904-21). In the following excerpt, More discusses Jewett's works in the context of New England literature.*]

Sarah Orne Jewett's tales and novels have been issued in seven peculiarly neat little volumes, which seem to reflect the delicate charm of the writer's work. These collected editions of an author that one has been reading for years in the magazines have sometimes a pleasant way of confirming and clarifying an opinion that has been floating vaguely in the mind. What was before ephemeral in the very nature of things, now appears to the eye as if dressed for an age of endurance. In external form at least it is not different from the eternal books, and one looks into it a little more seriously for its meaning.

Now, one has always felt that Miss Jewett's characteristic note was the spirit of [Elizabeth Gaskell's] *Cranford,* modified a little by New England weather, and the reading together of five of these new volumes (so far, good type has lured us over old paths) has strengthened this feeling, and added certain questions. Why is this Cranfordian manner so much more successfully followed in the two longish novels, *Deephaven* and *Country of the Pointed Firs,* than in the short tales? And why is the third novel, *A Country Doctor,* so much less interesting than the other two? A half-way answer to both questions has come to us with the questions themselves as we have read these volumes. It is the curious inability shared by Miss Jewett with the Brahmin writers of New England fiction generally to make passion or action real and vital. States of mind they can describe; the conscience of an individual or of a people they can analyze; characters petrified into some tragic or exquisitely pathetic or tender reminiscence they can make real; an aspect of nature they can portray as delicately as the human mood of which it seems a shadow; but in passion and action they have almost always failed. So one thinks of the twilight of passive reflection that broods over Whittier's "Leaves from Margaret Smith's Journal"; of the mistiness of grief in Longfellow's European tales and the remoteness, as of a holiday remembered from boyhood, of "Kavanagh"; of the amateurishness of Oliver Wendell Holmes's novels; of the magical glamour of Hawthorne, which to some readers conveys his world of people into a land where morality is only a sombre reminiscence and to others seems only inhumanity and bloodlessness. . . . Always we have the idyllic beauty of a scene that is petrified into motionlessness, and human moods in which the active passions remain as an echo from a remote distance.

And so in *Deephaven* and the *Country of the Pointed Firs,* which attempt no story in the proper sense of the word, but portray the very soul of fading villages on the sea and the life of people who move as if the motive fire in their hearts had long ago been covered over with ashes, Miss Jewett has almost rivalled the charm of *Cranford,* would quite have rivalled that charm, one feels, if she had only Mrs. Gaskell's constructive genius. On the other hand, in *A Country Doctor,* as soon as we get beyond first idyllic chapters and enter into the struggles and ambitions of the heroine, there is a flagging of interest and a sense of half-life; the passion and the action are unreal, almost as if imagined in the study of a school-girl. And this same lack mars many of the short stories. Even when these attempt to convey only a mood or a glimpse into dream-life, they are less successful than the longer idyls. They lack at once the point and dramatic situation needed in the short story and the cumulative friendliness, so to speak, of long association. (pp. 386-87)

Meanwhile, in her own world, what rare and exquisite entertainment Miss Jewett has provided. Perhaps only one who has himself been baptized in the still waters of New England faith can feel the perfect fascination of these people that move about so pathetically and speak with so subtle a humor in the village of *Deephaven* and in the towns and fields and islands of the *Country of the Pointed Firs.* Who is so immersed in the passionate game of life that he cannot for a while give his heart to Mrs. Todd, the quaint herb-woman and philosopher of the flowers, and to her mother and brother, the brave and beautiful hermits of Green Island?—

Cras amet qui nunquam amavit.

["Tomorrow let him love who has never loved."]

If the lives of these people seem very still, they are able somehow to arouse a strange warmth of friendship. (p. 387)

[*Paul Elmer More*], *"A Writer of New England,"* in *The Nation, Vol. XCI, No. 2365, October 27, 1910, pp. 386-87.*

MARTHA HALE SHACKFORD (essay date 1922)

[*Shackford was an American educator and critic. Her many works include studies of classical, medieval, renaissance, and modern literature, focusing on poetry and poets. In the following excerpt, Shackford discusses the strengths of Jewett's works.*]

It is a pity that Miss Jewett's tales are not better known in England. She, in her quiet fashion, has given a truer picture of the fundamental verities of American ideals than have some of our more notorious writers. And to-day, when so many of us are profoundly disturbed regarding the future of humanity, Miss Jewett's stories bring to the world a reassuring faith that man is both intelligent and trustworthy, that what was true in one corner of New England is true of mankind. It must be stated, at once, that she has little appeal to readers bent upon finding 'kinetic characters' and 'emphasis by direct action'. She was not circumscribed by the many rules which guide the present-day writer of short-stories. Her tales are disconcerting, tiresome to those whose logical powers are developed at the expense of their imagination and their love of romantic waywardness. The very lack of conspicuous 'efficiency' of method is one of her greatest charms, in this hour when the over-macadamized short-story sends the reader smoothly, swiftly, monotonously along, without a bump or a sight of grass-grown irregularity. Doubtless Miss Jewett's work might have been improved by more technique, but she had something better than formal skill,—wisdom, matured understanding of life, individual insight.

All of her stories are loosely woven narratives, picturing homely lives, yet she has so faithfully portrayed their strength, their tenderness, their response to primal duties, that she has lifted their existence to a high level of meaning. Her sea-captains, her fishermen, her housewives are like the persons in Sophoclean drama, deeply, ironically, aware of Fate. Their lives and their speech are shadowed by a consciousness of eternal truths. Only an artist, sensitive and meditative, endowed with the poet's vision, could have been content to suggest so quietly the meagre externals and the brooding inner life of these uninstructed, primitively real people. Herself a student of Wordsworth, she has given a Wordsworthian interpretation of austere, elemental feeling. (p. 20)

As a describer of the shore life of the state of Maine she is without an equal. The clear austerity of the air of northern New England is everywhere in these tales set among rocky shores and gray islands. The stimulating tang of salt breezes and the cool breath from the illimitable east meet here; for those who know it she pictures the visionary beauty of the northland's clarity of light, its mysterious distances touched with receding shades of blue and dim green glimmering and fading into crystalline colorlessness. That expectant, hesitant quality of atmosphere tone, described by Dorothy Wordsworth in her journal of a *Tour Made in Scotland,* and by Fiona Macleod in *Where the Forest Murmurs,* was perceived by Miss Jewett, giving her work a certain elemental majesty of background. She describes life on the open sea, the daily experiences of fishermen whose journeys out to the deep waters demand courage, hardihood, endurance, association with primeval wind and water and stars. The sea is continual in her stories, determining the life of the people dwelling at its edge and earning their livelihood from it. The fishermen who seem so commonplace, so unassuming, so normal, are the very embodiment of the strength of man's will, of his delight in matching his powers with the mighty forces of the ocean. When these men come back to live in local and temporal villages, their existence, seemingly monotonous, is vibrating all the while to past and future.

Always against backgrounds of distance and whelming ocean and eternal struggle one must see the scenes of domestic life in the dingy little kitchens, furnished with braided rugs, native oilcloth, and, often, rare imported china, if one is to get the right perspective for understanding. It is in these scenes that Miss Jewett shows her gift of presenting character in mild action. The situations are simple, not at all striking in opportunities for dramatic interest. There is nothing spectacular nor very tense in her presentments of life; she shows people living simple, normal, average lives, and the tissue of their existence is not external event but slow pondering of life, and still slower exchange of comment about it.

Miss Jewett's stories are always stories of character. Plots hardly exist in her work; she had little interest in creating suspense or in weaving together threads of varied interests. She presents people through mild desultory action, in situations seldom dramatically striking. The people interpreted live simple, inconspicuous lives, without great tragedy attending them, but made significant through the little things which, by reiterated irritation and pain, tax the spirit of endurance and shape character. The wisdom won from slow pondering of life is found on the lips of her men and women. And these persons speak the very thoughts and the very language of their region; thoughts expressed in a shrewd, picturesque, colloquial fashion, in a dialect directly true to life, not a romantic make-believe. But the best part, perhaps, of her delineation of these people is in her record of their silences. Miss Jewett has interpreted the impulse to reticence, has accounted for the temperament of these watchful, guarded folk who imitate the granite impenetrability of their natural surroundings. Also she has shown the extraordinary sense of justice to be noted in this district. So bound up with nature are these people that they feel accountable for nature's doings; they must help atone for nature's ravages and aberrations. But like the ocean's ebb and flow, the method of giving aid and comfort is somewhat indirect, oblique, attaining its end with the seventh wave.

Miss Jewett's most successful and probably her most representative work is *The Country of the Pointed Firs*, a series of chapters linked together loosely enough by the fact that one person records her experiences in a typical Maine village, on the edge of the sea, a village that reaches back to the land overgrown with the spruce trees that, in sharp spires, stand out against the blue sky. It is really a group of character-sketches, not a story, and the chief character is Mrs. Todd, a woman with a tragic past, fighting for her daily bread, yet brisk, hopeful, romantic to the last degree. Skilled in the lore of healing herbs, she seems like one of the Fates, endowed with portentous wisdom, stooping to pick sprigs of fragrant pennyroyal, in a sunshiny green pasture. Slowly, and with most delicate humor, Miss Jewett makes clear Mrs. Todd's endless curiosity, high-mindedness, and shrewd, inexhaustible kindness.

Another character is Captain Littlepage, whose experience on the deep waters of the Seven Seas has carried him into strange adventures. Many, in older days, were the men who had been around the world and had settled down in primitive seclusion to think over the scenes and events of a dramatic lifetime. This old man had a knowledge of foreign parts, his imagination was filled with brilliant pictures of the world; he was a thorough cosmopolitan, worldly-wise, efficient, yet an eternal child of mystery and romance; a mute, inglorious Marco Polo.

Joanna, in this story, was a young woman who, crossed in love, had gone to a lonely hermitage on a solitary island to spend her life, a combination of Ariadne and a mediaeval anchoress. The book is sheer reality both in setting and in character-study. The scattered bits of description give one the very look of green pastures, the scent of aromatic herbs, the fragrance of sun-smitten spruce-trees, the sting of the cool salt air, and the milder aspects of blue, sunshiny, safe harbors.

All through the casual recital of unimportant incidents the reader finds a spirit of gentle, appreciative humor. There is satire here, of the most charming sort, never unkind, never malicious, never condescending, but always quietly penetrating. Miss Jewett saw well the ironies, the whimsies of life, she watched with sympathy the interplay of human emotions; she knew how vanity, selfishness, obstinacy, and complacent virtue fail to recognize themselves in the tragi-comedy of social life. Her pages are full of keen pleasant enjoyment of the caprices of personality, the self-secured defeats, the amusing ignorance that calls itself knowledge. This humor cannot be illustrated by quotation, it must be recognized in the context, and is always the unspoken reflection of one silently pondering over the range of human life from the Age of Pericles to the day when the Bowden Family had a reunion.

Other stories have their individual charm, always preeminently the charm of character delineation. Mrs. Bonney in *Deephaven* is a tragic figure of Poverty, Labor, and Courtesy. "The White Heron" is a study of loyalty to Nature, a record of faithfulness to the wild, beautiful life which surrounds a little country girl. Repudiating money that would relieve her poverty, she keeps the White Heron's secret, sharing the bird's mysterious, lonely freedom, and remaining true to the primitive brotherhood between man and winged creature.

"The Neighbor's Landmark," in the same volume, encloses in itself a picture of another sort of loyalty to Nature and tradition. This concerns a man's balancing of beauty, association, sentiment, over against a profit which would greatly ease the struggle of an impoverished family. In these two stories are presented moral problems of absorbing interest to those who resent man's useless despoiling of the beauty of the natural world.

"The Queen's Twin" is a very subtly humorous study of a New England woman gravely concerned about the inner fortunes of her twin (by chronology), Queen Victoria. Here is a recognition of the fact that circumstances are accidental, that character, ideals, inward dignity are the realities of life. A sort of democracy of inner understanding and sympathy is pictured in this suggestive story of the bare, unlovely surroundings of one whose imagination carried her beyond space and courtiers.

Dozens of other stories, collected in various volumes, exist, and several more extended works make up the list of Miss Jewett's achievement. These stories have varying degrees of appeal. Some are frankly trivial, others are interpretations of the human 'predicament' where decisions must be made which involve surrender of personal desires, for the sake of some faith in the larger values of life. Through her record of interminable endurance, courageous patience, Miss Jewett has shown that in all the fluctuations of selfishness, something exists more stable than self, some sense of coercion exercised by ideals, some knowledge of the superiority of will over matter. A reader once attracted will wander on through these tales with increasing responsiveness. She arouses the reader to reflections, stimulates his curiosity, defies his conventionally and modernness, contributes to his faith in the worth of experience. The rugged and picturesque life of hardship is always a tonic to the jaded products of urbanity. (pp. 22-6)

Martha Hale Shackford, "Sarah Orne Jewett," in The Sewanee Review, *Vol. XXX, No. 1, Winter, 1922, pp. 20-6.*

LUDWIG LEWISOHN (essay date 1932)

[*A German-born American novelist and critic, Lewisohn was considered an authority on German literature, and his translations of Gerhart Hauptmann, Rainer Maria Rilke, and Jakob Wasserman are widely respected. In 1919 he became the drama critic for* The Nation, *serving as its associate editor until 1924, when he joined a group of expatriates in Paris. After his return to the United States in 1934, Lewisohn became a prominent sympathizer with the Zionist movement, and served as editor of the Jewish magazine* New Palestine *for five years. Many of his later works reflect his humanistic concern for the plight of the Jewish people. In the following excerpt, Lewisohn compares Jewett's writings with those of Mary Wilkins Freeman.*]

The sectional realism with which the period of national expression faintly began was in truth very feeble. The creative values left by these writers are few. They all or nearly all share one fatal mark; they were incapable of development; their first books remained their best. Thus, for instance, *Old Creole Days* and *The Grandissimes* of George W. Cable are still readable; his later books are not.... A lusciousness, lack of restraint and impertinent verbosity that characterized all the writers of what was then known as the New South are first observable in him.

New England, which always seems to decline and yet is never quite drained of creative energy, comes off better even in this period. It is fairly certain that all that will remain of it or be seen to have any but illustrative and disciplinary value will be a few pages by Sarah Orne Jewett and Mary Wilkins Freeman. These two cultivated the short story, not the short-story. Their field of observation was excessively limited; the society they had before them to depict was the least fruitful that human artists ever sought to treat. In these New England villages the old maid was the typical person; men, except the old and feeble or an occasional minister, were nuisances or intruders. A European would not credit the existence of such a society. He who truly knows America knows better. Upon the whole both Miss Jewett and Mrs. Freeman kept their eye on the object. They did not, to be sure, stand above or detachedly aside from the matter contemplated. Miss Jewett was capable of faintly ironic moments; Mrs. Freeman took a good deal for wool that had never seen a sheep's back. Yet both are scrupulous within the measure of their intelligence and the reach of their vision; their entire sincerity and formal simplicity make for a mildly classical quality, for a sobriety and completeness of delineation within the tiniest of frames.... Both Miss Jewett and Mrs. Freeman confined themselves largely to the short story. The thinness of their substance was such as to be palatable in highly concentrated portions; even the novelette, as witness, for instance, Mrs. Freeman's "The Jamesons," makes a demand they could not meet. I seem to be describing them in terms chiefly negative. But their virtue resides, in fact, in their avoidance of the vices of their period. What remains is thin but clear, narrow but unpretentious, infinitely restricted but sober and complete.

Miss Jewett's vein was the thinner, but the finer of the two. *Deephaven* is a little book that grows upon reflection in the memory. The decaying maritime village in Maine with its widows and spinsters and superannuated seafaring men, with its pride and its delicate aroma of the past lingers definitely in the imagination. If *Cranford* is a minor classic, so is *Deephaven*. The tints are unbelievably pale, but they have not at least faded in the weather of time. A few of Miss Jewett's stories are quite as fine and more substantial. In the very best she wholly avoids "plot"; she is content to render character—**"Miss Tempy's Watchers"**—or the pathos of frustrated lives—**"The Dulham Ladies"**—or a quality of the spirit—**"A White Heron"**—or, at her fullest, a complete tragedy in miniature, as in **"Marsh Rosemary."** She will find the universal in her little chosen plot, as in **"Law Lane,"** or as in **"An Only Son."** She has, too, an elegiac note in her prose, a sensitiveness to the spiritual overtone of rhythm, of form, that separates her from her crude contemporaries: "There was nobody to speak to him and the house was like a tomb where all the years of his past were lying dead, and all the pleasantness of life existed only in remembrance." If ever there came into being a library of American literature devoted to creative expression and not to document, a slender volume would assuredly be dedicated to Sarah Orne Jewett. (pp. 288-91)

Ludwig Lewisohn, "The Soil and the Transition," in his Expression in America, *Harper & Brothers, Publishers, 1932, pp. 273-309.*

OLIVE CROSS (essay date 1952)

[*In the following excerpt, Cross discusses Jewett's stylistic development from* Deephaven *to* The Country of the Pointed Firs.]

In 1929 a biographer placed Sarah Orne Jewett ... next to Emily Dickinson, and wrote of them confidently as "the two principal women writers America has had." Certainly a writer whose work was praised as was Miss Jewett's by Kipling, John Burroughs, James Russell Lowell, and Matthew Arnold; whose masterpiece *The Country of the Pointed Firs* was chosen in 1925 by Willa Cather to stand with *The Scarlet Letter* and *Huckleberry Finn* as one of the three American books destined for the longest life, must still hold a high place in a list that would now have to reckon with Edith Wharton, Anne Douglas Sedgwick, Ellen Glasgow, Mary Ellen Chase, Edna St. Vincent Millay, Margaret Mitchell, Marjorie Kinnan Rawlings, and Willa Cather herself. Certainly many of Miss Jewett's twenty-one volumes, ranging in date from 1877 to 1901, have grown in grace these more than fifty years, and in a time that has brought more change in attitude toward the values of life than the chronological period would indicate. Her best sketches quietly live on, saying to the future from the past that in one little section of Maine man has proven himself intelligent and honorable; saying this in universal language, implying that what is true in that little corner of the world may be true of mankind.

Miss Jewett wrote and published with only a few breaks from the time she was twenty until she was fifty-two. Since her work was in a sense not fiction at all, but a faithful recording of actual life around her as she saw it, it is interesting to note the gradual and subtle, though discernible, differences in the earlier and later writings, as the author herself saw her surroundings more and more clearly, and with a deeper sympathy and understanding. From the beginning she had unusual power of observation. This eventually grew into insight, a much rarer gift. This development from observation to insight, the way in which it was stimulated, yet at the same time limited, by her life and reflected in her writing, is the object of this study. (pp. 113-14)

> When I was perhaps fifteen (she records in an autobiographical fragment), the first city boarders began to make their appearance near Berwick, and the way they misconstrued the country people and made game of their peculiarities fired me with indignation. I determined to teach the world that country people were not the awkward, ignorant set those people seemed to think. I wanted the world to know their grand simple lives; and, so far as I had a mission when I first began to write, I think that was it.

There is something significant about this often repeated statement of Miss Jewett. It shows that even as a girl, she did not look upon herself as one of "these country people." She would observe and describe, even defend, but from the beginning she stood apart from her picture. (pp. 115-16)

All of this came out in *Deephaven,* Miss Jewett's first book. Published in 1877 when she was twenty-eight, it is a collection of sketches she had been contributing with great success to *The Atlantic* over a period of years. The very first sketch had received favorable comment from the New York *Nation,* the best critical journal of the time. William Dean Howells, editor of *The Atlantic,* had urged her to bring the papers together into a book. It was extremely well received. John Greenleaf Whittier wrote to the young author: "Dear friend: I must thank thee for thy admirable book *Deephaven.* I have given several copies to friends, all of whom appreciate it highly, and I have just been reading it for the third time. I know of nothing better in our literature of the kind." This book which Mr. Whittier read three times is by a girl, and much of it is about girls' doings. They row and swim and play on the beach and lie on the sofa in front of the fire and tell ghost stories. They rummage through the attic and through an escritoire where they find "a little package of letters; ship letters mostly, tied with a very pale and tired looking blue ribbon. They were in a drawer with a locket holding a faded miniature on ivory and a lock of brown hair, and there were also some dry twigs and bits of leaf which had long ago been bright wild roses such as still bloom among the Deephaven rocks."

The two young visitors who spend the summer in this imaginary seaport of New England engage two fish wagons to take a crowd of "natives" to the circus in the next town; they see "a dead snake, that must require an awful long grave and an elephant that looks as if he ain't got no animation."

But it is futile to try to give the flavor of *Deephaven* with scattered quotations. The collection of episodes "reminds me of the Dutch painters who presented the joy and sorrow of the common people in quiet colors." [Russell Blankenship, *American Literature* (1931)]. Here is the beauty of a civilization proud even in its decay, and uncompromising with progress. The delicate shades of social distinction which are preserved by the patricians who represent them and by the commonality who recognize them are touched with humor and yet with sympathy.

The best chapter is **"In Shadow."** There death is treated with impressive reality. The country people grieve, not so much over the dead as over the fact of death itself. In its presence they seem as deeply aware of Fate as if they were persons in a Sophoclean drama.

> Their faces were awed by the presence of death, and indifference had given place to uncertainty. Their neighbor was immeasurably their superior now. Living, he had been a failure by their own standards; but now, if he could come back, he would know secrets, and be wise beyond anything they could imagine, and who could know the riches of which he might have come into possession?

In this episode Miss Jewett gives prophecy of the insight that makes her later writings notable. But on the whole, *Deephaven* is just a pleasant story full of specific detail about out of door life and country people in the one small section well known and beloved by the author. (pp. 116-17)

[Miss Jewett] was never able to portray lovers convincingly in her writing. Her few sweethearts walk across the pages woodenly or foolishly. The nearest that she came to a life-like delineation of a lover was in William of *The Country of the Pointed Firs,* who courted Esther shyly for forty years by an annual visit to her house, a few miles away, with a gift of dried fish, William kept at home to attend his mother and Esther to attend hers. When they were both past sixty, Esther's mother died, and William married her at last,—in time for them to be buried, one assumes, side by side—though Miss Jewett does not carry the story to that extreme of intimacy. (p. 119)

[Miss Jewett's] style has been compared to that of Hawthorne and the earlier Howells, but she had nothing of Hawthorne's grasp of the powerful feelings that rock men's souls. Like Hawthorne, though, she did portray life in New England with genuine feeling.

A romantic realist if such is possible, she either did not see or refused to write about the coarse, the rough, the seamy side of life. She could delineate the pathetic, but could not grapple with tragedy. Since she was unable to plumb the depths of human misery, she likewise failed to reach the heights of man's bliss, and so left no stirring messages, inspired no truly great vision. Miss Jewett dealt only with the gentle because her experience was limited to gentle living. The only deep sorrow she seems to have suffered was the death of her father.

But with the years she grew in wisdom and insight, and the writing of her middle age reflects realism, even though it is well colored with optimism. When she was forty-seven she wrote *The Country of the Pointed Firs,* her most mature work. The structure of the book is almost the same as that of *Deephaven.* The people and events are seen through the eyes of a summer visitor. Again the situations are simple, sometimes even trivial; but the writer has gone far beyond mere observation and description that record facts correct in detail. Here she catches the lights and shadows that play upon the people, the freshness of the air they breathe. The writer has a new insight into the characters she portrays, and more sensitively communicates their feelings to the reader. One finds this in **"The Bowden Reunion":**

> "I don't ask no more," says Almiry Todd, the fisherman's widow and central character of the book; "I want to know if you saw mother walkin' at the head! It choked me right up to see mother at the head, walkin' with the ministers."

And there is a new, genial humor, that delightful flower of insight. "That's Sant Bowden; he always takes the lead, such days. Good for nothing else most o' his time; trouble is, he—stim'lates.''

In its procession across the field to the picnic grove, ''We were no more a New England family celebrating its own existence and simple progress; we carried the tokens and inheritance of all such households from which this had descended, and were only the latest of our line.''

Only a writer of insight could so portray Mrs. Todd, not only the ordinary, everyday housekeeper, droll gatherer of herbs, but while she walked up the rocky shore in her grief, ''something lonely and solitary about her great determined shape. She might have been Antigone alone on the Thebian plain.''

Even in his volume, full of the same sensitive feeling for characters as that which makes notable her story, ''**The White Heron,**'' Miss Jewett betrays the pre-war English attitude toward the country people, that of a lady writing of a beloved peasantry.

But these characters, shown through the simplest of happenings, are important; they are intelligent and trustworthy, forgetful of self, kind, shy, often silent, but full of a hidden fire of enthusiasm. Miss Jewett's finest tribute to them, perhaps, comes in the very beginning of ''**The Bowden Reunion**''; and here for once she identifies herself with the humble people of whom she writes:

> When at long intervals the altars to patriotism, to friendship, to the ties of kindred, are reared in our familiar fields, then the fires glow, the flames come up as if from the inexhaustible burning heart of the earth; the primal fires break through the granite dust in which our souls are set.

(pp. 120-21)

Olive Cross, ''From 'Deephaven' to 'The Country of the Pointed Firs','' in Florida State University Studies, *No. 5, 1952, pp. 113-21.*

ELEANOR M. SMITH (essay date 1956)

[In the following excerpt, Smith compares and contrasts Jewett's works with those of Willa Cather.]

Students of American literature are aware of a literary relationship between Sarah Orne Jewett and Willa Sibert Cather which goes beyond the obvious fact that each wrote of a period in American life which each had known and loved, and which no longer exists. (p. 472)

Probably the first link to be noted is that both are provincial writers. In this respect, however, as in all others, Miss Cather's works reach far and above Miss Jewett's and the reader must penetrate beyond the surface differences to reach the inner similarities. Miss Jewett never enlarges the scope of her work, and for the most part she tells of the incidents she saw about her. A drive through the country, a story told by a neighbor, an old person's visit to a nearby town, a chance meeting, the anticipations of the lonely, the plight of the town poor, a widow's ''dyin' spells,'' a flight from the poorhouse, a business failure, the unhappy romance of an elderly spinster, all became under her fertile imagination material out of which to weave a story. Miss Jewett was particularly interested in individuals, and her narratives abound in the presentation of old widows, spinsters, farmers, and fishermen. With charm, simplicity, and

not infrequent humor, she recaptures the character, ideals, and spirit of old New England.

The aging aristocracy would not let their poverty diminish their feeling of importance, and they walked up the church aisle ''proud as Lucifer and straight as a mast.'' The old fishermen, whose youth and strength had given way to rheumatic aches, eked out an existence with some offshore fishing. Every pleasant morning they could be found sunning themselves on the wharves, sitting close together to overcome their handicap of deafness and telling over and over again the stories of their adventures at sea. In their desire to be independent, the worn, tired bodies of the poor often made a pathetic picture. Old Mrs. Peet is but one of the many in this large group. The excited voice, with which she told that she was on her way to the city to look for work in the home of a relative, became a hollow mockery as she fearfully and silently sought to reassure herself it would not make a mite of difference that she looked quaint in her outmoded clothes so long as she willingly did her part. In *The Country of the Pointed Firs,* in the life of the widow, Mrs. Todd, Miss Jewett draws her most complete picture of the simple, yet dignified existence characteristic of the elderly people's home life. Mrs. Todd, in her matter-of-fact way, enjoyed small diversions as they came. A visit with her mother, a call to or from a neighbor, a visit from an old friend, all were important enough to give her a feeling of delight. In keeping with her restrained New England manner she was not sentimental, but her lack of sentiment did not keep her from being thoughtful of others and generous in doing kindly deeds.

From first to last Miss Jewett's unfailing characteristic is the sympathetic portrayal of old people. She never once lost sight of her purpose to show the good qualities of the poor and the old-fashioned and to point out the beauty of their efforts in maintaining as high a standard of dignity in living as was possible in their limited circumstances. Her altruistic purpose, however, did not blind her to amusing situations. And her lively, though always gentle, humor gives her stories much of their charm. In her portrayals it is not unusual to find humor and pathos interwoven, as, for example, in ''**The Dulham Ladies,**'' an account of two spinsters who tried to recapture their youth by buying false hair. The horrid shades and the long frizzy bangs, which became askew with a turn of the head, made the spinsters more pathetic looking than ever. But they rejoiced in their rejuvenation, happily unaware of the amused comment of a neighbor that they looked like poodle dogs.

Miss Cather covers a broader, more intricate, and more varied range of material, and the rugged influence of her background and her training in journalism give a vigor to her writing that is foreign to the sheltered atmosphere of Miss Jewett's works. In contrast to Miss Jewett's accounts of simple old-fashioned villages with their inhabitants steadfastly rooted in their way of life, firmly clinging to their inherited ideals, we find in Miss Cather's the struggles and achievements of the Western settlers set side by side with the shoddy aims, and often frustrated desires, of a commercial generation. As with Miss Jewett, character is predominant. But where Miss Jewett places stress on the idealism of fortitude in declining years, Miss Cather places stress on the idealism of youth's heroic endeavor. (pp. 478-80)

Since Miss Jewett's writings are limited in range and personality, deal with only one period, and use only one approach, the differences outweigh the similarities. It is both authors' unfailing stress on the necessity of ideals in living, which binds them—despite marked differences—in a distinctive, common bond. The prime relationship between Miss Jewett's emphasis on self-respect and Miss Cather's emphasis on the fulfillment of one's potentialities should not be overlooked, for the latter is the carrying of self-respect to a very high degree. Without respect for self one would not desire to fulfill one's potentialities. Therefore, it can be said that where Miss Jewett's elderly protagonists are concerned with self-respect in the sense of living as graciously and independently as their limited means will allow them, Miss Cather's youthful protagonists are concerned with self-respect in the sense of striving to make reality out of inner urgings to achieve a purpose in life. (pp. 481-82)

Some of Miss Jewett's elderly people brooded over their sorrows and became partially or completely insane. In telling of their peculiarities she never holds them up to ridicule. In Alexandra's kindly treatment of ''Crazy Ivar,'' Miss Cather reveals a similar attitude toward the mentally afflicted.

Miss Jewett's stories abound in native dialect and old-fashioned phrases. Such expressions as the beleaguered Captain Ball's '' 'I tell ye I feel as if I was tied in a bag of fleas. . . . Widders an' old maids, they're busier than the divil in a gale o' wind','' and Mrs. Bascom's remark to herself, '' 'I've been favoring myself till I'm as soft as an old hoss that's right out of pasture an' can't pull two wheels without wheezin' ','' are but two of the many expressions that are typical of the homely sayings of her people. (p. 483)

With both writers, even when there is a humorous touch, there is no suggestion of ridicule. The speech characteristics simply make the old folks stand apart from the group, and the reader is attracted to them because of their individual charm and simplicity.

Both writers also share a tendency to see in people a resemblance to the things of nature, and to attribute to nature the thoughts and feelings of people. Miss Jewett saw a little old widow with a ''cypress veil and big black bonnet'' and immediately thought of a ''thin black beetle.'' Miss Cather saw ''a tiny woman in high-heeled shoes and a big hat with nodding plumes, her black dress covered with bugles and jet that glittered and rattled'' and immediately thought of an ''insect.'' Miss Jewett's Captain Lant looked like a ''well-to-do old English sparrow.'' Miss Cather's Captain Forrester with his two canes and slow, careful steps ''looked like an old tree walking.'' (p. 484)

But the similarities do not end with characterization. A further tracing reveals that in the art of writing the same kind and degree of resemblances can be found; that is, beyond the differences there is an underlying common ground. To begin with, both authors aimed at simplicity and both achieved simplicity. It is evident, however, that where Miss Cather's simplicity is reserved and studied, Miss Jewett's is friendly and casual. That their identical aims did not produce identical effects is the result of difference of talent and temperament rather than of desire. The informal quality of Miss Jewett's writing springs from her ability to write spontaneously. Miss Cather recalls,

> She once laughingly told me that her head was full of dear old houses and dear old women, and that when an old house and an old woman came together in her brain with a click, she knew that a story was under way.

In Miss Jewett's later works, a careful choice of words and compactness of thought becomes apparent, but her stories never lose the warmth of her personality. In contrast, Miss Cather's

reserve is always evident. Too, she lacked the gift to write without conscious effort. (p. 485)

In the matter of structure the likeness is more pronounced, and the works of both writers can, speaking generally, be classified as stories of incident but little plot. For the bulk of her stories, Miss Jewett gives preference to the sketch as the type best adapted to local color and character delineation. Miss Cather also make skillful use of the sketch, although she does not confine herself to its limited possibilities. . . . For Miss Jewett to choose to omit plot follows naturally; for Miss Cather to do so in her varied settings and narratives points to a parallel that should not be disregarded.

The same parallel holds true with reference to drama. Neither is a dramatic writer, and T. K. Whipple's comment that Miss Cather prefers a picturesque scene to an exciting passage applies equally well to both authors. However, Miss Jewett does not employ the ingenious details and incidents to furnish dramatic scenes which Whipple attributes to the writings of Miss Cather. The few times Miss Jewett attempts a dramatic situation she is direct, though feeble, in its use. The presence of death to obtain a dramatic effect also marks a difference. Miss Jewett's reference is that of a sympathetic observer; she tells of the long funeral procession and the dignity of the mourners. Miss Cather describes the death of the individual to heighten dramatic atmosphere or to climax suspense. Since drama did not contribute to Miss Jewett's purpose in writing, it is not surprising that, as with plot, she made practically no use of it. Besides, she lacked the ability to dramatize situations. The same explanation can not be applied to Miss Cather; she could have made more frequent and effective use of the dramatic element had she wished to do so. That she chose otherwise is significant.

To apply the foregoing similarities to emotional responsiveness, only external revisions need to be made. Miss Jewett lacked the ability to portray complex emotions as she lacked the ability to portray drama. In her novel, *A Country Doctor,* she attempts a romantic setting for young love and fails miserably. In *The Tory Lover,* there is the same attempt with the same result. Yet her short stories do not suffer from this deficiency, for the treatment of love does not play an important part in them. In giving a portrayal of local manners and customs, she tells for the most part of the pride, grief, joy, fear, resignation, generosity, kindness, loneliness, and yearning which she saw revealed. True, she tells of an occasional romance that crept into the lives of the old people, but in keeping with their years and their repressed New England manner their love was sentiment rather than ardent affection. In contrast to Miss Jewett, Miss Cather does not lack ability. But she prefers to avoid the description of intense emotional situations. . . . Miss Cather is not squeamish, and her constant awareness of love in its varying aspects is far removed from Miss Jewett's infrequent and delicate treatment, but her indirect presentations indicate a common bond of reticence.

This bond of reticence can be extended to include selection of material, for both authors are criticized for evading realism. Although William Dean Howells could, and did, refer in his day to Miss Jewett's works as realistic, they can not be so classified today. The most cursory reading can not fail to reveal that the finer emotions of human nature are too pronounced and placed too much in the limelight for a realistic approach. She does not deny the existence of the unkempt slovenly family; she simply excludes them. She tells of sorrows and tribulations, but the manner in which her characters bear their trials colors her stories with idealism rather than with reality. The foibles of the old people, told with gentle humor, pop up here and there throughout her pages, but when it comes to telling of defects of character she is inclined to be silent. She does directly admit a few evidences of degeneracy as is found in *The Tory Lover,* "Marsh Rosemary," "The Failure of David Berry," and "In Dark New England Days." For the most part, however, she discloses only slight failings, and even these are rarely seen except in the shadows of the background. Mrs. Bonny's comment, "'I can't bear to see folks so pious to meeting, and cheat yer eye-teeth out Monday morning.'" is typical of Miss Jewett's method of treating human frailties. The reason for her evasions, no doubt, arises from the dominance of her purpose. Had she written of the mean, the sordid, and the contemptible, she would not have shown her people at their best. Also, it should not be forgotten that her refined touch is too gentle to emphasize the starker sides of life and the ruder elements of humanity. She does not disguise either; rather she reads into the scenes she sees her own interpretation of life, a life which was never subjected to hardship; therefore, instead of portraying its deprivations and pain, she stresses the nobility of character which it produces when cheerfully accepted. She was in the habit of seeing in all her acquaintances, rich and poor, a reflection of the dignity and pride characteristic of New England. (pp. 485-88)

An adverse comment on the writings of Miss Jewett, and one which upon casual thought removes her material from within the pale of Miss Cather's sphere, is her omission of social criticism. This charge seems somewhat unjust. Miss Jewett was neither by talent nor inclination a reformer, and her portrayal of village life is a reflection of what she valued, but she was not blind to changes. In a quiet way she lets her reader know that she is aware of the evils of poverty. In *Country By-Ways,* she speaks disapprovingly of education which does not take into consideration the ability or lack of ability in individuals. While she was not in sympathy with the removal of the high fences and the exposure of the homes to the bold gaze of curious passers-by, she realized that the changing home conditions were bringing about the equality of women and their active participation in public affairs. She regrets the effect, but approves the cause. She writes imaginatively of the old-established and once-prosperous lands, and she seems saddened at the passing of an era rather than aware of the economic significance of the crumbling houses, sagging barns, and neglected land slowly being reconverted into wooded areas; but at the same time she calls attention to the necessity of "tree laws" to curb the ruthless destroying of the forests and the resulting harm done to the farmlands by the drying up of the springs and brooks. The pollution of waterways from factory waste material, of which she voices criticism in *Strangers and Wayfarers,* is still an active issue today. Her criticism is slight, and perhaps for this reason it goes unnoticed. However, had Miss Jewett chosen themes of social reform, it is unlikely that her works would have met with the popularity they enjoyed. The period in which she lived was not a critical one, and the public showed little interest in the current reform movements. (pp. 489-90)

In the over-all picture of relationships, there is at least one surprising difference: the humor of Miss Cather, dry and detached and rarely present, has little in common with the bubbling, abundant spirits of Miss Jewett. In their response to the elements of nature and appreciation of its beauty, however, there is a close kinship. Both writers show a sensitive reaction to its moods and effects. As with characters, Miss Jewett's

New England is quiet and peaceful with the mellowness of age; Miss Cather's Western prairie is strong and challenging with the spirit of youth. Another strong link in their chain of relationship is the religious feeling which is evident in both writers. Miss Jewett expresses hers by inserting morals and maxims; Miss Cather reflects hers in the atmosphere of her religious settings.

Other developments of their literary relationships are possible. Miss Cather shifts emphasis from time to time, and a strong resemblance in one phase of her career may show only a slight resemblance in another. The similarities, therefore, fluctuate. But even with this acknowledgement of their limitations, the similarities indicate that despite marked differences there are definite literary bonds. Both Miss Jewett and Miss Cather were aware of the other's literary worth, and their close friendship was strengthened by their mutual appreciation of their ideals in life. It is from the reflection of these ideals in their writings that their literary relationship stems. In this relationship, both authors see the good in man, his high purpose, his courage, his sincerity, his faith in God and human nature. Both realize that it is the common, every-day events of life that determine the stature of man. In choosing to give emphasis to the ennobling, uplifting impulses, both writers lay stress on the character-forming qualities which set individuals apart and which elevate them above the mass of humanity. In their writings, both make use of the delicate, light touch of the idealistic artist, which covers the small outer flaws and reveals inner beauty.

The dissimilarities, though many, are not as important as they appear at first glance. Miss Jewett's writings reflect the late nineteenth century; Miss Cather's reflect the early twentieth century. In recording *personal* observations, Miss Jewett could not write of an America that had not yet developed, and Miss Cather could not write of an earlier America that she had never known. It is evident that their mutual purpose in writing—to re-create a passing phase of American life they had *personally* known—would result in a difference in content, in theme development, in social problems, in emotional depth, and in other aspects which were in keeping not only with the changes in the social and economic life of the nation, but also with the changes in the literary approach to contemporary problems. The attitude and social awareness of twentieth-century writers have made so violent a change in subject matter and style of modern fiction that the similarities in the writings of Sarah Orne Jewett and Willa Sibert Cather are remarkable in that they exist at all.

Some of the similarities in their writings are not readily evident, but that they do exist can not be denied. Indeed, it does not seem unwarranted to say that Sarah Orne Jewett paints a tiny segment in the broad landscape of Willa Cather's works and that in this fragment there is the same essential touch. (pp. 491-92)

Eleanor M. Smith, "The Literary Relationship of Sarah Orne Jewett and Willa Sibert Cather," in The New England Quarterly, *Vol. XXIX, No. 4, December, 1956, p. 472-92.*

HYATT H. WAGGONER (essay date 1959)

[*An American educator and critic, Waggoner has written extensively on American literature and literary figures of the nineteenth and twentieth centuries, and is particularly recognized for his numerous contributions to the field of Nathaniel Hawthorne schol-*

arship. In the following excerpt, he discusses thematic unity in
The Country of the Pointed Firs.]

Unity of tone has been sufficiently remarked in *The Country of the Pointed Firs,* and unity of setting is obvious enough not to require comment. The book is, after all, generally presented as an example, a high point, of the "local color" school, and it may be assumed that the specific locale is sufficient to supply a unified coloration. But there is a deeper and more difficult unity in the work, a unity emerging from symbolic texture and structure and partaking of the quality of a vision of life, that has not only never been adequately explored but that has sometimes been implicitly denied, as it would seem to be by the phrase Willa Cather used in her Preface, "the 'Pointed Fir' sketches" [see *TCLC,* Vol. 1].

I have no wish to denigrate the critical acumen of Miss Cather, whose Preface is criticism of a high order. But is it criticism of a special kind, personal, impressionistic, insightful but unsystematic. It leaves us wondering in what sense the work is, as she says, "tightly . . . built." Since I am convinced that the work is indeed tightly built, and since no one has ever shown us just *how* tightly built, I should like to trace some of the aspects of the thematic unity that, as I see it, accounts to a larger extent than we have realized for our impression that the work is truly a classic. It is finally, I think, chiefly unity of theme that transforms a group of semi-autobiographical sketches into a fiction that is at once a tribute to a way of life and an impression of life.

It effects this transformation in the first place by the way it manages partly through its evocative presentation of specific scenes and incidents, partly through suggestive grouping, organization, to transmute felt reality into symbol. The Maine town to which the narrator journeys in the summer is explicitly simply a vacation spot, a place one goes to "get away from it all"; but implicitly it is a haven in a changing world, an island of permanence in a sea, not just of mutability but of an essentially Victorian kind of mutability. *The Country of the Pointed Firs* foreshadows contemporary primitivism from Hemingway to Faulkner to the countless professors of the arts who journey farther and farther to find relaxation, refreshment, and renewed contrast with "reality" in Cuba or Vermont or Maine or wherever.

One leaves the "busy world" of an increasingly unsatisfactory "normality" for the re-creation offered by a stay in an "unspoiled" place. Since population and industry grow apace, one journeys farther and farther for the "unspoiled." But one knows where to go, for one knows what it is that "spoils" life. Miss Jewett knew: it was Boston, and what Boston and the great world stood for: commercialism, progress, and human busyness in which it was increasingly difficult to discern the purpose of the activity. Longfellow, at the height of the Victorian ethos, once urged his contemporaries to seek salvation by simple activity, to be "up and doing," without worrying about *what* they were doing. For Miss Jewett, at the end of the era, things were not so simple or clear: she wanted to know what and why. One can imagine literary historians treating her, with equal relevance, as a symptom of the continuance of the "romantic" idealization of the simple life, in direct line of descent from Wordsworth and his peasants; of the aesthetic reaction against an emerging megalopolitan mass society; of a nostalgic retreat from complexity to simplicity.

But these ways of cataloging the book, though relevant and, in some contexts, helpful enough, tend to obscure the reason for the book's continuing vitality as a work of art. The book is, no doubt, a symptom of these and other things, but it is much more. It is more because its nostalgia is controlled and its vision of life humane and coherent. The world it depicts, which "progress" has not yet touched, is a world where it is possible to perceive the essential human qualities clearly, in reduced and simplified form: and what is perceived as essential is life lived meaningfully. If it now seems necessary to label such a conception the product of a romantic haze that glorifies because it obscures, then so much the worse for us. The essential core of *The Country of the Pointed Firs* is finally neither romantic nor sentimental but humanistic and religious at once.

The essential core of the vision: it is important I think to insist on this just because there are other elements that enter now and then to constitute exceptions, qualifying elements; but they remain peripheral. There is, for instance, chiefly in the opening pages, a slight air of patronage toward the simple country folk who will be depicted so lovingly and with such admiration. They are, after all, judged by Boston standards, "quaint," picturesque. The cultivated woman of the world is aware not only of their virtue but of the virtue implicit in being sensitive to their virtue. The thorough-going worldling would see nothing but rusticity in them.

The essential quality of the feeling here in these opening pages may be pointed up by a comparison with Faulkner's *As I Lay Dying.* The difference is finally perhaps an aesthetic difference. Faulkner the man is presumably even less one of the Bundrens than Sarah Orne Jewett was one of her Maine villagers. But Faulkner the man does not enter the story in *As I Lay Dying.* If we have read Faulkner's other works attentively we can of course hear his voice and discern his values here, but by itself the story is independent, self-validating, the product of an impersonal conception of art. Miss Jewett, in contrast, is felt in her story—on the edges of it. She knows and loves these people, and studies them both tenderly and attentively, but she is not of course one of them. If we were to put the matter in its worst light, I suppose we should have to say that her attitude towards her people is compounded of a small remnant of class feeling—social condescension—and a larger portion of genuine affection and admiration. The result of the mixture is that when her presence is most felt the work tends to become what it has so often been called, simply an example of the "local color" school of early realism, which is to say, an example of a rather unsatisfactory, and certainly a minor, literary genre.

But to complete the necessary qualifications of what will be my final claim, that the book really is a classic, and perhaps almost as good a one as Miss Cather says it is, despite all necessary deductions: two of the sketches—but only two out of twenty-four—are likely, I think, to strike the modern reader as somewhat sentimental. They suffer, I should say, from just that ambivalence of point of view that I have just said is faintly discernible in the opening pages. Both sketches effectively advance the theme, and in both the sentimentality is more of attitude than of expression, so that it is not, strictly speaking, as much a literary defect as it is a reminder that this book is, after all, a nineteenth century work, so that, classic though it may be, it is not quite "timeless." Nevertheless, I suspect that most modern readers will agree with me when I say that **"The Queen's Twin"** and **"William's Wedding"** tend somewhat to break the spell the book casts over us. The former is rather Dickensian in its blurring of the lines between harmless idiosyncrasy and serious delusion, and the latter is dated by the lack of irony with which it produces the wished-for denoue-

THE COUNTRY
OF THE POINTED FIRS
BY SARAH ORNE
JEWETT

BOSTON AND NEW YORK
HOUGHTON MIFFLIN AND COMPANY
The Riverside Press Cambridge
MDCCCXCVI

Title page of the first edition of The Country of the Pointed Firs.

ment: to the extent to which it succeeds with us we feel warm and tender, but a little uneasy.

But the almost perfect purity and control of the work as a whole reduces these to minor flaws. They fall into place in the total unity of the work and are almost completely redeemed by their context. For the final meaning of the work as a whole cannot be called sentimental except from the point of view of a very cynical and rather childish materialism—"naturalism" of the happily now almost extinct variety. The vision of life that is in control here is, I have said, humanistic and religious. To be more specific is very difficult but the attempt must be made. A part of the theme—the first step in its progressive realization as it were—is that here at Dunnet Landing, where life is lived under simplified conditions, the permanent human situation may be discovered and the abiding human values discerned. (pp. 67-9)

There is—fortunately I should say—no explicit statement of theme in *The Country of the Pointed Firs*. It is a part of its lasting charm that its evocations are so delicately indirect. But a reflection of the narrator occasioned by William's wedding suggests a significant part of what she saw in Green Island:

> Santa Teresa says that the true proficiency of the soul is not in much thinking, but in much loving, and sometimes I believed that I had

never found love in its simplicity as I had found it at Dunnet Landing in the various hearts of Mrs. Blackett [matriarch of the family reunion] and Mrs. Todd and William.

But if love is the key to the theme, it does not exhaust the narrator's discoveries of the summer. There were plenty of "noisy women, with harsh clamorous voices" at Dunnet Landing, and a sufficient complement of the bereaved, the embittered, and the grotesque. It was not, we are told, the people who were different so much as a way of life, a total ethos and outlook, that made the perceptive see things differently and so ended by making them different. The quotation from St. Teresa continues, "The happiness of life is in its recognitions . . . ," and this too could be taken as close to an explicit statement of theme if indeed there were any one explicit theme.

There is none.

The theme emerges from the contrast between the funeral procession and the brightly lighted island far at sea, between the dark shore and all the outer islands, between the delusions of the grotesque like Captain Littlepage and the queen's twin and the well-founded and severely tested faith of William; and equally from the symbolic repetitions occuring in the captain's story, the visit to Green Island, the family reunion, and William's wedding. It emerges too from the total structural pattern of the book—for the sketches are *ordered,* they develop.

The pattern they make, as I see it, may be thought of in some such way as this. The first three sketches are introductory; if nothing followed them, or if what followed were simply more of the same, we should not be able to talk of any symbolic pattern in the work. The fourth sketch has a double function: it both prepares the way for the following two, which make up the first thematic group, and introduces the fundamental symbolic contrasts that are to dominate all the rest of the work—the funeral, the sea, the outer islands, the song sparrows. The two sketches devoted to Captain Littlepage follow naturally: if Dunnet Landing brings one into touch with fundamental truths, the Captain shows the danger of a too determined assault on the unknown. Whether man's insanity is God's sense or not is left undetermined.

The next group of five sketches, the largest group in the book, offers us the only kind of "certainty" we are likely to get short of Captain Littlepage's delusion—that the spheres were formed in love, not fright, to paraphrase Ishmael in *Moby Dick*. The inhabitants of the island *live* as though the captain's belief could be demonstrated, but they do not try to demonstrate it. On the island one finds "in the eyes a look of anticipation and joy"; Mrs. Todd's very aged mother looks youthful—"you felt as if she promised a great future, and was beginning, not ending, her summers and their happy toils." The two old inhabitants of the island, in short, conspicuously manifest faith, and hope, and love.

The next four sketches culminate in the narrator's visit to Shell-heap Island, where one is reminded of "hopelessness and winter weather, and all the sorrow and disappointment in the world" (the closing words of the group). We may call this the counter-theme. The next group of four sketches turns back to the Green Island theme—the sunlit islands as contrasted with the funeral on the dark shore of the fourth sketch—as we go to the family reunion. The next three may be called "bitter-sweet": they are concerned chiefly with frustration, loneliness, and bereavement, but the middle one of the group prepares for the fulfillment of **"William's Wedding,"** the last sketch in what we may call the body of the work. The final sketch, **"The Backward View,"** is *diminuendo;* it brings us back to the atmosphere of the opening sketches firmly reestablishing the sense of actuality, the felt presence of the real. If what I have said about the symbolic progression of the preceding sketches makes the work sound rather Melvillean, this last sketch could serve to remind us that Miss Jewett considered herself, and was, a realist, and her classic is symbolic in the way and to the degree that all really fine fiction is symbolic.

It might be argued that it is illustrative of the special quality of the work that even after one has noted some such symbolic pattern as I have just outlined, it remains extraordinarily difficult to state the theme. The book is delicate, subtle, elusive. Indeed, when I have used the expression "the theme," I have been using a kind of oversimplified short-hand expression. The mood is definable—I should call it tender—and the tone is definable—nostalgic—but "the theme" eludes precise definition. I have referred to the vision controlling and shaping the book as humanistic and religious, but it is quite possible to circle around it with other adjectives. It is, for instance, conservative in the sense that Hawthorne was conservative and Faulkner is conservative; or, perhaps more appositely, conservative as Willa Cather was later to be conservative, attempting to conserve the central humane values that both women saw as threatened.

"The happiness of life is in its recognitions." I shall risk—and in this time of reaction against the excesses of the symbolic analysts of literature it *is* a risk—I shall risk seeing a symbol in the ending. As the narrator sails away from Dunnet Landing on the steamer, "Presently the wind began to blow, and we struck out seaward to double the long sheltering headland of the cape, and when I looked back again, the islands and the headland had run together and Dunnet Landing and all its coasts were lost to sight." In this imagination geography Green Island, the outermost of the outer islands, is not, as we might expect, the last thing to be seen. Only from Dunnet Landing, looking seaward, is it discerned. When one looks toward the shore it and the mainland "run together," become indistinguishable, are lost to recognition.

But not to memory. The archetypal symbols we have been invited to glimpse have done their work. It is typical of the muted symbolism of the book that it should end in this way, with the summer's idyll over, the vision withdrawn, with an air of quiet honesty, of facticity. The vision has been withdrawn, not denied, not forgotten. Whether there may be a return to Dunnet Landing, or whether the values there perceived may be preserved once one has left the summer's "seaward view," these are further questions, on which the book offers no comment. Even the vision of life meaningfully lived which gives it its unity and so much of its value as a work of art is not so much presented as suggested. *The Country of the Pointed Firs* insists on nothing: it evokes: but we shall not be adequately responsive to all its evocations unless we note the singleness of its vision. (pp. 71-3)

Hyatt H. Waggoner, "The Unity of 'The Country of the Pointed Firs'," in Twentieth Century Literature, *Vol. 5, No. 2, July, 1959, pp. 67-73.*

WARNER BERTHOFF (essay date 1959)

[*An American biographer and critic, Berthoff is the author of numerous works on American literature and literary figures. In the following excerpt from an essay originally published in the*] New England Quarterly *in March, 1959, Berthoff praises the narrative structure and characterization in* The Country of the Pointed Firs *and discusses that novel's origins in American life and literature.*]

In *Deephaven* the summer visitors, two Boston girls, are the central figures, and the record of village life is the record of their self-consciously sensitive observation. They sympathize with the village in its evident decline into poverty and stagnation, and relish its lingering charm and beauty. But they are looking in from the outside. A positive class distinction between visitors and natives is all but asserted, and the visitors' patronizing approval, though well meant and not exactly offensive, is less attractive than Jewett seems to have realized. Similarly, though a part of her intention was clearly to pose, through the simple integrity of village manners, a pastoral criticism of the outer world, the fact that this criticism is delivered by outsiders, who will not stay, dissipates its force and leaves it vague and indecisive: "we told each other, as we went home in the moonlight down the quiet street, how much we had enjoyed the evening, for somehow [*sic*] the house and the people had nothing to do with the present, or the hurry of modern life."

In *Pointed Firs* the dispositions are altered. The emphasis is no longer divided, half on proving the observer's sensitivity. It is altogether on what she observes and apprehends—on the great presence of the natural landscape and on the figures in it who accept her into their community and tell her, enact before her, its almost buried life. Her sensitivity remains important in one respect only, that it opens the life of the village to her: her landlady, the herbgatherer Mrs. Todd, trusts her to keep shop; silent ruined men speak to her; she is allowed to be sympathetic with the "old ways"; and at the great tribal reunion which climaxes the book she may participate as an adopted member. But she never fully belongs, and there is no question of her staying. When she leaves in September, she must accept the rebuke implicit in Mrs. Todd's disinclination to stop for good-byes. The whole book has given an indelible impression of a community that is inexorably, however luminously, dying, but the narrator, as if to underscore what she is made to feel is a betrayal of privilege, of trust, now applies the metaphor of death not to the village but to herself:

> the little house had suddenly grown lonely, and my room looked empty as it had the day I came. I and all my belongings had died out of it, and I knew how it would seem when Mrs Todd came back and found her lodger gone. So we die before our own eyes; so we see some chapters of our lives come to their natural end.

The import of this, however, is equivocal: her departure is a kind of dying but one which, precisely in departure, she can outlive. And the final passage of *Pointed Firs,* though more simply staged and less obviously eloquent than the affecting ending of *Deephaven,* intensifies the ambiguity of feeling well beyond the pathos and nostalgic allegiances of the earlier book. Sailing out of the harbor and bay in early September, the narrator notices how rain had made turf and woods green again, "like the beginning of summer ashore"; and having thus established the still vital beauty of the place, she looks back to see that "the islands and the headland had run together and Dunnet Landing and all its coasts were lost to sight." The disappearance of the town into the landscape confirms its creeping decay; yet the beauty and vitality of the setting asserts a superior fortune; and we cannot say whether there is gain or loss in the departure, whether we are escaping death or being cut off from some rare, transforming condition of life.

What is notable here, in comparison with the ending of *Deephaven,* is both the greater emotional energy and also the greater spareness, the concentration, the restrictive simplicity of statement. Less seems attempted, more actually is secured. The advance is strictly formal: the basic materials which compose the *Pointed Firs* volume . . . are all in *Deephaven* . . . or in the stories Jewett collected in *Tales of New England.* . . . No new judgment is attempted, no different point of view arrived at. The difference comes, on the one hand, in a mode of narration suited as never before to the special nature of her apprehensions and, on the other, in a simple sustaining structure within which she could both elaborate and concentrate the thing she had to say.

It may be surprising, considering Jewett's reputation for craftsmanship, to observe how little she had been able, up to *Pointed Firs,* to master an art of narrative. . . . Her stories, even the most accomplished, are deficient precisely as stories; she simply does not manage narrative well. Her most scrupulous fidelity of observation, her most exactly suggestive delineation, cannot conceal and tend rather to underline the clumsiness and contrivance of the action. Sequences of unconvincing fantasy ("**A White Heron**"), coincidences and fatalities unsupported by a Hardy's positive intuition ("**A Lost Lover**"), clichés of melodrama ("**Marsh Rosemary**"), are what carry her stories along, from each carefully rendered situation to the next. It might be argued that she studied too exclusively the sentence of Flaubert which she kept pinned to her workdesk: "Ecrire la vie ordinaire comme on écrit l'histoire" ["To write of ordinary life as one writes history"]. She might better have taken note of Mark Twain's "How to Tell a Story." The suggestion is not made facetiously; the mode of narrative Jewett did finally come around to in *Pointed Firs* is much closer to that celebrated by Mark Twain (and stock-in-trade with a host of regional yarn-spinners, journalists and entertainers, apprenticed like Twain to a thoroughly artful popular tradition) than to the technique of Flaubert or Henry James. The first-person narrator in *Pointed Firs* tells no stories herself; rather, she sets down stories which are told to her. And much of their "meaning," in fact, is in the struggle of the teller, himself participant, to do justice to the thing he has to tell; and their truth is confirmed in the wavering rhythm of his effort to express himself as his story seems to require. It is in the stories-within-the-story that the major themes of the book are most fully registered; the narrator's part is simply to describe the teller and the situation, to provide the occasion, to give notice of the passing of time— and, at the beginning and end of the book, to lead the reader sympathetically into the legended world of Dunnet Landing and safely, if equivocally, out again when the time comes. Jewett, it might be said, solved her inability to master a Jamesian art of the short story by abandoning it.

Or she apprehended at last that what she had to tell was one story and one story only, one that all the earlier ones lead up to or provide analogies for. Another way of describing the achievement of *Pointed Firs* is to say, in these terms, that she had finally discovered within her materials—anecdotes, incident, scenes, special cases—the essential legend that was there for her to tell, and found for it an appropriate form. (pp. 145-48)

[Another] sign of the perfection of Jewett's utterance in *Pointed Firs* is her concentration on persons, her resistance to distracting details. Landscape and local custom, the anonymous picturesque, are strongly present but now in the background; the burden of meaning is carried by specific personal histories. The types of character she worked with would not have been unfamiliar to her readers. It is a commonplace concerning the later New England local-color writing that young people rarely figure in it—few children, almost no young men, even more rarely an ordinary young couple. In *Deephaven* an unusual passage of open satire describes an evening lecture on "Elements of True Manhood," an inspirational discourse "directed entirely toward young men, and there was not a young man there." Young men of energy and promise are sure to be from the outside, like the young hunter of "**A White Heron**"—and are likely to represent a certain coarseness, a positive danger to the delicate balance of backwater life. For the home-grown the one remaining hope of manhood is to break away into the great world—again with the imputation, usually, of coarseness and self-ruination, as with the "lost lover" of Miss Horatia Dane. Those who stay are the weak and pathetic, the halfmen, shiftless and full of "meechin' talk" like Jerry Lane of "**Marsh Rosemary**," whose "many years" older wife knows herself to be "the better man of the two." (p. 149)

There is no more striking symptom of the blight that has settled on the region than the recasting of customary social rôles particularly of the rôles of the sexes. The superiority of Jewett's work in the local-color genre—and here, too, *Pointed Firs* marks for her a distinct advance—appears in the combined bluntness and subtlety, the overwhelming indirection, with which she presents a norm of distorted, repressed, unfulfilled or transformed sexuality as an index to her essential story. When there is a marriage, it is like that of Ann Floyd and Jerry Lane—the weak boy marrying for protection and security the energetic spinster who has the competence and strength of a proper man; that the marriage is childless and ends in desertion does not come as a surprise. More usually there is no marriage at all, simply the desertion, as in "**A Lost Lover**": here the elderly heroine, whose lover was long ago supposed lost at sea but really has run away, has come to be regarded as a widow and, on the basis of this lie, a person of consequence in the village as well as in her own eyes; she has achieved position and respect, but at the cost of playing a woman's full part. The men do have the choice to go, though it may destroy them, and only the already defeated or crippled, the childish or womanlike, stay on. But for the women the only choice, the sacrifice required for survival, is to give up a woman's proper life and cover the default of the men, to be the guardians and preservers of a community with no other source of vitality and support. In a society without a future the woman's instinct to carry on the life of the tribe can only be fulfilled by devotion to what remains, and her energies must go to preservation of the past, to intercourse with nature, to disguising and delaying the inevitable dissolution. This is the ambiance even of a story like "**A White Heron**," in which the heroine is only a little girl. In the presence of the hunter "the woman's heart, asleep in the child," stirs with a premonition of the power and release of love; but in defense of her mysterious sympathy with wild creatures and her secret knowledge of the heron's sanctuary, she refuses his appeal like a profaning courtship (in his offering her money there is again the imputation of grossness); and the suggestion is made that her whole life will turn on this renunciation.

The story of the region, we may say, would not be honestly told if the sexual warping were not brought into it, but it would not be fully told if that were made the main, the climactic, theme of it. Sexuality figures, rather, as one among several of the great natural contingencies determining the forms life must take in this life-abandoned society. Old age and death are another: it is with the aged that the pessure of decay is registered most vividly. External nature provides the others—thus, perhaps, in the final clarifying of her vision and refining of its expression, Jewett's choice of title; and thus, in *The Country of the Pointed Firs,* the constant counterpointing of personal and tribal histories by the invoked presence not only of the landscape but of season and weather, too, and the incessant audible movement of the sea in its storms and calms, its tidal rise and fall. (pp. 149-50)

All form is "significant"—but some forms (to borrow a cadence) are more significant than others. A demonstration of structural wholeness does not prove, nor does it explain, the impressiveness of a piece of writing. Examining structure, we find ourselves judging substance and implication as well—and no doubt operating from pre-judgments (usually unspoken though not necessarily understood) as to interest and worth. There is nothing illegitimate in this. How else do we identify the specific gravity and bearing, the importance, of a work? We judge certain perceptions more commanding than others; we scarcely bother to *raise* questions of art or the lack of it unless our serious attention is commanded.

What is it then in Jewett's *Pointed Firs* that does so command attention, that secures the impression not only of integrity but of significance (and so of the durability Willa Cather claimed for it)? The book, we observe, proceeds through a sequence of personal histories and personal encounters. Yet the specific events, one by one, are too slight to produce much more than anecdotal pathos; what gives them body and interest is their insistent revelation of a more general order of existence. Particular persons have been put sharply before us, yet our feeling for their lives, though warm enough, is curiously impersonal; our interest in them is less as personalities than as examples, as case histories.

In this respect *Pointed Firs* is no special case. In most of the best "local-color" writing, as even in more ambitous work like Anderson's *Winesburg,* the interest in character is negligible—that is, as "character" is properly understood in fiction: persons moved through a convincing range of human response to moral decision or commitment. Instead there is an interest in linedrawing, or in caricature—a sociological interest, essentially. If *Pointed Firs* is exceptional as a work of art, it is so only through perfection of its *genre;* in substance and implication it is sociological, and historical. The powerful compulsions of American democratic life have always been too ambiguous and diverse—and too relentlessly novel—to be easily registered or immediately identified; what the restricted focus of "regionalism" has provided in our literature is a way of bringing them to expression and putting them in some sort of objective judgment. So a great part of what holds us to a *Pointed Firs* or a *Winesburg* is the clarity and accuracy of their testimony as to the experience of these compulsions and urgencies which in our civilization have traditionally worked (so witnesses as different as Tocqueville and Poe, Mark Twain and Henry Adams, Jewett and Anderson, have told us) to sap private morals, obliterate individuality, and transform persons into grotesque natural phenomena.

To say then that *Pointed Firs* is a masterpiece of the local-color school (its only peer would seem to be "Old Times on the Mississippi") is not at all to talk it down. The work of this school, the bulk of it produced between 1870 and 1900, constitutes a potentially powerful criticism of the main directions of American life. Set sometimes in the past and recalled from

the perspective of a transformed present, and sometimes in some backwater of the present seen from the turbulent main stream, these books hold up for inspection (occasionally satirical, more often affectionate and elegaic) some local pattern of community life which has already vanished or is on the point of vanishing and which in its isolation and decay gives off a luminous but pathetic (if not terrible) beauty—the flush of dying. These are the jolly corners of American life (Henry James, not equipped to look in the usual places, found them at Washington Square as well), and in the best of the literature that celebrates them there is not only a compassionate response to their ill fortune but also a knowledgeable criticism of what has overtaken them; in the very best the criticism returns upon the region itself—the jolly corner proves to be appalling, deadly, maleficent—and we find expressed a fatalism beyond nostalgia or irony, a sense of American life as requiring, as being *founded* upon, the pitiless extinction of the past, the violent extirpation of amenity and beauty and of every temporary establishment of that truly civil order which is the earliest of American dreams.

The art of *Pointed Firs* reaches this order of revelation—a rare enough achievement. The very condition in our civilization which provoke such books and such judgments seem to act also to deprive them of body and cogency. . . . Ours is a literature that springs, when it springs at all, from violent contradictions of idealized feeling, that makes a specialty of sudden fruition and melancholy aftermaths, that knows—with ambiguous exceptions like Henry James—no middle ground between extraordinary originality and equally extraordinary tastelessness, self-imitation, banality. A pragmatical literature, we might call it—one rarely able to live (and this is a source of strength as well as a limitation) except in immediate contact with its undistilled and unprinted sources of feeling. So all but a few of its finest books, and *Pointed Firs* is a perfect instance, ground their strength and appeal, and find their form, not in some objective order of thought or judgment but in a tenuous *ad hoc* balancing of intense and contradictory emotion—a balance or tension which, as it can give surprising authority to a style like Jewett's that otherwise follows a conventional rhetoric, requires in the first place a rare artfulness to get control of and maintain; which may achieve for the space of a single work the creating and sustaining force of some deep-grounded formal idea, yet will barely submit to argument or rational analysis.

Jewett's ultimate art in *Pointed Firs* is to sustain this creative balance of crossed feelings—to make for her materials a claim of value and permanence but to show it as hopeless. Readers of her letters and other work know that she was not free of certain "hysterias" of her time and society. Her judgments of present and past antedated her proving them in her art. But prove them she did—by making them as impersonal as the sympathy we are brought to feel for her characters; by suffusing them with the durable colors of legend, the solemnity of history. *The Country of the Pointed Firs* is a small work but an unimprovable one, with a secure and unrivaled place in the main line of American literary expression. (pp. 157-60)

Warner Berthoff, "The Art of Jewett's 'Pointed Firs'," in Appreciation of Sarah Orne Jewett: 29 Interpretive Essays, *edited by Richard Cary, Colby College Press, 1973, pp. 144-61.*

DAVID BONNELL GREEN (essay date 1962)

[*Green is an American educator and critic whose writings focus chiefly on nineteenth-century subjects. In the following excerpt, he discusses the four Dunnet Landing stories that were added to posthumous editions of* The Country of the Pointed Firs.]

Two excellent critical articles, Warner Berthoff's "The Art of Jewett's *Pointed Firs*" and Hyatt H. Waggoner's "The Unity of *The Country of the Pointed Firs*" [see excerpts dated 1959], that appeared during the fiftieth anniversary of Sarah Orne Jewett's death have done much to enlarge our understanding of her masterpiece. Both critics have in part, however, overlooked one of the central aspects of her achievement. Both are uneasy over the additional stories, "The Queen's Twin," "A Dunnet Shepherdess," and "William's Wedding," that were included in editions of the book published after Miss Jewett's death—and rightly so, for there is no indication that she authorized their inclusion. But the three stories are obviously related to *The Country of the Pointed Firs,* and a fourth story, "The Foreigner," quite as good as the other three, has an equally close connection with the book, although it has never been absorbed into it. Indeed, we learn more about Mrs. Todd's past in "The Foreigner" than we do anywhere else, even though some of the action takes place beyond the confines of Dunnet Landing.

The relationship of the four stories to *The Country of the Pointed Firs* supplies the necessary clue to the central aspect I have referred to, for Miss Jewett's triumph is in her creation of a fictional world, like Trollope's or Thackeray's or Faulkner's, a world that is fully imagined and realized, in its way more "real" than the world of actual experience. Usually, the creation of such a fictional world requires at least a novel, and often a series of novels, but Miss Jewett performs the feat in a volume of twenty-one sketches or episodes—the right term is hard to choose.

She had not come to the task unprepared. As both Berthoff and Waggoner suggest, the whole sequence of her fiction readies her for the crowning work. It is almost as though in the earlier books and stories, especially *Deephaven* . . . and *A Marsh Island* . . . , she had been rehearsing for the great final performance, in the course of which a world would be created. Once it had come into being, this fictional world could be entered again, and so it is that the four later stories are part of and extend *The Country of the Pointed Firs* without breaking its larger unity. (pp. 412-13)

Approximately two-fifths of the fiction devoted to the characters and setting found in *The Country of the Pointed Firs* appears outside that volume. Once Miss Jewett had established her fictional world, she could enlarge it in a number of ways. She could, for example, extend the map in a literal physical manner. The Hights in "A Dunnet Shepherdess" live "up country," "way up back o' the Bowden place"; Abby Martin, the Queen's twin, lives "over toward the Back Shore," and in "The Foreigner" we are told of "the coast beyond Monhegan," the mention of an actual place providing a distant link with the real world.

More importantly, Miss Jewett could extend and deepen the general milieu, giving the whole greater density and richness. She could do this not only by exploring new if adjacent localities but by introducing new characters and by revealing new facets in the lives or traits of familiar ones. New formative circumstances such as William's long devotion to Esther Hight in "A Dunnet Shepherdess" and "William's Wedding" are introduced, and we are allowed glimpses of previously undisclosed aspects of character such as William's sly humor or given deeper understanding of those already seen. In "The

Foreigner" Captain Lorenzo Bowden, Mrs. Todd's uncle, is representative of the old seafaring life and provides an interesting implicit contrast to Captain Littlepage. Mrs. Thankful Hight in "A Dunnet Shepherdess," with her pathos and selfishness, suggests new facets of the harshness of life in the region. We see further into Mrs. Todd's wise tact and humanity in her relations with the heroine of "The Foreigner," and Mrs. Blackett's active and practical kindness in the same story help to explain her effect upon other characters—and the reader— in *The Country of the Pointed Firs*.

> Mother happened to be there [at the parting of Captain Tolland and his wife—the foreigner] and she went an' spoke, and I remember what a comfort she seemed to be. Mis' Tolland clung to her then, and she wouldn't give a glance after the boat when it had started, though the captain was very eager a-wavin' to her. She wanted mother to come home with her an' wouldn't let go her hand, and . . . so they walked off together, an' 't was some considerable time before she got back.

From "The Foreigner" too we learn the origin of Mrs. Todd's dislike of Mari' Harris, when in her narrowness and prejudice she reproaches Mrs. Blackett. And in "The Queen's Twin" we are reminded concerning Mrs. Todd that "life was very strong in her, as if some force of Nature were personified in this simple-hearted woman and gave her cousinship to the ancient deities. She might have walked the primeval fields of Sicily."

Finally, Miss Jewett could reinforce old themes and introduce new ones, or rather perhaps add new dimensions to the old. One important group of themes, for example, is the question of time and eternity, of the finite and the infinite, or the relation of life and death, of mortality and immortality. Miss Jewett seldom introduced the supernatural into her stories, although she was greatly interested in it, but in "The Foreigner" she does use the supernatural at the climax of the story. It is far more, however, than a ghost story, for she is exploring the possibility of two realms of being and suggesting the means through which they may on occasion intersect. The supernatural element may possibly have embarrassed editors in 1910 and prevented them from collecting "The Foreigner" along with the other Dunnet Landing stories, but the story deserves to have its place among the rest.

The relationship of these four stories to each other and to the original group of sketches is, needless to say, reciprocal. We cannot read one sketch without being aware of the others, and the four later ones depend quite frankly if implicitly on the reader's knowledge of the principal group. The narrator remarks in one of the less effective passages of "William's Wedding," after seeing Mrs. Todd's happiness: "I felt something take possession of me which ought to communicate itself to the least sympathetic reader of this cold page. It is written for those who have a Dunnet Landing of their own: who either kindly share this with the writer, or possess another." We may not necessarily feel that these extensions of a fictional world are of equal merit, but they cannot be ignored in any assessment of the whole, and in their way "A Dunnet Shepherdess," "The Foreigner," "The Queen's Twin," and "William's Wedding" are vital parts of the world of Dunnet Landing. (pp. 414-17)

David Bonnell Green, "The World of Dunnet Landing," in The World of Dunnet Landing: A Sarah Orne Jewett Collection *by Sarah Orne Jewett, edited* by David Bonnell Green, University of Nebraska Press, 1962, pp. 412-17.

MARGARET FARRAND THORP (essay date 1966)

[Thorp was an American journalist and critic. In the following excerpt, she discusses prominent characteristics and techniques of Jewett's fiction.]

[Sarah Jewett's] first book was published in 1877 when she was twenty-eight. It was William Dean Howells who suggested to Miss Jewett that she collect the Maine stories the *Atlantic* had published, rearrange and add to them, and issue them as a book. They were all set in Deephaven, a seaport town which, she was careful to explain in her Preface, she had invented. (p. 17)

Deephaven does not have a plot in the usual sense of the term. It is a series of impressions of a little Maine coastal town and its inhabitants, as they are received by two lively girls in their early twenties who decide to spend the summer there because one of them has at her disposal the house of a great aunt who has recently died. Miss Brandon was so much respected in Deephaven that everyone welcomes her niece as an old friend. It seems to the young people that the society and way of life of the town are just what they were fifty years ago when it ceased to be an important seaport, but they find this a good way of life, full of interest and devoted to high standards.

The niece's friend, who tells the story, describes first ''The Brandon House'' (which resembles in many ways the Jewett house in Berwick), its furnishings, its treasures, its memories. Then she gives accounts of the various kinds of people she and her friend come to know in the town: **''My Lady Brandon and the Widow Jim,'' ''Deephaven Society,'' ''The Captains.''** The sketches present individuals of different types and the girls' relations with them. We listen to their conversation and hear the stories they tell, ranging from the history of their neighbors to adventures at sea to tales of second sight. There are Miss Brandon's aristocratic friends; there are old sailors—each must be addressed as Captain; there are fishermen; there are housewives of various degrees of social importance. The men are full of wisdom and salty talk, but they tend to blur a little into one another. The women are more distinctive. There is the lady of the old school, Miss Honora. There is the Widow Jim who has ''an uncommon facility of speech'' but has endured, courageously, hard years with a drunken husband and is known as ''a willin' woman,'' always respected. There is Mrs. Bonny who comes down from the hills in the summertime riding on her rough-coated old horse with bags and baskets of ''rosbries'' tied to the saddle. There is old Miss Chauncey, her mind so dim that she thinks herself still rich and elegant as she lives in her denuded, neglected old house, sustained by the charity of her neighbors. There is Mrs. Kew, the lighthouse keeper's wife, with a fine original gift of wit and speech.

There are lively accounts, too, of **''Cunner-Fishing,''** of sailing and cross-country walking, of going to church, attending a lecture, driving to **''The Circus at Denby''** where the girls hear an illuminating conversation between the Kentucky Giantess and the lighthouse keeper's wife, who had gone to school together.

There seems to be no particular order in the telling of events or in the presentation of characters—that was an art Miss Jewett learned much later—but the young women's enthusiasm for their new friends and new experiences is refreshing and contagious. The tempo and tone of the town become very clear.

The device by which she held these people and events together Miss Jewett was to use again and again. It bears some resemblance, though it is less subtle, to Henry James's central intelligence. A visitor—usually a woman—from Boston or some other part of the outside world comes to Maine and settles for a time in Deephaven, or Grafton, or Dunnet Landing. She meets the most interesting inhabitants of the village, learns their histories, and often makes them into friends. She delights in the old houses she visits and is captivated by the beauty of the austere fields, woods, and sea, so that she presents both narrative and background.

In *Deephaven,* unfortunately, the actual narrator, who is fairly self-effacing, is concerned not only to tell her stories but to make us love her companion, Kate, and admire the way in which she endears herself to different types of people. This puts, from time to time, more emphasis on the double central intelligence than is good for it, but the device of an observer slightly detached but interested is admirable. The weakness is that this central intelligence cannot really function alone; too many of the episodes to be related occurred long before her arrival. It becomes necessary to add an assistant intelligence, an older relative or some long-time resident of the community who knows all the history and legend and can impart them to an eager newcomer.

As a variant on the summer visitor Miss Jewett liked to send back to Maine someone who had roots there but had not lived in the state for a long time. Important among these is the **''Native of Winby,''** now senator from Kansota, who makes a surprise visit to his old school and then to an elderly widow whom he might once have married.

Nineteen years later, when she was writing *The Country of the Pointed Firs* ..., Miss Jewett was using her visitor device with real skill. The intelligence there is a woman from Boston who has settled in Dunnet Landing as a quiet place to write during the summer. Her response to the people and the stories she encounters is swift and warm but this is not insisted on, as it is in *Deephaven;* it is only implied, so that she does not intrude upon the tale she is telling. Involvement and detachment are beautifully balanced. The assistant narrator, the local herb-woman, is the most interesting of all the narrator assistants, one of the best characters, in fact, Miss Jewett ever drew.

Another literary instrument for which she was to be much admired Miss Jewett used first in *Deephaven;* her accurate and effective employment of Maine speech. Her ear and her memory had been recording it unconsciously ever since she was a little girl and when she came to reproduce it on the printed page she devised a simple method of presenting it to the reader without the cumbersome misspellings so frequently resorted to by the local colorists, even sometimes by a writer as accomplished as Harriet Beecher Stowe.

Miss Jewett's chief tool is the apostrophe, to indicate a dropped final *g* (goin'), or a blurred *a* (same's I always do), or the pronunciation of a word like v'y'ge. She uses it, too, to indicate the shortened vowel sound so characteristic of Maine; co't, bo't, flo't. In addition to this she has a rich knowledge of characteristic words and phrases, some of them very old: ''They beseeched me after supper till I let 'em go''; ''bespoke''; ''master hard''; ''master pretty''; ''a power of china''; ''I'd rather tough it out alone.'' ... (pp. 18-21)

One is impressed often by the subtle variations her dialect presents, differences in education and culture, between the young and the very old, between men and women. Sometimes Miss Jewett remarks on the relative social position of two characters she is presenting and this distinction within democracy is reflected by differences in speech.

In the handful of Irish stories the language is not nearly so convincing. Miss Jewett had heard the brogue all her life, chiefly from family servants, but she did not think in it or even, apparently, take an interest in it. As she sets it down it seems correct enough but contrived, not overheard. She records it with a fair amount of restraint but it seems always a little thicker than it ought to be, as though the personages were moving on a stage, not along a country road.

With the occasional French-Canadian characters at whom she tried her hand she is very timid. . . . In **"Little French Mary,"** a very slight sketch of a six-year-old daughter of French-Canadians whose pretty affectionate ways charm the old men who sit about the post-office stove in a Maine village, the child has French manners and features but she speaks scarcely two sentences. In **"Mère Pochette,"** set in a French-Canadian village, there is very little dialogue though a good deal of direct report of the dominant character's thinking. The phraseology falls too often into the tiresome form of English translation of the French idiom: "She will be incapable . . . to bring up an infant of no gifts." The story is an uninteresting one, anyway, of a grandmother who finally repents her mistake in breaking up a true love affair.

These dialects never became a serious problem, for Miss Jewett wrote only a few stories about the Irish and the Canadians. What mattered in *Deephaven* and in the later stories was the Maine speech, and her use of that, as I have said, delighted both her readers and the editors who were interested in her literary development. . . . One of the points on which she differed with her advisers most strongly was the matter of plot. . . . "I have no dramatic talent," she wrote to [editor Horace] Scudder in 1873. "It seems to me I can furnish the theater, and show you the actors and the scenery, but there never is any play." When she tried to make a "play" the result was either sentimental or melodramatic. She contrived sudden inheritances, unfaithful lovers, missing young men who return suddenly rich, wayward daughters who come home to die. There are even thieves and drunkards.

Yet sometimes a preposterous situation produces a convincing story. In **"A Lost Lover"** all the town of Longfield knows that Miss Horatia had a lover who was lost at sea. The young cousin who comes to visit her one summer is full of curiosity about the romance but Miss Horatia is thoroughly reserved and only a few facts are to be gleaned from Melissa, the devoted family servant. The affair, if it was a real love affair, took place very rapidly many years before when Miss Horatia was on a visit to Salem. The young man went off to sea and his ship was never heard from again.

One morning during the young cousin's visit a tramp comes by asking for food. While he eats he talks freely with Miss Horatia about himself, his bad luck, shipwrecks, craving for drink, and general discouragement. He does not recognize her but she gradually becomes aware who he is. When he leaves she faints, but tells her cousin it is the heat. "God forgive him," she says to herself and takes up her lonely life again.

"A Lost Lover" is an exception. The components of a Jewett story are usually much simpler. The incidents evolve perhaps from two characters in a conversation or from a character in relation to an old house or a community. A typical plot is **"Miss Tempy's Watchers"** in which two elderly women keep the traditional guard, the night before the funeral, over the body of a mutual friend. They install themselves in the kitchen, work at their knitting, and talk about Miss Tempy to whom both of them had been devoted. The circumstances make them speak more openly than they normally would. Nothing happens, but from the conversation emerge three definite and interesting New England characters and some illuminating information on the qualities of generosity and "closeness."

This construction from everyday materials makes the Jewett stories seem more durable than the in many ways comparable tales of Mary E. Wilkins Freeman and Rose Terry Cooke. The plots these writers contrive are ingeniously interesting or amusing, but the joints of their manufacture are too often evident. They are made; they do not grow. Miss Jewett's plots seem inevitable, not something she has invented but something she has seen or overheard or been told of by a friend. It is because she had to manufacture the plots of her Irish and French-Canadian stories that they lack the authenticity of her tales of Maine.

The way in which her Maine stories seemed to grow of themselves never ceased to astonish her. "What a wonderful kind of chemistry it is," she wrote to her close friend Mrs. James T. Fields, "that evolves all the details of a story and writes them presently in one flash of time! For two weeks I have been noticing a certain string of things and having hints of character, etc., and day before yesterday the plan of the story comes into my mind, and in half an hour I have put all the little words and ways into their places and can read it off to myself like print. Who does it? for I grow more and more sure that I don't!" (pp. 21-4)

Miss Jewett worked happily and well and volumes of collected stories appeared steadily. Eventually there were twelve of them. After the fourth, *The Mate of the Daylight* . . . , she attempted her first novel. She did not suppose that she had developed any skill in plotting but she wanted to make a portrait of her father and the sketch did not give her scope enough. The portrait is interesting and fairly successful; her story is not.

The family setting invented for Dr. Leslie in *A Country Doctor* . . . is quite different from Dr. Jewett's—Dr. Leslie is a lonely widower, cared for by a faithful servant—but otherwise Sarah Jewett makes him as like her father as she can. We see him comparing experiences with a much-traveled professional friend, with a charming aged lady he has known from childhood, with patients who desperately need his sympathy and his encouragement as well as his skill, and with others who simply enjoy the importance of being sick. His compassion, adaptability, and quick wit in handling a situation are attractive. His young ward has much the same relation to him that Sarah had to her father but Nan is not an attempt at a self-portrait though she expresses many of Miss Jewett's ideas.

The novel is not well proportioned. The first half, which pictures Nan's early life in the village of Oldfields, is much longer than it needs to be, though it is the best part of the book with its skillful Jewett sketches of country friends and neighbors. There is some of the charm of the later *Country of the Pointed Firs*. The real plot, the choice the heroine makes between marriage and a medical career, at a time when few people thought it possible to combine the two, has the substance for a good novel of the day but the conflict is never made sharp enough to be exciting. Nan realizes very early that she is not the sort of woman intended for matrimony (Sarah Jewett states her own case here, as we have seen) and the young man who would like to dissuade her is too pale a character to seem much of a loss. Other difficulties are not strong enough to be very interesting.

The possibilities she neglected here indicate quite clearly that, though she had vigorous and sometimes radical opinions, Sarah Jewett was not a reformer or a propagandist. She did not want her writing to plead a cause but to explore the relationship between an individual and the life in which he found himself. (pp. 30-1)

Immediately after *A Country Doctor* Miss Jewett tried another novel, *A Marsh Island*. . . . Its proportion and structure much better than the first novel's, it moves along quite smoothly, but neither the story nor the characters are very interesting. The plot is trite. A well-to-do dilettante landscape painter boards for part of the summer at the marsh island farm. He almost falls in love with the farmer's daughter and enjoys imagining how she would blossom in a richer cultural environment. He almost alienates her from her real lover, a fine metalworker-farmer, whose jealousy is aroused by Doris' interest in the painter. The situation is saved when Doris hears at the last moment that Dan, in his unhappiness, has signed on for a long voyage. She makes a dangerous trip across the marshes in the

Page from the holograph manuscript of A March Island.

early morning before the ship leaves to assure him of her true feelings. He does not sail and marries her soon.

The best thing about the novel is its picture of the marsh island farm, isolated and quite different from the others in the neighborhood. The farmer and his wife are estimable hardworking people whom the young painter grows to like and admire but they have little of the savor Miss Jewett usually manages to get into her secondary characters. The contrast between the marsh people and the painter's rich relatives, who are spending the summer further along the coast, has comparatively little force.

Sarah Jewett's only other attempt at a novel [*The Tory Lover*] was made sixteen years later. . . . (pp. 32-3)

The *Atlantic* ran the novel in serial form before its publication as a book and many people liked it despite its faults. The rather violent action—fighting, imprisonments, escapes—was quite beyond Miss Jewett's scope nor was she successful in her attempt to present the complex character of Jones, but the book has two virtues which have not been sufficiently noticed: the talk of the sailors, which Miss Jewett made, probably quite correctly, like the talk of the seafaring men she knew; and the hero, the most lively and attractive young man she ever drew. She sympathized with the conversatism which attached him to the mother country—he enlists with Jones finally to please his lady love—and the exposition of his Tory inclinations is unusual and interesting. (p. 33)

The Country of the Pointed Firs . . . is not a novel and not much seems to be gained by calling it, as some modern critics are inclined to do, a para-novel, but it does have a definite and effective unity. This is achieved by methods reminiscent of *Deephaven* but employed with far more sophistication so that the community of Dunnet Landing is not only a definite seacoast village but an epitome of the whole state of Maine. Between the covers of this remarkable little book one can find, indeed, almost the whole of New England, its landscape, its social changes, its people and their special qualities. Sarah Jewett did not deliberately set out to do anything of the kind but it was at this moment that her long observation and study of her country, her long practice in writing of everyday life as though it were history, came to its climax. It is with *The Country of the Pointed Firs* that one should begin to read the work of Sarah Orne Jewett. (pp. 41-2)

Four later sketches set in Dunnet Landing, which were added to the book in posthumous editions, are perfectly consistent in tone but fall outside the time sequence of the pattern, which runs from June to September. One is always conscious of the background, the firs, the balsams, the rocks, the birds and bushes, the constantly changing aspects of the sea, but it is never overemphasized.

The narrator is played down so that she provides only the necessary curiosity, questions, and responses. The important figure is the assistant narrator, one of the best characters, as I have said, Miss Jewett ever drew. She is the narrator's landlady, Mrs. Almira Todd, herbwoman of the village, and much of the book is told in her distinctive and effective speech. (pp. 42-3)

As the narrator has been made less conspicuous than she is in *Deephaven* and the language of the book has been made simpler and more precise, so the number of subsidiary characters has been reduced to a few of real significance. In all these characters Miss Jewett is presenting the New England qualities she has been describing in her other stories: endurance, courage, independence, industry, conscientiousness, and her own belief in the happy interest to be found in the commonplaces of day-to-day living.

The clearest exponent of Dunnet Landing's decline since it ceased to be a seaport is Captain Littlepage, long retired but full of pregnant ideas as well as strange fanciful thoughts. According to Mrs. Todd his mind has been unhinged by too much reading. He is devoted to Milton and Shakespeare. A curious experience in an Arctic shipwreck has left him with the conviction that he knows the location of a strange city, the waiting place for spirits between earth and heaven, but about the changes in the Landing he is quite lucid. "In the old days a good part o' the best men here knew a hundred ports and something of the way folks lived in them. They saw the world for themselves, and like's not their wives and children saw it with them. . . . they got some sense o' proportion." (pp. 43-4)

Most important of all is Mrs. Todd's octogenarian mother, Mrs. Blackett, who lives with her shy fisherman son on one of the outer islands. Its name, Green Island, suggests that it is a kind of little paradise. Mrs. Blackett enjoys nature and her daily life so thoroughly that she refreshes every friend with whom she comes in contact.

The Country of the Pointed Firs brought Miss Jewett enthusiastic approval both from the critics and from her friends. The most precise assessment of all came in a letter from William James. The book, he said, has "that incommunicable cleanness of the salt air when one first leaves town," and this is a quality one is refreshed by in most of Miss Jewett's work. (p. 44)

Margaret Farrand Thorp, in her Sarah Orne Jewett, *American Writers Pamphlet No. 61, University of Minnesota Press, Minneapolis, 1966, 48 p.*

ROBERT D. RHODE (essay date 1968)

[*Rhode is an American poet, critic, and educator. In the following excerpt, he examines the prominence of setting in Jewett's works.*]

Henry James, in a personal letter to his younger fellow-New Englander, Sarah Orne Jewett, took the liberty of advising her to return to her New England subjects—to "come back to the palpable present intimate that throbs responsive, and that wants, misses, needs you, God knows, and that suffers woefully in your absence" [see excerpt dated 1901]. James was saying in 1901 what numerous subsequent critics have since observed—that Jewett's relationship to her material was exceptional, if not unique—that she illuminated it with a kind of magic or intuition not evident in the work of other local colorists of her generation. (p. 146)

To understand Miss Jewett's unique contributon to the art of local fiction, it is necessary first to take note of her particular manner of employing setting as an element in narration. Some of Miss Jewett's critics seem to feel that she succeeded as a novelist and story writer without really mastering the art—that she could manage neither characterization nor plot in the usual sense of the terms, and that she could not muster a serious interest in theme—at least not from the standpoint of social criticism or reform. Most critics, on the other hand, credited her with a special sensitivity toward, and an intimate knowledge of, her specialized material. They also recognized her other qualifications: aesthetic taste and judgment, imagination, power of concentration and discipline as a writer. Almost all of the elements of strength in her art, it may be noted, had

little to do with character, plot, and theme, but much to do with the fourth quantum of narrative art—namely, setting.

All of the American local colorists, to a degree, were specialists in setting. Some, like Mary N. Murfree and George Washington Cable, distorted their fiction with lavish and sentimental descriptive backgrounds; a few, like Mark Twain and Hamlin Garland, used setting organically rather than obtrusively. They were able, through their skill in the management of setting, to add historocity—or credibility—to their fiction and thus to increase the total impact of their art. Jewett could not produce a story, as she herself admitted, that did not rely almost entirely on setting power—in the broadest sense of the phrase—to carry the burden of the narrative. (pp. 146-47)

Though setting generally plays a secondary rather than a major role in great works of fiction, it must be granted that a sufficient and appropriate intensification of setting can be sufficient, as was the case with Jewett, to sustain a high level of reader interest in a story and thus to make up for weaker or under-emphasized plotting and characterization. Many of Miss Jewett's stories are so slightly plotted, however, that it is impossible to analyze precisely the functions of their settings in terms of narrative structure.

There are ample instances in Miss Jewett's stories of conventional local-color descriptions. Her enthusiasm for New England fauna and flora occasionally trapped her into artistic excesses of descriptive catalogues and scenic painting, especially in her Deephaven period. But by 1896, the date of *The Country of the Pointed Firs,* she had come to recognize the superiority of developing setting by brief suggestion and implication rather than by lengthy description. But more important, she was developing an awareness of nature as a living force rather than as an inanimate, amorphous background.

Miss Jewett's feeling for nature has been appropriately compared with Wordsworth's and also with Hardy's, but neither comparison is an exact one. She has more humor than either, and is more at home amid the commonplace. She was aware of dark environmental and sociological forces being exerted upon her rustic characters, but, as already said, she was not conspicuously interested in reform, either to improve man so that he might survive, or to conserve an environment in which he might postpone his extinction. She recognized that nature—in the form of trees, water, and wind—was virile and waiting to repossess the land that the New Englanders, a dying society, must ultimately relinquish. She accepted the world as she found it; "we can use its forces, and shape and mould them, and perfect this thing or that, but we cannot make new forces" (*Country By-Ways* . . .). Through long struggle the New Englander was adapted to his environment, at least to the old one, now dying out. He was magnificent in his struggle, and his posture of hardiness, in Miss Jewett's stories, is not blurred by sentimentality or melodrama.

The new scientific notions of man embattled with his environment, a product of American Darwinism, which took an unrelenting hold on James Lane Allen, had little effect on Miss Jewett. Her response to her rural environment was more emotional than rational, and she was not preoccupied with scientific or sociological processes of heredity and environment. Her sense of literary art, as well as her humanity, saved her from the errors of James Lane Allen and other contemporary local colorists who followed the Darwinians into the fallacy of portraying man in indeterministic, depersonalized processes. Quite to the contrary, Miss Jewett seems to have accepted the idea

of "forces" in nature as merely part of the conventional teleological world of contemporary Christianity. Her strong characters—usually women—were free agents, with a strong will
to be themselves, within the limits set by natural law, divinely
decreed.

The secret of Miss Jewett's success as an artist lies in the
techniques which she developed for handling her settings. Like
Emily Dickinson, she had "learned to think New Englandly."
The relationship of people to place is not one of cause-and-
effect, but rather of identity. Man and environment merge,
with the result that people are portrayed in so low a key as to
be immersed into landscape, background, and tradition; and at
the same time the settings are vitalized by a vague sense of
humanity. There is ample evidence that the power of personification, often exercised at the subliminal level, accounts for
much of Miss Jewett's extraordinary skill as a setting specialist.

Though a large majority of Miss Jewett's stories are mere
descriptive sketches of scenes and people, they are highly charged
with human interest. "It is but seldom, as yet," she realized,
"that people really care much for anything for its own sake,
until it is proved to have some connection with humankind"
(*Country By-Ways* . . .). She does not allow her descriptive
muse to stray from the character situation, as do some local
colorists. Skilled at creating human interest by personifying
natural objects. Miss Jewett showed an advancement in two
respects at least: first, she breathed life, so to speak, into the
most omnipresent of natural objects, the New England trees
and flowers; second, she aroused a deep sympathy for these
creations by assuming a fresh and personal companionship with
them in an intimate, unaffected style like Henry Thoreau's.

Miss Jewett's personifications of local fauna and flora are reminiscent of Allen's best work minus the symbolism, but she is
superior to him in constancy of viewpoint. She wrote to Annie
Fields at various times that "hepaticas are like some people,
very dismal blue, with cold hands and faces"; that "There is
nothing dearer than a trig little company of anemones in a
pasture, all growing close together as if they kept each other
warm, and wanted the whole sun to themselves besides"; that
she is "neighborly with the hop-toads" and "intimate with a
big poppy"; and that she has been carrying on a sort of silent
intrigue with "a very handsome little bee" who "understands
things" and knows she "can do him no harm." In **"Cunner-
Fishing,"** a Deephaven sketch, she has one of her characters
observe that.

> the more one lives out of doors the more per-
> sonality there seems to be in what we call in-
> animate things. The strength of the hills and
> the voice of the waves are no longer only grand
> poetical sentences, but an expresson of some-
> thing real. . . .

There is no end of strange personalities among Miss Jewett's
trees. **"In Shadow,"** another Deephaven piece, contains a description of some gnarled pitch-pines which "looked like a
band of outlaws; they were such wild-looking trees. They seemed
very old, and as if their savage fights with the winter winds
had made them hard-hearted." . . . (pp. 147-50)

In **"A Neighbor's Landmark"** . . . , which has more plot than
most Jewett stories, two tall pines play a silent character role
of considerable importance. They have been serviceable in
guiding seamen into port; "they felt their responsibility as
landmarks and sentinels" (*The Life of Nancy* . . .). In a weak
moment John Packer forgets how they have served his people

and his ancestors and sells them to a conscienceless lumber-
man. The community circulates a petition to save the lives of
the Packer Pines, but in the meantime old Packer himself regrets his sudden promise and rows home across the bay just
in time to prevent their "murder."

> "I should miss them old trees," he said; "they
> always make me think of a married couple.
> They ain't no common growth, be they, Joe?
> Everybody knows 'em. I bet you if anything
> happened to one on 'em t'other would go an'
> die. They say ellums has mates, an' all them
> big trees." . . .

Miss Jewett's bird and flower characters are so much overshadowed by her tree patriarchs that they may easily be overlooked. Occasionally there is a magnificent personification of
some of the smaller plants, as in this selection from **"An
October Ride"** . . . :

> I passed some stiff, straight mullein stalks which
> stood apart together in a hollow as if they wished
> to be alone. They always remind me of the rigid
> old Scotch Covenanters, who used to gather
> themselves together in companies, against the
> law, to worship God in some secret hollow of
> the bleak hill-side. Even the smallest and
> youngest of the mulleins was a Covenanter at
> heart; they all had put by their yellow flowers,
> and they will still stand there, gray and un-
> bending, through the fall rains and winter snows,
> to keep their places and praise God in their own
> fashion, and they take great credit to themselves
> for doing it, I have no doubt, and think it is
> far better to be a stern and respectable mullein
> than a straying, idle clematis, that clings and
> wanders, and cannot bear wet weather. I saw
> members of the congregation scattered through
> all the pasture and felt like telling them to hurry,
> for the long sermon had already begun (*Country
> By-Ways* . . .).

As this and the preceding examples show, Miss Jewett sometimes introduces her wood folk not as mere figures of her poetic
fancy, but as creatures of rather durable personality. Such personifications do not spring wholly from figurative speech; they
are fruit of the author's conviction that trees are sentient beings,
not differing from human beings except in language. Wild
things do have a language of their own, she believes, and it is
our fault, not theirs, that so few of us can understand it. If we
would forget our conceit and make a serious effort, we might
be able to bridge the language breach that separates us from
the thought of these creatures. . . . In **"A Winter Drive"** Miss
Jewett pauses in train of thought to reveal a philosophical basis
for her conviction; and, incidentally, to reveal her occult
knowledge:

> There was an old doctrine called Hylozoism,
> which appeals to my far from Pagan sympa-
> thies, the theory of the soul of the world, of a
> life residing in nature, and that all matter lives;
> the doctrine that life and matter are inseparable.
> Trees are to most people as inanimate and un-
> conscious as rocks, but it seems to me that there
> is a good deal to say about the strongly marked
> individual characters, not only identified with
> a home, or a familiar bit of landscape or an

event in history, but of those that are crowded together in forests. There is a strange likeness to the characteristics of human beings among these, there is the same proportion of ignorant rabble of poor creatures who are struggling for life in more ways than one, and of self-respecting, well-to-do, dignified citizens. It is not a question of soil and of location any more than it is with us. . . .

It is impossible for one who has been a great deal among trees to resist the instinctive certainty that they have thought and purpose, and that they deliberately anticipate the future, or that they show traits of character which one is forced to call good or evil. How low down the scale of existence we may find the first glimmer of self-consciousness nobody can tell. . . . Man was the latest comer into this world, and he is just beginning to get acquainted with his neighbors, this is the truth of it [*Country By-Ways* . . .].

From this point Miss Jewett observes that the primitive pagans were wrong in inventing an imaginary race of spirits to inhabit the trees. Trees have their own souls and personalities that are analogous to, but not identical with, those of human beings. For this reason, she points out, "the true nature and life of a tree can never be exactly personified." . . .

Because of the absence of plots in most of her stories, Miss Jewett's personifications cannot be shown to have a dramatic function, yet they stand on an equal basis with many human characters serving as points of interest. Only occasionally does she attempt to lend a personality to nature as a whole. Though she sometimes uses, in a conventional way, the "mechanistic" phraseology of modern natural science, she never resigns her complete faith in a conventional teleological and dualistic world, in which the forces of nature are roughly identified with the will of the Author of the Universe. She may say casually that "Nature repossesses herself surely of what we boldly claim," but she does not neglect to add, in the same paragraph: "But it is only God who can plan and order it all,—who is father to his children, and cares for the least of us." . . . The impact of modern natural science upon her mind may have stimulated her curiosity in botanical and biological knowledge, but always she conceived of natural law as "the thoughts which He writes for us in the book of Nature" (*Deephaven* . . .). Her taste for the mystic aspect of plant life was hardly comparable to that of Allen, but occasionally a note of this kind is struck, as in a forest in **"The Gray Man,"** where

> There is everywhere a token of remembrance, of silence of secrecy. Some stronger nature once ruled these neglected trees and this fallow ground. They will wait the return of their master as long as roots can creep through mold, and make way for them. The stories of strange lives have been whispered to the earth, their thoughts have burned themselves into the cold rocks.

Innumerable examples and comments by the author herself support the conclusion that the personification of landscape is clearly the most distinctive feature of Miss Jewett's landscape art. Yet there is a second, less important, feature that deserves to be noted in passing, and that is her use of a time dimension, which adds depth to her scenes and thus reinforces the weight of her settings. Not being a dramatic artist, Miss Jewett did not create immediacy by a sudden emotion or by dramatic intensity. Like Wordsworth she presents "emotion recollected in tranquility," suffused by time and subsequent growth. She might have described Dunnet Landing with Coleridge's description of Tryermain: "The spring comes slowly up this way." The tempo of grief and forgetfulness, the emotions associated with Miss Jewett's bleak Maine landscapes, is slow, like the seasons of nature. The washing of ocean storms upon lonely islands, the snowstorms' encroaching upon winter forests, and lush summer green erupting upon the lonely farms—such changes are on a geological rather than a diurnal time scale.

Against such a temporal background, the stubborn Maine folk cling to their ways; the encroachment of modern technology, however certain, is very slow. In fact, there is almost no progress except decay, a kind of solemn death march as the process of civilization is reversed. Miss Jewett's superiority as a regional writer was achieved by the dimension of depth in her scenes. A sense of tradition highlighted her people and gave meaning to their actions.

In conclusion, it may be stated that Sarah Orne Jewett's ability to create "the palpable present intimate" was primarily derivative from a highly developed skill in her management of setting as an element of narration. In one sense she was a typical local colorist writing in the vogue of her generation. At the same time, she was successful in a more classical and abiding sense; she achieved a dimension of permanence and depth through a highly creative and novel use of setting—an element that is rarely raised to foremost importance in a story without a derangement of narrative equilibrium. Miss Jewett accomplished, mainly through her personifications of nature, a quality of personality that compensated for her lack of suspenseful drama. Having succeeded where many of her contemporary local colorists failed, she made a contribution to the art of fiction quite apart from her contribution to the body of the literature of New England. (pp. 151-55)

Robert D. Rhode, "Sarah Orne Jewett and 'The Palpable Present Intimate'," in Colby Library Quarterly, *Series VIII, No. 3, September, 1968, pp. 146-55.*

MARY ELLEN CHASE   (essay date 1968)

[*Chase was an American novelist, essayist, biographer, autobiographer, and critic. Partly inspired by Jewett, Chase wrote popular novels of the Maine coast and its seafaring families. In the following excerpt from her introduction to* The Country of the Pointed Firs, *Chase discusses characteristic traits of Jewett's fiction.*]

The Maine coast under [Sarah Orne Jewett's] hand and her imagination becomes more than a collection of seaside parishes, more than merely a place. Her care and vision unite in revealing its incomparable loveliness and its distinctive contribution not only to the state but to the country at large. Through that care and that vision the coast and its people merge into each other until they cease to be mere literary material and become a part of life itself.

Maine coast parishes, because of their location and the calling of most of their men, have given to the state, as Captain Littlepage well knew, both enlargement and enlightenment as sturdy gifts of untold value. (p. ix)

And Miss Jewett in perhaps the finest of her stories, **"The Queen's Twin,"** reveals clearly her own understanding of this unparalleled Maine coast background when she writes:

> The coast of Maine was in former years brought so near to foreign shores by its busy fleet of ships that among the older men and women one still finds a surprising proportion of travelers. Each seaward-stretching headland with its high-set houses, each island of a single farm, has sent its spies to view many a Land of Eschol: one may see plain, contented old faces at the windows whose eyes have looked at faraway ports and known the splendors of the Eastern world. They shame the easy voyager of the North Atlantic and the Mediterranean; they have rounded the Cape of Good Hope and braved the angry seas of Cape Horn in small wooden ships; they have brought up their hardy boys and girls on narrow decks. . . .

> More than this one cannot give to a young State for its enlightenment. The sea-captains and the captains' wives of Maine knew something of the wide world, and never mistook their native parishes for the whole instead of a part thereof. They knew not only Thomaston, Castine, and Portland, but London and Bristol and Bordeaux, and the strange-mannered harbors of the China Sea.

In her language, as these paragraphs richly prove, Sarah Orne Jewett is sure and certain, preserving for a long time, let us hope, those crisp, idiomatic terms of speech which are, alas! threatened with disappearance as television dims our differences and as easy transit from one place to another foretells a dismal conformity. The speech of all her characters is as inimitable as it is exact; yet perhaps Mrs. Almira Todd, her housekeeper and hostess at Dunnet Landing, provides the best lexicon. Even fifty years ago Mrs. Todd's speech would be easily understood anywhere along the coast of Maine; yet she and her language are bound to become anachronistic, unconscious contributors to the social history of a region.

In Miss Jewett's faithful hands Mrs. Todd's Maine verbs are precise and memorable. When one takes the arm of another, one *sleeves* him. When one wants something very much, one *lots* on it. When people or animals frequent a place, they *bange around* it. Those who like to be alone *hive away* in their own houses. (pp. x-xi)

Her adjectives are quite as charming. *Liable* is always used for *likely* as one hears it used today in many isolated coastal regions. . . . People who are eager are *wishful* instead of *wistful;* those who are ill are *dwindling,* or *puny,* or *peak-ed;* those who want something are the *coaxing sort.* Odd souls are *stray-away folks;* and those not quite sane are *scatter-witted,* not *scatter-brained* as elsewhere.

Mrs. Todd's exclamations are still commonly used among older coast people. That hardy expletive *There!* accompanies much of her conversation. Just what it means or why it seems necessary is a mystery; but it is always effective. "But—there! They enjoy it." "Well—there! I'm glad Mother's well." "There! How times have changed!" She is generous, too, with *Land sakes alive!* (pp. xi-xii)

Affirmatives and negatives emphasize Mrs. Todd's speech. Again and again she uses these with no necessity whatever save her obvious desire and habit. "There's nothin' like it. No, there's no such pennyroyal in the State of Maine." "There was good singers there; yes, there was excellent singers." "No, she ain't a mite considerate." "Yes, it's a real mercy there's a lobster." (p. xii)

With her many other fine qualities as an author Miss Jewett possessed a rare sense of humor—a humor which Willa Cather defines as archness. Sometimes this archness springs from a situation, as it does when the two Dulham ladies in the story called by their name decide on wigs to conceal their thin hair, or when Mrs. Hand in **"Aunt Cynthy Dallett"** diverts her weary self by killing the "brood o' moths" in the worsted mat on Mrs. Fulham's table while she waits for her hostess to prepare a long-deferred supper. At other times the archness lies in a neatly turned dialogue like that in *The Country of the Pointed Firs* where Asa gives unwelcome advice to Mrs. Todd about the loading of her dory.

> "Your bo't ain't trimmed proper, Mis' Todd. You won't never git out to Green Island that way. She's lo'ded bad, your bo't is—she's heavy behind."

> Mrs. Todd turned with difficulty and regarded the anxious adviser.

> "That you, Asa? Good mornin',' she said politely. 'When'd you git back from up country?"

And a third and most delicate use of this same humor, this same archness, which really means sensitiveness, of course, is seen in her apt comparison of Mrs. Todd to Antigone alone on the Theban plain, a "renewal of some historic soul" in spite of a daily life "busied with rustic simplicities," or in the quick consciousness of the old man in **"Decoration Day"** that he has become someone extraordinary because Abraham Lincoln has once shaken his hand.

Miss Jewett's singular awareness of people accounts, of course, for Willa Cather's contention that her portrayal of women illustrates her art at its best. One remembers with gratitude Esther Hight with her sheep, Susan Fosdick, "the same old sixpence," and the always immortal Almira Todd. Nevertheless, one remembers, too, with almost equal appreciation those seafaring men of the pointed fir country, who could hardly be drawn with greater skill—Captain Littlepage, Elijah Tilley, and William Blackett, the last of whom is treated at length and with rare understanding. (pp. xiii-xiv)

It is, indeed, this rare sensitiveness which sets Sarah Orne Jewett apart not only from all other Maine writers, but from many, if not most writers of all time and of many a place, gives her an enviable stature, makes her in short, the deeply desired, if unreachable, model for us all.

One likes to remember that Willa Cather, when asked to name three American novels "deserving of a long, long life," unhesitatingly selected *The Country of the Pointed Firs* to share this honor with *The Scarlet Letter* and *Huckleberry Finn* [see TCLC, Vol. 1]. How unhesitatingly those of us who know and love it echo her wise choice! (p. xiv)

Mary Ellen Chase, "Sarah Orne Jewett and Her Coast of Maine, an Introduction," in The Country of the Pointed Firs and Other Stories *by Sarah Orne Jewett, edited by Mary Ellen Chase, W. W. Norton & Company, Inc., 1968, pp. vii-xiv.*

HELEN V. PARSONS (essay date 1970)

[*In the following excerpt, Parsons compares and contrasts* The Tory Lover *with two historical novels set in the same period,* Richard Carvell *(1899) by Winston Churchill and* Oliver Wiswell *(1940) by Kenneth Roberts.*]

[Sarah Orne Jewett's] old friend Charles Dudley Warner, editor of the Hartford *Courant,* suggested that she consider writing an historical novel with Berwick for its setting. This idea appealed and, against her better judgment, she turned aside from her sketches of country people and everyday happenings in coastal Maine to produce *The Tory Lover.*

Although Miss Jewett was eager to preserve the historic Berwick names and places, they became pawns which she rearranged and shuffled to embellish a fiction. (p. 220)

It was almost incumbent on Miss Jewett that she choose John Paul Jones as the national heroic figure in *The Tory Lover* for during one portion of his eventful life he had been well-known along the Portsmouth docks while he had made ready the *Ranger* for its first crossing to France, in 1777. The presentation of Jones, however, is strictly romantic; a man of saccharine yearnings that were a far cry from his actual materialistic emotions.

Miss Jewett's departures from accuracy in her depictions of Berwick, its people, or of Jones, were not the real reasons for the lukewarm reception accorded the novel. The violent temper of the times never explodes in *The Tory Lover;* the heartbreaking separation of two lovers never develops into a warm love story. Reared in a gentle Victorian atmosphere, Miss Jewett was quite unable to portray an unknown violence; embued with her cameo portraits of the elderly, she did not understand and could not realistically portray youthful love. These faults were the basis for unfavorable criticism of the novel when it appeared in 1901.

A later critic, John Eldridge Frost, observed that although "*The Tory Lover* compared favorably with the fictionalized treatment of American history by Sarah Jewett's contemporaries," it would be forgotten because "Readers were soon to demand in historical fiction strict fidelity to fact based upon intensive research, and plots that followed a logical sequence instead of turning upon coincidence." Throughout *The Tory Lover* the plot turns upon an act of fate, of providence, or by the hand of God. Riders appear to dispense the mob just in time to save Madam Wallingford and her property from harm; letters written by Master Sullivan, who had been in America for nearly fifty years, miraculously reach men in important positions in England's government, men who just happen to be in positions that enable them to help Mary Hamilton; the hand of God leads Captain Jones and Mary to a particular English Church on a particular day; and luck, fate, or God enable the captain to locate Roger Wallingford within a few hours. Effortlessly and inexplicably the story unfolds.

Materials for Miss Jewett's plot offered no problem, for the history of the colonies was filled with the Tory-Whig conflict. Stories of individual conflicts over the issues existed in every town and city on the Atlantic seaboard. These conflicts arose between three distinct groups. There were those people who had gained security and affluence in America and were reluctant to sever their allegiance to the mother country in exchange for an uncertain existence in a crude, unformed society. There were those who had achieved no great success; they found it easy to oppose the mandates of a ruler that threatened their very existence. Then there were those leaders in the young country whose allegiance to the country of their birth was much stronger than the remote ties with the mother country.

With these three choices for the characters in her novel. Miss Jewett selected the prominent family of Wallingfords, known for their Tory sympathies, and another prominent family, the Hamiltons, whose patriotic sympathies lay with the country of their birth. Skillfully she introduces the thoughtful leaders of the community, whose patriotism for America superseded their loyalty to England. At the Hamilton House party which is being given in honor of John Paul Jones on the eve of his departure on the *Ranger,* Judge Chadbourne expresses the feelings of those present: "Our Counry is above our King in such a time as this, yet I myself was of those who could not lightly throw off the allegiance of a life-time." Major Haggens, speaking of Roger Wallingford's indecisiveness, adds: "I have always said that we must have patience with such lads and not try to drive them." . . . Thus, Miss Jewett sets the tone for her novel, a tone of tolerance for people of position, regardless of their sympathies. This tone she maintains to the end of the story with little or no regard for the temper of the times.

The weakness of such a novel is made clearer by a comparison with two other novels written about the same period of history: *Richard Carvel* (1899) by Winston Churchill and *Oliver Wiswell* (1940) by Kenneth Roberts. The Tory-Whig conflict in these two novels is similar to that in *The Tory Lover,* but the handling of it is significantly different. There is a surface parallelism in the love stories, but the feeling and development of them is much more consistent than in *The Tory Lover.* Some similarities in style exist in the two nineteenth-century novels, but in general the style of both *Richard Carvel* and *Oliver Wiswell* is much more vigorous than that of *The Tory Lover.* The plots in the first two novels are worked out in great detail, whereas Miss Jewett's contains many unexplained situations.

The patriots, aroused to action by men like Sam Adams, were not passive in expressing their dislike of the Tory sympathizers. Yet, when there is an actual confrontation, Miss Jewett draws back from disgusting situations or physical violence. She makes it clear that many of the dispossessed Tories have fled to Halifax or to England where they exist under miserable conditions. She carefully describes their "sad faces" and "idle days" and concludes that "a poor page of English history was unfolded before their eyes." . . . (pp. 221-23)

When Madam Wallingford's house is threatened by a mob of patriots, Miss Jewett neatly turns aside from violence and destruction by having a group of elderly gentlemen, mounted on horses, come to their neighbor's rescue, although these gentlemen are staunch patriots. Even some of the town authorities are present: "The town constable was bawling his official threats as he held one of the weaker assailants by the collar and pounded the poor repentant creature's back." . . . The total damage of the Wallingford estate is one broken window. . . .

In each book the mobs are unruly, illiterate and rough; but whereas Miss Jewett's mob can be turned aside and is "repentant," the mobs in *Oliver Wiswell* riot unchecked, are pitiless, fanatic, and unrepentant. Nor are they hindered by any friends of the family. Anyone who assists a Tory can expect to have his own property destroyed, and can expect bodily harm. (p. 224)

All three authors choose to place their young lovers in prominent families with opposing political views. There is a marked parallelism, however, between Mary Hamilton and Roger Wallingford of *The Tory Lover* and Sally Leighton and Oliver

Wiswell of the Roberts novel. Mary is the sister of a ship owner and a patriot; Sally is the daughter of a ship owner and a patriot. Roger is the son of a successful business man and is sympathetic to the Tory cause; Oliver is the son of a successful lawyer and also sympathizes with the loyalists. In both novels the young people have been friends and neighbors since childhood, and both young men have become romantically interested in the girls. Here the parallelism ends.

Roger returns to Berwick from Portsmouth to tell Mary that he has finally taken the patriot's oath and is to sail on the *Ranger.* Mary is sharp and impatient with him. Willfully she refuses to listen to any protestation of love: "'Stop; I must hear no more!' said the young queen coldly . . . 'Farewell for the present.'" When he begs to see her after he has proved his loyalty, she answers proudly: "'Then you may come, Mr. Wallingford.'" She leaves him and "had not even given him her dear hand at parting". . . . The cold, unfeeling attitude of "the young queen" does not suggest a romance. Here is a girl more interested in herself, her position, and her popularity than in the future of a good friend. It is unbelievable that she would address an old and dear neighbor as "Mr. Wallingford." This is the one romantic scene in the book, and it is totally lacking in warmth, to say nothing of passion. (p. 225)

Miss Jewett fails to develop a convincing romance. Her hero mouths the word "love" but neither a physical nor a spiritual awareness between the two young people is evident. Mary Hamilton does sail to England with Madam Wallingford to begin the long search for Roger but the feeling is not so much one of love for Roger as love for his mother. Mary declares that she has told her brother that she will never leave Madam Wallingford and finally announces: "'Dear friend, you must let me have my way. I could not let you go alone . . . I am going with you wherever you may go'." . . . Miss Jewett chooses to make her heroine queenly and imperious. She attempts to describe emotions by having Mary's "heart beat fast" as she "listens sadly" with "eager bravery" to "words that are hard to bear." At other times Mary exhibits "a majestic air," "a proud indifference," or "a great sweetness." Frequently Mary "sighs," her face "pales and flushes." Eventually Mary's great hidden love emerges in the "light of heaven on her lovely face." . . .

The detached approach to romance in *The Tory Lover* is neither as persuasive nor as realistic as the ardent rendition in *Oliver Wiswell* or the light progression in *Richard Carvel.* The sense arising from the pages of *The Tory Lover* is that the author is enamored with the idea of nobility and is slightly contemptuous of romantic weakness in the young male. When Roger is with Mary he appears to be callow, overwhelmed by her beauty, tongue-tied by her presence, and completely submissive to her demands. However, as he prepares to board the *Ranger,* he is a "gallant-looking fellow . . . in his face all the high breeding and character of his house." . . . A curt greeting and harsh order from the captain sends him scuttling to his cabin, but he returns to the deck as the ship is leaving the harbor. In the words of the author: "He may have gone below a boy, but he came on deck a man." . . . Just how one sharp command can bring forth such a change is not made clear. But from that moment Roger is a man, jealous of his love for Mary, sometimes moody over his precarious romance, and always a man of honor, as befits his position as a gentleman. He becomes the confidant of the notoriously aloof captain; he suffers injury at the hand of a traitor. Courageously he experiences hardships which eventually lead him back to Mary so that at the end they

can stand "hand in hand" waiting to step ashore at Hamilton House.

Roger, away from the regal Mary, acquires the stature of a man with a maturity that is more acceptable to the author. Throughout the book, however, Miss Jewett adheres to her own advice to Willa Cather about writing on a man's character: "it is safer to write about him . . . and not to be he!" Roger's moods are faithfully described by her, but he comes alive as a real person only twice: first, when he is stabbed, captured and imprisoned; later, when he faces the villain at the Inn. In these two brief moments Miss Jewett refrains from dictating his reactions and allows him actually to experience hardship and suffering, and to express his own violent indignation when he faces Dickson, the villain. . . .

There is little to be gained from comparing the literary style of a nineteenth-century novel with that of a twentieth-century novel; besides, the style employed by a woman is inescapably different from that of a man. Winston Churchill and Sarah Jewett were contemporaries, however, and each wrote an historical novel of the Revolutionary War period. Was it a trait of nineteenth-century writers to worship position and nobility? Was it necessary in that period for an author to introduce his own philosophical views through lengthy explanations of appearance, thoughts, and deeds? (pp. 227-29)

Plot in *Richard Carvel* and *Oliver Wiswell* moves forward strongly and reasonably from the opening conflict of views, through historic events and fictional situations, to a happy ending. In *The Tory Lover* events are often unexplained. Colonel John Langdon, former member of the Marine committee of Congress and the local Navy Agent, appoints the officers who are to serve on the *Ranger;* from him Roger Wallingford receives his commission. Immediately after Roger tells Mary of his commission she pleads with Captain Jones to allow Roger to sail with him. Furiously, he refuses her request, but as he "watches her face fall and all light go out of it," . . . he reverses his decision. Why is it necessary for Mary to plead with the captain? Why is the captain so opposed to her request? Scarcely an hour had passed since he had cried out to the assembled Berwick men: "Send your young men to sea! . . . Send me thoroughbred lads like your dainty young Wallingford!" . . .

In England, Mary becomes very despondent over her fruitless search for Roger. On a late summer afternoon she goes into a church seeking courage to face her trial. How does it happen that John Paul Jones appears before her? Jones has been a wanted man in England ever since the Whitehaven incident in April. His picture is posted in public places and a reward is offered for his capture. How does he, a ship's captain, turn up in this particular church in broad daylight in a hostile city? His reason: "I do my own errands,—that is all." . . . Then he attributes this most unusual encounter to "the hand of God." . . . All the logical questions are left unanswered.

During this brief meeting Jones learns for the first time the entire story of Roger Wallingford after his supposed desertion from the *Ranger* and realizes finally the probable duplicity of Dickson. That very night he appears under Mary's window singing a Berwick sailor song to attract her attention. He promises that she will have news of Wallingford if she goes to Old Passage Inn the next night. . . . How does Captain Jones find out so much about Wallingford in so short a time? If Miss Jewett had furnished answers to all of these questions concerning Jones's activities in England, she would have had at least one chapter of her book filled with intrigue and excitement and danger. That would not have been consistent with her gentle art. Yet, by deftly disposing of these questions as machinations of fate, she strains credence.

Many doubts surround Madam Wallingford also. The mob is gathering for an attack on the Wallingford house but is apparently dispersed by the news that Roger is sailing on the *Ranger*. . . . Later the mob does attack, screaming, "We want no Royalists among us, we want no abettors of George the Third; there's a bill now to proscribe ye and stop your luxury and pride." . . . In spite of all this, Madam Wallingford sails from Portsmouth two days later in her own timber-laden vessel bound for Halifax, a British colony, and no effort is made to detain her or to strip her of all that will make her financially secure. . . . One year thereafter, with the war still in progress, she sails back to Portsmouth in her own brig, the *Golden Dolphin*. Evidently she intends to take up her life on the Wallingford estate exactly as if nothing had happened. . . . How could Madam Wallingford have been so serenely unaware of the violence of the day?

The importance of family and good breeding governs the characters in *The Tory Lover;* gentle tolerance furnishes the tone; feminine distaste for violence curbs the action; unfamiliarity with romance restricts the love story; and only fate—exemplified in William Cowper's "God moves in a mysterious way / His wonders to perform"—ties sections of the story together to create a semblance of unity of plot. (pp. 229-31)

Helen V. Parsons, " 'The Tory Lover', 'Oliver Wiswell', and 'Richard Carvel'," in Colby Library Quarterly, *Series IX, No. 4, December, 1970, pp. 220-31.*

JOSEPHINE DONOVAN (essay date 1980)

[*Donovan is an American biographer and critic whose works study women in literature and women writers from a feminist viewpoint. According to Donovan: "In much of Western literature the moral being of women has been denied or repressed. Feminist literary criticism points this out and looks for works (often by women) in which women characters seek to achieve fullness of being." In the following excerpt, Donovan offers a new interpretation of several subjects, themes, and characteristics prominent in Jewett's fiction.*]

Many critics have remarked an elegaic mood in the work of Sarah Orne Jewett. They have attributed it to the fact that the world she was describing was one whose time of economic prosperity had passed. It is true that New England in the late nineteenth century was a world on the wane; nevertheless it is not sufficient to explain Jewett's elegy in this way. The reason lies deeper. It lies in the fact that Jewett, as a woman, identified with the world around her. The sense of lost or missed opportunity, the sense of unrealized dreams, the sense of isolation from the communal mainstream, which one finds in so much of her work, express a feeling with which she was quite familiar.

Indeed, the moralistic urgings to make the best of one's lot that one finds in her early work—especially **"A Guest at Home"** . . .—reveal most poignantly their author's struggle to transcend the boredom and isolation of rural life. If one had no other clue, the impassioned feminism of her semi-autobiographical *Bildungsroman*, **A Country Doctor** . . . , would be enough to legitimate an assertion that Jewett was keenly aware of the limitations to woman's lot, and that she did not accept them gracefully. And, while she herself eventually participated

in a rich and rewarding community of women, she must, nevertheless, in her early years have been aware of the emotional strait-jacket forced upon unmarried women.

It is her sense of the absence or failure of community that makes Jewett's tone elegaic. She is lamenting not only the lack of economic opportunity her region suffered from, and not only her own lack of political and social opportunity; perhaps most of all she is lamenting the lack of emotional possibility which cursed the world she knew. In this sense she is a modern: her theme is alienation—especially as it affected women.

An authorial comment in *The Country of the Pointed Firs* . . . illustrates this concern. It comes at the Bowden family reunion; the narrator is amazed at how Mrs. Todd has come to life in the community of her friends.

> The excitement of an unexpectedly great occasion was a subtle stimulant to her disposition, and I could see that sometimes when Mrs. Todd had seemed limited and heavily domestic, she had simply grown *sluggish* for lack of proper surroundings. . . .
>
> It was not the first time that I was full of wonder at the waste of human ability in this world, as a botanist wonders at the wastefulness of nature, the thousand seeds that die, the unused provision of every sort. . . .—a narrow set of circumstances had caged a fine able character and held it captive.

A central concern in Jewett's work issues, therefore, from her intimate awareness of the limited emotional and social condition of women; most of her stories deal with women's efforts to transcend their condition. One may make several statements about the ways in which Jewett's women do cope, the ways in which the theme of transcendence is handled.

1) One is the way of the independent woman, or what today we would call the career-woman. These are women who are not afraid to take on a male role, if necessary, to survive. The majority of Jewett's stories deal with some aspect or other of this kind of woman.

2) In mid-career, however (by the mid-'80s), Jewett begins to deal with women who live with other women or who are seeking to find a community. Several works are framed on a companionship between women; their conversations in themselves provide a kind of transcendence.

3) What finally emerges as a theme of isolation vs. community reaches its culmination in Jewett's later works, especially *The King of Folly Island and Other People* . . . and *The Country of the Pointed Firs*. . . .

4) The ultimate transcendence which Jewett presents seems to lie in a kind of women's religion; one in which the herb-gatherer-healer functions as a beneficient witch and wherein community is sustained by women and their ethos of hospitality. It is a kind of matriarchal Christianity. (pp. 365-67)

Critics have not been remiss in drawing attention to the purposeful, self-reliant women in Jewett's stories. Richard Cary in his *Sarah Orne Jewett* lists eighteen of them off the top of his head (there are many more), and entitles one major section of his critical study "Self-Reliant Women." In general, these women cope by exerting their will over adverse circumstances. Often this simply means getting economic control over their lives. It means dealing with men who are either false [**"A Lost**

Lover," "Marsh Rosemary"] . . . or incompetent ["Tom's Husband," "Farmer Finch," "A Village Shop"]. . . . In nearly all cases the women turn out to be shrewd businesswomen; one of the most delightful of these is "The Growtown 'Bugle'" . . . wherein a woman who lives alone makes a fortune speculating out West by mail, outwitting con men at their own game.

Occasionally, women take on a male role. The theme of role reversal reaches its culmination in *A Country Doctor* . . . , but it is a theme Jewett returned to throughout her career. Indeed, one of her earliest published stories, **"Hallowell's Pretty Sister"** . . . is a farcical piece about what would today be called a fraternity prank wherein one of the boys dresses up as a girl, Hallowell's "sister." "She" sets out to seduce one of Hallowell's friends who falls for "her," much to the amusement of Hallowell and the others.

The theme is picked up quite a bit more seriously in **"Tom's Husband."** . . . In this story Tom's wife, Mary Dunn, decides that she would be better at running the factory and he better at running their home. They decide to try reversing the roles and do so, with considerable success. Mary makes a go of the factory and Tom becomes absorbed in the details of being a housewife. Jewett reverses the expected conventions throughout: Mary, for example, becomes the tired businessman, coming home too exhausted to listen to Tom's housewifely complaints about the daily trivia. Finally, he grows exasperated with his role and demands that they give up the experiment, which they do.

Cary has read this as an "anti-feminist" ending, however, I believe it should be read rather as an example of Jewett's awareness of the tedium of housework and of how no man would endure it—a decidedly feminist point. Tom in fact develops

> . . . an uneasy suspicion that she could get along pretty well without him. . . . He seemed to himself to have merged his life in his wife's . . . he felt himself fast growing rusty and behind the times, and to have somehow missed a good deal in life . . . One day the thought rushed over him that his had been almost exactly the experience of most women and he wondered if it really was any more disappointing and ignominious to him than it was to women themselves.

"Farmer Finch" . . . is another story that deals quite consciously with role reversal. In this case a young woman takes over the farm management because her father is ill and otherwise incompetent. She makes a great success of her venture, much to the surprise of all concerned. We find a similar theme in **"The Stage Tavern,"** . . . wherein a recent Radcliffe graduate works competently as a tavern manager.

Jewett's own ambivalence between the "unnaturalness" of a woman pursuing a career versus the boredom and restrictions of the traditional role may be seen most clearly in **"A Guest at Home"** . . . and *A Country Doctor*. . . . Both are semi-autobiographical. The story involves the return of a young girl, Annie Hollis, to her parents who live on a bare, isolated farm. She has come home from the city where she was being educated, primarily in painting. Annie is dismal at having to leave the refinement, luxuries, and excitement of the city but determines to make the best of it at home—which she does by continuing to paint, using local subjects, and by selling her paintings to a dealer in New York. Jewett's somewhat heavy-handed moral to the story is: ". . . where there is a will there is a way, and there is certainly a great difference between making life and taking it."

A Country Doctor is ideologically feminist, indeed is so informed with feminist fervor—the work is really a series of feminist declamations—that it could be made into a feminist opera. Jewett once replied that it was perhaps her favorite work, possibly because it was so unorthodox a plot and so close to her own youth.

The plot involves the education and coming to womanhood of Nan Prince. Nan, an orphan, is raised by Dr. John Leslie. He being her only role-model, she not surprisingly decides to become a physician. The plot is built upon a series of challenges to Nan's unorthodox project. The last of these is a suitor, George Gerry, whom apparently she loves, but eventually rejects so as to carry out her life dream. Dr. Leslie encourages her to stick to her ambition. His defenses of her plan, like hers, read like feminist speeches. In rejecting her suitor, for example, she declaims, "still standing, and looking taller than ever":

> It is not easy to turn away from him . . . It is something that I have found it hard to fight, but it is not my whole self longing for his love and companionship. If I heard he had gone to the other side of the world for years and years, I should be glad and not sorry. I know all tradition fights on his side, but I can look forward, and see something a thousand times better than being his wife, and living here in Dunport keeping his house, and trying to forget all that nature fitted me to do.

(pp. 367-70)

Jewett's feminist awareness may be seen as well in some of her critical comments, which show her to be especially cognizant of the problems of the woman artist. In her discussion of the artistic chemistry in the mind of the writer, Jewett notes how important it is that irrelevant distractions not be allowed to intrude.

As an example of a case where they did interfere, she cites Harriet Beecher Stowe's *The Pearl of Orr's Island*. Jewett laments that the author has been unable to sustain the original "noble key of simplicity and harmony" through to the end. "A poor writer," she notes, "is at the mercy of much unconscious opposition." (*Letters* . . .) A writer must, she continues, "throw everything and everybody away at times, but a woman made like Mrs. Stowe cannot bring herself to that cold selfishness of the moment for one's work's sake." (p. 371)

Some of Jewett's most interesting and significant critical remarks were made to Willa Cather, who became a fast friend and devoted admirer in the last years of Jewett's life. In my opinion, indeed, the influence of Jewett on Cather cannot be overestimated.

In 1908 Jewett gave Cather three major pieces of advice: one was, not surprisingly, that she should absent herself from the newspaper world in order to devote her full attention to her art. "You don't have time and quiet to perfect your work . . . you must find a quiet place . . . your own quiet centre of life, and write from that . . ." (*Letters*. . . .)

Second, she advised Cather to write about material that she knew intimately—her "Nebraska life," for example. Third, and perhaps most significant, she criticized the use of a male *persona* in one of Cather's early stories.

> The lover is as well done as he could be when a woman writes in the man's character,—it must always, I believe, be something of a masquerade. I think it is safer to write about him as you did about the others and not try to be he! And you could almost have done it yourself—a woman could even care enough to wish to take her away from such a life, by some means or other (*Letters* . . .).

(p. 372)

Jewett herself had treated relationships between women in her fiction from the beginning . . . , but with more frequency by the mid-'80s. Perhaps *A Country Doctor* was a kind of turning point; or perhaps Jewett's own growing involvement with Annie Fields (and other women artists) is reflected in her fiction.

Two of the stories in *A White Heron and Other Stories* . . . deal with women couples. One is a comic masterpiece. **"The Dulham Ladies"** . . . , and the other, **"Mary and Martha,"** . . . deals with the resourcefulness of two women in establishing their economic security.

Another story published at this time, but never collected, is **"A Garden Story"** . . . , a somewhat sentimental piece about an older woman who lives alone in the country and who is joined by a young orphan girl from the city through a social welfare program, and the growing intensity of their attachment. This theme is picked up later in **"A Village Shop"** . . . wherein the younger woman eventually marries the brother of the older woman, much to the misery and jealousy of the latter.

In **"Fair Day,"** . . . a relatively unnoticed story, Jewett brings the theme of sisterhood to a level of significance not seen in earlier stories. It involves the re-establishment of a connection between two women in-laws who had been alienated for forty years due to a quarrel. The central episode is their decision to patch things up between them. This is a most positive step in Jewett's world, for community is a central value and women are its prime sustainers.

Several of Jewett's stories deal with pilgrimages made by women in quest of community and/or significance. These include ["**Miss Becky's Pilgrimage," "Going to Shrewsbury," "The Flight of Betsy Lane,"**] . . . , and the pilgrimage of Mrs. Todd and her mother to a family reunion in *The Country of the Pointed Firs.*

While stories featuring women couples continue, including [**"Miss Tempy's Watchers," "The Town Poor," "The Guests of Mrs. Timms,"** and **"The Green Bowl"**], the theme of woman love reaches its culmination in one of Jewett's greatest stories, **"Martha's Lady."** . . . This piece, somewhat reminiscent of Flaubert's "Un Coeur simple," involves a servant woman Martha, who develops an intense attachment to a young woman visitor who is kind to her. Promising soon to return, the visitor leaves and proceeds through life, not coming back for twenty years. Throughout this period Martha worshipfully follows the events of her life, thinks of nothing but her, dreaming of her return. Finally, the woman does return and in a joyous moment of reunion realizes the devotion and love that Martha has bestowed upon her from afar through the years. Again, the tone is markedly elegaic for the waste of human emotion potential.

It is in stories like this that Jewett leaves the company of good storytellers like Daudet and Maupassant and enters the ranks

From a letter to Horace E. Scudder on his succeeding Thomas Bailey Aldrich as editor of the Atlantic Monthly *in 1890.*

of Flaubert, Turgenev and Tolstoi. Oddly enough, Jewett worried about the "dullness" of this story and revealingly commented that Martha was Jewett herself. (pp. 373-74)

In her next collection after *A White Heron, The King of Folly Island and Other People* . . . , the theme of isolation versus community assumes major significance. Two of the stories in this work deal with male-dominated households wherein women are held in hermetic isolation from their friends.

In the title story the "king" is George Quint, a recluse who has "reigned" over a remote barren island, allegorically named Folly Island, for many years. His only "subjects" have been his wife, now dead, of emotional starvation effectively, and his daughter, who is dying of consumption. Her father refuses to return to the mainland for reasons of ego (he had vowed years before that he would never leave the island alive) and thus she is denied medical care.

It is clear to the narrator visiting the island that the girl has really been kept a prisoner by her father; at one point the girl wistfully watches a funeral procession on a neighboring island through spyglasses, longing to participate in community affairs. This story is a dramatic example of what Edward Garnett called the "isolated masculine understanding" tyrannizing over, and ultimately killing, the women who long for a social support system, for community. It illustrates what is becoming a central

Jewett theme—the yearning (by women) for a transcending community and the sense of loss at its lack.

In **"The Landscape Chamber,"** . . . also in this collection, we find a similar situation. Here a miserly father has kept friends at bay for years, forcing his daughter to live in solitude and poverty with him. When the shocked narrator, a young woman who has happened upon their farm during a trip, realizes the situation, she exclaims,

> "You surely have friends?"
>
> "Only at a distance," said she, sadly. "I fear they are no longer friends. I have *you*," she added, turning to me quickly, in a pathetic way that made me wish to put my arms about her. "I have been longing for a friendly face. Yes, it is very hard," and she went drearily out of the door. . . ."

In an earlier story, **"A White Heron,"** . . . Jewett had also dealt with the clash between women's loyalty to community versus the male will to destroy and isolate. In this story a young country girl, who is intimately familiar with her natural environment, is visited by a young man who hunts animals and birds for trophies. He realizes her knowledge and asks her to lead him to the bird that has succeeded in eluding him, a white heron. At first she is flattered, as she finds him romantically appealing, but in the end, though she knows exactly where the heron is, she keeps silent, refusing to betray her natural companion. Here, as in *A Country Doctor*, the young woman rejects a potential suitor in the name of loyalty to the sanctity of the natural community to which she belongs.

Sandwiched between the two stories of isolation in *The King of Folly Island* we find a joyous tale, **"The Courting of Sister Wisby,"** . . . that implicitly provides an alternative sense of community. As in *Deephaven* . . . , Jewett's first published collection, and *The Country of the Pointed Firs* . . . , the story is framed upon the relationship between two women. In *Deephaven* the women were young tourists spending the summer together in a family home on the Maine coast. The "plot" invokes their encounters with various sea-coast "characters" who will tell them their "stories." In *The Country of the Pointed Firs*, the frame relationship is between the narrator, an author who has come to the area for the summer to write, and Mrs. Todd, her landlady. In **"The Courting of Sister Wisby"** the narrator is, as usual, a thinly disguised *persona* for Jewett, and her companion is Mrs. Goodsoe, an herb-gatherer who prefigures Mrs. Todd in *The Country of the Pointed Firs*. Mrs. Goodsoe tells the narrator the story of Sister Wisby, a marvelously comic tale about a woman with a mind of her own.

The relationship, however, between the narrator and Mrs. Goodsoe is quite developed; indeed, it takes up more than half the story. The strength and joy of their conversation while gathering herbs stands as a stark contrast to the miserable isolation depicted in the stories that surround it, and provides as well a contrasting sense of community.

The theme of isolation versus community reaches its culmination in *The Country of the Pointed Firs*. This work presents a series of solitaries who are seen as lonely, shipwrecked souls who long for companionship and communion. These include William, Joanna, and Captain Littlepage. On the other hand, the work also provides high emotional points and these come when people are engaged in relationship, in visits, in conversations, at reunions, in social rituals. These are the only thing that give human life significance, that enable a measure of transcendence.

The final parting between the narrator and Mrs. Todd fittingly summarizes the theme of the preciousness and transitoriness of relationships—the fragility of community—and exemplifies Jewett's elegy at its most poignant.

> With this last word Mrs. Todd turned and left me as if with sudden thought of something she had forgotten, so that I felt sure she was coming back, but presently I heard her go out of the kitchen door and walk down the path toward the gate. I could not part so; I ran after her to say good-by, but she shook her head and waved her hand without looking back . . . So we die before our own eyes; so we see some chapters of our lives come to their natural end.
>
> (pp. 374-77)

The ultimate significance of the theme of women's communion emerges in *The Country of the Pointed Firs*. . . . It is prefigured in **"The Courting of Sister Wisby,"** . . . and continued in **"The Foreigner,"** a story published in 1900 but never reprinted. In these works we find that the connections between women form a kind of secret society, that womanly lore is handed down from mother to daughter in a continuing matrilineal tradition of healing and hospitality. It is the woman's function to be a loving center of community. This is the ultimate transcendence Jewett presents: a kind of matriarchal Christianity, a woman's religion.

In **"The Courting of Sister Wisby,"** we find in Mrs. Goodsoe a person similar to Mrs. Todd of *The Country of the Pointed Firs*. Both are herb-gatherers and medicine-makers. Both have an esoteric knowledge that has been handed down by women for centuries. Mrs. Goodsoe learned her knowledge of herbs from her mother, and Mrs. Todd learned hers primarily from a foreign woman (as reported in **"The Foreigner"**).

Both women have, if not open feelings of contempt toward men, at least an opinion of their general incompetence. Mrs. Goodsoe is presented as being wiser than most doctors, who, though they be "bilin' over with book-larnin' . . . is truly ignorant of what to do for the sick . . ." "Book-fools I call 'em," she adds. She, on the other hand, with her subtle knowledge of the art of herb-healing is "truly" able to cure the sick.

Mrs. Todd expresses a similarly dim view of men in general, although she harbors a certain nostalgia for her own dead husband. Her attitude comes across most clearly when she is preparing to journey over to the island where her mother lives. Significantly, she wishes to make the voyage with no male companion.

> . . . we don't want to carry no men folks havin' to be considered every minute an' takin' up all our time. No, you let me do; we'll just slip out an' see mother by ourselves.

Both Mrs. Goodsoe and Mrs. Todd have an extensive knowledge of the doings of their community and its history. Both pass on this information to the narrator who in turn sets down this oral history in writing. It is Mrs. Todd, however, who is presented as a figure of nearly legendary proportions, and it is really in *The Country of the Pointed Firs* where the concept of a woman's religion begins to emerge.

Mrs. Todd is one of Jewett's most enduring characters, anticipating in many respects Cather's Antonia. She is compared continually to great figures of ancient Greece. She had "the look of a huge sybil." She "stood there grand and architectural, like a *caryatide*." "She might have been Antigone alone on the Theban plain."

The narrator sees her as a kind of priestess of some ancient cult, "an enchantress," . . . expressed in her vast knowledge of herbs. She is the town healer; she is a beneficent witch. In her herb garden

> there were some strange and pungent odors that roused a dim sense and remembrance of something in the forgotten past. Some of these might have belonged to sacred and mystic rites, and have had some occult knowledge handed with them down the centuries.

The central person in Mrs. Todd's life is her mother. Indeed, two of the central episodes in *The Country* revolve around the mother: one is a visit the narrator and Mrs. Todd make, out to the island where her mother lives; the other is a family reunion over which Mrs. Brackett, the mother, reigns. ("'Mother's always the queen,' said Mrs. Todd.")

Significantly, her mother, when first presented in the narrative, is associated with transcendence.

> Mrs. Todd was looking off across the bay with a face full of affection and interest. The sunburst upon that outermost island made it seem like a sudden revelation of the world beyond this which some believe to be so near.
>
> "That's where mother lives," said Mrs. Todd.

The mother is an angel of hospitality and has not only the gift of sympathy but the "highest gift of heaven, a perfect self-forgetfulness." (pp. 377-79)

The reunion itself takes on religious significance.

> Such a day as this has transfiguring powers, and easily makes friends of those who have been cold-hearted, and gives to those who are dumb their chance to speak, and lends some beauty to the plainest face.

And it is women like Mrs. Todd and her mother who effect this transfiguration. It is this sense that they take on the function of magicians or beneficent witches. They seem to have the power to help people to overcome isolation and poverty.

> . . . it seemed sometimes as if love and hate and jealousy and adverse winds at sea might also find their proper remedies among the curious wild-looking plants in Mrs. Todd's garden.

"The Foreigner" is the story of a woman Mrs. Todd had known in her youth, forty years earlier, who had taught her much herbal lore and who at her death had bequeathed all her earthly belongings to Mrs. Todd. In this piece the matrilineal con-

nection and the hospitality theme are quite pronounced. When she first arrives in Dunnet Landing, the woman is a bride of Captain Tolland. She does not speak English, is from "the French islands" and generally feels like a "stranger in a strange land."

Mrs. Todd's mother recognizes the obligation of hospitality.

> What consequence . . . is your comfort or mine, beside letting a foreign person an' a stranger feel so desolate; she's done the best a woman could do in her lonesome place, and she asks nothing of anybody except a little common kindness.

Thus begins a bond among the women.

On the night of Mrs. Tolland's death occur mysterious happenings that can only suggest once again the dim outlines of a matriarchal religion. Mrs. Todd is sitting with Mrs. Tolland as she is dying. Suddenly a ghost of Mrs. Tolland's mother appears; both Mrs. Todd and Mrs. Tolland see her.

> "You saw her, didn't you," she said the second time, an' I says, "Yes, dear, I did; you ain't never goin' to feel strange an' lonesome no more."

Then Mrs. Tolland died.

Jewett had dealt with the supernatural in earlier stories. In **"Lady Ferry,"** . . . she treated the "wandering Jew" theme. The woman of the title seemed to be blessed/cursed with immortality. In **"Miss Tempy's Watchers,"** . . . Jewett dealt with the haunting presence of a corpse at a wake. While the fascination with the supernatural is characteristically New England, Jewett's interest seems finally to go beyond the level of the ghost story. Rather, as seen in her final works, it points in the direction of a woman's religion of healing, hospitality and community.

In her life Jewett found "transfiguration" through friendship. One of the central themes of her works is the quest for such "transfiguration." The resolution of this seeking lies in Jewett's intuition of woman's religion. This is the personal vision—the "heart"—of her most serious work. (pp. 379-80)

Josephine Donovan, "A Woman's Vision of Transcendence: A New Interpretation of the Works of Sarah Orne Jewett," in The Massachusetts Review, *Vol. XXI, No. 2, Summer, 1980, pp. 365-80.*

ADDITIONAL BIBLIOGRAPHY

Bender, Bert. "To Calm and Uplift 'Against the Dark': Sarah Orne Jewett's Lyric Narratives." *Colby Library Quarterly* XI, No. 4 (December 1975): 219-29.
    Calls for a critical reappraisal of Jewett's narrative style and analyzes the lyrical organization of "The Foreigner."

Commager, Henry Steele. "Transition Years in Literature and Journalism." In his *The American Mind: An Interpretation of American Thought and Character since the 1880s*, pp. 55-81. New Haven: Yale University Press, 1950.
    Includes a discussion of New England local colorists, including Jewett and Mary E. Wilkins Freeman. According to Commager, the characters in Jewett's *Deephaven* "may have been frustrated

and inhibited, but they cherished their frustrations, as it were, and respected their inhibitions. The line of literary succession, it is well to remember, leads from Miss Jewett and Miss Wilkins to Robert Frost rather than to Eugene O'Neill, to 'Mending Wall,' rather than to *Desire under the Elms*."

Donovan, Josephine. "The Unpublished Love Poems of Sarah Orne Jewett." *Frontiers: A Journal of Women's Studies* IV, No. 3 (Fall 1979): 26-31.

Discusses love relationships between women in the nineteenth century, focusing on such relationships in Jewett's life as they may be understood through thirty love poems that Jewett apparently addressed to women.

————. *Sarah Orne Jewett.* New York: Frederick Ungar Publishing Co., 1980, 165 p.

Biographical and critical study.

————. "Silence or Capitulation: Prepatriarchal 'Mothers' Gardens' in Jewett and Freeman." *Studies in Short Fiction* 23, No. 1 (Winter 1986): 43-8.

Offers a contemporary feminist reading of "A White Heron" and Mary E. Wilkins Freeman's "Evalina's Garden."

Frost, John Eldridge. *Sarah Orne Jewett.* Kittery Point, Maine: The Gundalow Club, 1960, 174 p.

A comprehensive, largely biographical study.

Humma, John B. "The Art and Meaning of Sarah Orne Jewett's 'The Courting of Sister Wisby'." *Studies in Short Fiction* X, No. 1 (Winter 1973): 85-91.

Summarizes and critiques this story from the collection *The King of Folly Island and Other People.*

James, Henry. "Mr. and Mrs. James T. Fields." *Atlantic Monthly* 116, No. 1 (July 1915): 21-31.

Reminiscence of Boston's celebrated literary couple and of their friend Sarah Orne Jewett. James praises Jewett, calling her the "mistress of an art of fiction all her own, even though of a minor compass, and surpassed only by Hawthorne as producer of the most finished and penetrating of the numerous 'short stories' that have the domestic life of New England for their general and their doubtless somewhat lean subject."

Jobes, Katharine T. "From Stowe's Eagle Island to Jewett's 'A White Heron'." *Colby Library Quarterly* X, No. 8 (December 1974): 515-21.

Considers Jewett's reworking, first as a poem and later as a short story, of the Eagle Island episode from Harriet Beecher Stowe's *The Pearl of Orr's Island.* According to Jobes: "Retaining their common belief in the artist's sensitive spirit and their common use of New England materials, Jewett develops independently a quality of gentle questing in place of Stowe's dogmatizing. She seeks in nature what Stowe finds in God."

Levy, Babette May. "Mutations in New England Local Color." *The New England Quarterly* XIX, No. 3 (September 1946): 338-58.

Compares and contrasts the works of Jewett with those of Harriet Beecher Stowe, Rose Terry Cooke, and Mary E. Wilkins Freeman.

Magowan, Robin. "Fromentin and Jewett: Pastoral Narrative in the Nineteenth Century." *Comparative Literature* XVI, No. 4 (Fall 1964): 331-37.

Examines Eugène Fromentin's *Dominique* and Jewett's *The Country of the Pointed Firs.* According to Magowan: "Instead of becoming a vehicle for social criticism, nineteenth-century pastoral is able to present its vision of the good life as a limited personal ethic, a journey for each man within himself, a journey achieved through his ability to accept the grace of what has become a kind of involuntary memory."

Matthiessen, Francis Otto. *Sarah Orne Jewett.* Boston: Houghton Mifflin Co., 1929, 159 p.

The first critical biography of Jewett.

Mawer, Randall R. "Setting as Symbol in Jewett's *A Marsh Island*." *Colby Library Quarterly* XII, No. 2 (June 1976): 83-90.

Maintains that "together, the events and the place (geographical and social) where these events transpire illuminate the novel's theme, the hard-won triumphs of loyalty to house and home."

Pratt, Annis. "Women and Nature in Modern Fiction." *Contemporary Literature* 13, No. 4 (Autumn 1972): 476-90.

Compares and contrasts the epiphanic episodes and nature visions in Jewett's "A White Heron" and James Joyce's *A Portrait of the Artist as a Young Man.*

Quinn, Arthur Hobson. "Place and Race in American Fiction." In his *American Fiction: An Historical and Critical Survey,* pp. 323-73. New York: D. Appleton-Century Co., 1936.

Contains a brief survey of Jewett's works. Of Jewett, Quinn notes: "She was right, from the very beginning of her career, in refusing to imitate any changing fashion of literary method and in cultivating her own limpid and distinctive style."

Renza, Louis A. *"A White Heron" and the Question of Minor Literature.* Madison: University of Wisconsin Press, 1984, 221 p.

Explores Jewett's short story from various critical perspectives.

Roosevelt, Theodore. "How I Became a Progressive." *The Outlook* (12 October 1912): 294-96.

Notes Jewett and Mary E. Wilkins Freeman as particularly praiseworthy authors. Roosevelt says: "From Mary E. Wilkins to Sarah O. Jewett, in story after story which I would read for mere enjoyment, I would come upon things that not merely pleased me but gave me instruction—I have always thought that a good novel or a good story could teach quite as much as a more solemnly pretentious work."

Stevenson, Catharine Barnes. "The Double Consciousness of the Narrator in Sarah Orne Jewett's Fiction." *Colby Library Quarterly* XI, No. 1 (March 1975): 1-12.

Analyzes the perceptions of Jewett's narrators in *Deephaven,* "A White Heron," and *The Country of the Pointed Firs.*

Thompson, Charles Miner. "The Art of Miss Jewett." *Atlantic Monthly* XCIV, No. DLXIV (October 1904): 485-97.

A biographical and critical sketch of Jewett, focusing on her literary motives, characteristics, and achievements. Thompson concludes: "So far as she goes, she tells the absolute truth about New England. There are sides of New England life from which, as a gentlewoman, she shrinks, and which, as an advocate, she finds no pleasure in relating. As an interpreter of the best in New England country character she leaves in shadow and unemphasized certain aspects of the life which she does describe. Hers is an idyllic picture, such as a good woman is apt to find life reflecting to her."

Weber, Carl J. "Whittier and Sarah Orne Jewett." *New England Quarterly* XVIII (September 1945): 401-07.

Includes an account of the friendship between Jewett and John Greenleaf Whittier and briefly discusses "The Eagle Trees," a poem written by Jewett as a tribute to the New England poet.

Westbrook, Perry D. *Acres of Flint: Writers of Rural New England, 1870-1900.* Washington, D.C.: Scarecrow Press, 1951, 199 p.

Contains critical analyses of Jewett's works, comparing them with the works of Willa Cather, Alice Brown, and Helen Hunt Jackson.

Wilson, Edmund. "The Chastening of American Prose Style; John W. De Forest." In his *Patriotic Gore: Studies in the Literature of the American Civil War,* pp. 635-742. New York: Oxford University Press, 1962.

Sketches a brief outline of similarities and differences in the works of Jewett and Harriet Beecher Stowe. According to Wilson: "If we read Sarah Jewett's remarks on the carelessness and lack of selection that prevented Mrs. Stowe's Maine novel from being successful as a work of art and if we compare the two writers' renderings of similar seascapes in Maine, we can see how the slack of the earlier writer was taken up by the latter. Mrs. Stowe has no sense of proportion and . . . flings out handfuls of words like confetti; *The Country of the Pointed Firs* consists of small finely shaped units in which every word has been weighed.''

Wood, Ann Douglas. "The Literature of Impoverishment: The Women Local Colorists in America 1865-1914.'' *Women's Studies—An Interdisciplinary Journal* 1, No. 1 (1972): 3-45.

Discusses Jewett and her works in the context of other women regionalist writers. Wood contends that writers such as Mary E. Wilkins Freeman, Kate Chopin, and Jewett "could scorn the falsities of the sentimental tradition in part because they did not feel the drive, the push, the ambition which . . . [sentimentalist writers] had used such fripperies to hide. Essentially, the women local-colorists could chart the demise of the sentimental heroine and her habitat, the home, but the only new beginning they could find was in her ending, and that could not take them far.''

Attila József

1905-1937

Hungarian poet and essayist.

Deeply influenced by the works of Karl Marx and Sigmund Freud, József was the author of poetry that explored the ills of society and the human psyche. Often referred to as a poet of the proletariat, he is best known for the many poems in which he vividly depicted the misery of the working class; however, critics consider his greatest poems to be those in which he sought to understand and overcome his own mental illness. In the years since his death József has come to be recognized as one of the most important Hungarian poets of the twentieth century.

József's life was characterized by poverty and emotional torment. His father was a day-laborer who left the family when his son was three years old, whereupon the boy was sent to an orphanage. Four years later he and his two sisters moved to the slums of Budapest with their mother, a cleaning woman, who died shortly thereafter and to whom József later paid tribute in numerous poems. He supported himself by odd jobs all his life, working during his school years as a shepherd, movie usher, newsboy, and waiter, and later earning a living as a janitor, railroad porter, dock worker, and tutor. When he was seventeen his first poems were published in *Nyugat,* Hungary's leading literary magazine, and later that year he published his first volume of poetry, entitled *A szépség koldusa.* In 1924 József received a scholarship to the University of Szeged, where he enrolled as a student of Hungarian and French literature. He was soon forced to resign, however, upon the publication of his poem "Tiszta szívvel" ("Song of Innocence"), which caused a nationwide scandal for its anarchistic tone. During the next few years he briefly attended universities in Vienna, Budapest, and Paris. While in Paris he read and was strongly influenced by the works of Marx and G.W.F. Hegel, and after his return to Hungary in the late 1920s he joined the then-illegal Hungarian Communist party. However, the unorthodox nature of József's Marxism—which included aspects of Freudianism and rejected the concept of "proletarian art"—earned him the distrust of communist leaders, and in 1932 he was expelled from the party for "Trotskyist leanings." During the early 1930s József's mental health began to deteriorate, as his natural instability was exacerbated by his acute consciousness of social injustice, the memory of a harsh childhood, and emotional crises including failed love affairs and his rejection by the socialist movement. József's last years consisted of bouts of madness alternating with periods of lucidity, during which he composed many of his most important poems. In 1937, after a brief stay in a mental institution, he committed suicide.

In what Arthur Koestler referred to as a "miraculous union of intellect and melody," József's poetry combines Marxist and Freudian concepts in a form modeled on the Magyar folk song. Additional influences on his poetry include the work of Hungarian poet Endre Ady, the French Surrealist poets, and German novelist Thomas Mann, whose dedication to truth József praised in the poem "Thomas Mann üdvözlése" ("To Thomas Mann—A Salutation"). József's portrayal of the urban poor has been called the most intimate portrait of proletarian life in

Hungarian literature, and critics observe that his work far surpasses that of other proletarian authors in its poetic artistry. According to Koestler, "his songs of the slums show no trace of the dreary naturalism and 'socialist realism'" that was prevalent in the 1930s; "they are pure and fresh and lyrical, even at their most terrifying." The poetry of József's later years is dominated by images of death, God, and madness. Andras Sándor writes that József's "effort to maintain his conscious grip on the world and to master the unconscious by the conscious" resulted in "great poems of exceptional intensity," and many critics praise these works for their power and craftsmanship. Other prominent topics in József's poetry include his childhood, erotic love, and personal obsessions related to his mental derangement. Joseph Reményi encapsulates the range of his poetry when he writes that József was "the poet of the slums, city-peripheries, the hungry and static village, of the insipid, tame, but also intransigent destiny of the proletariat, of his own vulnerable and irreconcilable spirit, of animals, things and nature, of fulfilled and frustrated love, of uprooted urbanity and folkish childishness, of family recollections."

Despite József's identification with the proletariat and his utilization of the Hungarian poetic tradition, critics maintain that he achieved in his works a universality of theme that transcends barriers of nation and class. Although he is virtually unknown abroad, József's reputation within Hungary has grown steadily since his death, and his work has exerted a considerable influence on Hungarian poetry since World War II.

PRINCIPAL WORKS

A szépség koldusa (poetry) 1922
Nem én kiáltok (poetry) 1925
Nincsen apám, se anyám (poetry) 1929
Döntsd a tökét, ne siránkozz (poetry) 1931
Külvárosi éj (poetry) 1932
Medvetánc (poetry) 1934
Nagyon fáj (poetry) 1936
József Attila összes müvei. 4 vols. (poetry and essays) 1952-67
Poems (poetry) 1966
Selected Poems and Texts (poetry and prose) 1973

JOSEPH REMÉNYI (essay date 1948)

[*Reményi was a Hungarian-born American man of letters who was widely regarded as the literary spokesman for America's Hungarian community during the first half of the twentieth century. His novels, short stories, and poetry often depict Hungarian-American life, and his numerous translations and critical essays have been instrumental in introducing modern Hungarian literature to American readers. In the following excerpt, Reményi examines dominant characteristics of József's poetry.*]

Attila József made no concessions to the ruling classes of his native land. They repaid him with lack of interest or with hostility. He was spied upon by the police as a dangerous rebel. His poetry expressed the plight of the pariah-elements of his country; it showed the stumbling blocks of their existence and their harassed spirit, the glaring unfairness of their individual and social position. The squalor, grief and invectives that emerged from his work were resented by those who considered his strong condemnation of social disparities as detrimental to the general welfare and historical prestige of the nation. He has been compared with Frederico Garcia Lorca, the Spanish poet. The gypsy-like freedom and affection that were abundant in the works of the Spanish poet have their counterpart in the writings of the Hungarian creator. Nevertheless, the true folk-feeling accompanied by an ingenious musical sense and the attributes of the *cante jondo* (deep song), a Spanish gypsy manner of poetry consisting of repeated phrases, are missing in the works of the Hungarian poet. To be sure, Attila József was motivated by "folk-feeling," but it was not the essence of his poetry, despite his championing of the abused and the oppressed. His "musical sense" was not an equivalent of Hungarian gypsy music; it was individual, occasionally sophisticated in its turbulence and recklessness. Shocks of traumatic meaning, such as the memory of a depressing proletarian childhood and adult awareness of unpardonable social injustice mingled to shape a world of creativeness in which the poet refused to surrender to the detestable and villainous mixture of reality. He never ran out of emotional ammunition, but he did not always succeed in integrating the forces of his being into authentic poetry. Sometimes—contrary to his better aesthetic judgment—his writings were marked by ill-tempered versification, by an excessive desire to even scores with his adversaries, by an irascible or irate attitude that lacked the redeeming quality of verbal charm

or completely realized poetic strength, by the incapacity to extricate himself from confusion.

Since his death, Hungarian society has undergone a sweeping change. The destructive estimate of his poetry has been replaced by extravagant approvals, which have led to a new interpretation of his work and to favorable comparisons with other poets. Attila József's high-strung, excitable, Jacobinic disposition, affected by years of misery and by the mockery of unadaptability, by experiences in which bread and milk seemed a fairy tale, suggest parallels with the pitiful existence of other unfortunate poets. Other poets too, driven by pauperism, wrote about feelings, ideas and things which in relation to subject matter and in the light of plutocratic self-assurance made their works "unattractive." At present clever and aggressive reasons are advanced in favor of his political poetry; various arguments are developed against the stifling atmosphere of the previous Hungarian regime when the beggarly subsistence of the poet impelled him to shout words of damnation into a persecuting and tedious universe; and the "dirty" words of his poems ("dirty" in the sense that Francois Villon was apt to use words) appeared in the perspective of changed conditions not as objectionable terms, but as protections and protests against environmental malice and social discriminations.

But while critics who are in sympathy with him insist upon environmental causality regarding Attila József's individual and social lot, on closer inspection his personality reveals paranoiac compulsions in his early life which, no doubt, became more noticeable, as reactions to provocative social circumstances increased. Attila József was not afraid to be confronted with reality and all its bitterness and unmitigated unfairness, but one must accentuate the fact that in several of his poems—especially in those written shortly before his death—there are disturbing images indicative of mental disorders and verbal twists by which the poet wished to be delivered from the prison of human fate, from all its vileness, terror and horror, regardless of positive social implications. But in such poems too he could recapture—in a line, a word—the courage of his spirit, a kind of illuminating toughness, vigor and gentleness combined. Poetry could not elude him, not even in the shadow of suicide.

Attila József had words and images at his disposal which help one to evaluate the scope of his contribution to literature not only in a timely, but timeless sense. In the terminology of Herbert Read, the English critic, he could be called a poet of "organic form," that is, his art followed "its own inherent laws"; whatever "abstract form" he applied—and this rarely happened—it was representative of an age of sharp transition in which combinations of expressive patterns and arrangements seemed unavoidable rather than of innate need for employing abstract form. It is unlikely that future critics will discover in him hitherto unknown qualities; it is reasonable to assume that he will never appeal to conservative or reactionary readers. The pictorial and musical elements of his poetry and its social-revolutionary ideology are now accepted without critical objection. Parts of his work are rudimentary affairs of potential poetry, an egocentrically conceived and socially projected attempt to place his singular poetic personality in the line of Hungary's progressive movements. Many of his poems seem like the *salto mortale* of a creative individual, endowed with instinctive sagacity, but victimized by an erratic temperament. One is reluctant to emphasize his human and artistic deficiencies as one is constantly aware of a life which was a sacrifice to integrity, a torrent of sorrow, an existence intoxicated by its own sense of individual and social truth. Even his infrequent euphoric or humorous utterances seem but relieved sadness and not expressions of a natural state of well being. His boldness is not always artistically relevant, and his poetic idiom does not consistently produce the kind of effect which he, as a poet, expected.

Attila József possessed qualities which were his own. He could not alter them, but he was not the only major Hungarian poet between the two World Wars, as some of his admirers wish to convince the world. His "personal" freedom resembled that of the Roman slave who during the Saturnalia was waited upon by his masters. Attila József never received such consideration from the Hungarian ruling class, except in so far that at times he was not interrupted in his quest for values. The unyielding antagonism that he felt against the ruling class was consistent, but his sense of aesthetic values—instinctively and consciously—asserted itself even when he was fed up with social conditions. He was threatened by the engulfing force of negation, but he combatted this nihilistic temptation, with disdain and perseverance. In the chaotic mess that surrounded him he experienced a sensation of independence that came from the feeling of well-expressed, honest convictions. The extent of his vocabulary was not overwhelming, but imaginative. He remained metrically fresh and refreshing, despite a certain topical monotony. Generally, he understood the technique of his craft very well. He seldom knew the niceties of life, he never stood on the platform that wealth erects for its literary exponents, he adhered strictly to the depth of his rebellious personality. In his fitful poetry he manifested a giddy, somewhat ironically pathetic, energy. In some of his poems breathing seems difficult, the poem, like the body of a tubercular patient, seems to shiver, yet in its totality it has the warmth of fire and its heart-beat is not dull. Some of his poems seem like a strange cough of the soul, or like a piercing whistle, startling in its unexpectedness, violent in its true meaning. If honesty is the *faculté maitresse* of poetry, Attila József's poems certainly reveal him in the light of such concept; that is, they are intellectually and emotionally honest, perfectly sincere in their gleams of hope and in their darkness of agony, in the free and playful, pensive and restive engagement of the poetic spirit.

He was the poet of the slums, city-peripheries, the hungry and static village, of the insipid, tame, but also intransigent destiny of the proletariat, of his own vulnerable and irreconcilable spirit, of animals, things and nature, of fulfilled and frustrated love, of uprooted urbanity and folkish childishness, of family recollections. How well he sang about his poverty-stricken father who worked in a soap factory and migrated to America, of his mother, the washwoman, whom in his beautifully intimate poems he liked to call in a child-like tone "mama," of truthfulness and falsehood, of social identification and social isolation. When the charge was leveled against him that he succumbed to propaganda methods, he parried the accusation by saying that it was form primarily that excited him. This "proud beggar of beauty" could write hexameters like a classical poet, and sing like a nervous lark. His succinct, scornful and often harsh poetry—first recognized by Gyula Juhász, the lyrist and later by Ignotus, the critic—is now regarded as a creative experience of special psychological, sociological and aesthetic interest, yet little of his poetry is known abroad. (pp. 55-9)

Attila József was never impersonal. He did not write refined and spiritualized poetry; at times, however, he used stylized expressions. He battled the pride and conceit of his intellect with an instinctual fervor, as a child struggles against the stubbornness of adults. An almost mythical consistency characterized his yearning for truth. As a rule his lyrical visions and anxieties were coherently realized, although the unconscious flow of his deepest self was disinclined to recognize its limitations: In moments when life seemed utterly worthless he remembered his mother. "All week long I've been thinking of my mother. . . ." This is not saccharine poetry, not even in the degree of its sweetness; it expresses love and concern, tenderness and a son's simple and complex passion for his mother, who worked hard and whose poverty placed her in a frame of martyrdom. He "stole chickens for her," but could not share them because she died "too soon." He reproached her on account of her early death. He could be savage in his unhappiness. At first reading some of these "mother" poems seem trivial; but after the second or third reading they penetrate into one's heart, and reveal a mastery of feeling, imagination and form that makes of them an aesthetic and social experience. Gábor Halász, the Hungarian critic, aptly stated that Attila József expected the kind of gentleness he associated with the memory of his mother from every woman he cared for.

There is an uncanny mixture of vital and hectic utterances in his poetry. "On the lips of the poet words clatter freely. . . ." "You know there is no forgiveness—therefore it is useless to sorrow." "In the twilight soot floats on soft wings like tiny bats." "I've been gazing at the river Danube for one hundred thousand years, and I really see it now for the first time. In one second I see time everlasting." He speaks about dusk, this "sharp, pure greyness," or about the night, "the blue, iron night." He sings about "the wealthy who do not favor him," and implores the Lord "to intimidate him as he needs his anger." In a love poem he tells his sweetheart, who is knocking at his door, to use caution as he will place her on a strawtick "where the rustling straw sighs with dust." In one of his frankly erotic poems he turns to her and says: "I hold you in my mouth like a dog his whelp." In another poem "the landscape groans, then it recalls its stillness and finds joy in it." Ronsard-like, but more vehemently, he reproaches the woman he loved and who turned him down, and portrays the day when she will be old and "will be suffering pangs of guilt for having hurt him—regrets for what makes her now proud." He called himself "freedom's beautiful, serious son," who strove for "order and brave words" and "who dared everything." (pp. 60-1)

There was much willfulness in Attila József, undisciplined intensity, although, strangely, some critics accused him of "coldness." Sometimes Dostoevsky's "underground man" ensnared in the warped psychology of the twentieth century, spoke through his verses. Certain phrases of his poems remind one of the Gyula Juhász, Lajos Kassák, Gyula Illyés and other contemporary Hungarian poets. Essentially, however, his poetic realm was an indivisible world, his own. He was an island of instinctual purity and candor surrounded by waves of skepticism, cynicism, abysmal spiritlessness. His dauntlessness and tenderness should be regarded as a congenital preoccupation with life in which the instinctive and conscious forces of his personality demanded the consolation of creativeness. He had little power over his inherent traits; improved social conditions might have softened his anger, but would not have eliminated it, as his whole being—that of a schizoid individual—vibrated unconquerable discontent. Here and there in his poetry one discerns self-depreciation, some form of atonement for a life discredited in the eyes of the "successful," but his fundamental impulse was in the opposite direction. The iniquities of his surroundings contributed to his misery; his organic complexities added to his defiant manner. (p. 62)

Joseph Reményi, "Attila József, Contemporary Hungarian Poet," in Voices, No. 133, Spring, 1948, pp. 55-62.

ARTHUR KOESTLER (essay date 1954)

[Koestler was a Hungarian-born English novelist, essayist, and political philosopher. Initially a dedicated communist and supporter of the Soviet Union, he grew disillusioned with the repressive nature of Soviet communism under the leadership of Joseph Stalin and became a prominent critic of totalitarianism. Koestler was a personal friend of József. In the following excerpt from his reminiscences of the poet, Koestler praises József's later poems.]

The unique quality of the poems of [József's] later years lies in their miraculous union of intellect and melody. In this respect I can think of no contemporary poet to whom he could be compared. His most complex and cerebral Marxist and Freudian poems read like folksongs, and sometimes like nursery rhymes; "ideology" is here completely distilled to music which, whether adagio or furioso, is always eminently cantabile. His rhythm almost automatically translates itself into song; his rhymes are virgin matings of rolling four- and five-syllable words. . . . (p. 4)

Arthur Koestler, "Attila, the Poet," in Encounter, Vol. II, No. 5, May, 1954, pp. 3-6.

ZOLTAN L. FARKAS (essay date 1959)

[In the following excerpt, Farkas presents characteristics of József's earlier and later poetry.]

The poems of Attila József can be broken down into two broad categories. The first, from 1922 to 1932, are typically loose in form and, like "Innocent Song," generally pessimistic in nature. There are notable exceptions: "Brides' Song," written in 1926, is a pure lyric piece. Other poems written in this period were escapes from the confusion of József's world and dealt with beautifully simple pastoral themes. It was during these first ten years of József's creativity that all of his Socialist Realist poetry was written. Along with his affiliation with the Hungarian Communist Party at this time, these poems were his most direct attempt to emancipate what he considered to be a populace enslaved by the Fascist government of Admiral Horthy. József's connections with the Party and with strict Socialist Realism came to an abrupt end with his expulsion from the Party for Trotskyite leanings. His criticism of the government continued, however, until his death in 1937.

From 1932 on, József became more and more plagued by periods of complete mental derangement. The many refusals which he had sustained during his youth began taking serious effect both on his naturally delicate mental equilibrium and on his poetry. His later poems abound with dark premonitions of his fate: his greater concern with death, madness, and the futility of his existence. In these later works, József adopted a more typically Hungarian form, the Magyar folk-song, which he studied and whose metres and rhymes he learned to imitate to perfection. His poetic subject broadened to include a more subjective, introvertive form of expression, with much of his symbolic vocabulary drawn from nature and an ineffable sense

of the Hungarian past. These poems were the flowering of his entire career and remain as the most famous poems he had ever written. Due to his use of folk-styles, the poems appear to be light, with child-like simplicity, yet they contain the record of his mental deterioration. (pp. 587-88)

Zoltan L. Farkas, "Poems of Attila József," in The Literary Review, Vol. 2, No. 4, Summer, 1959, pp. 586-88.

MIKLÓS SZABOLCSI (essay date 1964)

[In the following excerpt, Szabolcsi discusses the principal themes and techniques of József's poetry.]

The themes of Attila József's mature lyric poetry are highly varied. The poems conceived at the time of the volume Chop at the Roots were written in a mood of impatient expectation of an eagerly desired coming revolution: in some of them, nature—both living and dead—is charged with suspense; in other poems the poet is preparing himself for the coming struggle, while in another group of poems he strikes a direct political note, addressing the masses. "Night in the Slums" was only the first of his great meditative poems in which he surveys the condition and ponders on the historic mission of the working class and considers the whole process of world-wide progress. In those years, also, were written the poems brooding on various evils afflicting Hungarian life and society, and the Hungarian countryside. Besides his passionate interest in wider issues, his personal sorrows and passion were given expression—ardent life, sudden sadness, and memories of childhood years are all voiced in his poems. He reached the depths of desperation in the years 1935-36, when his mental suffering, his neurotic depression (and often obsessions) were expressed in a number of poems. In the summer of 1936 there followed a new soaring rise: a succession of great poems depict Europe drifting into war, the darkening horizon, and his anxiety for the future of his native Hungary writhing in the stranglehold of German nazism; he proclaims far and wide his belief in the power of his poetry and his confidence in the strength of humanity and in a better future for mankind.

All that has been said, is, of course, no more than a cursory survey of the themes treated by the great lyricist. Now, in an equally cursory survey: what are the characteristics of József's lyrics? Their most salient characteristics are a profound knowledge of conditions and a fundamental realism. Absolute loyalty and devotion to realities; an awareness of the most distinguishing traits of landscape and humanity, of groups of people; the permanent urge to season his imagination with reality, even if that reality is frustrating and disillusioning. Attila József, for instance, discarded certain features fairly common in working-class lyrics, the superficial and stylised representation of working-class types. He speaks in the voice of a poet who, even in the lyrical representation of his own class, had the capacity of discerning the contradictions as well as distress and predicament, and the greatness of mind never to varnish human conditions. It is this quality that renders his historical optimism, his confidence in the historical mission of the working class, so convincing.

But he does not leave it at that. He takes the bits and fragments of reality and fits them into a single system of reasonable thought, builds them into a single intellectual conception. Reality and a speculative quality; minute details and broad conceptions; the unity of accurate observation and the ability to see reality in full; and a harmony underlying it all—those are the makings of his unique greatness. He is a typical and yet original intellectual poet; "Order," "Reason" and "Knowledge" are his favoured words and by these key-words he means that harmony of a higher order under which man, released from class oppression, economic and social (and having put things to rights about his instincts and spiritual life), will find his place. With him, this fundamental intellectual approach is built on Marxism—the Marxist concept of the world and of society pervades his poetry. With him this means that he looks at the world through the eyes of the working class; that individual and universal, personal and public find an integration in every line; that his joys and sorrows, that his loneliness and release all reflect those of a whole class and beyond that—of an entire people. That is why Attila József deserves to be called a socialist realist poet.

His devotion to pure reason is an instrument to restrain the poet's seething emotions. It also served, of course, as a shield against nazi barbarity.

He adopted as the motto of one of his volumes a stanza from a Hungarian folk-song:

> He who would do his piping well
> Must descend the very depths of hell
> Only there can he hope to tell
> What to do to blow the pipe well.

Attila József had gone through hell—the inferno of destitution, solitude, of isolation. He was compelled to compile in his mind a list of the missed joys of childhood. From this inferno, there arose an image of his poor beloved mother and—so often and with such compelling force—a tormenting, terrifying vision of his childhood. And, even as a grown man, he had to descend to hell—the inferno of his mind, down deeper and deeper abysses of his aggravating sickness, his worsening schizophrenia. Besides the inferno of his individual troubles and sufferings, he had to endure that of his nation and his class. After 1932, in an age of steadily darkening horizon and growing barbarism, to the accompaniment of creaking boots marching towards the abyss of war, he had to probe the hell of the downtrodden peasantry and humiliated working class, the struggling intelligentsia and impoverished lower middle class, of Hungary—of his entire, beloved nation. It is a most amazing experience to watch him go down and rise again, and awake to a realisation of his sickness (and thereby conquer it); to admire his ability to explain the debasement of people and to face and throw light on his most tormenting trouble. The yearning for the revolution, the evocation of a more humane, a more just social system, confidence and perspective are never absent from his lyric poems.

He is not always brooding and pensive: playfulness, mockery and irony, a fondness for the grotesque and play as a part of human life are always present in his poetry. A Mozartian fulness, a rope-walking above the dark abyss, endows many of his poems with a poignant, dramatic quality.

All these elements are brought out by means of an extremely keen artistic instinct for condensing and fashioning. His mature lyrics—whether it is his great speculative poems or his "Freudian folk-songs" that one considers—are examples of poetic experience pressed into severe form. For Attila József there was a strict connection between the structure of poetry and that of the world. And since he regarded the structure of the world as fundamentally rational he preferred his own verse rational. He wanted to see the solution of the problems of reality in poetry and looked upon poetry as "a superfluous thing that is

Holograph copy of József's poem "Song of Innocence." From Attila József, English *by Anton N. Nyerges. Edited by Joseph M. Ertavy-Barath. Hungarian Cultural Foundation, 1973. Courtesy of Artisjus.*

absolutely necessary." Accordingly, in his compositions every word is put into its place with the precision of a surveying engineer. In his last few years, József frequently had recourse to the most classic forms, such as the sonnet or the distich. The throbbing of rhythm was for him a basic experience; he had a highly susceptible musical ear—many of his poems carry suggestions of remembered tunes. His poems present an endless array of verse-forms, strophic structures and airs, as though he were aware of the intellectual power and disciplinary force, the anti-irrationality, of regular forms. A good deal of his imagery is drawn from the life of the toilers, the workers and the peasants. It is a measure of his great intellectual power that, twenty years after his death, a wealth of condensed lines, formulated in something approaching proverb-like finality, had found its way not only into the Hungarian poetical idiom, but also into colloquial speech. (pp. 289-92)

Miklós Szabolcsi, "Between Two World Wars (1919-1944)," in History of Hungarian Literature *by Tibor Klaniczay, József Szauder, and Miklós Szabolcsi, edited by Miklós Szabolcsi, translated by József Hatvany and István Farkas, Collet's, 1964, pp. 229-308.*

ANDRAS SÁNDOR (essay date 1967)

[*Sándor is a Hungarian-born American educator and critic who has done research in Hungarian and German literature. In the following excerpt, he examines the reflection in József's poetry of the poet's intellectual and emotional torment.*]

The word carrying the greatest momentum in József's basic vocabulary is "order." Order in itself is ambiguous or inane unless it is further qualified. For order, expressing only the formal aspect of a state or situation, can be either good or bad. The Hungarian word has a number of connotations that it rarely has in English. One of them is "régime" or "system" in the sense of political systems. It is a word expressing "the order of the day." József believed that the "order of the day" in Hungary and in the world at large was a wrong order, and to emphasize this he often used the word in both of its contradictory connotations. In the poem, **"Enlighten Your Child,"** his irony is quite clear.

> You should perhaps mutter a new fairy tale,
> One about Fascist Communism.
> For the world needs order,
> and order demands
> that children are not born at random
> and what is good should not be free.

His idea of order is best expressed in a fragment of two lines:

> Where freedom is order,
> I always feel the infinite.

This is vague enough to sound like *unio mystica*, but his idea becomes a little more tangible if we realize that the paradox expressed in this couplet is linked with the concept of "playing" as defined, for instance, by Schiller and many others after him. When József explains in another poem, "Come freedom, you bear me order," he qualifies the content of his wish by saying, "teach your beautiful serious son with good words, and let him play too." And we can learn still more about his good order from its contrast with the wrong one:

> I saw blue, red, yellow
> smeared images in my dreams
> and felt that this was order—
> not a drifting speckle of dust was amiss.
> Now my dream hovers in my limbs
> like dimness, and the order is the iron world.
> A moon rises in me at daytime
> and at night a sun shines here within.

The poem suggests—as does the coalescence of freedom, order and the infinite in the former couplet—that this order is dynamic, animated, living. József emphasizes these qualities by contrasting his order with an iron order, with a world made of iron. "Iron" too is one of the key words in József's poetry. It has an utterly negative role; he frequently associates it with rigidity and coldness, winter and ice. The analogies are obvious, as is the symbolism they constitute. But the power and suggestiveness of this symbolism can only be properly recognized when reading given poems, or when thinking of his nearly sacrificial death on cold iron rails and under iron wheels late in November.

The destruction of Attila József began in 1932 when he was expelled from the illegal Communist Party. He came from a working class family (with peasant relatives on his mother's side), and he never turned his back on it. His poems tell us all we need to know about his people. His parents did not teach him political radicalism. After long searching, wading through nihilism and various kinds of radicalism, he became a Marxist in about 1930. It is not impossible that he made contacts with Communists earlier in his Paris years. (He studied at the Sorbonne, financed by a progressive-minded aristocrat who recognized his genius, after he had studied Hungarian and French literature four years at Szeged.) He approached Marxism slowly, as did Gorky, whom he resembled in some other respects. In other words, his attachment was not a matter of infatuation; it was not easily won, and therefore, it was neither uncritical nor unconditional. What *was* unconditional was his feeling of identity with the working class and the peasants, and his commitment to the spiritual-ideological quest for the solving of a situation he could well consider desperate.

He joined the underground Communist Party and worked for it, conducting seminars, doing whatever had to be done. In this period, from 1930 to 1933, he wrote a great number of poems in support of the working class movement. They served a propaganda purpose, but they were not "revolutionary posters" like many of Mayakovsky's poems. They pose problems and explain *why* they must be solved, not how. He never writes about the Party. His subject is the workers; he speaks in their name, trying to express their problems. His protest, therefore, is never an individual protest.

> Seething and wild,
> we are poured into the casting die
> of this terrible society
> to stand for mankind on the eternal ground.

But József extends his protest to all the oppressed—peasants, small shopkeepers, office workers—to the bulk of the nation. Considering the international output of this kind of poetry, these are quite exceptional poems. They provide an analysis of social and economic circumstances in a thoroughly poetic way, combining community and personal protest. Bertold Brecht was a bourgeois by origin and refrained from writing personal poems in order to write community protest, but József could say "us, the children of matter," and could say that "peasants, while plowing; have me in mind, and workers are sensing me between two rigid movements."

And yet he was expelled from the Communist Party, apparently for his deviation from the Party line. (pp. 128-30)

This happened in 1932. During the next year, his destruction advanced one stage further. The incredible happened. The German Communist Party, the strongest political party in the country, the strongest Communist Party in Europe, collapsed, and the National Socialists came to power. If his expulsion from the Party had raised questions of intransigence and of party policy, this time the problems were deeper. József presents them in [his essay] **"Hegel, Marx, Freud"** with perceptible alarm. "Marx writes that mankind only sets himself tasks that can be achieved with the available prerequisites. How can it then happen that half of a country of sixty million people regards the purity of the race as its historical goal? . . . Where is the error in the calculation? How can it happen that the so called 'objective prerequisites' are available, but the subjective ones are missing?" He could not reconcile this with Marx. He found that there were powers at work in the people, independent of the forces of production and of the class struggle. He suggested that the instincts and the subconscious can be suppressed also in a community, in a people. He says Marx has to be corrected with Freud in order to save the people from their inhibitions and the revolt against them. At the same time, he was persuaded that the working class, his own class, was not conscious of itself by definition, but had to achieve this consciousness—a view that he might have read in Georg Lukacs' heretical book, *History and Class-Consciousness*. But if his people and their (Communist) leaders could not be unconditionally trusted, he had to sever his direct ties, to remove himself from them in order to serve their interest. Discipline had to take the place of direct emotional attachment. After the withdrawal of the party, the people "withdrew" as well, and he found himself more lonely than ever before. In 1933 he wrote **"Without Hope"**:

> In the end you come to level country:
>   wet sands and sadness.
> You look around musingly and nod
>   with knowing head, do not hope.
>
> I too try to look around like that,
>   without deception and with ease.
> Silver stroke of an axe
>   hovers on the poplar leaves.
>
> My heart perches on the twig of nothing,
>   its little body shivers without a noise.
> Stars gather around it tamely
>   and look at it, just look at it.

This poem cannot be understood without knowing that József established a symbolic analogy between iron and ice on the one hand, and discipline and thought on the other. He established it about this time and maintained it to the end of his life. "Be disciplined. Summer has flickered out," he begins the poem **"Winter Night"** in which he also says "The winter night glitters like thought itself." He suggests that in winter time, or in the winter of time (history), one must resemble winter in order to survive. Under oppression, be it social-economical or psychological-instinctive, only discipline can give freedom, both to resist the oppression and to get rid of it. And thinking, of course, is the discipline of the spirit. There is an immense regret in József's sigh:

> O why must I forge
> a weapon of you, golden self-consciousness?

The implication is that if freedom *were* order, it would not be necessary to convert gold into iron. Spirit would not have to present itself so as to defend itself in the form of an intellectual discipline. But the order József faced was not made of "golden" freedom; it was the "iron" world.

The poem **"Without Hope"** presents this net of symbolism in a unique way. The "knowing head" is that of the intellect and discipline. It perceives without deception and with ease. In harmony with it, the axe of iron swings with ease. Its silver stroke—ice too is silvery—still hovers on the poplar leaves while the poplar itself is felled. This tree, nature, actual reality, is felled by the well-disciplined intellect, and now the heart perches on the twig of nothing and shivers without noise. For this is a poet's heart, a singing bird, in the winter of Time.

At this point (in 1933), József was alone, but he still possessed a heart of one piece which could direct its flight, unconditionally pure and innocent. But soon enough he came to think and feel differently. He had psychic disturbances and turned to psychoanalysis. He turned to it with his trust in Freud, a faith in intellectual disciplines which could cure maladies of the mind. But in his case, Freud proved as unsatisfactory as Marx. He was psychoanalyzed several times, but with no positive result. (pp. 130-31)

József never rejected Freud, as he never rejected Marx. But he had to accept that psychoanalysis could not help him personally. With a greatness characteristic of him, he concluded that something was wrong with him. The seeming failure of the system whose validity he trusted could only lie in a defect of his own—in this case, in a sin which he must have committed, but which he could no longer identify. "Why have I no sin, if I have one," he asks in one of his poems dealing with this obsession. Apparently he felt that if he could identify it, he would be liberated from it according to the rules of psychoanalysis. He could not find it, however, and as time went on, his situation deteriorated, and his hope dwindled. . . . (p. 132)

The feeling that nobody could help him did not mean his situation was completely hopeless. It left open the possibility of his eventually finding that knot and releasing himself. It is frightening that the idea that he must have sinned because he could not be cured endowed him with a deeper insight. It was at this time that he began to write strange poems about God.

> I stood on all fours and my standing God
> looked down upon me and did not lift me up.
> This freedom made me understand
> there will be power in me to raise myself.
>
> He helped me by not being able to help.
> He could be the flame, but never its ashes.
> As many kinds of truth, as many kinds of love.
> He stayed with me by leaving me alone.
>
> My body is weak, fear should protect it.
> But my companion I await here smiling,
> for faithfulness is present with me
> in this world reeling in an empty void.

The relationship between this God and his sin, the cause of his suffering, is quite intrinsic. The sin that exists though it does not exist is paralleled with an absolution—solution, release, God—that exists though it does not exist. The link between the non-existence and the existence of God, the solution, is the effort that can raise a man.

> I don't believe in God, and if there is a God
> he shouldn't care for me.
> I'll manage my own absolution,
> and he who lives will assist me,

he said when he still felt more powerful and energetic, suggesting that he was speaking of his personal problem in terms of the human condition. The God who had left him alone and the God who should not care for him are similar notions. In both cases he believes that a solution exists and he must come to it by himself. What he calls "faithfulness" is his commitment to the effort of achieving it.

His task to raise himself was a mental task. It meant the shaping of his own mental activity, holding out for consciousness and control against unconscious and irrational forces. He was still carried by the hope that man can shape his own fate. If his commitment to this hope was not complete because of his fears, at least his commitment to the effort of controlling himself was complete. Out of this effort to maintain his conscious grip on the world and to master the unconscious by the conscious, to tame and absolve it, come great poems of exceptional intensity. In his last two years, he wrote more poems than in any other since 1928; he had not written more in his youth, when he frequently poured them out in haste. Now, however, the intellectual quality of his work and his craftmanship were at a level that his own poetry, and Hungarian poetry generally, has rarely reached. The power, penetration and shrewd simplicity of his last poems are unique. The only poet with a comparable output who comes to my mind is Yeats. It is hard to believe that these poems were written by the same sick man described in his sister's book and in the accounts of his friends.

During his last years, he developed schizophrenia and lived in a disturbed state. (pp. 132-33)

But the astonishing thing about his mental disorder was that it did not affect his work. We do not have a single line by him that shows the loss of his consciousness as an artist, and while time and again certain obsessions appear in his poems, he controls them by treating them symbolically. Some of his best work was written in his last year, and even in the last days of his life. Desperately clinging to his ideal of order, he has never preserved it more faithfully than at the time of impending catastrophe.

József's final collapse, however, was due to yet another blow. He said in his **"Ars Poetica"** that man had two parents, two guardians: Spirit and Love. Now after spirit had betrayed him, love betrays him too. The blow that destroyed his innermost being took the form of two hopeless love affairs, one in 1936, the other in 1937.

In his love for a woman, he encountered nature, the world. Nature means attachment, living contact. The world gives meaning, and a being is human and loving in his capacity to attain that attachment and that meaning. Love and humanity are synonymous for József, as are spirit and humanity. His beloved gave him "the door-knob of the locked world," and he could step out into the open, into nature and the world. This, then, is the "warm world" in contrast to the cold one wrought in iron and discipline. In the human gift of love, the poet's eyes perceived the microcosm hidden in the beloved, and by perceiving this microcosm, he could see himself in a world of living order, of warmth.

This miracle involved two loves. Hers was giving, and that was important; but his was receiving, and that was equally important, for it makes the act of giving possible. Applying here József's metaphor, the wooden door that locked him in suddenly changed by the touch of his vision into a glass door, and he could perceive the world of living order, though he still could not be within it; he was still locked out. Her uniqueness was not enough; it only proved that there *was* a warm world.

To understand what such love meant for József, it is necessary to recall his desperate love for his mother, who died when he was still a boy. She represented nature:

> Only now do I see how immense she is:
> her grey hair flutters in the wind,
> she dilutes blue in the waters of the sky.

She was the warm world that abandoned him when she died. And she was a woman:

> You lay down at the side of death,
> like a slender easy girl when given a sign.

> You are a bigger cheat than any woman
> that deceives a man and feeds him with hopes.

Psychoanalysis further deepened this attachment of József to his mother, indeed it may have evoked its real force. But if it evoked it or deepened it, it was only because his original vision, the special quality of his imagination was working in that di-

rection. His ideal of order, his attitude toward the woman he loved, his love for his mother can only be understood as three aspects of the same basic attitude. Sometimes they appear intricately interwoven, as in this desperate love poem:

> My mother locked me out—I lay on the threshold—
> and wanted to crawl into myself, but in vain—
> stones below me and emptiness above.
> I want to sleep. I knock at your door.

The horror of being alone, abandoned, and locked out is powerfully suggested by his wish to crawl even into himself, so as to be in a safe place, in a warm world. In this stanza, the world cannot open up for him and accept him unless there is a woman who, in the role of his mother, accepts the man in the role of a boy.

The significance of love, not intrinsically, but rather its momentum, increased for József as his immediate hope in the social as well as the psychic spheres degenerated. It was his final tragedy that the two women whom he loved in his last two years did not love him. As far as he was concerned, they failed in their humanity when they were unable to come to his rescue; and through them, humanity was proved defective. He did not lose faith in love, just as he did not lose faith in Marx and in Freud, but he felt ultimately abandoned, and died, because there was really nothing left for him. (pp. 133-35)

József was aware of the symbolic implications of his life, and he expressed them in his poetry. But it is better to say that he grew aware of them in and through his poetry. In his case, life and poetry were dialectical—he lived his poems' insights. To be a socialist for him was to be a man freed from the tyranny of his unconscious. In his **"Causal Poem About the Standing of Socialism"** he says,

> Passion is wasted into passing fits
> Unless reason in advance pervades it.

The Hungarian word for "pervading" also suggests absolution. What he called Order was a state in which reason pervaded and absolved passion, and his poetry reflects such a synthesis. He died when he saw he could no longer maintain it. (pp. 135-36)

Andras Sándor, "Attila József," in TriQuarterly *No. 9, Spring, 1967, pp. 127-36.*

ANTON N. NYERGES (essay date 1973)

[*In the following excerpt, Nyerges surveys József's career.*]

The term "proletarian" as applied to a poet must seem strange to Americans. Only Hart Crane with his roots in the depression and his love for machines, manual workers, and melody may suggest a recognizable case. Recent American Negro writers have sought to create an immediacy between poet and common man. It would be premature to judge with what success. They may be the only potential source of such greatness, however, since other workers in general show little interest in literature as a political instrument.

Attila József is one of the very few genuine proletarian poets whom Western civilization has produced. Some others—Aragon, Eluard, Hikmet, Neruda, and Ady—were sympathetic to the workers' cause but not of it in the same intimate sense.

Poetically, József's greatness rests on having brought into verse a specificity and concreteness about social and economic life that was not there before. As he moved from contemplation of the physical environment to ideas and philosophy, this quality, while assuming many forms, remained with him as an indelible hallmark. Imagery is not the lifeblood of his poetry; reality is. He employs striking images to which we react perhaps as human beings have since the dawn of civilization, but generally his poetry is so close to reality that we may often wonder why we like it. He is not, however, an "engineer of the soul" as Stalin called writers. This remarkable man is rather the Spinoza or Russell of the lyrical world. Drawn by certain of his poems, some have called him the creator of the Freudian folksong and the Hegelian/Marxist lyric. But in fact, he designed a world view and a tragic outlook credible to Modern Man which make him a poet who cannot be fit into formal systems. He points the way out of the introversion and particularism of modern poetry which have raised doubts in the minds of intellectuals and public alike whether it has a place in our life.

Some of Attila József's most profound poems were written after a clinical diagnosis of schizophrenia. Although this does not make him a unique writer, his social background raises questions about the relationship of mental disorders and creativity to environment and culture. He is a poet of new psychological as well as aesthetic and social significance. (p. 9)

The earliest József is a blend of poets whom he studied and liked, primarily Ady, but also Juhász—the eremite of Makó—and Walt Whitman. This is reflected in **"Power Song."** . . . In the course of his development, however, József never abandoned his role as host to many sources. The overpowering influence of Ady diminished, but others took over at least in part, particularly impressionists, expressionists, and writers of free verse.

By 1923-1924, concreteness was becoming dominant in his poetry. Two of the best examples are **"The Weary Man"** and **"A Soft Summer Night."** The former still has imagery in the more traditional sense, but there are the lines

> the river and I: we lie
> side by side
> new grass dormant beneath my auricles,

and the impression as a whole is that the student at Makó wrote a poem that *is* the river, not about it.

"A Soft Summer Night" is all real—to anyone with ESP. The poet sits by his door and hears

> the soft turn of a
> pickpocket's wrist
> and the munching of a solitary peasant
> who ripped a fat one from his neighbor's.

All that is left of traditional poetry is the ironic title, used also as the opening and closing lines.

The real world which József discovered so early he saw essentially with the eyes of optimism. Certainly, there is no pessimism like in much poetry of our times. He dwells, although by no means exclusively, on the essential goodness of man and sees him "at the beginning of creation." Man need not go back to nature; he is still there developing into a superior biological and psychological being. Attila József, as he described himself, was at this stage a "poetic fool" with the

"simpleness that simmers in grass." The playfulness so characteristic of his early years is evident. His lovers are still happy:

> we sleep with a girl we do not know
> Who stirs with a caress when the cover slowly slips.

But when they laugh, the sound carries

> to the neighbors
> the quiet laborers,
> and they smile in their weary and shattered dreams.

The "insipid poet" is aware something is wrong with mankind. His problem is formulating it in terms of poetic reality. He tries in **"Fire!"** but the results are abstract and uncertain. He is more successful in **"Who Shrieks? Not I"** and there is the genuine Attila József touch in the lines:

> Why wash your face?
> It only washes in the face of others.

József's poetry is more or less representative of his early period through 1929 with the completion of his student days in Vienna and Paris. He brings to full development, however, his statements on the distortions that exist in modern life. He is the master of the grotesque as Ady is of the macabre. The earliest and most famous example is **"Song of Innocence."** There are many others, notably **"Without Knocking"** and **"Sit and Stand and Kill and Die"** with its opening lines

> Push the standing chair away
> squat before a coming train.

Most literary production is interchangeable and producible by this man or that. As a contemporary American writer once said, most poets today are busy writing one another's poems. It must have been evident to József very early that the order into which he was born was not meant to encourage him, the people he came from, or their outlook. He lived in a society in which established success was equated with superiority. An expanding awareness of this state of affairs became the source of the Attila József grotesque. Relatedly, he was also writing poems of expressionism and surrealism. However, he was obviously not only a French-type avant gardist but was digging deep into the bedrock of modern problems. When he turned his back on the grotesque with **"Medallions,"** he was unnecessarily, although imaginatively, harsh about his previous poetic experience.

By 1926, Attila wrote **"Socialists"** and the famous **"Proem"** describing himself as the "city kin of Batu Khan" and concluding with the lines

> Ay middle class, ay workingman,
> I Attila am here.

He was clearly groping after a more program-like view of society. Because of its dramatic quality and striking use of proper names, **"Proem"** has been particularly overquoted creating an impression of truculence. But if there is a single trait, next to the grotesque, which characterizes his poetry at this period, it is the quality of forgiveness. Any study of Attila József which fails to stress this as a dominant note from the beginning (and as we saw, to the end) of his career is widely amiss of the mark. It shows in poems on personal relationships—**"Why Ill Words? Sleep Silently,"** and **"It Was Summer"** and on God, which are about a forgiving (and forgiven) being—**"Not to Strike Back," "Only the Sea Has Come . . . ,"** and **"God"** (1926). Moreover, he looks at the world with an air of gentleness rare in modern poetry, as in **"Young Worker,"** **"Worker,"** **"The Scatter Skies Unsown,"** and **"Ant."**

Significantly, tools are prominent in his poetry, at first the hoe; then abstract ones (''steel-browed tools''); and finally specifics of industry like the jackhammer, scissors, and the ax (later the dynamo). And all about, we see common household objects— bench, stove, table, dough, paddles, bucket, and laundry soap (''she washes laundry, soap bubbles dreaming along her arms''). The God he was creating was as calm as a shoemaker at his last.

He suffers from an obsession with his mother which in American context would bring on him charges of ''momism.'' He recalls that she saw him in the nude, or visualized him in a pair of long pants. She patched his clothes, and he sees the scissors and cloth she used as the tool and materials for tailoring a new world. However, the dominant note is a firm and precise hold on reality as he so clearly demonstrates in his handling of the two ''Bethlehem'' poems.

From the earliest stage of his creative life, Attila József was searching to build a philosophical infrastructure for his poetry. Nothing was easy for he was seeking new insights and social frontiers. This was true when his experiences were still limited to Szeged/Makó, a few villages, and the outskirts of Budapest, and it became increasingly true as his experiences encompassed the intellectual atmospheres of Vienna and Paris and he became more and more aware of the disharmony between the theoretical bases of civilization and its practices. From this time on, his poetry became a heroic attempt at harmonization as his melodies deepened and his subject matter grew intensely complex. (pp. 23-5)

Between 1930 and 1935 Attila József produced a body of proletarian poetry which is outstanding by any standard, and likely the greatest the world has known. He broke the hold of ''priests, warriors, and the middle class'' on an art form which perhaps more than any other has shaped the best minds from Gilgamesh to the present day. In a world bent on industrialization, his achievement is a key intellectual and cultural development of our time. He did it during one of the most reactionary periods, politically and socially, in the history of a contemporary people and in the face of a powerful proletarian party operated illegally from outside the country. Perhaps no other modern poet can wear the terms ''heroic'' and ''anti-heroic'' as gracefully as this man who was the equivalent of a janitor for the ruling class and less for the illegal Communist Party. As far as the world in which he lived was concerned, he could have perished unfulfilled from the face of the earth without the help, over extended periods, of his sisters (Jolán and Eta), his mistress (Judit Szántó), a few friends (Gyula Juhász and the Szeged coterie, Andor Németh, the Hatvanys, Ignotus), and nameless ordinary people (a tailor's apprentice, a printer's devil, peasants). With or without name, they were Hungary's best in a black hour.

During the three years he spent unidyllically in the Communist Party, he wrote one or two out-and-out Party poems—**"Dialog"** and **"The Busted"** (the latter for ''Red Aid,'' an organization to help jailed communists). But his most important ''communist'' poem was **"Stricken,"** written after he was attacked by certain Party members shortly after his admission. As an expression of organizational experience, it is a unique poem. Although sometimes mistakenly explained as a description of his sorrow over expulsion, it is in fact a very early way station

on a course that was trouble-filled and of dubious value for both sides.

Attila József's great works from this period are **"Winter Night,"** **"Factory District: Night,"** **"What Is He Storing Up,"** **"The Masses,"** **"Elegy,"** and **"The City Limits."** They extend poetry to the industrial class for the first time in the sense that these poems are not merely about proletarian life, they *are* their life. With industrialization and increasing accumulation of wealth, affliction receded, in the eyes of fortunate people, as the instrument whereby man is made fit for God. Almost alone among modern poets, József brings us back to that world view which is older, and perhaps more durable, than civilization itself.

The general characteristic of these poems is a concreteness brought to full and remarkable development. **"Winter Night,"** for example, begins with the imperative ''Be disciplined!'' and concludes:

> A rustbrown tree
> leans from the fog,
> and I measure night
> like an owner
> his property.

The great achievement, however, is **"The City Limits"** with its opening lines:

> On the city limits where I live
> in twilight of fallout and glow
> the soot settles
> softwinglike, batlike
> and ossifies like guano
> hard and slow,

and the closing lines of the poet who

> . . .
> sees into a conscious future
> and creates a subjective harmony of cheer
> as you in the objective sphere.

The problem which he was unable to formulate in his early stage, he now saw as the harmonization of the productive forces within and forces of production without. It was this and similar attempts at a Hegelian synthesis that brought on him Party suspicion of heresy for seeking to reconcile Marxism and Freudianism, but it is difficult to read **"The City Limits"** and rest satisfied with a simplistic interpretation. An illumined man is writing who is profoundly concerned with veiled secrets of social and individual development. He is making relevant use of the trends and science of his time. The sufferings of the class in which he is primarily interested are an essential part of his world view. But József would have had no difficulty in accepting Donne's statement that ''he that hath least hath enough to waigh him down from heaven'' if he lacked subjective harmony.

The role of the intellect is eminent in József. He is one of the few poets who successfully link science and beauty. This is the secret of how he took Freud's ideas (not Freudian symbols) and made poetry of them. Regarding particularly **"The Sin,"** one of the most famous of the Freudian lyrics, Arthur Koestler writes: ''The unique quality of the poems of his later years lies in their miraculous union of intellect and melody. In this respect, I can think of no contemporary poet to whom he could be compared. His most complex and cerebral poems read like folksongs, and sometimes like nursery rhymes; 'ideology' is

DÖNTSD A TŐKÉT, NE SIRÁNKOZZ

JOZSEF ATTILA UJ VERSEI

új európa könyvtár

k i a d á s a

Title page of József's poetry collection Döntsd a tökét, ne siránkozz. *From* Attila József, *English by Anton N. Nyerges. Edited by Joseph M. Ertavy-Barath. Hungarian Cultural Foundation, 1973. Courtesy of Artisjus.*

here completely distilled to music which whether *adagio or furioso* is always eminently *cantabile* [see excerpt dated 1954].

But there is another, less well known, side to József's interest in form and melody. During the period of his most intensive concentration on proletarian life he became at least partially aware that the new subjects might well call for new poetic forms. Some of his best poems like **"Winter Night,"** **"Elegy,"** **"The Masses,"** **"An Occasional Poem,"** and **"Ode"** are ample evidence of this and represent the finest flowering of modern poetry in the language. At the same time, he did not break away from his dependence on the classics. For example, he wrote **"Dialog,"** a poem about a shoemaker's strike, in hexameters (!) despite an intuitive awareness of the incongruity.... His schizophrenia literally extended to problems of form.

The outstanding cerebral poem of this period is **"Consciousness,"** a remarkable synthesis of Villon, Freud, existentialism, and Hegel-Marx. In a book length treatment of this relatively short poem of 96 lines, Miklós Szabolcsi points out these various elements, concluding that basically the work is still Marxist in style, formulation and thought. But whatever the elements of the synthesis and their priority importance, the fundamental

image is that of a little boy in a freight yard stealing wood and fearing the police. The final and summary lines of this poem

> I stand in the flash of compartments,
> and leaning on my elbows I listen

shows the poet as a cerebral and reflective problem solver like in the much earlier **"A Soft Summer Night."** While undeniably beautiful and in keeping with the internal logic of the poem, the passage appears wanting in power. A much more forceful and relevant close appears to have been written in **"Stolen Lumber."** It was, after all, under the stress of almost superhuman suffering and not in intellectual exercise that the poet achieved his fullest measure of greatness and clearest insight into the mystery of social ways. (pp. 30-3)

Attila József gave birth during his late period to marvellous and strange poetic creations. He describes with new explicitness the anxieties of schizophrenia—the fear of loss of one's identity, the disintegration of the ego, and the disappearance of the distinction between self and outer world.

A major "schizoid" poem **"You Made Me Child"** is striking for the desire to "incorporate" the lost object:

> I hold you in my mouth like a dog his pup,
> and I would run to keep from choking on you.

It recalls the "I should have eaten you" in an earlier "mother" poem. Other poets (Donne, as Joan Riviere points out [in her study *The Unconscious Phantasy of an Inner World Reflected in Examples from Literature*]) have dealt with the phenomenon of "incorporation" but not often with József's explicitness.

An assertion of "badness" and "aggressiveness" is another important characteristic of his "schizoid" poetry. A close definition of its source is hardly possible because for the poet himself the mystery was: What is the "unforgivable sin" that has brought me to where I am? The phenomenon is intriguingly discussed in Joan Riviere's study: "The bad objects within take their origin from our own dangerous and evil tendencies, disowned by us; characteristically therefore they are felt as 'foreign objects,' as an incubus, a nightmare, an appalling, gratuitous and inescapable persecution. The classical and emotionally most significant example of these unconscious phantasies of inner activities with and by inner objects (i.e., 'cannibalized' objects) is that of the primal scene, the parents in intercourse, typically of a monstrous and unutterably terrifying character, inside one. By the child originally they are felt as enacting what one set of urges in him is aiming at with each of them, but these aims are denied as his own and transferred to them."

In Attila's fatherless circumstances, there were no re-enactments of the primal scene. Badness and sin are also a curse of inaction, the inability to perform. Gyertyán (*The Poet and His Age*) also moves in this interpretative direction although via a different path, or at least different language: "(Sin) is the characteristic of the man who cannot accept the fact that he is damned to impotence, the humanist who knows rationally that he rebels in vain and that his destiny and ultimate end are inaction, but he is still to his very roots a revolutionary."

The introjection of badness, whatever the source, brings on a fear of retaliation (punishment) and accompanying aggressiveness. **"They Say"** is the most suggestive of József's poems on aggressive phantasies, which, he says, were born with him (that is, when he was "thrown out" by his mother) and which he has been acting out ever since.

Perhaps the broadest statement of the psychological drama is in **"A Greendown of the Sun."** Melanie Klein sheds considerable light here: "My analytic experience has shown me that processes of introjection and projection in later life repeat in some measure the pattern of the earliest introjections and projections; the external world is again and again taken in and put out—re-introjected and re-projected."

József's unsuccessful attempts to find himself a place in the middle class or in the Communist Party and to establish an enduring relationship with a woman are all a part of this drama, for a drama now it is, and the lifeline always appears to lead back to his mother and the afflicted.

We are nearing a clue to the poetry more relevant to its deepest meaning than others we have followed so far. József is not the author of lyric, epic or dramatic poetry. His life *is* the drama. In the Hegelian sense we are witnesses of a vast and universal Collision, a passing phase of which is the political and social upheavals of our time which we sometimes simplistically interpret in terms of the protagonists—capitalism and communism. There is also something here of Hebbel's theory of tragedy as a conflict between the individual and Idea as a social institution. But Attila József's poetry cannot be reduced to a dialectical process. His view of life is a tragic one—new for Modern Man but springing from the most ancient layers of man's consciousness. This is the Tragedy of the Theft, the boy who carries a burden of stolen lumber throughout his life and finds that he has stolen with it the guards:

> Was it these hard men,
> these throwers of lumber I idolized and feared?
> I carry them now like stolen wood
> in this homeless world full of cops.

This is the tragedy that builds, as Bertrand Russell said, "the shining citadel in the very center of the enemy's country" by winning over the guards of human misery and degradation. This is why Attila József loved to teach the poor; why he opposed revolutionary violence; why he lived with a "Freudian" sin; why he identified his mother with a whole afflicted class; why he threw himself under a train; and why the quality of forgiveness was so important to him. This was the tragedy that the militant left could not see and identified with impotence because it is a world view that refuses to repeat the old answers to the question who is to control, and how, the materials built with the fire Prometheus stole. This was the unique poet who had the courage to say "I come as a thief" and mean it in the sense of the writer called the Divine.

Schizophrenia and myth do not make up all of József's poetry of the years 1936-1937. He had extended periods of lucidity and wrote, for example, **"Ars Poetica"** . . . , a poem of almost pure cerebration consisting of eleven quatrains, each apparently a poetic interpretation of the eleven-point "Marx's Theses on Feuerbach." In a sense, the "schizoid" poems are also witness to this lucidity because no matter how close to the reality of his disorder, they are still works of art. But he was lucid in a more conventional sense. His sister Jolán describes how he took command of the household at Balatonszárszó during a destructive rainstorm and gave out practical and effective instructions to save the structure in which they lived. These were the years of some of his genuinely human political poems—**"On the Gravestone of a Spanish Peasant," "Air!," "By the**

Danube," "Welcome Thomas Mann," "Gorgeous Dream," "An Atavist Rat," and a masterpiece of clarity with the opening line

> I need the precision and purity of this dusk.

Much of this poetry is based on logic which the poet loved as much for what it conceals as what it reveals. The wood pile harmonizes logic with the Tragedy of the Theft and recurs again and again as an image for the fantastic structure of the present. It can be dismantled by removing, however stealthily, a single stick. It represents order assembled by certain men in their own interests not a moral and ethical harmony. This man-made pattern is to the harmony of reality like a wood pile to the bare boughs of a tree sustaining the atmosphere.

Attila József is that rare combination of Thinker and Emotional Man, who have become separate entities. The world outlook that he tried to build was the ordonnance of a poet, not a philosopher or even a philosophical poet. Thus far only Marxists have recognized this, but naturally they attempt to shape József to their mould, as the chiliasts of a communist state subordinating the boy with a stolen plank to the adult who could make Marx sing. The Tragedy of the Theft extends from the Cave of Prometheus to a railroad yard in an industrial suburb of Budapest and includes dialectical materialism as a way station, but not as the course itself. The relationship of his poetry to existentialism, Christianity, surrealism, and rationalism, to mention the most important, may also be way stations but require objective exploration. It remains one of the tasks of literary criticism as a whole to discover Attila József's true human course. The relationship of József and his works to Sylvester, one of the two greatest figures of Petőfi's imagination, has been perhaps the most overlooked area. This may be because of a misunderstanding about József's station among European poets and an unbalanced evaluation of the complex influences in his work. (pp. 36-9)

Anton N. Nyerges, in an introduction to Attila József; *poems by Attila József, translated by Anton N. Nyerges, edited by Joseph M. Értavy-Baráth, Hungarian Cultural Foundation, 1973, pp. 9-39.*

LÓRÁNT CZIGÁNY   (essay date 1984)

[*In the following excerpt, Czigány discusses technical and thematic aspects of József's poetry.*]

Attila József, the foremost Hungarian socialist poet, like Petőfi and Ady is usually ranked by critics and scholars alike as one of the greatest poets Hungary ever produced; and one is struck immediately by the maturity and completeness of József's poetry. Although he died at the age of thirty-two, one can speak of his late poetry; the last poem he wrote is a final poetic statement. (p. 350)

His early poetry already showed signs of far more seriousness of mind than could be expected from the conventional defiance of an "angry young man." He incessantly searched for "order" in a seemingly chaotic universe, with a determination to accept the truth, whatever result his relentless probing of the world might bring. For him order was beauty and truth helped him to discover order. Moreover, he had a morbid obsession with minute details, for he believed the same universal truth to be manifest in the laws pertaining to the tiniest detail to the same extent as in the laws governing the order of the macro-cosmos. "Be the tiny blade on a leaf of grass / and you will be bigger than the axis of the world"—he claims in **"It's Not I Who Shouts,"** the title-poem of his second volume. . . . Jó-zsef trained himself to receive simultaneously the sights and sounds of a swirling world, a world for which he is ready to provide order by setting it in a frame (**"A Fine Summer Evening"** . . .); yet the bewildering choice of action weighs on his mind at all times in his early poems (**"To Sit, To Stand, To Kill, To Die"** . . .).

While József was undoubtedly a committed poet, he never became a "national poet" in the sense that Petőfi or Ady was, for his commitment tied him first of all to the "have-nots" (cf. his numerous early "poor man" poems), and secondly to the working-class movement, irrespective of national considerations [cf. his volumes *I Have Neither Father, Nor Mother, Fell the Tree-Trunks,* and *Night in the Slums*] . . . ; but he always had an awareness of universal significance, and linked whatever he wrote to his personal experiences—or rather he saw his personal experiences always in a universal context. It was due perhaps to his gift of identification with the social aims of the lower classes that his own despair never became exaggerated, but ran parallel to his collective social protest. True, he was maladjusted all the time, and he followed an inner urge to project his maladjustment on to the outside world, but his personal failure did not discredit for him the idea of structured order in the universe, and he did not try to alleviate his own plight by believing that there was no hope for mankind.

Quite early in his poetic development József became fascinated by the technique of free association, which remained a distinct feature of his poetry until the end and which assisted him in expressing hitherto unexplored states of mind. The best examples are his **"Medallions,"** . . . twelve eight-line couplets (except for the last piece), a grotesque poetic assessment of totality, resembling the whirling visions induced by the use of psychoactive drugs, yet with a curious sense of order and inevitability in the sequence of the bizarre associations, in spite of the seemingly abrupt ending.

The longer pieces, however, written in the early 1930s, are a series of large-scale *tableaux,* describing a desolate world of factories, dark warehouses, slums, empty lots, and heavy freight-trains, always permeated by a dull sadness. **"Night in the Slums,"** . . . an ode with impressionistic images, is the first of the sombre and depressing "maps of poverty," in which the only redeeming quality, József's revolutionary optimism, is kept effectively in the background till the end. **"On the Outskirts of the City,"** . . . another great fresco, is more personal and, at the same time, more imbued with political jargon; in it, however, József actually managed to paraphrase ideological concepts of Marxism poetically. **"Elegy"** . . . witnesses the poet's identification with slumland; and **"Winter Night"** . . . offers a more universal view of the human environment—the mood is defined by words suggesting cold, clear, firm images (e.g. "blue, iron night," "the molecules shiver," "silence cools off"). His preoccupation with hard objects (diamond, steel, crystal, or glass) is a striking feature, and recurs in many of his poems: József's world is often relentlessly rigid and yet fragile.

József best explained his ideas concerning the complex totality of his age in **"Consciousness,"** . . . a poem of twelve stanzas (with the simple rhyme scheme ABABBABA) written in the ballad form employed by Villon in his "Grand Testament." In this work he created a unity of three spheres: of direct experience, of autobiographic inspiration, and of abstract notions of the world. While claiming that the ultimate cause of suffering is of an objective nature, he is able to confront the hostile external reality by grasping it in its movement and as a whole, thereby preserving internal freedom:

> See, here inside is the suffering,
> out there, sure enough, is the explanation.
> Your wound is the world—it burns and rages
> and you feel your soul, the fever.
> You are a slave so long as your heart rebels—
> you can become free if you don't indulge in
> building yourself the kind of house
> which a landlord settles in.

In other words, the ultimate source of enslavement is a subjective *vis inertiae*—a lack of consciousness. Stanza XI shows an ascetic attitude in rejecting personal happiness, which may seem somewhat strange from a poet whose personality and poetic attitude were basically tender and playful. Yet "mere happiness" is rejected here as inhuman, since it is below the level of consciousness.

In his later **"Ars Poetica,"** . . . József has become aware, at the price of much suffering, that human existence is guarded by the watchful eye of its parents, spirit and love; but while his intellect would explain and understand personal and social conditions and problems, the feeling that nobody could help him, because he was unloved, overwhelmed him; the heart again produced its reasons with which the mind could not cope: "The bargain's off—let me be happy / Or else anybody will insult me; / growing spots of red will mark me out, / fever will suck my fluids dry."

His increased sense of being unloved created a nostalgia for the primeval motherly love, as witnessed by the numerous poems written about and to his mother. Her portrait in **"My Mother"** . . . is idyllic and serene, and she represents "Mother Nature" in **"Mama"** . . .—a poem which moved Benedetto Croce to hail József as possibly one of the greatest poets of the poor and of all humanity, and which clearly shows a growing obsession with his sense of irreparable loss. In **"Belated Lament,"** written in 1935 (a singularly unproductive year), accusations, already present in **"Mama,"** are aggravated by curses, but end on a note of final resignation: "My mind is enlightened, the myths are dispersed: the child clinging to his mother's love realizes how stupid he has been. Every mother's son is let down in the end, either deceived or else trying to deceive. You die either of trying to fight or of resignation."

His love affairs were unhappy; either the class-barrier, or wrong choice (e.g. he became infatuated with his psychoanalyst), prevented his finding emotional security in women. In his mature love poetry, however, he created an entirely new imagery for describing the most ancient of poetic subjects. In **"Ode,"** . . . for example, metaphors conjure up the internal world of the body with its "rosebushes of the bloodvessels," "the soil of the stomach," "the foliage of the lungs," or the "tunnels of the bowels," where "timeless matter moves serenely." The biological details of the internal organs, far from being revolting, create a unique landscape, not unlike those photos of human tissues magnified a thousand times, of which modern electronic photography is justly proud. Moreover, there is a unity of the perceptible world and the microcosmos achieved by the all-pervading love-declarations. Of the poems written to Flóra in 1937, **"Flóra"** stands out on two counts; by the sudden thawing of József's wintry imagery in Part One (**"Hexameters"**), and by the introduction of social references in Part Three (**"Already Two Thousand Millions"**): "I need you Flóra as villages / need electric light, stone-houses, schools, wells," which is rather uncommon in love-lyrics.

In his last two years, József wrote more poems than in any other period since 1928. The power, penetration, and shrewd simplicity of the last poems make it hard to believe that they were written by a mentally sick person, especially as there is not a single line that shows the loss of his consciousness as an artist. Yet he was in the final stage; his last volume, *The Pain Is Great,* . . . the only one to appear after his selected poems (*Bear's Dance* . . .), is a final attempt to grasp totality. The title poem talks about the "loss of the last refuge," it says that "there is no place for me here, among the living," and connects the stanzas with the outburst: "The pain is great!" But social awareness never left the poet; he reacted sharply to the signs of hostile external reality. He came to see—as many other renegades were to see a generation later—that for all their noble ideals, the Communists' methods were hardly distinguishable from those of the Fascists they were so valiantly combating, for they believed that "the world needs order, and order exists . . . to ban what is good." This ironic "new tale of fascist-communism" became the reality of the Stalinist era (**"Enlighten Your Child"** . . .).

When József assumed the authority of a spokesman of the people his vision became a complete fusion of personal experience and history seen simultaneously. **"By the Danube"** . . . is an expression of this totality, inspired by watching the river flow by while reflecting on the complex co-relationships of personal and collective existence. This most impressive statement of existential and social relevance is the realization that in his person both oppressor and oppressed, victor and the vanquished are embodied within the larger context of mankind, making nonsense of the conflict between self and society. **"A Breath of Air!"** . . . is an eloquent protest against all forms of dictatorship, a protest which has not ceased to be relevant in Eastern Europe: "They can tap all my telephone calls / (when, why, to whom.) / They have a file on my dreams and plans / and on those who read them. / And who knows when they'll find / sufficient reason to dig up the files / that violate my rights."

Children figure often in his similes, as in **"Welcome to Thomas Mann"** . . .—written when the novelist, a fugitive from the Fascism that also threatened Hungary, came to lecture in Budapest; here the audience is compared to a child pleading to be told another story. The touching simplicity of the child-like plea for beautiful tales as humanity is devoured by "monster-states," is effectively counterbalanced by the cultivated dignity maintained throughout the poem.

Until the end of his life József continued to plead for "fine words," as if he sought to counteract the grim reality of the times, and to make good the arrears of happiness outstanding to him from his childhood (as in **"Lullaby,"** . . . a beautiful poem written for little Balázs, the son of a composer friend).

Another feature of his work which remained till the end was the flippant humour with which, for example, he summarized his abortive career in **"For My Birthday,"** . . . as "a present to give myself a surprise in the corner of the coffee-house." Describing the clash with Professor Horger, who sent him down from Szeged University, thus ending his hopes of becoming a teacher, he concludes the poem on a note of sublime defiance: "I will teach all my people, not at high-school level!" The rhyme structure of the poem is a *tour de force;* the last two lines of each stanza consist of only two syllables. They are effortless pure rhymes which lend the poem its irreverent tone, and the climax coincides with a climax of virtuosity, the dividing of the infinitive of the verb *tanítani* (to teach), with its rhyming halves forming the last two lines of the stanza.

His dream of a world where order is maintained by human reason and conscience, had been eroded in the confrontation with reality. Nothing much remained to sustain his life, except to record his last states of mind: "Why should I be honest? I shall be laid out in any case! / Why should not I be honest? / I shall be laid out then too!" he argues in **"Two Hexameters."** . . . "In the guise of Knaves, Kings and Queens / we await silently what fate is in store for us" (**"After the Cards are Dealt,"** . . .)—he reports in a sonnet, and then admits defeat: "I am Crushed." . . . Once more he summarizes his *ars poetica:* "Eat, drink, hug, sleep! / Measure yourself with the universe!"—but there is now only one possibility left: death. His mood is summed up very soberly in the last stanza of his last poem, written probably on his last day:

> Spring is fine, and so is summer,
> but autumn's better, and winter is best
> for one who finally leaves his hopes
> for a family and a home to others.

His death was a symbolic sacrifice; at least that was how the next generation understood it, and it was also symbolic within the context of his poetry. Trains were of paramount importance in his imagery; he had already "put his hat on the rails" in 1926, and in the background of countless poems goods trains shunt, locomotives whistle, as they did on the outskirts of Budapest where he had grown up. The last freight train was due with its rigid iron wheels on a cold day in December.

József's poetic legacy consists of about 600 poems which he wrote in fifteen years. During his lifetime he achieved little recognition, he was known only to a handful of friends and intellectuals; his influence, however, became significant for the generation which attained consciousness in the 1950s, that is, for those intellectuals who were born in the 1930s. It is somewhat ironic that he became the master of those whom he should have taught at "high-school level" had he been allowed to graduate; it is still a greater irony that his poetry, which became widely available in school-books, also became an intellectual weapon against the regime which proclaimed him its "official poet." It can mean only that his ideas put into effective verse form a legacy pointing far beyond the manipulations of any regimes, to "where freedom is order," and as a result, he is still an active force in Hungarian literature. (pp. 354-60)

Lóránt Czigány, "The Avant-Garde, Class Consciousness, and Alienation," in his The Oxford History of Hungarian Literature: From the Earliest Times to the Present, *Oxford at the Clarendon Press, Oxford, 1984, pp. 343-60.*

ADDITIONAL BIBLIOGRAPHY

András, László, and Sutter, Ruth. "Translating Attila József's Poetry." *The New Hungarian Quarterly* VII, No. 24 (Winter 1966): 164-70.
> Assesses the quality of the translations in the 1966 collection *Poems* and discusses particular problems that József's poetry presents to the English translator.

Gőmőri, George. Introduction to *Selected Poems and Texts,* by Attila József, edited by George Gőmőri and James Atlas, translated by John Bákti, pp. 13-18. Cheadle, England: Carcanet Press, 1973.
> Biographical essay.

Lotz, John. *The Structure of the Sonetti a Corona of Attila József.* Stockholm: Almqvist & Wiksell, 1965, 22 p.
> Structural analysis of József's sonnet cycle "A kozmosz éneke."

Vladimir (Galaktionovich) Korolenko

1853-1921

(Also transliterated as Koroliénko) Russian short story writer, novelist, autobiographer, and journalist.

Best known as a journalist and activist for social justice, Korolenko was also the author of novels and short stories which reflect his sympathy for the outcasts of Russian society and his faith in human nature. His optimism stood in direct contrast to the predominantly pessimistic mood of late nineteenth-century Russian authors; nevertheless, his work was praised by many writers of this period, including Anton Chekhov, who called Korolenko his "favorite contemporary writer."

The son of a provincial judge and his wife, Korolenko was born in the Ukrainian village of Zhitomir. Upon graduation from secondary school he attended the St. Petersburg Technological Institute and the Moscow College of Agriculture and Forestry, supporting himself by tutoring and odd jobs. During his years as a student he remained independent of political factions and opposed the revolutionary terrorism advocated by his more radical peers. However, his liberal sympathies were well known, and in 1876 he was expelled from the agricultural college on the charge of engaging in revolutionary activity and exiled to Kronstadt, an island in the Gulf of Finland. A year later he was allowed to return to St. Petersburg, where he attended the Mining Institute and published his first sketches. During his residence in St. Petersburg Korolenko was arrested on several occasions, but each time was released without being charged. In 1879 he was sentenced without a trial to "administrative exile," a measure taken by the government against those suspected of political dissidence. He spent the next six years in exile in a series of villages in European Russia and in the Siberian settlement of Amga, which was populated by Yakuts, Tartars, and a variety of Russian outcasts and political exiles. This environment was a decisive influence on his fiction, which often depicts characters modeled on the convicts, refugees, and native tribespeople he met in the Siberian wilderness. Released from exile in 1886, he continued to write fiction centering on the disenfranchised as well as journalism on social issues. During this period he became actively involved in the humanitarian causes he promoted, including: a campaign to abolish the death penalty; the legal defense of several members of an Asian tribe who were falsely accused of ritual murder; the exposure of governmental complicity in anti-Jewish pogroms; a campaign to reform the corrupt and inefficient Russian judicial system; and the organization of relief for famine victims. In addition, Korolenko served as editor of the liberal journal *Russkoe Bogatstvo* from 1904 to 1918. As a result of these activities, he earned a reputation as Russia's foremost champion of the oppressed, and rose to such prominence that the years of his social activism have been called the "age of Korolenko." Upon his death in 1921, S. M. Dubnov observed that "the last embodiment of the conscience of the Russian people . . . has disappeared."

Korolenko's best fictional writings are those derived from his experiences in Siberia. These stories frequently utilize a framing device whereby a narrator resembling the author relates a tale told to him by a traveler, who is often a smuggler, murderer, tramp, or other individual in flight or desperate straits.

Typical of these is "Sokolinets," in which a political exile is visited by a Siberian settler who recounts his escape from a penal colony. Described by Chekhov upon its publication as "the most outstanding work that has appeared of late," "Sokolinets" has been praised for its skillful creation of mood through description of natural setting. Korolenko called himself "a fanatic devotee of Turgenev," and critics note Turgenev's influence on Korolenko's lyrical descriptions of the Siberian countryside. Lauren G. Leighton maintains that "Korolenko achieved the peak of his power of lyric expression" in his most famous story, *Son Makara (Makar's Dream)*, a work which also exemplifies the author's brilliant rendering of spoken language, including dialect, prison argot, and personal eccentricities of speech. *Makar's Dream* relates the life, death, and heavenly judgment of the peasant Makar, combining Christian mythology and Asian folklore in a manner common to the Siberian peasantry. Critics observe in Korolenko's fiction a tendency toward journalistic documentation of his rural subjects' customs, beliefs, and way of life. While some have dismissed his works as "mere ethnography," others have praised the literary artistry with which he rendered such ethnographic detail. Most, however, agree that Korolenko's attention to journalistic detail is of secondary importance to his treatment of human dilemmas and tragedies. Serge Persky, for example, maintains that "in spite of the importance of the background in Korolenko's work, it is really in the conscience of his characters that the essential drama takes place.'' Critics also observe that while Korolenko carefully rendered the brutality of Russian rural life, his stories are nevertheless pervaded by sympathy for humanity and faith in mankind's ultimate goodness. According to D. S. Mirsky, ''Korolenko's world is a fundamentally optimistic world, for man is good by nature, and only the evil conditions created by despotism and the brutal selfishness of capitalism make him what he is—a poor, helpless, absurd, pitiful, and irritating creature.'' This faith in the essential nobility of humankind has been assailed by some critics, who dismiss Korolenko's stories as sentimental romances. More than one commentator has maintained that the author's own moral integrity was detrimental to his literary development in that it undermined his ability to depict the baser side of life; Chekhov, for example, asserted that ''the trouble with Korolenko is that he will never write better unless he deceives his wife. He is too noble.''

In addition to his stories about Siberia, Korolenko wrote fiction set in southwestern Russia, historical legends, and allegories on such philosophical themes as determinism and nonresistance to evil. As his career progressed, Korolenko gradually abandoned fiction for journalism and nonfiction. He wrote several books on social issues, including *V golodny god*, a record of his work among victims of the famine of 1891 and 1892. His autobiography, *Istoria moego sovremennika (The History of My Contemporary)*, is considered by some critics to be his greatest work. According to Mirsky, the book contains ''wonderfully vivid, grotesque figures of cranks and originals, perhaps the best in his whole portrait gallery,'' and is free from what some critics consider the excessive lyricism and sentimentality of his earlier writings.

Commentators diverge over the relative importance of Korolenko's social activism and literary writings. While some consider his fiction to be of secondary importance to his advocacy of social justice, others find his enduring merit to lie in his contribution to Russian literature. Most agree, however, with the assessment of Korolenko made by Leighton, who maintains that during a period in Russia that was characterized by social upheaval and literary pessimism, Korolenko ''held out a hope and promise, a realistic optimism, which few other writers detected in the conditions of the time.''

PRINCIPAL WORKS

Son Makara (short story) 1885
   [''Makar's Dream'' published in *Makar's Dream, and Other Stories*, 1916]
Les shumit (short stories) 1886
   [*The Murmuring Forest, and Other Stories*, 1916]
The Vagrant, and Other Tales (short stories) 1887
Slepoi muzykant (novel) 1888
   [*The Blind Musician*, 1890]
In Two Moods. In Bad Society. (novellas) 1891
V golodny god (nonfiction) 1893
Bez iazyka (short story) 1895
   [*In a Strange Land*, 1925]
Istoria moego sovremennika. 4 vols. (autobiography)
   1909-22
   [*The History of My Contemporary* (partial translation), 1972]
Makar's Dream, and Other Stories (short stories) 1916
Birds of Heaven, and Other Stories (short stories) 1919

Sobranie sochineniy. 10 vols. (short stories, novels, and journalism) 1953-56
Korolenko's Siberia (short stories) 1954
Selected Stories (short stories) 1978

ANTON CHEKHOV (letter date 1888)

[*Considered the most significant Russian author of the literary generation to succeed Leo Tolstoy and Fedor Dostoevsky, Chekhov was one of the greatest short story writers in world literature and a personal friend of Korolenko. In the following excerpt from a letter to Korolenko, he praises the short story ''Escapee from Sakhalin.''*]

I find your **''Escapee from Sakhalin''** the most outstanding work that has appeared of late. It is written like a good musical composition in accordance with all the rules an artist's instinct suggests to him. Throughout the book you show yourself to be such a powerful artist, such a powerhouse, that even your biggest faults, which would be the death of any other writer, pass by unnoticed. Women, for instance, are stubbornly absent from the entire book, and I have only just managed to detect it.

Anton Chekhov, in a letter to Vladimir Korolenko on January 9, 1888, in his Letters of Anton Chekhov, *edited by Simon Karlinsky, translated by Michael Henry Heim with Simon Karlinksy, Harper & Row, Publishers, 1973, pp. 89-90.*

THE ATHENAEUM (essay date 1890)

[*In the following excerpt, the critic favorably reviews* The Blind Musician.]

The strain of melancholy which pervades, more or less, all modern Russian fiction is not wanting in this charming little idyl of one of the most modern and one of the most promising of Russia's writers. But if *The Blind Musician* be a melancholy work, it is at least not morbid. Totally different in this respect from the languid fragrance of Tourguénief's style, and the desperate misery which seem the inevitable Nemesis of Count Tolstoi's characters, this sketch of Korolenko's carries with it an air of healthy manliness and bracing energy. Instead of commencing brightly, joyously, and even wittily, as do the novels of Tolstoi, and those of the great French writers whom he imitates more or less unconsciously, *The Blind Musician* begins sadly. As we open the pages, and read how the mother knows by presentiment, what the doctor only discovers much later by experiment, that her son is blind, we feel that we have come across only another of the numerous pessimistic, lackadaisical stories with which the *fin de siècle* novelists imagine they entertain us. But as we go on we discover that this poor blind boy, with his nervous susceptibility and his introspection, which are marvellously rendered, is after all no morbid creature, but may teach us a lesson of healthy usefulness which we may be the better for; and when in the end the young man is taught by his grim but kind-hearted uncle to realize that he has fellow creatures more miserable than himself—when he rouses himself from his lethargic self-concentration, and devotes his splendid talents to the benefit of his brethren in affliction—when he at last discovers that even for him there is a place in this world, and that even he can lead a useful life—

we feel that we have not read the book in vain. It is conceivable that in Russia especially, which is at present almost paralyzed by pessimism and despair, the stirring words of Korolenko possess more than a purely literary value. After a generation or two of gloom and darkness it is pleasant to get a ray of light, to hear a voice proclaiming that there is a place in this world for one. . . . As a beautiful study beautifully written, displaying a wonderful knowledge of the human soul and conveying a healthy and stimulating lesson, *The Blind Musician* is perfect. But as a story, as we English vulgarly regard a story, it is nothing. It is a short record of the growth and early marriage of a blind boy with a talent for music. It is even devoid of thrilling love passages. A girl in the neighbourhood marries him more from pity than love. And yet this simple record of an uneventful boyhood is intensely interesting, and much better reading than all the shilling ''shockers'' that were ever printed. . . . To English readers *The Blind Musician*, apart from its inherent charm, should be interesting as showing that Count Tolstoi is not the only Russian novelist, and that pessimism is not the last word of Slavonic literature.

> *A review of "The Blind Musician," in* The Athenaeum, *Vol. 2, No. 3272, July 12, 1890, p. 60.*

K. WALISZEWSKI (essay date 1900)

[*In the following excerpt, Waliszewski discusses the artistic achievements and failings of Korolenko's works.*]

[Koroliénko] has hitherto published only one really considerable story. It numbers 150 pages, and is entitled *The Blind Musician.* This, with his *The Forest Whispers,* and *Iom-Kipour,* forms part of a cycle of compositions, the scene of which is laid in South-Western Russia, whereas his *Tales of a Siberian Tourist* call up the snow-covered landscapes of the north, and the exiles and convicts there to be found. Koroliénko himself made involuntary acquaintance with exile, brought about by the most trifling of political peccadilloes. In all these stories the moral teaching is identical, and strongly resembles that . . . of Garchine—sympathy felt with the weak and the hardly used, and no clear distinction drawn between the innocent and the guilty.

The novelist's reputation dates from the publication of his . . . [''Makar's Dream'']—a fanciful story, which winds up with the judgment of a drunkard peasant by a heavenly tribunal. Whether the heaven be that of the Gospel or that of Siberian legend is not made abundantly clear. The Russian public thirsts for poetry; it eagerly quaffed the cup offered it by Koroliénko, without looking too closely at the bottom. That which lies at the bottom of the cup does not, in this author's case, possess a perfect lucidity. His figures are like Murillo's beggars. But he possesses the art of escaping triviality by never lingering over external detail longer than is absolutely necessary to the realisation of his types. Dostoïevski's influence is clearly visible in the *Tales of a Siberian Tourist.* To it we owe some very doubtful portraits of *good* ruffians. But this is a mere passing error. The tales entitled ''The Old Ringer'' and ''An Easter Night,'' which belong to the same group, betray nothing of this kind. The exquisite language, the transparently brilliant colouring, and the picturesque imagery of these stories recall Tourguéniev's *Poems in Prose,* and no greater praise can be ascribed to any author. The soldier of the guard, who, in spite of himself, becomes the murderer of the escaped convict, whom he brings down by a shot from his rifle, just as the distant bells ring out the Easter vespers, attracts our sympathy even more

strongly than his victim. Koroliénko reached a height, here, which he was unfortunately not destined to maintain. The men of his generation soon lose their breath; it may be because they find so little air that they can breathe. In *Iom-Kipour* (the Jewish Day of Expiation), which relates how a Little-Russian miller, good Christian though he is, narrowly escapes being carried away by the devil, in the place of the Jewish tavern-keeper Iankiel, because, like him, he has tried to make money out of the poor peasants—a very true and deep idea is embodied in a most delightful description of local manners and customs. But all the other pieces in the same collection are pale in colour and empty in conception. *The Blind Musician,* who attempts to reproduce the sensations of sight by means of sounds, is an attempt, and a fresh failure, to work out a psychological subject, which had attracted many writers before Koroliénko's time.

The Russian novelist has hoped to replace the lack of substance in his writings by lyrical fire; but his enthusiasm is cold and without emotion.

In ''On the Road'' and ''Two Points of View,'' Tolstoï's influence, following on that of Dostoïevski, impels the author in his search for some moral principle as the basis of our common existence. The traveller who has lately escaped from a Siberian prison, and is straining every nerve to escape innumerable dangers and regain his home, stops suddenly short. A doubt has overwhelmed him. Why should he fly? Why go there rather than elsewhere? and Koroliénko is soon deep in the analysis of the wavering spirit of the men of his generation. A young man sees one of his friends killed in a railway accident; so struck is he by this event that he arrives at last, through a series of questions, at a completely mechanical conception of existence. What is the use of thought or love? and he forsakes a young girl, whose affections he has won, until the unhappy creature's sufferings reveal the true meaning of life to his case-hardened soul.

All this, finished as it is as far as the form goes, is very incomplete in conception, and for some years past Koroliénko seems to have taken a fancy to a still more slipshod method of work. He has published notes collected in the Government of Nijni-Novgorod, in the course of one of those famines which from time to time afflict the provinces of the great empire; and after a journey to England, he made known his impressions of a stormy sitting in Parliament. But all this may not unfairly be called mere reporter's work. (pp. 422-25)

> *K. Waliszewski, "Contemporary Literature," in his* A History of Russian Literature, *1900. Reprint by D. Appleton and Company, 1910, pp. 403-40.*

CHRISTIAN BRINTON (essay date 1905)

[*In the following excerpt, Brinton praises the sympathy for humanity evidenced in Korolenko's works.*]

Korolenko is an exponent of social pity. He has never penned a line that does not thrill with love for human kind or radiate an abiding tenderness for the frail and the forlorn. Instead of being embittered by his experiences, he has been broadened. Among cripples or convicts, among navvies or thieves, along the icebound Lena or the slumbering Volga, in filthy *kabak* or in tumble-down *izba*, he has always found sparks of kindness and of courage. He does not concern himself with those who indulge in sentimental self-analysis but with those who are hungry or sick unto death. Women seldom flit across his pages, for women are plastic, adaptable and easily appeased. It is more apt to be a blind child or a man shattered by suffering or blighted by ignorance who becomes his pathetic and appealing hero. There is hardly a character in the entire range of his work that has not been taken direct from the teeming, troubled life about him. He has never had to invent a situation nor to manufacture a tragedy. The material for innumerable plots lay seething before his eyes, and heart-racking scenes were daily enacted in his presence. Yet despite everything he has remained a mellow, sunny Little Russian, transfusing all he saw with sympathy and with a playful, endearing commiseration, that nothing could obscure.

"Makar's Dream," Korolenko's first story of importance, which appeared in the *Russkaya Mysl* while its author was still in exile, opened the eyes of Russia to a new man and to a new field. It is a prose epic, fanciful, yet real, depicting with colour, precision and expansive humour life among the Yakuts of the Siberian Taïga. The effect of the story was tonic. It came at a time when Tolstoy was confusing the public with *My Confession* and *My Religion,* and when Garshin's *Red Flower* was adding to the general hysteria. Here at last was a sane, jovial talent, a man who had not forgotten how to laugh. *Sketches of a Siberian Tourist* followed, and they, together with "A Saghalinian," "At-Davan," and a score of kindred tales quickly assured Korolenko's reputation. For consummate poetic realism and for pure descriptive beauty, Turgeniev himself never surpassed certain of these sketches, and for poignant humanity they often recall the agonising pages of *Crime and Punishment.* With later stories the range of character and incident became almost infinite. The grotesque terror of Makar was followed by the tremulous aspiration of little Joachim in "The Blind Musician," the demoniac cruelty of Arabin in "At-Davan" found antithesis in the garrulous solicitude of old Tiburzhy. "In Bad Company" and "A Paradox" are two of the most exquisite bits of child analysis in any language, and "At Night" and "The Old Bell-Ringer" show a power of evoking the supernatural that has rarely been equalled. The appeal to sympathy which persists through all these stories is infectious, not obvious. It is almost unwillingly that Korolenko touches the heart-strings, and yet he never fails to do so. No words of praise can be too high for the very latest stories which have come from Korolenko's pen—"The River at Play" and "The Siberian Carriers." They rank with his best work, which is, indeed, saying much.

It is natural that a man with Korolenko's civic temperament, his broad political humanism, should at times forsake fiction and devote himself to a closer study of actual conditions. Such is the spirit that prompted him during the great famine to visit the stricken districts, where for months he went from village to village dispensing the meagre aid at his command. *A Year of Famine,* in which he described his experiences, was a book without literary alloy, and was so fearless a record of fact that it was immediately suppressed by the censor. Korolenko has always loved the restless fermentation of humanity, and frequently journeys to various parts of the Empire in order to mingle with turbulent dock hands or pallid mystics. "Pavlovo Sketches," "The Eclipse" and "Judgment Day" are the best among these miscellaneous studies, and are filled with accurate detail and illuminating observation. (pp. 25-6)

Christian Brinton, "Korolenko, Apostle of Pity," in The Bookman, New York, Vol. XXI, No. 1, March, 1905, pp. 24-6.

G. H. PERRIS (essay date 1906)

[*Perris is the author of* Russia in Revolution, *among other works. In the following excerpt, he discusses psychological analysis and pictorial art in Korolenko's stories.*]

[Korolenko's] love of Nature and the humble folk who live very near to the earth-mother, his deep feeling for truth and justice are shown throughout his work; and his sense of the need of a wise and patient altruism is worked out in the larger stories both in personal and social applications. In *The Blind Musician* he offers us a minute study of a mind whose chief channel of communication with the outer world has been completely blocked from birth. The problem here is a purely individual one; and the intensity and command of detail with which it is described give it a terrible reality. One mental condition merges gradually into another. The fresh idealistic stage is followed—when the first collision with the pre-occupied and seemingly heartless world brings about the collapse of this egoistic Paradise—by black despair; and here some of Korolenko's eminent countrymen would have left it. But for blind Petrik there is a third mood. A state of "balanced melancholy" had succeeded to the early smart, and this in turn had deepened into the utter wretchedness and despair of baffled egoism. Where, however, love fails to touch this deep-seated disease, the appreciation of a deeper misfortune succeeds; and a solution at once moral and artistic is obtained. "In Two Moods" is not without an equal significance for the individual; but it has also a broader interest as a study in the psychology of a movement—the early phase of revolt commonly though inaccurately called Nihilism. Gavrik is no mere lay figure; but he is not too strongly individualised to stand for a type. The tragic death of a fellow-student strikes a dividing line between two characteristic periods of youthful experience. The first is a dreamland of vast aspirations and enterprises, honest and generous, but also undefined and untried.

> We were to develop into something quite special—altogether new and exceptional people. . . . I merely dreamt that in me and my fellow-students there existed, as it were, buds wherein lay hidden, and ready to unfold and come forth, the bright future, the full, new life.

Nature breaks in upon the childish comedy in her sharp, unceremonious way. Suicide makes a horrible sight, before which the inexperienced brain staggers. Is life and all its loves, sufferings, thoughts, resolvable, then, into mere physical processes, all ended when a single cog in the complex machine is broken? The familiar old questions succeed, albeit in a newly real form. Every phase of self-complacent pessimism is mercilessly analysed; Gavrik becomes more and more isolated, and the horror deepens till, having repelled his friends and insulted his girl-lover, a climax is reached. Then the spell is suddenly broken; to the blind eyes sight is at length given. Happily there is a contagion of self-sacrifice.

> Now I have faith—first of all in her, next in humanity. And beyond these glimmers the dawn of yet other faiths. This is the golden cloud of a new mood; into whatever shape it may unfold, my heart tells me that at least it will be life.

But Korolenko is at least as great in his pictorial art as in his psychology. In these two leading characters it may be said that we have mental types rather than beings of flesh and blood; but in the shorter stories the actors have generally distinct and sometimes vivid personalities. An astonishing wealth of impressionist material is expended upon these sketches; yet there are so many charming touches that we witness the kaleidoscopic review without a moment of weariness. **"Makar's Dream"** is one of the most delightful fables ever penned. (pp. 6-9)

All the mixed shrewdness and stupidity, the generosity, and sloth, and ignorance, the little shiftiness and great honesty of the Mujik, are in the picture, the cruelty and beauty of nature, the cruelty and nobility of man. Withal, there is a warm humour, tone of energy and health and hope, that add to Korolenko's Slav characteristics a distinct new note, a new message to young Russia.

In **"The Last Ray"** . . . we have the same vivid depiction of the Siberian wilderness, with its little group of unconquerable prisoners. The author's delightful humour is lacking; but, for the Russian reader at least, there is always food for hope in such a heroic legend as that of the lost Decembrist and his faithful old servant.

Korolenko has done much of the more substantial kind of journalistic work and has written several volumes on social subjects. In *The Year of Famine* he describes a journey through the districts affected by famine in 1894, and also his connection with a well-known case in which a man, whom he vigorously defended, was charged with "ritual murder." More recently he visited Kishiniev, and described one of the periodical massacres of Jews in that unhappy town. (pp. 12-13)

[Korolenko] occupies in his own country an honoured and influential position. He has not established any new school either of thought or style; but through much labour and suffering he has preserved a rare and most delicate charm, a steady faith in his own people, in their undeveloped power, a tender pity for all maimed and tortured souls, a calm assurance that only in the pursuit of truth and justice can permanent satisfaction be found. It is a noble creed, and rarely in our day has it received more beautiful expression. (p. 13)

> *G. H. Perris, "Vladimir Korolenko," in* Temple Bar, *Vol. 133, No. 1, January, 1906, pp. 1-13.*

SERGE PERSKY (essay date 1912)

[*Persky is a French critic. In the following excerpt, originally published in France in 1912, he discusses the themes, techniques, and philosophical bases of Korolenko's works.*]

In all of Korolenko's works we distinctly feel the living breath that inspires the artist, and the ardor of a fervent ideal. His god is man; his ideal, humanity; his "leitmotiv," the poetry of human suffering. This intimate connection with all that is human is to be found in his psychological analysis as well as in his descriptions of natural phenomena. Both God and nature are in turn spiritualized and humanized. Korolenko looks at life from a human standpoint; the world which he describes is made up wholly of men and exists for them only. He has a very clear philosophy, and a conscience aware of the duties it has to perform. If he has not opened up hitherto unknown paths, nor made new roads, he has himself nevertheless passed through terrible experiences; he has been a prey to profound sorrows and doubts, and in spite of all, he has kept his love for the people intact, and deeply pities their ignorance and abasement. His work constantly recalls to our minds the theory that the cultivated classes are in debt to the people for the education which they have received at the people's expense. This is the great moral principle which governs the conscience

of the Russian "intellectuals." It is in this sense then, that Korolenko may be said to continue the literature of 1870, and to be the successor of Zlatovratsky and Uspensky. But he has reincarnated this past in new forms, which naturally result from the activity of his far-sighted, powerful intelligence. We do not find in his work either the nervousness, often sickly, which pervades the works of Uspensky, or the optimism of Zlatovratsky, which often excessively idealizes the life of the Russian peasant, who is the principal hero of all his works. Korolenko, because he puts a high value on human personality, perfectly appreciates the terrible struggle that man has to make in order to secure his rights. A desire for justice on the one hand, and a defence of man's dignity on the other, form the very essence of the talent of this author, and it is with these feelings that he observes the people on whom injustice weighs most heavily and who have merely remnants of human dignity left in their make-up,—for in general, these people are not those whom fate has overcome. Most of them lead a hard and gloomy life beset with misfortunes. Many of them are vagabonds, escaped convicts, drunkards, murderers, who are bowed down with misery, and have no wish except to escape the mortal dangers of the Siberian forests and marshes. On opening any of Korolenko's books we find ourselves, to use his own words, in "bad company." He does not flatter his heroes, he does not make gentlemen of them; they are not even men, but rather human rubbish.

"Because I knew a lot about the world," he writes,

> I knew that there were people who had lost every vestige of humanity. I knew that they were corroded with vice and sunk deep in debauchery, in which they lived contented. But when the recollection of these beings surged through my mind, enveloped in the mists of the past, I saw nothing but a terrible tragedy, and felt only an inexpressible sorrow. . . .

This author does not give any judgment on life; he does not condemn it and does not nourish a preconceived spite against it, but his sad heart overflows with pity, and, if he approaches this life, it is with the balm of love, in order to try to dress its terrible wounds.

For Korolenko, the sufferings of existence atone for its injustice; he does not perceive the iniquities that surround him except through the prism of sorrow.

From the very beginning of his literary career, in his first book, *Episodes in the Life of a Seeker,* Korolenko shows himself to be a seeker after truth. With him, the understanding of life, so ardently sought after, is never summed up in a single solution. He dreams of it constantly; at times, he seems to have found it, but he loses track of it again and starts all over.

This groping about resulted in a moral crisis in which he looked forward to death with joy. Beset with the thought of suicide, he often prowled around railroad platforms and looked at the car-wheels.

"I went there and came back again," he writes,

> depressed by my realization of the stupidity of life. The snow was falling all around me, and shaping itself into a frozen carpet, the telegraph poles shivered as if they were cold through and through, and on the other side of the road, on a slope, shone the sad little light of the watchman's tower. There, in the darkness, lived a

whole family. Through the shadows the little red fire seemed to be as desolate as the family. The children were scrofulous and suffered; the mother was thin and sickly. To procreate and to bury! Such was the life of the father, probably the most unfortunate of all, because the household depended wholly upon him, and he saw no gleam of hope anywhere. He bore this condition of things, because, in his simplicity, he believed in a superior will, and thought that his misery was inevitable. The resignation of this man, the terrible bareness of his obscure existence, oppressed me. If I could bear the sight of it, it was only because I hoped; I thought that we should soon find the road which makes life happier, more agreeable to every one. How, where, in what manner? What a mystery! But the future beauty of life was in the search for it.

The observations that Korolenko was able to make were many and diverse. By going all over Russia he gathered inexhaustible riches, in the form of anecdotes and actual experiences. This can be easily realized when we consider the sumptuous variety of his descriptions. Where do we not go, and whom do we not meet in his books? First, we are in a peaceful little town of the southwest, then in the thick woods of Poliyessye, in the snow-covered and frozen Siberian forests, or in the valleys of Sakhaline, inhabited by half-breed Russians and escaped convicts, not to mention the innumerable sectarians who fill the Siberian prisons. And Korolenko never repeats. Not even a detail occurs more than once. Each of his works is a little world in itself. The author, moreover, unlike other writers, is never satisfied with pale sketches; each character is shown in full relief, each picture is absolutely finished. This wholeness, this finish which does not hurt the harmony of the proportions, is a precious quality, very rare in our time.

The *Sketches of a Siberian Tourist,* published in 1896, in which bandits of various odd types tell thrilling tales of nocturnal attacks and other adventures, is a kind of artistic novel. The postillion is the most original character in the book. Huge of stature, audacious and clever, he exercises a mysterious influence over the brigands, whom he inspires with a superstitious terror. Most of them, thinking him invulnerable, do not dare attack the travelers whom he is driving.

That same year another work of Korolenko's appeared, called: *In Bad Company,*—a sort of autobiography which added to his renown. (pp. 82-8)

Another short story, called "**The Murmuring Forest,**" which was published in the same year, made as much of a success as *Bad Company.*

But it is in *The Blind Musician* that Korolenko attains perfection. This masterly psychological study does not present a very complicated plot. From the very start the reader is captivated by a powerful poetic quality, free from all artifice, fresh, spontaneous, and breathing forth such moral purity, such tender pity, that one literally feels regenerated. (p. 91)

Korolenko belongs to the school of Turgenev. In all of his works he remains true to the principles which his master summed up in a letter:

> One must penetrate the surroundings, and take life in all its manifestations; decipher the laws

by which it is governed; get at the very essence of life, while remaining always within the boundaries of truth; and finally, one must not be contented with a superficial study.

Korolenko lives up to all of these principles. Without tiring, he watches life in all of its phases. He uses a large canvas for his studies of inanimate nature, as well as of individuals in particular and the masses in general. That is why his work gives us such an exact reproduction of life.

Like Turgenev, he describes nature admirably. His descriptions are not irrelevant ornaments, but they constitute an organic and integral part of the picture. In both Turgenev and Korolenko the surrounding country reflects the feelings and emotions of the heroes, and takes a purely lyric character. One might almost say that these country scenes breathe, speak a human language, and whisper mysterious legends.

Korolenko has given us several splendid landscapes. In some of these nature seems to be in a serene mood, like a good mother whose harmonious strength attracts man and shows him the need of reposing on her bosom. In others, nature is like a strong, free element which incites man to lead an independent life. Thus, in the beautiful prose poem, "**The Moment,**" in which the action passes in Spain, it is the ocean beating against the prison walls that arouses Diatz from his torpor and makes him attempt to escape.

But, in spite of the importance of the background in Korolenko's work, it is really in the conscience of his characters that the essential drama takes place. More than anything else, it is psychology that beguiles the artist; it is only through psychology that Korolenko depicts men and their mentalities. He studies the strong and the weak, the simple and the complex; exaltation, triumph, revolt, and downfall all interest him equally. (pp. 95-7)

Korolenko does not try to reconcile us to reality, but to mankind. In all of the catastrophes in his books, in the most sombre descriptions, he comforts us with a consolation, an ideal, a "little fire" that burns in the distance and attracts us. But to get to that fire we have to fight against evil. And it is perhaps in answer to Tolstoy's doctrine of passive resistance that Korolenko wrote that beautiful story called, "**The Legend of Florus,**" the subject of which was probably taken from *The War of the Jews,* by Flavius Josephus.

This work takes us back to the time when Judaea was bowed down under Roman rule. The Jews bear their lot without a murmur, and this resignation encourages Florus, the governor of Judaea, to oppress them more.

Soon there are two parties formed: the "pacifics" want to rid themselves of Roman cruelty by humble submission, while the others advise opposing this cruelty to the utmost. The chief of the latter party is Menahem, the son of a famous warrior who has inherited from his father his generous passions and his hatred of oppression. Menahem's words inspire respect even in his enemies. But he does not succeed in making peace among his people. In vain he cries to them, as his father before him had cried: "It is disgraceful to bow down to sovereigns, especially since these sovereigns are men; no human being should bow down to any one excepting God, who created men that they might be free." With great trouble he finally succeeds in rousing a part of the people to rebellion. Then he leaves the city with his followers, resolved to defend his country. Menahem has no illusions as to the outcome; he knows that he will be conquered by the Romans. Nevertheless he is fearless, for his whole being is filled with a single thought,—the idea of justice, which imposes upon men certain obligations which they must not scorn.

During his stay in Siberia Korolenko had a very good chance to observe the deported convicts. Most of them are thieves, forgers, and murderers. The others, urged on by a heroic desire to live their own true lives, have been sent to this "cursed land" because of "political offences."

Korolenko is not resigned to the sadness of life, he is not an enemy to manly calls to active struggle, but he neither wants to, nor can he, break the ties that bind him to the real life of the present. He does not wish either to judge or to renounce this life. Nor does he try, by fighting, to perpetuate a conflict which is in itself eternal. If he struggles, it is rather in discontent than in despair. Not all is evil in his eyes, and reality is not always and entirely sad. His protestations hardly ever take the form of disdain or contempt; he does not rise to summits which are inaccessible to mankind. In fact, his ideal is close to earth; it is the ideal which comes from mankind, from tears and sufferings. If the thoughts and feelings of the author rise sometimes high above the earth, he never forgets the world and its interests. Korolenko loves humanity, and his ideals cannot separate themselves from it. He loves man and he believes that God lives in their souls. (pp. 99-101)

As a publicist, he has written some very valuable articles. Among them are observations on the famine year (he spent two months in one of the worst districts). In other articles he has analyzed a moral malady peculiar to our state of society:—honor. In the recent Russian duels he studied the perverse notions of honor and the moral changes produced by sickly egotism. He has studied the causes that bring about the complete loss of individuality. Finally, in 1910, he published under the title, *Present Customs (Notes of a Publicist under Sentence of Death)* a series of documents gathered here and there, which constitute an eloquent and passionate plea in favor of the abolitionist thesis.

When the great Tolstoy read the preface of this work, he wrote to Korolenko, "I often sobbed and wept. Millions of copies of this work ought to be distributed; it ought to be read by every one who has a heart. No discourse, no novel or play, can produce the effect that your *Notes* do."

But above all, it is as the pure artist that Korolenko merits most attention. It is his talent that has already made him famous, and it is his talent that will make him immortal in Russian literature. (p. 106)

> *Serge Persky, "Vladimir Korolenko," in his* Contemporary Russian Novelists, *translated by Frederick Eisemann, John W. Luce and Company, 1913, pp. 76-107.*

D. S. MIRSKY (essay date 1926)

[*Mirsky was a Russian prince who fled his country after the Bolshevik Revolution and settled in London. While in England, he wrote two important and comprehensive histories of Russian literature,* Contemporary Russian Literature (1926) *and* A History of Russian Literature (1927). *In 1932, having reconciled himself to the Soviet regime, Mirsky returned to the U.S.S.R. He continued to write literary criticism, but his work eventually ran afoul of Soviet censors and he was exiled to Siberia. He disappeared in 1937. In the following excerpt from* Contemporary Russian Literature, *Mirsky discusses the salient features of Korolenko's works.*]

Korolénko's work is very typical of what the eighties and nineties called "artistic.". . . It is full of emotional poetry and of nature introduced in Turgénev's manner. This lyrical element seems today a little stale and uninteresting, and most of us will prefer to all his earlier work his last book, [*The History of My Contemporary*], in which he has almost freed himself of this facile poetry. . . . Korolénko's poetry may on the whole have faded, but his best early work still retains much of its charm. For even his poetry rises above the level of mere prettiness when he has to do with the more majestic aspects of nature. The northeast of Siberia, with its vast and empty spaces, its short sub-polar days, and its dazzling wilderness of snow, lives in his early stories with impressive grandeur. But what gives Korolénko his unique flavor is the wonderful blend of poetry with a delicate humor and with his undying faith in the human soul. Sympathy and faith in human goodness are characteristic of the Russian populist. Korolénko's world is a fundamentally optimistic world, for man is good by nature, and only the evil conditions created by despotism and the brutal selfishness of capitalism make him what he is—a poor, helpless, absurd, pitiful, and irritating creature. There is a mighty poetry in Korolénko's first story, **"Makár's Dream,"** not only because of the suggestive painting of the Yakút landscape, but still more because of the author's profound, indestructible sympathy with the dark and unenlightened savage, whose mind is so naïvely selfish and who yet has in him a ray of the divine light. Korolénko's humor is especially delightful. It is free from all satirical intent and sophistication. It is wonderfully easy and natural—it has a lightness of touch that is rare in Russian authors, and in which he is surpassed only by that wonderful and still unappreciated author Kuschévsky. In Korolénko this humor is often subtly interwoven with poetry—as in the delightful story **"At Night,"** in which a family of children discuss in their bedroom the absorbing question of how babies are made. **"The Day of Atonement,"** with its funny old Jewish devil, has that blend of humor and phantasy which is so delightful in Gógol's early stories, but Korolénko's colors are mellower and quieter, and though he has not an ounce of the creative exuberance of his great countryman, he has much more human sympathy and warmth. The most purely humorous of his stories is **"Tongueless"** . . . , the story of three Ukrainian peasants who emigrated to America without knowing a word of any language but their own. Russian critics have called it Dickensian, and this is true in the sense that in Korolénko, as in Dickens, the absurdity of his characters does not make them less lovable.

Korolénko's last work is an autobiography, which seems to be even a singularly exact and truthful account of his life but which for some supersensitive scruple he called the history, not of himself, but of his contemporary. It is less poetical and barer than his early work, but his two principal qualities—humor and sympathy—are very much present. He gives a delightful picture of life in yet semi-Polish Volynia—of his scrupulously honest but willful father. He records his early impressions of country life, of school, of the great events he had to witness—the Emancipation and the Polish revolt. It is full of wonderfully vivid, grotesque figures of cranks and originals, perhaps the best in his whole portrait gallery. It is certainly not thrilling, but it is a deliciously quiet story told by an old man (he was only fifty-five when he began it, but there always was something of the grandfather in Korolénko) who has ample leisure and good will and who finds pleasure in reviving the vivid memories of fifty years ago. (pp. 356-58)

> *D. S. Mirsky, "The Eighties and Early Nineties," in his* A History of Russian Literature from Its Be-

ginnings to 1900, *edited by Francis J. Whitfield, Vintage Books, 1958, pp. 347-83.*

R. F. CHRISTIAN (essay date 1954)

[*Christian is an English educator, translator, and critic specializing in Russian literature. His translations include the short story collection Korolenko's Siberia. In the following excerpt, he surveys Korolenko's writings in order to assess the author's lasting contribution to literature.*]

"Korolenko is not for all time," observed Yury Aikhenval'd (Eichenwald), while the author was still alive. Now that the centenary of his birth has been celebrated it may be an appropriate occasion to review the accuracy of this statement in the light of the more than ephemeral recognition he has won in his own country.

That Korolenko is still read and enjoyed today is in great measure evidence of the debt owed by the artist to the man. Here surely is a case where character and personality were greater than literary talent and yet have survived primarily by virtue of their expression through the medium of letters. His biography is the sum total of his stories, essays, letters and publicist articles, and their volume is an indication of the fullness of his life. While none may discredit the exemplary nature of that life, few would claim for Korolenko the stature of a great writer. But we may legitimately ask as a prelude to this essay how far his talent as a writer suffered from the discipline and rigid self-control which characterised his way of living. For a reading of his fiction suggests not only the obvious thought that conscientiousness and the utmost moral integrity are in themselves insufficient to make the good writer great, but also the unwelcome corollary that they may even be prejudicial to his development. Can it be argued that if the power of the really great novelist to recreate life (albeit with imagination) derives ultimately from the broadest possible acquaintance with all its diverse manifestations, the author who elects on principle to remain aloof from, or is by nature disinclined to probe into, the baser sides of life will for that reason be unlikely to attain universal recognition? Can it be said in fact that a man is "too good" to be a successful novelist?

Such is the charge that has been levelled against Korolenko, and not by the Decadents alone. When Chukovsky says that Korolenko is so good and we are so bad, he is echoing the sentiment of but a small group of fashionable literary sinners. But when Chekhov confides to Bunin that in his opinion Korolenko would write better if he would only "go and be unfaithful to his wife," he raises a more serious problem. Korolenko was puritanical in his way of life. His profound distaste for immoral excesses of any kind is confirmed by the total absence of sin and passion from his writings. (pp. 449-50)

Let us . . . see how Korolenko's character found its expression in his literary career and how the raw material of his experience was moulded into literary shape. Here we shall have to deal with short stories and novelettes, essays and autobiography; but before going into detail we may hazard a generalisation which holds good for the greater part of Korolenko's fiction, namely, that there is in it a little of God, more of nature, but most of man. Gor'ky, for whom the word "man" had a proud ring about it, would probably not have subscribed to [Yury Aikhenval'd's] remark that the atmosphere of Korolenko's stories is "sultry and stifling from the constant presence of man and man only." By disposition a lover of travel, conversation, observation and description, Gor'ky's older contemporary was

pre-eminently the purveyor of men's experiences as witnessed by him or narrated to him. The characters of his stories are simply the men he has met, spoken to, interrogated even. In so far as they were often unusual men in unusual places they provide him with a subject matter which is always interesting and often absorbing. Siberia was unquestionably the source of his finest inspiration as a writer, and the best of his early stories draw extensively on his accumulated knowledge of the country and the people. It is significant that he returned to that source in middle age. His terms of imprisonment brought him into the closest proximity with common criminals and fanatics; his journeys by road from stage to stage gave him the opportunity to extract from his drivers the stories of their lives; enforced halts *en route* would throw him into the company of a Siberian "Voltairean" or some enterprising trafficker in spirits. Escaped convicts told him their stories. With such people Korolenko was perfectly at ease. He was a good listener and a sympathetic companion. His retentive memory aided by a score of notebooks enabled him to store and reproduce at will some local dialect or prison *argot,* some speech mannerism or personal eccentricity, and to live through again, in his writings, episodes from the recent past. Among his most vivid characters are simple people who have suffered—the peasant who has been goaded all his life, the coachman impelled by an unjust society to take upon himself a prison cross, the zealot persecuted for political or religious nonconformity. Seldom do we meet women in his stories. Dostoyevsky's Nastasyas and Aglayas, who are snares and sphinxes for some Myshkin or Rogozhin, never entered the world of his experience, and it is no surprise to find that he did not care for the author with the "cruel talent." Such women as appear are sentimental girls or tenacious heroines.

When Korolenko left the rich, but narrow field of simple folk and endeavoured to describe the inner pyschological states of maturer individuals he was far less successful. The intellectual, the professional classes, the gentry did not attract him sufficiently to make him wish to write about them, or if he was tempted, as in *Slepoy muzykant,* to venture into more exalted social circles than those frequented by his peasants and convicts, there was Merezhkovsky to contend with. What has been said of Dickens may be said of Korolenko also: "He cannot draw complex, educated or aristocratic types." It is man in his more primitive condition—not, it should be observed, in his pristine innocence, but often in his elemental brutishness—who is the focal point of Korolenko's stories. Nature is the periphery.

What was it that interested him in his characters? We are reminded of the critic's observation on Andreyev, in almost all respects the exact antithesis of Korolenko. "The typical scheme of a story by Andreyev consists of the drab life of a commonplace person illuminated by a flash of thought which sublimates grey existence into tragedy." With Korolenko too it is the flash, the moment, the awakening, which count. Makar, patient and passive, suddenly finds himself possessed of eloquence to inveigh against his unjust lot. Tyuhn, the hero of **"Reka igrayet,"** is roused from his lethargy at a time of crisis. In **"At Davan,"** the memory of better days inspires the puny and timid Kruglikov to exercise an unwonted authority. Even the most apathetic of men is never quite devoid of that restlessness, that stimulus which comes into play now and again and transforms him, however temporarily, into something bigger than himself. We may discern a fairly typical pattern for a Korolenko story, or more exactly a Siberian story. There is usually a narrator. He is often on a journey. He meets a ferryman, a coachman, a smuggler. This person tells his tale. Perhaps he has murdered a man; perhaps he has escaped from prison; perhaps he is the victim of political persecution. For a moment he holds the stage. He has his hour of glory. His voice is heard and his presence felt before he passes on. In the background a frozen river begins to thaw; the taiga murmurs; water is swirling in a ravine. The individual comes to life, and with him his environment. But sometimes he is too obtrusive, too clearly drawn; for Korolenko loved detail and rarely selected from it with discrimination. Hence the prevalence in the stories of the passport technique—height, colour of eyes, visible marks of distinction. In the interests of accuracy nothing must be omitted. This approach betrays a lack of subtlety, which is further evidenced by the frequent need to underline, to interpret, to "point a moral or adorn a tale." The fastidious Pater acknowledged that a pleasurable stimulus can be derived by a strenuous mind from a style not too obvious. It is by labouring the obvious that Korolenko sometimes gives offence.

But at his best he could overcome his caution and write a little masterpiece like **"Son Makara."** Here he is drawing as much as anywhere else on his Siberian experiences, for Makar is avowedly a close portrait of his Amga host, and his little hut with icicles for window-panes, the Tartar horse thieves, the local *plashchki* for catching hares and even the drunken priest who falls into the fire are alluded to in letters or in diaries. But Korolenko transfers the prosaic and often unpleasant details of Siberian reality to a world of fantasy, a world more suited to the family hearth at Christmas time, where in his dreams Makar is transported after death. There God is a Yakut *toyon* in plush boots, warming himself before a silver stove in the middle of a Russian-style *izba*. His son has been down to earth and "knows what things are like there." His winged hosts are busy labourers. Conceived in earthly terms, they are all persuaded to judge Makar by his own earthly standards of justice. The clever blend of the mundane and the exalted, of fact and fantasy, is enhanced by a polished style and a delicate feeling for words. Whether the subject is the uncouth Makar with his stammering, truncated delivery or the metamorphosis of Makar before the judgement seat, the simple, solemn description of the approach to Toyon's residence or the brusque greeting in the conventional Yakut idiom, Korolenko can convey admirably the appropriate mood in a language which is as varied as it is meticulously chosen. Although using an unembellished and restrained vocabulary and an unsophisticated syntax he can nevertheless paint word pictures which are more reminiscent of the Turgenev tradition than of the *narodnik* style of *bytopisaniye*, to which he was by choice of subject more closely allied. A brief passage from **"Son Makara"** may support this contention in so far as a translation can ever effectively reproduce an original style.

> Makar had not previously noticed that day was beginning to dawn on the plain. First of all, a few dazzling rays shone out over the horizon. They soon spread across the sky and dimmed the bright stars. And the stars died and the moon sank. And the snowy plain grew dark.
>
> Then the mists rose above it and stood round the plain like a guard of honour.
>
> And in one quarter, in the east, the mists grew brighter, like warriors clad in gold.
>
> And then the mists began to stir, the golden warriors bowed down their heads.

> And from behind them rose the sun and stood upon their golden backs and surveyed the plain.
>
> And the whole plain shone forth with a dazzling, blinding light.
>
> And the mists rose triumphantly in an enormous round, broke up in the west and floated hovering aloft. . . .

This is the glow of the dream-like world of Korolenko's creating, the bright light which invariably shines in the darkest places to illumine suffering and to inspire hope. The Siberian stories, when not removed from the realm of what is, to what might be or what should be, are essentially grim records of actual people on whom fortune has seldom smiled. At times approximating to mere *reportage,* they do not allow much rein to the imagination. No doubt the author felt himself bound by the sentiment he expresses in his preface to the **Istoriya moyego sovremennika:** "There shall be nothing here which I have not encountered in real life, nothing I have not experienced, felt or seen." Such an attitude is of course a restrictive influence to the story-teller only so long as he is dealing with contemporary events. Should he wish to romanticise, he is perfectly at liberty to transfer his story to another world, where time and place are no longer relevant. Even Makar enjoys the privilege of dreaming.

Recourse to the dream is one means of giving latitude to the imagination of the prose-writer, troubled by a too conscientious urge to tell the truth. Korolenko made use of another means also—not what might be, but what has been in the remote historical past, what may have been at a time when personal observation and empirical evidence were not the author's prerogative. This brings us to a group of stories which are basically legends or fantasias on an historical theme. Chukovsky has drawn attention to Korolenko's gift of stylisation, of reproducing the essential features of a genre, whether it be a Ukrainian or Jewish legend, a Platonic dialogue, a Latin chronicle or an oriental fable. In such settings he can indulge his imagination without fear of the crafty workings of that treacherous faculty, inappropriate to the honest-to-goodness *bytopisatel'*—a fear he was prone to, as Gorodetsky has observed. It is interesting to see in what channels his unhampered imagination ran.

Korolenko had an essentially legalistic mind. He would rather capture by argument than surrender to impressions. He strove always to convince and used allegory to do so. He was usually neat and orderly, if a little long-winded. He loved the tidy progression of *vo pervykh, vo vtorykh.* **"Teni"** takes him back to classical Greece and owes something in construction to the Platonic dialogue. It is a plea for ceaseless mental enquiry, for the urge to follow the argument wheresoever it may lead. If the gods are unjust, they must be rejected. **"Neobkhodimost'"** is an Oriental fable in which two wise men, incarnating active volition and passive contemplation, come in search of truth to the temple of the god of necessity. Here the argument is directed against determinism; it is better to pretend to make our own decisions and accept responsibility for them, even though we cannot prove them to derive from our own free will, than to deny that the will is free and therefore make no decisions. A third version of the dialectical legend is the **"Skazaniye o Flore, Agrippe i Menakheme, syne Iegudy,"** which is Korolenko's contribution to the perennial problem of non-resistance to evil. The background is Judaea under Roman occupation; the main stylistic feature is the parable. The point at issue, namely whether to submit to the Roman yoke or to rise in rebellion against it, is treated as a sort of forensic exercise between a counsel for the prosecution and a counsel for the defence. Argument by analogy is crowned by a fanciful parable, and again we see the juxtaposition of the writer's imagination and the assertiveness of the publicist.

There is another type of story which also belongs to the legendary category, but in which the publicist element of the quasi-historical romance is relegated to the background. **"Les shumit"** is totally free from the sententious. The active intervention of the devil in human affairs and his eventual discomfiture make **"Sudny den'"** more than superficially reminiscent of Gogol''s ''Vechera na khutore bliz Dikan'ki.'' But it may be noted that even here Korolenko does not miss the opportunity of scoring a point in favour of his cherished cause of racial equality by portraying the traditional Jewish vice of usury as the common failing alike of Jew and Gentile. In all these legends we feel the presence of the warm-hearted, whimsical author of **"Noch' yu"** eavesdropping on the little children discussing how babies are made. When he temporarily abandoned the short story for the novelette, the result was inevitably a sentimental romance. The ''blind musician'' grows up in an atmosphere of family affection, learning to overcome his physical handicap and striving towards the light with manly determination and the encouragement of a woman's love. Such a situation, as is the case with nearly all Korolenko's stories, is essentially simple and potentially lachrymose. True they are seldom without an element of tragedy. But it is not an inner tragedy, a tragedy of the individual's own making or resulting from the innate sinfulness of man. It may be material impoverishment and its attendant miseries (**"V durnom obshchestve"**), or it may be a physical ailment such as deformity (**"Paradoks"**) or congenital blindness. Such is the curse of fate. But fate does not relentlessly destroy. There is no inevitability here. Fate is an antagonist for the individual to wrestle with and overcome. No human being, however grave his bodily defects, is ever devoid of some compensating faculty which at worst lies dormant and at best transforms his life. Although Pyotr is blind he has a heightened appreciation of sound, an abnormally sensitive musical gift. The dwarf is deformed but he acts on the belief, in the much-quoted phrase, that ''man is born for happiness as a bird for flight.'' The doubts and torments of the physically disabled are but palely reflected in their stories. Korolenko was no analyst of spiritual and emotional crises. Rather did he set off with an *a priori* contention—such, for example, as an inner striving towards the light inherited from a kind of group soul and operative in all human beings—and then proceed to describe the successive phases through which the individual passes. Consequently there is no drama, only narrative interest. It is perhaps an explanation of his popularity that when he treats of such transparent themes and concrete situations he enshrouds them in a nebulous haze which obscures the prosaic and lulls the senses of his readers who might otherwise demand more mental stimulation. ''Something,'' ''somehow,'' ''somewhere,'' ''it seemed,'' ''it was as if''—all these expressions are fundamental to his vocabulary. Lights flicker rather than shine. Objects flash by. Colours merge into one another. There is a goodly lexicon of light and sound, half-light and muffled noises, remote and imperfect sense associations. The frequent intrusion of the dream is in itself suggestive of the somnolent atmosphere created. The use of exclamatory dots slows down the tempo, provides pauses not for thought, but for wonder—opportunities for the mind to run free without concentrating on the immediate object. And so the tragedy is softened, and it is gradually revealed that Pyotr's blindness is a trivial thing. For after all, his lot is

in no way so hard as that of the blind beggars he meets, and indeed he can help them and derive inspiration from their courageous lives. Korolenko's longest novelette *Bez yazyka* is compounded of much the same ingredients as *Slepoy muzykant*. This time the physical handicap, dumbness, is only metaphorical, the speechlessness of a Russian peasant stranded in America, separated from friends, incapable of communication, not understanding and not being understood. It would indeed be difficult to agree with those Soviet critics who interpret the story as an actual or prophetic indictment of the soulless inhumanity of the American way of life. Korolenko may enjoy his sallies against Tammany Hall, the law courts, the press and particularly the hustle and intensity of life in New York. They provide him with material for what are often his most purely humorous narrative episodes. But the fact remains, he is more unhappy at the breakdown of human intercourse than embittered over material institutions. The temper is nostalgic, not polemical, and Matvey Lozinsky, simple warm-hearted giant that he is, yearns for his native land. The latent tragedy of the inability of human beings to understand each other never emerges through the thick layer of sentiment for hearth and home. From the character of the hard-working, clean-living, generous, unsophisticated Russian peasant we can learn something too of the author's personality.

The descriptive powers of Korolenko's talent and the lack of a profound analytical ability are most clearly evinced in the largely autobiographical *Istoriya moyego sovremennika*. In this work literary elements are almost entirely absent, and the ill-defined borderline between literature and *reportage* becomes increasingly more indeterminate as volume succeeds volume with the record of as much information as can be recollected about as great a number of people as possible. It is tempting to ask why Korolenko veered more and more away from imaginative fiction (grounded as it often was in actual experience) to journalism and non-fictional narrative, why his best short stories were virtually confined to the 1880's and why his exceptionally promising literary career never fully matured. It is not an uncommon phenomenon in Russian literature for poetic inspiration to be subordinated to civic responsibility. The theme of the poet and the citizen is an old one. We are reminded of Nekrasov's couplet: ''the fight kept down the poet in me; my songs kept down the fighter.'' Mayakovsky expresses the same thought when he speaks of ''stamping on the throat of his own song.'' There is no doubt that Korolenko with his abnormally sensitive conscience felt impelled to make a more direct contribution to society than was possible by creative literature, but that is not in itself a sufficient explanation. He had not the temperament of a great writer. He reached his full stature early in life and never grew. He was too dispassionate, too cautious, too even in quality. Like himself, his main characters are seldom tempted and never succumb. Again the question arises: Is the ''good man'' inherently unsuitable raw material for fiction? Dostoyevsky, when confiding to his niece that ''the main idea of *Idiot* was to portray the positively noble man,'' added that he feared for its outcome, since other writers who had essayed a similar task had succeeded only in making their hero ridiculous. The qualities of piety, unselfishness and the conscientious performance of duty, which in a public figure are invariably esteemed, are too easily regarded in a literary hero as priggish or pedestrian. As Korolenko's interests tended more and more towards contemporary social problems and the active struggle for justice, his attempts at creative literature were strongly influenced by the urge to plead a morally edifying and responsible cause. Under these circumstances his fiction seldom rose far above the level of polished journalism, while his journalism never lost its distinctive literary flavour. In the "autobiography" it is the early volumes which show the author to best advantage. Some of the brief character-sketches and pen-pictures of his schoolmasters, friends and casual acquaintances (the "actor-elocutionist" of **"Pervyye studencheskiye gody"** comes to mind) are vividly drawn and full of human interest. There is a spontaneous humour about his schoolboy anecdotes as there is a natural pathos about tales such as that of Antos the coachman (**"V derevne"**). We are given glimpses of some of the important issues of the day, the nationality problem, educational policy, the populist *(narodnik)* movement. Subsequently we have his unembellished account of his singularly unmerited victimisation at the hands of the authorities, an entertaining recollection of the lighter side of prison life and a regrettably deficient and unpolished version of administrative exile in Amga. Korolenko was too honest and too modest to excel in autobiography. His own person remains submerged. He does not draw attention to his individual problems or reveal his innermost thoughts. He is neither self-adulatory nor self-abasing. Nor is he given to touching up his memoirs. His *Kto ya?* ["who am I?"] is not, like Tolstoy's, an enquiry into the purpose of life but a question of nationality admitting of an answer. *Zachem?* ["why?"] is relevant, but *potom?* ["what comes after?"] is unimportant. For if we take care of the present, the future can safely be left to take care of itself. It is unfortunate that declining health and considerable physical suffering prevented him from doing justice to the latter sections of his work, for although it lacks the penetration of Tolstoy's autobiographical trilogy and the urbanity of Herzen's memoirs, it can nevertheless, in its early stages, be read with pleasure for its own sake and with profit as a source of period information at all times.

It may be appropriate here to mention an aspect of Korolenko's writing which some critics have rated especially highly in his contribution to Russian literature, namely the essay-memoirs of his greatest literary contemporaries, which recall impressions and record conversations illuminating his own nature no less than that of his subject. In the case of Chekhov boyish enthusiasm and exuberance are the first impressions, tempered later by melancholy and at times even a fatalistic acceptance that nothing can heal the sickness of the soul. In Tolstoy he admired above all his practical attitude and his quest of truth. "We educated people," he writes in the first of his two articles on his most venerable contemporary, "know a great deal, but very little of what we accept as the commonplace, elementary truth is realised in our lives." Tolstoy contrived both to give new vigour and originality to the presentation of universally recognised truths and also to narrow the gap between theory and practice. His very first words to Korolenko on the latter's return from Siberia, quoted in the same article, will bear repetition: "How lucky you are, you have suffered for your convictions! God does not grant me that. People are exiled because of me, while I am not troubled at all." Besides such snippets of conversation, felicitous judgements grace the pages of these essays. The slapdash Uspensky is likened to a builder admitting tenants to his house before the timber is cleared from the construction site. The veteran Chernyshevsky suggests the archaic figure of an 18th-century Pole on the macadamised pavements of Russian Warsaw. Korolenko liked to choose, when reminiscing over a fellow-writer, some phrase or *mot* of his which was simultaneously characteristic of his way of thought and aptly directed in itself. Thus Cherynshevsky, speaking of the post-*Confession* works of Tolstoy, confides to Korolenko that their author "blows his nose like a count." Or again, G. I. Uspensky is recalled as having in his curious manner of speak-

ing alluded to Dostoyevsky as piling into a doorway big enough for a pair of goloshes enough baseness and human suffering to fill four stone houses. Korolenko's literary judgements were not profound. He set Tolstoy head and shoulders above all rivals, but he did not care for Dostoyevsky. Nevertheless he can fill out for us the personalities of the authors he himself had known, and as they include Chekhov and Uspensky, Chernyshevsky and Tolstoy, the memoirs are both interesting and valuable. (pp. 452-60)

Korolenko made his greatest impact on Russian society as a journalist and moulder of public opinion. As a collaborator and eventual successor of N. K. Mikhaylovsky in the task of editing *Russkoye Bogatstvo,* his articles here and in the provincial press were of a consistently high standard of integrity and outspokenness. From his early protest against the abuse of disciplinary powers at the Petrine Academy in Moscow to his ultimate correspondence with Lunacharsky over post-revolutionary atrocities, never published in the Soviet Union and conveniently forgotten by Soviet critics, he was frequently in the public eye, and his fame spread far beyond the provinces where most of his work was done. (pp. 460-61)

In attempting to sum up Korolenko's contribution to Russian life, one may perhaps be at first inclined to think of the old debating rider—whether it is preferable to be the tail of a lion or the head of a mouse. But while it is true that Korolenko was infinitely more at home in the provinces than in the capital, to which his editorial colleagues on *Russkoye Bogatstvo* unsuccessfully sought to attract him, it would be quite unjust to regard his influence as merely provincial. His name and work were known throughout educated Russia. Content as he might temperamentally have been to belong to a small community where he could be consultant and adviser (and Gor'ky is not the only writer to acknowledge his debt to Korolenko's personal encouragement), setting a high moral standard and being able to make his presence felt in the lives of those about him, he was thrust by circumstances into the limelight, to speak vehemently and courageously on issues of national concern. Not that he was an outstanding writer or a profound thinker. But he could and did demonstrate the power for good of the individual personality divorced from party and creed, yet vigorously assertive and steadfastly purposeful. When he approached theoretical problems he tended to seek a compromise. As a literary ideal he envisaged a fusion of romanticism with realism stripped of its naturalistic excesses. He noted Carlyle's avowal and Tolstoy's denial of the importance of great men and believed that the new "synthesis" must reveal the significance of personality against the background of the importance of the masses. But when it was a question of action he never compromised, never surrendered his individuality. "I believe in individual people," wrote Chekhov; "I see salvation in individual personalities scattered here and there throughout Russia, whether they be intellectuals or peasants. It is in them that strength lies, though they are few in number. . . . The individual personalities of whom I speak play an unobtrusive role in society; they do not dominate, but their work leaves its mark." And Korolenko's work will leave its mark. (pp. 462-63)

R. F. Christian, "V. G. Korolenko (1853-1921): A Centennial Appreciation," in The Slavonic and East European Review, *Vol. XXXII, No. 79, June, 1954, pp. 449-63.*

CARL R. PROFFER (essay date 1969)

[*With his wife Ellendea Proffer, Carl Proffer was the founder of Ardis Publishers, the largest publishers of Russian literature out-*

side the Soviet Union. This venture has been responsible for the publication of works by dissident and exiled Russian authors who would otherwise have remained unknown. In addition, Proffer is recognized as an important critic and translator of modern Russian literature. In the following excerpt, he examines "Makar's Dream."]

Korolenko's best work is his autobiographical trilogy *The History of My Contemporary*. But the grandfatherly dispassion which makes his autobiography a delight evirates most of his fiction. . . . I am disinclined to make **"Makar's Dream"** an exception, but for some tastes there may be "mighty poetry" in the story, as D. S. Mirsky suggests [see excerpt dated 1949]. Originally, Makar's dream was a real dream—comparable to "The Dream of a Ridiculous Man" or the original version of Gogol's "The Nose." At the point where it now ends, Makar woke up, went out, and was met by the same series of hardships and torments he had always known. This would have weakened the poetry of the ending in favor of direct social comment. Even as it is, there is no doubt that the story belongs in the philanthropic tradition. Makar is one of the many "little men" of Russian literature. His name itself is symbolic—it is that of an unfortunate peasant in several proverbs. This Makar drives his calves measureless distances; all "acorns" and woes fall upon his head.

The populist literature of the 1880s and 1890s was often burdened with ethnography. The local color of the romantics degenerated into dull *ocherki* (sketches) describing the customs and surrounds of various social types from the lower classes. Korolenko uses his ethnographic detail much more artistically than most of these writers. The presentation of Makar's character governs the use of such material; only that which is essential for understanding Makar is introduced. As Korolenko discovered when he was a political exile to Siberia, the naïve mixture of Christianity and pagan beliefs was one of the amusing aspects of Yakut culture. For example, like a Siberian, Toyon lives in a hut with a fire burning all the time. And we at once laugh at and pity Makar when he tries to use simple Yakut trickery on Toyon—not yet realizing you can't con God. Makar's naïve view of the world at times affects the narration itself, as when Korolenko writes: "Everyone felt sorry for kind Father Ivan; but since all that was left of him were his legs, no doctor in the world could cure him." But in the end Makar's naïveté and meek acceptance of hardship fall away. Korolenko has not presented a Christian moral. Makar is not saved by humility; it is only when he gets angry that injustice is adverted. God is not an altogether sympathetic character, and even his son (recall it is a "Christmas story") is somewhat ineffectual.

Korolenko's style is in the tradition of Turgenev. The descriptions of the taiga are written in lyrical prose marked by "poetic" inversions and frequent use of personification. For example: "Bright, kind stars peeped through the thick branches and seemed to be saying: 'There, you see, a poor man has died.'" Nature comes alive, especially when Makar is drunk and delirious. In the old Karamzinian manner, the emotional involvement of the narrator is shown by rhetorical questions or exclamations such as: "Heavy is the work of a man from Chalgan!" At the end of chapter five, the series of exclamatory single-sentence paragraphs, with the incantatory repetition of "and" (polysyndeton), changes the tone from lyric to triumphant. This section and the ending are the most heavily rhetorical passages in the story. Perhaps it is just twentieth-century criticism that make such writing seem overly sentimental, but even Chekhov said, "The trouble with Korolenko is that he

will never write better unless he deceives his wife. He is too noble." (pp. 32-4)

Carl R. Proffer, "Practical Criticism for Students," in From Karamzin to Bunin: An Anthology of Russian Short Stories, *edited and translated by Carl R. Proffer, Indiana University Press, 1969, pp. 1-52.*

LAUREN G. LEIGHTON   (essay date 1971)

[*In the following excerpt, Leighton discusses theme and technique in Korolenko's stories about Siberia.*]

At a time when Russian literature was noted for its pessimistic naturalism, Vladimir Korolenko . . . was conspicuous as an optimistic writer whose warmth and humour were greatly appreciated by Russian readers of the late 19th century. He had a firm faith in the goodness of men, and his essential humanity is further emphasised by the fact that he began his literary career while suffering administrative exile in Siberia. "Try to see things from a more expressive point of view," he advised young Maksim Gor'ky in 1895, "much of your work is oversimplified. Life is dreary, but it has been even more dreary before, and if it is to become brighter with time, then, of course, it will not become so through despondency and misanthropy, but through active efforts to do what can be done with it as it is." Between 1880 and 1915 Korolenko wrote a cycle of sixteen stories of Siberia which were remarkable for their precise balance between social message and literary achievement. As the art of short story writing was greatly admired in Korolenko's time (Chekhov once remarked, "this is my favourite contemporary writer") the Siberian cycle is worthy of attention both as an illustration of a writer's development of this skill and as the continuation of a traditional Russian literary theme. (p. 200)

Chekhov greatly admired Korolenko's talent and made some perceptive comments about his friend's craftsmanship. "His colours are light and lively," he remarked about the Siberian tales in 1888, "his language is irreproachable, even if in places it is marred, and his images are well-devised." And in another letter of the same year to the author himself, he noted: "Your **'Sokolinets'** seems to me the most salient literary work of recent times. It is written like an excellent musical composition, in accordance with all the principles revealed to an author by his instinct" [see excerpt dated 1888]. What Chekhov admired particularly about Korolenko's stories was their structural conformity with techniques of composition, intuitively applied, and this assessment is born out by close analysis. For each story of the Siberian cycle is an elegant, polished, graceful and harmonious composition. Yet, in spite of the careful structure of the stories, the use of such devices as contrast and parallel, the creation of mood and setting, the fusion of contrasting styles and modes of narration, and the use of language in characterisation is instinctive.

The stories of the Siberian cycle are not identical in structure, but it is evident that Korolenko preferred the frame story, and he used the technique of *skaz*—particularised narration—in close conjunction with this form. A good example of this is the story mentioned by Chekhov, **"Sokolinets."** The narrator is a perceptive member of the intelligentsia, a stylised Korolenko-exile. Alone in his hut in the taiga, he is visited by a strange and desperate young man, a neighbouring settler. During the long winter night the guest tells a story of his escape from a penal colony on Sakhalin Island. It is the story of harsh imprisonment, of the escape of twelve convicts, the violent

Portrait of the original Makar. The handwritten notes are by Korolenko.

murder of a soldier, wanderings through Siberia, and finally the secondary narrator's settlement in the lonely taiga. Told in a dignified peasant vernacular sprinkled with prison and tramp slang, the story is framed by the main narrator's conclusion, the story's resolution with the desperate visitor's return to the violent, but free life of a tramp. Thus, in this simple frame structure there is told a "brodyazh'ya epopeya, poeziya vol'noy volyushki," the story of a man so haunted by freedom that he chooses the deprivation of tramp life to the comparative comfort of settlement.

"**Sokolinets**" is especially attractive for the way in which Korolenko establishes mood. The story opens with the main narrator lying in his hut sunk in apathy. With that instinct admired by Chekhov, Korolenko centres not on the narrator's frame of mind, but on the dreary, foreboding Siberian twilight. The fire is unlit, there is "silence and gloom," the brief winter day expires in the cold fog, light retreats through the windows until the gloom begins creeping from the corners of the hut, the walls seem to lean in menacingly from above. This mood is developed for fully two pages, with descriptions of fog and frost in the fading twilight, and is then contrasted suddenly with a new, cheery setting appropriate to the arrival of a guest. The fire is lit, the hut fills with its chatter and crackling, "something bright, lively, quick and restlessly garrulous burst into the hut," the corners and crannies light up, and the burning wood cracks forth like pistol shots. The contrast of mood and setting is both startling and natural, and the way is prepared for the lusty sub-story.

A frame story which employs *skaz* to perfection is "**Chudnaya**," the first story of the cycle and the first of Korolenko's

literary efforts. Like "**Sokolinets,**" this story is introduced by the stylised Korolenko, this time as he journeys to Siberia in the company of a guard, the simple and kindly peasant Gavrilov. The story itself—Gavrilov's account of a disillusioned and dying young woman, obviously a populist—is told and resolved by Gavrilov, and his conclusion is elaborated upon by the main narrator to complete the frame and restate the significance of the story in more educated terms. More important than the structure of the work, however, is the use of *skaz* narration, the establishment, from the onset, of Gavrilov's speech mannerisms. (pp. 201-02)

Particularised speech is used by still another secondary narrator, the hero of "**Ubivets**" who narrates one of the story's several short chapters. (p. 203)

"**Ubivets**" also shows that Korolenko was not exclusively dependent on the frame story. Mikhaylov is a coach driver who, having become involved with a band of robbers, redeems himself by killing its leader in defence of a woman and her children. Thanks to the stupidity of the Tsarist bureaucracy, however, Killer cannot leave the province until his trial, and he must earn his living by driving a coach through the taiga inhabited by the revenge-seeking robbers. Through the use of *skaz* Mikhaylov is permitted to tell one part of his story, his involvement with the robbers and his murder of their leader, but the events leading to his own murder are narrated by the stylised Korolenko. The result is a series of chronologically ordered chapters to develop the main story and, incidentally, to depict the corrupt relationship between Siberian officials and local criminals, with a single flashback to make the main narrative more meaningful. Through this adroit use of *skaz* in secondary narration, the reader becomes more intimately familiar with the chief hero than would otherwise be possible. Given the basic theme of cumbersome and corrupt Tsarist justice—Mikhaylov asks only to be condemned or acquitted of the murder, but the band's justice is swifter than the government's—such a familiarity with Mikhaylov dramatises the theme more effectively. Moreover, it involves the reader in the desperation of a brave man determined to go his own way, using only his reputation as a ''killer'' to keep his foes at bay.

''Son Makara'' is not only the best known of Korolenko's stories, but is structurally unique within the Siberian cycle. The story is told entirely by the stylised Korolenko, but it is told in two parts which are contrasted in form and integrated by structural parallels. The first part, in conventional story form, tells of the brutal life and death of Makar, a descendant of Russian peasants who has become as primitive as his Yakut neighbours. The second part is an allegory of Makar's journey to the judgment of Toyon, a mythical god-figure. Just as the story is dependent on passages filled with concrete nature imagery, the allegory is built on a fusion of folkloristic and pseudo-Christian mythology. The setting of the story in the snow-filled taiga—''silent and full of mystery''—is paralleled by the setting of the allegory in a vast snow-covered plain over which ''the moon, exactly like the bottom of a huge gold barrel, shone like the sun, illuminating the plain from edge to edge.'' Taken together, the two parts dramatise the brutal harshness of life in the wilderness and the optimistic promise of consolation after death.

The allegorical form of **''Son Makara''** is distinct from the story form, yet there are structural parallels which reveal the precision with which Korolenko composed his works. The first part is structured initially on a consideration of Makar's hard life and then of his sinful action, the plundering of another man's traps. This is followed by him losing his way in the woods and wandering through the bitter cold to his death. The structure of the allegory parallels that of the story in reverse. It begins with Makar's awakening after death, continues with the journey across the plain to judgment, and ends with the judgment and Makar's salvation. The entire work is thus structured on a full circle through two different hemispheres. The structure is lent further sophistication by the erasure in the story of the lines separating dream and reality, life and death. Only subjectively, unconsciously, does the reader realise that both the death in the lonely woods and the allegory are two parts of a single dream. The true line of reality is thus drawn not between story and allegory, but between the description of Makar's life and the point where he falls asleep and dreams that he awakens to begin the quest into the woods for stolen furs.

''Son Makara'' lacks *skaz*, but the use of particularised language is an essential ingredient. The narration is conducted by the stylised Korolenko, but not only does he tell the story from Makar's point of view, he does so with Makar's own speech mannerisms and, at the same time, uses this speech level to develop Makar's character. The result is both a deeply sympathetic treatment by the narrator of the main hero and a feeling on the part of the reader that he is listening to Makar himself. Thus, in describing Makar's life, the narrator observes: ''Whenever he was drunk, he could cry. 'What a life we have,' he would say, 'O Lord!' Besides this, he would sometimes say he would like to cast it all aside and go away to the 'mountain.' There he would neither till nor sow, would not chop and haul wood, would not even grind wheat on the hand

mill. He would only be saved.'' With perfect tact Korolenko pictures Makar's heaven in exactly the same terms—tilling, sowing, chopping, hauling, grinding—that Makar would use. Makar's simple interpretation of the Sermon on the Mount is conveyed from his own naive and primitive point of view.

It is also in this story that Korolenko achieved the peak of his power of lyric expression, and this is seen clearly in his treatment of Makar's dream-death. Again, as if by instinct, Korolenko focuses not so much on Makar himself as on the lonely taiga. As Makar wanders aimlessly through the bitter night, he slowly freezes to death. It becomes darker, and the moon disappears, the taiga falls silent, the night offers neither illumination, nor hope. ''Makar became bitter in his heart . . . the frost grew more bitter . . . the last echoes of the bell drifted to him from the distant settlement . . . the sound of the bell expired . . . and Makar died.'' What started as a bright moonlit night becomes darker, more alive, more hostile, and then vanishes together with Makar's consciousness.

The use of allegory distinguishes **''Son Makara''** sharply from the other stories of the cycle, and does much to enhance its individuality. Korolenko was very much aware of V. M. Garshin's cultivation of the allegory, and in a ''Literary Portrait'' of Garshin, written in 1888, he devoted particular attention to his predecessor's *Attalea princeps,* an allegory of a hothouse palm which seeks its freedom by growing through the glass roof of its comfortable prison. What was important about the work to Korolenko was that ''Garshin does not say, 'such is the lot of all that is beautiful on this earth, such are the inescapably eternal laws which punish all strivings toward light and freedom.' He says merely, 'this is the way it is' with beautiful exotic plants in harsh conditions.'' There is little in common between Garshin's allegory and **''Son Makara,''** of course, but Korolenko's evaluation does indicate a basic feature of his own approach to the allegory, and in fact all of his approach to literature. Whatever Korolenko's concern for social message, he was above all a writer, and he did not preach didactically. His allegory of Makar's journey to Toyon is a statement of ''this is the way it is'' in the view of a primitive person. It is a sympathetic story told in the fantasy of both dream-world and folkloristic-Christian myth. The reader's sympathy, even pity, for Makar is aroused not by direct pleas, but by Korolenko's own sincere sympathy for his hero and by his depiction of the intimate inner-being of one human person. (pp. 204-06)

Undoubtedly the shortest story in Russian literature is Korolenko's allegory **''Ogon'ki.''** Defined as ''a poem in prose,'' the work is brief and simple. The familiar narrator, while travelling by night in a rowing boat down a Siberian river, sees lights which seem to be close but turn out to be far away— ''but nevertheless . . . nevertheless, ahead there are lights!'' G. A Byaly, who has done extensive work on the life and works of Korolenko, has gone so far as to assert that **''Ogon'ki''** ''provides the key to an understanding of the entire Siberian cycle—life flows along between gloomy banks, but nevertheless . . . nevertheless, ahead there are lights.'' Russia's revolutionary youth received the work as nothing less than a manifesto, and given Korolenko's known optimism and social conscience, it was interpreted as an affirmation that Russia and the world were on the verge of revolution and social happiness. Korolenko's optimism was not so detached from reality, however, and he interpreted the allegory quite differently. ''In the essay **''Ogon'ki''** I did not mean to say that after an arduous transition there would come about a final calm and general happiness,'' he wrote in a letter of 1912. ''No—up there ahead begins a new stage. Life consists of constant striving, achievement and new striving. . . . In my view, humanity has already seen many 'beacons,' reached them and striven on.'' Beyond the work's social optimism and its impact on the young generation of the time lies the story's literary value, for in both its charm of idea and beauty of tone it amounts to a tiny vignette, a prose poem which justifies the effort of all those Russians who have since added it to the repertoire of their memory.

Closely linked to Korolenko's adept use of different levels of language in the structure and characterisation of his stories is his effective and unusual fusion of two apparently irreconcilable styles. His stories of Siberia stand as a synthesis of the lyric expression of Turgenev's *Zapiski okhotnika* and the documentary exposition of Dostoyevsky's *Zapiski iz myortvogo doma*. Many of the stories are thus characterised by a mixture of journalistic passages and lyrical descriptions. The achievement of a unity of exposition on the basis of such contrasting styles is no mean feat, and it is relevant to note here that Korolenko sub-titled many of the stories ''essays'' *(ocherki)* to signify his dual, literary-journalistic, motivation in writing the Siberian cycle.

Lyrical descriptions seem to serve three purposes in the stories of Siberia. First, they cement the structure, making what would otherwise be simple essays into short stories with a fictional appeal. Second, they establish mood and setting. And third, as has already been demonstrated by the treatment of Makar's dream death, they dramatise the human situation, emphasising the basic theme of human existence amidst the most terrifying physical deprivations.

It is evident, for example, that the stories share a single mood. In contrast with the charming and placid steppe setting of Turgenev's *Zapiski okhotnika*, the settings of Korolenko's stories are imbued with a mood of gloom which is in keeping with the ominous natural milieu of the Siberian forests. One illustration of this is in the descriptions of the black night through which Killer Mikhaylov of **''Ubivets''** journeys to his eventual death. The night has thickened into ''an utterly dark gloom'' of autumn, ''the sky is completely covered with heavy clouds,'' it is impossible to distinguish forms even a few feet away. ''It was drizzling lightly, with a gentle sound in the trees . . . the rain fell in the dense taiga with a rustle and a mysterious murmur.'' Much of Korolenko's lyrical power lies in such intuitive use of contrasts. A striking example of this is in the story part of **''Son Makara.''** Korolenko apparently felt the need of a contrast to his descriptions of the snow-filled night and the silent solitude of the taiga, and he found it in a description of a Tartar inn filled with the drunken inhabitants of the settlement. ''Within the close hut it was stifling. The acrid smoke of makhorka hung in a single cloud, drawn sluggishly toward the hearth fire.'' The room is filled with drunken men whose ''faces were sweaty and red.'' In the corner sits a drunken Yakut, swaying back and forth on a pile of straw: ''He dragged from his throat savage, grating sounds, repeating in sing-song that tomorrow is a big holiday, but today he is drunk.'' Here the hazy stifling atmosphere contrasts—and thus dramatises—the stark black and white colouring of the taiga setting, yet, at the same time, its depressing mood is contrary to the clear purity of the winter night outside. Curiously, Korolenko originally intended to dramatise the contrast between the dreary monotony of Siberia and the quick pace of life in Petersburg. Having once abandoned this theme, however, he dis-

carded an opening description of the bustling capital and replaced it with this more modest substitute.

Although there is an obvious difference between Korolenko's Siberia and Turgenev's steppes, there is a perceptibly Turgenevian quality to Korolenko's lyrical nature passages. Byaly is well justified in the statement that Korolenko considered himself ''a fanatic devote of Turgenev.'' The Siberian stories are thus filled with descriptions of the ''angry . . . unusually swift and sullen'' Lena with its ''looming cliffs, abysses, gorges.'' A ''chill dampness'' reigns over the river and ''there is an almost uninterrupted twilight.'' When the frost strikes, the mountainous banks ''become lighter, more ethereal'' and they ''slip away into the vague, luminous distance, scintillating, almost illusory.'' The last rays of *Posledniy luch* are described in a lyrical passage reminiscent of the sunrise in Turgenev's *Bezhin lug*: ''Several brilliant golden rays spluttered wildly in the depths of the cleft between the two mountains, piercing an aperture in the dense wall of the woods. Fiery sparks spewed down in wisps, into the dark deeps and ravines, tearing out of the chill blue dusk now a tree, now the crest of a schistous crag, now the tiny mountain meadow.''

The influence of Turgenev's *Zapiski okhotnika* is detectable not only in the lyrical descriptions, however, but also in narrative techniques. This is not true of mode of narration at all times, since Korolenko uses diverse modes where Turgenev used one narrator with one point of view. But it is true in the general use of a stylised author-narrator, and there are many similarities between the two narrators. Both narrators are perceptive members of the intelligentsia, both are detached, almost clinical observers of predominantly human situations, both have a similar sense of humour, both are keenly conscious of their natural milieu, both convey distinct personalities without intruding rudely on the action being narrated, both have the artistic good sense not to force their point of view on their characters, and both, without losing their objectivity, betray deep sympathy for their characters. The stylised Korolenko differs from the stylised Turgenev-hunter in the absence of the tone of superiority in narration. Moreover, whereas the stylised Turgenev's treatment of the *narod* is somewhat idealised, with only a few glimpses of stark brutality among his peasants, the stylised Korolenko makes an effort to ''de-idealise'' the *narod*, showing their cruelty with an almost brutal naturalism. This is the difference between Korolenko's description of the Tartar tavern in **''Son Makara''** and Turgenev's earlier description of the drunken bout in the inn of *Pevtsy*. Where Turgenev ascribes much of the brutality to the serf-owner of *Zapiski okhotnika*, Korolenko does not hesitate to reveal the savage, as well as the kind, features of his Siberian people. In **''Moroz''** the local people laugh at the sight of a stranger freezing to death; in **''Ubivets''** a coachman describes the torture of a thief in detail; in **''Sokolinets''** the desperate tramp describes the murder of a Russian soldier by the convicts. Quite obviously, the personalities of the two narrators are different, and each has a different perception of reality.

Korolenko learned from Dostoyevsky the value of straightforward documentation of facts. This is evident in most of the Siberian stories, but it is an overwhelming feature of the composition of **''Yashka.''** The story deals with the magnificent persistence of a possessed sectarian who, locked in a cell, completely isolated from other human beings, is determined to be recognised as an individual. Tied to this basic theme of human endurance is the narrator's careful documentation of prison life, and detailed descriptions of the physical milieu of the prison itself. The empty corridors, the high windows, the small square court-yard, the cell-chambers, the blackened doors, and the grey dirty wall, have none of that lyrical expressiveness of Turgenev. Instead, there is the emotionless recital of bare facts so characteristic of Dostoyevsky in *Zapiski iz myortvogo doma*. The other stories are also filled with documentary descriptions. In "**Moroz**" is a sober and factual description of the incredibly bitter Siberian frost. In the same story a *skyokla*, or community meeting, is described, and in "**Feodaly a rezidentsiya**," an administrative office usually found at the junction of river and road, is described in the full aura of bureaucracy. Much documentary attention is paid to the Siberian scene, and it is possible to learn about the customs and caste system of coachmen in both "**At-Davan**" and "**Gosudarevy-yamshchiki**," of which the latter is based entirely on exposition. In contrast to the many lyrical descriptions of staging posts in the stories there is a straightforward documentary account in "**Cherkes.**"

When Korolenko's methods of characterisation are considered, a curious similarity to Dostoyevsky's structural methods becomes apparent. Whether or not Korolenko was aware of the polyphonic composition of Dostoyevsky's novels—the conflicts between characters embodying irreconcilable metaphysical ideas—certain of the Siberian stories are built on diaphonic debates between conflicting social types. Korolenko created or developed many social types—the convict, the sectarian, the desperate man *(otchayannyy)*, the populist, the tramp, the coachdriver—and they are in large part the *raison d'être* of the cycle. They are not always in conflict because of the way in which the stylised Korolenko always establishes a rapport with his secondary narrators. But diaphonic debates are crucial to the structure of many of the stories and the composition of some is based entirely on this duality of characterisation.

The story "**Yashka**," for example, is built on the conflict between Yashka and the prison bureaucracy, which attempts to isolate him, and prevent him from disrupting the *status quo*. The means by which he persists in recognition of his dignity as a human being is to bang constantly on the door with his feet, thus irritating the guards and encouraging his fellow prisoners. Even though his feet swell from the constant banging, and he knows he will eventually be taken off to a lunatic asylum, where his legs will be broken, he persists in his magnificent struggle for recognition. In contrast to and in conflict with Yashka is Mikeich, the prison guard who represents the pettiness of the prison bureaucracy, draws clear lines of obligation and privilege between his "social position" as a caretaker and the social position of his charges. In his petty beliefs and cheap behaviour, he is the antithesis to the fanatic sectarian. (pp. 207-11)

A story whose characterisations and structure are dependent on the diaphonic method is "**Chudnaya**." As has been stated, Gavrilov's narrative deals with his relationship with a disillusioned young woman of the Populist movement, a dying young girl appropriately named Morozova. One Korolenko scholar, L. S. Kulik, has pointed out that "in this story Korolenko put two worlds into conflict, the world of the strange young woman continually amazes and attracts Gavrilov." This attraction is demonstrated by the simple peasant-soldier's naive first impression of his charge. He is impressed that she carries books, and the absence of any other belongings leads him to conclude that her parents are not wealthy. She seems like a child to him, and her pale complexion and red cheeks arouse his pity. The irony of "**Chudnaya**" is that the roles of *narod*

and intelligentsia are reversed by Gavrilov's pity for the girl, and all of his attempts to comfort her—to "go to the intelligentsia," so to speak—are rudely and resentfully rejected. No matter how hard Gavrilov attempts to console her, Morozova rebuffs him bitterly. She dies without realising that her former ideals were made a reality by this simple peasant who does not even understand her ideological debates with another Populist.

Beneath this social plane lies that concern for individuality that raises Korolenko above the level of a mere ideologist. Although Gavrilov does not understand Morozova as a social being or as an intellect, and he ultimately fails to communicate with her, he bridges the gap between them with his own sympathy for, and thus his intuitive understanding of her. She dies without consolation, but the experience transforms him, and he is haunted by his memory of that pitiful figure of the "strange woman."

The characterisation of the desperate man and the tramp, who are usually one and the same person in the writings of Korolenko, is a prominent feature of the stories of Siberia. The type was of intense concern to the writers of Korolenko's time, and his interpretation of the character is relevant to the similar types created by Chekhov and Gor'ky. (pp. 211-12)

[Korolenko's] stories of Siberia reveal an emphatic attitude on the author's part toward freedom and its relationship with property. To Korolenko the denial of property is always an act of desperation. Man is great, he seems to say, because he loves freedom so much that he will even surrender property. But the pursuit of freedom at the expense of property is always a cruel and violent action, and thus his tramps are always desperate men. The hero of "**Sokolinets**," for example, has long since settled down to a productive and comparatively secure life as a settler, but he is haunted by his past freedom and becomes increasingly desperate. Both his glory and his doom are bound up with his final decision to return to the life of a tramp. In "**Cherkes**" the lines of conflict are clearly drawn between Chepurnikov and the Circassian because the latter has possession of the gold, and could not care less, while the gendarme is petty because he counts copecks and covets gold. In "**Gosudarevy yamshchiki**" a chief character, Ostrovsky, burns down his home and property after the death of his wife and children in the cruel wilderness. So terrifying is this act to the neighbouring Yakuts that he is able to bully them and take revenge on them for their indifference to his family's survival. It is clear throughout the Siberian cycle that Korolenko's sympathies lie with the desperate and homeless and that he has contempt for the acquisitive, the smug and the propertied characters. But the act of seizing freedom is always an act of desperation, and it almost inevitably leads to deprivation, even self-destruction. Freedom, in Korolenko's terms, is a quality which costs human beings a terrifying price.

And this is the final and most fundamental feature of Korolenko's stories of Siberia. For the most distinctive and enduring feature of his talent is the subordination of all other techniques to characterisation. In structure, in mode of narration and point of view, in mood and tone, in fusion of styles and use of varying speech levels, and in means of expression, the stories deal first and always with human beings. All of Korolenko's compositional techniques are aimed at the dramatisation of human dilemmas, personal tragedies. The brave determination of Yashka, the pitiful figure of the strange girl, the bitter life of Makar, the impractical character of Ignatovich, the senseless death of Killer Mikhaylov, the desperate character of the Circassian—these are the fundamentals which determine the composition of the stories of Siberia. With that curious combination of reasoned composition and instinctive talent, Korolenko held out a hope and promise, a realistic optimism, which few other writers detected in the conditions of the time. (pp. 212-13)

> Lauren G. Leighton, *"Korolenko's Stories of Siberia," in* The Slavonic and East European Review, *Vol. XLIX, No. 115, April, 1971, pp. 200-13.*

NEIL PARSONS (essay date 1972)

[*Parsons is the English translator of Korolenko's autobiographical* History of My Contemporary. *In the following excerpt from an introduction to that work, he praises the autobiography as a historical document and a work of literature.*]

Korolenko's works—stories, novelettes, essays, articles, *The History of My Contemporary*—present a broad and detailed picture of Russia during his lifetime. He was always a keen observer of his environment, and his best fiction is based upon autobiographical material, many stories having obvious echoes in the pages of *The History.* Thus, for example, the episode of the doll in Chapter I of this book served as the dramatic climax for the story **"In Bad Company"** The direct dependence of his Siberian stories—the best stories he wrote—on his experiences and impressions in exile is particularly obvious.

Korolenko was a convinced advocate of the social purpose of literature. "Just as a man's legs carry him, let us suppose, from the cold and darkness towards habitation and light, so the word, art, literature help humanity in its progression from the past to the future." He continually reminded young writers of their duty not only to portray life, but to portray it in its most characteristic guise, "condemning or blessing."

Given the nature of the man and the times in which he lived, it was inevitable that he should turn increasingly away from imaginative literature to journalism and non-fictional writing. "Such a diversification may be right or wrong, but I never conceived of my literary work in any other way. It was second nature with me, and I could not do otherwise." *The History,* which Korolenko came to regard as his "most important task" and on which he laboured intermittently over a period of more than seventeen years, is a monumental work which crowns his career as a writer. It is at one and the same time a valuable historical document and a work of outstanding literary merit. (pp. viii-ix)

The title of the work is somewhat curious, and stems from the fact that Korolenko did not regard the work as a simple autobiography. "These notes," he wrote in the Preface to Volume I of the work,

> are not a biography, because I have not been particularly concerned about full biographical information; they are not a confession, because I do not believe either in the possibility or the usefulness of a public confession; they are not a portrait, because it is difficult to draw one's own portrait with any guarantee as to its likeness. . . . Here there will be nothing that I did not encounter in reality, nothing that I did not undergo, feel, or see. Yet I repeat: I am not trying to paint my own portrait. Here the reader will find only features from the history of "my contemporary," a man better known to me than all other people of my time.

First page of the manuscript of History of My Contemporary.

In a draft-version of this same Preface he had written that, while all the facts, impressions, thoughts and feelings set out in the work were facts of *his* life, were *his* thoughts, impressions and feelings, he had nevertheless only included those he considered bore some relation to things of general interest. In other words, the autobiographical material had been sieved, use being made only of what was judged to be significant. In this Korolenko was helped, as he realized, by the fact that he was separated from what he was describing by several decades. Enough time had elapsed for things to be seen in a truer and wider perspective. Unimportant things had had time to fade away. (p. ix)

The History covers virtually the whole of the reign of Alexander II—a reign that began with great expectations and ended with the Tsar's assassination at the hands of revolutionaries. In Volume I . . . Korolenko shows the impact of some of the great events of the first half of the reign on provincial life. He writes at length of his recollections as a child of the Emancipation of the Serfs, of the ill-starred Polish Revolt of 1863. He also shows how his acceptance as a child of established ways of life, of the existing order, was replaced by a gradual critical awareness, which ultimately developed into a bitter consciousness of social injustice. His pictures of school-life in Russia in the 1860s are unique in Russian literature. Some are highly amusing (in **"The Yellow-Red Parrot"** we are presented with an unforgettable portrait-gallery of his teachers), but there is always an undertone of seriousness, for these chapters also reveal the gradual stifling of all independence and initiative in education. Korolenko's early youth coincided with the emergence of Populism—the first revolutionary socialist movement in Russia. Volume II opens in 1871 with his first journey to Petersburg as a student. During the next few years (in Petersburg, then in the Petrovsky Academy just outside Moscow) he becomes caught in the ferment of Russian student-youth. His pictures of student life at this period are, again, very detailed and very finely drawn. (p. x)

The History is a many-sided work. As well as chapters devoted to important events, or to school-, student-, and prison-life, there are others which deal with such topics as his brother's short-lived career as a provincial correspondent, his own experiences as a proof-reader in Petersburg, or colourful individuals he met. These chapters are pervaded by a gentle, indulgent, often wistful humour. The work contains a wealth of fascinating portraits, episodes, and anecdotes which are of great human interest, and offer a view behind the pages of history, a view of what life was really like in Russia in the reign of the Tsar-Liberator.

The work possesses, finally, one remarkable, underlying quality: Korolenko presents his reader with a constantly changing view of life. He was able to evoke with consummate skill the world of a child, a boy, a youth, and a man, and it is this artistic gift which makes *The History* much more than memoirs. It is literature, and worthy to stand with the autobiographical trilogies of Tolstoy and Gorky. (pp. xi-xii)

> *Neil Parsons, in an introduction to* The History of My Contemporary *by V. G. Korolenko, edited and translated by Neil Parsons, Oxford University Press, London, 1972, pp. vii-xii.*

ADDITIONAL BIBLIOGRAPHY

Babenko, Victoria. "Nature Descriptions and Their Function in Korolenko's Stories." *Canadian Slavonic Papers* XVI, No. 3 (Autumn 1974): 424-35.
  Demonstrates that the literary merit of Korolenko's short stories outweighs their value as journalism or ethnography.

Christian, R. F. Introduction to *Korolenko's Siberia*, by Vladimir Korolenko, pp. 3-27. Liverpool, England: Liverpool at the University Press, 1954.
  Recounts Korolenko's years in exile.

Good, Jane E. "'I'd Rather Live in Siberia': V. G. Korolenko's Critique of America, 1893." *The Historian* XLIV, No. 2 (February 1982): 190-206.
  Maintains that Korolenko's trip to the United States "forced him to confront what could happen when democracy was abused," and that in his subsequent writings on America he sought to warn Russia of the dangers of hypocrisy, materialism, racism, and commercialism.

Gorky, Maxim. "Vladimir Korolenko and His Times" and "Vladimir Korolenko." In his *Literary Portraits*, pp. 169-219, 220-56. Moscow: Foreign Languages Publishing House, n.d.
  Reminiscences of Korolenko and of the years between 1886 and 1896.

Kolb-Seletski, Natalia M. "Elements of Light in the Fiction of Korolenko." *Slavic and East European Journal* 16, No. 2 (Summer 1972): 173-83.
  Analyzes Korolenko's symbolic use of light and darkness, maintaining that his works "reveal what seems to have been an almost innate drive towards light as reflected in his constant tendency to use words and phenomena suggesting light or its absence."

Lavrin, Janko. "The Chekov Period." In his *An Introduction to the Russian Novel*, pp. 135-45. New York: McGraw-Hill Book Co., 1947.
  Calls Korolenko "one of the most genially humane Russian authors," maintaining that "his mellowness may verge now and then on sentimentality, from which he is saved by his humor, his common sense, and most of all by his personality—simple and lucid as the style of his prose." Lavrin adds that "whatever theme he chooses, he invariably imbues it with that human warmth which compensates for a certain lack of creative verve in his works."

Moser, Charles A. "Korolenko and America." *The Russian Review* 28, No. 3 (July 1969): 303-14.
  Discusses Korolenko's visit to the United States, the writings derived from this experience, and the author's largely negative assessment of American social and political conditions.

O'Toole, L. Michael. "Fable." In his *Structure, Style, and Interpretation in the Russian Short Story*, pp. 84-112. New Haven, Conn.: Yale University Press, 1982.
  Analyzes technical aspects of "Makar's Dream" and demonstrates their importance to the story's thematic development.

Shub, David. "Lenin and Vladimir Korolenko." *The Russian Review* 25, No. 1 (January 1966): 46-53.
  Examines Korolenko's critical view of the socialist regime in Russia and notes V. I. Lenin's attempt to reconcile Korolenko to Soviet rule.

Slonim, Marc. "The Modernist Movement." In his *Modern Russian Literature*, pp. 79-102. New York: Oxford University Press, 1953.
  Brief survey of Korolenko's career which maintains that while he "was both an excellent narrator and an expert at drawing northern landscapes in the suffused manner of Turgenev," it was his "benign attitude toward mankind, his warm humor, and his faith in a better future that won him thousands of grateful readers."

Eugene (Jacob) Lee-Hamilton

1845-1907

English poet and dramatist.

Lee-Hamilton is best known for his emotionally penetrating poems about physical and mental suffering. Debilitated by paralysis for twenty years, he displayed a proclivity for the macabre in his works and conveyed the physical and emotional pain of the invalid with a dramatic power born of first-hand experience. In addition to his sharp pictorial delineation of a tortured mind and body, Lee-Hamilton is noted for his innovative development of the sonnet sequence as a form of dramatic monologue.

Born in London, Lee-Hamilton was still an infant when his father died; his mother later married Henry Paget, an English engineer whom Lee-Hamilton came to despise. Mrs. Lee-Hamilton believed that exposure to diversified cultures would provide her children with a broad education, and so she tutored them during travels in Germany and France. At nineteen, Lee-Hamilton went to Oxford University on a scholarship, majoring in modern languages and literature. Although he did not receive a degree, in 1869 he entered the British diplomatic service, where his proficiency in French was instrumental in his appointment as assistant to the British ambassador in Paris, a post that took on great significance from 1870 to 1871, the period of the Franco-Prussian war. When he began experiencing health problems in 1873, Lee-Hamilton was assigned to a less-demanding position as secretary to the legation in Lisbon, but shortly afterward he became partially paralyzed and was diagnosed as having a cerebro-spinal disease, which left him completely paralyzed by the following year. For the next twenty years he lived in Florence, Italy, under the care of his half sister, Violet Paget, a fiction writer and essayist who wrote under the pseudonym Vernon Lee. At their home Paget received many literary figures of the day, but only the most important—such as Oscar Wilde and Henry James—were allowed to meet with Lee-Hamilton, who found even brief conversation painful.

To take his mind off of his acute pain, Lee-Hamilton began to compose poetry in his head as a diversionary mental exercise; ironically, many commentators argue that his best works are artistic expressions of the fear and pain he tried to suppress. Of the works in his first six collections, all composed in his sickroom, the most successful are the sonnets and dramatic narratives. Following the moderate critical and popular success of *Sonnets of the Wingless Hours* in 1894, and the death of his stepfather the same year, Lee-Hamilton began what seemed a remarkable recovery: this coincidental timing has led some commentators to presume that his illness was psychosomatic, with Harvey T. Lyon diagnosing it a "textbook version of the Oedipal complex." Regardless, most agree that when he regained his health, Lee-Hamilton's poetic impetus waned. In 1898 he married Scottish novelist Annie E. Holdsworth, with whom he wrote the mawkish honeymoon collection *Forest Notes*. The couple's only child, born in 1903, died before her second birthday, and over the next three years Lee-Hamilton worked on a sonnet sequence in tribute to her entitled *Mimma Bella: In Memory of a Little Life*. Critics discern in these sonnets a return to the verbal clarity and emotional sincerity which inform the poet's best works in this form. Lee-Hamilton died in 1907 before the collection was published.

In the volumes *The New Medusa, and Other Poems* and *Apollo and Marsyas, and Other Poems,* Lee-Hamilton established the themes and central concerns of his best poetry: the penetrating exposure of psychological tragedy, the realistic horror of nightmares and hallucinations, pessimistic resignation to suffering, and the dramatic contrast between beautiful natural landscapes and grotesque situations for which they are backdrops. In the first collection, such poems as "The New Medusa" and "The Raft" launched Lee-Hamilton's reputation as an individual poetic voice so powerful in its emotional conviction that even treatments of vampires, gorgons, and dopplegängers had the ring of plausibility. Regarding *Apollo and Marsyas,* most critics agree with John Addington Symonds that the best poetry in the collection displays the poet's power for identifying himself with "abnormal personalities exposed to . . . unusual circumstances or exceptional temptation." Two of the best known works of the collection are "Ipsissimus," a dramatic dialogue about a man haunted by ghostly reflections of himself, and "Sister Mary of the Plague," a narrative which satirizes the Catholic church, the medical profession, and romantic conventions. Despite the attention given the dramatic strengths of the poems, critics note numerous technical weaknesses, including the use of trite vocabulary, a flawed sense of meter and rhyme, and mishandling of the caesuric effect in blank verse. Such flaws are minimized in Lee-Hamilton's sonnets, which are universally considered his most successful poetic works. Critics posit that the brevity of the sonnet allowed the poet to revise his work more carefully and that the severe restrictions of the form demanded disciplined attention to meter and rhyme.

According to the poet George MacBeth, *Imaginary Sonnets* "marks the period of Lee-Hamilton's maximum development." In particular, MacBeth regards Lee-Hamilton's invention of the sonnet-monologue for the volume a major technical innovation. Comprised of soliloquies delivered during critical periods in the lives of historical and mythical figures of the medieval and Renaissance periods, *Imaginary Sonnets* has been praised for an emotional urgency that critics consider a reflection of the poet's own self-absorption with his personal suffering. His next collection, the autobiographical *Sonnets of the Wingless Hours,* omits the guise of fictionalized personae and frankly confronts the loneliness, pain, and anxiety that obsess the poet. Called by Robert K. Rosenburg "his most important and characteristic work," it successfully evokes the life of an invalid, one of the best sections minutely detailing his daily amusements, preoccupations, and fantasies.

Although Lee-Hamilton was a minor poet who, according to critics, was limited in his stylistic range and central concerns, he exploited his strengths in his best works, which forcefully portray the effects of physical and psychological suffering.

(See also *Contemporary Authors,* Vol. 117.)

PRINCIPAL WORKS

Poems and Transcripts	(poetry)	1878
Gods, Saints, and Men	(poetry)	1880

THE ATHENAEUM   (essay date 1878)

[*In the following excerpt, the critic praises Lee-Hamilton's translations in* Poems and Transcripts, *but notes the absence of lyrical ability in the original poems in the volume.*]

Mr. Lee-Hamilton's *Poems and Transcripts* are finished with thoroughly artistic care, and are indeed admirable in all respects. His employment of classic metres is singularly happy, and his renderings of Goethe and Leopardi are among the best translations we have recently seen. . . . The original poems are strong and vigorous. . . . All that seems wanting to Mr. Lee-Hamilton is a larger measure of lyrical faculty. His verses, admirable as they are in some respects, do not run easily. We can fancy Sir John Suckling, in some new Sessions of the Poets issued from Parnassus, classing Mr. Lee-Hamilton with Carew,— no very dishonouring association.

> Tom Carew was next, but he had a fault
> That would not well stand with a laureate;
> His muse was hide-bound, and the issue of his brain
> Was seldom brought forth but with trouble and pain.

> *A review of "Poems and Transcripts," in* The Athenaeum, *No. 2651, August 17, 1878, p. 201.*

GEORGE SAINTSBURY   (essay date 1883)

[*Saintsbury has been called the most influential English literary historian and critic of the late nineteenth and early twentieth centuries. He adhered to two distinct sets of critical standards: one for the novel and the other for poetry and drama. As a critic of novels, Saintsbury maintained that "the novel has nothing to do with any beliefs, with any convictions, with any thoughts in the strict sense, except as mere garnishings. Its substance must always be life not thought, conduct not belief, the passions not the intellect, manners and morals not creeds and theories. . . . The novel is . . . mainly and firstly a criticism of life." As a critic of poetry and drama, Saintsbury was a radical formalist who frequently asserted that subject is of little importance, and that "the so-called 'formal' part is of the essence." In the following excerpt, Saintsbury praises Lee-Hamilton's portrayal of suffering in his poems but questions his technical prowess.*]

The power which every capable reader of *Gods, Saints, and Men* must have recognised in Mr. Lee-Hamilton is still more apparent in *The New Medusa*, though it cannot be said that its manifestation is likely to give universal pleasure. The author has made no secret of the fact that the phrase about learning in suffering and teaching in song is, in his case, no metaphor, but the expression of a grim reality. And the Introduction,

which is not the least good piece in the book, states the case clearly enough.

> What work I do, I do with numbed, chained hand.
> With scanty light, and seeing ill the whole,
> And each small part, once traced, must changeless
>   stand
>   Beyond control.
>
> The thoughts come peeping, like the small black mice
> Which in the dusk approach the prisoner's bed,
> Until they even nibble at his slice
>   Of mouldy bread.
>
> The whole is prison work: the human shapes
> Are such fantastic figures, one and all,
> As with a rusty nail the captive scrapes
>   Upon his wall.

After this confession no one need expect rose-pink and sky-blue from Mr. Hamilton's pencil, and they will not get either. "The New Medusa" is the story of a woman found chained on board a deserted vessel. One of her captors, or rescuers, struck with her beauty, buys her from his companions, and falls desperately in love with her, till at last he finds that her hair changes nightly to snakes. He kills her; we do not think he should have killed her, but that is a matter of individual taste, and, as such, irrelevant. The important point is that Mr. Lee-Hamilton has rendered the nightmarish atmosphere of the story excellently. His art is not quite perfect; there are lapses into the colloquial and bathetic here and there, such, especially, as the use of "I'll," "we've," and so on, which a little pains might have smoothed out. But this lack of application of the file is probably due in part to the writer's physical trials. The "Idyl of the Anchorite," which tells how a solitary, brooding constantly on ghostly enemies and temptations, mistook a belated traveller for a fiend, and drove her out to the night and the frost and the wolves, is also good, but would have been better if it had been in iambic decasyllables, which Mr. Lee-Hamilton can write with not a little stateliness and power, rather than in the very trying anapaestic tetrameter, which, in nearly all hands, sometimes lumbers and sometimes slips into burlesque. A similar objection (that the metrist is not master of the metre) may be thought to apply to two so-called ballads of the "Plague of Florence" and the "Sack of Prato," though each has merits. But the best piece of the book, to our thinking, is "The Raft." In this, the actor (and teller of the tale) commits in a half-dreamy fashion, and without any distinct or deliberate purpose, a hideous crime by cutting adrift, in a rapid and dangerous river, a raft which has been moored to the bank, and on which travellers are sleeping. Here, as elsewhere, the workmanship is not flawless, but the imaginative power which reproduces and dramatises a certain mood of mind is very noteworthy. It is in this faculty of what may be called psychography, of drawing the landscape of moods with atmosphere and environment suitable and complete, that Mr. Lee-Hamilton's poetic power chiefly consists. But this very fact and the occasional flaws in detail which have been noticed make him rather difficult to quote. Landscapes of any kind are not satisfactorily to be "sampled" by the square inch. . . . It would be almost heartless to say that his book has given us pleasure, for its appeal lies mainly, if not wholly, in the faithful revelation of the author's pain and in the reproduction—not in the mere vulgar fashion of the realist, but with something of the artistic treatment which nightmare and delirium themselves apply—of his sufferings. But this is a kind of art of which it is hardly selfish to prefer vicarious to direct enjoyment.

George Saintsbury, in a review of "The New Medusa, and Other Poems," in The Academy, *Vol. XXIII, No. 559, January 20, 1883, p. 36.*

THE ATHENAEUM (essay date 1884)

[In the following excerpt, the critic discusses the themes and techniques of the poems in Apollo and Marsyas.*]*

Inartistic in form as was Mr. Lee-Hamilton's previous volume [*The New Medusa*], it displayed so true a power of expressing emotion—dramatic emotion as well as personal—that another book from him deserves special attention. There is nothing in [*Apollo and Marsyas*] more powerful than **"The Raft"** or **"The New Medusa."** There are some poems, however, that are worthy to rank with them. This is especially so with the narrative in rhymed couplets called **"The Wonder of the World,"** a poem which for originality of conception and power of treatment must take a high place among dramatic monologues.

The story is this. Two young tourists, passionately fond of art, discovered in the crypts beneath the ruins of a temple the gold and ivory "Pallas" of Phidias, which was supposed to have been destroyed by the Crusaders at the sacking of Constantinople. One of the tourists was left to guard the treasure while his companion went to ask from the friendly pasha of the province a guard of men. Left alone in charge of a relic which to him was more precious than all the gems of Golconda, the young man who tells the story became alarmed, and took what seemed all necessary precautions to conceal the traces of the fissure in the crypts where the treasure was concealed. . . . [The] lonely tourist was soon seized, bound, and gagged. He was told to choose between death and discovery of the spot where the statue was concealed. Knowing but too well that the object of the ruffians was to demolish the statue on account of the gold, . . . the motive of the poem is the conflict between the man's desire to save the wonder of the world from destruction and the natural workings of the instinct of self-preservation. . . . (pp. 764-65)

The imagination at work in this poem is of so high an order that, had the execution been adequate, Mr. Lee-Hamilton's position among contemporary poets would have been clear and assured. The movement of the lines, however, lacks fluency, and the realistic method of narration reminds the reader too strongly of "Julian and Maddalo." Still the poem has a merit which is in our day rare, the merit of business-like conciseness. What the poet sets out to do he does; he tells in verse a story which has the grip and the realism of a prose narrative, and yet with all its shortcomings the narrative is a poem. **"Apollo and Marsyas,"** the poem that gives the name to the volume, is not the most successful. The Apollo is much too conventional a god for such advanced days as these, but the landscape is remarkably good. In the **"Pageant of Siena"** the writer calls up imaginative pictures of the past history of the city. It is a fine poem, and with a little more attention to certain requirements of art—requirements which are as easy as they are obvious—it might have been rendered finer still. In the descriptive poetry of our time it would be difficult to find a better piece of landscape. . . .

"Abraham Carew," a story in blank verse of religious monomania, is less successful than **"The Wonder of the World,"** though it certainly is not a failure. This kind of work requires a strength of hand and an acuteness of analysis such as Mr. Browning alone could have shown, and to compete with this great master of psychological monologue is hardy.

The merit of the sonnets is considerable, but again the merit lies in the substance rather than in the form. In no other kind of poetry is artistic perfection so imperiously demanded as in the sonnet. Blemishes which in other forms would easily be passed unnoticed are in the sonnet thrown up into sharp and painful relief. . . . The worst portion of the book consists of the ballads. With no ear whatsoever for anapaests, Mr. Lee-Hamilton seems to have an irresistible passion for writing them. Such lines as those in **"Hunting the King"** (a serious poem actually written in the metre of "Alonzo the Brave") show decisively that the author should never attempt another anapaestic verse. Nor can we say much in praise of his blank verse. There are laws of caesuric effect in blank verse—laws as obvious as inexorable—of which he seems to have not the slightest notion. Yet it is, we would assure him, only by bending to these laws that the poet's vehicle of blank verse becomes distinguishable from prose. The young poet is always and necessarily a courageous creature, or how would he become a young poet at all? But his courage is never so clearly shown as when he rushes into blank verse. The difficulty of writing in this measure becomes apparent enough when we consider that notwithstanding the splendid mastery over rhymed measures shown by our contemporary poets—notwithstanding the countless new metres that have been invented by poets subsequent to Shelley—the resources of English blank verse have not been materially added to since the publication of Wordsworth's "Prelude." Nay, it might not be too rash to say that while in rhymed metres there has been in the nineteenth century a growth and expansion that can only be called marvellous, there has in blank verse been no growth and expansion at all since Milton, while almost every cadence even of Milton himself may be found, if not in Marlowe (his great model), in Shakespeare or in Fletcher. Before a poet can hope to write in so difficult a measure as English blank verse he must undergo a training in rhymed metres such as Mr. Lee-Hamilton has certainly not undergone.

He is at his best in iambic rhymed measures, especially in the heroic couplet. And if he could overcome those defects of style which marred the verses in the previous volume, he would, we believe, excel in this noble metre. Even in prose such phrases as "but which" . . . , "and which" . . . , "and who," "but whom" . . . , are objectionable enough; in poetry they are really intolerable. The word "weird," too, which occurs over and over again, was always a prose word, and to steal it from the sentimental novelists, who have so little to lose, is cruel. The truth is, however, that what we call grace—that indefinable and ineffable quality which in Greek literature shows itself as surely in the wild ravings of Cassandra as in the most glowing prose passages of Plato, the most level prose passages of Xenophon—seems to be now less than it ever was a quality of English style. (p. 765)

A review of "Apollo and Marsyas, and Other Poems," in The Athenaeum, *Vol. 2, No. 2981, December 13, 1884, pp. 764-66.*

RICHARD Le GALLIENNE (essay date 1891)

[Le Gallienne was an English poet, essayist, and novelist who was associated early in his career with the fin de siècle movement of literary aestheticism that is commonly referred to as the Decadent movement. The literature of the Decadents, which grew out of French aestheticism, displays a fascination with perverse and morbid states; a search for novelty of sensation (the frisson nouveau, or "new thrill"); a preoccupation with both mysticism and

nihilism; and the assertion of an essential enmity between art and life implicit in the "art for art's sake" doctrine. In their writings the Decadents routinely violated accepted moral and ethical standards, often for shock value alone. In the following excerpt, Le Gallienne discusses what he considers the few strengths and many weaknesses of The Fountain of Youth.]

The supernatural is, as a rule, dangerous material for drama. Even in the novel it can only be made interesting by association with incongruous conditions, as the author of *Thoth* knows how to make it piquant; or as the means of pointing some forcible moral, that of *The Strange Case of Dr. Jekyll and Mr. Hyde,* for example. If a background of modernity be not a necessity, that of humanity certainly is. A drama entirely of supernatural interests is impossible, for the breath of drama is complexity of character, and supernatural beings lack that kindly human quality; they are either colourless or self-coloured as the scarlet of Mephistopheles. . . .

The only real figure, however, in Mr. Lee-Hamilton's drama [*The Fountain of Youth*] is the historical Ponce de Leon himself, though his, as it was bound to be, is but the reality of a familiar stencil. All the other figures, including his daughter and her lover, are shadows, and the villain Agrippa fails to convince from very excess of villainy. He is like one of Marlowe's inhuman monsters.

All this says nothing except against Mr. Lee-Hamilton's choice of a subject. His power as a poet is too well recognised to suffer from candour, and his possession of the dramatic gift has likewise been no question since his *Imaginary Sonnets.* But neither have a fair chance in this volume. The theme weighs them down. It had no inspirational interest for either. One seems to see the author in a struggle with it throughout, and it is not to be wondered at that the strain to be forcible by mere will, instead of impulse, should sometimes result in a treatment which out-Marlowes Marlowe, and occasionally "falls on the other side," in bathos. Indeed, in its piled up horror from beginning to end, *The Fountain of Youth* reminds one no little of *The Jew of Malta,* while it does not lack the occasional lurid effectiveness of that play. (p. 169)

Richard Le Gallienne, in a review of "The Fountain of Youth: A Fantastic Tragedy," in The Academy, *Vol. XL, No. 1008, August 29, 1891, pp. 169-70.*

JOHN ADDINGTON SYMONDS   (essay date 1893?)

[*Symonds was an English poet, historian, and critic who wrote extensively on Greek and Italian history and culture; he also made several highly praised translations of the literature of the Italian Renaissance. In the following excerpt, Symonds discusses the dramatic power and formal weaknesses of Lee-Hamilton's poetry.*]

[Eugene Lee-Hamilton] became subject to a cerebro-spinal malady, which has forced him, like Heine in his latter years, to assume the attitude of supine inactivity, a condition he makes pathetic reference to in the . . . sonnet "**To the Muse.**" . . . (p. 241)

Under these painful conditions the poet awoke in him; and though he now can only dictate what the ardent brain indites, though he can scarcely bear to receive verbal communications in more than sentences of a few words at a time, the many years which have passed across his manhood stretched upon a couch of suffering, are marked by a succession of volumes testifying to the ever vivid and unconquerable spirit of the man.

[*Poems and Transcripts, Gods, Saints and Men, The New Medusa, Apollo and Marsyas, Imaginary Sonnets, The Fountain of Youth*] . . . are the titles of six milestones on his road to a well-earned place in English poetry. (pp. 241-42)

Toward the criticism of Mr. Lee-Hamilton's poetry I cannot perhaps advance anything beyond what I wrote in *The Academy* upon the appearance of *Apollo and Marsyas.* At that time the study of these earlier volumes had enabled his readers to form a definite conception of his peculiar ability. His most salient quality appeared to be a power of identifying himself through the imagination with abnormal personalities, exposed to the pressure of unusual circumstance or exceptional temptation. Without being formally dramatic, he makes the men and women of his fancy tell their own tale, or tells it for them in narrative that has the force of a confession. The reality of his studies of character not unfrequently amounts to revelation; so completely, so painfully, has he absorbed the psychical nature of the subject he is dealing with into his own. While forcing the reader to see what he has seen in mental vision, he is aided by a vivid faculty of picture-painting. This faculty of suggesting scenes and images is always potent in his work; most remarkably so when it is employed in creating the environment of some dark psychological tragedy. As a fine example of its simple strength I may cite the "**Letter Addressed to Miss Mary Robinson.**" . . . It is still more prominent in a poem called "**The Raft,**" and in the ballad of "**The Death of the Duchess Isabella.**" These powers of dramatic insight and pictorial presentment are further qualified by a pronounced partiality for the horrible, the well-nigh impossible, the fantastically weird. His imagination delights in realising states of mind and caprices of the fancy which lie outside healthy human experience. "**The New Medusa**" may be cited as an illustration. Sometimes, too, he dwells on subjects which, in naked prose, are too revolting to bear the application of descriptive art in poetry. Such is the ballad of "**The Sack of Prato.**" Such, too, is the acutely painful study of an anatomist preparing for the vivisection of a man, called "**A Rival of Fallopius.**" Here Mr. Lee-Hamilton might claim Poe for master; but Poe's dry manner lent itself more appropriately to literature which aims at being ghastly or uncanny. The disciple's dissection of cruelty and madness is too subjective to be otherwise than repellent.

Technically, Mr. Lee-Hamilton commands a wide and picturesque vocabulary, and is not without considerable power over both rhyme and metre. His language is direct, spontaneous, unrestrained. But, in diction and versification alike, he is apt, when not working under severe restraints of form, to be more careless than befits an artist in the present age. His effects suffer also, in my opinion, from a want of reserve, an inattention to the advantages of compression. This accounts for the fact that he succeeds so well in the sonnet, which imposes limitations on his luxuriance. His volumes contain some of the best pictorial and dramatic sonnets in our language. (pp. 242-44)

The volume entitled *Apollo and Marsyas* takes its name from the Greek legend of the rivalry between the Satyr and the Olympian. Marsyas, for Mr. Lee-Hamilton, symbolises all that is remote, wild, pain-compelling, orgiastic, in the music of the world. Apollo represents its pure, defined, and chastened melodies. To Marsyas belongs the thrilling Phrygian, to Apollo the bracing Dorian mood. Of his personal susceptibility to the influence of Marsyas Mr. Lee-Hamilton makes no secret; and one of the most striking of his poems in this book, "**Sister Mary of the Plague,**" illustrates the extent to which he has submitted to that fascination of the terrible. Sister Mary is a nurse in a Belgian hospital, assiduous in her duties, and venerated by the people. Yet her patients, in spite of her best care, are apt to die of slow exhaustion. We soon perceive that all is not right; nay, that there is something horribly wrong about her. The power of the poem consists in this: that Sister Mary herself awakes with agony to the conviction that she is a vampire, one who had died of the plague, and has arisen to protract a hideous existence by draining the life-blood of the living. This motive would be too repulsive but for the tragic moral situation thus created. The vampire is herself the victim of a destiny she abhors, and obeys somnambulistically. So her story becomes an allegory of those psychological aberrations which are known as moral insanity, where the sufferer from some abnormal appetite is terror-stricken in his lucid intervals by what his morbid impulses have forced him to enact. A somewhat similar study of the tormented conscience is attempted in "The Wonder of the World" and "Ipissimus." (pp. 244-45)

While reviewing Mr. Lee-Hamilton in 1889 I ventured to express the hope that in the future he would pay his vows with greater assiduity to Apollo; Marsyas had controlled him long enough, and not without some detriment to his artistic faculty. His volume, *Imaginary Sonnets* has to a large extent shown that he can submit to the saner impulse of the Olympian deity. It consists entirely of sonnets, each written upon a noticeable personality in the world's history, setting forth some decisive incident or turning-point of action in the individual's life. Considered as a *tour-de-force*, the series must be reckoned remarkable in a very high degree. It illustrates the poet's leading faculty for penetrating and expressing moods, and for presenting these dramatically and pictorially. Still, there is a sense of effort, a want of rest, in this long picture-gallery of thrilling moments. We feel, when we close the book, the force of that Greek proverb: "The half is more than the whole." *The Fountain of Youth, a Fantastic Tragedy in Five Acts* . . . deals with the legend of Ponce de Leon, well known for its romantic fascination. Here the poet appears to have concentrated all his faculties and qualities on the production of the work; the lyrical passages showing a variety of form and a freedom of handling which had hardly been anticipated in previous performances. (pp. 245-46)

> John Addington Symonds, "Eugene Lee-Hamilton,"
> in The Poets and the Poetry of the Nineteenth Century: Robert Bridges and Contemporary Poets, *edited by Alfred H. Miles, George Routledge & Sons, Ltd., 1906, pp. 241-46.*

WILLIAM SHARP (essay date 1903)

[*Sharp, a Scottish poet and literary biographer, was a leading figure in the Celtic Renaissance of the late nineteenth century. A fine stylist, Sharp wrote his most distinguished tales and poems after the manner of Celtic romances and under the pseudonym Fiona Macleod, who was purported to be a highland poetess and Sharp's cousin; he kept his authorship a secret until his death, going so far as to compose a fictitious biography of Macleod. In the following excerpt from his introduction to* Dramatic Sonnets, Poems, and Ballads: Selections from the Poems of Eugene Lee-Hamilton, *Sharp examines the poet's works and artistic development.*]

During the first three years of his painful and disabling malady, Lee-Hamilton revised some of his youthful productions in verse, and, having selected and amplified, published his first volume, *Poems and Transcripts.* . . . His early book is interesting as a prelude: all the author's qualities are foreshadowed, if some-

times dimly. It reveals an indifferent accomplishment in technique, but the poet-touch is often evident and convincing. Even if the volume had not appeared at a time when the cult of deft metrical artifice was absorbing the attention of poets and critics, it is certain that *Poems and Transcripts* could have had no great measure of success. Yet one may turn to the book with pleasure, though the author has travelled a long way in the twenty-five years which have passed since its publication.

Two years later . . . the poet's second volume appeared. *Gods, Saints, and Men* showed an unmistakable advance. It was evident that a new craftsman in dramatic verse, in the dramatic ballad and lyrical narrative, had entered the lists. The touch was still unequal, the art often interspaced with disillusioning phrase, or dragged by the prosaic clay of the overworn or colourless word, the jejune epithet. But it was a poet and not merely a verse-writer who challenged criticism. And this, in itself a distinction, was still more manifest in *The New Medusa* and *Apollo and Marsyas.* . . . If in the later of these two volumes is no ballad to surpass in dramatic intensity "The Raft" in the earlier, the narrative and ballad poems show a more scrupulous art and compelling power. Their author loves a terrible subject as a gourmet loves a delicacy: it is the rich food and strong wine most beloved of his imagination. In "Sister Mary of the Plague," . . . he has a theme which has the demerit of fundamental unreality, but the merit of intensely dramatic possibility. This theme is one which might easily be treated repulsively, but which Lee-Hamilton has rendered in beauty, and as to whose imaginative reality he convinces us. But if in this tale of a vampire-woman to whom the enormity of her hidden life and frightful destiny are accidentally revealed, a revelation met not only with despair but with spiritual abhorrence, the poet has succeeded where most would fail, he has not always the like good fortune. Personally I find the flaws in workmanship more obvious in these dramatic narratives and ballads than in his sonnets, where the discipline of the form has for this poet ever exercised a salutary influence. Perhaps his finest achievement in this kind is the vivid dramatic narrative, "Abraham Carew," a Puritan fanatic who was wilfully murdered his only and dearly loved daughter under the terrible obsession of the idea that the sacrifice is required of him by the Almighty. It is refreshing to turn from sombre and tragical studies such as "Sister Mary of the Plague," "Abraham Carew," "The Wonder of the World," "Ipsissimus," and others, to a romantic ballad so strong and spirited as "Hunting the King" (based on the historic episode of Drouet's night-ride to Varennes). Yet even in the volume containing these noteworthy ballads and dramatic poems, the most memorable part is not that which comprises them, but that where a score of sonnets reveal a surer inspiration and a finer technique. As in *The New Medusa* one after a time recalls only vaguely "The Raft" and other strenuous compositions, one remembers sonnet after sonnet. One of these, "Sea-Shell Murmurs," is already accepted as one of the finest contemporary achievements in its kind— and none the less because that the central image is familiar: the more, indeed, from the triumph of imparting to an outworn poetic symbol a new life and a new beauty.

A genuine if limited success came to Lee-Hamilton with the publication . . . of his *Imaginary Sonnets,* despite its equivocal title. Here, in truth, it was realised, was a poet who had won the right to be considered seriously. On the other hand, his next volume, the poetic drama called *The Fountain of Youth,* though containing some of the poet's finest passages, and with the advantage of one of those deep-based themes which ignite the imagination of all of us, was almost ignored by the reading public. It is difficult to understand why this fine book failed to win wider appreciation than it did. The fault cannot lie wholly with the might-be readers, or with the critics—several of whom spoke of it highly. Probably the reason in part lies in that monotony in handling which characterises many of the author's narrative poems; and in the like tendency to wed fine and commonplace lines and passages in an incompatible union. Possibly the real reason is that "the reader" does not wish to be led to any Fountain of Youth, even if by Ponce de Leon himself (the author's "hero"), unless it be to a revelation of hope. The fountains of disillusion are dreaded by most of us. (pp. 334-38)

Eugene Lee-Hamilton's finest book, with its beautiful and appropriate title *Sonnets of the Wingless Hours,* convinced even those who had hitherto shown indifference, that here was a true and fine poet with an utterance all his own, an inspiration that none could gainsay, and a gift of beauty worthy indeed of welcome. The collection was not, it is true, of wholly new poetry: many of the sonnets had already appeared in earlier volumes. But here, it was realised, was brought together the most unalloyed ore that the poet had to offer: old and new, the collection was at once unique, beautiful, and convincing. (pp. 338-39)

In order to understand Eugene Lee-Hamilton's work, and properly to estimate it, one must know the conditions which shaped and the circumstances which coloured its growth. . . . For a fuller understanding of the mind and spirit of the poet one must look to the poems themselves, and particularly to the sonnets, naturally so much more a personal expression than the dramatic ballads and narrative poems, or than the "imaginary sonnets"—*i.e.,* sonnets imagined to be addressed from some historic individual to another, or to living or inanimate objects, or to an abstraction, or from some creation of the poetic imagination to another. . . . Above all, the reader will find what Maeterlinck calls both the outward fatality and the inward destiny, in many of the sonnets contained in *The Wingless Hours.* So simple and vivid is this poetic autobiography that few readers could fail to grasp the essential features of the author's life, and of the brave, unselfish, and truly poetic spirit which has uplifted it.

And this brings me to a point that has from the first been in my mind. No work of art can in the long run be estimated in connection with the maker's circumstances or suffering. Work in any of the arts is excellent, good, mediocre, poor, or bad: we may know the conditional reasons: we may be biassed in sympathy: but we must judge only by the achievement. There can be no greater literary fallacy than to believe that Leopardi's poetry owes what is enduring in it to the pathos of his brief and sorrowful life; that Heine's lyrics are unforgettable because of his mattress-grave; that the odes of Keats are more to be treasured by us because he died young and was derided by an influential critic; that the poems of Shelley are sweeter because he was of the stricken hearts, and was drowned in early manhood; or that the songs of Burns, or the lyrics of Poe, are supreme in kind because of the tragical circumstances in the lives of both poets. The essential part of the poetry of Leopardi, Heine, Keats, Shelley, Burns, Poe, is wholly independent of what has been called the pathetic fallacy. Each of these great artists would inevitably refuse to take any other standpoint. (pp. 341-43)

It is not, therefore, on account of what the author has suffered in body and endured in spirit that I would say, "Read: for here is verse wonderful as having been written in circumstances of almost intolerable hardship: verse moving and beautiful because the solace of a fine mind in a prolonged martyrdom of pain and hopelessness." That would be to do an injustice to the author's fine achievement. I would say first and foremost, "Read: for here is true poetry." The rest is incidental. It is right that we should be biassed by sympathy, and inevitable that the atmosphere wherein we approach should be coloured by that sympathy and an admiring pity; but when we come to the consideration of any work of the imagination, we have to judge of it solely by its conformity with or inability to fulfil these laws. Sorrow and suffering have given their colour to these "little children of pain." We feel their pain the more acutely because we know they are neither imagined through dramatic sympathy nor clad in rhetoric. Each is a personal utterance. But each is more than a statement, however pathetic in fact and moving in sentiment: each is a poem, by virtue of that life which the poet can give only when his emotion becomes rhythmical, and when his art controls that rhythm and compels it to an ordered excellence. Were it not so, these sonnets would merely be exclamatory. They might win our sympathy, they could not win our minds: they might persuade us to pity, they could not charm us with beauty. Look, for example, at the first sonnet one may perchance see: **"Lost Years."** A little less of discipline, and the octave would resolve itself into prose: already the ear revolts against the metallic iterance of "went"; but, suddenly, the poetry of the idea and the poetry of the idea's expression becomes one:

> And now my manhood goes where goes the song
> Of captive birds, the cry of crippled things:
> It goes where goes the day that unused dies.

In some of those chosen sonnets the infelicitous, because not the convincing or unconsciously satisfying word, leads perilously near disillusion. Others have an all but flawless beauty; and we hardly realise whether we are the more moved by the beauty of the poet's thought, and the sadness whence the thought arises a lovely phantom, or by the hushed air and ordered loveliness of the sonnet itself. . . . (pp. 343-45)

William Sharp, "Eugene Lee-Hamilton," in his Papers Critical & Reminiscent, *edited by Mrs. William Sharp, William Heinemann, 1912, pp. 321-47.*

THE ACADEMY AND LITERATURE (essay date 1903)

[*In the following excerpt, the critic discusses the strengths and weaknesses of Lee-Hamilton's poetic technique, and praises his skill as a sonneteer.*]

Mr. Lee-Hamilton has a certain eclectic reputation among cultivated lovers of poetry, though to the great indifferent public, ruffled into attention only by the loudest winds of rumour, he is unknown. Nor, though we welcome [*Dramatic Sonnets, Poems and Ballads,* a selection] made (we are told) by the author himself, can we complain that his fate is undeserved. For his is a singularly limited, quiet, and slow-ripening gift. Practically, it is confined to the sonnet. We would not say that the lyrics in various kinds, which compose a small final proportion of this little volume, are without their merit. But it is an artistic merit, lacking spontaneity or any marked original quality. The longer and more ambitious lyrics, such as those in the ode form, or tending that way, are apt to have a very plain Swinburnian stamp as regards style. One comes back to the sonnet as the form in which alone—or so chiefly as alone to be worth considering—Mr. Lee-Hamilton attains his measure of personal power, puts forth what is recognisably an individuality.

And these sonnets predominate in and dominate the book with an exclusiveness quite unusual. This engrossment with a single form is very peculiar among English poets of our day; and that a form which, despite the modern favour, remains something of an exotic in English verse. Yet in this self-imposed limitation Mr. Lee-Hamilton is manifestly justified. The sonnet fits his studious and artful gift. It needed not Mr. Sharp to tell us what his poems tell, that (like Mrs. Browning) he is a lifelong invalid [see excerpt dated 1903]. Unlike her, his suffering has depressed his vitality. There is a lack of central ardour which handicaps his poetry in sheer motive-power, so that the shorter the demand on his energy the more likely he is to sustain it. Even the brief burthen of the sonnet he does not attain to uplift all at once. His strength slowly and by practice grows equal to it—that is noticeable in this volume. From the outset there is delicacy of art, there is refinement of feeling and of reflection, there is pictorial—almost too painter-like—perception. But the emotion is a little thin, the emotional thought (and the poet must "think in his heart," or his poetry is made desolate) not deep and *red* enough. In these early sonnets the imagery, while it shows the poetic mind, is often somewhat trivial, ingenious, artificial, touched with the associations of a petty modernity. The ball-room and the band (for instance) yield imagery to one sonnet. . . . ["**Eagle of Tiberius**"] is good, but the later "**Sonnets of Life and Fate**" and "**Imaginary Sonnets**" are still better. Here at length the poet has reached a fulness of emotional thought which gives his best sonnets a true distinction. They have passed the subtle bound which divides poetic verse from absolute poems. Mr. Lee-Hamilton's favourite method is to expound in the sestet an image set forth in the octave. This is done with extreme skill, so that the application strikes home with an effect of almost dramatic and sometimes solemn surprise. It may not be the highest and austerest form of the sonnet; but the effect is fine and self-justifying. (pp. 529-30)

> "A Distinguished Limitation," in The Academy and Literature, *Vol. LXIV, No. 1621, May 30, 1903, pp. 529-30.*

ROBERT K. ROSENBURG (essay date 1946)

[*Rosenburg is an American poet and essayist. In the following excerpt, he discusses the themes and techniques of Lee-Hamilton's works.*]

[In] the twenty years of his illness [Lee-Hamilton] published some four volumes of poems and a drama, not an inconsiderable amount of work in view of his malady. His best poems are those that reveal his plight and his attitude toward it. *The Sonnets of the Wingless Hours,* . . . containing selections from previous collections as well as new material, is his most important and characteristic work, for it may be regarded as his *apologia pro vita sua*—if we consider the word "apology" to mean "explanation" rather than the usual sense of an "excuse." This sonnet sequence is a most personal revelation, and within the restrictions of this poetic form he created a thing of beauty, throbbing with life and emotion.

What was Lee-Hamilton's philosophy of life? It can hardly be said that he had a comprehensive view on the matter, for his statements are usually connected with his problems. However, one extract from *The Fountain of Youth* reveals his thoughts on nature and they are somewhat similar to the pessimism of Hardy:

> The two great ruling principles of Nature
> Are cruelty and Beauty-Pain and Sunshine
> And even as her tendrils grasp
> The monthly wretch we give her to devour
> So Nature in her placid beauty murders
> Through sea and air and earth. The world is like
> The walls in which we stand: Above the flowers;
> And catacombs of dungeons underneath
> All choking full.

It is in the self-revealing sonnets that the poet shows his real distinction. They are plaintive and sometimes hopeless in content, but they have none of the questioning of Job, the philosophizing of Omar, nor the bitter resentment of Housman. They are laments for the remembrance of a happy and active past.

Existence in a continually prostrate position becomes almost intolerable:

> To keep in life the posture of the grave
> While others walk and run and dance and leap;
> To keep it ever, waking or asleep,
> While shrink the limbs that Nature goodly gave:
> .   .   .
> 'Tis hard, 'tis hard.

The menace of the years does not find him completely unafraid, for in their passing he knows that hope of recovery is slowly diminishing, and still more surely the ability to participate in youthful activities is already past. . . . (pp. 165-66)

There were compensations, the love of books, especially of poetry. But even these pleasures have their bitter side. In "**Fairy Godmothers**" Lee-Hamilton tells how at his birth there came evil spirits bearing baleful gifts, but one came bringing the love of verse, which ironically became the most heavy load. (p. 167)

The slow passing of time and the accumulation of years are recurring themes of the sonnets. Thus he addresses the snail as the personification of slowness and the tortoise as a model of longevity. His spirit struggles against the infirmities of his body and he compares himself to the eagles of Tiberius, who were chained to slaves and forced to fly over the sea, the dead weight of the human bodies making it impossible for the birds to soar.

Not all of Lee-Hamilton's sonnets are of such a melancholy nature. He has a delightful whimsy as is exhibited in such poems as "**King Christmas**" and "**Elfin Skates.**" "**The Death of Puck**" reaches the height of fancy, and it may be ranked with any of the charming passages from *Midsummer Night's Dream*. These poems indicate the abiding youthfulness of the author, about which several of his friends have commented.

The Imaginary Sonnets are links between Lee-Hamilton's more personal utterances, his dramatic monologues and historical ballads; for they are written in the same form as the former group and yet possess the characteristics of the latter. These poems are addressed by famous characters of the past to some other person or to some inanimate object. Thus we hear da Vinci addressing his snakes, and Stradivarius speaking lovingly to one of his violins. In fourteen lines the poet is able to bring alive a character and even in some instances to throw light on an entire epoch. However, even in these sonnets Lee-Hamilton's fate is mirrored, for the best of them concern men and women who must spend their lives in confinement or who have died young, deprived of the enjoyment of youth. Few things are more pathetic than Lady Jane Gray's address to the birds and flowers on the day of her execution; we hear the voice of the invalid poet behind the words of the unfortunate princess and their complaints are the same.

The fantastic and the horrible predominate in the metrical narratives. Continual lack of sleep, coupled with the heightened sensitivity which often accompanies pain, may have caused the poet's imagination to tend in this direction. **"The Mandolin"** combines the Renaissance background of Browning with the revolting elements of "The Cenci," while **"Sister Mary van der Deck"** employs the age-old superstition of vampires, the frightfulness intensified by the creature appearing as a kindly, tireless, ministering nun. These poems, as well as the more happy **"The Fiddle and the Slipper"** and **"Prince Charlie's Weather-Vane,"** are somewhat imitative of Browning's method. They do not plumb the philosophical depths and they present their problems from one angle alone. Yet the direct unencumbered manner of presentation makes these poems a delight to read. They are the least introspective segment of Lee-Hamilton's works; they do not reveal any of his own sufferings and hopes, for their only purpose is to tell an engrossing tale and to set it forth in its proper historical background.

The same is not true of the *Fountain of Youth* for in this drama the poet associates Ponce de Leon's quest and disillusion with similar events in his own life. The technique employed is interesting; the poet combines the unrhymed verse of Elizabethan drama with the still older classical device of the chorus. Despite its disregard of known facts and the almost too conscious efforts to introduce fantastic blood-curdling elements, the play has genuine appeal and true pathos. (pp. 167-69)

After almost twenty years of agony, a miracle began in Lee-Hamilton's life; pain slowly diminished and the use of his muscles gradually returned. . . . [He] met the novelist Annie Holdsworth and in 1898 they were married at Rome, spending their first weeks together in England's famed New Forest. (p. 169)

A greater happiness came to them in 1903 with the birth of a daughter, Persis, whom the Italians poetically renamed Mimma Bella, the Beautiful Little One. . . . All his spare time was taken up in planning a beautiful, happy childhood for his daughter; a period in which he hoped to recapture some of the pleasures he had missed. Like his love of poetry, his devotion to his daughter was to have its drops of gall, for in less than two years Mimma Bella was dead.

All the hopelessness and frustration which he felt, Lee-Hamilton expressed in the twenty-nine sonnets which he published under the title *Mimma Bella: In Memory of a Little Life.* This sequence is a heart-rending book to read, for each turn of season reminds the bereaved parent of some incident in the child's short span. The depth of despair is reached in these lines:

All's well? O God, why bring into the world
A living thing, whose smallest dainty parts
Exceed man's nicest art; and then and there,
Tortoise or babe, or blossom half unfurled,
Crush it beneath the fatal foot that starts
None knows from whence, and hurries none knows where.

Mimma Bella was the poet's last publication. (pp. 169-70)

Lee-Hamilton's poems are only great when they concern his sorrows and sufferings. And this limited range may explain why he is now almost forgotten. How beautiful his verses would be, if we had no knowledge of his tragic life, is doubtful. Any work of art that depends on external things for its distinction, loses some of its value, but even in these cases we should not wholly dismiss the beauty contained in such products.

The poet knew some of his verses were crude and some of the words jarred on the ear, but the brief periods he was allowed for composition were his excuse. . . . But unfortunately he and his work have passed into the night; yet there is always the assurance which Eugene Lee-Hamilton has expressed in the closing lines of the Epilogue to the *Sonnets of the Wingless Hours:*

> But if it is of gold it will not rust;
> And when the time is ripe it will be brought
> Into the sun and glitter through its dust.
>
> (pp. 170-71)

Robert K. Rosenburg, "Full Many a Flower," in Poet Lore, Vol. LII, No. 2, Summer, 1946, pp. 163-71.

HARVEY T. LYON   (essay date 1957)

[*In the following excerpt, Lyon discusses the sources of Lee-Hamilton's poetic themes and his technical abilities.*]

Lee-Hamilton is a poet who was made, not born. The remarkable fact about the first thirty years of his life is that he was not remarkable. He was an ordinary Oxonian, beginning an ordinary career in the diplomatic corps. But at the age of twenty-nine he collapsed, apparently a hopeless paralytic. His collapse as a man was the beginning of his career as a poet. The paralysis continued for twenty years, the result of a textbook version of the Oedipus complex.

Unable to read or write, he began to frame lines of poetry in his mind, at first as a way of keeping his mind off his illness. His first book, *Poems and Transcripts* . . . , perhaps as unpromising a first book as any poet has ever brought out, was a collection of conventional verse, the product of the ordinary Oxonian. But by the appearance of his third book, *The New Medusa,* . . . he had emerged as a poet with a voice of his own, a voice that did not harmonize with his prose voice or personality.

As a prose man, he was a prudish late-Victorian gentleman, distinguishable from hundreds of others mainly by the fact that he was an atheist. In matters of civil polity, economics, and especially of sexual propriety, he held to the most repressive versions of conservatism. But as a poet, he dealt with themes that shocked and outraged his critics, and startled his friends. One of the most illuminating aspects of his career is that involved in following out the almost complete break between the prose man and the poet. In his poetry, he went far beneath the surface of the life his prose personality upheld. Nor could he himself control or understand the nature of his poetic gift. Poetry gave substance and objectivity to unconscious motivations; it permitted him to impose the order of rhyme and meter on the nightmare world he found within himself.

He could not control his imagination, but he could refine it. His career shows a slow but steady movement toward an exactness of form and intensity of conception which eventually brought him, after experiments in many forms, to the sonnet, a form in which over two-thirds of his 350-odd poems are written. Few poets have used the sonnet for so many different purposes. His first published sonnets, in *The New Medusa*, were philosophic. In *Apollo and Marsyas* . . . , he began to use the sonnet to describe paintings and sculpture. In *Imaginary Sonnets* . . . , he essayed to make the sonnet do the work of the dramatic lyric, in a series of soliloquies devoted to critical moments in the lives of historical and mythical figures. His seventh and last book, composed and published while he was paralyzed, *Sonnets of the Wingless Hours* . . . , was hailed by many as a book of unusual range and quality in an age which had seen a tremendous increase in the writing of sonnets.

The split within himself, which he had earlier expounded under the title of "*Apollo and Marsyas*," is everywhere evident in his poems, particularly in the series of sonnets addressed to writers like FitzGerald, Rossetti, Leopardi, and Baudelaire. He detested Swinburne, whose work he considered indecent, yet his own work has a marked Swinburnian flavor, especially in his early poems and in his play, *The Fountain of Youth*. . . . (pp. 141-42)

During his years of paralysis, he had steadfastly refused to acknowledge that his illness was anything but physical. His recovery, however, following the death of his hated step-father and preceding that of his adored mother, was effected by "auto-suggestion." Pain had made him a poet; his health recovered, his career as a poet seemed ended. . . .

In 1902, his only child, a daughter, was born. In 1904, she died. During the last three years of his life, he worked slowly at a series of sonnets to her memory. For almost the only time in his career, the man and the poet were not opposed to each other. *Mimma Bella* . . . is his last and finest book. The virtues of his earlier sonnets and poems came together: a vivid pictorial sense; powerful conceptions combined with plain, clean speech; a fluid command of the Petrarchan form. He did not live to see the book published. (p. 142)

The main themes of his poetry are the horror allied to beauty in nature, and the mystery of identity. He wrote very little amatory verse, but his steady subject was the oblique and hidden side of life. In spite of this interest, his poetry is marked by lucidity and clarity. His attempt to follow, so to speak, both Pater and the Queen bewildered him as well as his commentators. His best poetry occurs when Apollo and Marsyas complement rather than compete with one another. (p. 143)

Harvey T. Lyon, "A Publishing History of the Writings of Eugene Lee-Hamilton," in The Papers of the Bibliographical Society of America, *Vol. 51, first quarter, 1957, pp. 141-59.*

GEORGE MacBETH (essay date 1962)

[*MacBeth is a Scottish poet whose work characteristically examines personal suffering in a macabre and satiric manner akin to black humor. MacBeth's work is most often praised for its formal dexterity and criticized for its occasionally insubstantial themes. In the following excerpt, MacBeth examines the grotesque and macabre nature of Lee-Hamilton's poetry, concentrating his attention on the effect illness and self-analysis had on the poet's work.*]

Lee-Hamilton is an essential link in the chain of nineteenth century pessimism. He stands between Arnold and Housman as one of the most important English classical poets of the later nineteenth century. (p. 141)

He is one of the best exemplars in English literature of the writer whose work is conditioned and refined by the fact of his being bed-ridden. No other important writer lay in bed so long or made such good use of his time there. Of course, Lee-Hamilton didn't take to his bed by choice—at any rate, in the usual sense of the term. It's the forced confinement of his period in bed which gives his poetry its compression and its anguish. (pp. 141-42)

Contrived or inevitable, Lee-Hamilton's illness does provide both the key to his poetry and the batteries of its power. And if he built his own bed of nails he certainly made sure they weren't blunt ones. (p. 143)

Now I don't want to suggest that Lee-Hamilton's poetry has an interest solely as a kind of text-book of abnormal psychology; but this *is* the least of its merits, and no small one. The therapeutic motive of the writing, to exorcise phantoms as well as to pass time and soothe the urge for fame, made Lee-Hamilton his own psychiatrist. It was his developing skill as a metrist, together with his imaginative power as a constructor of adequate and various symbols, which enabled him to externalise the horrors of a tortured mind and the pains of a tormented body in classically clear and symbolically resonant poetry. Personal experience is never a sufficient condition of good poetry, but it is a necessary one.

One of the most successful poems in *The New Medusa*, and an excellent example of Lee-Hamilton's use of the dramatic monologue in a lyric metre, is the title poem of the book. The date of the poem's action is 1620, the scene England, and the speaker is a man who has just returned from travelling abroad: he is imagined as telling his story to his silent brother. He describes how he had become the lover of a "new Medusa," a girl picked up at sea on a raft, whose hair turned to snakes as she slept in punishment for some foul crime of poisoning, and whom he'd killed in horror at his discovery. The significant point is the man's uncertainty about whether this really happened, whether she was an embodiment of some evil spirit, or whether he only imagined it, whether she was a figment of his disordered mind. The poem is perhaps based in part on one of the author's own nightmares or periods of hallucination whose reality troubled him. (p. 144)

A later passage describing the Gorgon's head is a seminal one in Lee-Hamilton's work and one which he developed twice later in sonnets on Leonardo da Vinci and once in his play *The Fountain of Youth*:

> All round the face, convulsed in sleep and white,
>   Innumerable snakes—some large and slow,
>   Some lithe and small—writhed bluish in the light,
> Each striving with a kind of ceaseless flow
>   To quit the head, and groping as in doubt;
>   Then fast retained, returning to the brow.
> They glided on her pillow; all about
>   The moonlit sheet in endless turn and coil,
>   And all about her bosom, in and out;
>
> While round her temples, pale as leaden foil,
>   And fast closed lids, live curls of vipers twined,
>   Whose endless writhe had made all hell recoil.

The suppressed sexual connotations of such a passage as this need no stressing, but the skill with which the metre is handled is no less evident. The undulation and inward-turning of the terza rima gives a peculiarly apt sense of the constant coiling of the snakes; and the heavy alliteration, particularly of "v" and ''f'' and ''l'' sounds, together with the long ''i'' assonance (an abused kind of criticism but fair here, I think) also mimes the oozing, slow movement of the snakes. The choice of the word ''viper'' rather than ''adder'' or ''cobra'' or just plain ''serpent'' is symptomatic. (p. 145)

In his next book, *Apollo and Marsyas,* . . . Lee-Hamilton made an attempt to separate and comment on the darker side of his nature in the myth of the book's title. He seemed to realise that he might be fighting a Jekyll versus Hyde battle against his fascination for the macabre. He says a little plaintively in his Introduction:

> Apollo's name is sweet, and I were loth
>   to let the name of Marsyas stand alone
> Engraven on this book, while I can own
> Allegiance to both lords and love them both.

Fortunately for Lee-Hamilton's reputation today his illness prevented him from demonstrating any very marked allegiance to Apollo in his verse. (pp. 145-46)

The two best poems in *Apollo and Marsyas* are irredeemably macabre. **''Sister Mary of the Plague''** is perhaps the best of all Lee-Hamilton's narrative poems which is not a dramatic monologue. It describes in remarkably well-handled Hiawatha-metre how a nursing sister in the Middle Ages gradually comes to realise that she's a vampire and is undoing during the night the good work she'd set in train during the day. This Hammer-film formula enables Lee-Hamilton to indulge in some sharp implicit satire at the expense of the medical profession (from whom he no doubt believed he had suffered much) and also at the expense of the Catholic church, because Sister Mary is, of course, a nun. There's a grotesque power in some of the stanzas. . . . There's also a swing at conventional notions of sex, beautifully brought out in the final stanza, the sting in the scorpion's tail which is one of Lee-Hamilton's favourite weapons. The dying patient whose blood Sister Mary has sucked is speaking:

> Sister Mary, I have loved thee,
>   Is it sin to tell thee this?
> And I dreamt—O God, be lenient
> If 'tis sin—that thou didst give me
>   On the throat a long, long kiss.

This is a splendid take-off of one of the clichés of Romantic love, the kiss given to the desired maiden while she's sleeping; and of course it provides a macabre instance of Wilde's maxim that ''you always kill the one you love.'' Though in Sister Mary's case it's perhaps the converse.

The best of the dramatic monologues in *Apollo and Marsyas* is **''Ipsissimus.''** It's cast in the form of a confession by a Venetian gondolier who describes to his confessor how he tried to kill his deserving enemy but was always baulked by a ''masked and unknown watcher'' who later turns out to have been his doppelganger ''stiff with some frightful death's grimace.'' The end of the poem is a masterpiece of the macabre, and of psychological suggestiveness, when the Priest turns out to be his doppelganger too:

> Stretch out thy hands, thou priest unseen,
> That sittest there behind the screen,
>   And give me absolution quick!
>
> O God, O God, his hands are dead!
>   His hands are mine, O monstrous spell!
> I feel them clammy on my head,
>   Is he my own dead self as well?

> Those hands are mine—their scars, their shape:
> O God, O God, there's no escape,
>   And seeking Heaven, I fall to Hell.

The bitter satire on the confessional, the deeper suggestion that belief is impossible since the props of the Church's faith are all shams and delusions and the sheer terror and energy of the emotions make this one of Lee-Hamilton's most powerful poems. It has many incidental merits in its description of the apothecary's shop with its ''baleful philters, withering spells'' and ''the yellow dust that rings the knells'' and the enemy of whom the gondolier says:

> He makes my daily soup taste sour,
> He makes my daily bread taste salt.

We think perhaps of ''The Laboratory'' or ''Soliloquy of the Spanish Cloister'' but the differences are as instructive as the similarities, the diseased classicism of the borrowings is all Lee-Hamilton's own.

The publication of *Imaginary Sonnets* . . . marks the period of Lee-Hamilton's maximum development. . . . The invention of the sonnet-monologue for this book is Lee-Hamilton's major technical innovation, and one which has still not been fully exploited. The degree of flexibility and absence of strain in handling the metre is almost as great as Meredith's and far beyond for example, Charles Tennyson Turner's. The kernel of the idea may have come from the *Hortorum Deus* group of sonnets in Hérédia's collection *Les Trophées,* which Lee-Hamilton could have read in French magazines or in MSS before their publication in book form. The style and handling of the metre, however, is all Lee-Hamilton's own, and quite unlike Hérédia's; indeed, it forms a natural growth from the two wings of his style which had so far proved most successful—the dramatic monologue in blank verse or lyric stanza and the autobiographical sonnet in the first person singular.

Many of the sonnets in this collection are marked by Lee-Hamilton's characteristic preoccupation with the darker passions. Once or twice, however, as in **''Henry I to the Sea, 1120''** he can strike a note of pathos more commonly found in his autobiographical work. The poem forms an interesting comparison with Rossetti's ballad ''The White Ship'' commemorating the death of the prince in a storm at sea. . . . The Nietzschean violence is . . . nicely muted by the skilful balancing of the enjambement against the steady beat of the Petrarchan rhyme-scheme, so that the poem has the air of a telescoped speech from one of Shakespeare's Histories.

The last book of any importance published by Lee-Hamilton was the *Sonnets of the Wingless Hours,* which . . . enjoyed a moderate popular and critical success. It consisted of revised versions of autobiographical sonnets published in earlier books together with much new material. The twenty three poems in the sequence ''A Wheeled Bed'' run over the day to day amusements of the invalid poet—setting snails racing, composing his poems, longing to skate and fish again. The most interesting are those in which he is able to infect the descriptions with his own fever, as he does in **''Twilight.''** . . . Imagery, symbolism choice of epithets and direct statement all here combine to inject the author's sickness into the natural scene. (pp. 146-49)

Lee-Hamilton wrote his next book on his honeymoon in the New Forest in 1897. *Forest Notes,* with the dedication ''to each other and to the little velvet-coated creatures of the Woods,'' came out in 1899. It may seem unkind to begrudge Lee-Hamilton his happiness at the last, but there's a studied mawkishness about these poems which marks a tragic decline in the taste and energy of an impressive poet. It's a far cry from the self-lacerating irony of the snake image to the giggling silliness of his treatment of sex in this kind of thing:

> And all the elves that play at night have bent,
> From where they lurk beneath their mushroom hoods,
> Wee roguish eyes on us, whom Love has sent
>   To summer woods.

It would be hard to match this elephantine playfulness in the most extreme of Betjeman's progenitors, like Robert Brough; but Lee-Hamilton himself no doubt felt pleased to be in a position to write "nice" poetry which would please the taste of the frustrated and straight-laced middle-class whose approval he craved.

The career of Lee-Hamilton provides us with a classic case of a poet made by misfortune and unmade by return to normal life. His success both with direct and with indirect exploitation of his painful physical situation, his psychological disorders, nightmares and hallucinations, his repressed sexual energy and his militant atheism all mark him out as an individual voice in an age of giants. He is fit to stand comparison at different points with Housman, with Meredith, and even with Browning. He is a better poet than Stevenson or Henley and in his preoccupation with the dark passions a more contemporary poet that Rossetti or Patmore or Swinburne. (pp. 149-50)

George MacBeth, "Lee-Hamilton and the Romantic Agony," in Critical Quarterly, *Vol. 4, No. 2, Summer, 1962, pp. 141-50.*

ADDITIONAL BIBLIOGRAPHY

Brown, Robert W. "Eugene Lee-Hamilton's 'The Phantom Ship': Broad Popularity and Maturing Skill." *The Papers of the Bibliographical Society of America* 71 (Third Quarter 1977): 356-59.
    Discussion of the poem's development and publishing history.

"From Florence to Colby by Way of Kansas." *Colby Library Quarterly* III, No. 13 (February 1954): 217-18.
    Announces the addition of *Pictures on My Wall: A Lifetime in Kansas,* by Florence L. Snow, to the file on Lee-Hamilton in the Colby Library. The work contains a chapter, "In Regard to Eugene Lee-Hamilton," about the English poet's visit with Snow in Kansas, in 1897.

Pantazzi, Sybille. "Eugene Lee-Hamilton." *The Papers of the Bibliographical Society of America* 57 (First Quarter 1963): 92-4.
    Reprints a letter written by Lee-Hamilton to Oscar Wilde that discusses their association.

(Antoine Louis) Camille Lemonnier

1844-1913

Belgian novelist, short story writer, biographer, historian, and essayist.

Lemonnier was one of Belgium's foremost authors during the late nineteenth and early twentieth centuries. His novels and stories celebrate the spirit of the Belgian people and the beauty of their homeland with a realistic sensuality that has been compared to the work of Flemish painters. This reference to visual artists is not without justification; Lemonnier was a prominent art critic, and his literary style clearly manifests his interest in the accurate depiction of objects and the conveyance of physical impressions. Although Lemonnier was also profoundly influenced by the ideas of Emile Zola and the French Naturalists, his work differs from theirs in its optimism and its lyrical exuberance.

Lemonnier was born in Ixelles, a suburb of Brussels. His father, a lawyer, hoped Lemonnier too would practice law, but when the young man displayed no interest in that profession he was removed from the university and placed in civil service. Lemonnier, however, was determined to write and began composing essays which were published in local periodicals. In 1864 Lemonnier left his government post, planning to earn his living as a journalist. His interest in art and literature first led him to write commentaries on artists and their works, and soon after to begin creating the fiction for which he is best known. In 1869, Lemonnier's father died, and the small inheritance he left allowed his son to rent a chalet in the Belgian countryside. This event was pivotal for Lemonnier, who had always lived in or near the city and who was overwhelmed by his initial encounter with the beauty and majesty of the natural world. From that point on he devoted himself to the creation of fiction that would vividly and honestly portray the wonders of nature. His honesty was apparently distasteful to some, for Lemonnier was prosecuted three times for obscenity, although the second and third trials resulted in acquittal. His literary reputation, however, was unmarred by these litigations, and he was held as a model by the young writers who eventually comprised the Belgian literary renaissance of the early twentieth century. Lemonnier died in 1913, having written nearly thirty novels, several volumes of stories, and countless essays and articles.

Critics agree that Lemonnier's work exhibits three distinct phases. The first, described by critic Léon Bazalgette as the period of unconscious pantheism, is dominated by Lemonnier's intense and unquestioning love of nature. It was during this period that he created markedly sensual works such as *Un mâle (A Male)*, considered by many to be his best work. In *A Male*, Lemonnier portrayed the idyllic existence of a man who lives unfettered by social restraints in the primeval forest setting which is, according to the author, the proper environment for human beings. Lemonnier also felt compelled to present a complete picture of the natural world, and in other novels of this period he portrayed its harsher aspects. Lemonnier's unqualified acceptance of nature eventually gave way to the more sophisticated and speculative attitude which characterizes the novels of his second phase. These works display an intellectual dimension not generally present in the earlier fiction, exploring

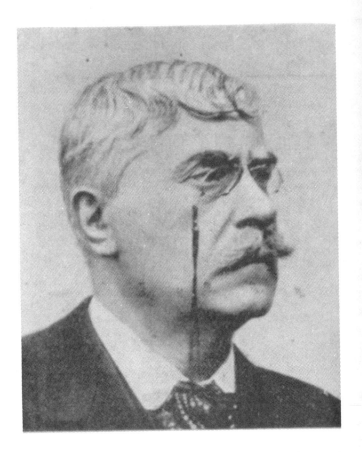

social and psychological themes such as capitalism, crime, and sexual perversion in a distinctly naturalistic manner. The novels of this period, which include *Le possédé* and *La fin des bourgeois,* are generally considered inferior to those of the earlier and later periods, inviting unfavorable comparison with the work of other Naturalist writers in general and Emile Zola in particular. In contrast, several of the novels written during the third phase of Lemonnier's career, most prominently *Le petit homme de Dieu* and *Le vent dans les moulins,* are ranked among the masterpieces of Belgian literature. These late novels, written after Lemonnier had reached fifty years of age, mark the author's return to the celebration of the beauty of nature and, by extension, of rural life. Many critics theorize that in his later years Lemonnier, dissatisfied with and sickened by his metaphysical exploration of overwhelming social problems, returned with renewed vigor and increased awareness to the pantheism of his youth. In addition, these later works display most clearly the influence of the visual arts, depicting colorful and somewhat voluptuous scenes of country life.

During his lifetime Lemonnier was a literary figure of enormous importance, and he was called "the marshal of Belgian letters." Critics believe that he was primarily responsible for the renaissance of Belgian literature, and while a scarcity of translations has severely limited knowledge of Lemonnier's work in non-French-speaking countries, his works remain an important contribution to modern Belgian literature.

PRINCIPAL WORKS

Salon de Bruxelles   (criticism)   1863
Nos flamands   (essays)   1869
Contes flamands et wallons   (short stories)   1875
Les charniers   (novel)   1881
Un mâle   (novel)   1881
   [*A Male,* 1917]
Le mort   (novel)   1882
L'hystérique   (novel)   1883
Happe-Chair   (novel)   1886
Histoire des beaux-arts en Belgique   (history)   1887
Madame Lupar   (novel)   1888
Les peintres de la vie   (criticism)   1888
Ceux de la glèbe   (short stories)   1889
Le possédé   (novel)   1890
Dames de volupté   (short stories)   1892
"Brussels"   (essay)   1893; published in journal *Harper's Weekly*
La fin des bourgeois   (novel)   1893
La faute de Madame Charvet   (novel)   1895
L'homme en amour   (novel)   1897
Adam et Eve   (novel)   1899
Au coeur frais de la forêt   (novel)   1900
Le petit homme de Dieu   (novel)   1902
Comme va le ruisseau   (novel)   1903
Le vent dans les moulins   (novel)   1903
Emile Claus   (biography)   1908
Félicien Rops, l'homme et l'artiste   (biography)   1908
La chanson du carillon   (novel)   1911
Birds and Beasts   (short stories)   1944

THE ATHENAEUM   (essay date 1898)

[*In the following excerpt, the critic discusses French novels of the day and comments on* Adam et Eve.]

The successful French novels of the last two years have been read by no one. Much as they differ in every other point, they have this in common, that they "drag" and are too long. That their writers do not read them we know, or they would correct their proofs. That the public who buy them and make their success do not read them we are convinced. They read bits here and there. We doubt whether any one, except our unfortunate reviewer, read the whole of *Les Déracinés*. We are certain that no one has read the clever, but outrageous *En Fête*, which the young firm of Simonis Empis has published for M. Auguste Germain, and which shows the "smart" set of Paris inextricably entwined with the "half-world." *Adam et Eve* is also a work of much talent, but it is also long-winded and barely readable. We prefer to all the new French novels a tiny volume in which three little sketches out of one of Bourget's early books have been brought together. But this deserves reprobation, for it is published without aught to show that it is not a new book, and, under a new title, forms a deception upon the public. *Adam et Eve* deserves notice as a really fine prose-poem. A man and a woman alone in the woods resuscitate the golden age of a most material Paradise which knows no Fall.

A review of "Adam et Eve," in The Athenaeum, *Vol. 112, No. 3712, December 17, 1898, p. 862.*

JETHRO BITHELL   (essay date 1915)

[*In the following excerpt, Bithell describes and discusses Lemonnier's major works.*]

In all Belgian literature there is no more outstanding figure than Camille Lemonnier. He is not merely the greatest Belgian novelist, he is the greatest Belgian prose-writer; and even if he had been a lesser artist, if he had lost ground to the sustained fierceness of Georges Eekhoud, or been out-classed by the subtle imagination and the exquisite refinement of Eugène Demolder, he would still have loomed large as a great fighter for the recognition of Belgian literature, as the general, in short, who set the young men of letters on their feet and led them to victory. "He alone perhaps," says Edmond Picard, "symbolises the Belgian literary activity in the French language in its entirety. He was the centre of it, the trunk, the backbone: nearly everything has issued forth from him, or directly or indirectly leaned on him." (p. 62)

Les Charniers, Lemonnier's first masterpiece, may be said to open his first creative period. Léon Bazalgette, in his authoritative monograph, divides Lemonnier's work into three distinct periods.

> The first, in which there triumphs a rich and opulent art, uncompromising and swollen with sap, plastic above all, filled his youth from twenty to forty. The second, dominated by the quest of originality and an inquiring and experimental psychology, is the result of his maturity, from his fortieth to his fiftieth year. At fifty he returns to the instinct of his youth, but to an instinct which, having traversed all the experiences of a lifetime, now appears enriched, fortified, more supple and wider of range, controlled by an unerring will—a magnificent period of plenitude and of triumphant fecundity, an age of re-birth ripening some of the noblest fruits of his art.

The fine flower of the first period is ***Un Mâle,*** which appeared in 1881, and at once placed Lemonnier in the first rank of contemporary novelists. It is the novel by which he is best known: he wrote some sixty books, but to the major part of the reading public he is "the author of *Un Mâle.*" There would be no risk in saying that this is the best, as it certainly is the most famous Belgian novel. But it is more than a novel, it is a lyric ecstasy, a poem in prose, a panegyric of forest and farm, a litany of instinct. The book, which was written at a farm, opens with a wonderful description of dawn in an orchard, where Cachaprès, a poacher famed far and wide for his prowess and agility, has spent the night. When he awakens he sees, from where he lies, the farmer's daughter, Germaine, opening her bedroom window. "Then something extraordinary happened. He looked at her, with his great teeth bared. On his cheeks there was a broad, cajoling smile, and his eyes seemed lost in a mist. A beast awoke in him, wild and tender." The story follows up the pursuit and the capture of this sturdy wench; but the love events are not more exciting than the detailed description of the poacher's life in the forest, his snaring of animals by night, his daring excursions to the neighbouring town to dispose of the game he has killed, his hair-breadth escapes from the gamekeepers who are on his track. It is all realism; but the realism is mellowed with poetry.

There are many things in *Un Mâle* which the memory will not let go. There are the *kermesse* scenes, full of gluttony and lust. There is a Homeric description of a fight in an inn: every phase stands out with the vigour of Meissonier's *Une Rixe*. But all the interest centres round Cachaprès in his defiant and full-blooded outlawry. "Some folks chop wood," he says to Germaine, "others plough; some have trades. I'm fond of animals." Brute as he is, he is a fascinating character, modelled to the mystery of the forest; and when the nets of his fate close round him, when at last he is hunted down and hit by the bullet of a gendarme, the novel gathers all the elemental force of a great and inevitable tragedy. He drags himself through the briars of a thicket to die as a wounded beast might die; and in his death-throes he is tended by a ragged little wench who has grown up like a squirrel in the woods and has helped him in his poaching. He has hardly noticed the little thing; but she with her wild heart has loved him. She will not leave him. (pp. 66-9)

Sad and terrible as the ending of *Un Mâle* is, it is not a depressing book. It is saturated with health; it throbs with virility; and it has the inspiriting force of all healthy and virile things. *Le Mort,* on the other hand, has the statuesque lugubriousness of a *Dance of Death*. *Le Mort* is just as much a hymn to Death as *Un Mâle* is a hymn to Life. To this extent they are companion volumes—the medal and its reverse. *Le Mort* appeared a year after *Un Mâle,* in 1882. It is the long drawn-out agony of remorse of two brothers, who have been driven by avarice to murder.

The psychological series opens with *L'Hystérique* .... This, the best of the series as well as the first, is the lurid story of the guilty love of a perverted priest for one of his flock, an anemic girl whose retarded puberty, breaking forth at last when she has whipped herself into ecstasies of religious fervour, plunges her into mystic hallucinations, in the spasms of which she believes that her seducer is Jesus. Splendidly drawn is the figure of the cleric, with his sexual disgrace motived by his descent from the Spanish conquerors of Flanders. This priest, however, is not wholly guilty of his hellish crimes; there is a note of discreet sympathy in the characterisation. It is the system, the cloistering, which is wrong—this strong man, who is overcome by his blood and the hypnotic suggestiveness of the rising sap in springtime, might have been a stalwart soldier, a headlong man of action.

L'Hystérique was followed by *Happe-Chair* ..., a documented study of the life of workers in rolling-mills. This novel, which owes something to Meunier's plastic art, has often been compared with Zola's *Germinal,* but according to Bazalgette Lemonnier's novel was "historically anterior." *Germinal* had, however, appeared the year before; and *Happe-Chair* is dedicated to Zola. It would be hard to prove that Lemonnier was not directly influenced, in the novels of his second period, by Zola. There is, for one thing, the exaltation of the *milieu* into a grandiose symbol. The life of the *béguinage,* sordid, and centred in creature comforts, in *L'Hystérique* is not excessively enforced; but in *Happe-Chair* the rolling-mill is as much an obsession as the coal-mine is in *Germinal*. Nevertheless, Lemonnier does not belong with a disciple's devotion to the school of Médan; he follows the lead, but with independence. He is less pedantic; he is more alive. It is difficult for him to keep the poet down: where his work is Zolaesque, it reminds one of *La Faute de l'Abbé Mouret,* that intense poem. The only

novels of Lemonnier which can fairly be censured as being in Zola's unpleasant manner are *Madame Lupar* ... and *La Fin des Bourgeois*....

In 1888 Lemonnier was fined one thousand francs and costs in Paris for his short story "L'Enfant du Crapaud," which had appeared in *Gil Blas,* to which he contributed many of the short stories collected in various volumes. "L'Enfant du Crapaud" was reprinted in *Ceux de la Glèbe* ..., perhaps Lemonnier's best collection of short stories, with its description of the dragging horror of the lives of those who till the soil. "L'Enfant du Crapaud" was condemned in spite of the eloquence of Edmond Picard, who had gone to Paris to defend his fellow-countryman. Lemonnier was not frightened into modifying his realistic method, and the next novel of his which appeared, *Le Possédé* ..., might not unreasonably have shocked conservative minds, although in justice to Lemonnier it must be said that he was never a pornographer—he was merely a great writer who, at all events during this psychological period which stretches from *L'Hystérique* to *La Faute de Madame Charvet,* thought it his duty to dive into the motive forces of disease and perversion and to describe life as he found it, without palliation. Realism and Satanism were the fashion, that is all; and Lemonnier in his prose went no farther than, for instance, Iwan Gilkin in his verse. *Le Possédé* shows the genesis and rapid growth of perverted sex instincts in an old man, a magistrate who has lived honourably till his fiftieth year.

A few years later Lemonnier was again prosecuted for immoral writing, this time at Brussels. He was defended by Edmond Picard again, aided by the novelist Henry Carton de Wiart; and he was acquitted. It was again a short story which had given offence. "L'Homme qui tue les Femmes" (reprinted in *Dames de Volupté* ...), quite a harmless presentation of the crimes of Jack the Ripper. Lemonnier was prosecuted for the third time, at Bruges, for the publication of *L'Homme en Amour* ...; and he was acquitted in triumph, the occasion being seized by his friends and sympathisers to do honour to his art. *L'Homme en Amour* and *Le Possédé* are really variations of the same theme; but the later novel is more universal in its application, and more in the nature of a protest against the atrophy of the sex instinct. It forms a diptych with another novel of protest, Georges Eekhoud's *Escal-Vigor*. The trial at Bruges inspired Lemonnier with *Les Deux Consciences,* an avowedly autobiographical novel in which he pleads his own case against his judges and justifies his literary method. Lighter in texture is *Claudine Lamour* ..., the history of a Parisian music-hall star. *L'Arche* ..., a fireside idyll, a glorification of motherhood and family life, points forward to the noble novels of the third period. It is a feminist novel, eloquent of the great future in store for woman when her emancipation is complete. *La Faute de Madame Charvet* ... is the opposite picture to *L'Arche:* ruthlessly it exposes the naked bones of adultery.

Now a new period, Lemonnier's third period, begins. It is as though he were sick of the depravities he has been painting with such conscientious truth, as though he had turned his back on perversion and adultery and taken refuge in the haunts of his youth, in the open country, at the heart of the forest. He is again the Lemonnier who wrote *Un Mâle;* but chastened by his long pilgrimage through the labyrinth of dingy streets and with a new message intense as the religion of an apostle. This message has all the freshness, in his glowing presentation of it, of a new and miraculous discovery; and yet it is essentially Rousseau's preaching of the return to nature, to instinct. There is no pretence of "philosophy": Lemonnier does nothing more than expound a view of life which amounts to a robust futurism. He writes *L'Île Vierge* . . . , which was to be the first part of a trilogy showing the progress of man through tribulation to the consciousness of divinity. Here Lemonnier had intended to lead up to the same conception of the man-god as informs the later work of Verhaeren and Maeterlinck. No other part of the trilogy was completed—perhaps the plan seemed too deliberate to Lemonnier, who was first and foremost an artist impelled by the mood of the moment, and always more attached to the character than to the idea. But in *Adam et Ève* . . . the legend is continued—a man who has suffered greatly flees to the forest, and finds calm and content in the physical activity of primitive existence. There is the spirit of *Robinson Crusoe* in *Adam et Ève; in Au Coeur Frais de la Forêt* . . . there is the witchery of *The Blue Lagoon*. Two waifs, a boy and a girl, find their way from the slums of a city to the heart of a mythical forest; here they learn to use their hands and their brains; here they have their first child, and from here they set forth to found the ideal city of the future.

If in this series of novels there is one tendency more evident than another, it is the tendency to socialism—not the socialism of parties, but a doctrine of brotherly affection and of the nobility of labour, an intuition of the future. Socialism is thrust openly into the foreground in *Le Vent dans les Moulins*. . . . This is more a poem than a novel: it is a hymn to "Mother Flanders." This Flanders, however, is not defined by names and drawn with clear-cut lines: it is all a dreamland, a land drowned in mists, a land of shy and awkward dreamers, a land of kitchen gardens and orchards, creeping canals, farms with green shutters and red-tiled roofs, roads that run between lines of poplars, with the river Lys meandering through the landscape. What a different country is this to that painted with opulent colour in the early novels, that country of teeming fertility and ruthless violence! The characters, too, have grown gentle; they are another race. Even the militant socialists, who, at the bidding of the gentry, are attacked with stones at their meetings, have more of milk and honey than of gall.

Le Vent dans les Moulins is Flemish through and through: it is informed, not by French realism, but by Flemish mysticism. These taciturn peasants, who "are shaken to the marrow by life and yet say things which belie the force of their emotion," are akin to those of Stijn Streuvels. A Fleming to the core is the hero, Dries Abeels, the son of a flax merchant. Dries is a socialist; but he is also a *rentier*. The intention is fixed in his heart to give all he has to the poor; he is convinced that it is his duty to learn some manual trade and live by the exercise of it, as those do who live and toil around him. But, well-nourished as he is, with his "bullock's blood," he is fond of good eating; he is idle; he does not like early rising. In the end his better nature prevails; he shakes his sloth away, rises heroically before the sun, and binds himself apprentice to a carpenter. What follows is a healthy glorification of manual labour, as in the other novels of this period. He is no longer Dries the gentleman of means; he is Dries the carpenter—and a good carpenter at that, for he works with love, reading poems into the wood he handles. Now he is conscious that "the man who does not work has no right to the bread he eats." Now, and now only, he has the right to preach socialism to the labourers—a hard task, even when fortified by personal example: for clergy and gentry are leagued against progress, and to teach the dignity and the rights of labour is like driving nails into beechwood.

There is scarcely a hint of sensual things in *Le Vent dans les Moulins*. There is a love story; but it is one of great restraint and chastity. The novels of primitive life at the heart of the forest are pure in intention; but their very purpose, the hymning of natural life, leads to scenes of initiation and marital passion. *Le Vent dans les Moulins* ends with an engagement which is likely to be long; and with Dries content to wait for his little housekeeper. Equally pure in tone is *Le Petit Homme de Dieu*. . . . It may be called a companion volume of *Le Vent dans les Moulins;* both are "local" novels, hymning the soul of Flanders. But whereas *Le Vent dans les Moulins* generalises the landscape, *Le Petit Homme de Dieu* centres in one dead city—in Furnes-la-Marine (Furnes by the Sea), with its old church of Saint Walburga, its old houses, and its age-old customs. The dominant picture is that of the *Ommegang*, the procession which from time immemorial has been seen every year in Furnes—the chief inhabitants proceed through the town in solemn state, clad as New Testament figures. (pp. 70-80)

The old city is described with meticulous accuracy, with the quaint realism of old Flemish *genre* pictures. But mysticism, not realism, emanates from the whole. The *Ommegang* has a subtle influence: the influence which the Passion Play has on the villagers of Oberammergau:

> In this strange little town of Furnes, people never knew exactly in what period things were happening: all the events of the day took on a sacred appearance.

The characters call one another by the names of the personages they represent: thus, the locksmith is Pilate to his cronies in his very shop, and the Wise Kings from the East cannot divest themselves of their regal dignity even when they sit down to their beer in the inn. But the one who is most conscious of his sacred character is Ivo Mabbe, the little ropemaker who takes the part of Jesus and is for that reason known as "Le Petit Homme de Dieu." In the intensity of his simple piety he grows close to the mind of the Saviour, so close that he begins to identify himself with the part he plays. This phase of religious mania has often been described: by Gerhart Hauptmann among others in *The Apostle* and *The Fool in Christ Emanuel Quint*. Hauptmann's Christs are mad: Ivo is merely on the way to madness. He only takes Christ's teaching literally, and shocks his fellow-townsmen, who are nothing if not "respectable," by associating with outcasts, to whom he preaches the Gospel, which in his mouth is identical with socialism. But the good burghers of Furnes do not approve of socialism, which to their minds is very far removed from Christianity. They turn against "the little Christman." . . . Ivo grows the more determined in his Christianity, and he persists in his ministrations to the outcast of the earth, considering that he has the right to repeat Christ's words. This extreme Christianity of his, however, as he comes to see, degenerates into a moral pride. In the end he realises that he is not and cannot be Christ; and that he must first of all practise humility. Now he returns to Cordula, the rich farmer's daughter from the dunes, who had long been betrothed to him, but whom he had kept at a distance because she played the part of Mary Magdalene (how could Christ marry the sinner?).

Another novel of Lemonnier's, *La Chanson du Carillon*, has its scene in a dead city, in Bruges. Of his other novels *Le Sang et les Roses* . . . should be mentioned. The theme is daring: a childless husband agrees to let his wife be loved by another man, for the sake of the child she desires and for which her nature cries out.

Lemonnier was not a French novelist. He was essentially a *Flemish* novelist: he is as much the novelist of Flanders as Verhaeren is the poet of Flanders. Not that he situated his novels entirely in Flemish districts: in such novels as *Happe-Chair* he has described the Walloons, and painted Walloon scenes with perfect precision. But his whole character was Flemish, violently Flemish, both in the realism of the earlier novels and the mysticism of those which came later. Lemonnier travelled little, only in France, Belgium, Holland, and Germany. His impressions of Germany he described in *En Alle-magne,* which contains valuable art criticism of the galleries in Munich. Even when he had become famous in Paris, when he was acknowledged in Paris as one of the most distinguished of French writers, he continued to live in Brussels, a guide counsellor, and friend to the tyros of literature, encouraging the diffident to plunge into the whirlpool, instilling his own breezy courage into those who drew back.

Lemonnier was a great optimist. But, unlike Verhaeren and Maeterlinck, he had not to pass through a stage of pessimism. His optimism was a part of his constitution; it is the optimism of a healthy man. (pp. 80-4)

> *Jethro Bithell, "Camille Lemonnier," in his* Con-temporary Belgian Literature, *Frederick A. Stokes Company Publishers, 1915, pp. 60-84.*

G. TURQUET-MILNES (essay date 1917)

[*In the following excerpt, Turquet-Milnes assesses Lemonnier's work, taking exception to the idea expressed by some critics that his fiction is simply an inferior imitation of the Naturalism of Emile Zola.*]

In 1895 M. Bernard Lazare wrote a book called *Figures Con-temporaines*, in which he tried to sum up and dismiss Camille Lemonnier in five pages. Here are some of the more vitriolic passages—

> In his own opinion M. Camille Lemonnier represents Belgian letters, at all events he spares no pains to convince us that this is so. Yet he does not succeed in making us ignore Georges Eekhoud, Emile Verhaeren, Maurice Maeter-linck and many others, not to mention Georges Rodenbach, who has been Parisian for a long time now.

> No author is safe from his depredations, he goes to everybody, to rich men like Hugo, or to the poor ones like Droz. . . . He wrote *Les Char-niers* for those readers who wanted some Hugo, just as at another time he obliged the admirers of *Monsieur, Madame et Bébé*. When many of us were delighting in Cladel's painting of the peasants of Quercy, we were given *Un Mâle*. When Zola held sway, we had *Le Mort* and *L'Hystérique* which took us back to *Thérèse Raquin* and *La Conquête de Plassans*, and to the early work of Céard and Hennique. . . . Then this growth of naturalism calmed down. . . .

> Lemonnier cultivated Mallarmé, and brought all his ingenuity to bear on the creation of awk-ward neologisms and distorted prosopopeia. At the present moment he is busy with *des Es-seintes*, and in this rôle he is a blacksmith smit-ing with all his might on a delicate jewel, and

taxing his wit in torturing filagree and fragile glass. . . . He piles up the gold of rare adjectives and the purple of strange words, and out of it all he fashions a mosaic which is without life, without delicacy and without charm.

These passages are a masterpiece of malevolent inaccuracy. It may be necessary to recognise that you can see in Lemonnier the influence of Chateaubriand, Gautier, Hugo, Baudelaire, Flaubert, Cladel, Zola and even Gustave Droz (Lemonnier's *Derrière le Rideau* bears some resemblance to Droz's *Monsieur, Madame et Bébé*), and doubtless there is a pedant or two living, who will be pleased to trace these successive influences. The fact remains that there is no more original Belgian artist than Camille Lemonnier. A powerful and fertile writer, he repre-sents Belgian literary activity for more than forty years, until his death in 1913, and even if he reflect the various tendencies of the French mind, and adapt himself to his surroundings, he is Flemish to the backbone in his mystico-sensual leanings, in his pious materialism, with its tendency towards pantheism, in his Rubens-like fertility and love of colour, dash and force.

It is true that he reminds the reader of Zola, and even of Dickens; but it is above all of Rubens and Jordaens that he makes us think, because, like them, he paints his imagination in the form of ever sensitive emotions. The moment Lemonnier states a fact, he feels obliged to magnify it, falsify it, he becomes inflamed with it. In *Au Coeur Frais de la Forêt* pub-lished in 1900, just as in *Un Mâle* published in 1881, he is faithful to his exuberant nature. His soul is in a continual state of unrest. Whether he describes a *Kermesse*, or a supper party or a free fight, he puts all his heart and soul into it, and always manages to communicate his enjoyment to the reader. His gift of perpetual invention appears nowhere to such advantage as in his descriptions of scenery; under his brush a forest becomes a living, breathing reality.

So that Lemonnier offers us a very interesting study: that of the Flemish artist, the poet-painter endowed with a rare blend-ing of the gifts of the realist and idealist. In the end the poet gains the day. He set out with symbol in *Un Mâle* and returns to symbol in *Au Coeur Frais de la Forêt*, the truth being that he is always true to himself, always guided by his feeling, and that, although perhaps he never wrote a line of verse, he is a lyrist and a great idealist. The contrast is piquant, when one thinks of the brutes he painted. (pp. 86-8)

Lemonnier shows in all his work an ever alert and almost feminine fineness of feeling, a very flexible, and thereby im-itative, temperament, fed by a sensitive and sensual love of nature, and—a minimum of thought, as we shall see.

The susceptibility which enabled him to write *Un Mâle* (one of the most interesting novels of the period) was certainly harmful to his other faculties. Not that it falsified his knowledge of life, but it rendered it incomplete, led him to over-cultivate and exaggerate his power of expression, for he had a kind of voluptuous feeling for words and sometimes allowed them to encumber his work. This same feature led him into boisterous explosions, into the bursting open of already open doors, and made him a very passionate writer: first realist, then socialist (in name at least), but always unsatisfied and with a taste for experiments. It made him a member of that family of which Baudelaire speaks: "Thou shalt love the place wherein thou art not; the lover whom thou dost not know." It made him the pilgrim of every school. A very courageous writer, yes. A great writer, if you will. But realist or scientific writer, no.

He is too overladen with emotion to see things steadily and in their scientific whole; emotion weighs him down and keeps him from rising above his own time. His characters are for the most part rustic demi-gods, or fauns pure in heart, who have strayed into our civilisation. Thence also it follows that Lemonnier must not be required to disentangle the interlaced threads which make a human soul. He will try willingly, but will fail. He is not a Marivaux, nor a Bourget, nor a Barrès.

In the same way his portraits are drawn in with broad strokes, without any very great insight. There again he is like Rubens whose portraits, as Fromentin so justly says, are all rather alike, and all rather like Rubens himself, but deficient in a life of their own and thereby lacking moral resemblance. His characters are drawn by means of vigorous acts and conversations. The dialogue is always clear, precise, and very often inimitable: that gift must be recognised, for it at once puts Lemonnier far above Zola, who always gives his peasants a townsman's loquacity.

When we come to examine what it is that constitutes the dominant characteristic of Lemonnier's heroes, we see that it is the same quality which he himself possessed above all others: the faculty of seeing, and delighting in what he sees. His gallery of "Mâles" is filled with various Lemonniers, wide-eyed, and keenly alive to the appeal of nature, conscious pantheists, intoxicated with the beauty of words and of things.

Take, for example, his two most famous novels, **Un Mâle** and **Le Vent dans les Moulins**. The poacher Cachaprès is—Lemonnier. For it is quite impossible that Cachaprès should have had all those feelings with which his creator credits him, especially since we are shown him in other aspects as a perfect brute. Would you care to know how Lemonnier's hero learnt to love Nature? Your thoughts will probably go to the boy in Wordsworth's *Prelude,* in which case you are most certainly on the wrong tack. When Cachaprès was still quite small, he was a terrible birdsnester. No foliage was too thick, no tree too difficult of ascent for the tiny brood to escape his eye. Then when he had caught his prey he carried it off to his mother, who wrung the baby birds' necks, cooked them over a wood fire, and the tender morsel quickly disappeared under Cachaprès' greedy young teeth. And it is this "mâle" (who gives several other instances of his brutality) of whom Lemonnier says, after a wonderful description of the sunrise:

> He became more and more the mate of the earth—he for whom she makes the lacework of her foliage, for whom she distils the scent of thyme and mint and lavender, for whom she makes the birds sing, the insects hum, and the streams flow under the moss with a sound of rustling silk.

That would pass, were Lemonnier ironical, but here he has no humour, he takes himself with all the seriousness of a man in full revolt.

In the same way in the opening pages of **Le Vent dans les Moulins,** Dries Abel, who is a peasant, again has the eye and imagination of the author. He thinks that his pigeons look like the pictures of the Holy Ghost descending when they fly over the church, and that the roofs are as blue as the eyes of his oxen, and that a humble dwelling has aches and pains in its joints like a rheumatic farm labourer.

It would be easy to continue this enumeration. It therefore follows that in Lemonnier's novels there will be much that is artificial, much that is conventional, much that is displeasing.

Truth to tell, it could not well be otherwise, since Lemonnier was born "a man for whom the actual world exists." If we run over his tales and novels in our minds, we see that it is always a *picture* which we remember: the awakening of the forest, the death of a faun, a cottage inhabited by toil-worn peasants, the red-hot furnace in the rolling-mill, paths in Flanders, exquisite nooks of greenery in the woods.

His first works were his Salons: **Salon de Bruxelles**, . . . ; **Salon de Paris**. . . . And his **Les Charniers** is a collection of pictures, a *Salon,* in fact, of the most fearful horrors of war. Lemonnier's reputation as an art critic will live as long as his reputation as a novelist. When his second *Salon* appeared in 1866 (he was born in 1844), Alfred Stevens went to see him, and said to him, "You are now the critic to whom we all look."

But this painter's eye, which enabled him to distinguish the characteristic detail everywhere, and which, given his profound sensibility, procured him endless and ever-fresh sensations, was bound to lead him to loving words for their own sake, because words were to enable him to render the multiplicity, the charm, the astonishment and the magic of his sensations. That is a feature which critics have been very slow to recognise in Lemonnier. But it is nevertheless true that for him, as for Victor Hugo, words were living beings. And he loved them so well that he could not bring himself to choose from among them, but welcomed them all, beggar and prince, introducing into literature the most richly picturesque terms of slang or patois. His work is like the seashore of those distant lands where the stones and shells cast up by the sea, with the traces of the waves still upon them, glint in the sun. Some are common pebbles, others shells worth polishing and carving, while here and there you may light upon a pearl, and on all you feel the great breath of the vast ocean.

On the subject of his style, Lemonnier has left us an important document in his Preface to Gustave Abel's *Le Labeur de la Prose.* Words, he tells us, were for him a revelation of the universe, and he speaks of the pleasure he gained by declaiming them in the solitude of his little room. Sometimes he would amuse himself by imagining all the possible variations of a simple idea, such as "the moon is shining." And he makes a significant statement: "A writer is a creator of forms, and these are the product of the extent and suppleness of his vocabulary rather than of the plenitude of his ideas." He advises all would-be writers to work hard at studying their dictionary—for "le mot accouche l'idée" ["the word gives birth to the idea"]. Then again, style is intimately connected with sensation, since he tells us that in the summer he thinks in luxuriant arabesques and happy music, the resulting words being clear, light, tender, but that he would never allow himself to express in the same way the frozen silences of winter. "Le style," he says, "est un rythme, et ce rythme est le mouvement même de mon âme en correspondance avec l'univers" ["Style is a rhythm, and this rhythm is the very movement of my soul in correlation to the universe"].

There you have the explanation of his way of writing. It is the outcome of an ardent and voluptuous curiosity. He makes his pictures out of the enumeration of an infinity of detail—as Zola did, but with much greater care and far greater delicacy, the master-mason's trowel is replaced by an extremely dexterous brush. Zola's is the descriptive novel, Lemonnier's is the picturesque novel. . . . When [Lemonnier] talks of peasants in dire poverty laying wagers of a hundred francs, and their womenkind plunging their teeth into enormous hunches of *tarte au riz* ["rice pie"], we feel that he is emulating Rubens, and trying to intoxicate us with the riotous strength of the earth. But, it should be observed, he is very careful not to let his heroine yield after the kermesse, as Zola would have done. That is the touch of an artist who is very sure of himself and for which much will be forgiven.

Since the epithet of "Zola of the Belgians" has been so often hurled at Lemonnier's head, it is perhaps not out of place to point out that *Les Charniers* preceded *La Débàcle* by more than twenty years, that if *Happe-Chair* came a year after *Germinal*, Lemonnier, in his ingenious style, the curiosity of his thought, his Flemish common-sense, and that indefinable touch of optimistic pride, is singularly different from the father of the Rougon-Macquart. It would be fairly easy to compare *Un Mâle* with *La Terre*, and the palm would not go to the high priest of naturalism. In all *La Terre*, full as it is of the most brutal rhetoric, you will find no scene comparable to the selling of the cow in *Un Mâle*. Zola has created nothing so true as Lemonnier's old peasant Hulotte. Lemonnier saw the beauty in the peasant's life; Zola quite overlooked it.

It would nevertheless be untrue to say that Lemonnier could not express the terror of life. He wrote *Le Mort,* which is as fine in its way as *Un Mâle*. This sinister book tells how the brothers Baraque kill a man, throw him into a ditch of liquid manure; and how, in spite of their efforts, he always reappears on the surface. It is in this book that he reminds us of Dickens. His portraits of the three brothers—Balt and Bast, thin as nails, with enormous hands and sticks of legs, Bast with his interminable cough and furtive eyes, Nol the idiot, with body all swollen by the damp in the house, and his flaxen wig stuck on with pitch—are pure Dickens. But Lemonnier certainly never thought of imitating the English master, he merely followed the bent of his own nature just as Dickens followed the bent of his. Any accusation of plagiarism falls to the ground, unless the accuser is prepared to uphold the absurd idea that Dickens begot Zola who begot Lemonnier.

Happe-Chair, another of Lemonnier's more famous works, is a romance of the Black Country. In order to write it Lemonnier lived for many weeks at Marcinelle and at Couillet, in the dreary villages, observing the existence of the miner. He was accompanied by the artist, Constantin Meunier. The result of this visit was the working-class art of Constantin Meunier, and Lemonnier's novel *Happe-Chair,* with its pictures of factory life. (pp. 89-95)

Lemonnier was a man of extremes. Like his Cachaprès, he was a born rebel. Clearly, then, he was bound to become obsessed at a given moment by the idea of the importance of rebellion, bound to become attracted by the swarming life of the lower grades of nature and to regard it as essential to life and human activity. All those writings, which certain critics consider as running counter to his other work, are, on the contrary, the typical product of his thought. The creator of Cachaprès, given the state of contemporary thought, was bound to become the author of *L'Hystérique, le Possédé, l'Homme en Amour,* and the rest. They are books of rebellion, books written by a poacher who has a grudge against all gamekeepers. He might be called a Flemish Bakounine *in petto,* when in *La Fin des Bourgeois* he announces the downfall of the bourgeoisie and the triumph of democracy. When he shakes his fist at society he is a good representative of the Belgian thought of his day—and of to-morrow, he shows us not only man's natural need of grumbling, but the need of improving the situation which is ingrained in the Belgian. We must never forget, as Professor Ashley reminds us: "Originality of social insight is

still alive in the land, for it was from Ghent that the modern State learned in recent years to think out practicable measures of insurance against unemployment." There is nothing astonishing, then, in the apparition of Lemonnier as a disciple of Jean Jacques, and in his declaration more than a century later than the Geneva philosopher, that Society has corrupted man, and that we must throw ourselves into Nature's arms to be calmed and purified. It is always the same with these blind, passionate flights towards the ideal: they impose excessive tasks upon man, which in reality only lead him into the pitfalls of his baser instincts—"Be my brother, else will I kill thee!" (pp. 96-7)

G. Turquet-Milnes, "Camille Lemonnier," in his Some Modern Belgian Writers: A Critical Study, *Robert M. McBride & Co., 1917, pp. 86-99.*

BENJAMIN MATHER WOODBRIDGE (essay date 1930)

[*In the following excerpt, Woodbridge discusses several of Lemonnier's most representative works, pointing out both positive and negative qualities.*]

[Lemonnier's] best known novel is probably *Un Mâle.* . . . This book is an epitome and an anthology of his art. As landscape painting, the awakening of the poacher, Cachaprès, in an orchard, remains unequalled. . . .

The theme of the novel is the loves of Cachaprès and Germaine, daughter of a rich farmer; still more it is the love of the author for the large and free life of the woods of which Cachaprès is the symbol. The forest remains faithful when his mistress deserts him; shot by officers, he drags himself to the thicket to die, and the spirit of the wild, personified by a vagabond child, watches over him. This scene, like the first, is unforgettable; it would be gruesome without the poetry which presides over the return of the splendid body to the universal life. As accessories, there are a kermess and a free-for-all bout of young peasants in a tavern, portrayed with the rich joy of the old masters in these brawny scenes; there are vividly drawn rustics who display all their ruses in the purchase of a cow, and finally there is the old Cougnole, a mistress of all trades who can show herself complacent to handsome young lovers. The lusty amours of the protagonists become chaste and sculptural, thanks to the benediction of the primitive forest which shelters them. The meetings of the lovers are described soberly with no insistance on lascivious detail. And that is characteristic of the best work of Lemonnier. He was hailed three times before the courts on charges of immoral writing, but there is found very rarely in his work what the critics of Zola called *putrid literature.* It would be difficult to outdo him in outspoken frankness: for him love is in the natural order; it has its natural beauty which is lost when treated with refined subtlety; it has its place—a large one—in the symphony of nature. (p. 59)

In 1878 Lemonnier published a study which is still regarded as authoritative, on Gustave Courbet. The influence of this brutally realistic painter is plainly marked in a short novel, *Le Mort,* which is dated October 1878. It is a sombre drama of murder committed by two depraved peasants, and of the ever increasing debasement which followed in them. The most sordid of the realists might envy him certain scenes of this story, yet it is told with a sobriety which confers a certain tragic beauty on its very hideousness. Published the year after *Un Mâle,* this triumph of death brought out in striking relief the Protean genius of the author. Cachaprès is perhaps only a "quat'chemins-la-potence-au-bout," but the perennial heart of the forest is beating joyously in his breast and it is plain that he is the ideal of his creator. Balt, Bast and Tonia of *Le Mort* are evocations of a nightmare in which the author sees and seeks to see only the beast. The conception of the characters recalls Thérèse Raquin and Laurent of Zola. But Lemonnier had too much judgment to attach himself or his book to a preconceived theory. He realizes that life is too complicated to be compressed into any formula and that it shatters all systems. He is content to paint it now under one now under another aspect. He will commune to-day with the realists or naturalists,—and once more I believe that Courbet first revealed to him the beauty which their method may offer,—on condition of fleeing to the idyll to-morrow.

Un Mâle may suffice as an example of the first period noted by Bazalgette, that of unconscious pantheism. The best of the psychological novels is undoubtedly *La Faute de Madame Charvet*. . . . Here Lemonnier has traced the evolution of the personality of his heroine to the threshold of her complete development. The novel is purely psychological, almost without action, of Racinian simplicity. Three characters hold the scene: the husband, the wife and their child. The lover does not appear; he is not even accorded a proper name. And to eliminate all which might detract from the universality of the study, there is no indication of the place of the action. The author has put aside his painter's brush to concentrate on the analysis of the reaction of the wife's infidelity on herself, on the child and on the husband who gradually acquires moral certainty of her fault. Charvet is calm, absolutely honest and inspired by a rare generosity. He will not question his wife nor spy upon her: "On n'a pas le droit de violer le secret des âmes" ["One has no right to violate the secrecy of another's soul"], he says. The story opens on the evening of Madame Charvet's return from her first rendez-vous. The author analyses the changing sentiments which her adultery arouses in her. At first there is the astonishment of the wife who had believed herself utterly honest; she has been irreproachable during the ten years of her married life. She asks herself whether she is not the victim of a hallucination; then she is flattered by the thought that she is still desirable, and she seeks to justify herself. . . . But almost immediately a desolating thought crosses her mind: "En espérant s'appartenir, elle n'avait fait qu'aliéner la forme intime de sa personnalité" ["In hoping to possess herself, she had only alienated the most intimate part of her personality"].

The power of the book is then in its stark simplicity: the very dialogue is reduced to a minimum; the characters speak almost incoherently, as in certain of the plays of Maeterlinck, but every word is pregnant with emotion. Thus a rather vulgar situation assumes the proportions of a tragedy in the grand style. In such a study we expect to find an effort at least to imitate the occasionally artificial complexity of Paul Bourget, and we are happily surprised to find nothing of the sort. The suffering of the husband and wife is portrayed with the utmost reserve and without any intrusion of the author's subtlety to distract our attention. The plot is a commonplace in the French novel, but the reader of *La Faute de Madame Charvet* will remember it among a thousand. With no formal confession or dramatic scene, the guilty wife feels the necessity of an expiation and she leaves her home to make her life anew." "A présent il y a trop de choses entre nous" ["At present, there are too many things coming between us"], she says, and Charvet answers: "Toi seule sais ce qu'il faut faire pour apaiser les voix en toi. Quand tu auras fini d'être en paix avec toi-même, moi aussi j'aurai oublié depuis longtemps" ["You alone know what must be done to appease the voice within you. By the time you are at peace with yourself, I too will have long forgotten"].

Lemonnier has happily avoided any intrusion of a thesis, but an idea pervades the entire book: it is the respect due to every individual, even when that individual happens to be a woman. (pp. 60-2)

There is a certain feminism in this novel and others of the same period. It takes different forms, but the essential trait is always the right of women to create their own lives without allowing themselves to be bound by the routine of a hypocritical society. Lemonnier's interest in feminine personality may well owe something to his studies of two painters of women, Alfred Stevens and Félicien Rops. He wrote appreciative essays on both.

The prelude to the novels of conscious pantheism, the third period indicated by Bazalgette, contains a very distinct sociological thesis. Critics are generally agreed that *La Fin des Bourgeois* is one of Lemonnier's books that is destined to oblivion. I have said that he was an artist and painter rather than a thinker. The story is of a family which rose from poverty to wealth only to fall, in the third generation, into hopeless degeneration. The characters reason interminably, for the novel is a sort of résumé, in a single volume, of the entire series of the *Rougon-Macquart*. (p. 62)

[*L'Ile Vierge* and *Comme va le ruisseau* are] characteristic of [Lemonnier's] later work. *L'Ile Vierge* has the freshness of an idyll of Theocritus, with something of the sweep of biblical and epic poetry in addition. The scene is far from the real world and symbolic characters express the author's ideal of a return to nature. . . . The title of *Comme va le ruisseau* is a symbol of the imperious destiny of the heroine who has devoted herself to the care of destitute orphans and refuses marriage in order to continue her work. Her character is thrown into strong relief by the indolent life of the rustics who surround her. . . . In this as in others of the author's novels of this period, there are delightful pictures of the life of the country folk. And in *Comme va le ruisseau* he has put the calmest and most complete expression of his pantheism. Noémie Larciel is resting in the shade after having helped with the haying, and she allows her thoughts to drift. "Un frisson religieux l'agita. Si c'était cela Dieu tout de même, . . . si Dieu était le vent, la lumière, le petit brin d'herbe, l'insecte et toute la vie en moi et en dehors de moi!" ["A religious shudder shook her. If it was all God, . . . if God was the wind, the sunlight, the little blades of grass, the insects, and all the life within me and outside me!"] (pp. 63-4)

I shall not attempt any résumé of these books of which the charm is hidden in subtle touches. Lemonnier has put here all his love of the quiet beauty of the rustic life of his country. I know nothing comparable in French literature; some of the idylls of George Sand come nearest, but she deliberately idealized her peasants. Lemonnier had been a realist, even a brutal realist: he has not forgotten it, and truth, even in poetry, gains by being told entire.

I have left but little space to speak of the short stories which alone would entitle the author to a place of honor among writers of fiction. The sub-title of the first collection, *Scènes de la Vie Nationale*, applies to the best of them all. He presents this life now in a sympathetic, even idyllic light, as in the *Contes Flamands et Wallons* . . . , now in its dark, cruel and brutal aspects, as in *Ceux de la Glèbe* . . . , or *Le Bestiaire*. . . . If I had to choose a single story, I should pick **"Le Thé de ma Tante Michel"** in which he gives a very vivid picture of a beloved relative.

In order to paint sympathetically rustic and popular manners, a large dose of humor is essential. Now humor, rare in France where wit is enthroned, is widespread in Belgium, and Lemonnier had received his full share. But there is a danger: humor cannot exist without sympathy for the unfortunate and for the ridiculous; this sympathy runs the risk of becoming ridiculous sentimentality. Such a phenomenon may be seen occasionally in Dickens, and Lemonnier, who has been compared to Dickens for a part of his work, does not always escape unscathed.

Lemonnier was a very successful practitioner of the difficult art of writing for children. It is surprising to find in this painter of kermess and rude peasant life a highly developed and subtle understanding of delicate children. These stories may also interest grown-ups, and at times the author seems to forget his juvenile audience and speak only to their elders. Children's stories, written by Protean hands, are nearly always *cousins germains* to satiric tales and this kinship is noticeable in Lemonnier. There are a few psychological stories, as in **Dames de Volupté** . . . , and the psychology is almost always morbid. Perhaps this lead him to attempt studies in the vein of Maeterlinck and of Poe. In **La Vie Secrète** we find exalted, half-unconscious sentiments; the characters move in an atmosphere of mystery doubled with horror. We are too far from reality here to speak of psychology.

Lemonnier stands forth now as a romantic artist, passionately fond of color and provocative shading. In his quest for variety and studied style, he is all too inclined to subordinate matter to form. A phrase from Montaigne will point the contrast with the classics: "Qui a dans l'esprit une vive imagination et claire, il la produira, soit en bergamesque, soit par mimes, s'il est muet" ["He who has in his spirit a lively and clear imagination will show it, be it in tapestry, or be it in mime, if he is mute"]. But Lemonnier belongs to his time: hence his incontestable influence over the new Belgian literature and his title of "le maréchal des lettres belges." (pp. 64-5)

Benjamin Mather Woodbridge, "Camille Lemonnier (1844-1913)," in The French Quarterly, *Vol. XII, No. 2, June, 1930, pp. 57-65.*

ADDITIONAL BIBLIOGRAPHY

Mallinson, Vernon. "La Jeune Belgique." In his *Modern Belgian Literature,* pp. 23-36. New York: Barnes & Noble, 1966.
    Brief discussion of the controversy surrounding *A Male.*

Pope, F. Russell. *Nature in the Work of Camille Lemonnier.* New York: Columbia University, 1932, 148 p.
    Discusses the relationship of humanity and nature in all Lemonnier's works.

H(oward) P(hillips) Lovecraft

1890-1937

(Also wrote under pseudonyms of Ward Phillips, Humphrey Littlewit, Gent., Lewis Theobald, Jr., Augustus T. Swift, Albert Frederick Willie, Edgar Softly, Richard Raleigh, and others) American short story writer, novelist, poet, critic, and essayist.

Lovecraft is widely considered the most important literary supernaturalist of the twentieth century and one of the greatest in a line of authors that originated with the Gothic novelists of the eighteenth century and was perpetuated throughout the nineteenth century by such figures as Edgar Allan Poe, Ambrose Bierce, J. Sheridan LeFanu, and Arthur Machen. Like these literary forebears, Lovecraft practiced what began as and remained an essentially popular form of writing, the evolution of which he traced in the critical history *Supernatural Horror in Literature*. Combining elements of the lowest pulp melodrama with the highest imaginative artistry, Lovecraft's "weird tales," a term he invested with special connotations, have become classics of an enduring branch of literature, and among authorities in this province he is regarded as a peer of his Gothic predecessors.

Lovecraft was born in Providence, Rhode Island, at the home of his maternal grandfather, Whipple V. Phillips, a prosperous industrialist and New England gentleman who was the dominant intellectual influence on his grandson's early life, both personally and through his extensive library of works by eighteenth and nineteenth century authors. Of the Victorian mansion on Angell Street, Lovecraft wrote: "Here I spent the best years of my childhood. The house was a beautiful and spacious edifice, with stable and grounds, the latter approaching a park in the beauty of the walk and trees." A precocious child whose delicate health allowed him only sporadic attendance at school, Lovecraft flourished in a world of cultured adults who fostered his interest in Greco-Roman antiquity, astronomy, eighteenth-century literature and history, and Gothic tales of terror. This milieu, and the traditions on which it was founded, served as the prime mental and emotional coordinates of Lovecraft's life, whose auspicious beginnings gradually devolved into a lethargic procession of loss and unfulfilled promise: Lovecraft's father, a handsome, syphilitic traveling salesman who was effectively a stranger to his son, died in 1898 after spending the last five years of his life institutionalized with general paresis; Lovecraft's grandfather died in 1904, and subsequent illmanagement of his financial holdings forced Sarah Phillips Lovecraft and her only child to move from their family home into a nearby duplex. In his published letters, Lovecraft unfailingly celebrates his mother's refinement and cultural accomplishments; in biographies of Lovecraft, his mother is portrayed as an intelligent and sensitive woman, a neglected wife, and an overprotective parent who instilled in her son a profound conviction that he was different from other people.

In 1908 Lovecraft suffered a nervous breakdown that prevented his attaining enough credits to graduate from high school, and, rather than entering Brown University to pursue the professorship that he had formerly assumed would occupy the rest of his life, he continued his program of self-education. During this period Lovecraft in large part existed as the semi-invalid

recluse of his popular legend. In 1914 his isolation was alleviated when he joined the United Amateur Press Association, a group of nonprofessional writers who produced a variety of publications and exchanged letters. A voluminous writer from an early age, Lovecraft now directed his efforts toward these amateur journals, with his own magazine, the *Conservative*, appearing from 1915 to 1923. He also became involved in the network of correspondence which for the rest of his life provided a major outlet for personal and artistic expression. In these letters, Lovecraft discussed an encyclopedic range of subjects in essay-like length and depth; here he also vented his lifelong obsessions, most prominently his love of the past and of scientific truth, and his aversion for the modern world and for all peoples who were not of the Anglo-Nordic cultural stream, although several biographers maintain that he moderated some of his extremist views later in his life. Lovecraft's contributions to amateur journals were almost exclusively in the form of poems and essays, the former being imitations of such eighteenth-century poets as Alexander Pope and James Thomson, and the latter displaying a style strongly influenced by such eighteenth-century prose writers as Joseph Addison and Samuel Johnson. Although Lovecraft wrote several horror stories after his first reading in 1898 of the tales of Poe, he destroyed most of these efforts and wrote no fiction from 1908 to 1917. In the latter year he was encouraged by editor W. Paul

Cook to resume fiction writing, resulting in the successive composition of "The Tomb" and "Dagon," the first of what are considered Lovecraft's mature works. After further encouragement from other friends, these two stories, along with three others, were submitted to the pulp magazine *Weird Tales,* which afterward became the principal publisher of Lovecraft's fiction during his lifetime.

Beginning around 1919, Lovecraft began to socialize with other amateur journalists, and in 1921 he met Sonia H. Greene, a Russian Jewish businesswoman from New York City who was active in amateur journalism. They married in 1924 and Lovecraft went to live with his wife in New York, where he hoped to find employment that would enable him to abandon the disagreeable and insubstantial living he previously earned as a literary reviser and ghostwriter. Ten months later the couple separated for reasons which Lovecraft described as largely financial, although the situation was aggravated by Lovecraft's hatred of a city with such a conspicuously mixed racial and ethnic population. In 1926, Lovecraft returned to Providence, where he lived for the remainder of his life. To supplement his dwindling inheritance he was forced to continue his revision work. Despite his nearly destitute financial state, Lovecraft managed to travel extensively, documenting these excursions in his letters and in such essays as "Vermont: A First Impression," "Charleston," and *A Description and Guide to the City of Quebeck.* He also produced what are considered his greatest works, including "The Call of Cthulhu," *The Case of Charles Dexter Ward,* "The Colour out of Space," "The Shadow over Innsmouth," and *At the Mountains of Madness.* Lovecraft died of intestinal cancer at the age of forty-six.

While an account of the outward events of Lovecraft's life may suggest some of the character traits which critics have found of immense value in explicating his works, it must fail to convey the full range and intensity of his convictions, preoccupations, and eccentricities. As revealed in his letters, Lovecraft's most important experiences were blatantly those of a self-sustaining and isolated imagination. The solitary worlds that he inhabited in childhood—based on his reading of the *Arabian Nights,* classical mythology, and Georgian authors—were fortified and augmented throughout his life, providing him with a well-defined set of interrelated roles which he sometimes facetiously, sometimes tenaciously assumed: the Anglophile gentleman who upheld the most staid conventionality and lamented the "tragic rebellion of 1775-83," the Nordic warrior who reveled in dreams of adventure and blood, the proud citizen of the Roman Empire, the anemic decadent immersed in every form of human and metaphysical abnormality, the frigid scientist seeking truth by the strictest criteria of logic, the generous and brilliantly humorous friend, the xenophobic admirer of *Mein Kampf* who evolved into a quasi-socialist supporter of Franklin Roosevelt's New Deal, and the "cosmic-minded" dreamer of imaginary spheres that transcend the brief and aimless episode of human history. The last-named quality of cosmic-mindedness was perhaps less a discrete component of Lovecraft's temperament than the relatively stable foundation upon which his numerous personae were constructed. Philosophically, Lovecraft was a strict scientific materialist who held that the universe is a mechanical assemblage of forces wherein all human values are simply fabrications having no validity outside the context of human imagination and that humanity itself is merely an evanescent phenomenon without any special dimension of soul or spirit to distinguish it from other forms of animate or inanimate matter. At the same time Lovecraft wrote that his strongest feelings were connected with

a sense of unknown realms outside human experience, an irrationally perceived mystery and meaning beyond the world of crude appearances. It is particularly this tension between Lovecraft's sterile scientism and mystic imagination—whose contradictory relationship he always recognized and relished— which critics find as source of the highly original character of his work.

Lovecraft's stories are commonly divided into three types: those influenced by the Irish fantasist Lord Dunsany, a diverse group of horror narratives set in New England, and tales sharing a background of cosmic legendry usually referred to as the "Cthulhu Mythos," a term coined by August Derleth and never used by Lovecraft himself. The Dunsanian stories begin with "Polaris," which Lovecraft actually wrote the year before his first reading of Dunsany's works. Nevertheless, his discovery of Dunsany was a crucial impetus to continue developing narratives more or less related to a tradition of fairy tales and typified by wholly imaginary settings and characters with otherwordly names. Stories in this vein are "The White Ship," "The Doom That Came to Sarnath," "The Cats of Ulthar," and *The Dream-Quest of Unknown Kadath.* Contrasting with these dreamlike romances are tales in which the central element of supernatural horror originates and is circumscribed in a realistic New England setting. Throughout his life Lovecraft was captivated by the architecture, landscape, and traditions of New England. In a letter of 1927, he wrote: "Sometimes I stumble accidentally on rare combinations of slope, curved street-line, roofs & gables & chimneys, & accessory details of verdure & background, which in the magic of late afternoon assume a mystic majesty & exotic significance beyond the power of words to describe. . . . All that I live for is to capture some fragment of this hidden & unreachable beauty; this beauty which is all of dream, yet which I feel I have known closely & revelled in through long aeons before my birth or the birth of this or any other world." To some extent, the fantasy realms of the Dunsanian stories are transfigurations of this New England of ideal beauty. On the other hand, Lovecraft simultaneously perceived and devoted much of his work to depicting a different side of his native region: the degeneracy and superstition that flourish in isolated locales, as described in "The Picture in the House" and "The Unnameable"; the survival of unearthly rites practiced in the quaint, colonial town of Kingsport in "The Festival"; the clan of ghouls that inhabits modern Boston in "Pickman's Model"; the horror interred beneath "The Shunned House," which was inspired by an actual home in the district of Providence where Lovecraft resided; and the foul aspirations of an eighteenth-century wizard which are recapitulated in twentieth-century Providence in *The Case of Charles Dexter Ward.* In other stories, those of the Cthulhu Mythos, Lovecraft provided literary travelogues to a New England that departed even further from the sites of his antiquarian wanderings, revising the geography so familiar to him to create the fictional world of Arkham, Innsmouth, and Dunwich. As he wrote to one of his correspondents: "Yes— my New England is a dream New England—the familiar scene with certain lights and shadows heightened (or meant to be heightened) just enough to merge it with things beyond the world." Among these "things" are the primeval and extra-stellar pantheon of a body of myth that, although irregular in its details, is highly consistent as Lovecraft's expression of humanity's insignificant and unsteady place in the universe.

One of the most important and controversial issues in Lovecraft criticism is that regarding nomenclature for his Mythos stories. Various labels have been employed, from the broad designations of "horror" and "Gothic" to more discriminating terms such as "supernormal" and "mechanistic supernatural." At the source of this diverse terminology is the fact that, while these works clearly belong to the tradition of Gothic literature, Lovecraft did not make them dependent on the common mythic conceits associated with this tradition—such as the ghost, the vampire, witches, werewolves, and other figures of folklore— and even when they do appear in his work, these entities are often modified to function against a new mythical background, one whose symbolism emphasizes the philosophical over the psychological. For example, Keziah Mason in "Dreams in the Witch-House" has all the appearance and appurtenances of a seventeenth-century New England witch; but instead of serving the demonic forces of Christian mythology, she is in league with extraplanetary forces wholly alien to the human sphere and ultimately beyond good or evil, superterrestrial entities blind to either the welfare or harm of the human species. This order of alien existence and its imposing relationship to human life is similarly displayed in such works as "The Call of Cthulhu," "The Dunwich Horror," "The Whisperer in Darkness," and "The Shadow over Innsmouth," while *At the Mountains of Madness* and "The Shadow out of Time" offer more elaborate development of cosmic civilizations whose non-human nature violates all earthly conceptions of reality, forcing upon the protagonists of these narratives an esoteric knowledge which they can neither live with nor disregard. The question of how to describe tales whose effect derives from the violation of the laws of nature rather than those of personal or public morality was somewhat resolved by Lovecraft himself when he applied the term "weird" to such works. In a letter of 1926, he wrote: "As to what is meant by 'weird'—and of course weirdness is by no means confined to horror—I should say that the real criterion is *a strong impression of the suspension of natural laws or the presence of unseen worlds or forces close at hand*." The literary consequences of this distinction between weirdness and horror may be noted in the remarks of critics who find horrific effects minimal in Lovecraft's stories, their power relying more on an expansive and devastating confrontation with the unknown.

Critical reaction to Lovecraft's work displays an unusual diversity, from exasperated attacks upon what are judged to be the puerile ravings of an artistic and intellectual incompetent to celebrations of Lovecraft as one of the greatest writers and thinkers of the modern era. His severest detractors regard him as an isolated neurotic, and even something of an imbecile, whose writings merely betray a pathetic estrangement from the concerns of adult society. For the most part admitting Lovecraft's eccentricity, his defenders find in his fiction, and more obviously in the five volumes of his *Selected Letters*, a complex vision of reality which could only be formed by a mind of exceptional independence. Summarizing his perception of existence and the implications this had for the outward aspect of his life, Lovecraft explained: "I preach & practice an extreme conservatism in art forms, society, & politics, as the only means of averting the ennui, despair, & confusion of a guideless & standardless struggle with unveiled chaos." While this reaction has been called pathological, and its manifestation as literature uninteresting for readers whose psychic functions remain sound, it has also inspired empathy, even admiration, as an existential ploy not without relevance for a world in which "chaos" has become a key word. With regard to the literary consequences of Lovecraft's character, a great deal of controversy has persisted over his prose style which, reflecting the division between his reactionary code and his sense of universal discord, varies from a highly formal, essay-like discourse to

manic outbursts wherein rationality may be sacrificed for poetic effect. Briefly, Lovecraft's prose has been derided as labored and archaic by critics who regard plain-spoken realism as the modern standard for fiction; at the same time, it has been praised by those who perceive its calculated suitability for the idiosyncratic nature of Lovecraft's fictional universe, which demands artificiality and a remoteness from the familiar as paradoxical requisites for a vivification of the unreal and the impossible.

The debate concerning the value of Lovecraft's work is, of course, hardly unique in the history of literature. Lovecraft himself was the first to argue both sides of this controversy, which often extends beyond his own work and calls into question the validity of all weird literature. As he described his position to one correspondent: "Doubtless I am the sort of shock-purveyor condemned by critics of the urbane tradition as decadent or culturally immature; but I can't resist the fascination of the *outside*'s mythical shadowland, & I really have a fairly respectable line of literary predecessors to back me up." Elsewhere Lovecraft defended the weird tradition when he noted shared traits in his fiction and that of his contemporaries, contending that this similarity "illustrates the essential parallelism of the fantastic imagination in different individuals—a circumstance strongly arguing the existence of a natural & definite (though rare) mental world of the weird with a common background & fixed laws, out of which there must necessarily spring a literature as authentic in its way as the realistic literature which springs from mundane experience." For most of those concerned with this "world of the weird," Lovecraft has long taken his place among its most dedicated explorers and supreme documentarians.

(See also *TCLC*, Vol. 4 and *Contemporary Authors*, Vol. 104.)

PRINCIPAL WORKS

The Shunned House (short story) 1928
The Shadow over Innsmouth (short story) 1936
*The Outsider, and Others (short stories, novel, and criticism) 1939
**Beyond the Wall of Sleep (short stories, essays, poetry, and novels) 1943
Marginalia (short stories, essays, and juvenilia) 1944
Supernatural Horror in Literature (criticism) 1945
Something about Cats, and Other Pieces (short stories, essays, and poetry) 1949
The Shuttered Room, and Other Pieces (short stories, essays, and juvenilia) 1959
Collected Poems (poetry) 1963
Selected Letters. 5 vols. (letters) 1965-76
The Dark Brotherhood, and Other Pieces (short stories, essays, and poetry) 1966
The Horror in the Museum, and Other Revisions (short stories) 1970
To Quebec and the Stars (essays and travel essays) 1976
A Winter Wish (poetry and essays) 1977

*This collection includes the novel *At the Mountains of Madness*.

**This collection includes the novels *The Case of Charles Dexter Ward* and *The Dream-Quest of Unknown Kadath*.

H. P. LOVECRAFT (essay date 1921)

[*In the following excerpt from an essay written in 1921 but not published until 1985, Lovecraft propounds his views on weird fiction in the course of defending his short story "Dagon." The critics mentioned by Lovecraft are fellow members of the Transatlantic Circulator, a casual group of English and American writers who exchanged and commented upon one another's manuscripts.*]

In replying to the adverse criticisms of my weird tale **"Dagon,"** I must begin by conceding that all such work is necessarily directed to a very limited section of the public. Fiction falls generally into three major divisions; romantic, realistic, and imaginative. The first is for those who value action and emotion for their own sake; who are interested in striking events which conform to a preconceived artificial pattern. These readers will accept psychological improbabilities and untruths, and even highly distorted objective happenings, but they demand a background of literalism. Romanticists are persons who on the one hand scorn the realist who says that moonlight is only reflected wave-motion in aether; but who on the other hand sit stolid and unmoved when a *fantaisiste* tells them that the moon is a hideous nightmare eye—watching . . . ever watching. . . . They will say to the realist that he forgets the emotional influence of moonlight; but they will not be able to follow up subjectively a fantastic conception involving myth-making, so will be equally opposed to the teller of strange legends.

The second fictional school—the realism which rules the public today—is for those who are intellectual and analytical rather than poetical or emotional. It is scientific and literal, and laughs both at the romanticist and the myth-maker. It has the virtue of being close to life, but has the disadvantage of sinking into the commonplace and the unpleasant at times. Both romanticism and realism have the common quality of dealing almost wholly with the objective world—with things rather than with what things suggest. The poetic element is wanting. Romanticism calls on emotion, realism on pure reason; both ignore the *imagination,* which groups isolated impressions into gorgeous patterns and finds strange relations and associations among the objects of visible and invisible Nature. Phantasy exists to fulfil the demands of the imagination; but since imagination is so much less widely diffused than are emotion and analytical reason, it follows that such a literary type must be relatively rare, and decidedly restricted in its appeal. Imaginative artists have been few, and always unappreciated. Blake is woefully undervalued. Poe would never have been understood had not the French taken the pains to exalt and interpret him. Dunsany has met with nothing but coldness or lukewarm praise. And nine persons out of ten *never heard* of Ambrose Bierce, the greatest story writer except Poe whom America ever produced. The imaginative writer devotes himself to art in its most essential sense. It is not his business to fashion a pretty trifle to please the children, to point a useful moral, to concoct superficial "uplift" stuff for the mid-Victorian hold-over, or to rehash insolvable human problems didactically. He is the painter of moods and mind-pictures—a capturer and amplifier of elusive dreams and fancies—a voyager into those unheard-of lands which are glimpsed through the veil of actuality but rarely, and only by the most sensitive. He is one who not only sees objects, but follows up all the bizarre trails of associated ideas which encompass and lead away from them. He is the poet of twilight visions and childhood memories, but sings only for the sensitive. All moods are his to reproduce, be they bright or dark. "Wholesomeness" and "utility" are to him unknown words. He mirrors the rays that fall upon him, and does not ask their source or effect. He is not practical, poor fellow, and sometimes dies in poverty; for his friends all live in the City of Never above the sunset, or in the antique rock temples of Mycenae, or in the crypts and catacombs of Egypt and Meroë. Most persons do not understand what he says, and most of those who do understand object because his statements and pictures are not always pleasant and sometimes *quite impossible.* But he exists not for praise, nor thinks of his readers. His only [goal is] to paint the scenes that pass before his eyes.

Now far be it from me to claim the honour of being a real imaginative artist. It is my privilege only to admire from the abyss of mediocrity, and to copy in my feeble way. But what I have said of imaginative literature may help to explain what it is that I am feebly and unsuccessfully *trying to do.* It may explain why I do not tag my tales with copy-book morals or try to confine the events to cheerful, every-day happenings of unimpeachable probability. As to criticism—I ask only that my reviewers observe the basic law of their craft; a comparison between design and achievement. No one is more acutely conscious than I of the inadequacy of my work. Nothing exasperates me more than the failure of my written products to duplicate the visions and nightmares that lie behind them. I am a self-confessed amateur and bungler, and have not much hope of improvement—but the visions clamour for expression and preservation, so what is one to do?

To come to details—Miss Taylor says that **"Dagon"** "does not awaken any responsive quiver of horror or repugnance" in her. A writer in the September *American Amateur,* referring to my efforts, said:

> I recall that one night I let the moon shine in my eyes because I was afraid to get up and pull down the shade after reading one of his stories—**"Dagon,"** I think it was.

"Who shall decide, when doctors disagree?" I paint what I dream, and will let the public settle the rest amongst themselves! About the bottom of the sea—one must use imagination in picturing the effect of an oceanic upheaval. The essence of the horrible is the *unnatural.* The thought of a *rock walking* is not necessarily repulsive, but in Dunsany's *Gods of the Mountain* a man says with a great deal of terror and repulsion, "Rock should not walk in the evening!" In estimating the effect of the sea-bottom on the man in **"Dagon,"** we must remember that it has just been raised beneath his feet by some mysterious force—unnaturally raised from its age-long sleep in the darkness of ancient waters—and that it extends all around him as far as he can see. He does not know its extent—all is doubt, wonder, and unnatural mystery. This man might not be afraid to watch the tide go out on the beach at home; but under the circumstances of the tale, he is likely to be a rather badly scared sailor. . . . Probably the worst thing is *solitude in barren immensity.* That has unhinged more than one mind. As to the fish—the assumption is correct. The earthquake killed some, and the rest died for want of water after the ocean bed rose to the air.

Mr. Brown is "unimpressed as to the reality" of **"Dagon,"** since to him it seems quite impossible. In reply I might say that realism was not the desired effect, although in past geological ages large bodies of land have both risen above and sunk beneath the waves. Does Mr. Brown recall the legend of "Atlantis"? I have written a long story on that theme. About the ocean bed—I shall have to disagree with Mr. Brown, summoning the facts of physical geography to my aid. The deep-sea bottom is smooth and monotonous—a rolling plain with few topographical features. There is no life—water-pressure is too great—but there is a deposit of "ooze" consisting of the tiny shells of simple marine organisms which live near the surface. One physiographer—to choose a book almost at random from my shelves—says:

> The monotony, dreariness, and desolation of the deeper parts of this submarine scenery can scarcely be realised. The most barren terrestrial districts must seem diversified when compared with the vast expanse of ooze which covers the deeper parts of the ocean.

Shallow-water conditions are not true of the deep sea.

Why should the hero of **"Dagon"** wish to escape from the Germans if well-treated? For one thing, he might prefer the chances of rescue to the certainties of a Hun prison-camp at the end of the voyage.

Miss Fidlar's remark that war horrors have exhausted the capacity of the world for receiving new horrors may be answered in two ways—(1) I do not write for any particular age—I wrote as much before the war as after, and **"Dagon"** was written about the middle of it. (2) The physical horrors of war, no matter how extreme and unprecedented, hardly have a bearing on the entirely different realm of supernatural terror. Ghosts are still ghosts—the mind can get more thrills from unrealities than from realities!

Mr. Bullen's criticism is greatly appreciated, and I am glad that poor **"Dagon"** did not bore *everyone*! He overestimates the didactic element a trifle—like Dunsany I protest that except in a few cases I have no thought of teaching. The story is first, and if any philosophy creeps in it is by accident. **"The White Ship"** was an exception. As to the criticisms—the hero-victim *is* sucked half into the mire, yet he *does* crawl! He pulls himself along in the detestable ooze, tenaciously though it cling to him. I know, for I dreamed that whole hideous crawl, and can yet feel the ooze sucking me down! Possibly my description lacked clearness. As to the expression "completeness of the stillness"—I wish to emphasise a peculiar condition paralleled only by that in Poe's "Silence; a Fable," and also to *balance* the phrase "homogeneity of the landscape." (pp. 11-14)

Mr. Munday asks the *raison d'être* of **"Dagon"**—I will give it—purely and simply to reproduce a mood. Its object is the simplest in all art—portrayal. (p. 14)

> H. P. Lovecraft, *"The Defense Reopens!"* in In Defense of Dagon, edited by S. T. Joshi, Necronomicon Press, 1985, pp. 11-21.

JACQUES BERGIER (letter date 1937)

[*Bergier was a French scientist, critic, and translator, and the author of works examining the common ground between science and occultism. During the 1950s he was instrumental in the introduction of Lovecraft's works to France, and in 1969 he published a French translation of* Supernatural Horror in Literature. *In the following excerpt from a letter to* Weird Tales, *Bergier expresses his high estimation of Lovecraft's work.*]

I deeply and sincerely mourn the passing of H. P. Lovecraft. I believe that Lovecraft was one of America's greatest writers, an equal to Poe. I believe that recognition of this fact will come after a lapse of years, as with Poe. Such tales as **"The Music of Erich Zann," "The Dreams in the Witch-House"**

and **"The Temple,"** as well as his cycle of the Elder Gods and strange civilizations, and the extraordinary **"Through the Gates of the Silver Key,"** will remain, marking a writer of extraordinary power, to be placed with Poe, Wells, Machen and Blackwood. The passing of Lovecraft seems to me to mark an end of an epoch in the history of American imaginative fiction, an history that begins with Poe, continues with Bierce's *Can Such Things Be?*, Chambers' *The King in Yellow*, Merritt's "The Moon Pool," and then the era of fantastic story magazines of which only *Weird Tales* and a science-fiction magazine now continue to print real fantasy. I think that many of the stories published in this last year—and among them, almost all of Lovecraft's—were great and will endure. And in spite—or perhaps because—of my scientific training I sometimes think that perhaps Lovecraft had a glimpse across 'undreamable abysses,' of facts about the structure of the universe that science will one day discover. . . .

> *Jacques Bergier, in a letter in "Weird Tales," September, 1937, in* H. P. Lovecraft *in "The Eyrie," edited by S. T. Joshi and Marc A. Michand, Necronomicon Press, 1979, p. 50.*

ANTON SZANDOR LaVEY (essay date 1972)

[*LaVey is the founder of the First Church of Satan, a religion devoted to spiritual and carnal fulfillment through the development of individual will. In the following excerpt from his* Satanic Rituals, *LaVey remarks on the likeness between the worldview implicit in Lovecraft's work and the philosophy of present-day Satanism.*]

Even to his most intimate acquaintances, Howard Phillips Lovecraft . . . remained frustratingly enigmatic. From the pen of this ingenious New Englander came a collection of the most convincing and thoroughly terrifying works of macabre fiction in modern times. His tales were uniquely embellished with painstaking pseudo-documentation and meticulous description of character and setting. It is frequently said that, once one has read Lovecraft, one disdains the efforts of the competition. This statement has been consistently difficult to refute.

As might be expected, Lovecraft was lionized and extensively imitated by a number of writers whose imaginations were sparked by his celebrated "Cthulhu mythos"—a term commonly given to a series of stories based upon a supernatural pantheon of Lovecraft's own invention. He had a firm conviction that reference to the classical mythologies would undermine the atmosphere of cyclic and spatial disorientation he sought to create. Lovecraft created his own beings, whose prehistoric activities on Earth set in motion the forces of man's civilization and genius, as well as the horrors of his educated imagination. While Freud and Einstein wrestled with their respective disciplines in the isolation of academic specialization, Lovecraft was describing the astonishing influence of physical and geometric law on the psyche. While he might have hesitated to style himself a master of scientific speculation, he is no less deserving of that title than are Asimov and Clarke.

What has puzzled many of Lovecraft's admirers is the author's almost casual attitude towards his work. He repeatedly referred to it as a mere means of financial subsistence. To people who suspected that he entertained a private belief in the mythos, he would reply that an objective detachment from one's material was necessary for effective writing. He was wont to mention the most nightmarish of his narratives with a levity bordering upon scorn, as though he did not consider them of genuine literary substance. As an author, Lovecraft enjoys an established reputation, but what of Lovecraft the philosopher?

Perhaps the most significant clues to the philosophy in the Cthulhu mythos derive from the author's fascination with human history, particularly that of the classical eras. That much of his work used material taken from Egyptian and Arabian legends is well known. There is evidence that he was acutely aware of civilization's effects upon mankind—both educational and repressive. His tales constantly remind the reader that humanity is but a short step from the most depraved and vicious forms of bestiality. He sensed man's drive toward knowledge, even at the risk of sanity. Intellectual excellence, he seemed to say, is achieved in concert with cataclysmic terror—not in avoidance of it.

This theme of a constant interrelationship between the constructive and destructive facets of the human personality is the keystone of the docrines of Satanism. Theism argues that the integrity of the individual can be increased by a rejection of the carnal and an obedience to morality. Lovecraft recorded his aversion to conventional religious dogma in **"The Silver Key,"** and he regarded with a similar scorn those who, rejecting religion, succumbed to a controversial substitute, i.e. the popular notion of witchcraft. The concept of worship *per se* is strikingly absent from the Cthulhu mythos. Nyarlathotep, Shub-Niggurath, Yog-Sothoth and Cthulhu are all honored through bizarre festivals, but their relationship to their followers is invariably that of teacher to students. Compare the description of a Lovecraftian ceremony to that of a Christian mass or a Voodoo rite, and it is clear that the element of servility is definitely lacking in the first.

Lovecraft, like the Miltonian Satan, chose to reign in Hell rather than to serve in Heaven. His creatures are never conclusive stereotypes of good or evil; they vacillate constantly between beneficence and cruelty. They respect knowledge, for which the protagonist of each story abandons every prudent restraint. Critics who consider the Old Ones as Aristotelian elementals—or as a collective influence of malignancy which man must destroy if he is to prevail—suggest a philistine disposition. Lovecraft, if he tolerated such analyses, can hardly have been impressed by them.

Assuming that Lovecraft was an advocate of Satanic amorality, what might have been the content of the ritual observances in Innsmouth, R'lyeh, or Leng? In his work he only goes as far as an occasional lurid line from some "nameless rite" or "unspeakable orgy" celebrated by grotesque apparitions amidst sulphurous caverns of fluorescent, decaying fungi, or against titanic monoliths of disturbing aspect. Perhaps he thought understatement to be more effective in freeing the imaginations of his readers, but clearly, he had been influenced by very real sources. Whether his sources of inspiration were consciously recognized and admitted or were a remarkable "psychic" absorption, one can only speculate. There is no doubt that Lovecraft was aware of rites not quite "nameless," as the allusions in his stories are often *identical* to actual ceremonial procedures and nomenclature, especially to those practiced and advanced around the turn of the last century.

The Innsmouths and Arkhams of Lovecraft have their counterparts in seaside hamlets and forlorn coastal areas all over the world, and one has but to use his senses to spot them: the Land's End sector of San Francisco; Mendocino on the Northern California coast; from the Hamptons to Montauk in New York; between Folkestone and Dover on the English Channel;

the Cornish coast west of Exmouth, and numerous points along the coast of Brittany in France. The list is endless. Where men have stood at earth's end contemplating the transition from sea to land with mingled fear and longing in their hearts, the lure of Cthulhu exists. Any offshore oil drilling platform or "Texas tower" is a potential altar to the Spawn of the Watery Abyss.

Lovecraft seems to have correlated the monsters of the canvasses of a hundred Pickmans—the great Symbolist painters of the 1890's—into a twentieth century scenario. His fantasies may well have been a conscious projection of the idea expressed so eloquently by Charles Lamb in his *Witches and Other Night Fears:*

> Gorgons, and Hydras, and Chimeras may reproduce themselves in the brain of superstition—but they were there before. They are transcripts, types—the archetypes are in us, and eternal.

One cannot help speculating upon a reality suggested by the fantasy—the possibility that the Old Ones are the spectres of a future hman mentality. (pp. 175-78)

Anton Szandor LaVey, "The Metaphysics of Love-craft—'The Ceremony of the Nine Angles' and 'The Call of Cthulhu'," in his The Satanic Rituals, *Avon, 1972, pp. 173-207.*

DIRK W. MOSIG (essay date 1973)

[*An American educator and critic, Mosig is one of the pioneering figures in the study of Lovecraft's work, and much subsequent scholarship and criticism was inspired by his contributions to this field. In the following excerpt, first published in* Whispers, *December, 1973, Mosig examines the view of humanity implied by Lovecraft's work, particularly the story "The Outsider."*]

Howard Phillips Lovecraft has finally achieved what appears to be a secure niche in Anglo-American literature, and is widely acclaimed for his fantastic creations in the worlds of the bizarre and the macabre. In addition, the publication of his brilliant letters is gradually earning him recognition as one of the greatest epistolarians of all time. Nevertheless, one aspect of Lovecraft has remained strangely neglected—his value as a significant thinker.

Lovecraft's greatest forte was perhaps his lucid and objective materialistic philosophy, so well exposed in many of his letters and in essays such as **"Idealism and Materialism," "The Materialist Today," "A Confession of Unfaith," "Nietzscheism and Realism,"** and others. These pieces, expounding his cosmic-minded mechanistic materialism, reveal him as a profound *penseur* and provide a unique framework for the understanding and interpretation of his memorable fiction.

In his conception of Life, Man, and the Universe, Lovecraft considered himself a *realist,* in the sense that Richard Upton Pickman was a realist. . . . He abandoned all cherished myths, all explanatory fictions, all dreams and illusions, and faced reality as he perceived it, with utmost objectivity and a total lack of emotional involvement. In this sense he was truly an Outsider, able to become an intellectually detached observer of the futile antics of men and beasts, standing aside and watching the stream of time flow by, like some mythical intelligence from Outside, amused by the abysmal insignificance of Man and the purposelessness of the cosmos. He coldly analyzed the beliefs in the perfectibility of man, and in science as the panacea of all evils, as well as the naive expectations of a utopic future,

Lovecraft's childhood home at 454 Angell Street, Providence. From left to right: Annie Phillips Gamwell, Mrs. Winfield Lovecraft, Sr., Winfield Lovecraft, Sr., and Sarah Phillips Lovecraft.

and found them equally unfounded on fact. Even though he was a scientist at heart, a rationalist for whom knowledge was the ultimate good, he prophesied with unique insight the general rejection of iconoclastic Science by horrified Man, unwillingly confronted with reality, and desperately refusing to accept the truth about his own meaninglessness and lack of destiny in a mechanistic Universe. As early as 1921, he clearly foresaw what we know today as "future shock," the recoil of Man from the revelations of the future which he is not ready nor willing to accept.

Future shock and man's retreat into insanity or the safety of a new Dark Age were clearly predicted in the introductory paragraph of **"The Call of Cthulhu,"** to which the reader stands referred, as well as in several other tales and passages, long before the publication of Alvin Toffler's bestseller. Consider, for example, the following lines from **"Arthur Jermyn"**:

> Life is a hideous thing, and from the background behind what we know of it peer daemoniacal hints of truth which make it sometimes a thousandfold more hideous. Science, already oppressive with its shocking revelations, will perhaps be the ultimate exterminator of our human species . . . for its reserve of unguessed horrors could never be borne by mortal brains if loosed upon the world.

For Lovecraft, "the most merciful thing in the world is the inability of the human mind to correlate all its contents," that is, the avoidance of cognitive dissonance by the compartmentalization and lack of communication between facts stored in the human brain. It is merciful because complete awareness of reality would almost certainly result in mental disintegration and psychosis. The consequences of such an instant of total realization form the theme of one of Lovecraft's early masterpieces, **"The Outsider."** In this peerless work of philosophical allegory, he grimly prophesied the outcome of Man's confrontation with the revelations of the Future. (pp. 9-10)

Three main stages are clearly discernible in **"The Ousider."** The first is the time spent in the subterranean castle, which stands for the *PAST*. Here the narrator, who represents MAN, lives in the security of ignorance, surrounded by the countless musty books of the great library—the storehouse of mythical lore and budding scientific knowledge accumulated through the ages. Completely unaware of reality, he dreams endlessly of the many marvels to come, of the happiness and blessings promised by the bright pictures in the mouldy volumes, and of the ultimate freedom that must result when the Light of day—the knowledge of Science—dispels the "brooding shadows" of fear and ignorance. His yearning for Light grows so frantic that he decides to climb the single black tower pointing the way to the Utopia that must lie above the "terrible trees" that keep him rooted in the past. His emergence through the monolithic tower into the level ground, symbolizes Man's birth into the *PRESENT*. The ensuing wanderings under the moonlight represent Man's frantic but hopeful quest for his idealized goals—freedom, happiness, perfection. . . . Man is convinced that all his dreams will come true through the miracles of Science in the not too distant future. The third stage shows Man coming face to face with reality in the Castle of Lights, representing the *FUTURE*. But the future is not what he expected, and instead of the fabled golden utopia of his dreams, he finds only the most bitter of disappointments. The future has not brought the happiness and security he yearned for, but instead has revealed the reality about Man—a meaningless accident in an unfathomable cosmos, lasting an instant in eternity, devoid of purpose, destiny, dignity, glory. . . . A filthy vermin polluting a grain of sand in a purposeless universe, the abominable disease of a negligible planet that did not exist a moment ago and which will have been forgotten an instant hence—all this, and much more, he sees in his fateful reflection on the mirror of Science with the golden frame of his dreams, in the castle of the Future.

Faced with the unutterable horror of total realization, Man is overwhelmed by the traumatic level of cognitive dissonance, and to reduce it, not only denies reality, but also changes his belief in science, in progress, and in the future. As he madly recoils and tries to regain the lost security of the past, attempting to return to the subterranean castle, he finds the trap door immovable: there is no return. His final flight is into the new freedom of insanity and the security provided by the unknown feasts of Nitokris—the superstitions of a new Dark Age. . . . The Outsider is alienated Man, ''dazed, disappointed, barren, broken,'' victim of ''future shock,'' condemned to a meaningless existence in the ever changing present, faced with traumatic revelations from which the only escape is self-deception and the regression of psychosis. . . .

Lovecraft did not share the naive humanistic beliefs in the unlimited perfectibility of Man and his unbounded ability to adapt to the revelations of the future. His view of the future went beyond Huxley's and Orwell's in terms of its detached objectivity and cold realism, and he predicted in many of his tales and essays the bleak consequences of man's inability to cope with reality and with the advancing tide of progress.

The accuracy of this pessimistic prophecy and the validity of his critique of progress are attested to today not only by the devastating super-abundance of maladaptive reactions to the unbearable stresses of modern life—with mental patients taking up over one-half of all hospital beds—but also by the wholesale escape into the ''cancer of superstition,'' the countless *fads* of pseudo-mysticism, astrology, palmistry, phrenology, numerology, occultism, religion, witchcraft, voodoo, transcendental meditation, satanism, psychic phenomena, psychedelic drugs . . . anything to regain the lost sense of security, to escape from the cold and unbearable reality emerging like a phoenix from the ashes of the crumbling edifices of traditional beliefs and cherished myths shattered by the efforts of the great iconoclasts: Galileo, Copernicus, Darwin, Freud, Einstein, Skinner, and many others. But it is a barren phoenix, rejected and despised, because the new Dark Age has already begun. . . . (Parenthetically, it is interesting to observe here that the rejection of Lovecraft's mechanistic materialism by readers of this article is an implicit confirmation of the validity of his prediction.)

Throughout the Lovecraft opus are scattered references to his philosophical *Weltanschauung*, as well as impressive glimpses of his vivid vision of the intellectual crisis of the future, felt today more than ever before. His works, like those of Franz Kafka, are full of allegories, analogies, parables, and symbols, resulting not from a hollow didacticism, but from the deep undercurrents of philosophical thought which permeate his writings and make them extremely relevant today. The time is right for a greater appreciation of this deeper, more serious aspect of Lovecraft's fiction, as well as of his many philosophical essays, which deserve being collected in a single volume together with excerpts from his prolific correspondence. The ground is particularly ready in Europe, where his works are held in highest esteem. For instance, two recent collections of Lovecraft's tales published in Spain appeared in a literary series including works by Nietzsche, Unamuno, Freud, Malthus, Pavlov, Jung, Kafka, Kant, Schopenhauer, Karl Marx, Bertrand Russell, and others.

Ultimately, Lovecraft's fame should rest not only on his value as a master of dramatic fiction, a skilled poet, and a brilliant epistolarian, but also on the depth and significance of the philosophical insights of his superior intellect. (pp. 10-11)

> *Dirk W. Mosig, ''The Prophet from Providence,'' in* Crypt of Cthulhu, *Vol. 4, No. 8, August 1, 1985, pp. 9-11.*

LARRY McMURTRY (essay date 1975)

[*An American fiction writer and critic, McMurtry has been called the best regional writer the Southwest has yet produced. While earlier ''cowboy'' novels were idealized epics of courage and nobility, McMurtry's works demythologize the American West, using satire and black humor to portray characters who share the basic human experiences of frustration, loneliness, and loss. These works have been especially praised for their realistic detail and skillful prose style. In the following review of L. Sprague De Camp's* Lovecraft: A Biography *(1975), McMurtry attacks Lovecraft and his works, the Gothic literary tradition, and pulp fiction of the 1920s and 1930s.*]

The long-awaited Lovecraft biography is finally here. Frankly, I could have awaited it 20 or 30 more years without serious discomfort, but there is a large and perennially adolescent subculture in America that will no doubt be grateful to have the book now. As a biography it is, at best, of sparse interest, but as a kind of casebook on the history of a phenomenon—i.e., the popularity of a totally untalented and unreadable writer—it is not without its curiosity.

L. Sprague De Camp is a scrupulous writer, honest to a fault. It is honesty, rather than his scholarship or his literary judgment, that gives this book its interest. Few biographers can have been forced to testify so constantly against their subjects. Almost every sentence De Camp quotes from the work or the correspondence of Howard Phillips Lovecraft (1890-1937)— and he quotes thousands—reveals the man to have been a hopeless and rather pitiful literary crank. It is quite clear that, emotionally and intellectually, Lovecraft never progressed beyond adolescence, and it is thus not surprising that adolescents have kept his name alive. Weird-fantasy, the genre in which Lovecraft worked, has always been a weak strain in Western literature; Lovecraft's antecedents were the German and English Gothics of the early 19th century—some of the most unreadable books ever written. Poe took this strain up and brought a certain thin genius to it, but it clearly peaked with him.

What the pulp writers of the '20s and '30s did was to achieve a kind of marriage of Gothicism a la Poe with the boy's adventure story, a la Henty, Kirk Monroe, etc. This was an awful mixture then and it is still an awful mixture, but it appeals precisely to adolescent morbidity and the adolescent need for the private and the arcane. The private kingdoms of the weird-fantasiasts offer adolescents an escape from their sense of misfittedness; if they didn't, the genre would have died with Monk Lewis.

There were a number of pulp writers who at least managed to write plain prose—Frank Gruber, Ernest Haycox and the prodigious Frederick Faust. Lovecraft, unfortunately, was the master of the turgid and the inflated. His chief gift seems to have been for the creation of vaguely Druidic vaguely Celtic nomenclature. What is one to make of a man, for example, whose sonnet sequence is called **"Fungi from Yuggoth"**? One of his most famous stories is called *The Dream-Quest of Unknown Kadath.* It contains dholes, ghouls, gugs, ghasts and small furry creatures called zoogs. De Camp admits that these names lend a juvenile flavor, but he appears to feel that they are offset by the story's atmosphere. Yet this famous Lovecraftian atmosphere—it is all he really ever had to offer, since, as his biographer admits, he was totally uninterested in the creation of character—seems to me to consist largely of more names. In that one story, for example, we find such names as Barzai, Hatheg-Kla, Pnakotic, Atal, Mount Ngranek, the isle of Oriab and something called Nyarlathotep. And if the reader thinks those names something, let me assure the reader that they are nothing compared to the names of Lovecraft's one-act Cthulhuvian operetta *Fen River.*

In 1945, writing in the *New Yorker*, Edmund Wilson said all that needed to be said about H. P. Lovecraft as a talent. What Wilson said was that Lovecraft had no talent [see excerpt in *TCLC*, Vol. 4]. De Camp tries to refute this judgment; his refutation is to insist that Edmund Wilson was a snob. Yet Wilson was clearly right. Lovecraft's prose is terrible, a third-rate imitation of Poe; and, as to content, he really has none. Even his fabled letters, about which one has heard so much, are the letters of a sad, silly, juvenile, self-deluded introvert. His reading, like his writing, was very limited; he seldom ever mentions having read a good book.

Finally, one might say that attempts to respectabilize the pulp writers of the '20s and '30s just don't work. The pulp writers were phenomenal producers but terrible writers; take away Raymond Chandler and the pulps were zilch, an almost totally sub-literary medium. They survive as a collecting fad largely because of their cover art, and not because of the writing between their covers.

> *Larry McMurtry, "'Master of the Turgid'," in* The Washington Post, *February 17, 1975, p. D4.*

URSULA LE GUIN (essay date 1976)

[*An American novelist and critic, Le Guin is considered one of the most important authors in contemporary science fiction and fantasy literature. Her works have been especially praised for their literate style, rich inventiveness, and deep humanism. In the following excerpt, Le Guin condemns Lovecraft's prose style while nonetheless recognizing the emotional power of his work.*]

H. P. Lovecraft of Providence, Rhode Island, the author of such works as **"The Dunwich Horror"** and **"Fungi from Yuggoth,"** is the object of a small but tenacious cult. It would be fun for anyone allergic to cultism to go through Lovecraft's works selecting a nosegay of fungi, collecting bigotries and infelicities, perhaps enlisting a computer to determine how many times he used the word "eldritch." Fun, but far too easy. One could quote almost at random. Lovecraft was an exceptionally, almost impeccably, bad writer. He imitated the worst bits of Poe quite accurately, but his efforts to catch Dunsany's sonorous rhythms show an ear of solid tin. Derivative, inept, and callow, his tales can satisfy only those who believe that a capital letter, some words, and a full stop make a sentence.

But though dissatisfied, one may be fascinated, as by any extreme psychological oddity. There cannot have been many writers who surrendered themselves so helplessly, so unprotestingly, to their daemon. Lovecraft dangles like a rabbit from the jaws of his unconscious. Seldom in his life and never in his writing did he try to fight back, to summon up a shred of coherent reasoning, a scrap of authentic prose, as a bulwark against the terrors and compulsions that tyrannized his mind. But Lovecraft's feebleness gave his writing its one strength: his tales can be frightening. Read late at night alone, they give the genuine chill. The house creaks; the cat stares fixedly at something about three feet tall which you cannot quite see, there behind the armchair. Is there, perhaps, a webfooted person in the basement?

Indeed there was, in Lovecraft's basement. His works beg for psychiatric analysis. They probably would not give a Jungian much scope of the kind that Rider Haggard gave Jung himself: Lovecraft's was a case of arrested development, and Freudian repression-hunting is what is called for. It might, however, be good hunting. At six, the gifted, coddled child of a syphilitic father and a hysterically protective mother wrote down his dream of "a boy who overheard some horrible conclave of subterranean beings in a cave." . . . He went on writing it down for the next forty years.

There was wit and intelligence in him, which went mostly to waste. He said: "All my tales are based on the fundamental premise that common human laws and emotions have no validity or significance in the cosmos-at-large." His effort was "to achieve the essence of real externality." That is no mean ambition, and the phrase provides a useful clue about the nature of the "horror story." For if we seek to be horrified, now and then, by stories, it is surely worth asking why, and how, and what it is that we are afraid of. . . .

> *Ursula Le Guin, "New England Gothic," in* The Times Literary Supplement, *No. 3863, March 26, 1976, p. 335.*

BARTON LEVI ST. ARMAND (essay date 1977)

[*St. Armand is an American critic and educator specializing in American literature and literary figures, particularly such New England authors as Nathaniel Hawthorne, Emily Dickinson, Sarah Orne Jewett, and H. P. Lovecraft. His studies of Lovecraft are considered among the most significant in the field. In the following excerpt, St. Armand discusses the sources and significance of horror in Lovecraft's fiction.*]

In his long historical essay entitled *Supernatural Horror in Literature,* the modern fantasist and master of the macabre, H. P. Lovecraft, tells us that "Children will always be afraid of the dark, and men with minds sensitive to hereditary impulse will always tremble at the thought of the hidden and fathomless worlds of strange life which may pulsate in the gulfs beyond the stars, or press hideously upon our own globe in unholy dimensions which only the dead and the moonstruck can glimpse.'' This insight is framed in typical Lovecraftian hyperbole, yet it appears in a study that, while both exhaustive and suggestive in the scope of its erudition, actually reveals little about the roots of horror itself and nothing about those particular eldritch roots of horror in Lovecraft's own work. Indeed, although he thought of himself as an eighteenth-century mind born into the wrong world, Lovecraft neglects to make a basic discrimination between ''horror'' and ''terror'' first formulated by Mrs. Ann Radcliffe, whose exquisitely horrid novels, *The Mysteries of Udolpho* and *The Italian*, titillated many a delicate Gothic sensibility in the 1790's. Lovecraft goes on to devote two long paragraphs to Mrs. Radcliffe in *Supernatural Horror in Literature,* noting that her ''genuine sense of the unearthly in scene and incident . . . closely approached genius'' and that ''A few sinister details like a track of blood on castle stairs, a groan from a distant vault, or a weird song in a nocturnal forest can with her conjure up the most powerful images of imminent horror; surpassing by far the extravagant and toilsome elaborations of others.'' . . . Yet, HPL's mention of Mrs. Radcliffe remains only a polite gesture, just as his reading of the interminable *Mysteries of Udolpho* must have been an extended act of scholarly homage and a supreme test of his own Chesterfieldian sense of honor.

The definitions in question appeared, as Bonamy Dobrée notes in his introduction to the most recent Oxford University Press edition of *Udolpho,* in a posthumous article entitled ''On the Supernatural in Poetry,'' in which Mrs. Radcliffe says:

> They must be men of very cold imaginations with whom certainty is more terrible than surmise. Terror and horror are so far opposite, that the first expands the soul, and wakens the faculties to a high degree of life; the other contracts, freezes, and nearly annihilates them. I apprehend that neither Shakespeare nor Milton by their fictions, nor Mr. Burke by his reasoning, anywhere looked to positive horror as a source of the sublime, though they all agree that terror is a very high one; and where lies the great difference between horror and terror, but in uncertainty and obscurity, that accompany the first, respecting the dreader evil?

Dobrée goes on to add that ''Her distinction would seem to gain support from the *New English Dictionary,* where terror is defined as 'intense fear, fright, or dread,' while horror is 'compounded of loathing and fear; shuddering with terror and repugnance.'''

Thus, there are two different directions or dimensions associated with these two different emotions if we accept Mrs. Radcliffe's initial premise about their essential dissimilarity. Terror expands the soul outward; it leads us to or engulfs us in the sublime, the immense, the cosmic. We are, as it were, lost in the ocean of fear or plunged directly into it, drowning of our dread. What we lose is the sense of self. That feeling of ''awe,'' which traditionally accompanies intimations of the sublime, links terror with experiences that are basically religious in nature, like those annihilating confrontations with the numinous that [Rudolph] Otto explores in *The Idea of the Holy.*

Lovecraft touches on this connection between the terrific and the numinous when, in his general discussion of fear, he writes, ''There is here involved a psychological pattern or tradition as real and as deeply grounded in mental experience as any other pattern or tradition of mankind; coeval with the religious feeling and closely related to many aspects of it, and too much a part of our innermost biological heritage to lose keen potency over a very important, though not numerically great, minority of our species.'' . . . (pp. 1-3)

Yet the archetypal patterns that Lovecraft associates with fear apply most precisely not only to the springs of terror in his fiction (although, as we shall see, there surely is an approach to the religious in his Descartian preoccupation with the sublimity of the void) but to those roots of horror—especially traditional Gothic horror—with which the fiction began. For if terror expands the soul and leads to an overwhelming, potentially destructive, sense of cosmic outsideness in Lovecraft's later and longer science-fiction works, then horror is equally annihilating, but from a dramatically different direction. Horror overtakes the soul from the inside; consciousness shrinks or withers from within, and the self is not flung into the exterior ocean of awe but, sinks in its own bloodstream, choked by the alien salts of its inescapable prevertebrate heritage.

Terror entails a quest for the wholly other, the outside. I should like to demonstrate that in Lovecraft's fiction horror demands a parallel descent into the subconscious, the inside, which reveals an added archetypal and psychological dimension to his own use of Mrs. Radcliffe's Gothic tradition. In semantically proper terms, terror is a means of evolution toward the ineffable; horror is a species of devolution toward—to use another appropriately Lovecraftian phrase—''the unspeakable.''

Horror and terror are also the visionary means by which Lovecraft manages to break the cosmic laws of time and space and so accomplish that rupture of the ordinary which he considered to be the great secret of the best supernatural fiction. Terror is the springboard that can hurl the soul and the self beyond the coordinates of daylight reality; horror is the plank in reason that can break and plummet the individual into the profoundest pit of his own darkest dreams. Writing at the beginning of *Supernatural Horror in Literature,* Lovecraft reiterates this doctrine, which can often be found in his letters to younger disciples who aspired to the making of superior weird tales. Here Lovecraft is speaking of ''cosmic fear'' and that kind of science-fiction fantasy he came to write only after experimenting with the possibilities of Gothic horror, that interior domain of the shuddery and the repugnant. ''The cosmic,'' he writes,

> must not be confounded with a type externally similar but psychologically widely different; the literature of mere physical fear and the mundanely gruesome. Such writing, to be sure, has its place, as has the conventional or even whimsical or humorous ghost story where formalism or the author's knowing wink removes the true sense of the morbidly unnatural; but these things are not the literature of cosmic fear in its purest sense. The true weird tale has something more than secret murder, bloody bones, or a sheeted form clanking chains according to rule. A certain atmosphere of breathless and unexplainable dread of outer, unknown forces must be present; and there must be a hint, expressed with a seriousness and portentousness becoming its subject, of that most terrible conception of the human brain—a malign and particular suspension or defeat of those fixed laws of Nature which are our only safeguard against the

assaults of chaos and the demons of unplumbed
space. . . .

(pp. 3-4)

Lovecraft tried to abandon his early dream-quest of the dreadful
because he felt his first, traditionally Gothic pieces were too
derivative and "mundanely gruesome." Much has been made
of the slow development of his "Cthulhu Mythos" and the
tales of cosmic outsideness, such as **"The Shadow Out of
Time"** and *At the Mountains of Madness,* yet the full scope of
Lovecraft's work cannot really be understood without also understanding what he was trying to achieve in these increasingly
longer productions. This was nothing less than a mating of
Gothic horror and cosmic terror, an unholy marriage of inside
and outside—hence the presence in these tales of a whole
pantheon of outside gods (Cthulhu, Azathoth, Yog-Sothoth)
as well as such entities as the viscous Shugoths of Antarctica,
or what Edmund Wilson called the "invisible whistling octopus" of the forbidden city in **"The Shadow Out of Time,"**
both of which come from subterranean caves deep below the
desert of the ice. A kind of monstrous theory of relativity is
operating in these longer fictions: one can go so far outside
that the result is a return or emergence at the farthest point
inside. (p. 4)

Like the short stories of Lovecraft's great mentor, Edgar Allan
Poe, Lovecraft's tales operate on at least two levels: the first,
an instinctive Gothic one calculated to produce in the reader
what Victor Hugo called a *frisson nouveau;* the second, an
archetypal, psychological, or metaphysical level that (to use
one of Poe's favorite metaphors) "has a depth greater than the
well of Democritus." The primary level is precisely that of
Poe's famous unitary and preconceived "effect," the effect of
sheer sensation and radical dislocation of the psyche. But as
we have noted, this initial disruption of the sense of self,
dictated by the prime coordinates of our mundane, daylight
world of space and time, leads in both artists to a contemplation
of the meaning of space and of time and ultimately to a consideration of the place of man in an alien and indifferent universe.

Thus, through the first circle of fear or horror (to utilize the
Radcliffean dichotomy I stated at the beginning of this discussion) we are launched toward ever-widening maelstroms of
terror or the sublime. Otto has explored in depth this connection
between these two extremely polar yet inextricably linked states
of the soul, taking as one of his principles the maxim propounded by the French metaphysician Récéjac in his *Essai sur
les fondements de la connaissance mystique,* where he states
that: "Mysticism begins in fear, in the feeling of a universal
and invincible domination, which later becomes a desire for
union with that which dominates" (Otto . . .). Although Lovecraft, dedicated materialist that he was, would have shuddered
at having either his works or himself labeled "mystical," still
in his own rationalistic terms he fully believed that fear or
horror was allied to a realm of primitive vision "coeval with
the religious feeling and closely related to many aspects of it,"
as he wrote in *Supernatural Horror in Literature.* This can be
easily seen if we substitute the term "sublimity" for his own
vague and elusive words "alienage" and "outsideness," staples of his critical vocabulary.

Much like one of the old Cabbalists, who forbade pronouncing
or writing the true and awful name of God, Lovecraft himself
had a certain horror of defining his concepts too rigidly. He
was at his artistic best when he matched the majesty and inef-
fability of his idea of the unholy with poetic and equally "sub-

lime" prose. Thus he could write Wilfred Blanch Talman,
advising him on the composition of a horror story, that "if any
suggestions are in order, I suppose the thing to urge would be
a more bizarre, cosmically external, and utterly non-human set
of motives and phenomena—in order to achieve that effect of
the *unknown outside clawing at the rim of the known* which
forms spectral horror in its acutest form." . . . (pp. 34-5)

It is a critical truism with Lovecraft, and an unfortunate one,
that the more realistic and detailed his monsters grow, the less
convincing and the less horrific they simultaneously become.
He was conscious of this tendency himself, and wrote one
correspondent that "Most of my monsters fail altogether to
satisfy my sense of the cosmic—the abnormally chromatic entity in **'The Colour Out of Space'** being the only one of the
lot which I take any pride in." . . . The fascination of the
cosmic outside, of what might lie hidden in the spaces between
the stars or beneath one's very feet (which, as Lovecraft explained in a letter to Elizabeth Tolridge in January, 1931, was
the very spot that "lies ultimately beyond the deepest gulf of
infinity") held for him all the emotion he needed for the creation of what Mrs. Radcliffe would have termed a "sublime
transport." As he wrote:

> . . . one of my strongest and most persistent
> wishes [is] to achieve, momentarily, the illu-
> sion of some strange suspension or violation of
> the galling limitations of time, space, and nat-
> ural law which forever imprison us and frustrate
> our curiosity about the infinite cosmic spaces
> beyond the radius of our sight and analysis.
> [My] stories frequently emphasize the element
> of horror because fear is our deepest and stron-
> gest emotion, and the one which best lends
> itself to the creation of nature-defying illusions.
> Horror and the unknown or the strange are al-
> ways closely connected, so that it is hard to
> create a convincing picture of shattered natural
> law or cosmic alienage and "outsideness"
> without laying stress on the emotion of fear.
> The reason why TIME plays such a great part
> in so many of my tales is that this element
> looms up in my mind as the most profoundly
> dramatic and grimly terrible thing in the uni-
> verse. CONFLICT WITH TIME seems to me
> the most potent and fruitful theme in all human
> expression.

The doubleness which runs through all of HPL's thought must
be, by this point, blatantly apparent, for he is at once a defender
and upholder of a strict universe of natural law as well as its
secret saboteur. As we shall see, this attraction-repulsion syn-
drome is at the root of the horror tale itself, but for now it is
enough to state that the subtle progression in Lovecraft's best
work is always from the ordinary to the extraordinary, the
particular and detailed to the monumental and the epic, the
mundane to the sacred, unholy, or archetypal. It is HPL's
cosmicism that provides the unique resonance of his fiction,
which, like **"The Rats in the Walls,"** reverberates with meanings that go far beyond the surface conventions of weird tales
and Gothic props. What Lovecraft accomplishes in his work
is to take the old Gothic machinery and invest it with new,
archetypal meaning. (pp. 35-6)

Lovecraft formed a whole mythology of the outside and a
philsophy of the outsider hidden in every human being. He
liked to think of himself (in the terms of a Schopenhauer or a

Nietzsche) as a mechanistic materialist living in an age whose total result was, in the words of the latter philosopher, "a chaos, a nihilistic sigh, an ignorance as to where or whence, an instinct of fatigue." But Lovecraft found himself in the position of modern man as Jung defined him: a being who spurned the sacred and the religious as a defense mechanism against a sterilized existence, only to find that he could not help scaring himself almost to death for his own good. "We have stripped all things of their mystery and numinosity," Jung writes, "nothing is holy any longer":

> In earlier ages, as instinctive concepts welled up in the mind of man, his conscious mind could no doubt integrate them into a coherent psychic pattern. But the "civilized" man is no longer able to do this. His "advanced" consciousness has deprived itself of the means by which the auxiliary contributions of the instincts and the unconscious can be assimilated. These organs of assimilation and integration were numinous symbols, held holy by common consent. (*Man and His Symbols* . . .).
>
> (p. 87)

In spite of his protests to the contrary, H. P. Lovecraft was modern man *par excellence* because he was also the most extreme example of what contemporary psychologists call "the divided self": the most civilized of conversationalists and the most violent of xenophobes, the most rational of scientists and the most fantastic of visionaries, the most controlled of authors and the most extravagant of artists. This inextricable doubleness runs through all of his work and his thought, for such doubleness is the hallmark of archetypal power, the paradox of numinous symbols assimilated in his art. Vainly, Lovecraft tries to restore an epic sense of man's essentially precarious and ultimately tragic position in the cosmos by setting up a polarity between frail humanity, on the one hand, and the force of a willful pantheon of deities (not unlike the Greek gods who gaze down and occasionally intervene in the events of the *Iliad* or the *Odyssey*), on the other. But the god, the monster, is always a mirror of its creator, as Mary Shelley's Dr. Frankenstein finds out to his woe.

"I believe that no honest aesthetic canon," Lovecraft wrote to Frank Belknap Long in 1922, "can exclude that highest of organic faculties—the pure, ice-cold reason; which gives man his sole contact with things outside himself, and which must be superimposed upon emotion before anything like *imagination* can be produced." . . . Reason may always hold the reins in H. P. Lovecraft's fiction, but the spectre rides in harness.

It was the "creation of a given sensation" that, in *Supernatural Horror in Literature* remained "the all important thing." . . . He begins that work with the "admitted truth" that "the oldest and strongest emotion of mankind is fear, and the oldest and strongest kind of fear is fear of the unknown." . . . More and more HPL realized that it was emotion and feeling, not the intricate dovetailing of a plot, that made for the success of weird fiction. Writing to E. Hoffman Price (who provided the impetus for the composition of **"Through the Gates of the Silver Key"**), HPL acknowledged, ten years after his praise of reason to Long, that:

> When a writer succeeds in translating these nebulous urges into symbols which in some way satisfy the imagination—symbols which adroitly

The "Shunned House" on Benefit Street in Providence, R.I. Photograph copyright by Steve Mariconda.

suggest actual glimpses into forbidden dimensions, actual happenings following the myth-patterns of human fancy, actual voyages of thought or body into the nameless deeps of tantalising space and actual evasions, frustrations, or violations of the commonly accepted laws of the cosmos—then he is a true artist in every sense of the word. He has produced literature by accomplishing a sincere emotional catharsis. . . .

(pp. 87-8)

No better defense of weird fiction in general or his own accomplishment in particular could be devised. (p. 89)

> *Barton Levi St. Armand, in his* The Roots of Horror in the Fiction of H. P. Lovecraft, *Dragon Press, 1977, 102 p.*

ANGELA CARTER   (essay date 1978)

[Carter is an English fiction writer and critic whose works are noted for their rich prose style and a self-conscious Gothicism reflected in their fantastic, violent, and erotic subjects. In the following excerpt, she discusses the significance of setting and landscape in Lovecraft's fiction.]

Since Lovecraft's geography is that of dream, it has the uncanny precision of dream. We know far more about the book of his world than we ever could know of the real world precisely because Lovecraft himself invented it all and knows all there is to know about it. The abhorrent plateau of Leng; the haunted forests of New England; witch-haunted Arkham; the cities of dream or of nightmare or of dream subtly modulating into nightmare, whose blue-prints were drawn up without the aid of Euclidian geometry—any competent map-maker could chart the world of H. P. Lovecraft in microscopic detail. But, not quite—Lovecraft moves at ease in an assemblage of picturesque constructions in space and time, yet, since these landscapes are primarily the projection of, or models of, states of mind, they take on a special kind of ambiguity.

The very precision with which Lovecraft notes the structure of rock formations, the age and type of a windowframe, the dimensions of a hallucinatory plaza, is the excessive precision of paranoia. The twisted shapes of the trees in the woods above Arkham are emanations of the menace they evoke—menace, anguish, perturbation, dread. The cities themselves, whether those of old New England or those that lie beyond the gates of dream, present the dreadful enigma of a maze, always labyrinthine and always, the Minotaur at the heart of this labyrinth, lies the unspeakable in some form or else in some especially vile state of formlessness—the unspeakable, a nameless and unnameable fear.

Lovecraft's is an expressionist landscape of imminent dread; his very world is inimical to man. But these landscapes, although man is never at home in them, can sicken and die, as a man does. Worse, they can go mad. Even the stars above them are rendered in human terms. "Still the Pole Star leers down from the same place in the black vault, winking hideously like an insane watching eye which strives to convey some message, yet recalls nothing save that it once had a message to convey."

There is a generalized dread everywhere in Lovecraft's landscapes; there's also a specific, regional horror which he places in localities already filled with echoes of antique paranoia, the New England of the early colonists, or, occasionally, in the Catskill Mountains in upstate New York, a far wilder region given its literary credentials as a supernatural place by Rip Van Winkle's lengthy nap there.

Lovecraft's New England derives in part from literary sources, also; if the ghost of Poe stalks through his Boston, then there's a lot of Nathaniel Hawthorne (himself born in Salem of the witch trials) in those gambrel-roofed colonial towns and, especially, in the woods above Arkham—those same woods, tangled, obscure, in which the protagonists of *The Scarlet Letter* made their assignations with the emissaries of Satan. This is the scenery of virgin America that Lovecraft refers to in his essay, *Supernatural Horror in Literature,* the "vast and gloomy virgin forest in whose perpetual twilight all terrors might well lurk."

The woods above Arkham, very typical of the haunted forest fairy-tale, are inhabited by an inbred and genetically suspect breed whose ancestors frequently fled the witch-trials of seventeenth-century Massachusetts, where phantoms are frequently those of the Indians most cruelly dispossessed by the newcomers to the strange land. This is primordial forest where time past dominates time present and will remain unmodified by the future; man has no business here and, if he makes it his business to visit, it will be the worse for him. Lovecraft speaks of the "inherent weirdness of the American heritage"; in these infernal forestscapes, he touches something very deep in the consciousness of those first settlers. He's touched a hidden vein of archaic paranoia. The woods above Arkham are an exact image of the fear of the unknown country which lay outside the hastily-erected fences of the first settlers, the land they came to subdue but which, for the moment, showed no signs whatsoever of submission.

There's legendary fear of forests, the panic fear which Pan himself inspired in those who entered his domain. The Roman soldiery, fearless in the face of every enemy, were overcome with stark terror by their first sight of the untrodden forests of Germany. It is a reasonable fear in the face of massive evidence of a tumultuous form of life which is not human, the world of giant vegetables.

"West of Arkham, the woods rise wild and there are valleys with deep woods where no axe has ever cut." Here flow brooks that have never caught the sun; the tumbled stones of abandoned farmhouses suggest how unwelcome a visitor man was when, in his hubris, he thought he might come to live here and how precipitate, how ignominious was his departure. This is the home of the Black Goat of the Woods with a Thousand Young, these "solid, luxuriant masses of forest among whose primal trees whole armies of elemental sprites might well lurk" (**"The Whisperer in Darkness"**).

The moment it is blasted by a meteorite, this landscape throws off any lingering aspect of superficial benevolence. Now the grass is greyish and withered, vines have fallen from the walls of a decaying farm in "brittle wreckage" and "great bare trees claw up at the grey November sky with studied malevolence" (**"The Colour out of Space"**). This anthropomorphized terrain exudes poisons; the cultivated land has turned into a blasted heath, is in the process, in fact, of transforming itself into a version of the utterly barren and benighted plateau of Leng in Lovecraft's mythology. A landscape based, in however a stylized way, on real forms is becoming pure invention, or else a sinister prefiguration of a landscape devastated by a more explicable blast than that of those oddly coloured globes that came from the sky. This is the landscape of post-nuclear despoliation. Mircea Eliade says: "The forest is a symbol which contains death."

Man is excluded from the forest, where beings and objects, plants and animals, mingle and blend their forms. In the woods above Arkham, in the deep forests of Massachusetts and Vermont, may be found those caverns which lead to the home of the unnameable and the black stones graven with curious hieroglyphs that will invoke the Elder Beings Lovecraft subsumes to the witch-folklore of New England. Here, also, live on, horned phantoms in the green dark, the mythologies of the Indians who originally lived here in perfect harmony with the forests we only fear because we do not know. Man is excluded from the forest but the Indians are not because they are not human; perhaps they lived here as angels before the Europeans came but now some Luciferan fall has converted them to beings of darkness. Similarly, the witch-tribe from Salem/Arkham can find a home in woods which are not forests before creation, the abode of innocence, but forests after the Fall, realms devised by a demented nature whose instinctual life has extinguished reason.

The Narangasset Indians are often evoked by Lovecraft as servants to the eighteenth-century savants and necromancers whose descendants are forced to carry such vile hereditaries of damnation with them into the age of the internal combustion engine. The Indians themselves exist in the twentieth-century as ghosts or as place names, the names of rivers . . . the Miskatonic, the Pawtuxet. Yet their absence itself suggests the presence of death. The Pawtuxet is a long river "which winds through many settled regions abounding in graveyards'' (*The Case of Charles Dexter Ward*). The very absence of the Indians from their own forests embodies the estrangement of the alien country. Darkly Satanic, they are in league with Satan himself who is, himself, no more than a metaphor for the Elder Beings or, the unnameable. They are not men, but part of the landscape, beings of the same substance as the twisted and malign trees, as the rampant foliage which might, at any moment, sprout carnivorous flowers.

Evil is part of the structure of ''those ancient and cryptically brooding hills,'' ''the wild, haunted hills behind hoary and witch-accursed Arkham.'' But the black magic of those hills is not that of the Sabbath, however often Lovecraft refers to Cotton Mather; those carven archways in the forest depths (c.f. *The Case of Charles Dexter Ward*) are ''the gates certain audacious and abhorred men have blasted through titan walls between the world and the absolute outside'' (**''Through the Gates of the Silver Key''**). The antique savants used cabbalistic methods to escape from time, into the nether realm of the Cthulhu mythology; the forest holds these secrets in its vegetable maze.

For the forest is a kind of maze. But it is a sentient one; it has a ''hideous soul'' (**''The Tomb''**). The forest is a ravenous and multiform being capable of passions, which expresses itself in the movement of the branches, unexpected, causeless, and in the stirrings of a wind that moves the leaves but which we ourselves cannot feel upon our faces.

Lovecraft's townscapes are also mazes. A maze is an architechtonic structure, apparently aimless in intention, and of a pattern so complex that, once inside, it is impossible or very difficult, to escape. Some antique labyrinths may have been designed as traps for demons; once the malign creatures had been enticed inside, they'd be trapped as effectively as a djinni in a bottle. More significantly as regards Lovecraft's weird mazes, Waldemar Fenn suggests some prehistoric labyrinths should be interpreted as images of the apparent motions of astral bodies. There is an illustration in *De Groene Leeuw* by Goosse van Wreeswyk (Amsterdam, 1672) which depicts the sanctuary of the alchemists' stone, encircled by the orbits of the planets as walls, suggesting in this way a cosmic labyrinth; since a maze is a positive emblem of existential anguish, the presentation of innumerable choices only one of which is, or can possibly be, the *right* choice, the labyrinthine cities, towns and catacombs in Lovecraft, transposed to a cosmic scale, suggest the possibility of eternal and infinite panic.

The maze is the symbol of interiority, of inwardness, of the tormented journey towards the centre of the unconscious, the core of the dark. In this darkness, blindness is enlightenment: ''The nethermost caverns are not for the fathoming of eyes that see,'' Lovecraft quotes from the *Necronomicon* of the mad Arab. A very early story of Lovecraft's begins: ''I was lost, completely, hopelessly lost in the vast and labyrinthine recess of the Mammoth Cave'' (**''The Beast in the Cave''**). There is no maze without a minotaur as its central secret. One must lose oneself in order to find oneself; forest, maze and huddled slums of a great city all serve the same function, landscapes of concrete perplexity in which, oldest and most potent of fears, one may lose one's very self. The maze is the way *in;* outside, in the light of day, in the senior common room of Miskatonic University, say, there is nothing to fear.

The description of the city of Providence, Rhode Island, in *The Case of Charles Dexter Ward,* offers a specific declension

of outwardness, of the safe public world, and a descent downwards, into the dangerous maze. The young Ward lives in a great Georgian mansion, built in the age of reason, on top of a hill, in the clear untainted air of public being, an externalized and hence safe landscape. The United States, politically the child of the French Enlightenment with its conviction in the inherent virtue of man, created, in Providence, the architecture of enlightenment itself, of classical rational proportions, a city that would be free of the ghosts of the past who lurk in the cluttered corners of European cities. But Ward's Providence, which, from the windows of his rambling home, has the look of one of Lovecraft's lovely cities of dream with its ''clustered spires, domes, roofs,'' is confined largely to the summit of the hill. Descend lower. Leave the public city, the abode of outwardness. Put behind you the ''exquisite First Baptist Church of 1775, luxurious with its matchless Gibbs steeple, and the Georgian roofs and cupolas hovering by.'' Go down the little ancient lanes, ''spectral in their many peaked archaism,'' descend to the ''riot of incandescent decay'' of the waterfront, with its rotting wharves, its polyglot vice and squalor. As in an engraving by Piranesi, the lucid lines of Palladian architecture turn, by a process of progressive paranoia, into the maze of unknowing and anguish. Red Hook, in Brooklyn, ''is a maze of antique squalor near the ancient waterfront,'' ''a tangle of material and spiritual putrescence,'' where, as in Providence, the presence of the ocean, the begetter of monsters, the ''abysmal abode,'' home of Dagon and Lovecraft's weird amphibians, suggests the horror of formlessness.

New York undergoes the same declension in **''He.''** Seen by a newcomer for the first time from a bridge at sunset, the city looks like Eldorado, a fabled city of dream with ''its incredible peaks and pyramids rising flowerlike and delicate from pools of violet mist.'' But closer acquaintance with it reveals a city which is ''quite dead, its sprawling body imperfectly embalmed and infested with queer inanimate things which have nothing to do with it as it was in life.'' The necromancer, the ''he'' of the title, takes the narrator backwards in time to an innocent city of the colonial past and then reveals to him, in a magic mirror, the city of the future.

''I saw the heavens verminous with strange flying things, and beneath them a hellish black city of giant stone terraces with impious pyramids flung savagely to the moon and devil-lights burning from un-numbered windows. And swarming loathsomely on aerial galleries I saw the yellow, squint-eyed people of that city, robed horribly in orange and red, and dancing insanely to the pounding of fevered kettle-drums. . . .''

The dream Eldorado has turned into one of the nightmare cities of black rock that also lie beyond the walls of sleep. The narrator escapes from the necromancer's house, which was the heart of a maze, the central space in which the ghastly secret was preserved. ''I never sought to return to those tenebrous labyrinths.'' He will go home to an innocent New England, up whose lanes ''fragrant seawinds sweep at evening.'' However, considering the significance of the ocean in Lovecraft's mythology, this innocence is illusory; at any moment, it may be invaded by the formless denizens of the deep. (Don't the bearded and finny Gnorri build ''singular labyrinths in the sea below the town of Ilek-Vad''? (**''Through the Gates of the Silver Key''**).

Innocent New England, whose farmland Lovecraft occasionally invokes as an emblematic rusticity, is, however, the abode of demons. Arkham, with its tangle of unpaved and musty-smelling lanes, ''the changeless, legend-haunted city of Arkham with its clustering gambrel roofs that sway and swag over attics where witches hid from the King's men," is in itself a labyrinth. The secret this labyrinth contains is the spectre of human sacrifice and cannibalism, which appears to have haunted Lovecraft to an unusual degree.

In the house in Arkham where once a witch lived, the student Gilman, dreams of an infernal city, one of "outlandish peaks, balanced planes, domes, minarets, horizontal discs posed on pinnacles"—all glittering in the blistering glare from a polychromatic sky. The maze pattern is transposed from the slums of Arkham and becomes the blueprint for Lovecraft's wholly imaginary cities, with their names that look like typing errors. Ilek-Vad, R'lyeh, Sarnath, Ulthar, Thalarion, "that fascinating and repellent city . . . where only daemons and mad things that are no longer men walk." Flesh is not the substance of which the beings who inhabit these places are composed.

When we glimpse the majestic sky-lines of these cities, we know we have left far behind us the terrors rooted in the real world of forest and slum and waterfront. The architecture is absolutely nonfunctional and often represents a confusion of styles—Gothic arches, Renaissance doorways, Aztec pyramids, Moorish domes—that suggest a wholesale ransacking of all the cities that ever existed, or might ever have existed.

Sometimes this uninhabitable architecture resembles those towns of mist and lace drawn by Paul Klee; "the walls of Sarnath were of glazed brick and chalcedony, each having its walled garden and crystal lakelet" (**"The Doom That Came to Sarnath"**). Others have the metaphysical sonorisity of the perspectives of de Chirico, like Atlantis, the city beneath the sea, in **"The Temple"**: "an extended and elaborate array of ruined edifices," mostly of marble, "untarnished and inviolate in the endless night and silence of an ocean chasm." These are cities to be seen, not to be lived in.

These dream cities often begin as visions of loveliness executed with all the kitsch hyperbole at Lovecraft's disposal; but the dream will soon turn sour, the paranoid complexity of the colonnades (which Max Ernst would probably have called "phallustrades"), the alleys, the ramps, the turrets, begins to distill its own darkness. The hallucination turns into delirium. The terraces crumble; the foundations fall away; we perceive the residue of nightmare as we sense the imminence of catastrophe. There's a lurking disquiet in the very peristyles. We are forced to recall how very, very few dreams are actually totally pleasurable.

There is a sound that always accompanies the transformation of these landscapes from dream to dread; it is the piping of flutes. Lovecraft's own neurasthenia, as sensitive to sounds, textures and temperature as that of Roderick Usher himself, utilizes this piping sound again and again, as the prelude to a crisis of the imagination that will bring the formless beings from their caves or change a quiet New England mansion into a place of terror. Gilman, the student, in **"The Dreams in the Witch-House,"** identifies the source of this sound as "the throne of chaos where thin flutes pipe mindlessly."

The sound of flutes herald the approach to the door of the inner world in **"The Festival."** In the antarctic mountains, the rocks themselves emit a thin, high, piping due to the way the wind blows through them; they are a set of stone pan pipes. "Through the desolate summits swept raging, intermittent gusts of the terrible antarctic wind whose cadences sometimes held vague suggestions of a wild and half-sentient musical piping, with notes extending over a wide range, and which for some sub-

conscious mnemonic reason seemed to me disquieting and even dimly terrible" (*At the Mountains of Madness*). This piping sound, whether of flutes, or the wind, or bull-frogs, is always the prelude to terror. It is disquietingly similar to the atrocious high, held violin note in Smetana's autobiographical string quartet, *My Life,* which he uses to illustrate the thin, agonizing sound which heralded to him his own deafness.

Lovecraft's Antarctica is the most truly terrible of all his landscapes. This bleak realm of ice and death, the place where came "both mist and snow" to the Ancient Mariner, is at once a heightened version of the real Antarctic; and a vision of the abhorrent plateau of Leng, the roof of the world; and the labyrinthine city of the Elder Beings. It is a symphone structure of landscaping. According to de Quincy, Coleridge, before starting "The Rime of the Ancient Mariner," has planned "a poem on delirium, confounding its own dream scenery with external things and connected with the imagery of high latitudes." To some similar plan, Lovecraft brought his own fears; he had a horror of, and an allergy to, any temperature lower than twenty degrees and, frequently, in later life, below thirty degrees.

If there is too much life in the convulsive forest, then there is none at all in the land of mist and snow. The mist mirages of "the great unknown continent and its cryptic world of frozen death" transform the icebergs into "battlements of unimagineable cosmic castles," places of perpetual exile. The whiteness of the snow is the infinite blankness of true mystery; the discovery of a range of mountains in the subcontinent reveals to the explorers "a gateway to a forbidden world of untrodden wonder." Under a cryptic sky, the landscape itself becomes a vast cryptogram which, once it is unravelled, reveals to man his insignificance in the cosmic scheme of things.

In the spectacle of the mountain peaks, "there was a persistent, pervasive hint of stupendous secrecy and potential revelation." They look like a mandala. They form the entry into an oracular cavern. "It was as if these stark, nightmare spires marked the pylons of a frightful gateway into forbidden spheres of dream and complex gulfs of remote time, space and ultradimensionality"; these are the mountains of stark dementia, whose farther slopes look out over some accursed, ultimate abyss. (The sexual element in Lovecraft's imagery need hardly be stressed.)

This is the landscape of abandonment, of desolation, of death. This is the gateway to the plateau of Leng, a metaphor for utter barrenness; and here, once again, we find a maze, a labyrinth of "geometrically eurythmic stone masses" built in "fiendish violation of natural law." No human hand helped chisel the stones of this vast, derelict city. Once again, its architecture features towers and interconnecting bridges; Lovecraft must have admired the futurist architecture in Fritz Lang's *Metropolis.*

This ultimate stone puzzle is "a complex tangle of twisted lanes and alleys, all of them deep canyons and some little better than tunnels because of the overhanging masonry of overarching bridges." The entire city composes the elaborate hiding place of a world, or anti-world of dark secrets; the ghastly minotaur at its heart is a complete and hitherto unknown prehistory of this planet, in which man has no place at all.

The architecture is of "endless variety, preternatural massiveness and utterly alien exoticism," featuring cones, terraces, broken columns, and a recurring five-pointed star motif, with its qabbalistic overtones. And this city, with its monuments and murals, is utterly dead. "In stark certainty, we were wandering amidst a death which had reigned at least five hundred thousand years.''

The narrator, and his companion, Danforth, now the only survivors of the team of explorers who set out, with such hubris, from the rational world of Miskatonic University, go into the labyrinth itself. Like Hansel and Gretel in the forest, they mark their path with dropped pieces of paper until at last they arrive at a monumental gateway—''chiselled avenues to the black inner world of whose existence we had not known before but which we were now eager to traverse.'' The labyrinth has brought them to the gateway to a perfect darkness, to a steeply descending shaft which will bring them to the brink of a great abyss. The only fauna in these regions are blind, albino penguins, foetal-like beings. This is the authentic landscape of interiority, of the archetypal Inner Place, the womb. The intrauterine imagery is made all the more startling by the presence, in this gulf, of the ruined remains of an immense tower. In this landscape of devastated sterility, they find concrete evidence of a life which is not human life—the corpse of their fellow-explorer, Gedney, and one of the team's husky dogs, preserved with great care, as if they were laboratory specimens. As, indeed, for the Elder Ones who inhabit these regions of interiority, the black pit beneath the mountains of madness, they are; interesting examples of an unknown form of being.

This elementary fear of non-being shapes the paranoid perspectives of Lovecraft's landscapes. (pp. 173-81)

> *Angela Carter, "Lovecraft and Landscape," in* The Necronomicon, *edited by George Hay, Neville Spearman, 1978, pp. 173-81.*

BARTON LEVI ST. ARMAND (essay date 1979)

[*St. Armand's* H. P. Lovecraft: New England Decadent *demonstrates Lovecraft's connections to the Puritans of seventeenth-century New England on the one hand and to the Aesthetic and Decadent artists of nineteenth-century Europe on the other. In the following excerpt from that study, St. Armand establishes a relationship between Lovecraft's fiction and pictorial artists representing Decadence and Puritanism, then discusses three of Lovecraft's stories within the framework of Puritanism, Aestheticism, and Decadence.*]

It is as an artist of the afterglow of Decadence, the twilight of the Gods, that Lovecraft must be judged. Here a paradox exists relative to Lovecraft's connection with the tradition of weird and fantastic art, of which he had little or almost no knowledge until relatively late in his career. Rather, the brilliance of Lovecraft's emerald cities and non-Euclidian worlds came instead from the vividness of his dreams and the actual cosmic horror of his nightmares, which alternated between scenes reminiscent of Coleridge's "Kubla Khan," at one pole, to the apocalyptic canvasses of a Hieronymous Bosch, at the other. He once wrote Rheinhart Kleiner that he was puzzled why a certain individual had to turn to drugs in order to perceive "an ideal world of gorgeousness and sublimity" because it seemed to him that "a man of active imagination ought to be able to behold vividly before his closed eyes any vision whatever that his mind is capable of conceiving, independent of external stimulation." He had "gazed on vistas as strange, as terrible, and as magnificent" as most of the pipedreams detailed to him "without having ever partaken of any drug or stimulant." . . . In truth, Lovecraft had only to shut his eyes in order to enter that Poesque dreamland which was alluringly "out of Space" and "out of Time."

Still, Lovecraft despaired from childhood on because he had not inherited his mother's gift as a painter of landscapes, lamenting that "I always wanted to be able to draw, but I have no talent, and in one of my pictures you cannot tell a cow from a locomotive." . . . "I ought to have been a pictorial artist instead of a would-be writer," he admitted in a moment of self-deprecation, and it was from others that he received a tutelage in the history of Decadent art, which he found with great surprise paralleled but did not exactly reproduce the particular cosmic character of his own nightmare landscapes. This aesthetic education was inculcated by his "gang" of reactionary ("We are certainly a gallery of anachronisms") and largely auto-didactic American Decadents: Frank Belknap Long, who "as a poet obviously belongs to the aesthetic nineties"; Samuel Loveman, who "really forms part of the romantic movement of a century ago—being akin to Keats & Walter Savage Landor"; and, most importantly, the California sculptor and prose poet, Clark Ashton Smith, who "is, in all but race & language, a French symbolist or Parnassian of the middle 19th century— closer to Baudelaire than any other American I know." . . . It was Loveman who first introduced Lovecraft to the weird drawings and writings of Smith, of whom HPL wrote to the genteel Elizabeth Toldridge:

> He has translated Baudelaire into English prose, & also writes poems in French which have been substantially praised even by French critics. One Paris editor told him that he could scarcely believe that French was not his mother-tongue. Smith's drawings & paintings range from realistic subjects with an aura of strangeness about them to the very peaks & depths of livid nightmare, hashish-ecstacy, & polychromatic madness. . . .
>
> (pp. 36-7)

Lovecraft's 1922 discovery of Smith's talent while leafing through the rare books and pictures in Loveman's Cleveland apartment had a decisive effect on his own art, for Smith was an eclectic who had absorbed, through Aubrey Beardsley and others, the entire tradition of Western and neo-Decadent grotesque art. HPL's immediate (and uncharacteristic) reaction was to fire off a "fan letter" to Smith in California, confessing that "Of the drawings & water-colours I lack a vocabulary adequate to express my enthusiastic admiration."

> What a world of opiate phantasy & horror is here unveiled, & what an unique power & perspective must lie behind it! I speak with especial sincerity & enthusiasm, because my own especial tastes centre almost wholly around the grotesque & the arabesque. I have tried to write short stories & sketches affording glimpses into unknown abysses of terror which leer beyond the boundaries of the known, but have never succeeded in evoking even a fraction of the stark hideousness conveyed by any one of your ghoulishly-potent designs. . . .
>
> (p. 37)

Because of this overwhelming pictorial talent, in which Lovecraft believed himself to be so lacking, HPL admired Smith to the point of idolatry, finally sending him his tale "**The Lurking Fear**" for the purposes of illustration and revealing that "You are a genius in conceiving & rendering noxious, baleful, poisonous vegetation, & I veritably believe my descriptions were excited by some of your drawings which Loveman shewed me.'' . . . The same year, Loveman brought Lovecraft's attention to some illustrations by the British nineteenth-century artist of the grand, the sublime, and the catastrophic, John Martin. Lovecraft was "enthralled by the darkly thunderous, apocalyptically majestic, and cataclysmically unearthly power of one who, to me, seemed to hold the essence of cosmic mystery; notwithstanding the blandly low estimate placed upon his work by the tamely & urbanely correct artists & critics of his time." . . . Whereas Smith appealed to Lovecraft's chastened sense of the numinously decadent, Martin, "a Milton among painters," satisfied his more frigid hunger for the "vast space-suggestions" and "colossal effects of ancient architecture" which he experienced in his own dreams. Thus, Lovecraft equally delighted in Martin's "daemon-dowered mastery of subtle and unearthly lighting effects amidst an all engulfing gloom—the ravenous gloom of the outer void, whose *fluctus decumanus* beats so periously on the frail dykes of our little world of light." . . . (p. 38)

Lovecraft's taste in art, then, typically polarizes into the warm and the cold, the soft and the hard, the Decadent and the Puritan, which yield, alternately, phantasmagoric details of an artificial paradise and "oneiriscopic glimpses of other worlds." These coordinates define, as well, both the limits and the perils of the artist as Lovecraft presents him in three of his best tales, **"The Horror at Red Hook," "Pickman's Model,"** and **"The Music of Erich Zann."** Thomas Malone, of the first-mentioned story, is a New York detective, a detective in the tradition of Poe's C. Auguste Dupin and Doyle's Sherlock Holmes. Like these great questers, he is a seeker after bizarre and stimulating varieties of crime, a connoisseur of the possibilities of human sin and transgression, whose personality is divided between the dreamy fantasizing of the Aesthete and the active probing of the master of ratiocination. Malone, is therefore, a mystic as well as a rationalist—a graduate of Dublin University who has dabbled in the occult, managing to retain "the Celt's far vision of weird and hidden things" as well as "the logician's eye for the outwardly unconvincing." Like Lovecraft himself, Malone is a believer in the possibility of reversion to type and an armchair anthropologist who is convinced that bestial patterns of behavior are perpetuated in the obscure rituals and cult-practices of the genetically unfit. Malone is a Des Esseints who has found his *frisson nouveau* in the dregs of human horror; he is a Decadent visionary who uses as the materials of his art the permutations of corruption to be observed in his fellow man. An Aesthete who worships at the Satanic altar where burns "the hellish green flame of secret wonder," he reveals a proper taste for fellow limners of the terrible and the obscene:

> To Malone the sense of latent mystery in existence was always present. In youth he had felt the hidden beauty and ecstacy of things, and had been a poet; but poverty and sorrow and exile had turned his gaze in darker directions, and he had thrilled at the imputations of evil in the world around. Daily life had for him come to be a phantasmagoria of macabre shadow-studies; now glittering and leering with concealed rottenness as in Beardsley's best manner, now hinting terrors behind the commonest shapes and objects as in the subtler and less obvious work of Gustave Doré. (**"Horror at Red Hook"** . . .)

(pp. 38-9)

A reader of Margaret Murray's book, *The Witch-Cult in Western Europe* (which Lovecraft had recommended to Clark Ash-

ton Smith as "a work which ought to be full of inspiration for you"), Malone has made the connection between Satanism and sexual license—the breaking down of all orthodox limits—that also so fascinated the outwardly genteel HPL. It is a confrontation with this Satanic vision that simultaneously so appalls and beckons Malone: his is the pagan desire to look upon the naked body of the Dark God, as it is inversely the Hebrew-Christian blasphemy of confronting Jehova face to face, and the Romantic-Faustian urge to acquire a forbidden knowledge of unutterable things. Malone's opponent is Robert Suydam, who is a genius of crime like Doyle's Moriarty and Poe's "Man of the Crowd." He is also the supreme hierophant who inducts Malone into the depths of unspeakable mysteries. Suydam, the aged scion of an ancient Dutch colonial family, has formed an unholy alliance with the alien population of the Red Hook district of Brooklyn, as he has also entered into a pact with the alien spirits of the universe, incarnate in the Lilith of the Kabbalists—the legendary evil first wife of Adam. For his part in reviving her cult, Suydam has gained the Faustian gift of the Elixir of Life (that theme that rules Nathaniel Hawthorne's late, unfinished American romances) but, for this privilege, he must ultimately sacrifice his earthly existence and enter into an unholy marriage with the succubus herself.

There is thus a peculiar connection between Malone, the questing Aesthete, and Suydam, the full-fledged Decadent, as there is in Poe's detective stories of the pursuer and the pursued, a mirrored doubleness of temperament and even of habit. Malone, who "had many poignant things to his credit in the *Dublin Review,*" admires Suydam's own darker occultism, in particular, "an out-of-print pamphlet of his on the Kabbalah and the Faustus legend, which a friend had quoted from memory." Both men might have conceivably been, like Algernon Blackwood, William Butler Yeats, Arthur Machen, and Aleister Crowley, members of an occult secret society like the Order of the Golden Dawn, save that while Malone remains a dreamer of decadence and a curious voyeur of its perversities, Suydam has become (like Crowley, "the Beast 666") an active participant in the destructive magic of sin. Suydam also illustrates, tangentially, Philippe Jullian's observation that with the Decadents, "Thanks to Péladan and Villiers de l'Isle-Adam, the old families came to be regarded as the repository of strange secrets" and "The idea of aristocracy became linked with the idea of death" (*Dreamers of Decadence* . . .). The old Dutch families of the Kaatskills, whom Washington Irving used to so delight in for their quaint and picturesque qualities, have, with Lovecraft, become obscene, inbred, and hermetic, linked symbolically with the constantly declining progeny of Poe's House of Usher.

It is typical, too, that the place of the performance of these Satanic rites is an old church which has been made over into a dancehall. Just as the **"Haunter of the Dark"** inhabits a deserted Providence cathedral in the story of the same name, so does Lovecraft make his horror topographical, locating it in places which have become desanctified and then inversely consecrated to the unholy through prolonged contact with the forces of perversity. "There are sacraments of evil as well as of good about us" are the words which Lovecraft quotes from Arthur Machen as an epigraph to **"The Horror at Red Hook."** HPL's profanation of the sacred is similar to the backwards recitation of the Pater Noster, which forms a central motif of the Black Mass, while it follows a long tradition of Gothic fiction that invests sanctuaries supposedly dedicated to the reverence of the light with a Decadent darkness (i.e., M. G. Lewis's cursed monasteries and evil nunneries in *The Monk*).

But Lovecraft's desacramentalization of the holy always carries with it Puritanical consequences. The profane act produces cosmic resonances, which in **"Red Hook"** open up the possibility of not only a particular reversion to type but also the revelation of an epic knowledge that entails the diminishing and disparagement of the stature of mankind in general. Thus, the void which Thomas Malone confronts is not totally outside but, rather, inside and below as well. As Lovecraft himself explained in an unpublished letter to Elizabeth Toldridge discoursing on Einstein's theory of relativity, it is the spot beneath our very feet which is ultimately the farthest reach of infinity. Breaking through the locked cellar door beneath the crumbling church, Malone watches as "A crack formed and enlarged, and the whole door gave way—but from the *other side;* whence poured a howling tumult of ice-cold wind with all the stenches of the bottomless pit, and whence reached a sucking force not of earth or of heaven, which, coiling sentiently about the paralysed detective, dragged him through the aperture and down unmeasured spaces filled with whispers and wails, and gusts of mocking laughter" (**"Horror at Red Hook"** . . .). (pp. 39-42)

That wind we have noted before: it is the frigid New England wind which whips and buffets the dark tapestry of the Puritan consciousness, while the bottomless pit is the "dreadful pit of the glowing flames of the wrath of God," "Hell's wide gaping mouth open," which Jonathan Edwards thundered about in *Sinners in the Hands of an Angry God* (1741), warning his listeners that "you have nothing to stand upon, nor anything to take hold of; there is nothing between you and hell but the air; it is only the mere power and pleasure of God that holds you up." This pit is also that shadowy gulf which Jung called "the collective unconscious," the darkness hidden in the psyche of every man. No angry God presides over Lovecraft's version of this nightmare landscape, for instead it is ruled by the tittering, naked, phosphorescent form of the beckoning Bride of Evil, Lilith, Queen of the Succubae. The sight which Malone beholds is a Litany of Satan made manifest:

> Avenues of limitless night seemed to radiate in every direction, till one might fancy that here lay the root of a contagion destined to sicken and swallow cities, and engulf nations in the foetor of hybrid pestilence. Here cosmic sin had entered, and festered by unhallowed rites had commenced the grinning march of death that was to rot us all to fungous abnormalities too hideous for the grave's holding. Satan here held his Babylonish court, and in the blood of stainless childhood the leprous limbs of phosphorescent Lilith were laved. Incubi and succubae howled praise to Hecate, and headless mooncalves bleated to the Magna Mater. Goats leaped to the sound of thin accursed flutes, and AEgyptus chased endlessly after misshapen fauns over rocks twisted like swollen toads. Moloch and Ashtaroth were not absent; for in this quintessence of all damnation the bounds of consciousness were let down, and man's fancy lay open to vistas of every realm of horror and every forbidden dimension that evil had power to mould. The world and nature were helpless against such assaults from unsealed wells of night, nor could any sign or prayer check the Walpurgis-riot of horror which had come when a sage with the hateful key had stumbled on a horde with the locked and brimming coffer of

transmitted daemon-lore. (**"Horror at Red Hook"** . . .)

(pp. 42-3)

This is not the radiant *hieros gamos* or sacred marriage of Isis and Osiris, of full moon and full sun, but rather the obscene nuptials of Lucifer and Lilith, or of Asmodeus and Nahemah, false star and dead orb. Such is the Decadent vision which blasts and withers Malone's consciousness, just before the glassy-eyed, gangrenous corpse of Suydam manages to topple the carven golden pedestal, the very throne of Evil itself, from its onyx base and so initiate the final collapse of the grotto and its hideous rites. But it is precisely this knowledge of a whole other universe of malevolent spirits pressing coldly upon our own which must remain, for the good of mankind, secret and truly *occult*, truly hidden. If such knowledge drives the staid Malone to distraction, phobia, and neuraesthenia, it would wreak a havoc of mass psychosis and hysteria among the larger family of man if ever made known. That is the moral of **"The Horror at Red Hook,"** for, in spite of Lovecraft's much-touted ethical relativism, moral it has—as much as the Puritan Thomas Hooker's sermon "A True Sight of Sin" (1659) warns that "suppose thou heardest the devil's roaring, and sawest hell gaping, and the flames of everlasting burnings flashing before thine eyes? It's certain it were better for thee to be cast into those inconceivable torments than to commit the least sin against the Lord." What Malone learns is that "Age-old horror is a hydra with a thousand heads, and the cults of darkness are rooted in blasphemies deeper than the well of Democritus," a final metaphor which Lovecraft borrows from Poe, ("Ligeia" and "A Descent into the Maelstrom") who, in turn, borrowed it from Glanvill. The image of the abyss is simply an extension of the old New England belief in what Jonathan Edwards called "the hell within of the natural man" or that sin which Hooker, again, claimed had "ruined and laid waste the very principles of reason and nature and morality, and made [man] a terror to himself." Or, as Lovecraft's New England contemporary, Robert Frost, said of these same "unsealed wells of night":

> . . . They cannot scare me with their empty spaces
> Between stars—on stars where no human race is.
> I have it in me so much nearer home
> To scare myself with my own desert places.

This ambiguous wisdom about his own desert places converts Malone into a wandering Ancient Mariner, compelled to brood endlessly on the terror which he has experienced. The corollary of this terror is the fact that "The soul of the beast is omnipresent and triumphant" but that "beast" also has particularly Decadent connotations. In the works of a writer who usually does not deal at all with women characters, Lovecraft's vision of the lascivious Lilith is doubly intriguing. If the tale as a whole forcibly embodies HPL's paranoid hatred of New York, the "polyglot abyss" and its alien hordes, may it not also express, obliquely and subliminally, his twin horror at that marriage which brought him there in the first place? The repeated references to the Kabbalah remind us that Lilith is primarily a Hebraic succubus and also that the asexual, xenophobic Lovecraft must have experienced many anomalous emotions in the arms of his Jewish bride, Sonia Haft Greene. But, more than this, the Lilith of **"The Horror at Red Hook"** is in the long tradition of the Decadents' worship at the feet of a destroying bitch-goddess. Swinburne's Faustine, Wilde's Salomé, and Rossetti's Lady Lilith, are only a few of the avatars of Lovecraft's "Great Beast," a Whore of Babylon who expresses all the equivocal fantasies of the Puritan's iconoclastic soul even as she fulfills Huysman's pronouncement that ''Woman is the great vessel of iniquity and crime, the charnel-house of misery and shame, the mistress of ceremonies who introduces into our souls the ambassadors of all the vices'' (*Dreamers of Decadence . . .*). (pp. 43-4)

What Lovecraft continues to stress in his fiction, in spite of the imaginative revels we are presented with here, is precisely the effect of this confrontation with ancient evil. There is a terrible reality to Lovecraft's conception of the imminence of the unspeakable, a Puritan terror expressed by Cotton Mather in *Wonders of the Invisible World* (1692) or his *Discourse on Witchcraft,* that sermon preached during the winter of 1688, ''after Goodwife Glover of Boston was hanged for bewitching John Goodwin's children,'' wherein Mather warned his audience that ''Christian, there are *Devils:* and so many of them, too, that sometimes a *Legion* of them are spared for the vexation of *One Man*. The *Air* in which we breathe is full of them. Be sensible of this, you that *obey God:* there are troops of *Tempters* on every side of thee.'' Thomas Malone, who meets these legions, registers their effects by suffering a nervous breakdown and developing a phobia which causes him to collapse at the sight of brick buildings, proving Mather's further contention that ''The Effects [of Witchcraft] are dreadfully real. Our dear neighbors are most really tormented. Really murdered & really acquainted with hidden things, which are afterwards proved plainly to have been Realities.'' Lovecraft, in fact, tried to be as authentic as possible about the details of this kind of supernatural reality, writing to Clark Ashton Smith about his new tale **''The Horror at Red Hook''** that:

> I have a nest of devil-worshippers & devotees of Lilith in one of the squalid Brooklyn neighborhoods, & describe the marvels & horrors that ensued when these ignorant inheritors of hideous ceremonies found a learned & initiated man to lead them. I bedeck my tale with incantations copied from the ''Magic'' article in the 9th edition of the *Britannica*, but I'd like to draw on less obvious sources if I knew the right reservoirs to tap. Do you know of any good works on magic & dark mysteries which might furnish fitting ideas & formulae? . . .
>
> (p. 45)

Malone, who begins as a contemporary Dorian Gray, becomes through his confrontation with this Puritan reality a latter-day version of Hawthorne's Young Goodman Brown. Like Brown, Malone is baptized into a soul-shattering knowledge of universal malignancy. His Decadent sense of evil (and we remember here Lovecraft's contention that the Puritans ''were the only really effective diabolists and decadents the world has known''), of contagious and preteroriginal sin called forth by ''the chanting, cursing processions of bleary-eyed and pockmarked young men which wound their way along in the dark small hours of morning,'' predestines him to defeat and disaster. All Lovecraft's heroes are Puritanically predestined; their fates are immutably decreed by their own exotic temperaments and insatiable, Faustian curiosity. Those who are rationalists become emblems of human reason seized by the irrational nightmare of man's insecure and essentially ephemeral place in a universe which is, at best, glimpsed through a glass, darkly. Malone seeks to penetrate beyond that glass, but what he sees is only a mirror-reflection of man's basically demonic nature—to use Arthur Machen's words in the epigraph—''A place where there are caves and shadows and dwellers in twilight''—and the vacant void beyond, the *néant* of ''unholy dimensions and fathomless worlds.'' This is Lovecraft's ultimate reality, and Lovecraft, like Poe, is a realist simply because any glance at the newspapers provides convincing evidence that for every anonymous John Doe there exists also a Roderick Usher, a Robert Suydam, or a Thomas Malone.

In **''Pickman's Model,''** that other tale of art, horror, and reality, which Lovecraft called ''one of my very tamest and mildest effusions,'' . . . the Decadent artist is also fully a realist, while the narrator, Thurber, is the genteel Aesthete whose vague notes for a monograph on weird painting lead to a traumatic apprehension of the omnipresence of a very palpable Evil. Of Richard Upton Pickman, master of the macabre, the narrator remarks, for example, that ''Morbid art doesn't shock me, and when a man has the genius Pickman had I feel it an honour to know him, no matter what direction his work takes. Boston never had a greater painter. . . .'' What Thurber really admires is the precision with which Pickman delineates his grotesque vision, observing that:

> You know, it takes profound art and profound insight into Nature to turn out stuff like Pickman's. Any magazine-cover hack can splash paint around wildly and call it a nightmare or a Witches' Sabbath or a portrait of the devil, but only a great painter can make such a thing really scare or ring true. That's because only a real artist knows the actual anatomy of the terrible or the physiology of fear—the exact sort of lines and proportions that connect up with latent instincts or hereditary memories of fright, and the proper colour contrasts and lighting effects to stir the dormant sense of strangeness. I don't have to tell you why a Fuseli brings a shiver while a cheap ghost-story frontispiece merely makes us laugh. There's something those fellows catch—beyond life—that they're able to make us catch for a second. (**''Pickman's Model''** . . .)
>
> (pp. 45-7)

Here Lovecraft is actually describing his own approach to ''the physiology of fear'' for did he not speculate on the nature and evolution of the dreadful in his *Supernatural Horror in Literature,* and was he not, like Poe, an anatomist of the imagination who reduced the tale of horror to its fundamentals, devising theories of effect and the breakdown of cosmic limits? The Decadent artist, possessed by a corrupting devil and gifted with an unholy talent, is a recurring theme in his fiction, while the power of art itself to evoke diabolical consequences remains one of his central ideas (i.e., **''The Picture in the House''**). Surely Lovecraft identified himself with these doomed fantasists whose type once again is the musician-poet Roderick Usher, and he delights in sprinkling throughout **''Pickman's Model''** references not only to Fuseli, Doré, and Goya (who ''could put so much of sheer hell into a set of features or a twist of expression'') but to more contemporary artists as well— ''Anagarola of Chicago,'' Sidney Sime, and Clark Ashton Smith. Even the hideous canvasses which Pickman paints, for example, reveal Lovecraft's new education in the history of fantastic and Decadent art, for ''the things shown leaping through open windows at night, or squatting on the chests of sleepers, worrying at their throats'' are obviously based on Fuseli's *Nightmare* series, while the ''colossal and nameless blasphemy with glaring red eyes,'' that ''held in bony claws a thing that had been a man, gnawing at the head as a child nibbles at a stick of candy'' is directly borrowed from Goya's chilling *Chronos Devouring his Children*. Acting on the hints given him by Long . . . , he could have found this latter work reproduced in the collections of the Providence Athenaeum, a private library which was one of Lovecraft's favorite local haunts, for the place itself was doubly sanctified by its associations with the courtship of Edgar Allan Poe and Sarah Helen Whitman. . . . (pp. 47-8)

It is paintings such as these which begin to overturn Thurber's mild contention that "I should say that the really weird artist has a kind of vision which makes models, or summons up what amounts to actual scenes from the spectral world he lives in," for Pickman's "model" *is* the real world, and no fanciful *moi intérieur* of the imagination. Pickman himself, who "comes of old Salem stock, and had a witch ancestor hanged in 1692," inhabits, significantly, the Decadent North End of Boston, where a residue of evil has been allowed to build up insidiously over the centuries, becoming part of the very substance of the crooked alleys, "crumbling-looking gables, broken small-paned windows, and archaic chimneys that stood out half-disintegrated against the moonlit sky." So many of these skewed structures which we find in Lovecraft, like Pickman's studio in the North End (the Ultima Thule of Boston) or the old Witch House in Salem (in **"The Dreams in the Witch House"**), with their gambrel roofs and rotten timbers and rooms tilted at crazy or obtuse angles are, of course, psychic allegories of decadent and tumbled-down minds, twisted to exquisite and picturesque degrees of insanity by the ponderous forces of age and heredity. Here the dreamland which makes "colonial New England into a kind of annexe of hell" or populates modern Boston with ghouls and living gargoyles is no longer an antiuqarian fancy but rather immediately beneath the cellar door or around the nearest corner:

> It was not any mere artist's interpretation that we saw; it was pandemonium itself, crystal-clear in stark objectivity. That was it, by Heaven! The man was not a fantaisiste or romanticist at all—he did not even try to give us the churning, prismatic ephemera of dreams, but coldly and sardonically reflected some stable, mechanistic, and well-established horror-world which he saw fully, brilliantly, squarely, and unfalteringly. God knows what that world can have been, or where he ever glimpsed the blasphemous shapes that loped and trotted and crawled through it; but whatever the baffling source of his images, one thing was plain. Pickman was in every sense—in conception and in execution—a thorough, painstaking, and almost scientific *realist*. (**"Pickman's Model"** . . .)
>
> (pp. 48-9)

The reality which Richard Upton Pickman paints is Lovecraft's mechanistic, materialist universe combined with his dream world of shuddering unnameabilities and nightmare, cosmic landscapes. The narrator, Thurber, pays for his glimpse into this wasteland by the same kind of psychological maiming that afflicts the Thomas Malone of **"Red Hook"**—he develops a peculiar form of spelunkaphobia—an insane dread of caves and cellars that also afflicted HPL himself . . . after he discovers that Pickman's *immediate* models are undeniably real and that the scrap of paper affixed to his most demonic canvas "*was a photograph from life*." Lovecraft's tales of art and artists

continue to underscore his basically Puritan moralism, for, while the casual voyeur suffers a merely mental trauma, the price which the artist himself must pay for dabbling in the decadence of the underworld is to become part of it, to be locked behind the cellar door with the burrowers from beneath who constantly hurl themselves against it. To find "a way to unlock the hidden gate" is also to be condemned to enter its one-way portals, as so many of Lovecraft's "gloomy heroes" discover. Richard Pickman, Randolph Carter, and Walter Gilman of **"The Dreams in the Witch House"** all break the bounds of natural law, but the transgression carries with it a karmic penalty. All buy the gift of superhuman prowess and the satisfaction of their Faustian curiosity at the price of becoming one with that "nether-world which no mortal unsold to the Fiend" should know, the price of ultimate corruption which Wilde's Dorian Gray cedes for his prolonged dalliance with sin and excess.

It is the same, finally, with the old musician, Erich Zann, who is actually the earliest of Lovecraft's portraits of the artist, composed in 1921 before HPL had made real contact with the mainstream of Decadent painting. Here we see more clearly the cosmic backdrop of Lovecraft's instinctive fascination with Decadence, for this mute Parisian violinist, an exile and an émigré who dwells in the tottering Rue d'Auseil (partially modeled on the steep Meeting Street or ancient "Gaol Lane" of Lovecraft's native Providence), has made an unnatural contact with the forbidden music of the spheres. Zann, too, has broken natural law by hearing and then expressing what no mortal should, and his fate is to become part of that cosmic, atonal, cacaphonous orchestra of the exterior darknesses, where, as Scripture warns us, there shall be much "weeping and gnashing of teeth" (Matt. 8:12). Like E.T.A. Hoffmann's demonic violinist, "Rath Krespel" (1818), Zann too is "only the magnetizer who has the power of moving his subject to reveal of its own accord . . . the visions of his inner nature." HPL's narrator, once again, has only a glimpse of the void to which Zann has condemned himself:

> Then I remembered my old wish to gaze from this window, the only window in the Rue d'Auseil from which one might see the slope beyond the wall, and the city outspread beneath. It was very dark, but the city's lights always burned, and I expected to see them there amidst the rain and the wind. Yet when I looked from that highest of all gable windows, looked while the candles sputtered and the insane viol howled with the nightwind, I saw no city spread below, and no friendly lights gleamed from remembered streets, but only the blackness of space illimitable; unimagined space alive with motion and music, and having no semblance of anything on earth. And as I stood there looking in terror, the wind blew out both the candles in that ancient peaked garret, leaving me in savage and impenetrable darkness with chaos and pandemonium before me, and the demon-madness of that night-baying viol behind me.

Paris, the City of Light itself is extinguished, for even the Rue d'Auseil (a street much like the Rue de la Vielle-Lanterne, where the visionary French poet Gérard de Nerval hanged himself in 1855) is haunted by a New England consciousness of the imminence of the pit. We have seen that as he matured, Lovecraft in fact abandoned the literary pose which he had assumed as a young man, so that as early as 1923 we find him writing to Frank Belknap Long that "I believe Mortonius [Ferdinand Morton] is right in considering me no true decadent, for much that decadents love seems to me either absurd or merely disgusting" and that "I despise Bohemians, who think it essential to art to lead wild lives." . . . HPL wished to sustain, at any cost, his Genteel heritage—which perhaps was the greatest of all his fantasies. Increasingly, he saw the Modernist English writers, whom he abominated, as the true inheritors of *fin de siècle* traditions, and he predicted that "This sickly, decadent neo-mysticism—a protest not only against machine materialism but against pure science with its destruction of the mystery and dignity of human emotion and experience— will be the dominant creed of twentieth century aesthetes, as the Eliot and Huxley penumbra well prognosticate." . . . But, unknown even to himself, he had already absorbed and expanded all that the *fin de siècle* could teach him. Writing to Maurice W. Moe in 1932, in a curious flash of self-revelation he declared that "Wilde, Flaubert, Gautier, and many others were sensationalist-extraverts. I am inclined to think I am." . . . A "sensationalist-extravert" in his art, in his introverted day-to-day existence HPL adopted the poetic strategy of his ancestors, and "set up a life in Gothick design, with formal arches and precise traceries" and "austere spires." In sum Lovecraft remained until his death that most remarkable and anomalous of twentieth-century trinities: a Providence Aesthete, a New England Decadent, and a Cosmic Puritan. (pp. 49-52)

Barton Levi St. Armand, in his H. P. Lovecraft: New England Decadent, *Silver Scarab Press, 1979, 76 p.*

S. S. PRAWER (essay date 1981)

[*Prawer is a German-born English critic and educator specializing in German literature, particularly the work of Heinrich Heine. He is also the author of* Caligari's Children: The Film as Tale of Terror *(1978), which examines the masterpieces of Gothic cinema and theorizes on the function and significance of the artistic expression of horror. In the following excerpt, Prawer examines the distinctive traits of Lovecraft's stories and offers a defense of his prose style.*]

[Fritz] Leiber has called Lovecraft "the Copernicus of the horror-story": "He shifted the focus of supernatural dread," Leiber maintains, "from man and his little world and his gods, to the stars and the black, unplumbed gulfs of intergalactic space" [see excerpt in *TCLC*, Vol. 4]. He did so, we might add, without writing "Space Westerns" like *Star Wars* and without succumbing to the lure of the many cranky theosophists who tried to recruit him for their narrow heterodoxies. Nor did he write "science fiction" in the usual sense, despite his smattering in many sciences and his thorough knowledge of astronomy. He sought, rather, to compose what he called "weird tales," adopting the title of the pulp magazine which published many of his writings. "The crux of the *weird* tale," he explained to Derleth in 1931, "is something which could not possibly happen. If any unexpected advance of physics, chemistry, or biology were to indicate the *possibility* of any phenomena related to the weird tale, that particular set of phenomena would cease to be *weird* in the ultimate sense because it would become surrounded by a different set of emotions." That, it will be realized, suggests a spirit radically opposed to the spirit of Jules Verne or any other pioneer of what we regard as science fiction today.

But what Lovecraft called "the alluring and provocative abysses of unplumbed space and unguessed entity which press in on the known world from unknown infinities and in unknown relationships of time, space, matter, force, dimensionality, and consciousness" constitutes only one of five co-ordinates that may be discussed in his narrative universe. At the opposite extreme, and in significant tension with the cosmos-centred view just described, is the delicate, precise evocation of New England settings in many of his tales—the streets, the buildings, the surrounding countryside, of his native Providence, of Boston, and of the imaginary town of Arkham which we may imagine not many miles away from either of these centres. Unlike Poe (with whom he had much in common, whose work he expounded sensitively and imaginatively, and whose manner he imitated in more than one tale), Lovecraft did not select European settings for his characters; he chose, rather, to follow the lead of Hawthorne's *Young Goodman Brown* and the *The House of the Seven Gables*. "The heritage of American weirdness," he said of Hawthorne in *Supernatural Horror in Literature*, "was his to a most intense degree, and he saw a dismal throng of vague spectres behind the common phenomena of life . . .". Lovecraft's "cosmic feeling," his experience of "the lure of unplumbed space, the terror of the encroaching outer void, and the struggle of the ego to transcend the known and established order of time, space, matter, force, geometry, and natural law in general" (writing to C. A. Smith, November 7, 1930)—these were firmly anchored in the topographic and architectural particulars of his beloved New England. In this he resembled the *"epicure of the terrible"* whom he placed at the centre of his frequently anthologized tale **"The Picture in the House":** a character who praises the New England backwoods as able to lead towards a "perfection of the hideous" which lures and fascinates as much as it frightens or repels.

We have now reached the third co-ordinate of Lovecraft's world, the point at which cosmic vision and a keen appreciation of one small corner of our earth come together. This is, of course, the mind of a particular kind of person whom Lovecraft chooses as narrator or protagonist of his tales. He is usually a scholar or a scientist (the narrator of **"The Shadow out of Time"** characteristically abandons political economy for non-Freudian psychology), who pursues knowledge beyond the bounds of the explored world and thus comes into contact and collision with forces that overwhelm and often destroy him.

If the mind of such narrators or protagonists, with its yearning to transcend ordinary space and time, with its "dreams of some Unknown Kadath," forms the third of our five co-ordinates, then the fourth is a place where this mind can find the food it craves and the wings it needs to transcend our everyday limitations. This place, of course, as Borges well knew, is a *library*. Libraries, the stored wisdom of the ages, therefore play a vital part in the perdition, and—occasionally—in the salvation, of Lovecraft's characters. They range from Boston Public Library to the imagined library of Miskatonic University and thence to a vast library beyond known space and time whose treasures one of the more fortunate of Lovecraft's narrators is allowed, not only to read, but also to annotate in his own earthly handwriting. In these libraries may be found books that actually exist—the writings of Cotton Mather, for instance, which can summon up an atmosphere Lovecraft described as follows in *Supernatural Horror in Literature*:

> The vast and gloomy virgin forests in whose perpetual twilight all terrors may well lurk; the hordes of coppery Indians whose strange saturnine visages and violent customs hinted strongly at traces of infernal origin; the free

rein given under the influence of Puritan theo-
cracy to all manner of notions respecting man's
relation to the stern and vengeful God of the
Calvinists, and to the sulphurous Adversary of
that God, about whom so much was thundered
in the pulpits each Sunday; and the morbid introspection developed by an isolated backwoods life devoid of normal amusements and
of the recreational mood, harrassed by commands for theological self-examination, keyed
to unnatural emotional repression, and forming
above all a mere grim struggle for survival. . . .

But Lovecraft's libraries also contain a number of imaginary
works, "forbidden books" that turn up in tale after tale, pseu-
dobiblia, some of whose titles he invented himself, while he
took over others from friends and correspondents. Their frac-
tured German and Arabic would have made a professional
scholar like M. R. James squirm—the autodidact in Lovecraft
shows through rather blatantly on some occasions. Chief among
these "forbidden books," which allow contact to be made with
other worlds and transhuman entities, is the *Necronomicon*,
whose name combines *necros, nomos* and *eikon* to suggest an
image of the order, or the law, of the dead. It is wholly characteristic of the bookish Lovecraft that in *The Case of Charles
Dexter Ward* he should substitute intellectual vampirism for the
more obviously sexual variety of Stoker's *Dracula* to which
his tale consciously alludes. His ghouls seek to reconstitute the
brains of the world's most eminent thinkers in order to harness
their capacity for clear, profound and novel thoughts to their
own purposes. The New England wizard Joseph Curwen and
his fellow conspirators from Prague and Transylvania seek to
read minds like books, in order to gain power by means of the
knowledge and the capacities they thus hope to acquire. There
is no question whatever of traditional blood-sucking, though
blood plays an eerie role in depictions of sadism like that in
"The Picture in the House."

The symbolic import of such tales is usually not too difficult
to fathom, and it may serve to introduce the fifth and last co-
ordinate of Lovecraft's weird world: the mind, the personality,
of the author himself. There can be no doubt that Lovecraft's
well-documented xenophobia and uneasy sense that white Anglo-
Saxon enclaves were being invaded, or were about to be invaded, by yellow, black and swarthy races of various kinds
have influenced, on many occasions, the form which his visions
of horror took; and so have his sexual inadequacies or hang-
ups, his sense of women as dangerous entities that could threaten
and overwhelm. But there is nothing simple or one-way about
these influences, just as there is nothing simple and one-way
about the personality of this xenophobe and believer in Nordic
superiority who chose to marry a Jewish wife of East European
ancestry; this convinced materialist who knew, better than anyone, the "oceanic feeling" characteristic of the religious temperament; this self-proclaimed loather of romanticism who wrote
fiction the romantic antecedents of which are clear for anyone
to see. Lovecraft's compelling visions, which ranged from the
backwoods of New England to "unknown Yuggoth," are neither devalued nor explained away by the personal phobias,
prejudices, anxieties and human inadequacies, of their originator. They have been transmuted into characters, actions and
reflections within the work.

The Case of Charles Dexter Ward is Lovecraft's only novel: a
skilful interweaving of themes and characters which makes
excellent use of elements from the detective novel (with Dr

Willett acting as detective as well as Van-Helsing-like dispeller
of malign influences) within the overall pattern of a supernatural horror-tale, a tale of daemonic possession. The rest of his
fiction takes the form of the short story or that of the "Novelle"
with its one central turning-point and its starting climactic
event. All this fiction is admirably constructed, often leading
inexorably to a clinching final sentence which brings a thrilling
but long expected and adroitly prepared revelation. Narratorial
voices are well sustained; "documents" are introduced in convincing ways, helping to support verisimilitude and further the
story while maintaining or increasing the tensions the author
constantly builds up; and Lovecraft's thorough knowledge of
other horror-fiction, from the Gothic novel to Meyrink and
Ewers, enables him to draw a great mnay themes and devices
worked out by earlier writers into the service of his "haunted
regionalism." Goethe, it will be remembered, lauded America
because unlike Europe it had no ruined castles and no basalt,
keine Basalte, and expressed the hope that the new continent
would therefore be spared the tales of knights, robbers and
ghosts, the *Ritter- Räuber- und Gespenstergeschichten,* that
were the curse of the old world. Lovecraft, in **"The Shadow
out of Time,"** deliberately introduced "basalt ruins" into the
cosmic landscape of his Great Race—and he frequently showed,
discursively or by example, that in despite of Goethe the dark
traditions of the European supernatural tale were alive and well
and living in New England.

What, then, of Lovecraft's style? Let us listen . . . to Edmund
Wilson. "One of Lovecraft's worst faults," Wilson tells us
[see excerpt in *TCLC,* Vol. 4], "is his incessant effort to work
up the expectations of the reader by sprinkling his stories with
such adjectives as 'horrible', 'terrible', 'frightful', 'awesome',
'eerie', 'weird', 'forbidden', 'unhallowed', 'unholy', 'blasphemous', 'hellish', and 'infernal'. Surely one of the primary
rules for writing an effective tale of horror is never to use any
of these words—especially if you are going, at the end, to
produce an invisible whistling octopus." Well, yes, the realistically described non-human entities, different though they
are from the usual Bug-Eyed Monsters of crude science fiction,
do occasionally provoke ribaldry; but this is, I think, a calculated effect, for Lovecraft's is a grotesque art that deliberately sets up tensions between horrified recoil and the impulse
to laugh. And yes, Lovecraft does, in many of his fictions,
pile up the adjectives Wilson lists, as well as more precious,
recherché terms like "gibbous" and "eldritch."

But is this necessarily indefensible? Even those who justifiably
squirm at phrases like "the ghoul-pooled darkness of earth's
bowels" in such minor works as **"The Nameless City"** may
soon reconcile themselves to the use Lovecraft's personae make
of the adjectives Wilson condemns so unequivocally. What
these suggest to me is narrators and protagonists imprisoned
by the walls of normal human speech; narrators and protagonists who have experienced transcendent visions, and suffered
aural or (very frequently) olfactory assaults never known before, and who must now strain to convey all this to others by
means of the hackneyed and plainly inadequate adjectives Wilson has listed. "The words reaching the reader," one of them
is made to say, "can never suggest the awfulness of the sight
itself." It is not just their *parole* which is deficient, but also
the *langue* which enshrines the whole repertoire on which they
can draw. The "horrendous" adjectives in Wilson's list, and
the nouns that go with them, are therefore supplemented, again
and again, by verbal gestures of inadequacy: "I cannot tell
you . . . ," "nothing can convey . . . ," ". . . surpassed description" and so on. Characteristically, it was Lovecraft who

The Halsey Mansion in Providence, R.I., which served as the model for the Ward family home in The Case of Charles Dexter Ward. *Photograph by Henry L.P. Beckwith, Jr.*

hit on the title **"The Unnameable"** for one of his fictions, long before Beckett made it his own. One may prefer the gentlemanly understatements of M. R. James, of course, or the subtle indirections of Henry James, which Lovecraft dismissed as unfairly as he dismissed the poetic innovations of T. S. Eliot; but Lovecraft's way seems to me a wholly legitimate one.

"You may laugh," Wilson sums up his impression of the terror-narratives he so heartily dislikes, "or you may be disgusted; but you are not likely to be terrified." I rarely laugh, and am even more rarely disgusted, at Lovecraft's fictions; but it is equally true that I am never terrified by them. My reaction is rather one of *fascination*. I am perennially fascinated by the way personal obsessions are absorbed and transmuted in these skilfully constructed tales—obsessions which range from dislike of fishy foods, of certain smells, of draughts and cold temperatures, to a radical dissatisfaction with the boundaries of time and space that our normal perceptions impose on us. I am no less intrigued by the manner in which a small corner of the known world is linked to inconceivably vast cosmic spaces with the help of the system of co-ordinates that I have already described. I admire the strange association of Gothic horrors with modern ideas of a space-time continuum; the amalgamation and reworking of many past modes of horror-fiction in the very personal and individual mode of a man writing in the second, third and fourth decade of the twentieth century;

the use of pulp-magazine format and conventions for conveying, in fictional form, the complex psychic constellation of an idiosyncratic and by no means uncultured personality.

I am fascinated, above all, by the way in which Lovecraft unites the appeal of the *fantastic*—defined by Theodore Ziolkowski as "a mode whose effect is an epistemological perplexity stemming from the momentary irruption of the seemingly supernatural into our world"—with the appeal of *fantasy*, described by the same perceptive critic as "a literary genre whose effect is the ethical insight which stems from our contemplation of an otherworld governed by supernatural laws." We may distance ourselves from such "ethics" as may be implicit in Lovecraft's fantastic tales, and may question the conclusions his protagonists draw from their "insights." We may even, in some of the tales, hold that there are natural explanations of apparently supernatural experiences, explanations in terms of delusion, hysteria, or insanity. All this does not, however, detract in the least from the appeal of Lovecraft the *fantaisiste* who (to adapt Tolkien's celebrated definition), "makes or glimpses Other-worlds."

Edmund Wilson's memorably formulated charges, then, neither can nor should be forgotten; but they may, I think, be countered in ways I have tried to suggest. Even this, however, is not important—for . . . this body of fantastic tales will always attract new readers who feel that it conveys, in satisfying literary form, feelings and sensations to which they too are not strangers. I venture to prophesy that *The Case of Charles Dexter Ward,* "The Colour out of Space," "The Haunter of the Dark," and other fictions discussed in [*H. P. Lovecraft: Four Decades of Criticism*] will remain in print, and be read with fascinated appreciation, longer than that famous essay in *Classics and Commercials* which has induced many a literary jury to return a negative verdict in the case of Howard Phillips Lovecraft. (pp. 687-88)

S. S. Prawer, "Allurements of the Abyss," in The Times Literary Supplement, No. 4081, June 19, 1981, pp. 687-88.

S. T. JOSHI (essay date 1982)

[*An American educator and critic, Joshi is the leading figure in the field of Lovecraft scholarship and criticism. As an editor, his publications include several volumes of Lovecraft's uncollected or unpublished works, critical editions of Lovecraft's major fiction, a collection of essays surveying Lovecraft's critical reputation, the journal* Lovecraft Studies, *and the definitive bibliography of Lovecraft's works and Lovecraft criticism. As a critic, he has published numerous essays on Lovecraft's life and work as well as a full-length biographical and critical study. In the following excerpt from that study, Joshi discusses the foundations and characteristics of Lovecraft's philosophical thought.*]

In forty-six-and-a-half years, Lovecraft wrote some of the most memorable fantasy fiction of this century, some powerful essays and poetry, and more letters that anyone in the history of world literature. Lovecraft's life and character, however, cannot be so summarily dismissed. We must now not merely explore some hitherto untouched or misunderstood facets of his personality, but also the philosophical thought upon which he himself claimed to base all his literary work.

The central tenet in what Lovecraft called his "cosmic indifferentism" is mechanistic materialism. The term postulates two ontological hypotheses: 1) the universe is a "mechanism" governed by fixed laws (although these may not all be known to men) where all entity is inextricably connected causally. There can be no such thing as chance (hence no free will but instead an absolute determinism) since every incident is the inevitable outcome of countless ancillary and contributory events reaching back into infinity. 2) All entity is material (Democritus' "atoms and void"), and there can be no other essence, whether it be "soul" or "spirit" or any other non-material substance. Einstein's discovery that matter is only one form of energy not merely does not overturn this system, but is in fact "*the materialist's trump card,*" since it now appears that "*matter . . . really is exactly what 'spirit' was always supposed to be.* Thus it is proved *that wandering energy always has a detectable form*—that if it doesn't take the form of waves or electron-streams, *it becomes matter itself;* and that the absence of matter or any other detectable energy-form indicates *not the presense of spirit, but the absence of anything whatever*" [= void]. . . . Moreover, the universe has always been and will always be. There can be no such thing as any purpose or goal toward which the universe as such is directed: the idea of purpose is a purely human concept.

In this way Lovecraft dispensed with religion. For not only did he find (and this beginning so early as the age of five) that no religion was congruent with the facts of science, but—through later readings in anthropology, notably Tylor's *Primitive Culture* and Frazer's *Golden Bough*—he learned how the religious

instinct is inbred in primitive man far before the advent of science and philosophy. Since religion is merely the savage's awe and wonder at the mystery of a Nature whose workings he cannot understand save by the postulation of anthropomorphic gods, it can be no indicator of objective truth. Darwin's theory of evolution, too, helped to free Lovecraft from the intellectual shackles of religion; for if man has a "soul" and beasts do not, at what point in man's evolution from the apes did he suddenly gain this new, divine, and undetectable trait? (pp. 13-14)

With cosmic teleology firmly eliminated and determinism espoused, what possible ethical code could Lovecraft recommend on the human scale? Here Lovecraft countered with the notion of *proximate values.* Given that there is no absolute or objective morality (for this would imply teleology), Lovecraft nevertheless felt that, on the human scale, men should retain the moral code which they have gained by being members of a given culture-stream since this cultural inheritance is the only thing which can provide the illusion of meaning and purpose in an otherwise aimless cosmos. Lovecraft therefore embraced the standards of conduct instilled in him by the Anglo-American Victorian culture to which he belonged, although augmenting and substituting parts of this ethic through his absorption of ancient philsophy (notably that of Epicurus, "the leading ethical philosopher of the world" . . . , and the traditions of Republican Rome and Augustan England. Nevertheless, Lovecraft made it clear that his ethics was not self-supported nor a direct outgrowth of his metaphysics (for this could not be possible, since ethical precepts are redundant in a deterministic system), but was founded upon *aesthetics.* Here Lovecraft has made a fundamental and innovative break with the whole Western philosophical tradition from Plato onwards:

> So far as I am concerned—I am an aesthete devoted to harmony, and to the extraction of the maximum possible pleasure from life. I find by experience that my chief pleasure is in symbolic identification with the landscape and tradition-stream to which I belong—hence I follow the ancient, simple New England ways of living, and observe the principles of honour expected of a descendent of English gentlemen. It is pride and beauty-sense, plus the automatic instincts of generations trained in certain conduct-patterns, which determine my conduct from day to day. But this is *not ethics,* because the same compulsions and preferences apply, with me, to things wholly outside the ethical zone. For example, I never cheat or steal. Also, I never wear a top-hat with a sack coat or munch bananas in public on the streets, because a gentlemen does not do those things either. I would as soon do the one as the other sort of thing— it is all a matter of harmony and good taste— whereas the ethical or "righteous" man would be horrified by dishonesty yet tolerant of coarse personal ways. . . .
>
> (pp. 14-15)

This importance which Lovecraft attached to *culture,* and the preservation of it, is the foundation for his entire political philosophy. His politics underwent the most significant changes during the course of his life of any aspect of his thought. However, the basic desire to maintain culture—and by "culture" he meant the ability of a given political unit or civilization to produce not only enduring art (whether it be painting, sculpture, music, literature, or architecture) but also an harmonious milieu for those of the higher mental caliber—underlies all the changes. For the first forty years of his life, Lovecraft felt that only aristocracy and oligarchy could produce sufficient leisure for the highest intellectual classes who always set the tone of a civilization. Here Lovecraft was supported by his knowledge of history, for he could point to Periclean Athens, Augustan Rome, Elizabethan and Georgian England, and the France of the *ancien regime*—all oligarchic and aristocratic—as creators of the greatest levels of civilization known to Western man, Democracy is "a mere catchword and illusion of inferior classes, visionaries, and dying civilisations." . . . In the United States it "gradually induced the notion of diffused rather than intensive development. Idealists wanted to raise the level of the ground by tearing down all the towers and strewing them over the surface—and when it was done they wondered why the ground didn't seem much higher, after all. And they had lost their towers!" . . . (p. 15)

In the end, however, Lovecraft became convinced that socialism could (if implemented properly) maintain as high a level of culture as aristocracy, since both systems emphasized "a set of qualities . . . whose merit lay only in a psychology of non-calculative, non-competitive disinterestedness, truthfulness, courage, and generosity fostered by good education, minimum economic stress, and assumed position" . . .—qualities not advocated by bourgeois capitalism which valued speed, money, and mechanization. Lovecraft's was not, however, the doctrinaire socialism of the Marxists—he saw only horror in the cultural devastation of Russia after the October Revolution—but the moderate form embodied in Franklin D. Roosevelt's New Deal, whereby the fundamental bases and traditions of Anglo-American culture would be preserved. Among the reforms suggested by Lovecraft were shorter working hours for all so that more people could have employment, government control of important resources and utilities, unemployment compensation, and a higher level of education for the majority so that the greater amount of leisure time could be used profitably in intellectual and aesthetic appreciation. But while *economic wealth* would thus be spread more equitably amongst the many, *political power* would be correspondingly limited to the few. The complexity of government in a technological age rendered it impossible for any but experts to have a real grasp of the political situation. Hence only technicians would be elected by a limited voting body consisting only of those individuals who could pass certain intellectual and psychological tests. Universal suffrage was outmoded in a technological age. In this way Lovecraft created his theory of "fascistic socialism." . . . (pp. 15-16)

Still, Lovecraft saw little of good in store for Western civilization, and the cause of its decline was clearly mechanization:

> But nothing good can be said of that cancerous machine-culture itself. It is not a true civilisation, and has nothing in it to satisfy a mature and fully developed human mind. It is attuned to the mentality and imagination of the galley-slave and the moron, and crushes relentlessly with disapproval, ridicule, and economic annihilation any sign of actually independent thought and civilised feeling which chances to rise above its sodden level. It is a treadmill, squirrel-trap culture—drugged and frenzied with the hasheesh of industrial servitude and mate-

rial luxury. It is wholly a material body-culture, and its symbol is the tiled bathroom and steam radiator rather than the Doric portico and the temple of Philosophy. Its denizens do not live or know how to live. . . .

(p. 16)

As a result, the intelligent man can only keep aloof from the throng and immerse himself in the culture-stream of the past. For Lovecraft, this meant plunging intellectualy and aesthetically into Graeco-Roman antiquity and eighteenth-century England; not only because he had grown immeasureably fond of these periods of Western culture but because the later age "was the *final* phase of that perfectly unmechanised era which as a whole gave us our most satisfying life." . . . The nineteenth century (especially in the England of Victoria) was simply a "mistake" . . . a "desert of illusions, pomposities, and hypocrises" . . . whose only virtues were its "manners and conceptions of life as a fine art." . . . The twentieth century, recoiling from the hypocrisy and repression of the nineteenth, had gone too far in radicalism—hence Lovecraft's distaste for avant-garde architecture, music, literature (although he recognized that such works as Joyce's *Ulysses* and Hecht's *Erik Dorn* represented a healthy if excessive aesthetic *sincerity* which partially redeemed them), manners, and politics. Lovecraft espoused the theory of a "decline of the West" years before he read Spengler's monumental treatise, and his attitudes had been reached independently of his later readings of Joseph Wood Krutch (*The Modern Temper*), Bertrand Russell, and George Santayana.

It is again the desire to preserve culture that accounts for Lovecraft's "racist" (better "racialist") stance. The America of Lovecraft's day was experiencing an enormous flood of immigration and no longer from the "Anglo-Saxon" branches (England, Ireland, Germany, Scandinavia) but from Eastern Europe and Asia. Through his readings of Social Darwinists, such as Spencer and T. H. Huxley, Lovecraft came to feel that each culture—whether inferior or superior to his own—must preserve its own distinctive fabric in the interests of world civilization. Hence, only those aliens ought to be admitted into a culture who will at once relinquish their own cultural stance and adopt that of the dominant civilization. Lovecraft saw that many minorities (the Jews of New York, the Italians and Portuguese of Providence) were refusing to do this, and were thereby (in Lovecraft's mind) helping to undermine the distinctive Anglo-American culture of the nation. As for the Negro, Lovecraft felt—with the best scientists of his day—that the problem here was not so much cultural as biological, since the Negro and native Australian appeared demonstrably to be biologically inferior to the other races of the world. They ought, as a result, to be clearly segregated from the dominant stock lest miscegenation corrupt the whole culture. These views of Lovecraft's did not so much *change* during the course of his life (as many have believed) but were merely *rationalized* and *synthesized*, a circumstance which some critics find unpalatable, but which we can accept intellectually if we regard Lovecraft as an historical figure susceptible to the intellectual and social trends of his time.

We have so far explored most of the major branches of Lovecraft's philosophical system with the exception of his aesthetics. We have seen that aesthetics—the eighteenth-century standard of "good taste"—was the foundation of his ethics, but what were his aesthetic views themselves? In particular, how did he envision the nature and function of literature? His views are of some subtlety and complexity, but we can begin by noticing that *pleasure*—the Epicurean ideal of rational intellectual pleasure and tranquility—was the desideratum; this means that art is not to provide a mere titillation of the senses but is instead to fulfill a profound psychologial need:

> False or insincere amusement is the sort of activity which does not meet the real psychological demands of the human glandular-nervous system, but merely affects to do so. Real amusement is the sort which is based on a knowledge of real needs, and which therefore hits the spot. *This latter kind of amusement is what art is.* . . .

This puts a great burden upon the creative artist: His goal must not be the pandering of the herd with cheap, formula-ridden hackwork but instead must be *self-expression* in the profoundest sense. The artist must strive to capture those fleeting images of beauty or terror that clamor within him demanding an outlet. And because Lovecraft adopted Poe's belief that art must reflect not abstract or objective *truth* (for this is the realm of science or philosophy) but emotional and aesthetic *beauty*, Lovecraft did away with any didactic motive in art. This is not to say that art is to be philosophically vacuous. A profound artist, in fact, cannot help but reflect his own vision of reality in one form or another, and . . . even some of Lovecraft's tales are openly and primarily philosophical or moral in nature, while all his work directly or indirectly conveys the tenets of his own philosophy. However, this didactic or philosophical element must be subordinated to the principal objective of conveying moods or images. The primacy of self-expression in art caused Lovecraft to repudiate the attempt to write for money. Writing for money was for Lovecraft a paradox, or rather it was a *business* not associated with art at all: "It's a legitimate business, just like insurance or banking or engineering, which somebody has got to do." . . . Indeed, it makes no difference whether a work of literature is even published after it is written, for its fundamental goal—"the mental and emotional satisfaction of self-expression" . . .—has already been reached. "There are probably seven persons, in all, who really like my work; and they are enough," wrote Lovecraft in 1921. "I should write even if I were the only patient reader, for my aim is merely self-expression." This belief—instilled in him by his genteel upbringing, bolstered by his years in amateur journalism, and intellectualized as part of his general aesthetic theory—accounts for Lovecraft's "uncommercial" attitude towards his own work. This attitude made him reluctant to submit any work to *Weird Tales* at all upon its founding in 1923, made him stick to *Weird Tales* as a market despite frequent rejections of his best work, made him feel (perhaps rightly) that *Weird Tales* had insidiously corrupted his style by causing his work to become too explicit and obvious, and made him unwilling to prepare either *Dream-Quest of Unknown Kadath* or *The Case of Charles Dexter Ward* for book publication (and this in spite of several publishers' requests for a novel-length work from his pen) because he was so discouraged as to their quality. This attitude is the more remarkable and admirable since Lovecraft failed to compromise his high standards in the face of his abject poverty. That we, his readers, are vastly the beneficiaries of this aesthetic integrity is now abundantly clear not merely by the high accord granted to his work worldwide but by the corresponding neglect and vacuity of the work of his colleagues who felt no such qualms in catering to the mob. Many critics have been exasperated at these attitudes of Lovecraft's and would like to have seen him enjoy some of the success which

his "posthumous triumph" (as L. Sprague de Camp aptly termed it) has accorded his work. However, Lovecraft was willing to make personal sacrifices in the name of his work, since it was not material prosperity but his writing itself which meant the most to him: "Writing after all is the essence of whatever is left in my life, and if the ability or opportunity for that goes, I have no further reason for—or mind to endure—the joke of existence." (pp. 16-18)

> *S. T. Joshi, in his* H. P. Lovecraft, *Starmont House, 1982, 83 p.*

DONALD R. BURLESON (essay date 1983)

[*Burleson is an American educator and critic whose* H. P. Lovecraft: A Critical Study *is the most extensive consideration to date of Lovecraft's fiction, nonfiction, and poetry. In the following excerpt from that study, Burleson examines some of Lovecraft's philosophical precepts and analyzes "The Call of Cthulhu" and "The Dunwich Horror," two of the most important stories in Lovecraft's fictional mythology.*]

[It] is interesting to consider . . . the views of the man who gave the world the Lovecraft Mythos, especially his views as they concern art, the artist, and the universe to which the artist must respond. (p. 11)

Lovecraft's view of the universe was essentially that of a "mechanistic materialist." The cosmos for him was a pointless, random collocation of atoms, winding down toward total entropy like an expiring clock. This view did not make him morose, for he took the attitude that one may as well enjoy beauty and aesthetic stimulation and the warmth of friendship even in a meaningless world. His view, however, did seem to give him a sort of objectivity or aesthetic distance in which his fictive pantheon could flourish; since he had no belief in the supernatural, he was emotionally free to imagine any sort of ultimate cosmic entities he liked.

Further, his world-view was such that mankind was, to him, incidental and wholly insignificant, and this view is the thematic key to much of Lovecraft's fiction. The horror, ultimately, in a Lovecraft tale is not some gelatinous lurker in dark places, but rather the realisation, by the characters involved, of their helplessness and their insignificance in the scheme of things—their terribly ironic predicament of being sufficiently well-developed organisms to perceive and feel the poignancy of their own motelike unimportance in a blind and chaotic universe which neither loves them nor even finds them worthy of notice, let alone hatred or hostility. The true horror, for example, of **"The Shadow out of Time"** is not the Great Race, or even the older, intangible entities that the Great Race fears; rather, it is the crushing realisation by the protagonist that he and all mankind, far from occupying the centre of the cosmic stage even on earth, are scarcely important or long-enduring enough to occupy that stage's shabbiest corner. The protagonist finds that there are vast cycles of time and immensities of space that reduce human concerns to the merest atoms. Thus was Lovecraft able to play upon the central idea of utter cosmic alienage, removing the spotlight from mankind and playing it upon the blindly wheeling cosmos itself. Lovecraft makes his own central statement of literary philosophy in a 1927 letter to Farnsworth Wright:

> Now all my tales are based on the fundamental premise that common human laws and interests and emotions have no validity or significance in the vast cosmos-at-large. To me there is

nothing but puerility in a tale in which the human form—and the local human passions and conditions and standards—are depicted as native to other worlds or other universes. To achieve the essence of real externality, whether of time or space or dimension, one must forget that such things as organic life, good and evil, love and hate, and all such attributes of a negligible and temporary race called mankind, have any existence at all. Only the human scenes and characters must have human qualities. *These* must be handled with unsparing *realism* (*not* catch-penny *romanticism*) but when we cross the line to the boundless and hideous unknown—the shadow-haunted *Outside*—we must remember to leave our humanity and terrestrialism at the threshold.

Lovecraft further remarks, in a 1931 letter:

> The only things I can conceive as worthy protagonists of cosmic drama are *basic natural forces and laws,* and what spells *interest* for me is simply the convincing illusion of the thwarting, suspension, or disturbance of such forces and laws. To me a climax is simply an effective demonstration of a temporary defeat of the cosmic order. I use human puppets as symbols, but my interest is not with them. It is the situation of defeat itself—and the sensation of liberation therein implicit—which provides me with the thrills and catharsis of aesthetic endeavour.

Nevertheless, Lovecraft of course had to operate on the basis that fiction is a human activity—that the horrors to be experienced are experienced vicariously by the reader through the subjective reactions of the fictional character. One finds these character reactions to be highly significant; the horror is not really some unspeakable external reality, but rather the protagonist's emotional reactions to his glimpses of that reality, and his realisation of the awesome implications for mankind. In **"The Colour out of Space,"** for example, it is not so much the "blasted heath" that one finds horrific; rather, it is the narrator's ponderous fear of that site and its implications, in his mind, of unspeakable alienage. Thus, one may term Lovecraft's approach to fiction a sort of "ironic impressionism"—impressionism because it is the act of perceiving and feeling and pondering the implications of glimpsed external realities that finds emphasis, rather than those realities themselves; ironic because Lovecraft on the one hand makes the human capacity for fear and other emotional responses the conduit of effectiveness in presenting his ideas, while on the other hand reducing this very feeling and thinking human creature to self-understood insignificance by the implications of that creature's glimpses of what lies beyond his previous understanding of the cosmos. The "blasted heath" is not so much a physical phenomenon as a psychological process, a fear-response and an awe, in a mind that by the very experience discovers its own minuteness and precariousness in a cosmos far vaster, far more indifferent to human concerns than that mind has ever imagined. This ironic capability to *sense* one's own vanishingly small place in the universe is the central feature of the Lovecraft Mythos and constitutes an effect virtually unprecedented in literature. (pp. 12-14)

Lovecraft . . . remarks in a 1930 letter: "My own attitude in writing is always that of the hoax-weaver. . . . For the time being I try to forget formal literature, & simply devise a lie as carefully as a crooked witness prepares a line of testimony with cross-examining lawyers in his mind." Thus, he obviously gives great weight to consistency, plausibility, and realism—realism in the sense that in order for the reader to be emotionally prepared to "suspend disbelief" at the moment necessary, when the unreal horror enters and gives the illusion of violating cosmic law, the writer must lead the way with a realistic backdrop which serves as a foil to the unreal eventualities. Lovecraft depends on the psychology of fear for his effects, and remarks (. . . in **"Notes on Writing Weird Fiction"**):

> Horror and the unknown or the strange are always closely connected, so that it is hard to create a convincing picture of shattered natural law or cosmic alienage and "outsideness" without laying stress on the emotion of fear. The reason why *time* plays a great part in so many of my tales is that this element looms up in my mind as the most profoundly dramatic and grimly terrible thing in the universe. *Conflict with time* seems to me the most potent and fruitful theme in all human expression.

Lovecraft emerges, by his own pronouncements and from the evidence of his fictional creations themselves, as a writer with well-thought-out philosophical principles and deep convictions about the nature of the properly conceived and executed weird tale, and a writer closely in touch with the nature of fear. Well in evidence also is his inclination to revere the integrity and beauty of language, after the classical and eighteenth-century models that he so much admired. (pp. 15-16)

During the summer of 1926 Lovecraft wrote a story which, considering the directions of his work from this point on, was to be of great importance in the Lovecraft canon, **"The Call of Cthulhu,"** a tale with interesting mythic overtones. (p. 115)

In manuscript, the story provides a colophon after the title: "(Found Among the Papers of the Late Francis Wayland Thurston, of Boston)." This has been omitted in most printed texts of the story, and the first-person narrator is not otherwise named. The story, in part set in Lovecraft's College Hill area of Providence, is divided into three titled sections, and in the first, "The Horror in Clay," the narrator opens with a philosophical statement embodying what may be called Lovecraft's "forbidden knowledge" or "merciful ignorance" motif:

> The most merciful thing in the world, I think, is the inability of the human mind to correlate all its contents. We live on a placid island of ignorance in the midst of black seas of infinity, and it was not meant that we should voyage far.

Science, he continues, may someday usher in our collective madness by piecing together for us the underlying horror of reality, only our ignorance of which keeps us sane. (Lovecraft has previously, though far less effectively, suggested this notion in **"Facts Concerning the Late Arthur Jermyn & His Family."**) The narrator has himself stumbled on the dreadful truths of the story by "an accidental piecing together of separated things . . . an old newspaper item and the notes of a dead professor." The professor was the narrator's nonagenarian grand-uncle Professor Angell of Brown University, who has died "after being jostled by a nautical-looking negro" but whose death has officially been ascribed to natural causes. The narrator, as his uncle's executor, finds among his possessions a box of exceedingly curious things, including a bas-relief in clay, and various "cuttings" (Lovecraft's habitual term for "clippings") and other papers. The bas-relief features a monstrous form "which only a diseased fancy could conceive"—a sort of octopus-dragon—and the accompanying papers bear the title "CTHULHU CULT." (p. 116)

The narrator finds the "Cthulhu cult" manuscript divided into two sections. The first tells the story of a study related to the dreams of a young artist named Wilcox; the second relates the experiences of a New Orleans police inspector named Legrasse. Throughout, Lovecraft maintains a high level of realism by making the narrative rely heavily on newspaper items, scholarly notes, and the like. (p. 117)

In the story's second section, "The Tale of Inspector Legrasse," the reader is made aware of the Legrasse data; again the narrative milieu is one of control and scholarly verisimilitude for heightened realism, the realism needed to serve as a balance or foil for the fantastic disclosures to come. Professor Angell, we are told, attended the 1908 annual meeting of the American Archaeological Society in St. Louis, meeting Inspector Legrasse, who carried with him "a grotesque, repulsive, and apparently very ancient stone statuette" which he sought to identify. In this story within a story, there is related a story within a story within a story . . . of how Legrasse came to possess the statuette, which represented "a monster of vaguely anthropoid outline, but with an octopus-like head whose face was a mass of feelers"; the thing sat on a "pedestal covered with undecipherable characters" of which even the grand assembly of scholars found it impossible to "form the least notion of even their remotest kinship." Thus, Lovecraft cleverly establishes the absolute externality of the thing, which is seen as "frightfully suggestive of old and unhallowed cycles of life in which our world and our conceptions have no part." (pp. 117-18)

Legrasse related a long tale of his investigating a bizarre sacrificial cult ritual in voodoo country, breaking up the rites, seizing the idol, and questioning the prisoners: "Degraded and ignorant as they were, the creatures held with surprising consistency to the central idea of their loathsome faith." From this questioning the reader learns an essential notion underlying the Lovecraft Mythos:

> They worshipped . . . the Great Old Ones who lived ages before there were any men, and who came to the young world out of the sky. Those Old Ones were gone now, inside the earth and under the sea; but their dead bodies had told their secrets in dreams to the first men, who formed a cult which had never died. This was the cult, and the prisoners said it had always existed and always would exist, hidden in distant wastes and dark places all over the world until the time when the great priest Cthulhu, from his dark house in the mighty city of R'lyeh under the waters, should rise and bring the earth again beneath his sway. Someday he would call, when the stars were ready, and the secret cult would always be waiting to liberate him.

Thus, Lovecraft begins to develop in earnest a central idea hinted at as long ago as **"Dagon"** and **"The Doom that Came to Sarnath"**—that man is relatively recent among earth's lords

and holds but a tenuous position in the cosmic scheme of things. The Lovecraft Mythos makes its debut firmly rooted, as all substantial literature must be, in myth, for clearly Cthulhu is Lovecraft's expression of the archetypal motif of death and rebirth of a god, the mythic motif of the god whose return is gloriously awaited. Cthulhu, not a "water elemental" of the Poseidon type as August Derleth has claimed, has been trapped in his watery tomb by the sinking of the primordial temple-city of R'lyeh in the Pacific, and his death is not true death; for Lovecraft now revives with a vengeance the *Necronomicon* couplet from **"The Nameless City"**:

> That is not dead which can eternal lie,
> And with strange aeons even death may die.

The narrator, digesting all these records, interviews the artist Wilcox at the youth's lodgings in the Fleur-de-Lys Building in Thomas Street (7 Thomas Street, a real Providence locale faithfully described); Wilcox's dream of a slimy Cyclopean city parallels the accounts of R'lyeh, "whose geometry . . . was *all wrong.*" Lovecraft places his fictive events outside of *all* human comprehension by denying them a part in the familiar world so basic as traditional geometry.

In the tale's third and decisive section, "The Madness from the Sea," the narrator experiences the coincidental piecing-together of things destined to be the end of him. He visits a "learned friend of Paterson, New Jersey; the curator of a local museum and a mineralogist of note" . . . and sees among the shelf-papers an article from the Australian *Sydney Bulletin*. Lovecraft gives the text of this article in full for considerable realism, though one may notice that the style in which the supposedly journalistic piece is written is not sufficiently different from the Lovecraftian style of narration of the story itself. At any rate, the article tells the tale of a Norwegian sailor, Gustav Johansen, who has survived some horrendous incident at sea involving "a horrible stone idol of unknown origin" and a calamity on an uncharted island. (Lovecraft's choice of Norway is probably significant in that his description of Cthulhu would appear to owe much to Tennyson's poem "The Kraken," based in turn on a Norwegian myth.) The narrator draws correlations from the dates mentioned, noting parallels with Wilcox's period of delirium. Eventually he visits Johansens's home in Oslo, finding that the sailor has died rather mysteriously; Johansen's wife discloses that he has left a long manuscript "written in English, evidently in order to safeguard her from the peril of casual perusal." The reader's credulity is somewhat strained here—the narrator could not have read the document in Norwegian; the English is a trifle too convenient. It is strained even more by the fact that the narrator is allowed to carry the manuscript away; Lovecraft could have made this detail more persuasive.

The diary, like the later Smith diary in **The Case of Charles Dexter Ward**, is a good device, nonetheless, for keeping distance between the reader and the horror. According to Johansen's account, he and his men encountered the mysteriously upheaved island and "nightmare corpse-city" (R'lyeh) in S. Latitude 47°9', W. Longitude 126°43'—in keeping with Lovecraft's penchant for realistic detail, indeed a forsaken spot in the Pacific, and one south of the Valparaíso ocean route as stated. Like the locale of Wilcox's dreams, the place was one whose geometry was "abnormal, non-Euclidean, and loathsomely redolent of spheres and dimensions apart from ours." The sailors found a vast door; effectively, Lovecraft says that "they could not decide whether it lay flat like a trap door or slantwise like an outside cellar-door," but they managed to get it open, only to hear "a nasty, slopping sound down there." And they were listening still

> when It lumbered slobberingly into sight and gropingly squeezed Its gelatinous green immensity through the black doorway. . . . What wonder that across the earth . . . poor Wilcox raved with fever in that telepathic instant? . . . The stars were right again. . . . After vigintillions of years great Cthulhu was loose again, and ravening for delight.

Johansen and one companion reached the ship and prepared to get under way, and "the titan Thing from the stars slavered and gibbered like Polypheme cursing the fleeing ship of Odysseus," and gave pursuit. Johansen rammed the monstrosity with the ship; here Lovecraft indulges in extravagant yet controlled description by simile: "There was a bursting as of an exploding bladder, a slushy nastiness as of a cloven sunfish, a stench as of a thousand opened graves, and [the effective modicum of restraint] a sound that the chronicler would not put on paper." However, Cthulhu's "scattered plasticity" recombined as the ship fled. The narrator ends the tale in a potently suggestive and alliteratively poetic fashion:

> I have looked upon all that the universe has to hold of horror, and even the skies of spring and flowers of summer must ever afterward be poison to me. But I do not think my life will be long. As my uncle went, and poor Johansen went, so I shall go. I know too much, and the cult still lives. Cthulhu still lives, too. . . . What has risen may sink, and what has sunk may rise.

Following this sonorous chaismus, the narrator expresses the final hope that "if I do not survive this manuscript, my executors may put caution before audacity and see that it meets no other eye."

Although **"The Call of Cthulhu"** is marred by some minor problems of credibility—ironically, the reader is probably more willing to "believe" in Cthulhu and the momentary surfacing of R'lyeh than to believe that the narrator was allowed to depart with Johansen's manuscript—it is a tale of skillfully balanced realism and fantasy, of carefully prepared horrors which . . . have awesomely cosmic implications and which ominously survive beyond story's end. . . . **"The Call of Cthulhu"** marks a distinct turning-point, a turning toward the precepts of the now-developing Lovecraft Mythos, by which man is a helpless and insignificant newcomer in a cosmos too old and too vastly unplumbed to be other than indifferent, at best, to his wellbeing. (pp. 118-21)

During the summer of 1928, a summer of very eventful travel, Lovecraft wrote **"The Dunwich Horror,"** one of his most widely read and, as it turns out, most critically problematical works. Lovecraft says of the story just written:

> . . . The title is **"The Dunwich Horror,"** & it belongs to the Arkham cycle. The *Necronomicon* figures in it to some extent.

(Curiously, the term "Arkham cycle" is not one that Lovecraft in other known letters ever employs.) Later he remarks of **"The Dunwich Horror"**:

> I used considerable realism in developing the locale of that thing—the prototype being the

decaying agricultural region N.E. of Springfield, Mass.—especially the township of Wilbraham, where I visited for a fortnight in 1928.

Lovecraft neglects to mention that his travel impressions, transmuted deftly into the fictive Dunwich region, also stemmed from a stay in Athol, Massachusetts, just before visiting Wilbraham; he is consistently silent on this point, but as will be shown, there can be no doubt that his Dunwich is an imaginative blend of impressions from both Athol and Wilbraham, or that this story is a striking instance of the extent to which Lovecraft could practice fictional adaptation of his place-impressions.

On the face of it, **"The Dunwich Horror"** appears to be a vivid horror tale oddly flawed by certain crudities of characterisation and plot; but there is more than meets the eye. The story deals with the breeding of a monstrous, invisible entity in a decadent Massachusetts backwater, and of the efforts, in the end successful, of Miskatonic University's Dr. Henry Armitage to put down this local horror. In a surface-level reading, one wonders that the tale can fit at all into a Lovecraft Mythos in which such human concepts as "good" and "evil" are meaningless, and the cosmos is portrayed as awesomely indifferent to human interests, for in **"The Dunwich Horror"** there appears to be a sort of "stock" struggle between good and evil, between Armitage and the blasphemous monstrosity which he rushes in like a movie hero to quell. Indeed, Armitage comes off as an oddly conventionalised character, with lines so corny that one may wonder how Lovecraft could have suffered such a lapse. However, to read the story on this level is to miss much of what it has to offer; for it turns out that with a reading in the light of *mythic* interpretation, one sees a vastly different picture, one in which Armitage sounds like a buffoon because, in mythic context, he *is* a buffoon.

Like **"The Colour out of Space,"** this work begins (after an epigraph from Charles Lamb suggesting that monstrous traditions are archetypal in the human mind) with an atmospheric study of the locale in which the story will be set: "When a traveller in north central Massachusetts takes the wrong fork at the junction of the Aylesbury pike just beyond Dean's Corners he comes upon a lonely and curious country." (The reference to "north central" Massachusetts is patently a tip of the Lovecraftian hat to Athol.) This country, the omniscient narrator continues, is singularly wild, remote, and decadent. The description waxes symbolic as well as colourful: "Gorges and ravines of problematical depth intersect the way, and the crude wooden bridges always seem of dubious safety." The gorges are suggestive of mysterious, untrammeled nature; the bridges are suggestive of the feebleness of human attempts to deal with what cannot be fathomed.

Dunwich itself is described as a village having a "cluster of rotting gambrel roofs bespeaking an earlier architectural period than that of the neighbouring region." Its denizens are "a race by themselves, with the well-defined mental and physical stigmata of degeneracy and inbreeding." The place is one of much local folklore. In particular, the numerous whippoorwills of the region are said to be "psychopomps lying in wait for the souls of the dying," timing their cries "in unison with the sufferer's struggling breath." When they catch a fleeing soul, they "flutter away chittering in daemoniac laughter"; when they fail, "they subside gradually into a disappointed silence." Lovecraft is here making use of a local legend he imbibed during his stay in Wilbraham, Massachusetts, with his friend Edith Miniter and her cousin Evanore Beebe in their "Maplehurst'' family home. Much Dunwich legendry also centres about Sentinel Hill, atop which the ill-famed Wizard Whateley performs shocking rituals in the midst of a circle of stones. (pp. 140-41)

The narrator tells of the birth of Wilbur Whateley (the name Wilbur being a probable echo of Wilbraham) on 2 February 1913—''Candlemas, which people in Dunwich curiously observe under another name''—born to the unwed, ''somewhat deformed, unattractive albino woman'' Lavinia Whateley, daughter of old Wizard Whateley. The boy's grandfathher utters a prophecy at the general store, that ''*some day yew folks'll hear a child o' Lavinny's a-callin' its father's name on the top of Sentinel Hill!*'' (The reader may erroneously assume at this point that the child referred to is Wilbur, but there are surprises waiting.) The boy grows and learns at an uncanny rate, and has repellent, ''goatish-looking'' features. With foreshadowing, the narrator remarks that dogs abhor Wilbur. Old Whateley buys astonishing numbers of cattle, and repairs and locks a long disused toolshed, also boarding up the upper story of the house; a singular stench hangs about the place, quite beyond its simple lack of cleanliness. About ten years later, when the old man dies, the whippoorwills gather and chirp but do not seem to catch his soul, and the attending physician hears ''a disquieting suggestion of rhythmical surging or lapping, as of waves on some level beach'' from the upper portions of the house. The old man, just before dying, enjoins Wilbur:

> More space, Willy, more space soon. Yew grows—an' *that* grows faster. It'll be ready to sarve ye soon, boy. Open up the gates to Yog-Sothoth. . . . [But] dun't let it grow too fast fer the place, fer ef it busts quarters or gits aout afore ye opens to Yog-Sothoth, it's all over an' no use. Only them beyont kin make it multiply an' work. . . . Only them, the old uns as wants to come back.

He dies. Thus grows not only the implied monstrosity upstairs but also the Lovecraft Mythos itself; the notion (first glimpsed in **''The Call of Cthulhu''**) is more firmly establishcd that there are primordial entities (ultimately symbolic of *chaos*) lying in the great Outside who must once have held sway and now want to re-establish their dominion, aided by sorcery. Soon afterward Wilbur is busy removing timbers from the house, gradually turning it into a hollow shell to hold what is growing inside it—Lovecraft keeps the creature tantalisingly hidden—and is off to Miskatonic University to consult their complete text of the Latin *Necronomicon* for chants needed. By this time he is almost eight feet tall, and he is met at the university library by a naturally apprehensive librarian, Henry Armitage, who grudgingly allows him to look at the forbidden volume but refuses to let him take it home. Wilbur reads a long passage which Lovecraft makes Biblically sonorous, the most impressive and substantially illuminative peek inside the tome to be found anywhere in the Lovecraft *oeuvre*:

> Nor is it to be thought that man is either the oldest or the last of earth's masters. . . . The Old Ones were, the Old Ones are, and the Old Ones shall be. Not in the spaces we know but *between* them. They walk serene and primal, undimensioned and to us unseen. *Yog-Sothoth* knows the gate. *Yog-Sothoth* is the gate. *Yog-Sothoth* is the key and guardian of the gate. Past, present, future, all are one in *Yog-Sothoth*. . . . Great Cthulhu is Their cousin, yet

can he spy Them only dimly. Iä, *Shub-Niggurath!* As a foulness shall ye know Them. . . . Man rules now where They ruled once; They shall soon rule where man rules now. After summer is winter, and after winter summer.

With this passage, so poetically balanced by the device of chiasmus, Lovecraft implies the cyclic cosmicism of his Mythos conception.

Later Wilbur tries to steal the forbidden book but is torn to shreds by the guard dog. Lovecraft describes what is found, in great detail; one might be tempted to say too much detail, but it should be kept in mind that the tentacled, saurian horror that lies turning into whitish ichor on the library floor is not *the* horror of the tale—that horror, Lovecraft's eternal ''something worse waiting,'' is yet to come, and will be kept more tastefully vague. When Wilbur dies, Lovecraft gives a nice twist to the whippoorwill legend; the birds chirp in anticipation of the departure of Wilbur's soul, but are panic-stricken when they behold it: ''Against the moon vast clouds of feathery watchers rose and raced from sight, frantic at that which they had sought for prey.'' The narrator remarks that ''the really human element in Wilbur Whateley must have been very small.''

In Wilbur's absence the horror back at the Whateley farmhouse in Dunwich bursts forth to scatter death and terror through the region. The monstrosity is invisible—Lovecraft continues to make the reader wonder about its exact nature. It descends into Cold Spring Glen, a ''great sinister ravine,'' as a sort of lair, emerging from time to time to attack the farm families. (pp. 142-44)

Henry Armitage, deciphering a Wilbur Whateley diary . . . dcvises some counter-sorcery, aided by a chemical spray to make the monstrous entity visible. He engages two colleagues, Professors Morgan and Rice, to accompany him to Dunwich to put down the horror. (p. 145)

Armitage and his cohorts follow the enormous invisible entity up Sentinel Hill, leaving the townsfolk to watch through a telescope; Lovecraft thus arranges effective distance between the reader and the horror. The delegation from Miskatonic intones a chant designed to send the creature back to Yog-Sothoth, its father, and the monstrosity bellows:

> *Eh-ya-ya-ya-yahaah—e'yayayayaaaa . . . . . .*
> *ngh'aaaa . . . ngh'aaaa . . . h'yuh . . . h'yuh*
> *. . . HELP! HELP! . . . ff—ff—ff-FATHER! FA-*
> *THER! YOG-SOTHOTH!*

One almost expects, ''Why has thou forsaken me?'' The scene is a clear tongue-in-cheek parody of the crucifixion; the monstrous entity returns to the father. Below, the farmers have espied the thing fleetingly, describing it as ''a octopus, centipede, spider kind o' thing [but] *they was a haff-shaped man's face on top of it, an' it looked like Wizard Whateley's only it was yards an' yards acrost.*''

Armitage lectures the men about the thing called out of external spheres and sent back, finally giving utterance to the revelation: ''You needn't ask how Wilbur called it out of the air. He didn't call it out. *It was his twin brother, but it looked more like the father than he did.*''

Despite this powerful ending, Armitage comes off in the end as a curiously hokey and seemingly un-Lovecraftian character, mouthing such corny lines as ''*But what, in God's name, can we do?*'' and giving utterance to a sort of moralising good-versus-evil mentality that seems to run mawkishly contrary to the precepts of the Lovecraft Mythos: ''We have no business calling in such things from outside, and only very wicked people and very wicked cults ever try to.'' But to read the story only on this level is to miss much of its interpretative potential, because the most compelling view of the tale is that which emerges in terms of *myth* and the mythic motif of the questioning hero. Seen in such terms, the story undergoes a startling reversal in meaning.

The question arises: who is the hero? In mythic terms it turns out that only one character has all the requisite characteristics: Wilbur Whateley and his twin brother, regarded—as is commonly done in such contexts as the Twin Cycle of the hero myth in Winnebago Indian mythology—as *one* entity. Typically, the twins in such hero mythology seem invincible at first, but eventually succumb to an overreaching hubris or ambitious pride; this is clearly the case with the Whateley twins. Typically, also, the twins are separated, and it is difficult to reunite them; witness the separation of Wilbur and his brother in the quest for the *Necronomicon*.

Thought of as a unified entity, the Whateley twins remarkably well fit the mythic pattern known as the *hero monomyth,* an archetypal pattern present in varying degrees in all hero mythology. The monomyth consists of eight stages:

(1) Miraculous conception or birth, as in traditional accounts of the virgin birth of Quetzalcoatl and Jesus, or of the immaculate conception of Buddha, Lao-Tzu, and Horus.

(2) Initiation of the hero, who commonly evinces uncanny wisdom as a child, as in the case of Jesus or Buddha; frequently a disguised god sires the hero, who is threatened and must be hidden.

(3) Preparation, meditation, and withdrawal of the hero, as in the withdrawal of Buddha to the Bodhi tree, or Moses to his mountain, or Jesus to the wilderness, or Mohammed to his cave.

(4) Trial and quest; the hero embarks on some such quest as that of Gilgamesh for the plant of life, or Percival for the Holy Grail, or Sir Gawain for the chapel of the Green Knight.

(5) Death of the hero because of his quest, often by dismemberment as in the cases of Osiris, Dionysos, and Orpheus.

(6) Descent to the underworld, as in the case of Jesus; typically, one sees here the theme of overcoming the forces of death, as in the case of Hercules and Cerberus.

(7) Resurrection and rebirth, as in the cases of Dionysos, Buddha, Adonis, Osiris, and Jesus.

(8) Ascension, as in the case of Jesus.

It is generally significant to find even half of these things in any one account; Wilbur Whateley and his twin brother fit all eight stages quite closely:

(1) The twins are products of a sort of miraculous conception and birth, sired by the ''god'' Yog-Sothoth in May-Eve rites on Sentinel Hill; Wilbur is shunned by townsfolk and threatened by dogs, and must conceal his teratological form under his clothing, while the brother is hidden in the farmhouse, a symbolic second womb in which he grows and prepares for ''rebirth.''

(2) Wilbur is ''initiated'' by being allowed to take part in Sentinel Hill rites at May Eve and All Hallows Eve with his mother and grandfather. As is typical in myth, we are told little of his childhood; here, the narration skips from Wilbur's fourth to tenth year. Wilbur exhibits uncanny early wisdom and growth, developing rapidly both in physical and mental stature, beginning to talk at the age of eleven months, becoming a ''fluent and incredibily intelligent talker'' by nineteen months, and reading fluently and avidly by the age of four.

(3) Wilbur's withdrawal and ''meditation'' consist of his studies out of ancient books with his grandfather ''through long, hushed afternoons'' ensconced in the farmhouse. The grandfather acts as the sort of ''tutelary figure'' common in hero mythology, a guardian or mentor who offsets the hero's early inability to act independently; in **''The Dunwich Horror''** he is protector to the twin upstairs as well.

(4) Wilbur's trial or quest ensues, after his intellectual preparations under the tutelage of the old wizard, when he sets out to obtain the full Latin text of the *Necronomicon* to aid in his sorcery; this quest, beset with the difficulties in the form of Armitage and the guard dog, is embedded in the grander quest to open the gates to Yog-Sothoth.

(5) Wilbur's death comes as a direct consequence of his quest, when he is ripped to pieces by the university guard dog. Ironically, it is really this dog that saves the world from unthinkable horrors, for in Wilbur's absence, the twin, though capable of much local mischief, is essentially ineffectual in cosmic terms. The dog has saved the world—so much for the messianic vision in Lovecraft's fictive cosmos.

(6) The descent to the underworld is suggested symbolically by the descent of Wilbur's twin into Cold Spring Glen, the ''great sinister ravine'' described in such hellish terms.

(7) Rebirth, when Wilbur and his brother are regarded as one entity, is symbolically but clearly given by the emergence of the monstrous twin from the ''womb'' of the farmhouse when Wilbur dies; the Yog-Sothoth spawn is not only reborn, but reborn in stronger form. The notion of death and rebirth is also suggested and reinforced by the descent into and emergence from the ravine, like the symbolically significant leap of Hamlet into and out of the grave.

(8) Ascension comes when the twin returns to his place of conception, the great table-rock atop Sentinel Hill, and is returned to the father.

Thus, the Whateley twins have all the characteristics of the mythic archetypal hero. Armitage, whom one might have supposed to be a ''hero,'' has none of these qualities, and operates essentially as a sort of fictional prop; his corny utterances are thus quite befitting. Although he has rushed in to "save the day," it is quite clear from the quotation from the *Necronomicon* that the Old Ones are eventually to regain dominance; there are cosmic cycles not to be denied, and Armitage's local "victory" is in larger terms a hollow and meaningless one indeed. It is not humankind but the ineluctable forces of the outer spheres that will prevail; man cannot forever resist the onslaught of a universe that is chaotic from his point of view because indifferent to his well-being.

Thus, regardless of the question of how much of the mythic-level meaning Lovecraft consciously contrived, the story when viewed mythically forms a sardonic reversal of its surface reading. . . . The twins, for whom one is presumably to feel loathing, are archetypally heroic; Armitage, whom one is presumably supposed to admire, is essentially a cipher; and thematically the tale gives articulation to the Lovecraftian view that man is but an evanescent mote in the universe of stars. Seen in this way, **"The Dunwich Horror"** ceases to appear to be a "good versus evil" moralising tale that fits only awkwardly into the Lovecraft canon, and becomes a work centrally expressive of the *Weltanschauung* underlying all of the Lovecraft Mythos. (pp. 145-49)

> *Donald R. Burleson, in his* H. P. Lovecraft: A Critical Study, *Greenwood Press, 1983, 243 p.*

ROBERT M. PRICE (essay date 1984)

[*Price is an American educator and critic whose writings are principally devoted to his two main fields of expertise: Christian theology and the works of H. P. Lovecraft. He is the editor of* Crypt of Cthulhu: A Pulp Thriller and Theological Journal, *which publishes both facetious and serious essays on Lovecraft and other authors of the* Weird Tales *school. In the following excerpt, Price applies the hermeneutic principle of "demythologizing" to Lovecraft's fiction in order to arrive at a more valid understanding of his invented mythology than is allowed by either literal occultist belief or symbolic literary interpretation.*]

Just how seriously did H. P. Lovecraft mean us to take his Cthulhu Mythos? How seriously did he take it himself? Was his use of the "Great Old Ones" and their terrors merely some kind of stage setting, something "he chanced to mould in play"? Or were the blasphemies of the *Necronomicon* actually nightmares haunting Lovecraft, to which his fiction was the nervous response of a "whistler in darkness"? Of late, these theories have made the rounds among fans and scholars of Lovecraft's work. Both alike are unsatisfying. Cthulhu and his cousins are surely more than stylistic accessories. Yet equally certainly, Lovecraft does not seem to have so taken leave of his senses as to have actually given credence to the monsters of his imagination. Perhaps surprisingly, the answer to this dilemma is to be found in the "demythologizing" hermeneutic of New Testament scholar Rudolf Bultmann. To anticipate, Lovecraft's tales of the Great Old Ones are real myths, and thus to be taken seriously but not literally.

The debate as to the intent and nature of the Cthulhu cycle strikingly parallels the contest that raged over the miracle stories of the gospels, beginning with Lessing's publication of the *Fragments* of Hermann Samuel Reimarus between 1774 and 1778. For centuries, apologists for the Christian faith had relied on the so-called "proofs from prophecy and miracle" to convince unbelievers. If Jesus could be demonstrated to have fulfilled Old Testament prophecies and to have worked super-

natural miracles, then any rational person should acquiesce to his claims to have been the Messiah and the Son of God. Such a convincing case could only be made, of course, as long as all parties assumed that the gospel texts recording his words and deeds were composed by eyewitnesses, and thus contemporaneous with what they described.

Reimarus pointed out numerous indications within the texts that they were not in fact accurate. Among these were the presence of divergent understandings (political vs. spiritual) of the "Kingdom of God" preached by Jesus, and embarrassing contradictions among the resurrection narratives. Reimarus and other rationalist critics after him thus rejected the Christian apologists' claim that the gospels were historically accurate. But they did not think to question the twin claim that the texts were eyewitness accounts. The seemingly inevitable conclusion was that the wonder tales of the gospels were deliberate lies, intended to capture the allegiance of the gullible. Now this would not have been out of the question. Such "pious (and not so pious) frauds" have always been present in religious history. The second-century satirist Lucian chronicles a famous instance in his "Alexander the Quack Prophet," wherein one Alexander of Ablonuticus establishes a phony oracle, a large snake wearing a mask resembling a human face, and set back from the crowds in the shadows. Alexander collected considerable revenue from the manufactured marvel, and even sent out apostles to advertise the new god to more prospective customers! In our own day, the clever hoax-miracles of Reverend Jim Jones provide a parallel. (For instance, the late Jeannie Mills, once an advisor to Jones, recounted to this writer how Jones engineered walking on water!)

Nonetheless, the supernatural stories of Jesus in the New Testament do not seem to fall in this category. David Friedrich Strauss, in his epoch-making *The Life of Jesus Critically Examined* (1835), broke the "hoax or history" deadlock by indicating a third possibility. He simply pointed out that the common assumption of apologists and skeptics, that the gospels were the product of eyewitnesses, was erroneous. Instead, several considerations led to the conclusion that the texts represented the legend-mongering propensity of first- and second-generation religious enthusiasts who had themselves witnessed little or nothing of the activities of their founder. Pious imagination, not cynical deception, was the determinative factor.

But so what? Wasn't the whole enterprise debunked either way? Orthodox apologists thought so, and thus resisted Strauss' conclusion. Strauss himself, on the other hand, was sure that the gospel story of Jesus' incarnation, miracles, and resurrection did enshrine an important truth—the essential unity of humanity and God. This truth, and adjacent ones, were presented in the New Testament in pictorial form. The important thing for our purposes is that Strauss had indicated that myth, even if not *literally* true, may be true in an important sense nevertheless. It remained for others to describe more accurately the way in which myth serves to communicate truth. In the present century, the work of two scholars in particular stands out. E. R. Dodds and Rudolf Bultmann moved beyond Strauss, rejecting the "intellectualist bias" present in his view of myth.

Anthropologists James Frazer and Edward Tylor in their theories of the origins of religion from magic and animism, respectively, had imagined primitive man as a kind of early theorist, positing explanations (magic, etc.) for natural phenomena. Even so, Strauss envisioned the early Christians as setting forth philosophical abstractions in mythical terms. Dodds and Bultmann realized instead that myth was an unconscious representation (via externalizing projection) of one's conception of his manner of existence in the world. In his famous essay "New Testament and Mythology," Bultmann argued at length that

> The real purpose of myth is not to present an objective picture of the world as it is, but to express man's understanding of himself in the world in which he lives. Myth should be interpreted not cosmologically, but anthropologically, or better still, existentially. Myth speaks of the power or the powers which man supposes he experiences as the ground and limit of his world and of his own activity and suffering.

He goes on to describe how the New Testament sees the existence of man as dominated by evil "powers" (demons and evil angels) whose power he can never hope to resist by himself. E. R. Dodds in his *Pagan and Christian in an Age of Anxiety* shows this pessimistic perspective to have been endemic in the Mediterranean world at this time. This perception might have been expressed in terms of disparate religious mythologies or philosophical world-views, but the underlying sense of guilt, anxiety, and frustration was pretty much the same.

> "The whole world lieth in [the grasp of] the Evil One," says the author of the First Epistle of John; it is "the dominion of fear and terror, the place of distress, with desolation," according to a psalm from Qumran; it is "the totality of wickedness," according to a pagan Hermeticist; for the Gnostic Heracleon it is a desert peopled only by wild beasts; in the Valentinian *Gospel of Truth* it is a realm of nightmare in which "either one flees one knows not where, or else one remains inert in pursuit of one knows not whom."

The key to all these dreary cosmological visions is that "they are very largely an hypostatisation, a dreamlike projection, of their authors' inner experience."

Basically, people found themselves, in their everyday existence, to be at bay—confronted with a snapping pack of disasters including "barbarian invasions, bloody civil wars, recurrent epidemics, galloping inflation and extreme personal insecurity." Where could they turn for relief? If their subconscious had projected their fears in the form of demonic "powers," it also provided redemptive hope, assuming the form of various salvation schemes. The hope of astrology, oracles, and dream interpretation was that even if one could not divert the blows of Fate, at least one might roll with the punches if he were forewarned. The "mystery cults" of Serapis, Isis, Mithras, and others promised actual deliverance from the power of Fate. Gnosticism supplied its adherents with the secret knowledge to slip past the evil *archons* keeping mankind prisoner in this dark vale of tears. And of course Christ was depicted as "having disarmed the powers and authorities . . . , triumphing over them by the cross" (Colossians 2:15).

For moderns, the proper response to this mythology is not to reject or subtract it, but rather to "demythologize," i.e. *interpret* it. For, though the myths may be factually untenable, the self-understanding, the view of existence in the world, may still merit our attention. The "demonic powers" may find their counterparts in today's ideologies, slogans, "isms," conven-

tions, propaganda, public opinion, inherited prejudices, orthodoxies, etc. They still hold man prisoner.

So the imaginative pictorial projection of existential self-understanding we find in ancient mythos can still be powerful and effective, even when we no longer believe the myths literally.

Now how does any of this bear on Lovecraft's Cthulhu Mythos? The dilemma with which this article began, it should now be clear, is closely analogous to that which led to the demythologizing of the New Testament. In each case the deadlock was created by the assumption that the myths (of Christ or Cthulhu) must be either dismissed as mere fiction (Christ as a fraud, Lovecraft as a mere storyteller) or taken literally (Christ as a real miracle-worker, Lovecraft as a real occultist). In fact Lovecraft can be seen as a modern myth-maker, expressing in fictional terms his pessimistic, materialistic world-view. Lovecraft's work can be elucidated in two interesting ways in light of Bultmann's demythologizing program, first by way of analogy, and second by way of contrast.

What might at first seem to be a stark difference between the two men is actually a fascinating similarity. This concerns the manner in which the Christian and Lovecraftian mythologies originated. Bultmann follows Strauss in rejecting the notion that early Christian miracle-stories and supernatural myths were anyone's conscious inventions. But Lovecraft, obviously, artificially created his myths. In view of such a difference, can Bultmann's conceptuality be appropriately used to understand Lovecraft? Yes indeed; remember that for Bultmann the most important thing about myth is what it tells us about the myth-maker's (or the myth-believers') existential self-understanding. And in an era when myths may be accepted only as they are "deliteralized," the only way to create new myths is to create them "artificially," or as already demythologized; they will be wittingly non-literal, but true on a deeper level—true to the myth-maker's experience. And this is what Lovecraft (along with some other recent fantasy writers) has done. Lovecraft is a genuine, though "artificial," maker of myth.

The important point of contrast to Bultmann's conception of myth is that Lovecraft's schema is entirely pessimistic with no redemptive element. A great step forward in understanding the Cthulhu Mythos was the removal of the accretions of August Derleth. Derleth had misread Lovecraft and made the Mythos into a cosmic epic of good vs. evil, of fall and redemption. Lovecraft, by contrast, had depicted a bleak scenario wherein man is in danger of being crushed by cosmic forces whose existence he does not comprehend, and which in turn are indifferent to his welfare. Clearly, Lovecraft's "Great Old Ones" are mythological figures corresponding to the "powers" and "archons" of the Age of Anxiety in Mediterranean religion. Like them, the Old Ones represent blind social and natural forces that toss us about like flotsam and jetsam. But the Cthulhu Mythos leaves mankind at the mercy of the powers. There is no one to save us. Lovecraft would have regarded Derleth's benevolent "Elder Gods" as an instance of childish wish-fulfillment, as he did the Christian story of salvation. Thus Lovecraft's mythology, though a real mythology expressive of his existential self-understanding, disregards Bultmann's stipulation that "myth expresses man's belief that . . . he can be delivered from the forces within the visible world."

In this Lovecraft's mythos would seem to be unique not only in terms of religious myth, but also in the field of fantasy literature. Not only is it to be contrasted with the work of other

writers like Robert E. Howard, who do seem to use mythological elements (Crom, Mitra, the Hyborian Age, etc.) simply as exotic stage-setting, but also with others like J.R.R.
Tolkien who also craft modern myths. Tolkien's heroic fantasy
mythologizes his existential self-understanding whereby the
threatening forces of evil (Sauron, Saruman, Smaug) are finally
vanquishable by the heroic efforts of the mundane "common
man" (Bilbo, Frodo, Sam Gamgee). For the Catholic Tolkien,
the aid of a martyred-and-risen savior (Gandalf) may be necessary, but at the end of the day, the portly little bourgeois
can triumph. Tolkien's myth is one of optimism, of "euca-
tastrophe," but Lovecraft's is one of inevitable, and pointless,
catastrophe.

Finally, the fatalistic and absurdist thrust of the Cthulhu Mythos
makes evident the fallacy of occasional claims that Lovecraft
actually believed in his myths, whether he acknowledged it or
tried unsuccessfully to repress this belief, as Kenneth Grant,
Robert Turner, Colin Wilson, and Ron Goulart have suggested.
(Here one thinks of a cute piece of self-parody by Lovecraft:
"God! I wonder if there *isn't* some truth in some of this? What
is this my emotions are telling me about Cthulhu? Ya-R'lyeh!
Ya-R'lyeh—Cthulhu fhgthagn . . . n'ggah . . . ggll . . . Iä! Iä!"
[letter to Frank Belknap Long, November 22, 1930 . . .].)
Grant and Turner suggest that Lovecraft had unwittingly tapped
in on cosmic reality, though he made the mistake of dismissing
it as fiction, as if to deny what he knew, deep down, to be the
terrible truth. Significantly, Lovecraft almost seems to have
foreseen that someone would say this: "Who can disprove
any . . . concoction [of the imagination], or say that it is not
'esoterically true' even if its creator did think he invented it
in jest or fiction?" . . .). So if anyone wants to maintain that
the Cthulhu Mythos is literal truth, there would seem to be no
stopping him. But surely this theory runs aground on the fact
that the "truth" actually expressed in Lovecraft's fiction (i.e.,
pessimistic materialism) would seem to be much more terrible
than that envisioned by occultists like Grant and Turner! Belief
in occultism implies an optimistic attempt to escape the kind
of absurdist determinism espoused by Lovecraft. It implies that
"supernature," like nature, is predictable and manipulable by
anyone who knows the proper technique. As Bultmann notes,
"Even occultism pretends to be a science." Who is the escapist
here—the fatalist Lovecraft, or the occultists who would co-
opt his popularity in the name of their superstition?

In conclusion it is plain that both those who see Lovecraft's
mythology as only a dramatic prop, and those who take the
Mythos literally (or believe Lovecraft did), are alike wide of
the mark. Modern New Testament scholarship has transcended
a similar set of unrealistic assessments of the gospels (as either
literal truth or mere hoaxes) by means of demythologizing.
Applying this hermeneutical key to the Cthulhu Mythos, Lovecraft's work can be seen to represent *real though artificial*
mythology. Thus it is to be taken *seriously* as an expression
of Lovecraft's existential self-understanding, but not *literally*
as an expression of occult belief. And as a *pessimistic* myth,
Lovecraft's fantasy is seen to be not only unique among religious mythology and fantasy literature, but also completely
alien to the world-view of literalistic occultists who would
initiate him posthumously into their number.

It remains for us to ask whether Lovecraft himself had anything
like demythologizing in mind. As it happens, he did. In fact
the concept enables us to recognize and understand an important
development in his writing that can be pinpointed in the year
1929. In short, Lovecraft began at this point to demythologize

his own mythos and to hit the reader directly between the eyes
with his bleak vision of cosmic isolation. Lovecraft's narrators
begin to "spill the beans," explicitly admitting that the sham-
bling monsters of the *Necronomicon* are primitive myths, inadequate allegories for the real horrors of science and its di-
sorienting revelations.

The first intimation of the new approach is found in **"The
Mound"** (1929). Here the gods Tulu (=Cthulhu) and Yig are
demythologized in terms reminiscent of Bultmann. "Religion
was a leading interest in Tsath, though very few actually believed in the supernatural. . . ." "Great Tulu [was] a spirit of
universal harmony anciently symbolized as the octopus-headed
god who had brought all men down from the stars. . . ." On
the other hand, "Yig [was] the principle of life symbolized as
the Father of all Serpents. . . ." Here the truths masked under
the names of the Great Old Ones are not so horrifying, but
Tulu and Yig are said to be myths symbolizing abstract truths.

In **"The Whisperer in Darkness"** (1930), we hear of the "monstrous nuclear chaos beyond angled space which the *Necronomicon* had mercifully cloaked under the name of Azathoth." Thus the gibbering daemon-sultan of the *Necronomicon*
was merely a cipher for the much more frightening revelations
of science. In this case it is the advanced science of the Outer
Ones, the living fungi from Yuggoth. Extra-terrestrials occupy
center stage again in *At the Mountains of Madness,* written the
very next year (1931). The crinoids of ancient Antarctica "were
above all doubt the originals of the fiendish elder myths which
things like the Pnakotic Manuscripts and the *Necronomicon*
affrightedly hint about. They were the great 'Old Ones' that
had filtered down from the stars when earth was young." Thus
the occult and transcendent Great Old Ones of **"The Call of
Cthulhu"** and **"The Dunwich Horror"** were simply a race of
space aliens. The import of this fact is still supposed to be
horrifying, since these creatures had created humanity "as a
jest or mistake" dim ages ago. Man's cosmic insignificance
is once again underscored.

"The Dreams in the Witch House" (1932) was clearly written
with the new demythologized outlook in mind. Over-zealous
student Walter Gilman penetrates the legends of medieval sorcery and witchcraft to discover that they really cloaked a knowledge of advanced mathematics and physics. The Arkham witch
Keziah Mason had mastered interdimensional travel. Gilman
follows in her footsteps, reaching an alien plane inhabited by
beings identical to the Old Ones of *At the Mountains of Madness*
except for their winglessness. Some readers might feel inclined
to dispute our interpretation of this tale on the grounds that
nowhere else in Lovecraft do we find so much of traditional
magic and the supernatural. For instance, Keziah Mason is
obviously supposed to have been a casualty of the Salem witch
trials. She has a rodent-like familiar (Brown Jenkin) and com-
ports with the satanic "Black Man." She even shuns a crucifix!
Yet the narration is clear that the real secret of all this is
Keziah's precocious discovery of non-Euclidean calculus. The
accoutrements of witchcraft are there simply to say that witchcraft's horror was real after all, but with the reality of science.

The same year (1932) Lovecraft collaborated with E. Hoffmann
Price on **"Through the Gates of the Silver Key."** In it Randolph
Carter explores transcendental states of mystical consciousness. Carter refers derisively to the superstitious depiction of
such experiences in ancient legend, including the *Necronomicon*. Encountering the transfigured bodhisattvas who have made
the inner journey before him, "He wondered at the vast conceit
of those who had babbled of the *malignant* Ancient Ones, as

if They could pause from their everlasting dreams to wreak a wrath on mankind." Going on to experience the disorientation of the void of "destroyed individuality," he guesses that this "All-in-One and One-in-All" state "was perhaps that which certain secret cults of earth had whispered of as Yog-Sothoth, and which has been a deity under other names . . . yet in a flash the Carter-facet realised how slight and fractional all these conceptions are." Pity poor Henry Armitage who actually believed in a literal Yog-Sothoth.

Finally, in 1934, Lovecraft demythologized the mythos of the Old Ones again in **"The Shadow out of Time."** There we discover that certain old myths dimly reflected the truth about the Great Race of Yith, another band of extraterrestrials. "In the *Necronomicon* the presence of . . . a cult among human beings was suggested—a cult that sometimes gave aid to minds voyaging down the aeons from the days of the Great Race." The context implies that this is not quite what the writer of the *Necronomicon* actually thought was going on. Rather, it is implied, Abdul Alhazred entertained some primitive notion such as that the Old Ones might beget their progeny upon mankind. Again, the dreadful truth is a scientific, not a magical, one. In the same story, it is the discovery of the incredibly ancient Australian ruins, with their implication of intelligent pre-human life, that terrifies the archaeologist Mackenzie: "These blocks are so ancient they frighten me." (pp. 3-9, 24)

> *Robert M. Price, "Demythologizing Cthulhu," in* Lovecraft Studies, *Vol. III, No. 1, Spring, 1984, pp. 3-9, 24.*

STEVEN J. MARICONDA (essay date 1986)

[In the following excerpt, Mariconda explains how Lovecraft's fiction and philosophical thought reflect a reconciliation between his nihilistic view of human existence and the illusions and values necessary for psychological survival.]

The seemingly antithetical elements of cosmic outsideness and New England local color in H. P. Lovecraft's fiction may be traced, paradoxically enough, to the same source: his philosophy of cosmic indifferentism. The universe was to him a purposeless mechanism, one which mankind, with its limited sensory apparatus, can never fully comprehend. The cosmic horror of Lovecraft's fiction—the horror of unknowable forces or beings which sweep men aside as indifferently as men do ants—stems from this philosophy. Though Lovecraft evidently found intellectual and imaginative satisfaction in this bleak position, one inevitably wonders how he sustained himself emotionally. In fact, it was the same sceptical analysis behind Lovecraft's metaphysics which led him to the concept of relative values and to his one great source of emotional fulfillment: his "background," the rich heritage of New England tradition and culture which we find so often used as the setting for his tales of cosmic intrusion. The concept of background is a central one in Lovecraft's life and work, and our understanding of both may be increased by examining it.

As is true with most delvings into Lovecraft's thought, we should begin with his metaphysics. The seeds of the latter seem to have been, in a sense, innate—he was a born analyst, by nature inclined to approach the world on an intellectual level. Taking an early interest in the sciences, he was dabbling in chemistry at age eight, and he equally early applied the same sort of rigorous analysis to religion. At five years Lovecraft was asking if God was a myth in the manner of Santa Claus; soon after he was questioning his Sunday School teachers so

vehemently that they were undoubtedly glad to see him go when his mother allowed him to discontinue attendance at age twelve. By seventeen, following on the heels of profound study of astronomy and other natural sciences, he had adopted the essentials of his philosophical orientation, following Democritus, Epicurus, and Lucretius; that of a mechanistic materialist who saw the cosmos as "a meaningless affair of endless cycles of alternate electronic condensation & dispersal—a thing without beginning, permanent direction, or ending, & consisting wholly of blind force operating according to fixed & eternal patterns inherent in entity." Such an outlook eliminated the possibility of deity and afterlife, but the positivist Lovecraft found he could come to no other conclusion: science provided no evidence to support such beliefs, instead explaining their origins with anthropological and psychological theories.

Lovecraft's philosophy thus left him adrift in a universe that cared neither for him nor anything else, an emotionally unpleasant situation at best. Joseph Wood Krutch, in *The Modern Temper* (1929)—a volume Lovecraft thought of highly—expressed the problem this way:

> The world of modern science is one in which the intellect alone can rejoice. The mind leaps, and leaps perhaps with a sort of elation, through the immensities of space, but the spirit, frightened and cowed, longs to have once more above its head the inverted bowl beyond which may lie whatever paradise its desires may create. . . . Thus man seems caught in a dilemma which his intellect has devised.

The Providence dreamer's mind certainly did leap with elation through space, but nonetheless realized that his emotional stability would have to be found elsewhere.

The same sense of rationality or objectivity which caused Lovecraft's emotional dilemma, however, also provided its solution. Though human concerns were of no importance to the universe at large, this need not mean that they were of no value to the individual psyche:

> I have the cynic's and the analyst's inability to recognise the difference in *value* between the two types of consciousness-impacts, *real* and *unreal* . . . [and] to retain the illusion that their actual vast physical difference gives them any difference *in value* as psychological agents impinging on man's consciousness. My one standard of value is imaginative suggesting-power or symbolising-quality.

Thus we have Lovecraft's pragmatic adoption of relative values: "What gives us relative painlessness and contentment we may arbitrarily call 'good' & vice versa." The necessity of such an adoption amidst the bleak cosmos of modern science was also evident to Krutch:

> The most ardent lover of truth, the most resolute determination to follow nature no matter to what black abyss she may lead, need not blind one to the fact that many of the lost illusions had, to speak the language of science, a survival value.

Lovecraft's notion that "*the satisfaction of our own emotions is the one solid thing which we can ever get out of life*" need not lead us to believe that he was a hedonist or amoralist, for the notion was moderated by his Apollonian insistence that such satisfaction might take place only by the "intelligent manipulation" of the "raw material" of emotion. Lovecraft, then, drew upon those emotions which gave him pleasure but *did not* conflict with his intellectual perception, while rationally minimizing the effects of their unpleasant counterparts.

But where did Lovecraft, who found human beings no more or less interesting than any other phenomenon, find his emotional sustenance? The answer, documented explicitly in innumerable letters and implicitly in the bulk of his fiction, poetry, and essays, is his "background," a term he used to describe his cultural heritage in its very broadest dimension.

> No one thinks or feels or appreciates or lives a mental-emotional-imaginative life at all, except in terms of the artificial reference-points supply'd him by the enveloping body of race tradition and heritage into which he is born. We form an emotionally realisable picture of the external world, and an emotionally endurable set of illusions as to value and direction in existence, solely and exclusively through the arbitrary concepts and folkways bequeathed to us through our traditional culture-stream.

Lovecraft saw his background not merely as simple traditions passed down from father to son. Aside from components normally associated with tradition such as social customs, attitudes, and institutions, he described background as including "material from my immediate blood-ancestry and personal milieu—habit-patterns, spontaneous likes & dislikes, standards & phenomena—gland functionings & nerve patterns." This last implies something beyond the mere influences of Lovecraft's upbringing: the action of the environmental factors upon his heredity. He felt that his ancestors' agrestic lifestyles had, to some extent, affected his psychological makeup. "My instincts," he wrote, "were formed by the functioning of a certain line of germ-plasm through a certain set of geographical & social environing conditions . . . & so I continue to react spontaneously & unconsciously in the manner of my forefathers, liking the same superficial forms & types & attitudes they liked, except when such things conflict with the fundamental laws of truth & beauty."

As far as specifics go, Lovecraft saw his background as consisting of layers of different intensity, most distantly his Aryan heritage, followed in increasing strength by his Western-European heritage, his Teuton-Celtic heritage, his Anglo-Saxon heritage, and his Anglo-American heritage. As is well known, Lovecraft especially revered the life of the eighteenth century of old and New England. (pp. 3-6)

Defending his emotional kinship with the period in later life, he explained its lure in more impersonal terms:

> What the eighteenth century really was, was the *final* phase of that perfectly unmechanised aera which as a whole gave us our most satisfying life. . . . Its hold upon moderns is due mainly to its *proximity* . . . it is the *nearest* to us of all the purely pre-mechanical periods; the only one with which we have any semblance of *personal* contact (surviving houses and household effects in large quantities; association [for Americans] with high historic tension; fact that we can still talk with old men who in their youth talked with living survivors; vestigial customs and speech-forms in greater num-

ber than from earlier periods, etc., etc.) and whose ways are in any manner familiar to us save through sheer archaeological reconstruction.

This proximity Lovecraft felt most potently in youth, both in the houses, churches, and brick sidewalks of Providence, and the conservative mores of his family. It served to create in him a strong sense of background which would last throughout his life.

Aside from the purely old New England ways of life, there was also a strong agrestic or pastoral component in Lovecraft's upbringing. . . . Providence was at the turn of the century a city of only 175,000; and Lovecraft's house was not far from the wooded countryside, where he loved to wander. In his neighborhood were several small farmsteads which strongly affected him emotionally, and he later boasted that he "knew the old New England country as well as if I had been a farmer's boy." More astonishing is the little-known fact that Whipple Phillips himself pastured a milk cow and planted potatoes and corn on the property of 454 Angell Street. Lovecraft avidly read all the old Farmer's Almanacs he could find around the house—he continued to be a collector throughout his lifetime—and became devoted to the pastorals of Thomson and Bloomfield, of Virgil and Hesiod.

Lovecraft valued his background highly, and the concept figures greatly in his thought. His racialist stance, for example, was partly based in his wish to keep his culture-stream—his one last emotional anchor—safe from erosion by an influx of foreign tradition. More importantly for our purposes, background played an important part in Lovecraft's thoughts on the nature of art:

> My theory of aesthetics is a compound one. To me beauty as we know it, consists of two elements; one absolute and objective, and based on rhythm and symmetry; and one relative and subjective, based on traditional associations with the hereditary culture-stream of the beholder. The second element is probably strongest with me, since my notions of enjoyment are invariably bound up with strange recallings of the past.

This passage has important repercussions in both Lovecraft's fiction and poetry. There is, in his finest work, an adherence to the traditional values of simplicity, proportion, and restraint; in these qualities we may trace the influence of the ancient classics filtered through the art of the Georgian age. But more explicitly, the substance of Lovecraft's art is often concerned with "recallings of the past."

Lovecraft's poetry is an obvious example. His work in this area has often been condemned as soulless imitation of Augustan verse. This is true to a point, as Lovecraft himself realized:

> I wrote only as a means of re-creating around me the atmosphere of my beloved 18th century favourites . . . everything succumbed to my one intense purpose of thinking & dreaming myself back into that world of periwigs & long s's which for some odd reason seemed to me the normal world.

Lovecraft here admits that he wrote much of his early poetry merely as an exercise in recapturing the ethos of his background. This is true in both its form (primarily rhymed couplets in the manner of Pope) and, often, in its subject matter; examples include **"On a New England Village Seen by Moonlight"** (1913), **"An American to Mother England"** (1916), and **"Old Christmas"** (1917). The last, a seemingly interminable 324-line paean to the traditions of his ancestors, begins:

> Would that some Druid, wise in mystic lore,
> Might waft me backward to the scenes of yore;
> Midst happier years my wandring soul detain,
> and let me dwell in ANNA's virtuous reign:
> Warm in the honest glow of pure content,
> And share the boons of rustic merriment.
> Awake, Pierian Muse! and call to view
> The snow-clad groves and plains my grandsires
>   knew. . . .

Happily, Lovecraft largely shed his affected approach to poetry in the mid-1920s. It is ironic that when he eventually composed a verse on his concept of **"Background,"** in the *Fungi from Yuggoth* (1929-30), he did so not in his beloved Augustan couplets but in a simple and understated sonnet form.

The background concept can help us explicate another of the *Fungi*, **"Continuity."** Lovecraft writes that certain objects hint "of locked dimensions harbouring years gone by" concluding:

> It moves me most when slanting sunbeams glow
> On old farm buildings set against a hill,
> And paint with life the shapes which linger still
> From centuries less a dream than this we know.
> In that strange light I feel I am not far
> From the fixt mass whose sides the ages are. . . .

Lovecraft at such times felt an almost mystical sense of *identity* with his native and hereditary tradition. One such instance was his first sight, from high ground, of the colonial seaport Marblehead, Massachusetts, in 1922:

> In a flash all the past of New England—all the
> past of old England—all the past of Anglo-
> Saxondom and the Western World—swept over
> me and identified with me the stupendous to-
> tality of all things in such a way as it never did
> before and never will again.

Note the emphasis on the sense of unity, the feeling that one may "merge oneself with the whole historic stream and be wholly emancipated from the transient & the ephemeral." This *acute realization* of background, typically incited by regional scenic vistas, is what Lovecraft labelled "continuity."

Turning to Lovecraft's fiction, we may better understand his use of realistic local color when we recall his emphasis on the importance of background in aesthetics. An author, he felt, "does best in founding his elements of incident & colour on a life & background to which he has a real & deep-seated relation." As he viewed it, the creative process is more natural—and the result more powerful—when an author uses the raw materials he knows best: the social customs, attitudes, institutions, geographical points of view, and other components of his background. The subjective or associative component is also vital to the work from the reader's perspective—the latter may relate more poignantly to the events of a tale when realistic detail is used, for such details will be instantly recognizable and set off a chain of personal associations in his mind.

The New England background figures in many of Lovecraft's stories to some extent. In a few (such as **"From Beyond"** . . .),

it has little or no role in the tale. For the most part, though, the local color of the region plays a pivotal part in the proceedings. The first tale to exploit the approach was **"The Picture in the House"** . . . , whose first paragraph suggests that in certain isolated dwellings common in desolate areas of the region, "strength, solitude, grotesqueness, and ignorance combine to form the perfection of the hideous." The narrator of the tale is forced by a storm to seek shelter in such a dwelling—despite his bias, acquired from "legends" he has heard, against such places. He finds that the interior, with its relics of Revolutionary days, would but for its condition be "a collector's paradise." The occupant soon descends from the floor above; with his ragged clothing and "weak voice full of fawning respect" which speaks "an extreme form of Yankee dialect," he at first seems merely a New England eccentric. We soon discover, though, that he is nothing less than a cannibal who is several hundreds of years old.

In this tale we see Lovecraft using elements of his background in the local color of the story. In later works he would make yet more extensive use of the history, folklore, speech, dress, mannerisms, beliefs, and topography of New England and its people. Tales such as **"The Shunned House"** . . . and *The Case of Charles Dexter Ward* . . . are inextricably intertwined with regional history. The latter is mixed so deftly with the events of these tales that scholarship has not yet been fully able to decide exactly what is fact and what fiction. (pp. 7-10)

[**"The Colour out of Space," "The Dunwich Horror," "The Whisperer in Darkness," "The Shadow over Innsmouth," "The Haunter of the Dark,"**] . . . and others also make pivotal use of New England locales. They describe, with an insight only a native can possess, the loneliness and grandeur of the primal countryside, as well as villages spanning from the "ridiculously old" Dunwich to contemporary Providence.

Special note should be made of Lovecraft's use of regional characters. It has often been said that Lovecraft was unable to draw convincing characters, but this is belied by many of his rural portraits. The farmer Nahum Gardner in **"The Colour out of Space"** is one among many vivid Lovecraftian figures. (pp. 10-11)

How can we reconcile the seemingly disparate elements of cosmic horror and background in Lovecraft's fiction? The answer may be found in his explanation of the difference between his brand of cosmicism and that of his fellow fantaisistes Clark Ashton Smith and Donald Wandrei. The latter two authors often began and wholly conducted their tales in other dimensions or the far reaches of space; but Lovecraft felt his cosmic voyagings were most affecting when shown relative to the small realm of mankind, and to New England in particular. Again he refers to background as the basis of his excursions, this time not merely emotional but also imaginative:

> I recognise the impossibility of any correlation
> of the individual and the universal without the
> immediate visible world as a background—or
> starting-place for a system of outward-extending
> points of reference. I cannot think of any in-
> dividual as existing except as part of a pattern—
> and the pattern's most visible and tangible areas
> are of course the individual's immediate en-
> vironment; the soil and culture-stream from
> which he springs, and the milieu of ideas,
> impressions, traditions, landscapes, and archi-

tecture through which he must necessarily peer in order to reach the "outside" ... I begin with the individual and think outward—appreciating the sensation of spatial and temporal liberation only when I can scale it against the known terrestrial scene. . . . With me, the very quality of being cosmically sensitive breeds an exaggerated attachment to the familiar and immediate—Old Providence, the woods and hills, the ancient ways and thoughts of New England.

The cosmic vistas of Lovecraft's tales, then, are made even more meaningful when juxtaposed with the solid, familiar scenes and traditions of his regional background. The terrible alienness of Lovecraft's outside beings and realms is emphasized by their antipodal difference from the narratives' settings. (pp. 11-12)

> *Steven J. Mariconda, "Lovecraft's Concept of 'Background'," in* Lovecraft Studies, *Vol. V, No. 1, Spring, 1986, pp. 3-12.*

ADDITIONAL BIBLIOGRAPHY

Carter, Lin. *Lovecraft: A Look behind the "Cthulhu Mythos."* New York: Ballantine Books, 1972, 198 p.
Offers a thorough background on the nature and evolution of the Mythos stories.

Carter, Paul A. *The Creation of Tomorrow: Fifty Years of Magazine Science Fiction*, p. 7 ff. New York: Columbia University Press, 1977.
Discusses Lovecraft's place in the early development of science fiction.

Conover, Willis, Jr. *Lovecraft at Last*. Arlington, Va.: Carrollton-Clark, 1975, 272 p.
Personal chronicle of Conover's correspondence with Lovecraft during the last months of Lovecraft's life.

Cook, W. Paul. *In Memoriam: Howard Phillips Lovecraft*. 1941. Reprint. West Warwick, R.I.: Necronomicon Press, 1977, 75 p.
Reminiscences of Lovecraft by a longtime friend and fellow amateur journalist.

Davis, Sonia H. *The Private Life of H. P. Lovecraft*. West Warwick, R.I.: Necronomicon Press, 1985, 25 p.
Reminiscences of Lovecraft by his wife.

De Camp, L. Sprague. *Lovecraft: A Biography*. Garden City, N.Y.: Doubleday & Co., 1975, 510 p.
Controversial biography that is informative and opinionated, designed to offer little extended criticism on the work though much information about the personal life of its subject.

Faig, Kenneth W., Jr. *H. P. Lovecraft: His Life, His Work*. West Warwick, R.I.: Necronomicon Press, 1979, 36 p.

Biographical sketch followed by a chronology of important dates in the life and literary career of Lovecraft and a chronology of selected fiction, nonfiction, and poetry.

Fresco: Howard Phillips Lovecraft Memorial Symposium 8, No. 3 (Spring 1958): 68 p.
Reminiscences, essays, and a bibliography by Samuel Loveman, Matthew Onderdonk, Thomas O. Mabbott, David Keller, and others.

Joshi, S. T. *H. P. Lovecraft and Lovecraft Criticism: An Annotated Bibliography*. Kent, Ohio: The Kent State University Press, 1981, 473 p.
Comprehensive primary and secondary bibliography, with an introductory essay on the development of Lovecraft's critical reputation.

――――. "Topical References in Lovecraft." *Extrapolation* 25, No. 3 (Fall 1984): 247-65.
Details references in Lovecraft's fiction to events and figures of his time.

――――, ed. *H. P. Lovecraft: Four Decades of Criticism*. Athens, Ohio: Ohio University Press, 1980, 250 p.
Collection of seminal essays on Lovecraft, including studies by Barton Levi St. Armand, J. Vernon Shea, and Dirk W. Mosig, with a survey of Lovecraft criticism by the editor.

――――, and Blackmore, L. D. *H. P. Lovecraft and Lovecraft Criticism: An Annotated Bibliography*. West Warwick, R.I.: Necronomicon Press, 1985, 72 p.
Supplement to Joshi's 1981 bibliography, documenting primary and secondary publications from 1980 to 1984.

Ketterer, David. "Somebody Up There." In his *New Worlds for Old: The Apocalyptic Imagination, Science Fiction, and American Literature*, pp. 261-66. Bloomington: Indiana University Press, 1974.
Discusses elements in Lovecraft's stories that link them to science fiction.

Miller, Rob Hillis. "On Humour in Lovecraft." *Riverside Quarterly* 7, No. 1 (March 1980): 50-2.
Provides examples from "Herbert West—Reanimator," "Pickman's Model," and "The Strange High House in the Mist" to illustrate Lovecraft's use of humor in his fiction.

Pattee, Fred Lewis. Review of *Supernatural Horror in Literature*, by H. P. Lovecraft. *American Literature* 18, No. 2 (May 1946): 175-77.
Descriptive summary of Lovecraft's survey of horror literature, which Pattee calls a "brilliant piece of criticism."

Schweitzer, Darrell, ed. *Essays Lovecraftian*. Baltimore: T-K Graphics, 1976, 114 p.
Collection of reprinted essays, including pieces by Fritz Lieber, Richard Tierney, Dirk Mosig, and Arthur Jean Cox.

Wilson, Colin. "H. P. Lovecraft." In *Science Fiction Writers: Critical Studies from the Early Nineteenth Century to the Present Day*, edited by E. F. Bleiler, pp. 131-37. New York: Charles Scribner's Sons, 1982.
Frequently disparaging survey of Lovecraft's fiction.

Thomas (Mokopu) Mofolo

1876-1948

(Also Mopoku) Lesothan novelist.

Mofolo is considered the first great author of modern African literature. Written in the Sesotho language, his three novels are concerned with the radical effect of Christian teachings on traditional African society. *Chaka*, Mofolo's most highly regarded work, is often interpreted as a depiction of the negative moral consequences of paganism unchecked by Christian ethics; however, a respect for traditional African customs and beliefs pervades the work, especially in the heroic portrayal of the Zulu king Chaka. This respect, in part, caused missionary publishers to suppress Mofolo's manuscript until thirteen years after its completion. Today the novel is considered an epic tragedy of literary and historical significance and has served as the model for numerous subsequent works about Chaka, one of the most celebrated legendary figures in African literature.

Mofolo was born in Kojane, Basutoland (now Lesotho), a small country surrounded by the Republic of South Africa. The third son of Christian parents, he was educated at local religious schools and then sent to Morija to work as a houseboy for the Reverend Alfred Casalis, who headed the Bible School, printing press, and Book Depot there. In 1894 Casalis enrolled Mofolo in the Bible School, and two years later Mofolo entered the Teacher Training College, earning a teaching certificate in 1899. He then began work as an interpreter at the printing press, but the operation was suspended during the South African War (also known as the Boer War or Anglo-Boer War) which began in October, 1899 and continued until 1902. Mofolo studied carpentry for two years and taught at various schools until 1904, when he returned to Morija as secretary to Casalis and proofreader for the press.

Exposed to a variety of books at the Morija Book Depot, Mofolo read religious works, African and European histories, and novels by such writers as H. Rider Haggard and Marie Corelli. Several missionaries encouraged him to write works of his own, and his Christian allegory *Moeti oa bochabela* (*The Traveller to the East*), published in 1907, became the first novel written in Sesotho. His next novel, *Pitseng*, the story of two exemplary youths inspired by an African Christian teacher, was published in 1910. During this period Mofolo also began research for a novel based on the life of the Zulu warrior-king Chaka. Traveling to Pietermaritzburg, the former Zulu capital Mgungundluvu, Mofolo visited Chaka's gravesite and collected historical data, recollections, and legends which had persisted in oral literature. The manuscript of *Chaka* was submitted to the Morija printers around 1912. Despite acknowledgment of the novel's extraordinary qualities, the missionaries were deeply divided over whether to publish the work, with those who opposed it citing their fear that the novel's depiction of traditional Africa would entice the indigenous reader to return to a non-Christian way of life. After a campaign by supporters and the excision of some material, *Chaka* was published in 1925. Mofolo, however, had left the Morija press after the novel was rejected. Disillusioned and feeling betrayed, he gave up writing.

He afterward held various jobs, including recruiter and labor agent for diamond mines, sugar plantations, and large farms, manager of a postal route, and trade store proprietor. In 1933 Mofolo returned to his home district, where he purchased a large farm from a white landowner; however, the farm was confiscated by the government under provisions of the Land Act of 1914 because one end of the property touched that of another African landowner. Mofolo spent several years and much money in an unsuccessful court fight to regain his land. In 1940, impoverished and ill, he retired to live on a pension until his death in 1948.

Mofolo's *Chaka* has been called by many critics a masterpiece of world literature. Regarded by contemporary reviewers as an "Africanized" Christian tract, the novel has more recently been assessed as a sophisticated fusion of Christian philosophy, African praise-poetry and myth, and elements from Western literatures. Although it is a fictionalized historical biography, *Chaka* retains much that is factual. The story depicts the rise and decline of the early nineteenth-century Zulu monarch Chaka, who systematically conquered Natal and by 1824 ruled over 50,000 subjects. The illegitimate son of chief Senzangakona and Nandi, a woman from a neighboring tribe, Chaka is ostracized by his father, maligned and physically brutalized by his peers, and, in retaliation, resolves to lead a life of vengeful aggression. He becomes an innovative chief and then a warrior-king whose egoism and bloodlust give rise to a reign of terror that ends when he is murdered by his half brothers.

There are many Christian readings of *Chaka* as an illustration of the battle between good and evil. In such interpretations, Chaka's death at the hands of his brothers is considered a just punishment for his sinful paganism. Many critics, however, note that much of the so-called Christian morality in the novel is in fact based on African traditions in which nature, the tribal community, and the gods are indivisible. Chaka's illegitimacy, for example, is fateful according to this tradition, because it opposes tribal law, a law established before the introduction of Christianity to Africa. Similarly, Chaka ensures his destruction when he murders his mother, which breaks the ultimate taboo against shedding the blood of kin. Ben Obumselu contends that a critical reading of the work as Christian morality cannot sufficiently account for the novel's complexity, which is most apparent in the portrayal of Chaka's psychological development. While this careful attention to the events of Chaka's early childhood and his reaction to them does not excuse his behavior, it does provide an explanation for his actions which goes beyond that of a simplistic pagan symbolism promoted by those who read the novel as a Christian allegory. Several critics have also commented on the sympathetic nature of Mofolo's eulogy for Chaka and the Mazulus at the end of the novel. Daniel P. Kunene, for instance, believes that the passage reveals Mofolo's conscious or unconscious loyalty to Sesotho culture and its traditions of heroism and virility. Albert S. Gérard similarly considers the eulogy a passage wherein Mofolo sets aside religion to reflect on the Mazulu empire, pondering the "past greatness of his race and its present subjugation."

Mofolo employed several diverse stylistic elements in *Chaka*, including the rhythm and narrative devices of African praise poems, which were performed to honor Bantu monarchs; the didactic elements of African oral narratives, which traditionally served as vehicles for moral instruction; and Biblical terminology, which reflected his missionary schooling. Because the novel form is not intrinsically African, Mofolo also utilized some of the conventions of the Western novel. He combined these various stylistic forms throughout *Chaka,* shifting from one to another when appropriate for dramatic or thematic emphasis. Mofolo's use of witch doctors in the novel is an instance demonstrating the extent to which these various traditions are skillfully synthesized. Essential to the portrayal of Chaka's drive for power, the role of the witch doctor has been interpreted as: a literal commentary on good and bad witch doctors in the tribal community; a symbolic revelation of Chaka's personality traits and true desires reminiscent of the witches in *MacBeth;* and an allegorical rendering of a Mephistophelean devil with whom the Faustian Chaka makes a pact.

Mofolo's *Chaka* demonstrates the author's respect for Chaka and traditional African ways of life, unlike the negative depictions of these subjects by white historians. For this reason, Mofolo has profoundly influenced such African authors as Léopold Sédar Senghor, Abdou Anta Ka, and Djibril Tamsir Niane, whose works go even beyond his novel in celebrating Chaka's military and political genius. Translated into English, French, German, and several African languages, *Chaka* remains one of the great works of African literature.

PRINCIPAL WORKS

Moeti oa bochabela   (novel)   1907
   [*The Traveller to the East,* 1934]
Pitseng   (novel)   1910
*Chaka   (novel)   1925
   [*Chaka: An Historical Romance,* 1931]

*This novel was written between 1909 and 1912.

HENRY NEWBOLT   (essay date 1931)

[*Newbolt, one of the most popular English poets of the early twentieth century, is best known for his poems on naval and patriotic subjects. In the following excerpt from his introduction to* Chaka, *Newbolt discusses the novel's literary, historical, and cultural value.*]

Rome had her African colonies, and there were born in them writers who are still remembered. But there is a wide gulf between cultivated quasi-Romans such as Apuleius or Augustine, and the life of the primitive African world of the veld and forest. Mofolo takes us little more than a century back in time, but the society whose secrets he reveals to us [in *Chaka*] is literally and in the deepest sense a prehistoric, or even a timeless society. In it we may see our own origins and the magnified image of our own spiritual conflicts.

It is unfortunate that we cannot read his work in the language in which it was written. Translation is here more than usually thwarting, because the book is not a mere record of events, or a historian's analysis of motives, but a piece of imaginative literature. It has the persuasive charm, we are told, of a fine language finely written, and this naturally cannot be reproduced adequately in English. (p. x)

It is right I think to speak of Mofolo's book as an imaginative work, but there can be no doubt that in the author's own view it is a serious contribution to history. His first four pages are enough to prove this, and his intention is further shown by the fact that he has made more than one journey into Natal to ascertain dates and other details for his narrative. The result is certainly an interesting and convincing record, probably a valuable one. If it is put side by side with accounts of the same events in such books as Miss Gollock's *Lives of Eminent Africans,* Sir Godfrey Lagden's *The Basutos,* and the Rev. A. T. Bryant's *Olden Times in Zululand and Natal,* it will be found to differ from them very seldom on points of fact, while it shows, as might be expected, more intimate knowledge of native life and thought, and a more serious attitude towards the character and motives of the African peoples and their chiefs. In Mofolo's pages not only Chaka himself, but all the persons in the drama (except the witch-doctors) are treated as inheritors of human feelings and an ancient culture: they are shown in turn as kindly or cruel, faithful or faithless, single-minded or ambitious, but they are never judged from a political standpoint, and still less are they ever portrayed as beings of an inferior race, childish or ridiculous even in their most violent and criminal moments. From any such misrepresentation Mofolo is saved as well by his moral sense as by his artistic instinct. He is a soul by nature Christian, and sees in every crisis the clash of good and evil, of gentleness and militarism, of chivalry and brutality. For him Chaka's irresistible career is the perfect and unanswerable example of the ruin of human life by the rule of force, deliberately adopted and consistently followed. Dingiswayo is chosen to heighten the effect by contrast. He is not on the same scale as Chaka, and in battle he was probably no less whole-heartedly a fighting man; but his principal characteristic is skilfully brought out. In Chapter X, after the capture of his enemy Zwide, we are told that "Dingiswayo detained his prisoner a few days and then released him, and sent him to his home in peace, as if he had paid a friendly visit and was never a prisoner." In Chapter XXV we find Chaka on the last night of his life dreaming the last of his terrible dreams. Among them "he saw his chief Dingiswayo, and the noble acts he did when he tried to instil a spirit of humanity into the tribe: and he saw himself bringing to naught those high endeavors." By his conquest of the whole African world he had raised himself to almost superhuman rank: "he had become the originator of all that was evil."

But this is not the whole account of the matter: it is only the vision of the sinner, agonized by remorse. Mofolo looks more deeply into it: he looks behind the crimes to the source of them. Chaka's guilt is the working out of a Nemesis: as the son of Nandi and Senzangakona he was "a sin incarnate, damned from birth." The tragedy falls naturally into five Acts. In the first we see the trials and triumphs of the boy, hated and ill-used by his more legitimate half-brothers. In the second he flies from home, in danger of death, and on the open veld he meets the witch-doctor Isanusi, the tempter from nowhere, the visible symbol of his own hardening ambition. In the face of this mysterious stranger Chaka sees at one moment unbounded malice and cruelty, at the next compassion and the truest love. In a sweet voice which is not the voice of a deceiver he offers Chaka deliverance from his oppressors, and a chieftainship greater than that of his father. But the gaining of this will demands great sacrifices. Chaka accepts the bargain without hesitation.

In the third Act Chaka comes to the capital of Dingiswayo, falls in love with his new chief's sister Noliwe, and distinguishes himself in war. Isanusi's promises are all coming true: Senzangakona dies, and Chaka is appointed by Dingiswayo, as overlord, to succeed him. In the fourth Act Dingiswayo is murdered by Zwide, the enemy whom he had spared. Chaka steps into his place as overlord, and is tempted by Isanusi to aim at a still wider lordship, to make himself the supreme chief of the African world. The sacrifice for this must be the life of his betrothed, Noliwe. Again he accepts without hesitation, and kills the victim with his own hand, in a scene which could not be surpassed for tenderness and horror. Nor could any hand better the art with which Isanusi persuades him to this final and fatal decision.

The fifth and last Act traces with great power the change which now comes upon Chaka and his world. The tragedy is no longer concerned merely with the fated fall of an ambitious chieftain: it becomes the apocalyptic vision of a monstrous beast, consumed by an all-destroying blood-lust. To quench this unquenchable thirst Chaka's own child, his own mother, his own faithful warriors in thousands must all be sacrificed: and at last he cannot sleep till he has slaughtered with his own hand. His deliverance can only come by death: his own brothers drive their spears into his heart, and as he falls dying his evil genius Isanusi is suddenly present to demand his reward. He is gone again as suddenly; we hear no more of him. Being but a symbol, an attribute, the evil part of the man's nature, he inevitably passes away with him. (pp. xi-xiv)

I have drawn only the essential outlines of the drama, the mere bones of it: and this can give no idea of the richness and vitality of the whole work. It has many characters in it, and none of them are more curious than the two servants, Ndlebe and Malunga, whom Isanusi gave to Chaka for his attendants and guardians. They are gifted with sub-human faculties—animal cunning and acute animal senses—and they are clearly intended, like Isanusi himself, to symbolize faculties or instincts of Chaka's own nature. The whole business of the witch-doctor's profession is thus raised from the contempt which commonly attends it among our own writers, its real origin is hinted at, and its effects at least partly accounted for. At any rate it has become a fit subject for serious art. It is only upon these terms that magic can find an entrance into our Western scheme of thought. What we have hardly yet realized is that feelings or beliefs or practices which cannot claim any sanction from our religion, our science, or our philosophy may yet have a traceable origin and a psychological value: but not until they have been studied in their native environment. Some of our explorers have discovered this. . . . Isanusi in his striking appeal to Chaka . . . to act according to his true nature, tells him that there is another life, and that "all that a man does here the Sun when it sets takes with it to that great city of the living, the city of those who, *ye* say, have died and are dead: and his acts await him there." Yet this does not in Mofolo's mind clash with that other passage on a later page: when Noliwe dies we are told that her spirit fled and went to Dingiswayo "to the place of glory above." So Mofolo . . . belongs not only to the Africa of the future, but to the Africa of the past: he can write of both with perfect sincerity, because his feeling is identical with both. This double sympathy is no small part of his claim on our attention—he belongs to an intermediate age which may be quickly passing. It would be well if we could ensure that his successors shall not be tempted to gain a more advanced civilization at the cost of becoming less characteristic Africans. (pp. xiv-xv)

Henry Newbolt, in an introduction to Chaka: An Historical Romance *by Thomas Mofolo, translated by F. H. Dutton, 1931. Reprint by Oxford University Press, London, 1967, pp. vii-xv.*

THE SPECTATOR   (essay date 1931)

[*In the following excerpt, the critic reviews* Chaka.]

The name of Chaka is familiar to most readers, but there is something distinctive and intimate in this account of his life [*Chaka*] which is missing in the more formal histories. For his whole life was a romance, and the author has succeeded in keeping an even balance between historical accuracy and the romantic tragedy that was Chaka. It is an epic subject containing situations both of horror and pathos, while the author has legitimately exploited the contrasted characters of Chaka, the sadist, and Dingiswayo, the merciful. Chaka's rise to power, the insatiable restlessness of his tortured spirit driven from cruelty to cruelty, his sublime egotism and lust of conquest, all these move with the true inevitability of drama to the last tragedy of his madness and death.

Only one criticism suggests itself. Chaka is sometimes represented as being almost an automaton in the hands of the "witch-doctors." We should be the last to minimize the importance of magic in the scheme of African life, but we doubt whether Chaka, with his vast political ambitions and his Napoleonic designs, was the man to let magic ever be his master. His was rather the spirit of the Roman admiral who, when told by the priest that the sacred chickens refused to eat, ordered them to be thrown overboard to see whether they would drink. In this point, perhaps, his education may have predisposed the author to read more into the influence of the witch-doctors than Chaka would have admitted.

"Nemesis," in The Spectator, *Vol. 147, No. 5381, August 15, 1931, p. 222.*

MELVILLE J. HERSKOVITS   (essay date 1932)

[*Herskovits was an American anthropologist and scientific explorer who has written studies based on his travels in West Africa, South America, and the Caribbean. The author of* The American Negro: A Study in Racial Crossing (*1928*) *and* The Myth of the Negro Past (*1942*), *Herskovits was an early promoter of Afro-American studies and was particularly concerned with the consequences that result from moving African cultures to environments where other cultures were already established. In the following excerpt, Herskovits discusses* Chaka *as a fascinating literary achievement that presents African history from an African point of view.*]

[*Chaka*] is a distinguished contribution to recent biography. (p. 119)

The life of Chaka has fascinated all those who have touched upon it. An outcast boy, with the stigma that attaches to the child born of a Zulu mating before marriage, Chaka overcame obstacle after obstacle, ending his life in a debauchery of bloodshed, his name to go down in history as one of the world's great warriors and conquerors. He lived at about the time of Napoleon, and his exploits on the battlefield fully warrant the title of "the black Napoleon" he has been given by white historians.

Nothing of the point of view of the white man is found in Mr. Mofolo's book, where the author is above all an African writing in terms of his own civilization. The characterizations of Isanusi the witch doctor, of Ndlebe and Malunga, sent by Isanusi to help Chaka, are superb. The development of the plot, which shows how Chaka in his lust for power sacrificed everyone who was dear to him—his beloved, his benefactor, and finally his mother; the manner in which his growing suspicion and insistence on reverence toward his person are shown to have made him more and more bloodthirsty; the description of the disintegration of the character of the man under the influence of the witch doctor—all of these show the touch of a skilled hand.

Books of this character are rare enough, but books of this character that achieve the standard set by Mr. Mofolo have hitherto not been found at all. The biography is to be recommended as a tale fascinating enough for any reader. But for the person who is interested in gaining insight into the thought processes of a people whose civilization is entirely different from his own, and whose behavior springs from traditions with which his own have nothing in common, a reading of this life of Chaka will give a point of view that no work by a European observer, however well trained, can possibly give. (pp. 119-20)

Melville J. Herskovits, "African Biography," in The Nation, Vol. CXXXIV, No. 3473, January 27, 1932, pp. 119-20.

EZEKIEL MPHAHLELE (essay date 1962)

[*Mphahlele, an expatriate South African critic, novelist, and short story writer, is considered one of Africa's leading literary figures and a significant contributor to the development of African writing in English. While his criticism deals with the growth of African literature throughout the continent, his fiction most commonly examines the tragic lives of black people in South Africa. In the following excerpt, he examines the witch doctor Isanusi in* Chaka *as a symbol of the protagonist's deepening moral depravity.*]

Mofolo's first novel, *Moeti oa bochabela* (**The Pilgrim of the East**) gives an account of African life in ancient days. It is about a boy who wanders away from his home in search of "the unknown Creator." He believes that the Creator does not like the brute behaviour of his people, disgust in whose drunkenness, hatred and other moral lapses has caused him to leave home.

His next novel, *Pitseng,* also in Sotho, is set in a village that is built in a hollow (*Pitseng*—at the pot). It is a love story telling of the education and courtship of a modern African. It is a classic in its language and idiom.

In his introduction to *Chaka,* Sir Henry Newbolt says Mofolo's first novel is something like a mixture of *Pilgrim's Progress* and Olive Schreiner's *Story of an African Farm* [see excerpt dated 1931]. Although it is not likely that Mofolo was acquainted with Christopher Marlowe, *Chaka* is an interesting mixture of Tamburlaine and Dr. Faustus. (p. 170)

Chaka is in a sense a religious king. He might not feel that he is the scourge of the ancestors, but he believes that his witch-doctor, Isanusi, is an efficient intercessor between his people, epitomized by himself, and his ancestors; inasmuch as the witch-doctor in traditional African society is not a mere dealer in charms and potions, but is the moral conscience of his people. It is to him that the people appeal when they want to know what to do so that they do not offend the community and thereby the spirits of the ancestors.

Mofolo's king commits tyrannical acts in alarming succession. But he has his moments of "psychic conflict." His career began as a compensatory response to people's despise of him which arose from the fact that he was a chief's illegitimate child. It was also a response to his brother's lust for his own blood, and to his father's ill-treatment of his mother (she was expelled from the royal house). After the last attempt by his brothers to take his life, "he resolved that from that time on he would do as he liked: whether a man was guilty or not he would kill him if he wished, for that was the law of man. Chaka was always a man of fixed purpose. . . . But until now his purposes had been good. Henceforth he had only one purpose—to do as he liked, even if it was wrong, and to take the most complete vengeance that he alone would imagine." We can almost hear Edmund in *King Lear* or Richard III speaking.

This is where the Faustian element comes in. Chaka meets Isanusi, the witch-doctor, who is to "work on him," so that he conquer the chieftainship which he believes rightly belongs to him. Isanusi tempts him further and confronts him with the "moral problem of choice." Chaka can procure another kind of medicine which will make him king of a much bigger empire than he ever dreamed of. "It is very evil, but of great power," says the witch-doctor. "Choose." He asks Chaka to give this serious thought first, because he will have to murder and shed much blood in the process of becoming the desired monarch. Isanusi provides Chaka with two attendants: Ndlebe (ear) with long ears that could catch the faintest whisper from miles away and report back to the king; Malunga, whose work was to doctor the regiments so that they are brave and obedient.

Chaka succeeds to the stool. He has been to the river and seen a serpent which came out of the water, coiled itself round him, licked his body, and receded, staring at him. This is the messenger of the ancestors, which is to assure Chaka that his career deserves their watchfulness and assistance.

Isanusi comes up again with that suggestion of a potent medicine. The king must give the blood of one he loves most, to be mixed with the medicine.

"I Chaka had no need of deep thought. I have decided upon the chieftainship of which thou hast spoken. But I have no children and I do not know if the blood of my mother or my brothers would be sufficient. But if it is, I will give it you that ye may compound your medicines of it."

"But among those whom thou has promised there is not included the one thou dost love with the love of which I spoke. *Her* thou hast passed over. Think of *her* and tell us thy decision."

"Apart from these, the one I love is Noliwe."

"So be it. Think well which thou dost desire. The chieftainship without Noliwe. . . . But thou wilt not win it unless thou kill Noliwe, thou thyself, with thy own hand. [Isanusi smiles and continues.] Today, Chaka, we are teaching thee the highest kind of witchcraft when men kill their children or their parents so that the spirits may receive them and prosper them."

Isanusi is a symbol of Chaka's other self. Whenever he is in a tricky situation he need only shout, "Isanusi," and the witch-doctor will be there to assist. The decision is confirmed, and Noliwe, who has already delivered Chaka's child (unknown to him) is killed by his own hand in a scene that is full of pathos.

Chaka makes several reforms and gathers a number of small tribes under him and they become part of the Zulu nation, protected against the plundering expeditions of men like Zwide and Matiwane. Chaka's military genius creates the most formidable army in Africa at the time.

At the peak of his power and manhood, Chaka begins to be plagued by nightmares. He leaves his homestead in order to be "alone" outside the city. Even then he continues in lust for blood and sends one division of his army to destroy another. Bodies continue to feed a very large pit just outside the city. But he feels the approach of death. (pp. 170-72)

Chaka knows death is near and he cannot flee. In his . . . dream he sees Noliwe, the woman he loved; Dingiswayo, now dead, who was against unnecessary bloodshed and forgave those he conquered; the trusted soldier of whose popularity he was so jealous that he sent him to distant lands to fetch a stone from which metal is made so that he perish, and who dragged his living corpse back to his king.

Isanusi does come to claim his price in cattle. Chaka's attendants, Ndlebe and Malunga, simply disappear without a word of explanation. Chaka must pay the supreme price. His brothers murder him. The hyenas do not touch him; they merely circle round his body.

Indeed Chaka's life story stripped of all the romance still reads like a romance, as can be seen in E. A. Ritter's magnificent biographical epic, *Shaka Zulu*, which was published in 1955. Mofolo tells his story as a Christian, who is concerned with the battle between Evil and Good in Chaka. The manner of telling it is in the tradition of African oral literature—interspersed with songs and snatches of moralizing. (p. 173)

> *Ezekiel Mphahlele, "The Black Man's Literary Image of Himself," in his* The African Image, *Faber & Faber, 1962, pp. 166-203.*

CLAUDE WAUTHIER (essay date 1964)

[*Wauthier is a French critic and the author of* The Literature and Thought of Modern Africa: A Survey, *which examines the writings of African intellectuals in the post-colonial era. In the following excerpt from that work, originally published in 1964, Wauthier praises Mofolo's characterization of the protagonist of* Chaka.]

The first [African author] to have devoted a book to Shaka was the South African writer, Thomas Mofolo. His book has been translated from Sesotho into English, French and German. It is well known that Shaka was a pitiless chief, and Pastor V. Ellenberger, who translated the book into French, sees in his fate "the story of a human passion, an uncontrolled and then uncontrollable ambition which grew and developed fatally, as though fanned by some implacable Nemesis. Gradually it enveloped the whole personality, consuming all before it, until it led to the moral destruction of the character and inevitable punishment." Mofolo, a fervent Christian, saw the tragic death of Shaka, assassinated by his brothers who were weary of tyranny, as a just punishment for his sins and paganism.

This paganism is personified by the witch-doctor Isanusi, who teaches him, from his adolescence, the magic formulae of power. Shaka becomes a great chief, extending his power over tribes and territories. He marries the beautiful Noliwe and this is the period of reforms which make him a loved and respected sovereign, founder of a new nation, the Zulus, "people of heaven," forged from the tribes he had subjugated and unified. But the thirst for power was stronger. Neither love nor pity can have any place in the warrior's heart. Isanusi, the soothsayer who had taught him the first secrets of success, reappears and summons Shaka to choose: "Which dost thou choose—Noliwe or absolute power?" And Shaka answers, "Absolute power." The witch-doctor's face lights up. Shaka is of the stuff of heroes whom nothing will stop. Isanusi can confide to him the last magic formulae of omnipotence. Then Shaka plunges into a welter of blood and death: he kills Noliwe and his mother; then, suspecting his warriors, makes one regiment annihilate another. Like Caesar, he dies without attempting to defend himself from the assegai thrusts of his brothers. But before breathing his last, he hurls this curse at them: "It is your hope that by killing me ye will become chiefs when I am dead. But ye are deluded; it will not be so, for the Umlungu [white man] will come and it is he who will rule, and ye will be his bondmen." In spite of this welter of blood—and here perhaps is Mofolo's greatest strength—the character of Shaka remains fascinating throughout. To such an extent, indeed, that according to Jahn [see Additional Bibliography], the missionaries who employed Mofolo refused for many years to publish his manuscript for fear of awakening the flicker of some unknown pagan response. Mofolo had to wait twenty years for his book to be published. (p. 96)

> *Claude Wauthier, "To Each His Own Truth," in his* The Literature and Thought of Modern Africa, *translated by Shirley Kay, second edition, Heinemann, 1978, pp. 77-103.*

O. R. DATHORNE (essay date 1966)

[*Dathorne is a Guyanese-born English novelist, short story writer, and critic whose fiction satirically examines the lives of expatriate black people in England and Africa. In the following excerpt, Dathorne discusses Mofolo's stylistic synthesis of Sotho and biblical traditions in his novels and his pioneering treatment of the divisive, alienating influence of metaphysical Christian thought on the members of a secure tribal society.*]

Thomas Mofolo . . . , the greatest Sotho writer, was a product of Morija and even worked for the Paris Evangelical Mission there at one time. Perhaps Mofolo's work more than any of his contemporaries, shows what Jahn [see Additional Bibliography] has called "the synthesis of Sotho tradition and Christianity." The New Testament had been rendered into Southern Sotho as far back as 1868, a Southern Sotho-English dictionary had been produced at Morija in 1876, and an anonymous collection of folklore had been published at nearby Platberg in 1850. It is therefore no cause of surprise that Mofolo published *Moeti oa bochabela (The Traveller to the East)* in 1907.

In the story Fekisi is disgusted with the life round him. He begins to ask certain questions about the source of cloud and rain, the origin of the sun, the nature of God. He finds that the world of nature seems by contrast to be happy and more pleasant. An old man, Ntsoanatsatsi, tells him that men formerly originated from the place where the sun rises every morning, and in a vision he sees a man rising out of a pool, brighter than the sun. It is this he decides to seek.

Mofolo's form is the familiar hero-quest story found in the tale. But the impetus for the hero's departure is never the disgust that Fekisi feels; this alienation is a direct result of the Christian presence which had driven a wedge in tribal society and divided kinsmen on the question of ideology. It is interesting that to seek the Christian ideal Fekisi has to leave the familiar haunts of his tribe and his gods and to travel far away across open fields and deserted lands. It is as if the thoughtful, honest Mofolo were telling the reader that Christianity was far removed from the African plane of realism and was an elusive, insubstantial phantom which had to be sought. But his hero up to the time of setting out remains very much a Mosotho; appropriately he sings a praise-song to his father's cattle before he finally departs.

The first stages of his journey are disappointing; the people he encounters are no better than those he has left behind. It is with relief that he leaves all human company and treks across desert until he reaches the sea. There he meets three white elephant hunters who convert him and incidentally return to him some of the happiness he had lost. Mofolo adds that his hero "accepted all they told him, he believed them." On the occasion of receiving the first sacrament he sees Christ at the altar and rushes forward. He is found dead.

Mofolo had altered the hero-quest tale in an important way; not only was there little link with nature but, as has been shown, there was an abomination of man. In addition the whole allegorical interpretation was centred on the protagonist; it was *his* search, for *his* needs, for *his* boon. Nothing like this had existed in traditional oral literature and perhaps Mofolo was really visualising this as the only possibility for the new emerging individual consciousness, that it should bear the consequences of egocentricity. The burden of the responsibility of the tribe could be carried by one man in the oral tales, because behind him and ahead of him there was the *wholeness* of the tribe. It was from where he had come and it was the place to which he was returning. His adventures only made him more loyal, more readily able to appreciate what he had left behind; they confirmed the superiority of the tribe. But Mofolo's hero is alienated because he has lost the ability to pivot within the consciousness of the tribe which is itself disintegrating. His death confirms his pointless vacillations and the illogicality of alienation.

By contrast *Pitseng* is a disappointment. All his life Mofolo had to choose between the amiable offerings of Christian cameraderie and the set diet of an uncompromising art. The difficulties of the situation were made even more emphatic especially as he was an employee of Morija. It is only by taking this into consideration that one can accept the second novel at all; it was an attempt to pacify his teachers, employers and publishers. For the third, *Chaka,* the world had to wait until 1925, owing to its outright rejection by the missionaries. Another, *Masaroa,* still remains unpublished.

The second novel is named after the village of Pitseng in which it is set. Mr. Katse has brought Christianity to the village and soon has a very large following, including Alfred Phakoe and Aria Sebaka. Katse, rather arbitrarily, dispenses the benefits of the good life and he decides that the two children should in time marry. Alfred goes off to a training school and Aria becomes an assistant at the school. Alfred withstands all temptations and returns to marry Aria. This is the bare bones of the highly moral story and it is not really possible that the author of *Moeti oa bochabela* was capable of seeing the world in such unequivocal and obvious terms.

What however seems to deserve some mention in the book is the relationship that the hero has with nature. It is a relationship that is to become more evident in *Chaka.* The rejection of nature that had been noticed in the first novel, as well as in the work of Mangoela, Segoete and Motsamai was part of the rejection of their tradition. In the oral literature there is rapport between man and nature and therefore nature is never rhapsodised nor objectified. It is intrinsic, whole and consummatory. After the initial rejection, Mofolo's return to nature is to do with its rediscovery through Europe; it is now seen with European eyes. For instance as Alfred journeys to Aria's home:

The finches again flew up in a swarm and passed by quite close to them, but a little distance away they wheeled and rushed past them and settled in the reeds. It was as though they were trying to greet him in this manner.

The hesitation "as though" is important; in the world of oral literature they would have greeted him. Mofolo hesitates because, like his hero of the first novel, he had journeyed away from his people's ethos on a voyage of repudiation.

This is the key to an understanding of *Chaka.* It is no simple debunking of legend, but in Noni Jabavu's words "it becomes the apocalyptic vision of a monstrous beast, consumed by an all-destroying blood-lust." The historical Chaka is only the impetus for Mofolo's psychological study of the nature of repudiation. Mofolo reverts to the theme of the first novel—and this was his testament—the individual could not survive. Both Christian and pagan needed the props of tribal security. It is no accident that both Fekisi who saw Christ, and Shaka who connived with the devil, had to die.

Chaka is forced into individuality; he is the illegitimate son of Senzangakona, chief of the Ifenilenja tribe, and Nandi. Hated by his jealous brothers he is forced to flee from home. He grows up quite alone but brave and his mother wants to ensure that her son inherits the chieftainship. She has him anointed by the great serpent of the deep and he is put in the care of the evil Isanusi. His brothers never let up against him and finally his own father orders that he should be killed. This marks the turning point in Chaka's alienation. . . . *Chaka* has suffered from being too closely regarded as historical reconstruction and too little as a great novel, apart from its melodrama. A *Times Literary Supplement* review in 1931 thought it was a partly accurate and partly imaginary account and Mphahlele sees Chaka as a king given the moral problem of choice [see excerpt dated 1962]. But *Chaka* is neither pure history nor ethics; it is part of the tradition of the praise-poem and the hero monomyth but both of these have undergone a startling blend and a unique transformation. The catalytic effect of the missionaries had caused a renewal of concepts; a new melancholy has entered the African soul and no longer can the natural world, gods and man be accepted *in toto,* without question.

To say that Mofolo's two great novels belong to the *genre* of *Pitseng* and are mere exercises in the complacency of missionary teaching is to misunderstand them and Mofolo. They are above all the quests of befuddled individuals, catapulted from the security of tribal consciousness into the personal uncertainty of metaphysical speculation. What should concern the reader of today is not the individual enquiry but the tragic necessity for it. (pp. 152-53)

    O. R. Dathorne, "Thomas Mofolo and the Sotho Hero," in The New African, Vol. 5, No. 7, September, 1966, pp. 152-53.

ALBERT S. GÉRARD (essay date 1971)

[*Gérard is a Belgian essayist and scholar who has contributed to surveys of African literature and to literary journals in the Congo and South Africa. In the following excerpt from his* Four African Literatures: Xhosa, Sotho, Zulu, Amharic, *Gérard notes the importance of Mofolo's novels in African and world literature and discusses their embodiment of Christian philosophy, African culture, and Western literary conventions.*]

[The] foundation of the novel in Southern Sotho must be ascribed to a man of remarkable genius, who belonged to the same generation as Mqhayi among the Xhosa: Thomas Mofolo. (p. 108)

[In] 1905-1906 he composed the first Sotho novel. His sponsors were fully aware of the novelty of the thing. One of them said that it was "an absolutely original work of imagination," and F. H. Dutton, one-time director of education in Basutoland was later to describe it as a "surprise": "it was a new product—not a history, but a novel describing native life in ancient days." The book was *Moeti oa bochabela (The Traveller to the East)*, which was first serialized in *Leselinyana* in 1906, and appeared in book form in 1907.

Actually, it is more than a mere ethnographical novel. It is a quest story set in Lesotho before the coming of the white man. The hero, Fekesi, is an idealistic young man who is prompted by two impulses. One is of a moral nature: he is horrified at the evil ways of the village people, who live in drunkenness, quarrels, and sexual promiscuity; the other is intellectual, and has to do with the mystery of the origins of the universe. (p. 109)

Moeti oa bochabela is, of course, a Christian tract, ostensibly based on the antithesis of Africa—"clothed in great darkness," "a fearful darkness," Africa is the place "in which all the things of darkness were done,"—and the radiant light of the white man and of his religion, "the light that has come." This somewhat obvious symbolism involves a measure of suppression, perhaps of insincerity. By the beginning of this century, the Sotho people had been in touch with Europeans far less commendable than their devoted French missionaries, and Mofolo certainly knew that the white man's society was no faithful materialization of the City of God. Although the overall symbolism is simple and rather inadequate, Mofolo is by no means insensitive to the more subtle relations between Christianity and African culture. His highly unfavorable presentation of allegedly actual African mores may have prompted, as a reaction, the glorification of old-time Lesotho in Segoete's *Raphepheng*, which was to appear in 1913. But the fact remains that underneath the disparaging depiction of the minor characters of the novel, there is—illustrated by the elder's speeches, the mythical story of Kgodumodumo, and the motivations of Fekesi himself—the memory of and the aspiration to a life of orderliness and virtue that are presented as independent of any Christian teaching. So that the hero's discovery of Christianity is, as much as a conversion to a new faith, a return to beliefs and manners that had antedated both the introduction of Christianity and the degradation of morality exemplified in the early chapters of the book. Mofolo's ideal, then, may be said to be less one of rejection of traditional values in favor of Christian standards, than one of syncretism. Christianity is the new way toward the restoration of ancient purity. Mofolo has his white characters themselves point to the similarity between the legend of Kgodumodumo and the story of Jesus Christ. As Miss P. D. Beuchat has written, "*Moeti oa bochabela* is interesting in that it shows the merging of Sotho beliefs and Christian thought."

Sotho readers can enjoy the outstanding style of that first novel. But everyone can appreciate its careful two-part structure of search and discovery, hankering and fulfillment, evil and good. Moreover, the writer makes skillful use of the allegorical vision. Miss Beuchat goes on to claim that "the novel ends with a highly mystical scene, a dream or revelation which little resembles anything that Mofolo might have been taught by the rather austere Protestant faith in which he was brought up."

Yet, he could have drawn his inspiration from the Bible and/or from Bunyan. Jack Halpern has wondered "just what the Basuto of the 1860s made of *Pilgrim's Progress,* the first work to be translated and published." The reply seems to be that they found it congenial to their own mode of thought, as did countless African readers in about three dozens of languages. And there is little doubt that Mofolo's example encouraged his former teacher Segoete to make use of the same technique—albeit with less skill—in *Monono ke moholi, ke mouoane,* which was to be printed three years later.

It is in character depiction that the book—like so many African novels—is defective. In tribal societies, little attention is paid to individual inwardness. A person's awareness of self is primarily as a member of the group, and not—as is the case in Western society—as an autonomous individual whose chief legitimate preoccupations are with his own personal identity, rights, and privileges. This fundamental culture trait has many literary implications. Not only are African writers notoriously clumsy in the expression of strictly personal emotions such as love but also, more generally, their interests are ethical rather than psychological, and they are seldom able to present convincing individual characters. Their societal outlook drives them to turn character into type, so that the reader's response is one of moral edification rather than imaginative empathy. . . . This particular cultural trait makes it very difficult even for Europeans versed in the African languages to provide a balanced appraisal taking into account both the conscious purposes of the writer and his society's notion of the function of literature. To illustrate the kind of patronizing ethnocentricity to which white readers are liable, I cannot resist quoting a pronouncement made on *Moeti oa bochabela* by Professor W. A Norton of the University of Cape Town in 1921. He called the book "a charming odyssey . . . which, with a little more bloodshed, might have been saga, or, in verse, an embryo epic"!

Mofolo next embarked on a second novel, which was to have been entitled *The Fallen Angel* (Sotho title unknown). According to the *Livre d'Or*, the purpose of the book was to disprove some unspecified theory of Marie Corelli's; whether this was actually so or not is open to doubt. As we have seen in connection with *Moeti oa bochabela,* and as we shall see again when dealing with *Chaka,* at least some of the missionaries displayed complete lack of understanding in their interpretation of Mofolo's intentions. Anyhow, the author showed his manuscript to a missionary who disapproved of it; the work never reached print, and its whereabouts are unknown, if in fact it still exists.

Mofolo's second published novel was *Pitseng,* which was serialized in *Leselinyana* before it appeared in book form in 1910. The title refers to a village in the Leribe district. One of the chief characters in the book is the Reverend Katse, preacher and schoolteacher in Pitseng. He is a portrait of Mofolo's former teacher, Segoete, and the writer insists on his selfless dedication to the task of converting the pagans and educating the young. There is, however, little connection between Katse's career and the love plot on which the book is flimsily built, except that a considerable amount of Katse's preaching has to do with love and marriage. (pp. 110-13)

The many disquisitions on courtship and marriage in the book illustrate the confusion that, in Lesotho as in many parts of Africa, resulted from the intrusions of Christian ethics. The new ideal of genuine feeling, sexual restraint, and monogamy is extensively described in Katse's sermons and is enacted in the story of Alfred and Aria. These two, however, can hardly be said ever to come to life, so that there is a wide gap between the edifying purpose of the book and the realistic description of actual mores as observed by Alfred. Whereas Mofolo's earlier volume was marked by the unquestioning identification of European mores with the Christian ideal, *Pitseng* strongly emphasizes the contrast between this ideal and actual behavior among Christians, both black and white. In Pitseng and in the Cape Colony, he notices that native Christians do "like most white people who put God last in everything," and indulge in aimless flirtations and desultory promiscuity. And he comes to the unpalatable conclusion that "the heathens are telling the truth when they say that the evil influences come from the Whites and come into Lesotho with the Christian converts, because this habit whereby a young man decides independently upon marriage, consulting only with his girl friend, started with the converts. This attitude has completely destroyed the youth of Lesotho."

Noting that proper respect for the sacredness of courtship and marriage is more often found among heathens than among Christians, Mofolo extols the time-honored ways of the Sotho. . . . But traditional marriage customs have other aspects than this restraint and this symbolic indirection in conveying personal desires. . . . [Two] elements in traditional marriage, the bride-price and polygamy, are precisely those to which Mofolo takes exception, dutifully following the teaching of the missionaries, like so many of the early writers. His objection to polygamy is of course consonant with the overall Christian and Western concept of marriage. But his criticism of the bride-price seems to be more specifically an echo of French Protestant policy in Lesotho. . . . (pp. 113-15)

The main source of African puzzlement in this matter is of course the fact that "objectionable" traits cannot be separated from "approved" features in either of the two main conceptions that Christianization brought face to face. This appears clearly—although, no doubt, unintentionally—in the development of the love plot in *Pitseng*. Although Alfred and Aria avoid the "reprehensible" aspects of African courtship practice, that is, the bride-price and polygamy, and although they refrain from the promiscuity so widely spread, according to Mofolo, among the Christian village youth, yet they do not conform to the aspect of custom that the writer explicitly extols, namely, the total submission to parental will. Alfred and Aria select each other from the depth of their personal feelings, without previously seeking their parents' approval. Nor could it have been otherwise: the Christian insistence upon inner feeling and personal responsibility, and therefore upon personal freedom, was bound to disrupt the traditional morality. It is noteworthy that a similar critique was to be raised by Jolobe in *Thuthula* and, much later, in a Rhodesian novel, *Nhorvondo dzokuwanana (The Way to Get Married* [1958]) by a Shona author, Paul Chidyausiku.

While it is quite true, as Daniel Kunene points out [see excerpt dated 1976] that the two young people "are, for most of the time, portrayed as statues of virtue, sitting upon their high pedestals and looking with disapproval and even dismay at the goings-on of ordinary mortals," *Pitseng* contains all the data of the dilemma that the new view of marriage raised in most African societies. And although Mofolo fails, as he was bound to do, to provide a convincing picture of the ideal syncretism he advocates, this novel has more realistic subtlety than the previous one, because it is based on something that was fast becoming fundamental in the African mind: a clear perception of the antinomy between Christian theory and Christian prac-

tice. "Christianity," Mofolo writes, "is very good, it is better than anything on earth, if only all Christians would behave as this man [Katze] does."

While he was composing *Pitseng,* presumably in 1909, Mofolo was journeying through Natal on a bicycle, gathering historical background information for a new novel, to be based on the life of the early nineteenth-century Zulu conqueror, Chaka. . . . The result was *Chaka,* a genuine masterpiece of insight and composition, and perhaps the first major African contribution to world literature. (pp. 115-16)

It is . . . not surprising that Mofolo, as an African and as a Sotho, should have been interested in the momentous career of that Zulu Napoleon. What is less expected, however, in view of the strictures legitimately leveled at the deficiencies of most modern African fiction both with regard to character depiction and plot organization, is that Mofolo's research and meditation and genius should have produced a work that is remarkable for the clarity of its structure, the sharpness of its psychological insight, and the depth of its ethical approach. Although *Chaka* has been variously described as "an historical romance" and "a Bantu epic," it is really a tragedy, both in terms of construction and significance. Peter Sulzer perceptively observed that "while it has the rhythm of an epic, its inner structure and tragic content bring it near the sphere of the dramatic." *Chaka* can be defined as a narrative tragedy in prose, built along the simple curve of growth and decline which defines the structure of classic tragedy at its best. (pp. 116-17)

With great psychological acumen, Mofolo, in the first four chapters of the novel, goes to the very roots of his hero's fate. As Ezekiel Mphahlele rightly observed, "His career began as a compensatory response to people's despise of him which arose from the fact that he was a chief's illegitimate child. It was also a response to his brother's lust for his own blood and to his father's ill-treatment of his mother" [see excerpt dated 1962]. In tribal societies, estrangement from the group is the worst fate that can befall an individual. The numerous outlaw stories in the Icelandic sagas are cases in point. Chaka's suffering at being rejected by the tribe is the primary conditioning factor of his later development. His sense of alienation and frustration kindles an unquenchable thirst for revenge and domination, which he will be able to gratify as a result of the bravery and resilience he has acquired in resisting the most cruel persecutions.

Chaka's boyhood comes to an end when he decides to seek redress at the court of his father's overlord, Dingiswayo, head of the Mthethwa. Historically, this took place in the early years of the nineteenth century. On his way through the forest, "he reviewed all his life since his childhood, and he found that it was evil, terrifying, fearsome." . . . The philosophy experience has taught him is that "on earth the wise man, the strong man, the man who is admired and respected is the man who knows how to wield his spear, who, when people try to hinder him, settles the matter with his club." . . . The realization leads him to the ethics of unlimited self-assertion which accounts for all his subsequent behavior. "He resolved that from that time on he would do as he liked: whether a man was guilty or not he would kill him if he wished, for that was the law of man. . . . Until now his purposes had been good. Henceforth he had only one purpose—to do as he liked, even if it was wrong, and to take the most complete vengeance that he alone could imagine." . . . From a reluctant victim, Chaka deliberately turns himself into an unscrupled revenger. It is at that moment he has his first meeting with one Isanusi, whose name means "witch doctor" in Zulu.

The status of this supernatural character in the novel was bound to cause considerable attention among the critics, not least because the beliefs of Africans are usually supposed to be just crude superstitions. (pp. 117-18)

[Early] critics appraised the book against the backdrop of the traditional image of Chaka as a bloodthirsty monster of motiveless malignity. They were struck by the fact that Mofolo's interpretation seemed to turn him not only into a human being with definable and intelligible human motivation, but almost into a victim of his malignant fate. Hence, presumably, they show a proclivity to overemphasize the role of Isanusi and to load him with full responsibility for Chaka's evil deeds. As late as 1947, we find M. Leenhardt still claiming that "les magiciens exigent la maturation du projet criminel" ["the witch doctors demand the fulfillment of the criminal designs"]. But in 1948, Luc Decaunes, in what was at the time the best discussion of *Chaka,* hardly mentioned this supernatural element, but analyzed the book in terms of fate and freedom. . . . (p. 119)

[We] still find the notion that Isanusi is a genuine supernatural being and the decisive causal agent in Chaka's career. In 1953, without discussing the witch doctor himself, Sulzer stated that the two envoys whom Isanusi places at the disposal of the Zulu warrior "are personifications of the bestial features which take ever greater hold of Chaka." Nevertheless, as late as 1963, Miss Beuchat wrote that in the person of the witch doctor "we are presented with a supernatural explanation for Chaka's succumbing to evil," because "at the most crucial moments, when subsidiary crises occur, the power is there to challenge Chaka's decisions and remind him of his previous undertakings." And in the same year the Soviet critic L. B. Saratovskaya claimed that "Mofolo's book is permeated with the concept of fate, of a mysterious higher force which controls Chaka's actions." Other recent commentators, however, have preferred to work along lines that had been suggested by Sir Henry Newbolt when he wrote that Isanusi is "the visible symbol of [Chaka's] own hardening ambition" [see excerpt dated 1931]. "The witch doctor," said Mphahlele, "is a symbol of Chaka's other self" [see excerpt dated 1962], and Claude Wauthier viewed him as a "personification of paganism" [see excerpt dated 1964]. More recently, Kunene has shrewdly noticed that "if we compare the thoughts of Chaka at the time he hears the wailing in the village while he is hiding in the forest, with Isanusi's words during his first meeting with Chaka, we see identical sentiments, almost identical words."

It is as irrelevant to ask whether Mofolo actually conceived of Isanusi as a real supernatural being within the Chaka-world, as it is to discuss whether Shakespeare believed in witches. The point is that the Sotho sorcerer fulfills exactly the same function as do the witches in *Macbeth:* he helps crystallize the hero's impulses; he coaxes him into articulate awareness of his own desires and of their implications. When Isanusi, speaking of Chaka's ancestor, says, "If thou dost not spill blood he will take no pleasure in thee" . . . , he simply confirms the philosophy of status through strength to which the young man had come unaided during his earlier meditation. And when the sorcerer adds, "The medicine with which I inoculated thee is a medicine of blood. If thou dost not spill much blood it will turn its potency against thee and compass thy death. Thy work is to kill without mercy, fashioning thyself a road to thy glorious chieftainship," he merely makes Chaka fully conscious of the logic and of the dangers inherent in the course he has already decided to take.

At that point, we must observe, Isanusi assumes that the young man merely wants to be reinstalled into his birthright as the eldest son and successor of Senzangakona. Chaka's ambition so far has nothing that could be called illegitimate. It is Chaka himself who makes Isanusi understand that his aspirations are of wider scope. . . . (pp. 119-21)

At Dingiswayo's court, Chaka's story branches off into three narrative trends: his bravery against the chief's enemy, Zwide, earns him the honor of being placed at the head of Dingiswayo's army; he falls in love with the king's sister, Noliwe, who loves him too; at the death of Senzangakona (which actually occurred in 1816), Chaka is made chief in his father's stead, much to the fury of his half brothers. In each case, his success is facilitated by the intervention of Isanusi's mysterious delegates—Malunga, who represents bravery and strength, and Ndlebe, who represents intelligence and cunning. Thus far, however, Chaka's overt purposes have been legitimate. Nor has any actual evil been involved in their materialization, devious and uncommon though the devices of Isanusi's envoys may be. (pp. 121-22)

When Dingiswayo dies (this was in 1817), Chaka is not aware that Isanusi's henchmen have made arrangements for the king to be conveniently killed so that the young chief can succeed him at the head of the Mthethwa. In a sense, this is a climax in Chaka's career. Although he has acquiesced in evil, he himself bears no actual guilt for the murderous treachery that has brought him to the throne.

The point of no return is reached when Isanusi reappears after Dingiswayo's death as he had reappeared at the grave of Senzangakona. He explains to Chaka that further progress in power entails a new dedication to evil. . . . "It is a difficult matter, for it is thou who must provide the right medicine, and not I." . . . This medicine, it soon turns out, is the blood of Noliwe, which must be mixed with the food of the warriors. And although Chaka is willing to sacrifice his beloved instantly, the witch doctor insists that he wait for a period of nine months, "in which to confirm his decision so that he might not wish to turn back too late when the work had begun." . . . The true nature of Chaka's longing is made clear when he changes the name of his tribe from Mthethwa to Zulu (which means "People of Heaven"), "because I am great, I am even as this cloud that has thundered, that is irresistible. I, too, look upon the tribes and they tremble"—and Mofolo, for once, intervenes in the story to comment: "we . . . must wonder at the arrogance and ambition of this Kafir who could compare his greatness to that of the Gods," . . . adding, "Then it was that he sacrificed his conscience for his chieftainship." . . . (pp. 122-23)

It is important to understand the peculiar significance with which the murder of Noliwe is endowed in the total symbolism of the work, for the character of the girl and everything that is connected with her seem to be of Mofolo's own invention.

Describing Chaka's reform of the army, Mofolo mentions that he forbade his soldiers to marry at the usual early age:

> He said that the married man . . . thought of
> his wife and children, so that he ran away and
> disgraced himself. But the unmarried man fought
> to kill instead of being killed, and to conquer,
> so that he might enjoy the praises of the maidens. All the same, Chaka did not forbid them

absolutely. He promised that the troops that surpassed the others in war would be released first from this bondage of celibacy, even if they had not remained long in that state: more, they would be given wives by the chief himself. . . .

And the writer adds the following, highly meaningful, generalizations:

> The reader must remember that above all else on the earth the Black Races love to marry. Often in speaking of the good things of life people do not mention marriage, because *marriage is life*. Therefore we can understand well how hard the warriors of Chaka worked to gain this reward. To set his regiments an example, Chaka remained a bachelor till the end of his life. (. . . italics mine)

Mofolo provides another reason for Chaka's rejection of marriage. Marriage, Isanusi had advised him, "is a hindrance to a chief, and brings dissension in his house." . . . Indeed, it was sometimes the custom in Africa for a newly enthroned monarch to kill, or otherwise dispose of, all potential pretenders. Chaka's bachelorhood and his enforcement of celibacy on his warriors are part of a pattern that culminates in the murder of Noliwe and signals the victory of the values of war and death symbolized by Isanusi over the values of love and life. (p. 123)

Self-imposed sterility, as in the case of Chaka, is viewed as so unnatural an attitude in the African culture context that it can only stir puzzlement and awe. But Mofolo turns it into an image of evil, the symbolism of which is clinched by the murder of Noliwe. As Chaka's beloved, as a woman, the instrument of human perpetuation, Noliwe is truly the embodiment of the forces of love and life in Chaka. His falling in love with her was the sign that, at that early stage in his evolution, he was still capable of redemption; it stood on a par with his devotion to Dingiswayo. On the level of Chaka's psychology, her murder illustrates his complete surrender to the evil impulses of self-assertion. In the wider symbolism of the work, it brings to its highest intensity the antinomy of fame and love, of power and life. It is the most repellent aspect of the overall destruction that is the only way to worldly glory and might.

In the introduction to his French translation of the work, Victor Ellenberg writes that *Chaka* is "the story of a human passion, ambition, first uncontrolled, then uncontrollable, which fatally grows and develops, as if fanned by some implacable Nemesis, and consumes everything until it ruins the moral personality and leads to the unescapable punishment." This Nemesis, however, is no outward power. It is the very same immanent logic of crime and punishment which was at work in *Macbeth*. The murder of Noliwe marks the moment of Chaka's rupture with human nature, as does the murder of Banquo for Macbeth. From that point on, bloodshed becomes an addiction. The tyrant's downfall is linked to his rise by an inexorable chain of cause and effect. The growing extent of his power also increases the number of his enemies and compels him to impose ever sterner control upon his warriors. He is, therefore, threatened from two sides: by those who resent his ruthless authority, and by those who want a larger share of its benefits—until his two half brothers, from whom he had wrenched the chieftainship at the death of their father, pluck up enough courage to kill him. (pp. 124-25)

It is obvious that Mofolo had fully assimilated the Christian view of man as a free agent, totally responsible for his acts. Among Chaka's deeds, he makes a perfectly clear distinction between those that are prompted by legitimate justice, and those that result from a fiendish lust for power. At every decisive point, the meaning and consequences of contemplated actions are fully described by Isanusi, and Chaka always makes up his mind in complete awareness of what he is doing. Few African works exhibit such a profoundly integrated sense of the meaning of freedom and guilt in Christian ethics. (p. 125)

[While] the central idea of *Chaka* is coherently and impressively Christian, it would be an over simplification to suggest that any other types of outlook were altogether foreign to Mofolo. Indeed, the last page of the novel is unobtrusively marked by the emergence of two other standards of valuation.

It is all too often forgotten that as a Sotho, Mofolo participated in the vivid legacy of bloody memories that his nation had inherited from the times of the Wars of Calamity. The Sotho people had suffered grievously as a result of Chaka's imperialism, and national feeling may well have played its part, side by side with Christian inspiration, in Mofolo's choice of this particular evil hero. Some patriotic satisfaction, one presumes, was involved in illustrating the workings of immanent justice, not only on Chaka, but also on the Zulu nation as a whole. Before dying, Chaka prophesies for the benefit of his half brothers: "It is your hope that by killing me ye will become chiefs when I am dead. But ye are deluded; it will not be so, for Umlungu (the White Man) will come and it is he who will rule, and ye will be his boundmen." . . . Writing those words, Mofolo may have felt some complacency at this reversal of fortune for the enemies of his people, particularly in view of the fact that Zulu resistance to white occupation had finally been put down in 1906.

But Mofolo was not only a Christian and a Sotho. He was also an African, whose native continent was being increasingly and irresistibly incorporated into the white man's sphere. Awareness of their identity and of the need to overcome tribal definitions and differences was spreading fast among African intellectuals in those early years of the century. . . . Owing to its privileged status as a British protectorate, Lesotho's active part in this movement was negligible. The feeling was there, however, and we catch a fugitive echo of it in the subdued pathos of the last paragraph of *Chaka*:

> Even today the Mazulu remember how that they were men once, in the time of Chaka, and how the tribes in fear and trembling came to them for protection. And when they think of their lost empire the tears pour down their cheeks and they say: "Kingdoms wax and wane. Springs that once were mighty dry away." . . .

It is difficult to escape the impression that at this final stage the Christian and the Sotho in Mofolo have made room for the African, who renounces, for a brief while, his tribal rancors and his new definitions of good and evil to ponder on the past greatness of his race and on its present subjugation, finding some undivulged hope, perhaps, in the notion that the white man's empire, too, will wane some day.

It may have been this final impression that, in later times, was to enable Senegal's Léopold Sédar Senghor and Mali's Seydou Badian to extol Chaka, in poetry and on the stage, as the heroic, self-denying ruler, who does not hesitate to sacrifice the tenderest passion of the heart in order to ensure the greatness and to defend the freedom of his people. Mofolo's conception of Chaka is entirely different and, as far as can be ascertained, much closer to historical fact. The Sotho author is by no means blind to his hero's inherent greatness, but he judges him and indicts him in the name of an essentially ethical view of life. Besides the technical skill and the depth of outlook which it evinces, Mofolo's novel is unique in its successful combination of traditional African and modern Christian elements.

But it is considerably more than a novel. Apart from the wider, universal ethical significance of the curve in Chaka's career—from innocence to evil, and from crime to punishment—the story also has that mysterious quality in which all myths partake. In his *Nachwort,* which is easily the most perceptive analysis of *Chaka* to date, Sulzer points out that the Zulu monarch is, in some respects, an inverted image of Christ, while exhibiting, in other respects, fundamentally Faustian elements. Ever since its inception in sixteenth-century Spain, the modern European novel has been essentially realistic. Yet, literary realism ignores the realities of mystery that are basic to human experience. However extensively the certainties of science and logic have grown, the fundamental questions—the whence, the why, and the whither—of human existence and behavior still remain unanswered. It is with these that myth deals, and the level of myth can only be reached through non-realistic, nonrational channels. The mystery in *Moby Dick*, the madness in *Don Quixote* and *Hamlet*, the magic in *Macbeth* and *Faust*, these are the elements that raise such works to the higher levels of myth. If they are so undefinably satisfying, it is because they beckon to the dim reluctant awareness within us that in all important matters uncertainty is still our lot. Whether Mofolo's *Chaka* can be claimed to rank with them is a matter for cultured Sotho readers and critics to decide. The mere fact that the question can be raised is in itself significant. (pp. 125-27)

Albert S. Gérard, "Literature in Southern Sotho," in his Four African Literatures: Xhosa, Sotho, Zulu, Amharic, *University of California Press, 1971, pp. 101-80.*

BEN OBUMSELU (lecture date 1975-76)

[In the following excerpt, Obumselu contends that in the novel Chaka *Mofolo unsuccessfully attempts to transform a traditional African myth celebrating cultural order into a realistic Christian moral fable by portraying the novel's protagonist as a demonic psychopath rather than as a political hero.]*

Chaka is not an easy work to classify. For, although the Zulu king has epic stature, his fortunes as Thomas Mopoku Mofolo . . . traces them, follow the curve of a tragedy. But as a tragic hero Shaka is not true to type. He is too much of a villain to raise and purge the sympathetic emotions of pity and terror; and Mofolo denies him that final self-recognition which enables the hero in defeat to recover his composure and some of his lost greatness. Mofolo is clearly working outside the Western conventions of tragedy and the epic.

Surprisingly, however, Shaka (and Sundiata also) resemble the legendary heroes of Euro-Asian epic whose family features Otto Rank and Lord Raglan have described. Both are conceived in abnormal circumstances and are destined to succeed their fathers on the throne. Cruelly persecuted as children, both go into exile and there become the chief counsellor and warrior of foreign kings. Both lose their kingdoms to a favoured half

brother. But they both return and with supernatural support win back their thrones and conquer vast empires. (p. 33)

Shaka is, in a sense, notorious. In Mofolo's novel . . . the Zulu king's greatness is a brilliant haze which shines through his tragic misdirection of amazing creative powers. . . . [The] Shaka legend was made by the king's enemies, Queen Nkabayi who planned his assassination, Dingane who carried it out, and the tribes whom he scattered. And quite unlike a traditional chronicler, Mofolo was an outsider. He was a Sotho writing about a Zulu, a Christian writing about pagans, a moralist describing the corruption of political authority. In its unusual line of descent, the Shaka legend crossed the frontier which separates tribal myths of origin (celebrating the creation of the cultural order by patron gods and fabulous ancestors) from ordinary moral fables in which actions, no longer conceived as primordial or normative, are judged as moral instances. It passed from the mythical time and communal symbolism of folk art to the realistic idiom of the novel. The point is, of course, that in Mofolo the crossing is incomplete.

Predictably, Mofolo did not concern himself with the political and heroic logic of Shaka's doings. With his individualistic and moral frame of reference, he was in no position to understand the struggle for Nguni paramountcy in early nineteenth-century Natal nor the splendid extravagances of the heroic temper. The use he made of Isanusi, Ndlebe and Malunga showed that Shaka baffled him. . . . Shaka was in fact the flower of South Africa's heroic age. Mofolo's imperfect sympathy and extra-tribal perspective prevented him from writing the great black epic of which the Zulu conqueror was such an apt subject.

It is usual to explain Mofolo's account of Shaka as a case of psychopathic vengefulness or demonic possession as the consequence of the writer's missionary background. The facts of Mofolo's life support this interpretation. . . . The four novels he wrote, *Traveller to the East* (1905/6), the unpublished *The Fallen Angel* (1907/8), *Pitseng* (1909), and *Chaka* (finished in 1911) fall in his second missionary period when he was a proof reader at the press and secretary to Casalis. *Chaka* remained unpublished for fifteen years because the mission thought that it "could do nothing but harm to its readers because of its defence of pagan superstitions."

If the long apprenticeship at the mission did not shape Mofolo's moral and religious sensibility, the demands of the press certainly conditioned his writing. Like other Morija or Lovedale authors he was obliged to appear Christian beyond the warrant of his own faith and beliefs. The pattern had been set by Ntsikana, Tiyo and the early Christians who wrote edifying pamphlets and hymns. In Mofolo's day that tradition was continued by Everitt Segoette's *The Patience of God with the Sinner* and Edward Motsamai's attack on paganism in *Five Pebbles from the Brook*. The first work of fiction published at Lovedale was indeed a translation in 1867 of *The Pilgrim's Progress* and of this, Mofolo's *Traveller to the East* is an imitation.

The plot and moral theme of *Chaka* arise logically, it is suggested, from the background we have just sketched. "The great crime which started everything was the sin of Nandi and Senzangakona" . . . , Mofolo says. What clouds Shaka's childhood would appear to be the original sin of his illegitimate conception. The careful psychology of this opening section shows how that sin prevents Senzangakona from being the affectionate parent it is in his nature to be. Frustrated, Shaka as "a hare whose ears are struck, an orphan, a buffalo who stands alone'' . . . moves inevitably to his fated pact with the devil. The identification of Isanusi as the devil of Christian doctrine is unmistakeable: he seems to Shaka on his first appearance ''far more evil than any sorcerer, more cruel by far than any murderer—the very father of malice, wickedness and treachery.'' . . . If Isanusi is able to change his damning aspect immediately afterwards, that merely confirms his identity. He is, of course, also the diabolical African witchdoctor as missionaries see that much maligned village functionary; and at Senzangakona's grave the tribal cult of the ancestor becomes necromancy and black magic.

To complete the Christian reading of *Chaka,* it is argued that Mofolo himself does not credit Isanusi and his familiars; that he uses them as dramatic conveniences like Shakespeare or Goethe; that the novelist, in other words, is completely outside the tribal frame of reference. The earliest African commentators on the Sotho text of the novel took Isanusi quite literally, regarding him as the agent of a malign fate. But with the appearance of the English translation, Sir Henry Newbolt suggested that the warlock should be seen instead as the symbol of Shaka's perverse lusts. ''The whole business of the witch doctor's profession is thus raised from the contempt which commonly attends it among our own writers, its origin is hinted at, and its effect at least partly accounted for'' [see excerpt dated 1931]. This interpretation has been followed by Luc Decaunes, Peter Sulzer, Ezekiel Mphahlele and Albert Gérard among others. (pp. 33-5)

Comparing *Chaka* with *Macbeth* [Gérard] emphasizes the Zulu king's eventual rejection of creative and communal values [see excerpt dated 1971]. But in so far as the origins of the novel are missionary, it is more to the point that Shaka barters away his immortal soul. *Chaka* is a novel of infernal *hubris* and idolatry. One of the ideas that Mofolo returns to again and again is the impiety of the tribal name *zulu,* heaven. The idea was certainly present in the minds of Shaka's contemporaries, though to them *zulu* was not so much God's seat as the source of death-dealing thunder, lightning and, in a more auspicious mood, rain. The praise-singers called Shaka *izulu eliphezulu,* the heavens above, much as they called the Sotho king Joel

> Heaven, comrade of Kindler of fires,
> Comrade of the children of the Depriver, you are a
>   cloud.

Mofolo first uses the idea when Isanusi invites Shaka to choose a new name for his tribe. Hearing a rumble of thunder from the clouds, Shaka chooses the name *zulu.* Even Isanusi is filled with pious alarm; ''and we, too,'' Mofolo adds, ''must wonder at the arrogance of this Kafir who could compare his greatness to that of the Gods.'' . . . (p. 36)

As a king of morality play, *Chaka* is more like *Doctor Faustus* than *Macbeth.* Both are stories of giants fatally drawn to

> . . . a world of profit and delight
> Of power, of honour, of omnipotence.

The two heroes transgress all bounds to satisfy the lusts of a lawless imagination. In consequence both are cut off from human loves and joys. At the end of both lives the devil steps forward to claim the lost soul.

The effect of the Elizabethan parallels is to suggest that missionary sermons cannot account for the sophistication of plot and symbolism which *Chaka* achieves. Marie Corelli's imaginative procedures—Mofolo knew the work of the earnest best-selling novelist well—might have helped him, and so might any Elizabethans he came across. But he was himself remarkably fertile and resourceful, as the psychological observation of the early Noliwe episodes show. If he profited from his acquaintance with European works in mission libraries, he was surely exercising the artist's prerogative to use previous literature in shaping his own creations.

It seems to me, however, that although the above is a perceptive and useful way to read the novel, *Chaka* is a more interesting work when it is approached as folk narrative. Viewed in its own traditional setting, the offence of Senzangakona and Nandi is not the sin of lust but the violation of the tribal rules of *ukuhlobonga.* ''In those days in Kafir land an unmarried girl who bore a child was put to death. . . .'' Isanusi is evil not because he is the devil, but because he is neither an *isanusi* (diviner), nor an *inyanga* (healer), nor an *isangoma* (witchdoctor), but an *umthakathi* (sorcerer). Mofolo assumes these tribal distinctions when he implicitly endorses Nandi's early visits to an isangoma. Shaka too assumes it when he conceals his dealings with the sorcerer from his mother. Dr. T. C. Lloyd reports that among the offerings of the Mthethwa Lucky Stars in Durban in the early 1930s was *Umthakathi,* a play which turns on the distinction between good and bad witchcraft. Tribal hunts to expose and punish men like Isanusi were general throughout pre-Christian Africa. And heinous as the killing of Noliwe is, the roll call of Shaka's murders at the end of the novel . . . would suggest that Mofolo found matricide and child murder even more abominable. The final enormity for him is not the offence against love and life, but the breaking of kinship bonds. Shaka is not merely unloving; he is in Hamlet's pun, unkind. It is the breaking of the august taboo against the shedding of a kinsman's blood for which his own *imbongi* condemns Shaka.

> King, you are wrong because you do not dis-
> criminate
>
> Because even those of your maternal uncle's
> you kill

It is very likely that Mofolo did not think of his work as a novel but a biography. . . . Throughout the work he is at pains to accommodate all the known facts: Shaka's illegitimacy, his killing of the lion and the lunatic and the appropriate *izibongos,* his friendship with Dingiswayo, his military reforms and the plans of his campaigns, the layout of his capital, the deflection of Mzilikazi, the attempt to kill the king at a dance, his prophetic last words. . . . Even the departures from history, such as the episodes in which Shaka kills his mother and his only son, may have been taken for history in Mofolo's time. If the fictional method makes us think of the narrative as a novel, it should be remembered that E. A. Ritter, writing about the oral rendering of the legend among the Zulu, says that folk history enjoys the liberties of fiction.

From Ritter we learn also how alive Shaka was in the folk imagination of South Africa at the turn of the century. Old men, like Chief Sigananda Cube, could still be found who had served the king personally. But apart from eye witnesses, the legend with its marvels, dramatic dialogue and the swift action of folk narrative, was being propagated orally just out of earshot of Europeans. These were the sources which Mofolo, Motsamai and other African chroniclers of the period relied on. Twenty years later when Zulu writers appeared on the scene, the material was ready for their use. The first Zulu novel, John Dube's *Jege, the Bodyservant of King Shaka* (1930) drew predictably from the national legend. Starting from 1936, Rolfes Dhlomo wrote four fictional biographies of Shaka and his successors. Benedict Vilakazi's *Zulu Songs* (1936), the first volume of verse to appear in Zulu, had its expected Shaka poems; just as the author's only novel *UDingiswayo KaJobe* (1939), was about Shaka's patron. The interesting thing about the body of literature of which these are the signposts is that its judgement of Shaka is surprisingly uniform. He is the matchless, almost superhuman, hero whose perversions make him a fiend. Missionary indoctrination is not needed to explain an attitude which Mofolo shares with his contemporaries, an attitude accounted for historically by the unspeakable suffering of the *mfecane*.

To obtain a closer view of the folk elements in Mofolo's writing and the extent in which he modified the tradition he inherited, the presentation of the supernatural in the novel should be looked at in more detail. Gérard rightly observes that Isanusi and the other supernatural characters in the novel are not real people. They share the same symbolic virtuality as Noliwe and Mnyamana. For our purposes, they are in the work as expressions of the dramatic tensions which the story requires. But it would be wrong to infer from their lack of naturalistic truth that Mofolo imagined them differently from Dingiswayo and Nandi. Indeed the historical Shaka had an *inyanga yoku songa,* a war doctor, Mqalane, a foreigner from the Nzuza tribe; and Ngobozi, his drill master, the best known soldier in the Zulu army, was another foreigner from the Nsane tribe. These aliens were resented by the Zulu; and during the witch hunt of 1817 Ngobozi and Ndlaka, a general, were accused of sorcery. From these foreign associates of the king believed to be sorcerers, popular tradition must have thrown up hints which the novelist took up.

The first supernatural agent in the novel is, of course, the river monster which appears to Shaka during his ritual bath in the river. To prepare the reader for this event, Mofolo points out early in the novel that among the Nguni "the snake is a well-recognized messenger bringing tidings from the dead to their decendants." . . . After the event, the water serpent is spoken of as "a great chief coming from the dead" . . . , "the great chief who visited thee in the river." . . . We can speak of Shaka's supernatural election in his culture just as in the world of *L'Enfant noir* the association between the black python and Kamara Komady is the visible sign of his spiritual grace, and in *Sundiata* the association with the buffalo of Do makes the founder of Mali the elect of the gods. Though Shaka's experience in the river is Gothic in its outlines, it is not unnaturalistic for that reason. It is an event which in the culture is believed to occur from time to time to the spiritual elite. The *tikoloshi* itself and the setting in which it appears come from traditional folklore; and I would suggest that it is the background of belief and dread which gives them their astonishing reality. Although in a sense conventional, both the snake and its ambience are far from being fantastic. The chill winds, the caves, the mist, the waterfalls and the other Gothic apparatus are natural enough at the foot of the Drakensberg mountains. And strange as the monster is, it is also very familiar. "It had long ears like those of a hare, but in shape they were more like the ears of a field mouse. Its eyes resembled great green hammer stones. . . ." The frisson we feel is not a response to vague adjectival appeals, nor is it related to any apprehension that Shaka stands in moral, as distinct from physical, peril. It depends on the novelist's command of realistic detail: the snake winds itself round Shaka, stares him in the eyes, licks him over from head to foot; "its hot foul-smelling breath covering him with steam." . . . (pp. 36-40)

In the boldness and the visual immediacy of the writing, there is no hint of that subordination of what is presented to a moral generalization which we would expect if Mofolo thought of the serpent as a symbol. But his expansive realism is, of course, different from the rapid impressionism of the folk narrator. In the wonderful Sotho story of Thakane's raid on underwater dragons to obtain their shining hide for her brothers' initiation gear, we have an illustration of the very different approach of the folk artist. He hardly describes the monsters at all; apart from a single simile he leaves visual effects to his audience's imagination. . . . The storyteller is before his audience. By gesture, tone, and ideophones he can summon from them the required emotion. Mofolo, on the other hand, is writing a novel which each reader faces alone; he must orchestrate detail and imagery which will create the experience he wants to evoke.

The portraits of Ndlebe and Malunga are artistic triumphs. Whereas in describing the tikoloshi of the deep waters Mofolo handles horror remarkably well, Isanusi's two assistants show him controlling horror as symbols of moral experience. The description of Ndlebe illustrates the point. . . . Mofolo starts from Ndlebe's head and works systematically down to the feet. But despite this callow thoroughness, character and significance shine through every feature. The symbolism is bold. But so splendidly observed is the man that he is not a mere symbol. Moreover, the whole scene is full of action and drama although nothing happens. When Shaka gazes at Ndlebe, his ears "become bigger and rounder than ever, his eyes still more full of guile and falsehood. He stepped round like an ostrich and sat down again."

The artistic strength of **Chaka** lies in qualities of this kind. The moral outlook at the novel has the force of sober commonplace, a commonplace which is obvious enough, the perverse insistence of Western commentators notwithstanding, to both missionaries and tribesmen. But in the use of bold fantastic symbols to mirror these august commonplaces, Mofolo relies on the artistic idiom of his own culture. On every page we find him enriching his inheritance with a new sense of fact, a more realistic psychology and his peculiar dramatic effects. But the basic forms are those of folk art; Ndlebe, for instance, is at bottom the trickster.

Ndlebe differs, however, from Malunga. As the Medicineman Malunga is less dramatic. In presenting him Mofolo uses the same epic style he adopts in a number of passages describing Shaka in the first half of the novel. It is important to recognize that Sotho praise poetry is a formative influence on Mofolo's rhetorical method. . . . But citations, of *lithoko,* proverbs and folktales, are only incidentals. What is essential is the novelist's tendency to slip into the mood and cadences of the praise singer whenever his subject requires epic heightening. The effect is not amenable to brief illustration but can be observed in the passage describing Shaka's exploits during the first Ndandwe war . . . and on the occasion of his enstoolment. . . . (pp. 40-1)

Isanusi, Ndlebe and Malunga are the only actors in **Chaka** who are as vivid and interesting as the hero of the novel himself. The vigour with which they are imagined and presented derives from the tradition of magical narratives which the novelist shared with his audience. Mofolo wrote in Sotho for a public who were used to witchcraft and magic in life and literature. Fiction, even to the most sceptical among them, was inconceivable without the miraculous. The occurrences of daily life, in a cattle raid, a hunt or a battle, must be re-interpreted before it could enter poetry or any recreational narrative.

The technical correlatives of this approach to fiction can be seen in the description of Shaka's battles. It is apparent that Mofolo learnt something, expectedly inaccurate, of what actually happened in the nineteenth-century battle fields of Nguniland.

Chapter fifteen of the novel appears, for instance, to be based on authentic history: Shaka's evacuation of the theatre of war before the third Ndandwe campaign; his retreat from Zwide until hunger, exposure to cold and sleeplessness forced the enemy to give up the pursuit; the Zulu king's shock swoop on the Ndandwe as they were halfway across the Umlutuze river; and his sending a party to cut off their retreat and head them away from their home. Mofolo reproduces the first step in this sequence faithfully. Then he makes Zwide, the invader with superior numbers retreat from the tiny Zulu army which proceeds to encircle the innumerable Ndandwe. Mofolo obviously did not understand what he was told, nor did he bother to imagine a reasonable alternative. He is not a realist and cannot organize a large body of circumstantial detail. For the kind of episode he can handle he needs Isanusi, Ndlebe and Malunga. His writing belongs in a culture where the supernatural is the true substance of art. He is more at home with fantasy and myth than with the imitation of life. Typically he substitutes the simple formulae of folklore for densely textured individual actions and motives. Just as the griot telling the story of Sundiata's victory at Krina reduces the long campaign to one mighty shout and the shooting of a fateful arrow; so Shaka's use of Zwide's treacherous counsellor and the Dlimini as sources of information is replaced by Ndlebe's enormous ear, and instead of adopting superior training and tactics the king has only to shout Isanusi's name to rout his enemies.

This formulaic method should not be regarded as a symbolic shorthand affected by folk artists to disguise their lack of diligence. They believed, as did their audience, in a supernatural order which shapes the destinies of men. To imagine experience as a whole and communicate its participating nature, folk narrative needed to relate the seen with the unseen, the efficient human cause with its occult pre-conditions, the natural with the supernatural. The curious thing was, of course, that the universe of the missionary was very similarly constituted. The psychological interpretation of Isanusi, Ndlebe and Malunga has the effect of collapsing the tiered system of the religious world picture unto a single plane, an inevitable critical procedure in a sceptical age but quite invalid for either the Sotho writer or his Christian sponsors. Owing to their mistaken belief in the unity and rationality of the West, Sir Henry Newbolt and Professor Gérard would probably not admit that in some essentials they were further removed from Casalis and Jacottet than Mopoku Mofolo ever was. (pp. 41-2)

Ben Obumselu, "Mofolo's 'Chaka' and the Folk Tradition," in Sheffield Papers on Literature and Society *Vol. 1, 1976, pp. 33-44.*

DANIEL P. KUNENE (essay date 1976)

[*Kunene is a South African critic, scholar, and poet who has written extensively on South African literatures and on the novels of Mofolo. In the following excerpt, Kunene discusses the employment of Basotho literary traditions in Mofolo's novels and analyses the degree to which Mofolo's works oppose or uphold the ethics of African and Christian societies.*]

The schools through which Mofolo learned to read and write and to define his relationship with his fellowmen and with the cosmos, were established and controlled by the missionaries with the specific aim that they be used as aids to facilitate and accelerate the process of Christianization. Christianity, therefore, became a powerful factor in Mofolo's life, in his view of the world, and in his judgement of his fellowmen. And a severe judge he was.

At the same time, the Basotho continued to live according to their traditions, which stood strong against the vicious onslaughts of the new religion and its new set of values. Mofolo was thus simultaneously immersed in a virile Sesotho culture marked by an uninhibited relationship of people, both to themselves as physical and spiritual beings with bodies and souls that needed to be revealed and admired and given expression, rather than hidden in some dark recesses of a guilty conscience, and with those around them who constituted their social environment and provided them not only with companionship, but also with solace and comfort when the need arose.

Mofolo's admonitions to his characters are therefore seen to be often motivated by a combination of the traditional and the new, the Sesotho and the Christian, sometimes even while he himself consciously thinks that he is committing himself to a definite choice. (pp. 243-44)

As a participant in the oral literature of the Basotho, Mofolo carried on a tradition that, in its folk narratives, sought to maintain harmony in society. This harmony could only be achieved and sustained through the observance of the social mores that then applied. In that all the Basotho of premissionary times subscribed to these ideals, the social function of art was that of integration. The people's behaviour in all its varied aspects was seen by the artist as being polarized around the social ideal. On the one hand there was the majority of the people who not only subscribed to this ideal, but also strove to keep it alive and meaningful. These were the heroes of the narratives. There were, on the other hand, also the few who, while subscribing to the ideal, none-the-less fell victim to various temptations that brought them into direct confrontation with their society. These were the villains of the narratives, social misfits who were either rehabilitated or banished or destroyed. The oral artist synthesized all these elements in society and told a narrative in which they all contributed to the total didactic purpose of the story. Being himself a member of the society, the artist took sides. He liked those characters who were constant and steadfast in maintaining the integrity of the social ideal, and disliked those whose antisocial actions placed this ideal in jeopardy.

Christianity introduced a new and very powerful element into the moral fabric of Basotho society. It created new loyalties, destroying some of the old ones in the process. It brought into being new factions. The verbal artist of this time had a much more difficult task trying to sort out things so that his message could make some sense to his audience. We are talking, in specific terms, about the writer who, in the process of acquiring literacy, was placed, willy nilly, in the forefront of the movement for change. Circumstances turned him into the most vocal and vehement advocate of the new order. Basically he still considered himself the keeper of the conscience of society, of the people who constituted his audience. This time, however, heroes and villains found new definitions, and many who were the heroes of the old Basotho society became villains solely for their refusal to accept the new dispensation. In the eyes of the writer, much of the old beliefs and customs that the old narratives had sought to hold together were now to be dismantled. Therefore there was need to destroy the old edifice before building the new one. Indeed the new one could only be built on the ground left vacant by the old one. The writer's loyalty was therefore largely alienated from his traditional society and allied to the forces of change, specifically to the missionaries. Again we see how the verbal artist takes sides. He likes those of his characters who accept the new ethical code that he now advocates, and dislikes those who don't.

We can therefore identify the didacticism of the traditional artist as being integrative, and that of the writer of Christian times as being disintegrative.

For our purpose at this point the important consequence of all this is that the writer is involved with his characters as well as the events and conflicts in his story. We see certain very important features of his style arising directly from this involvement.

Now, to come specifically to Mofolo, we have first of all to see how he fits into the picture described above. Basing our judgement solely on his three published novels, we can say that in **Moeti oa bochabela** he displays the greatest degree of conscious rejection of Sesotho traditional values. The missionaries of the Paris Evangelical Missionary Society welcomed his manuscript with overflowing enthusiasm not, as it turned out four or five years later when they evaluated **Chaka,** primarily because of its literary merit—indeed they referred to it condescendingly as "a kind of little masterpiece"—but because of its Bunyanesque message of escape from a corrupt society and the search for perfection, a message calculated to advance the cause of Christianity.

In **Pitseng** Mofolo's earlier enthusiasm for the ways of the Whites begins to be tempered by an advocacy of caution. The mystique of the white man's superiority in all things has begun to be replaced by the discovery that he (the white man) is not so perfect or infallible after all, but is sometimes wrong, at times indeed alarmingly so, as in the case of his attitude to love, courtship and marriage.

Mofolo shows much empathy with the Zulu diviner, the Isanusi who, next to Chaka, is the most central figure in **Chaka,** Mofolo's third published novel. This despite the fact that the Isanusi is a traditional Zulu medical doctor-cum-spiritualist. Mofolo is neither apologetic nor condescending as he demonstrates the powers of the Isanusi.

Despite surface indications of alienation in his first two novels, there is no doubt that Mofolo retains a strong, if unconscious, loyalty to Sesotho culture and traditions as well as its definitions of heroism. There is an irrepressible enthusiasm about things Sesotho or, indeed, things African, which surfaces at moments of emotional excitement. Thus we see how, even after declaring over and over that Chaka has lost his claim to humanity and has become totally a beast, especially after his murder of Noliwe, Mofolo still admires certain qualities in him which appeal to his (Mofolo's) sense of manhood, of virility and masculinity. So, towards the ends when Chaka is weakened by his evil dreams and frightening nightmares, Mofolo still bubbles over with pure admiration. . . . (pp. 244-45)

Mofolo's reference to Chaka at the very end of the book is in eulogistic terms when he says:

> Ho bile jwalo ho fela ha Chaka, mora wa Senzangakhona . . .
>
> So it was, the end of Chaka, son of Senzangakhona

The associative reference son-of-Senzangakhona is a powerful affirmation of Chaka as a person of worth. Also, there is an unmistakable tone of nostalgia on Mofolo's part strongly suggested by the inversion of the syntax, which brings about subtle shifts of emphasis, in *So it was, the end of Chaka.* This nostalgia comes out a great deal more strongly as a national sentiment of the contemporary Zulu people when Mofolo concludes his powerful narrative with the words:

> MaZulu le kajeno a bokajeno ha a hopola kamoo e kileng ya eba batho kateng, mehleng ya Chaka, kamoo ditjhaba di neng di jela kgwebeleng ke ho ba tshoha, le ha ba hopola borena ba bona boo weleng, eba ba sekisa mahlong, ba re: "Di a bela di a hlweba! Madiba ho pjha a maholo!" . . .
>
> To this very day the Zulus, when they remember how they were once a great people, in the days of Chaka, and how the nations lived in mortal fear of them, and also when they remember their kingdom that fell, then tears well in their eyes, and they say, "They ferment, they curdle! Even mighty pools do dry away!"

Mofolo's sentiments of admiration and nostalgia are doubly significant in that they come from a severe judge who has previously expressed such negative feelings about Chaka. . . . (p. 246)

There is thus an intense relationship between Mofolo the author and Chaka the character, a relationship whose vicissitudes between love and hate are paralleled by the author's changing attitudes towards his character. These attitudes in turn are motivated by a variety of stimuli including Mofolo's new Christian ethic, the old Sesotho ethic, and the traditional admiration for the qualities of manhood.

There are syncretist tendencies in **Moeti oa bochabela,** in which Mofolo is most severe in his criticism of Basotho society, and in **Pitseng.** For example, the symbolism of light and darkness in **Moeti,** where Fekisi goes from a morass of darkness in search of light, the light that he first espies in a dream, which is to be his guiding light throughout his journey, comes out of Ntswanatsatsi, the place from which, according to Basotho myths of origins, all the people and living things originated, a place of birth and renewal. Thus in Fekisi's search for the Christian God, tradition intervenes, to point the way he is to go. In **Pitseng** Christian and traditional values are jointly responsible for the upright and virtuous lives of Aria Sebaka and Alfred Phakoe, which is important since these two characters are the models against whom the intemperate, reckless love lives of the other characters are seen and judged.

It is therefore not a simple context within which Mofolo defines his ethical standards and on which his judgement of his characters is based. Yet, despite its complexity, this context still yields but two basic types of character, namely ones that the author likes, and ones he does not like. There are, of course, other relationships the author may have with his characters. For example, he sometimes shows pity for a character who is overwhelmed by events; he may also display a paternalistic amusement at the foibles of a character; he may reflect the humility of a character. But all these are manifested within the broad framework of his affection or disaffection for the character in question.

This relationship of the writer to his characters is at the very center of the total experience that begins with him and ends with the reader, with the characters and their words and thoughts and deeds serving to bind them all together in what the author perceives as the pursuit of a common ideal. Like the oral narrator, the writer not only narrates, but he also reacts to the story, cuing the audience in the process. Indeed he sometimes becomes part of the audience and exclaims at the events in the story. This is what happens in *Moeti* where Mofolo writes that Fekisi has to find shelter in a hole to escape from a lion and a lioness that are attacking him. The lion pushes its head into the hole in an attempt to reach him, and he stabs it in the ear with his spear. Mofolo immediately switches roles and sees the whole scene from the point of view of the audience. He exclaims:

> Joo! Joo! Joo! Ruri jwale ya batla ho hlanya
> ke kgalefo. . . .

> Joo! Joo! Joo! Truly now it nearly went mad
> with anger.

One page later he repeats a closely parallel scene in which Fekisi stabs the lioness in the eye. Again Mofolo reacts in the same manner as he says:

> Ao! Ao! Ao! Ke re ruri ya etsa ntho tsee tsha-
> behang. . . .

> Ao! Ao! Ao! I say truly it did fearful things.

Before going into a detailed examination of the relationships described above, it is relevant to ask, Why does the author not simply narrate his story and let the characters and their actions speak for themselves? Why does he not detach himself from the action and give the reader an objective, non-partisan view of the story? At the very base of it all lies the fact that the author subscribes to a certain set of moral values which he regards as the *sine qua non* of his society. Like his oral narrative performer counterpart, he believes that justice must always prevail in the end, murder must out, evil must be punished and virtue rewarded. He believes that it is the business of all those who are involved in this human drama—the narrator, the actors and the audience—to ensure that these ends are achieved. The people must sit in judgement over the actions of the characters, with the narrator presiding over this court, so to speak. All through the story they observe the actions and sayings of the characters, they approve or condemn as the case may be. And throughout the story it is the narrator who, by description and impersonation, and by various kinds of reactions, brings together all the participants in the drama, and guides the people towards a fair and just assessment of the situation.

This is communalism at work, operating within the broad framework of humanism. For the writer does not approach his story with the cold detachment of a journalist. On the contrary, he never sees himself as anything but a human being who cannot help reacting, indeed must react, with sympathy to a human situation. Therefore throughout his story he closely watches every move and every syllable of his characters, and he comments on them. He manifests a relationship of Affection/Disaffection with them, loving those who do what he considers to be right, and hating those who do not conform to his patterns of behaviour.

The first indication of Mofolo as a severe judge of human character comes in the very opening sentence of his first book, *Moeti*, and is repeated several times within the first chapter of that book. In *Moeti* as well as in *Chaka*, Mofolo establishes a standard by which he rigorously distinguishes man from beast. Here are the first two sentences of *Moeti*:

> Lefifing le letsho lee reng tsho, mehleng ya ha ditjhaba di sa ntsane di jana jwale ka dibatana tsa naha, motho o ne a le teng yaa bitswang Fekisi. . . .

> In the black darkness that was pitch black, the days when the nations still ate each other like the wild beasts of the veld, there was a human being called Fekisi. . . .

Having told us that this human being was a "child-who-is-getter-up-with-the-heart-of-yesterday," that is, one who has a consistently good disposition towards other people, Mofolo reinforces his definition even further. . . . (pp. 247-49)

This "human being" is Fekisi, the hero of the story, the righteous young man who, having struggled in vain to correct what he perceives as the evils of his society, goes in search of a Utopia and of God. He finds both—and dies.

At the same time as he introduces his ideal human being, Mofolo tells us of "the nations" that "ate each other like the beasts of the wilds." A little later he singles out a neighbour of Fekisi's parents, one Phakoane who "was a human being when he had not taken any drink. But when he was drunk, he was wild beast." Phakoane is a regular drinker and a wife beater who ends up killing his wife in a drunken rage.

The world Mofolo creates for us in his books, then, is a world of human beings and beasts. But since, in fact, Mofolo gives us ample evidence of his admiration for the real beasts, namely the quadrupeds that roam the wilds in pristine innocence, the term *man-beast* more accurately describes the depraved people of his stories. Indeed, . . . animals which play a significant role in a story often arouse feelings of great admiration in the author, who then conveys his affection for them in the same way he does for a character he loves. Mofolo's message is, consistently, that to be a human being is all right; to be a beast is all right; but to be a man-beast is not all right, in fact, it is abominable.

One of the ways that are open to an involved author like Mofolo to express his involvement, is digression. When a writer uses this method, he has, of necessity, to interrupt his story, to temporarily suspend all action. In this interval he comes out from behind the scenes and speaks direct to his readers. We have a good example of this in *Chaka*. The fighting that follows Chaka's killing of a hyena to rescue the girl the hyena is carrying away, results in serious injuries for Mfokazana and Dingana, Chaka's half-brothers. Senzangakhona's senior wives are so furious that they demand that Chaka be killed. Senzangakhona gives the order: "Kill him!" This is a critical moment in Chaka's life, a moment of separation. The umbilical cord is snapped, and he is truly on his own. Mofolo concludes this chapter in true Aesopian style when he says:

> Kgaohanyong ena re fumana hore efela ruri tholwana ya sebe e le bohloko ka mokgwa oo makatsang, hobane ha re bone tshito ya Chaka tabeng tsena, empa le ha ho le jwalo ntat'ae o laela hore a bolawe. Molatolato, sesosa, ke hobane Nandi hammoho le Senzangakhona ba ne ba na le modimo; mme Senzangakhona, moo a tshabang ha ditaba tsa hae di tsejwa, a ba a rera ho bolaya mora wa hae. Athe hoja Senzangakhona a se etse ditaba tsena tsee dihlong

botjheng ba hae, Chaka a ka be a le hae ha
habo, Nobamba, e le ngwana wa mpowane,
ngwana yaa hlokolotsi haholo ho ntat'ae. . . .

In this chapter we find that it is indeed true that
the fruit of sin is bitter to an amazing degree,
because we do not see any transgression on
Chaka's part in these matters, yet, even though
this is so, his father commands that he be killed.
The real issue, the cause of it all, is that Nandi
and Senzangakhona suffer from guilt, and Senzangakhona, fearing lest these secret matters
should become known, went so far as to kill
his own son. Yet, if Senzangakhona had not
committed this shameful deed in his youth,
Chaka would have been at his home at Nobamba, a precious child, truly beloved of his
father.

The detrimental effect of this digression as an interruption of
the narrative is mitigated by the fact that it occurs at the end
of a chapter, where there is a natural division. The only other
such Aesopian conclusion in this book comes at the end of
chapter 9 where Mofolo expresses surprise that Chaka fails to
tell his mother the whole story about Malunga and Ndlebe,
making no mention at all of Malunga and only a casual reference to Ndlebe, making no mention at all of Malunga and
only a casual reference to Ndlebe by saying simply that he had
"found himself a fool who will carry his blankets." (pp. 249-50)

Most of the digressions in *Chaka* occur in the bodies of the
chapters where they are more likely to jolt the reader as intrusive elements. Yet, so much is Mofolo is control of his narrative
that the reader tends to be oblivious of these interferences.

Whether, or to what extent, digression can be considered as
having a potential for enhancing a writer's style, is a moot
point. One incontrovertible fact is that a digression is a very
convenient potential vehicle for moral lessons. Indeed, all the
digressions we have quoted or referred to so far have no other
purpose but to carry a homily. Therefore while it would, perhaps, be rash to consider them totally without any aesthetic
potential in fiction, one must nevertheless point out the unlikelihood of this being the case, and simultaneously the danger
that they could be used as propaganda vehicles. There is abundant evidence of this where African language writers plead the
cause of the Christian missions and of the westernization process to their readers, while condemning their own.

Further, it should be pointed out that to separate narrative from
digression is not always as easy as it might seem. For example,
at the end of the first war Chaka fights for Dingiswayo, namely
the war against Zwide, Mofolo refers to the songs composed
for him by the women. . . . There is here a mixture of Mofolo's
parenthetical reaction to a situation in the story, combined with
a narrative of that very situation.

But, even with all things considered, it remains nevertheless
true that a digression creates a dangerous vacuum in the story,
one that is liable to suck in the nearest thing to it. And that,
usually, is the message that the writer is either incapable of
building into his narrative, or considers to be so important that
it needs to be singled out and "told like it is."

A resourceful Sesotho prose writer, however, does not have
to rely solely, or even mainly on digression and other interruptions of narrative to convey his reactions to the events and
characters in his story. The Sesotho language— its idiom, its

syntax, its store of emotive words; the Sesotho tradition that
lays so much store on the relationship of a person to other
people, and to places of abode or of origin as contextualizing
factors that give him strong affirmation as a social being, one
who belongs, who has antecedents; the Sesotho traditional communalism that makes every man his brother's keeper—all these
factors, as well as others . . . , are often used by the writer
within the stream of his narrative. They then serve the triple
purpose of defining the writer's relationship to his characters,
advancing the narrative, and enhancing its aesthetic appeal.
(p. 251)

> *Daniel P. Kunene, "Writer, Reader and Character
> in African Language Literature: Towards a New Def-
> inition," in* Neo-African Literature and Culture: Es-
> says in Memory of Janheinz Jahn, *edited by Bernth
> Lindfors and Ulla Schild, B. Heymann, 1976, pp.
> 243-57.*

DONALD BURNESS   (essay date 1976)

[*In the following excerpt from his* Shaka, King of the Zulu's, in
African Literature, *Burness provides a detailed analysis of Chaka's character and examines Mofolo's novel as a masterpiece
which makes selective use of elements from African and Western
literary traditions and Christian philosophy.*]

Mofolo's *Chaka* has been called "the first historical novel in
modern African literature and a masterpiece." Yet the narrative
does not fit into a convenient generic category. It can be considered an extended praise song singing the deeds of this heroic
Zulu leader; it can be regarded as an African epic celebrating
the founding of an empire; it can be treated as a five act dramatic
prose tragedy. In fact, Ezekiel Mphahlele has compared it to
Tamburlaine, Dr. Faustus, King Lear and *Richard III* [see
excerpt dated 1962]. Such comparisons are not exaggerated as
I shall show in this chapter. Mofolo himself definitely felt that
his work was a serious presentation of the history of a people:

> The country of South Africa is a large peninsula
> lying between two oceans, one to the east and
> one to the west of it. Its inhabitants belong to
> many and various tribes speaking different lan-
> guages, yet they all fall easily into three main
> divisions. . . . The differences are so striking
> that any one travelling from west to east feels
> them at once, and when he arrives among the
> Basuto of the midlands he realizes . . . that he
> has come into a different country among dif-
> ferent people. He feels the difference further
> when he crosses the mountains and comes down
> among the Matebele living on the other side.
>
> Our story is concerned with the eastern tribes,
> the Kafirs, and before we begin it we must
> describe the state of these tribes in the early
> days, so that the reader may be able to follow
> the narrative in the succeeding chapters.

Certainly the style of this passage is direct and clear. It lacks
the variety and eloquence of language characteristic of many
fictional works. It seems that Mofolo's intent is non-literary,
that the author is an historian of his people. But the tone and
ostensible purpose established in the early pages of his *Chaka*
are not continued throughout the book. I suggest that such
discrepancies in generic interpretation are neither novel nor
inexplicable. The western reader who has been schooled in the

tradition of Aristotle and Boileau often tends to judge literary merit on the basis of European artistic ideals. (pp. 2-3)

Mofolo's *Chaka,* it must be remembered, is not a European work. The author synthesizes the tradition of African story telling with its songs and bits of moralizing and Christian philosophy. Mofolo is writing for an audience largely unfamiliar with tribal ritual. Therefore, he must make explicit those patterns of behaviour that a native Zulu or Sotho would understand implicitly. For instance, he explains the intricacies of the custom of witch-doctors prescribing medicines as follows:

> It is the rule in cases like this or in prescribing medicines for sterility or disease that the witch-doctor should insist that his patient undertake to carry out his orders, although, if he thinks what he commands is too difficult, he can refuse. The rule is thus, because if the patient leaves without having definitely refused to obey, the witch-doctor can claim his fee even if his services have been of no avail.

Mofolo's work, as well as much of modern African literature, constitutes a fusion of native culture and Western literary tradition. Since the novel is not endemic to Africa, the African writer of narrative finds himself free to experiment with form. The *Chaka* of Mofolo represents the African genius borrowing what is artistically useful from African and alien traditions. Such contemporary novelists as Gabriel Okara, Yambo Ouologuem, Chiekh Hamidou Kane, and Wole Soyinka can be equally baffling to the reader conditioned to see the novel as a purely Western genre.

The Bible was the principal model that existed for Sotho writers in the early part of the twentieth century. Although *Pilgrim's Progress* had been translated into Xhosa and Zulu by the turn of the century, there was no translation of Bunyan's Christian allegory in Sotho. Certainly, Mofolo must have studied the Bible in great depth for there are distinct stylistic and thematic parallels between *Chaka* and tales in both the Old and New Testaments. The simplicity of language, the elevated tone, the use of the second person 'thee' and 'thou' (probably inspired by the editors of the Morija Press or by other missionary supporters; certainly such usage is alien to any African spirit that I know), the tendency to begin sentences with 'and' as well as the justification of Christian goodness are Biblical elements common to Mofolo's historical novel. Certainly the moral basis of Mofolo's judgments resulted from his Christianity.

Yet it is a diversity of composition rather than a homogeneous style that characterizes Mofolo's writing. Such a stylistic cocktail is evident in the following passage:

> When it had made an end, it raised its head to the level of Chaka's eyes and looked closely at him, and its hot foul-smelling breath covered him like steam; then it licked his eyes again and his whole face, and went backwards into the water, still keeping his eyes fixed upon him.

> Chaka did not see where the body of the snake ended, for there was always part of it hidden in the water; that is to say, not even Chaka knew how long it was. When it finally disappeared the water of the river was agitated in a fearsome manner and swelled up again: a cold wind blew and the reeds waved and twisted, and a thick mist rose from the pool like a col-

umn of cloud and enveloped Chaka, so that he could see nothing even of things near him, and in the reeds something sang in a voice loud and deep:

> "Mphu-mphu ahe-ee
> Kalamajoeng, Kalamajoeng.
> Mphu-mphu ahe-ee
> Kalamajoeng, Kalamajoeng.
> There is a great monster in the water,
> Kalamajoeng, Kalamajoeng.
> Seen only by the favoured,
> Kalamajoeng, Kalamajoeng.
> Seen only by those who are born to rule the
> nations,
> Kalamajoeng, Kalamajoeng."

The words were repeated twice, and then there was silence. And then a very gentle voice sang,

> "Ahe, ahe. The world is thine, child of my
> own people,
> Thou shalt rule the nations and their governors,
> Thou shalt rule all the nations of men,
> Thou shalt rule all the winds and the storms of
> the sea
> And the deep pools of the mighty rivers,
> And all things shall obey thy word.
> They shall kneel down beneath thy feet.
> E, oi, oi. But beware thou takest the right path."

The fusion of concrete description and supernatural mystery has its source in African oral storytelling and the song in the reeds sung by beautiful voices is pure African. To emphasize the fact, the author does not translate those African words that are part of the chant. This tendency to introduce musical elements in a literary work manifests a characteristic element of many African people. Leopold Sedar Senghor, the apostle of "Negritude," has proclaimed on various occasions that music is an integral part of the African personality. The German Africanist Janheinz Jahn has demonstrated structural elements common to certain African praise songs and some blues form in America. Praise songs are spontaneous oral poetic creations, which often celebrate the deeds of particular individuals. Such poems are most frequently created in the presence of the entire community so that the celebration is communal rather than individual. In Mofolo's novel Shaka's ego finds satisfaction from hearing, on numerous occasions, his feats praised by particular singers or poets. The recurring patterns in the song in the reeds, I suppose, parallels those of various Zulu praise songs. Repetition is common to this form of the praise song. The initial ten lines include repetition of "Kalamajoeng, Kalamajoeng" on five occasions. The first and third lines as well repeat one another. (pp. 3-5)

The episode of the meeting between Shaka and the serpentine Lord of the Deep Waters suggests another traditional African cultural element—the inclination to explain human behavior and natural phenomena through fable, legend or myth. Ulli Beier has edited, for instance, a remarkable collection of colorful and inventive creation myths which are culturally as valid as those Christian myths we cherish so much. Despite his Christian upbringing, Mofolo is an African personality who goes to great lengths to convince the reader of the importance of witch doctors and sorcerers as viable forces at work within traditional Zulu and Sotho societies. (pp. 5-6)

The second part of the song in the reeds differs considerably from the first. Although it begins with a spontaneous shout 'Ahe, ahe,' the song is more Christian than traditional. There are no African words nor is there a distinct pattern of repetition even though the second, third and fourth lines begin alike. The moral warning at the conclusion of the chant and the frequent use of the 'thou', 'thine' and 'thy' have a Biblical source. Mofolo has succeeded in incorporating both traditional and Christian concepts into one prose song.

Another example of stylistic variety occurs on those occasions when the author breaks away from his narrative to speak directly to the reader:

> I do not think that anyone's life was ever so involved in mystery as was Chaka's. Dingiswayo's life is obscure and hidden, but when the facts are known they can be easily understood. But with Chaka all is mysterious. . . .
>
> (p. 6)

Mofolo's feeling towards Shaka is best characterized as ambiguous. There is a curious mixture of contempt for his cruelty and malice, and respect for his awe inspiring deeds. Shaka is not merely a brutal tyrant; Mofolo deliberately provides the reader with pertinent background information which in part may explain Shaka's mania for killing. Two primary sources of the Zulu leader's proclivity to violence are suggested: his illegitimacy and his father's unwillingness to help him overcome social ostracism. In fact, his father directly contributes to his childhood isolation. Shaka's father, Senzangakona, who rules the little tribe of Mazulu, has three or four wives, none of whom has produced a male child for the chief. Senzangakona is grievously upset, as he desperately desires an heir. He is not among fortune's minions. Out of despair and lust for Nandi, a girl from a neighboring village, he gets her pregnant. They are married soon thereafter and a son, Shaka, is born. However, the conception of a child out of wedlock is an egregious violation of tribal law to the extent that a guilty party can be punished by death. The messenger who announces to Senzangakona the birth of his son comments, "A child is born to thee, an ox to feed the vultures." What supreme irony, for those souls who are directly or indirectly slain by Shaka are to be eaten by vultures. After Shaka's birth Senzangakona knows only trouble and discontent. It was thought that witchcraft prohibited his wives from being able to bear male children. Yet soon after Shaka's entrance into the world three other sons are born to Senzangakona—Mfokazana, Dingana, and Mhlingana. The mothers of these legitimate children grow most hostile to Nandi as her son has been declared heir. The wives challenge Senzangakona to abandon Nandi and Shaka. Moreover, they refuse to recognize Shaka's right to the chieftainship. They go as far as to send for a witch-doctor to turn Senzangakona's heart from Nandi so that his conscience will trouble him whenever he contemplates visiting her. Mofolo does not present this specific witch-doctor as the one whose power causes Senzangakona to go so long without producing a male child. Nevertheless, the mention of his existence presages the triptych of witch-doctors whose roles cannot be overestimated in the novel. Senzangakona surrenders to his wives who threaten to declaim in public the facts relating to Nandi's pregnancy.

As a young child Shaka is remarkable in that he seldom shows signs of weakness. . . . Moreover, when he is still quite young,

a woman witch-doctor at Pokoni, renowned for bringing good luck, visits Shaka to doctor him with medicines that he may be fortunate in all things. . . . (pp. 6-7)

Shaka's childhood somewhat resembles that of Jacob's favorite son, Joseph, in the Bible. He is ill-treated by most of the other boys. When he is herding calves he is continually tormented and abused by other herdboys. They often pounce upon him, giving the poor boy terrible thrashings. They are inspired by the community itself which feels that it would be a good thing if the illegitimate Shaka were killed. Because of his frequent battles Shaka becomes a skilled combatant. His lithe body and quick reflexes aid him in developing his capacity for self-defense. Shaka's grandmother, distressed at his pugilistic activities that are causing him frequent injuries, takes him away and gives him work scaring birds from the cornfields. Still, he is mocked and teased by the other bird scarers. In fact, the herdboys, having grown accustomed to their ritualistic beating of Shaka, seek him out in the corn fields where they seize him and beat him. Shaka loses consciousness and, like his Biblical counterpart, is thrown into a ditch where he is left for dead. Fortunately, a passing woman rescues him. The arduous childhood of Shaka is emphasized by Mofolo so that the reader can better understand his transformation into a raving killer.

As frustrating as are his confrontations with his peers, Shaka refuses to lament his plight. He is able, with the aid of witchcraft, to overcome his aggressive coevals. The witchdoctor provides him with two kinds of medicine: one enables him to become brave and warlike; the other gives him courage and makes him fearless. From that time Shaka loves fighting. He is able to defeat the gang of herdboys who then let him alone. Shortly thereafter, he becomes their leader. Yet his travails are merely beginning. His brothers, jealous of his strength and his ever increasing fame, plot to murder him. Mfokazana, the eldest, is especially envious, for Shaka once threatened his dignity. He remembers how a wild hyena entered Mfokazana's hut and seized his lover. She gave forth screams of agony, but all in the hut were too petrified to move, for they had always trembled upon hearing the hyena's praise song. . . . (pp. 7-8)

That particular night Shaka was sleeping in a separate outhouse with a few others. Upon hearing a girl scream, he immediately sought out the feared beast and killed it with his spear. The companions of the girl sang songs extolling Shaka and ridiculed the disgraced Mfokazana. Rage consumed Mfokazana whose wrath demanded the death of Shaka. In a passage reminiscent of battle descriptions in *The Iliad*, Mofolo describes with truculent realism the conflict between the brothers. . . . But the final straw was yet to come. Senzangakona arrived on the scene and without questioning the cause of the conflict ordered Shaka to be killed. . . . (pp. 8-9)

Mofolo concludes this pivotal scene by remarking that Shaka was not the culpable aggressor but rather the unfortunate victim of moral and physical injustice. Mofolo postulates that had Senzangakona not betrayed Shaka, the son would have lived with his father and become his beloved darling. It is no wonder that Shaka feels himself a pariah in a hostile universe where his presence threatens the security of those around him. It is necessary to realize that Mofolo seeks to explain (not to justify) the evolution of Shaka's barbarism. To this extent *Chaka* is a psychological novel wherein character motivation is not gratuitous, but rather the result of specific childhood experiences. . . .

Mofolo has carefully laid the groundwork for Shaka's fateful encounter with . . . [a] witch-doctor. It is not until Shaka has abandoned all belief in the efficacy of moral virtue that he is visited by Isanusi. (p. 10)

Shaka recognizes at once the evil in Isanusi; he sees in his eyes unbounded hatred and cruelty. The witch-doctor is described as the "very father of malice, wickedness and treachery." If we remember that Mofolo is a believing Christian, then it is safe to assume that Isanusi is a devil-figure, destined to tempt the souls of all who abandon faith in virtue. He is an African Mephistopheles. But to explain his function in purely allegorical terms does not suffice. *Chaka* does contain elements of a medieval Christian morality play in which the writer teaches the society that evil is to be avoided and that goodness is to be preferred. In his introduction to *Chaka* Sir Henry Newbolt affirms that "he (Mofolo) is a soul by nature Christian and sees in every crisis the clash of good and evil" [see excerpt dated 1931]. True enough. However, Mofolo as a writer does not permit his religious convictions to detract from his art. Isanusi is evil incarnate; yet, like the supernatural witches in *Macbeth*, his power depends upon the abnegation of conscience in his intended victims. On a psychological level the witch-doctor symbolizes all that is evil within Shaka's personality. "Isanusi is a symbol of Shaka's other self," a ubiquitous force that has gained dominance in the heart and soul of the future leader. It is no less than a stroke of genius that Mofolo succeeds in creating out of this witch-doctor a psychological embodiment of malice and at the same time an archetypal symbol of the devil.

I am not suggesting, however, that Mofolo's novel be seen as an African morality play, for, despite the use of allegory for didactic purposes, *Chaka* is an African work. In a European Christian world it is God who ultimately rewards or punishes. Such eschatological concern is anathema to African societies, where the community itself is the ultimate judge of the individual's fate. Certainly Mofolo is a Christian, but he is not a European.

Shaka immediately becomes convinced that Isanusi is his only ally in a world that has neglected him. The witch-doctor's command is direct and simple; he assures Shaka that he can fulfill all promises if Shaka binds himself to whatever commandments Isanusi may give. Shaka at once swears allegiance to his new acquaintance, for he feels that at last fortune has provided him with a means to gain the chieftainship that his brother and father have sought to deny him. The witch-doctor proceeds to doctor Shaka with a variety of potent medicines. (pp. 10-11)

It is significant that Isanusi cannot bestow power unless Shaka willingly desires it. Shaka, not Isanusi, chooses death over life. Such a simple choice in the hands of a bloodthirsty tyrant eventually produces repression, fear, torture and a tendency towards a personality cult. Mofolo's Shaka is an historical confrere of Hitler, Stalin and other modern political leaders whose ambition for personal glory was accomplished by a rejection of life-giving forces. The latter two-thirds of *Chaka* is a working out of Isanusi's command that Shaka must kill mercilessly in order to gain greater power and fame. Isanusi appeals to Shaka's manhood. . . . (p. 11)

[A] masculine ideal and its relationship to fame is a major theme in African literature recalling life in the pre-classical period. For instance, the conduct of Okonkwo, the hero of Chinua Achebe's first novel, *Things Fall Apart,* conforms to the view that a man must at all times be aggressive, valiant and brutally cruel.

Isanusi provides Shaka with two witch-doctor guardians, Ndlebe and Malunga. The former is a bestial, repulsive man whose unique capacity for ferreting out secrets makes him a valuable ally. On various occasions, Ndlebe warns Shaka of the plans of an enemy force or an incipient revolt among his own ranks. Malunga, on the other hand, doctors the regiments so that they are valorous and obedient. Shaka's two attendants, like their master, Isanusi, desert him when death is near, for their ultimate goal is possession of his spirit. Ezekiel Mphahlele's assessment that ultimately Shaka is a religious king must be taken with a grain of salt [see excerpt dated 1962]. It is true as Mphahlele asserts that Shaka believes that Isanusi, his personal witch-doctor, is an efficient intercessor between the living and the ancestors. It is also true that in traditional African society the witch-doctor is not only a dealer in charms but is the moral conscience of his people. We find examples of this in Achebe's *Arrow of God,* Peter Abrahams' *Wild Conquest,* and Flora Nwapa's *Efuru.* Modern day religious "witch-doctors" are satirized by Wole Soyinka in *The Trial of Brother Jero* and *The Interpreters.* But Isanusi only reflects the inner nature of Shaka. He is as much Shaka's servant as Shaka is his. If Shaka is a religious king then his religion is that of self-glorification and brutality.

Mofolo's antithesis to Isanusi and his evil companions is Dingiswayo, the chief under whom Senzangakona serves. The gentle ruler represents the ideal king as seen from a humanistic viewpoint. He is what Shaka might become were he of a generous nature. . . . (p. 12)

Time and again we see the moral integrity and compassion of Dingiswayo whose actions are never motivated by revenge or personal glory. Years before Shaka's birth, Senzangakona harassed the youthful Dingiswayo and even planned to kill him. Since that time Senzangakona secretly feared that his chief was determined to punish him. Such was not the case, however. When Shaka, on the other hand, learns that his uncle is plotting against him, he orders him killed with dispatch.

Mofolo carefully recounts only those events in the life of Dingiswayo that illuminate by contrast the character of Shaka. The mysterious death by illness of Senzangakona is a case in point. Upon hearing from Ndlebe of his father's demise, Shaka's immediate concern is the vacant chieftainship and the fulfillment of Isanusi's promises. Dingiswayo in contrast, is saddened at the loss of his subordinate. He feels compelled to restrain the impetuous Shaka for six months from the active pursuit of his goal so that the latter will not dishonor his dead father by immediately waging war with Mfokazana who has been installed as chief in his father's stead. Shaka reluctantly accepts Dingiswayo's counsel.

Like Shakespeare's Prospero, Dingiswayo's goodness fails to capture the fire and imagination of his people. He is a civilizing agent in a world that prefers power and animal destructiveness to human virtue and wisdom. That Dingiswayo's goodness is not reciprocated either by his followers or his enemies offends the sensibilities of political and moral humanists. The unfortunate man meets his death at the hands of his enemy, Zwide, after he has been taken prisoner. Mofolo carefully establishes a moral contrast to such brutality, for formerly Zwide was captured by Shaka for Dingiswayo: "The noble king detained his prisoner only a few days, and then released him, and sent him to his home in peace as if he had paid a friendly visit and were never a prisoner." The juxtaposition of Dingiswayo's mercy with the total lack of human sentiment on the part of Zwide and Shaka heighten the contrast Mofolo is making.

Chaka is a political work. Mofolo is concerned with the nature of power and the destiny of African peoples. Because of this, his novel has much in common with contemporary African literature. Mofolo's Dingiswayo is an ancestor of Ezeulu, the chief character in Achebe's *Arrow of God,* and Roland Medo and Biere Ekonte in John Munonye's novel of the Biafran war, *A Wreath for the Maidens.* He is a thinker who tries to understand history and seeks above all the welfare of his people. But historical forces and human nature are such that he fails. This is his tragedy in a novel that deals primarily with a man very much unlike him.

The untimely death of Senzangakona provides Shaka with the opportunity he has longed for. . . . Dingiswayo provides his celebrated warrior with one of his own companies to help him in the inevitable battle. In the fight Mfokazana is overcome and slain. Shaka intends to destroy Dingana and Mhlangana as well but Ndlebe begs that their lives be spared. Mofolo innocently claims that Ndlebe's conduct is incomprehensible. . . . (pp. 13-14)

It is only towards the end of the novel that Ndlebe's apparently inconsistent behavior is understood. Dingana and Mhlangana are unwittingly agents of the malevolent witch-doctors in their scheme to capture the soul of Shaka. Ndlebe's seeming mercy is a ploy to spare the men who will murder Shaka in the future.

Having attained his father's chieftainship, Shaka is visited again by Isanusi. There is a distinct pattern to the timing of the great diviner's visitations. He comes to Shaka at pivotal moments when the Zulu warrior's soul is most susceptible. On this particular occasion Isanusi advises Shaka to wet his spear with blood if he desires a chieftainship as great as that of Dingiswayo. Like Macbeth, Shaka has come to believe that supernatural forces are guarding his destiny. Shaka is not satisfied with his father's chieftainship. He desires greater fame and Isanusi is there to stimulate and encourage his lust for power. . . .

Zwide captures and kills Dingiswayo. Isanusi's promises to Shaka are now to be realized. Shaka is chosen chief by Dingiswayo's regiments on condition that he marry his beloved Noliwe, sister of Dingiswayo. Such a union would join the tribe of Shaka to that of Dingiswayo. Thus, the unwanted youth who was abandoned by his father ascends another step in his quest for fame and glory.

In recording Shaka's rise, Mofolo, the historian, emphasizes the mysteriousness of the man. The author seems at a loss to explain certain events in the life of the ruler whose very essence defies complete understanding: "I do not think that anyone's life was ever so involved in mystery." The effect of Mofolo's personal confusion lends to the mystique of Shaka's mythical qualities. Shaka becomes more than a mere mortal; his life is as fantastical as it is real. (p. 15)

There is less doubt and confusion in Mofolo's mind as he recounts the period of Shaka's greatest triumphs and most horrendous cruelties. The success of Shaka's rule stems from his knowledge that fear alone on the part of the masses assures a workable totalitarian government. (p. 16)

[It] is clear that either through instinct or careful consideration he recognizes the practical necessity of terror as a means of coordinating disparate tribal elements into a cohesive force whose "raison d'etre" is the glorification of Shaka's name. Therefore, Shaka instigates a series of reforms and regulations. The captured forces of Zwide are given the opportunity to join Shaka's regiment. His ambition is to make them Zulus in heart

and soul. It is characteristic of his chieftainship that conquered forces augment his own army. Secondly, the education of children excludes parental influences. At an early age a young male child is taken to the regiments where he learns true manhood. His entire education concerns itself with preparations for a military career. Spears, battle axes and shields become his toys. Thirdly, Shaka puts an end to the tribal custom of circumcision, saying that the art of killing rather than circumcision makes a man. One cannot underestimate the revolutionary impact of such a decree. Circumcision was among the most characteristic rituals of many pre-Colonial African societies. Modern novelists as diverse as James Ngugi in *The River Between* and Camara Laye in *L'Enfant Noir* emphasize the cultural significance of circumcision. Ngugi juxtaposes Christian teaching that circumcision is a heathen and unsanitary act with the Kikuyu belief that circumcision represents initiation into manhood or womanhood. In fact, in his novel, the circumcision conflict becomes emblematic of the dissolution of a way of life. It is ironic that Shaka advocates eliminating circumcision long before the invasion of the white colonialists. Fourthly, Shaka forbids his regiments to marry for many years, for he feels that an unmarried man will not be thinking of his wife and children in the heat of battle. This reform is perhaps as striking as that condemning circumcision, for as Mofolo states:

> The reader must remember that above all else
> on earth the Black Races love to marry. Often
> in speaking of the good things of life people
> do not mention marriage, because marriage is
> life.

Fifthly, Shaka revolutionizes the art of warfare. He teaches his forces to abandon the accepted techniques of throwing the spear at an enemy. Instead, he encourages them to use the spear as a stabbing instrument. If a warrior returns from war without his single spear or without a captured spear to go along with it, he is put to death. Lastly, Shaka teaches his regiments a term of greeting him, "Bayete", which means "He that is between God and man" or "The little God through whom the Great God rules all the chiefs and tribes upon earth."

This concept of the King being God's (be he Nkulunkulu or the Christian God) representative on earth has a distinct parallel in European thought. In the plays of Marlowe, Shakespeare, and Corneille, for instance, the audience assumes the king to be a divine servant of God. The idea of the great chain of being in which, after God and the nine branches of angels, the king constitutes the highest level of existence in the universe, flourished from before the Middle Ages until recent times. Mofolo raises the same question in metaphysical terms as Shakespeare in his history plays and in *Macbeth*—what is to be done when the highest and most divine being, the king, turns out to be a criminal? An interesting and complex problem with no easy solution. . . . Mofolo, the historian, refuses to see in Shaka a divine spirit. On the contrary, the Zulu ruler's satanic egocentrism elicits Mofolo's opprobrium.

Shaka's cruelty goes beyond the bounds of political necessity. The deliberate murders of Noliwe, his betrothed, and Nandi, his mother, shock even the sensibilities of the modern reader, accustomed to the horrors of wars and natural disasters. Internecine slaughter, more than anything else, refutes the vision of man as a civilized animal.

Shaka's marriage to Noliwe has been delayed because of a rather unusual problem. Since Shaka is the chief of the various tribes, to whom is he to pay a bride price for Noliwe? This dilemma has to be resolved as Noliwe has become pregnant. Upon visiting Shaka again Isanusi proposes to him the possibility of greater conquests and increased power but only upon the condition that he slay Noliwe.... (pp. 16-18)

Isanusi is overjoyed at Shaka's response referring to him as "a man after my own heart." Shaka has decided that fame, glory and untold riches are of more value than friendship, morality or love. Mphahlele's comparisons of Mofolo's *Chaka* with Marlowe's *Tamburlaine* and *Doctor Faustus* merit explanation. Like Faustus, Shaka "sells his soul" to a devil-figure with magical powers, in order to learn the innermost secrets of the universe. Of course Faustus' desire to repent is stronger at the end of his life than Shaka's, whose impending death does not bring forth a hunger for spiritual redemption. Nevertheless, Shaka's loss of reason, his insanity, can be equated with Faustus' hysteria. The differences, of course, are many, for Mofolo's world, in contrast to Marlowe's, is equally "pagan" as it is Christian. Whereas *Dr. Faustus* is a play concerned primarily with sin and redemption, *Chaka* is the history of a tyrannical ruler who firmly believes destiny to be his helper. In this sense, Mphahlele's comparison between *Chaka* and *Tamburlaine* is understood. Tamburlaine, Richard III, Macbeth, Iago, Edmund and Claudius are Elizabethan portraits of ambitious men willing to use whatever means possible to insure the success of their stratagems. Shaka belongs to this gallery of literary men of ambition.

The murder of the innocent Noliwe is followed immediately by that of her girl-in-waiting. Shaka blames her in public for not revealing the putative illness of Noliwe that supposedly caused her death. The murder of his mother is equally horrible for Isanusi in no way influences Shaka's decision to kill her. Shaka has many concubines whom he discards at will, often having them killed. On many occasions children are born to Shaka's concubines. He orders all such infants immediately put to death as well as the mothers who weep for them. Nandi, who has longed for grandchildren, steals one of Shaka's pregnant concubines and hides her far off until her child is born. Then the girl returns to Shaka and leaves the child where it is. Ndlebe, of course, knows of the birth of the child and reports to Shaka that he has become a father. The Zulu chieftain becomes angry and immediately kills his mother with a needle in the same way he killed Noliwe. He is relieved to rid himself of her nagging voice, for she particularly irritated him when he wanted to kill.

Shaka is now so completely dominated by suspicion, doubt and insecurity that he is only able to ease his tormented mind by further killing.... Whenever he conquers a people Shaka kills all who are married as well as the old people and children, for the former are too set in their ways to become true Zulus and the latter will evoke pity if they are left when their parents are gone. The young boys are to become Zulu soldiers while the young girls are made slaves to serve the soldiers. No wonder neighboring tribes flee Shaka's batallions. As a result of this peripatetic activity and mass slaughter, famine becomes more common. Because of the famine people first begin to eat one another. Mofolo recounts that the first cannibal was a Kafir named Undave who lived near where the city of Durban is today. Many tribes are completely wiped out including the Amaqwabe, the Amafunze, the Abatembu, the Amacunu, the Amakunze, and Abakwamacibise, the Amabomvu and the Amatuli. Mofolo makes it clear the Shaka's great conquests result in a more barbaric society than existed before his political ascension.

Mofolo never directly states that Shaka becomes insane; however, there are various overt references to his mental disorder.... (pp. 19-20)

The sources of Shaka's nightmares and terrible doubts are not psychologically explained by Mofolo. Certainly neither an overwhelming sense of guilt nor a sudden religiosity (in the Christian sense) alters Shaka's psychic state. On the contrary, his insatiable blood lust increases proportionately as his kingdom expands. It seems to me that Shaka's increased fears and suspicions are almost inevitable, for in a totalitarian state the king or chief or prince becomes a victim of his own tactics. Government by fear historically breeds a state of mistrust and insecurity. Shaka comes to see potential enemies in his most faithful lieutenants; he becomes hysterically jealous of the successes of his military leaders. No one is safe from his wrath, especially after Umziligazi, his commander-in-chief, deserts him to establish his own kingdom in a distant land.

To insure his position Shaka kills, at random, Nongogo, a leader of one of the regiments and a man who lives only to please his chief, but has the misfortune to be loved by the people. (p. 20)

Shaka's unquenchable thirst for violence results in a loss of confidence on the part of his soldiers and his people. No longer is he praised for his wisdom and the righteousness of his judgments; no longer is he the infallible prime mover of his society. This lack of confidence in him increases the tempo of his killings. Thousands of his own men are executed on the grounds of participating in a putative conspiracy.

Shaka's decreasing mental health is accompanied by a severe physical illness. Seeing that their brother is now vulnerable, Dingana and Mhlangana plan to assassinate him. It is without difficulty that their plot is carried out. Mofolo implies that had he not been assassinated, Shaka might very well have died from the disease that was afflicting him.

Even in death, Shaka is portrayed as a heroic figure on the one hand and as a moral failure on the other. As Shaka breathes his last, Isanusi comes to collect his reward. Both Ndlebe and Malunga permit the assassination, for they could very easily have warned Shaka and protected him, if necessary. But as servants to Isanusi they are not going to defy the wishes of their master. Isanusi's gestures of friendship to Shaka are not gratuitous; Isanusi knows full well that at his death Shaka's spirit will never ascend to an abode of peace. Yet even in death Shaka inspires fear.... (pp. 21-2)

The novel closes with a recollection that in Shaka's epoch the Africans had dignity and self-respect. Mofolo, like contemporary African writers, celebrates dignity. (p. 22)

Mofolo's basic optimism and sense of dignity has not been lost in Africa. The fact that his novel has served as a source for various heroic treatments of Shaka is ample evidence that the spirit of affirmation is still strong.

Ultimately, Thomas Mofolo's contribution to African literature cannot be overestimated. He has succeeded in creating a world, both Christian and African, that speaks of the best and noblest instincts in man while recognizing human failings. In this sense we can understand *Chaka*'s being called a masterpiece, for it belongs among the major works of twentieth century literature. (p. 23)

Donald Burness, "Thomas Mofolo's 'Chaka'," in his Shaka, King of the Zulus, in African Literature, *Three Continents Press, 1976, pp. 1-24.*

ADDITIONAL BIBLIOGRAPHY

Armah, Ayi Kwei. A review of *Chaka. Black World* XXVI, No. 4 (February 1975): 51-2.
    Discusses Mofolo's characterization of Chaka.

Franz, G. H. "The Literature of Lesotho." *Bantu Studies* IV (1930): 145-80.
    Bibliographical information, plot summaries, and criticism of Lesothan literature, including Mofolo's novels.

Gleason, Judith Illsley. "The Heroic Legacy in Africa." In her *This Africa: Novels by West Africans in English and French*, pp. 41-68. Evanston, Ill.: Northwestern University Press, 1965.
    Examines the influence of the African oral tradition upon the historical romance in modern African literature. In the essay, Gleason also discusses historical and imaginative elements in *Chaka*.

Gollock, G. A. A review of *The Traveller to the East. Africa* VII, No. 4 (October 1934): 510-11.
    Plot outline and review.

Ikonne, Chidi. "Thomas Mofolo's Narrator." In *Aspects of South African Literature*, edited by Christopher Heywood, pp. 54-65. New York: Africana Publishing Co., 1976.
    Analyses the narrative voice as a key to understanding characterization in *Chaka*.

Jahn, Janheinz. "The Tragedy of Southern Bantu Literature." In his *Neo-African Literature: A History of Black Writing*, pp. 100-20. New York: Grove Press, 1968.
    Analyses the effects of Christian missionary education on the works of Bantu writers. Jahn includes a discussion of Mofolo's changing attitude toward the sincerity of Western Christianity and the ways it affected his works and his opportunity to publish them.

Kunene, Daniel P. *The Works of Thomas Mofolo: Summaries and Critiques*. Los Angeles: African Studies Center, University of California, 1967, 28 p.
    Plot summaries with critical comments.

——. "The Imagery of Darkness and Light in Thomas Mofolo's *Moeti oa Bochabela*." In *The Commonwealth Writer Overseas: Themes of Exile and Expatriation*, edited by Alastair Niven, pp. 255-64. Brussels: Librairie Marcel Didier S. A., 1976.
    Discusses imagery of light and darkness in *The Traveller to the East*, a novel Kunene considers to be in the tradition of John Bunyan's *Pilgrim's Progress*.

——. "Towards an Aesthetic of Sesotho Prose." In *Exile and Tradition: Studies in African and Caribbean Literature*, edited by Rowland Smith, pp. 98-115. New York: African Publishing Co., 1976.
    Considers the influence of French missionary values on the motives and function of the Lesothan writer. Kunene asserts that Mofolo's novels take the form of classical fables which promote Christian ethics.

McDowell, Robert E. "The Brief Search for an African Hero: The Chaka-Mzilikazi Story in South African Novels." *Discourse: A Review of the Liberal Arts* XI, No. 2 (Spring 1968): 276-83.
    Contends that historical literature such as *Chaka* reveals a psychic struggle to impose order in a chaotic present by writing of a "romantic past which obliterates the white man or at least shows the black man still holding dominion over the land."

"A Kafir Chieftain." *The New York Times Book Review* (29 November 1931): 7.
    Review containing a plot summary.

Spronk, Johannes M. "Chaka and the Problem of Power in the French Theater of Black Africa." *The French Review* LVII, No. 5 (April 1984): 634-40.
    Details the direct influence of Mofolo's *Chaka* on other works about the Zulu chieftain written by dramatists of black Africa's French theater.

Werner, A. "A Mosuto Novelist." *The International Review of Missions* 14, No. 6 (April 1925): 428-36.
    Plot summary of *The Traveller to the East*, which Werner compares with John Bunyan's *Pilgrim's Progress*.

Giovanni Papini

1881-1956

(Also wrote under pseudonym of Gian Falco) Italian essayist, journalist, editor, biographer, autobiographer, novelist, short story writer, and poet.

As an editor and journalist, Papini was instrumental in shaping modern Italian culture during the early years of the twentieth century. At this time Italian art and thought were considered static and decadent, depending heavily upon the traditions of the past. In the pages of his journal *Leonardo,* Papini emerged as a leader of radical and intellectual youth anxious to revolutionize Italian letters, arts, and social thought. He also helped to bring about great changes by introducing the literatures, philosophies, and arts of other nations into his own country and by providing editorial encouragement to many innovative young writers, artists, and thinkers. In his own iconoclastic writings, Papini examined many different literary, philosophical, and artistic movements, helping to advance them all, and ultimately rejected his earlier intellectual causes when he became a convert, albeit an unorthodox one, to Catholicism.

Papini was one of three children born to a lower-middle-class Florentine family. His father, a furniture maker, was an atheist, while his mother was a devout Roman Catholic. Until his conversion to Catholicism at about forty, Papini adhered to his father's atheism and dislike of the commercial middle class, a social category that Papini avoided by marrying a peasant woman and living with her in an isolated rural area until he moved back to Florence late in his life. Papini's parents wanted him to enter his father's furniture business; his refusal led to bitter arguments, and he left home before he was eighteen. This circumstance, combined with uncertain finances, limited Papini's formal schooling.

In the first years of the twentieth century Papini was at the center of a group of young essayists, artists, and philosophers who gathered regularly to exchange ideas and to discuss new and innovative movements in literature, philosophy, and the arts. Although nationalistic in their political beliefs, these youthful intellectuals perceived Italian culture as too narrow and too overly reliant upon the past, and sought to introduce the cultural achievements of other nations into Italy. Primary forums for the dissemination of new ideas were the many periodicals that began appearing around the turn of the century. During this period, which is often called "the age of journals in Italian literature," Papini was instrumental in founding and contributing extensively to a number of the most influential literary, philosophical, and political publications, beginning with *Leonardo.* Cofounded by Papini and Giuseppe Prezzolini in 1903 and appearing through 1908, *Leonardo* proved an important intellectual force in the crusade for *rinnovarsi,* or renewal, of Italian cultural life. The writers connected with *Leonardo* opposed the prevailing creed of Positivism in Italian literature, disagreeing in particular with the Positivist desire to reproduce the actual world as realistically as possible in literature and art, electing instead to employ fantastic or transcendental interpretations of reality. The young writers of the *rinnovarsi* also opposed the extreme Naturalism prevalent in European literature of the time, preferring an idealized image of the solitary, rebellious figure over the Naturalist tendency to view the in-

dividual primarily as part of the social body. According to Carlo L. Golino, the journal *Leonardo* "set about its destructive task by tearing down the existing idols beginning . . . with Positivism." Golino further notes that Papini's personal need for a transcendental vision of life made the "unimaginative nature" and "suffocating materialism" of Positivism abhorrent to him, thus encouraging him to explore the literatures and philosophies of other countries for more compatible beliefs. Giovanni Gullace has written that Papini "battled, from the beginning of his literary career, against Positivism which had stagnated Italian culture, and he sought cultural and spiritual renovation first in new philosophical trends, such as Bergsonism and Pragmatism, and later in Christian thought." Under Papini's editorial direction *Leonardo* promulgated the tenets of William James's philosophy of Pragmatism, a body of thought in which James allowed that ideas may be deemed true solely on the basis of their utilitarian value. Around 1904, James became aware of Papini's introduction of Pragmatism into Italy, and later praised the "enthusiasm, and also [the] literary swing and activity" of the contributors to *Leonardo.* On the strength of Papini's work in *Leonardo* and the essays in *Il crepuscolo dei filosofi,* James hailed him as "the most radical conceiver of Pragmatism to be found anywhere."

Papini eventually abandoned his promotion of Pragmatism and discontinued publication of *Leonardo,* as he and Prezzolini concluded that the formerly iconoclastic publication had become too highly regarded, and thus a part of the establishment it had been created to question. He went on to serve as chief editor of the nationalistic periodical *Regno* and to contribute extensively to *La voce*, Prezzolini's new political and literary magazine. Papini eventually left *La voce* to found, jointly with Ardengo Soffici, the avant-garde journal *Lacerba*, which soon after its inception became the mouthpiece for the burgeoning Futurist movement. Although Papini soon abandoned both Futurism and *Lacerba*, he remained an important contributor to many significant Italian literary and political publications.

Papini's literary career reflects his lifelong search through many philosophies, creeds, and systems of belief, adopting and discarding, for example, Pragmatism, Futurism, and atheism, until at a midpoint of his life he came to the acceptance of the Catholic faith that colored his subsequent works. Critics writing about Papini generally differentiate between these two major phases of his career. The earlier phase they find characterized by extremes of egoism and vituperation against those writers and ideas that he opposed, as well as adulation and hero-worship of those individuals and philosophies that he admired. The later phase, encompassing the years immediately preceding his religious conversion and thereafter, is characterized by Papini's conviction that history is best approached through biography. Still devoted to telling the stories of strong individuals, he now chose to write about those whose lives, like his, resembled a long search for truth and ended in sanctity. Domenico Vittorini has noted that Papini's oeuvre "is a document of two distinct phases of his life: one, in which he destroys all that comes within his reach, tradition, philosophy, religion; the other . . . in which he finds a concrete basis for his thought together with a sense of harmony and repose."

Critics concur that the most representative works of the first part of Papini's career are his essay collections *24 cervelli*, *Stroncature*, *Testimonianze*, and *Il crepuscolo dei filosofi*, in which he reexamined the ideas of the major nineteenth-century philosophers and rejected what he saw as their oppressive influence on modern thought. William James assessed *Il crepuscolo dei filosofi* as "a settling of the author's private accounts with several philosophers (Kant, Hegel, Schopenhauer, Comte, Spencer, Nietzsche)"—each of whom, having failed to provide Papini with a comforting doctrine that he could wholeheartedly embrace, he rejected as inadequate for the philosophic needs of the twentieth century. Critics generally agree that Papini's prose style was at its best in his essays, which are vigorously iconoclastic, intensely personal, and often bitterly polemical, but always insightful, demonstrating a probing, inquisitive mind and reflecting Papini's committment to broadening the scope of narrowly nationalistic Italian arts and letters. The masterpiece of the early phase of Papini's career is his autobiography *Un uomo finito* (*A Man—Finished*; also published as *The Failure*), a pessimistic and defeatist work that he concluded with the words "I am nothing because I tried to be everything!" This autobiography has been characterized by Vittorini as having greater significance than merely the personal record of Papini's own stormy youth: in many ways it is a typical account of the inward search for purpose so common among young intellectuals of the era, and will continue to be read for that reason.

The acquisition of religious faith seemed to impart a sense of peace and acceptance to Papini; his vituperative attacks gave way to concilatory and even adulatory biographies of historical figures whom he perceived as "the only people one can really admire or tolerate in this world . . . saints and artists: those who imitate God, and those who imitate the works of God."

He treated the lives of Michelangelo, Saint Augustine, and Dante in this way: largely disregarding their works in order to examine their actions and ideas, drawing a comparison between their search for ultimate meaning and his own spiritual quest. In these works Papini was often too uncritical and too eulogistic to produce the balanced view and historical perspective necessary to good biography. This second phase of Papini's career is perhaps best exemplified by his *Storia di Cristo* (*The Life of Christ*), an internationally popular work that attempted to humanize Christ and make his life accessible to the average modern reader. Although in subsequent years the *Life* has been sharply questioned for its highly subjective interpretations of certain events—for example, the literalism of Papini's acceptance of miracles performed by Christ—*The Life of Christ* took its place as one of the best-selling, most famous, and most widely read of the many similar religious works that were enormously popular in the United States and Europe in the 1920s through the 1940s.

Long before his death Papini had fallen out of favor with the youngest generation of Italian writers. His shift from atheism to Roman Catholicism was accompanied by an equally extreme reversal of his previous conviction that Italian culture could best be advanced through a break with its past. In such works as *Italia mia* and *Storia della letteratura italiana*, Papini began a vigorous defense of national roots in literature, philosophy, and the arts—just those areas wherein he had earlier advised a more international and less parochial approach. *Italia mia* also professed support of the foreign policies of Italy's fascist government, and this, together with Papini's religious conservatism, met with the approval of the fascist regime. Thus, the once rebellious and iconoclastic Papini ended his career as a member of the cultural establishment that he had once so enthusiastically attacked. Papini's reputation today rests largely on both his *Life of Christ* and other post-conversion works, as well as his place as a primary force in the intellectual history of modern Italy.

PRINCIPAL WORKS

Il crepuscolo dei filosofi (essays) 1906
Il tragico quotidiano (essays and short stories) 1906
 [*Life and Myself*, 1930]
Il pitota cieco (essays and short stories) 1907
L'altra metà (essays) 1912
Le memorie d'Iddio (short stories) 1912
 [*The Memoirs of God*, 1926]
24 cervelli (essays) 1912
Un uomo finito (autobiography) 1912
 [*A Man—Finished*, 1924; also published as *The Failure*, 1924]
Pragmatismo (essays) 1913
Buffonate (essays and short stories) 1914
Cento pagine di poesia (essays) 1915
Stroncature (essays) 1916
Polemiche religiose (essays) 1918
Testimonianze (essays) 1918
L'uomo Carducci (biography) 1918
Storia di Cristo (biography) 1921
 [*The Life of Christ*, 1923]
Four and Twenty Minds (essays) 1922
Gli operai della vigna (essays) 1929
 [*Laborers in the Vineyard*, 1930]
Sant'Agostino (biography) 1929
 [*Saint Augustine*, 1930]

Gog (novel) 1931
 [*Gog*, 1931]
Dante vivo (biography) 1933
 [*Dante vivo*, 1934]
Storia della litterature italiana (criticism) 1937
Italia mia (essay) 1939
Lettere algi vomini di papa Celestino VI (novel) 1946
Vita di Michelangelo (biography) 1949
 [*Michelangelo*, 1952]
Il diavolo (treatise) 1953
 [*The Devil*, 1954]
Il guidizio universale (history) 1957
Tutte le opere di Giovanni Papini. 10 vols. (essays,
 biographies, history, philosophy, autobiography, novels,
 short stories, and poetry) 1958-62

*This work contains translations of essays from the earlier *24 cervelli,
Stroncature,* and *Testimonianze.*

WILLIAM JAMES (essay date 1906)

[*James was one of the most influential figures in modern Western
philosophy and the founder of Pragmatism as a philosophical
school. Despite formidable resistance to James's ideas during his
lifetime, his works have become recognized as landmarks in the
development of modern thought. In opposition to the tenets of
scientific materialism and philosophic idealism, which had prevailed in Western philosophy throughout the eighteenth and nineteenth centuries, James attempted to comprehend and to describe
human life as it is actually experienced, rather than formulating
models of abstract reality far removed from the passion and pain
of life. Among the best-known and most controversial examples
of the tolerant and liberal spirit in James's work is "The Will to
Believe." In this essay, as well as in his writings that expound
the Pragmatic theory of truth, James attempted to resolve one of
the oldest questions of philosophy—what can or cannot be known
as "true"—by viewing any given truth as something that not only
differs from person to person and is subject to change over a
period of time, but also as something that may depend upon an
individual's willing belief. This philosophy of the diversity and
changeability of truths, which James later developed as the doctrine of "radical pluralism," stood in contrast to the monist
absolutism of such thinkers of the time as F. H. Bradley, Charles
Sanders Peirce, and Josiah Royce, who held that ultimate truth
was unchanging and that reality was an immutable transcendent
unity known as the absolute. These philosophers, who found James's
view of the universe overly literal and materialistic, comprised
one of two principal groups that attacked James's ideas. The
other group was made up of such figures as G. E. Moore and
Bertrand Russell, strict materialists and logicians who saw James's
Pragmatism as simply indefensible in rational terms. While the
doctrines of this latter group would dominate Anglo-American
philosophy throughout the twentieth century, rather than those of
either James himself or his most illustrious successor, John Dewey,
as an individual thinker James continues to be regarded among
the most important in Western intellectual history. Papini propounded James's theory of Pragmatism at a time when American
cultural influences were rarely felt in Italy. James met Papini in
1904 and, learning that Papini and other contributors to* Leonardo
*were responsible for the introduction of Pragmatism into Italy,
followed Papini's subsequent career with interest. In the following
excerpt from an essay originally published in the* Journal of Philosophy, Psychology, and Scientific Method *in 1906, James praises
Papini's interpretation of Pragmatism and explores his "Man-
God programme," a theory that omniscience and omnipotence
should be strived for by humankind.*]

American students have so long had the habit of turning to
Germany for their philosophic inspiration, that they are only
beginning to recognize the splendid psychological and philosophical activity with which France to-day is animated; and as
for poor little Italy, few of them think it necessary even to
learn to read her language. Meanwhile Italy is engaged in the
throes of an intellectual *rinascimento* ["renaissance"] quite as
vigorous as her political one. Her sons still class the things of
thought somewhat too politically, making partizan capital, clerical or positivist, of every conquest or concession, but that is
only the slow dying of a habit born in darker times. The ancient
genius of her people is evidently unweakened, and the tendency
to individualism that has always marked her is beginning to
mark her again as strongly as ever, and nowhere more notably
than in philosophy.

As an illustration, let me give a brief account of the aggressive
movement in favor of "pragmatism" which the monthly journal *Leonardo* (published at Florence, and now in its fourth
year) is carrying on, with the youthful Giovanni Papini tipping
the wedge of it as editor, and the scarcely less youthful names
of Prezzolini, Vailati, Calderoni, Amendola, and others, signing the more conspicuous articles. To one accustomed to the
style of article that has usually discussed pragmatism, Dew-
eyism, or radical empiricism, in this country, and more particularly in this *Journal,* the Italian literature of the subject is
a surprising, and to the present writer a refreshing, novelty.
(pp. 459-60)

In this Florentine band of Leonardists . . . , we find, instead
of heaviness, length, and obscurity, lightness, clearness, and
brevity, with no lack of profundity or learning (quite the reverse, indeed), and a frolicsomeness and impertinence that
wear the charm of youth and freedom. Signor Papini in particular has a real genius for cutting and untechnical phraseology. He can write descriptive literature, polychromatic with
adjectives, like a decadent, and clear up a subject by drawing
cold distinctions, like a scholastic. As he is the most enthusiastic pragmatist of them all (some of his colleagues make
decided reservations) I will speak of him exclusively. He ad-
vertises a general work on the pragmatist movement as in press;
but the February number of *Leonardo* and the last chapter of
his just published volume, **Il Crepuscolo dei Filosofi,** give his
programme, and announce him as the most radical conceiver
of pragmatism to be found anywhere.

The *Crepuscolo* book calls itself in the preface a work of "passion," being a settling of the author's private accounts with
several philosophers (Kant, Hegel, Schopenhauer, Comte,
Spencer, Nietzsche) and a clearing of his mental tables from
their impeding rubbish, so as to leave him the freer for constructive business. I will only say of the critical chapters that
they are strongly thought and pungently written. The author
hits essentials, but he doesn't always cover everything, and
more than he has said, either for or against, remains to be said
about both Kant and Hegel. It is the preface and the final
chapter of the book that contain the passion. The "good rid-
dance," which is Papini's cry of farewell to the past of philosophy, seems most of all to signify for him a good-by to its
exaggerated respect for universals and abstractions. Reality for
him *exists* only *distributively,* in the particular concretes of
experience. Abstracts and universals are only instruments by
which we meet and handle these latter.

In an article in *Leonardo* last year [April 1905], he states the
whole pragmatic scope and programme very neatly. Fundamentally, he says, it means an *unstiffening* of all our theories

and beliefs by attending to their *instrumental* value. It incorporates and harmonizes various ancient tendencies, as

1. *Nominalism,* by which he means the *appeal to the particular.* Pragmatism is nominalistic not only in regard to words, but in regard to phrases and to theories.

2. *Utilitarianism,* or the emphasizing of practical aspects and problems.

3. *Positivism,* or the disdain of verbal and useless questions.

4. *Kantism,* in so far as Kant affirms the primacy of practical reason.

5. *Voluntarism,* in the psychological sense, of the intellect's secondary position.

6. *Fideism,* in its attitude towards religious questions.

Pragmatism, according to Papini, is thus only a collection of attitudes and methods, and its chief characteristic is its armed neutrality in the midst of doctrines. It is like a corridor in a hotel, from which a hundred doors open into a hundred chambers. In one you may see a man on his knees praying to regain his faith; in another a desk at which sits some one eager to destroy all metaphysics; in a third a laboratory with an investigator looking for new footholds by which to advance upon the future. But the corridor belongs to all, and all must pass there. Pragmatism, in short, is a great *corridor-theory.*

In the **Crepuscolo** Signor Papini says that what pragmatism has always meant for him is the necessity of enlarging our means of action, the vanity of the universal as such, the bringing of our spiritual powers into use, and the need of making the world over instead of merely standing by and contemplating it. It *inspires human activity,* in short, differently from other philosophies.

"The common denominator to which all the forms of human life can be reduced is this: *the quest of instruments to act with,* or, in other words, *the quest of power.*"

By "action" Signor Papini means any change into which man enters as a conscious cause, whether it be to add to existing reality or to subtract from it. Art, science, religion, and philosophy all are but so many instruments of change. Art changes things for our vision; religion for our vital tone and hope; science tells us how to change the course of nature and our conduct towards it; philosophy is only a more penetrating science. . . . Instead of affirming with the positivists that we must render the ideal world as similar as possible to the actual, Signor Papini emphasizes our duty of turning the actual world into as close a copy of the ideal as it will let us. The various ideal worlds are here because the real world fails to satisfy us. They are more adapted to us, realize more potently our desires. We should treat them as *ideal limits* towards which reality must evermore be approximated.

All our ideal instruments are as yet imperfect. Arts, religion, sciences, philosophies, have their vices and defects, and the worst of all are those of the philosophies. But philosophy can be regenerated. Since change and action are the most general ideals possible, philosophy can become a "*pragmatic*" in the strict sense of the word, meaning a *general theory of human action.* Ends and means can here be studied together, in the abstractest and most inclusive way, so that philosophy can

resolve itself into a comparative discussion of all the possible programs for man's life when man is once for all regarded as a creative being.

As such, man becomes a kind of god, and where are we to draw his limits? In an article called **"From Man to God"** in the *Leonardo* for last February Signor Papini lets his imagination work at stretching the limits. His attempt will be called Promethean or bullfroggian, according to the temper of the reader. It has decidedly an element of literary swagger and conscious impertinence, but I confess that I am unable to treat it otherwise than respectfully. Why should not the divine attributes of omniscience and omnipotence be used by man as the pole-stars by which he may methodically lay his own course? Why should not divine *rest* be his own ultimate goal, rest attained by an activity in the end so immense that all desires are satisfied, and no more action necessary? The unexplored powers and relations of man, both physical and mental, are certainly enormous; why should we impose limits on them *a priori?* And, if not, why are the most utopian programmes not in order?

The programme of a Man-God is surely one of the possible great type-programmes of philosophy. I myself have been slow in coming into the full inwardness of pragmatism. [F.C.S.] Schiller's writings and those of Dewey and his school have taught me some of its wider reaches; and in the writings of this youthful Italian, clear in spite of all their brevity and audacity, I find not only a way in which our English views might be developed farther with consistency—at least so it appears to me—but also a tone of feeling well fitted to rally devotees and to make of pragmatism a new militant form of religious or quasi-religious philosophy.

The supreme merit of it in these adventurous regions is that it can never grow doctrinarian in advance of verification, or make dogmatic pretensions.

When, as one looks back from the actual world that one believes and lives and moves in, and tries to understand how the knowledge of its content and structure ever grew up step by step in our minds, one has to confess that objective and subjective influences have so mingled in the process that it is impossible now to disentangle their contributions or to give to either the primacy. When a man has walked a mile, who can say whether his right or his left leg is the more responsible? and who can say whether the water or the clay is most to be thanked for the evolution of the bed of an existing river? Something like this I understand to be Messrs. Dewey's and Schiller's contention about "truth." The subjective and objective factors of any presently functioning body of it are lost in the night of time and indistinguishable. Only the way in which we see a new truth develop shows us that, by analogy, subjective factors must always have been active. Subjective factors thus are potent, and their effects remain. They are in *some* degree creative, then; and this carries with it, it seems to me, the admissibility of the entire Italian pragmatistic programme. But, be the God-Man part of it sound or foolish, the Italian pragmatists are an extraordinarily well-informed and gifted, and above all an extraordinarily free and spirited and unpedantic, group of writers. (pp. 460-66)

William James, "G. Papini and the Pragmatist Movement in Italy," in his Collected Essays and Reviews, *1920. Reprint by Russel & Russel, 1969, pp. 459-66.*

GIOVANNI PAPINI   (essay date 1918)

[*The following excerpt is taken from an essay originally published in Italian in* Testimonianze *and translated into English by Ernest Hatch Wilkins for inclusion in the collection* Four and Twenty Minds. *In it Papini sarcastically and negatively assesses his own character and his essay collection* Stroncature.]

Giovanni Papini does not need to be introduced to our readers. Every one knows, his friends with even more certainty than his enemies, that he is the ugliest man in Italy (if indeed he deserves the name of man at all), so repulsive that Mirabeau would seem in comparison an academy model, a Discobolus, an Apollo Belvedere. And since the face is the mirror of the soul, as the infinite wisdom of the race informs us in one of its proverbial condensations of experience, no one will be surprised to learn that this Papini is the scoundrel of literature, the blackguard of journalism, the Barabbas of art, the thug of philosophy, the bully of politics, the Apaché of culture, and that he is inextricably involved in all the enterprises of the intellectual underworld. It is also well known that he lives sumptuously and gorgeously, and of course like a Sybarite, in an inaccessible castle; and that he derives his usual means of sustenance from theft, blackmail, and highway robbery. We may add, though it is scarcely necessary, that his favorite food is the flesh of fools and his favorite drink is warm, steaming human blood.

It is a matter of common knowledge that this creature is the worst of all the churls and boors that feed on Italian soil: rumor has it that he has sworn a Carthaginian hatred against every past or future treatise on good behavior. This shameful rascal goes even so far as to say what he actually thinks. Worse still, he has the audacity to turn on the critics when they annoy him:

> Cet animal est très méchant:
> Quand on l'attaque il se défend!
> ["This animal is very naughty:
> When you attack it, it defends itself!"]

This Giovanni Papini, this sinister chameleon of the zoölogy of the spirit, has just published a new book, a thick book, an abominable book. (pp. 318-19)

The volume in question, which the author shamelessly entitles *Slashings,* opens appropriately with several pages of "Boasts," in which Papini insinuates that indignation as well as love may lead to knowledge, since only our enemies clearly perceive our defects and our failings. But this Tamerlane of literary warfare does not keep to the promise of his title. Of his twenty-four chapters, in fact, there are only eleven that can fairly be called "slashings." The other thirteen are either eulogies of men alive or dead, or cordial presentations of men famous or unknown. And this again is scandalous, and sheds the clearest electric light on the fundamental dishonesty of Papini. Any one who has been so unfortunate as to spend five *lire* in the hope of witnessing a massacre (and in view of the common human instincts one cannot deny *a priori* that such a purchase is possible) would be justified in suing the slasher for an attempt to collect money under false pretenses. For this wretched book contains pages so steeped in affection and so warm with love—and this not only in the chapters in which he is talking of his friends—that it is hard to believe them written by the same murderous hand that wrote the other pages. If the men praised were acquaintances of Papini, the phenomenon might easily be explained as a case of bribery or blackmail. But in almost all these instances the men are dead, and in many cases they have been dead so long that Papini cannot possibly have known

them. We confess that we are powerless to solve this enigma, and we console ourselves with the thought—an ancient and excellent idea—that the soul of man is an abyss where lights and shadows mingle in conflict, to the confusion of the psychologists.

But we must not let this impudent Proteus deceive us. We must not forget that he spends more than fifty pages in an onslaught on that Benedetto Croce, whom the young men of forty-five and fifty years regard as their standard and their lighthouse, that Croce whom all revere—from the *Giornale d'Italia* to the Senate, from Pescasseroli to Texas—as the ultimate intuition and expression of the truth. We must not forget that this Zoilus in the form of Thersites allows himself to attack Gabriele d'Annunzio, our great national poet, novelist, dramatist, and orator, our champion intellectual importer, who, like Ferrero, his only rival in this respect, lives on the results of a most profitable exportation. . . . The devouring hunger of this hyena is so boundless that he has even attacked unreal beings, imagined by the fancy of peoples and of poets. Incredible though it may seem, there are pages here in which, with an unprecedented refinement of malignity, he tears to bits the learned Dr. Faust and the melancholy Prince Hamlet.

The case is all the clearer since the men whom he praises are themselves calumniators: Swift, who calumniated man; Weininger, who calumniated woman; Cervantes, who mocked idealism; Remy de Gourmont, who performed the autopsy on Philistine thought; Tristan Corbière, who ridiculed the whole of humanity, including himself.

Giovanni Papini knows only hatred. His one motive is wrath. He deals only in invective; he delights only in blasphemy. (pp. 320-23)

It is perfectly right that boneheads should be given a drubbing, that undeserved reputations should be reduced to their true level, that the mediocre should be exposed, that bubbles should be pricked, and so on. That is all right. But this is not the way it should be done. (pp. 323-24)

The author of this detestable book is still young, and has given evidence of ability to do things not so bad as this. We will remind him, therefore, of a great truth which our fathers have handed down to us, and which we shall entrust as a precious thing to our sons: "Criticism is easy, but art is difficult." And if this stubborn wretch should reply that even criticism may be art, and should persist in his wickedness, we shall retort with a saying of the immortal Manzoni, a saying that is somewhat out of date, but still convenient: "Don't worry, poor creature, it will take more than you to turn Milan upside down." (p. 324)

Giovanni Papini, "Giovanni Papini," in his Four and Twenty Minds: Essays, *edited and translated by Ernest Hatch Wilkins, Thomas Y. Crowell Company Publishers, 1922, pp. 318-24.*

JOSEPH COLLINS   (essay date 1920)

[*Collins is an American physician and essayist who has written the literary studies* The Doctor Looks at Literature *(1923),* Taking the Literary Pulse *(1924),* The Doctor Looks at Biography *(1925) and* The Doctor Looks at Love and Life *(1942). In the following excerpt, he discusses Papini's writings and explains why he considers Papini an overrated author and thinker.*]

Signor Papini is an interesting literary figure, particularly as a sign of the times. During the past generation there has been in Italy a profound revolt against what may be called satisfaction with and reverence for past performances and against slavish subscription to French, German, and Russian realism. It is to a group of writers who call themselves Futurists and who see in the designation praise rather than opprobrium that this salutary, beneficial, and praiseworthy movement is due.

Signor Papini has publicly read himself out of the party, but apostasy of one kind or another is almost as necessary to him as food, and most people still regard him as a Futurist, though he refuses to subscribe to the clause in the constitution of the literary Futurists of Italy bearing on love, published by their monarch Signor Marinetti in that classic of Futuristic literature "Zang Tumb Tumb" and in "Democrazia Futurista."

It is now twenty years since there appeared unheralded in Florence a literary journal called the *Leonardo,* whose purpose in the main seemed to be to overthrow certain philosophic and socialistic doctrines, Positivism and Tolstoian ethics. The particularly noteworthy articles were signed Gian Falco. It soon became known that the writer was one Giovanni Papini, a contentious, self-confident youth of peculiarly inquisitive turn of mind, and of sensitiveness bordering on the pathological, an omnivorous reader, an aggressive debater. He was hailed by a group of youthful literary enthusiastics as a man of promise.

In the twenty years that have elapsed since then he has written more than a score of books, short stories, essays, criticisms, poetry, polemics, some of which, such as *Un Uomo Finito (The Played-Out Man), Venti Quattro Cervelli (Twenty-four Minds),* and *Cento Pagine di Poesia (One Hundred Pages of Poetry),* have been widely read in Italy and have known several editions. Save for a few short stories, he has not appeared in English, though there seems to be propaganda in his behalf directed by himself and by his friends of his publishing-house in Florence to make him known to foreigners. Like other Italian propaganda it has not been very successful and this is to be regretted. It is due in part to the fact his advocates have claimed too much for him.

Signor Papini is like Mr. Arnold Bennett in that they both know the reading public are personally interested in authors. From the beginning he and his friends have capitalized his poverty of pulchritude and his pulchritudinous poverty. Signor Giuseppe Prezzolini, in a book entitled *Discorso su Giovanni Papini* has devoted several pages to his person, which, he writes, "is like those pears, coarse to the touch but sweet to the palate," yet I am moved to say that the eye long habituated to resting lovingly upon somatic beauty does not blink nor is it pained when it rests upon Giovanni Papini.

In one of his latest books—it is never safe to say which is really his last, unless you stand outside the door of the bindery of *La Voce*—in one of his latest books, entitled *Testimonials,* the third series of *Twenty-four Brains,* he reverts to this, and says that his person is "so repugnant that Mirabeau, world-famed for his ugliness, was compared with him an Apollo" [see excerpt dated 1918].

He does not get the same exquisite pleasure from deriding his qualities of soul, but, as the face is the mirror of the soul, no one is astonished to learn that "this same Papini is the gangster of literature, the tough of journalism, the Barabbas of art, the dwarf of philosophy, the straddler of politics, and the Apache of culture and learning." Nevertheless, no prudent, sensitive man should permit himself to say this or anything approximating it in Papini's hearing, for not only has he a card index

of substantives that convey derogation, but he has perhaps the fullest arsenal of adjectives in Italy, and has habituated himself to the use of them, both with and without provocation.

I have been told by his schoolmates and by those whom he later essayed to teach that as a youth he was inquisitive about the nature of things and objects susceptible to physical and chemical explanation. His writings indicate that his real seduction was conditioned by philosophic questions. Early in life he displayed a symptom which is common to many psychopaths—an uncontrollable desire to read philosophical writers beyond their comprehension. In the twenty years that he has been publishing books he has constantly returned to this practice, as shown by his *Twilight of the Philosophers, The Other Half,* and *Pragmatism.* (pp. 90-2)

Signor Papini is never so transparent as he is in his . . . excursions into the realm of philosophy. His attack on Nietzsche is most illuminating. In fact, Giovanni Papini is Frederick Nietzsche viewed through an inverted telescope. "Nietzsche's volubility (indication of easy fatigue) makes him prefer the fragmentary and aphoristic style of expression; his incapacity to select from all that which he has thought and written leads him to publish a quantity of useless and repeated thought; his reluctance to synthetize, to construct, to organize, which gives to his books an air of oriental stuff, a mixture of old rags and of precious drapery, jumbled up without order, are the best arguments for imputing to him a deficiency of imperial mentality, a reflex of the general weakness of philosophy. But the most unexpected proof of this weakness consists in his incapacity to be truly and authentically original. The highest and most difficult forms of originality are certainly these two: to find new interpretation and solution of old problems, to pose new problems and to open streets absolutely unknown."

No one can examine closely the writings of Signor Papini without recognizing that he has shown himself incapable of selecting from that which he has written and thought and of setting it forth as a statement of his philosophy or as an Apologia pro Sua Vita. Constant republication of the same statements and the same ideas dressed up with different synonyms is a charge that can be brought with justice. It can be substantiated not only by his books but by *La Vraie Italie,* an organ of intellectual liaison between Italy and other countries directed by Signor Papini, which had a brief existence in 1919, a considerable portion of which was taken up with republication of the old writings of the director.

Even the most intemperate of his admirers would scarcely contend that he merits being called original, judged by his own standards. At one time in his life Nietzsche was undoubtedly his idol, and I can think of the juvenile Papini . . . suggesting that he model himself after the Teutonic descendant of Pasiphae and the bull of Poseidon. Thus did he appease his morbid sensitiveness and soothe his pathological erethism by enveloping himself in an armor made up of rude and uncouth words, of sentiment and of disparagement; of raillery against piety, reverence, and faith; of contempt for tradition. In fact, he seemed equipped with a special apparatus for pulling roots founded in the tender emotions. He would pretend that he is superior to the ordinary mortal to whom love in its various display, sentiment in its manifold presentations, dependence upon others in its countless aspects are as essential to happiness as the breath of the nostrils is essential to life. In secret, however, he is not only dependent upon it, he is beholden to it.

When he assumes his most callous and indifferent air, when he is least cognizant of the sensitiveness of others, when in brief he is speaking of his fellow countrymen, Signore D'Annunzio, Mazzoni, Bertacchi, Croce, and up until recently when he speaks of God or religion, he reminds me of that extraordinary and inexplicable type of individual whom we have had ''in our midst'' since time immemorial, but who had greater vogue in the time of Petronius than he has to-day.

Although the majority of these persons are *au fond* proud of their endowment, the world at large scoffs at them; and in primitive countries such as our own it kicks at them; therefore they are quick to see the advantage of assuming an air of crass indifference and, with the swagger of the social corsair, to express a brutal insensitiveness to the aesthetic and the hedonistic to which in reality they vibrate. They never deceive themselves, and Signor Papini does not deceive himself. He knows his limitations, and the greatest of them are that he is timid, lacking in imagination, in sense of humor, and in originality. He is as dependent upon love as a baby is upon its bottle.

When writing about himself he hopes the reader will identify him only with the characters whose thoughts and actions are flattering, but the real man is to be identified with some of the characters whom he desires his public to think fictitious. In one of his short stories he narrates a visit to a world-famed literary man. He describes his trip to the remote city that he may lay the modest wreath plated from the pride of his mind and his heart at the feet of his idol. He finds him a commonplace, almost undifferentiated lump of clay with a more commonplace, slatternly wife and even more hopelessly commonplace children. His repute is dependent wholly upon the skill with which he manipulates a card index and pigeon-holes. Papini fled to escape contemplation of himself and the fragments of the sacred vessel.

Signor Papini has been an omnivorous reader along certain lines; he has been a tireless writer, and he is notorious for his neologistic logorrhea, but the possession which stands in closest relation to his literary reputation is his indexed collection of words, phrases, and sentences. This, plus knowing by heart the poetry of Carducci, and his envy of Benedetto Croce for having obtained the repute of being one of the most fertile philosophic minds of his age, and his advocacy of the gospel of strenuousness, is the framework upon which he has ensheathed his house of letters.

No study of the man or of his work can neglect one aspect of his career—his constant change of position. He knocks with breathless anxiety at the door of some new world, and no sooner does he secure entrance and see the pleasant valley of Hinnom than he feels the lure of black Gehenna and is seized with an uncontrollable desire to explore it. When he returns he hastens to the public forum and announces his discoveries, preferring to tell of the gewgaws which he discovered than to expatiate on the few jewels which he gathered.

His last production augurs well for him, because it indicates that finally he will bathe in the pool of the five porches at Jerusalem, the World War having troubled its water instead of an angel. November 30, 1919, he published in the most widely circulated and influential newspaper of Central Italy, the *Resto del Carlino*, an article entitled **"Amore e Morte"** (**"Love and Death"**), which sets forth that he has had that experience which the Christian calls ''seeing a great light, knowing a spiritual reincarnation,'' and which those whom Papini has been supposed to represent call a pitiable defalcation, a spiritual bankruptcy.

On February 21, 1913, he proclaimed in the Costanzi Theatre of Rome that ''in order to reach his power man must throw off religious faith, not only Christianity or Catholicism, but all mystic, spiritualistic, theosophic faiths and beliefs.'' Now he has discovered Jesus. (pp. 99-103)

Were [Papini] a genius and at the same time had the industry that he has displayed, he would be the equal of H. G. Wells, possibly the peer of Bernard Shaw, but he is neither. He is simply a clever, industrious, versatile, sensitive, emotional man of forty, whose mental juvenility tends to cling to him. He has so long habituated himself to overestimation and his admiring friends have been so injudicious in praising his productions for qualities which they do not possess and neglecting praiseworthy qualities which they do possess, that he is like an object under a magnifying-glass out of focus. (p. 106)

Joseph Collins, ''Giovanni Papini and the Futuristic Literary Movement in Italy,'' in his Idling in Italy: Studies of Literature and of Life, *Charles Scribner's Sons, 1920, pp. 88-106.*

UGO OJETTI (essay date 1921)

[*Ojetti was an Italian journalist, essayist, critic, short story writer, novelist, and dramatist. Best known for his literary and art criticism, he was a regular columnist for leading Italian periodicals from 1898 through 1934. Many of his critical columns were collected and published in the six-volume* Cose viste (1923-34; some of which were translated as As They Seemed to Me, 1928). Despite his sometimes fragmentary journalistic style, commentators praise Ojetti's insight and the cosmopolitanism he brought to his assessments of Italian literature and art. In the following excerpt from an essay written in 1921, Ojetti mocks Papini's religious conversion.*]

Napoleon III, when, almost at Papini's age, he was head over heels in love with Eugenia Montijo, and she was still holding back, took refuge, during a ball, in a window-recess, pricked up his courage and put the question to her: ''Tell me, then, by what road can I reach your heart?'' ''Sire, the only way is through the church,'' the blonde calmly answered. I do not say that Giovanni Papini, in order at last to wed the big public and the adored big editions, had no other way; but after all the smoothest, surest and straightest way was that recommended by the Montijo to the frantic Emperor. And Papini too has taken it, boldly, wondering, like all lovers who are young no longer, that others should be at first a bit taken aback and murmur at him.

Papini is unable to doubt. He knows every kind of fever, but not the fever of doubt, which after all may sometimes not be a fever, but a sort of well-aired peace cradled between ''yes'' and ''no.'' This peremptory certitude of his has perhaps in the course of years become for him a defence even against himself: a wall erected in haste, with all the stones that come to hand, if only to find a shelter from opposed gusts and unpleasant vistas. Perhaps it is also the easiest way, if not to convince one's neighbours, at least to proselytize and to dazzle them. Papini's dialectic was formed during many years at the café, which is in a way a public meeting and where every opinion is a kind of wager. The pace of his Pegasus, in short, is never an amble: either a gallop, or even a charge, or else a grazing in the clear sunshine of Heliconian meadows. (Rare moments; but few as Papini's bucolic pages are, I enjoy them, and savour them, more than any other pages of his.) Did he have to enter the Church? He crossed it all at a run with his head lowered, whether to gather momentum or from piety is not known, from the door to the apse, even into the sacristy; and then upstairs as far as the priest's little room with a chromo of the Sacred Heart, and into the parlour of His Grace the Bishop, with the portrait of Pope Benedict himself.

"C'est une barre de fer," said Renan of Catholicism, when he too was on the edge of a conversion, but in the other direction. *"On ne raisonne pas avec une barre de fer."* Papini at once gave up reasoning, happy in having at last found something on which to lean and rest after so much journeying, in which to enjoy the illusion of resting and breathing in front of a great horizon. The iron bar is for him to a certain extent the bar of a railing.

He has accepted from the Church all the loves and hates, and the very dislikes which the sternest of the orthodox would have allowed him to forget. He was not satisfied with forgetting, or rather demolishing, Zeus and Apollo, Caesar and Augustus; he finished off also Socrates and Horace, Seneca and Renan. A century after Christ there were Fathers of the Church like Justin who considered Heraclitus and Socrates to be Christians. In this apocalyptic year of grace of 1921 the apologist Giovanni does not pardon even them; he is just willing partly to forgive himself because it seems to him right to attribute the blame of his long error to this convulsive and voluble era. A putrid epoch, an abject epoch, like none other that has ever been, if you hearken to Papini, who, by one of the numerous unexpected tricks of the evil one, does, after all, feel a certain satisfaction and pride in having chanced upon the earth precisely in this superlative epoch.

Something similar to this he experiences when he boasts of the supreme ugliness, under his dishevelled hair, of his pallid face, and of his bulging forehead and emaciated cheeks and blood-shot short-sighted eyes; and that straight deep furrow between the eyes which looks like the scar of an arrow. He will not admit polite attenuations, Lavateresque interpretations. He wants to be ugly, and especially to be called ugly; even in this he is faithful to his *Carducci the Man* who so enjoyed playing the orge: "I know, and in my heart it amuses me, that I am so ugly as to be frightening. . . ." The pride of humility, which forces you to note the evident beauty of the contrast between face and spirit. *Carducci the Man.* Has anyone observed that the *Storia di Cristo* is after the same pattern? In the *Carducci,* it was obvious that Papini was trying to find himself; here, in the *Life of Jesus,* this search is less manifest and less permissible. But read one chapter, the *Overturner:* "The greatest overturner is Jesus, the supreme paradoxist, the radical fearless Overturner—" He too.

I think that we should bring ourselves gracefully to forgive Giovanni Papini, even now that he is all Christian from head to foot, for this minimum of pride, and, if you will, touchy and fierce pride. It is, after all, a churchman's quality, the quality of all the chosen of the people or of God. *"Non tibi sed Petro." "Et mihi et Petro."* He who will humble himself shall be exalted. Perhaps that is why he humbles himself. And as a writer I am all the more willing to grant Papini this right to be proud, because he is a master in the art that I serve. "We are condemned to perpetual literature, to the harsh prison of the dictionary," he once wrote; but it is a dear prison, after all, in which, with the diminution of the crew imposed by democracy, he still has a just claim to one of the few posts as boatswain. And besides, as a Roman, I like these rare Catholics, survivors or neophytes, still convinced that the love of man to man must be imposed by authority, even with a few thoroughly dry faggots and well-greased ropes; that authority

in short precedes and controls love and prevents it becoming stupid and drunk. "I like them better than all the stuffy sacristans of affected Christianity," who are in fashion to-day, to borrow a phrase from Domenico Giuliotti, another ruthless Catholic who, if I am not mistaken, divides humanity into three sections: the good ones; the ones that we can still hope to convert or enchain; and those without any hope, whom one must quickly send into the other world, nearer to God, so that He who is omnipotent may attend to them in person. But I have never dared to ask Giuliotti how many men the good section consists of nowadays. Were I to ask him to count them for me on his fingers, I fear he would at once stick one of his hands in his pocket.

In short, if there is one thing that I admire in Giovanni Papini's conversion, it is precisely what others do not admire: that is, the sudden and complete way in which he was converted, not only because thus he has been true to himself and to that constant risky and even generous habit of his, of surrendering all himself in order to receive all in an embrace or a swallow, but also because in so doing he revealed, without formulating it in so many words, his own inner tragedy: the tragedy of his weariness. In every phrase of his new book I feel the strain of a man who was at the end of his tether. He could no longer endure his solitude, his failure, in so many years of intellectual and moral hunger and thirst, to find a substantial and nourishing food—in so many years of vagabondage from one idea to the other, and from one book to the other, to find an abode for his soul. Of course, here too, a share of the effect must be attributed to the war, to this war which every one swore would not change anything in men's heads and in their hearts. Just as in their bodies it caused all their hidden afflictions to break out and hastened all forms of decay, so in their souls as well. Without the war, without the earthquake and the convulsion of the bloody terror of the war, Giovanni Papini would have gone on with his rope-dancing gambols on the shining steel cord of his strained intelligence. Instead of that, here you see him taking refuge in the Church, in a mad rush, like a man who has hurried in to seek asylum and shelter from pressing mortal danger, and now touches the walls, the pillars, the altars, the gates, and cries out, to comfort himself most of all: "They are of granite, they are of iron, they have endured for centuries, they will endure always, they will defend me for ever."

But for him the difficulties are now beginning. The gate is of iron, I allow; but it has closed behind him. (pp. 76-80)

Ugo Ojetti, "Papini Converted," in his As They Seemed to Me, *translated by Henry Furst, E. P. Dutton and Company Publishers, 1928, pp. 76-80.*

GIUSEPPE PREZZOLINI (essay date 1922)

[*Prezzolini was an Italian critic, journalist, essayist, and editor who cofounded the noted literary and political periodical* Leonardo *together with Papini, and edited or contributed to many other important Italian journals. In 1930 Prezzolini became a professor of Italian at Columbia University in New York. A published collection of his lectures from this time proved instrumental in sparking interest in Italian studies in the United States. In the following excerpt, he discusses Papini's career and character.*]

In January, 1901, there appeared in Florence, unheralded by any barometer, a strange literary magazine, printed on hand-made paper, illustrated with original woodcuts, and written entirely by youths unknown up to that time. In the contents each month, an editorial, and critical notes appeared, signed

"Gian Falco," pregnant with poetry and passion, irony and romanticism, color and sensitiveness, treating in the most independent spirit philosophic and moral problems of all kinds, far from any preoccupation with actuality, and often in direct and abrupt conflict with the current ideas then prevalent in Italy, such as "Positivism" and Christian and Tolstoyian Socialism.

This periodical soon became greatly renowned, perhaps more renowned than read, and was called *Leonardo*.

The founder and editor who gave it importance and character, revealing in its pages those strange attitudes and violent passions, this spirit of extravagance and insolence, was Giovanni Papini since known in Italy as a writer, read and admired by the young—the most hated and the most loved. (pp. 239-40)

The many witticisms, the epithets hurled by him at writers of his and other times, the scoffing and the irony which have filled his magazines and books, are not the corrosive acid of an intelligence consciously setting out to do harm to others, but the natural expression of a fresh mind which conceives with great rapidity and in lightning flashes,—with that scintillation which is possessed by romantics such as Schlegel, an accompanying characteristic of the true genius. If he has been able more often to see the ridiculous side and to point out the defects, rather than the good qualities of the people about him, shall we attribute it to the fact that these phases are the more obvious? Or, is it an inclination of his spirit which has suffered overmuch, which has not been loved enough, which has become sour, desiring above all to appear locked, closed, diffident, deaf, willing rather to lose the possibility of finding a beautiful soul, than to let itself be defrauded by one having in reality, only its semblance? It seems to me evident that the latter is the case. His life as narrated by himself is not a happy one. And perhaps he has not disclosed the very depths of his bitterness. (p. 241)

There are cries of tenderness, and a seeking for love growing from the same sentiment, in the first fantastic-romantic period of Papini's work. He is interested in philosophical and moral problems, but these assume a purely literary expression taking spontaneously the form of legends and myths. These remind one of the methods of Baudelaire and Poe, the moral essays of Maeterlinck and the travesties of Laforgue. The classic book of this period is the *Tragico Quotidiano;* in the last editions, *Il Pilota Cieco* has been added. In this vein also is a third and inferior work, *Buffonate,* which represents the tired remnants of the inspiration of that type. These writings have a glitter of false antique gold, artificial, yet seductive. The device is nearly always original, the gesture a happy one, but there is a rudeness in the style, and at the same time a little of affectation when compared with his later writings, which are much more human and solid.

One notes here two probable reasons for his change (not overlooking the principal one—that of his constant development, his continual unveiling of himself and the perpetual effort of writers to fathom the depths of themselves): on the one side, his life in the country and his marriage; on the other, his careful study of the classics. Bulciano and the collection of *Scittori Nostri* (*Our Writers*);—already this "Our" was the beginning of a new phase of Papini's—coming as it did at a time when he had only been speaking of international literature, Spanish and German; Arabian and Chinese. It was for him a renewal of a life lived; to find again, or find for the first time, human experiences, and to enlarge his vocabulary of people and au-

thors, which up to that time was poor, abstract and often common.

Blessed be the poverty which compelled him to live in Bulciano, and the need which forced him to become an editor—and we need not look too closely at the punctuation of his text.

The conclusion of this movement was a book of confessions, the masterpiece of Papini, *l'Uomo finito* (*The Finished Man*). One need no longer refer to Hamlet or the Devil, to invent characters, or feign extraordinary adventures when wishing to recount the torments of a life. One says, finally,—that torment, that life, the l'Uomo Finito, is Papini himself—his own story, his life, his own intimate thoughts—from childhood to his final confessions. He has tried everything—and succeeded in nothing. He has sought always the impossible, the too great, the too high. As a child he dreamt of compiling the encyclopedia of encyclopedias; so as man, he dreamt of becoming the revealer of a new religion. But everything has failed him: family affection, the understanding of the spirits who surrounded him, help of friends, the ecstasy of real love. Here he is, discontented, disheartened, broken. Another man, of mediocre mentality would be satisfied with his fame, with his success, with his "position"—but Papini aspired to a greater glory—that of a genius who spiritually overturns the world.

What he wished most to have written, was a "universal judgment," and the entire book is a cry of dissatisfaction, a clamour toward the unattainable. It is his masterpiece because it is the most honest and sincere of his works. His other books are more often those of the Papini "who wishes to hide his secret." His secret is his weakness. Papini is not a strong man, and as he knows his vulnerability, he isolates himself, entrenches himself behind a breast-plate. There he remains with the audacity of the timid—attacking, scoffing, engaging in polemics, denouncing. Not only does he say impertinences; he writes and publishes them. In this manner he has won his fame as an "enfant terrible" of literature. If there is a scandal to instigate, he thinks of it at once; he is ready to speak of a rope in the house of the hanged; to talk of anti-semitism at the home of a Jew; and of divorce with a divorcee.

He has acquired this reputation a little through his natural temperament and a little through his desire of making it so—and of augmenting it. If there be an unmentionable word, he speaks it at once. And in certain of his shorter works, we find five or six of the worst substantives ever used by writers, from Dante to Carducci. There is in him a little of Bernard Shaw, but of a Shaw less contented with himself and his impertinences; above all, Papini is more unsatisfied—and therefore changeable. And perhaps dissatisfied because of being obliged to be changeable.

This reproach of being changeable is the most common and perhaps the most true of the many reproaches flung at him. Nothing could be more evident. With the exception of a few strong antipathies, such as the one for Croce which has always remained, one might say that every two or three years, Papini changes his opinions. He has been positivist, idealist, pragmatist; has believed in philosophy and then scoffed at it; has combatted, then embraced and finally abandoned futurism; was passionately in favor of the war—then soon tired of it; has been anti-Christian and now apparently has become Christian. In his writings, one can find mockeries of all opinions—and reasoning in favor of all faiths.

All this is quite true—but . . . And there is a "but". An analysis of the mutability of Papini's temperament brings important results. First of all, it is disinterested; secondly, it denotes an extreme prosensitiveness to whatever the times demand, and finally, it reveals still another secret aspect of Papini's mind. His mutability is that of a lyric spirit ready to enthuse for that which is not yet realized, and incapable of undertaking afterwards the more arduous task of dominating the real obstacles. Papini's weakness is here also demonstrated. There is in him an intense desire for truth and faith, of living in contact with that reality which he missed when young; of feeling himself convinced; and all this is in direct opposition to what he so often appears to be, a cynic, a mocker, a sceptic. He is sceptical, but suffers from being so; a cynic, but his cynicism hides a sorrow; he is a mocker, but how he would love to be mocked providing he had a faith.

His revolt against the ideals he once loved is not the expression of the malcontent toward those faiths that have not held him enough, have not totally inflamed him. His movements toward ideas, groups, literary fashions, problems of the day, are quick at first—and reach their goal in one jump. It is his readiness to accept a new subject, a new ideal, that reveals the genial aspect in him. But the conquests of Papini, if they are quicker than those of others, are also less durable. He is as a child who sees far above him a little rose cloud, climbs the mountain quickly to touch it—and finds upon nearing it, that it has become grey. The realized reality does not satisfy him, and he becomes bitter, critical, ironical and aggressive. This has been the fate of the ideas and movements of which he has hoped the most: idealism, futurism, his war-enthusiasm.

As often happens, Papini is known more for his "ideas"—that is, those ideas he caught here and there and soon abandoned, than for having given to these ideas, life, character, importance, relations, logic (sometimes elementary), which they had not in themselves. He has been, and this is not the first example, more admired for his unworthy and passing

Papini with his daughter Viola. From Giovanni Papini, *by Vintila Horia. Wesmael-Charlier, 1963. Reproduced by permission of the publisher.*

actions than for his better and profound; for his clamorous discordant manifestations rather than for his penetrating and silent ones. On the whole, his fame was chiefly won during the period of futurism and *Lacerba*.

However, he has derived the greatest benefit from one characteristic of his mentality, notable especially in his articles: an extraordinary capacity for grasping in all problems the three or four chief points of importance and developing them with the greatest simplicity and often, ingenuity, using phrases of such an imaginative quality as to completely capture the reader. The power of rhetoric that some men possess over the masses is also in the hands of this man. His ingenuity has rendered it possible for him to approach the mentality of the humblest and to find readers among the lowest classes.

And in the meanwhile, so few have noted the great progress made by Papini in his writing. Generally, one asks for the "Papini"—without distinction or hierarchy; one also judges him without discerning the deep from the superficial, or even his progress through and beyond his varied methods. His career, if one may so express oneself, is a succession of leaps, followed by long periods of lassitude and stagnation, during which the forces for a new jump seem to mature. Arrived at the summit again, he seems, after a little while, to lose his footing and fall back once more. At the very beginning of each of these periods, his productions are the best.

Meanwhile, he is making constant progress in his instrument: the language. This is mainly notable since his seclusion in Bulciano and his study of the classics. He has even temporarily adopted rhythm and rhymes to show how easy it was for the Tuscans to compose in a given traditional line. Of course, I do not believe that in this lies proof of his genius; rather, he has measured with them the extreme elasticity of his natural talent.

Papini is primarily an artist—but one of a special character: he is an artist of "ideas". His world of colours and forms (the external world) has presented itself to him a little late perhaps, and with a few exceptions, the rest of his work is that of talent, literary science, and we might say, is more academic than lyrical. His is a moral lyricism, the lyricism of one who is always preoccupied with logical and ethical problems. Without enclosing them in their proper philosophical forms, he presents them, following the method of certain foreigners, in their sentimental and aesthetic aspects.

This may again recall to us Papini's mutability and dilettantism, but can easily be explained. For him, it is not the ideas which sustain his spirit. These are only considered lyrical occasions. This also explains his minute erudition, which has never satisfied the men of learning, but which has served to give to many of his writings an appearance multicolored and interesting; comparable to the appearance of the drawing-room of a gentleman of good taste, in which are gathered together—masks of savages, impressionist paintings; Etruscan vases and Greek robes; tables of the 5th century and Chinese drawings. (pp. 242, 244-46)

We now find no more detractors of Papini; but battalions of people more dangerous—his admirers. We call them dangerous, but they are only temporarily so, for no critic, favorable or unfavorable, can stifle the flow of a poet's life. A poet who has natural inspiration and perseverance, though men swear his incapacity, forges ahead, always ahead.

Papini is the strongest and most original prose writer of our generation, in addition to being the representative of all the good and the bad that is ours,—the torments, the changeableness, the uncertainty, the aspirations. His torment has passed into others—awakening their spirits without being able to give them rest. He has been a man tormented who torments, an impregnator of doubts and questions which he leaves unanswered. The answers will be sought for by the young of his period and by those who follow.

Papini will remain as a type. In his extravagances and insolences, in his gestures whose sincerity we sometimes doubt, in his angers and disagreements, and in his more equivocal sympathies—he still radiates about him something sympathetic; which explains why anger has been pacified and wounds have been healed, and why Papini is now considered to be above the melange and more or less accepted by the crowd.

His name will be known as the name of a good writer. It will be easy for the future generations to recognize in him one of the purest followers of Carducci, one of the rungs of that chain which tomorrow shall stretch between the writers of the past and the writers of the future. His periods of indignation and his revolutionary proposals will be forgotten by all. His place will be among the powerful literary figures; among those from whom Italian culture has fed its brain. It will happen to him as it has to certain painters, called "exception" painters, whom to-day we admit in the perfect line of tradition.

His geniality, his inspired poetic sense in carrying on an argument, describing a scene or drawing a character (the latter rarely), will always be characteristic of him. Above all, he is a writer of movement. In his manner of opening a paragraph and of closing it, after elaborating his thought; in his personal participation in the dramas of life or of social problems, there is always evident that clear energy which one misses in the style of Pascoli and d'Annunzio, and which is the characteristic of our best Italian tradition. In this lies his power, his distinctive personality.

And in the depths of Papini's soul, there are still unexplored and unsatisfied regions of tenderness—his need of love—to which all have turned a deaf ear—and for which no one of us has done enough. (pp. 247-48)

Giuseppe Prezzolini, "Giovanni Papini," in Broom, *Vol. 1, No. 3, January, 1922, pp. 239-48.*

HUTCHINS HAPGOOD (essay date 1922)

[*In the following excerpt, Hapgood notes the charm and color of Papini's literary style as demonstrated in the essays from* Four and Twenty Minds.]

It is a sceptical time, as far as systematic thought goes. Whether it is in the field of metaphysics, politics, economics, the phenomena of general doubts are observable. The best minds no longer think that any system or thing is applicable in any exhaustive way to life. So-called conservative and so-called radical alike are wary of the generalizing habit of the mind and tend to cultivate the garden of personality and its genial though unprincipled reactions to experience. The conscious mind itself is somewhat in disrepute, and more relative emphasis is put on its intuitions, instincts and artistic impulses. Giovanni Papini represents this tendency of the time. Years ago, in his *Twilight of the Philosophers,* he showed how the supposedly objective thought of the metaphysicians sprang not from unchanging and universal reality but from the idiosyncrasies of

each philosopher's personality, and was really, therefore, lacking in metaphysical value. William James recognized Papini as the Italian pragmatist of his time.

In [*Four and Twenty Minds*] . . . , Papini frankly reveals himself as a literary rather than a metaphysical thinker. This remark is not intended as a limitation of his philosophic understanding. The essays on Berkeley, Spencer and Hegel show that thorough grasp of abstract and universal conceptions which mark the philosopher. That Papini's treatment of these large views is clear and simple indicates the depth and thoroughness of his thought. When the metaphysician shows himself as such through the complicated confusion of thought he is least so. Through intensity of thought and philosophic learning the thinker works through metaphysics as through a cloud into the clear and luminous spaces beyond. In the present volume, Papini moves about in these clear spaces with incisive charm, with no attempt not to be personal, with, in fact, an engaging willingness to reveal himself, his loves and his hates, even his prejudices. But into these frankly personal reactions he inevitably inserts the color of philosophy, which is rare in general literary essays. One feels, as a rule even in the best essay work, a lack of background. There is hardly a literary article in our contemporary journalism which suggests the eternal passions of the general thinker. Without that, the essay becomes a matter of mental and temperamental agility, and of little value to the poet, the philosopher and the human being as such. It is for that reason that Papini's essays are deeply amusing. The mind and spirit are entertained primarily by the ultimate meanings applied to passing and specific things. Freed from the dogma of speculative systems, the mind turns to a deeper, more conscious treatment of the specific fact. So Papini writes charmingly, colorfully, significantly, about the Unknown Man, about Walt Whitman, Nietzsche, Dante, Leonardo Da Vinci, Ghiberti, Croce, Shakespeare, Don Quixote, Calderon, Maeterlinck, Remy de Gourmont and several relatively unknown Italians.

To judge from the free English translation, there is a genuine style to Papini's prose. It is a style that does not spring from any conscious attempt to ornament, but even when gay and epigrammatic, is a result of the release of thought. So it is Papini's thought which intrigues us. And that thought is rich and constant—the volume is full of ideas and the feeling that the writer enjoys them for their own sake. It is an easy thing for Papini to live in the world of thought, and his reaction to it is inevitable. Nothing pompous or solemn, nothing tortuously unclear. A beautifully lucid Latin mind throughout. And a mind unconventional and uncontrolled.

The only marked limitation that we have been able to find in this philosophic essayist is the lack of understanding for Shakespeare. It seems to be the rock on which the validity of Latin thought is traditionally wrecked. Papini, perhaps unconsciously, demands a centralized point of view in the literary artist. He needs to feel that a man's work is a man's life, means *one* thing predominantly, that some stable principle, some contribution to the spirit or to thought has been definitely added to the world's store. . . .

The intense modernity of Papini's thought is indicated by his attitude towards the lyric. He feels all other literary forms, even drama, to be barbaric and naïve. . . .

The only democratic thing about Papini is that he heralds the glorious contributions of the Unknown Man, to which he devotes an essay, and in the essay on Dante continues the thought:

"Every man who reads a great work, even though he be a poor spirit, adds to it some meaning, some pause, some intonation of his own; something of what he feels enters into it and is borne on to others who are to read thereafter."

Hutchins Hapgood, in a review of "Four and Twenty Minds," in The New Republic, Vol. XXXII, No. 412, October 25, 1922, p. 228.

THE DUBLIN MAGAZINE   (essay date 1923)

[In the following excerpt from an essay devoted to the works of Benedetto Croce, Gabriele D'Annunzio, and Papini, an anonymous critic discusses Papini's perception of himself as "the standard-bearer of new programmes in literature." Unexcerpted portions of the essay discuss the careers of the other two writers and offer some comparisons and contrasts between the three.]

Both in Italy and outside, the consensus of opinion "places" D'Annunzio, Croce, Papini as the three most interesting and accomplished of living Italian writers. In conjunction, they remind us of the individualistic nature of the Italian. In talents and feeling no three men could well be more dissimilar than D'Annunzio, poet, novelist, and excessive patriot; Croce, the philosopher, with his disentangling mind, vast erudition, his rock-like adherence to certain cardinal ideas; Papini, a restless, sceptical searcher for some certainty of belief, whom no modern movement has satisfied or left untouched. In practical life, too, these men have been divided. Croce was a Neutralist in 1914; he has been a member (Minister of Fine Arts) in the Cabinet of old Signor Giolitti, who had once to hide from the interventionist fury of the Roman populace. D'Annunzio's admirers claim that it was he chiefly who brought Italy into the war; and the romance of the poet's achievements at Fiume stirred two continents. Papini has talked of politics, as he has talked of everything else under the sun; but he is an Italian Hamlet, and does not proceed to action. With his bitter tongue he has lashed at times the theatricality, as it seems to him, of D'Annunzio, the self-content of Croce and his school of erudite critics.

Of the three, Papini is the youngest; now a man of between forty and fifty he started early to write, and had material for a spiritual autobiography when still in the early thirties. I do not think this autobiography, *Un Uomo Finito*, has yet been translated into English; yet it is Papini's most remarkable book, with the possible exception of his recent *La Storia di Cristo*. He has also written prose poems and innumerable essays; he has constituted himself at moments the standard-bearer of new programmes in literature—he is a Florentine, and Florence has been the home of new movements, including the programme of the Futurists. In *Un Uomo Finito,* a very vigorously written work, Papini tells us of many things; of the various phases of belief and disbelief, despair and hope through which he passed from childhood onwards; of the mediocre conditions in which he was nurtured; of his enormous reading; of his early literary efforts; of Tuscany, the countryside that was his own—not rich, tropical, perfumed like D'Annunzio's; but naked, melancholy, *moral*, with its "strong and clear rock"; its plain, "honest" flowers, "resolute cypresses," that seemed to him so much more beautiful than any southern landscape of palms, oranges, and whitened dust. A bitter and gloomy temper did not preclude the cloudiest ambitions; Papini was born, like Nietzsche, who was at one time his master, with the "malady of grandeur"—

This is my first recollection: I must have been eight or nine years old. . . . I found one day the story of Petrarch's coronation in the Capitol, and I read and re-read it. "I, too, I, too," I kept saying to myself, although I knew not precisely why the crown had been put on the head of the corpulent poet. . . . I made my father take me to the Viale dei Colli. When I got there, I picked from the low shrubs some evergreen foliage. I was not sure that it was the famous laurel; but that did not matter. Returning home, I shut myself in my little room . . . and made from the foliage a sort of crown which I put on my head, throwing over my shoulders a great red rag, and commenced to walk along the walls singing a mournful drawn-out ditty which to me seemed quivering and heroic.

Un Uomo Finito is not among the greatest of books; but as an accurate account of the inward processes of so many of Papini's contemporaries, it will be always read and valued by the men of Papini's generation, in every country. There are wonderful things in it, particularly those that picture the effect on the nervous system of intellectual subjects, of certain philosophical ideas, when comprehended for the first time—the chapter on the discovery of Berkeley and the passage to an absolute solipsism, is a good example. But from the various essays and reviews which Papini later on collected and published, essays and reviews touching on all the systems of thought, every attitude towards life, ancient and modern, this mood of surrender and docility is wholly absent. He plays skittles with all the philosophers, particularly with the most respected of the moderns, most particularly of all with his own contemporary and countryman, Bendetto Croce. Only Nietzsche and Bishop Berkeley (a strange conjunction) retain a certain measure of his respect. There is an interesting allusion in the essay on Berkeley, showing Papini's wide range, on the effect of Irish atmosphere on the Bishop's views of the Catholic Church. In the same volume, which contains the essay on Berkeley is a picturesque account of the overwhelming influence of Whitman's poetry on a young man; we note once more Papini's responsiveness to northern influences—yet, look at his portrait, surely he is a Mediterranean man, if ever there was one! These essays, with their delight in argument, in the besting of an opponent, reveal the pugnacious side of Papini's personality. In *La Storia di Cristo* alone Papini tries to be persuasive, to "convert" the reader to his own thought and mood. It is the book of a Catholic, without reservations. But it is written not for those of simple faith, who have never doubted, but for "the indifferent, the profane, the artists." A book that is to be classed a work of piety, a devotional work, distinguished from such other works of modern date in that its author has (as he observes modestly) "some notion of the art of writing and of poetry!" (pp. 61-3)

M. P., "Three Italians: Papini—Croce—D'Annunzio," in The Dublin Magazine, Vol. 1, No. 1, August, 1923, pp. 61-6.

JOSEPH WOOD KRUTCH   (essay date 1924)

[Krutch is widely regarded as one of America's most respected literary and drama critics. A conservative and idealistic thinker, he was a consistent proponent of human dignity and the preeminence of literary art. His literary criticism is characterized by such concerns: in The Modern Temper (1929) he argued that *because scientific thought has denied human worth, tragedy had become obsolete, and in* The Measure of Man *(1954) he attacked modern culture for depriving humanity of the sense of individual responsibility necessary for making important decisions in an increasingly complex age. In the following excerpt, Krutch reviews Papini's* The Failure.]

With the *Life of Christ* Giovanni Papini first swam into the ken of the vast public which is now acclaiming him with that unanimous and whole-hearted enthusiasm it reserves for the authors of those books which it accepts, not because they are forced upon it by clamor of some sort or other, but because it finds them truly congenial. Those who knew before something of this spectacular *enfant terrible* of ideas were few, but the rest are no doubt anxious to learn more of their idol, and *The Failure*, his autobiographical novel, will tell them much—though hardly of the sort of thing likely to assure any but the most uncritical. The book clearly reveals the character of the man, but it is less the character of a philosopher than of a romanticist, and a romanticist of a somewhat old-fashioned Byronic sort. With a more remarkable if not altogether intentional frankness he gives himself completely away, proudly parading both his uninterrupted search for the sensational and that boundless ambition of his which, at times, looks disconcertingly like Ambition's idiot sister, Vanity.

"Byronic" is the only word that describes fitly his grandiose dramatization of his character and of his actions from the moment when, as a child, he realized with a gloomy exaltation that he was "different," through his violent championships of all the most spectacular philosophies, to the moment when, at the end of [*The Failure*], he has exhausted the possibilities of the more startling heresies and is ready to assume his present role of Catholic conservative and vitriolic denouncer of everything which has appeared in the world since the Renaissance. "It is not hard to see that these eyes were never intended to reflect the blue of the heavens," he says in describing himself as a child. "And these lips, so tightly, so wilfully closed, were never made to be parted in a smile. They are the lips of a man who will suffer pain, but never betray it with a cry. They are lips that will be kissed too late in life." This passage sets the key, and Childe Harold and Manfred seem to live again. Papini's eye is fixed always on himself, and no human task is great enough to express his sense of his own importance. As a child he dreamed of composing an encyclopedia of encyclopedias which should include all knowledge, as a youth he planned a radical review which should set all Italy aflame, and then later he imagined himself the leader of some band of revolutionary doers who should upset and then remold the world. But he never knew for long at a time what it was that he was going to do; only the thirst for notoriety was constant, for, as he frankly confesses, he was determined to be "founder of a school, leader of a faction, prophet of a religion, redeemer of souls, author of a best seller, anything so long as I was first, foremost, greatest in Something."

I do not wish to imply that Papini has no brain or even that he has not in the past expressed some interesting ideas, but in any estimate of his work it is necessary to remember that he is first of all a romantic egoist to whom truth cannot seem for long more important in itself than as a means of self-exploitation. Often he is violent and vulgar, occasionally he is brilliant, but his dominant manner is excited, nervous, declamatory, florid—in a word, operatic, with bravura arias taking the place of passion. Sometimes, perhaps, he suggests the philosopher but far more often the tenor.

Once more, it seems, the super-subtle Italian has proved himself too much for the honest Saxon. Thousands of pious souls have accepted the *Life of Christ* in all simplicity and, entirely ignorant of the past of this matinee idol among philosophers, have been completely unaware of the sizzle of the spotlight and the smell of the grease paint which betray the theatrical character of the book. God works in a mysterious way and it will not do to question too closely the motive of a conversion, but when a man puts himself at the foot of the cross chiefly for the purpose of holding the center of the stage the joy in heaven over a sinner saved may well be tempered with a little skepticism. Papini was Atheist, Positivist, Pragmatist, Pyrrhonist, Nietzschian, and Theosophist before assuming the part of Medieval Catholic. This latest has been announced as positively his final appearance in his last and greatest role, but actors have a way of giving many farewell tours, and a wise public will always ask, What next? (p. 483)

Joseph Wood Krutch, "Two Actors and a Tragedy," in The Nation, *Vol. CXVIII, No. 3068, April 23, 1924, pp. 483-84.*

ARTHUR LIVINGSTON   (essay date 1931)

[*In the following excerpt, Livingston assesses* Gog, *Papini's only novel to be translated into English, as an antimodernist satire.*]

For some years past Giovanni Papini has been making no secret of the fact that his current address was the Mansion of Truth, where he could be found, ready for business, at all hours. On the background of Papini's whole biography as a fascinating spiritual adventurer this experiment in voluntary cretinism was certainly interesting; though the literary efforts that expressed it were often dull. To be sure those who had eyes sharp enough to penetrate the clouds of incense could see that something besides "spiritual regeneration" was going on. If Papini was dipping, with no special competence or enthusiasm, into ecclesiastical, apologetical and polemical literature, he was also following the movement of Continental, English and even American, letters. If he was loving Jesus and hating Jews he was also seeking in his old nationalistic formulae some "squared circle" in which he could again put on the gloves with his old-style fondness for slugging with his guard down. The only question was whether Papini, after a decade of softening in the sanctuary, could make a comeback, and, in the affirmative case, when he would do so.

In these last days he has published *Gog* . . . , and the book seems to answer the question. Papini has come back. One is half inclined to suspect him of having been spoofing part of the time in the interval; for if he has memorized a large part of the Gospels he must also have been reading Voltaire, or at least Anatole France. *Gog,* in fact, is a sort of *Candide*. It is a "conte philosophique" of the French eighteenth century. Even the style is there—that short, crisp, transparent sentence, made up of nouns, verbs, a few indispensable adverbs and still fewer adjectives, which the French call "analytical." If Papini will not confess to Voltaire he must confess at least to Leopardi, the Leopardi of the *Prose*. In some guise or other the Devil must have been among his callers at the Mansion of Truth.

To be sure *Gog* has a thesis of "antimodernism." It would not be fair to say that it is "anti-American." The fact that "Gog" (short for Goggins) is an American, "one of the richest men in the United States" at the end of the war, is merely incidental. He is a Melanesian halfbreed by birth. Papini has him educated in the United States only because in America the disease of modernism happens to show its most characteristic virulence. For the rest "Gog" travels all about the world, and everywhere, we are led to believe, he finds modernism (the "machine-age" stuff), and the modernism, we are also led to believe, is, when not grotesquely crazy, very, very bad.

This doctrine Papini diffuses through his book. It is the tithe he pays to the Truth. For in the other nine-tenths he is Papini, the old and very real Papini. That is saying a great deal: Giovanni Papini is a writer of genius.

In his journeys about the world (after retiring from business in Chicago) Gog has some seventy adventures, which are reported in that many brief, witty, unfailingly interesting "talks," which one may call stories, essays, or even editorials, as one may prefer. There are fantastic interviews with Henry Ford, Gandhi, Einstein, Freud, Lenin, Edison, Wells, Shaw, Frazer, Knut Hamsun and even a Spaniard—Ramon Gomez de la Serna. Some of the paragraphs show a very Papinian trait at its best: a free play of fancy, half childlike (in Papini's enjoyment of it as pure fun), always ingenious: a sculptor who makes statues out of smoke; what does it feel like to be a cannibal? What would music be like if the sounds were suppressed? . . . To his dying day, I believe, in one of the most attractive aspects of his genius he will be the "child sublime," adorable even when he is naughtiest. I do not know whether others have remarked an aspect of Papini's imagination where he is kindred with Poe. The lugubrious, the terrible, the "Gothic" allures him now and again, in pure imagination. And at such moments he is infallibly excellent.

As a "philosophical tale" *Gog* is a collection of tales. They have a cumulative effect of some power. This modern world of ours when it is examined fragment by fragment may be thought of as a sort of Babylonic chaos monstrous, portentous, mighty, insane. . . .

Whether the character of "Gog" is coherently conceived one may well wonder. Perhaps Papini deliberately leaves us wondering. As a typical spirit of this modern world, as contrasted with Papini, who, presumably, exemplifies the sanity of some other world (the Medieval?), "Gog" should look at things from the modern point of view. We understand him, in fact, when he speaks most sacrilegiously of the great classics of world literature. What appreciation could a Melanesian half-breed educated in the United States have of Dante, of Goethe, of Dostoievsky? But to invert judgments to this extent would be a difficult formula even for a man of Papini's talent to use. He deserts it almost at once and for the greater part of the volume. "Gog" would seem to be Papini. Perhaps the solution of the inconsistency is to be found in the fact that Papini, as a poet, likes ideas merely because they are ideas and quite irrespective of their truth. That is why, as Papini earnestly explains in his introduction, "Gog" is talking on his own responsibility exclusively, without danger or compromise to Papini! In other words, "Gog" may sometimes artistically and in all seriousness expound ideas of which Papini does not approve! But, in this case, one has a right to ask: is it only in *Gog* that Papini's love of ideas is so Platonic? Is he equally Platonic in his love of the truth?

And one might voice one little lament. "Gog," being the millionaire that he was, bought a library in the United States just after the war. As an American of the period he surely bought one of those half-million copies of the *Life of Christ* that Giovanni Papini sold in this Magog of the Machine Age. It would have been interesting to have his opinion of it.

By virtue of its mood (chaos, insanity, violence), its restless intellectuality, and its resort to pure fancy, *Gog* might be classified, by those who insist on classifications, with the present-day Italian "modernistic" trend toward irrationality, or better non-nationality, a term that is clearer on its negative side as a denial of naturalism. This development in the arts is, of course, general throughout Europe. It is even world-wide. In letters, however, the Italians early took the lead in it, and they are still holding their ground, if the bulk of their "modernist" production and the average excellence of their results be taken as standards of measurement.

Arthur Livingston, "Italian Humor," in New York Herald Tribune Books, *January 25, 1931, p. 9.*

WILLIAM P. GIULIANO   (essay date 1946)

[*In the following excerpt, Guiliano traces the growth of religious feeling in Papini as demonstrated by his constant examination and ultimate rejection of all nonreligious philosophies, a process which culminated in his religious conversion.*]

Giovanni Papini, rather late in life, finally achieved Christianity and gave us the *Storia di Cristo,* one of the finest accounts of the life of Christ written in modern times. His inspiration, the warmth of his account, may come from the fact that he found Christ only after a long, bitter, struggle against Him, yet towards whom he always felt himself irresistibly drawn. . . .

Papini's writings are characterized by a search for truth. He reminds one of a man searching for a lost object. He walks along, pounces on a thing which resembles it, shouts for joy, but examining it closely he realizes that it is not the thing he is seeking and dejectedly throws it away, continuing the search with fearfully beating heart. This search for truth is epitomized in *Un uomo finito,* a spiritual autobiography of his intellectual investigations up to the year of its publication, 1912.

This desire for truth is the motivation of all his speculations, but it in turn is generated by an infinitely potent desire to make himself great, to raise himself above the multitude, to become immortal at any price, in any field of speculation. He himself, affirms this fact in *Un uomo finito.* . . .

This egoism took an intellectual direction, perhaps because he began reading voluminously at an early age, and also because he was very conscious at an early age of his physical unattractiveness and wished to compensate for it by making himself intellectually attractive. In order to avenge himself on the rest of the world because of its aversion towards him, he decided to make himself a great man. He definitely alludes to this in *Un uomo finito.* (p. 304)

The youngster had made a decision. He was to become an immortal. His greatest asset and his keenest weapon was his intellectual capacity. Therefore, he wanted his name to be placed alongside that of Dante, Shakespeare, Cervantes, Goethe, Aristotle, etc. to be revered for all time by all men. His first god was Papini. His first church was the library. Later he enrolled under the banner of pragmatism and appropriately called his ultimate goal l'Uomo-Dio.

According to Papini, man wants to become l'Uomo-Dio in order to attain perfect and lasting peace. He can reach this state of beatitude in two ways; by simply renouncing all desire, Nirvana, or by becoming omnipotent and thus so satiated with power as to be bereft of desire, also Nirvana. The first, the

Nirvana of Buddhism, Papini says, is a failure. Consequently man must make himself omnipotent.

By means of metaphysics, religion, the arts, occult arts, and performances of miracles, he must make himself capable of doing anything, and, upon knowing that he has the capacity to do anything, he will have no further desires. Hence, he will have achieved Nirvana, eternal peace, perfect immobility and absolute cessation of all action.

Papini of course did not succeed in making himself omnipotent. He wished to attempt the impossible precisely because it was impossible. Finally, even he made no further attempts to attain the unattainable. Philosophy had failed him, not only in his pragmatism, his Uomo-Dio, but also in the philosophies he had so joyously embraced before that venture. He had been a Schopenhauerian pessimist, a positivist, a monist, an idealist, a mystic, and an occultist. He had discarded them one by one. He had no further use for philosophy, and he took his leave of it in *Crepuscolo dei filosofi*. . . .

In *Crepuscolo dei filosofi* he discusses Kant, Hegel, Schopenhauer, Spencer, Nietzsche, and Comte and reduces their systems to mere plays on words. He attempts to prove that all their speculations are devices to justify their own beliefs by dialectics based on unproven premises. These were the men who had previously impressed him most, and by crushing them, he had liberated himself.

This is the first of his disillusionments. He now turned to creative writing. He had not succeeded in the realm of the logical, the real, so he was constrained to direct his efforts to the illogical, the unreal, the fantastic. He could not fathom the real world so he had to create a world of his own. He then wrote [*Il tragico quotidiano, Il pilota cieco, Parole e sangue, Buffonate, Le memorie d'Iddio, La vita de nessuno*, and *Cento pagine di poesia*]. . . . The first four books are collections of articles written by Papini in many newspapers and magazines. The first two from 1904-1906, *Parole e sangue* from 1907-1910, *Buffonate* from 1912-1914.

All of them contain a series of short stories written in a very fantastic vein. While they are fantastic to the point of absurdity, they retain an element of reality, and each one has a message to tell. They are the battleground of his thoughts, an attempt to liberate himself from the ideas he has rejected by putting them on paper. For example, in *Il tragico quotidiano* ("L'uomo che volle essere imperatore") and No. 3. of *Parole e sangue* ("L'uomo desireoso"), we see a return to idealism. In No. 5 of *Il tragico quotidiano* ("Il demonio tentato") he wants the devil to make the whole world one homogeneous substance (monism). In No. 9 of the same work, ("L'ultima visita del gentiluomo malato"), there is the desire to annihilate himself (Schopenhauerian pessimism). In No. 11 of *Il tragico quotidiano* ("Non voglio esser più quel che sono") he has reached the depths of pessimism and wishes to transform himself into an entirely new person. *Memorie d'Iddio* is an acknowledgment of the failure of his Uomo-Dio. In it he achieves omnipotence but he is still unhappy.

Papini by this time has reached a state of complete and profound pessimism. He hates everything human and material. In many stories his characters die, led to their death by a relentless chain of circumstances. Papini is like Mattia Pascal. He strives incessantly to destroy his former self, but he cannot escape from his past. His past must forever be reflected in his existence at any given moment.

In some of the stories, however, he merely wishes to stimulate men into thinking. This is especially true of those in *Buffonate*. It may be said that all these stories are written with a double purpose; a mental catharsis, and the desire to reveal problems to those who have never stopped to consider them.

Of this group, *Cento pagine di poesia* stands out as an example of Papini's great lyrical qualities in his prose. One is carried away by its flowing rhythm and strikingly beautiful imagery. The content is also strikingly different. Papini here rejects mankind and turns to nature and animals for consolation. In No. 1 ("I miei amici") he shows a great love for a serpent, a toad, a scorpion and a jay. Only his immediate family is exempted from this scorn towards humanity, and he devotes two tender episodes to the eulogy of their charms. No. 3 ("Il mio fiume") is a masterpiece of lyrical description. He vividly and beautifully describes the immortal life of a river. Man's life is short by comparison. Man is impotent against the great forces of nature. Each story of this work is an expression of Papini's innermost thoughts, told in an incomparably beautiful, rhythmic prose.

Papini still did not find the peace he was seeking. He had rejected almost everything of positive value, therefore he made one last effort to find himself by examining negative values in *L'altra metà*, first published in 1912. In it Papini starts from this premise:—every proposition begets its opposite. Consequently since we have failed to divine the real essence of Being, let us study Diversity, the Impossible, the Non-existent; for Knowledge we must study Ignorance, Error, and Insanity; for Action we should investigate Inaction, Evil and the Useless.

Papini devotes the entire book to the inquiries concerning these negative values. He is always logical and often makes significant and important observations, but he can never accomplish his objective. The last chapter, "Rimorsi," is written in true Papinian style. He realizes the futility of his quest and says:

"Chi crede insomma, che in questo libro c'è la verità, un buon dato di verità, sarebbe uno stupido anche agli occhi miei, di me, padre ingrato e disconoscente" ["Who believes on the whole, that in this book there is truth, a good quantity of truth, would also be a dunce in my eyes, by me, thankless father and ingrate"].

The nature of the book clearly shows the desperate, abject pessimism of Papini. He has tried every field of knowledge to ascertain a rational truth, but again he has failed. In *L'altra metà*, however, the beginning of the acceptance of Christianity can be seen. Papini himself later had the book reprinted because it represented the initial stages of his conversion. (pp. 305-07)

Thus Papini, unable to find a rational absolute truth, rejects reality and begins to look towards the supernatural. The event which finally made Papini a firm Catholic, however, was World War I. During the period 1914-1917, he was preoccupied mainly with matters concerning the war. He urged the Italians to fight on the side of the Allies and tried to enlist himself. He was greatly disappointed on being rejected because of physical defects. He soon learned, however, that war was a grim game. The innumerable massacres, and the destruction of countless lives and property filled him with horror, and thus for a second reason he rejected the world of reality and looked towards the supernatural. He was now a Catholic in every sense of the word. He did not explain the reason for his conversion until many years later when he published an article in 1932 (published in *La pietra infernale* later), entitled "Il Croce e la croce." . . .

It would seem that the World War, and his philosophical dis-illusionments led to Papini's conversion rather late in his life but such is not the case. From the moment he took his pen in hand he was destined to be led to Christianity, for in his very earliest writings when he was very far from calling himself a Christian he showed a great deal of respect for the Church. (p. 308)

Throughout his writings Papini constantly uses the terminology of the church; e.g. l'Uomo-Dio, Santo, etc. His means of reaching the state of l'Uomo-Dio are precisely those which lead to the canonization of holy men, that is, the working of miracles, fasting, solitude, chastity, and concentration of the spiritual faculties.

He also wrote a number of articles from 1908-1914 which, if read without reference to his other works, would lead one to believe that he had always been a staunch Catholic. He later collected them and edited them in a book, *Polemiche religiose.* A brief summary of the more important ones follows:

I. **"La religione sta da sè"** (1908). He defends Catholicism against Croce as a system independent of philosophy and in no way subservient to it.

III. **"Ecce homo"** (1912). He defends the literal interpretation of the Gospels against W. P. Smith who believed them symbolical.

V. **"I liberi cristiani"** (1910). He is hostile to the Modernists.

VI. **"Puzzo di cristianucci"** (1913) and

VII. **"Esistono cattolici"** (1913). He exposes the hypocrisy of many Catholics.

VIII. **"Risposta a Benedetto"** (1914). This is a diatribe against Pope Benedict XVI for his incompetence in trying to end the war, and against the weaknesses of the church in general.

Papini during these years was strongly anti-religious, yet one cannot help thinking, after reading these articles, that his criticisms were not destructive ones, but rather were attempts to purify the Church by pointing out its faults.

As was pointed out in the beginning of this article, Papini's great inspiration was always the desire to make himself great, to create a new creed with himself as the head. After years of fruitless effort he gave up. He was no longer anxious to be the prime mover himself but was now content to accept a position as a pillar of the church, to strive to achieve his greatness within the framework of the Church, to become a saint. He no longer wished his name to be placed alongside that of Goethe, Shakespeare, and Cervantes but alongside that of St. Thomas Aquinas, and St. Augustine. (p. 309)

[Ironically] enough, Papini's first step into the fold brought him more fame than any he had ever achieved while striving to remain outside of it. The *Storia di Cristo* . . . deservedly merits the praise it provoked. It has a fresh vividness which brings it very close to the reader and makes Christ a very close friend of his. Throughout the book there is evident a strong love for Christ, a nostalgia to behold Him and adore Him which reaches its climax in the epilogue, a fervent prayer to Christ.

Christ's greatest and most important axiom was, for Papini, "Love thine enemies." It is the leit-motif of the whole story; the doctrine Papini wishes to teach a war-torn world that all peoples might unite in everlasting peace.

The key to the new Papini lies in his book *Sant' Agostino.* Papini felt very close to Saint Augustine because Saint Augustine had exalted the intellect, and had been converted from a life of sin to Christianity. He says as much in his preface. . . . (p. 310)

Papini then proceeds to devote most of his time to the propagation of the faith. He writes of the lives and works of great Catholics both ancient and modern, that we might emulate them (*Scala di Giacobbe,* a collection of articles written between 1919-1930 . . . , *Sant' Agostino, Gli operai della vigna* . . .). He even takes Dante to task in *Dante Vivo* . . . , for not following the road he has shown to others. He takes pains to point out the contradictions between Dante the poet and Dante the man. He says that Dante could never be an imitator of Christ because he was proud, revengeful, lascivious and cruel. He condemns him as a Christian but admires him as a poet and as a Catholic who indicates the good road to others.

Papini is relentless in his attacks upon the enemies of the Church, and unstinting in his praise of the great Catholics. He is now a firm pillar of the Church.

In 1931 the old Papini rose up once again to face the new one and he wrote *Gog.* All the conflicting ideas and emotions which had so tormented him before he had found peace in the Church, visited him again. *Gog* is a worthy and suitable companion for *Il tragico quotidiano, Il pilota cieco, Memorie d'Iddio, Vita di nessuno, Parole e sangue,* and *Buffonate.* It is again fantastic but at the same time critical and purifying. All of his discarded ideas return to torment him and perhaps by writing them down he thought he could liberate himself from them just as he had freed himself from his previous philosophical beliefs in *Crepuscolo dei filosofi.* In the story entitled "Filomania" (study of insanity) we see the return of *L'altra metà.* "Egolatria" seems a regeneration of l'Uomo-Dio. "Siao Sin," and "Sir C. Frazer e la magia" are a return to occultism. "Il viale degli dei" savors of the old anti-Catholicism. In "Caccavone" he reduces Being to *il Nulla,* and lastly "Ripulitura difficile" is the re-birth of the desire for the complete extinction of our species (Schopenhauer). He adversely criticizes poetry, music, the theater, our ideas of progress and our institutions. We see traces of his former idealism, pessimism, and fatalism. He is still the seeker of glory. . . . (pp. 310-11)

Thus the militant Catholic Papini still retained some of the elements of his former self just as the atheist Papini had in him the seeds of Christianity.

Papini may not be canonized by the Church he has so well attacked and defended, but he has left his mark in the literary world and he can rightfully say that he has fulfilled the wish he so determinedly expressed as a child:

"Son piccino, povero e brutto ma ho un'anima anch'io e quest' anima getterà tali gridi che tutti dovrete voltarvi e sentirmi" ["A small child, poor and ill-favored, but I too have a soul, and this soul will let out such a cry that all must take notice"]. (p. 311)

William P. Giuliano, "Spiritual Evolution of Giovanni Papini," in Italica, *Vol. XXIII, No. 4, December, 1946, pp. 304-11.*

CARLO L. GOLINO (essay date 1955)

[*In the following excerpt, Golino examines the development of Papini's Pragmatist thought, contending that Papini's presenta-*

tion of William James's philosophy of Pragmatism in the journal Leonardo *was the first instance of a general introduction and acceptance of American culture into Italy.*]

Giovanni Papini was one of the very few Italian writers well known outside of Italy long before the recent *discovery* of Italian literature made the names and works of contemporary writers of that country commonplace knowledge throughout the world. His **Dante Vivo** and particularly his **Life of Christ** have been translated into practically every known language. But these books are the fruit of the mature Papini and give us but a glimpse of his brilliant and versatile intellect. It is this unique personality which gives him such an outstanding and peculiar place in the history of Italian letters. A powerful writer endowed with a vivid and lucid style, an inveterate satirist who preferred bluntness to subtlety, an acid critic who spared neither friends nor admirers, a patriot who missed no chance to curse his countrymen, a sentimentalist who analyzed human feelings with clinical objectivity, a man of deep religious feeling who professed atheism for a good part of his life, this man of paradox and contrast never waivered from his ultimate goal, that was the search of truth. So far he has given us no great masterpiece; but whether as a creative writer, as a critic, as an editor, or as an instigator of intellectual controversy, he has always played the role of a leavening agent in Italian intellectual life, and in his indefatigable search for truth he has explored all realms of human thought and experience, bringing to light and disseminating through Italy innumerable and varied currents from abroad, and reexamining with new criteria the more traditional and fundamental Italian trends.

This desire to break from tradition, "di rinnovarsi," as he was fond of saying, is probably the strongest characteristic of the young Papini, and it found its earliest sustained expression in the review *Leonardo*. (pp. 38-9)

Since the concern of the *Leonardo* was not with literature *per se,* but rather with life as a whole, philosophy became its prime concern and, in fact, its first attack was directed against the then prevailing school of philosophical thought, that is, Positivism. In this respect Papini was very fortunate for he had as a collaborator Giuseppe Prezzolini, who, though not an original philosopher, possessed that keenness of mind and that perceptive ability so necessary to philosophical analysis. It is well to remember at this point that both of these men were very young. Papini was then twenty-two and Prezzolini twenty-one. It was probably because of their youth that they were able so recklessly to challenge the world, for that is what their program amounts to. I need not emphasize that the reception the journal received was hardly joyous or flattering. The serious scholars of the responsible academic world dismissed it with a shrug of the shoulders and some mumbling about the impudence of today's youth. The more open-minded and intellectual resented the haughty tone of the journal and only the intellectually unemployed sensed something in the air and made themselves comfortable for a good spectacle. They were not disappointed. After the first three or four issues of *Leonardo* had appeared, it became obvious that this magazine could not be easily dismissed. Both its editor, Papini, and its chief contributor, Prezzolini, brought to it an erudition and a preparation well beyond their years. This intellectual preparation plus the above-mentioned aggressive spirit which animated the magazine made it indeed a formidable destructive instrument. For the chief function of *Leonardo* through its initial period was that of destructive criticism. The situation well justified this function. The desire to break from the past, to find new horizons and new directions was well evident throughout Italy, and *Leonardo*

was one of the first concrete and articulate expressions of this fast-developing spirit. It is no mere coincidence that two other reviews, *La Critica* of Benedetto Croce and *Il Regno* of Enrico Corradini, both extremely significant for a comprehension of Italian culture of the period, began publication at about the same time.

These three magazines initiated the period which has been called the age of journals in Italian literature. After them, literally hundreds of reviews, usually short-lived and normally revolutionary, have come and gone on the Italian scene and, if they have not left any evident profound traces, they clearly indicate a period of radical change in Italian culture. The main theme in this new orientation is the *esame di coscienza,* that is, an introspective examination by the intellectual and the artist in order to discover new and original thoughts and inspirations, to find as a substitute for the fast-disappearing set of values inherited from the 19th century a new concept of life, a new philosophical interpretation of existence. Naturally, the inevitable fragmentation of views and directions led to such absurd excesses as Futurism. But even this movement had ultimately a beneficial result, for it helped to break once and for all Italian intellectual provincialism by projecting the Italian artist in front of world problems and by leading Italian culture from the cozy shelter of the provincial culture club or elegant literary salon into the currents of international intellectual life. Thus, if nothing more, Papini and his *Leonardo* had the merit of being instrumental in starting off this much-needed revival of Italian cultural life. More specifically, *Leonardo* set about its destructive task by tearing down the existing idols beginning, as I mentioned, with Positivism. Papini's personal need for a more transcendental vision of life, the unimaginative nature of Pos-

Papini in Florence. From Giovanni Papini, *by Vintila Horia. Wesmael-Charlier, 1963. Reproduced by permission of the publisher.*

itivism, the suffocating materialism which this philosophy preached, made it abhorrent to Papini who, even then, perhaps unconsciously, felt himself attracted toward the explanation of life in terms of God, a feeling which was eventually to become the prevalent one in his mind and lead him back to Catholicism. On the other hand, the new idealism which Benedetto Croce was beginning to disseminate, while it attracted Papini momentarily, could not fill his spiritual vacuum. [The critic adds in a footnote that "the early relations between Papini and Croce were very cordial. The latter praised the early numbers of the *Leonardo* in his *Critica*. But as Papini drew farther and farther from Croce's idealism, his criticism of the 'celebre accademico pontaniano,' as he sarcastically called Croce, became sharper and sharper until all direct contacts ceased entirely."] Papini objected to its basic immanentism and monism, and he felt that it afforded him no opportunity for the realization of his intense desire for activity which was one of his primary motivations. True, this desire for action, we have seen, had manifested itself in a negative fashion by undermining existing and traditional concepts. But this was due chiefly to the lack of anything positive, any definite concept out of which he could find an ultimate goal. . . . As has been suggested, the spirit of *Leonardo* might be synthesized in one word, "insofferenza"—a word which can mean dissatisfaction, intolerance or impatience with existing conditions, and a desire for change. It was at this point that Papini discovered Pragmatism, and from then on *Leonardo* became identified with this philosophy. Papini first came in contact with it through the writings of William James which only shortly before had begun to appear in Europe and were as yet hardly known in Italy. What appealed to Papini was that Pragmatism, without denying the possibility of transcendental flight, left the door open for immediate and practical activity. . . . Pragmatism has been defined as the utilitarian or practical philosophy. Some have gone so far as to deny that Pragmatism is a philosophy at all, but that it should rather be regarded as a psychological attitude in which the utilitarian results are the basis for all measurements. At any rate, according to it nothing in life has an absolute value, neither matter nor spirit. Everything, instead, has a practical value; that is to say, our ideas are true only in as much as they are susceptible of practical realization. Objective truth does not exist; truth exists only as a utilitarian criterion. For example, since it is useful to believe in God, and since this faith can create in the believer a great vital energy, it is good to believe in God, without stopping to ask oneself whether God actually exists. One must therefore believe in order to act and because believing is useful to life. (pp. 39-42)

Once Papini had accepted Pragmatism he proceeded to give to it a peculiar turn through his intellectual background, and *Leonardo* became the outstanding exponent of Pragmatism not only in Italy but in Europe, where this review had begun to acquire a very respectable reputation. In fact, in 1907, after four years of life, the *Leonardo* was an all-around success; it even became economically solvent. It was just at this point—that is, at the height of the magazine's success—that all of a sudden Papini and Prezzolini decided to stop its publication. In announcing this decision, Papini gave as a chief reason the very success of the review. He felt *Leonardo* was becoming too respectable, too solid, too conventional, and that its earlier sense of urgency of reform, its zeal for action and its originality were being overwhelmed by its success. Actually, Papini and Prezzolini were coming to the parting of their ways and their common pragmatic experience was to lead them toward different directions. By the same token they felt that the mission of the *Leonardo* had been carried out. They had set out to awaken in

Italy an interest in new trends of thought; they had sought to break down the barriers of tradition and stimulate new activity in Italian intellectual life. This they had accomplished. . . . (pp. 42-3)

This, then, was the extent and life of the *Leonardo*. All the polemics and discussions on Pragmatism which Papini had published in the *Leonardo* he finally synthesized into two volumes. One, **Il crepuscolo dei filosofi,** is a résumé of the earlier or more destructive period of Papini's activity. It is, as William James himself remarked:

> . . . the settling of the author's private accounts with several philosophers (Kant, Hegel, Schopenhauer, Comte, Spencer, Nietzsche) and a clearing of his mental tables from their impeding rubbish, so as to leave him the freer for constructive business [see excerpt dated 1906].

The second work, **Pragmatismo,** is the synthesis of the positive or constructive part of Papini's thought during the *Leonardo* years and it represents the actual sum total of Papini's pragmatic experience.

Exactly how did Papini assimilate, transform or change the basic tenets of Pragmatism? Perhaps no one can answer our question better than William James, the first inspirer of Papini, and the international prophet of this philosophy. On April 30, 1904, there took place in Rome the Fifth International Congress of Psychology; William James attended this meeting and delivered a paper which was immediately translated and published by *Leonardo* in the June number of the same year. After his visit to Rome, James went to Florence and there met Papini in person. His impressions of the young Italian intellectual were most favorable and far-reaching [see James entry in Additional Bibliography]. . . . In the following year, still much impressed by Papini's contribution to Pragmatism, James devoted a long article to him [see excerpt dated 1906]. . . . James stated that . . . "[Papini] has a real genius for cutting and untechnical phraseology. He can write descriptive literature, polychromatic with adjectives, like a decadent, and clean up a subject by drawing cold distinctions, like a scholastic." In general, wrote James, Papini has accepted the basic ideas of Pragmatism. He has shown his originality and contributed to the clarification of its concepts in many ways. Most original is Papini's explanation of Pragmatism with his so-called corridor theory. Pragmatism, according to Papini and as explained by James:

> . . . is only a collection of attitudes and methods, and its chief characteristic is its armed neutrality in the midst of doctrines. It is like a corridor in a hotel, from which a hundred doors open into a hundred chambers. In one you may see a man on his knees praying to regain his faith; in another a desk at which sits someone eager to destroy all metaphysics; in a third a laboratory with an investigator looking for new footholds by which to advance upon the future. But the corridor belongs to all, and all must pass there. Pragmatism, in short, is a great corridor-theory.

The other and more significant addition of Papini to the theory of Pragmatism is a more definite and articulate expression of that transcendental tendency which I have already pointed out existed in Papini originally. This new concept Papini had explained in an article in *Leonardo* called **"Dall'uomo a Dio,"** and it represented his most original conribution to Pragmatism. Starting with the assumption that since change and action are the most general ideals possible, "philosophy can become a 'pragmatic' in the strict sense of the word, meaning a general theory of human action." In other words, in Papini's line of thought:

> Ends and means can here be studied together, in the abstractest and most inclusive way, so that philosophy can resolve itself into a comparative discussion of all the possible programs for man's life when man is once for all regarded as a creative being.
>
> As such, man becomes a kind of god, and where are we to draw his limits?

James was impressed by Papini's novel attempt and he stated that he was unable to treat it otherwise than respectfully, for he saw great possibilities for the opening of new and unforeseen horizons for Pragmatism through Papini's views.

> Why should not the divine attributes of omniscience and omnipotence be used by man as the pole-stars by which he may methodically lay his own course? Why should not divine *rest* be his own ultimate goal, rest attained by an activity in the end so immense that all desires are satisfied, and no more action necessary? The unexplored powers and relations of man, both physical and mental, are certainly enormous; why should we impose limits on them *a priori*? And, if not, why are the most utopian programs not in order?
>
> The programme of a Man-God is surely one of the possible great type-programmes of philosophy. I myself have been slow in coming into the full inwardness of pragmatism. Schiller's writings and those of Dewey and his school have taught me some of its wider reaches; and in the writings of this youthful Italian, clear in spite of all their brevity and audacity, I find not only a way in which our English views might be developed farther with consistency— at least so it appears to me—but also a tone of feeling well fitted to rally devotees and to make of pragmatism a new militant form of religion or quasi-religious philosophy.

Coming from the one person who was above all responsible for the diffusion and wide understanding of Pragmatism, these were very complimentary words, particularly for a young and still relatively unknown intellectual such as Papini. But as we have seen, a few months after James wrote these words, *Leonardo* ceased publication and the pragmatistic parenthesis in Papini's intellectual development began to draw to an end. A year after *Leonardo* disappeared, Prezzolini came out with another periodical, *La Voce*, which was to have even greater effects than the former on Italian culture. But it was a different Prezzolini. He had definitely abandoned Pragmatism and shifted toward, and finally embraced, Croce's idealism. Papini, after *Leonardo*, went along with the new Futurist movement but quickly broke away to found still another review, *Lacerba*, which retained only in part the orientation of the earlier *Leonardo*.

It is now time to ask ourselves what significance did this pragmatic experience have in the formation of Papini and his associates of *Leonardo*, and by reflection, how it affected Italian cultural trends of the period. Obviously it was not a paramount influence. It was rather a point of departure which was offered to them when the deteriorating concept of Positivism and the resurgent Idealism seemed to have nothing to offer on which to build. Equally, it did not leave any lasting traces on Italian culture because it never left the limited and exclusive circle of intellectuals and was never changed into a manner of life for the people in general. But the particular overtone of the necessity of action which is fundamental in Pragmatism did have definite repercussions on the Italian scene through the personalities of Papini and the other members of *Leonardo*, and this gave a powerful jolt to the sense of complacency and lethargy and to the somnolent provincialism which had afflicted a great part of Italian cultural life to that time. True enough, the sense of urgency for action we have seen to exist in Papini, but Pragmatism offered him the first opportunity to channel this tendency into concrete results. However minor these considerations may be in themselves and when seen within the restricted framework of the life span of *Leonardo*, they acquire a different light if observed from the wider point of view of American influences on Italy. The *Leonardo* and Pragmatism are the first sustained and successful effort to introduce American intellectual trends in Italy. The longstanding prejudice that America could not play the role of intellectual mentor to European culture suffered a heavy blow from Papini. . . . It is perhaps a coincidence that a definite interest in American culture begins to awaken in Italy shortly after *Leonardo*, but it is definitely true that what was to become in later years a veritable *flood* of American culture and customs in Italy found its first expression with the penetration of Pragmatism into Italian soil. (pp. 43-7)

Carlo L. Golino, "Giovanni Papini and American Pragmatism," in Italica, *Vol. XXXII, No. 1, March, 1955, pp. 38-48.*

GIOVANNI GULLACE (essay date 1962)

[*In the following excerpt, Gullace discusses* The Devil.]

Papini's first dealing with the Devil goes back more than fifty years to the time when the author was twenty-four. In 1905, in fact, he wrote two stories—**"The Devil Said to Me,"** and **"The Tempted Devil"**—which should be credited to his youthful contacts with Satan. Since then his mind had almost constantly been concerned with the fallen angel. But his conception of Satan underwent radical changes over the years, especially after his conversion to Christianity in 1921. (He began his *Life of Christ* with a Voltairian smile and ended it in tears, moved to the depths by his own story.) Prior to his conversion Papini's interest in the Devil had been rather literary: his Christian faith gave him a new outlook. But strangely enough he always felt sympathy rather than hatred for the terrible fate of the once most perfect of all angels. Papini's lively sense of charity brought him to desire and to hope that God's infinite mercy might finally prevail over His supreme justice, and that the cursed angel might be restored to his celestial seat. Some of his desires and hopes concerning Satan were expounded in 1950 in a short drama in three acts, **"The Tempted Devil,"** which was twice presented on radio in Italy. But the thoughts springing from his long years of study and meditation were to take form in his 398-page book, *Il Diavolo*, which appeared in Florence in December 1953.

The thesis of Papini's book constitutes a serious challenge to official doctrine and reveals a new and unsuspected dimension of the Catholic writer—that of Papini, apologist of Satan. The author maintains, however, that his book is neither a history of beliefs about the Devil, nor an erudite survey of ancient and modern legends, nor a Scholastic treatise, nor a collection of holy invectives, nor a metaphysical lucubration on the problem of evil, and so on (actually his disclaimer is true only for "holy invectives"). He warns that his book is not an apology for the Devil, but rather a painstaking and unprejudiced study on: 1) "the true causes of Lucifer's revolt (which are not those commonly believed)"; 2) "the true relations between God and the Devil (far more cordial than imagined)"; 3) "the possibility of an attempt on the part of mankind to have Satan returned to his original status, thus freeing us all from the temptation of evil." . . . Different, however, is the impression the book leaves on the reader. Rather than Christianlike, the author appears in his pages as the ambassador of Satan, stubbornly determined to defend his master at all costs. His intent is evidently a triple one: 1) to show what he thinks to be the whole truth concerning the fallen angel and disprove all misrepresentation; 2) to explain the necessity of his presence in the world and the injustice of our hatred toward him; 3) to demonstrate conclusively that the Devil deserves to be saved, and that, as good Christians, we ought to work toward his redemption in the way Papini suggests.

It is hard to understand how one can be a good Christian while working for the salvation of Satan, whom God damned and cursed. But Papini, as a keen dialectician, has a great deal to say on this matter. His whimsical book is a small encyclopedia of diabolic discussions, sometimes surprisingly banal, inconsistent, or contradictory. The author seems determined to use every bit of information and the resources of his mind to build, in Papinian style, this paradoxical and controversial monument to the Devil. Many people wonder whether Papini is possessed. When he was about to write the last chapters of the book, which are the crucial ones, his right hand was suddenly stricken by paralysis. Was it a warning? But the author did not surrender: he continued his work dictating the rest of it to his niece with astonishing determination. (pp. 233-35)

Many Catholics still wonder why Papini, who knew Christian thought so well and who had been its tireless defender for over thirty years, waged this attack against the eternity of infernal punishments which is part of the fundamental dogma of the Catholic Church. Papini's answer is very clear: he candidly holds that he is not dogmatizing, but that he is simply expressing a hope—according to him, a very legitimate hope for any true Christian. The doctrine of the reconciliation of all creatures with God is not a part of the teaching of the Church, but Papini maintains that, in its historical development, the doctrine underwent many changes. Through the years new opinions have been accepted, while others have been abandoned, if not condemned. A similar renewal may occur in the centuries to come. Provided that the essence of the dogma is not altered or denied (apparently Papini refuses to admit the evident alterations of the dogma which his book advocates), it is always possible to enrich it with new experiences, and to deepen it with new and more authentic interpretations. Christians who follow orthodox doctrine faithfully in its eternal meaning cannot deny the existence of Hell, but they would be more Christian, says the author, if they desired. Hell to be depopulated: an empty Hell and an overcrowded Paradise! Papini holds that it is impossible to conceive of God, who is the true Father, as eternally torturing His children. God, whose all-embracing love is manifest in Christ, cannot eternally deny His forgiveness even to the first rebel. Mercy, thinks the author, finally must prevail over justice; otherwise we must conclude that the Father of Christ is not a perfect Christian.

> We cannot pretend, says Papini, that these sentiments and thoughts may be accepted today as official doctrine by the ruling Church and much less do we pretend to speak either for it or in its place. But that which may not be taught as sure, certain truth may and must be admitted as Christian and human hope. The treatises of theology continue to say "no" to the doctrine of total and ultimate reconciliation but the heart "which has its reasons that reason does not know" will continue to yearn for and to await a "yes." In the school of Christ we have learned that the impossible is above all the credible. . . .

Papini stresses several times that he is not expounding a well-established truth, but only a hope. Consequently, the crux of the whole question is to be found in the two terms: Truth, Hope. Theologically, truth is a fixed formulation, a definite dogma which admits no internal antinomies, and which is not susceptible to further development. In the order of fixed truth—dogma—it is impossible to allow the redemption of Satan without weakening the dramatic tension through which the Christian achieves his destiny. The existence of Hell and the eternity of infernal punishments are thus unalterable truths of the Christian doctrine which are at the basis of man's action and give eternal meaning to his choice. But while Truth is actuality, Hope is potentiality: it is a sort of dynamic force within the soul impelling it toward a different state. Within the order of Hope nothing appears in the form of rigid definition, but everything is in motion, in a state of dramatic expectation. This élan toward universal restoration, the vision of an empty Hell and an overflowing Paradise, are motifs and experiences that the Church has never rejected, leaving in mystery the definition of final punishment. St. Paul, in fact, seems to extend to all rational beings the benefit of redemption. The mysterious sense of certain Scriptural texts leaves the door open to man's hope. In expressing this hope, however, Papini comes to preemptory conclusions. He applies all the resourcefulness and sharpness of his mind to show that there are many things in Christian doctrine which are inexplicable, since our mind cannot penetrate God's final designs. Thus it is not illegitimate to conclude that things which seem illogical in the eyes of man may happen nevertheless. God with His absolute power can do what to man seems impossible. To justify his hope, which eventually leads to a Christian conception beyond the dogma and which presents serious and delicate problems, Papini offers in his book a series of surprising arguments, building up a curious mosaic full of contradictions and banalities. He takes advantage of all kinds of literature to prove his thesis. He digs up theories abandoned or condemned by the Church, and sometimes, forcing the sense of passages, draws his own unorthodox conclusions. When the religious writers and theologians are not enough, he resorts to poets, even though he well knows that on questions of doctrine any discussion should be based on accepted theological texts rather than on the fancy of poets.

Throughout the book the reader sees in Lucifer, rather than the cursed angel, a noble and unfortunate figure. Sympathetic light is shed upon him to prove that he should be pitied rather than cursed. Some critics have maintained that Papini's thesis is true, since it indicates a broader aspiration of the Christian conscience, widespread in our time: namely, the propensity to see reconciliation prevail over the eternal antithesis. (pp. 236-38)

With emotion-laden voice [Papini] invites us to pity the crushed angel and to try to help his redemption instead of hating him. "The Christian," says the author, "cannot and must not love rebellion, evil, and sin in Satan; but he can and must love in him, the most dreadfully unfortunate creature in all creation, the leader and symbol of all enemies, the Archangel who once was nearest to God. Perhaps only our love can help him save himself, help him become again what he once was, the most perfect of heavenly spirits." . . . Christ loved everyone, even the most rebellious and corrupt, and He died for all, so Papini maintains. (Must we assume, then, that He loved Satan and died for him as well?) Might it not be possible, queries the author, that Christ redeemed men so that they could, through the practice of His precepts, some day bring about the redemption of the fiercest and most stubborn of all enemies? (May we ask whether there is any such example in Christ's life?) But Papini now becomes cosmic: the tragedy which started at the beginning of Time, he says, has not yet ended. This tragedy has three stages: the Empyrean, the Earth, and the Abyss; and five acts: 1) Satan rebels; 2) Satan is defeated and thrown into the Abyss; 3) Satan robs man from God; 4) Christ takes man away from Satan; 5) Satan, using his last resources, tries again to recapture man, but he will be defeated for ever. We are now at the fourth act. What will the end of the fifth be? Will Satan be chained for all eternity, or will he be won by the power of God's love and return to his celestial seat? According to Papini, no one can say. Man, the weakest protagonist of the tragedy, will perhaps have something to say before the end of the drama. A true Christian, maintains the author, should not be wicked, not even with the wicked; should not be unjust, not even with the unjust; should not be cruel, not even with the cruel: but he must be the temptor of good even with the temptor of evil. He must approach Satan with charity; only love can disarm and redeem him. If he caused the fall of man, man, following the Christian doctrine in its profound meaning, should help the salvation of the great enemy. The salvation of Satan would alleviate God's grief for His miserable creature. And Papini adds, as a conclusion to his book, his short drama in three acts, *The Tempted Devil,* which sounds like a poetic appeal to mercy and love toward the helpless Satan.

The author's religious zeal has brought him beyond the concept of Christian charity, and his ideas are fraught with serious consequences. If they were brought into the official doctrine, they would shake it from the very depths. The moral principles of Christianity are mostly based on the concept of reward and punishment. If everyone is finally saved, there will be no need to follow the straight and narrow path in this world, since there will be no special merit. Consequently, man would feel free to do whatever he wished, and Christian morals would be in danger of being swept away from our society.

Moreover, if Papini's ideas are unorthodox, his method of treatment is dangerous. The most familiar concepts are questioned in a manner which, in many regards, is similar to that of eighteenth century philosophers—Bayle, Voltaire, etc. To prove that his hope for Satan's final salvation is not to be discarded, despite the straight "No" of the Church, the author engages in discussions which tend to discredit the official doctrine on the matter. He is especially guilty of trying to show, in many instances, what seems to him logical contradictions in the *Scriptures* and in other religious writings, in order to demonstrate that at many points official doctrine rests on bases fully as debatable as the fate of Satan. Furthermore, what makes Papini's book a suspect work is not so much his hope of universal restoration (which being a simple aspiration to go beyond the common concept of Christian charity could be tolerated, if not accepted), but the stubborness of the author in maintaining that after all Satan is not alone responsible for his situation, and that in the arrangement of the universe he is a necessary character. Some critics have conceded, however, that *Il Diavolo* presents a positive aspect: namely, in an epoch unconcerned with man's spiritual destiny and deeply penetrated by materialism, the book calls the attention of the world to one of the most terrifying truths before which humanity passes with beatific indifference: the fires of Hell. But if this is true to some extent, it is also true that the unorthodox treatment of the matter and the assumptions of the author may lead to deleterious conclusions. One could be in error at the time of Origen when the doctrine was in its making, but after two thousand years of Christian thinking and experience, and the unifying action of the Church, it seems absurd to return to old mistakes, never accepted in the official doctrine, and to embellish them with fancies of modern poets. (pp. 249-51)

> Giovanni Gullace, "Giovanni Papini and the Redemption of the Devil," in The Personalist, Vol. XLIII, No. 2, April, 1962, pp. 233-52.

MIRCEA ELIADE (essay date 1966)

[*Eliade was a Romanian essayist, novelist, and critic who wrote extensively on religious history, mystical thought, and comparative religion. His works are most concerned with examining, in both fiction and nonfiction, the nature of sacred experiences which give meaning to human existence. In the following excerpt, Eliade examines several volumes in the complete works of Papini with an eye to the constancy of Papini's religious feelings prior to his actual conversion.*]

It is becoming increasingly evident that Papini was a religious writer even before his conversion. A case in point is the series of articles which was written between 1908 and 1914 and collected in a small volume, *Polemiche religiose.* . . . Although at that time Papini was still a vociferous unbeliever, in a long essay, **"La religione sta da se,"** . . . he emphasized the autonomy of religious experience, taking issue with Croce and Giovanni Gentile, who looked upon religion as an imperfect philosophy. Papini stated that the validity of a religion does not depend upon the "theory" or the moral philosophy which it implies. Moreover, he insisted on the paradoxical character of the religious experience. "Religion reveals (to the believer) an infinite Being manifested as person; an eternal and spiritual God made flesh and mortal man. . . . These experiences, which are absurd for abstract thinking, even for the philosophical thought elaborated by Hegel, are simple, living realities for a saint. The religious *life* conceives and realizes syntheses which are inconceivable and impossible even for the most audacious dialectics." . . . (p. 333)

The book on the Devil [*Il Diavolo*] has both an autobiographical and a theological interest. Papini was in the process of completing his chef d'oeuvre, the enormous and ambitious *Giudizio universale,* when he suddenly decided to write *Il Diavolo.* A few months later he was struck down by a rare and mysterious illness which, as it were, buried him alive in his own body. Thus, *Giudizio universale* was never finished; his *opus imperfectum* was brought out posthumously in 1957. *Il Diavolo* is a significant book theologically; it reintroduces into contemporary literature the idea of universal reconciliation. Papini's contribution to the solution of the problem of evil is audacious. He analyzes the possibilities for man's *forcing* Satan to reintegrate his primeval, angelic, mode of being—and thus to deliver mankind from the very temptation of evil. . . .

The Twilight of the Philosophers was Papini's first book. Today it seems to have lost most of the exuberance and brilliance which so vividly impressed his readers sixty years ago. The book on pragmatism [*Pragmatismo*] is momentous both for the history of ideas in Italy and for the role that it played in Papini's life. Almost all of his subsequent "experiences"—magic, occultism, nihilism—developed from his rather personal understanding of pragmatism. . . .

One of the most provocative pieces [collected in *Filosofia e Letteratura*] is *L'Altra Metà,* which has as its subtitle: "Essay of a Mephistophelic Philosophy." Papini discusses some problems which, in 1912, were not yet popular with Western philosophers: nothingness, ignorance, madness as a philosophical problem, the paradoxical nature of evil, etc. *L'Altra Metà* exemplifies the extreme limits of nihilism and despair. One can well understand how, after this book, the author could only commit suicide or accept a "conversion." It is surprising, not that he wrote *Storia di Cristo,* but that he wrote it only seven years later and only after many other, unexpected "experiences" (futurism, the vitriolic iconoclasm of *Lacerba,* the political campaign for Italy's entrance into war against the Central Powers, etc.). *L'Altra Metà* has a most revealing postscript entitled "Remorse." There one can read such sentences as: "But how arid and bitter is my soul, coming out from these regions of the void, the darkness, and the negative!" Or: "And still, how much belief is in this unbelief, how much hope is in this desperation, and how much tragedy in this clownishness! It is the tragedy of him who wants to believe and cannot, of him who loves the truth more than himself, and cannot find it." . . .

The volume *Cristo e Santi* brings together all of Papini's Christian writings, the most important being *Storia di Cristo* . . . , *Sant' Agostina* . . . , and *I Testimoni della Passione*. . . . After a long period of gestation, Papini wrote the four hundred pages of *Sant' Agostino* in less than a month. This amazing feat is not without relationship to the autobiographical elements latent in the book. Papini wrote the life of Saint Augustine as he would have liked to have written and interpreted his own life.

Also reproduced in *Cristo e Santi* are quite a number of other minor but significant texts; among them are the last fragments dictated by Papini during his long agony. Reading these beautiful pages again, one cannot doubt that the author of *Felicitá dell'infelice* was the most important Italian religious writer after Manzoni. (p. 334)

> *Mircea Eliade, in a review of "Tutte le Opere: Testimonianze e polemiche religiose; Filosofia e Letteratura" and "Cristo e Santi," in* The Journal of Religion, *Vol. XLVI, No. 2, April, 1966, pp. 333-34.*

WILLIAM A. SESSIONS (essay date 1970)

[*In the following excerpt, Sessions surveys Papini's major works.*]

The name of Giovanni Papini would seem today to belong to that catalogue of "high camp" compiled by Susan Sontag some years ago. If one adds the fact that Papini is best known for a life of Christ that in the 'twenties and 'thirties enjoyed an international vogue and had the disadvantage of being accepted

piety for Catholics and Protestants alike, his relevance to the list zooms astronomically. If, further, the reader of the last third of the twentieth century should view the strange shapes of egoism stamping his work from its agnostic beginnings to the rhapsodies of the mythical Pope Celestine VI and the mystical defenses of the Devil, what else but "camp" of a very special grade could describe this forgotten Italian writer?

Yet in 1904 William James, having just met the twenty-five-year-old Papini, wrote to Schiller at Oxford:

> Papini is a jewel. To think of that little Dago putting himself ahead of every one of us at a single stride. And what a writer! and what fecundity! and what courage! and what humor, and what truth.

The next year James wrote an essay "Giovanni Papini and the Pragmatist Movement in Italy" [see excerpt dated 1906] in which he showed himself indebted to the young "Dago" for two evidences of his critical acuity, evidences that would recur in almost every line of Papini's until his death in 1956: the brilliant image and the insight into the possibilities of transcendence. James, for example, appreciated Papini's explanation of Pragmatism "like a corridor in a hotel, from which a hundred doors open into a hundred chambers." The Italian's "most original contribution to Pragmatism," however [according to Carlo Golino (see excerpt dated 1955)], concerned—typically—the movement of human action into transcendence. Inspired by Papini, James wrote: "man becomes a kind of God and where are we to draw his limits? . . . The program of a man-God is surely one of the possible type-programs of philosophy."

Already, therefore, Papini had evinced that power of intellect and personality that would sometimes appear like the self-glorification of his contemporary D'Annunzio or the more sinister swagger of Mussolini, with whom he cooperated on the *Popolo d'Italia* in a campaign for the intervention of Italy in the First World War. But Papini's mask of egoism—as self-conscious as the other two—has roots more complex and more clearly probing into the whole secret of human action. . . . Papini stands bizarre and toweringly alone in an age of computer anonymity; but, similarly, he echoes other possibilities for human existence in the last part of the twentieth century. Giovanni Papini's greatest literary achievements are his biographies or, more exactly, his critical studies of human actors. Like his contemporary Pirandello—but with entirely different results—Papini tends to see all forms of human action through the mask that the actor wears, or is. The personality is all-important; the achievement is the result of the passion of that personality. "My book," says Papini in his preface to his biography of Michelangelo, ". . . aims to tell the story of Michelangelo the man, searching into his soul, his character and his spirit. . . ." His famous study of Dante is called *Dante Vivo* and "is an essay of investigation about the things in Dante which really matter to us today." Similarly he admires Ignatius Loyola because he is a soldier of Christ whose *Spiritual Exercises* "are not meant to be *read* but *done*" and whose genius in constructing the method of the *Exercises* was to give back what Renaissance art had lost: "familiarity by sight, hearing, almost by touch and breathing, with Christ the Son of the Living God." It is Petrarch's personality that makes all his works "an intimate diary for the public, written in ten styles," magnificent in its "sapphire brilliance of the right word inlaid into the right harmonies of rhythm," and dominated by the passion of nostalgia "which gives consistency to Petrarch's mind." Both the fictitious Pope Celestine VI and the real Pope Pius XI offer heroic solutions to their ages, solutions born of their personalities. Finally, at the end, the Devil himself becomes for Papini a passionate hero. It is as though Papini—from the beginning, even though with different terms—saw that human action as opposed to its transcendence is a mask, or that, as he might have said later, all men, even Christ (or especially Christ), in the eyes of God, are performing actors.

As one might expect, Papini's origins are important to the development of this concept of vitalism. Giovanni Papini was born on January 9, 1881, into a lower-middle-class family in Florence. His father was a furniture maker, philosophically a product of nineteenth-century Italy. He was an atheist and a patriot while, in the traditional fashion, his wife was a simple woman, a Catholic devoted to her three children. Papini's origins, then, were somewhat proletarian, but with his marriage in 1907 to Giacinta Giovagnoli, a peasant girl from Bulciano in Tuscany, Papini escapes the social force he most despises in all his work: the commercial middle class. Papini is really unique in stories of conversion in that he continues to attack this class until the very end. Neither Pope Celestine nor Papini's Devil is a product of the genteel middle class of Europe in the early twentieth century or of the technological capitalist class of the mid-century. Papini is, in many ways, his father's son until the very end of his life in that the established is no friend of his.

But it is Florence that primarily created the man. The ancient city reminded Papini in all his metamorphoses that human action could transcend the limits of twentieth-century life. Papini's biographies of Dante and Michelangelo constantly recall the reader to the importance of this "holy" city where the great egoists of spirit achieve transcendence through the action of art. His study of Dante, says Papini in his introduction, is "the book of an artist about an artist, of a Catholic about a Catholic, of a Florentine about a Florentine." The city taught him from the beginning that the positivism and scientific industrialism of nineteenth-century Europe were not enough. "I knew him when I was still a child," writes Papini in the last lines of **Michelangelo**, "walking on the uneven cobblestones of San Miniato; his David was among my earliest and most eloquent teachers." But the transcendental nature of Florence—its part in his redemption from twentieth-century materialism—is evidenced most forcefully in the last part of Papini's introduction to his biography of Christ:

> This book is written, if you will pardon the mention, by a Florentine, a son of the only nation which ever chose Christ for its King. . . . [Even] today after four hundred years of usurpations, the writer of this book is proud to call himself a subject and soldier of Christ the King.

But the Florence the young Papini knew had, like Europe, become, in the fashionable phrase, post-Christian. In his introduction to his study of the African saint, Papini cites two early discoveries of Augustine. The impression given is somewhat like that of a modern Russian student staring at an icon in the Hermitage or at the ghostly domes of Saint Basil's in Red Square. Augustine existed for the young Papini not in any religious context at all, but in a Botticelli accidentally discovered in the Uffizi and in the glimpses of frescoes at the top of his school gymnasium, formerly a convent.

It was natural, then, that the period of *Sturm und Drang* so vividly described in his early autobiography **Un Uomo Finito** should follow. Where in modern Europe was a system that could govern life by providing it with a vision large enough or stable enough to allow human action to move into transcendence as it clearly had at one time in Florence? In 1903 the remarkable journal *Leonardo* edited by Papini and Prezzolini had as its prime desire a renewal of modern life, "di rinnovarsi." In the same way the early works, **24 Cervelli, Stroncature,** and **Testimonianze,** probe contemporary and past heroes of the intellect like Croce, Hegel, Bishop Berkeley, Spandini, Walt Whitman, Spencer, and Remy de Gourmont. Papini is never neutral in these studies: the negative is as much a method of finding reality as the positive. Similarly, in his editing of various journals like the futuristic *Lacerba,* his desire for true renewal led to violent attacks by "the wild man," as he was called, and ultimately to a kind of nihilism that coincided with the First World War.

The terrors of the First World War may seem remote to us today, but its devastation of modern Europe and its consequent technological horrors sparked, as much as any one social force, Giovanni Papini's conversion to Christianity as the one teaching left in the modern world capable of giving human action the dimension in which it could truly be itself—that is, in which it could transcend itself. Of course, Papini's conversion was a shock to the Italian intellectual world, as Prezzolini himself has noted. But those who doubted Papini's sincerity did not understand "the will to believe" or the stages of any metamorphosis as well as Papini himself. (pp. 221-25)

Immediately, there was no startling change in subject matter. Rather, as Papini might have shown from that Platonism which increasingly served him, he moved up the ladder of ascent. That is, the great individualists—the heroes of his intellect, the egoists of reality like Nietzsche, Swift, and Don Quixote—become heroes of another type. The heroes of art remained just that, and the heroes of the intellect remained themselves or they became what was for the new Papini a higher reality, heroes of faith. This faith, however, always remained carefully circumscribed by a tough realism, either of the intellect or of the social context. In other words, there were now two great egoists for Papini: the saint and the artist. In his volume of critical studies, **Laborers in the Vineyard,** Papini defines the only true forms of individualism possible for him in the modern world (or the world at any time):

> For I confess that in my view the only people one can really admire or tolerate in this world are saints and artists: those who imitate God, and those who imitate the works of God.

It was inevitable, therefore, that biography should be his most successful literary form. Papini began writing at fourteen and produced no fewer than sixty-five volumes of fiction, poetry, philosophy, literary criticism, theology, and history. His poetry is quite negligible; his novel **Gog** is the only one translated into English and its primary interest is its repetition of Papini patterns and themes. Only when Papini turned to historical human action—the philosopher or artist or saint in time—did he draw upon his fullest resources as an artist himself. This human action moving into transcendence was seen, however, not by the imagination of a poet or novelist but by an exalted critical intelligence. As vivid as are the fictional cries of Pope Celestine before a world gone mad or the anguish of Jesus in

His last days, they are, in the most magnificent sense, commentaries. They do not offer the immediate realities of Raskolnikov or Alyosha. In fact, the great achievement of Papini's biography of Christ is that it leads us, at every turn, back to the Gospels.

Early in the 'twenties, in the first flush of conversion, Papini wrote his greatest biography, *Storia di Cristo*. It was a tremendous success on all continents. His books, then, won him fame, fortune, prizes, and academic positions. But the remarkable ferment of Papini did not allow stasis of any kind. At the end of his life, in 1953, he published the result of years of meditation, *Il Diavolo,* which shocked the Catholic world and was promptly put on the Index. (pp. 225-27)

If it is through his biographies that we can know Papini best, his study of Saint Augustine . . . would seem to offer some understanding of his conversion. In a sense, as with so many of his biographies, Papini seemed destined to write a study of the African saint. For Papini's Christianity is essentially Augustinian. Indeed, it is his subtle understanding of the intellectual and sexual temptations besetting Augustine that makes the book relevant to a twentieth-century audience. Its weakness lies, perhaps, in its chosen limits: "a story of a soul" in which "his vast labors are but examples necessary for a better understanding of his spiritual nature." . . . It is, like all his biographies, however, carefully appointed in its research; and his examination of the intellectual ferment of the day, the heroes like Ambrose and the heresies like the Manichaean and Pelagian, is made all the more conclusive by its restatement in modern terms. Similarly, his analysis of Augustine's sexuality may be exaggerated, but the idea of Augustine as homosexual in one phase of his early life is certainly contemporary. It thus illustrates more vividly the dramatic conflict of the ascent toward Grace, or, in Papini's terms, "the deeper the valley, the stronger the light upon the heights." (p. 227)

Papini's biography of Michelangelo was not published until the very end of his life . . . , but in it he sounds very much like the fiery critic of his youth. Acidly denouncing "contemporary Italian criticism" for its dissecting "to infinity" the work of a great man, and then ignoring the great man himself in his time and place, Papini repeats his whole theory of biography:

> We must acknowledge the fact that the life of
> a great artist, that is, a man who is set apart
> from the herd of men and who is distinguished
> by his extraordinary qualities and virtue, has
> an historical and spiritual value in itself, and
> the study of that life can be a guide in a discerning analysis of human nature.

The development of the book logically follows from this theory. Michelangelo is viewed in a painstakingly created context of individuals and events in Renaissance Italy. The method is not so simple as it appears, for behind the erudition lies the vitalism of Papini's view of existence. Michelangelo, not some abstract theory, is allowed to appear amid the clutter of humanists, popes, wars, murders, and general horror.

The weakness of the book, as critics noted, is that, like the study of Augustine, the works themselves of the hero are not sufficiently analyzed. In the immense mosiac of facts of *Michelangelo,* the lack of such analysis does indeed take direction from the glittering existential ferment surrounding the Titan.

Especially one feels this loss in the short chapters that mark the movement of the book. Their splendid ingenuity in evoking a life in which the great artist naturally emerges is finally dissipated by the authorial failure to summarize, to direct the reader to abstractions from which he can return, with relief, to the vivid picture of developing heroism by which Michelangelo created art in his period.

This picture, however, is considerably enhanced by the larger themes that do appear—as, for example, the neo-Platonism of Renaissance Florence and its influence on Michelangelo or the religious influence of Savonarola, who is viewed as a prophet amid papal lust, adultery, sodomy, and greed. Similarly, when the art works are seen in terms of paradox, a paradox at the root of Michelangelo's being, the details gain momentum. The incredible multitude of sharply etched vignettes—often as bitter as the early personal essays—approach a kind of unity by virtue of their relevance to the central paradox, Michelangelo himself, the artist-hero whose human action moves into the idealization of art, towards a greater transcendence.

Dante's influence on Michelangelo is a major part of this biography, and the logical relationship of the three Tuscans is focused by Papini in his concept of prophecy. The Sistine Chapel, the *Divine Comedy,* and his own volumes are works, in Papini's eyes, fraught with the Hebraic vision of God's voice in history. This concept of prophecy in Italy is remarkable and is proof of Papini's originality, once converted. That is, prophecy in Italy was hardly new; Papini superbly demonstrates the effect of Joachim of Flora on Dante in *Dante Vivo,* and in *Michelangelo* the tragic attempts of Savonarola to reform a papacy gone mad. . . . But it was Protestantism that brought back the vision of the prophetic to modern Europe, with accompanying neo-Platonic overtones. Only in Vatican Council II did the role of individual prophecy receive a restated validity; and here, therefore, years before, Papini is certainly pioneering, especially in Italy.

This insight into Dante the prophet is one of the richest sections of the popular *Dante Vivo*. . . . Dante is, of course, the great egoist-hero for Papini whose poetry most nearly approaches transcendence. To create before the modern reader all the living individualism of Dante, Papini again used the method of short chapters organized here with the loosest unity under the general headings of "Life," "Soul," "Work," and "Destiny" so that themes could be inductively developed or simply presented.

But Dante is no saint. In a staccato series of chapters on Dante's "Soul" and in a later chapter "The *Commedia* as Revenge," Papini cuts almost cruelly into the weaknesses of the poet. His use of the negative here does give insight into the failure of Dante as a person, but this valuable insight is blurred by a bad critical method: he commits too often the critical mistake of "the intentional fallacy." It is a real mistake here, for we are reduced to a level not above the art but below it, for the simple reason that the poet's consequent idealizations are seen not as art but as personal action. Such analysis will not work with Dante, and, therefore, when Papini turns to an analysis of the language and its form, he is gratuitous and falls back on the worst kind of Platonic analysis. Poetry, says Papini pompously, "is also, to speak plainly, a craft; nor is it thereby degraded" but "if the soul is lifeless, what it produces is also lifeless." In his reaction against Thomism, Papini seems never to have read the *Poetics*.

But this same Platonism which fails him in criticism of form deepens that analysis of Dante the prophet. The section on Dante's image of the greyhound, the Veltro, allows Papini to state here what will be repeated in the later works and was first stated in *Storia di Cristo:* the imminent descent of the Holy Spirit. Like Dante, Papini expects a renewal before the final judgment, and, aware of Dante's own false dreams of emperor and purified church, he nevertheless will preach as Pope Celestine VI the necessity of the Veltro in the modern world. (pp. 228-31)

[Papini's *Life of Christ*] was the first important work after his conversion, and he turned from another work to write it. He also wrote it in the country, most likely in the isolated Tuscan landscape of Bulciano, his wife's home. This fact is important for it is obvious that the simplicity of the Gospels converted Papini as much as anything else. Papini had always sought a kind of primitivism—vigorous and medieval and not Rousseau's, if we judge only by the agnostic essays. Here, in the narratives of the life of the God-man, the completest expression of human action as transcendence, Papini found a synthesis of never-ending complexity and immediate simplicity: a paradox, in short, that gave life. The beauty of the rural Tuscan landscape (and there are many sensual echoes in Papini's narrative) is the physical expression of the humility that lies at the root of this greatest of his biographies. The egoist, the searcher, the Nietzschean (there is an attack on Nietzsche in the first pages) are here balanced by the humility of the Incarnation in which paradoxically transcendence seeks human action. Christ therefore becomes, for Papini, the human actor *par excellence,* the only one whose mask was simply His naked face, it alone masking divinity. The great Egoist who drew all to Him, who was the Way, has at the source of His Titanic program the irony of humiliation or death or the utter giving away of human action for complete transcendence. Needless to say, Papini in this work demonstrates the depth of his conversion, for the whole book is suffused with the wonder of discovery.

Most of Papini's themes as a literary artist either culminate or are discovered in this work. The same is true of his concept of form. His method of the short chapters, of the vignette instead of the detailed analysis, of the image instead of the abstraction, of the method of the loose unity, originates in this book; and clearly it is the Gospels which have provided the pattern. His introduction is extremely important, for it gives us the kind of vision the reader must bring. It is a vision of personality, a focus of temperament; and this introduction immediately tells us how different the life will be from those great studies of Christ in the twentieth century by Guardini and Daniel-Rops. Unlike the others, Papini is consciously the apologist, consciously the Augustinian convert (unlike Guardini and Daniel-Rops), and consciously answering the world of *Un Uomo Finito.* "We live in the Christian era, and it is not yet finished," says Papini in his introduction. A new Gospel must be written, therefore, and he has attempted such "for the Gospel's sake." . . . Fortunately, the personally perceived Jesus of this narrative was not that of an illiterate or a Rousseau primitive but of a Florentine. The result is a pictorial marvel; and the details show what Auden says of the old masters, an awareness of the human position of suffering. In the section "Four Nails" the impersonal spring morning is described; in "Perfumes in the Rock" the job of taking Jesus from the cross and burying Him is precisely described with Flaubertian realism; in "Return by the Sea" the lake is "rendered," to use

Henry James's phrase, in its various appearances and serves as a kind of symbol for that metamorphosed Jesus who will soon appear to the disciples. But while certain scenes have the tightness and yet bold treatment of Sienese primitives, other scenes, the trial of Jesus and the descriptions of those ruined by wealth and materialism, have the piercing caricature of a Rouault or Daumier. Similarly, in his satiric attacks on money (verbally echoing Sir Thomas More's attack on money, in the *Utopia*), his vignettes of corruption seem like chapters of Mauriac.

But it is the human realism that is the center of the book. The actors of that momentous narrative become modern—literally, when Pilate is seen as an English governor of Asia or Africa but more subtly in the depiction of the disciples:

> Fate knows no better way to punish the great for their greatness than by sending them disciples. . . . Here is one of the most tragic elements in all greatness: disciples are repugnant and dangerous, but disciples, even false ones, cannot be dispensed with. Prophets suffer if they do not find them; they suffer, perhaps more, when they have found them.

As a result, his portrayal of these disciples, notably Matthew, is superb in its ability to draw their human dimensions. Peter especially fits the Papini love of paradox:

> His surname "Cephas," stone, piece of rock, was not given him only for the firmness of his faith, but for the hardness of his head. . . . And yet he was the first to recognize Jesus as the Christ; and this primacy is so great that nothing has been able to cancel it.

But it is in the long analysis of Judas' torment and anguish that Papini evokes the kind of psychological realism that, as in the great novels, finally cannot be defined:

> The mystery of Judas is doubly tied to the mystery of the Redemption and we lesser ones shall never solve it.

Each of Papini's commentaries on the parables also illustrates this quintessentially human—one might even say Italian—concern. . . . There are also the inevitable baroque scenes, and, with a writer prone to excess, the simplicities that really seem simplemindedness.

But Christ as hero is best found, in Papini's version, not on the Cross or Resurrected, but on the Mount of Transfiguration and in the Sermon on the Mount. Throughout the work, although subdued and properly placed in relation to the personal emphasis of the book, the reader finds Papini's erudition. At times it is combined with exegesis for a maximum effect as in Papini's explication of Jesus' prophecy in "Judea Overcome" and "The Parousia." But in these two crucial scenes of the hero on the mountain, where the Greatest Actor is as exalted as Zarathustra, knowledge and critical intelligence are used and subsumed. In these scenes Papini shows, with the skill of an old master himself, the personality of the God-man literally transfigured and transcendent in one scene and, in the other, the personality of God transfiguring human action.

In two works of his last period, Giovanni Papini seems almost obsessed with the figure of the grand egoist. *Lettere agli vomini di Papa Celestino Sesto* . . . is a work of fiction devised, like his novel *Gog* fifteen years earlier, as a series of confessions. In *Gog* Papini satirizes the modern world through an American super-millionaire, Goggins; and his method is a series of miscellaneous papers in which the millionaire records his searching for novelty, strange adventures, the great and near-great, and his cynicism on such searching in the modern world. The fictional Pope Celestine also expresses his observations on an insane world, and the essay-letters are the same series of chapters first explored as method in the early essays and *Storia di Cristo.*

In many ways the old man Pope Celestine is the most forceful of all Papini's masks. Papini obviously wrote this work during the Second World War, and his work is a voice from the apocalypse. (pp. 231-35)

How else could Papini the egoist respond to a technological leveling—literally and spiritually—of the world except to choose, for him, the supreme individual whose mask as hero was given by God? In his essay on Pius XI, Papini had admired the papal encyclicals. Therefore, in his fiction, Papini invents a pope who "lived in a terrible era of storm and blood" and who "died a martyr during the last days of the Great Persecution." Clearly Papini is again in the realm of the Veltro, and prophecy now becomes history through a series of letters to Christians, priests, monks, theologians, the rich, the poor, the rulers, the subjects, the women, the poets, the historians, the scientists, the separated Christians, the Hebrews, those without Christ, those without God, and finally to all men. The prayer to God that ends the work is a formal rhapsody that merely reflects the rhapsodic tone of the whole work.

What is significant about the work is that it attacks not only the modern world—Papini's task since the *Leonardo*—but the mechanism of the Church itself. It is a prophetic call for renewal (and, a few years after Papini's death, Pope John XXIII in a mysterious, sudden impulse called the Vatican Council for just that purpose of renewal). Old Pope Celestine's revolutionary theology would de-emphasize Mariology and would lead to new inventiveness, as illustrated in an old monk's theory of the redemption of the Devil. It would emphasize the Holy Spirit and would fully condemn all wealth and all capitalism. It would be an eschatological theology that realizes that there are "only two types of men today: economic man, with all his appetites; and the man of God, with all his certainties"; that "we have arrived at the ultimate dilemma: Love or Death." Papini has, in short, compiled the theology of all his heroes, Francis of Assisi, Joachim of Flora, Savonarola, and even of artists like Dante and the Michelangelo of the "Last Judgment."

The Devil, in Christian theology, is *the* destructive egoist— the greatest actor who must always wear a mask to cover his hideousness. In his *Il Diavolo* . . . Papini will not accept this loss of supreme action, this colossal failure of transcendence, that is the traditional Christian Devil. The thesis of his book, therefore, is that the Devil and all the fallen will be forgiven by a God who if He "is really the Father cannot torture his children into eternity" or, if Satan is not redeemed, "we should have to think that the Father of Christ himself were not a perfect Christian." Papini's arguments turn to the past as well as to the present and future. Furthermore, adding a note that does not appear in the arguments of Origen and other theologians (which Papini minutely but not always carefully examines), man must be the instrument of Satan's salvation. In one of

those aphoristic paradoxes that abound in the book, Papini sees the ultimate liberation of man in this possibility: "If Satan can be freed from the hatred of Christians, men would be forever freed from Satan."

The organization of the book provides a veritable encyclopedia of diabology, but the whole still remains a series of notes, another kind of biography in which the real force of Satan can be seen in literature, in art, in history, in theology, and in France, Satan's "promised land"! Unfortunately, this sort of study demanded the tight thesis and the controlled level of argument. Fascinated by the aesthetic and, in his mind, prophetic possibilities of paradox and a dualism that he had admired in Augustine, Papini moves from sublime mystical defenses to trivial fallacies and plain stupidity. Nowhere is there the precision of image that dominates the earlier work, and clearly, without a human subject, Papini does not succeed.

It is precisely the vitalism of his concept of action, however, that seems to betray him. Anyone as *alive* as Satan must *necessarily* be redeemed by Complete Life or God. From his early Pragmatic origins through his visions of saints and artists, the heroes who imitate the God-man Hero (a Hero vitally and completely masculine, one might add, with the role of the Father strongly centered and the role of the Virgin barely perceptible), Papini was predestined to deal with the mysterious negative presence called Satan, a vital presence felt so acutely during the Second World War and in the decade before when, if we can judge by Pope Celestine's remarks, these meditations on the Devil began.

It is easy to attack Papini's thesis. But the shock that it gave the Catholic world (to the delight of Italian Communists) was anticipated by Papini himself when he clearly pointed out that the Church of Rome did not hold such teachings and, furthermore, that his book had as subtitle: "Notes for a Future Diabology." Papini, like Pope Celestine in the same instance, was merely calling out for inventiveness in discussing dogma in an era when practically no dogma is deemed worthy of serious discussion. Similarly, Papini was calling for that universal charity which he held to be the one source of that vitalism at the heart of all action and which, in fact, gave human action its very transcendence. The great individualist Papini, essentially inheriting a Romantic Devil (and certainly creating one in his book as well), could not bear to keep that transcendence sustaining all action from the greatest of egoists. For Papini to do so would be to deny that living transcendence within himself, himself as egoist.

The world of Giovanni Papini is clearly gone. Hitler has given way to the Central Committee, and lonely hero-egoists are largely "camp." That impulse of individualism begun by the Renaissance and Reformation died in this century, and Papini's Pope Celestine (like his Devil) seems a sad relic. But what about his egoism? No matter what the historical context of Papini's personalism, there remains the seemingly enduring fact that the moment one rises above the ant society—that is, to a conception of vitalism as opposed to sheer motion—personality enters in. Or, if human action follows its own tendency as either human or action, it will end up transcending itself through a mask of personality. Transcendence is always personal, says this seemingly inexorable law of human society (whether cavemen or moon-emigrés); and it is a law tiresome at times and capable of wild excesses of egoism. But as Papini's biographies tell us, societies seldom transcend themselves—

only the heroic human being or, in Papini's terms, the egoist Pope Celestine who "hurled his words like arrows of light into the hearts of all men." (pp. 235-38)

> *William A. Sessions, "Giovanni Papini, or, The Probabilities of Christian Egoism," in* The Vision Obscured: Perceptions of Some Twentieth-Century Catholic Novelists, *edited by Melvin J. Friedman, Fordham University Press, 1970, pp. 221-40.*

ADDITIONAL BIBLIOGRAPHY

Boyd, Ernest. "Giovanni Papini." In his *Studies from Ten Literatures*, pp. 167-76. 1925. Reprint. Port Washington, N.Y.: Kennikat Press, 1968.
  Survey of Papini's principal works.

Forman, Henry James. "Giovanni Papini—A New Apostle." *The Bookman*, London LXIII, No. 377 (February 1923): 232-37.
  Enthusiastic response to Papini's *Life of Christ*, including an interview with Papini and a brief overview of his career.

Frank, Glenn. "The Next Great Biography." In his *An American Looks at His World*, pp. 344-50. Newark: University of Delaware Press, 1923.
  Decries the nonhistoricity of Papini's *Life of Christ*.

Gullace, Giovanni. "The Pragmatist Movement in Italy." *Journal of the History of Ideas* XXIII, No. 1 (1962): 91-105.
  Indicates the importance of Papini and *Leonardo* in introducing the philosophy of Pragmatism into Italy.

———. "Giovanni Papini Resurrected." *Forum Italicum* X, No. 3 (September 1976): 265-72.
  Discussion of Papini's profound influence on Italian literary and cultural life.

James, William. Letter to F. C. S. Schiller. In his *The Letters of William James*, edited by Henry James, Vol. II, pp. 245-46. Boston: Atlantic Monthly Press, 1920.
  Letter of 7 April 1906. James writes with enthusiasm of Papini's intellectualism, humanism, and *uomo-dio* (Man-God) concept.

Phelps, Ruth Shepard. "The Poet in Papini." In her *Italian Silhouettes*, pp. 79-95. New York: Alfred A. Knopf, 1924.
  Approbatory examination of the poetic nature of Papini's prose style.

Riccio, Peter Michael. "Giovanni Papini." In his *Italian Authors of Today*, pp. 87-96. 1938. Reprint. Freeport, N.Y.: Books for Libraries Press, 1970.
  Overview of Papini's literary career, noting the extremes of critical reaction to Papini.

Vittorini, Domenico. "The Novels of the New Generation" and "The Novel of Ideas: The Group of *La Voce*." In his *The Modern Italian Novel*, pp. 156-71, 172-99. Philadelphia: University of Pennsylvania Press, 1930.
  Establishes Papini's importance as the ideological leader of one of two major intellectual movements in early twentieth-century Italian literary, philosophical, and cultural thought, calling for revolution in these areas rather than the gradual evolutionary change recommended by Benedetto Croce.

Ziolkowski, Theodore. "The Resurrection: A Motif from Nineteenth-Century Thought in Twentieth-Century Fiction." In his *Varieties of Literary Thematics*, pp. 152-74. Princeton: Princeton University Press, 1983.
  Discusses Papini's treatment of the Resurrection in his *Life of Christ*.

Kōda Rohan

1867-1947

(Pseudonym of Kōda Shigeyuki) Japanese novelist, short story writer, poet, essayist, lexicographer, critic, historian, and biographer.

A highly influential figure in late nineteenth-century Japanese literature, Rohan is considered one of that country's greatest authors. His works, written at a time when Western ideas dominated Japan's arts, clearly manifest Rohan's rejection of the prevailing Naturalist and sociopolitical realist trends and reflect his devotion to the themes and techniques of classical Chinese literature. Concerned primarily with questions of metaphysics, Rohan created highly idealistic fiction using an ornate, traditional style which had been rejected as archaic by other members of his generation. Nevertheless, Rohan's works were enormously popular during his lifetime, and he is still revered as an erudite scholar and a creative genius.

Born in Tokyo, Rohan was the fourth son of a prominent shogunate official. As a member of the samurai, or warrior nobility, he was expected to be a scholar and a gentleman, and his education was structured accordingly. Although the young Rohan excelled in math and science at school, he preferred classical Chinese literature and philosophy, and his first attempts at literature were Buddhist-influenced poems written while he was in his teens. Soon, however, he abandoned poetry in favor of prose. While working in a paper shop, Rohan became acquainted with other writers who liked his work and who encouraged him to submit his writing for publication, with the result that in 1889 his first short story, "Tsuyu Dandan," appeared in a prominent literary journal. The story was universally applauded and Rohan was acknowledged as a master of fiction, even though he was only twenty-two years old. Rohan devoted many years to the writing of fiction, producing a large number of stories and several novels, but his inquisitive nature and diverse interests gradually led him to explore other areas, including literary criticism, lexicography, natural science, and philosophy. He published his last work of fiction in 1919, but continued to write essays and to compile dictionaries until his death at the age of eighty.

As a student of both Confucianism and Buddhism, Rohan sought to create works that were morally and metaphysically enlightening as well as aesthetically pleasing, and critics agree that he achieved his goal. His characters represent idealized human types, reflected in such names as Illusory Hook, Virtuous Beauty, and Master Humanity, while their conflicts are intended to illustrate their function in and duty to the cosmos. For example, in Rohan's best known work, "Gojū no Tō" ("The Pagoda"), the conflict between two artisans allows each to rise to a new level of virtue, one relinquishing a coveted commission for the benefit of a colleague, the other taking full advantage of an opportunity to strive for perfection in his craft. Critics consider the celebration of masculine heroism typical of Rohan's stories, although his conception of the heroic is distinctly Japanese and involves not only courage and physical prowess but also sincerity, wisdom, and creativity. Mystic visions and supernatural phenomena often play a major role in Rohan's fiction, generally serving as a warning or terrifying punishment for those who choose to stray from the path to enlightenment. However, in

keeping with his conviction that literature is above all an art form and as such should not be relegated to a merely hortatory function, Rohan presented his ideas in an elegant prose style and observed the many conventions of traditional Japanese literature, including the frequent use of Buddhist symbolism, to convey thematic content.

Although Rohan's prose style renders his work inaccessible to many modern Japanese readers, and a scarcity of translations has limited his international reputation, his work is highly esteemed among critics of Japanese literature. In particular, they praise Rohan's great erudition and his ability to vividly relate his transcendent vision of reality. Moreover, while Rohan's writings gained him a prominent position in the literary world of his day, through his exemplary life, devoted to the pursuit of wisdom and virtue, he has earned the enduring reverence of the Japanese people.

PRINCIPAL WORKS

"Tsuyu Dandan" (short story) 1889
"Fūryūbutsu" (short story) 1889
"Dokushushin" (short story) 1890
"Fūjibumi" (short story) 1890

"Taidokuro" (short story) 1890
   ["Lodging for the Night" published in *Representative
   Tales of Japan*, 1914; also published as "Encounter
   with a Skull" in *Pagoda, Skull, and Samurai*, 1985]
"Gojū no Tō" (short story) 1891
   ["The Pagoda," 1909; also published as "The Five-
   storied Pagoda" in *Pagoda, Skull, and Samurai*, 1985]
Isanatori (novel) 1891
"Kekkōsei" (short story) 1891
Fūryū Mijinzō (novel) 1893
"Shin Urashima" (short story) 1895
"Higeotoko" (short story) 1896
   ["The Bearded Samurai" published in *Pagoda, Skull, and
   Samurai*, 1985]
Suijō Goi (dictionary) 1897
"Futsuka Monogatari" (short story) 1898-1901
"Wankyū Monogatari" (short story) 1899
Sora Utsu Nami (unfinished novel) 1903-05
Shutsuro (poem) 1904
   [*Leaving the Hermitage*, 1925]
Unmei (novel) 1919
Rohan Zenshū. 41 vols. (novels, short stories, essays,
   poetry, dictionaries, and catalogues) 1950-58
Pagoda, Skull, and Samurai (short stories) 1985

The majority of Rohan's works were published serially in literary
journals of the day. This accounts for multiple publication dates, except
in the case of *Rohan Zenshu*, which is a multivolume collection of his
works.

CHIEKO IRIE MULHERN (essay date 1977)

[*Mulhern is a Japanese-born American critic. In the following
excerpt she discusses several of Rohan's principal works, focusing
in particular on the themes in "Gojū no Tō" ("The Five-storied
Pagoda"). English titles provided in the text are the critic's free
translations.*]

[Rohan's first published work, **"Tsuyu Dandan"** (**Dewdrops**)]
is unlike any of Rohan's subsequent works in many respects. . . . The imagery is obviously Western. . . . The scene
is set in contemporary New York and China, but it is an idealized America envisioned and aspired to by the Japanese of the
early Meiji. The characters, all Americans and Chinese except
for one Japanese, do not yet exhibit typically Rohanesque forceful
individualities.

Yet sincerity, which was to become the core of Rohan's "ideal,"
already plays an important, even central, role here in close
connection with the plot development. The subplots involving
the tests and a substitute suitor were transposed from a Chinese
popular story, "Master Ch'ien Wins Miss Feng Unexpectedly," included in *Chin-ku-ch'i-kuan*, a collection of Ming
period tales. The difference between the Chinese story and
Dewdrops is most revealing. The Chinese father of the intended
bride was a wealthy money lender seeking a son-in-law superior
in looks as well as in scholarly aptitude, which in China of
the day directly related to social and financial success. The
protagonist was accepted even after he was discovered to be a
substitute for his rich but unattractive cousin, solely because
of his handsome appearance and his reputation as an excellent
student. The Chinese story offered neither love theme nor emphasis on personal integrity, and did not contain the concept

of *fūryū* (poetic enjoyment of nature and emotional freedom)
as submerging of the self into the universe.

Such a nebulous relationship between Rohan's works and their
sources was to become a pattern throughout his career. It is
generally quite difficult to pinpoint sources of influence on
Rohan, because any similarities found between his stories and
possible sources are usually indecisive and partial. In his own
preface to **Dewdrops**, however, Rohan acknowledges that "despite its plot reminiscent of Lytton and Thackeray, this story
has a source that must be obvious to learned readers." . . . (pp.
36-7)

The themes which were eventually to blossom in his later and
more representative works are already suggested in **Dewdrops**.
The love between [the central characters] Rubina and Shinzia
is not only descriptive of the new and ideal mode of love
conceived in the mind of early Meiji youth, but it also heralds
Rohan's theory of love, which embraces an innocent, spiritual,
and fairy-talelike aspect. And the concept of *fūryū*, as practiced
by the carefree Japanese poet and the worldly-wise, open-
hearted Bunseimu, was later developed into a very complex
view of art, man, and nature. **Dewdrops** may at first glance
appear to echo the exoticism and Westernization craze prevalent in that period, but more careful reading will reveal Rohan's critical attitude toward such contemporary taste. (p. 37)

It was with this idealistic story that Rohan launched into a
career through which he intended to define the moral order of
the universe. Thanks to its novel plot, exotic setting, expansive
vision, accomplished *gazoku setchū bun* (a mixture of poetic
and colloquial styles), and unique theme, **Dewdrops** was received with enormous enthusiasm. (p. 38)

Rohan's place in the literary world was firmly established with
his next work, [**"Fūryūbutsu"** (**Love Bodhisattva**)]. . . . **Love
Bodhisattva** tells of a Buddhist sculptor called Shu'un who sets
out on a journey in quest of artistic perfection. He comes upon
a house where Tatsu, vendor of preserved flowers, is held
prisoner by her violent uncle who is planning to sell her to a
brothel. When Shu'un brings her back to his inn, the kindly
innkeeper takes it upon himself to arrange matrimony between
Shu'un and the grateful Tatsu. . . . On the night of their wedding, however, Tatsu is forced to leave Shu'un by a messenger
from her long lost samurai father, now a viscount.

Brokenhearted, Shu'un carves an image of Tatsu. . . . When
he reads a newspaper article announcing Tatsu's impending
marriage to a young nobleman, he tries in anger to destroy the
almost lifelike statue. Finding himself unable to touch his own
work, he breaks down in tears. Suddenly the statue appears to
move. . . . In the last chapter, Shu'un and Tatsu ascend to
heaven man and wife, followed by believers in Tatsu the bodhisattva, including even her evil uncle.

The synopsis may read like a melodrama, but the impact of
Love Bodhisattva was immense. (pp. 39-40)

Love Bodhisattva caused a sensation for two reasons: one was
its striking style, the other, its intensely poetic imagination. . . .
Love Bodhisattva was Rohan's answer to the stylistic confusion
of the time. (pp. 40-1)

In **Love Bodhisattva**, Rohan successfully employs two vastly
different styles: a facile, vernacular, humorous, fluent style for
the first eight sections; and after Shu'un begins to carve the
image, a terse, rhythmic, intense style. The latter . . . is better-
known as typically Rohanesque. . . . (p. 41)

The flexible and dynamic style of **Love Bodhisattva** contributed immensely to the flourishing of *gazoku setchū* style in its time.

In this tale, Rohan pursues the theme of love and sincerity to an artistic and mystic crystallization. Despite its first impression of classicism, this story deals with a new view of love, unexpectedly rendered in classical guise. The setting is contemporary Meiji society, where a traditional horror of love as delusion (as preached to Shu'un by the innkeeper) was still deep, concurrent with a Western-inspired awareness that one must be true to one's own emotions. (p. 42)

["Taidokuro" ("Encounter with a Skull")] is a tale of mystical beauty and haunting visions. A brash young man called (Young) Rohan loses his way in the mountains beyond Nikko. He stumbles into a lonely hut and spends a disquieting night with an unearthly beauty, who unnerves him with an invitation to share the only bed in the house. He manages to stay up by asking her to tell the story of her life. The woman, Tae, had been a wealthy, happy girl until her mother died, leaving a letter which condemned her to a celibate life. A young nobleman fell hopelessly in love with her and finally died of a broken heart. One day Tae in feverish madness followed the young man's phantom into the mountains, where a saintly hermit taught her to accept all things with good grace. Young Rohan asks what was written in her mother's letter which so drastically altered her life; her only reply is that it revealed the accursed fate of her family. With the first sign of sunlight, the house and the woman vanish, leaving Young Rohan in a desolate field with a bleached white skull at his feet. Upon reaching a village, Young Rohan learns from an innkeeper that a mad leper woman disappeared into the mountains some time earlier in the year.

There is little wonder that "Encounter with a Skull" should have earned Rohan many admirers. (The most enthusiastic of them was Tanizaki Jun'ichirō, who wrote similar stories of eerie visions.) Its structure is reminiscent of *Nō* plays, in which the protagonist undergoes metamorphosis, usually from a humble disguise to the spirit of a dead nobleman suffering because he is still undelivered from his former self, revealing the pathos of this world and visions of the life after death. Rather than an aged traveling monk as in most *Nō* plays, it is a still immature young man who encounters the heroine in this story. The metamorphosis of the charming hostess of the night is more complex and philosophical than the typical *Nō* version. A beauty changes into an abomination in reality, and a grotesque skull projects an image of a perfect, ideal woman transcending the limitations imposed by the flesh. Even beyond simple relativism or contrast, Rohan penetrates into human existence not only to delineate it but to pursue its ultimate meaning. (pp. 47-8)

In 1891, Rohan wrote two major works: [*Isanatori* (**The Whaler**)], the only one of his three long novels to be completed; and "**The Five-storied Pagoda,**"perhaps his greatest accomplishment. (p. 72)

The most famous sections [of **The Whaler**] are the descriptions of the whalers' life, the scene of whale catching by premodern methods (perhaps the only one of its kind in Japanese literature), and the portentous apparitions of his victims haunting him in the violent sea storm. In **The Whaler**, Rohan's idealistic tendencies are beginning to blend with his attempts at objective and descriptive techniques. Characterization is more natural and plausible with a certain psychological depth; and the plot development is intricately related to the personality of each character involved

To a great extent, this novel reveals Rohan's views on human nature and karma. (p. 73)

In **The Whaler**, Rohan describes the vicissitudes of life not so much as records of particular events and people's lives as concrete examples to illustrate the workings of the law of cause and effect. In his view, fate is closely related to man's self-cultivation and almost equivalent to manifestation of man's will. The main messages conveyed in this novel are that the law of cause and effect exists as unequivocally and perceptibly as reality itself and that man must endure suffering by the strength of his will in order to turn adverse karma into good fortune. (p. 74)

The Whaler is a remarkable work in which events are closely related to the personality traits of each character, and a reader can easily apply modern psychological analysis to the story.... Far from being simplistic, Rohan observes life with penetrating yet sympathetic eyes, for in his view, the real human tragedy is not that a man may be born weak and beyond salvation but rather that he is desperately bound in the intricate and mysterious web woven by his own emotions and karma.

Although Rohan's literary techniques had not yet fully matured, **The Whaler** shows a markedly improved unity of idealistic theme and realistic approach. Such changes in novelistic techniques culminated in creating his best work, "**The Five-storied Pagoda.**" (pp. 75-6)

"**The Five-storied Pagoda**" ... is a work perfect in its own way: Rohan's idealistic tendencies and literary skill matured to the extent that [the protagonist] Jūbei is unmistakably a personification of Rohan's ideals—dedication to art and confidence in man's ability—yet at the same time quite believable as a simple carpenter with a personality of his own. This story manifests all the characteristics that distinguish Rohan's works in general, as Seki Ryōichi enumerates them: (1) the author's strong desire to express himself through protagonists; (2) artist-artisan heroes (especially in early phases); (3) disregard of, or aloofness from, mundane conventions; (4) mystic and allegorical tendencies; (5) propensity toward traditionalism; and (6) denouement through the use of *deus ex machina* (such as the Abbot Rōen) evoked by the sheer force of a protagonist's desperate determination and willpower.

"**The Five-storied Pagoda**" has no superfluous characters, for even foil characters are well-developed and memorably individual. The primary emphasis is focused on characterization rather than effective verisimilitude, yet the emotional impact is heightened by realistic descriptions and dramatic scenes, leading in a crescendo to the final climax of the storm. (pp. 77-8)

Involved in "**The Five-storied Pagoda**" are a number of critical issues. First of all, Jūbei can be considered a champion of new Meiji individualism, which encouraged lofty aspiration beyond the confines of a traditional class system. By 1891, Japan's modernization was in full swing, accompanied by an inevitable social state of "the survival of the fittest" and individual rivalry to supersede the earlier, unified national effort and cooperation. On the one hand, Jūbei is a personification of egoism and exclusiveness innate in artists and modern technicians. The pagoda, in this sense, is a symbolic expression of the Meiji aspiration. At the same time, Jūbei is also a modern hero with the unswerving conviction, "All or nothing." Rohan eagerly read Plutarch's *Parallel Lives* and Carlyle's *On Heroes* and *The French Revolution;* he wrote detailed headnotes and annotations for Takahashi Gorō's translations of *Parallel Lives* (1925) and *The French Revolution* (1926). Rohan's idealistic characters echo heroism such as found in the lives of great historical figures whose human frailties and idiosyncrasies seem to intensify the significance of their achievements.

It was Rohan's belief that "man by nature must have an ambition or an ideal, for ambition is what separates man from animals".... Moreover, "ambition must be of the grandest magnitude and of the most sublime order".... "A man cannot expect to control his desires, resist temptations, correct himself, or take command of his mind, if his ambition is too meager or weak; and for this reason, [the ancient Confucian philosopher] Wang Yang-ming taught his disciples to aspire to sagehood. Man should set his aim at the apex." ... The ideal or the ambition of the Confucian *kunshi* (scholar-gentleman) was to become a sage—a man who has perfected himself morally and spiritually to be harmonious with the absolute. The Confucian gentleman was by no means an idle intellectual dilettante, for his ambition was inseparably conjoined to the betterment of society as a whole. The *kunshi* could bring salvation to society by acquiring virtues that were believed to be self-propagating. Successful realization of his ambition, therefore, hinged upon self-perfection, which involved two processes: moral discipline and intellectual activities.

Rohan wrote three commentaries on the *Analects,* one each during the Meiji, Taisho, and Showa periods. In the first of them, **Commentary on "Government"** ..., he describes the *kunshi* as a well-rounded, versatile man in contrast to a mediocrity who is limited to a certain fixed function (just as a small saké cup cannot serve as a soup bowl). And in **Joy and Pleasure** ..., Rohan contends that a *kunshi,* with his multiple talents, is by no means a simple jack of all trades; as even a great writer cannot boast of unwritten masterpieces, a man is not a *kunshi* unless he employs his talents for the purpose of serving society. Such an idea may sound peculiar to today's readers, but Rohan's ultimate ambition was well understood by his contemporaries, as attested by the poet Kitamura Tōkoku (1868-1894), who in 1892 exclaimed: "It is my ardent wish that, rather than trying to imitate realist writers, a poet of ideals such as Rohan foster his imagination and perfect his philosophy of idealism so as to enlighten us, the ignorant mass."

Rohan was, of course, aware that ambition could not be uniform or identical for all men. In **Mediocre Men and Superior Individuals,** he suggests that every person according to his caliber aspire to accomplish the highest goal in his own field to contribute to the entire society. Once he was asked why he often chose artists and artisans for his heroes. He replied that loath to produce superfluous characters, he had tried to depict people "who would be able to function outside of the artificial world of fiction as well. They happened to emerge as the artist-artisan type, but it was simply a consequence of my determination to draw on real people, that is, people with real work to perform." As the Rohanesque heroes pursue their goal with such intense passion and by all possible means, they stand in marked contrast to the superfluous heroes—the basically skeptical, unproductive protagonists dominating modern Japanese literature (such as Bunzō in *Ukigumo,* Kōyō's courtesans, Shimamura in Kawabata Yasunari's *Snow Country,* or even Sōseki's dilettante).

The nature of the artist's work—to create something new—has a great deal to do with Rohan's choice. The Confucians, es-

pecially during the Ming period, saw the fundamental characteristic of the universe (or the Way) as creativity or productivity, and they considered man as similarly creative in his very essence. Wang Yang-ming's idea of sagehood was, moreover, "to stop relying on external standards, to become completely identical with the principle of nature (or Heaven) within oneself and thus become self-sustaining." An artist can, as Rohan saw it, become a sage by creating a self-contained organic work of art. Without waiting for the introduction of the organic theory of art from the West, Rohan established his own organic view based on Oriental philosophies.

In the social context of the early Meiji, moreover, "ambition" was a prominent word: the most widespread form of ambition was typified by the slogan *risshin shusse* ("advance yourself socially"), which was applied to national purposes and needs as much as to individual aspiration. The literary historian Itō Sei (1906-1969) notes that Rohan's artisan stories illustrate a poetic aspect of *risshin shusse shugi* ("social successism") in the Meiji period. He points out that until about 1900, aspiration for social success was still parallel and compatible with idealism; for, during the early stages of modernization, one was directly contributing to society by becoming a success in one's own field.

More concretely, Rohan's positive hero portrays an image of a new Japanese youth envisioned by the leaders of the national essence movement during the Meiji twenties. They severely denounced what they called the "sneering youth," who emerged with the disillusioning decline of the people's rights movement; and the "kowtowing youth," who conformed to the system by selling their souls to social successism. As their antitheses, Tokutomi Sohō extolled the industrious youth (*rikisa-kugata seinen*); and Miyake Setsurei called for the "Japanese of truth, goodness, and beauty" (*shinzenbi Nihon-jin*). Rohan's artists embody the aesthetic beauty of Japanese tradition and the new positive youth driven by a sense of mission.

The new youth must be assiduous in his work and adventurous in his spirit. Adventure, says Rohan, is "not a reckless, senseless action nor an ignoble attitude expecting a lucky chance ..., but it simply means to be unafraid of danger or difficulty in one's pursuit of the sublime goal." ... In fact, the will to suffer in creation is essential in an artist's life. "I shall undertake painstaking endeavor in my writing career," declares Rohan, "for I would be infinitely ashamed to spend my life shunning hardships." ... Creation is a lonely struggle, for an artist has only his own individuality and uncompromising conviction to rely on. At a meeting of Seinen Bungaku Kai (Literary Association of Young Men, a youth branch of the romantic Bungakukai group) in 1891, Rohan made a speech entitled **Conquest of Bookcases.** He warned the aspiring young writers that no great literature would be born until a writer freed himself from bookcases (past literature) and nurtured his own creativity. He advocated that a writer or a poet build bookcases of his own to overshadow the past literature and to produce works long-lasting and universal, that is, true to human nature rather than to himself alone.

In an article on Saikaku, to quote one of Rohan's most famous passages, he cries out, "Born in the glorious era of Meiji, why should I worship the dried residue of the past masters?".... Similarly, he asserts in another discourse, "Of course, we must respect history, which none of us have the right to wantonly destroy. At the same time, we are children of history, not its slaves." ... In pursuit of freedom from the limitations and expectations of contemporary society, Rohan admired Takizawa Bakin (1767-1848; the master writer of late Edo didactic historical romances) for his ethical stand that was shared by Rohan himself: "Bakin's life cut a horizontal line across his own time, while other writers lived parallel to their times. Not a man to drift along with the fashions of his period, he passed critical judgment on his era, applying a set of intransigent criteria." . . . Man must establish his ideal, asserts Rohan, to use it as though it were a rigid ruler made of steel, not of rubber, if he expects to maintain independence of mind and accurate judgment: everything must be measured by such a ruler and corrected accordingly. Hence the principle of "all or nothing" by which Jūbei refuses compromise of any sort.

The second motif in **"The Five-storied Pagoda"** is the immortality of art. Jūbei represents romantic aestheticism, which had been gathering momentum in Japan since around 1887, to be stimulated all the more by the works of the English Pre-Raphaelites (especially Dante Gabriel Rossetti) and the critical theories of Walter Pater, the spokesman for the art-for-art's-sake movement. Rossetti's name was mentioned for the first time in Japan by Mori Ōgai in a phrase "Rossetti's neoromantic poetry" (*Ima no Igirisu Bungaku,* March, 1890). A more detailed introduction came much later in December, 1893, when *Waseda Bungaku* carried an article based on W. Basil Worsfold's critical review of Rossetti found in the British journal, *Nineteenth Century* (renamed *Twentieth Century*).

Preceding it by two years, Rohan had independently achieved in **"The Five-storied Pagoda"** the Pre-Raphaelite ideal of "combining realistic fidelity in detail with a romantic mysticism in the general effect." Rossetti's influence blossomed later in the poetry of the full-fledged Japanese romanticists (*Nihon Rōmanha,* for example, Shimazaki Tōson, 1872-1943; and Yosano Akiko, 1878-1942) but chiefly in sensuous beauty and vague symbolism. Even before Walter Pater became fashionable in Japan, Rohan had written a work embodying one of the general ideals of both classical and romantic schools of the West, such as reaffirmed by Pater: "the organic union of form and content, in which the end is not distinct from the means . . . the subject from the expression."

Nevertheless, Rohan was by no means a believer in the art-for-art's-sake idea. The *raison d'être* of art, as he saw it, must be identical with that of religion—aspire to Buddhahood and enlighten mankind; for art can inspire and educate man, show visions of perfection, and convey the knowledge of the absolute. Art as artificial creation serves as *hōben* (*upaya* or "means") by which man can be led to the ultimate knowledge. A poem in the *Vimalakīrti Sūtra* declares that *pāramitā* ("wisdom") is the mother of all bodhisattvas, and *upaya* ("means") their father. (*Upaya* is believed to require intellect, supposedly a male virtue.)

The *Lotus Sutra* (in which "*Hōbenbon,*" or the *Upaya* Chapter, teaches the usefulness of expedient devices such as "*jūnyoze,* ten such-likenesses" in explaining the universe) compares the Buddha's love to a father's love for his sons, as illustrated in the Parable of the Burning House. Japanese artists were traditionally regarded as heirs to their masters either by blood or by superior skill. It is not for a sentimental effect that Rohan describes the episode of Jūbei's young son building an imitation pagoda. The boy is an acolyte learning the sacred art to become a future bodhisattva-errant.

In Rohan's view, art discriminates against no one, for creativity is man's very nature; and artistic accomplishment is the most sublime of all human achievements. Through it, man can compete with nature and may even be able to win. Jūbei's pagoda is a testimony to the beauty and sublimity of art as a crystallization of man's spiritual essence. The storm that threatens and tests the pagoda signifies, at the same time, the contest between man and Nature. Only when Jūbei and Genta together stand by the pagoda representing mankind, in order to protect man's creation, does Nature concede defeat. (This is clearly indicated by the Abbot's final inscription.)

At the same time, the storm also mirrors the psychological conflict between Genta and Jūbei generated by idiosyncratic dissimilarities; but it is not petty personal antagonism. While Jūbei is undoubtedly his ideal hero, Rohan is simultaneously identifying with Genta. Halfway through the writing of **"The Five-storied Pagoda,"** Rohan himself circled the Tennō Temple pagoda in a fierce storm fearing for its safety, and he incorporated this experience into the storm scene. Furthermore, Rohan's own **Dictionary of Current Personal Names** (1900) discloses that "Genta" meant "lumber" in the dialect of Owari (present-day Nagoya).

Genta as a man of lumber can be considered a representative of all carpenter-architects. The storm, then, signifies the relentlessly critical appraisal by nature and by fellow artist-artisans to which a work of art is subjected, as well as mankind's desperate and concerted effort to preserve one possible proof of man's spiritual immortality. The pagoda is a symbol of man's supreme challenge to nature and impermanence.

Art as artificial creation may even be superior to nature in its power to enlighten man. **Viewing of a Painting** . . . deals with the case of a student of mature age nicknamed Taiki Bansei Sensei (Master Late Bloomer). After many years of hard work and saving, Bansei finally enters college but soon suffers from a neurosis. On a journey to nurse his mind back to health, he spends a night in a bleak temple in the gloomy mountains during a fierce rain storm. Suddenly he realizes that all the sounds in the world, past and present, are contained in the sound of falling rain: in the single steady tone, "zaaaa," he can distinguish the train whistle, cattle mooing, children singing, people laughing, quarreling, rejoicing—all the sounds audible to man. Muttering to himself, "Oh, well," he falls asleep.

Awakened later, he is led to a hut higher on the mountain to escape the encroaching flood. Almost covering one wall of the small room is a large painting of a magnificent city by a beautiful river, with mountains, houses, valleys, boats, and people going about their business peacefully. As he attentively examines the picture, he sees and actually hears a ferryman open his mouth wide and announce, "Last call!" Just as Bansei is about to answer, "I'm coming!," a draft of cold air causes the light to flicker, and the ferry and the ferryman recede into two dimensions. "It was just one moment, without beginning or end." . . . Bansei's neurosis is cured, and he is said to have become a farmer. "Whether the great talent failed to bloom at all or he had already bloomed, it probably no longer mattered to Bansei," . . . concludes Rohan.

Hearing the sound of the rain, Bansei is able to attain a partial enlightenment, merely enough to ascend one more level (higher on the mountain); but through contemplation of the picture (as in religious training), he reaches the ultimate state where the distinction between reality and illusion (art) ceases to exist. The life in the painting is actually his life, for he has come to live in "a moment without beginning or end," that is, the eternal present. What art can create is not a static, conceptual plane but a dynamic moment embracing time, space, self, others, existence, emptiness—all opposites and antitheses. It is significant that Bansei acquires the knowledge of this eternal moment by entering into a painting, which by nature exists in eternal time. Art is greater not only because it outlives man, as John Keats noted with envy, but also, and more intrinsically, because it is a cosmic entity existing in the eternal moment for Rohan. Whereas Keats's Grecian urn is a "foster-child of silence and slow time," Rohan's painting is the eternal, omnipresent, vital, eloquent cosmos in itself, for by the principle of undifferentiation of all things, every moment is identical with eternity.

Such inexorable belief in the power of art (man's creation) is naturally accompanied by an equally limitless confidence in man. The third issue presented in "The Five-storied Pagoda" is humanism. The supreme Buddhist goal is revealed in the bodhisattva concept of Mahayana philosophy. It is the postulate without which life has no meaning for a Buddhist; it is both man's innate wish (gan) to be delivered from the miseries of existence and the Buddha's Original Vow (hongan) to save mankind. The bodhisattva concept is summed up in the familiar words, jōgubodai gekeshujō ("aspire to Buddhahood and enlighten mankind").

The term bodhisattva has multilevel meanings. In early Buddhism, it referred to Gautama Buddha in his former lives as a "being of enlightenment" (bodhi-sattva) in the sense that he was destined for enlightenment. Historically this term designated laymen who tended the stupa in which the Buddha's remains were enshrined: they were "seekers of enlightenment," for they worshipped the stupa as the embodiment of the Buddha himself. On the metaphysical level, the bodhisattva is viewed as having attained a stage of enlightenment surpassed only by Buddhahood. One can become a bodhisattva through bodhisattva practices, such as genuine love of mankind, endurance of all persecutions, and attainment of the knowledge that all things are empty. Finally on the most familiar, but not the least significant, level, the bodhisattva is revered as one who has attained enlightenment but chooses to postpone his entry into Nirvana until all sentient beings on earth have been saved. It is in this sense of the potential Buddha who denies himself Nirvana in order to help man save himself that the bodhisattva concept has made the greatest impact on the Japanese mind.

Illustrated in the famous Parable of the Burning House in the Lotus Sutra is the idea of gan—man's innate wish to be saved, and the bodhisattva's vow to help man. A chōja (elder who is wealthy as much in virtue and wisdom as in material riches) returns home to find his house on fire with his three sons inside, unaware of the danger. The father urges them to come out of the burning house, but they are too preoccupied with their game to heed his advice. The father coaxes them out by promising to give them treasure carts drawn by a sheep, a deer, or an ox. Once outside, each of the sons receives, instead of three different lesser carts as promised, a white-ox cart laden with precious gifts.

This parable teaches the principle of the Great Vehicle, by which the universal salvation of Mahayana is achieved, in contrast to Hinayana beliefs in hierarchically selective, limited salvation by the Three Small Vehicles. (The Shrāvaka vehicle for the direct disciples of the Buddha; the Pratyeka-Buddha vehicle for those pursuing enlightenment on their own without a master; and the Bodhisattva vehicle.) At the same time, it is a story illustrating the bodhisattva's love for man and his means of guidance that is sometimes expedient but always justified

by the purpose: the father (bodhisattva) saves his son (man) by luring him out of a burning house (complacent life) with the reward of treasures (truth). Man must wish to be saved before it is possible for the bodhisattva to save him. The Abbot's tale in "The Five-storied Pagoda" is Rohan's version of this parable. Only if man learns the futility of selfishness will a pebble appear identical with a jewel, and will he realize that all things are the same in essence. Rohan's version emphasizes universal salvation through the selfless, unified efforts of mankind.

For Rohan, the bodhisattva concept was a feasible ideal, by no means merely a philosophical abstraction. In the person of Ninomiya Sontoku (1787-1856), for example, Rohan found substantiation of the bodhisattva vow and wrote his biography (1891) for the inspiration of young readers. (Sontoku was a true Confucian scholar-gentleman who aided farmers by providing technical advice on such matters as agricultural improvement and reclamation of land as well as spiritual guidance. He stressed the virtue of labor, planned agrarian economy in a communal order, and a view of life as a continuing act of thanksgiving for the Heaven, earth, and man.)

Rohan further asserted that a writer, being an artist, cannot by nature help but aspire to be a bodhisattva. He expressed his admiration for Bakin's "great talent, remarkable energy, and artistic view fused with his staunch sense of justice—his fierce artistic conscience with which he worked for scores of years on the principle of 'reward the good and chastise the evil.' " . . . In Rohan's **Evil Wind in the Chaotic World** . . . , a beautiful woman sends a letter of indictment to the attorney general of a fictitious country, deploring the moral confusion of the people. She denounces scholars for not educating the people, politicians for being indifferent to widespread moral chaos, priests for not being virtuous enough to lead the people. But above all, she reproaches writers for their superficiality and myopic vision, because they "ought to be the light illuminating the world inside and out for eternity and ought to raise their sight beyond one generation and one country" . . . . (pp. 82-91)

The artist charged with the mission to lead the people, demands Rohan, must perfect himself first so he may save others. The long arduous process of self-perfection is often expressed in literature by the metaphor of a journey. In his second story, **Love Bodhisattva**, Rohan sets his sculptor hero on a journey to seek inspiration from great works of art. The journey is a traditional means of religious and artistic training that figured large in the lives of great poets such as Bashō and Saigyō, whom Rohan loved. But at the same time, it also suggests a gradual yet dramatic approach toward the secrets of art, religion, or the universe itself. **Love Bodhisattva** begins with a section entitled nyozegamon ("So I have heard"). For the heading of the ten succeeding chapters, Rohan borrowed from the Lotus Sutra a philosophical concept known as jūnyoze ("ten such-likenesses," or ten categories of supreme truth as manifested in mundane experience, that is, ten relative truths). The story ends with the twelfth section called shohō jissō (all dharma reflects the true state). Shu'un's journey is, therefore, the spiritual ascent of a man's soul seeking knowledge and self-perfection.

A man confident in advancing such a view must be a humanist who loves and applauds man as well as a romantic optimist who believes in the ultimate perfectibility of man and society. This point did not escape Rohan's contemporaries, who classified Rohan, together with Mori Ōgai, as a rare Apollonian type in contrast to the numerous Dionysian types who fill the pages of Japanese literary history. The Apollonian type (at least in the Japanese sense) is identified with intellect rather than instinct, and in Rohan's case, also approbation and healthy adoration of life, and a humanistic glorification of man.

Rohan's apotheosis of man arises from an affirmative, optimistic view of man as possessing an innate ideal nature that corresponds to religious and moral ideals. Rohan is in this regard an orthodox Confucian who sees human nature as basically good. Confucianism dealt quite exclusively with man's life in this world here and now, aspiring to improve and perfect society and man. Humanism is the basic tenet of Confucianism, the central concept of which is *jen* ("humanity"), the universal common nature in man. Moreover, even a Neo-Taoist book, *Pao-p'u Tzu,* affirms that man has an innate wisdom by the power of which he can perceive cosmic mysteries and attain immortality. Within the Japanese tradition, the concept of *makoto* ("sincerity," "fidelity to genuine emotion") predominating the *Man'yōshū* (an eighth-century anthology of poetry) derives also from the belief that a spontaneous expression of the human heart would reflect the unadulterated, therefore ideal, state of human nature.

True insight, or the ultimate wisdom, in Buddhist terms is called *prajñā,* which the Heart Sutra equates with great compassion. Man can attain self-perfection by means of *prajñā,* affirms Mahayana Buddhism, because all things (animate and inanimate) possess the Buddha Nature in them. The Bodhisattva Kannon is conceived as the symbol of mercy who appears in the guise of any being that serves best to save a particular person in a particular situation. This concept metaphorically embraces the reverse truth that every being possesses the potential to become a Kannon. The *Lotus Sutra* tells an episode of a man named Sadâparibhūta, who bowed to everyone, saying, "I do not slight you, for you are all future Buddhas." He eventually became the Slight-No-One Bodhisattva through such awareness of the universal Buddha Nature and determined observance of bodhisattva practices, the most important of which is veneration of man. One must revere man, believed Rohan, because every man is a potential Buddha worthy of veneration; and a man is sinful only when his Buddha Nature is clouded or obstructed by desires and weaknesses. That is why even the murder of Hikoemon the whaler is expiated through dedicated labor, and the villainous uncle in **Love Bodhisattva** repents in the end and follows his niece-turned-bodhisattva to heaven.

Rohan advocates self-help or man's will to save himself by performing good deeds, by doing penance, or even by making the effort simply to say prayers; for no man is beyond salvation and Buddhist love is all-inclusive. In a sense, Rohan's egalitarian view reflected the mood of early Meiji society, in which all four classes (samurai, farmers, artisans, and merchants) were declared equal by the Constitution. It is owing to Rohan's humanistic belief in the social equality of all people that Tae in **Encounter with a Skull** can reject the love of a nobleman, and Jūbei is allowed to bid for a job against his master.

Based on a story in *Shuryōgon-gyō (Sūramgama Sutra),* Rohan wrote **"Purakurichi"**. . . . An Indian girl named Prakritī falls in love with Ananda, a handsome disciple of Gautama Buddha, after Ananda unhesitatingly drank water handed out by her, an untouchable. In her agonies of mad longing, she appeals to the Buddha to grant her love, whereupon the Buddha dispels her illusion of love by teaching the emptiness of the flesh. She becomes a nun, and the religious community is scandalized by the entry of an untouchable among their ranks. Thereupon, the Buddha expounds the truth of the equality of all castes by revealing the former existences of all concerned.

Rohan's faith in man's capability did not lead to egocentric individualism. Jūbei's desire to build the pagoda is motivated by the artist's instinct for self-expression and his urge to create a perfect work of art. He is, moreover, ordered to build it by a mysterious figure who appears in his dream. While Genta is concerned with the judgment of posterity, Jūbei is pitting himself against the destructive forces of nature and the ultimate perfection personified by the Demon King and the Abbot Rōen. It is not by an arbitrary choice that Rohan pictured the storm as an assault of the host of demons rather than as natural forces of wind and rain, and the sea storm in **The Whaler** as apparitions of Hikoemon's slain victims haunting him. In most religions, divine beings are visualized in human form. Rohan presents the forces of retribution also in human form, whether ghost, devil, woman, or apparition. Rohan the poet was able to humanize and personify the abstract ideals conceived by Rohan the philosopher. And Rohan the writer had only one subject matter—mankind, unlike most Japanese writers who were only concerned with their own limited personal worlds.

In **The Blood-red Star** . . . , a mad poet called Kaihi (All Negative) is invited to the moon palace. Arrogantly expecting heavenly applause, he asks for a subject on which to compose a poem. The exquisite moon princess says, "Here on the moon, the only object of our love and worship is man. We would like you to compose on the subject of Man. If it is too broad, please narrow it down to Mr. Kaihi, yourself."

> Instantly, his brain boiled, heart burst, liver split; his chest froze in the ice of awe, entrails singed in the fire of remorse; half his muscles were limp from despondence, the other half twitching in rage; hot blood sprayed out of his pores, and black smoke billowed through his gnashing teeth. His eyes blazing and his body engulfed in flames, he uttered a piercing scream. Then, he plunged, a blood-red star, hurtling headlong through the infinite space. . . .

The poet Kaihi's entire existence was annihilated the moment he realized that he had failed to understand himself, not to mention mankind. A failure to depict the real man is, at least in Rohan's view, a fatal flaw in literature, the *raison d'être* of which is to help man understand his own true nature and attain enlightenment.

It is in an attempt to delineate the divine aspect of human nature that Rohan humanizes and personifies divine beings while deifying and mythicizing human beings. Tae in **"Encounter with a Skull"** is a Benzai Tennyo (Heavenly Maiden Benzai), who is usually depicted in Buddhist and secular art as a beautiful girl dressed in grass robes living in a humble mountain hut far from the madding world. The heroine of **Venomous Coral Lips** in a mountain retreat is in love with the Buddha, for he has written the sutras, the most beautiful poems in the world. (This is not a sacrilegious concept but rather reminiscent of Christian nuns' ritual marriage to Christ.) The Buddha is a poet moved by the pathos of things (*mono no aware*), and sutras are all poems expressing his love for mankind; the Buddha and sutras are all the more sacred for that reason. In Rohan's eyes, the one who is best able to save mankind is the poet. Then, who else is the greatest of the poets if not the Buddha?

Rohan, however, was far from being a shallow-minded optimist. He was aware that reality was not quite so tractable in the face of ideals. The liberated man must still fight and often taste defeat in reality, and his defeat may be all the more tragic for his self-awareness. It was necessary, therefore, not only to point out the evils and vices to guide people away from indulgence, but most positively, to show the glimpses of hope and the world attainable beyond reality. Rohan's best works are his attempts to picture such ideal worlds as an incentive to encourage the aspiration toward self-enlightenment. There are two methods of achieving enlightenment. Man can reinforce and enlarge his individuality by means of willpower and innate ability till his own self coincides in part with the universal, ideal Self: Rohan's artist heroes improve their fate through dedication to their arts and eventually attain the ideal. The alternative is the conquest and elimination of man's self so as to submerge into the universal Self: it is by such sublimation of the superficial identity that Tae, after her body has been consumed by leprosy, arrives at the realm of perfect composure to be related to all times and all souls.

Eternity and cosmic vision constitute the fourth issue in **"The Five-storied Pagoda"**—the religious symbolism. On this level, Jūbei takes on a role comparable to that of a savior: he builds a perfect object of religious worship believed to be endowed with the power to purify and enlighten recreant mankind; and it is he who courageously confronts the legion of demons while apostate people cower and panic. Romantic mysticism is exalted to a sublime plane until man is placed in a supernatural cosmic realm with superhuman beings in this story. Many a Japanese critic has been reminded, especially by the storm scene, of Milton's *Paradise Lost*. In 1906, Rohan named five great literary figures who had influenced him most: "Shakespeare, Milton, Goethe, Ssu-ma Ch'ien, and Tu Fu." . . . Milton's name was first mentioned as early as in 1853 (*Igirisu Kiryaku*, or *An Outline of English History*) and 1861 (*Eikokushi*, or *History of England*). Nevertheless, exactly when Rohan read *Paradise Lost* has yet to be determined. **"The Five-storied Pagoda"** itself proves its Buddhist origin: the demons are not rebels against God but rather beings who come to protect the Law and punish the arrogant; and above the moral chaos and human struggle, there is a realm of peace, harmony, and wisdom attainable by man, as exemplified in the person of the Abbot (whose name means "Radiant Sphere").

Eternity and cosmos are symbolized by a stupa in the *Lotus Sutra*. When an ancient Buddha called the Abundant Treasure Buddha finished his course and approached the entry into Nirvana, he instructed, "After my extinction, those who desire to worship my whole body should erect a great Stupa," and he vowed, "If in any country in the universe there be a place where the Lotus Flower Sutra is preached, let my Stupa arise and appear there, in order that I may harken to that Sutra, bear testimony to it, and extol it." In a dramatic scene, a magnificent vision of a stupa appears in midair over the crowd witnessing the Abundant Treasure Buddha entering Nirvana.

Jūbei's pagoda is thus a symbol of the Buddha's whole body, and its construction is a religious rite in itself. It takes absolute concentration and negation of all other desires as well as a concerted effort of all mankind. Only when the entire crew works in unity (as after Jūbei's injury) can the pagoda escape the fate of the Tower of Babel. The vision of the Stupa, moreover, is to appear exclusively on the occasion when the teaching of the Lotus is being preached, testifying, "All is true that thou sayest." Conversely, the building of a pagoda was tra-

ditionally believed to signify efficacious preaching of the *Lotus Sutra*. Viewed in this context, Jūbei's role takes on a sacerdotal significance, and the storm implies a divine test of Jūbei's true faith.

The symbolism of the stupa in the *Lotus Sutra* is by no means limited to the religious level. As Gautama Buddha is expounding the gospel of the White Lotus, a mystic stupa does indeed spring from the ground into the air. When its doors open, an emaciated figure of the Abundant Treasure Buddha is seen within. He moves over to one side and invites Gautama Buddha to sit next to him. The stupa in which the two Buddhas are seated side by side symbolizes the eternal cosmos, with the ancient Buddha and the present Buddha bearing testimony to the identity and unity of all times and all beings. The ending of **"The Five-storied Pagoda"** indicates that Rohan did in fact mirror this mystic, cosmic stupa in Jūbei's pagoda.

The present Buddha, from a curl of white hair in the middle of his forehead, sends forth a ray of light to project visions of all Buddhas and all Buddha Lands in the air. The Abundant Treasure Buddha, who is already extinct yet immanent, has become emaciated in proportion to the decline of faith in the world. As noted by an early translator of the *Lotus Sutra*, Hendrik Kern, the present Buddha is the symbol of the sun, and the ancient Buddha the moon. Jūbei's pagoda, which is seen launching the moon and swallowing the sun, is undoubtedly the Abundant Treasure Stupa; and it is the universe, where man has the hope of salvation by the help of the merciful Buddhas who vowed to save mankind. It may even be Nirvana itself or the Western Paradise, whence the ancient Buddha returns to lead mankind and whither the present Buddha is headed after his extinction. (Rohan deliberately makes the moon rise from Jūbei's pagoda and the sun set into it, reversing the familiar imagery of the rising sun.) Art is thus magnified and elevated by Rohan to symbolize the hope, the purpose, and the essence of man's existence in the universe.

Rohan may be considered a didactic writer to the extent that his works usually convey some meaningful messages. Nonetheless, he was not a moralist in the strict sense. His heroes transcend the dictates of conventional moral codes without a trace of guilt feeling. Driven by an artistic aspiration that is not a take-it-or-leave-it playful pursuit but an intense and serious inner calling, Jūbei must transcend the customary heroics such as the typical Edoite generosity displayed by Genta or the human sentiments by which his wife lives. As Zen Buddhism teaches, "If you meet your parents, kill them. If you meet the Buddha, kill the Buddha as well," mundane human relationships and preconceived ideas only stand in one's way to enlightenment.

Shu'un rescues Tatsu and allows himself to be put in the position of her guardian out of chivalrous spirit, which demands an act without expectation of reward. But his own emotion (budding love for Tatsu) and outside pressure (Tatsu's father claiming her) interfere with his gallant action. He surmounts this crisis by immersing himself in artistic concentration. Rohan's ideal character is no doubt Jūbei, who typifies uncompromising commitment to art, absolute confidence in his own skill, total abnegation of unartistic aspects of life, and undeflectable passion for achievement. Tsubouchi Shōyō observed in 1892:

> Rohan expressed the view that every man must
> preserve his own individuality, never allowing
> himself to be assimilated into anything to the

point of losing it. He expounds the virtue and the benefit of individuality, asserting that it is the only means available for a man to save himself. I have not yet ascertained whether or not Ibsen's individualism is similar to Rohan's. But in stressing the individual will and in believing that the will is intensified and energized by each obstacle to be virtually omnipotent, Rohan does resemble Browning, who accords so much significance to the power of emotion.

More specifically, some modern scholars detect certain parallels between Rohan's Jūbei and Ibsen's hero in the idealistic play *Brand* . . . , in their unmitigated passion, their total commitment, and their earnest response to the calling from the absolute. They each build a religious monument to awaken morally complacent people, and both suffer persecution by society. As incarnate will itself, Jūbei is an embodiment of individualism, as is the clergyman Brand. Yet their dissimilarities are more revealing than their affinity. Brand's uncompromising demand for "All or Nothing" alienates him from everyone except his boy child (whose frail life is claimed by the cold climate) and his faithful wife (who dies of anguish), sacrificed to his mission; whereas Jūbei's votive offerings are an ear (severed by an irate colleague) and possibly his own life. Brand's is a lonely tragic struggle after he repudiates his new church as a temple of idolatry, but Jūbei is a divinely inspired artist-priest protecting the pagoda—a symbol of human willpower and the Buddha's body itself. Brand is destined to die alone in an avalanche, defeated by nature, while Jūbei triumphs over nature's test and succeeds in his mission.

Brand, facing death, asks God whether he has earned salvation by virtue of his dedication to the mission. A voice calls through the thunder of the snow and ice, "God is Love!" As for this mystifying ending, there are three possible interpretations: first, he is being punished for his lack of love for fellowmen; second, he is granted salvation by the grace of God, who shows more compassion than Brand ever practiced; and the third answer is offered by Irving Deer, who emphasizes the theological explanation that Brand's uncertainty about the merit of his absolutism reveals his essential humanity and earns him salvation, for man is inherently doomed to failure precisely because he is a man and not God.

Herein lies the fundamental distinction between the Christian martyr and Rohan's bodhisattva hero. An irrevocable chasm separating God and man nullifies any hope for man to become God. Brand can be called a tragic hero who failed due to character flaws (such as lack of human compassion) or his opposite—a villain afflicted with the supreme hubris of absolutism, as Brand was labeled by George Bernard Shaw in *The Quintessence of Ibsenism* (1891). Jūbei is decidedly not a tragic hero: aside from his final triumph, his seeming eccentricity and extremism are never meant to be tragic flaws; on the contrary, they are the very essence of Jūbei the man and indispensable qualities in a bodhisattva hero.

Before becoming a bodhisattva, Rohan believed, man must first become a nonhuman, a social outcast by conventional standards but a being with fewer human limitations. Ibsen's Brand, a Christian, may be saved because he is human in his self-doubt, but the Buddhist Jūbei must paradoxically transcend humanness in order to be truly humane. Astounded by Jūbei's adamant refusal to accept his master's offer of a joint project, his wife asks, "Without a doubt you will be ostracized as an ingrate, a social deviate, a beast without human feelings, a

dog, a crow. What glory is there in undertaking a job if you must turn yourself into a dog or a crow?" Jūbei later confides in her: "Well, I just can't help myself. It is my very obstinacy that makes me what I am. It makes me Jūbei the Slow-wit." Not only is personal glory or satisfaction quite meaningless for a Rohanesque hero but he must transcend it that he may bring true glory to the world.

If Rohan's individualism resembles Ibsen's, then, it is only in the single-minded drive to respond to a calling at the risk of self-extinction as in *Brand,* but never in the hedonistic, self-indulgent pursuit of one's own desires typified by *Peer Gynt,* the better-known counterpart of *Brand.* Ibsen was introduced to Japan by Tsubouchi Shōyō in his article, "Hendrik Ibsen" (*Waseda Bungaku,* November, 1893). Rohan's **"The Five-storied Pagoda"** was serialized in the *Kokkai* Newspaper from November, 1892, to March, 1893. It is improbable that Rohan had been exposed to Ibsen's works before 1893.

Rohan's individualism is closer to the Ming Neo-Confucian concept of individuality. "Neo-Confucianism brings to recognition an evident but difficult truth, namely, that individuality in the human being will be unique, not alone in what he is, but in what he does. His life may be expected to yield something significant—not only different—and something which *no one else can do.* In this deed, the individual is realized." Rohan's heroes are not only action-oriented but also self-confident and intrepid. From a Neo-Confucian point of view, "one's mental and moral capacities greatly depend on one's physical powers and drives for their development. Even the so-called [Buddhist] School of the Mind does not see the mind as a disembodied spirit but rather as a vital power manifested through the physical aspect of man, his material force or ether [*ch'i*]."

Most of Rohan's heroes are depicted as powerfully built, tall, and masculine. Kiken the Rare Man, Kasai Dairoku the Bearded Man, and Hikoemon the harpooner are typical examples. Jūbei's name can also mean "a heavy man," and his nickname "Nossori" describes the rather slow movements of a massive man as well as slow-wittedness. Even Shōzō the swordsmith, after three years of utter concentration, still has an enormous figure. Not to be overlooked is Rohan's article, **On Great Men,** in which Rohan illustrates metaphorically: a great man is a person who is not easily or quickly fulfilled and therefore continues to pursue a more distant, greater goal, just as the larger the bowl, the longer it takes to fill it. The titles of Rohan's works also add to the masculine, therefore dynamic, impression by their male imagery as well as their Freudian symbolism, in sword, star, towering pagoda, whaler, gun, statue, and the like.

His tendency toward masculinity, however, is not an expression of contempt for, or condemnation of, women. On the contrary, there are few other Japanese writers who endowed their female characters with more heroic spirit, humanistic cultivation, and insight than Rohan did Rubina of **Dewdrops,** Tae of **"Encounter with a Skull,"** the Madonna-Eve, mystic lady in **Enlightenment of Love,** Rikyū's wife, and others. If his heroines seem to be equipped with typically male virtues, it is because such virtues are, in Rohan's eyes, the fundamental ideal qualities in any human being. In fact, Rohanesque heroines are as much bodhisattvas as their male counterparts.

While man is fighting against the evil in himself and in society toward the remote goal of enlightenment, he needs to be armed with an indomitable spirit and an unswerving ambition. Without them, man cannot survive hardships nor follow the rules in religious discipline. The way to immortality is so simple and easy, says *Pao-p'u Tzu*, that only lack of ambition and insufficient faith prevent a person from achieving it. Buddhist enlightenment is impossible, nevertheless, without the knowledge that suffering is an inevitable part of life. And more crucially, enlightenment requires an acceptance of suffering. If the positive hero is inspired by a mission of mercy to save mankind, his pursuit of the goal must be resolute and relentless.

The definition of mercy or great compassion is not a simple matter. *Hagakure*, the Nabeshima Clan house codes recorded around 1716, lists four sacrosanct pledges of the samurai: first, not to fail in the way of the warrior; second, to serve one's lord with good faith; third, to be pious toward one's parents; but the fourth is, rather unexpectedly, to practice great compassion to serve people. It is not farfetched, accordingly, to see Rohan's samurai heroes as practicing the way of the bodhisattva as much as his artisan heroes. The bodhisattva helps man in the spirit of mercy but man can be led astray by false compassion as well. Whereas the Devil tried to tempt Christ in the wilderness with the visions of glory and power the Buddha meditating under the bodhi tree was approached by a devil Namuci, who wept in false compassion urging the Buddha to terminate his agonizing contemplation and fast. True compassion sometimes lies in denying the sufferer immediate relief or perhaps even in a combative attitude as Nichiren believed.

Jūbei's stubborn refusal to compromise is reminiscent of the most extreme and aggressive faction of Nichiren Sect known as the *Fujufuse-ha* (Receive-not—Offer-not faction). It originates with Nichiō (1565-1630), who urged his followers not to receive alms from, nor to give religious services for, nonbelievers of the *Lotus Sutra*. Nichiō saw this as the purest form of the bodhisattva way, refusing any type of compromise in his effort to turn Japan into the Buddha Land here and now. Jūbei's obstinacy is true mercy in this sense, for in compromising he would jeopardize the fate of mankind. Rohan's heroes, nevertheless, have no conscious intention of becoming bodhisattvas. They suffer, struggle, endeavor, and eventually succeed, simply as human beings without an awareness of their symbolic role.

Rohan advises, "To value individuality does not entail rejection of others. Man must be like a well-ploughed field, soft and moist, ever ready to soak up light, heat, or cold. . . . A man without furrows of belief cannot be disciplined in his emotion". . . . For the truly ambitious and the able, however, Rohan extols the "pleasure of independence": "It is the rebel of one age that heralds a new age; and it is the adversary of one era that formulates the thought of the next era. . . . Very few can endure the anguish and loneliness of independence to stand heroically alone, but history is invariably bejeweled with such men of independent mind". . . . (pp. 91-103)

When Rohan is successful, as in "**The Five-storied Pagoda,**" his bodhisattva-errant hero personifies mankind in its sublime essence, and his work of art is a manifestation of man's immortal spirit—a supreme unity of passion, faith and intellect. At this point, man's creation, including literature, signifies at once man's confrontation with the absolute and the perfect, not to challenge their existence but to become part of them. Such union is possible, in Rohan's view, for a work of art into which man's entire being is submerged must naturally come to bear a mystical spiritual force. Thus, Rohan idealizes human power to a degree that it appears potent enough to render the impossible possible and his positive heroes emerge as bodhi-

sattva-errants striving, if unwittingly, to fulfill the bodhisattva vow to enlighten mankind. (p. 103)

[Rohan's] experiments in realistic techniques culminated in [*Sora Utsu Nami* (**Waves Dashing Against Heaven**)] (1903-1905), which was welcomed by the literary world with immense enthusiasm. Yet this novel was also fated to remain unfinished. (p. 131)

Waves Dashing Against Heaven concerns seven young men who make a pact to achieve success each in his own way. They all come to Tokyo and realize their dreams—becoming a ship's captain, a stock speculator, an army lieutenant, a journalist, etc. The finished portion in 462 pages deals chiefly with one of them, Mizuno, who alone has not accomplished his ambition, that is, to write but a single poem to offer to the world. He is a school teacher hopelessly in love with a woman colleague who is critically ill but somehow loathes him, refusing even to receive his help. When Mizuno in desperation begins to supplicate gods and bodhisattvas, he is dismissed from his post as a superstitious regressionist unfit to teach. In his financial and emotional crisis, a beautiful and sympathetic woman appears to help him. Just as this woman goes to live with another attractive woman who is the mistress of an influential industrialist, Rohan laid down his pen. (p. 132)

In his 1900 article, **The Ocean and Japanese Literature,** Rohan laments the absence of true "sea literature" in Japan—an archipelago. In Rohan's own words, **Waves Dashing Against Heaven** was intended to be a study of an intellectual, modern-day, Japanese Robinson Crusoe. The central character Mizuno was to commit a murder and leave Japan in a ship commanded by his friend; and they would be forced to live on a desolate island after a shipwreck. Rohan chose seven men of different professions to represent various aspects of the capitalistic, utilitarian Meiji society so that the descriptions of their aggressive and dynamic life would amplify the contrast with the major portion of the story, in which human existence isolated from civilization would be explored with dramatic effects and psychological depth.

Rohan's last novel yielded two new literary devices. One is his style effectively harmonizing a softened classical language in the narrative portion with vernacular employed in the dialogues. The other is a new technique in characterization. Isoko, who is the primary motive for Mizuno's actions, is never once described directly: she is presented only through the references made by other characters or Mizuno, who is in fact constantly barred from seeing her in her sick bed from the beginning of the story. Even though she is decisively a moving force, her personal features and emotions are rather nebulous, except for her intense dislike of Mizuno. It was Rohan's intention to keep Isoko a "shadow character" by means of this unique presentation to the end of the originally planned novel. Mizuno himself, moreover, is a new type of protagonist for Rohan: unlike the massive and sanguine heroes of earlier works, Mizuno's "face is sallow, his slanted eyes murky, and under his thin long nose, his pale straight lips are tightly drawn as if never to open again. Though his features are grimly handsome, he has an air about him that would frighten a child to tears." . . . (pp. 132-33)

Waves Dashing Against Heaven would have been an ambitious modern version of **The Whaler**, for Mizuno's voyage was to be undertaken so that he would be able to pass a severe judgment on his entire being, to give a definitive interpretation of his existence, and eventually to kill himself in compliance with a self-pronounced death sentence. Mizuno is still an ideal character inasmuch as he reflects the self-analytical conscience of the Meiji intellectual youth, but he is more realistic and human than the Rohanesque samurai and artisan heroes, in his painful self-doubt, emotional anguish, and helplessness. (p. 133)

[*Shutsuro* (*Leaving the Hermitage*)] was Rohan's attempt at creating a national poetry (*kokushi*) to sing the poetic thoughts of the Japanese in the language of the Japanese, at a time when the so-called new style poetry (*shintaishi*) was deliberately imitating Western models. The new style poetry (written in classical poetic diction but not in the traditional short forms such as haiku or *waka*) originates with *Shintaishishō* (1882), a collection of Western poems in translation and some original Japanese poems. The term *shintaishi* was invented by Rohan's friend and philosopher, Inoue Tetsujirō (1855-1944), who stated in the preface to "Song of Life" in this collection that Meiji poetry must be poetry of Meiji Japan, not Chinese poetry nor Japanese classical poetry. Even though *shintaishi* still relied on the traditional Japanese 7-5 or 5-7 meters and poetic styles, its devotees were strongly inclined toward romanticism, as typified by Shimazaki Tōson, who betrays the influence of such English poets as Shelley and Wordsworth. Gotō Chūgai extolled *Leaving the Hermitage* in his article "My First Encounter with National Poetry" (*Shin Shōsetsu*, May, 1904), defining national poetry as poems that have the power to communicate sincere emotions and sincere thoughts through the indigenous, living language.

Leaving the Hermitage is a significant and even a unique poem in terms of the stylistic innovations and philosophical concepts integrated into it. This poem in 267 pages utilizes all manner of poetical devices and styles: Chinese parallel construction, haikulike cryptic expressions, Japanese meters; stanzas and chapters and parts of varied lengths; mixture of diction—classical, literary, vernacular, Chinese, abstruse; varieties of forms—verses, narratives, dialogues, antiphonic songs, lyric poems; characters of all types—gods, goddesses, children, youth, old men, poets, hermits, soldiers, shadows, visions.

Issues are also diverse. The impermanence of the universe is attributed to a mythical lady in Part I, who healed Heaven's battle scars with a medicine made of five stones kneaded together. She thereby gave the universe sincerity (the white stone), compassion (blue), beauty (red), hope (yellow), and strength (black), but she overlooked the permanence of the colorless stone, which never takes on other colors nor loses its own transparency. In Part II, every man is a knot in nature's net called the world, ineluctably related to every other man and affected by others' movements, just as Indra's net in the *Kegon Sutra* illustrates. The moral crisis of the poet at the time of national emergency is dramatized in the dialogue between the Shadow (aspiring toward celestial visions of poetry) and the Form (stirred by its body made of the country's very soil) in Part III. In the final part, the conflict is finally resolved by the realization that poetry is the impermanent world as it is, not because a thing is more beautiful by reason of its impermanence, but simply because the universe is poetry in itself as it is.

This poem may appear to be a confutation of art-for-art's-sake views and an affirmation of naturalistic approaches to literature, but it must be remembered that Rohan had never taken any antinaturalism stands. If the naturalist writers were trying to depict the sordid dark aspects of reality, as they were in Japan, Rohan was seeking to exemplify in his works such ideal characters as actually lived in Meiji society. Since there was no Platonic ideal world apart from reality for Rohan, his idealistic stories were at once products of his objective study of the world, long before naturalism came into vogue in Japan, and *Leaving the Hermitage* must be considered a summation of his consistent belief rather than a declaration of change. (pp. 140-41)

Rohan's standing in modern literary history may be summed up in a few words: a grand antithesis. Rather than representing modern Japanese literature, he signified the ideal that his age could have attained both in literature and society. Early Meiji literature was dominated by prose, Western concepts, realistic techniques, objectivism, descriptions of phenomena, and mundane settings. In direct contrast, Rohan's works offer intensely poetic tone and style, Oriental transcendentalism, idealistic plot and characterization, humanistic individualism, visions of inner reality, and realms of imagination and mystery. Rohan's literary idiosyncrasies, which place him outside of the dominant currents of Japanese literature, paradoxically make his works relevant to and reflective of his contemporary society. Alone among the alienated, self-destructive, cynical, and superfluous heroes of Japanese literature, Rohan's positive, idealistic, and active hero typifies the fiery vitality and constructive idealism of early Meiji society.

Rohan's distinction is attributable also to the transitional nature of his works: the last bloom of Japanese classical traditions and the early budding of Japanese romanticism and symbolism. His view of love as spiritual, religious, aesthetic inspiration exerted crucial influence on the romantic literary group associated with the magazine, *Bungakukai* (1893-1898), which boasted such diverse types of writers as Kitamura Tōkoku, Shimazaki Tōson, and Higuchi Ichiyō. Rohan's transcendental humanism provided an initial impetus to their attempt to liberate humanity from the vulgar confines of reality.

As Okazaki Yoshie observed, furthermore, Rohan's symbolism is echoed in the symbolist poems of Kanbara Ariake (1876-1952), the plays of Kinoshita Mokutarō (1885-1945), and the symbolic short stories of Akutagawa Ryūnosuke (1892-1927), though they failed to achieve the masculine demonic force of Rohan's visions. (pp. 157-58)

Chieko Irie Mulhern, in her Kōda Rohan, *Twayne Publishers, 1977, 178 p.*

DONALD KEENE (essay date 1984)

[*Keene is one of the foremost translators and critics of Japanese literature. In the following excerpt, he presents a discussion of Rohan's major works. English titles provided in the text are the critic's free translations.*]

The 1890s have often been referred to as "the age of Kōyō and Rohan." The phrase aptly suggests the dominant position that these two men occupied in the literary world of the time, though there was little else connecting them, whether in their writings or their lives. It is true that Kōda Rohan . . . , like Ozaki Kōyō, was born in Edo just before it became Tokyo, and that both men early fell under the spell of Saikaku, but that is about the limit of their resemblances. Kōyō was the central figure of a literary group; Rohan remained a solitary writer almost untouched by the work of his contemporaries. Some of Rohan's early stories were such popular favorites that, in the old phrase, "the price of paper rose," but his writings tended increasingly to be directed at small groups of connoisseurs and not at the mass audiences that acclaimed Kōyō's works.

Indeed, the dissimilarities are so striking that critics now tend to see these two men as opposing poles, and they contrast especially Kōyō's "realism" with Rohan's "idealism." This contrast can be expressed in other terms: Kōyō's "femininity" (especially in such novels as *Passions and Griefs*) as opposed to Rohan's "masculinity"; Kōyō's indebtedness to Japanese literature, as opposed to Rohan's lifelong devotion to Chinese literature; Kōyō's subjectivity, as opposed to Rohan's objectivity. Kōyō's novels lie squarely in the mainstream of modern Japanese literature, though the current has long since passed them by and there is little likelihood he will ever again influence writers. Rohan's writings, especially those of his later years, are acclaimed for their grandeur and nobility of style, but are so far removed from the mainstream that they are almost totally forgotten by the public today. Some critics even ridicule Rohan's stiff-necked adherence to the modes of the past; but if ever the Confucian concept of literature—history, philosophy, and moral essays—is revived in Japan, Rohan will be seen not as a last survivor of a forgotten tradition, but as the prophet of a literature that rejected the undistinguished realism that has characterized the mass of Japanese fiction in the twentieth century. (pp. 150-51)

[Rohan's first published work, "Tsuyu Dandan" (Drops of Dew)], is intriguing because it is so unlike Rohan's later writings. It is set mainly in America. The central character, an eccentric millionaire named Bunsame, places an advertisement in a newspaper for a man to marry his daughter Rubina. There is only one requirement: the prospective son-in-law must never lose his good humor. No questions are to be asked about his education, finances, profession, appearance, race, or religion. Various candidates present themselves, but Bunsame manages in one way or another to irritate each man. At this point a Japanese poet answers the advertisement. He has been paid by a Chinese to serve as his stand-in, the Chinese knowing of the unfailing cheerfulness of the poet. Bunsame attempts to provoke him by making insulting remarks about China, but they have no effect on the Japanese. We learn that the millionaire's original purpose in placing the advertisement was to test Rubina's fiancé, the young Unitarian minister Mr. Sincere, but the latter refuses to enter so unseemly a contest. By default, the young lady is awarded to the smiling Japanese, but the latter, embarrassed by this undesired good fortune, flees to Hong Kong to consult his employer. In the meantime Rubina and Sincere are married, and Bunsame, who is delighted by the Japanese's affability, invites the poet to take a round-the-world journey with him.

The germs of inspiration for **Drops of Dew** were provided by the sixteenth-century Chinese collection of ghost and strange stories *Chin Ku Ch'i Kuan,* but Rohan masked his sources so completely, even to the use of foreign-sounding expressions, that many readers supposed **Drops of Dew** was the translation of some European novel. The following passage is typical:

> The sun sinking in the western sky had turned a steadily deeper hue. "Ah, that is a ruby set in the ring of God!" thought a nursemaid pushing a perambulator, an interesting observation. Tiers of clouds, drifting to the south, formed many layers. "Ah, that must be the lace on Apollo's robe," thought a young man with a Greek book under his arm, an amusing turn of phrase. This evening the voices of locusts dinned in the woods where the trees were in first leaf. A gentle breeze, crossing a pond graced by a fountain, brought a touch of cool.

The parallelism of this prose immediately suggests Rohan's familiarity with classical Chinese; the diction (especially the omission of normal grammatical particles) owes much to Saikaku; and the imagery, though drawn from the West rather than from traditional China and Japan, anticipates the pedanticism of the mature Rohan. **Drops of Dew** is otherwise notable for its unembarrassed treatment of distant places, ranging from New York to Hong Kong, an indication perhaps of the influence of *Chance Meetings with Beautiful Women,* which Rohan had read in Hokkaidō. Read today, the work is probably funnier than Rohan intended, but it is not without novelistic skill.

Drops of Dew was well received, perhaps because the idealized picture of America appealed to Japanese of the time, and Rohan was accordingly commissioned to write the fifth in the "New Series of One Hundred Works," which had been inaugurated with Ozaki Kōyō's *Confessions of Love.* "Fūryū Butsu" (The Buddha of Art . . .), a story of a sculptor who finds in art a deliverance from the bitter disappointments of this world, brought Rohan critical acclaim, and established his reputation as an "idealist." The style of **The Buddha of Art** combined descriptive passages in an idiom reminiscent of Saikaku's with colloquial conversations. The language was sometimes almost perversely obscure; Masaoka Shiki, Masamune Hakuchō, and other distinguished critics of the period confessed that they had trouble deciphering Rohan's complicated phraseology. But even if not all readers could parse Rohan's elaborate sentences, the general meaning was clear enough, and with re-reading the language gradually unlocked its treasures, leaving an impression of richness that could not have been achieved with more straightforward expression. The style was marred, however, by an occasional archness that is perilously close to the contrived manner of the Ken'yūsha.

The story of **The Buddha of Art,** riddled though it is with implausibilities and unplugged holes, is saved by the pervading tone of unreality. Once the style has disarmed us into accepting the sculptor's vision of his beloved Otatsu as the bodhisattva Kwannon, we are not likely to quibble over the likelihood of a messenger arriving from Otatsu's father on precisely the day of her wedding. Nor will we question Otatsu's failure to write the sculptor Shu'un, whom she so eagerly wished to marry, either before her precipitous departure or after her arrival in Tokyo; nor her father's claim that he was so frantically busy for twenty years that he never had a chance to write even one letter inquiring about his wife and daughter; nor the author's failure to indicate how Otatsu felt about her marriage to the marquis. We can overlook what would be intolerable faults in a realistic story because we understand that the author's intent is not to portray life as it actually is lived, but to present in idealized form the emotions and aspirations of an artist. The story has dated badly, but it is not hard to imagine why it was so popular in its time.

The vision of the nude bodhisattva at the end of the story contributed an erotic element to **The Buddha of Art,** which undoubtedly appealed even to earnest Meiji readers. Rohan's next important story, **"Tai Dokuro" ("Encounter with a Skull"** . . .), on the surface at least also provided a romantic element that intrigued young Japanese. This story opens as a youth (called Rohan), who has been traveling in distant mountains, takes refuge in a lonely hut where a strange but beautiful woman entertains him. She invites him to share her bed, but the moral young man asks her to tell her story instead, and she complies. As she nears the end of her long recitation, the first rays of the sun enter the cottage, and at once both house and woman disappear, leaving behind only a skull. Later the young man discovers that a mad woman, a leper of revolting appearance, had disappeared in the mountains, and he realizes that it was she who had appeared before him in his vision. The element of fantasy recalls Ueda Akinari's *Tales of Rain and the Moon* and the world of the Chinese romances; but the Buddhist rejection of lust and the ideals of love inspiring the tale are typical of Rohan, especially at this time.

Rohan's most popular work, the story **"Gojū no Tō" ("The Five-storied Pagoda"** . . .), treated a typical theme, the enlightenment that can be achieved through art. The abbot Rōen of the Kannō-ji, a temple in Edo, decides after his temple has been rebuilt that the remaining funds should be used to erect a pagoda. Genta, the craftsman who built the temple so magnificently that it cannot be faulted, is the obvious person to entrust with building the pagoda, but the carpenter Jūbei, a man known as "lazybones" because of his indolence and ineffectualness, begs the abbot to let him design and build the pagoda; he claims that it is his only way to redeem his life and give it meaning. The abbot is stirred by this unexpected request, but hesitates to deprive Genta of his commission. He summons the two men and relates the parable of two brothers who had been unhappy as rivals but found joy in yielding to each other.

Genta, after pondering the parable, proposes to Jūbei that they build the pagoda together, with himself as the chief architect and Jūbei as his assistant. Jūbei politely refuses. Genta, making another effort to emulate the yielding brother of the parable, offers to serve as Jūbei's assistant, but once again Jūbei refuses, insisting that the entire work must be planned by one man. Genta declares angrily that he will build the pagoda himself.

That night Genta cannot sleep. The next day he visits the abbot and announces he is willing to let Jūbei build the pagoda alone. The delighted abbot asks Genta to help Jūbei, but when Genta offers to reveal to Jūbei the secrets of the builder's trade, Jūbei spurns him. He is determined not to rely on anyone else.

Jūbei sets about erecting the pagoda. The workmen, loyal to Genta and resentful of the upstart, try in every way to impede Jūbei, and even attack him with a carpenter's adze, cutting off one of his ears. The next morning Jūbei goes as usual to the building site. Impressed by his determination, they at last throw their efforts behind him, and the pagoda is soon completed.

Soon afterward a terrible storm strikes Edo. Houses are blown down and the temple trembles under the wind and rain. The priests are apprehensive about the pagoda, which seems especially vulnerable. Jūbei climbs to the top of the pagoda, resolved to kill himself if so much as one nail is shaken loose by the storm. But even as he stands in the fierce wind, another figure is seen pacing around the pagoda, watching it intently, indifferent to the storm. It is Genta, his rival, who is ready to kill Jūbei for his insult to the temple-builder's trade if the pagoda he erected with such arrogant confidence is damaged. But when the storm clears the next day, the pagoda stands triumphantly whole, and Jūbei's skill is acclaimed. The abbot goes to the top story of the pagoda and, wielding a great brush, writes the inscription, "Built by Jūbei and achieved by Genta."

The abbot's inscription pays tribute both to Jūbei's skill and to the Confucian virtue of yielding, which Genta displayed, but **"The Five-storied Pagoda"** is above all a paean to art. Twentieth-century Japanese fiction is populated with artists of different kinds, most of them thinly disguised representations of the author. In these works the novelist or painter or actor is rarely successful and even more rarely derives satisfaction from his art. Usually the fact that he is an artist means little more in the story than that he is not tied down to a job that might interfere with nonprofessional activities or hours of brooding over his alienation from the world. The heroes of these novels tend to be in the mold of Futabatei Shimei's Bunzō, superfluous to society and incapable of justifying their own existences. But Rohan's heroes, beginning with Shu'un, belong to quite a different breed of artist; their art brings them salvation.

Rohan's masculinity, often contrasted with the introspective, "feminine" manner characteristic of much Japanese literature, is also evident in these stories. In part this reputation comes from his preference for describing the harsh aspects of nature— the snow and searing cold of **The Buddha of Art,** the fierce mountain landscapes of **"Encounter with a Skull,"** or the celebrated storm in **"The Five-storied Pagoda."** Nature, as Rohan described it, was not observed in a garden or through windowpanes, but tasted by his flesh in painful confrontation. Rohan's works are masculine in another sense: his heroes do not spend their time brooding over emotional involvements because their minds and energies are fully occupied by their work. Shu'un, it is true, yields to despair when Otatsu leaves him, but this grief is sublimated into the masterpieces he carves. Jūbei's life has been a total failure until he begins building the pagoda, and once this enterprise takes possession of him, nothing can deflect him from carrying it to completion. These men obviously cannot be dismissed as being "superfluous." Even if Jūbei's pagoda had collapsed in the storm, bearing him to death, he would have fulfilled his artistic vision in a manner inconceivable to a less masculine hero.

Rohan's characters tend to be two-dimensional, in the traditional manner of Japanese and Chinese fiction. They lack a "dark side," the contradictions in their natures that would make them fully rounded human beings. One cannot imagine Jūbei being tormented by doubts as to the ultimate value of the pagoda he built, or suffering the shock of disillusion when he realizes that the pagoda has become no more than a tourist attraction. If Rohan's characters are unhappy, it is a wholesome unhappiness that can be resolved by masculine determination; it is not a wasting grief, like Sumi Ryūnosuke's, feeding on itself. Such characters are not necessarily untrue to life, but Rohan's may not move us as characters with greater flaws. Rohan's heroes, no matter how humble their station in life, are giants, and they are rewarded for their strength by miracles. Shu'un is lifted from this world by the ideal Otatsu; their love proves stronger than the force of gravity. The young Rohan in **"Encounter with a Skull,"** though strongly tempted by the beautiful woman who invites him into her bed, fortifies himself by reciting admonitions against lust, and thus escapes the evil fate that seems to be in store for him. Jūbei has never before planned the construction of a building, but his consecration to art and his powerful desire to give meaning to his life produce a miracle: his is the only pagoda in Edo to stand undamaged through an unparalleled storm. These heroes are seen whole by their creator, and the critic can add little to what Rohan himself informs us, though sometimes it requires several readings before we can perceive his full intent. If his characters lack a "dark side," the ideals that inspire them give them grandeur, and it is pointless to search for a third dimension.

Rohan's early novels and short stories appeared at a time when many Japanese were beginning to feel disenchanted with the West. Apart from the atypical **Drops of Dew,** Rohan's works were conspicuously "oriental" in inspiration, whether set in the Japanese, Chinese, or Indian past, or based to some degree on personal experiences. They tended to appeal mainly to intellectuals who were familiar with literary and philosophical traditions, rather than to the general public, though Rohan's early works enjoyed surprising popularity. His later works, quite apart from their intrinsic value, were esteemed by the intellectuals because they were so conspicuously free of the appurtenances of popular fiction, and because their lean style had a dignity reminiscent of Chinese writings of the past. An admiration for Rohan has usually been coupled with a dislike for the Japanese fiction that has especially been influenced by the West, notably the novels of the Naturalist school.

Rohan had no use for Naturalism as a literary technique. Even works of his that seem to be no more than straightforward descriptions of minor incidents create a totally different impression from Naturalist fiction: the unspoken overtones, the quiet manner and, above all, the ''oriental'' reserve impart a dignity not found in typical Naturalist writings. ''Tarōbō'' . . ., written in the gembun itchi style, describes a quite ordinary event: a middle-aged man, having accidentally broken a saké cup, is moved to tell his wife for the first time about his love for the girl he associates in his mind with the broken cup. It is easy to imagine how a member of the Naturalist school would have set the scene: a middle-aged man, frustrated by the meaningless routine of his life, returns slumping home, his battered briefcase under his arm. He is met by his wife, a harridan who complains that she cannot keep the household going on the meager salary he brings home. She produces a meal, still grumbling, slapping down his dinner tray so hard that his saké cup, the one object of beauty in his life, is smashed. At that moment, he recalls the past. . . .

Rohan's story begins as the man, having lovingly tended his garden, goes over to the public bath, as he does every day. When he returns he sits on the veranda for a while, contentedly puffing on a cigarette. His meal, served on a black-lacquered tray, is set before him. A paper lantern casts a cool light. His wife brings saké in a container of Izumi pottery. As she pours him a cup she remarks, ''You must be tired.'' Rohan comments, ''The words were extremely simple, but her voice carried a suggestion of the gratitude she felt as she looked out on the garden, which looked cool after the watering.'' Every touch confirms the impression of a quietly happy, incontestably Japanese scene. The food is in no way unusual, but the man can detect little details that bespeak his wife's thoughtfulness. He accidentally drops his saké cup, which he has given the affectionate name Tarōbō, and for a while he is dejected by its loss. Then he tells his wife the story of the cup and of the girl who was his first love. For unstated reasons he was unable to marry the girl. The wife, far from resenting this revelation of love for another woman, expresses her sympathy. But soon the husband shakes off his momentary grief and gives a laugh. He says he has had all the saké he wants. The story concludes: ''He looked out on the garden. A sudden gust of wind made the lamp flicker. The cool of evening filled the room.''

The little pleasures of ordinary Japanese life, the understanding between husband and wife, the unsentimental manliness of the husband's recollections of an old affair are all presented with the light coloration associated with the Chinese conception of the gentleman and scholar. The incident described is small but not unimportant; it is the transference to ordinary, daily life of some of the themes Rohan had more strikingly conveyed in his stories of larger-than-life heroes and their dedication to their ideals.

Rohan's career underwent a conspicuous change in 1905, indicated by his decision to break off unfinished the long novel *Sora utsu Nami* (**Waves Striking the Sky**), which he had begun publishing serially two years earlier. Rohan apparently felt that the writing of fiction was incompatible with the national emergency of the Russo-Japanese War, which broke out that year. In his long poem *Shutsuro* (*Leaving the Hermitage* . . .), he expressed his conviction that the poet cannot remain secluded in a hermitage when his country is in danger. This belief was in consonance with the patriotism displayed by many Chinese poets of the past, though in Japan the hermit ideal was usually stronger than the sense of civic duty.

Rohan came in this way to reject fiction as a means of expressing his ideals. During the rest of his long life he devoted himself to writing historical or biographical works that displayed his extraordinary learning. These later works are nevertheless described as ''novels'' (*shōsetsu*) by many critics, perhaps for want of a more appropriate term. Among these ''novels'' *Unmei* (*Fate* . . .) is considered by many to be Rohan's masterpiece. This is an account of the brief reign of the second Ming emperor, Chien Wen, his defeat at the hands of forces led by his uncle (who succeeded him on the throne as Emperor Yung Lo), and his subsequent life as a monk who must wander from place to place, avoiding the spies sent by his uncle. Rohan made no attempt to develop the historical facts novelistically. Far from inventing touching details or modern motivations for the actions performed by the characters, in the manner typical of historical novels, he deliberately remained at a great distance from the events, treating them as the workings of destiny. Rohan naturally chose materials that contributed to his grand theme, and did not hesitate even to rely on Chinese histories of dubious authenticity, especially in his descriptions of the life as a fugitive of Chien Wen, who probably perished when his uncle took the capital. Rohan's use of such materials was dictated by his artistic purpose and his sense of drama; even when he seemed to be merely recounting the unadorned facts of history, he was shaping them to artistic ends. But this is still a far cry from the flights of imagination in which writers of historical fiction more commonly indulge.

Fate is not a novel in a usual sense, but it belongs squarely in the domain that the Chinese had traditionally considered to be ''literature,'' and Rohan's manner of narration evokes the grandeur and spaciousness of the dynastic histories. The characters in **Fate** are two-dimensional, presented only in their public aspects, but they are affecting, as figures briefly mentioned in an epic poem can be affecting, picked out from the crowd by a few telling phrases. The transformation of a powerful monarch into a fugitive priest who lives in constant fear for his life is a tragic theme, no matter how treated, and behind the griefs of a particular man Rohan was able to detect the relentless motions of fate.

Rohan employed in **Fate** a severely formal style suggestive of literal translations into Japanese of the Chinese classics. The effect is dignified and sonorous, poles apart from the informal (and often inartistic) prose of the Naturalist school, still influential when **Fate** was written. The manner is intensely masculine: Rohan does not even allow Chien Wen to reflect sadly on the changes in his life brought about by the passage of time, though we might expect this of an emperor who, like Richard II, lost his throne to a usurper. Everything is linear and spare: the battles fought and the deeds of bravery recounted do not invite individual attention but serve to carry forward the inevitable catastrophe. The masculinity is further emphasized by the virtual absence of women among the hundreds of figures mentioned by name.

In most of his works after **Fate** Rohan employed the colloquial, yielding to the times, but this had little effect on the contents. He had by now acquired the reputation of a great literary figure, and magazines fought for the privilege and prestige of publishing his works, even those least likely to appeal to their readers. Only a few of the later works enjoyed popularity, and then generally for the wrong reasons. *Gendan* (**Supernatural Tales** . . .) received an enthusiastic welcome, no doubt because the readers were delighted to be able at last to understand a work by Rohan without effort; but his masterly use of language and atmosphere was probably overlooked by those who enjoyed the ghoulish details of the story of a drowned man who clung to his fishing pole even in death.

Renkanki (**Chain of Circumstances** . . .), Rohan's last major work, is in much the same vein as **Fate,** but the style is freer, even digressive, and there is little effort to focus the incidents on a central theme. Although the book suggests at times the garrulousness of an aging writer, Rohan skillfully led his incidents back to the point of departure, making a necklace of touching beads. The story deals mainly with the circumstances that caused two quite dissimilar Heian statesmen to abandon their high positions and take orders as Buddhist priests. The narration is anecdotal, but the incidents are sufficiently absorbing to retain the reader's interest, and at the end, as Rohan slips the last bead into place, we become aware of a curious unity provided by a theme we may not have noticed earlier, the power of fate.

Rohan's erudition, revealed in historical studies and in a massive commentary on Bashō's seven collections of linked verse, is sometimes marred by the pedanticism of the autodidact and he reveled in difficult terms drawn from philosophical texts. But even though his works could be fully appreciated only by a relatively small number of readers, he was accorded the respect that the Japanese offer to the most eminent men. He received every honor the government could bestow, and his writings, even the most forbidding, were printed in newspapers and magazines of wide circulation.

Rohan remained apart from the mainstream of modern Japanese literature. At a time when most other Japanese novelists were eagerly pursuing different European literary movements, he unperturbedly continued to produce works that revealed no trace of European influence. He had few close associations with the rest of the Japanese literary world, but when he died in 1947 his loss was felt by writers of many different literary persuasions. He stood for traditions that the Japanese have long respected, even though they have found them difficult to maintain in the twentieth century. (pp. 152-61)

Donald Keene, *"Kōda Rohan," in his* Dawn to the West, Japanese Literature of the Modern Era: Fiction, Vol. 1, *Holt, Rinehart and Winston, 1984, pp. 150-64.*

ADDITIONAL BIBLIOGRAPHY

Nakamura, Mitsuo. "Kenyusha." In his *Modern Japanese Fiction,* pp. 51-63. Tokyo: Japan Cultural Society, 1968.

  Discussion of Rohan's role in the development of modern Japanese fiction.

Morrison, John W. "Translators and Early Naturalists." In his *Modern Japanese Fiction,* pp. 33-49. Salt Lake City: University of Utah Press, 1955.

  Mentions Rohan's "ornate classical style" that places him in the movement of reaction against the Naturalism favored by earlier Japanese writers.

Putzar, Edward. "Contemporary Period A.D. 1868 to 1945: Neo-Classicism." In *Japanese Literature: A Historical Outline,* adapted from *Nihon bungaku,* edited by Hisamatsu Sen'ichi, pp. 179-81. Tucson: The University of Arizona Press, 1973.

  Briefly notes Rohan's "crisp pseudoarchaic style" and his achievements in characterization and the idealistic novel.

(William) Olaf Stapledon

1886-1950

English novelist, short story writer, essayist, philosopher, and poet.

Stapledon is regarded as one of the most important English science fiction writers of the early twentieth century. Although he considered science fiction primarily a vehicle for the propagation of his philosophical ideas, Stapledon is acclaimed for the inventiveness of his works and is credited with introducing many of the themes that have since become staples of the genre. According to Sam Moskowitz, his imagination was "the most titanic . . . ever brought to science fiction."

Born in England, Stapledon spent most of his childhood in Egypt, where his father managed a shipping agency. When he was eight years old he and his mother returned to England, where he was educated at the Abbotsholme School and later at Oxford University. After his graduation in 1909 with a degree in modern history, Stapledon worked as a shipping clerk and as a schoolteacher but found neither of these occupations suited to his talents and personality. In 1912 he found more congenial work lecturing on history and English literature for the Worker's Educational Association and for the University of Liverpool. According to Patrick A. McCarthy, Stapledon found this occupation "especially welcome since it provided him with a forum for expounding his socialist interpretation of industrial history." In 1914 he published *Latter-Day Psalms,* an undistinguished poetry collection in which appeared many of the concerns that would dominate his fiction, including contemporary social issues and the search for transcendent spiritual truths. Despite pacifist leanings, Stapledon served in World War I as a driver for the Friends' Ambulance Unit in France and Belgium; he called his decision to join the unit the result of "two overmastering and wholesome impulses, the will to share in the common ordeal and the will to make some kind of protest against the common folly." After the war he resumed his work with the Worker's Education Association and with the University of Liverpool, where he also completed a doctoral program in philosophy in 1925. Four years later he published his first philosophical study, *A Modern Theory of Ethics,* which received little critical attention. In 1930, however, Stapledon received both popular and critical acclaim for his first novel, *Last and First Men.* For the next twenty years he alternately published works of philosophy that were largely ignored and highly-praised science fiction novels. In addition to writing, Stapledon was active in numerous political and social groups, including the League of Nations Union, the Progressive League, and the Association for Education in Citizenship. He died in 1950.

Stapledon's works often criticize dominant twentieth-century views of religion, politics, and socioeconomic systems. Central to his thought is the conviction that the "painful rediscovery and restatement of 'spiritual values' [is] the most important feature of our time." He rejected both capitalistic deification of the individual and communistic suppression of the individual as means to that end, contending that true spiritual growth is only possible through "personality-in-community," the development of the individual through interaction with other members of his community. At the same time, Stapledon's

writings often assert the inadequacy of human intellect for apprehending spiritual truth. According to Mark Adlard, it was this "conviction which provided the springboard for the writing of his fiction: all the fiction, by some speculative device or other, strives to overcome the congenital deficiencies of the ordinary human being."

Best known among Stapledon's fictional works is *Last and First Men.* In this novel a being from two billion years in the future uses the "docile but scarcely adequate brain" of a 1930s earthman to telepathically relate the rise and fall of eighteen races of humanity—of which humankind as we know it is the first. In the novel's preface, Stapledon asserted that his goal was to "achieve neither mere history, nor mere fiction, but myth," and a great deal of critical comment has centered on the "mythic-consciousness" informing the book. K. V. Bailey, for example, attributes the appeal of Stapledon's works to his "ability to shape, from the large problems of human ethics, cosmic dramas shot through with overtones of myth; and, in doing this, to give novel form and imagery to certain universal archetypes." The cosmic scope of *Last and First Men* has, however, also served as a basis for criticism: in the words of John Carter, "there is little humor in human history, taken in chunks of 500,000 years, and as Mr. Stapledon speeds up his mental time-machine and reels off the years by ten millions at a stroke, human interest is apt to falter." Stapledon's second major future history, *Star Maker*, is even broader in scope than *Last and First Men*, depicting over 100 billion years of cosmic evolution; however, critics note that the presence in *Star Maker* of a human protagonist lends a cohesiveness to the narrative that *Last and First Men* lacks. Nevertheless, both works have been criticized for stylistic flaws and weak narration. Mc-Carthy, who notes that Stapledon's novels are "often viewed simply as philosophical treatises masked by a thin veil of fictional narration," observes that "to Stapledon the ideas in his novels are all-important, the narrative line serving primarily as an imaginative device to provoke confrontation with the philosophical argument." John Kinnaird, however, defends Stapledon's frequently austere style as a function of his subject, maintaining that "the theme of the myth-histories necessarily demanded prose of a certain rarefied abstraction and austerity of feeling."

More conventional in style and form than Stapledon's future histories is *Odd John,* which is regarded among science fiction's greatest "superman" novels. The book treats several of Stapledon's favorite themes, including the alienation of a superior individual and the importance of personality-in-community: the novel's protagonist, who rejects and is rejected by society for his superhuman abilities, forms a utopian colony with other superior individuals who thereafter devote themselves to the pursuit of spiritual wisdom. *Sirius,* which is generally considered Stapledon's most artistically successful work, similarly depicts the alienation of a being with abnormal intelligence, in this case a dog with human capacities. Demonstrating what Curtis C. Smith calls "the Frankenstein theme in an exploration of the complex relationship between animal and human nature," *Sirius* has been widely praised for the sensitive portrayal of its protagonist. In addition, Leslie Fiedler has described the novel as "more coherent and elegantly structured than anything which preceded it or was to follow," as well as "more archetypally resonant, more genuinely pathetic, more truly a product of deep psychic impulses for once blessedly out of the author's control."

Stapledon's readership, however devoted, has remained small, perhaps due to what many consider the difficult style of *Last and First Men* and *Star Maker*. His works have nevertheless influenced such science fiction authors as Robert A. Heinlein, C. S. Lewis, Arthur C. Clarke, and Stanislaw Lem. Stapledon is also credited with either introducing or giving the first serious treatment to numerous themes that have come to be associated with the genre, including, in the words of Kinnaird, "future history, galactic wars and empires, sympathetic presentation of alien psychologies and cultures, science and technology conceived critically in their reaction upon society (and even upon sexuality), man's mind itself seen as radically mutating, evolving toward a trans-earthly destiny either tragic or superhuman (or both), and in that evolution exploring the depths of time and space in the quest to find some ultimate meaning in the Universe." In assessing Stapledon's importance, Basil Davenport has stated that "William Olaf Stapledon was not a great poet, nor even in some conventional respects a very good novelist; but he was a mythmaker, and as such he was unique. In his chosen field, his books stand absolutely unequalled in their combination of intellectual brilliance, imaginative sweep, and tragic dignity."

(See also *Dictionary of Literary Biography*, Vol. 15: *British Novelists, 1930-1959*.)

PRINCIPAL WORKS

Latter-Day Psalms   (poetry)   1914
A Modern Theory of Ethics. A Study of the Relations of Ethics and Psychology   (philosophy)   1929
Last and First Men: A Story of the Near and Far Future (novel)   1930
Last Men in London   (novel)   1932
Waking World   (philosophy)   1934
Odd John: A Story between Jest and Earnest   (novel) 1935
Star Maker   (novel)   1937
New Hope for Britain   (philosophy)   1939
Philosophy and Living. 2 vols.   (philosophy)   1939
Saints and Revolutionaries   (philosophy)   1939
Beyond the "Isms"   (philosophy)   1942
Darkness and the Light   (novel)   1942
Old Man in New World   (novella)   1944
Seven Pillars of Peace   (essay)   1944
Sirius: A Fantasy of Love and Discord   (novel)   1944
Death into Life   (novel)   1946
Youth and Tomorrow   (autobiography and philosophy) 1946
The Flames: A Fantasy   (novel)   1947
A Man Divided   (novel)   1950
Nebula Maker   (unfinished novel)   1976

LAURENCE SEARS   (essay date 1929)

[*In the following excerpt, Sears explicates Stapledon's ethical system as presented in* A Modern Theory of Ethics *and criticizes Stapledon's prescriptions for ethical behavior.*]

There are two respects at least in which [*A Modern Theory of Ethics*] represents a modern theory of ethics. It is concerned with the ethical concepts which are being so widely questioned in our day. Sacrifice, duty, obligation, self-fulfilment, happiness, all are brought before the bar for examination. And it is modern in that there is a definite attempt to use the results of recent biological and psychological research. Whether it is modern in the sense of being in line with present practice and trends is a more difficult question to answer.

The opening chapters are concerned with an analysis and criticism of certain ethical theories, in the midst of which the author's own view appears. He deals first with Bradley as an exponent of the idealist theory of self-fulfilment. He takes objection to Bradley's acceptance of pleasure as a sign or symptom of self-fulfilment, since that, he feels, would make morality an essentially egoistic business of saving one's soul, a matter primarily of subjective feeling rather than objective obligation. "The moral agent's obligation toward other conscious individuals can not be simply derived from his own will for self-fulfilment. It must be derived from that which is objective to him epistemologically, and in the last resort from that which is ontologically objective. If it is the world which imposes obligation on the individual, obligation can not be derived from the will to self-fulfilment. If, on the other hand, obligation is derived from the will to self-fulfilment, it is not imposed by the real world, and is not in strictness obligation at all." Over and over again in reading his criticism of Bradley one is driven to the view that it is something other than the individuals in the universe that sets our obligation and demands our loyalty.

"Ought we to seek to be the universal self simply because only so can we be our own true selves; or ought we to seek to fulfill the universe because *it* claims fulfilment?" "For moral conduct is not essentially self-increase any more than it is essentially self-destruction. . . . Its effect on the self is incidental." "Doubtless morality is loyalty not to an individual or a nation or a cause, but to the universe, or to whatever is believed to be the supreme good. But the point is that such loyalty is moral by virtue of its object, not by virtue of its being experienced as demanded for self-fulfilment."

His criticism of Hobhouse is made from the same general standpoint. He feels that the theory as set forth in *The Rational Good* is at heart hedonistic, since it holds that there can not be anything good which is wholly unrelated to conscious beings. As with Bradley, feelings are allowed to enter, and that makes absolute, objective standards impossible. "A man may say (and how is he to be confuted?) 'even though it cripple me for life, I *prefer* this moment's thrill to an age of humdrum health.' You may tell him he will be sorry later; but perhaps he won't. Perhaps he will successfully console himself with a dream life based on the past ecstasy. If his goal is pleasant feeling, in what is he imprudent? In what sense is he missing the good?" Bradley's theory breaks down when it is attempted to reconcile it with obligation. That is the all-important norm. "It would seem, then, that we must either reject the view that goodness is grounded in feeling, or exonerate the individual from moral obligation."

His own theory is based on the assumption of universal teleological activity, which he defines as "activity which . . . is as a matter of fact regulated in relation to a future state." It is the fulfilment of whatever capacities are inherent in the object, but he makes it clear that consciousness is not necessarily involved. "What we call 'good' is in the last resort the attainment of an end posited in the nature of some teleological process; but it is *not* essential to the goodness of such attainment that it should be related, either directly or indirectly, to consciousness." He criticizes the position that anything that is intrinsically good must be an "organic whole" consisting of a teleological process, conscious espousal of that process, and conscious fulfilment of the process. He holds that the fulfilment itself is essentially the sort of thing that we mean by good, and that any awareness of the process is irrelevant.

This objective character of goodness is fundamentally characteristic of his theory. "We habitually use the word 'good' in two entirely different senses, namely, sometimes as a predicate of the object valued." "If moral obligation is to be taken seriously and not as a mere delusion, we must, in ethics, stick to the second sense rigorously. . . ."

Ethics and a sense of moral obligation seem synonymous for him. When we say that a man ought to love his neighbors we should not mean that he needs to do it in order to fulfil his own nature. Even if it is true that he may not be able to attain fulfilment without perhaps sacrificing his life, none the less he does not do it because his fulfilment demands it. On the contrary the universe is such that it has a dominant need whose fulfilment demands these activities on the part of a man. He reiterates that the universe does not simply offer opportunities, it demands obligations. "Art, science, philosophy, and the loving community are demanded, we are tempted to say, by the universe itself: they are not merely means to the satisfaction of impulses."

As one reviews this theory he is impressed by the underlying metaphysical assumptions. It seems to be the "contract theory"

of morals, only in this case the contract is made with the universe. By virtue of being born into the world we assume cosmic obligations. In return for the privilege of birth we are obligated to further the ends of the universe whether we wish to do so or not. Morals are not experiments in adequate living: they are given the status of binding legal obligations, and that, not with other individuals, but with a total universe.

Another question which arises is as to the significance of self-fulfilment apart from any consciously achieved satisfaction. Feelings are rigorously excluded as being in any sense desirable or normative. "We must either reject the view that goodness is grounded in feeling, or exonerate the individual from moral obligation." But how is this fulfilment to be judged? In a given situation when a choice must be made, if feelings of pain or pleasure, satisfaction or dissatisfaction, either in the present or in the future, are excluded, by what standard is it possible to judge whether this objective self-fulfilment is taking place?

Even granting that we must not do what we want, but what the universe demands, when we try to put content into the idea of obligation, do we not find ourselves inevitably thrown back into the world of satisfactions? What happens is that instead of trusting our own judgment as to what seems good we accept the judgment of others, as though they had some special insight. The author of this book does not leave the concept of duty empty. He has his ideals, only he is desperately concerned with making them obligations rather than opportunities. He is apparently afraid that what seems good to him may not seem so to others, and he is concerned, therefore, to take what essentially *are* opportunities for *him,* and raise them to the height of absolute cosmic obligations. It is not enough that things seem good to him; they must be good for all.

Does such a theory provide for any genuine development of character? He recognizes to a degree its habit basis, but he gives no adequate reason how constructive, new habits may be formed. It would seem clear from recent psychology that habits are only formed on a basis of satisfaction. But he has ruled this feeling aspect out, and has stressed instead our obligation to ally ourselves with some objective, teleological trend. This may provide an excellent basis for judgments of blame, but it is certainly inadequate if what we are most concerned about is control. That can only come when we have learned that constructive, social habits will only be built up when genuine satisfaction results. The way out lies through satisfaction, not repression, of our fundamental needs.

Such a theory as presented in this book seems far removed from the every-day concerns of life. It does not furnish norms which will be of actual help in specific situations; it seems impotent to translate life into terms of a vivid, joyous experience. Indeed, for him, joy is irrelevant to morals, as irrelevant in the final analysis as consciousness.

The goal was set, so he would seem to say, without considering our desires; it is for us to run the race. It may not take us in the direction we wish to go, and we probably will not enjoy it. No matter; run! For the Universe tells us to. (pp. 470-73)

Laurence Sears, in a review of "A Modern Theory of Ethics: A Study in the Relations of Ethics and Psychology," in The Journal of Philosophy, *Vol. XXVI, No. 17, August 15, 1929, pp. 470-73.*

JOHN CARTER (essay date 1931)

[*In the following excerpt Carter reviews* Last and First Men, *describing the work as a masterpiece of imaginative mythmaking.*]

The author of this remarkable essay in scientific romance [*Last and First Men*] has triumphed in the field hitherto pre-empted by Jules Verne and H. G. Wells. His book, which is an imaginative forecast of human history for two billion years, is a monument to his versatility and imagination, and yet nowhere wanders into the merely plausible or the vague. He has conceived not only the future social, political and economic history of the present human race, but has also conceived no less than seventeen subsequent human races, with numerous sub-species, differing essentially from each other, and yet linked together genetically. He has imagined modes of life on Mars and Venus radically different to life on earth and to each other. He records the travail of humanity through planetary disasters, solar disorganization, from earth to Venus and from Venus to Neptune, and describes the cosmic disaster which engulfs the known universe and the eighteenth race of men two billion years from now. Yet at no point in his narrative does he stray far from what is already known of the mutation of species, of physical science and of biochemistry.

From this point of view it is a masterpiece, yet the very immensity of the theme and the vast scope of the narrative made it difficult reading. There is little humor in human history, taken in chunks of 500,000 years, and as Mr. Stapledon speeds up his mental time-machine and reels off the years by ten millions at a stroke, human interest is apt to falter.

However, the author insists that there is no attempt at prophecy, that he is only writing myth and that if humanity wishes to avoid a future of the sort which he describes it had better look to its interests. Man's "whole future, nay, the possibility of his having any future at all, depends on the turn which events may take in the next half century," he says. "Nothing can save him but a new vision, and a consequent new order of sanity, or common sense." His book assumes that man does not reform, but remains a prey to his own spiritual limitations and that it is not until the appearance of the fifteenth human race on Neptune, 1,500,000,000 years hence, that men "set themselves to abolish five great evils, namely disease, suffocating toil, senility, misunderstanding, ill-will." . . .

While this narrative is close-written and pessimistic in tone, it is infused by a consciousness that human tragedy is that of character and that human grandeur is that of the conquest of character as a prelude to the conquest of environment. The closing pages are suffused with an almost Biblical poetry:

> Great are the stars, and man is no account to them. But man is a fair spirit, whom a star conceived and a star kills. He is greater than those bright companies. For though in them there is incalculable potentiality, in him there is achievement, small, but actual. Too soon, seemingly, he comes to his end. But when he is done he will not be nothing, not as though he had never been; for he is eternally a beauty in the eternal form of things.

Last and First Men is an extraordinary achievement. If you have the patience to follow the author's admittedly mythical account of two billion years of humanity's future, it will repay you with a splendid vision of human relativity to the cosmos and will drive home the truth of the Hebrew poem which told that "seeing that is past is as a watch of the night."

*John Carter, "The Next Two Billion Years or So,"
in* The New York Times Book Review, *April 19, 1931, p. 2.*

V. S. PRITCHETT   (essay date 1935)

[*Pritchett is a highly esteemed English novelist, short story writer, and critic. Considered one of the modern masters of the short story, he is also one of the world's most respected and well-read literary critics. Pritchett writes in the conversational tone of the familiar essay, a method by which he approaches literature from the viewpoint of a lettered but not overly scholarly reader. A twentieth-century successor to such early nineteenth-century essayist-critics as William Hazlitt and Charles Lamb, Pritchett employs much the same critical method: his own experience, judgment, and sense of literary art are emphasized, rather than a codified critical doctrine derived from a school of psychological or philosophical speculation. His criticism is often described as fair, reliable, and insightful. In the following excerpt, Pritchett discusses* Odd John *as a work of philosophic speculation in the form of fiction.*]

Mr. Stapledon made a reputation for himself some years ago with an extraordinary and daring flight of speculation, entitled *Last and First Men.* Unlike Mr. Wells, who used his fantasies of life in the future in order satirically to expose life in the present, Mr. Stapledon seemed to push biological curiosity onward for its own sake. He showed us the collapse of this civilization as a mere incident in a vast stretch of time which saw the rise and downfall of the first World State, the rise and fall of Patagonia, the appearance of a new species, invasion from Mars and migration to Venus and Neptune. The present book [*Odd John*] is not so ambitious in scope, nor is its idea original. The treatment, however, is new.

Many writers have imagined a minority of supermen or Superior Beings who appear on the earth and make ordinary men and women look inadequate, muddle-headed and beastly.

Mr. Stapledon's creatures have not this godlike appearance. They seem to have immense ingenuity and inventive power, but they have certain vaguely defined but important spiritual resources and aspirations which, by an irony, inhibit those distinctive powers which might save them from the hostility of human beings. Faced with the alternatives of waging a world war in defense of their superiority or of destroying themselves and the island they have colonized, they choose the latter course.

Odd John is the leader. Born in England of ordinary parentage, he is a prodigy of mental accomplishment who can confute politicians, businessmen, writers, bishops and philosophers when he is a few years old. His morality is startling—almost non-existent by human standards—but he justifies it by the superior purpose by which he, as so much pure brain, is animated. Physically underdeveloped, never much more than a child even when he is grown up, this white, woolly-haired creature with large cat-like eyes gets through philosophy, natural science, mathematics and the mysteries of finance in a year or so, and after an acute crisis, when he disappears into Scotland to live like a wild animal in a cave, he gets into touch with other superior beings like himself all over the world.

The obvious difficulty in this kind of book is not to make the reader accept these phenomena, but to show what their life is, what their higher purpose is, and how their ideal life differs from our own. Mr. Stapledon is successful to some extent with this, but his success is limited. Again, it is one thing to write arguments, and another to create. Mr. Stapledon is primarily a maker of sociological, ethical and political arguments. There is only one real character in the book—no, perhaps there are two, Odd John's delightful mother and Lo, his fellow. Fantasy must be lived, one feels, and not argued.

Then, what is Mr. Stapledon's purpose? Are we reading a plea for pure intelligence? Or is the book a parable of the tragedy of pure intelligence in contemporary society? Again, has it some closer satirical bearing on present-day political ideas? Is it an anarchist argument against Communism and Fascism, the stand of an individualist who regards the old regime with horror and the new ones with contempt because of their lack of spiritual substance? Are we to take Odd John's final decision as a warning to the enlightened to reject war at all costs, however plausible the cause? The reader, at varying stages in the book may take his choice; for Mr. Stapledon is a man of theories and notions, daring and stimulating, yet sometimes surprisingly commonplace. His mind is in fact fantastic, rather than imaginative, and his interesting speculations are fundamentally erratic. He is a journalist and not a prophet. Still, those who like their speculation in fantastic disguise will find matter for entertainment and thought in this book.

V. S. Pritchett, "Fantastic Speculation," *in* The Christian Science Monitor, *November 6, 1935, p. 13.*

BERTRAND RUSSELL (essay date 1937)

[*A respected and prolific author, Russell was an English philosopher and mathematician known for his support of humanistic concerns. Two of his early works,* Principles of Mathematics *(1903) and* Principia Mathematica *(1910-1913), written with Alfred North Whitehead, are considered classics of mathematical logic. His philosophical approach to all his endeavors discounts idealism or emotionalism and asserts a progressive application of his "logical atomism," a process whereby individual facts are logically analyzed. Russell's humanistic beliefs often centered around support of unorthodox social concerns, including free love, undisciplined education, and the eradication of nuclear weapons. Regarding Russell, biographer Alan Wood states: "He started by asking questions about mathematics and religion and philosophy, and went on to question accepted ideas about war and politics and sex and education, setting the minds of men on the march, so that the world could never be quite the same as if he had not lived." In recognition of his contributions in a number of literary genres, Russell was awarded the Nobel Prize in literature in 1950. In the following excerpt he reviews* Star Maker *and discusses Stapledon's imaginative creation of the future.*]

Mr. Stapledon, through his *Last and First Men,* is known as a writer with a very remarkable cosmological imagination, who has taken seriously the prophecies of astronomers as to the immense future ages during which the human race may be expected to continue. To most of us, when, if ever, we try to picture the distant future, it appears as leading up to some sort of Utopia and then growing uninteresting. The thought of (say) a hundred million years of orderly government, virtuous living, and steady scientific progress somehow fails to be inspiring. Mr. Stapledon does not have this common imaginative defect. His future, however distant, remains dramatic and exciting, with an alternation of tragedy and victory; he credits the human spirit with an indomitable quality which I hope it possesses. His science is as correct as is compatible with the purposes of a romance, and his future, while just as probable as other men's, is much more interesting.

Compared to [*Star Maker*], *Last and First Men* was parochial: it confined itself to man and to the solar system, whereas this book deals with life throughout the universe. The author imagines that when wars have been brought to an end on each separate planet, there are wars between planets; when the planets of one star have achieved their League of Nations, they start

fighting those of another star; then whole clusters of stars fight other clusters and so on. Most of the most civilized parts of the universe are destroyed by causing their suns to explode; but they refrain from retaliation, on the ground that war will make them barbarous. In the end, however, the civilized remnant conquer through telepathy. But the second law of Thermodynamics defeats them, and the universe grows too cold to support life. By this time, however, the survivors have grown so completely philosophical that they find consolation in the prospect of new universes. The Star Maker, who is an artist rather than a philanthropist, is perpetually increasing in ingenuity, and our universe is only half-way up the scale of his creative efforts. The last shivering sages, as they expire, take comfort in the thought that some of the defects of this universe will be avoidable next time.

In general, Mr. Stapledon is very serious, but sometimes he allows himself a grim jest. He imagines each star to be a person, very conscious of rectitude in always obeying the law of Gravitation (in its Einsteinian form of course), but gnawed by a secret shame, the shame of having vermin on its surface—you and me, dear reader! Every star imagines that it is the only one thus afflicted, and believes the others to be all as wholly admirable as it pretends to be in its discourses with them. In general, however, there is almost nothing that could be called satire in this book.

Mr. Stapledon's writing has a quality of austere beauty, and by his large scope he makes present evils bearable. I cannot resist quoting his final thoughts, when, after his voyage through space and time, he returns to our earth at the present moment:

> It seemed that in the coming storm all the dearest things must be destroyed. All private happiness, all loving, all creative work in art, science, and philosophy, all intellectual scrutiny and speculative imagination, and all creative social building; all, indeed, that man should normally live for, seemed folly and mockery and mere self-indulgence in the presence of public calamity. But if we failed to preserve them, when would they live again?

He finds consolation in two things: the possibility of community between human beings, and "the cold light of the stars," in which "the human crisis does not lose but gains significance. Strange, that it seems more, not less, urgent to play some part in this struggle, this brief effort of animalcules striving to win for their race some increase of lucidity before the ultimate darkness."

There is in this attitude a fine intellectual courage, and something which, for certain types of mind, has all that is good in religion without any of the bad features of most historical creeds.

When confronted with the vastness of the cosmos and the smallness of our planet, different men react very differently. Some are merely made uncomfortable, and forget as soon as possible. Others set to work to make the universe cosy and friendly by the invention of myths. Yet others find that some of their purposes seem trivial when confronted with astronomical space-time, while certain impersonal aims survive the test. A man who wishes (let us say) to be rich can hardly feel that if he succeeds he will enrich the cosmos; but the man who attempts to understand the cosmos better than it has hitherto been understood can feel that, in some sense, his understanding, if he succeeds, is part of the world's understanding of

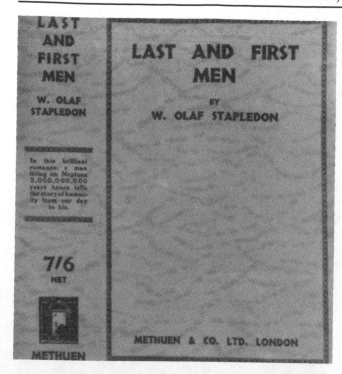

Dust jacket of Stapledon's first novel. Reproduced by permission of Methuen & Company Ltd.

itself, and is an achievement which is not merely personal. Perhaps this feeling is an illusion; I would not undertake to defend it against a critic. However that may be, it is a feeling which I share with Mr. Stapledon, and which I believe beneficial in relation to actual life. (pp. 297-98)

> Bertrand Russell, "War in the Heavens," in The London Mercury, Vol. XXXVI, No. 213, July, 1937, pp. 297-98.

E. W. MARTIN (essay date 1947)

[*Martin is an English critic and the author of social and historical studies that often focus on English rural life. In the following excerpt, he examines Stapledon's philosophical principles.*]

If a demonstration were needed of the futility and unwisdom of all classification in literature, the work of Olaf Stapledon might well provide it. He is not a Christian nor a Theist; though sympathetic to the method of Dialectical Materialism he is not a Marxist; a supporter of federalism, he has no facile scheme ready-made to save the world from wrecking itself on the rocks of a new group-imperialism. In his thought and writing he is steering a middle course, striving to keep his balance on the tight-rope of reality. In a recent lecture to the P.E.N. Club on **"What are 'Spiritual' Values?"** he has indicated what his position is: "It may be said that to take a position between the materialists who recognize no spiritual values and the theists who ground the spiritual values in their belief in God, is to go between the devil and the deep sea, and it is the only way of life in our day."

This is an emphatic statement which is not so unphilosophic as it sounds. Such a way of life is perhaps inevitable in times of recovery, when there is no knowledge but "probable knowledge" for the man who cannot accept any religious teaching, or has failed to discover either in himself or the world outside

him new allegiances that will command the support of the sublimated energy of the entire personality. It probably could never be true for the man who is first and last a politician, any more than it could be true for the preacher who is carried beyond the rational by his vision. Travelling in this path that is inescapably his own, Stapledon has brought to the problems which confront humanity, not only independence of judgment and an argumentative erudition, but an unusual and often disquieting fund of humility, reasonableness and insight.

Philosophy has obviously been the chief influence in shaping his personality; but it is philosophy of a rather special kind. It can never be associated with the academic intellectualism that plays with ideas, glorifies rationality and yet ends in futility because unrelated to action. Olaf Stapledon may not be religious in the orthodox sense of the term; his "compassion with insight," however, is akin to love because it carries with it the urgent plea that the ordinary person shall not spend spiritual energy on soul-saving for a heavenly reward but come forward to the task of to-morrow as one sufficiently fortified to exercise his spirit in the interests of the community. This activist tendency, this need to serve the community on all personal levels, is the corner-stone of Stapledon's philosophy.

Of his early ambitions and aspirations he writes: "I determined to create an Educated Democracy. Workington miners, Barrow riveters, Crewe railwaymen gave me a better education than I could give them. Since then two experiences have dominated me: philosophy, and the tragic disorder of the whole terrestrial hive." The lover of wisdom, the artist and thinker, is not to be cut off from life because his talents are not obviously of a practical utility; his knowledge is for the community and he relies upon it for sustenance, for a vision of the good that may come out of mediocrity. Devotion to the true philosophic spirit, the spirit of Kant, Spinoza and Lessing has given a freshness and integration to this modern ethic of creativeness and holiness.

"Philosophy," Stapledon says,

> "is a way of life"; it is not simply an intellectual discipline. Of course a rigorous intellectual discipline is included in philosophy; but no matter how rigorous, no matter how subtle and conscientious, intellectual activity alone is not by itself philosophy, in the fullest sense of that ambiguous but important word. Philosophy is an attitude taken up by the mind in relation to its whole world; a mental tone or temper which should affect the whole of man's practical living, giving it a sanity, a coherence, a constancy of direction, which it could not otherwise have. Philosophy, according to the original Greek meaning of the word and its common English usage, is the love and pursuit of wisdom, and wisdom involves action. A man who knew everything and did nothing about it would be no philosopher. Inevitably philosophical contemplation points beyond itself. It suggests an attitude to life, a mode of behaviour, appropriate in beings such as ourselves, faced with a universe such as ours; or as ours is tentatively judged to be when we have learnt to see it from the point of view of the informed and critical philosophical intelligence.

In his search for values of enduring personal significance, Stapledon has not allowed himself to be shifted from his course by pressure of events, or by rising and engulfing tides of popular emotion. All such possible outward determinants have not cut him off from that Lawrentian "otherness" of which he is conscious, nor deflected his mind from its known directions.

Even in his first book, *A Modern Theory of Ethics*, . . . it is evident that the writer's powers were ranging far beyond the confines of orthodox philosophy to the fringe of those territories that the mystics and devotees like Blake and Spinoza have touched with awe, and wherein the mind can be reduced to a state of doubting impotence or raised to a passionate exaltation in the transfiguration of personal belief. In this book he postulates three doubts, cosmological, psychological and ethical, which were beginning to make themselves felt just as the first World War began in 1914.

He passes over the cosmological doubt, as Kant would have done, on the grounds that no judgments can be formulated on cosmic questions because, since the nature of the "whole of being" remains a mystery to us, it is not possible to comment credibly upon it. War accelerated the process, quickening thought in the people through suffering; those who had previously accepted what they did not understand now refused to take spiritual medicine without questioning its value. They had rejected the dogmatic metaphysic. Once again it was the repetition of ancient story; it was a time of crucifixion of ideas by custom established; all things were called into question, and as "religious faiths waned, national faiths waxed." Those who experienced the reality of the idea-sacrifice, now looked for new absolutes, for the resurrected ideology that the historic will of man was creating. If life was gone out from the old gods crucified, man could create new ones. Or so it seemed then. . . .

Stapledon's account of the doubt and disillusionment of modern man in those years is still true in its essentials for us. The impact of scientific discovery was a destructive force for many; simple faith was lost irrecoverably and there was no law left beyond those that the self created. The time had come for man to live without loyalty in the old sense; but if there was to be no worship before an unremembered God, there could be ecstasy before the ideal which is comparable to religious deliverance. Probably Stapledon's god would be universal man in the universal community, culturally united by ideals that would provide a wider satisfaction than the arid individualism earlier offered as a religious substitute.

While Stapledon puts in a plea for an ethical science that will assist man in his effort to distinguish the good from the lesser good, he also begins to justify his own confidence—the confidence of necessity—in *intellectual scepticism*. There is a good deal of the stoic, perhaps something also of the Logical Positivist, in Stapledon's composition. "The stoic," he writes, "disillusioned with all other objects, is driven to conceive in his own mind an ideal of conduct and to achieve a precarious peace by pretending with all his might that this which he believes to be a figment of his personal taste is yet somehow of intrinsic and universal excellence." Man, that is to say, realizes himself not through contemplation of the ground and centre of things that is God, nor through metaphysical speculation, but through *acts* of love and creativeness.

When he considers personality in terms of world-community as he so often does, Stapledon turns to the theme which is basic in his work. He is in agreement with such critics of society as Dr. Reinhold Niebuhr and the late Dr. Temple in his belief that this age is dangerously cramped by technics, by subservience to false values of wealth and power. He sees that the dilemma of the age that cannot bring things to birth is really a clash between moral and mechanical forces, and while the mechanical forces progress, the moral forces stagnate. "The supreme goal," he writes, in *Waking World*, "in all our world-remaking or world revolution, must be the spiritual development of the human personality. The human race is to be recognized as a system of selves and the world-aim will be the perfection of those selves, for true reconstruction comes from the individual and not from the plans and blue-prints drawn up by those who are concerned with man as he is or should be, but with the balance of material forces, with questions of power and national expansion."

Following Gerald Heard, Stapledon has divided the human mentality into three categories, namely, the herd-mentality, the individualistic mentality and the mentality making for genuine community. He does not concur with Heard in respect of the continuity of psychical evolution, but takes the far more sensible view that the three types of mentality have been developing throughout history even as the human personality itself in all its aspects has been evolving and suffering temporary eclipses and set-backs through the rise and fall of a score of civilizations.

As many contemporary writers have seen, those technical advances which constitute a menace to the identities of men have themselves made the World-Community a proposition to be practically considered. Niebuhr has written of this new form of universality which is "the global independence of nations achieved by a technical civilization." Such a civilization ready-made through the effort of total war now awaits transformation in its nature, the shifting of emphasis from the field of technical design and practice to that of the separate selves of the nations as a whole. What must be infused into the technical society to save it from ruin are those activities by which man demonstrates his uniqueness and his humanity. Individualism, in Stapledon's view, is the dominating form of mentality in this age, and it is not the most fertile soil in which the true spirit of community can grow. The genuine communal personality of the future will see the problems of society imaginatively in terms of an ethic of truth, friendship and charity.

Stapledon's book *New Hope For Britain* shows how the national faiths which have waxed during the past two decades can be turned to good account by citizens who are knowing and striving beings anxious to realize the ideal of personality-in-community, to achieve that elusive harmony of togetherness.

He is insistent that loyalty must first of all be cultivated towards humanity, towards the human race rather than towards the nation-state. He wants to see a nation of world citizens whose minds, philosophically nurtured and disciplined, will rise above the petty idea of nationhood, and the tyranny of national sovereignty which may be classed as one of the basic causes of conflicts between states. But it is to the spiritual principle that devotion and service must be given, for in this way alone is it possible to leave behind the false conceptions which lead men into barbarism. The man who believes in true democracy will see to it that the freedom he desires for himself is extended to others. "In our day," writes Stapledon, "the true patriot's earnest desire must be that his country shall play an outstanding part in creating World Federal Union." Thus, he will be giving direct expression to that will for world-community which is the most obvious and fruitful moral answer to the challenge of the age of technics.

Although notable as a philosopher, nimble and charitable in speculation, Olaf Stapledon feels bound to distrust the findings of the intellect. It could be said of him, as it was said of Bergson, that he has used intellectual means to decry the intellect. But such a method may be metaphysically justified as a necessary means of ensuring that the natural rationality of Western consciousness does not wholly lose its capacity for imagination or vision. Having reduced his beliefs to a bare minimum he has become one of the most dependably lucid expositors of the sceptical temper of a scientific age and has consistently maintained that scepticism is a good thing in itself.

In certain circumstances Stapledon could be defined as an ethical sceptic; but in so defining him one could easily give a false impression. In the intellectual sphere Stapledon knows no certainty; he is, however, intuitively able to feel a security within himself which is like the Theist's trust in God. It is an awareness of a oneness and an otherness which is both beyond himself and of himself. He is conscious of what might be called a "becoming," in tune with emergent forces that remain vaguely seen. They are the values which give Stapledon his quality of persistence and his power of persuasiveness.

With his devotion to the communal personality he has been interested in the findings of the mystics who travel their narrow ways on the heights with dim lights. Yet he is unable to accept mystical interpretations, though he would not deny the reality of the mystical visions themselves. Stapledon is sensitively aware, however, of the necessity for spiritual values, and he has taken care to define with some precision in the lecture to the P.E.N. Club mentioned above, just where he stands among the increasing groups of "inners" and "outers," of yogis and commissars, priests and prophets. What he has to say about Christianity is revealing because, whatever view we may take of this writer's work, he does come close in many ways to the broadest and best form of Christianity:

> This painful rediscovery and restatement of "spiritual values" I believe to be the most important feature of our time. But it brings with it a great danger. Many who have found that, after all, pure materialism is not enough, are tempted simply to accept uncritically the teaching of some religion, generally the Christian religion, or at any rate, some kind of theism. But the spiritual problem of our day is not solved as easily as that. While we have indeed to outgrow simple materialism and ethical nihilism, we must not forget all that we have learnt from the great movement of scepticism.

The dangers Stapledon sees are not one but many. He has dealt with the subject in an important if little-known book, *Saints and Revolutionaries,* in which he considers the possibility of the recovery of fundamental guiding principles for himself and for society.

There are, he says, two heroic kinds of people in our world, advocating heroic policies, and a third kind advocating a policy, wiser, if less heroic. The first group tend to be otherworldly; to retreat into seclusion when the community stands in need of their counsel and guidance. These are the saints who are concerned with man for his own sake and look into the human personality for those solutions that shall redeem civilization. The second group are activists with a sense of comradeship and social responsibility. They are the revolutionaries and would change society in order to re-create man. The two types meet in their devotion to Everyman and their desire to contribute to his welfare. The less heroic type is the sceptic, more balanced,

but surely less effective spiritually or socially? Stapledon is not unaware of the total ineffectiveness of scepticism alone. He sees the danger there for the philosopher who is apt to be suspicious of all notions but his own.

> The sceptic's loyalty to the intellect tends to distract from all other values. Indeed one of the main causes of the distress of our age is the disintegration of morals caused by the triumph of scepticism, an emotional scepticism which sprang from a well justified but unbalanced revulsion against superstition and humbug.

Sceptics are those who reject whatever offends their intellectual conscience. Stapledon is himself, intellectually, a sceptic, with a bias in favour of the revolutionary. Such a bias is shown in several ways, but perhaps most clearly in the manner in which the claims of religious visionaries are ignored and the assertions of political revolutionaries turned into object lessons. It is not surprising, therefore, that this writer should come to look upon the Russian Revolution as a step forward in our spiritual progress. The social revolutionary, as he is presented to us by Stapledon, is a special type of reformer. It is possible that the leaven of his influence may cause the spiritual will of man to take precedence over his acquisitive impulses and thus become the controlling power in a freer society.

In his defence of the sceptic, Stapledon, for all his caution, is on stony and slippery ground. For he claims that the sceptic is suspicious of all emotion—"he rebels against his own emotion and emotion in others." To rebel against all emotion is to rebel against what is perhaps the mainspring of that creative action which is the centre of Stapledon's social faith, the admired characteristic of the dynamic individual. It might be a sign of emotional immaturity, but it is much more likely to arise out of the necessity for balance. It could not well be otherwise, for what is important for the natural sceptic is also paramount for the true philosopher.

Stapledon goes on to affirm that as human beings fall short of love and reason in their relationships so they will experience frustration. But love does not arise out of systematized suspicion; and development in emotion, in feeling, is as important as development in the intellect. If what the age needs is the synthesis of saint with revolutionary, then when this is attained the sceptic will have no place, for it is as mediator between the two as yet conflicting forms, that he fulfils his function.

In his plans for the awakening of the individual and in his devotion to the ideal of personality-in-community, Stapledon is comparable with such Christian writers as Albert Schweitzer, John Macmurray and Jacques Maritain. But because he is a creative artist as well as a philosopher, he goes a stage farther. He has clothed his abstract ideas realistically; given life and form to new types of personality and higher forms of community in those works of fiction and fantasy which are mostly symbolic suggestions hinting at the way in which humanity can progress or retrogress. All the fictional works, from *Last and First Men* to the new work which he has just published, are concerned with human possibilities and are never wholly divorced from reality, because it is Stapledon's natural urge as a conscious teacher to forecast only from the scientific knowledge now available about the destiny of man. His name has been coupled with that of the late H. G. Wells as a scientific romancer; but the comparison is misleading. Without Wells's gift of narrative or selection, Stapledon has greater philosophic reserve and is not subject to those irritations and explosions which have marred some of the works of one of the most truly creative men since Balzac.

Like Plato of old, Stapledon is anxious to impart his meaning as myth. In the preface to *Last and First Men,* he writes: "Our aim is not merely to create aesthetically admirable fiction. We must achieve neither mere history, nor mere fiction, but myth. A true myth is one which, within the universe of a certain culture (living or dead) expresses richly, and often perhaps tragically, the highest admirations possible within that culture." The myth is a tragic myth; it pictures the failure of man to achieve the Utopia he seeks. It is necessary to face tragic situations, and in this book the treasures of the spirit are finally surrendered by fatalists who see that all hope for man is lost. Such a book as this is not easy to read, and, in reading it, one realizes that even more than Aldous Huxley, Stapledon is a writer of tracts and not a novelist. His main concern is not to produce a work of art or to tell a tale, but to give form to his ideas, to invest them with the universal excellence which is the pleasure of the stoic.

With the philosopher-artist it is always possible that the art will be sacrificed to the philosophy. M. Jacques Maritain issued a warning to the serious artist when he said: "Do not separate your art from your faith. But leave distinct what is distinct. Do not try to blend by force what life unites so well. If you were to make your aesthetic an article of faith, you would spoil your faith. If you were to make your devotion a rule of your art, you would spoil your art." Stapledon is without faith in the sense in which it is understood by the French writer, but it is the desire to edify which has ruined Olaf Stapledon as a writer of fiction.

Stapledon would maintain that his fictional works are not intended as prophecy; but they would appear to have a broadly prophetic aim; even if incidentally unpredictive they serve to show in a general way the direction mankind could take, given certain circumstances. The most readable and unified work to date is *Darkness and the Light,* wherein the possibility for mankind to realize two futures—one through the will for darkness, the material inhuman will of the collective beast; the other through the will for light, the spiritual will of the creative person. The Tibetans in this volume remind us of Heard's neo-Brahmins; they are the *élite* without legislative power or commitments who will train others if not for seership, then for citizenship. The new Lama-class that arises in the peaceful unmechanized land of Tibet symbolizes the developed personality capable of sustained communal effort. They are both monks and revolutionaries; saints who do not desire to flee from the world, but rather to work in it as a eaven. The servants of light, therefore, decide that they must dispense with the "prop of celibacy" and meet normal biological and civic demands in a normal way.

"It was realized in the new monasteries that the two most precious social capacities were the disposition for genuine community and the capacity for intelligent action." For believing this the servants of light were excommunicated by the Grand Lama and they had to save themselves by force. Stapledon develops his story without dialogue and yet the structure is interestingly woven. Like Bunyan and the symbolists of our time Stapledon has realized the value of allegory, of preaching to the people through the use of the indirect suggestion and the concrete image. In a more recent fantasy, *Sirius,* he stages a symbolic struggle of nature with spirit; the dog Sirius is possessed of supernormal powers and in him are the forces which can ennoble and destroy. This book marks a stage in Stapledon's development. Technically and aesthetically it is perhaps his best effort; and if he continues to work in this way he will master a difficult medium which will always remain a vehicle subordinate to those ideas that mean so much.

Any sort of ethical judgment of Stapledon's work in both fields, the philosophic and the fantastic, must attempt to measure his scepticism. Although a genuine sceptic on the level of intellectuality, he is ready to point out the merits of any religious or political faith, and equally prepared to criticize what he considers a falling-away from the ideal he sees ahead. To that ideal of personality-in-community he is, as a moralist, passionately attached. He distrusts a too zealous display of emotion but his humanity has not been dissipated by the restraints necessary to the practice of philosophy.

The most serious defect in his doctrine is that he is asking the ordinary "plain man" to live and to act without any of the essential inner comfort which faith can give. The trained philosopher (for deny it as he will, that is what Stapledon is) cannot demand so much from the average man without being accused of the over-estimation of innate and normal capacity. All over the world religious substitutes have arisen because men demand them for the sake of sanity. It is to be doubted whether logic and scepticism can take the place of faith and vision in a world given over to the things of the spirit and a love of wisdom. (pp. 204-16)

E. W. Martin, "Between the Devil and the Deep Sea: The Philosophy of Olaf Stapledon," in The Pleasure Ground: A Miscellany of English Writing, *edited by Malcolm Elwin, Macdonald & Co. (Publishers) Ltd., 1947, pp. 204-16.*

BASIL DAVENPORT (essay date 1952)

[*Davenport was an American educator, critic, and editor who has compiled numerous anthologies of science fiction and fantasy, including* To the End of Time: The Best of Olaf Stapledon. *In the following excerpt from an introduction to that collection, Davenport discusses the vision of humanity expressed in Stapledon's novels.*]

Olaf Stapledon's first novel, *Last and First Men,* was written in 1930, when modern science-fiction (dating from the foundation of *Amazing Stories,* the first magazine in the field, in 1926) was only four years old. His last, *A Man Divided,* appeared in 1950. For twenty years he produced a series of science-fiction novels which reveal one of the few truly creative intelligences that have ever tried the medium—yet most of them have never been published in America, and, except to a handful of enthusiasts, are unknown in this country at first-hand. At second-hand, Stapledon's ideas and inventions turn up constantly. He has been an inspiration to good writers and a veritable quarry to hacks. The mutant who is both a prodigy and a monster; the dog whose intelligence is equal to man's; the ruin of a world by an atomic chain-reaction; the superman who is not the oppressor of *Homo sapiens* but his potential savior and actual victim; alien intelligences which are not even animal; controlled evolution and artificial brains—in a field so wide and unpruned and one which depends so much on the actual findings of science, which are open to everyone, it is not possible to be absolutely sure that any given book has not been anticipated by another, but certainly I first came on all these ideas in Stapledon, and have constantly come on them since, sometimes in a recognizably Stapledonian form.

Here, perhaps, is as good a place as any for a necessary parenthesis on the label *science-fiction*, which, like *detective story, ghost story,* and *fairy tale,* though a vague and not altogether satisfactory one, yet does well enough. Some purists in the field draw a distinction between science-fiction and fantasy-fiction. I have never been able to see much value in the distinction. There appears to be more objective evidence for apparitions of the dead—ghosts—which are fantasy-fiction, than for the possibility of time-travel, which is science-fiction. Both depend on taking some hypothesis contrary to present fact; both can be used as the vehicle of imagination and ideas. It does not matter which term is applied to Stapledon's work; the important thing is that it belongs to the imaginative and philosophic class.

That is not to say that Stapledon's novels are difficult or dull. Once the reader has captured the sweep and richness of his invention, and grown used to the fact that essentially the ideas in his major books are their characters, the reading becomes an experience which no imaginative person would wish to forgo. True, there are few of the narrative mechanisms of the popular novel, though the slighter books are full of scenes complete with dramatis personae and dialog. But the pleasure—perhaps I should use the word delight—of reading him is inward. The drama is the great drama of human fate. The tragic sense of life is expressed not in the death of an individual but in the destruction or superseding of an entire race, and what is lost is not so much a life as a whole mode of life. It would be forcing the matter to compare the narrative structure of Stapledon's fiction to a fugue in music, but the figure contains a suggestion of the truth.

It is significant that he came to science-fiction by way of philosophy. In an autobiographical note to one of his books, written in 1939, he says:

> My childhood, which lasted some twenty-five years, was moulded chiefly by the Suez Canal, Abbotsholme, and Balliol. Since those days I have attempted several careers, in each case escaping before the otherwise inevitable disaster. First, as a schoolmaster, I swotted up Bible stories on the eve of the scripture lesson. Then, in a Liverpool shipping office, I spoiled bills of lading, and in Port Said I innocently let skippers have more coal than they needed. Next I determined to create an Educated Democracy. Worthington miners, Barrow riveters, Crewe railwaymen, gave me a better education than I could give them. Since then two experiences have dominated me: philosophy, and the tragic disorder of our whole terrestrial hive. After a belated attack on academic philosophy, I wrote a couple of books on philosophical subjects and several works of fantastic fiction dealing with the career of mankind.

It is no disparagement to Stapledon's purely philosophical works to say that his philosophy is better expressed in his novels. In C. S. Lewis' Martian novel *Out of the Silent Planet,* Mars is inhabited by three rational races, two of which are the *séroni,* devoted to science and philosophy, and the *hrossa,* to hunting and poetry. A *hross,* trying to explain a philosophic idea to the earthman hero, says, "The *séroni* could say it better than I say it now. Not better than I could say it in a poem." Stapledon was one of the people who can best say what they have to say in a myth. Some of his deepest feelings, indeed, come

from the sort of mystic intuition which cannot be fully stated in logical terms, though in a work left in manuscript at the time of his death, *The Opening of the Eyes,* he was still trying to do so.

One theme that runs through all his work is of course "the tragic disorder of our whole terrestrial hive." He understands how much of man's misery he brings on himself, and how much of it he could avert—*if* he could! His last novel, *A Man Divided,* is about a man who suffers from a sort of divine schizophrenia; at times he is the mean sensual man, acting under the pressures of all the taboos and false values he has been taught, and all the petty self-seeking motives which he has learned to disguise from himself; then, for months at a time, he sees through all these pretences and falsities with angelic clarity, and acts for the Good, as Socrates said all men must if they could perceive clearly what the Good was. *A Man Divided* is one of Stapledon's weakest novels; yet there is something fine in the thought of Stapledon, at the end of his life, reining in his imagination from galaxies and aeons, to try to give once more the eternal unheeded message of how good life might be if man could learn to act sensibly and unselfishly.

There is a somewhat similar theme in *Last Men in London.* In *Last and First Men* he described the Last Men, a race which flourishes some two billion years hence; immensely more highly evolved than we, they have learned to traverse time telepathically, and to inhabit the minds of their inconceivably remote ancestors of today. The story is told by one of the Last Men who is making a study of the early twentieth century; he inhabits the mind of a young man named Paul, of the generation that fought in the First World War, and describes our society as it appears to a being from a world ruled by intelligence. Also, he tries to give his host the kind of enlightenment which the Man Divided received through some unexplained illumination. When Paul is suffering agonies of guilt because of his normal sexual impulses, the Last Man produces in him a vision of a society like ours, but one in which the act of eating is both sacramental and shameful, something to be performed only in private and never mentioned in polite society.

> He saw with the mind's eye an early Neptunian couple engaged upon an act which to them was one of shocking licentiousness and excrutiating delight, but to the Terrestrial eye was merely ridiculous. This guilty pair stood facing one another, their mouth-aprons removed. From mouth to crimson mouth there stretched a curious fruit, not unlike a much-elongated banana. With mobile lips both he and she were drawing the object into the mouth, and eating it progressively. They gazed into each other's kindled eyes, their cheeks aflame. Clearly they were both enwrapped in that exquisite sweet horror which is afforded only by the fruit that is forbidden.

Man could make a good life if he could act sensibly and unselfishly; but Stapledon has the gravest doubts as to whether he can do that. There is no explanation for the literally superhuman clearsightedness which at times visits the Man Divided: it is simply a miraculous change of heart such as H. G. Wells used to postulate for the race to account for his tiresome Utopias. Lacking such a miracle, Odd John says, "*Homo sapiens* is a spider trying to crawl out of a basin. The higher he crawls, the steeper the hill. Sooner or later, down he goes. He can make civilization after civilization, but every time, long before he becomes really civilized, skid!'' *Homo sapiens* must be superseded. *Homo superior* may come as a mutant, as a more successful Odd John; or by evolution, natural or directed, producing a new species, as in *Last and First Men;* or it may turn out, as in the vast cosmic sweep of *Star Maker,* that the whole genus *Homo,* with all its eighteen species, is but an unimportant eddy in the history of a universe filled with intelligence.

It is Stapledon's gift that he can contemplate the supersession of *Homo sapiens* without bitterness either toward *Homo sapiens* or his successors. Swift detested humanity, and would have been delighted to see it replaced by *Equus sapiens,* the Noble Horse; but Stapledon regards mankind with a grave pity. Odd John recognized that the beautiful stag which he knew and praised was a symbol of ''the whole normal human species, as a thing with a great beauty and dignity of its own, and a rightness of its own, so long as it was not put into situations too difficult for it. *Homo sapiens,* poor thing, *had* floundered into a situation too difficult for it, namely the present world-civilization. The thought of *Homo sapiens* trying to run a mechanized civilization suddenly seemed to him as ludicrous and pathetic as the thought of a stag in the driving-seat of a motor-car.'' And the whole of *Sirius,* the dog with an intelligence strictly canine in nature but human in power, might be an allegory of the same thing. Indeed, Sirius himself, who is more than brute and yet is still at the mercy of its brute instincts, is the Christian concept of Man with the Redemption left out.

For Stapledon, there was no Redemption, and therefore man must give way to some worthier, more fortunate race; and he accepts this, not merely with resignation, but with generous joy in the good life that can be lived, if not by Man, at least by his descendants, and not only his descendants, but his intellectual and spiritual kinsmen of whatever form. In *Out of the Silent Planet,* C. S. Lewis rightly denounces the underlying assumptions of so much science-fiction that alien races must necessarily be horrible, a ''monstrous union of superhuman intelligence and insatiable cruelty,'' and that it is the duty and the destiny of man to fight wars of extermination against other races, more intelligent and more highly civilized, simply because they are not human. Stapledon, a pioneer in this as in many of the ideas of present-day science-fiction, is entirely free from this jingoist patriotism of the human race. He perceives that what matters is neither bodily form nor blood-relationship, but a certain quality which can be recognized in all the vast variety, the arachnoid, ichthyoid, symbiotic or sessile races of *Star Maker.*

In one of his philosophic books Stapledon has said that what claims his allegiance is ''spirit,'' and he then devotes a page trying to define the word as he uses it. He does not do it very well, for it is after all the sort of thing which, like the *hross's* idea, can only be said adequately in a poem or a myth; but it is plain enough from the whole body of his writing what he means. It is a quality independent of form, or even of modes of thought, which might be called the *humanitas* of *Homo sapiens;* or it might be called his *divinitas.*

He himself must have had instinctive understanding of all creatures, of freaks like Odd John and Sirius, if he could have ever met them; and it is the lack of mutual comprehension and sympathy that is at the root of many of his tragedies—although, it is important to remember, not of all. For him, the inevitable, total want of understanding between the Second Men and Martian cloudlets was tragic as causing ''the ruin of *two* worlds,'' the one as great a loss as the other. His great wish and hope, his imaginative solution, is the perfect union that is to be found,

at its lower stages, in telepathy, and at the higher in that fusion of personalities which he described so often and so eloquently. He seems almost to have hoped—for we are now at the level where present symbolism and future possibility are fused—that Man might be saved by some telepathic intervention of a higher power, a Last Man from the future, an intelligent Flame from the sun. Even Odd John, the most *farouche* of his supermen (because the one who was born in a society that was not ready for him) might have had much to give to *Homo sapiens.* Perhaps, this time, before *Homo sapiens* blows himself up altogether, another Odd John will be born, and have better luck.

And if he does, *Homo sapiens* or *superior,* will have greater problems to surmount. ''Out of every victory shall come that which makes a greater struggle necessary.'' Stapledon's imagination is, from one point of view, profoundly tragic. Again and again he describes the good life, sometimes an almost Homeric life, sometimes a life whose activities strain our comprehension, but always felt to be profoundly good; and again and again, in *Last and First Men* and *Star Maker,* its expansion unwittingly challenges some greater force, or it meets some fatal accident, like that in *Last and First Men* which puts an end to *Homo*—accidents which, coming as they do, seem not to be accidental, but to express some quality of the universe. (pp. vii-xii)

Because of such allegories as [*Darkness and the Light*] and because of the succession of catastrophes that overtake all his many-formed races, I have said that Stapledon's imagination is from one point of view profoundly tragic. It is tragic only in the sense that makes *Hamlet* or *King Lear* an exalting and not a depressing experience, and perhaps it should not be called tragic at all. For side by side with his ability to conceive calamities that are galactic in their scope and ruthless in their detail, goes an insistence that (if we could only see it) everything that is, is good. From Odd John's enjoyment of what he calls ''the 'realness' and the *neatness* of my own pains and grief,'' and his horror-struck recognition that other people have to endure pains without this consolation, to the vastest speculations of *Star Maker,* the same theme is expressed: darkness and light are part of the same picture, the picture is beautiful, and the darkness is as necessary to its beauty as the light. It is a feeling that cannot be defended in strict rationalism; Stapledon's last, unpublished book, *The Opening of the Eyes,* a dialog between his mind and an inner voice which he does not dare to call God, is full of it. In this last book he states the rational objections, that wanton cruelty cannot be called beautiful, and that even if aesthetically it forms a part of a beautiful whole, still it is morally wrong to approve or admire it. This books states the objections, but it must be confessed that its author does not succeed in answering them on rational grounds. He is dealing with Spinoza's ''intellectual love of God,'' in which the individual realizes himself as a part of the living Universe,—and here, says an authority on Spinoza, ''we are on the verge of the mystical where all but the greatest poets cease to be articulate.''

William Olaf Stapledon was not a great poet, nor even in some conventional respects a very good novelist; but he was a myth-maker, and as such he was unique. In his chosen field, his books stand absolutely unequalled in their combination of intellectual brilliance, imaginative sweep, and tragic dignity. (p. xiv)

Basil Davenport, ''The Vision of Olaf Stapledon,''
in To the End of Time: The Best of Olaf Stapledon

by Olaf Stapledon, edited by Basil Davenport, Funk & Wagnalls Company, 1953, pp. vii-xlv.

CURTIS C. SMITH (essay date 1976)

[An American educator and critic, Smith has written extensively on Stapledon. In the following excerpt, he examines the dialectical pattern of history in Last and First Men *and* Star Maker.*]*

Olaf Stapledon is an oddity. He seems to defy classification either as a mainstream writer or a science fiction writer. He is respected, but he is not read, although a slowly increasing number of devotees now turn his intricately constructed pages. Stapledon certainly didn't consider himself a science fiction writer—he probably wasn't even aware of the existence of science fiction as a genre when he began to write—and he fits hardly any of the preconceptions most readers have of early science fiction. Political, religious, and philosophical ideas, rather than gadgets or adventure, are central to his works. To be sure, one can find gadgets and adventure in Stapledon, but it would be difficult to separate them from the philosophical significance given them. Stapledon makes one think. He doesn't write "real science fiction," many fans complain.

H. G. Wells's fate has not been dissimilar. However, it's just barely possible to look at Eloi vs. Morlocks as good guys vs. BEM's [bug-eyed monsters; a term used to denote the embodiment of trashy science fiction], rather than as capitalists vs. proletarians. It's just barely possible, in other words, to ignore the social commentary in Wells. By contrast, there are no potential BEM's in Stapledon's works, and no movies to be made starring Rod Taylor and Yvette Mimieux.

This is, in a way, as Stapledon would have wished it. He doesn't seem to have aimed at commercial success or a broad audience. He wrote for the people he called the "wide awakes," those few who would wish to join him in serving and glorifying "the spirit," a nexus of love, intelligence, and creative action. (pp. 44-5)

Stapledon's belief in absolute spirit tells us a good deal of his social and intellectual background. In *Youth and Tomorrow* . . . he reminisces about his late Victorian childhood, contrasting its feel to the feel of the world in 1945. Perhaps the Victorian period lingered in Stapledon's native Liverpool; for there is, in Stapledon's search for an absolute and in the slow rhythm of his neoclassical prose, much that could be labelled Victorian. As does Carlyle, Stapledon accepts religious terminology but casts off the "Hebrew old clothes" of conventional religion. Carlyle's "natural supernaturalism" is a phrase which might aptly describe Stapledon's metaphysics.

He shares Carlyle's revulsion, too, at mechanical materialism. And since he charges H. G. Wells with being a mechanical materialist, Stapledon could be said to write as much in reaction to Wells as in debt to him. There is still a sense, though, in which Stapledon is a materialist, since in his future histories he seems to accept Marx's materialistic inversion of Hegelian dialectic.

Thus he writes in several nineteenth century traditions. Outside the science fiction mainstream (and at first unaware of it), he nonetheless illustrates a major paradox of science fiction, the literature of the future: it is a conservative genre. Stapledon seems to have learned almost nothing from the twentieth century's experiments with stream of consciousness and point of view, and his tragic but orderly universe is as far as it could be from the absurd.

However, he can't be reduced to what he inherited from the past or what he did not learn from the present. Stapledon's concern for up-to-date scientific accuracy in *Last and First Men* was such as to lead J. B. S. Haldane to believe it the work of a scientist. *Last and First Men* is an attempt to extrapolate science as well as to extrapolate history. And there are other ways in which Stapledon's works were ahead of their time, as the Stapledonian elements in *2001* bear witness. Darko Suvin defines science fiction as literature of cognitive estrangement; and (if I understand him correctly) this is what he sees science fiction evolving toward rather than where it is. Clearly, Stapledon's works are fully evolved. They are estranged in that they are written from the fantastic point of view of the world beyond the hill (in Alexei Panshin's phrase), and they describe the evolution of norms and values remote from our own. Dialectically, Stapledon's works are also cognitive: they teach us things about our own world. The last man, who supposedly narrates *Last and First Men* from a point in the very remote future, is nonetheless a man talking to men of the present. The very estrangement of the point of view helps us to learn more about the present. Although he constructs a myth of the future, Stapledon is always talking simultaneously about what possibilities are open to human beings of the present. The imagined relationship between the last man and the first men is dialectical: "we can help you," says the last man, "and we need your help."

Last and First Men is dialectical also in the relationship it develops between humanity and its environment. Although it is a tragedy, the novel expresses an evolutionary rather than a closed and pessimistic view of human nature. The last man announces in the Introduction that "I shall record huge fluctuations of joy and woe, the results of changes not only in man's environment but in his fluid nature." . . . Humanity's physical and social environment acts on the fluid human nature, and human activity helps to transform and reproduce the physical and social environment, in an endless dialectical process. In effect, the last man's story is of humanity's increasingly successful but ultimately tragic attempts at *anthropogenesis.* Present human nature keeps forming future human nature, and increasingly this is a planned and conscious self-creation.

The vastness of the human future is intended, in one way, to impress upon us the littleness of the present. Still, the present is significant. In fact, Stapledon views the present and the near future as a point of crisis, the outcome of which will influence all future human history. A single incident in an Anglo-French war of the near future begins the fall of the First Men, ourselves. A stray French plane kills an English princess and quickens England to violence just as the English leaders had resolved upon unilateral pacifism and a peace message to the world. Had this accident not happened, Stapledon tells us . . . , England and France might not have destroyed each other, the human race might have achieved unity, and the first Dark Age might never have occurred. In the twentieth century the human race is delicately balanced between two futures. Chance is decisive, and "chance" (which is not really chance) is one of the motifs of the human struggle for self control.

As civilizations and species rise and fall, as human beings struggle with self and environment and succumb to chances which are not chances, the pattern of history slowly becomes apparent. At one point the last man summarizes the pattern as follows:

> The movement of world culture was in a manner spiral. There would be an age during which

the interest of the race was directed almost wholly upon certain tracts or aspects of existence; and then, after perhaps a hundred thousand years, these would seem to have been fully cultivated, and would be left fallow. During the next epoch attention would be in the main directed to other spheres, and then afterwards to yet others, and again others. But at length a return would be made to the fields that had been deserted, and it would be discovered that they could now miraculously bear a millionfold the former crop. Thus, in both science and art man kept recurring again and again to the ancient themes, to work over them once more in meticulous detail and strike from them new truth and new beauty, such as, in the earlier epoch, he could never have conceived. . . .

(pp. 45-8)

Accordingly, a theme may be expressed perversely on one level but fully and marvelously on another. Flight is wasteful and self-destructive as performed by the religious fanatics of the First World State, but beautiful when the Seventh (flying) Men "browse upon the bright pastures of the sky, like swallows." . . . When the Third Men perform the first conscious *anthropogenesis*, making the species of "Great Brains," their creation is grotesque and unfeeling; when the Fifth Men make Venus habitable for men, they must kill another intelligent species. But later species of men do the same things at different levels of the spiral. The Last Men, made artificially by those who lived before them and inhabiting a humanized Neptune, recapitulate all previous themes: they are both more fully animal and more fully human than any previous species.

Despite its immense spatial and temporal scope, *Last and First Men* is remarkably concentrated upon the vicissitudes of the human race, its collectively tragic "hero." Remarkably, too, Stapledon succeeds in transforming the few human individuals in his narrative into representatives of the entire species. The Patagonian civilization precipitates a worldwide nuclear disaster which leaves only a few survivors. "'We are ordinary folk,'" says one of them, "'but somehow we must become great.' And they were, indeed, in a manner made great by their unique position." . . . The tragic division which eventually overtakes these few survivors merely adds to our conviction that Stapledon is celebrating the potential greatness of ordinary people.

The Last Men are killed by an exploding star, which seems to be an inverse *deus ex machina;* but this is merely another chance which is not chance. The human tragedy is really a logical consequence of Stapledon's agnostic view of life and of the dialectical tension he develops between humanity and environment; for humanity's environment is, ultimately, too vast for men and women to humanize it. The Last Men struggle to disseminate the seed of future life. Lest we feel uninvolved in their struggle, the last man reminds us that our success in resolving our present world crisis in some way affects the outcome of the last men's final project.

Star Maker . . . continues—on a cosmic level and with a more complex time scale—the dialectical interrelationship between intelligence and matter. In this work, in many ways a sequel to *Last and First Men*, Stapledon inverts the point of view. In *Last and First Men* the future, estranged point of view comes to and asks the attention of the present; in *Star Maker*, a contemporary Englishman floats into the cosmos, and in an upward spiral of experience he learns the pattern of cosmic history. "Man" in *Last and First Men* always remains man; similarly, the narrator of *Star Maker* remains in some way an Englishman, even though his point of view becomes increasingly complex.

Only a book length study could begin to analyze Stapledon's fictionalized cosmology, and I wish to make only one approach to such an analysis. *Star Maker*'s estranged vision of plant men, nautiloids, and other wonders is once again used dialectically for cognitive evaluation of the human present. Surprisingly, perhaps, *Star Maker* is a political book. Satirizing certain aspects of (what he conceives to be) Marxist theory and practice, Stapledon also attempts to demonstrate the core of soundness which Marxism contains. In the partially autobiographical *Last Men in London*, Paul "tried to persuade the Communists that he knew their mind better than they did themselves . . . he was expelled from the Communist Party as an incorrigible bourgeois . . . the communistically inclined editor of a well-known literary journal, who at first hoped to bring Paul within his own circle, was soon very thankful to get rid of him."

Whether or not all or part of Paul's experience is Stapledon's, this passage describes the stance of Stapledon in relation to the Left; he is sympathetic, but he cannot accept the Party wholeheartedly. In the Preface to *Star Maker*, written in March 1937, Stapledon says that "our outworn economic system," not simply German fascism, "dooms millions to frustration." There is a worldwide crisis, the identical crisis which confronts every world the *Star Maker* pilgrims visit. Consequently "a book like this may be condemned as a distraction from the desperately urgent defense of civilization against modern barbarism." . . . Stapledon is aware of the charge that science fiction is bourgeois and escapist. But he accepts the challenge of such a charge. *Star Maker* is, among many other things, an attempt to demonstrate the political usefulness of estranged, visionary literature and to explore the cosmic implications of dialectics; to express, in short, the Left's core of truth better than the Left itself expresses it.

He develops a Marxist analysis of the first place visited by the narrator after he is snatched from his hillside, the "Other Earth"; but he is simultaneously satirizing Marxism. A small ruling class owns the means of production:

> The owners directed the energy of the workers increasingly toward the production of more means of production rather than to the fulfillment of the needs of individual life. For machinery might bring profit to the owners; bread would not. With the increasing competition of machine with machine, profits declined, and therefore wages, and therefore effective demand for goods. Marketless products were destroyed, though bellies were unfed and backs unclad. Unemployment, disorder, and stern repression increased as the economic system disintegrated. A familiar story! . . .

(pp. 48-50)

This ruling class uses race and class divisions to maintain itself in power. Race is determined by the taste of the sexual organs, taste being the dominant sense on the Other Earth. The lowest race-class, the pariahs, is kept alive only because workers are needed. Stapledon brilliantly extrapolates the ruling class use of radio and television as opiates. Sexual broadcasts are developed, and it becomes possible for a man to "retire to bed for life and spend all his time receiving radio programmes." . . . But Stapledon has the political sophistication to see, as so many writers of dystopias do not, that a capitalist ruling class might have ambiguous, contradictory attitudes toward soma. Part of the ruling class supports the broadcasts, citing their usefulness for social control; the other part turns against the very instrument they have created, for "their craving was for power: and for power they needed [conscious] slaves whose labour they could command for their great industrial ventures." . . . (pp. 50-1)

Marxist terminology and analysis, then, apply more accurately to the Other Earth than to any other world in *Star Maker*. But the Other Earth is condemned to cycles of civilization and savagery, with no dialectical advances out of the cycle. Since his distressed condition on the hillside forms a psychic bond downward, the pilgrim begins his journey on the one world of *Star Maker* which is less advanced spiritually than the Earth. It is as if Stapledon is saying that a purely Marxist analysis could apply only to a world more primitive or more simple than our own. The Communists on the Other Earth are merely a part of the hopeless battle between extremes, such as dogmatic religion and complete atheism, which are never transcended by a synthesis:

> Communism . . . still maintained its irreligious convention; but in the two great Communist countries the officially organized 'irreligion' was becoming a religion in all but name. It had its institutions, its priesthood, its ritual, its morality, its system of absolution, its metaphysical doctrines, which, though devoutly materialistic, were none the less superstitious. And the flavour of deity had been displaced by the flavour of the proletariat. . . .

(p. 51)

Despite his satire here of Communism's paradoxical rigidities and absurdities, Stapledon sees cosmic history as dialectical. Worlds in a crisis of economic and social individualism such as our own are transcended, after "a long-drawn agony of economic distress and maniac warfare," . . . by a new level which Stapledon calls the "waking world."

"In the loosest possible sense" all of these waking worlds "were communistic; for in all of them the means of production were communally owned, and no individual could control the labours of others for private profit. Again, in a sense all of these world-orders were democratic," . . . but democracy is the democratic centralism of a bureaucracy or even a dictatorship. Stapledon's waking worlds sweep aside both the machinery of economic control by a minority and the machinery of bourgeois representative government which prevents the true expression of the people's will while pretending to foster it.

Despite his generalizations, Stapledon recognizes the uniqueness of dialectical development. Not in every case does the dialectic lead to the waking world. More often than not, social and environmental factors end history altogether. Even when achieved, the waking worlds are very diverse: "this was, of course, to be expected, since biologically, psychologically, culturally, these worlds were very different." . . . Echinoderms (starfish-men) and Ichthyoid (fish)-Arachnoid (crustacean) symbiotic races quite obviously have histories very different from ours! The brilliance of *Star Maker* comes from Stapledon's ability to sketch scores of unique dialectical developments within a general framework, showing in each case the

mediation between physical and environmental forces and the resulting cultural and social forces.

Stapledon describes, too, the continuation of the dialectic beyond the level of the waking world. The formation of a classless society, while an immense step, does not mean the end of struggle. Certain "mad" worlds impede the formation of a galactic utopia. These worlds are waking worlds, but they have become perversely obsessed with the hunger for community; obsessed, too, with the technology of interstellar travel and with the possibility of empire-making which results from it. Probably Stapledon is satirizing what he conceives to be the U.S.S.R.'s mania for industrial development to the exclusion of the quality of life.

As the dialectic continues through galactic utopia and galactic symbiosis, to the cosmic mind and its symbiosis with the Star Maker, and to the final dialectical relationship between the Star Maker and its creations, we realize that Stapledon is trying to communicate the value of being able to experience and feel the size and complexity of the universe. And when the scene is suddenly shifted back to Earth, in the Epilogue, we realize that Stapledon is saying that this same value may be found on Earth. For the Earth, too, is vast; and as the narrator dimly sensed when he left it, "the vital presence of Earth [is] of a creature alive but tranced and obscurely yearning to wake." . . . (pp. 51-2)

The final dialectic is offered on the last page of the book. Thesis and antithesis are the two lights to guide by, the little atom of community on Earth and the cold light of the stars. The synthesis is a greater, not a lesser, significance to the human struggle. The contrast between man and star does not detract from our dedication to the struggle but in fact intensifies that struggle. Stapledon asserts, as ecologists now do, that only by feeling the value of the whole universe, including that which lies beyond humanity, will we feel the value of humanity and struggle to preserve it.

In some such way, then, Stapledon would defend himself against the charge of irrelevance and escapism. Is the defense successful? Fresh from the incredibly abstract rendering of the dialectical relationship between cosmic spirit and Star Maker, we may not be ready to feel what Stapledon is telling us to feel in the final pages. The Epilogue on Earth helps, but not enough. In *Last and First Men*, the concentration remains upon *anthropogenesis*, with humanity as subject and the cosmos as object. In *Star Maker*, as I began by saying, there is an inversion of point of view. Not only do we leave Earth with the Englishman, but in the "supreme moment" of the cosmos we leap again, to the Star Maker's point of view. With Star Maker as subject, each cosmos (including our own, past and future) becomes an object. *Last and First Men* is a tragedy, concentrating upon an upward and outward struggle which is never completed; *Star Maker* could not be called a tragedy, for it ends by leaping outside of all mortal struggle and looking back upon it from outside. "Time Scale Three" . . . presents the succession of the Star Maker's creations as a cycle from "immature" to "mature" creating—a repeating cycle, it would seem, in some paradoxical way. At the center of the cycle (which is represented by a circular graph of the creations) is the "view point of eternity." The emotional force of *Last and First Men* comes as a result of the weight of time; in *Star Maker*, time is in some way or sense unreal. Leaving *Last and First Men*, we remember the pathos of the last man's last words, about how good it is to have been man; leaving *Star Maker*, we remember the frosty ecstasy of the Star Maker, contemplating "his" creations from a point outside of time and space. *Star Maker* is a magnificent achievement on an almost unbelievably vast scale, but it is not a human book. As his Preface shows, Stapledon understood the dangers in what he was doing, and tried to compensate for them. He was not altogether successful. (pp. 52-3)

Curtis C. Smith, "Olaf Stapledon's Dispassionate Objectivity," in Voices for the Future: Essays on Major Science Fiction Writers, Vol. I, *edited by Thomas D. Clareson, Bowling Green University Popular Press, 1976, pp. 44-63.*

JAMES L. CAMPBELL, Sr. (essay date 1982)

[*An American educator and critic, Campbell has written extensively on Victorian literature. In the following excerpt, he surveys Stapledon's career and discusses his most important novels.*]

Stapledon's first published work was a slim, privately printed volume of verse entitled *Latter-Day Psalms.* It is of interest because it represents the first appearance of important ideas central to his later philosophical and science fiction works. One such theme is the moral irrelevance of a theology centered on the expectation of immortality. Also important is Stapledon's poetic description of a creative principle that evolves through time by experience. Such a figure greatly resembles the evolving God described in his novel *Star Maker.*

Stapledon's next book, *A Modern Theory of Ethics,* is also important as a source for ideas central to his science fiction. In his description of Stapledon and his writings in the *Science Fiction Encyclopedia* (1979), Mark Adlard identifies a number of important themes: "moral obligation as a teleological requirement; ecstasy as a cognitive intuition of cosmic excellence; personal fulfilment of individual capacities as an intrinsic good; community as a necessary prerequisite for individual fulfilment; and the hopeless inadequacy of human faculties for the discovery of truth." It is this last notion, Adlard argues, that most directly concerned Stapledon in his science fiction writing; for in each novel he wrote, the issue seems to be the often anguished attempts of the characters to overcome the limitations of normal human intelligence and perception.

In Stapledon's other political and philosophic books, some indication of his development as a thinker and social critic can be seen. *Waking World* shows his debt to Wells's social theories. In it Stapledon criticizes capitalism as a self-destructive, wasteful, and decadent economic system. As such, he argues, it ought to be replaced by a more humane and rational production system of a socialist type. Although Stapledon deplores violence, he is realistic enough to recognize that only through some form of social revolution can capitalism be replaced. In his next book, *Philosophy and Living,* Stapledon's philosophical views appear in their most comprehensive and elaborate form.

But for the general reader Stapledon's closing chapter in *Beyond the "Isms"* more clearly presents such important concepts appearing in his science fiction as spiritual crisis, spirit, and community. *Beyond the "Isms"* is particularly helpful in defining Stapledon's often-used phrase "the way of the spirit."

In it Stapledon discusses the major religious and political movements of his day. From this examination he asserts that a better life in the future can come about only through development of a new spirit that combines sensitive and intelligent awareness with greater love and creative action. Such a spirit would lead to the achievement of a new "personality-in-community."

New Hope for Britain is a well-measured philosophic discussion advocating direct political action to usher in an age of socialism in England. Such an age would be the first step in a larger program for creating a world state. *Saints and Revolutionaries* compares and contrasts historical figures traditionally depicted as saints or revolutionaries, or both. This work was one of the *I Believe* series written by such well-known authors as J. D. Beresford, Charles Williams, Gerald Bullett, and Kenneth Ingram as expressions of personal belief. In *Saints and Revolutionaries* Stapledon argues that in the future humanity may create its God-image only by achieving the "cosmic mind" level of awareness.

Youth and Tomorrow is in part autobiographical, describing Stapledon's childhood memories of Suez, and in part philosophical. In it he restates his earlier notions about human development through personality-in-community, and argues that humanity's ultimate hope lies in the biological improvement of the species. Transcribed from Stapledon's notes after his death, *The Opening of the Eyes* suggests that his long-term inner conflicts about religion and politics were resolved before his death. In this incomplete work he claims that it is far better to accept even the pretense of God's reality than to believe in stark nothingness. He also renounces collective revolutionary action, arguing that the only real progress toward social justice is made through each individual's independent growth toward enlightenment.

In Stapledon's fictional works the range of topics is both wide and richly imaginative. In *Last and First Men,* Stapledon describes the history of humanity from the close of World War I to some 2 billion years into the future. We follow mankind's agonizingly slow development on Earth, witness its forced migration to Venus, and observe its final brilliant days on Neptune. *Last Men in London,* to some extent, is a continuation of several themes introduced in Stapledon's first novel. In it, the narrator is a member of the last human civilization on Neptune, a brilliant utopian social order ruled by pure intelligence. But much of the story focuses on the growth and maturation of an artistically sensitive, somewhat neurotic young man in modern London. We are provided thereby not only with a detailed account of human life, social system, manners, and intellectual progress on Neptune, but also with commentary on the contemporary world.

The struggles of a supernormal human mutant is the subject of *Odd John.* In *Star Maker,* Stapledon depicts the history of the entire cosmos and more, covering more than 100 billion years. We observe not only the rise, maturation, and decline of countless diverse life forms on numberless planets and millions of galaxies, but also the creation and history of the entire cosmos, as one in a long series of progressively more mature cosmos. *Darkness and the Light,* another future history, describes two different worlds and two possible futures for man—depending on whether the forces of darkness or of light succeed. Central is the theme of superhuman development achieved through artificial life or mutation in which spirit overcomes animal and tribal instincts. Stapledon's short work *Old Man in New World* dramatizes some of the notions found in *Saints and Revolutionaries.* In *Old Man,* a group of intellectuals stages a strike on the eve of World War III, causing drastic policy changes in Russia and a revolution in America. Out of these events a world state is created that achieves a utopian social order. *Sirius,* a complementary novel to *Odd John,* features the adventures of a supernormal mutant dog with human intelligence who struggles to find meaning in his life.

In his narrative prose poem *Death into Life,* Stapledon describes the deaths of a bomber crew flying over Germany during World War II. Told from the viewpoint of the tail gunner as he dies, Stapledon's narrative moves from communication among the dead crew members to a mystical communion with the Spirit of Man. *The Flames,* a novella, treats contact between a psychically sensitive but insane human being and a race of flame creatures from the sun's surface. These supernormal flames have survived on Earth for ages inside igneous rocks. Now they want humans to assist them in creating a special colony on Earth around a radioactive belt near the equator. And Stapledon's last novel, *A Man Divided,* features a man with a split personality who alternates between intellectual brilliance and commonplace thinking. Much of this work is autobiographical in content, recounting scenes from Stapledon's life between 1912 and 1948. (pp. 93-4)

Among Stapledon's novels, four stand out as superior to the rest: *Last and First Men, Star Maker, Odd John,* and *Sirius.* All four are unified by a coherent informing philosophy. Seen from the view of content and literary construction, they complement each other. In terms of subject, *Odd John* and *Sirius* are companion novels, showing through parallel development the problems faced by two supernormal mutants—one a man, the other a dog. The relationship between Stapledon's two great future histories, *Last and First Men* and *Star Maker,* is far more complex. For example, the human narrator in *Star Maker* raises two important questions before he begins his cosmic pilgrimage. By what means, he asks, should mankind progress, particularly with respect to overcoming its present spiritual crisis? And if progress can be made toward a fuller notion of humanity, is such progress meaningful when contrasted with mankind's brief, self-tortured tenure in this world? From the short view, Stapledon's narrator refers mainly to those forces, clearly evident when the novel was written, that by 1939 would engulf much of the world in war; but Stapledon also intends these questions to be understood in the broader context of the totality of human history. The answers to both questions shape not only *Star Maker,* but also give clear meaning to *Last and First Men.*

In *Last and First Men*—that vast chronicle of mankind's 2-billion-year history on Earth, Venus, and ultimately Neptune, described from the cultural perspective of eighteen progressively but haltingly more advanced species of humanity—Stapledon presents a fairly straightforward thesis about human progress. No significant movement toward full humanity can occur until mankind undergoes significant biological—not just spiritual—modification. Humanity's tribalism, its self-destructive individualism, and its lockstep collective social organizations are doomed from the start by its biological limitations. The modification Stapledon has in mind, whether achieved naturally through evolutionary mutation or artificially by genetic engineering, must begin by removing the limits to human intellect and moral insight.

But larger brains and stronger bodies are not necessarily the way to a fuller humanity. As a first step toward greater human awareness, some manipulation of the brain is necessary to develop telepathic communication among all people. Greater human sympathy and understanding, achieved by better psychological communication, will ultimately lead to the creation of a group mind. But such a group mind must not eliminate the differences among individuals, as seen in the Martian group

mind, but must enrich the collective consciousness while preserving each member's unique individuality. At best each individual partakes of the cultural, or collective, mind of the species.

Through this spiritual multiplication of mental diversity, the subhuman instinct for tribal nationalism, for destructive individualism, and for debased collectivism becomes impossible. Waking to full potential, mankind can aspire to utopia and to both superindividuality and community with the great collective host. Although humanity may temporarily strive for utopia, banish hunger, eliminate disease, end class conflict, and prevent economic disaster, any hope for an awakened sense of community without biological modification will always end in failure.

Such a controlling thesis explains the continual rise and fall of one human civilization and/or species after another in *Last and First Men.* Aside from the ferocity of natural forces, cosmic accidents, and foreign invasions, mankind always is undone by its own biological contradictions. Stapledon's panorama of mankind's future is structured around a well-wrought historical myth. His novel is divided into two distinct phases of historical development: phases based on mankind before and after biological modification. The first phase describes a cyclical movement in human culture embracing several recognizable subdivisions—primitive subhuman savagery, agricultural tribalism, medieval mercantilism, nation-state industrialism, and some attempt to achieve a unified world-state.

Passing from the nation-state to the world-state phase inevitably brings about what Stapledon calls a "social and spiritual crisis." This is because the societal forces precipitating this crisis essentially stem from the limits imposed on man by his own biological backwardness. Conflicts between individualism and collectivism, between capitalism and socialism, between tribalism and cosmopolitanism, between behaviorism and spiritism, and between nationalism and world-statism cannot be bridged by the will of a minority whose intellect and moral insight outrun the biological retardation of the majority. Failure to undertake biological modification at the point where human civilization has both the technology and the leisure to alter human biology always leads to self-destruction. Such stagnant societies, failing to evolve to a higher stage of human awareness, regress into savagery or destroy themselves by worldwide holocaust.

The most telling dramatization of this social and spiritual crisis in the novel is the extended account of contemporary humanity—of the specific period in the history of First Men (*Homo sapiens*) when American hegemony triumphs throughout the world. Perhaps no European writer since Alexis de Tocqueville has so well understood the main currents of American thought as did Stapledon. The realism of his depiction made Stapledon fear some American displeasure. In the foreword to the original American edition, he admitted that in the early chapters of his book America is "given a not very attractive part."

Stapledon imagined the triumph of what he called the cruder sort of Americanism over all that is best and most promising in American life. While hoping that this cruder strain would not succeed, the possibility that it might was admitted, Stapledon claimed, by many thoughtful Americans. In these chapters America professes to have outgrown nationalism and to stand for political and cultural world unity. But such world unity is in reality a unity under American hegemony. The cultural unity in society stems from the fact that Americanism dominates other cultural traditions. Despised by the rest of the world, America nevertheless remolds the human species in its own image. Stapledon's narrator claims that such an event would not really have mattered, had America given her very best, but:

> . . . inevitably only her worst could be propagated. Only the most vulgar traits of that potentially great people could get through into the minds of foreigners by means of these crude instruments. And so, by the floods of poison issuing from this people's baser members, the whole world and with it the nobler parts of America herself, were irrevocably corrupted. . . .
>
> (pp. 94-6)

This "bright race of arrested adolescents," given the gifts to rejuvenate the planet, instead plunges it through spiritual desolation into senility and agelong night. Great wealth and bustling industry become concentrated upon ever more puerile ends. American life is organized around the cult of the powerful individual. Only wealth has the power to set things and people in motion. In fact, wealth came

> . . . to be frankly regarded as the breath of God, the divine spirit immanent in man. God was the supreme Boss, the universal Employer. His wisdom was conceived as a stupendous efficiency, his love as munificence towards his employees. . . . The typical American man of big business was one who, in the midst of a show of luxury, was at heart ascetic. He valued his splendour only because it advertised to all men that he was of the [spiritual] elect. . . .

A cult of activity—any kind of activity for the mere sake of activity—comes to dominate American life. God, according to this doctrine, appointed the great American people to conquer and to mechanize the universe. Such wrong-headed tribal lust for power propels the world into its first worldwide holocaust.

But in contrast to our own, a few future societies do achieve a higher level of human awareness. They do so because they succeed in modifying human biology, and thus pass beyond spiritual crisis. Yet in the second phase of Stapledon's historical myth, not all advanced societies create perfect utopias or maintain a vital sense of human community. In this second phase the direction of human progress is as uncertain as it is in the first. Mistakes in genetic engineering, the failure to strike a proper balance between brain and body, and between intellect and feeling, cause many of these civilizations to destroy themselves or to decline in vitality and to lose full human awareness. For example, Fifth Man's guilt, his loss of intellectual self-confidence, and his despair at not finding a scientific solution to the moon's impending approach, undermine his social order. Even when the proper balance is found and maintained in human psychology, as in the tragic case of Eighteenth Man, progress may be cut short by natural catastrophe. This sad end to some 2 billion years of human struggle to realize its full potential raises the question of whether striving for progress is worth the human price.

The youngest of the Last Men articulates Stapledon's other shaping notion in the novel: Humanity's fluctuating progress toward harmonious complexity of form and toward the awakening of the spirit into unity, knowledge, delight, and self-

expression is the proper goal of all human effort—even in the face of an uncertain future. As individuals, the Last Man asserts, we "earnestly desire that the eternal being of things may include this supreme awakening." For nothing less than this has been the goal of practical religious life and active social policy.

The Last Man sees the career of humanity in its successive planetary homes as a process of very great beauty. As individuals, humans regard the entire cosmic adventure as a symphony in progress, which may or may not achieve its just conclusion. Like a work of music, the vast biography of the stars is to be judged not solely by its final moment, but by the perfection of its whole form. But one thing is certain:

> Man himself, at the very least, is music, a brave theme that makes music also of its vast accompaniment, its matrix of storms and stars. Man himself in his degree is eternally a beauty in the eternal form of things. It is very good to have been man. And so we may go forward together with laughter in our hearts, and peace, thankful for the past, and for our own courage. For we shall make after all a fair conclusion to this brief music that is man. . . .
>
> (pp. 96-7)

This passage, which ends *Last and First Men*, is important not only as a clear reaffirmation of human struggle against an uncertain future, but also as one of the novel's central, controlling metaphors. Throughout *Last and First Men* we are told that the history of mankind is like a great musical symphony. Each of humanity's civilizations represents a movement in this symphony, and the totality of human existence is only a smaller theme in a larger, cosmic music of the spheres.

This notion becomes both the connecting complementary link with *Star Maker* and, in turn, *Star Maker*'s controlling metaphor. (In the short story "A World of Sound," Stapledon postulates a kind of telepathic music as the ultimate art form, as the ultimate form of sentience.) In addition, the questions shaping *Last and First Men*—how do we progress toward a fuller notion of humanity, and is such a struggle meaningful in an uncertain universe?—reappear in *Star Maker,* but are restated on a far greater cosmic canvas. Unlike its complement, *Star Maker* follows the progress not only of human creatures, but of all life in the cosmos. The human narrator, a contemporary Englishman, is swept up into the cosmos, where he proceeds on his pilgrimage-quest, searching for the meaning of life and for the creative principle behind all life in the cosmos.

Star Maker's narrative is structured around the human narrator's growing capacity to appreciate and to sympathize with unfamiliar life forms. The greater his sympathy, the greater the magnitude of his travels, in terms of time as well as distance. His first visit is to a planet similar to Earth, called Other Earth. Here the narrator telepathically shares the thoughts of the planet's inhabitants. These people, called Other Men, reproduce a tragically familiar world dominated by destructive individualism, heartless industrialism, and mindless tribal nationalism. Significant on Other Earth is a debilitating prejudice based on taste. Some races taste superior to others; violent arguments take place about what God tastes like. The narrator meets a wise philosopher named Bvalltu, who later joins him on his pilgrimage through the cosmos. Bvalltu makes possible contact with still other races, thus radically extending the scope of the narrator's journey.

Star Maker is shaped by the historical and moral thesis found in *Last and First Men.* We see myriad creatures in *Star Maker*— echinoderms, nautiloids, ichthyoids, arachnoids, bird composites, insectoids, mobile superherbs, and plantmen—who reenact the same form of spiritual crisis seen on Earth. Again and again various races throughout the cosmos rise from savagery and pass through barbaric culture into a phase of world-wide brilliance and sensibility. Entire populations achieve an ever-increasing capacity for generosity, self-knowledge, self-discipline, for dispassionate and penetrating thought and uncontaminated religious feeling.

But in time a general decline undermines even the most advanced societies. Where societies once were free and happy, where unprecedented mental clarity did away with all social injustices and private cruelties, later generations become less sincere, less self-searching, less sensitive to others, and less capable of community. Societies that once worked well are dislocated by injustice and corruption. Dictators and tyrannical oligarchies destroy liberty. Gradually the material benefits of civilization disappear; the entire culture reverts to barbarism, followed by protracted periods of subhuman savagery. Where earlier in this spiritual progression through time and space, the human narrator believed human history was shaped by a progressive improvement in the species and by a gradual awakening of the human spirit, he now sees cosmic proof against any such theory. He laments the horror that

> . . . all struggle should be finally, absolutely vain, that a whole world of sensitive spirits fail and die, must be sheer evil. In my horror it seemed to me that Hate must be the Star Maker. . . .

(pp. 97-8)

Eventually the narrator confronts the Star Maker, the elemental creative force in the cosmos. The Star Maker appears as a bright, blinding star who evolves to greater and greater insight by learning from his past experiences. We observe his detached and disinterested spirit as he creates progressively more brilliant and more complex stars, galaxies, and entire cosmos. The narrator sees the Star Maker and his creations as good, but he laments humanity's brief and tragic existence in the Star Maker's newly created worlds.

Despite such human misery, the narrator sees that had the Star Maker intervened and given mankind a carefree life and made the cosmos infinite, he would have disrupted their essential beauty. For their distinct virtues stem from their finitude and minute particularity, which maintain a tortured balance between dullness and lucidity. The narrator recognizes that even if the creator's primary motivating spirit is contemplative rather than loving or benign, he and his creative acts are good. He comes to understand these insights in a dream in which the Star Maker creates the Ultimate Cosmos, seen as the culmination of a vast cycle of many, many cosmos. But when the narrator awakes, he finds himself back on Earth, in the present. His final thought is that in the face of humanity's uncertain future and possible defeat in his own half-waking world, the coming human crisis

> . . . does not lose but gains significance. Strange, that it seems more, not less, urgent to play some part in this struggle, this brief effort of animalcules striving to win for their race some

increase of lucidity before the ultimate darkness. . . .

(p. 98)

Set in England and, later, on an unnamed island in the South Pacific, *Odd John* is a philosophic fantasy that describes how John Wainwright, a supernormal human mutant, comes to terms with his unique intellectual gifts. Yet from the start both his intellect and his physical appearance—he has a thin, spiderish body with large, sinewy hands; a large head covered with closely cropped white, wool-like hair; a broad, Negroid nose set in a Mongolian-shaped face; and a pair of large, greenish eyes nearly devoid of pupils—mark him as a subject of great curiosity. John early understands that his future rests in finding other supernormals like himself and, with them, establishing a colony somewhere away from normal humans. Most of the novel's action—told from the sympathetic point of view of a normal, middle-aged human journalist called "Fido, old thing" by John—depicts John's efforts to establish a colony where he and the others like him can create a social organization and a way of life that freely reflect their awakened sense of community.

But once the colony is established, it is the subject of curiosity among the great powers, whose contending policies soon lead to its destruction. Recognizing that the great powers intend to invade the island and arrest them, the members of John's community feel a fresh intensity of consciousness in all their personal relations and social activities. They see that the true purpose of the awakened spirit is to help in the practical task of building a new world, and that they should employ themselves, to the best of their capacities, in intelligent worship. In the time remaining, they strive to understand existence as precisely and as zestfully as they can. At one point they salute all in the universe that is of supreme excellence. Given a chance to preserve their utopian community through the use of superweapons, they refuse. Such slaughter, they recognize, would hopelessly ruin their awakened spirit. Adhering to its pacifist policy, the colony is overrun and destroyed.

In *Sirius,* Stapledon employs a number of recognizable themes found in *Odd John,* such as the love of life, even if life seems to be of no purpose; the necessity to confront reality squarely and to experience the ecstasy of the quickened spirit for its own sake; the pursuit of spirit-in-community; and the search for meaning in life. The central action describes how Professor Thomas Trelone crossbreeds a superior Alsatian-Great Dane pup by injecting a special hormone into the bloodstream of the pup's mother before she gives birth. This hormone reorganizes the pup's neural system, giving him the intellectual capacity of a human being. From the outset the pup, called Sirius, is handicapped by not possessing human hands, a disability that haunts him throughout his life. He learns to talk so that he can be understood by his creator.

Trelone vaguely resembles the cosmic creator in *Star Maker,* since he is contemplative and objective rather than loving and caring toward Sirius. Sirius is educated in Trelone's family along with Trelone's infant daughter, Plaxy. In time the relationship between Sirius and Plaxy moves toward an uneasy community-in-spirit. But this strange symbiosis is threatened by the instabilities in both their personalities and by the outside world's misunderstanding of their behavior. Sirius alternates between a lucid, thoughtful human intellect and a savage wolfishness brought on by his reactions to human cruelty as well as his ancestral instincts. Throughout the action, Sirius strives to bring these two attitudes into balance by discovering the true meaning of his life. But in the end he is destroyed by ignorant fanatics who think he is a Nazi spy and who question the nature of his sexuality. Yet, faced with an uncertain fate, Sirius tries to serve the spirit—to love, to give full expression to his intelligence, and to create. Yet his tragic death is inevitable. Sirius epitomizes in his life and in his death something universal, something that is common to all awakening spirits, on Earth and in the farthest galaxies. The music Sirius composes and his urge to live fully in the spirit illuminate the darkness that is seen by the quickened mind everywhere.

This quartet of Stapledon's major novels reflects the core of his philosophy and suggest both the diversity and the richness of his vast fictive imagination. The desire to express a heightened appreciation of life's beauty, to reaffirm the importance of the play of intellect, to argue the continuing significance of love as a shaping human force, and to urge us to seize the best expressions in the human spirit is no trifling world view. There is in Stapledon's tragic vision of man's bittersweet history, an ennobling effect, a catharsis of sorts. We are better for having shared his imaginative spirit. It is this particular power that makes Stapledon's writings endure. In science fiction he is a writer and thinker of the first magnitude whose influence and readership will continue to widen in the future. (pp. 98-9)

> *James L. Campbell, Sr., ''Olaf Stapledon,'' in* Science Fiction Writers: Critical Studies of the Major Authors from the Early Nineteenth Century to the Present Day, *edited by E. F. Bleiler, Charles Scribner's Sons, 1982, pp. 91-100.*

PATRICK A. McCARTHY (essay date 1982)

[*McCarthy is an American educator and critic specializing in modern English and Irish literature. In the following excerpt from his biographical and critical study* Olaf Stapledon, *he discusses Stapledon's examination of a superior individual's relationship to society in* Odd John *and* Sirius.]

The theme of the superior (and often alienated) individual, which is evident in many of Stapledon's works, became the focus of two of his finest novels: ***Odd John*** . . . , the story of a superman whose great intelligence is the result of a natural mutation, and ***Sirius*** . . . , which chronicles the life of a dog with superhuman mentality. For many of the ideas developed in these books, Stapledon drew upon two main sources: the Nietzschean concept of the *Übermensch* or superman, and the tradition of the superman in science fiction. Although these concepts are related, it will be most convenient to deal with them separately.

The influence of Friedrich Nietzsche on ***Odd John*** is both evident and complex. As a socialist, Stapledon would have had little sympathy for Nietzsche's aristocratic leanings, or for his contemptuous attitude toward the masses whom Nietzsche termed ''the much-too-many''; it is particularly difficult to imagine Stapledon praising Cesare Borgia, as Nietzsche did. Moreover, Stapledon believed that the spiritual development of man was inseparable from a general improvement in the conditions of life for all people, while Nietzsche argued that ''the abolition of these evils [vice, illness, prostitution, poverty] was neither possible nor even desirable, since they have belonged and will belong to all periods of human history.'' Yet like Nietzsche, Stapledon found himself in revolt against nihilism, against the conformist mentality of the bourgeois world, and against purely scientific and reductive views of mankind. It is also likely that Stapledon's concept of the re-

lation of man and superman was shaped partly by passages like the following from *Thus Spoke Zarathustra:*

> Man is a rope, fastened between animal and Superman—a rope over an abyss.
>
> A dangerous going-across, a dangerous wayfaring, a dangerous looking-back, a dangerous shuddering and staying-still.
>
> What is great in man is that he is a bridge and not a goal; what can be loved in man is that he is a *going-across* and a *down-going*.

Perhaps the two ideas which most closely relate Nietzsche and Stapledon are that the superman is certain to be misunderstood and distrusted by the great mass of humanity, and that the superman is not necessarily bound by the same code of morality that applies to other men. . . . [The] alienation of the superman from the rest of mankind is a theme found in science fiction novels ever since the publication of Mary Shelley's *Frankenstein* (1818). One of the ironies of *Frankenstein* is that the monster is in many ways superior to the people whose company and love he so desperately wants—Frankenstein and the others who fear and despise him: not only is he larger, faster, more powerful, and more intelligent than other people, but along with our awareness of his tragic loneliness comes a feeling that, as Harold Bloom puts it, ''the monster is *more human* than his creator.'' (pp. 54-5)

Narrated by a free-lance journalist who describes himself as ''a respectable member of the English middle class,'' ***Odd John*** is the history of a superhuman being whose very existence constitutes a challenge to ''normality.'' John Wainwright, the ''odd'' member of an otherwise unremarkable English family, develops erratically, conceiving a theory of relativity at the age of five but not learning to walk until the age of six. As he grows, he becomes increasingly aware that he is unlike most other people, but eventually he begins to establish contact with other supernormals from distant parts of the world. Gathered together upon a Pacific island, twenty-two supernormal children found a secret utopian colony, but after a few years they are discovered and harassed by governments of the world they have fled. Rather than abandon their colony and return to the ''normal'' world, the colonists commit mass suicide by exploding the island so that it sinks beneath the waves.

Odd John has been described as ''a powerfully evocative communication of the spirit in crisis,'' and the deaths of the colonists certainly suggest one aspect of the spiritual crisis of our age: the triumph of the doltish conformity or subhuman mentality of the millions over the superhuman intelligence of the awakened few. Yet . . . John Wainwright and his fellow colonists are motivated by an ecstatic acceptance of their fate, a conviction that they have played a significant role in the life of the spirit. . . . John finds beauty, love, and meaning in the twenty-three years of his brief but intense existence. Still, as an alien in the world of *Homo sapiens*, John suffers through a series of crises that symbolize the conflict of the subhuman and the superhuman (or, as Stapledon would have it, the ''truly human'') forces, both within him and within mankind generally.

Two incidents—the murder of a policeman and the slaying of a stag—will illustrate the nature of the spiritual crisis that John faces and the pattern of his spiritual development. Both events derive ultimately from John's estrangement from the rest of mankind and his search for his own identity apart from the norms of human society. The first occurrence, the murder of a constable, is the unforeseen outcome of John's brief career as a second-story man. Initially, at least, John has no doubts about the morality of burglary: he sees it as a way to gain money and experience at the same time, and he argues that "Mr. Magnate [a rich capitalist] and his like [are] fair game." . . . Yet his decision to rob the rich brings him to a more difficult, and unexpected, moral decision when he is caught by Smithson, a friendly police constable whom John knows. Faced with the choice of killing himself, going to jail, or murdering Smithson, John chooses the last alternative in the belief that the other choices would betray his task of advancing the spirit on Earth. He is motivated not simply by faith in his mission but by a sudden realization that there is a spiritual dimension to his superiority over the rest of humanity:

> I had already, some time before, come to think of myself as definitely of a different biological species from *Homo sapiens,* the species of that amiable bloodhound behind the torch [Smithson]. But at last I realized for the first time that this difference carried with it what I should now describe as a far-reaching spiritual difference, that my purpose in life, and my attitude to life, were to be different from anything which the normal species could conceive, that I stood, as it were, on the threshold of a world far beyond the reach of those sixteen hundred million crude animals that at present ruled the planet. . . .
>
> (pp. 57-9)

The justification for the murder, then, rests largely on John's belief in his superiority over other men and in the superiority of his mission. (The description of men in animal terms in the quotation above is echoed when John compares his regret over Smithson's death to the feeling he had once before when he killed a mouse . . . ; the suggestion is that from John's perspective, man is not much greater than the mouse.) In a superficial way this incident recalls Dostoevsky's *Crime and Punishment,* but the parallels only serve to highlight the crucial differences between Dostoevsky's self-styled superman and Stapledon's Odd John. For one thing, Raskolnikov kills the old pawnbroker woman largely to prove to himself that he is superior to others and that the ordinary moral laws do not apply to him any more than (in his mind) they apply to Napoleon. He steals money from her, but this seems an afterthought: he does not absolutely need her money, and in any case he is so afraid of being caught that he buries the money and never uses any of it. In short, Raskolnikov commits a senseless murder. By comparison, John's murder of Smithson is clearly motivated. A more important difference, though, is that Raskolnikov is really *not* superior to others—he learns, in fact, that he is in some ways inferior to other people and that he must suffer in order to redeem himself—while John is demonstrably superhuman.

At the time of the murder, John sees that he "must set about the more practical side of [his] task either by taking charge of the common species and teaching it to bring out the best in itself, or, if that proved impossible, by founding a finer type of [his] own." . . . Later, after carrying out a thorough examination of humanity, he declares "*Homo sapiens* is at the end of his tether, and I'm not going to spend my life tinkering a doomed species." . . . Retreating to a mountainous area, John learns to live entirely apart from human civilization and to rely entirely on his own devices. The climax of his retreat is the slaying of a magnificent stag, a symbolic action that Roger Brunet interprets as John's triumph over "the subhuman in man that refuses to be killed in generation after generation, causing war after war." Brunet notes that

> John is able to kill [the stag], to come at once to terms with nature and through nature to man and his own identity, because he is John, potentially 'fully human,' free of the repetitive cycle of self-destruction that is the fate of normal men. When John kills the stag he dominates nature (obtains food) and dominates on a symbolic level the *homo sapiens* species, the normal human. It is in fact the superhuman dominating the normal and the subhuman within himself: it is the achievement of self-mastery.

The death of the stag, then, represents a spiritual triumph, an awakening, just as the half-born and half-dead foal in *Last Men in London* represents the defeat of man's spirit and the triumph of the subhuman over the fully human in man. John's triumph leads to a new awakening, for he suddenly sees mankind from a new perspective. His disgust with *Homo sapiens* is replaced with a sudden understanding of man's spiritual plight: sensitive to pain but unable to achieve the detached viewpoint of the superman, man is doomed to suffer without being able to understand why. Having seen men merely as beasts, John comes to realize that man "was indeed a spirit of a higher order than any beast, though in the main obtuse, heartless, unfaithful to the best in himself." . . . Thus when his hideout is discovered by two mountain climbers, he recalls the beautiful but doomed stag: "suddenly the stag seemed to symbolize the whole normal human species, as a thing with a great beauty and dignity of its own, and a rightness of its own, so long as it was not put into situations too difficult for it." . . . Unfortunately, "the present world-situation" has proved to be beyond man's capacities: "The thought of *Homo sapiens* trying to run a mechanized civilization suddenly seemed to him as ludicrous and pathetic as the thought of a stag in the driving-seat of a motor-car."

Throughout this section, Stapledon's theme is reminiscent of his criticism of the First Men in *Last and First Men* and *Last Men in London.* In those books, Stapledon contends that man's animal nature is fundamentally in conflict with the demands of the world-community and of modern technology: again and again nationalism, militarism, chauvinism, and other subhuman elements prevent man's awakening into a higher awareness. Narrated by a superior being, one of the Last Men, both of the earlier novels are supposed to be aimed at First Men who cannot comprehend fully the meaning of the books but can be given glimpses of the future in order that they may become more alert to beauty and truth. The process is especially clear in *Last Men in London,* where the narrator gives Paul occasional glimpses of the future that subtly change his character as he adopts a more "Neptunian" point of view; *Far Future Calling,* of course, is devoted to the same principle. Likewise, in *Odd John,* after he is discovered in the cave, John performs a "miracle": he lifts a gigantic boulder and allows the two mountain climbers a clear look at the starry sky. . . . Later, called on to explain, John says that

> The important thing was that, when I did see the stars (riotously darting in all directions according to the caprice of their own wild natures, yet in every movement confirming the law), the whole tangled horror that had tormented me

finally presented itself to me in its true and
beautiful shape. And I knew that the first, blind
stage of my childhood had ended. . . .

(pp. 59-61)

The vision of the stars symbolizes John's awakening from the
dark night of the soul into the self-detached ecstasy of the
cosmic or "Neptunian" point of view. In sharing this vision
with normal men, John affirms his own humanity and his sense
of his mission in life. Reacting against the temptation to nihilism, John realizes that he must dedicate himself to the awakening of spirit throughout the world. From this point on he
concentrates on searching for and bringing together others of
his kind, and on creating the colony that will permit each of
its members to develop fully without the restraining and per-
verting influence of the "normal" or subhuman world.

John's search for other supernormals gives Stapledon an opportunity to describe a wide variety of responses to the normal
world. At one extreme are John's first two discoveries: James
Jones, a lunatic whose only coherent form of expression is a
music so subtle that it can only be appreciated by one like
himself, and a Hebridean cripple who has become so twisted,
frustrated, and filled with hatred that he tries to destroy John's
mind. Like Humpty, these beings find life among *Homo sapiens* a source of torment, just as we might be driven into insanity
if we were forced to live in a world controlled by apes or idiots.
At the other extreme are the particularly well-balanced beings
who, through good fortune, have escaped psychological scar-
ring: Jacqueline, a French prostitute who "combined in her
person the functions of harlot, psycho-analyst and priest" . . .
and who at the age of 165 still appears a young woman; Adlan,
an Egyptian who died thirty-five years earlier but still manages
to make mental contact with John; Langatse, a blind Tibetan
monk who is able to see telepathically by using the eyes of
other people; and dozens more. Among the others are the twenty-
two with whom John founds his colony.

Like the advanced societies of *Last and First Men,* the Pacific
colony of *Odd John* is an idealized world with all the best
features of communism and individualism. John criticizes the
standard brand of communism as too "rationalistic, scientific,
mechanistic, brass-tackistic," . . . that is, for failing to see the
spiritual impulse behind dialectical materialism, just as he might
have censured Nietzsche for not recognizing the need for an
economic basis for man's spiritual development. When a Russian ship arrives to offer the colonists sanctuary in the Soviet
Union, John spells out the differences between the form of
communism practiced on the island and the communism of the
Bolshevik state:

> "Yes," said John, laughing, "Comrades, you
> have the wrong approach. Like you, we are
> Communists, but we are other things also. For
> you, Communism is the goal, but for us it is
> the beginning. For you the group is sacred, but
> for us it is only the pattern made up of indi-
> viduals. Though we are Communists, we have
> reached beyond Communism to a new individ-
> ualism. Our Communism is individualistic. In
> many ways we admire the achievements of the
> New Russia; but if we were to accept this offer
> we should very soon come into conflict with
> your Government. From our point of view it is
> better for our colony to be destroyed than to be
> enslaved by any alien Power." . . .

(pp. 61-3)

On the broad level, then, the colony is a reaction against the
conformism both of the capitalist state and of the communist
state: John and the others are always aware that the group "is
only the pattern made up of individuals" and that their differences from one another are at least as important as their
similarities. The aim is to engender and nourish "personality-
in-community," an idea based on our recognition of the essential "otherness" of our fellows: as Stapledon says elsewhere, "In the truly human kind of social behaviour there is
clear awareness of the other as a person, different from oneself
in character, temperament, needs, capacities; and these differences are accepted, nay welcomed." Hence the relationship
of the awakened or superior individual and the utopian society
can be seen clearly, for "true community is impossible save
as the community of mutually aware and mutually respecting
persons. But on the other hand, personality itself cannot exist,
in any form worthy of the name, save as 'persons-in-com-
munity.'" If the refusal or inability of "normal" society to
recognize and accept the otherness of the supernormals is largely
to blame for the twisted mind of the Hebridean cripple and for
James Jones's lunacy, precisely the reverse is true in the colony, where the recognition and acceptance of differences helps
to create a symbiotic relationship among the colonists.

"The true purpose of the awakened spirit," the colonists tell
the narrator, "is twofold, namely to help in the practical task
of world-building, and to employ itself to the best of its capacity
in intelligent worship." . . . The colony itself is an attempt to
fuse the active and the contemplative aspects of the life of the
awakened spirit. The active side of their life consists of all the
outward life of the island: eugenic experimentation, research
into the relationship of mind and matter, the production of art
objects, and especially the reformation of the economic and
social life of the island along the lines of utopian communism.
But when the colony is discovered and is brought to the attention of the six "Pacific Powers"—Britain, France, the United
States, Holland, Japan, and Russia—the islanders realize that
they will not be allowed to proceed with their work toward the
remaking of man and his world. With a clear-minded and
ecstatic acceptance of fate (reminiscent of the attitude of the
Last Men before their minds are destroyed by the mad star's
radiation), they turn to the life of contemplation and praise,
hoping to "offer to the universal Spirit such a bright and peculiar jewel of worship as even the great Langatse himself,
alone and thwarted, could not create." . . . (pp. 63-4)

Whether or not the colonists create that "jewel of worship"
is not clear, for here (as in the conclusions of *Last and First
Men* and *Star Maker*) Stapledon is reaching for ideas so far
beyond the range of realistic fiction that they can be described
only in the most abstract terms. Constant interruptions from
the outside world—first by the navies of the Pacific Powers,
later by hired assassins—disrupt their concentration, forcing
them away from the life of contemplation and praise, but when
they commit suicide by destroying their island, the narrator,
following events from afar, hopes that they have achieved their
aim:

> I suspected that the islanders had been holding
> their assailants at bay in order to gain a few
> days for the completion of their high spiritual
> task, or in order to bring it at least to a point
> beyond which there was no hope of further
> advancement. I liked to believe that during the
> few days after the repulse of the third landing-
> party they accomplished this aim. They then

decided, I thought, not to await the destruction which was bound sooner or later to overtake them at the hands of the less human species. . . . They would not allow their home, and all the objects of beauty with which they had adorned it, to fall into subhuman clutches. Therefore they deliberately blew up their power-station. . . .

(p. 64)

Whatever the ultimate value of John Wainwright's life, it is clear that in the communal life of the colony, and particularly in his relationship with Lo, a supernormal girl whose love for him seems to be consummated only at the very end, he has discovered a meaning and purpose in life and in death. Yet John achieves his final attitude of ecstasy in the face of oblivion only through the awakened community of supernormal peers. By contrast, near the end of *Sirius* the great dog realizes that "There is no place for me in man's world, and there is no other world for me. There is no place for me anywhere in the universe." . . . Because he has no community of peers, because his divided nature is at home neither in the world of man nor in the world of the wolf, Sirius endures frustration and torment greater than John ever knows. And his story, which Aldiss half-ironically calls "the most human of all Stapledon's novels," reexamines from another (and a more original) angle all of the questions raised in *Odd John*.

In "Tobermory," one of the finest satiric fantasies of H. H. Munro ("Saki"), Cornelius Appin teaches a tomcat to speak. Appin considers his discovery more important than the invention of the printing press, but the experiment backfires when it develops that Tobermory knows, and loves to repeat, all of the things that nobody wants told: whose bedroom Major Barfield has frequented, what Lady Blemley said about Mavis Pellington, and the like. Saki's story is a recent example of a traditional plot motif that is perhaps best illustrated by *The Golden Ass* of Apuleius, in which Lucius is transformed into an ass and forced to remain in that condition for a year until he is released through the agency of Isis and Osiris. Like Tobermory, Lucius has ample opportunity to observe the worst in human behavior since people normally assume that an animal cannot understand, much less report, what they are doing and saying.

To a certain extent, the same possibilities are exploited in *Sirius*, Stapledon's novel about a sheep dog whose intelligence is at least human (and in some ways superhuman). The narrator observes that "One cause of Sirius's incipient contempt for human beings was the fact that since they thought he was 'only an animal,' they often gave themselves away badly in his presence." . . . Almost in the manner of an invisible man, Sirius watches the hypocrisy and cruelty of mankind and, from his alien point of view, develops a sophisticated understanding of the spiritual condition of modern man. Yet *Sirius* is not simply a satiric portrait of humanity. Rather, the novel is "a fantasy of love and discord," as Stapledon subtitled it, and its true value lies in the portrayal of the deep spiritual conflicts produced in the mind of this great dog who, like Frankenstein's monster, has no mate, no companion of his own kind.

The comparison with *Frankenstein* is suggested in part by a biblical analogy. In Mary Shelley's novel the creature finds and reads a copy of *Paradise Lost* and comes to see that "Like Adam, I was apparently united by no link to any other being in existence." Sirius regards himself in similar terms when he asks his creator, "Why did you make *me* without making a world for me to live in. It's as though God had made Adam and not bothered to make Eden, nor Eve." . . . In both books, too, the analogy has a darker side: Frankenstein's monster comes to see himself as Satan warring against the human world that has rejected him, while Sirius, who is thought by superstitious people to be a devil in the shape of a dog, periodically rebels against the same world of men. Yet the form of the monster's Satanic revolt—"Evil thenceforth became my good"—is at heart a simplistic reversal of values deriving from his exclusion from human society. Unlike Frankenstein's monster, Sirius is neither rejected by his creator nor deprived of human love and affection, but he is always a stranger in a strange land, completely at home neither in the human nor in the canine world.

Sirius is the creation of Thomas Trelone, a scientist who develops a method for stimulating brain growth in unborn animals through the injection of a hormone into their mothers. His research leads to the production of a series of "super-sheep-dogs," and through chance one dog, Sirius, proves so much superior to all the rest that he is raised with Trelone's daughter Plaxy, taught to speak and read, and treated at home with the respect due an intelligence comparable to man's. When he is older he is exposed to a variety of environments and experiences: he herds sheep on a farm in Wales, helps Trelone with his research at Cambridge, and lives for a time with a minister in a slum area of London. Throughout these years he begins to be aware of a split between what he calls his "wolf-nature" or instinctive, lower self, and his "human" or spiritual side. In his wolf-mood he can see man only as a repulsive tyrant with "the uncouth hairless features of a super-ape;" . . . fearing and despising mankind, he reverts to bestiality and kills a ram and later a pony. In the truly "human" mood, however, he desires what Stapledon's most awakened characters always seek: he wants to play a role in the quickening of the spirit, in whatever form it may manifest itself. After Trelone dies, Sirius enters into a kind of spiritual symbiosis with Plaxy; but the relationship is impaired by the hostility of the villagers, and it is broken up altogether when Plaxy is drafted into the national service during World War II. Left alone, Sirius turns wild and is killed.

Perhaps the most complex aspect of Sirius's life is his relationship with Plaxy. Believing that "the most valuable social relationships were those between minds as different from one another as possible yet capable of mutual sympathy," . . . Thomas Trelone raises Plaxy and Sirius as equals but respects their essential differences. The symbiotic nature of their bond is apparent even in childhood, when "Plaxy's hands [are] held almost as common property" in recognition of Sirius's lack of hands. . . . The relationship is strained by their awakening sexual interest in others of their own species, by long periods of enforced separation, and by the dog's growing disenchantment with the entire human race. Coming at a time of unusual tension between Sirius and Plaxy, the killing of the pony epitomizes Sirius's rebellion against the world of man, but when the conflict comes into the open both Sirius and Plaxy become more candid about their relationship:

> Sirius on his side told her of the conflict which was racking him, the alternating moods of respect and loathing for humanity. "You, for instance, are sometimes the dearest of all things in the world, and sometimes just a horrible monkey that has cast a filthy spell on me." She answered at once, "And *you* are sometimes just

my father's experimental dog that I have some-how got tangled up with and responsible for, because of *him*; but sometimes you are—*Sirius, the part of Sirius-Plaxy that I love."* . . .

(pp. 64-7)

The two come more and more to think of themselves as Sirius-Plaxy, "a bright gem of community" . . . whose value derives from their love for one another. There are suggestions that that love takes the form of sexual relations between Sirius and Plaxy, although Brunet errs in assuring us that "the text states that their intercourse is a fact." There are many sexual over-tones to the relationship, such as Sirius's tendency to refer to Plaxy as his "human bitch," but the passage Brunet cites is somewhat ambiguous: speaking to the narrator (her future hus-band, Robert), Plaxy says "No, dear Robert, you don't un-derstand. Humanly I do love you very much, but . . . super-humanly, in the spirit, but therefore in the flesh also, I love my other dear, my strange darling." . . . Perhaps stronger evidence of a sexual bond can be found in Robert's "imagining with horror how a beast had awkwardly mauled the sweet human form that I now so fittingly embraced," . . . or in the following passage: "At a later date both Plaxy and Sirius told me much about their life together at this time; but though after our marriage she urged me to publish all the facts for the light they throw on Sirius, consideration for her feelings and respect for the conventions of contemporary society force me to be reticent." . . . (pp. 67-8)

The implication of sexual relations in this last passage is all the stronger because of its similarity to a passage in *Odd John* where the narrator reveals—while pretending to refuse to re-veal—that at one point John engaged in an incestuous rela-tionship with his mother, thereby violating "one of the most cherished of all the taboos of [the human] species." . . . John, however, breaks the incest taboo for the sake of breaking it—because "he needed to assert his moral independence of *Homo sapiens,* to free himself of all deep unconscious acquiescence in the conventions of the species that had nurtured him"—while Sirius's action, although obviously a violation of man's moral code, must be seen quite simply as the physical em-bodiment of a spiritual bond that is essential to the sanity of this quasi-human dog. The relationship of Sirius and Plaxy is thus more logically compared to the love relationships that form the basis for John's colony than to John's incestuous relations with his mother. The community established between Sirius and Plaxy proves much more fragile than the community of supernormals in *Odd John,* however, for it is flawed by their different perceptions of the "human" condition and it is threatened by the fears and superstitions of other people from the beginning of their "marriage." Stapledon may be glancing at racial attitudes here, but the full force of his argument can be felt only if we see that he is asking us to disregard ap-pearances altogether and to focus on the spirit. The sexual theme in *Sirius* can best be understood as an extreme example of a recurrent motif in Stapledon's works: again and again we see individuals who appear homely or even grotesque or de-formed to the "unawakened" eye, but whose true beauty be-comes apparent to our awakened selves.

Stapledon, however, would be the last to deny a connection between the physical and spiritual aspects of being: Sirius's spiritual development, after all, is hampered by his lack of hands and his poor vision, but it is advanced by the keen perception of odors and sounds that makes him sensitive to realms of experience to which Plaxy is a stranger. The name

Sirius, suggesting the Dog Star, may itself imply a duality of subhuman and superhuman, canine body and celestial spirit; only at the end of the novel, when he dies and "the sun's bright finger set[s] fire to Sirius," can we view Sirius as pure flame or spirit. Meanwhile, Sirius's passion for the spirit man-ifests itself most clearly in his relationship with Plaxy and in his "singing," an odd form of music reminiscent of James Jones's playing in *Odd John.* In perhaps the most memorable scene in the novel, Sirius sings at a church service conducted by the Reverend Geoffrey Adams, a sympathetic pastor. His song, which Reverend Adams terms "a very lovely miracle," gives the parishioners a chance to view the struggle of man's spirit from a nonhuman perspective; but unlike the vision of the stars that John gives the two mountain climbers, this "vi-sion" is comprehensible to very few who experience it: "To most of the congregation it was an inconsequent mixture of music and noise, and moreover a mixture of the recognizably, comfortably pious and the diabolical." . . . Like Nietzsche's Zarathustra, who is misunderstood when he speaks of the super-man, Sirius finds that his great song falls on deaf ears.

The similarities between *Odd John* and *Sirius* are so striking that it is difficult not to view the two books as companion pieces. The central metaphor of *Sirius* is borrowed (in inverted form) from the earlier novel, where John continually sees hu-man beings as dogs: he refers to Constable Smithson as an "amiable bloodhound," . . . and when he is commencing sex-ual relations with a beautiful young woman he suddenly feels "as though a dog were smelling round me, or a monkey." . . . The narrator, whom John likes to call Fido, uses similar terms: he describes the mixed ethnic heritages of John's parents by saying that Pax "was no less a mongrel than her husband," . . . and when John ironically quotes Hegel in a conversation with a capitalist, he says that "like a dog encountering an unfamiliar and rather formidable smell, Mr. Magnate sniffed this remark, bristled, and vaguely growled." . . . In a broader sense, the pattern of the two books is the same: John's late physical development, his rejection both of orthodox religion and of pure materialism, and his awakening devotion to the spirit are all reproduced in the life of Sirius. Specific incidents also suggest a close parallel between John and Sirius. Thus John is first knocked down by a larger boy named Stephen, then teaches himself to fight, lures Stephen into a fight, and defeats him soundly. In *Sirius,* the same chain of events occurs, this time involving Sirius and a larger dog named Diawl Du (Black Devil). Both battles end in victories for the superhuman over the subhuman, for mind or spirit over brute instinct, and both presage the greater conflicts to come.

Other parallels between the two novels suggest contrasts as well as similarities. When Sirius kills the sheep and the pony, for example, his action is structurally parallel to John's killing of the deer, but the motives in the two cases are quite different from each other. The slaying of the great stag is the act of a superman who reverts to primitive conditions in order to triumph over the subhuman element in his own nature. John's attitude toward the stag is complex, for he sees something of himself in the animal: "With my soul I saluted him. Then I pitied him, because he was doomed, and in the prime. But I remembered that I too was doomed. I suddenly knew that I should never reach my prime." . . . Seeing his own death in the stag's, John nevertheless kills him, thereby signifying his acceptance of his own condition. In the case of Sirius, however, almost the reverse is true. Sirius kills the ram because "it was man's creature, and it epitomized all the tyranny of the sheep-dog's servitude" . . . ; that is, he kills him to symbolize his rejection of the human world. The murders of the sheep and the pony both demonstrate the increasing strain caused by Sirius's failure to fit into the human world. Thus, while John's act helps him to resolve the conflicts in his nature, Sirius can only respond with an action that aggravates the strife between his "wolf-nature" and his more "human" side.

Perhaps a stronger contrast can be drawn between the attitudes of John and Sirius toward the murder of human beings. For his part, John is directly responsible for the deaths of several innocent persons: first Smithson, the constable who catches him in the act of burglary; then two survivors of a shipwreck whose curiosity about John, the other supernormal children, and their boat causes John to fear the discovery and destruction of his plans to create a colony; and later still the primitive people who have the misfortune to occupy the island selected for the colony. The colonists even conspire in the murder of a Polynesian girl as part of an experiment in eugenics. The narrator is "convinced that John was far superior to the rest of us in moral sensibility," . . . but he remains deeply troubled. John, meanwhile, rests his defense on his superiority, and the superiority of his mission, over man and his society:

> Had we been members of your species, con-
> cerned only with the dreamlike purposes of the
> normal mind, what we did would have been a
> crime. For today the chief lesson which your
> species has to learn is that it is far better to die,
> far better to sacrifice even the loftiest of all
> "sapient" purposes, than to kill beings of one's
> own mental order. But just as you kill wolves
> and tigers so that the far brighter spirits of men
> may flourish, so we killed those unfortunate
> creatures that we had rescued. Innocent as they
> were, they were dangerous. Unwittingly they
> threatened the noblest practical venture that has
> yet occurred on this planet. . . .
>
> (pp. 68-71)

The distinction between "beings of one's own mental order" and beings of a lower order reappears in *Sirius*. When Sirius mates with another sheep dog, the products of the union are, from his point of view, worse than morons; and since he regards them as examples of an inferior species, he has no qualms about drowning some of them and selling others—that is, treating them exactly as a human being would have. On the other hand, at one point Sirius is put in the care of a particularly brutal farmer, Thwaites, whose "great cruel hands symbolized for [Sirius] the process by which the ruthless species had mastered all the living creatures of the planet." . . . When Thwaites strikes another dog Sirius knocks him down; Thwaites responds by getting a gun to destroy Sirius, and Sirius attacks and kills Thwaites, partly in self-defense but also in the insane belief that "In his symbolic act he would kill not only Thwaites but the whole tyrant race. Henceforth all beasts and birds should live naturally, and the planet's natural order should never again be disturbed by the machinations of this upstart species." . . . Yet when the battle is over and he is able to regard the issue more dispassionately, he comes to see himself as a Cain who has murdered his brother; and in a gesture that reveals the ambivalent nature of his feelings toward mankind, he licks "the forehead of his slaughtered brother." . . . (pp. 71-2)

It seems likely that in writing this episode in 1944, Stapledon was thinking about the war that was still to rage in Europe for another year. Stapledon's abandonment of pacifism for the duration of World War II meant that like Sirius, he "realized that the war had to be won, otherwise all that was best in the tyrant species would be destroyed." . . . The danger was that in the process of defeating the Nazis we might become so spiritually damaged that we will be incapable of building a more awakened society after the war. What is necessary is the recognition of our common humanity, just as Sirius recognizes that in some fundamental way he and Thwaites are manifestations of the universal spirit.

The example of the Nazis may well have caused Stapledon to reconsider some of the ideas advanced in *Odd John*. John's adaptation of the Nietzschean idea that the superman is above the moral code of *Homo sapiens* looks very different when it is seen against the background of Hitler's use of the same idea for his own perverse reasons. As William L. Shirer has noted, "no one who lived in the Third Reich could have failed to be impressed by Nietzsche's influence on it," and "in the end Hitler considered himself the superman of Nietzsche's prophecy." In particular, Hitler adopted from Nietzsche the idea that "the supreme leader is above the morals of ordinary man":

> A genius with a mission was above the law; he
> could not be bound by "bourgeois" morals.
> Thus, when his time for action came, Hitler
> could justify the most ruthless and cold-blooded
> deeds, the suppression of personal freedom, the
> brutal practice of slave labor, the depravities
> of the concentration camp, the massacre of his
> own followers in June 1934, the killing of war
> prisoners and the mass slaughter of the Jews.

Stapledon was coming to realize how easily the most "awakened" ideas could be warped into a new and more stifling orthodoxy. In *Odd John* there is no one capable of contesting John's political ideas, and the confidence with which he advances them reflects Stapledon's own assuredness. Writing about this period, Sam Moskowitz has commented that "Stapledon the philosopher is somewhat cocky, somewhat sure of himself. It is 1934 and everything is in a deplorable state. . . . His patient is the world and he precisely and confidently diagnoses its illnesses and cures." In contrast, *Sirius* reflects its author's growing awareness of his own fallibility. The debate in Stapledon's mind appears in the book as a political debate between Sirius and Plaxy . . . , in which Plaxy argues that "the people" must plan a better society while Sirius contends that planning should be left in the hands of the "wide-awake people." To Plaxy's argument that "that's the way straight to Fascism. There's a leader who *knows,* and the rest do what they're told. And there's a Party of faithful sheep-dogs who make them do it," Sirius replies that "a Fascist Party is *not* made up of wide-awake people"; but the riposte is not altogether convincing, and it is unlikely that it was meant to be. As Stapledon demonstrates in the depiction of the "mad worlds" in *Star Maker,* the line between the awakening of the spirit and its perversion is razor thin.

Sirius himself moves from one side of the line to the other after Plaxy is forced to leave him to complete her national service during the war. A series of events precipitated by a delusional girl who claims that Sirius raped her forces him into progressively open and violent conflict with the villagers, a conflict that culminates in vigilante action when it is discovered that Sirius has killed and half-eaten a man. Half-mad, he returns to his senses when Plaxy reappears but realizes that "There is no place for me in man's world, and there is no other world for me. There is no place for me anywhere in the universe." . . . (pp. 72-3)

Sirius's ambition has been to be "the hound of the spirit," . . . that is, a sort of prophet who will help to awaken mankind generally into a higher state of spiritual awareness. That this ambition never develops into a practical policy comparable to John Wainwright's founding of the colony is due partly to Sirius's greater isolation—John, after all, has peers while Sirius is unique—and partly to the deep and unresolved divisions in his nature. Still, his nature is ours regarded from another perspective, and if Sirius fails to resolve the conflict of spirit and world, superhuman and subhuman, in the way John does, we find him a more sympathetic character—and a more *human* one—partly because of his strange, tragic love for Plaxy and partly because of his failure to transcend his condition. As Barbara Bengels has observed "in leaving humanity behind, John has left us behind. In being driven to bestiality, Sirius has nevertheless achieved a kindred humanity for he is the beast—and the man—in us all." In an odd and rather ironic fashion *Sirius*, as its punning title implies, is one of the most *serious*—and certainly one of the most moving—of Stapledon's novels. (pp. 73-4)

> *Patrick A. McCarthy, in his* Olaf Stapledon, *Twayne Publishers, 1982, 166 p.*

LESLIE A. FIEDLER (essay date 1983)

[*Fiedler is a controversial and provocative American critic. Emphasizing the psychological, sociological, and ethical context of works, Fiedler often views literature as the mirror of a society's consciousness. Similarly, he believes that the conventions and values of a society are powerful determinants of the direction taken by its authors' works. The most notable instance of Fiedler's critical stance is his reading of American literature, and therefore American society, as an infantile flight from "adult heterosexual love." This idea is developed in his most important work,* Love and Death in the American Novel *(1960), along with the theory that American literature is essentially an extension of the Gothic novel. Although Fiedler has been criticized for what are considered eccentric pronouncements on literature, he is also highly valued for his adventuresome and eclectic approach, which complements the predominantly academic tenor of contemporary criticism. In the following excerpt, Fiedler discusses the themes and artistic weaknesses of two of Stapledon's last works of fiction.*]

Darkness and the Light was not the only futurist fantasy in which Stapledon responded to the personal crisis of finding himself an old man confronting death. In their titles, his two other World War II novels, *Old Man in New World* . . . and *Death into Life* . . . confess the troubled awareness of age and mortality which underlie the rather blithe sociology of the first and the fundamentally reassuring metaphysics of the second. *Old Man in New World*, moreover, ends with its venerable hero reduced to tears by the words of a privileged Jester, who at ceremonies honoring the thirtieth anniversary of a utopian New World order, reminds the celebrants "But death dogs you. . . . We are mere sparks that flash and die. . . ."

Yet it is finally the most optimistic of all Stapledon's books, as well as the briefest (some thirty-three pages of text, it seems scarcely more than a short story) and the most colloquial. It projects the triumph of worldwide revolution by 1968, and the development before the end of the twentieth century of a world state in which "psychosynthesis" and telepathy are well advanced, "sub-atomic" energy so developed that spaceflight seems to lie just ahead, and the air of the largest cities is sparkling clean. Moreover, monogamy (with, of course, extramarital privileges) had been "rehabilitated," and even the dread "decline in population" has been reversed—at least in

Britain, whose contingent in the Anniversary Procession is headed by "a rank of young mothers carrying babies." It is all a little too pat and propagandistic, perhaps; less a freely invented fiction than a fictionalized version of the pamphlet *Seven Pillars of Peace*, which Stapledon also published in 1944. But this seems fair enough in light of the fact that *Old Man in New World* was produced on request for the P.E.N., an organization left of center and dedicated to "freedom of artistic expression, and international goodwill."

Stapledon's "international goodwill" did not, however, at this point, extend as far as the United States. America emerges as the villain of the postwar years, which, in his imaginary future, endured a catastrophic super-Depression:

> . . . Everywhere there were ruined factories, deserted mines, streets of dilapidated houses, whole cities neglected and in ruins. Those that still functioned at all were inhabited by a few ragged and unhealthy, and mostly middle-aged, people who had lost all hope. The few boys and girls, moreover, seemed prematurely old and grim. . . .

To the Old Man of the story's title is entrusted the task of explaining that America bears the burden of guilt for helping this disaster come to pass:

> How I remember the wild hope when peace came! Never again should gangsters rule! Never again should money power mess up everything. . . . People really believed that the incubus of the old system could be shifted as easily as that! Unfortunately they forgot that everything depended on the Americans, and that those former pioneers were still stuck in the nineteenth century. The American money-bosses were able to bolster up our own tottering capitalist rulers and prevent our revolution.

To these charges, a young pilot, entrusted with flying the aged revolutionary to his place of honor in the reviewing stands, protests that "the Americans did well at first pouring food and goods into Europe without expectation of payment." But this, of course, does not satisfy the still resentful revolutionary:

> "Yes," replied the old man, "but think how the American rulers, the men of big business, when they had recaptured the state after the decline of the New Deal, used the power of the larder and the store-cupboard to establish swarms of their own people in charge of relief throughout Europe. These 'relieving' Americans settled down as a kind of aristocracy. . . . In the name of freedom and mercy they set up a despotism almost as strict as Hitler's."

Clearly the Old Man is not identical with Stapledon; since he is described as having been born during World War I to a working-class family, and having dedicated almost all of his eighty years to political activism. In many of his basic opinions, moreover, he differs radically from his author; distrusting, for instance, the institution of matrimony (a lifelong bachelor, he had experienced only a "late, desperate, childless marriage," which ended in a "stormy separation"). And he is stubbornly hostile not just to organized religion but to anything which smacks of "spirituality." He serves, nonetheless, as the author's mouthpiece on the subject of the United States. Without a clearly defined public enemy, some historical, secular embodiment of the Powers of Darkness, Stapledon was driven, as in *Darkness and the Light,* to self-hatred and the paranoic fear of occult, "titanic" forces. For his own mental health, then, Stapledon *needed* to return to the wholehearted hostility toward capitalist America with which he had begun in *Last and First Men,* and which was to sustain him in his public life right up to the 1949 Communist-inspired world conference of intellectuals at the New York Waldorf. In *Old Man in New World,* therefore, he imagines the American "bosses" not just as utterly hateful once more, but for the first time as totally defeated; and in some way the sanguine tone of the whole depends on his maintaining this Good Dream.

Yet the Old Man is in a sense the victim as well as the beneficiary of that dream; justifying in its name the rigid imposition of repressive discipline. Without such controls, he argues, the "precious old-dead-as-mutton liberal democracy" will be revived, with its hypocritical slogans: "Individual initiative, private enterprise, freedom of thought" and its long-compromised cant about "spirit," "that ancient opium." But the young man who pilots him remembers what the older one has forgotten: that the Revolution they both applaud triumphed not merely over the embattled capitalists of the United States, but over the corrupted bureaucrats of the Soviet Union as well, being led by "airmen, skilled workers *and*—the agnostic mystics . . . those modern saints . . . ," with their "purged and clarified *will for the light.*"

At this point, the younger man becomes the spokesman for Stapledon; "remembering forward," and therefore aware that "individual initiative" and "freedom of thought" must become the goals of society, once regimentation has become the chief threat. The new regime has, therefore, built into itself safeguards against rigidity and solemnity; institutionalizing, as it were, the anti-institutional principle. In the grand 30th Anniversary Procession, that principle is represented by "unattached individuals whose task it was to clown hither and thither beside the marchers. . . ."

> Each of these comedians was dressed in a stylized and extravagant version of some costume prominent in his own national contingent. All were clearly meant to represent the undisciplined individuality of the common man. . . . Sometimes they merely blundered along enthusiastically beside the column, vainly trying to conform to the regimented conduct of their fellows. . . . Occasionally one of them would attach himself to a leader of the column, mimicking his pompous bearing and military gait . . .

One of them finally speaks:

> The stars give no answer. But within ourselves . . . the answer lies. . . . And from the depth of each one of us, and from our community together, a will arises. . . . "Live, oh fully live!" it bids us. To be aware, to love, to make—this is the music that I command of all my instruments. . . . And we, little human instruments, though death will surely hunt us down, and though our species is ephemeral, we shall obey. Weak we are, and blind, but the Unseen makes music with us.

His is not the last word, however. Nor does it belong to the World's President, who takes the microphone from him to echo

the conclusion of Stapledon's first novel: "I say no more but that your leaders, who are also your comrades, will go forward with you to make the living music that is man."

The last words are reserved for the Old Man, speaking for what in a tired and aging Stapledon still resists waking to a wisdom that transcends social utility. "Oh yes, it was a great feat of stage-craft," he says of the interchange between Jester and President. "One could not but be moved. But it was dangerous, and subtly false to the spirit of the Revolution. . . . It was all a cunning bid for popularity. Worse, it was a reversion to religion. . . . Where would this thing end?" Yet even this response is not quite final; since the author, who is both the Old Man and the young, adds, in a muted prose, scarcely distinguishable from that of the Old Man's interior monologue, "But tears were in his eyes."

Clearly, Stapledon after his return to fiction found it hard to achieve a proper fictional voice, as well as to rediscover a viable fictional subject. The latter, however, seemed to him an easier problem. He would simply revive the formula which had brought him success: mingling macrohistory with a tragic vision that transcended time. It had worked well in *Last and First Men* and, following the failures of *Last Men in London* and the radio play, *Far Future Calling,* spectacularly in *Star Maker.* So why not once more? or twice? or three times, if he lived so long? But it did not work in either *Darkness and the Light* or *Old Man in New World,* the former turning out unendurably incoherent, and the latter unredeemably slight. In both, moreover, Stapledon was unable to recapture the temporal and spatial magnitude which his readers had come to think of as the hallmark of his fiction. In *Darkness and the Light,* the time span had shrunk . . . to the lifetime of a single human species, and the arena of action to our tiny earth; while the main plot in *Old Man in New World* occurs in one day. Even in retrospect (there is *no* prospect), it covers only half a century, and its events are confined almost entirely to the city of London.

Besides, in neither of these books does Stapledon manage to evoke the secular-mystic encounter with the ineffable Creator. In the former, he reaches no further than an apprehension of "ultimate horror" in the form of the "titanic" destroyers (there is a hint that beyond their seemingly final darkness, there may be "the true light," but it comes to nothing); and in the latter, ends with a couple of cryptic references to the "Unseen," who remains just that. He failed in both instances, moreover, to imagine a "possessed" or telepathically reinforced narrator capable of seeing any further or deeper. Finally, in neither case did he attain a level of language capable of evoking the old grandeurs. It seems, indeed, as if he had lost faith not only in the Far Future and the icy ecstasy, but in the old-fashioned high rhetoric which he had sustained in a time when its overstuffed Victorian virtues were being challenged, on one side by Ernest Hemingway and on the other by James Joyce. (pp. 166-71)

> *Leslie A. Fiedler, in his* Olaf Stapledon: A Man Divided, *Oxford University Press, 1983, 236 p.*

STANISLAW LEM (essay date 1984)

[*A Polish novelist and short story writer, Lem is the most prominent science fiction author of Eastern Europe. His works, which have been translated into over thirty languages, are characterized by surreal comedy and a preoccupation with ethical questions, and are praised for their transcendence of the conventions and limitations of science fiction. In the following excerpt from an essay which first appeared in the* New Yorker *(Vol. LIX, No. 50, January 30, 1984), Lem discusses the innovative nature of Stapledon's fiction.]*

As a reader of science fiction, I expected something like what is called, in the evolutionary processes of nature, "speciation"—a new animal species generating a diverging, fanlike radiation of other new species. In my ignorance, I thought that the time of Verne, Wells, and Stapledon was the beginning, but not the beginning of the decline, of the sovereign individuality of the author. Each of these men created something not only radically new for their time but also quite different from what the others created. They all had enormous room for maneuvering in the field of speculation, because the field had only recently been opened up and was still empty of both writers and books. Each of them entered the no man's land from a different direction and made some particular province of this *terra incognita* his own. Their successors, on the other hand, had to compromise more and more with the crowd. They were forced to become like ants in an ant hill, or industrious bees, each of which is indeed building a different cell in the honeycomb but whose cells are all similar. Such is the law of mass production. Thus, the distance between individual works of science fiction has not grown greater, as I erroneously expected, but has shrunk. The very thought that a Wells or a Stapledon could have written, alternately, visionary fantasies and typical mysteries strikes me as absurd. For the next generation of writers, however, this was something quite normal. Wells and Stapledon are comparable to the people who invented chess and draughts. They discovered new rules for games, and their successors have applied these rules with only smaller or larger variations. The sources of innovation have gradually become depleted; the thematic clusters have become fossilized. Hybrids have arisen (science fantasy), and the patterns and schemata of the literary form have been applied in a mechanical and ready-made way. (pp. 17-18)

> *Stanislaw Lem, "Reflections on My Life," in his*
> Microworlds: Writings on Science Fiction and Fantasy, *edited by Franz Rottensteiner, Harcourt Brace Jovanovich, Publishers, 1984, pp. 1-30.*

ROBERT CROSSLEY (essay date 1986)

[Crossley is an American educator and critic and the literary executor of the Stapledon estate. In the following excerpt, he examines Stapledon's ideas on the nature and purpose of science fiction in general and his own works in particular, basing this discussion on the unpublished manuscript notes to four lectures by Stapledon.]

Scholars looking for wider frames of reference for naming Stapledon's literary ambitions and assessing their products have been confounded by his apparent reticence on the whole subject of the scientific romance. There are scattered clues to his sources of inspiration to be found in references tucked away in odd pockets of his books: the acknowledgement of Gerald Heard in the prefatory note to *Last Men in London* . . . , or the allusion made by the narrator of *Odd John* to J. D. Beresford's 1911 novel *The Hampdenshire Wonder* . . . , or the homage to Edwin Abbott's Victorian mathematical fantasy *Flatland* in the description of dying stellar worlds in *Star Maker*. . . . But even a diligent collector of such fugitive references would not emerge with a very coherent picture of Stapledon's reading. (pp. 22-3)

Until recently the closest things we have had to an exposition of the poetics and ideology of Stapledon's fiction have been

the short Prefaces he attached to some of his books, notably *Last and First Men* and *Star Maker*. They are important for understanding his concern to write romances that are philosophically sound and socially responsible. . . . In introducing *Last and First Men* Stapledon outlines his central fictional principle that future-fiction is a medium for designing cultural myths. Because "the merely fantastic has only minor power," he writes, the mythic romance exercises "controlled imagination" in the service of a "serious attempt to envisage the future of our race" and "to mould our hearts to entertain new values." . . . The Preface to *Star Maker*, with the Spanish Civil War in the foreground and the prospect of a second Great War on the horizon, stresses the politics of fantasy and defends the exploration of imaginary worlds and distant times in a period of terrestrial crisis. The "attempt to see our turbulent world against a background of stars" may heighten awareness of human politics and "strengthen our charity toward one another." . . . Eloquent as they are, these two Prefaces remain tantalizingly vague on larger generic questions about science fiction. (p. 23)

There is now newly available evidence that Stapledon was not nearly so isolated from the tradition of the scientific romance as has been surmised. If he had no occasion to see into print his mature thoughts on the nature of the literary forms he worked with, he had another natural outlet for his accumulating reflections on the interplay of the literary and scientific imaginations. Long before his writing came to public attention, Stapledon had been a lecturer in the adult education movement in Britain, both formally as a tutor in the Workers' Educational Association and in ad hoc talks given to women's clubs, high schools, political societies, student organizations, soldiers' study circles, and a variety of philosophical, educational, and scientific conferences. The Stapledon Archive at the University of Liverpool contains 240 sets of detailed notes for lectures he gave between 1913 and 1950. Among them are several that bear on the ideas and aims of Stapledon's fiction and two that are central to his own theories and judgments about science fiction. On the basis of these notes some of Stapledon's silences can be filled in, and we can begin to learn how widely read and how thoughtful he was about science fiction.

In fall, 1937, a few months after *Star Maker* appeared and following critical successes in *Last and First Men, Last Men in London,* and *Odd John*, Stapledon prepared a talk called "Science and Literature." Jottings at the top of the first sheet indicate that he made the presentation at least three times in 1937 and 1938; as with all his lecture notes there are many interpolations and revisions as he kept adapting it to successive occasions. In "Science and Literature" Stapledon takes a historical view of the impact of scientific knowledge on poetry and fiction. Interestingly for critics who have linked *Star Maker* to the *Divine Comedy*, his analysis begins with Dante and itemizes a dozen writers from the Renaissance, the Enlightenment, and the nineteenth century whose works are shaped by incorporating or resisting scientific inquiry and experiment. Thus Dante's effort to envisage Ptolemaic astronomy and adjust it to Christian cosmography leads the way to Milton's struggle to reconcile mythology and Copernican astronomy, to Shelley's Prometheanism with its "medley of science and Greece," to Hardy's testing of humanist individualism against the cold and inhuman realities disclosed by modern astrophysics. "*Immensity—fear—fascination*," reads a telegraphic note on Hardy's *Two on a Tower;* not incidentally, this verbal configuration also contours the emotional situation of the narrator in the first chapter of *Star Maker.*

The roll call of scientifically venturesome poets and novelists in **"Science and Literature"** is the framework for Stapledon's construction of an iconoclastic tradition of writers who respond imaginatively both to words and numbers, to books and machines, and who try to unify the perspectives of the two cultures. The artists he names all seek, as he says of Dante, scientific "verisimilitude" according to the lights of their age. Even two writers whom Stapledon says display "no direct influence of science" are treated as examples not of pure fantasy but of scientific method applied to fictional procedure: Rabelais' Gargantua is not just a fantastic creature but an instance of "gigantism *realistically* worked out," and the worlds of Gulliver reveal how Swift "works out *consequences of novel ideas*—realism." Only the name of Wordsworth on the list represents literature's retreat from the scientific ethos. Citing a famous instance from "A Poet's Epitaph"—a scientist "botanizing on his mother's grave"—Stapledon characterizes Wordsworth's hostility to science: "alarmed, flies to perceived nature."

Stapledon's lecture finds ancestors for the modern scientific romancer in writers who combine fantasy with realism by logical extension and amplification of innovative ideas or imaginary hypotheses. They create not unreal worlds but imagined worlds "realistically worked out." In addition to the writers already mentioned Stapledon sees Bacon, Butler, Meredith, Rosny, Abbott, and Verne forming a line of prophet-critics who offer visions, fancies, and warnings in fictional speculations that are rooted in scientific discoveries and laboratory methods. The impact of all these writers on their audiences is what Stapledon, with a large X in his notes, attributes specifically to Swift: "Puts man in his place." Again, this note could serve to gloss Stapledon's own major fictions that, from premises different from those of the mostly Christian writers he cites, mount assaults on the limitations and pretensions of anthropocentrism.

The second part of **"Science and Literature"** moves from prototypes to "contemporary examples" of a dozen writers situated at the junction of the literary and scientific cultures. In addition to expected names such as Wells (identified as "the master") and Aldous Huxley, we find the then-little-known novelists M. P. Shiel and David Lindsay, the geneticist J. B. S. Haldane, the physicist Bernal, the pseudonymous Murray Constantine (Katharine Burdekin), and Régis Messac, whose futuristic fiction was at that time available only in French. Stapledon is more judgmental of his contemporaries than of his forebears, finding Shaw "hostile to science, medicine"; noting the antifascist myth developed in Joseph O'Neill's *Land under England* but regretting the narrative's "implausible mechanism"; approving James Hilton's combination of psychology, mysticism, and science in *Lost Horizon;* and condemning J. C. Powys's *Morwyn* for equating scientists with sadists and for its "faulty mechanism." At the high end of Stapledon's critical scale Wells's work is admired for its narrative powers of "scientific melodrama," for the "sheer *mind-stretching*" it requires of readers, and for the prophecies of "scientific utopia" to be found "in all his work." At the bottom end Stapledon is characteristically standoffish about the "crude human factor" in what he labels "Scientifiction: Wonder Stories, Amazing Stories, etc." There may be a few surprising absences from Stapledon's lists—notably *Frankenstein* from the earlier one and Zamyatin's *We* from the contemporary one—but the notion that Stapledon was insulated from other work in the fantastic mode should now be obsolete.

Perhaps most interestingly, **"Science and Literature"** ponders the cultural significance of the new hybrid of scientific literature. (Stapledon had not yet learned to call this hybrid "science fiction.") In 1937 the body of literature that was genuinely scientific seemed to him "v. small," but he was ready to name its distinctive virtues. He describes the new form functionally in terms now taken for granted in science fiction criticism but still fresh in the mid-1930s as "critical" and "speculative." Scientific literature provides a corrective to "the *specialist's fallacy*," a target he subdivides to include "abstraction, materialism, determinism, magnitude, myopic detail." He distinguishes it from the literature of escape and from literature that responds narrowly to the current moment and finds a place for it within what he calls "creative literature." As science infiltrates the literary imagination, fiction's prophetic powers are enhanced, and Stapledon indicates the two extrapolative directions such fiction can take: toward the visionary splendor of utopianism and the celebration of human potentiality or toward the literature of disaster and "*revulsion* against science."

Stapledon's climactic arguments concern the epistemological and spiritual effects of science's influence on literature. The new fiction, he says, encourages, a "*natural piety* toward the universe for its aloofness, for its potentiality," and it contributes to the "atrophy" of Alexander Pope's dictum that "the proper study of mankind is man." Because scientific literature tends philosophically to the "weakening of human interest," its "literary style" shifts in the direction of the "unemotional, unrhetorical, dry, concise, abstract." In this litany of stylistic markers that concludes the lecture notes we find a distinctively Stapledonian approach to the language of science fiction. The stylistic terms Stapledon uses do not at all fit either Wells's lively, colloquial storytelling or the unsophisticated purple prosiness of the fiction in American pulp magazines. But these terms describe accurately one side of Stapledon's style. His own fictions typically alternate between dispassionate and evocative language, between the clinical record and the startling metaphor, between the conceptual and the lyrical, between the numerical austerity of an astronomer's star catalogue and the sonorous grandeur of a Homeric catalogue. Stylistically his works behave in exactly the way one would expect of that symbiotic kind of text called science fiction. (pp. 24-8)

"Science and Literature" is the only one of Stapledon's lectures from the 1930s to explore so extensively the literary history and scientific inquiry that facilitated his own contributions to science fiction. But several other talks from that period have at least a tangential bearing on his fiction. In **"Living on Other Planets"** . . . he proposes an "exercise of imagination" for his audience: how would they react to a headline announcing the end of the world in 300 years? He then summarizes some conventional responses: the suicidal thrill in the idea of global annihilation; indifference bred of the assurance that the end will be deferred until after one is dead; the carpe diem impulse to self-indulgence and a last fling for the human race. But Stapledon fastens on the question that had preoccupied his first two romances: could the species preserve itself by seeking a new home for a remnant of homo sapiens on another world? . . . Near the end of the lecture, asking his listeners whether they could imagine life on stars, Stapledon may have wanted to try out the idea of the stellar and nebular beings he would invent for **Star Maker**. Essentially, though, **"Living on Other Planets"** is a digest of his ideas about space exploration, and it foreshadows the subject of what would be his most famous lecture and one that did achieve a life in print:

"**Interplanetary Man,**" delivered at the invitation of Arthur C. Clarke to the annual meeting of the British Interplanetary Society in 1948.

In a 1934 lecture, "**Man's Prospects,**" Stapledon considers the uses of forecasting. Speculation about the future, he says, "stretches the mind," helps us "distinguish the ephemeral & the permanent in human aims [and] problems," "brings out the essentials of the human drama," "makes for clear *orientation* of world policy," assists social evolution by preparing "the way for *long-range* planning," and "teaches *detachment* from humanity." As a critical exercise, forecasting helps us "realize the future" so that the next century becomes as vital to us as the next day or next year. In fact, Stapledon is more interested in forecasting as a discipline of the mind than as a tool for predicting particular technological or social events. His analysis of the value of speculation bears on his own fictions about the future that aim to be prophetic in the widest sense: educative, cautionary, eye-opening, stirring.

The notes for "**Man's Prospects**" are unusually full in analyzing seven "rules of the game of speculation." These principles offer some insight into the way Stapledon's mind works and into the kind of rigor he applies to his futuristic fiction. The game demands:

> 1) up-to-date knowledge from a wide variety of disciplines (sociology, astronomy, biochemistry, philosophy, and so forth);

> 2) imaginative freedom from the limitations of contemporary knowledge and the audacity to "peer beyond" those limits;

> 3) a comprehensive and balanced vision that avoids the one-dimensionality of a forecast that is merely economic, merely physical, merely psychological, and so on;

> 4) a "radical skepticism" on the part of the prophet who should acknowledge the unlikelihood of all specific anticipations of the future, including his own;

> 5) an ability to define the main questions about the future: questions of work, class, leisure, human interests, political organization, etc. (the usual utopian agenda);

> 6) a commitment to pursue "the fundamental question": "Will man be *more developed* mentally? or fallen into barbarism?";

> 7) working distinctions among the near future (measured in centuries), the middle future (thousands and hundreds of thousands of years), and the remote future (millions and billions of years).

Stapledon's rules are more comprehensive and even more intimidating than Wells's genial instructions to his readers on "how to play the game" of the scientific romance (though the first six of Stapledon's rules certainly fit Wells's practice in his utopian books). Where Wells emphasizes the tricks of the storytelling trade, Stapledon enumerates the philosophical requirements for a valid attempt at prophecy. Wells does not neglect the social and political issues of prophetic fiction—he was, after all, often pilloried for being too tendentious—but his rules give greatest weight to the pleasures of imagination. Stapledon's principles stress the obligations of the speculative imagination—at least in this instance, where he is thinking less of fiction than of epistemology.

The last of Stapledon's talks I want to consider, "**Science and Fiction,**" comes a full decade after "**Science and Literature**" and is his last formal presentation on his chosen literary genre. The circumstances of this talk were unusual for Stapledon. He delivered it in 1947 at a Book Exhibition in Manchester at the urging of his editor at Secker and Warburg. Because sales of his most recent fantasy, *The Flames*, were disappointing, the hope was that Stapledon might help himself by giving a public lecture on the genre to which it belonged. . . . The result is the unique case among his talks in which he offers an overview of his own fiction in relation to the history of the scientific romance. For the first time in his career we hear him using, a little awkwardly, the term "science fiction" to describe his work and that of other writers from Wells forward in whose fiction there are "scientific ideas *in the focus*." Unlike the 1937 talk, however, "**Science and Fiction**" emphasizes the art of science fiction rather than the science in scientific literature. His discussion here is often judicial, discriminating the "imaginative doodling" and "sheer marvels" found in "the science fiction mags" from what he calls "serious science fiction" that aims at "mind stretching" and giving "concrete life to abstract possibilities." Although careful to insist that "*orthodox novel standards* [are] *not applicable*" to science fiction, he does not hesitate to reject the standards of magazines that print stories "often scientifically poor & humanly atrocious."

Once more in "**Science and Fiction**" Stapledon sets up as legislator of the speculative imagination. The seven rules in "**Man's Prospects**" are replaced by three crisply stated "rules of the game of science fiction," all of which are directed especially to the demands of fictionmaking. Stapledon requires: 1) plausibility, achieved by the fiction's conformity to the best current scientific knowledge; 2) the imaginative creation of further possibilities developed by logical extension from current ideas; and 3) psychological and spiritual relevance to human readers in the present through the construction of "*Myths* for a scientific age." The first of Stapledon's rules is what separates science fiction decisively from tales of magic and the preternatural and other forms of fantasy. His second rule states what is now generally accepted as the extrapolative principle for writing science fiction. The last rule obviously addresses the particular aims of his own kind of fiction, though it works as a thumbnail description of the ambitions of a wide range of later authors from J. G. Ballard to John Brunner, from Ursula LeGuin to Octavia Butler, from Brian Aldiss to Doris Lessing, all of whom write what may be thought of as anthropological (if not anthropocentric) science fiction. (pp. 29-32)

For students of Stapledon's career the most teasing part of ["**Science and Fiction**"] must be the concluding fragmentary notes intended to prompt the speaker to assess "my own aims" as writer. . . . Because the lecture was composed after publication of *The Flames*, which turned out to be his last science fiction, this self-study is interesting as a summing-up of Stapledon's entire eighteen-year production of scientific romances. He frames his review with two large critical observations on his fiction—one by "L. H. Myers on *Last and First Men*," the other by Rebecca West comparing his work with Milton's. Myers corresponded frequently with Stapledon for thirteen years, and it is hard to be sure which comment Stapledon intended to cite. But because he kept a special file of letters about *Last and First Men* in his study—including Myers' first letter to him—and because the Rebecca West review with which Myers is paired concerns style, it is likely that Stapledon paraphrased this portion from Myers' letter of 6 June 1931:

> Lastly I must say something about your style & method. It is very difficult to make a strictly intellectualistic approach to beauty & grandeur with any effect, or rather without a poor effect. They have to be illustrated through Art with lyric or tragic fire rather than just talked about. Well, you have succeeded better than I shd have thought possible on intellectual lines as such, and this is a great achievement. What you have borrowed from Art, what recourse you have made to the emotions, has been strictly subordinated to the thinking mind and made a part of it, so that there is no violation of the mind's purity and austerity.

Myers extolled precisely the aspect of *Last and First Men*'s style that Stapledon would claim in his 1937 lecture as characteristic of scientifically inspired literature ("unemotional, unrhetorical, dry, concise, abstract"). Stapledon in 1947 epitomizes the alternative viewpoint with the note, "What *Rebecca West* said of *Star Maker*." Remembering clearly enough *what* she said, he forgot that her target was not *Star Maker* but the less successful novel *Darkness and the Light*. In her review of that book West applauded the splendor of its conception and the "apocalyptic power" of its closing vision, but she was devastating on its style:

> This book should be read, though it is unlikely to be read with any exhilaration, owing to a self-denying ordinance of the author. Mr. Stapledon has a Miltonic imagination. . . . But Mr. Stapledon has evidently a conscious abhorrence of the Miltonic phrase, and the effect is as if Milton had sent the completed manuscript of "Paradise Lost" to be rewritten by the author of Bradshaw's Railway Guide.

Having offered competing perspectives on his art, Stapledon turns to his own evaluation. Predictably, he puts greatest emphasis on his desire *"to write modern myths,"* though he believes that to a more sophisticated age his fictions "will seem very crude." In a running gloss on his works he notes his recurrent concern "to relate science to religion," and he lists the thematic centers of each of his romances: "man's vicissitudes" in *Last and First Men,* "glimpse of a super human" in *Odd John,* "spirit & the other" in *Death into Life,* "wild biology" and "spirit again" in *The Flames,* and so forth. The thematic tags are self-evident, and there needs no ghost come from the grave to tell us this. But there is one intriguing question in the margin, addressed either to himself or to his audience, about *Sirius:* "My best sc. fictn?" The question may have been prompted by a letter from Haldane shortly after *Sirius* was published, saying: "I regard it as a far more plausible futuristic book than 1st and last men, last men in London, etc." Whatever lies behind the question, it signals the kind of critical scrutiny of his work that he seems to have been ready to make.

One page of notes has been added to these minimal thematic comments, perhaps for a future expansion of the lecture. Here Stapledon limits himself to commentary on only four of his books—and they are the quartet that later critics almost unanimously agree are his essential body of work: *Last and First Men, Odd John, Star Maker,* and *Sirius.* The jottings on the

first are fairly cryptic, but it is possible to reconstruct the substance of what he talked about. One note reads: "Anglesey vision; stout Cortes." He alludes to the moment when the idea for *Last and First Men* burst on him during a holiday with his wife on the Welsh coast when they observed seals sunning on the rocks. The sight must have started a train of associations—life emerging from the ocean, the long pageant of evolution, the hugh spectacle of time imprinted on rocks creased and polished by the ceaselessly moving waters, wonderment about the biological forms that intelligence might inhabit in future ages. From the cliffs of Anglesey he looked down on the ocean and forward into time, and the sestet from Keats's sonnet on Chapman's Homer came into his head:

> Then felt I like some watcher of the skies
>   When a new planet swims into his ken;
> Or like stout Cortez when with eagle eyes
>   He star'd at the Pacific—and all his men
> Look'd at each other with a wild surmise—
>   Silent, upon a peak in Darien. . . .
>
> (pp. 34-7)

It is like Stapledon, however, not to stop with the glamour of a Pisgah view that would wrap in mystery the "wild surmise" that became *Last and First Men.* His notes move directly to the more mundane stage of composing fictions. After the flash of vision, he tells his audience, "'the artificer' gets to work." He consults "scientific friends" for technical advice and referees his imagination by the "rules of the game" so that his "successive species" of the human race from man to "superman" to the "extravagances" of Great Brains, flying Venusians, and other evolutionary marvels in the next 2,000,000,000 years of history will have scientific and narrative credibility. Stapledon reflects on the paradox of creating fiction about, as the subtitle of *Last and First Men* reads, "the near and far future." Plausibility about events millions of years ahead is won through scientific homework and carefully plotted extrapolation, but the reader's assent to the narrative illusion can be jeopardized by failures of forecasting in the near future. By 1947 the early chapters of *Last and First Men* had become obsolete as prediction, and Stapledon was in the position of having sheepishly to submit a scorecard to his audience. If in the aftermath of the death camps and a global war against fascism he had to confess that he had "missed Hitler," he could at least claim that he got "atomic power." The desire for "transcendence of time" is, as the lecturer points out, basic to the structure of *Last and First Men,* but time and history have a way of sabotaging the merely human and transient narrative artist.

With *Star Maker* Stapledon worked on a "larger canvas" and adopted a "more philosophical perspective." His most interesting note here reads: "fiction of the Maker—artist." This is the climactic entry in a short list of topics for discussion on *Star Maker,* and it suggests that the author wanted to look at his masterpiece not primarily as a theological romance but as a self-reflective parable about the nature of creativity in which the visionary spectacle of the star maker's drafting and redrafting of the universe becomes a macrocosmic emblem of the human artist's repeated struggle to achieve satisfying forms.

Like later critics of his work, Stapledon evidently viewed *Odd John* and *Sirius* as a pair of exercises in plausible speculation on a deliberately narrower and more intimate scale than his large cosmic histories. In the case of *Odd John* the "aim" was to depict a superman whose powers are rendered credibly by a direct "extrapolation" (Stapledon uses the term here himself) from existing human capabilities and by a more delicate ''hinting'' at powers that are ''qualitatively new.''

Sirius, Stapledon reveals, originated in ''Waddington's story of experiments on rats'' and is like *Odd John* in being problem-centered. The conceptual challenge, for which the novelist must ''work out the consequences,'' is the hormonal inducement of brain growth in a nonhuman mammal. The lecture emphasizes the sequence of steps in the making of *Sirius.* Only *after* the problem in its abstract form (''the conflict of natures'') has occurred to Stapledon does he turn to the specific ''choice of beast & of environment.'' For the reader the unforgettable images of the macrocephalic sheepdog, oscillating sometimes comically, often painfully between his canine instincts and his human education, are in the foreground of the reading experience; for the author the question of what sort of mammal Sirius would be was secondary. Waddington's rats produce Stapledon's dog; the idea generates the fiction. On precisely this point Arthur Koestler registered a reservation about *Sirius.* In a letter to Stapledon he questioned an episode in which the dog sings sacred music of his own devising in a medley of canine sounds with ''echoes of Bach and Beethoven, of Holst, Vaughan Williams, Stravinsky, and Bliss.'' . . . Koestler thought the narrative credibility had been sacrificed to intellectual coherence: ''I believe it is almost a great book, the 'almost' referring to those passages which I feel you wrote prompted by philosophical integrity against your own artistic taste—e.g. the dog singing Bach in the East End church.''

However one judges the particular moment Koestler objects to in *Sirius,* the larger issue in his critique persists. Stapledon's lectures only confirm what many readers besides Koestler have intuited about his books: that it is the idea of science fiction that commands his imagination, and all the narrative apparatus exists in support of that idea. C. S. Lewis, a much more polemical fantasist than Stapledon, and Ursula LeGuin, who owns as rich an anthropological imagination as Stapledon's, have described the origins of their stories in mental pictures. Lewis envisioned the floating islands and then created the locale for *Perelandra* . . . ; LeGuin saw the face of Shevek in her mind's eye; and the construction of *The Dispossessed* framed that face. . . . But for Stapledon the idea antedates the image. Even the ''vision'' he claims as inspiration for his first novel did not beget an episode or a picture; he saw seals on the Welsh coast, but the human image presides over *Last and First Men.* In Stapledon's fiction the idea also determines the voice. The sheer number of narrators who are explicitly mediums for messages is telling: the amanuenses who record the telepathically dictated texts of *Last and First Men* and *Last Men in London;* the Boswellian anonym who is induced to tell Odd John's ''biography'' under the guise of fiction; the doubting Thomas who transmits the epistolary prophecy of a mad, male Cassandra possessed by solar creatures in *The Flames.* That such taletellers should be instrumental to some other being who manipulates them to serve a higher purpose suggests the degree to which Stapledon was inclined to fabricate and manipulate fictions in order to make a point or to explore a hypothesis or to unfold the layers of a problem.

To say all this, however, is not to imply that Stapledon neglected the art of his science fiction. Neither the sequence in which he assembled his artifice nor the demonstrable prominence of ideas in his narratives argues against his status as a scientific and philosophical *romancer.* Certainly he did not shun Art as Wells pretended to, nor did he share Wells's habit of polemical disjunction: either it is Literature or Journalism.

The force of Stapledon's lectures is to consolidate rather than polarize, to argue for the uniting of literary and scientific perspectives, of moral designs and narrative play, of the inspiration of the visionary and the mechanisms of the artificer. The practice matches the theory. In his four most famous works, as well as the smaller triumphs of *Last Men in London, Death into Life,* and *The Flames,* Stapledon houses his ideas in powerful, innovative, and beautiful forms.

Stapledon was a teacher long before he became a novelist, and he remained a teacher after his fiction declined in popularity in the late 1940s. The commitment to teaching shows in his fiction and points to his place in the line of English didactic romancers—the line of Thomas More, Bunyan, Swift, Godwin, Carlyle, Butler, and, of course, Wells. Stapledon is always a writer with a purpose, fitting words to ideas and images to intellectual strategies, outfitting his readers for citizenship in the world, in the universe, in the days and eons to come. Because people at the present stage of human civilization are provincials in space and time, the task Stapledon marked out for himself as a writer required all the resources of art along with philosophical acuity and a breadth of scientific knowledge. In an undated lecture called **''Ourselves and the Future''** he speaks of the difficulty of teaching people to care about and prepare for the future. In the outline for that talk he jotted down what amounts to his artistic credo, the vital motivation of his writing career, the idea behind all the ideas in his science fiction: ''The improvident are to be got at by appeal to imagination.'' (pp. 37-40)

Robert Crossley, ''Olaf Stapledon and the Idea of Science Fiction,'' in Modern Fiction Studies, *Vol. 32, No. 1, Spring, 1986, pp. 21-42.*

JOHN KINNAIRD (essay date 1986)

[*An American educator and critic, Kinnaird is the author of the critical study* A Reader's Guide to Olaf Stapledon. *In the following excerpt from that work, he examines theme and technique in* Last and First Men.]

[*Last and First Men*] is so famous as the ancestor of all ''future histories'' that it takes an effort to remind ourselves that, in the most fundamental sense, the book is not prophetic history at all but a work, as Stapledon says in his preface, of ''myth.'' Some interpreters have seen the book as dramatizing Stapledon's theories of historical evolution—and so it does, of course—but I am inclined to agree with C. S. Lewis (Stapledon's philosophical enemy but an admirer of his imagination), who describes the book as ''pseudo history'' only in ''form,'' only insofar as it is not ''novelistic.'' Stapledon, he says, in adopting the ''pace'' and ''tone'' of ''the historiographer,'' was creating ''a new form,'' and this was ''the right form for the theme''; but that theme identifies the book as belonging to what Lewis calls ''eschatological'' fantasy, fiction about ''the last things,'' about man's destiny—in a word, to apocalyptic myth.

This dual character of the book is reflected in the fact that there are two Prefaces, written respectively by the historically actual author, ''Stapledon,'' and the transcendent or timeless—the eschatological—narrator, one of the Last Men. The decision to make the ''true'' narrator a voice from the end of time—a member of the last and most ''mature'' human species, whose culture has achieved telepathic communication with the entire human past, is one of the most brilliant variations of the *persona* device (the authorial ''mask,'' or narrational personality) in the history of fiction. This device not only enables Stapledon to lend an air of authenticity—indeed of godlike omniscience—to his narrative as history, but also to suggest to his readers that there may be another perspective entirely, even on twentieth-century events, than "history"—something more real, that is, than the simple socio-economic determinism which most science-minded intellectuals in his time regarded as the law governing all human destiny. Thus, within the narrative premises of the story, it is "Stapledon," the mind conditioned by the attitudes of historical determinism, who is the real *persona,* his imagination being manipulated by the "true" author, the representative of mythic vision, whose sense of the environmental "field" is the total "cosmic setting" and who sees the evolution of humanity as a universal whole, not merely as a temporal series. And the Last Man makes no secret of the fact that his intention is not to satisfy twentieth-century curiosity about the future but, through this vision of unprecedented change, to force his readers to acknowledge their "primitive" sense of reality and to begin imagining "loftier potencies" for humanity than any yet conceived. As the Last Man explains, "Though he (Stapledon) seeks to tell a plausible story, he neither believes it himself, nor expects others to believe it. Yet the story is true. A being whom you would call a future man has seized the docile but scarcely adequate brain of your contemporary, and is trying to direct its familiar processes for an alien purpose." . . . (pp. 39-40)

That purpose, being "alien," necessarily has to remain dark at first, but in the early chapters it almost disappears from view, as Stapledon, trying to engage the interest of history-minded readers, yields to the temptation to invent an intricate pattern of events, rather than concentrating on the drama of his mythic theme. Yet anyone familiar in advance with Stapledon's favorite metaphor, the "sleep" and "waking" of the mind, has no trouble picking up the thread that will take us through the labyrinth. The first human species, we are told, "sometimes stirred in its sleep, opened bewildered eyes, and slept again." Only in fleeting moments of their history did the First Men awaken to the true possibilities of their nature—as in the searching thought of Socrates, who first conceived the ideal of "dispassionate" truth, or in the loving spirit of Jesus, who first gave men the ideal of "passionate yet self-oblivious worship." . . . What keeps the First Men from awakening, as a species, from the sub-human state is less the pull of animal instincts and desires than the inability to recognize the difference between a true and false transcendence of animality. The First Men continually lapse into the nightmare of war, not through brute violence alone but through a deceptive will to transcendence—one that embraces idealism at the expense of our genuine animal needs, or one that pretends to aspire beyond the limits of self yet really flatters the insatiable vanity of self, and thus perverts both animal desire in man and his "impulses to a higher loyalty." . . . (pp. 40-1)

Nearly all the wars of the First Men are, we should note, provoked by incidents that center on sexuality. And nowhere are man's sexual energies being put to more perverse uses than in the brilliant scene, ironically modelled on Botticelli's painting *The Birth of Venus,* where a young Polynesian beauty suddenly swims into the Pacific Island cove where the heads of the American and Chinese empires are holding their summit conference to negotiate peace for the world. As she walks ashore, her uninhibited, frankly sensual beauty gradually penetrates the puritanical shell of the American—not, however, because his masculinity responds at last with throbbing vitality to the natural power of Eros, but because her voluptuousness appeals to his lust as it awakens his lust for power; he takes her under the banana trees less as an act of irresistible desire than as an act of triumph over his vain and rather effete Chinese rival. . . . Out of this incident is born the First World State, and this state, being without a spiritual basis in true will to community, owes its ultimate undoing to the same perversion of sexuality and its consequent undermining of intelligence. Though not himself a Freudian, Stapledon shows Freudian insight into the unconscious mind's equation of dream-images of flying with repressed desires for sexual intercourse. And precisely such repression motivates the new craze for aviation that soon sweeps the planet. The World State squanders, at an exponential rate, the resources of the earth (and is this really so unprophetic of what is coming to pass?), through mass-sublimations of sexual desire in an official world-religion of ritualized flight, and in other practices that reflect a fatal confusion of human vitality with technological prowess and compulsive ego-assertion.

At this point, with the gradual extinction of the First Men, it becomes especially important to recognize that Stapledon is not writing "prophecy." He is traditionally, and not incorrectly, recognized as a "pessimist," but he is not here predicting the doom of civilization and the fatal degeneration of our species; on the contrary, although he believed that such a fate was more than possible, his fictional projection of it was expressly designed to help prevent it. . . . What better way was there for Stapledon to rouse his First Men readers from "sleep" than by a cold, cathartic bath of their imaginations in this future of relentless progress toward technological self-destruction? And in the book itself, other specimens of humanity will find in the defeat of their hopes that spiritual strengthening which, as Stapledon believed, only an honestly tragic awareness of man's inescapable conflicts could provide. "The only way to an optimism of finer mood, if it be intellectually possible at all, is perhaps through heart-felt acceptance of pessimism." . . . (pp. 41-2)

After the devastation of the planet by the last Patagonian civilization of the First Men, a new human species gradually evolves over several millennia. Not until the emergence of these Second Men is it fully clear why the First Men have failed to achieve transcendence, although it will now be clear also that the mind's overcoming of self, when achieved, is precarious and holds its own dangers for "spirit." Thanks mainly to the volcanically altered environment, the new species is favored with a larger and stronger, Titan-like body and with improved sensory equipment—much better vision, for example. They are naturally more interested in the world and in each other; being no longer subject to the First Man's fears—fears rooted in the fragility of an inadequate body—they are no longer plagued by his craving for power, or by his constant temptation to make ideals serve the secret interests of a defensive self-love. In their Arcadian yet intellectual Utopia, these amiable, altruistic giants seem almost too good to be true—until their own hidden weakness is exposed by the unexpected advent of the Martians.

But why, we may wonder, have a Martian invasion at all—apart from the need to match H. G. Wells at his own game? The episode is necessary for three reasons: to introduce the cosmic aspect of Stapledon's theme; to suggest—by presenting a life-form that does not depend on organic biology or on "bodies" as we know them—that the potential for life and intelligence may inhere in all electromagnetic energy; and lastly, to develop a tragic situation in which two mutually alien species fail to recognize themselves in the strange mirror of the other.

The tragedy of both antagonists is that each possesses, though often to excess or in debased form, what the other lacks and needs. The Martian cloud-swarms have rudimentary individuality, but radiational union with other cloudlets does not produce transcendent awakening of individuals to true community but only a group-consciousness that tends to collective, authoritarian conformity. The Second Men, on the other hand, though capable of intense sympathy with each other as individuals, are incapable of achieving their own "super-mind," except as an ideal of community that they sincerely long for yet feel always to be unattainable, separated as they are within the extroverted but still self-enclosed nervous systems of their bodies. And it is their very capacity for dispassionate awareness, coupled as this is with a religious sense of tragic necessity (and even of a certain cosmic beauty in that fate)—a transcendent lucidity that the Second Men can achieve intellectually but cannot sustain emotionally in their separateness—which gradually weakens their animal loyalty to life in their war with the Martians. They are led to acquiesce in the dissemination of a lethal bacterium which insures the annihilation of the invaders (note the variation on the ending of Wells' novel) but guarantees also, as they well know, their own ultimate destruction.

A genuine and enduring transcendence, then, if the will that it generates is not to continue dividing man's consciousness from his vital animality, would seem to require a more secure basis in physical existence than man's natural body affords. Or to state the principle in positive terms, another body awaits man in the potentialities of nature and its energies—not a body essentially different from his original body but one that is capable of becoming part of a larger body, part of a community of being where mind and body may become one power, one in "spirit." The Second Men are the first to conceive seriously the ambition to remake man's nature; but it is, much later, the Third Men—aeons later, a multimillion-year half-inch down the Stapledonian time-scale—who bring the dream to its first reality. The concept of "artificial evolution" has always been associated in our culture with the sterile and the unnatural, with the proverbial insensitivities of the abstract scientific intellect, and perhaps this association of ideas explains why Stapledon gives his Third Men their special blend of qualities. They are, predictably, clever and manipulative, but they are also animal-like and animal-loving. Short-lived, they are naturally lovers of life. They are small and lithe and large-eared: blest with this fine motor and auditory equipment, they are enraptured by music; and their science is always subordinated to a "plastic vital art" based on intuitive reverence for biological nature. Thus the first artificial species of man is to be created by a culture that worships Life yet is intensely aesthetic. The redesigning of a body and a sensorium more commensurate with the true nature of man's mind is in Stapledon's myth a necessary step in the fulfillment of humanity—not a repudiation of the earthly past but the long-postponed outcome of man's growth from animal infancy to "maturity."

Yet what the Third Men finally create is an abominable monstrosity—the Fourth Men, the Great Brains. What goes wrong, and why? Here is transcendence with a vengeance; for these virtually bodiless Superminds, though confined physically (hands alone excepted) to a turret-like "cranium" of ferro-concrete, soon set about enslaving and destroying their creators. As hunters in the wilderness, the Third Men had always felt a secret attraction to pain, a feral delight in predatory energies mixed with the familiar human love of power, and the best of this *Schadenfreude* is that it leads to a certain transvaluation of

values, liberating the species from the self-regarding bondage of pleasure. Yet the dark underside to this range of sensibility is a "long-suppressed lust in cruelty"; because the Third Men sense that the evil really dwells within them, they are finally unable to oppose the tyranny of the unfeeling Brains and their merciless experiments. . . . It would be a mistake, however, to regard the Brains as utter abominations, or as monstrous parodies of the Mad Scientist legend. They remain human in their demonism, and it is a tribute to Stapledon's talent for mythic characterization that he makes us feel a human sympathy for them even at their most insanely monstrous. We feel their intellectual frustration as they discover that in learning everything, they know nothing, and then we are made to share their "cold jealousy" as they contemplate "the free movement, the group life, the love-making of their menials." . . . We may, and should, be reminded here of another artificial creature, Mary Shelley's monster in *Frankenstein,* but there is one significant difference. For although this monster, too, embarks on a suicidal course of revenge and destroys his Promethean creators, he becomes the next Prometheus: he creates his supplanters, the Fifth Men. He does this simply out of awareness that the very existence of a mind—since its only power lies in knowledge and understanding—would be pointless without a creation that would remedy its own inferred deficiencies. This is a staggering paradox but by no means an impossibility: "It was much as though a blind race, after studying physics, should invent organs of sight." . . . The story of the Brains is, in short, within the larger myth, a parable of the mind rediscovering, against all empirical odds, its true nature as the will to transcend the limits of its given being through creative intuition.

The Fifth Men, simply as characters, are much less successful. Titanically Utopian creatures, they are enormous in size and intelligence; they live an average of three thousand years; and with this much time at their disposal, they discover the Stapledonian science of "psycho-physics," a knowledge that provides the basis for telepathic communication. This new transcendence, though, is not yet a true "group-mind," for the telepathic union (made possible by Martian radiation-units incorporated into their brain cells) is still only a bridge between individuals. Their telepathy does accomplish a great breakthrough: it is capable of reaching individual minds in the past—not through "travel" down the time-stream, but through the ultimate participation of all minds in the timelessness of eternal being. The Fifth Men thus become the first species to discover that they belong to another human community than their own in time. And if this inspires, it also worries them; they feel guilty when they return to the comfort and security of their Utopia from the despair and agony of the past. They need not have worried, however, for in Stapledon's universe there is no such thing as immunity from change and suffering. Transcendence in Stapledon is never simply *of* something but *into* something: man bursts from the chrysalis of animal "sleep" not into Utopian happiness but into cosmic awareness—and *this* awakening is always a rude one. So again Cosmic Process comes calling on Utopian Man, and again the visitation is disastrous. Learning that their telepathic radiations have disturbed the electromagnetic field of the planet and are causing the moon's orbit to close in upon the earth, the Fifth Men gird themselves to undertake the greatest Exodus of all—migration to the planet Venus. From this point on, man in Stapledon's saga is to live in intimate conjunction—and strange confrontation—with the universe. Out of this interaction with the ultimate environment is to emerge a wholly new union of body and mind, whose achievement is to be both the victory and the tragedy of the Last Men.

First, though, there is a magnificent—and thematically important—interlude. Only a brief scherzo in comparison with the more extended movements of Stapledon's symphony (and the symphonic analogy is his own, often repeated . . .), the episode of the Flying Men nevertheless develops certain symbolic motifs that become thematically major in the concluding movement. After the hostile environment of Venus has been made more congenial through aeons of adaptive mutation and several cycles of civilization, a new species is artificially perfected for flight in the planet's densely buoyant atmosphere. Bat-winged, but bird-like in temperament, the Seventh Men exult in the freedom and self-expressive joy of flight. Like the First Men aviators, they go in for elaborate aerial choreography, but now the massed soarings are exuberant, wholly vital in their graceful beauty. And the sexual impulse in the imagination of flight is now explicit and pure, as "love-intoxicated pairs" of these winged beings are seen "entwining their courses" and then embracing to "drop ten thousand feet in bodily union." These are the most "care-free" of all the species; yet their joy is by no means thoughtless, for it is "the spiritual aspect of flight which obsessed the species." These fliers exult not only in their gift for aerial art but in the power of the sky over them: even when, "dismembered by the hurricane," they find themselves "crashing to death," they still exult with "aesthetic delight" in the living intensity of the experience—indifferent in that "ecstasy" to the body's destruction and even greeting it with intoxicated laughter. Only when, after surviving some disaster, they return to the ground are they overwhelmed with grief and horror, often to die from heart-failure or to lapse more deeply into that torpor which is their customary condition when not in flight. Always rediscovering anew, as they escape into flight, the tragic beauty of all fragile life in the cosmos, it becomes the tragedy of the species that they cannot learn to sustain this awareness, as an inspiration of the will, beyond the aesthetic moment of its perception. Just as the Fourth men, bound to one spot on earth, are fulfilled but perish through an overtranscendent mind, so the Seventh men, their physical contraries, alive only when on the wing, can at last realize their transcendence of the body's bondage only in an act of racial suicide. Temperamentally unable to endure the regimen of thought and will necessary to support civilization and increasingly persecuted by their successors (the technology-minded descendants of their crippled offspring), the Seventh Men, recognizing irreversible defeat yet too high-souled to surrender, take off on one last concerted flight and dive exulting, couple by couple, into the mouth of a volcano. . . . (pp. 42-6)

The great difficulty for all men in the Stapledon universe . . . is to combine tragic self-knowledge with creative will. And the saga of the Flying Men is there to remind us that this union must be accomplished without impairing either man's capacity for animal joy or his instinctive loyalty to life—the animal will to survive, no less important than the mind's will to transcend and create. This is the challenge that the Last Men recognize and accept; and although they too rise only to fall from the height of their triumph, they almost succeed in mastering the delicate balance of the human paradox.

After aeons of eclipse, during which man declines again and again into sub-human animality, another long upward spiral ensues, culminating in the supreme civilization of the Eighteenth men on Neptune. These are Stapledon's showpieces for his ideal of community, but I find them, on the whole, less

appealing in their super-Utopian aspect (about which the Neptunian narrator is a bit of a boaster) than in their character, which emerges only in the concluding pages, as the Last of Men. In general shape and physique they resemble the Fifth Men, but their bodies have far greater power, being composed entirely of super-strong artificial atoms. They have learned, moreover, from all the grim cycles of degeneration and rebirth, new respect for their animal heritage and are proudly animal-like, not only in certain features of their appearance but in their emotional genesis: their bodies, though artificial in substance, are sexually engendered and viviparously reproduced. Sexuality, indeed, provides the sympathetic basis for the entire culture: it is now polymorphous, the two principal sexes having diversified into ninety-six subsexes, whose subtle distinctions may be further refined and recombined in the life of the Neptunian individual through the changing memberships of "marriage groups"—a variety of experience which is fortunate, since each Neptunian lives as long as a quarter of a million terrestrial years! All the aspirations of the previous species are thus realized to near-perfection by the Eighteenth Men: they even make some approximation (with the help of flying suits) to the joy in flight of the Seventh Men. But the most distinctive achievement of this species is the development—through radiation from certain brain-cells in telepathic combination with the psychic sympathies of members in a "marriage group"—of a truly "super-individual" mind. These "group minds" in turn communicate telepathically and when fully united, linked together through the electromagnetic field of the planet, form "the racial mind," which constitutes Neptunian Man's supreme experience of "awakening."

Transcendence into purely human communion, though, is no longer the goal of "the racial mind." As his mind enters "the racial mode," an Eighteenth Man "apprehends all things astronomically," and not only his perceptions but his sense of values, and indeed his very sense of being, become "cosmical." From their vantage-point at the outer limits of the solar system (Pluto had only just been discovered, in March, 1930, and its existence was not yet confirmed when Stapledon was finishing his book), the Neptunians look out across the great impassable sea of the galaxy; their space-ships have ventured out into the void, only to return with the voyagers "crazed," stricken with fear of the stars. . . . Only the telepathic powers of "the racial mind" can penetrate galactic space, and what it learns is not encouraging. A few traces of intelligence and civilization are found among the stars, but man now seems alone in the galaxy and, with one possible exception, the other galaxies observed have nowhere "produced anything comparable with man." The cosmological metaphysic that results from millennia of searching yields no promise of an emerging wholeness of "spirit" in the universe. The only certain knowledge is that man is doomed to extinction: the universe is cyclical, and the life-cycle of the solar system is drawing inexorably toward an end, toward some new beginning that has no place for Man. . . . (pp. 46-8)

The Last Men thus learn that they are indeed Last, that they stand on the last possible frontier of the human future. Yet they are not crushed by this knowledge, and insofar as their minds retain the telepathic effects of the "racial mode," are even inspired by it; indeed, their entire culture is based on worship of the stars as they represent the beauty and "potency" of "spirit" redeeming the fatality of the cosmic process. In the practical sphere, they are inspired to design, for dissemination into space, "the seeds of a new humanity" . . . ; if man himself must perish and if his dream of "spirit" exists nowhere else in the universe, then, it may be his destiny to be himself the germinal source of the ultimate cosmic "awakening." The racial mind, though, is not "enslaved to this desire." More than in its continued identity as the human species, it values the "music" of the cosmos itself, as both "beautiful" and "terrible"; it seeks therefore to teach its individual members "the supreme art of ecstatic fatalism." Even as the racial mind wills to achieve an awakening of the cosmos, it yet "holds itself aloof from its own will, and from "all desire . . . save the ecstasy which admires the Real as it is, and accepts its dark-bright form with joy." . . . (p. 48)

Man's capacity for the ultimate self-transcendence is soon put to the ultimate test. The dark-bright Real is suddenly manifest in the form of a strange and beautiful supernova whose violent radiation soon infects the sun and insures the imminent destruction of all the planets. The Neptunian mentality has no trouble recognizing in both the menace and the "splendor" of the nova the perfect symmetry of man's fate within the cyclical cosmic process: "Man is a fair spirit, whom a star conceived and a star kills." . . . Yet this Olympian apocalyptic fire intensifies. For the very basis of Neptunian mind, whose telepathic connections depend on a planetary system of radiation, now begins to break down. The resources of tragic endurance must now become again more purely human than cosmic— must now be rediscovered in the past. Originally the Eighteenth Men, like their predecessors, had turned to the past out of altruism or curiosity, but now they have another motive, as the Neptunian narrator in his Preface had cryptically confided, without explanation, to his twentieth-century readers: "We can help you, and we need your help." . . . Just as their presence in the minds of certain First Men has helped those minds to understand experience or has given a nobler or more creative turn to certain actions, so now the favor can be returned in quite a different way. Habituated to transcendence, their minds keyed to accept all eventuality as necessary or even right, the "dispassionate" Last Men now "go humbly to the past to learn over again that other supreme achievement of the spirit, loyalty to the forces of life embattled against the forces of death. . . . (pp. 48-9)

Perhaps only in the spirit of this return to humanity can we understand the ending Stapledon devised for his myth and the significance of his title. That title does not simply mean, as most readers seem to assume, that the Last Men are communicating in spirit with the First Men, or that this is man's history from First to Last. The Last Men *are* really, in a tragically ironic sense, the First of Men—the first to achieve full humanity, to bring their distinctive powers as a species beyond their animal childhood to mature and integrated fulfillment. But they at last accomplish this feat less through their Utopian achievement of transcendent world-community, necessary though that aspiration is, than through their reunion in spirit with the historically First Men—through their rediscovery of the timeless resources of heroic strength in man's naked and spontaneous individuality. And this is why the last figure we meet in Stapledon's story is not a fully fledged, maturely "dispassionate" Last Man; he is the youngest and latest-born of the species, one who has not fully learned to subordinate to the group mind the native energies and instincts of his youth. Neptunian culture requires all young men to undergo the baptism of a long exposure to the ways of the wilderness ("the Land of the Young"), and this youngest Neptunian still retains the saving grace of that experience. He is both a First and a Last Man; he is strengthened by both his animal vitality and his tragic sense, which mingle in a "strange sweet raillery"

as he tries to cheer and rally the minds disintegrating into despair and madness around him. . . . He is the reincarnation of a familiar type, the Wise Child (*puer senex*) or Child-Prophet, a type that had so often appeared to rekindle hope among Stapledon's First Men. He is not unlike the self-sacrificing young Mongol scientist (worshipped as legendary "Gordelpus" in later generations) who destroyed himself rather than reveal the destructive secrets of nuclear power, or the Divine Boy who founded a religion of youth in the senescent culture of the Patagonians. But he is really the embodiment of all men who have ever lived, insofar as they retain in their lives the savor of the sweetness of life in youth—its hope, its courage, its beauty and love of beauty, its will to dream and its dreams of transcendent will. And so he speaks also, this youth who will never know fruition, or no other fruition than his identity as the Last Child, for the spirit of a life-form called Man that itself is dying young—that after two billion years has scarcely fledged its evolutionary wings: "Man," as he says, "was winged hopefully" and "had in him to go further than this short flight, now ending." Always inspired to the highest efforts of vision or intellect by the ages-old dream of "the music of the spheres," revelation of that quest forms part of the music of man's own being—a music that can be heard now only as it completes itself against the final silence. What we are hearing in these last notes from that music is, in one sense, simply another young man's dream, but as such its pathos brings back echoes of the "symphony" we have been tracing—the great cyclical fugue of human dream and disaster, with all its indomitable variations, as Stapledon's entire myth resonates in memory:

> Man himself, at the very least, is music, a brave theme that makes music also of its vast accompaniment, its matrix of storms and stars. Man himself in his degree is eternally a beauty in the eternal form of things. It is very good to have been man. And so we may go forward together with laughter in our hearts, and peace, thankful for the past, and for our own courage. For we shall make after all a fair conclusion to this brief music that is man. . . .
>
> (pp. 49-50)

John Kinnaird, in his Olaf Stapledon, *Starmont House, 1986, 107 p.*

BRIAN W. ALDISS (essay date 1986)

[*Aldiss is an English novelist, short story writer, critic, and editor who is best known for his science fiction novels and criticism. In the following excerpt, he discusses the themes and techniques of Stapledon's novels, focusing upon* Star Maker *as the author's most important work.*]

The atmosphere Stapledon generates is chill but intoxicating. Reading his books is like standing on the top of a high mountain. One can see a lot of planet and much of the sprawling uncertain works of man, but little actual human activity; from such an altitude, all sense of the individual is lost.

The best of Stapledon is contained in two long works of fiction and two shorter novels. His most famous work is the first he published: *Last and First Men: A Story of the Near and Far Future.* It appeared in 1930.

The author himself regarded—or said he regarded—his chronicle as expendable; for the next generation, it would "certainly raise a smile." Well, there is no doubt that Stapledon's version of events from 1930 to the present is ludicrous. It is worth close attention if one wishes to savour how wrong prediction can be, in both fact and spirit. Almost anything Stapledon says about Germany and America is incorrect. Only when one climbs through the leaden opening chapters of the book does one start to soar on the wings of inspiration—"myth," Stapledon called it. Politics then gives way to an inquiry into life processes.

One thing is never at fault: the invention. The Second Men, for instance, are bothered by Martian invasions; although the idea may have been derived from Wells, the Martians are cloudlike beings and derive only from Stapledon.

If the periodical catastrophes become mechanical, the successive panoramas of life which Stapledon unrolls are always varied and striking. They are variations on the theme of mankind as a creature like any other, fatally victim of its surroundings, so that whatever is godlike in the creature is brought to nothing by blind happenstance. Like Hardy, Stapledon was influenced by Schopenhauer's philosophy of being, as well as Spengler's philosophy of the cyclic nature of history; his view is at once more prideful and more pessimistic than Hardy's. The time-scale of the novel is unmatched in science fiction, except by the later Stapledon.

Here is one of his final visions, which science fiction readers find moving—though it is the kind of passage which annoyed C. S. Lewis:

> But in the fullness of time there would come a far more serious crisis. The sun would continue to cool, and at last man would no longer be able to live by means of solar radiation. It would become necessary to annihilate matter to supply the deficiency. The other planets might be used for this purpose, and possibly the sun itself. Or, given the sustenance for so long a voyage, man might boldly project his planet into the neighbourhood of some young star. Thenceforth, perhaps, he might operate upon a far grander scale. He might explore and colonise all suitable worlds in every corner of the galaxy, and organise himself as a vast community of minded worlds. Even (so we dreamed) he might achieve intercourse with other galaxies. It did not seem impossible that man himself was the germ of the world-soul, which, we still hope, is destined to awake for a while before the universal decline, and to crown the eternal cosmos with its due of knowledge and admiration, fleeting yet eternal. We dared to think that in some far distant epoch the human spirit, clad in all wisdom, power, and delight, might look back upon our primitive age with a certain respect; no doubt with pity also and amusement, but none the less with admiration for the spirit in us, still only half awake, and struggling against great disabilities. (Chapter 16)

Such a chilly vision is best conveyed as fiction or music; as architecture or government, it would be intolerable. (pp. 183-84)

His greatest work [*Star Maker*] appeared in 1937, when the shadow of another war was stretching over Europe. In his Preface, Stapledon makes an apology for writing something so far removed from the sounds of battle, and says of those in the thick of the struggle that they "nobly forgo something of that detachment, that power of cold assessment, which is, after all, among the most valuable human capacities"—a very suspect claim; there is no denying that he set great store by a detachment he probably could not help but feel. His was among those "intellects vast and cool and unsympathetic" to which Wells made reference in another context.

Star Maker begins, in some respects, where *Last and First Men* left off. An unnamed human being, the disembodied "I" of the book, falls into a kind of trance, a "hawk-flight of the imagination," while sitting amid the heather on a hill close to his home. The "I"'s essence is drawn away from Earth, into the solar system and then beyond, farther and farther, and faster.

This is a new—and so far unsurpassed—version of the spiritual voyage. A fresh generation has brought fresh knowledge. Einstein's perceptions, and the findings of astronomers, add calibre to Stapledon's new model of the universe. As in this poetic vision of the doppler effect:

> After a while I noticed that the sun and all the stars in his neighbourhood were ruddy. Those at the opposite pole of the heaven were of an icy blue. The explanation of this strange phenomenon flashed upon me. I was still travelling, and travelling so fast that light itself was not wholly indifferent to my passage. The overtaking undulations took long to catch me. They therefore affected me as slower pulsations than they normally were, and I saw them therefore as red. Those that met me on my headlong flight were congested and shortened, and were seen as blue.
>
> Very soon the heavens presented an extraordinary appearance, for all the stars directly behind me were now deep red, while those directly ahead were violet. Rubies lay behind me, amethysts ahead of me. Surrounding the ruby constellations there spread an area of topaz stars, and round the amethyst constellations an area of sapphires. Beside my course, on every side, the colours faded into the normal white of the sky's familiar diamonds. Since I was travelling almost in the plane of the galaxy, the hoop of the Milky Way, white on either hand, was violet ahead of me, red behind. Presently the stars immediately before and behind grew dim, then vanished, leaving two starless holes in heaven, each hole surrounded by a zone of coloured stars. Evidently I was still gathering speed. Light from the forward and the hinder stars now reached me in forms beyond the range of my human vision.
>
> As my speed increased, the two starless patches, before and behind, each with its coloured fringe, continued to encroach upon the intervening zone of normal stars which lay abreast of me on every side. Amongst these I now detected movement. Through the effect of my own passage the nearer stars appeared to drift across the background of stars at greater distance, the whole visible sky was streaked with flying stars. Then everything vanished. Presumably my speed was so great in relation to the stars that light

from none of them could take normal effect on
me. (Chapter 2)

The traveller moves ever on in quest for planets that might
support humanlike life, and eventually arrives on Other Earth.
A full description of its societies is given before the traveller
passes on; there is some mild satire of terrestrial behaviour, as
well as occasional comments which foreshadow the writings
of more intelligent modern SF writers, including C. S. Lewis
and James Blish. "Shortly before I left Other Earth a geologist
discovered a fossil diagram of a very complicated radio set,"
suggests the extraordinary reality-reversions of Philip K. Dick.

Travelling faster than light, the traveller meets other mental
cosmic adventurers. They explore endless worlds, endless modes
of life, in which Stapledon's ingenuity in creating varied species of men as demonstrated in *Last and First Men* is completely
eclipsed. Here, under all sorts of alien conditions, he shows
us many "strange mankinds," as he calls them—among them
centaurs, which are fairly common in the universe (recalling
Van Vogt's comment in his novelette *The Storm* that the centaur
family is "almost universal"), human echinoderms, and intelligent ships, as well as symbiotic races, multiple minds,
composite beings, mobile plant men, and other teeming variants of the life force. Utopias, interstellar-ship travel, war
between planets, galactic empires, terrible crises in galactic
history, telepathic sub-galaxies going down in madness . . .
until a galactic utopia becomes a possibility. In all this, the
history of *Last and First Men* appears as a couple of paragraphs,
lost among greater things. Stapledon is truly frightening at
times.

He keeps turning the volume up. We move to para-galactic
scale. Stars also have mentalities, and the minded worlds establish contact with them. As the galaxy begins to rot, there
is perfect symbiosis between stars and worlds. Meanwhile the
"I" observes "the great snowstorm of many million galaxies."
A full telepathic exploration of the cosmos is now possible,
yet the "I" still remains a mystery to itself.

The scale increases. The "I" is now part of the cosmic mind,
listening to muttered thoughts of nebulae as it goes in quest of
the Star Maker itself. This Supreme Creator is eventually found,
star-like and remote. It repulses the raptures of the cosmic
mind. The created may love the creator but not vice versa,
since that would merely be self-love of a kind. This emphasis
that God is Not Love was bound to upset Christians such as
C. S. Lewis.

This encounter brings a sort of dream to the cosmic mind. In
the most fantastic part of the book, the cosmic mind visits
earlier models of the cosmos with which the young Star Maker
experimented, now cast aside like old video cassettes in a
cupboard. These are toy versions of the universe. They cannot
be detailed here; their place is exactly where Stapledon sets
them. Suffice it to say that one of these "toy" cosmoses consists of three linked universes which resemble a Christian vision
of the world. In the first of these universes, two spirits, one
"good" and one "evil" dice or play for possession of souls
of creatures. According to whether they are won or lost, the
souls plunge into the second or third linked universes, which
are eternal heavens or hells, and there experience either eternal
torment or eternal bliss of comprehension. We in our cosmos
retain a dim memory of this regime.

The range of cosmoses is continued, up the scale, as the Star
Maker's own skill and perception are improved by his models.
Perpetually and tragically he outgrows his creatures. Later cre-

ations show greater economy of effort than ours, but suffering
is always widespread. The creations pour on successively, until
the cosmic mind is fatigued; then it comes to the ultimate
cosmos.

Beyond that, the cosmic mind wakes from its "dream" and
understands that it has encountered the consciousness of the
Star Maker, which comprehends all lives in one timeless vision.
Such contemplation is its greatest goal.

The "I" now returns to Earth, is back in the present, may take
refuge in littleness. The man may go home to his wife. Yet
private happiness remains mocked by public calamity. The
world is faced with another crisis. All we can do is fight for
a little lucidity before ultimate darkness falls.

Time scales complete this magnificent and neurasthenic vision.

Not only is the vision in *Star Maker* wider than in *Last and
First Men;* it has become less coarse. Not only does a continuity
operate among its parts which is much more various than the
somewhat crude cause-and-effect which serves to perform
changes of scene in the earlier book, but a concomitant flexibility works through the prose itself. The personal viewpoint,
however attenuated it becomes, is a help in this respect, adding
a cohesion which *Last and First Men* lacks.

Last and First Men is just slightly an atheist's tract, based
largely on nineteenth-century thought, and in particular on
Winwood Reade's *Martyrdom of Man*. In *Star Maker,* the atheism has become a faith in itself, so that it inevitably approaches
higher religion, which is bodied forth on a genuinely new
twentieth-century perception of cosmology. It therefore marks
a great step forward in Stapledon's art, the thought unfolding
with little sense of strain through chapter after chapter. It is
magnificent. It is almost unbearable.

Stapledon also published several slightly more orthodox novels, of which mention need only be made of *Odd John* . . . and
Sirius. . . . *Odd John* is a pleasant superman tale, relating how
John grows up, experimenting with his special powers until he
discovers others of his kind and founds a community on a small
island in the Pacific. Although this small and somewhat crazy
utopia is eventually wiped out, the mood of the book is light
and cheerful. The histories of all the supermen are different,
and Stapledon clearly enjoys himself inventing past histories
for them. Since this is the nearest the author ever came to "a
good read," it is a suitable Stapledon for beginners, a vernal
hill before tackling the dizzy and formidable heights beyond.

Sirius is the most human of all Stapledon's novels, perhaps
because its central figure is a dog. Sirius is a sheep dog that
has the brain and consequently the perceptions of a man, although in other respects it remains dog. The product of a
scientific experiment, the dog gradually wins its independence.
The scientist who develops Sirius's intelligence exclaims, "I
feel as God ought to have felt towards Adam when Adam went
wrong—morally responsible." By this and references to Milton's poems, the theme of *Sirius* is linked to *Frankenstein*, as
another critic has observed.

Unlike Frankenstein's monster, the great dog is allowed a mate.
Its life is made tolerable by a reciprocated love for the girl
Plaxy. Love is a rare thing in Stapledon's work; here, reaching
across species, it finds its warmest and most touching expression, to live on even when the mutated dog is killed.

The ordinary clamour of human affairs, the rattle of coffee
spoons, the marrying and begetting, lie beyond Stapledon's

compass; yet this harried canine life, with its struggle for self-realisation on lonely hillsides, does grow to represent, as Fiedler declares, "the condition of all creatures, including ourselves" [see excerpt dated 1983].

These two novels are fine of their kind; the name of Olaf Stapledon would be remembered by them alone in the science fiction field, where memories are long. But *Last and First Men* and *Star Maker* soar far beyond the accepted limits of science fiction. Or rather, one might say, Stapledon is the great classical example, the cold pitch of perfection as he turns scientific concepts into vast ontological epic prose poems, the ultimate SF writer. In particular, *Star Maker* stands on that very remote shelf of books which contains huge foolhardy endeavours, carried out according to their author's ambitions: Hardy's *Dynasts* stands there, the writings of Sir Thomas Browne, C. M. Doughty's epic poems, and maybe Milton's *Paradise Lost.*

How it is that the funeral masons and morticians who work their preserving processes on Eng. Lit. have rejected Stapledon entirely from their critical incantations is a matter before which speculation falls fainting away. His prose is as lucid as his imagination is huge and frightening.

Star Maker is really the one great grey holy book of science fiction—perhaps after all there is something appropriate in its wonderful obscurity and neglect! (pp. 185-88)

> Brian W. Aldiss, "In the Clutches of the Zeitgeist: Mainly the Thirties," in his Trillion Year Spree, Atheneum, 1986, pp. 165-194.

ADDITIONAL BIBLIOGRAPHY

Bailey, K. V. "A Prized Harmony: Myth, Symbol and Dialectic in the Novels of Olaf Stapledon." *Foundation*, No. 15 (January 1979): 53-66.
> Finds the importance of Stapledon's works to lie in "Stapledon's ability to shape, from the large problems of human ethics, cosmic dramas shot through with overtones of myth; and, in doing this, to give novel form and imagery to certain universal archetypes."

Bengels, Barbara. "Olaf Stapledon's *Odd John* and *Sirius*: Ascent into Bestiality." *Foundation*, No. 9 (November 1975): 57-61.
> Notes extensive similarities of theme and technique in the novels but concludes that *Sirius* far surpasses *Odd John* in artistic achievement.

Crossley, Robert. "Famous Mythical Beasts: Olaf Stapledon and H. G. Wells." *The Georgia Review* XXXVI, No. 3 (Fall 1982): 619-35.
> Discusses the authors' personal relationship as revealed in their letters and explores affinities between their works.

———, ed. "The Letters of Olaf Stapledon and H. G. Wells, 1931-1942." In *Science Fiction Dialogues*, edited by Gary Wolfe, pp. 27-57. Chicago: Academy Chicago, 1982.
> Prints thirty-three previously unpublished letters, with an introductory essay and notes by Crossley.

Elkins, Charles. "The Worlds of Olaf Stapledon: Myth or Fiction?" *Mosaic* XIII, Nos. 3-4 (Spring-Summer 1980): 145-52.
> Argues against Stapledon's claim in the preface to *Last and First Men* that his goal is to achieve "neither mere history, nor mere fiction, but myth," by asserting that "a) Stapledon is not creating myth, and b) to the extent that he tries, his works violate some of the very assumptions upon which science fiction rests."

Glicksohn, Susan. "A City of Which the Stars Are Suburbs." In *SF: The Other Side of Realism*, edited by Thomas D. Clareson, pp. 334-47. Bowling Green, Ohio: Bowling Green University Popular Press, 1971.
> Examines how *Last and First Men* and Isaac Asimov's *Foundation Trilogy* "explore the universal question of the nature of human history in terms of the future of man."

Goodheart, Eugene. "Olaf Stapledon's *Last and First Men*." In *No Place Else: Explorations in Utopian and Dystopian Fiction*, edited by Eric S. Rabkin, Martin H. Greenberg, and Joseph D. Olander. Carbondale, Ill.: Southern Illinois University Press, 1983.
> Discusses the novel's utopian and dystopian elements, concluding that Stapledon's "stories are fertile sources of ideas about men, of interest to people of humanistic philosophical interests as well as to writers and readers of science fiction, but they are deficient in the fictional concreteness and stylish felicity which give authority to works of the imagination."

Huntington, John. "Olaf Stapledon and the Novel about the Future." *Contemporary Literature* 22, No. 3 (Summer 1981): 349-65.
> Discusses Stapledon's rendering of future history in *Last and First Men*, maintaining that he "developed a form that is unique in literature, one that manages to engage the future without defusing its potential for the unforeseen."

Mackey, Douglas A. "Science Fiction and Gnosticism." *The Missouri Review* VII, No. 2 (1984): 112-20.
> Cites *Star Maker* in a discussion of science fiction novels exhibiting principles of gnostic philosophy.

McCarthy, Patrick A. "*Last and First Men* as Miltonic Epic." *Science-Fiction Studies* 11, Part 3, No. 34 (1984): 244-52.
> Examines the ways in which *Last and First Men* resembles John Milton's *Paradise Lost* in "its narrative strategies and its emphasis on the reader's education," maintaining that such parallels "suggest that Stapledon intended his novel to be read in the tradition of the Miltonic epic."

Moskowitz, Sam. "Olaf Stapledon: Cosmic Philosopher." In his *Explorers of the Infinite: Shapers of Science Fiction*, pp. 261-77. Cleveland: World Publishing Co., 1963.
> Discusses Stapledon's works and their popular and critical reception.

———. "Olaf Stapledon: His Son, His Daughter, His Political Perceptions." *Fantasy Commentator* V, No. 3 (Fall 1985): 151-62, 175.
> Biography based on interviews with Stapledon's children, supplemented by a brief essay in which Moskowitz assesses what he considers Stapledon's "biased and parochial political opinions."

Priestley, J. B. "J. B. Priestley Confesses Himself Fascinated by These Literary Leg Pulls." *The Clarion* (2 June 1934).
> Calls *Last and First Men* "far and away the best book of this kind in our time . . . a masterpiece. . . ."

Science-Fiction Studies 9, Part 3, No. 28 (November 1982): 235-321.
> Essays by nine critics, including Eric Rabkin ("The Composite Fiction of Olaf Stapledon"), Amelia A. Rutledge ("*Star Maker*: The Agnostic Quest"), and Roy Arthur Swanson ("The Spiritual Factor in *Odd John* and *Sirius*").

Shelton, Robert. "The Mars-Begotten Men of Olaf Stapledon and H. G. Wells." *Science-Fiction Studies* 11, Part 1, No. 32 (March 1984): 1-14.
> Examines Stapledon and Wells's reciprocal literary debt, arguing that *Last and First Men* was influenced by Wells's *War of the Worlds* (1898) and in turn influenced Wells's *Star-Begotten* (1937).

Smith, Curtis C. "Olaf Stapledon: Saint and Revolutionary." *Extrapolation* 13, No. 1 (December 1971): 5-15.
> Maintains that Stapledon "shows us how to transcend the distinctions between literature, history, political science, philosophy, physics, and astronomy" in that his works synthesize "all knowledge until it becomes useful and comprehensible and can help man to extend his nature to new levels of perception."

————. "Horror Versus Tragedy: Mary Shelley's *Frankenstein* and Olaf Stapledon's *Sirius*." *Extrapolation* 26, No. 1 (Spring 1985): 66-73.

  Explores the novels' thematic similarities and philosophical differences, concluding that "Stapledon's work affirms a transcendent order" while "Shelley's gives us what Susan Sontag calls the imagination of disaster."

Tremaine, Louis. "Historical Consciousness in Stapledon and Malraux." *Science-Fiction Studies* 11, Part 2, No. 33 (July 1984): 130-38.

  Compares Stapledon's fiction with André Malraux's *La Condition humaine* (1933; *Man's Fate*) in order to disprove the view that Stapledon's works are primarily concerned with issues that lie beyond the realm of human history. Tremaine concludes that "we are . . . reading Stapledon's fictional work most accurately when we read it as the expression of a fundamentally historical, rather than mythic or pseudo-mythic, narrative consciousness."

Leon (Davidovich) Trotsky

1879-1940

(Also transliterated as Davydovich; also Trotski and Troskii; pseudonym of Lev Davidovich Bronstein; also wrote under pseudonyms of Antid Oto, Arbuzov, G. Gurov, Lvov, Lev N., O'Brien, Pero, Petr Petrovich, L. Takhotskii, L. Yanovskii, Your Old Man, and many others) Russian political philosopher, historian, essayist, biographer, critic, and diarist.

David King Collection, London

Considered the principal strategist of the Bolshevik Revolution, Trotsky was also a brilliant and influential political theorist who contributed thousands of essays, letters, and political tracts to the literature of Marxism. Described by Alfred Kazin as "the most brilliant, the most high-minded, the most cultivated of the Russian Communists," he was furthermore a highly regarded historian, biographer, and literary critic. As the foremost critic of Joseph Stalin—the leader of the Soviet Union from 1924 to 1953, whose brutally repressive policies resulted in the deaths of millions of Soviet citizens—Trotsky became a figure of violent international controversy: vilified by Marxists who considered his opposition to Stalin counterrevolutionary, he was conversely held as a symbol of revolutionary purity by those who were disillusioned with the growing totalitarian nature of the Soviet Union. The passions engendered by the public image of Trotsky have tended to obscure his contributions to political and cultural thought, contributions which place him among the seminal thinkers of the twentieth century.

Trotsky was born in Yanovka, a village in the Russian Ukraine. His parents were industrious Jewish farmers who had achieved a measure of prosperity unusual for Ukrainian peasants, and Trotsky later wrote that while his childhood was not a "sunny meadow," neither was it a "dark pit of hunger, violence, and misery." His formal education was undertaken in Odessa under the guidance of Mossoi Filipovich Spentzer, his mother's nephew, a journalist and publisher with whom Trotsky lived from the ages of nine to sixteen. Trotsky was strongly influenced by the intellectual atmosphere of the Spentzer home, where visitors frequently included authors, artists, and journalists, and Trotsky's biographers trace his lifelong fascination with the written word to his experiences there. For his final year of studies Trotsky transferred to a secondary school in Nikolayev, where he first came into contact with members of the Russian socialist movement and, as a result of their influence, developed an interest in political and social issues. Drawn into a radical discussion group whose members espoused a variety of socialist doctrines, Trotsky initially resisted the tenets of Marxism, maintaining that a philosophy based on economic determinism was an affront to human dignity. He instead became an ardent proponent of populism, a movement whose adherents maintained that socialism in Russia could be achieved through agrarian revolution and that enlightenment of the peasantry was therefore the proper task of the revolutionist. Within a year of his arrival in Nikolayev, Trotsky had instigated the establishment of the Southern Russian Workers' Union, a clandestine organization of approximately two hundred laborers and students dedicated to improving the life of the working class. The Union achieved widespread influence, largely through the circulation of leaflets written, illustrated, and printed by Trotsky in which factory conditions were publicized and abuses by employers and government officials were exposed. The group's success drew the attention of larger, more established socialist organizations as well as that of authorities, and in early 1898 Trotsky and his companions were arrested for engaging in subversive activity.

Trotsky was held in a series of prisons for the next two years before being sentenced to four years of exile in Siberia. During his imprisonment he read widely, debated with fellow inmates, and produced a steady stream of political essays and pamphlets for clandestine circulation among prisoners. In exile he studied works by such political theorists as Karl Marx and V. I. Lenin, and gradually underwent a conversion to Marxism. Through frequent contributions of social commentary and literary criticism to Siberian newspapers, he achieved a reputation as a brilliant analyst and prose stylist and rose to prominence in the growing Siberian socialist movement. His reputation eventually reached the Russian émigré community in Europe, and upon his escape from Siberia in 1902 Trotsky was directed by leaders of the Russian underground movement to report to London. There he joined the circle of exiled revolutionists, including Lenin, George Plekhanov, and Julius Martov, who formed the editorial board of *Iskra,* the newspaper of the Russian Social Democratic Party. Trotsky was set to work writing for *Iskra* and lecturing in France, Switzerland, and Belgium, and within months was an established member of the Social Democratic leadership.

At the Social Democratic party congress of 1903, however, the leadership diverged over a combination of personal antagonisms and doctrinal differences, initiating what would eventually become an irreconcilable split between two adversary factions: the Bolsheviks, led by Lenin, and the Mensheviks, led by Martov. Principal among their doctrinal differences was the issue of party organization. While Lenin sought to limit party membership to a small, tightly organized group of revolutionaries, Martov favored a broader membership, including liberals and sympathizers. Although Lenin attempted to convert Trotsky to the Bolshevik position on this and other issues, Trotsky sided with the Mensheviks, thus initiating more than a decade of estrangement and mutual recrimination between the two men, much of which would be used by Trotsky's enemies to discredit him later in his career. Trotsky elaborated his support for the Mensheviks in the pamphlet *Our Political Tasks,* in which he wrote: "Lenin's methods lead to this: the party organization at first substitutes itself for the party as a whole; then the Central Committee substitutes itself for the organization; and finally a single 'dictator' substitutes himself for the Central Committee." In this observation some historians have seen a remarkably prescient anticipation of the rise of Stalinism in the 1920s and 1930s. Despite his insightful defense of Menshevik policy, however, Trotsky's affiliation with Menshevism was also short-lived. In 1904 he broke with the group over fundamental philosophical differences, which were compounded by an insult Trotsky had suffered at the hands of the Menshevik leadership. According to biographer Isaac Deutscher, Trotsky "sulkily" left Menshevik headquarters in Geneva and disappeared from public view for several months, during which time he came under the influence of A. L. Helfland, a Russian-born German Marxist theoretician. During the period of their association, which lasted for several years, Helfland exerted a formative influence upon many of Trotsky's most characteristic ideas.

In St. Petersburg in January, 1905, government soldiers fired into a group of citizens who had gathered in front of the Winter Palace to petition Czar Nicholas II for civil and political rights. Over a hundred people were killed, precipitating nationwide turmoil. Trotsky returned to Russia almost immediately, where he conferred with leaders of local underground organizations and produced essays, letters, leaflets, and pamphlets propounding his views and advocating armed insurrection. Student demonstrations, peasant uprisings, and industrial strikes continued throughout the year, culminating in a general strike in October that brought Russian industry, transportation, and communications to a standstill and led to the formation of the first elective body to represent the Russian working class, the Council (or Soviet) of Workers' Deputies. According to Robert Wistrich, Trotsky became "the moving spirit behind the St. Petersburg Soviet" and "its most effective leader," drafting the council's resolutions, appeals, and manifestoes as well as arguing and lecturing on its behalf at every opportunity. The Soviet gained extraordinary authority among the citizenry, coordinating activity and usurping a variety of governmental functions during the chaos of the general strike, and secured from the government the promise of concessions including free speech, free assembly, and universal suffrage. In December, however, the leaders of the Soviet were arrested for fomenting insurrection. With the dissolution of the Soviet the government regained its authority among the populace, and, through a combination of concessions and the imposition of martial law,

restored order. After a lengthy trial Trotsky was again exiled to Siberia, but he escaped en route, and as the Russian revolutionary movement entered a period of dormancy, he returned to Europe.

Trotsky spent most of the next decade in Vienna, editing the revolutionary newspaper *Pravda* and contributing political journalism to the European press. Although he occasionally attempted to effect a reconciliation between the feuding Bolsheviks and Mensheviks, he remained independent of both factions and made frequent public attacks on what he considered their misguided policies, incurring as a result the mistrust and outright antagonism of other party leaders. His principal intellectual work during this period was the development of the theory of "permanent revolution," considered his most important contribution to Marxist thought. According to traditional Marxist doctrine, socialist revolution consists of two stages: the bourgeois-democratic revolution, in which an economically and politically powerful middle class overthrows an autocratic government, abolishes feudalism, and institutes a constitutional democracy; and a proletarian revolution, in which an increasingly powerful working class overthrows the bourgeoisie to institute communism. Trotsky argued that in economically backward societies such as Russia, the middle class lacks the power and motivation to conduct the bourgeois-democratic revolution. In Russia, therefore, the revolutionary role of the middle class would be assumed by the proletariat, which would be unwilling and unable to confine the revolution within the limits of bourgeois democracy. Thus, Trotsky wrote, "the democratic revolution goes over immediately into the socialist, and thereby becomes a *permanent* revolution." Trotsky added that the survival of such a revolutionary society would be dependent on economic support from abroad, and in the event that international proletarian revolution did not immediately follow the revolution in Russia and such economic assistance was as a result not forthcoming, the permanent revolution was bound to degenerate into reaction. This theory, which was strongly influenced by the ideas of Helfland, departed radically from accepted Marxist doctrine and was scorned by Russian radicals. However, as Irving Howe observes, after the Revolution "Lenin tacitly acknowledged the prescience of Trotsky's theory, and in retrospect it seems no exaggeration to add that of all the Marxists it was Trotsky who best foresaw the course of events in Russia."

Threatened with internment by the Austrian government upon the outbreak of World War I, Trotsky left Vienna and for the next few years resided in Switzerland, France, and the United States. As the war progressed, Russia's domestic situation became increasingly unstable. By 1917 a combination of war-weariness, food shortages, increased political repression, and governmental ineptitude in relieving tensions prompted widespread anti-government activism, leading in February to the precipitous overthrow of the Czar. In place of the monarchy two rival political bodies came into being: the Provisional Government, a council made up of prominent public figures that held nominal power, and the Workers' and Soldiers' Soviets, local councils made up of elected representatives of the people. The Provisional Government, insecure in its authority and lacking a unifying political philosophy, was irresolute and ineffectual, and furthermore was opposed on virtually every issue by the Soviets. As a result, the overthrow of the monarchy was rapidly followed by the disintegration of administrative institutions throughout the country, creating political, economic, and military chaos. Trotsky, Lenin, and other exiled revolutionists returned immediately to Russia in hopes of turning the situation to Marxist revolution. Within a few months the theoretical differences that had divided Lenin and Trotsky for over a decade were rendered insignificant by the practical exigencies of insurrection, and Trotsky joined the Bolshevik Party. In the following months he distinguished himself as the most brilliant popular spokesman of Bolshevism, described by his contemporary Anatoly Lunacharsky as "probably the greatest orator of our times," and gained influence over the masses that was unrivalled by any other leader. According to Menshevik N. N. Sukhanov, Trotsky "spoke everywhere simultaneously. Every worker and soldier at Petrograd knew him and listened to him. His influence on the masses and the leaders alike was overwhelming." In July Lenin was forced into hiding under suspicion of being a German spy, and Trotsky assumed de facto leadership of the Bolshevik Party. Two months later he was elected chairman of the Petrograd Soviet, the most powerful and most radical Soviet in the country, and in that capacity prepared the mechanics of insurrection, mobilizing pro-Bolshevik military regiments under the guise of defensive action against impending counterrevolutionary attack. Under his direction the Bolsheviks seized power in late October in a virtually bloodless coup.

In the government formed after the coup Trotsky was offered the chairmanship of the ruling Council of People's Commissars, but he declined the post, offering instead to become the new regime's press director. The chairmanship was assumed by Lenin, who also retained leadership of the Bolshevik Party, and Trotsky was eventually persuaded to serve as Commissar for Foreign Affairs. In this capacity he led the Soviet delegation in the Brest-Litovsk peace negotiations with Germany after World War I. Shortly thereafter, when civil war broke out in Russia between supporters and opponents of the Soviet regime, Trotsky became War Commissar, assuming command of an exhausted, demoralized, and rebellious army that had dwindled to less than ten thousand soldiers. In what historian E. H. Carr calls his supreme achievement, Trotsky rebuilt the Red Army to over five million men, restored order and discipline, and within two and a half years achieved victory over the anti-Bolshevik White Army.

In early 1922 Lenin suffered a paralytic stroke that necessitated his withdrawal from active leadership of the Party and the state and precipitated a bitter struggle for succession among Bolshevik leaders. Although Trotsky was considered by many to be Lenin's logical successor, his brilliance as a theoretician, orator, and strategist was offset by a notorious incapacity for practical politics and by testy personal relations with other party members. Lunacharsky noted in Trotsky "a tremendous imperiousness and a kind of inability or unwillingness to be at all caressing or attentive to people, an absence of that charm which always surrounded Lenin," and historians observe that this perceived arrogance made it impossible for Trotsky to build a broad base of support. His principal opponent, Joseph Stalin, was a gifted political tactician who succeeded through a series of strategic moves in gaining control of the rapidly expanding party bureaucracy while effectively discrediting Trotsky and undermining his influence among party members. In a barrage of speeches, articles, pamphlets, and letters written between 1923 and 1927 Stalin appealed for support to the numerous enemies Trotsky had made during his period of exile, often citing Trotsky's attacks on Lenin during those years and his deviations from Bolshevik doctrine as evidence of counterrevolutionary beliefs and intentions. Trotsky's most important theoretical writings of this period—*Novyi kurs (The New Course)* and *The Lessons of October*—provoked further attacks, con-

stituting as they did a denunciation of the party's growing conservatism and increasing abuse of bureaucratic power, an analysis which implicitly and explicitly indicted Stalin and his associates. According to Wistrich, there ensued upon the publication of the latter work an "onslaught against Trotsky that . . . was unprecedented in its tone of slander and open vilification of his Bolshevik credentials and revolutionary biography." Historians often note a curious unwillingness on Trotsky's part to defend himself against this assault. His friend and translator Max Eastman observes that Trotsky preferred instead to maintain dignified silence, stating on one occasion, "Why, this is not an argument, it is a personal attack. I can't reply to a thing like that." This passivity, combined with Trotsky's tendency to alienate potential supporters, rendered him helpless against Stalin's machinations, and between 1925 and 1927 he was systematically forced to relinquish his political responsibilities. In 1927 Trotsky and fifteen hundred other "Trotskyists" were expelled from the Bolshevik Party, and early the next year Trotsky was exiled to Central Asia.

Trotsky spent the next twelve years in exile in Central Asia, Turkey, France, Norway, and Mexico. Deprived of an active role in politics he turned to literature and during this period composed many of his most important works, including *Istoriya Russkoi Revolyutsii (The History of the Russian Revolution)* and *Moya zhizn (My Life)*. His principal works of political theory attacked Stalin's betrayal of a Marxist society and his promotion of a "parasitic" administrative elite that sought to stifle dissent and perpetuate its dominance. In *The Revolution Betrayed,* his major analysis of Stalinism, Trotsky argued that this bureaucratic deformation of the socialist state was the result of the delay in worldwide revolution. In an elaborate historical analogy he compared Stalinism to the Thermidorian phase of reaction that followed the French Revolution, and maintained that the complete restoration of bourgeois hegemony could only be averted by a popular workers' uprising. While praising Trotsky's critique of Stalinist society as penetrating and insightful, critics have taken issue with virtually every aspect of his analysis. Deutscher, among others, rejects Trotsky's Thermidorian analogy as historically untenable, maintaining that the comparison served "more to obfuscate minds than to enlighten them." Other commentators point out Trotsky's mistaken contention that Soviet society under Stalin was in a period of transition that would result in either a progression to socialism as envisioned by Marx or a regression to capitalism. According to Wistrich, "the possibility that the U.S.S.R. might continue to ossify or else undergo a mutation into some new hybrid form of despotism escaped him." Some critics fault Trotsky with failing to locate the basis of Stalinism in classical Marxist doctrine, while others attribute the phenomenon to the Bolshevik centralism that Trotsky had assailed before the Revolution but later failed to acknowledge as a possible factor in the rise of Soviet totalitarianism. Despite such criticism of various facets of Trotsky's inquiry, *The Revolution Betrayed* remains a highly-respected work of political analysis. Deutscher, who calls the study "Trotsky's political testament," maintains that "because of the wealth of its ideas and its imaginative force, this has been one of the seminal books of this century."

Trotsky considered his most important work during his final period of exile to be the formation of a Fourth International, a federation of socialist organizations dedicated to worldwide revolution that would supercede the Third (or Communist) International, which had fallen under Stalin's direction and had become solely an instrument of Russian foreign policy. However, the Fourth International never achieved more than a small, isolated membership. Stalin's assault on Trotsky's reputation during these years remained unmitigated, and in 1936 Trotsky was tried in absentia in the Soviet Union for treasonable acts including murder, conspiracy, and espionage. Although convicted in Soviet courts, Trotsky was found innocent of all charges by a Western commission of inquiry made up of independent scholars under the chairmanship of American philosopher John Dewey. In 1940 Trotsky was killed by a Stalinist assassin.

Despite his renown as a political leader, Trotsky considered himself primarily an author, commenting that at many times in his life he felt that the revolution was interfering with his literary work. His writings have been widely praised by both Marxist and non-Marxist critics, and the union in Trotsky of the man of letters and the man of action has been a topic of fascination for commentators. Dwight Macdonald, for example, has observed that "of Churchill one thinks, 'remarkable that a politician should write so well'; of Trotsky, 'remarkable that an intellectual should be so gifted in politics'." Trotsky's combination of literary talent and political acumen is particularly evident in his historical writings, foremost among which are *1905* and *The History of the Russian Revolution. 1905,* Trotsky's first major work, was written early in his career and completed before the development of many of his important political ideas. Critics note that as a result, the work is free of the sweeping theoretical generalizations that characterize his later historical writings: according to Howe, *1905* "is not so completely at the mercy of a grand ideological scheme" as *The History of the Russian Revolution,* written twenty-five years later. At the same time, *1905* anticipates the later work in its broad scope and in the lucidity and forcefulness with which it relates the events of 1905. *The History of the Russian Revolution* is considered both Trotsky's masterpiece and the greatest Marxist history ever written. Described by A. L. Rowse as "a kind of prose-epic of the Revolution," the work portrays on an enormous scale the action and interaction of masses and individuals in the months between February and December of 1917. Trotsky maintained that "the most indubitable feature of a revolution is the direct intervention of the masses in historic events," and although the *History* is dominated by a Marxist perspective, stressing throughout the inevitability of the Revolution, the author's analysis places as much emphasis on the dynamics of mass psychology as on the importance of economic factors. According to Rowse, the book's principal theme is "the gradual self-realization of the people under the pressure of revolutionary circumstances." Critics are unanimous in praising Trotsky's compelling narrative style and skillful portraiture in the *History;* however, no consensus exists as to Trotsky's success in achieving the dispassion necessary to a work of historical scholarship. George Vernadsky, among others, calls the work "an impassioned invective against [Trotsky's] enemies" that is "undeniably permeated by ill-suppressed bias." Trotsky, however, distinguished between "objectivity" and "impartiality," writing in the work's preface that he sought the former while disdaining the latter, and many critics agree that he succeeded in achieving intellectual honesty without sacrificing his commitment to a particular ideological perspective. According to Deutscher, in the *History* "extreme partisanship and scrupulously sober observation go hand in hand."

The question of Trotsky's objectivity is even more central to criticism of *Stalin,* a scathing analysis of Stalin's personality and rise to power that is the most controversial of Trotsky's biographical writings. Left unfinished at the time of Trotsky's

death, the manuscript was pieced together from the author's notes by editor Charles Malamuth and submitted for publication in 1941. According to Bertram Wolfe, Malamuth's version differed enough on crucial issues from Trotsky's known views that the author's literary executors threatened legal proceedings to prevent its publication. This proved unnecessary, however, as the manuscript was voluntarily withheld by the publisher at the behest of the United States government, which was at that time allied with Stalin's Russia in World War II. Upon its eventual appearance in 1946, the work was viciously received by many critics who considered it a malicious and unjustified attack on Stalin and Stalinism motivated solely by personal vindictiveness. Such critics as Robert H. McNeal, however, offer a contrasting assessment, asserting that "it is rather to be wondered that the polemical reaction of a leader so naturally proud and combative as Trotsky was so restrained, considering the provocation that Stalin gave him." Although Trotsky's intellectual integrity in this matter has several prominent defenders, even those critics who consider the biography an accurate depiction of Stalin's personality and career agree that *Stalin* is largely unsuccessful as a work of literature and of political interpretation.

Trotsky's other biographical and autobiographical writings are more highly regarded by critics. His first work in this genre, *O Lenine (On Lenin),* was hurriedly compiled and published within a few months of Lenin's death. Intended to serve as the basis of a full-scale biography, the book contains fragmentary personal reminiscences and episodes from Lenin's life. Of the planned biography, only the first volume was completed. Entitled *The Young Lenin,* the work has been widely praised for its sensitive and poetic portrayal of Lenin's childhood and youth. According to Warth, "for sheer writing ability nothing that he wrote excels this study of Lenin's development into a young revolutionary." The opening chapters of Trotsky's autobiography, *My Life,* have been similarly praised for their vivid evocation of childhood, earning favorable comparison to self-portraits by Leo Tolstoy and Maxim Gorky. The later chapters of the work, however, have been criticized for their concentration on political and public matters to the exclusion of Trotsky's inner and personal life. According to Howe, *My Life* "is neither quite a personal narrative nor a comprehensive public record but alternates with brilliant uncertainty between the two." In his *Diary in Exile,* a journal kept during his exile in France and Norway, Trotsky noted that the diary was likewise dominated by political commentary and literary criticism. "And how could it actually be otherwise?" he wrote. "For politics and literature constitute the essence of my personal life." According to Renato Poggioli, the reflections contained in the diary prove Trotsky to be "one of the outstanding prose writers of his nation and time" as well as "an excellent critic."

Poggioli's assessment is echoed by Howe, who maintains that had Trotsky "devoted himself systematically (or better yet, unsystematically) to literature, he might have become one of the great critics of the century." Trotsky's most important work of literary criticism, *Lituratura i revolyutsiya (Literature and Revolution),* comprises a survey of prominent Russian authors and a controversial theoretical essay. Central to the latter is a refutation of "proletarian art," a concept championed after the Revolution by a group of writers and artists intent on fostering art and literature informed by class consciousness and Marxist values. Trotsky maintained that "proletarian culture and art will never exist," arguing that the Russian Revolution "derives its historic significance and moral greatness from the fact that it lays the foundation for a classless society and for the first truly universal culture.'' His theories were strongly opposed by a variety of factions, most notably by Soviet officials who sought to control intellectual life through regulation of the arts and by literary groups who sought official endorsement for their particular doctrines. In the years preceding Trotsky's exile to Central Asia, his opponents cited these ''anti-proletarian'' views of art and culture as evidence of the fundamentally counterrevolutionary nature of his thought. Among Western critics, however, *Literature and Revolution* is praised for its wit, originality, and insight, and is generally considered the definitive exposition of Marxist literary theory.

Although the controversy surrounding Trotsky has subsided in the years since his death, few public figures of the century have inspired such intense emotions from both admirers and detractors. He continues to be denounced in the Soviet Union as the arch-heretic of Marxism, as well as by Western commentators antagonistic to communism who consider him a ruthless, or at best, misguided, revolutionary fanatic. At the same time, he remains a hero to Marxists who consider him the embodiment of classical Marxist thought, and his many-faceted career, brilliant writings, and tragic life have inspired adulation by Western intellectuals who see in Trotsky the perfect union of thought and action. Due to the complexity of Trotsky's life, thought, and character, commentators often find it difficult to discuss his ideas independently from his career and personality. Robert Wistrich, among others, finds this very complexity to be the source of Trotsky's importance. Maintaining that Trotsky's ''singularity of style was related both to his character and to the content of his political discourse,'' Wistrich writes that ''it is here, at the crossroads of politics and life, literature and revolution, abstract theory and human experience, historical dialectics and personal fate, that Trotsky's enduring significance resides.''

PRINCIPAL WORKS

Nashi politicheskiya zadachi   (essay)   1904
Itogi i perspektivy   (essay)   1906
   [*Results and Prospects* published in *''The Permanent Revolution'' and ''Results and Prospects,''* 1962]
Terrorizm i kommunizm   (essay)   1920
   [*Terrorism and Communism*, 1961]
1905   (history)   1922
   [*1905*, 1971]
Lituratura i revolyutsiya   (criticism)   1923
   [*Literature and Revolution*, 1925]
Novyi kurs   (essays)   1923
   [*The New Course*, 1943]
O Lenine: Materialy dla biografa   (biographical sketches) 1924
   [*Lenin*, 1925; also published as *On Lenin: Notes toward a Biography*, 1971]
1917. Uroki Oktyabrya.   (speeches and essays)   1924
   [*The Lessons of October, 1917* (partial translation), 1925]
Pyat let Kominterna   (history)   1924
   [*The First Five Years of the Communist International*. 2 vols., 1945-53]
Kuda idet Angliya?   (essay)   1925
   [*Where Is Britain Going?*, 1926]
Sochinenia. 12 vols.   (essays, history, political philosophy, biography, and criticism)   1925-27
Moya zhizn. 2 vols.   (autobiography)   1930
   [*My Life*, 1930]

Permanentnaya revolyutsia   (political philosophy)   1930
   [*The Permanent Revolution* published in *''The Permanent Revolution'' and ''Results and Prospects,''* 1962]
Istorlya Russkol Revolyutsll. 2 vols.   (history)   1931-33
   [*The History of the Russian Revolution*. 3 vols., 1932]
Nemetskaya revolutsia i Stalinskaya burokratiya   (essay) 1932
   [*What Next?*, 1932]
Stalinskaya shkola falsifikatsii   (nonfiction)   1932
   [*The Stalin School of Falsification*, 1937]
Vie de Lénine, jeunesse   (biography)   1936
   [*The Young Lenin*, 1972]
The Revolution Betrayed   (essay)   1937
Their Morals and Ours   (philosophy)   1939
Stalin: An Appraisal of the Man and His Influence
   (unfinished biography)   1941
Diary in Exile, 1935   (diary)   1958
The Trotsky Papers, 1917-22. 2 vols.   (nonfiction) 1964-71
Writings of Leon Trotsky, 1929-1940. 12 vols.   (essays, political philosophy, history, and biography)   1972-78

ANDRÉ BRETON   (essay date 1925)

[Breton was a French poet, prose writer, and critic who is best known as the founder of Surrealism. One of the most influential artistic schools of the twentieth century, the Surrealist movement began in 1924 with Breton's Manifeste du surrealisme. *Strongly influenced by the psychoanalytic theories of Sigmund Freud, the poetry of Arthur Rimbaud, and the post-World War I movement of Dada, Breton proposed radical changes in both the theory and methods of literature. He considered reason and logic as merely repressive functions of the conscious mind and sought to draw upon the subconscious through the use of automatic writing, a literary technique closely related to the psychoanalytic technique of free association. Breton's theories, however, reached far beyond the limits of literature; he considered Surrealist art a means of liberating one's consciousness from societal, moral, and religious constraints, thereby enriching and intensifying the experience of life. While Breton's creative works are considered by most critics to be uneven, his importance as a literary theorist is unquestioned. In the following excerpt, Breton praises* Lenin.]

[At] last we are able to learn a little about [the Russian revolutionaries]. Here are the men we hear slandered and presented as enemies of everything we deem worthwhile, as fomenters of who-knows-what worse utilitarian disaster than the one facing us. Here, disengaged from any political afterthoughts, they come before us in full humanity, addressing themselves to us no longer as impassive executors of a forever-inexhaustible will but as men arriving at their destiny, discovering themselves unexpectedly, speaking to us, questioning themselves. I renounce describing our impressions.

Trotsky recalls Lenin; he passes with such brilliant reason over so many troubles that it is as if a splendid storm had come to rest. Lenin, Trotsky: the simple enunciation of these names still makes heads turn and turn. Do they understand? Don't they understand? Those who do not understand furnish their homes as before. Trotsky offers them, ironically, a few items from a desk: Lenin's lamp, from the old *Iskra*, the unsigned articles he rewrote in the first person and later—at last, everything that makes up the blind accounting of history. And I find nothing lacking, either in grandeur or perfection. Ah!

Certainly these are not mere statesmen, basely policing the peoples of Europe, whom we find this time!

Thus the great revelation of this book, and I cannot insist upon it too much, is that many of the ideas dearest to us, and on which we take the liberty of making strictly dependent the particular moral sense we employ, do not condition our attitude regarding the essential significance we seem to give ourselves. On the moral plane on which we have resolved to situate ourselves Lenin seems absolutely unimpeachable. And if someone objects that in this book Lenin is a *type,* and that *"types are not men"* (Lautréamont), I ask: which of our barbaric rationalisers could have the impudence to insist that there is something reproachable in the general assessments Trotsky makes of others and himself? Which of them could continue to despise this man, unmoved by his perfect tone?

One must read the brilliant, the *just,* the definitive, the magnificent pages of refutation given over to Gorky's or Wells's accounts of Lenin. One must meditate at length on the chapter discussing a collection of children's writings about Lenin's life and death, entirely worthy of commentary, and on which the author focuses so fine and desperate a critique: "Lenin loved fishing. On warm days he would take his tackle to the riverbank and sit down, thinking of ways to improve the life of the workers and peasants."

Then long live Lenin! I salute Leon Trotsky, who could without recourse to most of the illusions remaining with us and *perhaps without, like us, believing in eternity,* maintain for our enthusiasm this invulnerable slogan: "Should the tocsin resound in the west—and it *will* resound—we will respond without hesitation and without tardiness even though we be up to our necks in calculations, in balance sheets, in the NEP. We are, we have been, we will remain, revolutionaries from head to toe." (pp. 30-1)

> André Breton, "Leon Trotsky's 'Lenin'," *translated by Stephen Schwartz, in his* What Is Surrealism? Selected Writings, *edited by Franklin Rosemont, Monad Press, 1978, pp. 28-31.*

JOHN MAYNARD KEYNES (essay date 1926)

[*One of the most influential economists of the twentieth century, Keynes was among the first to argue against the concept of laissez faire, the theory that government should not interfere in economic affairs. He outlined his views in* General Theory of Employment, Interest, and Money *(1936), in which he advocated government expenditure and a cheap money policy to counteract deflation and depression. Highly controversial at the time of its publication, the work eventually revolutionized the field of economics and became the basis of the monetary policies of nearly every free-market nation. In the following excerpt from a discussion of* Where Is Britain Going?, *originally written in 1926, Keynes criticizes Trotsky's advocacy of force as a means to power for the British labor movement.*]

A contemporary reviewing [*Where Is Britain Going?*] says: "He stammers out platitudes in the voice of a phonograph with a scratched record." I should guess that Trotsky dictated it. In its English dress it emerges in a turbid stream with a hectoring gurgle which is characteristic of modern revolutionary literature translated from the Russian. Its dogmatic tone about our affairs, where even the author's flashes of insight are clouded by his inevitable ignorance of what he is talking about, cannot commend it to an English reader. Yet there is a certain style

about Trotsky. A personality is visible through the distorting medium. And it is not all platitudes.

The book is, first of all, an attack on the official leaders of the British Labour Party because of their "religiosity," and because they believe that it is useful to prepare for Socialism without preparing for Revolution at the same time. Trotsky sees, what is probably true, that our Labour Party is the direct offspring of the radical non-conformists and the philanthropic bourgeois, without a tinge of atheism, blood, and revolution. Emotionally and intellectually, therefore, he finds them intensely unsympathetic. A short anthology will exhibit his state of mind:

> The doctrine of the leaders of the Labour Party is a kind of amalgam of Conservatism and Liberalism, partially adapted to the needs of trade unions.... The Liberal and semi-Liberal leaders of the Labour Party still think that the social revolution is the mournful privilege of the European Continent.

> "In the realm of feeling and conscience," MacDonald begins, "in the realm of spirit, Socialism forms the religion of service to the people." In these words is immediately betrayed the benevolent bourgeois, the left Liberal, who "serves" the people, coming to them from one side, or more truly from above. Such an approach has its roots entirely in the dim past, when the radical intelligentsia went to live in the working-class districts of London in order to carry on cultural and educational work.

> Together with theological literature, Fabianism is perhaps the most useless, and in any case the most boring form of verbal creation.... The cheaply optimistic Victorian epoch, when it seemed that to-morrow would be a little better than to-day, and the day after to-morrow still better than to-morrow, found its most finished expression in the Webbs, Snowden, MacDonald, and other Fabians.... These bombastic authorities, pedants, arrogant and ranting poltroons, systematically poison the Labour Movement, befog the consciousness of the proletariat, and paralyse its will.... The Fabians, the I.L.P.ers, the Conservative bureaucrats of the trade unions represent at the moment the most counter-revolutionary force in Great Britain, and perhaps of all the world's development.... Fabianism, MacDonaldism, Pacifism, is the chief rallying-point of British imperialism and of the European, if not the world, bourgeoisie. At any cost, these self-satisfied pedants, these gabbling eclectics, these sentimental careerists, these upstart liveried lackeys of the bourgeoisie, must be shown in their natural form to the workers. To reveal them as they are will mean their hopeless discrediting.

Well, that is how the gentlemen who so much alarm Mr. Winston Churchill strike the real article. And we must hope that the real article, having got it off his chest, feels better. How few words need changing, let the reader note, to permit the attribution of my anthology to the philo-fisticuffs of the right.

And the reason for this similarity is evident. Trotsky is concerned in these passages with an attitude towards public affairs, not with ultimate aims. He is just exhibiting the temper of the band of brigand-statesmen to whom Action means War, and who are irritated to fury by the atmosphere of sweet reasonableness, of charity, tolerance, and mercy in which, though the wind whistles in the East or in the South, Mr Baldwin and Lord Oxford and Mr MacDonald smoke the pipe of peace. "They smoke Peace where there should be no Peace," Fascists and Bolshevists cry in a chorus, "canting, imbecile emblems of decay, senility, and death, the antithesis of Life and the Life-Force which exist only in the spirit of merciless struggle." If only it was so easy! If only one could accomplish by roaring, whether roaring like a lion or like any sucking dove!

The roaring occupies the first half of Trotsky's book. The second half, which affords a summary exposition of his political philosophy, deserves a closer attention.

First proposition. The historical process necessitates the change-over to Socialism if civilisation is to be preserved. "Without a transfer to Socialism all our culture is threatened with decay and decomposition."

Second proposition. It is unthinkable that this change-over can come about by peaceful argument and voluntary surrender. Except in response to force, the possessing classes will surrender nothing. The strike is already a resort to force. "The class struggle is a continual sequence of open or masked forces, which are regulated in more or less degree by the State, which in turn represents the organised apparatus of force of the stronger of the antagonists, in other words, the ruling class." The hypothesis that the Labour Party will come into power by constitutional methods and will then "proceed to the business so cautiously, so tactfully, so intelligently, that the bourgeoisie will not feel any need for active opposition," is "facetious"—though this "is indeed the very rock-bottom hope of MacDonald and company."

Third proposition. Even if, sooner or later, the Labour Party achieve power by constitutional methods, *the reactionary parties will at once proceed to force.* The possessing classes will do lip-service to parliamentary methods so long as they are in control of the parliamentary machine, but if they are dislodged, then, Trotsky maintains, it is absurd to suppose that they will prove squeamish about a resort to force on their side. Suppose, he says, that a Labour majority in Parliament were to decide in the most legal fashion to confiscate the land without compensation, to put a heavy tax on capital, and to abolish the Crown and the House of Lords, "there cannot be the least doubt that the possessing classes will not submit without a struggle, the more so as all the police, judiciary, and military apparatus is entirely in their hands." Moreover, they control the banks and the whole system of social credit and the machinery of transport and trade, so that the daily food of London, including that of the Labour Government itself, depends on the great capitalist combines. It is obvious, Trotsky argues, that these terrific means of pressure "will be brought into action with frantic violence in order to dam the activity of the Labour Government, to paralyse its exertions, to frighten it, to effect cleavages in its parliamentary majority, and, finally, to cause a financial panic, provision difficulties, and lock-outs." To suppose, indeed, that the destiny of society is going to be determined by whether Labour achieves a parliamentary majority and not by the actual balance of material forces at the moment is an "enslavement to the fetishism of parliamentary arithmetic."

Fourth proposition. In view of all this, whilst it may be good strategy to aim also at constitutional power, it is silly not to organise on the basis that material force will be the determining factor in the end.

> In the revolutionary struggle only the greatest determination is of avail to strike the arms out of the hands of reaction, to limit the period of civil war, and to lessen the number of its victims. If this course be not taken it is better not to take to arms at all. If arms are not resorted to, it is impossible to organise a general strike; if the general strike is renounced, there can be no thought of any serious struggle.

Granted his assumption, much of Trotsky's argument is, I think, unanswerable. Nothing can be sillier than to *play* at revolution—if that is what he means. But what are his assumptions? He assumes that the moral and intellectual problems of the transformation of society have been already solved—that a plan exists, and that nothing remains except to put it into operation. He assumes further that society is divided into two parts—the proletariat who are converted to the plan, and the rest who for purely selfish reasons oppose it. He does not understand that no plan could win until it had first convinced many people, and that, if there really were a plan, it would draw support from many different quarters. He is so much occupied with means that he forgets to tell us what it is all for. If we pressed him, I suppose he would mention Marx. And there we will leave him with an echo of his own words—"together with theological literature, perhaps the most useless, and in any case the most boring form of verbal creation."

Trotsky's book must confirm us in our conviction of the uselessness, the empty-headedness of force at the present stage of human affairs. Force would settle nothing—no more in the class war than in the wars of nations or in the wars of religion. An understanding of the historical process, to which Trotsky is so fond of appealing, declares not for, but against, force at this juncture of things. We lack more than usual a coherent scheme of progress, a tangible ideal. All the political parties alike have their origins in past ideas and not in new ideas—and none more conspicuously so than the Marxists. It is not necessary to debate the subtleties of what justifies a man in promoting his gospel by force; for no one has a gospel. The next move is with the head, and fists must wait. (pp. 84-91)

John Maynard Keynes, "Trotsky on England," in his Essays in Biography, *Harcourt Brace Jovanovich, 1933, pp. 84-91.*

A. L. ROWSE (essay date 1933)

[*An English historian, poet, and critic, Rowse is the author of numerous studies of Elizabethan history and literature, many of which have been highly controversial for their untraditional approach to conventions of historical and literary scholarship. At the same time, Rowse's works have been praised for their lively prose style and exhaustive knowledge of social and political life in Elizabethan England. In the following excerpt, originally published in 1933, Rowse discusses Trotsky's analysis of the Revolution in* The History of the Russian Revolution *and praises the work's artistic and intellectual achievements.*]

Reading [*The History of the Russian Revolution*] through from beginning to end—in itself no mean task, for there are three volumes of it and some thirteen hundred outsize pages—one feels that there is some consolation for the loss of such ability to the Revolution in Russia, when it is devoted to a task like this and so triumphantly achieves its purpose. Trotsky as Commissar of War at this moment might hardly add much to his political record; while with this book he opens up another field of influence to himself—a field that is often more important than a man's achievement in actual politics. Bacon, as the author of the *Novum Organum* and the *New Atlantis,* was better occupied than as Lord Chancellor, though he did not appear to think so; and it is to political exile that we owe the *History of the Peloponnesian War* and Clarendon's *History of the Great Rebellion,* no less than *Paradise Lost* to political defeat.

It is more difficult to define what *kind* of a book this is. Mr. Max Eastman, its translator, claims that "this is the first time the scientific history of a great event has been written by a man who played a dominant part in it." There is no doubt about the "dominance," but more doubt about the "science." For the real claim of this book is not that it is an impersonal, a scientific history; though, indeed, it is a brilliant example of a very rare species, a history that is inspired by the conception of society and the forces at work in it, implied by historical materialism. This, in short, is *a* Marxist history, but not *the* Marxist history of the Revolution; for that we shall have to wait for some future Pokrovsky, altogether more impersonal, more objective; but, no doubt, that will be a much duller affair. Whereas this is alive and tingling in every nerve. It has all the brilliant qualities, and the defects, of its author's personality. It has extreme definiteness of outline, a relentlessness towards his enemies that goes with it, dramatic sense and visual power, a remarkable sympathy for the moods of the masses with a gift for vividly portraying them—the qualities we should expect from a great orator; and, in addition, the political understanding of a first-rate political figure.

It was noted by Macaulay how incomparably superior in the understanding of politics any political pamphlet of Swift's was to one of Johnson's; just because of the intimate contact of the former with politics, and hence his correct judgment of the forces that as a writer he was estimating. The same holds good of Trotsky as an historian. He may not be impartial (neither for that matter is anybody else); but what a political grasp is revealed on every page, in the chance remarks thrown out as he proceeds, compared with the laborious irrelevancies of academic historians. (pp. 274-75)

It was impossible to expect Trotsky to suppress his own personality in the book; not only for the reason that he is Trotsky, but because, after all, he played such an important part in the Revolution. To have suppressed himself would be a falsification of history. But he does go much further towards impersonality than one would have thought possible from one of his temperament. He writes throughout in the third person; he keeps himself in the background of the picture. The book gives an impression of a highly exciting personality, but not one of egoism; and, with one notable exception, it leaves an impression of fairness, at least not of unfairness. In the light of events he seems justified in his merciless characterisation of the Tsar and Tsarina, Miliukov, Kornilov, Kerensky, and many of the Socialists. The exception is, of course, Stalin.

It is a pity that his personal feud with Stalin has prevented him from recognising Stalin's part in the Revolution. Whenever he comes near the subject, the history tends to turn into a political pamphlet; and one is tempted to think that Trotsky writes history, as the celebrated Dr. Clifford was said to offer extemporary prayer, for the purpose of scarifying his enemies. (pp. 276-77)

That said, one can pay tribute to the extraordinary and original qualities of the work. It is a kind of prose-epic of the Revolution. The Revolution is Trotsky's hero, and he displays an attitude of reverence towards it, very proper when one considers the vastness of the subject and the profundity of its issues, and singularly appropriate in so irreverent a character as the author. It is as if the Revolution were the one great revelation of his life, a kind of beatific vision which it must be very exasperating to be withdrawn from, even such a distance as Prinkipo is from Odessa. His sympathy with the masses, remarkable in so impatient a person, is surprising in its reality and imaginativeness. It is easy enough when, as in the February Revolution, the masses are on the up grade, feeling their way forward, carrying the soldiers with them; he picks out vivid, significant little episodes of the "struggle of the workers for the soul of the soldiers," the fraternising of the men from the factories of the Vyborg district with the old and famous regiments quartered in the capital. But in the more difficult days of July, when the Bolsheviks were defeated and Lenin driven into hiding, when the workers and soldiers were stupid enough to believe the slanders that were sedulously propagated by the Provisional Government to the effect that Lenin and Trotsky were German agents, he still defends them. He argues that it was only a superficial change in the minds of the people; that if they "really did change their feelings and thoughts under the influence of accidental circumstances, then that mighty obedience to natural law which characterises the development of great revolutions would be inexplicable." That, he implies with a superb rationalism, is quite inadmissible; in one place, he speaks of the "insulted reason of history"—a phrase so revealing in its optimism. The deeper the masses are caught up in the revolutionary process, he claims, "the more confidently you can predict the sequence of its further stages." Only—and he gets out of the difficulty by adding—"you must remember that the political development of the masses proceeds not in the direct line, but in a complicated curve."

Yet one wonders a little whether he does not over-estimate the intelligence and the willed activity of the masses as such; whether he does not dramatise them too much, having seen them in action when stirred up from the depths and at the top of their form? But this has its good side; there is no facile scorn of the people; he calls even scepticism with regard to their latent potentialities for action, "cheap." And he is fundamentally right: he remembers the source of their ineptitudes and mistakes, when one is tempted to think of their consequences in their own suffering. Even when the dregs of the population, the criminal elements, see their chance and come out of their holes, he says a little pityingly, Here is the barbarism that the barbarism of the old order created! When one considers the horror of a régime run by a Rasputin, the weak and cold-blooded Byzantinism of the Court, the criminal levity of the aristocracy, the disasters, the corruption, the repression, was not the Tsardom but a "crowned hooliganism?" Nor is the judgment of the masses so blind and credulous as is so commonly supposed, he says. They have a shrewd idea of the factors affecting their own action, he remarks concerning the conviction of the people that the responsibility for the July clashes was that of patriotic provocateurs. "Where it is touched to the quick, it gathers facts and conjectures with a thousand eyes and ears, tests rumours by its own experience, selects some and rejects others. Where versions touching a mass movement are contradictory, those appropriated by the mass itself are nearest to the truth." He goes on to pour scorn on those historians typified by Taine, who, "in studying great popular movements ignore the voices of the street, and spend their time carefully collecting and sifting the empty gossip produced in drawing-rooms by moods of isolation and fear.'' True enough; but the moods and thoughts of the people themselves are the most difficult of all historical material to collect; up to now, theirs has been a silent contribution, though their fate is the burden of history. Will the Revolution bring freedom and consciousness to them? Trotsky, with the Communists, believes so: it is for them, the whole justification for Revolution, the reward of intolerable effort and no less intolerable suffering— the end that he calls *''the spiritualisation of the inert mass.''*

It must be said that artistically the book is completely successful in developing its theme, the gradual self-realisation of the people under the pressure of revolutionary circumstances. It is as if one watches the people coming alive, thawing after the long winter of repression, shaking themselves free from the unmeaning and frozen gestures of the ages. It is a progress from the old Russia, when on the outbreak of war the Tsar went to find strength in prayer at the shrines of the Kremlin, and the people kissed the ground he trod on; when the War Minister declared to the Duma, as the whole front was caving in, in 1915, ''I place my trust in the impenetrable spaces, impassable mud, and the mercy of St. Nicholas Mirlikisky, Protector of Holy Russia''; a progress to the dream that inspired the whole lives of Marx and Lenin, that all these millions of beings might realise themselves as concrete conscious selves.

Intellectually, it is no less successful in its formulations, though here there is more scope for variety of interpretation and some dispute. He analyses the Revolution down to its roots in the backwardness of Russian economic development as a whole, cheek-by-jowl with the most advanced and concentrated industrialism in and around Petrograd and Moscow, the two great revolutionary centres. (pp. 277-80)

One does not need to halt over Trotsky's characterisation of the old régime; like the image of the stricken tree, in which Swift saw the premonition of his own fate, it was dying from the top downwards. What is more curious to observe is that Trotsky, who like all Communists would deny the primary importance of ethical motives, is really shocked by the putrescence at the top. The Emperor, who was unmoved when hundreds of people were crushed to death at his coronation, when thousands were shot down unarmed in the streets in 1905, but who wrote on a report that a certain officer was executing soldiers without any trial, ''Ah, what a fine fellow''; the Empress, who right up to the end, against the remonstrances of all her own family, was pressing the Tsar for extreme measures: ''Anything but this responsible ministry about which everybody has gone crazy. People want to feel your hand. How long they have been saying to me for whole years, the same thing: Russia loves to feel the whip. That is *their* nature.'' Of the one, Trotsky writes: ''This orthodox Hessian, with a Windsor upbringing and a Byzantine crown on her head, not only 'incarnates' the Russian soul, but also organically despises it. This German woman adopted with a kind of cold fury all the traditions and romances of Russian medievalism, the most meagre and crude of all medievalisms, in that very period when the people were making mighty efforts to free themselves of it.'' Of the Tsar, he says: ''This 'charmer,' without will, without aim, without imagination, was more awful than all the tyrants of ancient and modern history.''

The real importance of Trotsky's *History* does not lie in his power of word-painting, either of character or scene; though indeed his gift is so brilliant and incisive that one is continually reminded of Carlyle. There is something of the same technique, the same mannerism even, in the way the rapid lights shift across the scene and particular odd episodes are brought out in singular sharpness of relief and made to bear general significance; something of the same difficulty in following the sequence of events—the lights are so blinding—one may add. But where Carlyle had but his magnificent powers of intuition to rely on, Trotsky has a theory of history at his command, which enables him to grasp what is significant and to relate

Photographs of Trotsky taken by Czarist police upon his first arrest in 1899.

355

things together. The same point can be illustrated more appositely by comparison with Winston Churchill's *The World Crisis*, for the two men are not dissimilar in character and gifts of mind. But here again one notices the difference; for Mr. Churchill's *History*, for all its personality, its vividness and vitality—points which it has in common with Trotsky—has not a philosophy of history behind it.

What distinguishes this work is the basic attempt Trotsky makes to define his subject, to make clear the methods appropriate to understanding it, and to see it in relation to the whole historical perspective opened up by Marxism. He states in his Preface: "The most indubitable feature of a revolution is the direct interference of the masses in historic events." He explains how, in normal times, when society is not shaken up from its foundations, the events that happen on the surface of society, more or less in political circles, come to be identified with the history of the whole society. A case of mistaken identity that is all very well in quiet times when the surface is not too unrepresentative of what is going on beneath, but is entirely inadequate in time of revolution, when the old order has become too atrophied for the forces that are boiling up underneath, and the masses break through its framework to create a new régime. "The history of a revolution is, then, first of all a history of the forcible entrance of the masses into the realm of rulership over their own destiny."

Trotsky explains that the changes that are brought about in the economic bases of society and in the social substratum of classes in the course of the revolution are not enough alone to explain its creative activity. There is nothing mechanical or schematic about the course of revolution: "The dynamic of revolutionary events is *directly* determined by swift, intense and passionate changes in the psychology of classes which have already formed themselves before the revolution." On the other hand, neither is the process a spontaneous one, a sort of spontaneous combustion, arising for no known reason out of no discernible circumstances, as liberal idealism would give one to suppose. No; the revolution has its own logic, which is part and parcel of the logic of history, dynamic, living, flexible, capable of innumerable variants, but not without reason. The swift changes in the views and moods of the masses, so characteristic of revolutionary epochs, do not take place in the void, nor are they unrelated to the economic and social conditions that provide the field in which they move and which limits their effective variation.

The Marxist view of history provides a satisfactory correlation of these two elements—a correlation so close as to form one many-sided but homogeneous process. The danger lies in separating out the various strands in the one process, for the purposes of historical exposition. Nor has Trotsky entirely escaped criticism from other Marxists on this account. He sees the danger in the purely psychological approach, "which looks upon the nature of events as an inter-weaving of the free activities of separate individuals and their groupings"; and describes his own approach as that of

> the materialist method which disciplines the historian, compelling him to take his departure from the weighty facts of the social structure. For us the fundamental forces of the historic process are classes; political parties rest upon them; ideas and slogans emerge as the small change of objective interests. The whole course of the investigation proceeds from the objective

to the subjective, from the social to the individual, from the fundamental to the incidental.

In the course of his treatment of the Revolution, his activism of temperament, perhaps also the fact that he was a participant in the action, leads him to put a stress upon the psychological factors that laid him open to the criticism of Pokrovsky on the score of idealism. Trotsky writes:

> The immediate causes of the events of a revolution are changes in the state of mind of the conflicting classes. The material relations of society merely define the channel within which these processes take place. . . . It is impossible to understand the real significance of a political party or find your way among the manoeuvres of the leaders, without searching out the deep molecular process in the mind of the mass.

Does not this give the process too idealist a cast of character? Granted that the historian must search out the molecular changes and adaptations going on in the minds of the masses—since these things are happening to men, not blocks of wood; yet the changes in the course of events are determined by changes in the external situation—by the economic collapse between February and October, for instance, by the shortage of food, by the impossibility of carrying on the government on the old social foundations, *i.e.* by the inner contradictions of the existing order. This is the ground of Pokrovsky's charge, who looks for the motive force of the Revolution to the objective shifts in society rather than to the mental processes of the masses.

The real problem is how to correlate the two; and it may be that Trotsky and Pokrovsky are not in such direct opposition as they supposed, that their views are complementary rather than antithetical, and that much of their controversy is simply due to their being at cross-purposes with one another. It is only to be expected that Trotsky, as an active participator in the events, would be altogether more activist in his sympathies and his interpretation than the Professor. The danger on the side of the Professor would be that of under-estimating the part played by the conscious and willed activity of the masses—a tinge, perhaps, of fatalism. Nevertheless, one is inclined to think that the Professor sees the whole thing in the better and more balanced historical perspective; Trotsky's book is above all things a guide to action; the Professor is more concerned with adding to knowledge. Yet it is a great strength of Trotsky's book that he never forgets that the figures behind these great events are human beings. "Let us not forget," he says, "that revolutions are accomplished through people, although they be nameless. Materialism does not ignore the feeling, thinking, acting man, but explains him."

This very activism is a great asset when he comes to estimating the role of parties in the Revolution, in particular that of the Bolshevik Party, and the importance of Lenin's leadership in it. He remarks at the outset:

> Only on the basis of a study of political processes in the masses themselves, can we understand the role of parties and leaders, whom we least of all are inclined to ignore. They constitute not an independent, but nevertheless a very important, element in the process. Without a guiding organisation the masses would dissipate like steam not enclosed in a piston-

box. But nevertheless what moves things is not the piston or the box, but the steam.

Later on, when he comes to the crucial question of what was Lenin's contribution to the Revolution, how it would have developed without his leadership, Trotsky's view wins our complete agreement; the question itself provides a kind of test of the satisfactoriness or not of his general historical conception. He emerges from it triumphantly, in one of the most memorable passages of the book . . . ; though, indeed, it is only a vulgar misconception of historical materialism—alas, one that is all too common—that supposes it to exclude all possibility of individuals influencing the course of events. Of course, they have some scope of influence; the point is to know *how far* they may influence events. They cannot transcend the field of conditions within which they are acting; they do not start with a clean slate, as historical idealists suppose, upon which they may write anything; they are bound and limited at every turn by the forces that exist in the field of their action. But to understand this, is itself the greatest aid to effective action that there can be. It was the fact that Lenin understood what was possible on this basis, that his whole mentality was guided by this outlook and method, that made him incomparably superior to any other leading figure in the field. (pp. 281-86)

How, then, would the Revolution have developed if Lenin had not reached Russia in 1917? Trotsky has no difficulty in allowing that the role of Lenin was one of decisive importance at that time; it was a case of the perfect conjunction of circumstances and the man. There is no question of the man creating possibilities that were not given in the situation; the situation itself was ripening for further stages in the development of the Revolution, and the leader and the party to take advantage of it were there. Trotsky sums up:

> If our exposition proves anything at all, it proves that Lenin was not a demiurge of the revolutionary process, that he merely entered into a chain of historic forces. But he was a great link in that chain. The dictatorship of the proletariat was to be inferred from the whole situation, but it had still to be established. It could not be established without a party. The party could fulfil its mission only after understanding it. For that Lenin was needed.

But without him, is it possible to say with certainty that the party would have found its road?

> We would by no means make bold to say that. The factor of time is decisive here, and it is difficult in retrospect to tell time historically. Dialectic materialism has nothing in common with fatalism. Without Lenin the crisis, which the opportunist leadership was inevitably bound to produce, would have assumed an extraordinarily sharp and protracted character. The conditions of war and revolution, however, would not allow the party a long period for fulfilling its mission. Thus it is by no means excluded that a disorientated and split party might have let slip the revolutionary opportunity for many years. The role of personality arises before us here on a truly gigantic scale. It is necessary only to understand that role cor-

rectly, taking personality as a link in the historic chain.

(pp. 287-88)

Trotsky's great work draws to an end on a subdued note in which it is not difficult to detect a certain scepticism, or perhaps one should say, philosophical acceptance of the world's ways. Was it, after all, worth all the sacrifice? something seems to whisper in the intermittences of the heart. His first attempt to answer these promptings does not satisfy. "It would be as well to ask in face of the difficulties and griefs of personal existence: Is it worth while to be born?" These melancholy reflections are, he thinks, in general, unimportant. Perhaps so; but they may be important for certain exceptional people—as they must have been for Lenin himself at some stage of his life, before his decision was irrevocably made. But in general, since these things have to be, the only reasonable course is to direct them into the best channels and to minimise the suffering they involve. The suffering involved might have been greater if October had never been; and it need never have been so great if other forces had not prolonged the struggle needlessly against the solution that history itself indicated. For these forces had only a dead end, a blind alley, to offer; whereas, through the October Revolution, the future was made possible, and not for Russia alone.

That seems to be the answer Trotsky and the Communists would make. Nor can we doubt that the October Revolution is the most important world event of our time; it has the significance for us that the French Revolution had for the nineteenth century. It is evidently necessary to know where we stand in relation to it; and to know this we have to understand it. In spite of the deluge of literature on the Revolution produced to delude fools, there is now a reliable literature growing up, on the basis of which we may judge; and in Trotsky's *History of the Russian Revolution* we have had the unbelievable good fortune of a work worthy of that great event. (pp. 289-90)

> A. L. Rowse, "An Epic of Revolution: Reflections on Trotsky's 'History'," in his The End of an Epoch: Reflections on Contemporary History, *Macmillan & Co. Ltd.*, 1947, pp. 274-90.

JOHN DEWEY (essay date 1938)

[*Dewey was one of the most celebrated American philosophers of the twentieth century and the leading philosopher of pragmatism after the death of William James. Like James's pragmatism, Dewey's philosophy, which he named "instrumentalism," was an action-oriented form of speculation which judged ideas by their practical results, especially in furthering human adaptation to the changing circumstances of existence. Dewey criticized the detached pursuit of truth for its own sake and advocated a philosophy with the specific aim of seeking improvements in human life. Much of Dewey's influence has been felt in the fields of education and political theory. In the following excerpt, originally published in 1938 in the journal* New International, *Dewey disputes Trotsky's view in* Their Morals and Ours *of the relationship between means and ends.*]

The relation of means and ends has long been an outstanding issue in morals. It has also been a burning issue in political theory and practice. Of late the discussion has centered about the later developments of Marxism in the U.S.S.R. The course of the Stalinists has been defended by many of his adherents in other countries on the ground that the purges and prosecutions, perhaps even with a certain amount of falsification, was necessary to maintain the alleged socialist regime of that country. Others have used the measures of the Stalinist bureaucracy to condemn the Marxist policy on the ground that the latter leads to such excesses as have occurred in the U.S.S.R. precisely because Marxism holds that the end justifies the means. Some of these critics have held that since Trotsky is also a Marxian he is committed to the same policy and consequently if he had been in power would also have felt bound to use any means whatever that seemed necessary to achieve the end involved in dictatorship by the proletariat.

The discussion has had at least one useful theoretical result. It has brought out into the open for the first time, as far as I am aware, an explicit discussion by a consistent Marxian on the relation of means and ends in social action [*Their Morals and Ours*]. . . . I propose to discuss this issue in the light of Mr. Trotsky's discussion of the interdependence of means and ends. Much of the earlier part of his essay does not, accordingly, enter into my discussion, though I may say that on the ground of *tu quoque* argument (suggested by the title) Trotsky has had no great difficulty in showing that some of his critics have acted in much the same way they attribute to him. Since Mr. Trotsky also indicates that the only alternative position to the idea that the end justifies the means is some form of absolutistic ethics based on the alleged deliverances of conscience, or a moral sense, or some brand of eternal truths, I wish to say that I write from a standpoint that rejects all such doctrines as definitely as does Mr. Trotsky himself, and that I hold that the end in the sense of consequences provides the only basis for moral ideas and action, and therefore provides the only justification that can be found for means employed.

The point I propose to consider is that brought up toward the end of Mr. Trotsky's discussion in the section headed "Dialectic Interdependence of Means and Ends." The following statement is basic: "A means can be justified only by its end. But the end in turn needs to be justified. From the Marxian point of view, which expresses the historic interests of the proletariat, the end is justified if it leads to increasing the power of man over nature and to the abolition of the power of man over man." . . . This increase of the power of man over nature, accompanying the abolition of the power of man over man, seems accordingly to be *the* end—that is, an end which does not need itself to be justified but which is the justification of the ends that are in turn means to it. It may also be added that others than Marxians might accept this formulation of *the* end and hold it expresses the moral interest of society—if not the historic interest—and not merely and exclusively that of the proletariat.

But for my present purpose, it is important to note that the word *"end"* is here used to cover two things—the final justifying end and ends that are themselves means to this final end. For while it is not said in so many words that some ends are but means, that proposition is certainly implied in the statement that some ends *"lead to* increasing the power of man over nature, *etc."* Mr. Trotsky goes on to explain that the principle that the end justifies the means does not mean that every means is permissible. "That is permissible, we answer, which really leads to the liberation of mankind."

Were the latter statement consistently adhered to and followed through it would be consistent with the sound principle of interdependence of means and end. Being in accord with it, it would lead to scrupulous examination of the means that are used, to ascertain what their actual objective consequences will be as far as it is humanly possible to tell—to show that they do "really" lead to the liberation of mankind. It is at this point

that the double significance of *end* becomes important. As far as it means consequences actually reached, it is clearly dependent upon means used, while measures in their capacity of means are dependent upon the end in the sense that they have to be viewed and judged on the ground of their actual objective results. On this basis, an *end-in-view* represents or is an *idea* of the final consequences, in case the idea is formed *on the ground of the means that are judged to be most likely to produce the end.* The end in view is thus itself a means for directing action—just as a man's *idea* of health to be attained or a house to be built is not identical with *end* in the sense of actual outcome but is a means for directing action to achieve that end.

Now what has given the maxim (and the practice it formulates) that the end justifies the means a bad name is that the end-in-view, the end professed and entertained (perhaps quite sincerely) justifies the use of certain means, and so justifies the latter that it is not necessary to examine what the actual consequences of the use of chosen means will be. An individual may hold, and quite sincerely as far as his personal opinion is concerned, that certain means will "really" lead to a professed and desired end. But the real question is not one of personal belief but of the objective grounds upon which it is held: namely, the consequences that will actually be produced by them. So when Mr. Trotsky says that "dialectical materialism knows no dualism between means and end," the natural interpretation is that he will recommend the use of means that can be shown by their own nature to lead to the liberation of mankind as an objective consequence.

One would expect, then, that with the idea of the liberation of mankind as the end-in-view, there would be an examination of *all* means that are likely to attain this end without any fixed preconception as to what they *must* be, and that every suggested means would be weighed and judged on the express ground of the consequences it is likely to produce.

But this is *not* the course adopted in Mr. Trotsky's further discussion. He says: "The liberating morality of the proletariat is of a revolutionary character. . . . It *deduces* a rule of conduct from the laws of the development of society, thus primarily from the class struggle, the law of all laws" (italics are mine). As if to leave no doubt of his meaning he says: "The end flows from the historical movement"—that of the class struggle. The principle of interdependence of means and end has thus disappeared or at least been submerged. For the choice of means is not decided upon on the ground of an independent examination of measures and policies with respect to their actual objective consequences. On the contrary, means are *"deduced"* from an independent source, an alleged law of history which is *the* law of all laws of social development. Nor does the logic of the case change if the word "alleged" is stricken out. For even so, it follows that means to be used are not derived from consideration of the end, the liberation of mankind, but from another outside source. The professed end— the end-in-view—the liberation of mankind, is thus subordinated to the class struggle as the means by which it is to be attained. Instead of *inter*dependence of means and end, the end is dependent upon the means but the means are not derived from the end. Since the class struggle is regarded as the *only* means that will reach the end, and since the view that it is the only means is reached deductively and not by an inductive examination of the means-consequences in their interdependence, the means, the class struggle, does not need to be critically examined with respect to its actual objective consequences. It is automatically absolved from all need for critical examination. If we are not back in the position that the *end-in-view* (as distinct from objective consequences) justifies the use of any means in line with the class struggle and that it justifies the neglect of all other means, I fail to understand the logic of Mr. Trotsky's position.

The position that I have indicated as that of genuine interdependence of means and ends does not automatically rule out class struggle as one means for attaining the end. But it does rule out the deductive method of arriving at it as a means, to say nothing of its being the *only* means. The selection of class struggle as a means has to be justified, on the ground of the interdependence of means and end, by an examination of actual consequences of its use, not deductively. Historical considerations are certainly relevant to this examination. But the assumption of a *fixed law* of social development is not relevant. It is as if a biologist or a physician were to assert that a certain law of biology which he accepts is so related to the end of health that the means of arriving at health—the only means—can be deduced from it, so that no further examination of biological phenomena is needed. The whole case is prejudged.

It is one thing to say that class struggle is a means of attaining the end of the liberation of mankind. It is a radically different thing to say that there is an absolute *law* of class struggle which determines the means to be used. For if it determines the means, it also determines the end—the actual consequence, and upon the principle of genuine interdependence of means and end it is arbitrary and subjective to say that that consequence will be the liberation of mankind. The liberation of mankind is the end to be striven for. In any legitimate sense of "moral," it is a moral end. No scientific law can determine a moral end save by deserting the principle of interdependence of means and end. A Marxian may sincerely believe that class struggle is *the* law of social development. But quite aside from the fact that the belief closes the doors to further examination of history—just as an assertion that the Newtonian laws are the final laws of physics would preclude further search for physical laws—it would not follow, even if it were *the* scientific law of history, that it is the means to the moral goal of the liberation of mankind. That it is such a means has to be shown not by "deduction" from a law but by examination of the actual relations of means and consequences; an examination in which, given the liberation of mankind as end, there is free and unprejudiced search for the means by which it can be attained.

One more consideration may be added about class struggle as a means. There are presumably several, perhaps many, different ways by means of which the class struggle may be carried on. How can a choice be made among these different ways except by examining their consequences in relation to the goal of liberation of mankind? The belief that a law of history determines the particular way in which the struggle is to be carried on certainly seems to tend toward a fanatical and even mystical devotion to use of certain ways of conducting the class struggle to the exclusion of all other ways of conducting it. I have no wish to go outside the theoretical question of the interdependence of means and ends, but it is conceivable that the course actually taken by the revolution in the U.S.S.R. becomes more explicable when it is noted that means were deduced from a supposed scientific law instead of being searched for and adopted on the ground of their relation to the moral end of the liberation of mankind.

The only conclusion I am able to reach is that in avoiding one kind of absolutism Mr. Trotsky has plunged into another kind of absolutism. There appears to be a curious transfer among orthodox Marxists of allegiance from the ideals of socialism and scientific *methods* of attaining them (scientific in the sense of being based on the objective relations of means and consequences) to the class struggle as the law of historical change. Deduction of ends set up, of means and attitudes, from this law as the primary thing makes all moral questions, that is, all questions of the end to be finally attained, meaningless. To be scientific about ends does not mean to read them out of laws, whether the laws are natural or social. Orthodox Marxism shares with orthodox religionism and with traditional idealism the belief that human ends are interwoven into the very texture and structure of existence—a conception inherited presumably from its Hegelian origin. (pp. 51-6)

John Dewey, "Means and Ends," in Their Morals and Ours: Marxist versus Liberal Views on Morality *by Leon Trotsky, John Dewey, and George Novack, Merit Publishers, 1969, pp. 51-6.*

DWIGHT MACDONALD (essay date 1940)

[*An American essayist and critic, Macdonald was a noted proponent of various radical causes from the mid-1930s until his death in 1982. Founder of the journal* Politics *(1944-49), which welcomed "all varieties of radical thought," he pursued Trotskyism, anarchism, pacifism, and anti-communism before eventually settling on "conservative anarchism"—a humanistic libertarian ethic in which Thoreauesque civil disobedience plays a prominent part—as his personal ethic. In the following excerpt, he discusses Trotsky's prose style and his theory of permanent revolution.*]

It would take a long article, and one that I hope some day will be written, to consider adequately Trotsky's literary style. It would be exaggerating to say that all of Trotsky's immense literary production—a critical bibliography is another need—is written in a great style. But a remarkable amount of it is. The adjective that comes first to every one's mind is "brilliant." His turn for witty characterizations is well known, as in his description of the late Morris Hillquit as "the ideal Socialist leader for successful dentists." Or his comment on Nazi racial theories: "Rejecting 'economic thought' as a base, National Socialism descends a stage lower—from economic materialism it appeals to zoologic materialism." His metaphors are daring. Only a supremely self-confident writer could carry off the figure with which he describes Lenin's attitude at the Finland Station: "Lenin endured the flood of eulogistic speeches like an impatient pedestrian waiting in the doorway for the rain to stop." He knew how to contrast the general and the particular, how to unite grand historical abstractions with homely details, often in one sentence, as when he writes of "The pauperization of the German petty bourgeoisie, barely covered by ties and socks of artificial silk. . . ."

The chief defect of his writing, in fact, is perhaps an excessive energy and ingenuity of expression, so that the style sometimes obscures the development of the thought. Individual paragraphs, sentences, and phrases, distract attention from the general design by their brilliant display. But whether obscured or not, the structure is usually there: the most casual of Trotsky's articles are distinguished from most products of leftwing journalism in that they are equipped with a beginning, a middle, and an end. Even in his testimony before the Dewey Commission this instinctive sense of form appears. And always, informing the style and raising it to a high level, the historical imagination is at work. Has any better characterization of fascism been made than Trotsky's summary, tossed off in a long-forgotten magazine article: "Fascism has opened up the depths of society for politics. Today, not only in peasant huts but also in the city skyscrapers there lives alongside of the twentieth century the tenth or the thirteenth. A hundred million people use electricity and still believe in the magic power of signs and exorcisms. What inexhaustible reserves they possess of darkness, ignorance and savagery!''

As a polemist, Trotsky had few if any equals. Bernard Shaw, a competent judge in such matters, awarded Trotsky the palm over Marx himself: "In everything but length of wind, the pupil surpasses the master. . . . Trotsky has a much better temper. Marx hit where he could and often hit spitefully; Trotsky does not hit below the belt.'' Shaw also noted "the gaiety of his controversial style.'' Although Trotsky at times was guilty of the sort of venomous, turgid abuse which has become, unhappily, part of the Marxist tradition—as in his attack last year on Serge and Souvarine—Shaw's appreciation is on the whole a just one. His polemical style is considerably more civilized than Lenin's: he does not try to strip his antagonist of all human dignity; he usually maintains an easy witty, even genial, tone; there is more of Voltaire about him than of Jeremiah. A certain gaiety is indeed a feature of his style, as in this characterization: "Bukharin's nature is such that he must always attach himself to something. . . . You must always keep your eye on him, or else he will succumb quite imperceptibly to the influence of some one directly opposed to you, as other people fall under an automobile.'' Lenin would have denounced Bukharin as a "renegade,'' and not once but many times. Trotsky's method is not only more effective, but it is also less open to abuse. To some extent he moderated—often not enough—and humanized the sharp, almost brutal tone of Marxist polemics, a tone that has by now become a real debit to the movement.

Trotsky's claim to greatness as a political thinker rests on a long series of books and pamphlets, stretching from his history of the 1905 revolution through his writings on the Chinese revolution, the march to power of German fascism, and the course of the French Popular Front, up to his culminating exposures of the Stalinist degeneration in *The Revolution Betrayed* and his writings on the Moscow Trials. For international scope, for brilliance, solidity, and sheer volume, this body of work has no parallel in the literature of Marxism. But perhaps the most spectacular demonstration of his powers was his conception of "the permanent revolution.''

When the young Trotsky—twenty-seven years old—came out in 1906 with his theory of "the permanent revolution,'' he was almost universally considered an ultra-left visionary. Yet his was a remarkable intellectual achievement: a decade before the 1917 revolution, he predicted both its occurrence and the way in which it might degenerate. Not only did he insist it would be a proletarian socialist revolution, but also that, once it was made, it would prove possible to create a socialist order in Russia only if similar revolutions in more advanced nations came to the aid of the Russian workers. If this did not happen, he predicted degeneration and reaction in Russia—a prophecy which needs little underlining today.

For his theory Trotsky received no support in either wing of the Russian Social Democracy. While differing radically on the form of state to be set up after the next revolution, the Bolsheviks and the Mensheviks agreed that it would be a middle-class democratic regime, which would not, could not abolish private property. It seemed logical that, after feudal Czarism had been overthrown, backward Russia would first have to go through a bourgeois democratic stage of evolution before it would be ripe for socialist revolution. Trotsky, however, insisted that precisely because Russia was so extremely backward the revolutionary tasks that would arise after the Czar's downfall would prove too enormous to be coped with by the weak Russian bourgeoisie within the framework of middle class property relations. Just as the "law of combined development'' had enabled such Russian big industry as there was to leap over all historical intervening stages and at one bound to reach a level of technology and concentration equal to the most advanced European industry, so the same law would operate in politics, and backward, primitive "holy Russia'' would overleap bourgeois democracy and make the transition in one mighty bound from feudalism to the dictatorship of the proletariat. It was a daring conception and it is not surprising that no one took it very seriously—until it happened.

When the 1917 revolution came, Lenin, who had fought Trotsky's permanent-revolution theory for years, quickly came to see it was correct and adopted it, while Trotsky, who had long opposed Lenin's organizational views, saw that Lenin had built the political instrument to make the revolution and at once joined the Bolshevik Party. (One wishes, indeed, that Trotsky, whose pre-1917 objections to the undemocratic, bureaucratic features of Leninism sound prophetic today, had not accepted Leninism so uncritically, had not tried to become the firmest of firm Bolsheviks.) When Lenin produced his famous "April Theses'' soon after his arrival in Russia, the Old Bolsheviks quite correctly scented in them more than a whiff of "Trotskyism.'' For a time Lenin was as isolated as Trotsky had been for years, and, like him, considered an ultra-left dreamer. But events moved fast, even the Old Bolsheviks saw the drift, Trotsky appeared on the scene and joined Lenin's party, and the two leaders went on together to organize and lead to victory the October revolution.

Now the other part of the "permanent revolution'' theory came into play. Trotsky never attempted to deny that Russia was too backward to maintain for very long a political form so advanced as the dictatorship of the proletariat. Therefore, the revolution must be "permanent'' in the sense of spreading into the more advanced European nations. Unless the newborn Soviet state could break through the chain of capitalist nations surrounding it and establish contact, on a socialist basis, with some more advanced European nation, the battle was lost. "Without direct political aid from the European proletariat,'' Trotsky had written in 1906, "the workingclass of Russia will not be able to retain its power and to turn its temporary supremacy into a permanent Socialist dictatorship.'' The Russian revolution must be the spark that lit the fires of world revolution. Failing this, the revolutionary regime would degenerate. Against this theory, also accepted by Lenin, Stalin later counterposed the conception of "building socialism in one country.'' History has tested these opposing theories, and the verdict is no longer in doubt. (pp. 345-49)

> *Dwight Macdonald, "Trotsky Is Dead: An Attempt at an Appreciation,'' in* Partisan Review, *Vol. VII, No. 5, September-October, 1940, pp. 339-53.*

BERTRAM D. WOLFE (essay date 1946)

[*Wolfe was an American historian and biographer and one of the founding members of the Communist Party in the United States. Although he wrote extensively on Spanish and Mexican history and culture, he is better known for his numerous studies of Marxism, Soviet history, and Soviet political figures. Foremost among these is* Three Who Made a Revolution *(1948), a biography of Lenin, Stalin, and Trotsky. In the following excerpt, Wolfe examines Trotsky's analysis in* Stalin *of his subject's personality and rise to power.*]

In all literature there is no more dramatic relation between author and subject than in this biography of Joseph Stalin by Leon Trotsky. It is like Robespierre doing a life of Fouché, Kurbsky of Ivan the Terrible, Muenzer of Martin Luther, Sathanas of the Archangel Michael . . . with the world still beset with controversy as to which was Prince of Heaven and which Lord of the Powers of Darkness.

The hero, or anti-hero, of this biography has already after his own fashion done a life of his biographer: in the purge trials; in the burning of a succession of official party histories and the ultimate dictating of his own; in the retroactive editing of his past and Trotsky's on a scale possible only to the master of a state which possesses a monopoly alike of the production and distribution of goods and of the production and distribution of ideas. In Stalin's history of the Party Trotsky is drawn as "Judas Iscariot" betraying Lenin, opposing the Revolution of 1917 with which he somehow got identified, attempting to surrender the new Soviet state to Germany early in 1918, directing the bullet which struck Lenin down later in the same year, trying his hardest to lose the Civil War, and thereafter engaging in "the betrayal of state secrets and the supply of information of an espionage character to foreign espionage services, the vile assassination of Kirov, acts of wrecking, diversion and explosions, the dastardly murder of Menzhinsky, Kuibyshev and Gorky—all these and similar villainies over a period of twenty years."

Trotsky's *Stalin* is only fully understandable when we bear in mind that it is Trotsky's rejoinder, his last word in defense of his own career and in indictment of his powerful antagonist. A good part of it is chapter and verse refutation of Stalin's official and originally anonymous *History of the Communist Party of the Soviet Union.* Many arid pages are devoted to a detailed re-examination of the actual record, a resurrection of suppressed and flouted documents, an interminable going over the lists of committees in charge of this and that to show that they did not always consist of Lenin and Stalin alone, that Stalin's name was as a rule not even in second place, that often it did not figure in the list at all.

"History is becoming clay in the hands of the potter," exclaims Trotsky. But how different would his tone have been, how much more scornful and devastating his invective, had he known that he was quarreling not with the will-less potter's wheel, but with the potter himself. If he had lived until January 20, 1946, he would have learned from the columns of *Pravda* that Stalin is himself the author of this strange work of historical falsification, endless self-quotation and self-glorification, and that the anonymous *History* first published in 1938 will soon appear as Volume XV of Joseph Stalin's sixteen-volume *Collected Works!*

Read thus together, both Stalin's *History* and Trotsky's biography of Stalin take on enormously more meaning, tension and intellectual excitement. Many an obscure passage, so trivial-seeming that one wondered why Stalin even put it into a book, suddenly reveals itself as a cover for something far from trivial. Those episodes and passages in which Stalin's undocumented assertions seem wildest and most nonsensical turn out to be the places in Trotsky's book where the documents speak most eloquently. Even as these two men were polar opposites bound to each other by antagonistic energies in a single, highly charged magnetic field, so their two books are inseparably bound together as polar complements of each other. (pp. 109-10)

Leon Trotsky was a born writer (his earliest underground name was *Pero*—the Russian word for "pen"), with a strong sense of literary form and a fastidious pride in every line he wrote. Doubtless he would have worked hard to make this book, so important to him, more nearly equal to his best. But, in any case, the finished portions betray that it would have sagged far below his masterpieces, *The Year 1905* and *The History of the Russian Revolution.* The completed chapters are inferior, too, to the finished portions of a life of Lenin, likewise interrupted by death. This *Stalin* is not done—to put it mildly—*con amore*, but as a disagreeable duty by one with an obvious distaste for the machinations and falsifications which he feels obliged to follow with such painful and painstaking detail. The very grossness of Stalin's invective has impelled Trotsky, himself an undoubted master of powerful invective, to assume an unwonted dry and colorless restraint. Moreover, he is haunted by the fear that the unthinking and unconcerned will attribute his book to hatred rather than desire to restore the erased outlines of historical truth.

At times grudgingly, at times freely, Trotsky concedes to Stalin whatever strong points he can: "indomitable will (a will that always immeasurably surpassed his intellectual powers); firmness of character and action; grit; stubbornness; and to a certain extent even his slyness . . . ruthlessness and conniving, attributes indispensable in the struggle" with an enemy class; "personal courage; cold persistence and practical common sense."

But the mainspring of Stalin's personality Trotsky finds to be "love of power, ambition, envy—active, never-slumbering envy of all who were more gifted, more powerful, of higher rank than he."

Trotsky proves from incontestable documents that up to 1917 Stalin was not regarded as a leader, hardly even on a provincial scale, but as a second-string lieutenant, "a small time propagandist and organizer"; that in the fateful year 1917 when all the other leaders "went around with cracked voices" from addressing mass-meetings Stalin proved lacking in the fire and eloquence to stir the people; that "he emerged from the Civil War as unknown and alien to the masses as he had from the October Revolution." Stalin's secret and spectacular rise to power, Trotsky maintains, "began only after it had become possible to harness the masses with the aid of the machine." Through it all Stalin remained "what he is to this day, a mediocrity, though not a nonentity," with an inherent political "caution" in making up his mind, an utter "lack of initiative, daring and originality . . . never anticipating anything, never running ahead of any one, preferring to measure ten times before cutting the cloth. Inside this revolutionist always lurked a conservative bureaucrat."

In this psychological analysis there are some major difficulties which Trotsky never succeeds in surmounting. How did this incurable "mediocrity" rise to the position of most powerful single individual on the face of the earth? This is a problem comparable to the one so many analysts of Hitler have left unsolved: after they have exhibited the Dictator of Berchtesgaden as ignorant, psychopathic, a mediocre misfit in private life, they are at a loss to explain what forces elevated such a man to leadership of a great and cultured nation. Trotsky rightly shifts his ground from the psychological to the sociological, but his sociological schemata hobble his analysis rather than guide it. As Trotsky sees it, "Thermidorean reaction" was inevitable in Russia unless its revolution spread to the West. Stalin was "the best possible expression of this bureaucratic conservative reaction" and his rise to power inevitable, too. ("Lenin's recovery could not, of course, have prevented the supersedure of the Revolution by the bureaucratic reaction. Krupskaya—Lenin's wife—had sound reasons for observing in 1926: 'If Volodya were alive he would be in prison now.'")

But how can one lead a struggle against reaction under the slogan that reaction is inevitable? How unleash the resources of moral condemnation upon a phenomenon as natural and unavoidable as an earthquake? Clearly it is one of the secrets of Trotsky's defeat in the struggle with his antagonist, as it is one of the deficiencies of the present book that its author's mind was paralyzed by this self-disarming dogma of "inevitability."

Akin to it is Trotsky's underestimation of the capacities of the man with whom he had to deal. Trotsky's Jewish heritage as a descendant of "the People of the Book"; his Marxist heritage as a disciple of the greatest sociological thinker of modern times; his literary heritage as a lover of the Russian tongue and master of the written word; his revolutionary heritage as the pre-eminent tribune of the people, able by flaming eloquence to stir the masses, hearten them to struggle, lift them outside their petty personal concerns to the level of action on the arena of history—all these combined to make Trotsky set the highest possible value upon ideas, originality and theoretical clarity in their formulation, exactness in their expression, eloquence in writing and in speech, contagious personal magnetism and attractive force. In these respects Stalin always was and remains to this day what Trotsky calls him: a gray and colorless mediocrity. But as the builder of a political machine, or, if not as builder, then as master of the art of winning such a machine once opportunity offered and of utilizing it for his purposes, as a manipulator of men and a master of the art of disposing of his forces, Stalin has had few equals. Certainly, Trotsky was not one of them. All his life, when he was apart from Lenin, he proved unable to build a machine. When he entered Lenin's machine, he had no talents for taking possession of it.

If he had lived until 1946, could he have continued to call the master of the greatest state machine in history a mere "mediocrity"? Could he have continued to insist that this dictator was "lacking in initiative, originality, and daring" and "ever prone to take the path of least resistance" while Stalin was surprising his hesitant, would-be allies by making a pact with Hitler to win without war a fifth of Europe; while he was contriving to hold the same gains with Allied sanction when Hitler had broken the pact; while, all through the war and the peace which followed, he was continuing to make gains and to face his Allies with a dizzying succession of audacious *faits accomplis*?

The central problem of this book and of Stalin's career is one which Trotsky repeatedly touches on, yet leaves unsolved. It is the problem of Stalin's relation to Lenin: to Lenin's, or we may properly say Lenin's and Trotsky's Revolution, and to Lenin's Party machine. "Stalin," writes Trotsky at one point, "represents a phenomenon utterly exceptional. He is neither a thinker, a writer nor an orator. He took possession of power not with the aid of personal qualities, but with the aid of an impersonal machine. And it was not he who created the machine but the machine that created him." What was there in that machine which could create a Stalin? The author nowhere in these pages asks the question clearly or clearly answers it.

Yet there was a time, back in 1904, when Trotsky rose to the heights of brilliant prophecy, and warned Lenin that the machine the latter was creating (undemocratic, centralized, ruled and directed from above, naming professional agents to run each local organization, which nominees would in turn assemble in convention to confirm the Central Committee which had named them)—that such a machine would inevitably breed personal dictatorship.

"The organization of the Party," warned Trotsky, "will take the place of the Party itself; the Central Committee will take the place of the organization; and finally, the dictator will take the place of the Central Committee."

Why is it that in the present book Trotsky nowhere ventures to recall this brilliant example of scientific prophecy, so painfully verified by history? There are moments when that insight hovers on the threshold of consciousness. "In this connection," writes Trotsky at one point, "it is rather tempting to draw the inference that future Stalinism was already rooted in Bolshevik centralism, or, more sweepingly, in the underground hierarchy of professional revolutionaries." *"Rather tempting"*—but Trotsky refuses to be tempted.

When Trotsky and Lenin joined forces in 1917, it was on the basis of a political *quid pro quo*. Trotsky accepted once for all Lenin's machine, and Lenin accepted Trotsky's conception of the nature of the Russian Revolution. As Trotsky accepted Lenin's undemocratic machine, Lenin accepted Trotsky's no less undemocratic idea, first formulated in 1905, that the Russian Revolution might dispense with democracy and leap right over to a minority dictatorship by a single minority party acting in the name of a minority class.

An undemocratic machine to seize power and make an undemocratic revolution! That combination contained a mighty potential for totalitarianism: for a one-party dictatorship which would drain the soviets of their political content as parliaments of the working class; for a Central Committee dictatorship which would drain the Party of its political content as forum for planning and discussion; for personal dictatorship which would drain the Central Committee of its political content as leading body of the Party. Even as Trotsky had predicted in 1904, so with the fatality of Greek tragedy did the drama unfold, until it ended for Trotsky with a pickaxe in the back of the brain.

But there was a complement to Trotsky's warning of 1904, a warning and prophecy uttered at the same time by Lenin against Trotsky's concept of an undemocratic revolution. Wrote Lenin against Trotsky in 1905:

"Whoever attempts to achieve socialism by any other route than that of political democracy will inevitably arrive at the most absurd and reactionary results, both political and economic."

Also a brilliant foreseeing! But in 1917, when Lenin accepted Trotsky's concept of the Russian Revolution and Trotsky accepted Lenin's concept of the Party machine, they compounded each other's errors and raised the totalitarian potential to the second power. There was a world war on, and both men had reason to hope that a spread of the Russian Revolution to all warring countries might save Russia from the consequences which each of them had foreseen by halves. But in place of the World Revolution . . . came Stalin! That is the real meaning of Trotsky's "inevitability." Like a cuttlefish in a cloud of ink he shies away from its implications wherever they suggest

Lenin and Trotsky in 1920. David King Collection, London.

themselves in these pages. For he approaches Stalin as a loyal Leninist and Bolshevist, which reduces him, despite his angry scorn, to a species of loyal opposition. He dare not subject Lenin's machine to a real re-examination, that machine which lent itself so easily to the "usurpation" of "the driver's seat" by a totalitarian dictator; which even "created" that dictator; which, once such a man was in the driver's seat, became the juggernaut we know. And he dare not re-examine the seizure of power by a minority party in the name of a minority class or a fraction of that class, in November 1917. Only with this in mind can we understand how he can still describe the Russian totalitarian state as "a workers' state" albeit with "monstrous bureaucratic distortions." Only thus can we understand why he says that state ownership of all property, of the means of production of goods and the means of production of ideas, ownership by the state of the food, the jobs, the bodies and the minds of its subjects, is still "a progressive force."

The real deficiency of this book lies in the unconscious limitations that Trotsky has put upon his task of re-examination of the work of a lifetime. Those limitations reduce him from the role of a genuine critic to the role of a pretender denouncing "a usurper."

As a psychological and personal study of the dictator who was "created by the machine" and of the stratagems by which he contrived to "usurp the driver's seat," Trotsky's *Stalin* is sometimes brilliant and at all points highly informative and revealing. No one who would understand the character and actions of the man who wields greater power than any other on earth today can afford to miss this book. But those who

would understand the most important problem of our time— the problem of democracy versus totalitarianism in a world that is moving everywhere towards greater collectivism and greater state intervention—will have to go beyond its pages. They provide only raw materials. For Trotsky is so contemptuous of democracy that he can think of nothing more devastating to say of the master totalitarian of today than this:

"A plebian democrat of the provincial type, armed with a rather primitive 'Marxist' doctrine—it was as such that he entered the revolutionary movement, and such in essence he remained to the very end. . . ." (pp. 112-16)

Bertram D. Wolfe, "Trotsky on Stalin," in American Mercury, *Vol. LXIII, No. 271, July, 1946, pp. 109-16.*

ROBERT D. WARTH   (essay date 1948)

[*Warth is an American educator, biographer, and historian specializing in the Soviet Union and the history of Marxism who has written biographies of Lenin, Stalin, and Trotsky. In the following excerpt Warth surveys Trotsky's literary career, focusing on literary technique and political analysis in* The History of the Russian Revolution.]

As a writer and speaker Trotsky was at his best. He overcame his early floridity of style and developed an unsurpassed ability for incisive oratory and pamphleteering, illuminated by sparkling insight and withering scorn. Trotsky's polemical prowess, of course, was an integral part of Trotsky, the professional revolutionist, and pervaded all his literary work. To speak of him as a historian, then, would seem contradictory to perhaps a majority of persons whose profession is writing or teaching history instead of fostering proletarian revolution and whose ideal historian is the "impartial" compiler of "facts" in a reasonably logical and coherent narrative. It is therefore not surprising that the historical craft as a whole has shown marked coolness toward Trotsky's chief work, *The History of the Russian Revolution,* as merely a superior variety of special pleading. The *History* is clearly his most significant achievement in historical writing although his unfinished life of Lenin showed promise of surpassing the earlier work. His posthumous life of Stalin, despite its pretensions as a scholarly study, is markedly inferior both in style and in erudition to these ostensibly nonpropagandistic works. Trotsky's other writings are of a different nature; in many cases they do not lack genuine merit as historical analysis, but their value in this respect is purely incidental to their purpose. (pp. 27-8)

During the Russian revolution of 1905 Trotsky emerged as the outstanding revolutionary leader. As vice-president, and then president, of the Soviet of Workers' Deputies he labored at a furious pace—speaking incessantly, writing for three radical papers, and drafting all the documents of the Soviet. With the failure of the revolution, the arrest of the members of the Soviet was inevitable. Trotsky spent a year in solitary confinement before being placed on trial. There he made a notable speech of defense, which he skilfully turned into an indictment of the regime. Again sentenced to Siberia, this time for life, he escaped before reaching his destination. The colorful details of his adventures form the basis of his booklet, *My Flight from Siberia.*

The long years of reaction following the unsuccessful revolution Trotsky spent in exile. He wandered over most of Europe during this period, speaking, writing, and editing various social democratic journals and in general plying his trade as an intellectual revolutionary. Drawing on his experiences in the 1905 revolution, he wrote a series of essays entitled *Summaries and Perspectives,* which still stands as one of the major works of Marxian literature. A searching diagnosis of the reasons for the failure of the revolution was offered, but more important was the first systematic presentation of his theory of "permanent revolution." By this theory Trotsky meant a world proletarian revolution, whose success was necessary before socialism would be feasible in Russia. The more orthodox Marxists also looked forward to world revolution but predicted that a revolution in Russia would necessarily be bourgeois in character and would yield to the proletariat only when Russia caught up industrially with the rest of Europe. Since Trotsky was correct in foreseeing a socialist Russian revolution, he always alluded with ill-concealed pride to this prediction whenever his opponents pointed out his Menshevik affiliation in contrast with the "true Marxism" of Lenin and Stalin; but in defending his theory Trotsky was also forced to defend the questionable thesis that Russian socialism hinged upon the world revolution. As the years rolled by and this great event did not occur, Trotsky, instead of abandoning his thesis, revived it with even added zest after his expulsion from the Soviet Union. He brought it up to date and gave it a more elaborate presentation in a book called *The Permanent Revolution.* If the world proletarian revolution had not arrived, he insisted, in effect, then it was the socialism of the Soviet Union which was defective, not the theory of permanent revolution. This doctrine remained Trotsky's main intellectual prop throughout his life and even today approaches holy writ as a guide for the faithful of the Fourth (Trotskyite) International.

The unexpected overthrow of the tsarist regime in March 1917 found Trotsky in New York, where he had lived for ten weeks following his expulsion from Europe. Upon hearing the news he left immediately for Russia but did not arrive there until May because of his detention at Halifax, Nova Scotia, by the British. Joining the Bolsheviks in July, he became known second only to Lenin as a leader of the November Revolution. Later, as the organizer and commander of the Red Army during the period of civil war and intervention, Trotsky achieved fame as a great military leader. His immediate experiences in the Bolshevik Revolution stimulated a number of pamphlets and articles, some of which have been collected along with Lenin's literary work of the period into a fairly complete narrative analysis of the Revolution. At the peace conference of Brest Litovsk, where Russia withdrew from the first World War, Trotsky was the leader of the Russian delegation, and there he wrote two brief sketches, *The History of the Russian Revolution to Brest-Litovsk* and *From October to Brest-Litovsk.* The former, despite its title, contains little on the Revolution after October. Designed for popular consumption as a justification of the Bolshevik Revolution, the two together present a lucid narrative of events from July 1917 to February 1918 relatively free from Marxian clichés and still useful for those who prefer their history in shorter and simpler doses than that contained in Trotsky's three-volume offering on the Revolution.

A year later, in the thick of civil war, Trotsky found time to pen a notable polemic against Karl Kautsky's *Communism and Terrorism,* which has usually been published under the title, *The Defense of Terrorism.* Kautsky was a German Marxist of a mild persuasion, and he denounced the ruthless conduct of the Bolsheviks. To this Trotsky replied with a scorching rejoinder on the bankruptcy of Kautskyism and the necessity of force to save the Revolution. It was obviously not Kautsky personally who aroused Trotsky's ire; rather, it was the point of view which Kautsky represented. The Marxists of western Europe had long since diverged from the tradition of uncompromising class warfare and had adapted themselves to the parliamentary procedures of bourgeois democracy. That most of these leaders should view the Bolsheviks with distaste and horror was only to be expected. Yet, though Trotsky was on solid ideological ground in flaying Kautsky and his school for passing off their brand of anemic socialism as the genuine article, his naïveté in explaining their conduct in terms of treason to socialist ideals is curiously unhistorical and even "unMarxian." From the historian's standpoint Trotsky's most important literary output stemming from his experiences in the civil war is his valuable collection of materials and documents on the history of the Red Army, *Kak voorzhalas Revolyutsiya* (**How the Revolution Armed Itself**), which will likely remain a mine of information to specialists on the period long after many of his other works are forgotten.

The death of Lenin in 1924 precipitated a struggle for power in which Stalin's ability as an organizer was exceeded only by Trotsky's ineptness as a practical politician. In the same year the state publishing house began printing a lengthy edition of Trotsky's collected writings and speeches. Later three of his better-known works appeared: some sketchy recollections of Lenin, a study of literature and aesthetics called *Literature and Revolution,* and the historic *Lessons of October.* The book on Lenin was meant to be a modest contribution to the source material on the great Bolshevik leader but contains fully as much on Trotsky and other leaders as upon Lenin and, in any case, little that Trotsky himself did not expound more fully in his autobiography. It does, however, avoid the controversial tone of the latter, covering mainly the *Iskra* period (1902-3) and the revolutionary period (1917-18) in a pleasant, gossipy style. *Literature and Revolution* is perhaps the best illustration of Trotsky's literary versatility. This book, one of the few Marxian studies of the subject, briefly and critically examines Russian literature, especially its contemporary trends, rejecting a narrow emphasis upon specifically ''proletarian'' writing.

Lessons of October was originally published as an introduction to a two-volume collection of Trotsky's writings on the Bolshevik Revolution. It is a short but masterly analysis of party tactics in 1917, ostensibly written for the purpose of examining, in a purely objective spirit, the mistakes of the party with a view toward insuring sounder strategy in future revolutionary situations. Kamenev and Zinoviev, two leading Bolsheviks who had come out openly against the November insurrection as too risky, are the scapegoats of the piece. Stalin is nowhere mentioned by name, but it is obvious that the author had him in mind in certain disparaging passages. After carefully refraining from any indication of his own position at the time, Trotsky permits himself a few concluding remarks to the effect that he and Lenin, as opposed to the ''Right Bolsheviks,'' were in fundamental agreement on every major question in 1917. Notwithstanding its cautious approach, *Lessons of October* was an attack which Stalin and his followers did not choose to ignore. The specter of ''Trotskyism,'' real or fancied, was conjured up, and from that date onward its perniciousness, despite the vigor of the exorcists, increased to such an extent that by 1938 it was on a par with ''fascism'' to Communists the world over. Thus the brochure has since assumed a significance out of all proportion to its intrinsic value and has been reprinted in many editions and languages under the auspices of various Trotskyite groups.

Trotsky was forced to accede—outwardly at least—to party discipline. A proposal to expel him from the party was vetoed by Stalin. To prove his orthodoxy, Trotsky wrote *Whither Russia?* in praise of the accomplishments of Soviet economic planning—the last of his writings favorable to the Soviet Union. The truce lasted only so long as he refrained from active political struggle, a feat which he was temperamentally incapable of continuing for long. Not until 1927, however, did his open hostility to the ''Stalinist bureaucracy'' break into channels which the Communist party leaders considered intolerable. One of his pamphlets, presenting the program of the opposition and later published under the title *The Real Situation in Russia,* circulated secretly in mimeographed form. Trotsky was then expelled from the party and in 1928 exiled to Alma Ata, Turkestan, near the Chinese frontier.

In Alma Ata his output of oppositional literature, mostly in the form of ''political letters,'' reached staggering proportions. Of these works the best known are *The Draft Program of the Communist International* and *What Now?* Their predominant theme was a denunciation of the party bureaucracy for its dictatorship and for its emphasis upon socialism in a single country instead of world revolution. This thesis became the basis of nearly all Trotsky's later writings against the Soviet Union. Since he refused to discontinue his politico-literary activities and recant, as had most of the other leading oppositionists, he was exiled to Turkey early in 1929. (pp. 29-32)

Until his assassination in 1940, under circumstances as yet uncertain, he lived the good life as he saw it—a martyred but active apostle of the world proletarian revolution. But the ''logic of events'' led him into an almost entirely negative revolutionary role. Criticism of the Soviet Union and a hatred for

Stalin which bordered on the paranoiac became his emotional outlet in a world in which the original enemy, capitalism, seemed to bend but never to break. As a writer Trotsky retained all his old crusading zeal, and, if anything, his productivity increased. An indefatigable contributor to Trotskyite journals the world over, he also upon occasion wrote for the capitalist press. Of his longer works in the decade of the thirties, *The Revolution Betrayed,* a comparatively temperate treatise, was by far the most popular of his anti-Soviet writings. Its relative success may be ascribed to the absence, save in general terms, of that continual wrangling over the finer points of Marxist dogma and Soviet policy, usually so prominent a part of his work. Surprisingly enough, in view of his conviction which forms the title of the book, he says some complimentary things about the industrial growth of the new Russia, and, in comparison with his remarks on the capitalist countries, one might almost infer from the opening chapter that he was a staunch, if critical, supporter of the Soviet state. But the tone changes gradually thereafter though never does it reach the bitterness of the views ordinarily associated with Trotsky. By means of a brief historical survey the reader is gently led into the brutal realities of the Stalinist regime and is shown how it has brought about a retreat from the socialist aims of Marx, Lenin, and, by implication, Trotsky. The broad critique of Soviet society presented from a leftist approach was a fresh and compelling one to many who were inclined to doubt the actuality of the communist utopia and who were at the same time repelled by the monotonous diatribes of the critics from the Right. It would not be far wrong to say that during the late 1930's *The Revolution Betrayed* was the bible of the anti-Soviet intellectuals.

With the exception of the first volume of his projected life of Lenin, Trotsky confined his later works almost entirely to direct or indirect attacks upon the Soviet Union. That so talented a conspirator would be content with a purely literary offensive is difficult to believe, but the true extent of his activity is as yet an unsolved and perhaps unsolvable question, although the Moscow trials of 1936, 1937, and 1938, after which scores of ''Trotskyites'' were executed or imprisoned for treason and sabotage, were predicated upon the assumption (and testimony of defendants) that Trotsky was the guiding genius behind the oppositionist campaign. Indeed, it is entirely possible, perhaps probable, that the Lenin biography was suspended to make way for more pressing propagandistic activity and that Trotsky had every intention of completing it. For sheer writing ability nothing that he wrote excels this study of Lenin's development into a young revolutionary. Trotsky approached his subject through a lengthy historical introduction, and, when he came to Lenin himself, it was rather through a wealth of family and other environmental influences than by a detailed recital of every event in Lenin's youth for which there happens to be a record.

Not nearly so happy an example of biographical skill was the aforementioned *Stalin,* a prolix and unwieldy study which was unfinished at Trotsky's death and remained unpublished during the war years in deference, very probably, to the wishes of the American state department. The defect of such a book is both obvious and inevitable. The essential question in Trotsky's case is how well he has managed to conceal his bias and not *if* he is biased. For a work intended to be serious, the perfunctory nature of Trotsky's pretense to objectivity is surprising. In contrast with the bitter rancor of the biography, the hostile treatment of Stalin in the history of the Revolution is calm and detached. But the Trotsky who in 1924 could describe his future enemy as ''a brave man and a sincere revolutionary'' was not the Trotsky of 1930-32 and the *History* and still less the Trotsky of 1940 and *Stalin.* One might explain away the occasional stylistic lapses, the tedious piling-up of detail on insignificant points, and even the questionable, if not dishonest, projection of unwarranted hypotheses to discredit Stalin (e.g., his alleged poisoning of Lenin) as defects which Trotsky would have corrected had he lived; but what cannot be so easily excused is an end product so consistently malevolent and without the saving grace of being at least interesting or significant. Compared, for instance, with Boris Souvarine's scarcely less hostile study of Stalin, the book is hopelessly dull. To all but the specialist in Soviet history Trotsky's *Stalin* seems slated for oblivion. That it possesses even this redeeming feature is due perhaps more to the fame of the author than to the content of his book.

When one looks at Trotsky's enormous literary output as a whole, it is readily apparent that his tremendous intellectual energy was permeated by Marxist ideology and channeled into the active struggle for proletarian revolution, whatever one may think of his methods or of his success in achieving his end. His reputation as a historian, however, does not necessarily stem from his fame as a revolutionary, though it cannot be denied that his *History of the Russian Revolution* blends first-rate history with skilful propaganda to such good purpose that only the absolutely "objective expert" could be expected to pry them apart. The combination of writer and maker of history is hardly an unknown one; but rarer is the feat of composing "a scientific history of a great event . . . by a man who played a dominant part in it." If one may legitimately doubt the "scientific" validity of any history, including Trotsky's, it seems reasonable enough to agree that "it is the first time a revolution was ever retraced and explained by one of its leaders" with the literary artistry and dramatic power that characterize *The History of the Russian Revolution.* Stylistically alone it is a work of major distinction. Heightened by the suspense inherent in a revolutionary situation, the *History* forms a compelling narrative of events from the fall of the tsarist monarchy to the victorious "congress of the soviet dictatorship" in December 1917. To enhance the atmosphere of suspense, Trotsky has adopted a staccato rhythm which is well maintained in short, clipped sentences, and he has written the noninterpretative aspects of his history largely in the present tense. His mastery of ironic phraseology, both subtle and harsh, has no superior. . . . The dry, stereotyped manner of exposition found in much Marxian literature, not excepting Trotsky's, is notable by its absence. The extensive quotations, so often the sign of sterile pedantry, are handled with such skill that they increase rather than retard the pace of the narrative. Trotsky's particular delight is to quote from an opposition source to drive home a point favorable to the Bolsheviks.

As for the mechanics of research, Trotsky has concealed them as a good historian should, but he overdoes it to the extent of completely avoiding the traditional trappings of the scholar—footnotes and bibliography—in order not to bother the general reader. This offense against professional historical standards is partially atoned for by frequent source citations in the body of the text and a few remarks in the introduction and appendixes. Since the sources he mentions are all well known and library facilities in Turkey were probably limited in their collection of Russian materials, it is highly doubtful that Trotsky came near to exhausting the sources dealing with the Russian Revolution. But it is equally doubtful that he would have wished to do so had they been available, for he is clearly no research historian painfully laboring at the task of putting his documents together with the proper literary mucilage. His forte is interpretative history and sociological generalization; the particulars are well enough known so that the specialist cannot quarrel with him except over minor points; and the layman, as always, must take the facts as given or not at all.

This does not mean that in this work Trotsky has generalized from his own experiences, camouflaging his memoirs with the story of the Revolution, however valuable such a study might be. That he had already done in part in his autobiography and in several of his political writings. On the contrary, in order to avoid bias, he has so ostentatiously subdued his own major role in the Revolution that it becomes almost a bias in the opposite direction. For instance, his use of the third person and quotation when speaking of himself as a historical figure is all the more conspicuous for its attempt at inconspicuousness. From his personal life we know that Trotsky was never a self-effacing personality, so his excessive modesty becomes rather suspicious under the circumstances. The suspicion is confirmed when the reader is left with the impression that this unassuming fellow, Trotsky, was the only Bolshevik besides Lenin to diagnose the revolutionary situation correctly and prescribe without hesitation the proper remedy—proletarian insurrection. But to accuse Trotsky of hypocrisy is to ignore the more probable explanation that he thought he was offering a sufficient correction to the quite human impulse to expand one's own importance and defend one's actions. After all, Trotsky had a great vested interest in the *History,* and the amazing thing about it is its lack of personal bias in view of the unusual temptation it must have offered for self-glorification.

The problem of objectivity in writing history is, of course, not confined to the personal element. One way of reducing the subjective aspect is to be as completely neutral (and therefore colorless?) as possible. Another way is to set up a standard of judgment and consciously to exclude or criticize the false and irrelevant according to this standard. Trotsky manifestly chose the latter course in the *History.* There was no other choice, for to write about the Russian Revolution as a neutral would have been a rejection of his lifework.

Revolution is one of the most controversial topics that the historian can discuss. As a historian who justifies a victorious revolution, Trotsky has an obvious advantage over the one who rejects it. The latter, placed on the defensive at the outset, appears to swim against the historical current by having to minimize the defects of the old regime and explain away its downfall as the work of demagogues and conspirators. But a revolution is not merely an armed uprising. The old order falls from within more than from without, because, as Trotsky says, "No economic regime . . . has ever disappeared before exhausting all its possibilities." In short, Trotsky makes no claims to a specious "impartiality," a pose on the part of some historians which he thinks is but a cloak for the reactionary. "The coefficient of subjectivism," he insists, "is defined, limited, and tested not so much by the temperament of the historian, as by the nature of his method." On the other hand, he does not reject the ideal of objectivity, proof of which must lie in "the inner logic of the narrative itself." For him the inner logic of the historic process is the class struggle, and "if episodes, testimonies, figures, quotations, fall in with the general pointing of the needle of his [the historian's] social analysis, then the reader has a most weighty guarantee of the scientific validity of his conclusion." While such a method can never guarantee scientific validity, there can be no denying that, if we accept his premises, Trotsky has fulfilled his task to a superlative degree. That most will not accept history on such terms is not in itself necessarily a reflection on the trustworthiness of the historian who does.

Trotsky's defects as a historian follow rather from the very ambiguity of his method. Though espousing the superiority of dialectical materialism as the key to history's secrets, he nevertheless has contradictions in his *History,* at times psychological and at times moralistic, which an orthodox Marxist must find hard to accept. These contradictions might well be praised as showing Trotsky's flexibility, his rejection of rigid dogmatism, in which case his materialist philosophy of history would have to be discarded. This he has refused to do. Yet he can condemn the Marxist historian, Pokrovsky, for a "vulgar" economic interpretation of history with the same assurance that he can glorify the Petrograd proletariat in semimystical terms. The Petrograd masses are, in a sense, the real heroes of his revolution, and Trotsky becomes so engrossed in the party maneuvers and psychology of this proletariat that at times the rest of Russia seems lost in the thickening web of intrigue in the capital city. His probable reply that as Paris was to the French Revolution so Petrograd was to the Russian Revolution is no excuse for a protracted exercise in social psychology while relatively slight attention is paid to important economic problems.

Trotsky's moralistic approach is most evident in his treatment of the many personalities who sully the pages of his book with their villainies and stupidities. They are perfect foils for his biting irony. The savage delight with which he baits them makes fascinating reading; the devastating autopsy which he performs upon their political corpses shows brilliant insight; and the brief character sketches present his style to perfection. For example, Trotsky describes Kerensky, the social revolutionary leader, as follows: "Kerensky was not a revolutionist; he merely hung around the revolution. . . . He had no theoretical preparation, no political schooling, no ability to think, no political will. The place of these qualities was occupied by a nimble susceptibility, an inflammable temperament, and that kind of eloquence which operates neither upon mind or will, but upon the nerves. His speeches in the Duma, couched in a spirit of declamatory radicalism which had no lack of occasions, gave Kerensky, if not popularity, at least a certain notoriety." Assuming that all Trotsky's judgments as to Kerensky and other leaders are correct does not sufficiently explain why he has dwelt at such length and ferocity upon persons, who, from a purely Marxist viewpoint, must be only the mediocre by-products of class struggle. But he cannot let them escape so easily. A personality, he admits, grows out of its historical environment, but "as a rose does not lose its fragrance because the natural scientist points out upon what ingredients of soil and atmosphere it is nourished, so an exposure of the social roots of a personality does not remove from it either its aroma or its foul smell." Trotsky thus considers it his moral obligation to remove the odor with a proper dose of ridicule. But to spend so much time on "foul smells" seems a dispensable luxury for a Marxist historian supposedly concerned with exposing the "social roots of a personality," in so far as he deals in personalities at all. In any case, if the Revolution were as inevitable as Trotsky pretends, why this concern over bankrupt aristocrats and vacuous bourgeois politicians, who are only defending their class interests in a perfectly predictable manner? It is hardly to be expected that they would jump on the Bolshevik band wagon, or be welcomed if they did.

In his portrayal of the Bolshevik leaders, Trotsky is not quite so sure that all are heroes as he is that all non-Bolsheviks are villains. This inconsistency within the larger inconsistency of

his treatment of the problem of personality in history may be accounted for partly by his hero-worship of Lenin and partly by his attitude toward the Soviet leaders at the time he wrote the passages. It may be that Lenin's exalted position in the story of the Revolution is due as much to Trotsky's desire to expose such leaders as Stalin, Zinoviev, and Kamenev as "compromisers" (i.e., those Bolsheviks who advocated collaboration with other parties in support of the bourgeois government) as it is to his genuine respect for Lenin. By the time Trotsky wrote his *History,* Leninism had already taken its place beside Marxism as an infallible guide for the right-thinking Bolshevik, so it is inevitable that both Stalinism and Trotskyism should justify themselves with appeals to higher authority. Of Trotsky's boundless admiration for Lenin there can be no doubt. When discussing the master, Trotsky seems almost willing to forgo his theoretical conviction that personality in history is secondary to material considerations. His best effort to resolve the dilemma is interesting but equivocal.

> Is it possible . . . to say confidently that the party without him [Lenin] would have found its road? We would by no means make so bold as to say that. The factor of time is decisive here, and it is difficult in retrospect to tell time historically. Dialectical materialism at any rate has nothing in common with fatalism. Without Lenin the crisis, which the opportunistic leadership was inevitably bound to produce, would have assumed an extraordinary [*sic*] sharp and protracted character. The conditions of war and revolution, however, would not allow the party a long period for fulfilling its mission. Thus it is by no means excluded that a disoriented and split party might have let slip the revolutionary opportunity for many years. The role of personality arises before us here on a truly gigantic scale. It is necesssary only to understand that role correctly, taking personality as a link in the historic chain.

After approaching the brink of Marxian heresy with these statements, he beats a hasty retreat with an additional paragraph on Lenin as a product of the "deepest roots" of the "whole past of Russian history." Trotsky by no means indicates that his understanding of the role of personality is equal to the task of placing Lenin correctly in the "historic chain." If Lenin as an individual can affect the Revolution to the extent that Trotsky suggests, it is difficult to see how a mere "link in the historic chain" can influence the rest of the chain in such an important manner.

Besides Lenin the only other Bolshevik who consistently appears to good advantage is Trotsky himself. His late arrival in the Bolshevik fold was always an embarrassing handicap in the struggle with Stalin, an "Old Bolshevik." To compensate for his belated conversion, Trotsky constantly sought to stress his orthodoxy in contrast to the vacillating attitude of the other party leaders. This is particularly noticeable in the *History,* even though his show of impartiality, as previously pointed out, makes it much less obvious. The minor Bolsheviks, none the less weak by the canons of Leninism, Trotsky generally praises. His quarrel is not with the "small fry" but with the Stalin-Zinoviev-Kamenev triumvirate. His treatment of these leaders is an instructive example of current prejudice being injected into past events, for Trotsky apparently had no animus against them in 1917. Zinoviev and Kamenev he treats with a cavalier contempt. . . . Together they represent the "blocking tendencies of the party, the moods of irresolution, the influence of petty bourgeois connection, and the pressure of the ruling classes." The pair present a sorry contrast, one is led to believe, to the brilliant leadership of Lenin and Trotsky.

Quite different is the portrayal accorded Stalin. Here Trotsky is cautious, weighs his words carefully, and avoids sweeping denunciation, for he knows that indiscriminate mudslinging will not further his cause. There is hatred for Stalin, and contempt too, but mingled with it is a curious respect that he cannot accord Zinoviev and Kamenev. Whereas they are weak through character defects, Stalin retreats and compromises through "narrowness of horizon and lack of creative imagination." Inscrutable, patient, "suspiciously cautious," he "retires into the shadow" to wait and "insure himself" against all possible contingencies. This, Trotsky thinks, is due to Stalin's background as a practical organizer and "political primitive." Without a "theoretical viewpoint" and a "knowledge of foreign languages," he was "inseparable from the Russian soil"; as a "practical" he was distinguished for "energy, persistence, and inventiveness in the matter of moves behind the scenes"; and, "uniting insistence with rudeness," he stubbornly defended his "practical conclusions." In many ways Trotsky's reaction to Stalin is that of a cosmopolitan intellectual who is forced to acknowledge in spite of himself that his boorish adversary has a certain primitive ability along nontheoretical lines. Trotsky is never willing to admit, though, that these abilities are not somehow tied in with backstage conspiracies and perennial plots against Lenin and the Revolution, in spite of Stalin's support of Lenin upon every crucial issue. Trotsky, the "dispassionate" Marxist historian, could never quite reconcile himself to Trotsky, the bitter anti-Stalinist. If he thought that Lenin brought the role of personality into history upon a "truly gigantic scale," what must he have thought of Stalin, against whom Trotsky based his whole later career? Here, indeed, is a personality, if we are to accept the reality of Trotskyism, so gigantic that his perfidiousness can change the course of history by discarding the essential meaning and program of the Russian Revolution. Had Trotsky been willing to analyze himself in accordance with his own canons of historical evolution, he must have come to the inescapable conclusion that Trotskyism, like the bourgeoisie during the Revolution, "was caught historically in a blind alley."

Throughout his *History* Trotsky successfully weaves a spell of inevitability about the Revolution which, unless resisted, drugs the unwary into a highly receptive mood for his ideas. By use of constantly repeated phrases like "objective necessity" and "the inner logic of events," by emphasizing the decadence and corruption of the old regime and its leaders, by stressing the irresistible surge of the masses, and especially by his hypnotic style, Trotsky makes the Revolution almost a living, breathing reality, prepared to engulf the world if only the Social Democratic hirelings of the capitalists had not checked it. The problem of explaining how a proletarian revolution developed in such a backward country as Russia without passing through a bourgeois capitalist stage appears to aid instead of to mar Trotsky's majestic panorama. He summons to his rescue a pair of universal historical principles which he designates as the "law of unevenness" and the "law of combined development." By the first he refers to the process by which retarded countries assimilate the culture, institutions, and technology of more advanced nations, thus making it possible to skip whole eras of normal historical evolution. By the second he means the combined presence within a backward country of the archaic

Soviet propaganda print of 1922 depicting Trotsky as a red lion destroying the forces of counterrevolution.

and modern. In order not to frighten us with unfamiliar concepts, he assures us that the "laws of history have nothing in common with a pedantic schematism." He then brandishes his dialectical weapons to demolish two rival theories of how Russia jumped over the capitalist period: (1) that Russia was a nation too unique to explain in terms of the European pattern of development and (2) that Russia was really a more advanced capitalist society than has been heretofore admitted. In demonstrating how the Revolution came about under the aegis of these laws, Trotsky is less than convincing. As simply a modest hypothesis to fit the prerevolutionary situation his analysis may be warranted, but as "universal law" the theory can no more be substantiated than any other well-reasoned explanation.

In spite of all his impressive appeals to historic necessity, Trotsky is never sure that the course of any particular revolution is subject to prediction. The key to the success or failure of a revolution is ultimately narrowed down for us anyway. "There is no doubt," he says, "that the fate of every revolution at a certain point is decided by a break in the disposition of the army." To find this point, then, is the problem. Instead of the usual materialistic doctrines, Trotsky invokes a weird pseudo-psychological approach: "The psychological moment when the soldiers go over to the revolution is prepared by a long molecular process. . . . In this process there are many elements imponderable or difficult to weigh, many cross-currents, collective suggestions and autosuggestions." Out of this confusing welter of "material and psychic forces," the sole clear certainty is that the soldiers will join the rebels only if they are convinced that this is real revolution and not just another demonstration. Trotsky then performs the not inconsiderable feat of narrowing the fate of the revolution down to the "decisive second" of the "critical minute" of the "critical hour of contact" in a street skirmish "between the pushing crowd and the soldiers who bar their way." The very pinnacle of suspense is reached when the officer commands his soldiers to fire on the crowd; the soldiers hesitate; the crowd pushes; "the officer points the barrel of his revolver at the most suspicious soldier." If the officer is forestalled by a shot from the crowd, then the revolution succeeds; if not, the revolution fails. Manifestly, this exposition is remarkable for its dramatic portrayal of revolution in microcosm; but if this is the difference between success or failure in revolution, it is truly an interpretation of the role of accident on a scale seldom before envisaged in the history of historical writing.

In the light of the foregoing scene, what can we make of Trotsky's assertion: "Revolutions take place according to certain laws. This does not mean that the masses in action are aware of the laws of revolution, but it does mean that the changes in mass consciousness are not accidental, but are subject to an objective necessity which is capable of theoretic explanation, and thus makes both prophecy and leadership possible"? For a specialist in the theory and practice of revolution, Trotsky's discussion of the general causes of revolution is meager and scattered. But what little he does say is usually consistent and agrees rather closely with the conclusions of most academic authorities on the problem.

If Trotsky had been willing to examine some of his theories and "laws" without his extreme penchant for literary imagery and historical analogy, the value of many of his sociological interpretations might have been greatly improved. The unfortunate crowd scene, for instance, may have been due more to Trotsky's tendency to allow his literary brilliance to overpower his judgment as a scholar than to any inherent weakness in his materialist philosophy. His use of purely literary analogy is usually most effective, as when he compares the Bolshevik party leadership to Napoleon's army.

> If we were to unfold on a screen the most brilliant of Napoleon's victories, the film would show us, side by side with genius, scope, ingenuity, heroism, also the irresolution of individual marshals, the confusion of generals unable to read the map, the stupidity of officers, and the panic of whole detachments, even down to the bowels relaxed with fright. This realistic document would only testify that the army of Napoleon consisted not of the automatons of legend, but of living Frenchmen born and brought up during the break between the two epochs. And the picture of human weakness would only the more plainly emphasize the grandeur of the whole.

When Trotsky uses historical analogy to bolster his generalizations on the Russian Revolution, however, the results are less fortunate. There are a great many spread throughout the work, and, while most historians would probably be willing to accept the validity of a large majority of them, the ones which are controversial or doubtful and the few which are clearly false tend to weaken the usefulness of the remainder. Comments on past revolutions, above all the French Revolution, form the bulk of these arguments by analogy. Easily the most powerful for its propagandistic value is the comparison of the Stalinist regime to the Thermidorian reaction of the French Revolution. Trotsky does not use Thermidor for this purpose in his *History*, but its utility was amply demonstrated in *The Revolution Betrayed, Stalin,* and other writings. That the analogy is completely misleading seems not to have dis-

couraged its extensive use by both Trotsky and his sympathizers.

If the defects which have been pointed out impair Trotsky's significance as a historian—and they undoubtedly do—they are obscured in his *History* by a sustained power of vivid narration and cogent historical interpretation which has seldom been equaled and almost never surpassed. A masterly chapter like "The Art of Insurrection," which prefaces the story of the November Revolution, is in itself enough to compensate for the errors which inevitably creep into every work of comparable scope. Though we cannot with any assurance second the enthusiastic panegyric of one prominent liberal critic [Kingsley Martin], who declared that Trotsky (assuming his facts to be correct) is to most historical writing as Gibbon is to the medieval chroniclers, we nevertheless do not believe it is too bold a prediction to make that *The History of the Russian Revolution* is likely to remain a classic of historical literature. (pp. 32-41)

> *Robert D. Warth, "Leon Trotsky: Writer and Historian," in* The Journal of Modern History, *Vol. XX, No. 1, March, 1948, pp. 27-41.*

RENATO POGGIOLI (essay date 1959)

[*Poggioli was an Italian-born American critic and translator. Much of his critical writing is concerned with Russian literature, including* The Poets of Russia: 1890-1930 *(1960), which is one of the most important examinations of this literary era. In the following excerpt, originally published in the* Yale Review *in 1959, Poggioli discusses Trotsky's* Diary in Exile.]

The most vivid and lurid personal drama of contemporary history is the struggle between Stalin and Trotsky, which for one of the two rivals ended in crime and triumph, for the other in death and defeat. Future historians will be bound to consider the winner as the protagonist of that drama, and the loser as its antagonist. On the other hand, the poets of the future, if attracted by such a theme, will reverse the roles and assign to Trotsky the major and nobler part. This is another way of saying that they will be tempted to see a tragic agony in that struggle, and a tragic hero in the character who lost the fight and paid for this failure with his head. From the viewpoint of the personalities involved, they will be right in doing so. But from a more universal viewpoint they will be wrong. Taking Hegel's definition as a norm, tragedy is the conflict between a higher and a lower law. Yet in that struggle or drama Stalin and Trotsky represented and upheld one and the same law; and it matters little that the former played the same role far more crudely than the latter. The tragic hero is such in public as well as in private terms: his personal catastrophe warns us of the evils which threaten the social fabric, or the condition of man. But those evils would have equally affected the destinies of Russia, as well as those of the West and of the whole world, even if Trotsky had won the fight instead of losing it. That is why the drama of his life and career may be viewed as a tragedy only if we look at it from the perspective of individual, rather than of general, values; if we treat it as a biographical accident, not as a historical event.

Nothing proves this point better than the only extant journal of Trotsky, which, significantly enough, he kept during the sixth year of what he himself called his "third exile," which was also to be the last. That exile had started in 1929 when, deported from Stalin's Russia, he had found his first refuge in Turkey; and it was to end in 1940 when, unprotected even in his Mexican sanctuary, he literally fell under the ax of Stalin's executioners. Trotsky wrote this diary for the most of 1935 or, more precisely, from February 7 to September 8. The period so covered coincided with the closing phase of his two-year stay in France and with the opening phase of his stay in Norway, which was to last for more than another year. In all, seven months: four of which were spent in the French provinces, in a little town near Grenoble, and three in the surroundings of Oslo, the Norwegian capital. Because of this shift from one residence to another, as well as the worsening of his health, Trotsky was far less faithful to the daily task of diary writing during the second half of this period of time: he failed, for instance, to enter a single notation in his journal for the whole month of August. (pp. 264-65)

The importance of this diary is to be seen not only in the great figure who wrote it, but also in the events which dictated most of its entries. 1935 was, in the life of Trotsky, as well as in the history of contemporary Europe, if not a crucial at least a critical year. Having risen to power two years before, Hitler was then rearming Germany, while the Western powers were already blindly developing their suicidal appeasement policies. Frightened by the riots and the armed leagues of the Right, France was reacting to the internal and external menace by establishing the Popular Front and by signing a treaty of friendship with Stalin. Soviet Russia was becoming fashionable and respectable abroad, and seemed to be willing to serve the cause of peace within the framework of the League of Nations. Yet at home Stalin was submitting the revolution to a bloody Thermidor, and was destroying his enemies in the merciless purges which followed in the wake of Kirov's assassination during the preceding year. Not content with hounding Trotsky's followers, Stalin was about to persecute the relatives whom the exiled leader had left in Soviet Russia, including his son Seryozha, who was to be arrested while the diary was being written. The journal reflects all this, as well as the aging and the ailing of the writer, his material hardships, and his sense of psychological estrangement and moral loneliness.

Yet the author seldom treats these pages as if they were the report of a personal ordeal, or the mirror of his own intimate self. In the opening lines he defines this journal as a kind of political *pis aller:* "The diary is not a literary form I am especially fond of; at the moment I would prefer the daily newspaper. But there is none available . . . Cut off from political action, I am obliged to resort to such ersatz journalism as a private diary." A month and a half later, realizing again that he had been keeping "a political and literary diary rather than a personal one," the writer observes: "And could it actually be otherwise? For politics and literature constitute in essence the content of my personal life. I need only take pen in hand and my thoughts of their own accord arrange themselves for *public* exposition." Unable to write polemical pieces or political leaders for a mass audience, Trotsky writes here his own journalism for himself, while becoming at the same time a critical reader of the journalism written by others. This is why he fills this diary with pasted clippings from many newspapers, all of them unfriendly ones. After all, such a man cannot fail to be deeply interested "in the working of the deeper social forces as they appear reflected" in what he calls, with an image probably taken from Gogol's epigraph to *The Inspector General,* "the crooked mirror of the press."

We may define as journalistic in the best sense all the polemical pages in which Trotsky expresses his judgments, opinions, and attitudes in regard to the current political situation in the West. His *bête noire* is Western socialism, especially in its French

version, so typically represented for him by such a figure as Léon Blum. Its alliance with the Third International and Moscow confirms Trotsky's view that Western socialism is the accomplice of both Stalinism and Fascism. To prove, almost *ad absurdum,* this view, Trotsky does not hesitate to cite no less an authority than his main enemy: "Stalin once delivered himself of an aphorism: Social Democracy and Fascism are twins! Nowadays it is Social Democracy and Stalinism—Blum and Cachin—that have become twins. They are doing everything in their power to ensure the victory of Fascism." A Western reader not committed to Marxist and Trotskyite ideology can hardly accept this judgment, or approve of the ferocity with which Trotsky treats Léon Blum; yet to blame Trotsky for this, one would have to forget all that happened in the years that followed, from Munich to the Nazi-Soviet Pact.

This is another way of saying that Trotsky seems to have sensed the turn of events: and this is enough to save the diary from becoming entirely dated, as such documents usually do. Since these pages are already so many years old, it is no wonder that many of Trotsky's observations have grown stale and meaningless. History has run faster than ever in the last quarter of a century, as we know all too well. Even Trotsky's foresight may occasionally fare all too badly when confronted with a hindsight for which we are still paying dearly. Yet, in the main, one could apply to Trotsky's predictions what Trotsky himself says of Engels' "prognoses," as he calls them: "Not infrequently they run ahead of the actual course of events." But, "In the last analysis Engels is always right." Thus Trotsky's claim that "the machinery of neo-Bonapartism *was* evident" already in that stage of the French crisis he was then witnessing, although hardly valid for the Third Republic and the France of 1935, suddenly seems to hold true for the France of 1958, for that Fourth Republic which is now dying under our own eyes. Right as he is in seeing the coming apocalypse, Trotsky seems, however, to be wrong in his expectation of the palingenesis that should accompany or follow it. Of his prophecy of the ultimate triumph of that Fourth International, this diary speaks surprisingly little except for saying: "The cause of the new International will move forward." Trotsky's International, the only one wholly composed of good Marxists, resembles a little that International wholly composed of decent people of which the meek old Jew Gedali dreams in Isaac Babel's *Red Cavalry;* and such a likeness may well reveal the messianic and utopian side of the thought of the man who was perhaps the last representative of scientific Marxism.

This, after all, is not so strange when we realize that Trotsky's mind was of the kind which sees the forest better than the trees. This holds particularly true in regard to his attitude toward Stalin and Stalinism. Trotsky perceives and apprehends the abstraction better than the concrete figure at the center of the phenomenon itself. If I say so, it is because it does honor to Trotsky rather than discredit. It is obvious that, if finally Trotsky yields to the belief that "the motive of *personal revenge* has always been a considerable factor in the repressive policies of Stalin," he does so reluctantly and against his best judgment. An all too direct experience prevents Trotsky from denying that Stalin is now running down not only the political associates but also the relatives whom his rival had been forced to leave within the tyrant's reach, and that their persecution cannot be fully explained on the grounds of political expediency alone. Yet as long as he can, Trotsky tries to interpret in pure Marxist terms the devious behavior of his adversary, what Trotsky himself calls Stalin's "mode of struggle," his habit of waging political warfare "on another plane" than the ideological one.

This does not mean that in his diary there is no *ad hominem* criticism of Stalin and his servants, but that such a criticism is found in only limited quantity. As far as Stalin is concerned, it varies from the statement, both indulgent and supercilious, that the latter "underestimated the danger of a struggle purely on the plane of ideas," to a lashing indictment of his intellectual cowardice and spiritual barbarism: "that savage fears ideas." Yet normally Trotsky prefers to affirm that, if Stalin behaves as he does, it is only because the economic and social reality he represents forces him to act in that, and no other, way. "The very possibility of such a mode of struggle," says Trotsky, "had been created for the formation and consolidation of an elaborate and self-sufficient social milieu—the Soviet bureaucracy." If Trotsky chooses such an explanation, it is because it is the one which, in the long run, does least violence to his most cherished intellectual beliefs. It is out of a deep loyalty to those beliefs that he compels himself to look at his own individual plight, even at the tragedy of his family, from a high, unimpassioned, and impersonal standpoint. It is only fair to say that, by transcending any private concern or human anguish, Trotsky succeeds in judging even his own personal enemy according to his own lights, and yet as objectively or, at least, as little subjectively as possible.

Although he fails to realize that the method he has chosen is perhaps ill suited to understanding the personality of Stalin, if not the social reality of Stalinism, Trotsky is well aware that the perspective he could not fail to adopt involves great risks on his part. He knows in advance that his attempt to judge Stalin objectively may well end by legitimizing Stalinism, by providing it with the august sanction of historical necessity. Yet Trotsky faces this danger squarely, and does not shirk the harsh intellectual duty of acknowledging that Stalin and Stalinism are something more than mere deviations or oddities in the march of socialism. He is even willing to admit that "in view of the prolonged decline in the international revolution the victory of the bureaucracy—and consequently of Stalinism—was foreordained." After all, if Trotsky had tried to explain Stalin differently, or to explain Stalinism away, he would have been left with only two alternatives, both unacceptable. The first would have been a purely moralistic rejection of the new Soviet order as an error and horror, as the wicked creation of a willful monster whom the whim of chance, rather than the dialectics of history, had unexpectedly placed at the revolution's helm. Trotsky does not lose any time in refuting such a hypothesis; he does so when he defines Stalin "as the half-conscious expression of the second chapter of the revolution, of its 'morning after.'"

By that significant adjective, Trotsky explicitly rejects the view that Stalin was the evil genius of the revolution, a view still held by so many disappointed party members, fellow travelers, and parlor pinks. Yet, in a sense, the man who is really "half-conscious" here is Trotsky himself. One may even claim that, while uttering that definition, Trotsky speaks unconsciously or subconsciously: beyond and behind the evident intention to refute the sentimental and pathetic view of the idealists of the revolution, who condemn Stalin as a monster, what inspires these words may well be the latent desire to refute the opposite view, held by all the cynics and the opportunists of the Left, which attribute Stalin's victory to the fact that, whether good or evil, he was a genius after all. It is obvious that Trotsky can accept this alternative hypothesis even less readily than the

other one. His whole personality, or at least his most intimate being, reacts against it. This is why, almost in the same passage, he denies that very hypothesis again: this time not unconsciously or obliquely, but directly and deliberately, in a straightforward statement and in clear-cut words. It is worth remarking that he does so by attacking all those who hold that hypothesis, not as cynical opportunists, as for the most part they were, but rather as ignorant dolts: "The result which the idle observers and fools attribute to the personal forcefulness of Stalin, or at least to his exceptional cunning, stemmed from causes lying deep in the dynamics of social forces."

Trotsky may grant Stalin and his henchmen everything except a single blessing: what is for him the supreme endowment, that is, intelligence. At the same time, while denying them any sense and understanding as individual beings, he is willing to bestow a kind of superior, if cynical, wisdom on the social group to which they belong, although that group embodies all that Trotsky stands against. That group, which Trotsky calls a caste, is identical with what Milovan Djilas was later to label "the new class." Trotsky, the first to indict the "new class," seems to have recognized in the earliest manifestations of its class-consciousness so much self-awareness as to amount to a kind of insight. After evoking a meeting of the Politboro where Molotov, Rudzutak, and others behaved toward him as uncouth boors, Trotsky concludes: "But that, of course, was not the main thing. Behind the ignorance, the narrowness, the obstinacy and hostility of separate individuals, one could almost feel with one's fingers the social features of a privileged caste, very sensitive, very perceptive, very enterprising in everything that concerned *its own interests*." Notwithstanding the closing words, inspired by the most orthodox historical materialism, and significantly italicized in the original text, the writer's willingness to find a meaningful and purposeful intelligence even in the forces which represent a negative phase in the historical process, in the very antithesis to the thesis he professes, seems to suggest that Trotsky thinks here more like a Hegelian than like a Marxist.

Trotsky goes so far in his attempt to deny Stalin any intelligent or independent policy, any freedom of action even in the most restricted sense, as to claim that the very decision to deport Trotsky had been suggested to Stalin by Trotsky himself. To this purpose he tells a story which sounds both improbable and true. The story refers to the visit a Soviet engineer paid to Trotsky during the latter's banishment to the Kazakh city of Alma-Ata. Despite all appearances to the contrary, Trotsky claims that the visitor was an agent sent by Stalin "to feel my pulse." Trotsky sees the proof of this in the visitor's query whether his host thought that a reconciliation between him and Stalin was still possible. Trotsky quotes himself as replying that "at that moment there could be no question of reconciliation, not because I *did not want it,* but because Stalin *could not make peace with me*." Trotsky reports that he closed his reply with the prophecy that the matter could only "come to a sticky end," since "Stalin cannot settle it any other way." He maintains not only that his answer to that question was conveyed to Stalin, but that it determined, rather than precipitated, Stalin's decision to exile him.

The story itself could be viewed as a petulant anecdote that Trotsky tells merely to argue that he knew Stalin's mind even better than Stalin himself. I think, however, that it should be treated as a significant apologue, the moral of which is that Trotsky was a man who would rather be right than be president: in his own case, general secretary of the Russian Communist

Party, rather than leader *ex officio* and *de facto* of the international revolutionary movement. What this telltale episode shows in effect is that Trotsky's *amour propre* led him to believe retrospectively that he had foretold, as well as accepted in advance, his own defeat. As such, it reveals a chink in Trotsky's armor; but the weakness so bared is a noble one. In a sense this story proves the moderation and the limits of Trotsky's *amour de soi*, and points out how impossible it would have been for him to yield for his own benefit to that "cult of personality" of which Stalin stood accused in the Khrushchev report. Trotsky was made of the stuff of the Robespierres rather than the Napoleons: he could not conceive of action as divorced from right, as long as it was the right of the revolution. Above all, Trotsky could not admit of power except as a weapon fashioned by intelligence to defend or uphold ideas, and to rule with them.

The lesson that the whole of this journal teaches us is that, although he rationalized defeat, Trotsky never sublimated it. It is this ability to accept political reality even when distasteful that explains why he prefers one image rather than another to suggest the role of the Marxist, of the revolutionary, of the Trotskyite himself. Here Trotsky rejects Max Eastman's metaphor of the revolutionary as an engineer, because it implies an all too mechanistic conception of both social reality and political action: and the scorn of such a rejection may be due to the fact that the same metaphor had wide currency even in Russia, where Stalin was then defining the Soviet writers as "engineers of the human soul." At least thrice in these pages Trotsky replaces that metaphor with his favorite image of the revolutionary as a doctor, which he develops so movingly in the passage where he likens the purge of his own followers in Soviet Russia to the killing of their medical helpers by ignorant peasants during the cholera epidemics which affected the Russia of the Tsars: "Distractedly the masses watch the brutal beating of the doctors, the only people who know both the disease and the cure."

The fitness of the image of the Marxist as doctor may be seen also in the ultimate indifference with which both look at the effects brought about by the laws of necessity—violence in history and death in the natural world. It is indeed with a sort of medical impassivity that Trotsky rehearses again in his mind the attitude he took once and for all when he learned for the first time of the slaughter of the Imperial family, which had been decided on in his absence, primarily by Lenin himself. Even in retrospect, Trotsky approves of that decision without reservation, justifying or, rather, explaining it with the following words: "The execution of the Tsar's family was needed not only in order to frighten, horrify, and dishearten the enemy, but also in order to shake up our own ranks, to show them that there was no turning back, that ahead lay either complete victory or complete ruin." Later he adds, as an afterthought, that judicial procedure would have made impossible the killing of the Tsar's children, which was, however, required by the terrorism of the act.

Up to this point Trotsky thinks and speaks like a practitioner willing to save his patient through the ordeal of surgery, at the cost of one of his organs or limbs. But at the end Trotsky acts more like the anatomist who has performed or watched an autopsy, and wants to forget all that bloody mess: "When I was abroad I read in *Poslednie Novosti* ["The Last News," a Russian emigré newspaper] a description of the shooting, the burning of the bodies, etc. How much of all this is true and how much is invented, I have not the least idea, since I was never curious about *how* the sentence was carried out and, frankly, do not understand such curiosity." Here Trotsky becomes inhuman. What makes him unable to understand such curiosity is his outright insensitivity to either one of the two psychological impulses which may motivate it: on one side, the pathological urge of morbidity; on the other, a moral or religious concern, a sense of piety and pity. Thus Trotsky fails not only to shed a single tear, but even to murmur a single word, on the grave of the Tsar's children, whom the revolution chose as guiltless sacrificial lambs. Unaware of any contradiction, blind to the tragic irony of his position, Trotsky refuses to pay such tribute of compassion at the very moment he is deeply worried about the destiny of his son Seryozha, the only member of his family who always avoided any political commitment or responsibility, and whom Stalin was then about to sacrifice as the scapegoat for his father, as the victim of both Stalinism and Trotskyism.

There is a striking contrast between Trotsky's reluctance to pay attention even to the negative side of Stalin's personality and the eagerness with which he emphasizes the most touching aspects of Lenin's psychology. He likes to catch Lenin in the moments he would "fall in love" with a fellow worker or any human being deserving his affection or respect; or while exhibiting a rare sensitivity, an exceptional delicacy of feeling, as he did when he sensed that Trotsky would feel uneasy entering the tragic Moscow of the fall of 1918 with the pots of flowers a bodyguard had ceremoniously put into his car. Yet, despite these tender touches, he paints a portrait of Lenin which tends to impress us with the heroic stature, with the monumental greatness, of its model. Nothing is more significant in this regard than the passage where he avows that Lenin was the only indispensable man for the triumph of October 1917. By doing so, Trotsky makes Lenin the peer of Marx, while putting himself only on a par with Engels. In an extraordinary passage he likens the task of the latter to the mission of Christ, who came to bring God the Father nearer to mortal men: "Alongside the Olympian Marx, Engels is more 'human,' more approachable." This comparison may well be read like an unconscious autobiographical allusion to the kind of role Trotsky liked to think he had played vis-à-vis Lenin himself.

At times, Trotsky's reminiscences of Lenin are almost hagiographic, in effect if not in intent. What is even more remarkable is that, in all his references to Madame Trotsky, of which this diary is so full, he employs the language of devotion and the imagery of mysticism. His wife is the only person seemingly endowed with what Trotsky unashamedly calls a soul: a soul which reveals itself through an enchanting voice, echoing the unique magic of its own "inner music." The noble and wild charm of her youth, which this journal recaptures in two splendid occasions, re-evoking Natasha while performing an acrobatic feat during a Parisian visit and while submitting with both humility and self-respect to the indignities attending an immigrant's landing in New York, seems to have survived unchanged through that old age which Trotsky defines as the worst of all vices. That charm endures because it is a spiritual gift, and if her husband is still able to see it, it is because he looks at her with the eyes of the spirit. Trotsky's affection for his wife is not a mere attachment, but a profound, genuine love. And the man experiencing it knows that love can utter only religious and sacramental words: it is nature, not convention, that makes love speak in such a holy and symbolic tongue, and no other.

It is both strange and wonderful that Trotsky finds it fit to compare the ordeal he and his wife are now undergoing to the tragic lot of the rebellious archpriest Avvakum and his faithful spouse. Avvakum was deported to Siberia for his refusal to accept the ecclesiastical and ritual reforms of Peter the Great. And it is with a grief so pure as to allow of neither self-pity nor self-irony that Trotsky quotes from Avvakum's autobiography the words which the old cleric once exchanged with the companion of his life, while marching together in the snows of the Siberian winter: "she, poor soul, began to reproach me, saying: 'How long, archpriest, is this suffering to be?' And I said, 'Markovna, unto our very death.' And she, with a sigh, answered: 'So be it, Petrovich, let us be getting on our way.'"

It is this courage and patience, the courage of Trotsky-Avvakum and the patience of Natasha-Markovana, which dictate the manifold testament that appears at the end of this book. In that document Trotsky reaffirms again with moving eloquence both his loyalty to the revolutionary ideal and his love for his wife. There he also faces unflinchingly the cruel vision of death. He knows that his end is near, although he expects it not from the hand of man, but from the hand of God. He even conceives the possibility of a violent death, which he however envisages as self-inflicted, in case he should be threatened "with a long-drawn-out invalidism" and with the loss of his mental powers. Yet, while thinking and writing thus, while staring in the very face of death, he can look at once with a loving eye at the green grass beneath, and at the blue sky above, the walls of that Mexican house which is both his fortress and his jail, and which will be his tomb. Yes, "life is beautiful," even then and there, despite present misery and imminent death.

Both testament and diary prove again that Trotsky is a first-rate author, one of the outstanding prose writers of his nation and time. He is not only this; he is also an excellent critic, as shown by his penetrating comments on the books he has been reading. No unfriendly judge of Soviet letters ever found anything better than his mocking definition of proletarian fiction, of the all too official and all too edifying products of "socialist realism," as "assembly-line romance." Although primarily interested in ideas, Trotsky shows himself in this diary also a shrewd observer of the human comedy, even of its most farcical side.

There is no doubt that his power as a writer rests on what one might call a sort of imaginative journalism: on his ability to be at once a vivid reporter and a visionary essayist. Those who will try to give a final assessment of Trotsky's contribution to literature will have to face the issue implied in such an attempt, which is the problematic and controversial question of the man of action as a writer. To make their task easier, they will do well to compare Trotsky with other leaders who wielded the pen no less successfully than the sword. The most obvious contemporary parallel is with a figure whom Trotsky would consider the strangest of all his possible bedfellows: Winston Churchill. The utility of such a juxtaposition would be to emphasize not so much their similarities as their differences. Besides many other differences, Trotsky is the one of the two who is an intellectual. Churchill is an aristocrat, even in the sense that he feels hardly at home among ideas: he prefers to dwell among traditions and values, among *beaux gestes* and high deeds. We can imagine Churchill painting a powerful, personal portrait of Clemenceau the Tiger; but we would hardly expect of him to draw from that portrait such a generalized inference as Trotsky does: "The main impediment that prevented Clemenceau—as well as many other French intellectuals—from advancing beyond radicalism was *rationalism.*" This diagnosis, far from being merely ideological, is a highly

philosophical one, revealing the cosmopolitan range and the cultivation of Trotsky's mind, his awareness of the famous antinomy which Kant bequeathed to Romantics and Hegelians, of the sharp distinction between classical Gallic intellect (*Verstand*) and modern Teutonic reason (*Vernunft*). In brief, all that Churchill has ever composed is monumental (even if the monuments so erected celebrate something higher than mere self), while everything Trotsky wrote, despite the conflicts of his nature and the contradictions of his temper, of which this diary is such an eloquent proof, is always *illuministic,* in the better sense of that term. (pp. 265-76)

Renato Poggioli, "'Trotsky's Diary in Exile'," in his The Spirit of the Letter: Essays in European Literature, Cambridge, Mass.: Harvard University Press, 1965, pp. 264-76.

ISAAC DEUTSCHER (essay date 1963)

[*Deutscher was a prominent Anglo-Polish journalist, biographer, and historian. Active in the Polish Communist Party from the age of nineteen, he was expelled from the Party in 1932 for his activities as leader of the anti-Stalinist opposition in Poland. Throughout his life Deutscher opposed Stalin's policies while remaining an "unrepentant Marxist and socialist," and his numerous studies of Soviet political history reflect these convictions. Although non-Marxist commentators often criticize Deutscher's works for their leftist ideological perspective and Marxist critics frequently take issue with aspects of his Marxism, scholars are nearly unanimous in their praise for his scholarship, insightful historical analyses, and lucid and engaging prose style. Deutscher's three-volume biography of Trotsky—*The Prophet Armed *(1954), *The Prophet Unarmed *(1959), and* The Prophet Outcast *(1963)—is generally considered the definitive work on Trotsky's life as well as one of the best political biographies of the twentieth century. In the following excerpt from* The Prophet Outcast, *Deutscher discusses* The Revolution Betrayed, *examining Trotsky's indictment of the absolutism and bureaucracy that characterized Stalin's regime, his conception of "Thermidorian" reaction to the Revolution, and his predictions for the effect on the Soviet Union of a second world war.*]

The Revolution Betrayed occupies a special place in Trotsky's literary work. It is the last book he managed to complete and, in a sense, his political testament. In it he gave his final analysis of Soviet society and a survey of its history up to the middle of the Stalin era. His most complex book, it combines all the weakness and the strength of his thought. It contains many new and original reflections on socialism, on the difficulties with which proletarian revolution has to grapple, and on the role of a bureaucracy in a workers' state. He also surveyed the international position of the Soviet Union before the Second World War and tried to pierce the future with daring and partly erroneous forecasts. The book is a profound theoretical treatise and a tract for the time; a creative restatement of classical Marxist views; and the manifesto of the "new Trotskyism" calling for revolution in the Soviet Union. Trotsky appears here in all his capacities: as detached and rigorously objective thinker; as leader of a defeated Opposition; and as passionate pamphleteer and polemicist. The polemicist's contribution forms the more esoteric part of the work and tends to overshadow the objective and analytical argument. Because of the wealth of its ideas and its imaginative force, this has been one of the seminal books of this century, as instructive as confusing, and destined to be put to adventitious use more often than any other piece of political writing. Even its title was to become one of the shibboleths of our time.

The Revolution Betrayed was Trotsky's critical reaction to a crucial moment of the Stalin era. Official Moscow had just proclaimed that the Soviet Union had already achieved socialism—until recently it had contented itself with the more modest claim that only "the foundations of socialism" had been laid. (pp. 298-99)

Trotsky set out to refute Stalin's claims; and he did this by confronting the realities of Stalinism with the classical Marxist conception of socialism. He pointed out that the predominance of social forms of ownership did not yet constitute socialism, even though it was its essential condition. Socialism presupposed an economy of abundance; it could not be founded on the want and poverty that prevailed in the Soviet Union and that led to the recrudescence of glaring inequality. Stalin had invoked Marx's dictum about the two stages of communism, a lower one where society would reward its members "each according to his work," and the higher where it would reward them "each according to his needs"—it was at the lower stage, Stalin declared, that the Soviet Union found itself. Trotsky pointed out that Stalin was abusing the authority of Marx in order to justify the inequality he was promoting. While it was true that Marx had foreseen that inequality would persist in the early phase of socialism, it would not have occurred to him that it would grow, and even grow by leaps and bounds, as it did under Stalin's rule. Soviet society was still only halfway between capitalism and socialism. It could advance or slide back; and only to the extent to which it overcame inequality would it advance. The growth of inequality indicated backsliding.

The orgies of Stalinist absolutism were part and parcel of the same retrograde trend. Lenin had, in his *State and Revolution*, wrested from oblivion the Marxian notion of the "withering away of the state" and made of it the household idea of Bolshevism; and Trotsky now defended the idea against Stalinist manipulation. He insisted that socialism was inconceivable without the withering away of the state. It was from class conflict that the state had arisen; and it existed as an instrument of class domination. Even in its lower phase socialism meant the disappearance of class antagonisms and of political coercion—only the purely administrative functions of the state "the management of things, not of men" were to survive under socialism. Lenin had imagined the proletarian dictatorship as a "semi-state" only, modelled on the Commune of Paris, whose officials would be elected and deposed by vote and paid workers' wages, so that they should not form a bureaucracy estranged from the people. In backward and isolated Russia this scheme had proved unworkable. All the same, the advance towards socialism must be measured by the degree to which the coercive power of the state was on the decline. Massive political persecution and the glorification of the state in themselves refuted the Stalinist claim about the achievement of socialism. Stalin argued that the state could not wither away in a single country; to Trotsky this was only an indirect admission that socialism could not be achieved in a single country either. But it was not the "capitalist encirclement" that was the chief reason for the increased power of the state, for the Stalinist terror aimed primarily at "domestic enemies," i.e. at communist opposition.

To the non-Marxist much of this critique must seem "doctrinaire." To the Marxist it was vital because it stripped Stalinism of "ideological" pretensions and dissociated Marxism from Stalin's practices. Trotsky sought to establish for the Marxist school of thought a position, from which it could disclaim the

moral liabilities which Stalinism was creating for it, and from which it could declare that its ideas were no more responsible for Stalin's reign of terror than the Ten Commandments and the Sermon on the Mount had been for the Holy Inquisition. (pp. 300-02)

The Revolution Betrayed is Trotsky's classical indictment of bureaucracy. Once again, in the "conflict between the ordinary working woman and the bureaucrat who has seized her by the throat" he "sided with the working woman." He saw the mainspring of Stalinism in the defence of privilege, which alone gave a certain unity to all the disparate aspects of Stalin's policy, connecting its "Thermidorian" spirit with its diplomacy and the debasement of the Comintern. The ruling group shielded the interests of an acquisitive minority against popular discontent at home and the shocks of revolutionary class struggle abroad. Trotsky analysed the social composition of the managerial groups, of the party machine, of the civil servants and of the officer corps, who between them formed 12 to 15 per cent of the population, a massive stratum, conscious of its weight, rendered conservative by privilege, and straining with all its might to preserve the national and the international *status quo*.

Not content with indicting the bureaucracy, Trotsky considered again how and why it had achieved its power in the Soviet Union and whether its predominance was not inherent in socialist revolution at large. He went beyond his earlier answers and threw into bolder relief the objective causes for the recrudescence of inequality amid all the "want and poverty" in the Soviet Union. But he also stated with emphasis that some of these factors would recur in every socialist revolution, for none would be able to abolish inequality immediately. Even the United States, the wealthiest industrial nation, did not yet produce enough to be able to reward labour "according to needs"; it still suffered from a relative scarcity which would compel it, under communist government, to maintain differential wages and salaries. Consequently, tensions and social conflicts would persist, although they would be much milder than in an underdeveloped country. And so "the tendencies of bureaucratism . . . would everywhere show themselves even after a proletarian revolution." Marx and Lenin had been aware of this. Marx had spoken of "bourgeois law," safeguarding unequal distribution of goods, as being "inevitable in the first phase of communist society." Lenin had described the Soviet republic as being in some respects a "bourgeois state without the bourgeoisie," even if it were governed in the spirit of proletarian democracy. But only the experience of the Stalin era had revealed the full dimensions of the problem and allowed real insight into the contradictions of post-capitalist society. A revolutionary government had to maintain inequality and had to struggle against it; and it had to do both for the sake of socialism. It had to provide incentives to technicians, skilled workers, and administrators in order to ensure the proper functioning and the rapid expansion of the economy; yet it had also to aim at the reduction and the eventual abolition of privileges.

Ultimately, this contradiction could be resolved only by an increase in social wealth, surpassing all that mankind had hitherto dreamt of, and by the attainment of so high and universal a level of education that the gulf between manual labour and intellectual work would vanish. In the meantime before these conditions are fulfilled, the revolutionary state assumes "directly and from the very beginning a dual character": it is socialist in so far as it defends social property in the means of production; and it is bourgeois in so far as it directs an unequal, differential distribution of goods among the members of society. The clear formulation of this contradiction and duality as inherent in the transition to socialism is one of Trotsky's important contributions to the Marxist thought of his time.

Returning to the analysis of Soviet society he admitted that Lenin and he had not foreseen that a "bourgeois state without a bourgeoisie" would prove inconsistent with genuine Soviet democracy; and that the state could not "wither away" as long as there was "the iron necessity" for it to foster and support a privileged minority. The destruction of Soviet democracy was thus due not merely to Stalin's conspiracy, which was the subjective aspect of a wider objective process. He went on to say that the Stalinist government had preserved the "dual character" inherent in any revolutionary government; but that the bourgeois element in it had gained immense weight and power at the expense of the socialist element. The bureaucracy was by its very nature "the planter and protector of inequality"; it acted like a policeman who during an acute shortage of goods "keeps order" while crowds queue up at foodshops—when food is abundant there are no queues and the policeman becomes superfluous. Yet "nobody who has wealth to distribute ever omits himself. Thus out of a social necessity there has developed an organ which has far outgrown its socially necessary function, and has become an independent factor and therewith the source of great danger for the whole social organism.... The poverty and cultural backwardness of the masses have again become incarnate in the malignant figure of the ruler with the great club in his hand." (pp. 302-04)

It was against a "greedy, mendacious, and cynical caste of rulers," against the germ of a new possessing class, that Trotsky formulated his programme of a "political revolution" in the U.S.S.R. "There is no peaceful outcome . . ." he wrote. "The Soviet bureaucracy will not give up its positions without a fight . . . no devil has ever yet voluntarily cut off his own claws." "The proletariat of a backward country was fated to accomplish the first socialist revolution. For this historic privilege it must, according to all the evidence, pay with a second supplementary revolution—against bureaucratic absolutism." He preached "a political, not a social revolution," a revolution, that is, which would overthrow the Stalinist system of government, but would not change the existing property relations.

This was a completely new prospect: Marxists had never imagined that after a socialist revolution they would have to call upon the workers to rise again, for they had taken it for granted that a workers' state could be only a proletarian democracy. History had now demonstrated that this was not so; and that, just as the bourgeois order had developed various forms of government, monarchical and republican, constitutional and autocratic, so the workers' state could exist in various political forms, ranging from a bureaucratic absolutism to government by democratic Soviets. And just as the French bourgeoisie had to "supplement" the social revolution of 1789-93 by the political revolutions of 1830 and 1848, in which ruling groups and methods of government were changed but not the economic structure of society—so, Trotsky argued, the working class too had to "supplement" the October Revolution. The bourgeoisie had acted consistently within its class interest when it asserted itself against its own absolutist rulers; and the working class would also act legitimately in freeing its own state from a despotic stranglehold. A political revolution of this kind had, of course, nothing to do with terroristic acts: "Individual terror is a weapon of impatient and despairing individuals, belonging

most frequently to the young generation of the bureaucracy itself." For Marxists it was axiomatic that they could carry out the revolution only with the open support of the majority of the workers. It was therefore not with a call for any immediate action that Trotsky came out, for as long as the workers saw in the bureaucracy the "watchman of their conquests," they would not rise against it. Trotsky advanced the idea, not the slogan, of a revolution; he offered a long-term orientation for the struggle against Stalinism, not guidance for direct action.

This is how he formulated the programme of the revolution:

> It is not a question of substituting one ruling clique for another, but of changing the very methods of administering the economy and guiding the culture of the country. Bureaucratic autocracy must give place to Soviet democracy. A restoration of the right of criticism and genuine freedom of elections is the necessary condition for the further development of the country. This assumes a revival of freedom of Soviet parties, beginning with the party of Bolsheviks, and a renascence of the trade unions. The bringing of democracy into industry means a radical revision of plans in the interests of the toilers. Free discussion of economic problems will decrease the overhead expense of bureaucratic mistakes and zigzags. Expensive playthings— Palaces of the Soviets, new theatres, showy Metro subways—will be abandoned in favour of workers' dwellings. "Bourgeois norms of distribution" will be confined within the limits of strict necessity, and, in step with the growth of social wealth, will give way to socialist equality. Ranks will be immediately abolished. The tinsel of decorations will go into the melting pot. Youth will receive the opportunity to breathe freely, criticise, make mistakes, and grow up. Science and art will be freed of their chains. And, finally, foreign policy will return to the traditions of revolutionary internationalism.

He reiterated here all the familiar desiderata of the period when he still stood for reform. Only in one point did he make a new departure—namely, in his demand for "genuine freedom of elections." On this point, however, he was confronted with a dilemma: he had discarded the principle of the single party; but he did not advocate unqualified freedom of parties. Going back to a pre-1921 formula, he spoke of a "revival of freedom of *Soviet* parties," that is of the parties that "stood on the ground of the October Revolution." But who was to determine which were and which were not "Soviet parties"? Should the Mensheviks, for instance, be allowed to benefit from the "revived" freedom? He left these questions in suspense, no doubt because he held that they could not be resolved in advance, regardless of circumstances. He was similarly cautious in discussing equality: he did not speak of any "abolition" of "bourgeois norms of distribution"—these were to be maintained, but only "within the limits of strict necessity"; and dispensed with gradually, "with the growth of social wealth." The political revolution was thus to leave some privileges to managers, administrators, technicians, and skilled workers. As he himself sometimes, in polemical utterances, spoke loosely of the "overthrow" or "abolition" of bureaucracy, this gloss put the

Trotsky addressing members of the newly-formed Red Army.

problem in a more realistic perspective. What he envisaged on calm reflection was a drastic curtailment, not the obliteration, of bureaucratic and managerial privilege. (pp. 309-11)

Mention should be made here of the revision, which Trotsky carried out in *The Revolution Betrayed,* of his conception of the Soviet Thermidor. We have described earlier [in *The Prophet Unarmed;* see Additional Bibliography] the passions and the turbulence which this abstruse historical analogy had aroused in the Bolshevik party in the nineteen-twenties; and we have said that this was a case of *le mort saisit le vif*. About ten years later we find Trotsky, under a Norwegian village roof, still wrestling with the French phantom of 1794. We remember that as long as he stood for reform in the Soviet Union, he rejected the view, originally held by the Workers' Opposition, that the Russian Revolution had already declined into the Thermidorian or post-Thermidorian phase. Thermidor, he argued, was the danger with which Stalin's policy was fraught, but not yet an accomplished fact. He still defended this attitude against friend and foe alike in the first years of his banishment. But having decided that the Opposition must become an independent party and that political revolution was inevitable in the Soviet Union, he thought again and stated that the Soviet Union had long since been living in the post-Thermidorian epoch.

He admitted that the historical analogy had done more to obfuscate minds than to enlighten them; yet he went on elaborating it. He and his friends, he argued, had committed a mistake in thinking that Thermidor amounted to a counter-revolution and restoration; and having so defined it, they had been right in insisting that no Thermidor had occurred in Russia. But the definition was wrong and unhistoric: the original Thermidor had not been a counter-revolution, but only ''a phase of reaction *within* the revolution.'' The Thermidorians had not destroyed the social basis of the French Revolution, the new bourgeois property relations, that had taken shape in 1789-93; but they had on that basis set up their anti-popular rule and set the stage for the Consulate and the Empire. The comparable development in the Soviet Union occurred as early as 1923, when Stalin suppressed the Left Opposition and established his anti-proletarian régime on the social foundations of the October Revolution. With the calendar of the French Revolution before his eyes all the time, Trotsky went on to say that Stalin's rule having assumed a Bonapartist character, the Soviet Union was living under its Consulate. Within this perspective the danger of restoration appeared all too real—in France twenty years had passed between Thermidor and the return of the Bourbons; and Trotsky's call for a new revolution and a return to Soviet democracy echoed the cry raised by the Conspiracy of Equals for a return to the First Republic. (pp. 313-14)

The original Thermidor was one of the most involved, many-faceted, and enigmatic events in modern history; and this accounts partly for the confusion about it. The Thermidorians overthrew Robespierre after a series of internecine Jacobin struggles, in the course of which Robespierre, leading the centre of his party, had destroyed its right and left wings, the Dantonists and Hebertists. The end of his rule marked the downfall of his faction and of the Jacobin party at large. Soon after Thermidor the Jacobin Club was disbanded and ceased to exist.

The Thermidorians replaced Robespierre's "reign of terror" by the rule of "law and order" and inflicted final defeat on the plebs of Paris, which had suffered many reverses even earlier. They abolished the quasi-egalitarian distribution of food, which Robespierre had maintained by fixing "maximum" prices. Henceforth, the bourgeoisie was free to trade profitably, to amass fortunes, and to gain the social dominance which it was to preserve even under the Empire. Thus, against the background of ebbing revolutionary energies and of disillusionment and apathy in the masses, the revolutionary régime passed from the popular to the anti-popular phase.

It is enough to outline briefly these various aspects of Thermidor to see where Trotsky was wrong in his assertion that Russia had gone through her Thermidor in 1923. The defeat of the Opposition in that year was not in any sense an event comparable to the collapse and dissolution of the Jacobin party; it corresponded rather to the defeat of the left Jacobins which had taken place well before Thermidor. While Trotsky was writing *The Revolution Betrayed* the Soviet Union was on the eve of the great purge trials—in France the *épurations* were part and parcel of the Jacobin period; only after Robespierre's downfall was the guillotine brought to a halt. Thermidor was in fact an explosion of despair with the permanent purge; and most of the Thermidorians were ex-Dantonists and ex-Hebertists who had survived the slaughter of their factions. The Russian analogy to this would have been a successful coup against Stalin carried out, after the trials of 1936-8, by remnants of the Bukharinist and Trotskyist oppositions.

Another difference is even more important: Thermidor brought to a close the revolutionary transformation of French society and the upheaval in property. In the Soviet Union these did not come to a halt with Stalin's ascendancy. On the contrary, the most violent upheaval, collectivization of farming, was carried out under his rule. And it was surely not "law and order," even in a most anti-popular form, that prevailed either in 1923, or at any time during the Stalin era. What the early nineteen-twenties had in common with the Thermidorian period was the ebbing away of the popular revolutionary energies and the disillusionment and apathy of the masses. It was against such a background that Robespierre had sought to keep the rump of the Jacobin party in power and failed; and that Stalin struggled to preserve the dictatorship of the Bolshevik rump (i.e. of his own faction) and succeeded.

Admittedly, there was a strong Thermidorian flavour about Stalin's anti-egalitarianism. But that was not absent from Lenin's N.E.P. either. Curiously, when in 1921 the Mensheviks described N.E.P. as the "Soviet Thermidor," neither Lenin nor Trotsky protested. On the contrary, they congratulated themselves on having carried out something like Thermidor peacefully, without breaking up their own party and losing power. "It was not they [the Mensheviks]," Trotsky wrote in 1921, "but we ourselves who formulated this diagnosis. And, what is more important, the concessions to the Thermidorian mood and tendencies of the petty bourgeoisie, necessary for the purpose of maintaining the power of the proletariat, were made by the Communist party without effecting a break in the system and without quitting the helm." Stalin also made the most far-reaching "concessions to the Thermidorian moods and tendencies" of his bureaucracy and managerial groups, "without effecting a break in the system and without quitting the helm." In any case, an historical analogy which led Trotsky, in 1921, almost to boast that he and Lenin had carried out a semi-Thermidor, then to deny that any Soviet Thermidor

had occurred, and finally, in 1935, to maintain that the Soviet Union had for twelve years lived under a Thermidor, without Trotsky himself noticing it—such an analogy did indeed serve more to obfuscate minds than to enlighten them. (pp. 315-17)

The pessimism, real and apparent, underlying *The Revolution Betrayed* shows itself also in those pages where Trotsky tried to anticipate the impact of the Second World War on the Soviet Union. He noted that the new social system had provided "national defence with advantages of which the old Russia could not dream"; that in a planned economy it was relatively easy to switch from civilian to military production and "to focus on the interests of defence even in building and equipping new factories." He underlined the progress of the Soviet armed forces in all modern weapons and stated that "the correlation between the living and mechanical forces of the Red Army may be considered by and large as on a level with the best armies of the West." This was not, in 1936, a view generally accepted by western military experts; and the emphasis with which Trotsky expressed it was undoubtedly calculated to impress the Governments and the General Staffs of the western powers. But he saw the weakness of the Soviet defences in the Thermidorian spirit of its officer corps, in the army's rigidly hierarchical structure which was replacing its revolutionary-democratic organization, and above all in Stalin's foreign policy. He argued that Stalin, having first neglected the danger from the Third Reich, was now, to counter it, relying mainly on alliances with western bourgeois Governments, on the League of Nations, and on "collective security," for the sake of which he would in case of war refrain from making any genuinely revolutionary appeal to the armed workers and peasants of the belligerent nations.

"Can we . . ." Trotsky asked, "expect that the Soviet Union will come out of the approaching great war without defeat? To this frankly posed question we will answer as frankly: if the war should remain only a war, the defeat of the Soviet Union would be inevitable. In a technical, economic, and military sense, imperialism is incomparably stronger. If it is not paralysed by revolution in the West, imperialism will sweep away the régime which issued from the October Revolution." Divided though the West was against itself, it would eventually unite "in order to block the military victory of the Soviet Union." Well before the Munich crisis, Trotsky observed that France was already treating her alliance with the Soviet Union as a "scrap of paper" and she would continue to do so, no matter how much Stalin tried to secure the alliance through the Popular Front. Only if Stalin were to yield further to French, British and American economic and political pressures, would the alliance assume reality; but even then the allies would take advantage of the Soviet Union's wartime difficulties and seek to sap the socialist foundations of its economy and exact far-reaching concessions to capitalism. At the same time the peasantry's individualism, stirred up by war, would threaten to disrupt collective farming. These external and domestic pressures, Trotsky concluded, would bring the danger of counter-revolution and restoration closer to Russia. The situation was not hopeless, however, because the war would also bring revolution closer to Europe; and so, on balance, "the Soviet régime would have more stability than the régimes of its probable enemies." "The Polish bourgeoisie" could only "hasten the war and find in it . . . certain death"; and "Hitler has far less chance than had Wilhelm II of carrying a war to victory." Trotsky's confidence in European revolution was as strong as was his despondency about the prospects of the Soviet Union in the absence of such a revolution:

The danger of war and defeat of the Soviet Union is a reality, but the revolution is also a reality. If the revolution does not prevent war, then war will help the revolution. Second births are commonly easier than first. In the new war it will not be necessary to wait a whole two years and a half for the first insurrection [as it was after 1914]. Once it is begun, moreover, the revolution will not this time stop half way. The fate of the Soviet Union will be decided in the long run not on the maps of the General Staffs, but on the map of the class struggle. Only the European proletariat, implacably opposing its bourgeoisie . . . can protect the Soviet Union from destruction, or from an ''allied'' stab in the back. Even a military defeat of the Soviet Union would be only a short episode, if there were to be a victory of the proletariat in other countries. And, on the other hand, no military victory can save the inheritance of the October revolution if imperialism holds out in the rest of the world. . . . Without the Red Army the Soviet Union would be crushed and dismembered like China. Only its stubborn and heroic resistance to the future capitalist enemy can create favourable conditions for the development of the class struggle in the imperialist camp. The Red Army is thus a factor of immense significance. But this does not mean that it is the sole historic factor.

It is not under the banner of the *status quo* [which Stalin's diplomacy defended in the nineteen-thirties] that the European workers and the colonial peoples can rise. . . . The task of the European proletariat is not the perpetuation of boundaries, but, on the contrary, their revolutionary abolition, not [the preservation of] the *status quo* but a socialist United States of Europe.

The outcome of the Second World War was to be far less clear cut than this alternative; and nothing would be easier than to compile from *The Revolution Betrayed* a list of Trotsky's errors in prognostication. Yet each of his errors contains important elements of truth and follows from premises which retain validity; and so more can still be learned from his mistakes than from the correct platitudes of most political writers. Trotsky is in this respect not unlike Marx: his thought is ''algebraically'' correct, even when his ''arithmetical'' conclusions are wrong. Where his forecasts were erroneous, they were so because too often he viewed the Second World War in terms of the first; but his general insights into the relationship between war and revolution were deep and are still essential to an understanding of the revolutionary aftermath of the Second World War. (pp. 318-21)

> *Isaac Deutscher, in his* The Prophet Outcast: Trotsky, 1929-1940, *Oxford University Press, London, 1963, 543 p.*

PAUL N. SIEGEL (essay date 1969)

[*Siegel is an American educator and critic who has written extensively on English Renaissance literature and the works of William Shakespeare. According to Siegel, his criticism often examines* ''literature in relation to the intellectual and emotional environment created by changes in the economic basis of society,'' *as well as* ''the revolutionary events of our epoch and their reflections in literature.'' *In the following excerpt from an introduction written in 1969, he explicates Trotsky's literary philosophy and defends his theories against attacks by prominent Western literary critics.*]

Trotsky's ability as a literary critic may be gauged by his having hailed before they received general acclaim Malraux, Silone and Celine, the first two of whom wrote novels that affected so strongly the decade of the thirties and that are among the very few works which have survived it, and the last who wrote novels that have so strongly influenced subsequent European and American novelists. But a volume of Trotsky's literary criticism is justified not only by his taste and judgment as a literary critic. It is justified by the abiding value of what he has to say on the relationship between literature and society, by the fact that it is Marxist literary criticism written by one of the great Marxist thinkers. For just as Trotsky's Red Army, although it won the respect of the military experts by its achievements, was organized on revolutionary principles of which they had no understanding, so his literary criticism proceeds from a theory of literature concerning which most of the professional critics of the Western world, particularly those of the United States, have little knowledge.

The limited extent of this knowledge is indicated by the statement of Professor Rene Wellek in the 1952 brochure ''The Aims, Methods and Materials of Research in the Modern Languages and Literatures'' published by the Modern Language Association of America: ''Marx and the Marxists only admit the determining influence of economic and social conditions, attempting to establish definite causal connections between technological change and the stratification of classes on the one hand, and literary creation on the other. The majority of literary historians in the United States have, however, eschewed such extreme determinism and have not, on the whole, endorsed claims for complete scientific explanation.''

Trotsky, however, quoted the Italian Marxist philosopher Antonio Labriola against those who would simplify Marxist theory into crude economic determinism: ''By this method fools could reduce the whole of history to the level of commercial arithmetic and, finally, a new, original interpretation of Dante's work could show us *The Divine Comedy* in the light of calculations regarding pieces of cloth which crafty Florentine merchants sold for their maximum profit.'' (pp. 8-10)

The truth is that Marxist theory finds complex interactions to exist between what Marx called the economic foundation (the sum total of the relations into which men enter to carry on social production) and the ideological superstructure (the legal, political, religious, aesthetic and philosophical systems of ideas and institutions) which may develop on the basis of that foundation. As Engels wrote, ''Political, juridical, philosophical, religious, literary, artistic, etc., development is based on economic development. But all these react upon one another and also upon the economic base. It is not that the economic position is the *cause and alone active*, while everything else only has a passive effect. There is, rather, interaction on the basis of the economic necessity, which *ultimately* always asserts itself.''

The men engaged in the various spheres of ideological activity acquire their own special interests, their traditions, their rationale. These conditions of activity established by the disciplines themselves are only relatively independent, the course of their movement being subject to the more powerful movement of economic development, which alters social relations and thereby the social consciousness determined by these relations. "The ruling ideas of each age," as Marx said, "have ever been the ideas of its ruling class," but the web of thought is woven by the ideologists of that class from the materials bequeathed by the past and is a result of a process of interaction between the class and its ideologists.

Trotsky, therefore, far from minimizing the role of tradition in literature, insists upon it as much as does T. S. Eliot. He adds, however, that the continuity of literary history is dialectical, proceeding by a series of reactions, each of which is united to the tradition from which it is seeking to break ("artistic creation is always a complicated turning inside out of old forms"). Nor are these reactions merely mechanical, the eternal swing of the pendulum from "classic" to "romantic." They take place under the stimuli of new artistic needs as the result of changes in the psychology of social classes attendant upon changes in the economic structure. (pp. 10-11)

If, however, the most eminent literary scholars and critics in the United States are ignorant of Marxism, Trotsky the Marxist, writing more than forty years ago, has much to say which is relevant for the leading scholarly and critical schools in the United States today. What are the Russian formalists, of whom Trotsky speaks in *Literature and Revolution,* if not forerunners of our own "new critics"? Trotsky points out the empty pretensions of the formalists in seeking to make literature completely autonomous and in proclaiming themselves to possess the first scientific theory of literature, but he adds: "The methods of formalism, confined within legitimate limits, may help to clarify the artistic and psychologic peculiarities of form (its economy, its movement, its contrasts, its hyperbolism, etc.). . . . But the formalists are not content to ascribe to their methods a merely subsidiary, serviceable and technical significance. . . . The social and psychologic approach which, to us, gives a meaning to the microscopic and statistical work done in connection with verbal material is, for the formalists, only alchemy." So the "new critics," it has been observed by Professor Douglas Bush, have given American literary scholars a course in advanced remedial reading but have at the same time promoted an attitude of looking upon literary works as if they were specimens on microscope slides. As Trotsky long ago warned, "The effort to set art free from life, to declare it a craft self-sufficient unto itself, devitalizes and kills art."

"A work of art," says Trotsky, "should, in the first place, be judged by its own law, that is, by the law of art." But before we can judge we must understand, and before we can really understand, we must see the work in its historical context. This the various kinds of historical scholarship other than Marxism likewise seek to do. Marxism, however, claims to unite these kinds of scholarship into a single all-embracing system.

The literary historian looks at a literary work in relation to the development of literary form. But, says Trotsky, the development of literary form, like the individual literary work, is only relatively autonomous. Each literary work is the product of a living man handling the materials handed down to him by his predecessors and possessing a psychology that is the result of his social environment. "Between the physiology of sex and a poem about love there lies a complex system of psychological transmitting mechanisms in which there are individual, racial and social elements. The racial foundation, that is, the sexual basis of man, changes slowly. The social forms of love change more rapidly. They affect the psychologic substructure of love, they produce new shadings and intonations,

new spiritual demands, a need of a new vocabulary, and so they present new demands on poetry." To understand the love poetry of Donne, we have to understand how it grows out of and reacts against Elizabethan love poetry, as the orthodox literary historian tells us; we have to understand the life of the Jack Donne who became the clergyman John Donne, as the orthodox literary biographer tells us; we have to understand Donne, the man living at a time of social change and uncertainty consequent upon the growth in power of the middle class, and the way in which his expression of attitude toward love reflected his outlook on life and caused him to make a "revolution" in poetry, as the Marxist critic can tell us.

The other forms of literary scholarship—the study of literature in relation to the history of ideas, to the history of science, to the history of religion, to myth and ritual (Trotsky's discussion of the existence of enduring themes in literature is relevant to this latest scholarly vogue) and so forth—constitute what Trotsky called "a crossing or combining and interacting of certain independent principles [as it seems to those engaged in this scholarship]—the religious, political, juridical, aesthetic substances, which find their origin and explanation in themselves." For Trotsky, however, these spheres of ideological activity are "separate aspects of one and the same process of social development" which "evolves the necessary organs and functions from within itself." They interact among themselves and react upon the economic base from which they have evolved and upon whose development the general course of their development is finally dependent.

Trotsky does not claim, as Wellek states Marxists claim, that Marxism gives a "complete scientific explanation" for a literary work. Marx had drawn a distinction between "the material transformation of the economic conditions of production which can be determined with the precision of natural science" and the transformation of the cultural superstructure which follows this transformation. So too Trotsky states: "To say that man's environment, including the artist's, that is, the conditions of his education and life, find expression in his art also, does not mean to say that such expression has a precise geographic, ethnographic and statistical character." If we cannot, however, construct an elaborate formula that gives "a complete scientific explanation" why this work of art was written just that day by just that man in just that way, it remains true that, in the words of Marx, "the mode of production in material life determines the social, political, and intellectual life processes in general" and that a knowledge of how literature is governed in a general way by the functioning of the mode of production is essential for its fullest understanding.

T. S. Eliot, discussing Trotsky's statement that "Marxism alone can explain why and how a given tendency in art has originated in a given period of history," comments, "If Marxism explains why and how a given tendency in history originated, such as the tendency for Shakespeare's plays to be written, . . . then there seems to me to be a good deal left to explain" [see excerpt dated 1933]. He goes on to ask how Marxism explains the fact that great works of literature, while they are an expression of their age, continue to have artistic interest for future generations: "While recognizing the interest of the work of literature as a document upon the ideas and the sensibility of its epoch, and recognizing even that the permanent work of literature is one which does not lack this interest, yet [one] cannot help valuing literary work, like philosophical work, in the end by its transcendence of the limits of its age. . . ."

Trotsky, however, far from being concerned only with the historical origins of literature, speaks in **"Class and Art"** of the need for understanding "art as art." He attacks those who find the sole value of *The Divine Comedy* to be that it gives us "an understanding of the state of mind of certain classes in a certain epoch" and comments that such a view of it makes it "merely a historical document," not a work of art, which "must speak in some way to my feelings and moods."

How, then, does he explain the fact that Dante, "a Florentine petty bourgeois of the thirteenth century," speaks to him across the centuries? Before Eliot raised the question, Trotsky answered it. "In class society, in spite of all its changeability, there are certain common features." The expression of the feeling of love or of the fear of death has changed with changes in society, but the feeling of love and the fear of death remain. Literature, by articulating such feelings with intensity and precision, refines feeling and generalizes experience. It thus helps man to become aware of himself, to understand his position in the universe. The great literature of the past continues to fulfill this function for us because its expression of basic feelings and experiences, however these feelings and experiences have differed among different social classes at different times, is so powerful that it throws into relief features in them common to men of all times of class society. It thus still has the capacity to enrich our internal life.

F. R. Leavis thinks that he finds Trotsky in a contradiction in his acceptance of the great literature of the past while condemning the culture of which it is an expression:

> Like all Marxists, [he] practices, with the familiar air of scientific rigour, the familiar vague, blanketing use of essential terms. He can refer, for instance, to the "second of August, 1914, when the maddened power of bourgeois culture let loose upon the world the blood and fire of an imperialistic war." ... This, however is perhaps a salute to orthodoxy. And it would not be surprising if he had thought it wise to distract attention, if possible, from such things as the following, which uses "culture" very differently, and is hardly orthodox: "The proletariat is forced to take power before it has appropriated the fundamental elements of bourgeois culture; it is forced to overthrow bourgeois society by revolutionary violence, for the very reason that society does not allow it access to culture." ... The aim of revolution, it appears, is to secure this accursed bourgeois culture for the proletariat. Or, rather, Trotsky knows that behind the word "culture" there is something that cannot be explained by the "methods of production" and that it would be disastrous to destroy as "bourgeois" [see Additional Bibliography].

Trotsky, however, defines precisely the way in which he uses the word "culture" in the very *Literature and Revolution* that the editor of *Scrutiny*, an advocate of rigorously close reading, did not scrutinize sufficiently closely: "Culture is the organic sum of knowledge and capacity which characterizes the entire society, or at least its ruling class. It embraces and penetrates all fields of human work and unifies them into a system." The victorious proletariat, in seizing "the fundamental elements" of this sum of knowledge and skill, modifies it by rejecting that which it finds useless, by adding to it and in general by

putting its own stamp upon it. It serves a period of cultural apprenticeship, gradually mastering the whole of the culture before it can completely renovate it. By the time it will have left this period of apprenticeship to construct a culture of its own, it will have ceased to be a proletariat.

In **"Culture and Socialism"** Trotsky, in discussing the matter of the proletarian appropriation of bourgeois culture, from which it has been excluded, explicitly raises the question later raised by Leavis:

> Exploiters' society has given rise to an exploiters' culture. ... And yet we say to the working class: master all the culture of the past, otherwise you will not build socialism. How is this to be understood?

In raising the question, far from giving up the idea that culture is to be explained by the methods of production, as Leavis says he does in calling upon the workers to become the possessors of bourgeois culture, Trotsky insists upon it:

> Over this contradiction many people have stumbled, and they stumble so frequently because they approach the understanding of class society superficially, semi-idealistically, forgetting that fundamentally this is the organization of production. Every class society has been formed on the basis of definite modes of struggle with nature, and these modes have changed in accordance with the development of technique. ... On this dynamic foundation there arise classes, which by their interrelations determine the character of culture.

Trotsky's answer to the question is that the contradiction is not his but is the dialectical contradiction present in culture itself. Technique, the basis of class organization, has served as a means of exploitation, but it is also a condition for the emancipation of the exploited. The machine crushes the worker, but he can free himself only through the machine. What is true of material culture is also true of spiritual culture. After having conquered illiteracy and semiliteracy, the Russian worker must master classical Russian literature.

One cannot speak of a cultural revolution in the same way as one speaks of a social revolution. A social revolution is the birth of a new society. This new society grows for a prolonged period of time within the womb of the old society, but the seizure of power by the new class—the violent birth of the revolution—takes only a brief time. One cannot, however, build a new culture overnight, nor can one build a new culture without having mastered the old one.

Yet this is what the Chinese Cultural Revolution, outlawing the literature of past cultures, would do. Chiang Ching, Mao Tsetung's wife and a leader of the Cultural Revolution, has written: "If our literature and art do not correspond to the socialist economic base, they will inevitably destroy it." Thus, despite her access to the thoughts of Chairman Mao, she flies in the face of the elementary Marxist tenet that it is the economic base, not the cultural superstructure, which is the chief force in the interaction between them, that the economic base will sooner transform the cultural superstructure than the cultural superstructure will transform the economic base. As a result of such thinking, Shakespeare, who was read by Marx every year, is forbidden in China, as is Pushkin, who was a favorite author of Lenin's. For Trotsky, on the other hand, fear of the effect of the literature of a previous class is a silly bogeyman:

> It is childish to think that bourgeois *belles lettres* can make a breach in class solidarity. What the worker will take from Shakespeare, Goethe, Pushkin, or Dostoyevsky, will be a more complex idea of human personality, of its passions and feelings, a deeper and more profound understanding of its psychic forces and of the role of the subconscious, etc. In the final analysis, the worker will be richer.

However, while Trotsky does not fear the effect of bourgeois *belles lettres* in itself, he upholds the right of the proletarian dictatorship, when it is fighting for its life, to proscribe writing aimed at undermining the regime, even if it appears as *belles lettres*. If during a civil war the proletarian army has the right to destroy edifices of artistic value for military reasons (the same right which other armies arrogate to themselves without discussing the matter), so, he argues, the regime has the right under such or similar conditions to suppress counterrevolutionary literature. Its first obligation is to safeguard the new order, whose overthrow would mean an end to the cultural liberation of the masses. This right of the regime, however, should on no account be used against those not opposed to the revolution and should be exercised less and less as the regime consolidates its power. (pp. 12-19)

Does [Trotsky's] statement that the artist is the natural ally of revolution mean that he should make his art a propaganda art? Georg Lukacs, the renowned Hungarian Marxist critic, writing in 1934, when he was striving to maintain his critical independence while accommodating himself to Stalinism, attacks Trotsky as supporting propaganda art or " 'tendentious' portrayal" in order that Lukacs himself may oppose it [see Additional Bibliography]. Lukacs differentiates between partisanship, which is "not inconsistent with objectivity in reproducing and re-creating reality," and propaganda, "in which support of something means its idealist glorification, while opposition to it involves its distortion." Trotsky, he charges, speaks of an impossibly pure art, separated from society, in the socialist future but upholds a propagandist art in the here and now: "Trotzky writes: 'Revolutionary literature cannot but be imbued with a spirit of social hatred . . . [thus it is merely "propaganda art"—G.L.] Under Socialism solidarity will be the basis of society' (*Literature and Revolution* . . .). In other words, 'pure art' and 'true culture' are attainable."

But hatred of oppressors, with which the partisans of revolution must be filled, need not obscure the writer's vision so that it results in a distortion of reality, and social solidarity does not imply an art divorced from society. As a matter of fact, Trotsky had in *Literature and Revolution* dismissed the quarrels between the advocates of "pure art" and those of tendentious art as quarrels that "do not become us"—that is, that are unsuitable for Marxists to engage in because they are irrelevant, Marxism finding both supposedly pure art and frankly tendentious art to have social roots and to fulfill a social function. Those who seek to quarrel, however, will always find a reason to do so, even if they have to invent it.

Trotsky, like Engels before him, always objected to exaggerating the artistic worth of the purely propagandist literature which simplifies a complex reality in order to present an easy lesson. In 1922 he said of the French poet and dramatist Marcel Martinet: "One need neither expect nor fear from him purely propagandist activity." In 1939 he wrote of Jean Malaquais's *Les Javanais:* "Although social in its implications, this novel is in no way tendentious in character. He does not try to prove anything, he does not propagandize, as do many productions of our time, when far too many submit to orders even in the sphere of art. The Malaquais novel is 'only' a work of art."

But a literary work which has an avowed "message," if that work is deeply thought and felt so that it renders reality in all of its complexity and its "message" is organic to it, not an obtrusive appendix, rises from propaganda to art. Such is Ignazio Silone's *Fontamara.* It is, says Trotsky, "a book of passionate political propaganda," but it is "a truly artistic work" because "revolutionary passion is raised here to such heights" and because Silone sees "life as it is."

Although Trotsky calls upon the artist to become the ally of revolution, he does not guarantee that the revolution will enable him to produce masterpieces. The revolutionary view cannot be merely intellectually accepted; it must become part of the very being of the artist, if he is to give expression to it in art. "The artist," says "A Manifesto: Towards a Free Revolutionary Art," "cannot serve the struggle for freedom unless he subjectively assimilates its social content, unless he feels in his very nerves its meaning and drama and freely seeks to give his own inner world incarnation in his art."

He must freely seek to communicate his own inner world, not present a view of the world which has been dictated to him by anyone else or even by himself, not allow any internal inhibitions or external compulsions to cause him to withhold a part of his vision. Gorky, after beginning as a tramp poet, honorably turned toward the proletariat when the proletariat and the radical intelligentsia came into opposition with each other in 1905. However, he never organically assimilated the revolutionary view, and consequently his best period as an artist is that of his first days, when his work had a spontaneity it did not have when he was seeking to apply literary and political lessons. Mayakovsky, devoted to the revolutionary cause, squandered himself meeting the daily demands of newspapers and seeking to adhere to the "correct ideological line" that hack critics imposed on him. Malraux, after producing some significant works, found that his pessimism and skepticism made him need "some outside force to lean on, some established authority," and his novels about Germany and Spain became apologies for Stalinism.

These comments, written by Trotsky at different times, are crystallized in his words to André Breton: "The struggle for revolutionary ideas in art must begin once again with the struggle for artistic *truth*, not in terms of any single school, but in terms of *the immutable faith of the artist in his own inner self.* Without this there is no art. 'You shall not lie!'—that is the formula of salvation."

Artistic truth, Trotsky states in defending his *History of the Russian Revolution,* consists of the work of art following its own laws in the unfolding of the chain of events, in character development, and so on. To attain it the artist must be true to his own vision. Historical truth is analogous to it. Truth in history, as in art, does not demand impartiality, which indeed is impossible. It demands a rigorous regard for the facts and a scientific method through which "facts combine into one whole process which, as in life, lives according to its own interior laws. . . ."

In his wittily devastating analysis of Churchill's history of the period immediately after World War I and its portrait of Lenin,

Trotsky demonstrates how false to historical truth Churchill is: inaccurate in his facts, confused in his visualization of the time and persons he is describing, artificial even in his verbal antitheses. It is interesting to compare Churchill as historian and biographer with Trotsky. None of the political antagonists who attacked the *History of the Russian Revolution* and the biography of Stalin were able to challenge Trotsky's use of fact, for which he had a scrupulous concern. One may add that his attackers' attempt to hammer loose his causal connections between facts left them undamaged.

What is true of Trotsky in the quasi-literary arts of the historian and biographer is also true of him as a literary critic. He does not disguise his sympathies, he is devoted to accuracy of statement, he seeks to get at the essence of things through the Marxist method. Committed to the cause of revolution, he is especially interested in literature written by those of revolutionary tendencies. To the writers of this literature he is sympathetic and generous, but he is also honest and judicious. Despite Gorky's friendship with the leading Soviet bureaucrats, Trotsky pays tribute to him as a man and as a writer of great talent, if not of the genius for which he was uncritically lauded by the hacks in the service of the bureaucracy. In his obituary articles on Mayakovsky and Essenin he is warm and moving, yet discriminating. In writing to Jack London's daughter, he expresses his sincerely great admiration for *The Iron Heel* but refers to its artistic limitations.

Although Trotsky is especially interested in literary works written by writers of revolutionary tendencies and summons writers to the revolutionary cause, which he believes can save them from demoralization, he is appreciative of all kinds of literature. Political partisan though he is, he does not demand that writers be of his political camp or even of his general political sympathies for them to receive his acclaim. He is aware that, as Rosa Luxemburg said, "With the true artist, the social formula that he recommends is a matter of secondary importance; the source of his art, its animating spirit, is decisive."

The young Trotsky probes the social roots of the art of Tolstoy, who was then still alive, finding them to spring from the soil of his aristocratic upbringing, but he finds the animating spirit of Tolstoy's art to be his "priceless talent for moral indignation" and his "unbending moral courage." The Trotsky of later years, who had suffered unprecedented blows but had retained his youthful faith in life and the revolution, only tempered by experience, finds Celine's *Journey to the End of Night* a novel of the utmost pessimism, but a novel which in its relentless honesty in confronting life strips aside the official lies concerning society. It thus helps to bring about the future already manifesting itself in the present, to which the novel itself is blind. "Exposing the lie, he instills the want for a more harmonious future. Though he himself may consider that nothing good can generally come from man, the very intensity of his pessimism bears within it a dose of the antidote."

In his literary criticism, then, as in his other writing, Trotsky's revolutionary optimism and his fighting revolutionary spirit express themselves. He does not write either in the impersonal manner of the scientist or with the genteel enthusiasm of a taster of fine wines. He writes as one for whom literature is an essential part of human life and for whom humanity, despite the degradation, sordidness and misery which surround us, is grand in the heroism of its struggles and noble in its potentiality. His literary criticism, in short, has its origin in the vision of social humanism that animated his whole life. (pp. 21-6)

Trotsky in 1940.

Paul N. Siegel, in an introduction to Leon Trotsky on Literature and Art *by Leon Trotsky, edited by Paul N. Siegel, Pathfinder Press, Inc., 1970, pp. 7-26.*

BARUCH KNEI-PAZ (essay date 1977)

[*Knei-Paz is the author of* The Social and Political Thought of Leon Trotsky *(1978). In the following excerpt, he discusses Trotsky's theory of Russian backwardness as the basis of his theory of permanent revolution.*]

In 1905 . . . the conjoining of Marxian socialism and Russian backwardness still required a theoretical framework, one which went beyond the simple mechanical projection into Russia's future of the Western historical experience. And it was in that year, under the impact of its revolutionary events, that Trotsky became the first to begin to formulate such a framework—though initially he took his cue from one Alexander Helphand, better known by his pen-name Parvus, an expatriate Russian Marxist whom Trotsky had met a year earlier in Germany. Parvus had published a series of articles in 1904 the gist of which was that Russia, being the "weakest link" in the capitalist chain, especially during a time of war, was most vulnerable to being overextended by war, and thus most susceptible to internal upheaval. He appended to this the rather unexpected observation that such an upheaval stood every chance of culminating with the workers in power. And he concluded, therefore, that a revolution led by the workers could erupt in

Russia before it had done so in Western Europe. Parvus later made a brief attempt to explain this phenomenon on the basis of Russia's social development; but he did not go into this very deeply or systematically. And, in any case, when discussing the social character of the workers' government which might arise in Russia, Parvus had stopped short of defining it as a socialist regime; he appeared, rather, to envisage it as a radical vanguard pushing in the direction of the rapid democratization of the country.

The influence of Parvus upon Trotsky was nevertheless profound and Trotsky would in later years often acknowledge this intellectual debt. For, having taken the cue from Parvus and having then witnessed the turmoil in Russia during 1905, Trotsky proceeded, in a number of works written between the years 1905 to 1908—to which he would add refinements periodically, and especially many years later, in the 1920s and 1930s—to develop a theory of revolutionary change—more specifically socialist revolutionary change—in backward society. To do full justice to this theory it would be necessary to give an account of the careful and sometimes very detailed analysis which Trotsky made of Russian social history and development and of the peculiarities of Russian backwardness as these emerged in the wake of the economic changes at the end of the nineteenth century; but this is clearly impossible in the space afforded by this paper. Instead, therefore, I propose to reconstruct the conclusions which Trotsky, on the basis of his analysis of Russian backwardness, may be said to have abstracted about the phenomenon of backwardness in general. What follows is, admittedly, arranged in a manner more synoptic and systematic than it appears in Trotsky's writings; but the synopsis neither distorts nor oversteps the bounds of Trotsky's meaning and intentions. His theory of backwardness may thus be formulated as follows:

1. Backwardness is a condition (and a term) which characterizes or describes two essentially different types of societies. The one is a static, even stagnant, society whose internal mode of production and social structure remain what they have fundamentally always been and are incapable of generating change from within. This, roughly speaking, is the type of society called by Marx Oriental or whose "mode of production" he defined as Asiatic. The second type is a society which originally may have been of the first type but which in the course of time, and for various historical reasons (military confrontation, economic relations, colonialism), has been subject to the impact of other societies, defined as "advanced" or Western. In this case, change becomes a fundamental characteristic of backwardness and the interrelationship between this backward society and the advanced ones becomes crucial to an understanding of developments in the former particularly. Russia, for example, by virtue of her long interrelationship with the West, belongs to this second category of backwardness and it is this category which is the subject of sociological (and revolutionary) as opposed to anthropological analysis.

2. The impact of an advanced society on a backward one may be said to be traumatic: ultimately, it forces the backward society to adopt new forms of economic production, it undermines the traditional social hierarchy, it infects and transforms the existing elites, it introduces new patterns of thought and, throughout, it creates comparative norms. To a large extent all this is true even if the impact is the result of a "colonial-imperialist" relationship. But the effect is far more extreme and more rapid where the impact precedes the colonial period (as in the case of Russia) and where the backward society has

remained fundamentally independent. In that case, the very exigencies of the struggle for retaining independence lead to a more extensive adoption of new methods of economic and social organization and thus to a more widespread disintegration of the traditional methods and forms of life. The process whereby this occurs may now be traced.

3. The confrontation between the backward and the advanced initially leds the former to seek to adopt, in part at least, those aspects of the latter which are the source of its strength, since only in this way can the latter be withstood, i.e., on its own grounds. This involves primarily the copying of methods of economic production but the latter cannot be affected without simultaneously copying, or unleashing, those social relations which these methods demand. This presents a dilemma to the political authority—the state—of the backward society: how to change methods of production without overly disturbing traditional social relations. The state meets the dilemma by pursuing the former while attempting to take greater control of the latter, through bureaucratic interference, complete domination of the economy and especially capital formation, prevention of the growth of independent economic powers and, finally, force and oppression. In fact, however, new social relations can never be completely suppressed or even controlled and they develop in spite of the state's efforts.

4. In copying an advanced society, the backward society is working according to a ready-made model. This may suggest that it necessarily must reproduce both the paths followed by the advanced society in reaching that model as well as the actual model itself. In fact, of course, the advantage of a "late-comer" is that, with hindsight and through the experience of the "pioneer," it can move directly towards the end-product, skipping various stages, avoiding the *process* of development, imposing upon itself the result of it only. But this not only shortens the time-span; it introduces in fact a *different* process and leads in the end to the creation of a different model, which subsumes that of the advanced society and goes beyond it. This is so because of the previously mentioned disruption of old social relations, the innovative nature of the new ones and the peculiar intermixing of the whole:

> The laws of history have nothing in common with a pedantic schematism. Unevenness, the most general law of the historic process, reveals itself most sharply and complexly in the destiny of the backward countries. Under the whip of external necessity, their backward culture is compelled to make leaps. From the universal law of unevenness thus derives another law which, for the lack of a better name, we may call the law of *combined development*—by which we mean a drawing together of the different stages of the journey, a combining of separate steps, an amalgam of archaic with more contemporary forms. Without this law, to be taken of course in its whole material content, it is impossible to understand the history of Russia, and indeed of any country of the second, third or tenth cultural class.

5. The skipping of developmental stages creates curious results, for by leaping over forms of production the backward society is also by-passing social forms. Those social groupings which would have come into being had there been no skipping over stages, i.e., had there been an adoption of earlier forms of production, do *not* come into being. On the other hand, such

social groupings as are the pre-conditions of the latest model *do* crystallize. Simultaneously, the main elements of the traditional society remain: the old political authority, because of the power it has accumulated and its control over the economy; and the old agricultural sector because its break-up need be only partial and limited in order to make the new sector viable for immediate purposes, Thus, as in the case of Russia, the overall curious result is political absolutism, aristocratic privileges and a large agricultural population, together with advanced industry, urbanization, a working class, but—no middle class.

6. This situation is characteristic of the unique process through which the backward society has travelled, namely, "uneven and combined development." The situation may be broken down into the following attributes:

(a) Backwardness, far from being total, is only partial and in some ways the backward society is as advanced as any other.

(b) Conversely, sectors of the society have not changed at all, ostensibly at least, so that the overall impact is that of lopsidedness, uneven distribution of new forms of production, the polarization of society into various groups not directly or logically related to one another.

(c) The juxtaposition of very old and very new creates stark anomalies and a general non-rationalized economic and social structure, i.e., one that is in many ways counter-productive or self-defeating.

(d) The co-existence within one social framework of two fundamentally different and contradictory "models" of society arouses comparison, awareness of alternatives and, eventually, a *consciousness* of backwardness, i.e., a consciousness of the fact that the society is, in comparison with others, in some important senses defective.

(e) New methods of production create new goals and aspirations which are at variance with previous ones but since the former have not been wholly adopted and the latter not wholly abandoned there is both confusion over goals and a clash between them.

(f) The contradictions inherent in non-uniform development, the growth of a consciousness of backwardness and of alternatives, the conflict over goals, all these create disharmony, instability and a political situation which is potentially explosive. In fact, the peculiar nature and dynamics of backwardness make revolution inevitable. And this revolution, like the backward society from which it arises, will also have the character of an unprecedented, combined "amalgam," that is, one exhibiting both "archaic" and "contemporary" forms.

The conception of backwardness summarized above was at the basis of that theory of revolution with which Trotsky's name became universally identified, namely, the theory of the permanent revolution. Yet discussions of the latter theory have seldom related it to Trotsky's views about the social dynamics of backwardness; and the result, almost invariably, has been that the concept of the permanent revolution has been interpreted as a variant, albeit an intellectually more satisfying one, of the Bolshevik notion of vanguardism, that is, of radicalization from above, combined with the militant pursuit of revolution abroad. Nothing, however, could be further from the truth. Though the theory of the permanent revolution, like its author, came to be eventually linked to Bolshevism—for reasons I shall presently discuss—and though it *was* directly related to a general European conflagration, it was derived in the first place from what Trotsky took to be the objective character of social developments in a country such as Russia. Whatever its weaknesses—and these too will be presently mentioned—the theory did not divorce politics from society or revolutionary activity from social reality—habits of thought more justifiably associated with Lenin.

The summary I have given already indicates how Trotsky linked Russian politics with Russian society (and history). The central aspect of his view of backwardness was that social development was everywhere different, and nowhere more so than in Russia, and the notion therefore that all historical roads must eventually culminate in a repetition of the West-European experience—a notion so prevalent among Russian Marxists of the time—was for him a purely mechanical, and unhistorical, application of Marx's theories. The point about Russia, Trotsky believed, was not only that her history was unlike anything experienced in the West but that, having had so different a past, her future must also turn out to be unlike anything which had characterized the West. Plekhanov, Lenin and others had taken for granted that Russia must inevitably evolve into a capitalist phase. It is one aspect of Trotsky's originality that he dismissed this prospect as an absurdity of Marxist schematics. Capitalism, he argued, was in fact impossible in Russia; the view that it was taking root grew out of a confusion of capitalism with industrialization. The character of the latter provided, actually, the best evidence for the fact that the Russian economy was unique: industrialization was neither carried out by, nor did it create, a middle class; it had neither transformed Russian agriculture nor resolved the problem of the peasant population—for it had been simply "grafted on" from above, and it had been made to co-exist alongside the traditional agricultural economy, not intermix with it; and industrialization had left the political structure intact, in fact even more powerful, for the autocracy—the absolutist state—now controlled even greater economic resources.

This last, however, was, in Trotsky's view, a temporary phenomenon or rather an illusion created by the immediate, not final, impact of rapid industrialization. The latter had also set into motion longer-term processes of which the most striking was the—relatively—astronomical growth of a working class population; its strength was out of all proportion to its relative size within the population as a whole for it had the power to paralyze industry and thus the Russian state's capacity for pursuing its foreign policy objectives in general, its military ambitions in particular. In a parallel and obviously connected way, industrialization had given rise to significant urban centres; the city, Trotsky believed, was now imposing its hegemony over the countryside and would become the clue to revolutionary strategy. Finally, industrialization, though it had not grown organically via the countryside and the town, was having disruptive effects upon agriculture and the peasants, the ultimate pillars of the autocracy's traditional support. The first effect was economic: industrial capital had been mobilized by the state through huge foreign loans and these had to be serviced by higher taxation and more relentless exploitation of agriculture, so that the lot of the peasant had become worse as a direct result of the policy of industrialization. The second effect was social: industry took its labor force from the village but since the pace of industry was so great, the uprooting of those peasants who entered the industrial orbit was sudden—and in this sense violent—and at the same time both unassimilated and incomplete—thus the social phenomenon of peasants who found themselves simultaneously in two different worlds, the old and the new. The third effect was political: in the absence of a middle class, of a mediating force between city and country-side, between industry and agriculture, a basis had been created for a direct linkage between workers and peasants.

One other aspect of Trotsky's analysis must be touched upon before we conclude this discussion of the manner in which he conceived the relationship between Russian society and politics. This is what may be called the dilemma, which eventually confronted the autocracy and society in general, of modernization. The introduction of industry had created the need for such concomitant changes as would keep industry not only going but developing at a pace necessary to assure Russia's continued viability as a European and Far Eastern power. Could the autocracy afford to give its blessing to such changes—the most important of which was agrarian reform? Trotsky believed that it could not, for the simple reason that changes of this kind were tantamount to the autocracy committing suicide. Thus the Russian state at the beginning of the twentieth century was behaving in a manner reminiscent of its behaviour during previous centuries: having itself championed one element of modernization—in the present case industry—it suppressed and strangled all other elements.

It would be no exaggeration to say that Trotsky's concept of the permanent revolution—the revolution of backward society—was conceived by him as the only possible way out of the dilemma, that is, as the only way to modernizing Russia, and, moreover, as the only possible consequence of the emerging pattern of Russia's economic, social and political peculiarities. How else could Russia be transformed, and her anomalies erased, except through one, uninterrupted leap into the modern world? And who else except the working class could supervise this ongoing transition? The autocracy did not want to do it, the middle class—such as it was—could not do it, and the peasants had no idea how to do it. The Russian proletariat, Trotsky believed, however limited its relative size and resources, was in a position to seize power if it gained the support of the peasantry. But having gained this support and having seized power it would soon discover that it could not solve any of Russia's fundamental problems without organizing society on a collectivist basis. Thus the revolution of backwardness in the twentieth century would issue forth in the form of a combined revolution, bringing together two different, but now related in time, historical eras, that of the bourgeois-agrarian revolution and that of the industrial-socialist revolution.

But Trotsky was not so naive as to believe that out of the largely primitive and impoverished foundations of Russia's economy and society a modern, much less socialist, world could arise; the needs of society and the declared intentions of its revolutionary class, even if followed by immediate institutional changes, would not be enough to assure that the leap culminated with a landing in the socialist millennium. Had not Marx assumed that a pre-condition of socialism was man's capacity—already proven under advanced capitalism—for developing to its ultimate levels the means and organization of economic production? In this sense, Russia, whatever the industrial changes of the last decades of the nineteenth century, was merely an upstart and any attempt, in the post-revolutionary period, to rely on her internal resources alone would end, Trotsky thought, in disaster—either complete chaos or a bureaucratic tyranny. In the light of this premonition, therefore, it is not difficult to understand the emphasis which Trotsky, in the context of the revolution of backwardness, placed upon the European or world revolution. Without such a revolution,

he believed, the Russian revolution would be doomed to the vengeance of backwardness. Trotsky was indeed an internationalist by temperament and mentality, but his internationalism was not merely the idealistic frame of mind it has so often been made out to be; it was also an intrinsic part of his conception of the material needs of the *Russian* revolution.

In the event, the European revolution did not, of course, materialize and it is in fact one of the great weaknesses of Trotsky's theory of the permanent revolution that he could find no way of explaining why it *should* materialize (except by mouthing the standard, and in themselves insufficient, general Marxist assumptions about European capitalism). Nothing would be so amusing today, were it not so pathetic, than to parade Trotsky's obsessive misreadings, in the 1920s and 1930s, of developments at the time in Britain or Germany or France. But it would be too simple, and much too kind, to attribute the failure of his predictions for Russian socialism to the failure of the European revolution alone. There is a further, more important, lacuna in his conception of the Russian revolution—and of the revolution of backwardness in general—and it is worth considering briefly for it completes the picture of the scope and limits, and character, of his thought.

I have said nothing so far about Trotsky's view of revolutionary organization, more specifically the revolutionary party, and this is because for a long time the matter of party leadership and strategy played virtually no part in his formulation of the theory of permanent revolution. The whole subject of Trotsky's critique of Bolshevism is a story in itself, but suffice it to say that between 1903 and 1917 no one was more scathingly hostile towards—and, incidentally, more successful in laying bare—the ideas of Lenin. Why is it, then, that in mid-1917 Trotsky suddenly embraced what he had for so long and so convincingly rejected? The answer, I think, is not far-sought. Trotsky had always assumed—is *this*, perhaps, the reason why he has been called a "classical" Marxist?—that social, objective factors were both the necessary and the sufficient conditions for determining the character, the social content, of a revolution. And if the revolution were to be socialist, this meant, among other things, that it was to be led by the workers, or rather that the objective conditions were such as to catapult the workers into a position of leadership. It would be merely superfluous to dwell on the fact that this was too simplistic a formulation of the problem and that, even assuming the workers to be the force *behind* the revolution, it did not resolve two operative questions: firstly, in what concrete sense would the workers actually *lead* or organize the revolution; and, secondly, in what concrete sense were the Russian workers actually socialist. It is clear that these issues had suddenly dawned upon Trotsky after February 1917; and it is equally clear he then concluded that the somewhat glib manner in which he had over the years treated the issues could no longer be defended. It is clear, in other words, that he then recognized that his theory had assumed too much about the capacities of the Russian proletariat, that it had failed to provide for an operative, organizational link between social conditions—the objective revolutionary situation—and political consequences—the seizure of power. What happened in 1917 may thus be described as both a personal and theoretical coming together, between Trotsky and Lenin and between the theory of the revolution of backwardness and the theory of revolution-making in conditions of backwardness.

To put the matter thus is to reject the charge sometimes made against Trotsky that in 1917 he had succumbed to an instrumentalist view of revolution, to the view, in other words, that revolution was a function of personal, organizational factors, in this case Lenin and Bolshevism. In later years he would, it is true, admit that but for Lenin the October Revolution may never have taken place. And he would also argue that the main reason why a workers' revolution had not broken out in, for example, Germany was that the Marxist movement there had not succeeded in creating a Bolshevik-like party and leadership. But in both cases he meant only to say that neither the objective factor—social reality—nor the subjective one—revolutionary leadership—in itself constituted a sufficient condition for revolution. A combination of the two was essential. This, incidentally, is one of the central themes of his major historical work, *The History of the Russian Revolution,* in which he made so monumental an attempt to explain the events of 1917.

Nevertheless, his alliance with Lenin did commit him to an ambiguous position which in the course of time would press upon him but the implications of which he was never quite prepared to recognize, much less confess to, however much he himself did to make them credible. Before 1917, in his attacks against Lenin—particularly in 1903 and 1904—Trotsky had argued that Bolshevism was a form of Jacobinism—and a degenerate form at that—peculiar to a revolutionary movement in a backward society, that it was itself one reflection of backwardness. Its organizational principles, he had then claimed, like its attitudes to politics and society, were diametrically opposed to those of socialism. Were it to succeed in seizing power this would constitute proof not that socialism had triumphed but that it had been defeated, that the workers' cause was either betrayed or impossible in the first place. Following 1917, of course, Trotsky never raised this theme again; but it must surely have haunted him in the darkening days of the 1930s. It is not only the advantages of hindsight, therefore, which allow us to conclude that the revolution of backwardness which Trotsky had postulated as long ago as 1905 had ultimately assumed an ironic twist and one which he himself had not failed to anticipate; it was already inherent in his own understanding of Russia and of the dilemmas of backwardness in general. Trotsky, in his theory of the permanent revolution, had indeed gone a long way toward showing that the social and political conditions of backwardness were such as to make highly likely the emergence of a revolution in the name of socialism, for no other revolution, he had argued, could cope with the problems of backwardness. Elsewhere, however, he had also shown that such conditions were equally propitious to the growth of a Bolshevik-type party. In 1917, in fact, he came to recognize that the revolution in the name of socialism would emerge as a result, partly, of the existence and strength of such a party. In that case, however, in view of the character he had once attributed to Bolshevism, it could be said—though Trotsky was able to do so only inadvertently—that the conditions of backwardness were such as to make socialism—of the Marxist variety—itself impossible.

This same point may be put in a somewhat different form. Marx, it will be recalled, had frequently called attention to the "universalizing" force of capitalism, to its tendency to modernize the backward societies it came into contact with, and thus arouse them from their centuries-old stagnation. He made no systematic study of the pattern which this modernization assumed, but he claimed to see in it the self-reproduction of capitalism. Trotsky too, as we have seen, was fascinated by the processes of development set in motion by the impact of the West on a backward society. But Trotsky, in analyzing the peculiarities of these processes, may be said to have implicitly denied the truth of Marx's famous observation that capitalism

was everywhere creating "a world after its own image." On the contrary, Trotsky argued, capitalism in the West had the long-term effect of transforming backward societies in a direction historically unprecedented; modernization in such societies was thus by-passing the capitalist phase and would ultimately issue in a peculiarly twentieth century revolution. He believed this revolution would be the harbinger of socialism. It was not, and perhaps could not be; but the revolution of backwardness did bring forth a unique form of modern society, a unique form of collectivism. This last resembled nothing imagined in the Marxist canon; yet movements calling themselves Marxist have championed it. Why this should be so—and the irony of it—can in no small measure be comprehended and appreciated through the thought of Leon Trotsky. (pp. 69-79)

Baruch Knei-Paz, "Trotsky, Marxism and the Revolution of Backwardness," in Varieties of Marxism, *edited by Shlomo Avineri, Martinus Nijhoff, 1977, pp. 65-81.*

IRVING HOWE (essay date 1978)

[*A longtime editor of the leftist magazine* Dissent *and a regular contributor to the* New Republic, *Howe is one of America's most highly respected literary critics and social historians. He has been a socialist since the 1930s, and his criticism is frequently informed by a liberal social viewpoint. Howe is widely praised for what F. R. Dulles has termed his "knowledgeable understanding, critical acumen and forthright candor." Howe has written: "My work has fallen into two fields: social history and literary criticism. I have tried to strike a balance between the social and the literary; to fructify one with the other; yet not to confuse one with the other. Though I believe in the social approach to literature, it seems to me peculiarly open to misuse; it requires particular delicacy and care." In the following excerpt, Howe discusses* 1905, Literature and Revolution, My Life, *and* The History of the Russian Revolution.]

Though not so commanding in structure or rich in detail as the *History,* *1905* is a distinguished piece of historical writing—especially when one remembers that its author was under thirty when he wrote its somewhat disparate segments. *1905* lacks the sustained narrative line of the *History,* it does not venture upon the ambitious theoretical generalizations of the *History,* and only occasionally can it compare for vividness in the portraiture of major actors. Yet, at some points, *1905* seems to have a reliability as a record of events that is more persuasive than that of the *History.* It is not so completely at the mercy of a grand ideological scheme as the later book, nor so thoroughly subservient to the unfolding of a supposed historical progress. Event and interpretation are here somewhat ill at ease with one another, and precisely this roughness of execution, this occasional uncertainty and hesitation, lends *1905* a convincing air of verisimilitude.

Though in *1905* a short-breathed writer, Trotsky is admirably close to his materials, in touch with the swirl and chaos of the events he describes. The narrative rises and breaks; there are gaps in both story and idea; no Marxist enclosure or completion is possible with regard to a sequence of events still betraying uncertainty, inexperience, improvisation. Perhaps another way of saying this is that Trotsky does not here feel obliged to deal with the vexing problem of the relation between the Bolshevik party and the upsurge of the masses. The Bolsheviks played only a minor role in 1905 and Trotsky was by no means inclined to give them an inch more of credit than he had to. Instead of a schema of purposeful, indeed, almost inevitable revolution that controls the latter portion of the *History,* we find here elemental confrontations between an obtuse, sluggish oligarchy and masses of people suddenly thrust into political consciousness, testing for the first time the pleasures of opinion and speech. There is no "guiding hand," firm or shaky, from a "vangard party." There is only the improvised legislature of the masses, the Soviet or council, through which they seek coherence and legitimacy.

Trotsky's prose in *1905* is fresh, lucid, and, like all his historical works, remarkably free of Marxist jargon. The "*feuilleton* style" about which Lenin had complained is all but gone; the writer bows to his subject, finds his language through submitting to the momentum of fact. Occasionally he allows himself terms of insult and contempt when talking about the autocracy, terms he will no longer need in the *History;* for now, in the years after 1905, the autocracy still rules, and with a heavy fist, while after 1917 it will be no more than a pitiable relic. Elements of his later style are also present: the sardonic, gleaming passion, the eye searching out dramatic or revealingly incongruous moments (as in an astonishing vignette about his visit to a noblewoman's home where he is to lecture before a group of aristocratic officers).

Politically the greatest strength of *1905* lies not in its by now familiar rehearsal of the theory of permanent revolution but in Trotsky's stress—not nearly so evident in the *History*—upon the overwhelming, almost supra-class absolutism of the Tsarist state:

> Absolutism reached the apex of its power when the bourgeoisie, having hoisted itself on the shoulders of the third estate, became sufficiently strong to serve as the adequate counterweight to the forces of feudal society. The situation in which the privileged and owning classes, by fighting one another, balanced one another, ensured maximum independence for the state organization. Louis XIV was able to say, *"L'état, c'est moi."* The absolute monarchy of Prussia appeared to Hegel as an end in itself, as the materialization of the idea of the state as such.
>
> In its endeavor to create a centralized state apparatus, Tsarism was obliged not so much to oppose the claims of the privileged estates as to fight the barbarity, poverty, and general disjointedness of a country whose separate parts led wholly independent economic lives. It was not the equilibrium of the economically dominant classes, as in the West, but their weakness which made Russian bureaucratic autocracy a self-contained organization. In this respect Tsarism represents an intermediate form between European absolutism and Asian despotism, being, possibly, closer to the latter of these two.

Whether or not deliberately, Trotsky was here picking up a strand of Marx's thought—the Marx who wrote that in Louis Napoleon's France the state takes on a kind of independent life, "is an appalling parasitic body, which enmeshes the body of French society like a net and chokes all its pores." The view that the state can be not merely an agency acting in behalf of a ruling class but also, and sometimes still more so, an independent body weighing heavily upon all of society—this

view, so important to twentieth-century political thought, was not to be stressed by the classical Marxists. Trotsky turned to it in *1905* because he was seeking to explain the special features of Tsarist autocracy; later he devoted considerably less attention to this matter, not seeing sufficiently that the power of statist absolutism in Russia has been a phenomenon overarching particular modes of class rule and persisting, in fact, as a veritable constant of its backwardness. (pp. 22-5)

It was . . . in his writings about literature that Trotsky displayed his full intellectual virtuosity. Had he devoted himself systematically (or better yet, unsystematically) to literature, he might have become one of the great critics of our century. As it is, many of the pieces he wrote on literary themes are still fresh, still vivid with sharp insights and brilliant sentences. In one of his last critical pieces Trotsky wrote that the French novelist Céline "walked into great literature as other men walk into their own houses." The same could be said about Trotsky himself. He shows the mark of the true critic, which is not system, erudition, or opinion but the gift for evoking a writer's essential quality, his voice, inflection, accent, vision. (pp. 94-5)

Trotsky's major venture into literary criticism, *Literature and Revolution,* was composed during his summer vacations of 1922 and 1923, an extraordinary feat of concentration when one remembers the pressures under which he as working at the time. Not quite unified yet more than a mere gathering of essays, the book is marked by enormous verbal energy, a brilliance of phrasing that shines through even a somewhat erratic English translation. Away from the harshness of life under War Communism and free, if only for the moment, from the ugliness of Bolshevik factionalism, Trotsky seems to breathe a sigh of relief at once again entering that "world more attractive" he had always taken the arts to be.

The book divides into two parts: at the outset and in the concluding chapters a theoretical assault on the doctrines of Proletkult, which was then proclaiming the rise of a "proletarian literature" in the Soviet Union, and a series of chapters, often as acute as they are rash, on contemporary Russian writers, from Andrey Biely to Vladimir Mayakovsky.

Within the self-imposed bounds of Marxism, the theoretical chapters may be regarded as definitive. Trotsky begins with a strong appreciation of the role of tradition as it refers both to the slow, complex meshings of cultural experience and to the internal dynamics of literary history. It is an appreciation of tradition as keen in its way as T. S. Eliot's, but not, of course, derived from so intimate a participation in the actual life of literature.

Though Marx himself took for granted the power of tradition in his scattered remarks on cultural subjects, few Marxists have ever troubled to articulate this view with the care that Trotsky devoted to it. He understands that the tempo of cultural change, necessarily slow and at least partly determined by the inner life of culture itself, cannot be yoked to the tempo of political revolution. "The dramatic upheavals of political life must sooner or later affect the inner character of the arts but cannot drive them, cannot dictate to them, cannot issue edicts and demands. History shows that the formation of a new culture which centers around a ruling class demands considerable time and reaches completion only at the period preceding the political decadence of that class." That Trotsky fails here to specify what he means by "considerable time" is not nearly so important as his tacit warning against the assumption that a culture can be called into existence by fiat. Equally notable is the last part of the sentence, which links cultural upsurge with political decadence, an idea crucial to the serious study of modernism though not, unfortunately, elaborated by Trotsky.

At this point in his argument, the Marxist schema comes to appear excessively comprehensive and optimistic. So long as a "proletarian dictatorship" is necessary, there is little possibility that a distinctive proletarian culture can be created—there simply cannot be enough leisure, surplus, comfort, tradition. But once the conditions of material life improve significantly and sociopolitical tensions lessen to the point where the "proletarian state" begins to wither away, then "conditions for cultural creation will become more favorable, the proletariat will be more and more dissolved into a socialist community and will free itself from its class characteristics and thus cease to be a proletariat." If there is an element of troublesome utopianism in this vision of the future, there is also an insistence upon a powerful Marxist idea largely ignored during the dark age of Stalinism: that the historical mission of the proletariat is self-dissolution. Here Trotsky speaks cogently: "The proletariat was, and remains, a nonpossessing class. This alone restricted it very much from acquiring those elements of bourgeois culture which have entered into the inventory of mankind forever. . . . The bourgeoisie came into power fully armed with the culture of its time. The proletariat, on the other hand, comes into power fully armed only with the acute need of mastering culture."

Meanwhile, continues Trotsky, the transition to socialism is bound to entail difficulties of a kind inimical to culture in general and any effort to improvise a "proletarian culture" in particular. Since this transition must be seen as an experimental phase of man's history in which the lowly and the oppressed struggle toward self-determination, the culture of the transitional era should be largely free of party dictate. "The domain of art is not one in which the Party is called upon to command." If Trotsky was prepared to accept only conditionally the view that culture is an autonomous realm of human activity—he insisted that ultimately it remains dependent on "a material base" and that the party must retain the right to intervene against open political attacks—he sided, during the 1920s, with those Bolshevik intellectuals who took a relatively tolerant view of literary divergences.

But there is another side to Trotsky's book, a side that derives from both ideology and temperament. He can say, admirably enough, that "a work of art should, in the first place, be judged by its own law, that is, the law of art." But he then adds, "Marxism alone can explain why and how a given tendency in art has originated in a given period of history. . . ." This ideological arrogance, unbacked by evidence or argument, calls to mind endless and still more dubious claims that "Marxism alone" can shed light on this or explain that—though the shedding and the explaining do not often follow. A more personal source of Trotsky's historical arrogance is his infatuation with the spirit of dynamism, a fury of change. He keeps criticizing, though usually in a friendly spirit, writer after writer, work after work for lacking the "dynamic" tension, the urban thrust and drive that seem to him characteristic of a revolutionary era. It is as if he were in search of some quintessential poem or novel that will seize the spirit of the time—some new, shiny, functional work bearing within itself all the strengths of tradition yet rising into the glory of the future.

A touching hope but a vain one and, as it turned out, dangerous too. For such a demand could easily lead to impatience, im-

patience to intolerance, intolerance to proscription, and proscription to prison. Not that, in relation at least to literature, Trotsky slid down this scale of response. But one can't help noticing a clash between the cool good sense of his literary theory and the fiery ultimatism of his literary temperament. The "poem of the revolution" cannot be written, at least not in the form that Trotsky seemed to want. Precisely for the reasons he himself doubts the possibility of a "proletarian culture," so must that poem be marked, pocked, and graced by the bearings of the past. It grows uneasy before the high abstractions of the future, it lives most easily with the puzzlements and quiddities of the present. No wonder the poet Mayakovsky, in an untranslatable pun, joked that even the most cultivated of commissars remains a commissar.

Trotsky's hunger for a poem or fiction that would utterly embrace and reveal the spirit of the time—a hunger not exactly unknown among twentieth-century revolutionists of both deed and word—leads him at the end of his book into a utopian rhapsody about the spirit of a time not yet visible, the era of Communist man when "all the vital elements of contemporary art [will be developed] to the highest point." In that blissful classless future "man will become immeasurably stronger, wiser, and subtler. . . . The average human type will rise to the heights of an Aristotle, a Goethe, or a Marx. And above this ridge new peaks will rise."

Several decades ago this passage was lovingly cited by Trotsky's admirers as evidence of sublimity of vision. Now, in a somewhat cooler time, one may wonder about the relationship between such unqualified utopianism and the kind of politics, harsh with the authoritarian certitudes of Bolshevism in power, that Trotsky had been conducting since the revolution. Nor is it quite certain that a time in which "the average human type" will rise to the level of an Aristotle or Goethe would strike many of us as a prospect either attractive or even bearable.

The strength of *Literature and Revolution,* apart from its devastation of the notion of "proletarian literature," lies in the chapters on individual writers—quick, jagged, sardonic, affectionate, admiring, impatient. In writing about the enormously talented Mayakovsky Trotsky succeeds partly in slipping, so to say, under the poet's skin; he grasps imaginatively the poet's struggle to bring into some workable relation the clamor of self and the turbulence of the world; he notes the poet's weakness for large and grandiose phrases and, Marxist bias aside, celebrates instead the personal and nonpolitical lyrics. By certain readings Trotsky may well be wrong in his estimate of Mayakovsky's work, but that hardly matters when set against the penetration and sympathy of his criticism.

Trotsky is a master of the crisp summary, the synoptic evocation, of a writer's essential voice or spirit. Here he writes about the peasant poet Nikolay Kliuev:

> He promises paradise through the Revolution, but this paradise is only an exaggerated and embellished peasant kingdom, a wheat and honey paradise: a singing bird on the carved wing of the house and a sun shining in jasper and diamonds. Not without hesitation does Kliuev admit into his peasant paradise the radio and magnetism and electricity; and here it appears that electricity is a giant bull out of a peasant epic and that between his horns is a laden table.

A remark on the work of Biely:

It is absolutely irrefutable that the human word expresses not only meaning but has a sound value, and that without this attitude to the word there would be no mastery in poetry or in prose. We are not going to deny Biely the merits attributed to him in this field. However, the most weighty and high-sounding word cannot give more than is put into it. Biely seeks in the word, just as the Pythagoreans in numbers, a second, special and hidden meaning. And that is why he finds himself so often in a blind alley of words. If you cross your middle finger over your index finger and touch an object, you will feel two objects, and if you repeat this experiment it will make you feel queer; instead of the correct use of your sense of touch, you are abusing it to deceive yourself. Biely's artistic methods give exactly this impression. They are invariably falsely complex.

(pp. 96-101)

The most enduring portion of Trotsky's writings composed in his year of exile was not directly polemical or even narrowly political. It was directed to the world at large rather than the isolated sects of anti-Stalinist radicalism; it represents the culminating achievement of a major twentieth-century writer for whom the bitterness of defeat and the sufferings of persecution nevertheless brought an opportunity to fulfill his talent. The major books of these last eleven or twelve years are Trotsky's autobiography, *My Life*. . . , the lyrical fragment on Lenin's youth, the severely controlled biography of Stalin, the masterful compression of his basic views on Stalinism called *The Revolution Betrayed,* and above all, *The History of the Russian Revolution*. . . . (p. 152)

Written very soon after Trotsky began his exile in Turkey, *My Life* seems strongest in its first few chapters, rapid sketches of childhood, school, and early radicalism. In the very first paragraph Trotsky sets himself, with the self-consciousness of a seriously ambitious writer, against a major tradition of Russian literature: those spacious recollections of youth and portrayals of idyllic country life one finds in Akasov, Tolstoy, and Turgenev. But far from simply yielding himself to these predecessors, Trotsky strikes at the outset a note of respectful challenge, for he is after all a revolutionist:

> The idealization of childhood originated in the literature of the privileged. A secure, affluent, and unclouded childhood, spent in a home of inherited wealth and culture, a childhood of affection and play, brings back to one memories of a sunny meadow at the beginning of the road of life. The grandees of literature, or the plebeians who glorify the grandees, have canonized this purely aristocratic view of childhood. But the majority of the people, if it looks back at all, sees, on the contrary, a childhood of darkness, hunger, and dependence. Life strikes the weak—and who is weaker than a child?

Yet the tradition of "the grandees" is not to be dismissed so readily, not even by the revolutionist who helped destroy it; the early pages of *My Life* are rich with echoes of classical Russian literature, abounding with a serenity of space and air, an affection for the little things of daily existence, an immersion in the world of the senses that is rare in the Marxist canon. Trotsky writes, for example, about his childhood on his father's farm in a style that shows how well he remembered, and learned from, "the literature of the privileged":

> The barns, divided into bins, held fresh-smelling wheat, rough-prickly barley, smooth, almost liquid flaxseed, the blue-black beads of the winter rape, and light, slender oats. When the children played at hide-and-seek, they were allowed, on occasions when there were special guests, to hide in the barns. Crawling over one of the partitions into a bin, I would scramble up the mound of wheat and slip down on the other side. My arms would be buried to the elbows and my legs to the knees in the sliding mass of wheat, and my shirt and shoes, too often torn, would be filled with grain. . . .

The political sections of *My Life* lack the vividness of these early chapters, perhaps because Trotsky is covering ground that he has already touched upon in earlier books and expects to deal with more authoritatively in later ones. There are snapshots, often witty and malicious, of leading figures in the European Social Democracy; but about Stalin, still treated mistakenly as a mere bureaucratic mediocrity, and the significance of Stalinism as a social phenomenon *My Life* offers interpretations that, when compared with the books to come, seem rudimentary. About Trotsky's inner life, his private feelings, his relations with women and children, the book is stringently reticent, for he regards himself as a political man, he is writing a public autobiography, and the very thought of spilling out revelations would have been repugnant to him. Composed a little too early in his life, when some major elements of his thought had not yet crystallized, *My Life* suffers from a fault perhaps characteristic of the public autobiography: it is neither quite a personal narrative nor a comprehensive public record but alternates with brilliant uncertainty between the two.

The History of the Russian Revolution, an enormous three-volume work composed in thirteen months under the trying conditions of exile, is surely Trotsky's masterpiece, the single greatest work of history in the Marxist vein. Marxist not only in its terms of perception, so that the narrative unfolds as a great drama of the struggle between classes, but above all in its insistence that the mute objects of Russian oppression, the masses of proletarians and peasants, have now become active subjects, forging their own destiny on the streets, in the shops, and across the countryside. At times the masses are submitted to cool and dispassionate examination, shown in molecular drift, still more a potential of historical will than a cohered, purposeful force; at other times they take on an almost legendary strength, as if they have become a collective person, bound by class consciousness into a unity of power. Marxism serves here both as analytical method and political myth, a way of understanding and a way of transforming history. Later, Trotsky would pride himself on the claim that while the book was, of course, open to political and intellectual challenge, no serious errors of fact had been detected by its critics—even though he was forced, in Turkey, to write without access to libraries. He had tried, he said in the preface to the book, to be "objective" without pretending to be "impartial," and for once this seems really a distinction pointing to a difference.

The *History* is a work on the grand scale, epic in tone and proportion, brilliant in verbal coloring, quick with the passions of strongly remembered events. One sign of its superiority to *My Life,* which on a smaller scale also tells the story of the revolution, is that the piquant detail, the sardonic stroke, the brilliant summary characterizations are now firmly placed into a commanding structure. The great fault of Trotsky's early writing—bravura display for its own sake—is all but gone. The *History* is a work of high self-consciousness, parts tightly aligned with an eye toward a pattern of mosaic, incidents figured in behalf of an aura of inevitability.

The sharp, scornful sentences one has come to expect from Trotsky are there, of course. V. M. Chernov, the SR leader: "Abstention from voting became for him a form of political life." Kerensky: "Not a revolutionist; he merely hung around the revolution" indulging "the kind of eloquence which operates neither upon mind nor will, but upon the nerves." Martov: "The moment when the balance is still oscillating is his moment—this inventive statesman of eternal waverings." Lenin upon his return to Russia in 1917: "He endured the flood of eulogistic speeches like an impatient pedestrian waiting in a doorway for the rain to stop." The masses: "A revolution is always distinguished by impoliteness, probably because the ruling classes did not take the trouble in good season to teach the people fine manners."

Trotsky's tone is supremely self-confident, sometimes openly arrogant: it registers the voice of an *assured* victor. His strategy as narrator is to aim not for suspense but for an expected fulfillment. Trenchant observations and wicked thrusts: these are now at the bidding of ideology, or, more accurately, of an epic narrative being shaped in accord with that ideology.

I use the term "epic" intending more than an approximate suggestion of narrative sweep, heroic action, large consequence. I mean it to indicate that the book follows the curve of traditional epic narrative, not, probably, with deliberate intent or plan but as a consequence of the sheer magnitude of the task Trotsky set himself. The formation of a people, a great theme of the epic, becomes in Trotsky's book the emergence of a new historical epoch; the forging of nationhood becomes the breakthrough of the proletariat into self-awareness; and the testing of a hero becomes the steeling of the revolutionary party.

In still another way does the *History* resemble the epic: it ends on a note of fulfillment and high optimism. That the world has learned to recognize such terms as "Bolshevik" and "Soviet," writes Trotsky in his concluding sentence, "alone justifies the proletarian revolution, if you imagine that it needs justification." One has to remind oneself that the man writing these lines is an exile who in the book has refused that option of tragedy which carrying his story just a little further in time might entail. The epic tells of the early glory, not the later decline, of Rome; so too with Trotsky's account of the revolution. The choice of genre seems to reflect a world-view, or, perhaps, a decision to maintain that world-view at all odds. In the *History* the epic "hero" figures as the aroused maker of history shifting readily through three appearances: the newly triumphant proletariat, the newly triumphant party, the newly triumphant Lenin. Each, so to say, stands in for the other: the proletariat the arm of history, the party the fist of the proletariat, Lenin the brain of the party. At least until the next breakdown into a dialectic of struggle, history seems here well arranged, working according to plan, ending in a synthesis of triumph. For readers suspicious of visions or narratives clamped into excessive order, all this may constitute a certain sleight of hand; among later historians, this schema of necessary unfoldment has been a major ground for criticizing Trotsky's version of the revolution.

The tone is that of the epic, too: grand, soaring, assertive, all but willfully brushing aside the knowledge writer and reader share about what is to happen after the last page. Only a writer at the crest of victory, or determined to remember how it felt to be there, can long maintain this voice of historical exhilaration. Here, in a passage worthy of Dickens, is how Trotsky evokes St. Petersburg on the eve of revolution:

> All is changed and yet all remains as before. The revolution has shaken the country, deepened the split, frightened some, embittered others, but not yet wiped out a thing or replaced it. Imperial St. Petersburg seems drowned in a sleepy lethargy rather than dead. The revolution has stuck little red flags in the hands of the cast-iron monuments of the monarchy. Great red streamers are hanging down the fronts of the government buildings. But the palaces, the ministries, the headquarters, seem to be living a life entirely apart from those red banners, tolerably faded, moreover, by the autumn rains. The two-headed eagles with the scepter of empire have been torn down where possible, but oftener draped or hastily painted over. They seem to be lurking there. All the old Russia is lurking, its jaws set in rage.
>
> (pp. 153-58)

And earlier in the book, the workers from the radical Vyborg district come out on the Sampsonievsky Prospect, there to encounter a troop of Cossacks: the fate of the revolution seems to hang on this symbolic meeting.

> . . . the horsemen, cautiously, in a long ribbon, rode through the corridor just made by the officers. "Some of them smiled," Kayurov [a worker Bolshevik] recalls, "and one of them gave the workers a good wink." This wink was not without meaning. The workers were emboldened with a friendly, not hostile, kind of assurance, and slightly infected the Cossacks with it. The one who winked found imitators. In spite of renewed efforts from the officers, the Cossacks, without openly breaking discipline, failed to force the crowd to disperse, but flowed through it in streams. . . . Individual Cossacks began to reply to the workers' questions and even to enter into momentary conversations with them. Of discipline there remained but a thin transparent shell that threatened to break through any second. The officers hastened to separate their patrol from the workers, and, abandoning the idea of dispersing them, lined the Cossacks out across the street as a barrier to prevent the demonstrators from getting to the center. But even this did not help: standing stock-still in perfect discipline, the Cossacks did not hinder the workers from "diving" under their horses. The revolution did not choose its paths: it made its first steps toward victory under the belly of a Cossack's horse.

Epic but also idyllic. By the early 1930s the Bolsheviks, staggering under problems and failures, sometimes oppressed by their own handiwork, and more fearful of one another than they had ever been of the Tsarist police, were inclined to look back upon the October Revolution almost as a time of inno-

Cover illustration of the Soviet newspaper Krokodil *depicting Trotsky as a Nazi collaborator.*

was the role of *this* individual. Yet this is only an intellectual recognition, and it does not crucially interfere with the upward rhythm of the narrative. The book moves ahead steadily, inexorably: history's guardian. Because it acts in accord with the "agenda" of history, just as the epic hero acted in accord with the command of the gods, the triad of Progress—class/party/leader—reaches victory in a blaze of certainty. Anyone who surrenders himself even a little to Trotsky's narrative powers must find this story exhilarating, but a critical intelligence is likely to want stops for question and debate, likely to suspect that the actuality was more chaotic than Trotsky allows.

Of the problematic, the doubting, the hesitant, the tragic—of all these elements of the human enterprise the *History* has little to say, except when it turns for a glance at the vanquished, and then mainly to dismiss them as the refuse of history. There are great chapters on the sociology of dual power and the strategy of insurrection, but those who might look for reflection about the human lot, some touches of insight into the nature of mankind, are not likely to find them here. The power of mind in the *History,* and it is a very great power, is not of the kind that consorts with traditional modes of wisdom.

As historian Trotsky lacks the austere dispassionateness of Thucydides, the sense of watching a great action from a distance such that all human desire shrinks in scale and all human partisanship melts to transience. This, Trotsky would be the first to say, is precisely the kind of history he wishes not to write, a history of "wisdom" and resignation. He writes from another perspective, that of the embroiled participant who cannot, indeed would not, choose the detachment of tragedy.

By the same token, it can be said that Trotsky, unlike other great historians, refuses to grant his opponents dignity and, except perhaps with regard to Martov, hardly shows them respect. Again Trotsky might answer: who among these opponents had much dignity or merited much respect? The vain and hysterical Kerensky? The leaders of Menshevism who had missed their chance to bring Russia the social changes they knew it yearned for? The White Guard generals, some brave enough, but utterly uncomprehending of the historical storm that had swept them aside? Trotsky's tone of ironic contempt is a consequence not just of personal imperiousness or Bolshevik certitude but also of a thought-out verdict upon those who had been defeated. Whether this corresponds to our deepest sense of the human situation, or satisfies the greatest possibilities open to the historian, is another question. For even the reader prepared to yield himself to the triumphant absolutism with which the *History* moves toward its climax will sooner or later remember that its author too was one of the defeated. (pp. 158-61)

Nevertheless, I believe that a good portion of the writings of this extraordinary man is likely to survive and the example of his energy and heroism likely to grip the imaginations of generations to come. In the east European countries heretics turn instinctively to his forbidden books, not so much for precise guidance as for a renewal of the possibility for serious debate. In the West political thinkers must confront his formidable presence, parrying his sharp polemics and learning from his significant mistakes. His greatest books transcend political dispute: they are part of the heritage of our century. For Trotsky embodied the modern historical crisis with an intensity of consciousness and a gift for heroic response which few of his contemporaries could match: he tried, on his own terms, to be equal to his time. Even those of us who cannot heed his word

cence: the good, the great days. Trotsky's is prelapsarian history, or a simulation of it. And it is not hard to imagine that the more reflective among his enemies, huddling nervously in the Kremlin, would secretly turn to the *History* in order to share with its author a return to the "idyll" of their past. Later readers, still susceptible to the sonorities of October, would no doubt experience a similar need to relish the story unstained by denouement. Its sophistication notwithstanding, the *History* is not a book that shares the taste for the anxious and the problematic which has come to dominate serious thought in our century.

Still another literary comparison suggests itself: a comparison with myth. The *History* tells the story of the Russian Revolution as an unfolding and vindication of Bolshevik myth, which does not necessarily mean that it is untrue, only that it seems more persuasive as a work of imagination than of critical history. It is a book that ascends ineluctably from its own premises, everything hinged on the idea of necessity, every paragraph contributing toward a rush of fulfillment. With each page the aura of inevitability thickens. This is not, of course, something that can be maintained for three volumes without a break, and contradictions and doubts do sometimes show themselves. Trotsky is honest enough, for example, to face an important question: would the revolution have succeeded if by chance Lenin had been killed in the summer of 1917? His answer is a gingerly no, it probably would not have succeeded, so central may recognize that Leon Trotsky, in his power and his fall, is one of the titans of our century. (pp. 192-93)

Irving Howe, in his Leon Trotsky, *The Viking Press, 1978, p. 214.*

BARUCH KNEI-PAZ (essay date 1978)

[*In the following excerpt from his* The Social and Political Thought of Leon Trotsky, *Knei-Paz dicusses Trotsky's analysis of fascism.*]

Already in 1932 Trotsky had defined fascism as a political system to which the bourgeoisie resorts during the period of the "decline of capitalism." The notion that the bourgeoisie was tied to a parliamentary, democratic form of government was true, in his view, only of a particular stage of its development, the stage at which capitalism, having emerged from its Jacobinist, revolutionary struggle for dominance, settles into a period of unchallenged growth and maturity. During such a period orderly, democratic, and reformist government parallels, and facilitates, peaceful competition, the latter being the source of capitalism's growth. It is otherwise once the system begins to disintegrate. The commitment to democracy then emerges to be not axiomatic and eternal, but pragmatic and ephemeral. Since it is the economic system itself which is now at stake, all political measures needed to save it, including dictatorship, become legitimate. But the particular form of dictatorship which the crisis of capitalism encourages is not simply a political artifice hastily assembled to mete out force whenever necessary. It is that too, but it is first of all a reflection of the kind of social alliance which must be forged in order to deter the objective forces making for disintegration. These forces grow out of the conditions of mutual alienation and animosity, themselves a product of the decline of capitalism, which separate the three main classes: the big bourgeoisie (now mainly finance capital), the petty bourgeoisie, and the proletariat. Looked at in the context of the relationship among these classes during a period of the threat of economic collapse, fascism emerges as that political system which the big bourgeoisie finally must accept in order to effect an alliance with the petty bourgeoisie against the proletariat.

In order to give a more detailed explication of this, Trotsky's social analysis of fascism, we need turn to various articles which he wrote following the triumph of Nazism in 1933. Here Trotsky began with the observation that although Germany was once a comparatively backward capitalist country, she had in the decades prior to 1914 managed to build an industrial edifice which catapulted her into the forefront of the capitalist world. As in all backward countries which undergo rapid change, pockets of the agrarian, feudal past remained, retaining a partial hold over social and political power, and, in general, social anomalies were aggravated. But for all intents and purposes Germany had become an integral part of the capitalist orbit, and thus subject to the "ills" affecting this orbit as a whole: "over-ripeness" of the productive facilities—leading to the "imperialist" chase after markets and colonies and, eventually, to war—and the growth in the potential power of the proletariat. In a period of economic expansion, the big bourgeoisie was able to prevent the workers' power from becoming actual by applying placating measures—parliamentary enfranchisement, freedom of organization, economic rewards and so on. However, in a period of economic decline, the big bourgeoisie was more and more forced into a direct confrontation with the workers. At first, in the years following the World War, this took the form of suppression by force: thus the growth of a

Bonapartist regime, drawing its main office-holders from the army—Hindenburg, von Papen, etc.—and using the police and military as its main props. This, however, could only be a temporary measure; in an industrially advanced nation such as Germany, force could not in the end overcome the constant social pressures. What was needed was a more fundamental solution, one which took account of the reality and distribution of social classes and power.

The clue lay in the petty bourgeoisie which, during a period of economic depression, had become a huge element of discontent seeking a political vehicle for its grievances. Because of its threatened economic condition it leaned towards radical formulas, whether from the Left or the Right. Thus the struggle which developed between communism and fascism for the "soul" of the petty bourgeoisie and the workers, and which—for reasons Trotsky had elucidated in his criticism of communist tactics—was resolved in favour of fascism. Without the support of the petty bourgeoisie, the workers—and thus the communist movement—were unable to make a breakthrough; but the big bourgeoisie as well was unable to assert its hegemony without the petty bourgeoisie. And as for the petty bourgeoisie itself, now making up the main support of the fascist movement, it could not become a dominant political force on its own since it lacked real economic power.

In this situation of a polarization of the two "exploited" classes in separate and radical political movements, neither of which was strong enough to seize power yet both of which were large enough to prevent others from exercising it effectively, disorder, violence, virtual anarchy became normal everyday phenomena; "street politics" took over from institutional politics. This was obviously inimical to the interests of the big bourgeoisie; and the latter, though separated by an abyss from the petty bourgeoisie, and reluctant to share power with it, finally saw that its only salvation lay in an alliance with it. Thus did the big bourgeoisie, finance capital, join forces with fascism to produce the Nazi government of 1933.

There was no doubt in Trotsky's mind that the Nazi government scrupulously served the interests of big capitalism; although political power became monopolized in the hands of Hitler, the big bourgeoisie retained its economic power base. It is in this sense, therefore, that fascism became a new variant of capitalist government, albeit one appearing during the decline or degeneration of capitalism. That it almost immediately took on such an extreme form of brutality and oppression must partly at least, in Trotsky's view, be attributed to the main goal it set itself: the virtual liquidation of the proletariat as a social force. From this flowed all the main elements of totalitarianism: the ideological negation of class divisions, and the attempt to atomize society in one ubiquitous collective; a nationalist and racist ideology to provide the semblance of unity and homogeneity; economic and cultural regimentation; and state power personified in the figure of the *Fuehrer*. Because natural class divisions in German society were stronger than this new ideology could cope with, the Nazi government retained and refined the characteristic features of a Bonapartist regime, relying on the police and special organs of suppression. But it was more than just a form of Bonapartism, and thus more stable and more dangerous, because it represented the social and political union of both the higher and the lower bourgeoisie.

Trotsky's analysis of German fascism, for all the sweep and power of its generalizations, suffered from an exaggerated imposition of the Marxist theoretical framework. As a result it overemphasized the subsequent, if not original, role of big capital, and neglected the extent to which Hitler was ultimately able to exercise power, almost independently of particular economic interests, by creating autonomous political organs—the party, the secret police, the bureaucracy. Yet Trotsky was not entirely blind to this evolution of Nazi power; although he persisted in the view that economic interests remained supreme, it was just this Bonapartist tendency of Nazism which seemed to him to assure its eventual downfall. For the more politics became severed from economics and society, and the more terror replaced institutional government, the more did this signify that the regime was becoming isolated, and unable to cope with social problems and divisions. The need to resort with ever-growing regularity to force, the failure to cure society's ills, were not accidental. They grew, according to Trotsky, out of the fact that fascism, although it was meant to conceal the decline of capitalism, through its ideology and policies exposed all the underlying elements of capitalism's decay and degeneration:

> Fascism has opened up the depths of society for politics. Today, not only in peasant homes but also in city skyscrapers, there lives alongside the twentieth century the tenth or the thirteenth. A hundred million people use electricity and still believe in the magic power of signs and exorcisms. The Pope of Rome broadcasts over the radio about the miraculous transformation of water into wine. Movie stars go to mediums. Aviators who pilot miraculous mechanisms created by man's genius wear amulets on their sweaters. What inexhaustible reserves they possess of darkness, ignorance and savagery! Despair has raised them to their feet, Fascism has given them a banner. Everything that should have been eliminated from the national organism in the form of cultural excrement in the course of the normal development of society has now come gushing out from the throat; capitalist society is puking up the undigested barbarism. Such is the physiology of National Socialism.

(pp. 354-58)

Baruch Knei-Paz, in his The Social and Political Thought of Leon Trotsky, *Oxford at the Clarendon Press, Oxford, 1978, 629 p.*

ADDITIONAL BIBLIOGRAPHY

Bahne, Siegfried. "Trotsky on Stalin's Russia." *Survey*, No. 41 (April 1962): 27-42.
    Discusses Trotsky's interpretation of events in the Soviet Union under Stalin's rule.

Barker, Francis. "Some Problems in Trotsky's Literary Criticism." In *Literature, Society, and the Sociology of Literature*, edited by Francis Barker, John Coombes, and others, pp. 174-79. Colchester, England: University of Essex, 1977.
    Examines the "(unsuccessful) attempt of a leading Marxist to elaborate the relationship between literature and 'society' without resort to certain bourgeois aesthetic ideologies that threatened and invaded his work."

Bazelon, David T. "Trotsky: The Hero as Symbol." *Dissent* VI, No. 3 (Summer 1959): 288-94.

Cites entries from Trotsky's *Diary in Exile, 1935* to demonstrate that "what most characterizes Leon Trotsky, and the revolutionary generation he symbolizes, are: 1) the dominance of ideas; 2) the need and willingness to act on them; and 3) the fanatic belief in ideological purity."

Breton, André. "Visit with Leon Trotsky." In his *What Is Surrealism?: Selected Writings*, edited by Franklin Rosemont, pp. 173-82. New York: Monad, 1978.
    Recounts Breton's visit with Trotsky in Coyoacán during the summer of 1938.

Camejo, Peter. Introduction to *"The Permanent Revolution" and "Results and Prospects,"* by Leon Trotsky, pp. 7-23. New York: Merit Publishers, 1969.
    Outlines Trotsky's theory of permanent revolution, demonstrates the theory's relevance to political situations in Cuba and the United States, presents Bolshevik and Menshevik views of the issue, and asserts the importance of Trotsky's ideas to contemporary political problems throughout the world.

Churchill, Winston S. "Leon Trotsky." In his *Great Contemporaries*, pp. 197-205. Chicago: University of Chicago Press, 1937.
    Attacks Trotsky's political principles, role in the Revolution, and moral character, stating that "like the cancer bacillus he grew, he fed, he tortured, he slew in fulfilment of his nature."

Day, Richard B. *Leon Trotsky and the Politics of Economic Isolation*. London: Cambridge University Press, 1973, 221 p.
    Detailed analysis of Trotsky's economic policies.

Deutscher, Isaac. *The Prophet Armed. The Prophet Unarmed. The Prophet Outcast*. London: Oxford University Press, 1954-63.
    Three-volume biography which is considered the standard work on Trotsky's life.

——. Introduction to *The Age of Permanent Revolution: A Trotsky Anthology*, by Leon Trotsky, edited by Isaac Deutscher, pp. 13-39. New York: Dell Publishing Co., 1964.
    Discusses the principal tenets of Trotsky's political philosophy in relation to Soviet and world history.

Eastman, Max. "Trotsky becomes a Scholastic." *The Southern Review* VI, No. 2 (Autumn 1940): 317-35.
    Examines logical fallacies in Trotsky's explication of Marxian dialectics, maintaining that "like all religions, dialectic materialism rests fundamentally, not on investigation and rational calculation, but on the will to believe."

Eliot, T. S. "A Commentary." *The Criterion* XII, No. XLVII (January 1933): 244-49.
    Takes issue with the philosophy of art presented in *Literature and Revolution*.

Heyman, Neil M. "Leon Trotsky: Propagandist to the Red Army." *Studies in Comparative Communism* X, Nos. 1-2 (Spring-Summer 1977): 34-43.
    Discusses themes common to the propaganda that Trotsky used in three divergent military situations to boost Red Army morale.

Hook, Sidney. "Reflections on the Russian Revolution." *The Southern Review* IV, No. 3 (Winter 1939): 429-62.
    Takes issue with theoretical arguments in *The Revolution Betrayed*.

Institute of Marxism-Leninism of the Central Committee of the CPSU. *Against Trotskyism*. Moscow: Progress Publishers, 1972, 406 p.
    Excerpts from writings documenting the Communist Party's "unrelenting fight" against the "false and venemous ideology and pernicious practices of Trotskyism."

Katz, David H. "Trotsky's *The Revolution Betrayed*: A Reappraisal." *Midwest Quarterly* XVIII, No. 3 (April 1977): 287-97.
    Describes *The Revolution Betrayed* as a brilliant, "seminal study which influenced a whole generation of Sovietologists," but considers Trotsky's analysis inadequate as an explanation of the origins of Soviet totalitarianism.

Kern, Gary. "Trotsky's Autobiography." *The Russian Review* 36, No. 3 (July 1977): 297-319.
Argues that Trotsky was temperamentally and ideologically inclined to discount subjective factors of individual personality in his analysis of events, and attributes his fall from power to a resulting "inability to appreciate the personal element in Party relations and an utter vulnerability to personal attack."

Knei-Paz, Baruch. "The Political and Cultural Formation of Leon Trotsky: An Intellectual Portrait." *Il Politico* XLV, No. 3 (September 1980): 373-92.
Traces Trotsky's intellectual development, emphasizing his "simultaneous propensity towards ideas and action, towards the translation of one into the other and vice versa."

Kolakowski, Leszek. "Trotsky." In his *Main Currents of Marxism: Its Origin, Growth, and Dissolution*, pp. 183-219. Oxford: Clarendon Press, 1978.
Contends that "there was never any such thing as a Trotskyist theory—only a deposed leader who tried desperately to recover his role, who could not realize that his efforts were in vain, and who would not accept responsibility for a state of affairs which he regarded as a strange degeneration, but which was in fact the direct consequence of the principles that he, together with Lenin and the whole Boshevik party, had established as the foundations of socialism."

Krasso, Nicolas, ed. *Trotsky: The Great Debate Renewed*. St. Louis, Mo.: New Critics Press, 1972, 191 p.
Reprints a series of essays and rejoinders originally published in the *New Left Review*, including contributions by Nicolas Krasso, Ernest Mandel, and Monty Johnstone.

Leavis, F. R. "Under which King, Bezonian?" *Scrutiny* I, No. 3 (December 1932): 205-14.
Cites remarks from *Literature and Revolution* in a discussion of the relationship between culture and economic conditions.

Leon Trotsky: The Man and His Work. Merit Publishers: New York: 1969, 128 p.
Reprints essays and personal reminiscences written between 1925 and 1960. Contributors include Natalia Sedov Trotsky, George Novack, Rosa Luxemburg, Karl Radek, and Anatoly Lunacharsky.

Lichtheim, George. "Reflections on Trotsky." In his *The Concept of Ideology, and Other Essays*, pp. 204-24. New York: Random House, 1967.
Discusses Trotsky's life and thought, often disputing their representation in Isaac Deutscher's biography of Trotsky [see Additional Bibliography].

Lubitz, Wolfgang. *Trotsky Bibliography*. Munich: K. G. Saur, 1982, 454 p.
Comprehensive bibliography of writings about Trotsky through 1980.

Lukacs, Georg. "Propaganda or Partisanship?" *Partisan Review* 1, No. 2 (April-May 1934): 36-46.
Theoretical discussion of the nature of "proletarian literature" criticizing Trotsky's concept of culture in a socialist society.

Malraux, André. "Reply to Trotsky." In *Malraux: A Collection of Critical Essays*, edited by R.W.B. Lewis, pp. 20-4. Englewood Cliffs, N.J.: Prentice-Hall, 1964.
Takes issue with Trotsky's analysis in the essay "The Strangled Revolution" of Malraux's novel *Les Conquerants* (1928; *The Conquerors*), a novel set during the Chinese Revolution of 1925-27.

Mandel, Ernest. "World Revolution Today—Trotskyism or Stalinism?" *International Socialist Review* 31, No. 4 (June 1970): 34-9.
Argues that the Trotskyist movement remains a dynamic force in world politics because of the relevance of Trotsky's ideas to contemporary social and political problems.

———. *Trotsky: A Study in the Dynamic of His Thought*. London: NLB, 1979, 156 p.

Presents and analyzes Trotsky's most important contributions to Marxist theory, finding in Trotsky's works "nothing less than an attempt to provide a coherent explanation of all the basic trends of our epoch, an attempt to explain the 20th century."

McNeal, Robert H. "Trotsky's Interpretation of Stalin." In *Canadian Slavonic Papers*, vol. V, edited by G.S.N. Luckyj, J. St. Clair-Sobell, and others, pp. 87-97. Toronto: University of Toronto Press, 1961.
Assesses Trotsky's depiction of Stalin and Stalinism in various writings.

Molyneux, John. *Leon Trotsky's Theory of Revolution*. New York: St. Martin's Press, 1981, 252 p.
Analyzes the principal tenets of Trotsky's political philosophy in order to demonstrate "that . . . it is impossible to understand the world today without the aid of Trotsky, and that on the other hand, it is impossible to understand it (and, more importantly, to change it) on the basis of Trotsky alone."

Mudrick, Marvin. "Solzhenitsyn *versus* the Last Revolutionary." *The Hudson Review* XXXIV, No. 2 (Summer 1981): 195-217.
Demonstrates that Trotsky viewed the events and major figures of the Russian Revolution in much the same way that Aleksandr Solzhenitsyn does, but observes that Solzhenitsyn nevertheless "needs to demonstrate the hatefulness and baseness of the despotic regime *ab initio* and *ad nauseam* from Lenin through Stalin" and "can't bring himself to cite anything at all which oblige him to acknowledge Trotsky as in power and in exile the principled, untiring, and fearless opponent of Stalin."

Novack, George, and Hansen, Joseph. Introduction to *In Defense of Marxism*, by Leon Trotsky, pp. vii-xxii. New York: Pathfinder Press, 1973.
Discusses factional disputes in the American socialist movement in 1939 and 1940 and the writings in which Trotsky defended Marxist principles during these years.

Nove, Alec. "New Light on Trotskii's Economic Views." *Slavic Review* 40, No. 1 (Spring 1981): 84-97.
Presents Trotsky's most important economic theories and evaluates Richard B. Day's interpretation of Trotsky's views on the controversial issue of building socialism in one country [see Additional Bibliography].

Plamenetz, John. "Trotskyism." In his *German Marxism and Russian Communism*, pp. 281-305. London: Longmans, Green, and Co., 1954.
Delineates the theoretical arguments with which Trotsky denounced Stalinism in *The Revolution Betrayed*, contending that Stalin was not the "betrayer" of the Revolution, as Trotsky asserted, but that Stalinism was the inevitable result of a revolution that was effected prematurely.

Preliminary Commission of Inquiry. *The Case of Leon Trotsky*. New York: Harper & Brothers Publishers, 1937, 617 p.
Transcript of the hearings before the Dewey Commission.

Rahv, Philip. "Versions of Bolshevism." *Partisan Review* XIII, No. 3 (Summer 1946): 365-75.
Review of *Stalin*. While defending Trotsky against widespread accusations that the book's presentation of Stalin's personality and ascent to power are skewed by the author's personal feelings toward his subject, Rahv nevertheless contends that Trotsky's analysis of Stalinism is based on fallacious reasoning.

Rothstein, Andrew. "Trotsky on the Russian Revolution." *The Labour Monthly* 15, No. 12 (December 1933): 761-70.
Considers the *History* "a bulky, three-volume pamphlet against Leninism, and above all against Lenin's party."

Serge, Victor, and Trotsky, Natalia Sedova. *The Life and Death of Leon Trotsky*. New York: Basic Books, 1975. 296 p.
Memoir by a prominent Bolshevik and Trotsky's second wife.

Smith, Irving H., ed. *Trotsky*. Englewood Cliffs, N.J.: Prentice-Hall, 1973, 181 p.
Excerpts from Trotsky's works, from personal reminiscences by his contemporaries, and from examinations of his thought and

role in history by Soviet and Western historians. Contributors include Stalin, Grigori Zinoviev, John Reed, and Isaac Deutscher.

Solotaroff, Theodore. "Wrestling with Trotsky." In his *The Red Hot Vacuum and Other Pieces of Writing on the Sixties*, pp. 142-47. New York: Atheneum, 1970.
    Discusses Trotsky's status as hero to American liberals of the 1930s and examines the essays collected in a recent anthology of his works. Citing Trotsky's reputation as "the walking image of radical thought and action," Solotaroff concludes that "the relation of thought to action is ultimately the relation of truth to power" and in Trotsky's mind "the former is remorselessly subservient to the latter."

Steffens, Lincoln. Introduction to *The Bolsheviki and World Peace*, by Leon Trotsky, pp. 7-19. New York: Boni and Liveright, 1918.
    Maintains that Trotsky's advocacy of peace with Germany during World War I was the result of his international socialist perspective, in that he stood for "a democratic peace against imperialism and capitalism and the state everywhere, for the establishment in its stead of a free, worldwide democracy."

Steiner, George. "Trotsky and the Tragic Imagination." In his *Language and Silence: Essays on Language, Literature, and the Inhuman*, pp. 365-80. New York: Atheneum, 1967.
    Discusses the aspects of Trotsky's life that resemble elements of classical tragedy.

Vernadsky, George. "Trotsky Turns Historian." *Current History* XXXVIII (May 1933): 176-81.
    Early review of *The History of the Russian Revolution*.

Warth, Robert D. *Leon Trotsky*. Boston: Twayne Publishers, 1977, 215 p.
    Biography presenting an "alternative interpretation" to what Warth considers the "relatively benign view" of Trotsky in Isaac Deutscher's biography [see Additional Bibliography], stressing instead Trotsky's failings as an individual and as a politician.

Wilson, Edmund. "Trotsky Identifies Himself with History." In his *To the Finland Station*, pp. 428-44. Garden City, N.Y.: Doubleday, 1940.
    Examines Trotsky's personal and intellectual predilections and aspects of his political doctrines.

Wistrich, Robert. *Trotsky: Fate of a Revolutionary*. New York: Stein and Day, 1979, 235 p.
    Examines Trotsky's life and thought, attempting "to do justice to his undoubted qualities of heroism, energy, and creative imagination without concealing the darker side of his personality—the fanaticism, the Marxist dogmatism and intolerance with which he sought to impose his messianic vision on the world."

Wolfe, Bertram D. "Leon Trotsky as Historian." *Slavic Review* XX, No. 3 (October 1961): 495-502.
    Briefly outlines the theories put forth in the *History* and assesses the work's literary merit. Although Wolfe praises Trotsky's eloquent prose style and skillful portraiture, he finds the book marred by dogmatism and partisanship.

————. *Three Who Made a Revolution*. New York: Dell Publishing Co., 1964, 659 p.
    Biography of Lenin, Stalin, and Trotsky.

————. Introduction to *Lenin: Notes for a Biographer*, by Leon Trotsky, pp. 7-24. New York: G. P. Putnam's Sons, 1971.
    Discusses Trotsky's portrait of Lenin, the political relationship between the two men, and the circumstances under which the book was written.

Wolfenstein, E. Victor. *The Revolutionary Personality: Lenin, Trotsky, Gandhi*. Princeton, N.J.: Princeton University Press, 1967, 330 p.
    Psychoanalytic study.

Wyndham, Francis, and King, David. *Trotsky*. London: Allen Lane, 1972, 204 p.
    Pictorial biography.

Beatrice (Potter) Webb

1858-1943

Sidney (James) Webb

1859-1947

English political philosophers, sociologists, historians, and essayists.

Among the most outspoken and politically astute proponents of socialism in early twentieth-century England, the Webbs were the authors of numerous investigations into the history and nature of English institutions. Their remarkably comprehensive studies, many of which are still considered definitive, were the product of their conviction that ''no progress can be made except on the basis of ascertained fact and carefully thought out suggestion'' and were intended as a tool to be used in the restructuring of the British political system. The Webbs' concept of socialism was, however, evolutionary rather than revolutionary, and although they were frequently denounced by more radical elements of the socialist movement, their willingness to work within the parameters of parliamentary law and to cooperate with the established regime allowed them to exert more influence on the course of political reform than their less accomodating colleagues.

Beatrice Potter was the eighth of nine daughters born to a wealthy businessman whose family had become established among the gentry of the Cotswold region during the eighteenth century. Her upbringing was largely consistent with Victorian standards for a girl of her station; marginally educated in the schoolroom of her parents' home, she was prepared for the roles of helpmeet and hostess, and it was expected that she would marry a prominent man of her class. Beatrice, however, felt the need of some sort of occupation, and began in her teens to study history, philosophy, economics, and political science. Nevertheless, it was in the traditional Victorian female practice of performing charity work that she found the profession she had been seeking. Working among the poor, Beatrice became aware of the startling misery and destitution that existed alongside the opulent luxury to which she was accustomed. She perceived that the established systems of relief were largely ineffective, and, strongly influenced by her studies of Auguste Comte's positivism, she came to the conclusion that identification of the root causes of poverty would be necessary before effective reform could begin. Toward that end, she conducted a series of investigations into the condition of those at the lowest economic levels of English society, sometimes disguising herself as a working woman in order to establish a more confidential relationship. Already a prominent figure in London social circles, Beatrice quickly became a recognized authority on the plight of the poor. In 1890, while conducting research on the cooperative movement for her first book, she found she needed expert advice on reference materials, and a member of the socialist Fabian Society named Sidney Webb was recommended to her as a scholar of some standing. Beatrice's strong conviction that the condition of the poor was due primarily to gigantic flaws in the economic system had already led her to an interest in socialism and the Fabians, who were the intellectual vanguard of socialism in England, and she arranged a meeting with Webb at the first opportunity.

Sidney Webb was the son of lower middle-class London shopkeepers who realized that education was the key to a better future for their children. They accordingly provided Sidney with all the schooling they could afford, while the brilliant young man contributed substantially by earning a number of scholarships. After being awarded a law degree from London University, Webb entered the civil service, hoping eventually to become involved in politics. He was placed in the Foreign Office and, his duties being extremely light, spent most of his free time in lively political discussions at the London debating clubs which were a popular forum for such activities. It was through one such organization, the Karl Marx club, that Webb was exposed to the theories of socialism, and although he later developed major objections to certain of Marx's economic theories, he readily embraced much of socialist doctrine. It was also through the Karl Marx club that Webb met the man who became his closest friend and political ally, George Bernard Shaw. Soon after their first encounter in 1884, Shaw joined the newly formed Fabian Society, then under the direction of Frank Podmore and Edward Pease, and within a year he had persuaded Webb to do so as well. The combination of Shaw's brilliant iconoclasm and Webb's encyclopedic mind proved to be a dynamic force which allowed them to dominate the Fabians, and by 1890 they had become the guiding influence in the society.

Although dissimilar in almost every other respect, the Webbs shared a passionate concern for the plight of the masses which created a close relationship between them from their first meeting and ultimately led to their marriage in 1892. Typically pragmatic, they established the conditions of their union well before their wedding day: they would live on Beatrice's inheritance, which would allow them to devote themselves to their writings and investigations, while Sidney would take the additional step of pursuing the political career he desired. All went very much according to plan; in 1892, Sidney was elected to the London County Council, and two years later the Webbs' first joint work, *The History of Trade Unionism,* was published. The Fabian Society was at this point fast becoming a major force in English politics under the leadership of Shaw and the Webbs, and it was through their participation in the Society that the Webbs made known their plans for the government. Their preferred method of political action was a policy they called "permeation." Knowing that the formation of a third, strictly socialist party would be difficult at best and that once formed such a party would be much weaker than the firmly entrenched Liberal and Conservative parties, the Webbs planned to introduce socialist candidates into the existing parties and to influence nonsocialist representatives with their meticulously

documented arguments. The Webbs' attitude toward their position as political activists was, however, ambivalent. While they believed in the absolute necessity of the changes they advocated, both felt that their primary responsibility was the research upon which those changes should properly be based, and they regretted that so much of their time had to be spent in lobbying. Yet it was as a direct result of political activism that the Webbs made their most lasting contributions.

In 1895, Sidney was placed in charge of a large bequest left to the Fabian Society by a wealthy patron. Convinced through personal experience of the value of education, Sidney also believed that adequate study of social problems would naturally advance the cause of socialism, and he had long dreamed of founding a school based on the model of the French Ecole Libre des Sciences Politiques. He easily persuaded the other Fabians to use the bequest to establish such a university, and the London School of Economics was thus born. In addition, Sidney used his position on the London County Council to effect a thorough transformation of the public school system, adding art, technical, and polytechnical schools, substantially increasing funding for existing institutions, and restructuring London University in order to make it more accessible to students from lower income groups. Beatrice meanwhile continued with the research for their books, and she was often busy with the many publications of the Fabian Society, although her activities were limited by her always frail health. In 1905, she was given a unique opportunity to effect political reform when she was appointed to a royal commission formed for the purpose of studying the 1834 Poor Law. The result was the Minority Report of the commission, written by the Webbs together, recommending that the various administrative bodies established by the Poor Law be abolished and their functions assumed by related existing departments. Although the recommendations of the Minority Report were not implemented by the government at the time of their publication, they did in fact become an integral part of later reforms, and the Webbs were subsequently congratulated for their foresight.

Sidney's activities in the Fabian Society and his involvement in London local politics eventually placed him at the center of the Labour party, which arose during the first decade of the twentieth century in response to the decay and ultimate demise of the Liberal party. Moreover, his had been a consistently sober and moderating influence in the party's stormy inception, and more often than not his well-considered suggestions became incorporated into official Labour philosophy. This involvement culminated in his election to Parliament in 1922. Although Webb, at 63, had long before abandoned his youthful goal of a seat in Parliament, he felt he could not justly refuse the request of a group of northern coal miners to be their representative, and he agreed to stand for election. During the ten years Sidney sat in Parliament, much of his time was taken up in official duties, and he and his wife were forced to abandon their joint writings. Beatrice, however, took advantage of Sidney's frequent absences by beginning work on her autobiography.

The final phase of the Webbs' career was by far the most controversial. Long fascinated by the progress of socialism in the Soviet Union, the Webbs decided in 1932 to investigate for themselves the world's only Marxist state, and they made an extensive tour of Russia. There they saw what appeared to them to be an ideal state: unemployment was virtually nonexistent, the cities were clean and efficiently run and the citizens, provided for by the government, seemed well-ordered and contented. The Webbs' report to the West, published in 1935 as *Soviet Communism: A New Civilisation?*, was a glowing commendation of the Soviet system and promptly drew criticism from all quarters. Beatrice later admitted that she and Sidney had been deceived by the smooth surface of Soviet society and the facile lies of Joseph Stalin, and she attributed their mistake to the folly of old age.

The Webbs retired to their country home, Passfield Corner, in 1933. Plagued by a number of ailments, they were unable to resume their social research and writings, although Beatrice continued to keep a diary until her death in 1943. Sidney, however, suffered a severe stroke in 1938, and as a result was unable to do any sort of work during his final years.

The Webbs' concept of socialism was distinct from, and often directly opposed to, that of many of their contemporaries. Although they firmly believed in state control of the means of production, they felt expropriation was both immoral and unnecessary, and proposed instead a one hundred percent tax on corporate profits. This recommendation created conflict between the Fabians and the Syndicalists, who believed that the workers should use the power of trade unions to wrest control of industry from wealthy owners and to manage the various manufactures democratically. This is not to say that the Webbs discounted the importance of trade unions, but rather that they perceived the cooperation of unions, government, and factory owners to be the best way of ensuring both adequate production and equitable distribution of profits. Sidney, in a pamphlet produced by the Fabian Society during its formative years, specified the political philosophy upon which these industrial proposals were based: "We contend . . . that the whole produce of labour is due to labour alone—whether labour of hand or labour of brain—and that any form of society which enables idle monopolists of certain social products to extract for their personal consumption a toll from helpless fellow citizens, although perhaps useful in the earlier stages of social evolution, is now bad." Implicit in this statement is the essential feature of the Webbs' political philosophy: while not unconcerned with social and economic theory, their primary goal was simply to alleviate the suffering they had witnessed. While some critics charged that the Webbs' plans for society would necessitate the establishment of a gigantic bureaucratic state whose paternalistic control would present unwelcome intrusion into local affairs, the Webbs in fact considered local government the best unit for the implementation of government policy, and it was to the study of local government that the Webbs devoted much of their investigative work. Beatrice's experience in the Poor Law investigation had confirmed the Webbs' suspicion that highly bureaucratized administration of national policy was always ineffective, allowing for gross distortions of the original legislative intent. They believed that municipal authorities were far better equipped to deal with matters concerning the well-being of their constituencies than were representatives of the national government. Yet they clearly advocated legislative action on a national scale in order to ensure adequate standards of living for all and state involvement in the equitable distribution of wealth.

The moral dimension of the Webbs' theories has been the subject of some attention. Herb Greer has pointed out that many Victorians, faced with the sudden awareness of poverty through the efforts of social critics such as Charles Dickens, assumed that immoral persons must be taking more than their share of the nation's wealth and that moral persons must do something about it. Moreover, the prevailing progressivist philosophy of the period created the conviction that all social problems were indeed eradicable. Beatrice explained her decision to become involved in the crusade this way: "From the flight of emotion away from the service of God to the service of man and from the current faith in the scientific method I drew the inference that the most helpful form of social service was the craft of social investigator." Critics consider the religious aspect of this statement significant, since they generally view the Webbs' campaign for the alleviation of poverty as an essentially Christian endeavor, particularly in Beatice's case. Similarly, critics have discussed the middle-class Victorian morality of the Webbs' socialism, as exemplified in their plan to separate the deserving or morally upright poor from those who were simply malingerers. Critics find revealed in this idea the Webbs' inescapable artistocratic prejudice: while concerned with the welfare of all British citizens, they bore no great love for the poor as individuals and mistrusted the idea of pure democracy.

Although the Webbs devoted much effort to the formulation of political and economic theories, most notably in *A Constitution for the Socialist Commonwealth of Great Britain* and *The Decay of Capitalist Civilisation*, critics agree that they were most effective in the areas of research and reporting, and their eleven-volume history of English local government is often considered their finest work. Beatrice's independent writings, particularly her diaries, are also highly praised, and the comment is frequently made that she might have been a great novelist had she so desired. Many critics, however, feel that the Webbs' writings are insignificant when compared to their enormous impact upon English political development, citing as proof the fact that the modern British Labour party, still a powerful influence in policymaking, retains the essential features of Fabian socialism placed there by the Webbs during the opening decades of the century.

(See also *Contemporary Authors*, Vol. 117.)

PRINCIPAL WORKS

BY BEATRICE AND SIDNEY WEBB:

The History of Trade Unionism (history) 1894
Industrial Democracy. 2 vols. (nonfiction) 1897
Problems of Modern Industry (nonfiction) 1898
English Local Government from the Revolution to the Municipal Corporations Act. 11 vols. (history) 1906-1927
The Break-Up of the Poor Law (report) 1909
The Public Organisation of the Labour Movement (report) 1909
A Constitution for the Socialist Commonwealth of Great Britain (nonfiction) 1920
The Consumer's Co-operative Movement (nonfiction) 1921
The Decay of Capitalist Civilisation (nonfiction) 1923
English Poor Law History. 3 vols. (history) 1927-30
Methods of Social Study (nonfiction) 1932
Soviet Communism: A New Civilisation? (nonfiction) 1935
The Truth about Soviet Russia (nonfiction) 1942
The Letters of Beatrice and Sidney Webb. 3 vols. (letters) 1978

BY BEATRICE WEBB:

"The Dock Life of East London" (essay) 1887; published in journal *Nineteenth Century*
"Pages from a Work-Girl's Diary" (short story) 1888; published in journal *Nineteenth Century*

ANNIE G. PORRITT (essay date 1907)

[*In the following review of* English Local Government, *Porritt commends the comprehensive nature and historical objectivity of that work.*]

The first volume of **English Local Government** covers the government of the parish and the county, leaving the seignorial courts, the municipal corporations, and the various *ad hoc* bodies, created by Parliament for special duties, to future volumes. (p. 460)

The collection of the material for this great work has occupied Mr. and Mrs. Webb for eight years. During more or less of that time they have had the assistance of six trained helpers, to whom they acknowledge their indebtedness in the preface. Most useful for their purpose were the records—chiefly in manuscript—of the parish vestries and the courts of petty and quarter sessions. Next in value they rank the contemporary local newspapers and pamphlets, along with novels, plays, and even sermons. As a supplement to these, they searched the records of the State Departments, and the various Acts of Parliament—chiefly local Acts which were passed to alter the constitution or enlarge the powers of some individual local governing authority. These, with reports of law cases, and some very slight help from local and general histories, are the sources of information for Mr. and Mrs. Webb's volumes; and the notes taken from these manuscript and printed sources, each written on a separate sheet of paper, now form a collection of some fifty thousand pages.

The method of work is described by Mr. and Mrs. Webb in the preface: but even if it had not been mentioned, it would have been impossible to read a single chapter of the book without discovering that some such slip method had been used. When any subject was under consideration, all the slips relating to it were laid out and examined. Each chapter is thus a summary of information gathered from all parts of the country and from the most various sources. The method has the great advantage of accuracy of statement, and of an abundance of authorities; but with its use it is impossible to avoid some repetition or to produce an easy flowing narrative with any graces of style. The division of the the subject into the constitution and the functions of local governing authorities also leads to considerable repetition. This is especially marked in the second half of the volume, the County, in the description first of the rulers of the county—the justices of the peace—and then of the various phases of the judicial and administrative work of these justices. The same individuals and instances are frequently made use of to illustrate and elucidate various aspects of the subject—a method which, in spite of the repetition, is not without advantages of clearness and thoroughness of treatment.

The period covered in this great work of Sidney and Beatrice Webb's extends from 1689 to 1835. They do not seek to go back to the early beginnings of Anglo-Saxon or Norman local autonomy—that task was beyond their scope. The Revolution is chosen as a starting point, because it ushered in an era when the local authorities were left by Parliament to their own devices, and during which, consequently, we are able to see the local governing bodies in the various parts of the country slowly and laboriously working out the problems of government. (pp. 460-62)

Until the appearance of the first volume of Mr. and Mrs. Webb's **English Local Government,** this great subject had been left almost untouched by English writers. The Poor Law and the King's Peace had been the subjects of special treatises; but a comprehensive history of English Local Government had not been attempted. The two works on the subject which did exist, were both by Germans—Rudolf von Gneist and Josef Redlich. The great work of Gneist, which has never been translated, is written by a theorist with a definite thesis to maintain. The history is written to prove that self-government in England ceased to exist with the introduction of the ballot box. (pp. 462-63)

The work of Josef Redlich, which has been well translated by Francis W. Hirst, is concerned chiefly with local government since the Reform Act. On the ground covered by Mr. and Mrs. Webb he scarcely sets foot. . . . It will thus be seen that Mr. and Mrs. Webb are making a wholly new contribution to the history of England—a contribution which is invaluable on account of its thoroughness of research, the fulness of the authorities quoted for every important statement, and not least for the excellence of its arrangement and indexing. (p. 463)

Annie G. Porritt, in a review of ''English Local Government from the Revolution to the Municipal Corporations Act: The Parish and the County,'' in The Yale Review, *Vol. XV, No. 4, February, 1907, pp. 460-63.*

G. R. S. TAYLOR (essay date 1910)

[*In the following excerpt, Taylor examines Sidney Webb's approach to socialist reform.*]

One cannot easily believe that violent revolutions will ever happen in this sleepy England; so we have decided (somewhat hastily, perhaps), that revolutions are unscientific. Nevertheless, one of these days, after a course of better feeding and shorter working hours, it is just possible that even an English mob will forget its respect for science, and will do something rash. If it so happens, when the first messenger fights his way out of the rabble to carry round the great news of victory (we will assume that, for the moment), it will be interesting to hear how the leaders of Socialism receive his tale. "The Social Revolution is accomplished" he will shout. Mr. Bernard Shaw, in the confusion, will forget that he is a Fabian, and will wave an imaginary shillelagh round his head, as befits an Irishman. Mr. Hyndman and Mr. Keir Hardie will have heard the news already. But Mr. Webb will say: "The Social Revolution? I scarcely expected it. So it is really over. Then we can begin, at last." The reader must note that word "begin." It will seem a damp, unappreciative word to the messenger who has seen the last reactionary chased down Pall Mall and heard the last shot fired which cleared "law and order" out of Whitehall. "Begin, indeed; it is ended," he will pant with indignation. But Mr. Webb already will be on his way to take charge of a Department in Downing Street, where he can get to the work of "beginning" Socialism. He cannot think of a successful rebellion bringing Socialism any nearer; for in his mind Socialism can only come by an infinitely careful attention to an infinite number of points of detail. Socialism is the organization of society, and there can be no organization by a street riot.

Indeed, if Mr. Webb were told that Socialists had won—not merely a physical battle, but had captured every parliamentary seat and were in possession of the Houses of Parliament, and had swamped the Lords by raising Mr. Quelch and his friends to the peerage—Mr. Webb would still say: "Ah, then we can begin." Revolutions, either military or political, cannot bring Socialism; for that can only come by organization of the smallest details with the greatest pains. It is all a matter of administration, of putting into working order schemes which, however scientific, are only Utopian until they are actually in practice. Any Parliament could pass a law ordering the whole land to be nationalized, or the railways, or the bakers' shops and the coal mines, the telephones and the cycle trade. But it would be a matter for ceaseless thought and experiments to find out how best to cultivate the land; how to run the trains for the public good rather than for the good of the shareholders; how to bake bread, dig coal, arrange telephone wires, turn out cycles in the best possible way for the public advantage; that is, for the advantage of the whole people. In short, the organization of industry under the State will be no less a matter of careful business detail than it is under private control. Indeed, it will need infinitely more care; for it is only the profit to the masters with which private enterprise is ultimately concerned, whereas State industry must be undertaken for the good of the whole people, whether producers or consumers. The problem before Downing Street under Socialism will be the production of the greatest amount of wealth, in the most convenient way, and its distribution to the people in accordance with the laws of equity and social utility. When Mr. Webb starts off for Downing Street after the Social Revolution, he will ponder that he is going to take charge of a bankrupt business which must be reorganized from top to bottom; all his work will be before him. Vague ideals, lofty aspirations, generous sentiments, will not help him or his fellow ministers when they sit at their desks and write instructions for their subordinates. Only a precise knowledge of the facts and a clear idea of how to deal with them will make Socialism a working system instead of a Utopian desire. The thing which weighs on Mr. Webb's mind is the immensity of the problem before us and the depth of our ignorance. He has written, in 1894: "I am appalled when I realize how little attention we have yet been able to pay to what I may call the unsettled questions of democratic admin-

istration." He beseeches us "to work out the detailed application of Collectivist principles to the actual probem of modern life." Nothing is any good at all until the fine points of administration are properly settled.

Take the case of an Eight Hours Act; it is the simplest thing in the world to draft an Act which says "no one shall work more than eight hours in any one day or more than forty-eight hours a week." It is a grave problem to draft a scheme which will make that virtuous principle an accomplished fact. They have had regulation of the hours of labour in France for three-quarters of a century; but these regulations have not got much further than the statute book. In practical life they have been almost a dead letter, because they could not work out the details so that the masters (and the men, for that matter) could not evade them. We shall have exactly the same difficulty in England. It is easy to put Factory Acts on the statute book; it is the most difficult thing in the world to devise machinery which will ensure their enforcement. Then again, take the case of unemployment: it is useless to say "set the poor to work" unless you can suggest the kind of work which will be suitable for the odd collection of men who will apply to the local authority. When the State can organize labour for all, that will be Socialism. The problem is how to organize it. Mr. Webb probably conceives of Socialism as a sort of Chinese puzzle where you have to fit all the little bits together. He listens to his comrades heroically declaring for the nationalization of everything; he entirely agrees with them. Then he gets a bucket of water and pours it in the form of precise questions on the heads of these red-hot enthusiasts. When the steam has cleared away he demands, "By all means nationalize everything, but begin somewhere, and come, let us consider how we are going to do it." Mr. Webb is the wet blanket of the Socialist movement. Rodbertus said he thought we should get to Socialism in five hundred years; but Mr. Webb has not given us even that hope; there are so many details to think out. To all our passionate hopes and demands Mr. Webb answers with the chilly question: "Yes, but how shall we do it?" It is his contribution to the Socialist movement to have asked that question more often than any one else, and to have so often answered it as well.

He is so careful about details because he is sure that Socialism is coming by a process of instalments. He entirely disbelieves in sudden revolutions; he thinks that social organization will, very gradually, grow more and more complete, but it will never be possible to say exactly when the old system has gone and the new has come. Mr. Webb, if one reads him aright, teaches that Socialism will slowly develop out of the capitalist system. There will be no sudden break. There will be more and more control exercised over the master by the State until one day the much-controlled master will realize that he is merely the servant of the State. His wages list will be fixed by a Minimum Wage Act, his factories will have to conform to the requirements of stringent Factory Acts, his profits may be seized by a graduated Income Tax. Trade Unions will continue to protect the interests of the workers in their particular trade. Trusts will continue to develop, though here and there they will quietly pass from the unified ownership of Mr. Rockefeller to the ownership of the State. In short, Mr. Webb is a true Marxian in his belief that Socialism is the inevitable outcome of social evolution. He only leaves out the great revolution which Marx was inclined to put in his programme at first, but did not afterwards insist on as an essential thing. So that Sidney Webb shares with Karl Marx the honour of proving that Socialism is inevitably bound up with social development, a part of the social structure.

Marx puts more emphasis on the destruction of capitalists, Mr. Webb thinks more of the protection of the labourers. There is no lasting satisfaction in destruction, it is merely a negative good; the only finality is organization of something better. Mr. Webb is everlastingly preaching that the problem of Socialism is the organization of labour by the most careful attention to an unending number of details. And to think these out is Mr. Webb's business for Socialism. He is the quencher of all enthusiasms; the heartless arouser from all armchair dreams.

Now there is nothing to be gained by denying the danger of this kind of leadership, even though one admits its many advantages. "It behoves all true believers to watch and wait and diligently equip themselves for a warfare which must necessarily be harassing and protracted," he tells us. We are, it seems, always to be preparing for a war which will never begin. But it does not do to mistake the arsenal and the intelligence department for the seat of war; the fighting does not take place in these retired spots. There comes a time when the battle must begin, when we must form a Socialist army to use the Socialist ammunition. At least, that is the general opinion of every Socialist association in Europe; rather, of all but one—the Fabian Society, and the Fabian Society is Mr. Webb. Mr. Webb does not believe in fighting for Socialism. He thinks it will come most quickly by perpetual arbitration with the enemy. He thinks we should always "settle out of court," however hard the terms are. The Fabian ideal is "permeation," that is, never fight; if you cannot talk your opponent over to your side, then give way. It is impossible to ignore this side of Mr. Webb's leadership, and to carefully distinguish it from his theoretical side. He is the only great Socialist leader who has so completely severed his theory and his practice. In his grasp of the details of Socialism he is probably first; in his political practice he has thrown in his lot with the enemies and has deserted his friends, because he sincerely believes that it is better to permeate opponents than to found an independent army of one's own. So Mr. Webb went into the London County Council as a "Progressive," and is quite content that a large number of the Fabians should be warm supporters of the Liberals, or even Liberal members themselves. He is perfectly satisfied that Progressives, or Liberals, or Tories should get the credit if they adopt any of his Socialist schemes; and he does not apparently much mind if the people at large confuse Socialism with advanced Radicalism or Tory Democracy or County Council Progressivism. Nobody has the slightest objection to the enemy doing our work for us, only we are beginning to be ambitious and to think that we could do our work still better ourselves. Mr. Webb, by infinite cleverness, has undoubtedly linked the Socialist movement with the practical politics of the day; he has gone far towards giving Socialism a footing in the admin-

Standish House, home of the Potter family.

istrative machinery of the State and municipality. But that method has its definite limitations. It is not always an advantage to get a foot into machinery. The Fabian policy of wire-pulling has been successful in many ways; but we must never forget that it has been successful at the price of foregoing the foundation of a Socialist Party. Sooner or later we shall have to found that Party. Even to-day we have a Labour Party which is Socialist in all but name. Mr. Webb would be the best of leaders for such a party; but he has chosen, so far, to think that Liberals and Conservatives are sufficient to give us Socialism, and is apparently indifferent whether we have a party of our own or not. He is quite content that Liberals or Conservatives should reap the credit if they adopt his wise schemes, whereas he might get them all put down to the credit of the Socialist Labour Party if he would only take a place at its head. He stands alone amongst the leaders of Socialism in ignoring the necessity for an independent political organization. . . . He ignores the supreme advantage of having an army behind when one asks the enemy for terms. (pp. 74-82)

> *G. R. S. Taylor, "Sidney Webb," in his* Leaders of Socialism, Past and Present, *1910. Reprint by Books for Libraries Press, 1968; distributed by Arno Press, Inc., pp. 74-82.*

CHARLES A. BEARD (essay date 1920)

[*Beard was one of the most influential American historians of the early twentieth century. Through his numerous works he directed the course of historiography from the scientific formalism of his predecessors, who believed that natural law governs the course of history, toward the liberal reformism of the progressives, who viewed history as a record of social, economic, and intellectual choices made by individuals and groups, advocated political and social change based on their studies of the past, and thus sought to improve the future. Beard applied his reformist ideology to several areas of study, becoming widely recognized for his expertise in municipal government, educational development, and domestic and foreign policy. In his most famous and controversial work,* An Economic Interpretation of the Constitution of the United States, *he proposed the thesis that underlies most of his works: that America's past can be best interpreted through an examination of its economic forces. Although Beard's studies have been severely criticized for their economic bias, they have nevertheless exerted a profound influence on modern historical thought. In the following review of* A Constitution for the Socialist Commonwealth of Great Britain, *Beard compares the realistic expectations of the Webbs to the idealism of other socialist writers.*]

It is a far cry from the Republic of Plato, or for that matter from the Utopia of Sir Thomas More, to the Webbs's *Constitution for the Socialist Commonwealth of Great Britain.* Time and circumstance have wrought wonders even in Utopias. The trail of slag and soot lies across the face of the new realm of perfection. It is to be a kingdom of industrial workers, shop committees, craft rules, trade union standards, card catalogues, and balance sheets—no land of joyful hay tossers and merrymakers under the harvest moon pictured for us by William Morris in his *News from Nowhere.* (No one who ever pitched clover hay on a Kansas prairie under a brazen sky could read such news without laughter.) This is not quite fair; the Webbs do contemplate week-end trips into the country for the weary paving-rammers and lace-makers; but agriculture, the source of food and clothing, has a small part in this new scheme of things. The taxation of land values is mentioned, to be sure, and perhaps taxation will produce bumper crops of corn and potatoes.

Strictly speaking, the volume before us falls into three parts. The first is a survey of the existing signs and agencies of collectivism: the democracies of consumers (cooperative societies, friendly societies, municipalities, and national services); the democracies of producers (trade unions, copartnership concerns, and professional associations); and finally the political democracy of king, lords, and commons. Though the authors here traverse familiar ground, they make the sparks fly as they go. The king may stay, for aught they care, as a useful ceremonial symbol of unity; the lords must go as useless encumbrances; and the House of Commons is utterly unfit to undertake any large public services.

Those Americans who have recently been learning from men of light and leading that the cure for our political diseases lies in adopting the English system of responsible government, will be shocked to hear that the said government is a dictatorship and the responsibility is a sham. The real government of England, the Webbs tell us, is to be found in private conferences among the ministers, their principal officials, and the representatives of the interests to be affected by any proposed legislative or administrative action. Democratic control over the government is an illusory thing, for the government is elected in the midst of uproar and proceeds to do a hundred things not discussed or decided in the campaign. The cabinet is a body of dictators tempered by dangers of popular explosions; the M.P. is a fly on the wheel of the bureaucracy; and political parties confuse rather than clarify the issues.

The second part of the volume deals with the national structure that is to be set up in the socialist commonwealth. The lords are to be swept away and there are to be two parliaments— one political and the other social. Both are to be elected by universal suffrage but the idea of a vocational or economic soviet is utterly rejected. The political parliament will be very much like the present House of Commons with "responsible" ministers, and to it will be assigned foreign affairs, the maintenance of order, justice, colonies, and defense. To the second assembly, the social parliament, is to be given control over all social and economic matters vested in the state; it is to collect taxes, direct nationalized industries, and carry on technical administration through special committees. These assemblies are not to be two houses of the same parliament but separate organisms. They are to be balanced against each other, thus helping to safeguard individual liberty, and law courts are to decide when either of the parliaments has exceeded its powers.

In all this is to be seen the influences of many schools: old fashioned liberals who fear the state (and with reason), syndicalists, guild socialists, and disillusioned democrats. The philosophers of the new order looking upon the board of aldermen, the state legislature, or the national parliament, pronounce it stupid, inefficient, and not worthy to be intrusted with the management of a flock of chickens. Behold, they exclaim, we will not give it any economic responsibilities. Lenin says, with Cromwell, "Take the bauble away"; but liberals cannot be so ruthless. They must have their parliament for "political" and "ethical" functions; the real business is to go to another assembly empowered to deal with purely economic matters. Thus politics and economics are to be cleansed, put asunder, and all will be well in the New Jerusalem. To the present reviewer this seems pure and unadulterated innocence. The idea that foreign affairs, the maintenance of order, the administration of justice, colonies, and defense can be separated from economics seems utterly chimerical. The state is not and never has been purely "political"—whatever that may mean. It originated in economics and has gone into economic matters just to the extent which the classes dominating it have desired—no more and no less. Moreover, the idea that there would be no ''politics'' in an economic assembly seems equally unwarranted. Is there no politics in the American Federation of Labor or in the Central Federated Union of New York City? Who will dare to answer in the affirmative? Suppose there were an economic parliament and a political parliament with a court holding the balance between them; how long would it be before a contest would arise? Which assembly would dominate—the one dwelling in the windy realm of purified politics or the one possessing the real goods? Who would appoint the judges of the court? To the present reviewer one or two things seem clear. Wherever two or three are gathered together there is politics. A parliament made up of mere agents of guilds would burst any nation asunder. The hope of the future lies not in tinkering up assemblies but in the development of the ideal and technique of public service.

It is just this point which is fully treated in the third, and most important, part of the Webbs's book. The authors propose to administer nationalized interests through special committees of the social parliament—one committee for each. The administrative work, as such, is to be directed by boards representing the heads of administration, various vocations, and consumers in general; down the scale in the hierarchy are to be district councils and shop committees operating on principles of collective bargaining, vocational self-government, and accepted labor standards. The local government is to be reorganized; areas are to correspond to functions; the community spirit is to be encouraged; and the federation and emulation of local bodies are to be fostered. Voluntary cooperative agencies are to function in the new order very much as at present; but trade unions are to shift from a class-war basis to a new foundation. They are to be devoted to the elevation of the vocational status, the elaboration of vocational technique, the development of vocational ethics, the training of members, and the perfection of the science and art of the services. This part of the volume is real, stimulating, suggestive. Every page is illuminated by flashes that shoot to the bottom of the complex administrative technique which is to be the very foundation of the great society—if it is to endure at all. It is here that the Webbs have laid all students of government under a great debt. They do not speculate, but with clear eyes face the terrible tangle of realities that must make up any order new or old. It is their willingness to do this that distinguishes the Webbs from the whole army of socialist thinkers who when confronted with the question ''How will you do it?'' drop their hands with weary indignation and reply ''The guilds will do it'' or ''The dictatorship of the proletariat will do it'' or ''The soviet will display the necessary wisdom.'' The Webbs have really written a big book. If they could spend the next twenty-five years in agricultural economics, they would render a service almost immeasurable. (pp. 664, 666)

*Charles A. Beard, ''A Constitution before the Fact,''
in* The Nation, *Vol. CXI, No. 2892, December 8,
1920, pp. 664, 666.*

H. L. MENCKEN   (essay date 1923)

[*From the era of World War I until the early years of the Great Depression, Mencken was one of the most influential figures in American letters. His strongly individualistic, irreverent outlook on life and his vigorous, invective-charged writing style helped establish the iconoclastic spirit of the Jazz Age and significantly shaped the direction of American literature. As a social and literary critic—the roles for which he is best known—Mencken was the scourge of evangelical Christianity, public service organizations, literary censorship, boosterism, provincialism, democracy, all advocates of personal or social improvement, and every other facet of American life that he perceived as humbug. A man who was widely renowned or feared during his lifetime as a would-be destroyer of established American values, Mencken once wrote: ''All of my work, barring a few obvious burlesques, is based upon three fundamental ideas: 1. That knowledge is better than ignorance; 2. That it is better to tell the truth than to lie; and 3. That it is better to be free than to be a slave.'' In the following review of* The Decay of Capitalist Civilisation, *Mencken disagrees with the Webbs' contention that the egregious and inherent flaws of capitalism will inevitably cause its demise.*]

The Decay of Capitalist Civilization, by Sidney and Beatrice Webb . . . , is a book that is far too optimistically named—that is, considering that the authors are Socialists, and go to bed every night hoping that the millennium will come before dawn. What they describe as the ''decay'' of the ''civilization'' which now surrounds and kisses us, and whose speedy destruction they pray for, is nothing but a catalogue of imperfections, none of them fatal, nor even very painful. The worst, perhaps, are the ferocity with which war is waged under capitalism and the facility with which the more elemental varieties of producers, such as farmers and workingmen, are robbed and exploited by their masters. But it must be obvious to every calm man that neither has gone far enough to be unendurable. The horrors of war . . . are always greatly exaggerated by sentimentalists. Even in the actual trenches, as everyone who has been there knows, they are intermittent, and life in the intervals, to most of the men living it, is relatively easy and even amusing. After all, every conscript who is forced to go there is not killed, nor is every one wounded, nor is every one who is wounded hurt in any very forbidding manner. The killed simply anticipate the inevitable arrival of cancer, diabetes, pneumonia or syphilis, and in a swift and relatively painless fashion; the wounded, save for a small minority, are not seriously damaged, and have something to boast about all the rest of their lives. If the service were really as terrifying as stay-at-home romanticists say it is, then nine-tenths of the morons who face it would go crazy. (pp. 142-43)

The fact that capitalistic government facilitates the exploitation of the inferior masses is no argument against capitalism; it is simply an argument against all civilized government, which, as Prof. Dr. Franz Oppenheimer amply demonstrates in *The State* . . . , is always and inevitably no more than a vast machine for furthering such exploitation. Oppenheimer, true enough, dreams of a time when the exploiters will shut up shop, but that is only a dream, and of a piece with the one of Mr. and Mrs. Webb. We are living among realities, and one of the most salient of them is the fact that the inferior masses appear to have a congenital incapacity for self-government. They must be bossed in order to survive at all, and if kings do not boss them then they are bossed by priests, and if priests are kicked out then they submit to oligarchies of demagogues and capitalists, as now. It would not do them much good to get rid of either half of this combination, or of both halves. What Mr. and Mrs. Webb seem to visualize for the future is a sort of superior bureaucracy of experts, like the bureaucracy that has long run the American railroads. But what reason is there for believing that it would refrain from exploiting its vast mob of incompetent and ignorant employers? I can see none whatever. The railroad bureaucracy of today, facing a relatively small group of employers, always including a number of highly-trained specialists in the safeguarding of money, nevertheless manages to butter its own parsnips very neatly. Railroad presidents and other such high officials, of course, receive large salaries, but it is rare for one to die without devising to his heirs a sum greatly in excess of his whole professional income since puberty; the rest is the *lagniappe* that goes with his office. There is absolutely no indication that such experts would throw off their intelligent self-interest if they ceased working for their stockholders and began working for the great masses of the plain people. There is still less indication that the labor leaders who now live by petty graft and blackmail would suddenly become honest if turned into Senators, Ambassadors and Cabinet ministers; on the contrary, it is extremely likely that they would become worse sharks than they are today, and that it would be much harder to keep them within bounds.

I am surely no fanatical advocate of the capitalistic system, which has defects so patent that they must be visible even to . . . abject worshippers of money. . . . When the control of Christendom passed from kings and priests and nobles to pawnbrokers and note-shavers it was a step downward, if only because kings and priests and nobles cherished concepts of professional honor, which are always as incomprehensible to pawnbrokers and note-shavers, *i.e.*, to the bankers who now rule us, as they would be to pickpockets and policemen. There were things that a king would not do, even to secure his crown; there were things that a priest would not do, even to shake down the faithful for a good collection; there were things that a noble would not do, even to save his life. But there is absolutely nothing that a banker will not do to augment his profits, short of going to jail. It is only fear of the law that restrains him. In other words, the thing that keeps him relatively in order is the thing that keeps a streetwalker relatively in order, and not at all the thing that keeps a gentleman in order. But what of the Socialist "expert" nominated to follow him on the throne? Is this candidate, then, a man of honor? To ask the question is to answer it.

However, we need not even ask it, for there is absolutely no sign in the world today that capitalism is on its deathbed, as Mr. and Mrs. Webb hope, and, hoping, think. The example of Russia proves nothing. Capitalism went broke in Russia, and is now in the hands of the Jews, but it is by no means dead; once the country begins to accumulate new wealth, it will come out of hiding and begin to exploit the Russian masses once more; already, indeed, it ventures upon a few discreet experiments. France, Italy, Germany, the various component parts of Austria-Hungary, and all of the new republics save one or two are solidly capitalistic, despite occasional flares of communistic red fire. In England one hears doleful prognostications that the next government will be dominated by Labor, but that is but one more proof of the sad way in which words supplant realities in the thinking of man. Labor, in England, is now as tame as a tabby cat; capitalism has adopted it and put it out at nurse, as it has adopted Liberalism in the United States. The Labor party, if it ever gets into power, will be run by the same old gang of millionaires and professional politicians which now runs the Liberal party and the Tory party. There will be a change in the label, but none at all in the substance; Englishmen will continue to be exploited as they have been exploited ever since the first Norman hoof-print appeared on an English beach. But it is in the United States that capitalism really enters into Heaven. Here alone does belief in it take on the virulence of a state religion; here alone are men jailed, beaten and done to death for merely meditating against it, as they used to be burned for "imagining the king's

death." I doubt that in the whole country there are 50,000 native-born citizens who have so much as permitted their minds to dwell upon the theoretical possibility of ever supplanting it. That form of fancy, so instinctively abhorrent to the right-thinking Americano, is confined almost exclusively to foreigners—and, as everyone knows, a foreigner has no rights, even of cogitation *in camera*, by American law, and whatever he is in favor of is *ipso facto* felonious, immoral and against God. Nay, capitalism is planted as firmly in These States as the belief in democracy. It will never be shaken down while you and I breathe and hope and sweat and pray. Long before it feels the first shooting pains down the legs there will be nothing left of us save the glorious immortality of heroes.

For these reasons, though I have read the work of Mr. and Mrs. Webb with unflagging attention and great interest, I beg to suggest again that their title is unduly optimistic. (pp. 143-44)

> *H. L. Mencken, in a review of "The Decay of Capitalist Civilization," in* The Smart Set, *Vol. LXXI, No. 3, July, 1923, pp. 142-44.*

BEATRICE WEBB (essay date 1931)

[*In the following essay, Beatrice Webb explains her conception of the nature and function of sociology.*]

Out of the social environment and mental climate in which I was born and bred there seemed to arise two outstanding questions, questions perpetually recurring in my own consciousness from girlhood to old age. Can there be a science of social organization, in the sense in which we have a science of mechanics or a science of chemistry, enabling us to forecast what will happen, and perhaps to alter the event by taking appropriate action or persuading others to take it? Secondly, assuming that there can be, or will be, such a science of society, is man's capacity for scientific discovery the only faculty required for the reorganization of society according to an ideal? Or do we need religion as well as science, emotional faith as well as intellectual curiosity? In the following pages will be found my tentative answer to these two questions—that is, my philosophy of work or life.

The first of these questions, Can there be an applied science of society? led me early in life to choose a particular vocation—the study of social institutions by the methods of personal observation, actual participation in the organization concerned, the taking of evidence, statistical inquiry, and the examination of historical records. My reaction from this long-continued practice of the art of the social investigator has been an ever-deepening conviction of the supreme value in all social activity of the scientific method.

Let me give one or two examples of an applied science of society taken from the public administration of Great Britain during the past hundred years. In the early part of the nineteenth century the business of government, whether national or local government, was honeycombed with favoritism, corruption, and barefaced peculation. This wholesale dishonesty on the part of representatives and officials has been largely swept away by the adoption of a social invention of definitely scientific character, namely, the audit—a device which is scarcely a century old.

Another instance is the discovery, during the past three-quarters of a century, of what has been aptly called the device of the common rule. You see this exemplified in the advantage we all gain through the existence of fixed rules of the road. Because of the rule, whatever its terms, we all get greater safety and even greater speed of locomotion. Imagine the blocking of the traffic in the great cities—not to mention the accidents—if there were no rule of the road at all, if motor buses and lorries, taxis, cyclists, and pedestrians were left to scramble through as best they could.

It is this device of the common rule—a genuine social discovery—which has given us the factory acts and the public-health legislation about the pollution of rivers, the purity of food, and the prevention of the worst forms of overcrowding. One of the most recent of these common rules—summer or daylight-saving time—has astonished the world by the sudden and complete way in which it has borne out the prediction of its inventor, William Willett. By the simple expedient of insisting that all public clocks should, on a particular night, skip one hour, and that all transport undertakings and public bodies should accept this fiction, the whole population has been led to rise from bed one hour earlier every day during the hot months of the year. By this means each person enjoys some 200 additional hours of life-giving sunlight, while the community as a whole saves millions of pounds annually in the cost of artificial lighting.

Let me give one more instance of the advantage of the scientific study of facts in the way that I have described. A hundred years ago the accepted way of dealing with extreme poverty— what was called destitution—was poor-law relief. This relief took one of two forms—maintenance in the general mixed workhouse or a niggardly dole of unconditional outdoor relief. A century of experience has discredited both. As a result of extensive observation and experiment by all sorts of persons, officials and philanthropists, recorded in innumerable blue-books and scientific treatises, there has been gradually created a whole series of new social institutions vitally affecting human behavior—a veritable framework of prevention. Instead of threatening the sick person with the workhouse if he applies for relief, the public-health authority has come more and more to seek him out, in order to cure him and to prevent any spread of disease. The local education authority now welcomes every child to school, insists that the parents send the child to school reasonably clean, even feeds the child if it is found to require it, and prosecutes the parents who are guilty of wilful neglect. The infant-welfare center endeavors to look after every birth, instructs the mother how to rear the baby, and offers periodically to examine and weigh the growing infant so that the mother may know how it is progressing. This may seem a small matter. But the statistician proves to us that during the past thirty years, since these things have been done, only half as many babies die as in the previous generation. What is even more striking is the vast alteration for the better that has been effected by these preventive services in the behavior of the parents and the children in the way of healthy living, of cleanliness, and even of manners.

There are some of us who believe that it will yet be found practicable, through observation and experiment, to invent an analogous framework of prevention applicable to that terrible disease of modern industry, mass unemployment. And looking forward to a more distant future there is the science of the better breeding of the human race—eugenics is the name given to this department of social biology by its founder, Francis Galton—knowledge which, when we are wise enough and virtuous enough to apply it, may immeasurably improve the body and mind of man.

Have I succeeded by these few illustrations in making the reader realize why I believe that we have already a science of society—

a young and very incomplete science, but one that is steadily growing and that is capable of indefinite extension? But it is a science with limitations. Unlike iron and stone and machinery, human beings and social institutions are always changing, and such social changes are sometimes so catastrophic and far-reaching as completely to baffle our generalizations and nullify our predictions. No student of social facts, however competent, could have forecast the Russian Revolution or the nature of the Soviet Government. No one could have foreseen the sudden development of the Fascist state in Italy. No one could have predicted the rapid rise to prosperity and power of the Czecho-Slovak republic, the very name of which we can barely pronounce and the exact position of which is unknown to most of us. Here and there, from time to time, there emerges from the mass a man or a group of men whose uncommon qualities are exceptionally influential with the particular race of human beings with whom they come in contact. It may be a captivating personality, it may be religious exaltation, it may be superlative efficiency in the organization of war or in the administration of the state. William James called such great men "ferments," influences which change the course of life of a whole nation. We may recognize such a ferment in the great leader of the Czecho-Slovak race, Masaryk. Sometimes these potent individuals appear more like volcanic eruptions—as with Lenin in Russia and Mussolini in Italy and Gandhi in India. These are as unpredictable by science as is an earthquake. But woe betide the great man, be he prophet or warrior or statesman, who forges not only that the common man exists, but also that it is with the common man that he has to deal. If a Lenin, a Mussolini, or a Gandhi wants to reduce the infant death-rate or to adopt summer time, to create a universal system of public education or to build up a stable democratic state out of millions of men of different races and antagonistic creeds, in Russia, Italy, or India, he must, for all his volcanic power, learn from the knowledge of past and present social institutions the particular devices by which one or other of these things can be created. Before he died Lenin had to admit that in ignoring one common characteristic of the tens of millions of Russian peasant-cultivators—the desire to better their own circumstances—he had made a big mistake. He had, indeed, to reverse his policy of complete communism, and to permit, at least temporarily, a measure of individual accumulation and private trade. Mussolini may yet find that in suppressing all independence of speech and freedom of the press he has alienated an indispensable factor in a stable and progressive state.

To sum up: The generalizations and predictions of the science of society relate to that strange abstraction, the average human being. Here we recognize what might be termed the mystical element in the work of the statistician. What he tells us is the truth, even truth of a high order. But he does not deal with our individual peculiarities. He predicts what will be found true of what is common to all the individuals who make up the group or race of men with which he is dealing. The uncommon, the exceptional, the peculiar characteristics of the individual man, and the manner of his influence, are at present, and possibly always will be, outside the scope of a science of society.

I pass to the second question which has continuously confronted me in my passage through life. Is man's capacity for scientific discovery the only faculty required for the reorganization of society according to an ideal? Or do we need religion as well as science, emotional faith as well as intellectual curiosity?

Very early in my career as a social investigator I realized that science deals only with the processes of life; it has little to say of the purpose of life. We can learn through science how best to kill a man or slaughter a multitude of men; we can discover how to cure a human being of specific diseases and thus raise indefinitely the standard of health. But no amount of personal observation or statistical inquiry will tell us whether we *ought* to kill or to cure. Our behavior, as parent or child, as colleague or rival, as employer or employed, as private citizen or public official, is largely dictated to us by law or public opinion. But whenever we settle it for ourselves, it seems to depend on intuition or impulse, on likes or dislikes, or, to put it in another way, on our emotional outlook on life. Historically, codes of conduct, scales of value, patterns of behavior—to use the term of my friend, Graham Wallas—are intimately related to contemporary conceptions of man's relation to the universe, whether these notions are woven into magic rites, wrought into religious creeds, or expressed in systems of philosophy incapable of objective verification. My own experience is that in the nobler type of men these guides to conduct appear to rise out of emotive thought, connecting the purpose of individual man with the purpose of the universe, the visible with the invisible world. "Man lives in two worlds," Professor Haldane tells us in his brilliant exposition of What I Believe, "the visible world which changes with time, and an invisible world whose constituents do not change." "I have not very much use for people who are not in touch with the invisible world," he adds somewhat scornfully. The trouble is that when we ask to be put in touch with this invisible world we are given, by this eminent scientist, not the bread of spiritual guidance but the hard stone of pure intellect, and a short measure of that! "Among the components of the invisible world are the realities corresponding to mathematical statements like 16 + 9 = 25." This, literally, is all that he vouchsafes us! Memory recalls my friend Bertrand Russell arguing that the arithmetical proposition that two and two make four cannot be proved by pure logic, and is merely an empirical truth derived from experience, thus belonging to the visible and not to the invisible world. However that may be, to an undeveloped mind like mine Professor Haldane's exposition of the invisible world is meaningless. It arouses no response from my intellect or my emotions.

But why should we expect to describe the invisible world? All we can do is to explain our own state of mind, so that we may enter into communion with those of like temperament, and thus encourage and strengthen each other in our common pilgrimage through life. For my own part, I believe that the mind of man, as distinguished from the appetites and instincts which he shares with other animals, is divided into two parts—the intellectual and the emotional, each having its own methods and sanctions. What is called the scientific method is the highest expression of the intellect; by observation, verification, and reasoning we can discover how things happen and predict how they will happen under like circumstances, and, in many instances, by applying this knowledge we can alter this happening in the direction we desire.

The highest expression of the emotional side of human nature is the attainment of the beautiful and the good; the one represented by art in all its manifestations, the other by varieties of religious experience, leading to what is felt to be the right conduct of life. I have not the artistic temperament and I know not in what state of consciousness this may be embodied; what may be its discipline and its sanctions. But like the majority of the human race I have an incipient religious temperament—a yearning for the mental security of a spiritual home. Professor Whitehead says:

> Religion is the vision of something which stands beyond, behind, and within the passing flux of immediate things; something which is real, and yet waiting to be realized; something which is a remote possibility, and yet the greatest of present facts; something that gives meaning to all that passes, and yet eludes apprehension; something whose possession is the final good, and yet is beyond all reach; something which is the ultimate ideal, and the hopeless quest.

This vision of something which is real and yet waiting to be realized is associated in my experience with an intuitive use of prayer. A secularist friend once cross-examined me as to what exactly I meant by prayer; he challenged me to define the process of prayer, to describe its happening. I answered I would gladly do so if I could find the words. The trouble is, as Tagore observes about poetry, that words have meanings, or, as I prefer to say, predominantly intellectual meanings; and in prayer it is emotion, not reason, that seeks an outlet. It is by prayer, by communion with an all-pervading spiritual force, that the soul of man discovers the purpose or goal of human endeavor. That is why down all the ages of human development prayer has been intimately associated, whether as cause or effect, with the nobler and more enduring forms of architecture and music; associated, too, with poetry and painting, with the awe-inspiring aspects of nature, with the great emotional mysteries of maternity, mating, and death.

To Professor Haldane my longer string of words may seem as meaningless as his curt arithmetical formula does to me. Perhaps we can find common ground in "The Will to Believe," eloquently expounded by William James, or in "The Philosophy of 'As If,'" logically developed by Vaihinger. So far as I understand the conclusion of these eminent metaphysicians—a conclusion which I understand is also held by Einstein—it can be summed up in the proposition that wherever no hypothesis can be scientifically proved or disproved, and yet some hypothesis must be accepted as a starting-point for thought or as a basis for conduct, the individual is justified in selecting the hypothesis which yields the richest results in the discovery of truth or in the leading of a good life. Such a justifiable hypothesis seems to me the faith I hold: that man is related to the universe by an emotional as well as by a rational tie, that there is a spirit of love at work in the universe, and that the emotion of prayer or aspiration reveals to man the ends he should pursue if he desires to harmonize his own purpose with that of the universe; exactly as the working of his intellect discovers the means by which these ends may be best achieved. "Did I ever tell you," writes one of the greatest of British scientific thinkers, Francis Galton, "that I have always made it a habit to *pray* before writing anything for publication, that there may be no self-seeking in it, and perfect candor, together with respect for the feelings of others?"

But I realize that in the world of today science is in the ascendant, while the religious impulse is in eclipse. This decay of religious faith is, I think, a reaction from what is false in the current religious creeds. Throughout the ages, prophets and priests, saints and Sadducees, have dictated to the faithful mythical accounts of how things happen, how they have happened, and how they will happen—whether concerning the beginnings of life on this earth, or the course of the stars, or the diagnosis and cure of disease, or the better organization of society. This unwarranted intrusion of religion into the realm of science, this illegitimate attempt to supersede reason by emotion in respect to the processes of nature, has always led and will always lead, at best, to failure to attain the desired ends; at worst, to superstitious practices and degrading magic. Few believers in the scientific method accept as evidence of fact the Biblical narrative of the creation of the world in six days or that of the miracles of the Immaculate Conception and the resurrection from the dead of the physical body of Jesus of Nazareth. I am aware that these "dogmas" are deemed by some practicing Christians to be not statements of fact at all, but merely symbols of some invisible truth—appeals to the emotion and not to the intellect. This gloss on the creed of Christendom seems somewhat lacking in candor.

Thus, like many of my contemporaries, I am a religious outcast; I cannot enjoy, without sacrificing intellectual integrity, the immeasurable benefit of spiritual comradeship, the inner peace arising out of traditional forms of worship, the inspiration of noble motive—all of which I recognize as embodied in the disicpline of the great religions of the world, such as Christianity and Buddhism. And while I rejoice in the advance of science, I deplore the desuetude of regular religious services, with their encouragement of worship and prayer, for the good reason that personal experience and the study of history convince me that this absence of the religious habit leads to an ugly chaos in private and public morals and to a subtle lowering of the sense of beauty—witness the idol of the subhuman, the prevalence of crude animalism, in much of the music, art, and literature of the twentieth century.

But to my mind there is one hopeful portent. Men of science endowed with the religious temperament are today reinterpreting the mystical meaning of the universe; and it is they

Photograph of Beatrice Webb by Bernard Shaw.

who may bring about a new synthesis between our discovery of the true and our self-dedication to the beautiful and the good. (pp. 603-06)

Beatrice Webb, "What I Believe," in The Nation, Vol. CXXXII, No. 3439, June 3, 1931, pp. 603-06.

HAROLD J. LASKI   (essay date 1936)

[*A controversial figure with strongly held Marxian views, Laski was a noted English political scientist and author who, as a popular lecturer and teacher, maintained a large following of students throughout his career. In addition, he was an outspoken and active participant in the British Labour Party, advocating labor reforms that were in line with his socialist thought. In an assessment of Laski, Edmund Wilson stated that he was "not only a well-equipped scholar and an able political thinker but a fighter for unpopular ideals whose career as a whole is an example of singularly disinterested devotion." In the following review of* Soviet Communism: A New Civilisation?, *Laski objects to certain conclusions reached by the Webbs in that work.*]

Granted all the errors and crimes that have accompanied the Russian Revolution, it is the one civilization in the world today in which there is well-nigh universal hope, well-nigh universal exhilaration, the power to override the vested interest for the sake of corporate well-being. There is no unemployment. There is a continuous rise in the curve of material well-being. Illiteracy has been finally conquered. An end has been made of things like anti-Semitism and the color war. In such fields as crime and racial relations discoveries have been made, and applied, which I believe to be of seminal importance to the world. Although I shall make in later paragraphs important qualifications of the statement, I do agree, broadly, with the conclusion reached by Mr. and Mrs. Webb in their just published *Soviet Communism,* that the salvation of mankind depends upon its adoption of the principles of Russian social organization. It represents, in my judgment, the next stage in the evolution of any political society which wishes, first, to be the master of its own destiny, and, second, to make its relations of production correspond to the possibilities of its forces of production. Only by the acceptance of its premises can we hope to solve that paradox of poverty in the midst of plenty which is now the curse of capitalist civilization.

Soviet Communism is being deservedly hailed as by all odds the most remarkable book its great theme has so far produced. It has all the merits which have made the Webbs the supreme English sociologists of our time. It is based on massive investigation. It sees its subject as a whole. It has the Webb "flair" for the way the institutions work. There is hardly an aspect of Soviet civilization that is left untouched and it is fair to say that there is no aspect discussed upon which they do not shed illumination. No one is entitled to speak of Russia who has not read this book. It marks a definite epoch in the understanding of the greatest historical event since the French Revolution.

The substance of Mr. and Mrs. Webb's conclusions may be briefly summarized. They salute the results of the Revolution as definitely beneficent. They deny that the system is a dictatorship of the classic kind; on the contrary, they believe that a more real democracy exists in Russia than in any country in the world. They think that Soviet experience has demonstrated the possibility of successful planning, once the instruments of production are publicly owned. They are impressed by the depth and extent of Soviet experience in judicial work, in education, in public medicine, in the organization of technical and scientific research. They believe that what they happily term "the vocation of leadership" marks a turning point in the evolution of social forms. They clearly regard the appeal of communism as not less profound than that of the historic religions, which it has, indeed, been largely successful in replacing. They are satisfied that a generally classless society is in process of construction, and that only defeat in war can prevent its successful achievement. They argue that, sooner or later, the world will have to imitate the ends and the technique of the new Russia. How that imitation will be accomplished they do not attempt to decide. So stark a summary necessarily does grave injustice to the richness of the material with which the Webbs support their conclusions. For my own part, save for certain important exceptions, I see no answer to their case.

Having said so much, let me turn to one phase of the Webbs' book in which I think their treatment is defective. They speak with some sharpness of that "disease of orthodoxy" which afflicts the ruling party in Russia, and it is evident that they recognize the desirability of a greater intellectual freedom than Russia now enjoys. They are not, either, happy over some of the activities of the G.P.U., though I note that they accept the orthodox interpretation of what followed the recent Kirov assassination. On both counts, I think, Mr. and Mrs. Webb have taken the evidence far too lightly. Ideological differences have been penalized in Russia with a drastic severity it is impossible to defend. A controlled uniformity of thought has been produced by the relentless working of the party machine which is incompatible with the best creative work and difficult for the best of Russia's own friends to defend. I give two examples. I agree with the Webbs that in the doctrinal conflict between Stalin and Trotsky the former was right and the latter wrong; more, I think it probable that Stalin's victory was necessary to the salvation of the Revolution. But that does not justify the way in which post-1927 Soviet historians have deliberately falsified the history of 1917-22 in order to magnify the part Stalin then played and to diminish the role of Trotsky. Men who produce history to order must play with truth in a way fatal to honesty. Anyone who reads such party histories as those which go under the names of Yaroslavsky and of Popov and compare them with that produced some twenty years ago under official auspices by Linoviev will realize that the censorship the change has implied is definitely discreditable to the present rulers of Russia. It is also, I think, fruitless; for the pre-1927 evidence which exists outside Russia is fatal to the acceptance of such falsifications. I do not doubt that Stalin is a remarkable man. But I do not think, either, that his legacy to world socialism will be all that it might be if his supporters magnify his achievement by methods like these. He is, I believe, too big a man to need them; and men who stoop to these methods for the retention of power do profound moral injury to the cause they represent.

My second instance is the exile of political prisoners amid circumstances of great harshness. Some of them are Zionists—I write as one with little interest in Palestine—who ask only for the chance to go to Palestine. They are prevented from doing so and are often treated in a way that dishonors the regime. This is true, also, of the treatment of many social democrats, as I can myself testify from personal knowledge. Mr. and Mrs. Webb, I think, treat this body of evidence far too light-heartedly. They seem to have no conception either of the price mankind has had to pay for such liberty of thought as it has won or of the cost its suppression has always involved. A great deal of my energy is devoted to protest against German and Italian brutality to Jews and communists; I think I have

no moral alternative but to protest. For me, while Thälmann, Ossietsky, and their like remain in prison all of us remain in prison also. But how can I comfortably join with communists in attack upon their jailers, when, without any trial, hundreds of Russians, none of whom is guilty of any act against the Soviet government, have been imprisoned not less relentlessly there? Mr. and Mrs. Webb have no answer to this problem. It is one which makes their denial of a dictatorship in Russia futile; for if Russia were not a dictatorship it would not need methods of this kind to assure its authority.

That it is necessary to deal sternly with men who plot the overthrow of the regime I do not doubt; but a law of treason is amply effective for such men. Those of whom I speak are the victims of that "disease of orthodoxy" of which the Webbs write with justifiable contempt. Many of them would serve Russia gladly, given the opportunity. Do we who believe in the greatness of the new Russia serve her best by suppressing the true implications of this attitude? I cannot think so. On the contrary, I believe that were Stalin to reverse the policy for which the Communist Party in Russia now stands in this matter he would immensely increase its prestige and authority all over the world. But a communism which operates an inquisition on grounds indistinguishable from those of its predecessor does a disservice which the Webbs place in a wholly inadequate perspective to the greatest ideal of modern times.

One other aspect of this problem is worth annotation because, though the Webbs emphasize its reality, they do not treat it with sufficient emphasis. The "disease of orthodoxy," in the context of the communist international, is in no small degree responsible for those divisions in the working-class movement which in considerable part explain the ease of fascist triumph in Europe. That temper has produced in communists the world over a casuistry of method wholly indifferent on many—too many—occasions to simple honesty and objective truth. No one admires more than I do the superb courage they have so universally shown in the face of danger. But no one can seriously deny that their belief in the end has too often caused them to stoop to means incapable of justification on any showing. The price they have been compelled to pay for this is heavy; but the price the labor movements of Europe have paid is heavier still. What I should have liked to find in the Webbs' book—what is, I believe, absent from it—is a full explanation of what it is in communism that is responsible for this attitude. Sometimes one has been tempted to think that they preferred a fascist victory to a social democratic triumph. That, now, is officially contradicted by the new policy adopted last summer by the Congress of the Communist International. But it is a policy which comes only years after that same congress had built an abyss of suspicion and antagonism between itself and orthodox labor parties by its theory of social democracy as social fascism. How could a policy as futile as this ever have been urged by a man of the stature of Stalin? Mr. and Mrs. Webb do not even attempt to answer this problem. Yet for those who, like myself, believe that the united front of the left forces is the one way to save civilization, it remains a problem that it is urgent to answer.

One other general remark is worth making. Critics of Soviet Russia often insist that new classes are arising there, and point to the wide differences in income which exist in Russia as the proof of their argument. It is one of the best features of the Webbs' book that they decisively dispose of this view. The whole difference between the income-scheme of Soviet Russia and that of the rest of the world lies in the fact that in Russia income does not mean the possession of social power. No man in Russia is significant by virtue of the income he possesses; no man, either, can control the lives of others by virtue of that income. It is the outcome only of a social function assessed in value by its relevance to general well-being; and the opportunity of access to that function is more genuinely equal than in any other community in the world. The significance of this position needs no emphasis from me. It must be read in the context of the fact that the effective leaders of the party impose upon themselves a continuous and rigorous asceticism the more impressive the more fully it is known. From this angle, in my own judgment, Soviet Russia has discovered perspectives of motivation in matters of social constitution that open a new epoch in the history of mankind.

It is, I think, some fifty years since the Webbs made their first contribution to social theory. Looking back on the record of those years, it is difficult not to feel humble in its presence. Again and again they have set new horizons; again and again they have compelled new valuations of old ideas. There is a fundamental sense in which this is the greatest of all their works. Massive in conception, courageous in ideas, pioneering in method, it sets a new standard for works in this field. No one can afford to neglect it. The more widely it is read, the more hope there is that men will understand the perspective of their lives. (pp. 3-4)

> *Harold J. Laski, "Balance Sheet of a New Civilization," in* The Saturday Review of Literature, *Vol. XIII, No. 19, March 7, 1936, pp. 3-4.*

BERNARD SHAW (essay date 1941)

[*Shaw is generally considered the greatest dramatist to write in the English language since Shakespeare. Following the example of Henrik Ibsen, he succeeded in revolutionizing the English stage, disposing of the romantic conventions and devices of the "well-made play," and instituting the theater of ideas, grounded in realism. During the late nineteenth century, Shaw was also a prominent literary, art, and music critic. As Samuel Hynes has noted, Shaw was driven by a rage to better the world. A Fabian socialist, he wrote criticism that was often concerned with the humanitarian and political intent of the work under discussion. In the following excerpt from an essay originally published in* Picture Post *in September 1941, Shaw discusses the Webbs' careers and their contribution to English political thought.*]

The Webbs, Sidney and Beatrice, officially The Right Honourable the Baron and Lady Passfield, are a superextraordinary pair. I have never met anyone like them, either separately or in their most fortunate conjunction. Each of them is an English force; and their marriage was an irresistible reinforcement. Only England could have produced them. It is true that France produced the Curies, a pair equally happily matched; but in physics they found an established science and left it so, enriched as it was by their labors; but the Webbs found British Constitutional politics something which nobody had yet dreamt of calling a science or thinking of as such.

When they began, they were face to face with Capitalism and Marxism. Marxism, though it claims to be scientific, and has proved itself a mighty force in the modern world, was then a philosophy propounded by a foreigner without administrative experience, who gathered his facts in the Reading Room of the British Museum, and generalized the human race under the two heads of *bourgeoisie* and proletariat apparently without having ever come into business contact with a living human being.

Capitalism was and is a paper Utopia, the most unreal product of wishful thinking of all the Utopias. By pure logic, without a moment's reference to the facts, it demonstrated that you had only to enforce private contracts and let everybody buy in the cheapest market and sell in the dearest to produce automatically a condition in which there would be no unemployment, and every honest and industrious person would enjoy a sufficient wage to maintain himself and his wife and reproduce his kind, whilst an enriched superior class would have leisure and means to preserve and develop the nation's culture and civilization, and, by receiving more of the national income than they could possibly consume, save all the capital needed to make prosperity increase by leaps and bounds.

Karl Marx's philosophy had no effect on public opinion here or elsewhere; but when he published the facts as to the condition to which Capitalism had reduced the masses, it was like lifting the lid off hell. Capitalism has not yet recovered from the shock of that revelation, and never will.

Sixty years ago, the Marxian shock was only beginning to operate in England. I had to read *Das Kapital* in a French translation, there being no English version as yet. A new champion of the people, Henry Mayers Hyndman, had met and talked with Karl Marx. They quarrelled, as their habit was, but not before Hyndman had been completely converted by Marx; so his Democratic Federation presently became a Social-Democratic Federation. Socialism, in abeyance since the slaughter of the Paris Commune in 1871, suddenly revived; but Marx, its leader and prophet, died at that moment and left the movement to what leadership it could get.

Socialism was not a new thing peculiar to Marx. John Stuart Mill, himself a convert, had converted others, among them one very remarkable young man and an already famous elderly one. The elderly one was the great poet and craftsman William Morris, who, on reading Mill's early somewhat halfhearted condemnation of communism, at once declared that Mill's verdict was against the evidence, and that people who lived on unearned incomes were plainly "damned thieves." He joined Hyndman, and when the inevitable quarrel ensued, founded The Socialist League.

The younger disciple had followed Mill's conversion and shared it. His name was Sidney Webb. He was an entirely unassuming young Londoner of no extraordinary stature, guiltless of any sort of swank, and so naïvely convinced that he was an ordinary mortal and everybody else as gifted as himself that he did not suffer fools gladly, and was occasionally ungracious to the poor things.

The unassuming young cockney was in fact a prodigy. He could read a book as fast as he could turn the leaves, and remember everything worth remembering in it. Whatever country he was in, he spoke the language with perfect facility, though always in the English manner. He had gone through his teens gathering scholarships and exhibitions as a child gathers daisies, and had landed at last in the upper division of the civil service as resident clerk in the Colonial Office. He had acquired both scholarship and administrative experience, and knew not only why reforms were desirable but how they were put into practice under our queer political system. Hyndman and his Democratic Federation were no use to him, Morris and his Socialist League only an infant school. There was no organization fit for him except the Liberal Party, already moribund, but still holding a front bench position under the leadership of Gladstone. All Webb could do was something that he was forbidden to do as a civil servant: that is, issue pamphlets warning the Liberal Party that they were falling behind the times and even behind the Conservatives. Nevertheless he issued the pamphlets calmly. Nobody dared to remonstrate.

This was the situation when I picked him up at a debating society which I had joined to qualify myself as a public speaker. It was the year 1879, when I was 23 and he a year or two younger. I at once recognized and appreciated in him all the qualifications in which I was myself pitiably deficient. He was clearly the man for me to work with. I forced my acquaintance on him; and it soon ripened into an enduring friendship. This was by far the wisest step I ever took. The combination worked perfectly.

We were both in the same predicament in having no organization with which we could work. Our job was to get Socialism into some sort of working shape; and we knew that this brainwork must be done by groups of Socialists whose minds operated at the same speed on a foundation of the same culture and habits. We were not snobs; but neither were we mere reactionists against snobbery to such an extent as to believe that we could work in double harness with the working men of the Federation and the League, who deeply and wisely mistrusted us as "bourgeois," and who would inevitably waste our time in trying to clear up hopeless misunderstandings. (pp. 5-9)

One day I came upon a tract entitled "Why Are The Many Poor?" issued by a body of whom I had never heard, entitled The Fabian Society. The name struck me as an inspiration. I looked the Society up, and found a little group of educated middle class persons who, having come together to study philosophy, had finally resolved to take to active politics as Socialists. It was just what we needed. When I had sized it up, Webb joined, and with him Sydney Olivier, his fellow resident clerk at the Colonial Office. Webb swept everything before him; and the history of the Fabian Society began as the public knows it today. Barricades manned by Anarchists, and Utopian colonies, vanished from the Socialist program; and Socialism became constitutional, respectable, and practical. This was the work of Webb far more than of any other single person.

He was still a single person in another sense when the Fabian job was done. He was young enough to be unmarried when a young lady as rarely qualified as himself decided that he was old enough to be married. She had arrived at Socialism not by way of Karl Marx or John Stuart Mill, but by her own reasoning and observation. She was not a British Museum theorizer and bookworm; she was a born firsthand investigator. She had left the West End, where she was a society lady of the political plutocracy, for the East End, where she disguised herself to work in sweaters' dens and investigate the condition of the submerged tenth just discovered by Charles Booth and the Salvation Army. The sweaters found her an indifferent needlewoman, but chose her as an ideal bride for Ikey Mo: a generic name for their rising sons. They were so pressing that she had to bring her investigation to a hasty end, and seek the comparatively aristocratic society of the trade union secretaries, with whom she hobnobbed as comfortably as if she had been born in their houses. She had written descriptions of the dens for Booth's first famous Enquiry, and a history of Cooperation which helped powerfully to shift its vogue from producers' cooperation to consumers' cooperation. Before her lay the whole world of proletarian organization to investigate.

It was too big a job for one worker. She resolved to take a partner. She took a glance at the Fabian Society, now two thousand strong, and at once dismissed nineteen hundred and ninety-six of them as negligible sheep; but it was evident that they were not sheep without a shepherd. There were in fact some half-dozen shepherds. She investigated them personally one after the other, and with unerring judgment selected Sidney Webb, and gathered him without the least difficulty, as he had left himself defenseless by falling in love with her head over ears.

And so the famous partnership began. He took to her investigation business like a duck to water. They started with a history of trade unionism so complete and intimate in its information that it reduced all previous books on the subject to waste paper, and made organized labor in England class-conscious for the first time. It travelled beyond England and was translated by Lenin. Then came the volume on Industrial Democracy which took trade unionism out of its groove and made it politically conscious of its destiny. There followed a monumental history of Local Government which ran into many volumes, and involved such a program of investigations on the spot all over the country, and reading through local archives, as had never before been attempted. Under such handling not only Socialism but political sociology in general became scientific, leaving Marx and Lassalle almost as far behind in that respect as they had left Robert Owen. The labor of it was prodigious; but it was necessary. And it left the Webbs no time for argybargy as between Marx's Hegelian metaphysics and Marx Eastman's Cartesian materialism. The question whether Socialism is a soulless Conditioned Reflex *à la* Pavlov or the latest phase of The Light of the World announced by St. John, did not delay them: they kept to the facts and the methods suggested by the facts.

Finally came the work in which those who believe in Divine Providence may like to see its finger. The depth and genuineness of our Socialism found its crucial test in the Russian revolution which changed crude Tsarism into Red Communism. . . . The history of Communist Russia for the past twenty years in the British and American Press is a record in recklessly prejudiced mendacity. The Webbs waited until the wreckage and ruin of the change was ended, its mistakes remedied, and the Communist State fairly launched. Then they went and investigated it. In their last two volumes they give us the first really scientific analysis of the Soviet State, and of its developments of our political and social experiments and institutions, including trade unionism and cooperation, which we thought they had abolished. No Russian could have done this all-important job for us. The Webbs knew England, and knew what they were talking about. No one else did.

They unhesitatingly gave the Soviet system their support, and announced it definitely as a New Civilization.

It has been a wonderful life's work. . . . (pp. 10-14)

> *Bernard Shaw, "The Webbs," in* The Truth about Soviet Russia *by Sidney Webb and Beatrice Webb, Longmans, Green and Co., 1942, pp. 5-14.*

LEONARD WOOLF (essay date 1943)

[Woolf is best known as one of the leaders of the "Bloomsbury Group" of artists and thinkers, and as the husband of novelist Virginia Woolf, with whom he founded the Hogarth Press. The Bloomsbury Group, which was named after the section of London where the members lived and met, also included Clive and Vanessa Bell, John Maynard Keynes, Lytton Strachey, Desmond MacCarthy, and several others. The group's weekly meetings

were occasions for lively discussions of philosophy, literature, art, economics, politics, and life in general. Although the group observed no formal manifesto, Woolf and the others generally held to the tenets of philosopher G. E. Moore's Principia Ethica (1903), the essence of which is, in Moore's words, that "one's prime objects in life were love, the creation and enjoyment of aesthetic experience, and the pursuit of knowledge." A Fabian socialist during the World War I era, Woolf became a regular contributor to the socialist New Statesman *and later served as literary editor of the* Nation *and the* Athenaeum, *in which much of his literary criticism is found. Throughout most of his life, Woolf also contributed essays on economics and politics to Britain's leading journals and acted as an advisor to the Labour Party. In the following excerpt, Woolf describes the extent of the Webbs' influence in British society.]*

[Beatrice and Sidney Webb] did for both social thought and political practice in the twentieth century what Bentham had done in the nineteenth. There is, in fact, a queer resemblance between them and Bentham: their uncompromising intellectuality and rationalism; the aloofness, integrity, and asceticism of their life; their emergence as national "characters"; the way in which their theories influenced political practice by permeating or capturing the key politicians. The reason for this resemblance is, of course, that they, like Bentham, were thoroughly British in mind, method, and character; no other national tradition could produce that strange mixture of uncompromising ratiocination, practical common sense, and the courage of one's own absurdities. The Webbs developed a peculiar technique of social investigation. It was an attempt to apply the methods of science to the observation of human society, and in particular to contemporary social institutions, regarded not as static or historical phenomena, but as social processes. As Beatrice Webb herself put it: "Only by watching *the processes* of growth and decay during a period of time, can we understand even the contemporary facts at whatever may be their stage of development; and only by such a comprehension of the past and present processes can we get an insight into the means of change." Their technique was not an entirely new invention of their own. It was itself part of the general process by which the enormous developments in the "natural sciences" in the nineteenth century were changing men's attitude towards themselves and their institutions and had already had important effects upon the historian and the sociologist. They owed much directly to Herbert Spencer and to the great London investigation of Charles Booth, who, in Beatrice Webb's view, "was the boldest pioneer . . . and the achiever of the greatest results, in the methodology of the social sciences of the nineteenth century." But they differed from all other workers in their own field by the scale of their operations, the great intellectual power and imagination with which they handled their material, and that breadth and steadiness of social vision which enabled them never to forget that the ultimate object of "a comprehension of the past and present process" was always "an insight into the means of change." The result was that no British thinker or writer, no politician, no civil servant, however hostile to or critical of the Webbs he might be, could escape their influence, if he put a toe upon the territory which they had made their own. For over that vast territory, which stretched from Local Government to the Co-operative Movement, they ruled by right of conquest, and they taught us, whether we were professors, publicists, or politicians, whether we were Local Government officials or trade unionists or co-operators, not only to understand for the first time the society and institutions of which we were part, but the processes by which social evils might be abolished and social ideals attained.

Hence their immense influence upon political thought and action during the last forty years.

I do not believe it is possible to distinguish the contribution of each partner to this great work. No one who has himself worked with Sidney Webb on a piece of investigation can doubt that the method was part of himself or can fail to recognise the power of his brain, the mastery of material, the fertility of his historical and political imagination. Yet is is clear from Beatrice Webb's autobiography that, even before she met Sidney, she had already worked out for herself the Webb method of social investigation and had already applied it to the Co-operative Movement with the result that the nature and social significance of consumers' co-operation were revealed. All that one can say about their partnership is that by a rare miracle two great minds were enabled, not merely to think the same thoughts, but to think them for a lifetime together and for a common purpose.

They achieved another thing of equal importance. It was their personal influence. I do not refer only to their influence upon politicians and upon the workers, in the Labour Party, the Trade Union Movement, and in the Co-operative Movement—that was great and of great importance. I am thinking rather of their personal influence upon an unending series of younger generations. Their interest in the young, in any one who showed the slightest gift for political thought or social investigation, was unsleeping and undying. And they were tirelessly unselfish in offering to any young man or woman of the kind opportunities of learning and working. In this way they exercised a profound influence upon the minds and work of several generations of the politically conscious young, and not least upon those who rebelled against, and sometimes affectionately ridiculed, the Webbs. They achieved this partly by the power of their minds and characters, but also by a peculiar simplicity and integrity, which made any little-mindedness impossible for them. I have never known any one who met the opposition, violence, and ingratitude of youth with such complete fairness, sweetness, and tolerance as the Webbs.

Here again they acted as a composite personality. And yet . . . in one's memory Beatrice, as a person, is so distinct, so different from Sidney. She was, as her autobiography shows, a woman of strong emotions, and, though she would have denied this herself, she had in her the passions and imagination of an artist. There was, too, within her a deep-seated conflict between what she calls "the ego which affirmed" and "the ego which denied." But she chose for the work and object of her life social investigation, and she dedicated herself to it much as a nun or Buddhist priest is dedicated to a life of religion. She trained herself for her task intellectually with the greatest rigour, and somehow or other, with intense mental pain and effort, she reconciled the conflict within her and purged her passions. To succeed in this required pertinacity and courage of a high order. She had both. (It is characteristic of her that a passage in her diary in which she says: "Ah! me; there come times when one would recommend universal suicide," ends with the words: "Courage, my friend, courage.") When I first knew her, she had already completed her self-dedication and had become an intellectual ascetic. Superficially the extreme intellectuality and asceticism sometimes appeared rather bleak and arid, but the more one knew her, the more one realised how human and humane she was beneath the surface. As she grew old, this humanity seemed to me to increase, and it was noticeable in the gentle and rather amused distrust which she used to express of her own "aged" judgments. The last sentence in the last letter which I had from her, written last year, was: "I am afraid I am not very hopeful about the official Labour Party as it is at present constituted, but then the aged are apt to be pessimistic about the future in which they will not be concerned." (pp. 287-90)

Leonard Woolf, "Obituary: Beatrice Webb (1858-1943)," in The Economic Journal, Vol. LIII, Nos. 210 & 211, June & September, 1943, pp. 284-90.

G. D. H. COLE (essay date 1943)

[*Cole, an English economist and novelist, wrote widely on socialism and Marxism in a manner accessible to the common reader and was a prolific author of detective fiction. As secretary to the Fabian society and later economic advisor to the* New Statesman, *Cole worked closely with the Webbs, eventually becoming an intimate friend. In the following excerpt, he traces their career and explains how the individual ideas of each partner contributed to the Webbs' joint works.*]

Beatrice Potter, even before her meeting with Sidney Webb, knew very well what she was setting out to do, and had already formulated for herself both a critique of Political Economy and a constructive view of the functions and methods of Social Science. She was not, at this time, a Socialist: Socialism was, for her, the outcome of actual practice of the methods of social investigation which she had defined for her own use; and it follows that the Socialism at which she arrived was undogmatic, relativist, and regarded rather as an instrument of action than as a theory. She was as impatient of the dogmatic Marxism which took its stand on the labour theory of value as of the orthodox economics. Her own theory of value she defined in terms of "a correspondence or union between economic faculty and economic desire." "It is," she wrote in 1892, "so to speak, the marriage settlement of economic life, and like many other matrimonial arrangements it is not always to the advantage of both parties. And moreover, in this vale of tears many faculties and many desires do, as a matter of fact, remain unmarried; and thus fail to generate exchange value. Indeed, it should be one of the main objects of applied sociology to bring about the largest measure of unbroken continuity and mutual satisfaction in an ever-increasing stream of marriages between the economic faculties and economic desires of the human race."

Beatrice Webb linked this sociological theory of value to her conception of the integration of social structure. "Was it fantastic to suggest that this idea of the democratic government of industry as a joint affair of consumers and producers had some affinity with the idea of exchange value being the result of a correspondence or union between economic faculty and economic desire? The proper relationship of Trade Unionism and Cooperation is that of an ideal marriage, in which each partner respects the individuality and assists the work of the other, whilst both cordially join forces to secure their common end—the Co-operative State."

This passage was written in the actual year of Sidney and Beatrice Webb's marriage, and after his influence had begun to fuse itself with her thought. I think it is possible at this point to discover what was each partner's principal contribution to their long and latterly indistinguishable collaboration. Sidney Webb was already the mainstay of the Fabian Society, the principal source of the stream of social information which was

being poured out through its tracts and lectures, the very embodiment of the quantitative study which Beatrice had said should go hand in hand with qualitative study of social affairs. Her experience had been in this qualitative field, especially her work for Charles Booth's great London Survey. She had already published her small, but remarkable, study of *The Co-operative Movement in Great Britain;* he had written on *Socialism in England,* on *The Eight Hours Day,* and on *The London Programme,* and, in addition to *Facts for Socialists* and numerous other Fabian Tracts, had contributed to *Fabian Essays* the study of **"The Historic Basis of Socialism"** in which he gave the essence of the Fabian doctrine of Utilitarian Collectivism as the social structure appropriate to the age of machine production and surveyed the growth of the activities of the State as an organisation for the promotion of social welfare. He had moreover been very active behind the scenes in creating the Progressive Party on the newly formed London County Council, and was already deeply engaged in the study of local government as an agent for the provision of collective services for the people.

Thus, even at the time of their marriage, the work that lay before them as the outcome of their union was already defined. Sidney Webb drew from Beatrice a new interest in the achievements and possibilities of voluntary organisation and a conception of the need for a wide diversity of studies of forms of social and personal behaviour. She learnt from him to think more of the rôle of State and local government in the promotion of welfare, as well as a clearer appreciation of the forces of social evolution and the value of historical studies. In practice, she left the statistics to him, and he left the individual "case-work" largely to her; and they joined forces in an immense amount of documentary research which resulted, over a long period of years, in the great series of volumes on which their combined literary reputation securely rests.

In giving these studies their initial direction, Beatrice Webb evidently took the lead. Her relatively slight study of *The Co-operative Movement* . . . was followed . . . by their joint *History of Trade Unionism*—the first, and still the best, book that attempts any careful survey of the phases of Trade Union growth and of their significance. *Industrial Democracy* . . . was the sequel, studying and analysing in detail the current activities of the Unions in the fields of collective bargaining, social insurance, and the promotion of legal enactment, and in its concluding sections attempting an evaluation of the place of working class producers' associations in the society of the coming era. The companion pieces, following up Beatrice Webb's historical study of Co-operation, were long deferred. A part of them appeared in the special supplements on *Co-operative Production* and *The Co-operative Movement* issued in 1914 by the *New Statesman*—itself one of their children; but *The Consumer's Co-operative Movement,* the big volume in which they attempted to do for the Co-operative Societies what they had done in *Industrial Democracy* for the Trade Unions, was not published until 1921.

In the meantime, Sidney Webb had had his turn, of which the fruits appeared in the massive series of volumes on the history of *English Local Government* from the seventeenth century up to the reform of the Corporations in 1835. Unrivalled as history, in this field, these volumes were much more than a mere survey of the past. Although the story was not, save in the case of the Poor Law, carried beyond 1835, it was presented essentially as an introduction to the later development of local government as an instrument of collective welfare. The series culminated in the volume, unattractively and misleadingly called *Statutory Authorities for Special Purposes* . . . , in which, after recording the growth of the special Commissions which were the real forerunners of modern local government agencies, the Webbs attempted a social evaluation of the place of local governing institutions in the life of society. With this series of volumes go also their more specialised studies of modern local government, including the *New Statesman* supplement . . . on *State and Municipal Enterprise.*

During the years through which the Webbs were pursuing their intensive studies of Trade Unionism and local government the Labour Party was in the making, and the Fabian Society, which was one of its original constituents, was pouring out tracts and lectures developing its gospel of evolutionary Socialism. Sidney Webb, in addition to his work on the L.C.C., to which he had been elected in 1892, played a large part in the activities of the Society: Beatrice Webb but a small one, typified in her Fabian pamphlet on *Women and the Factory Acts* . . . and her editorship of *The Case for the Factory Acts.* . . . She, though a Fabian, still preferred to stand rather apart from politics, following up her special concern with the conditions of working women and her close connections with Trade Union and Co-operative leaders. This was the epoch of Fabian "permeation," when she and Sidney, in their several ways, were trying to influence the younger and more hopeful members of the existing governing class, and were still sceptical of the power of the working classes to create a powerful political party of their own. His field was primarily that of politics, local and national: hers, that of social reform, especially in connection with the growing agitation against sweated labour and the demand for a "national minimum" of wages and working conditions.

It was at this point that the appointment of a Royal Commission to enquire into the working of the Poor Laws gave them both a fresh field of social activity adjacent to the social studies which they had made their own. Beatrice Webb was made a member of the Commission; and she and Sidney Webb proceeded to devote the next few years of their lives to making the reform of the Poor Laws the point of focus for their practical social policy. The famous "Minority Report of the Poor Law Commission" (1909) was written mainly by Sidney Webb; and into it they put a large part of their social policy. Not content with proposing the abolition of the Boards of Guardians and the break-up of the Poor Law so as to merge it in with the developing duties of the local governing authorities in town and country, they proceeded in the second half of their report to deal at length with the problem of unemployment, advocating public works for the maintenance of the level of employment in bad times. State measures for the rehabilitation and training of the long unemployed, and many of the proposals which are now embodied in projects for the maintenance of "full employment" and the recognition by the State of responsibility for "Social security" among the people. They flouted convention by publishing, in face of official protests, their own annotated and edited issues of the "Minority Report"; they founded the National Committee to Promote the Break-up of the Poor Law (subsequently re-named the National Committee for the Prevention of Destitution) to spread abroad the doctrines of the "Report." They appealed for support to men and women of all parties, or of none; and they carried on together what was probably the most highly organised social campaign since the days of the Anti-Corn Law League. They addressed meetings and founded branches all over the country; they called in London a great conference at which they made the most of the support which they had been successful in

enlisting from all parties and from public men in a wide variety of spheres: they founded a journal, *The Crusade,* out of which developed the *New Statesman.* For several years their activity was unremitting; and Beatrice Webb, who had hitherto taken little part in the work of propaganda, took her full share in all these labours, and also made their home at 41 Grosvenor Road a centre of all manner of plots and entertainments. Their efforts were abortive. John Burns, the President of the Local Government Board, would have nothing to do with their proposals; and Lloyd George was following the different line that led to the National Insurance Act of 1911. The Poor Law remained unreformed save in secondary ways, right up to 1929. John Burns was able to boast that he had "dished the Webbs," though in fact the main responsibility was not his.

From 1911, when the Insurance Act became law and was accepted by the Trade Unions for the sake of their share in its administration, the failure was evident; and the Webbs had to decide what to do next. What they did was to found a Fabian Research Department, which they set to work on a series of inquiries relating their earlier work on Trade Unionism and Co-operation to the new winds of doctrine that were blowing about the working-class movement and making themselves manifest in waves of strikes, often against the wish of the Trade Union leaders, and in a widespread disillusionment with the achievements of the Labour Party, which had first appeared in force in the Parliament of 1906. They set on foot a new study of the control of industry, designed to further the idea of a partnership between the producers and the consumers, and to counteract on the one side Syndicalism and on the other the too exclusively political bias of the Labour Party leaders. Out of this new venture, in which Beatrice Webb played the leading part in organisation, while Sidney Webb took his full share in the writing, came the series of special supplements to the *New Statesman,* not only dealing with Co-operation in its various aspects but also embodying the first real study ever made of the forms and methods of organisation in the skilled professions—an exceedingly valuable pendent to their earlier account of the Trade Unions.

The outbreak of war in 1914 interrupted, though it did not wholly suspend, these researches. The Fabian Research Department found itself overwhelmed with current activities arising out of the war, and called up to serve as a daily adviser on emergency problems to the working-class movement. The Webbs themselves became immersed in war work—Sidney as a leading spirit of the War Emergency Workers' National Committee, Beatrice especially in connection with problems of women's employment and war service. When problems of reconstruction began to be taken into account, Beatrice Webb played an important part both on the War Cabinet Committee on Women in Industry and on various committees attached to the Ministry of Reconstruction—especially the Haldane Committee on the Machinery of Government, which enabled her to revive their proposals for the break-up of the Poor Law and for a reorganisation of the departmental structure designed to improve the equipment of the State for its task of promoting social welfare. Out of her work for the War Cabinet Committee arose her book, *The Wages of Men and Women: Should They be Equal?.* . . . At the same time she and Sidney Webb made use of such time as they could call their own to complete their series of books on local government, to begin work on their great history of the development of the Poor Laws, and to follow up Beatrice's earlier study of the growth of Co-operation with a full study of the contemporary development of the consumers' Co-operative movement.

Letter from Sidney to Beatrice.

The end of the war confronted them with the need to restate their social gospel of partnership between producers and consumer as the key to the right adjustment of social relationships. This they attempted to do in *A Constitution for the Socialist Commonwealth of Great Britain* . . .—the least successful of their major books. Sidney Webb had been mainly responsible for drafting the new Socialist programme with which the Labour Party, reorganised under his and Arthur Henderson's influence, appealed to the electors at the end of the war, and *A Constitution for the Socialist Commonwealth* was in the main an attempt to influence the formation of Labour opinion at a time when political and economic institutions alike seemed to be in the melting pot. Its proposals for a Social Parliament, distinct from the Political Parliament dealing with the affairs of government in the traditional sense, was an attempt to meet the attacks of Syndicalists and Guild Socialists on orthodox Fabian Collectivism without sacrificing the ultimate supremacy of the consumers in economic affairs. But its proposals were generally deemed too artificial; and it exercised little influence on the shape of public opinion. It appeared, indeed, at a time when the foundations of Syndicalist and Guild Socialist influence were being undermined by the postwar depression; and its ignoring of the challenge presented by the development of the Soviet system in Russia deprived it of any appeal to the working-class "Left" or to the new generation of Socialist intellectuals who were looking, still bemusedly, to Russia for inspiration. (pp. 424-30)

[The] Webbs followed up this unsuccessful essay in constitution-making with a very much better book, *The Decay of Capitalist Civilisation,* in which they analysed relentlessly the signs of capitalist decline and the growing tendency of capitalism in decay to resort to restrictive devices which were a blank denial of its claim to rank as a promotor of adventurous enterprise. Immediately thereafter, the accession of the first Labour Government to office drew them both away from writing to active participation in public affairs. Sidney Webb became President of the Board of Trade; and Beatrice Webb constituted herself hostess to the members of the new governing class and especially to the wives of the Labour Ministers and M.P.'s, for whose benefit she founded the "Half-Circle Club" in an endeavour to protect them at once from social isolation in London and from the insidious risks of patronage.

The fall of the first MacDonald Government at the end of 1924 gave the Webbs opportunity to resume their writing. . . . Beatrice published *My Apprenticeship,* the fascinating record, based on her diaries, of her mental and political development up to the time of her marriage. *My Apprenticeship* gave a wide public an idea of her personality quite different from that which had prevailed before among those who knew the Webbs only by their political writings. They had been dismissed often enough as inhuman, mechanistic, mere schemers of social projects into which men and women must be made to fit regardless of personality or private desire. Such a view of Beatrice Webb's outlook could not survive the publication of her candid and engaging record of the earlier phases of her pilgrimage. There were some who drew the conclusion that the inhumanity was Sidney Webb's, and that Beatrice was a great spirit thwarted by marriage to a machine. But none who knew Sidney Webb could have endorsed this judgment. Inhuman he never was, even if his part in their partnership was mainly that of quantitative analysis, while Beatrice attended to the qualitative elements in the social situations which they surveyed. They were too closely bound together in spirit for their thoughts and attitudes to be thus divided. In private conversation, either of them could at any moment begin a sentence with "We think" without fear of violating the other's mind.

The pause which followed the fall of the first Labour Government also gave them the opportunity to finish their great *English Poor Law History*. . . . *Methods of Social Study*, to which reference has been made already, followed. . . . (pp. 430-31)

At this point it seemed to many as if the Webbs had completed their life-work. The second Labour Government, in which Sidney Webb, now Lord Passfield, was Colonial Secretary, had called them back to politics in 1929; and Beatrice, who strongly objected to being called "Lady Passfield," had resumed her position as Labour hostess. The fall of the Government in 1931 had released them from these, on the whole, uncongenial tasks; and they withdrew from London to spend their latter years at their house, Passfield Corner, near Liphook, Beatrice announcing her intention of setting to work on *Our Partnership*, which was to be the sequel to *My Apprenticeship*, but was to be published only after their death. Their story was, however, to have an ending very different from that which most of their friends and admirers had anticipated. Experience of Labour politics over the dozen or so years since the end of the war had taught them much, and had above all roused in them an intense curiosity about the real significance of the immense Socialist experiment which was being made in the Soviet Union. In 1932, when Beatrice was 74 and Sidney 73 years old, they set off together to see for themselves what was really happening in the one country in which capitalism had been definitely overthrown and a form of Socialism set up in its place.

On the eve of their departure I was invited to write for an American magazine, *Current History*, a forecast of what they would make of the Russian experiment. Despite their reputation as "moderates," and their lifelong association in Great Britain with the cause of evolutionary Socialism—despite the association of their names with Sidney's *mot* about "the inevitability of gradualness," I was in no doubt what their conclusions would be. I felt sure they would come back enthusiastic for Soviet Communism, as it was working itself out in Russia, and that they would find in it something essentially consistent with their social ideals. I said so, and I was right; but I was taken by surprise by the thoroughness with which they were able to apply their methods of social investigation to the unfamiliar conditions of a new country and an unknown language. The two volumes of *Soviet Communism: A New Civilisation? . . .* were an astonishing *tour de force* for two ageing Fabians whose life-work many had deemed to be at an end. Astonishing, yes; but entirely consistent with the corpus of their previous writings. In the Soviet Union, Sidney Webb found the planned Socialist economy which he had been advocating steadily for the best part of fifty years; and Beatrice found a fascinating proliferation of social activity which she was able to interpret in terms of her interest in social behaviour and to study as a release of motives inhibited under capitalism but set free under Socialism to achieve miracles of individual and collective social effort. Neither of them was in any way appalled by the absence of many of the institutions which most people in England regarded as the essential hallmarks of political democracy. There were some who said this was because the Webbs preferred order and method to democracy; but anyone who reads their book can hardly fail to be struck by their continual insistence on the emergence of new forms of popular self-expression, on the efficacy of the appeal to new popular motives of collective service and aspiration in evoking new responses, and on the sheer number of persons actively participating in the work of government in the Soviet Union in comparison with supposedly more democratic countries. In effect, the Webbs believed that they had discovered in the Soviet Union a new kind of democracy, capable of serving as the basis for a new civilisation with values essentially different from those of the capitalist era. (pp. 431-33)

The Fabians have often been called "the modern utilitarians," as having taken the doctrines of Bentham and Mill and converted them from individualist to collectivist terms, using them to justify the extension of State activity in the social field and applying the "greatest happiness" principle in new ways corresponding to the changing technical conditions of the modern age. Thus stated, the Fabian doctrine is Sidney Webb's, rather than Beatrice's, contribution to the common stock. She, accepting it broadly, extended its meaning both by recognising that collective social action for happiness could manifest itself quite as fruitfully in voluntary as in statutory forms, and by insisting that the search for happiness must involve the creation of many-sided opportunity for the successful exercise of constructive faculties and the expansion of personal motives in socially productive actions as well as the satisfaction of passive consumers' needs or desires. Her curiosity about social *behaviour* had always the invigorating quality of a curiosity about individuals: it never reduced itself to a study of the institutions merely as social *mechanisms* apart from the motives which drove them on. That was why the Soviet experiment so deeply stirred her imagination—not mainly because it seemed to her to be solving the mechanical problems of productive organisation and releasing society from the inhibitions and restrictions characteristic of capitalism in decay, but principally because it was finding out new ways for the successful exercise of human faculty in the creative service of mankind. (pp. 435-36)

    G. D. H. Cole, "Obituary: Beatrice Webb as an Economist," in The Economic Journal, *Vol. LIII, No. 212, December, 1943, pp. 422-37.*

R. H. TAWNEY   (lecture date 1952)

[*Tawney was a prominent English economist and author who viewed economic matters from a Fabian socialist perspective. In particular, he urged the socialization of the English economic system while emphasizing the need to protect the civil liberties of individuals. In the following excerpt, he discusses the nature of the Webbs' sociological and political concerns.*]

The conventional portrait of the [Webbs] as bureaucratic energumens, conspiring to submit every human activity to the centralized control of an omni-competent State, is a caricature, which the subjects chosen for their researches should be sufficient to refute. Of the thirty odd volumes, apart from pamphlets and *brochures*, produced by them in the forty years between 1890 and 1930, five consisted of studies of working-class organizations; eleven of works on problems of Poor Law, Public Health, Education and industrial policy; ten of the successive instalments of the great history of English Local Government; and four, including the important *Decay of Capitalist Civilization,* of productions too heterogeneous for classification; while of books dealing at any length with the organization and functions of the Central Government I recall only one. It is not of such materials that idolators of the Great Leviathan are wont to build their altars to him. It is true, however, that the authors looked at the economic world from the planning, directing and managing end; envisaged their own task in intellectual terms, not as a mission of moral conversion, but as the discovery of realistic and practicable solutions for specific problems; and saw more hope in the dull Fabian war of attrition, with its succession of limited objectives, than in the spectacular strategy preached by more dogmatic or emotional creeds. Both had the fire at the centre without which great things are not done; but they took their work too seriously to be rhetorical about it. They regarded the Co-operative Commonwealth, neither as a distant Utopia, nor as the inevitable climax of an irresistible economic evolution, but as an edifice to be built piecemeal by hard practical labour—an edifice which, since its building was a long-term job, had better be begun here and now, and to the erection of which system, method, application, technical skill, a reasonable regard for the prejudices and susceptibilities of ordinary men and women, and, above all, knowledge, made a more serviceable contribution than untutored enthusiasm.

The Webbs' most massive work was done in the uncharted frontier region where History and Sociology meet. It is not an exaggeration to say that their books on Trade Unionism, Co-operation and Local Government revealed for the first time the full significance of a world of movements and institutions known, of course, to exist, but, before they turned their searchlights on it, not only obscure, but hardly thought deserving of systematic exploration. Time forbids me to illustrate the combination of exhaustive research with a power of illuminating generation which makes the works in question landmarks in the study of their respective subjects. Let me say something, however, of the relation between these predominantly historical investigations and the contemporary preoccupations in the interludes of which the fruits of the former saw the light.

The authors were commonly regarded, both in this country and on the continent, as the intellectual leaders of British Socialism. The paucity of their books specifically devoted to that subject—apart from pamphlets and articles, not more than four, including the reprint of the chapter "Towards Social Democracy" contributed by Sidney to the *Cambridge Modern History,* and together comparable in bulk with the first of the ten volumes on *English Local Government*—has sometimes caused surprise. In reality, it was not accidental or due to lack of time, but characteristic and deliberate. It expressed a considered verdict on the manner in which the supposedly neglected theme should be approached. Professor Oakeshott has remarked that "the systems of abstract ideas which we call ideologies are abstracts of some kind of concrete activity"; that such "activity . . . springs . . . not from general principles, but from the existing traditions of behaviour"; and that the function of political thought, if I understand him rightly, is to explore the intimations which such traditions convey. Provided that the word "tradition" be interpreted to include the great English tradition of breaking traditions, with reverential cries of devotion to them, then the view advanced by him seems sound sense. It is, at any rate, a faithful description of the Webbs' procedure. They conceived of Socialism, not as a system to be imposed, but as an organic growth from already vigorous roots. Tendencies long at work

on different planes of life, from colliery villages and cotton towns to municipal offices, Westminster, Whitehall and the business world itself, were creating, it seemed to them, a new fabric of rights and obligations, and with it a society more social and a civilization less uncivilized than the preceding generation had known. Their function as thinkers was not to draw designs for imposing new palaces on non-existent vacant sites. It was to reveal the significant features of the transformation under way about them; to elicit conclusions of general application from the mass of raw experience provided by it; and thus to make possible a progress no longer haphazard and halting, but deliberate and sustained.

Their views on the economics of Socialism, therefore, are rarely, if ever, cast in a doctrinal mould. They emerge as a synthesis of generalizations suggested by the institutions explored in their descriptive and historical works. Co-operation, with its lesson of the supremacy of the consumer; factory legislation and trade unionism demonstrating the case for a national minimum of life and work; social services, before 1914 a feeble plant, as a foretaste of an all-embracing system of provision for common needs; a still not steeply graduated income-tax as a precedent for the taxation to extinction of unearned wealth; Local Government and its expert officials, the eulogies of Mrs. Webb on whose transcendent virtues almost persuaded one to be an anarchist—such were the already half-fabricated bricks of which, when fixed in position by the firm's judiciously compounded mortar, the New Jerusalem would be built. The sources suggesting to the architects their methods of political construction were equally prosaic. The fathers of Socialist thought, both British and continental, had belonged, with few exceptions, to the pre-democratic era. Their theory of political strategy necessarily took its stamp from the realities of despotic, aristocratic, or bourgeois rule around them. The Webbs, whose entry on the tasks of adult life had begun in the decade of the third Reform Act, accepted in principle many of their predecessors' criticisms on the economic order, but rejected their political deductions as generalizations made obsolete by the movement of events. Nor, as far as Great Britain was concerned, did the Russian pilgrimage change their views. Their enthusiasm for Soviet communism, though qualified by a dislike of the espionage system of the secret police and of the atmosphere created by what they called "the disease of conformity," was genuine, profound and lasting; but, not being simpletons, they did not suppose that a political or social system born of one climate and soil could be transplanted to another. Their life-work for forty years before their visit had been to show how political democracy, once established, could grow, if it pleased, not, indeed, without arduous struggles, but without chaos or catastrophe, into social democracy. They continued, after their return, to believe that, given the will, Parliamentary government, whatever the limitations of its inevitable gradualism, could in this country do the job, and that, in British conditions, nothing else could.

It is of the nature of political thought that much of its best work is topical. Not only the subjects treated by it, but its method of dealing with them, are inevitably influenced by the intellectual styles at different periods in fashion. The contemporary triumphs of Natural Science profoundly impressed the Webbs. They attempted to apply an analogous procedure to the study of society, not always, as a friendly critic, Mr. Leonard Woolf, has remarked, with fortunate results. Their favourite categories of structure and function at once sharpened their vision and restricted its range. Invaluable in classifying institutions, they threw less light on such vital imponderables as the loyalties which sustain and the passions which, at times, destroy them. Relying, as it did, on great accumulations of documentary material supplemented, when possible, by personal observation, the Webbs' method of research achieved brilliant successes in interpreting a society whose unstated premises they already knew; but, applied to peoples whose histories, psychologies and values differed fundamentally from those familiar to them, it was liable to result in a combination of correct factual information with—to speak with moderation—questionable deductions from it. Some of the verdicts which surprised their friends after their Far Eastern tour of 1913—though not pretending, it is fair to say, to be more than a record of impressions—were, perhaps, minor cases in point. It may be suspected that similar misconceptions detract from the value of parts—especially the parts relating to agriculture and peasant life, where their urbanized minds were not at home— of their elaborate work on Soviet communism. A full-length portrait of a state in the making by observers so experienced as the Webbs could not fail to be instructive. Political systems, however, are a matter, not merely of machinery, but of the mentality expressed in them; and the remark made, in another connection, by Mrs. Webb, that "only by watching the processes of decay and growth over a period of time can we understand even the contemporary facts," suggests a comment on those two impressive volumes which readers, when studying them, ought not to ignore. The truth is that no sociologists, however gifted and industrious, can grasp the significance of a great body of institutions, unless by a prolonged study of their historical background, combined with an intimate familiarity with their daily operation, they have acquired an insight into those hidden springs of action which official reports and answers to questionnaires do not readily reveal. The authors' preoccupation with organization diverted their attention from some aspects even of the domestic scene not obviously covered by that rubric. It would have been invaluable to have their exposition of the Socialist attitude to the monetary, credit, and investment problems, which two wars were to make an obsession. Their admirers must always regret that, brought up, as they were, in an age accustomed to the seemingly quasi-automatic operations of a gold standard worked from London, they left those crucial topics to less sagacious heads.

Some of these defects and omissions were later to produce unfortunate results. Nevertheless, when due allowance is made for them, the contributions made by the Webbs, not only to social knowledge, but also to its practical application, remain unrivalled both in their day and our own. (pp. 8-12)

> *R. H. Tawney, in his* The Webbs in Perspective, *The Athlone Press, 1953, 21 p.*

JOHN STRACHEY (essay date 1962)

[*An English politician and author whose beliefs were strongly socialist, Strachey was an active member of the British Labour Party. In the following excerpt, he assesses the importance of the Webbs' contribution to twentieth-century political thought.*]

Most people would be inclined to say that the Webbs exerted more intellectual influence upon the British Labour Movement than anyone else has ever done. There was the influence of their books; and then there was the influence of their lives. Both were profound.

Their greatest book was one of their earliest: *The History of Trade Unionism*. . . . After more than half a century this remains a basic work of sociology. And in a way too it illustrates

how their books and their lives were really one. For the manner in which the Webbs went about this first major task of "their partnership," as Beatrice was to call it, set the noble pattern of their lives. They investigated the trade unions—the basic, indeed in the eighteen-eighties, almost the sole, organisation of the wage earners.

For the successful formation of the post-Chartist British trade unions was, as everybody can see now, one of the decisive events of modern history. These obscure molecular activities of the British wage earners, drab and prosaic compared with the revolutionary spirit of Chartism; feeble and precarious compared with the power of trade unionism today—these activities which had been thought below the dignity of social investigation—altered the course of history, and that not only in Britain.

Thus in investigating the "new unionism," as it was called at the time, this brilliantly good-looking young woman, born into the highest ranks of the new class captains of industry, and this strange, odd, awkward young civil servant from the lower middle class, united to accomplish one of the first major pieces of genuinely scientific field-work in sociology. They set out to discover how the British wage earners were organising themselves into stable and powerful association. Travelling indefatigably about the country, investigating the origins, the congresses, the disputes, the doctrines, the rule books of what were at that time obscure and unpopular organisations, they brought into the light of consciousness what was to prove one of the decisive social processes of modern times.

The establishment of trade unionism was one of the two decisive events which have modified the supposedly unalterable laws of capitalist development. The other decisive development was the establishment of political democracy under universal franchise; and, as the Webbs' book showed, these two events were linked together at a hundred points. It was out of and through the struggle of the trade unions, emancipated by the Cross Acts, struck down again by the courts, forming, in challenge and response, the Labour Representation Committee, and so the Labour Party, that the British wage earners won their political as well as their industrial influence. It was these two interlocked developments which falsified Marx's prediction that the fate of wage earners in a capitalist society must be "ever-increasing misery." And that has changed everything. But all this was far from obvious when the Webbs sat down to write *The History of Trade Unionism*. It was an act of faith to see that the obscure doings of rude men in Lancashire and Durham, or in the East End of London, were going to change the world. Yet by their exertions and their example, change the world they have.

It is curious to recall that Lenin translated the Webbs' book into Russian during one of his Siberian exiles. He evidently considered it of immense importance. But what did he think of its intensely cautious pragmatism, of the refusal of the Webbs to raise virtually any theoretical structure upon the immense factual groundwork of the book?

But let us turn to their lives. In the next period, in the Edwardian Age, in the nineteen-hundreds, it was the lives rather than the books of the Webbs which counted. From the turn of the century to 1914 they were the heart and core of the Fabian Society. In that brilliant, quarrelsome, extraordinary body, with Wells, Shaw, Leo Amery, and the young G. D. H. Cole, all brilliantly disputatious, the Webbs formed a central ballast and basis.

In the nineteen-hundreds, it is interesting to remember, the Webbs were by no means irrevocably committed to the nascent Labour Party. It was part of their Fabian philosophy of permeation that they were as willing to work towards socialism through the Liberal, or even the Conservative Parties, if those parties could be cajoled or persuaded into serving their purposes. It was not until what they regarded as the breakdown of the old social system in the First World War—it was not until after 1914—that Sidney became a practical political leader of the Labour Party as well as a Fabian theorist. In 1918, at the end of the war, he and Henderson played a decisive part in re-forming the Labour Party as a national party with individual membership, whilst yet retaining its original character of the "Labour Representation Committee" of the trade unions. And it was then that Sidney drafted Clause 4 of the Constitution which has been so much in the news in the last few years, that Clause which defines the common ownership of the *means* of production as a necessary basis for a reasonable and equitable distribution of the *fruits* of production.

Soon after this the Webbs produced what is to my mind their second best book, after *The History of Trade Unionism*. This is *The Decay of Capitalist Civilisation*. . . . They were convinced as early as the beginning of the nineteen-twenties, that capitalism, not merely as an economic but also as a social system, would never recover from its *felo de se* in the First World War. And this short book contains by far their sharpest—if you will by far their most left-wing—critique of the society which surrounded them. Its earlier companion volume, *A Constitution for a Socialist Commonwealth in Great Britain,* is frankly unreadable. It reveals the negative side, the limitations, of this great man and woman. There is a startling formalism, and a rigidly pedestrian spirit, about this attempt to foresee how socialism might be organised in Britain, a formalism which ignored many things which would, in fact, profoundly modify the real development of society. (pp. 183-86)

By the nineteen-twenties, Sidney was launched on his active political career. He was a member of the Labour Party Executive and he took office as President of the Board of Trade in the 1924 Labour Government. But his real test as a practical politician came five years later in the second Labour Government of 1929. In that Government he was Secretary of State for Dominion and Colonial Affairs. He was an industrious and competent departmental Minister.

But now another of the limitations of the Webbs came disastrously to the fore. Events, in their remorseless way, began to reveal the fact that both Sidney and Beatrice were great sociologists but by no means great economists. Their powers of economic analysis, as distinct from description, were severely limited. Sidney, no doubt, was a well-trained economist who knew extremely well economics up to and including Marshall. But somehow the subject had gone dead in his mind. He did not really believe that there was anything much new to say or think or do about economics.

Therefore when the catastrophe of the great slump struck the second Labour Government like a cyclone; when unemployment, which that Government had been elected to cure, or at any rate to combat, rose tidally to engulf it, the Webbs had nothing to offer. I was a young Labour M.P. at the time, and I, and other more important people than myself, tried desperately to make them and our other leaders face the issue. Keynes, it is true, had not then worked out the theoretical basis for the maintenance of full employment. Nevertheless, he had got the rough outline of how to set about the thing well in his mind.

We young people in the Labour Movement were in touch with him and we were convinced that whether he was right or wrong, an attempt to combat unemployment on some sort of Keynsian lines was the one hope for the Government. Such an attempt might very likely fail, but it was certain that if it were not even made the Government would go down, not only to defeat but to discredit.

As I remember it, the Webbs did not so much actively disagree with the Keynsian analysis and prescription; it was rather that they were not really interested in it one way or the other. It was the inequalities, wastes, and injustices of the capitalist system which had produced their socialism. Both theoretically and practically, unemployment was to them essentially a passing phase of the trade cycle rather than the centre of the picture. So the two leading theorists of the Labour Party failed even to see the necessity of making an attempt to find a way out along Keynsian lines.

On the other hand, when the crash came in 1931, as come it duly did, the Webbs' reaction was in the end far-reaching. For some time they seemed numbed by the political catastrophe; but, in the end, they came near to what was in effect the orthodox Marxist conclusion. By an extraordinary but logical process these arch-reformists, the very authors of that watchword of the British Labour Movement "the inevitability of gradualness," came, at the very end of their lives, to despair of the possibility of reforming the capitalist system. To them, just as to myself, in the nineteen-thirties, it looked as if the decay of capitalist civilisation had become irrevocable. We failed to see the extraordinary fact that Keynes's diagnosis and remedy, combined with the obstinate strength, industrial and political, of the wage earners, and combined, too, with the terrific jolt which the Second World War was to give to British society, would create a far more favourable opportunity for reformism in the latter part of the twentieth century than had ever existed before.

I never knew the Webbs well but I did occasionally go down to Liphook and see them during this period. I remember them telling me on one occasion that Keynes had been there the weekend before and that he was heartbroken by the fact that *The General Theory,* some time after its publication, had apparently fallen completely flat; that the economists were ignoring it; that nobody would pay any attention to it. I could not help noticing that Beatrice, at any rate, evidently thought that the book's apparent failure was inevitable; that it was a last despairing attempt to find a reformist way out which did not exist.

It was not that the Webbs had become communists. They still did not grasp, and were not really interested in, the whole massive body of Marxist theory; but they had despaired of reformism. Their reaction was to go to Russia and to write that extraordinary and, to be frank, preposterous book, *Soviet Communism: A New Civilisation?*, published in 1935.

I vividly remember the impression which it made on me, at the time. I was then much nearer to the communists than the Webbs ever became; but even I was staggered by the book's utter lack of any critical analysis of Russian society. It was not that the Webbs had seen Stalin's Russia as it was and had come to the conclusion that, nevertheless, since capitalism seemed to be dying, the Soviet system had to be accepted, with all its horrors, as the only remaining way out for human civilisation. That was a tenable proposition. But that was not the Webbs' reaction. Their huge, two-volume work gave the impression of taking Soviet society utterly at its face value. Their extraordinary formalism came out above all in their account of the political side of Soviet society. They described it as if it were in reality what it was on paper. Their formalism showed in their extraordinary belief that if a constitution said that democratic elections were to take place, that meant that they actually did take place. But there was also a fixed determination to see in Soviet Russia the hope of the world. They would not despair; therefore they had to have some repository for their hope. And they found it, not as many of the rest of us did, by concluding that the nightmarish features of Stalin's Russia had to be accepted as the inevitable birth pangs of a new civilisation: they found it by firmly shutting their eyes to the existence of any such features. Of course, they were old people by now.

It would be wholly wrong, however, to end this talk on a note of depreciation. The mistakes of a man and woman such as the Webbs are incidental and drop away in the tide of history. Their constructive achievements alone remain. It was said of a general in the last war: "To say that he made mistakes is merely to say that he made war." In the same way we may say of the Webbs: "To say that they made mistakes is merely to say that they made social history." Their theory deeply influenced what has become the major left-wing party in a virtually two-party system. The Labour Party might have been a very different thing without the life and theory of the Webbs.

Thus every British wage earner is profoundly in debt to the Webbs. They are concretely and financially in debt to them: for whether they know it or not, and whether they vote Labour or Conservative, the standard of life which the British wage earners now enjoy was in some measure built up by the lives of this man and woman. The strange partnership of this prosaic, ugly, able little man, with a woman in her own way intensely romantic, laid down many of the lines of action by which the wage earners have won full status in British society. (pp. 186-89)

> John Strachey, "The Webbs," in his *The Strangled Cry and Other Unparliamentary Papers,* *The Bodley Head,* 1962, pp. 183-89.

SAUL BELLOW (essay date 1963)

[*Recipient of the Nobel Prize in literature in 1976, Bellow is one of the most prominent figures in contemporary American fiction. Bellow is noted as an artist who upholds the traditional moral values of humanism and literary conventions of Realism, thus opposing the trend toward a modern literature that is nihilistic in temperament and experimental by conscious design. Critics find that Bellow's novels advance a basically affirmative sense of life and a belief in human dignity, attitudes that at the same time are thoroughly grounded in the complex and disturbing realities of the modern world. While recognizing the same world that many modern authors take for granted as declining and evil, Bellow has produced a body of work based on the possibility that "there may be truths on the side of life." In the following excerpt, he discusses the strengths and weaknesses of Beatrice Webb's portrait of American society.*]

The Sidney Webbs came to the United States in 1898 to have a look at American institutions; they had already published their study, in fifteen volumes, of local government in England. Crossing the Continent, they continued westward to Australia and New Zealand on a trip around the world. Beatrice Webb kept a daily record of her impressions, a document which might have been left to us by one of Shaw's beautiful bluestocking heroines. Mrs. Webb, gently bred, daughter of a railway mag-

nate, rejected the life (was it a life?) of a leisured Englishwoman and scorned the idea of a conventional and proper marriage. "When I turned to social investigation as my craft in life," she wrote in *My Apprenticeship,* "it was just my experience of London Society that started me with a personal bias effectually discounting, even if it did not wholly supersede, my father's faith in the social value of a leisured class."

Judging by [her *American Diary, 1898*], Mrs. Webb never quite succeeded in changing her social complexion. Congressional leaders in Washington, bosses in New York, Chicago, Denver and San Francisco she described with a note of patrician condescension, a sort of socialistic snobbery. She reminded me often of Tolstoy as he is described in Gorki's memoirs—the grand seigneur in peasant garb. Faultfinding, humorless, self-important, she was still a shrewd and observant woman, with a quick grasp of new and complicated situations. After a week in Boston she concludes a brilliant discussion of the political scene there with the following summary:

> Boston is administered by public spirited and well-informed brains, and corrupt and inefficient hands. The city of Boston is in fact governed by its aristocracy working through a corrupt democracy.

How she must have astonished the bosses, who thought they were entertaining—or giving the brush-off to—a pretty English visitor, and found the glad hand ignored by this formidable inquisitor who demanded information about the police, the voters, patronage, sewage and paving.

She quickly discerned the inordinate powers of Congressional committees, the dangers of bureaucracy, the complacency of the public toward graft, the power of business in government. She also noted "the American contempt for the vested interests or 'established expectations' of the individual citizen. Private enterprise is permitted to trample on the individual. . . ." She was shrewd, too, in her observations of the businessman and manager. She noted in Pittsburgh ("a veritable Hell of a place") the militant arrogance of the people who got things done at the Carnegie Mills, the "brainworkers." Carnegie himself she thought a "reptile." Her portraits of such types have nothing old-fashioned about them. The attitudes of "private power" are evidently little changed.

But she was not more flattering in her estimates of a man like Altgeld, who immediately seemed to her "a cross between a working man and a dissenting minister," who lacked "personal dignity and a certain 'savoir faire'." Mrs. Webb tended to judge the intellectual and moral qualities of people by the polish of their social harness. Woodrow Wilson pleased her; Teddy Roosevelt made her enthusiastic—he was "deliciously racy." Thomas Reed, Speaker of the House, she thought would make a "fairly good cashier." "He is said to be pious; he may be honest: but he does not matter." Idle American women she described as painfully dull creatures, hardly worth one's notice, "without intellectual curiosity or public spirit."

A word about her style. On the whole it is precise and sharp: Cornell students are "well-mannered but somewhat unhealthy looking youths, bad teeth, spotty complexions, narrow chests and sloping shoulders." Robert Lincoln "floated on his father's reputation into a position of importance. He had the ill-humour of continuous over-feeding and over-drinking: the hard uninspired intelligence of a complete materialist." Joseph W. Bailey, House minority leader, "to English eyes, looks a cad of the worst description, a strange combination of a low-class actor and rowdy stump orator.''

Her explanations of the American political setup are invariably lucid and to the point. The diary contains a memorable description of San Francisco, a brief history of Hawaii, and a lively, spirited and interested report of a meeting with one of the wives of a Mormon elder, who was herself a doctor and was running against her husband in an election for the state senate. Mrs. Webb allows the lady to tell her own story, a fascinating one, and concludes that she was a ''pure-minded little soul,'' but probably had no political ability and only a fragmentary medical knowledge. Mrs. Webb's high-mindedness here is redeemed only by her remark about polygamy— ''Only one bull is required for twenty cows.''

It would seem that the farther west Mrs. Webb traveled, the greater was her freedom from the self-imposed obligation to compare everything she saw with the English experience. Insular and provincial as she was, the crossing of the Rockies seems to have liberated her mind and her style. West of the Rockies, too, the Webbs were relieved of their single-minded pursuit of the facts of local government in the United States (Washington was something of a disappointment: ''An unfortunate time to be at Washington, seeing that all the politicians to whom we have introductions are completely absorbed in Cuba''), and Mrs. Webb could relax a little. Bryce and de Tocqueville looked more penetratingly into American institutions. Mrs. Webb was not a generous observer; what her journal does not lack, however, is intelligence and charm.

Saul Bellow, ''Beatrice Webb's America,'' in The Nation, Vol. 197, No. 6, September 7, 1963, p. 116.

SAMUEL HYNES (essay date 1972)

[An American critic and educator, Hynes has written and edited numerous studies of English literature and literary figures. In the following excerpt, he discusses Beatrice Webb's diaries as an outlet for her suppressed literary ambitions.]

''This last month or so,'' Beatrice Webb wrote in her diary in 1889, ''I have been haunted by a longing to create characters and to move them to and fro among fictitious circumstances. To put the matter plainly—by the vulgar wish to write a novel.'' There would seem to be no reason why a wealthy, intelligent spinster of thirty-one shouldn't indulge her wish, and write a novel, but for this spinster it was more than a wish, it was a temptation: she had a gift for descriptive writing and the analysis of character; she was widely read in both English and Continental fiction; and she had, as she later put in, ''intellectual curiosity and an overpowering impulse towards self-expression''; but she also felt a strong contrary pull, the imperative to Duty, which made mere self-expression seem unworthy.

The diary passage continues:

There is an intense attractiveness in the comparative ease of descriptive writing. Compare it with work in which movements of commodities, percentages, depreciations, averages, and all the ugly horrors of commercial facts are in the dominant place, and must remain so if the work is to be worthful. . . . The whole multitude of novels I have read pass before me; the genius, the talent, the clever mechanism or the popularity-hunting of mediocrities—what have

the whole lot of them, from the work of genius to the penny-a-liner, accomplished for the advancement of society on the one and only basis that bring with it virtue and happiness—the scientific method? This supreme ambition to present some clear and helpful idea of the forces we must subdue and the forces we must liberate in order to bring about reformation may be absurdly out of proportion to my ability. But it alone is the faith, the enthusiasm of my life, the work which I feel called upon to do. Other work would mean vanity and vexation of spirit: would begin in self-indulgence and end in a craving for popularity—for a day's fame!

The conflicts set down here, between Self and Service, and between Art and Science, were deep in Victorian life and thought, and Beatrice Webb was, as she recognized, a representative Victorian. She was beautiful, wealthy, and well-born, and might have been a leader of society. She was an imaginative writer of some promise, and might have become a novelist. But she rejected both society and art and chose instead the most uncreative, self-abnegating course—to give her life over to social research and to the writing, with her husband Sidney, of those ''solid but unreadable books'' that are in their way symbols of the life of Duty—admirable, but unappealing. In Mrs. Webb's public life Service and Science won; but self-expression, like Religion, if thrust out by the front door will come in by the scullery window, and the novels that Beatrice Webb would not write found a kind of private existence in her diaries. (pp. 153-54)

The world that Beatrice Webb observed was above all the world of a class—the governing class of England. There are some striking exceptions, some finely drawn working-class scenes, for example, but on the whole it was the governors—the political thinkers and doers—who engaged her attention, and got into the record. Over the nearly seventy years of her adult life, the governing class changed, and the dramatis personae of her diaries reflect that change (Sidney himself is the best example, a little tadpole-shaped man who turns up in an 1890 entry and becomes at the last a Cabinet Minister and a peer); but whatever their qualities and origins, the characters are public men, men from the corridors of power.

Her descriptions of these men are the best of her writing. She rarely deals with them in physical terms, except where she can treat physical details as significant of mental or moral qualities; it was the minds of men that mattered, and the ways in which their intellectual and moral natures impelled their public behaviour. (Private behaviour and scandal did not interest her as such; it was only when scandal became public, and thus a basis of public behaviour, as in the case of H. G. Wells, that she recorded it.) Her characterizations therefore tend to stand as examples or representatives of types—not because they are generalized over, but because they are analysed and explained. This was a habit of mind of which Mrs. Webb was entirely aware from early maturity; in 1884, at the end of her diary account of her relationship with Joseph Chamberlain, she wrote: ''I cannot feel, or think, or see, without a desire to formulate; and then desire is not satisfied unless the formula is as complete as I can make it and expressive of the whole experience.'' This seems an odd way to emerge from an unhappy love affair, but it is a true perception of her intellectual nature, and the formulating process is evident wherever she considered character (including her own). This does not prevent her portraits from being vivid and novelistic, but it does mean that they suggest a certain kind of novel, more philosophical than particular. (pp. 163-64)

She could caricature with a single trenchant phrase, as when she described Ramsay MacDonald as "a magnificent substitute for a leader"; and she could, with persons most dear to her, go on adding to a portrait so that it became a lifelong process. This is true of her account of Shaw, from her first meeting with him in the '80s through fifty years of observation. Shaw represented for her the route that she did not take—he was the artist, the humorous man of genius, the philanderer, with all the vanity and capacity for self-indulgence that she had suppressed in herself. She worked with him, cycled with him, argued with him, and probably spent more time with him than with any other man except her husband. She valued most highly his opinion of her own prose, and sought it whenever she could; but she did not like most of his plays, and had no great regard for his intellectual powers. It was Shaw-as-Shaw that she really admired: "Bernard Shaw's personality is a work of art," she wrote in 1933, "and grows more attractive with age—almost mythical!" Her running record of that work of art is one of the valuable things in the diaries.

Even more interesting, though, is the oblique and reticent portrait of Sidney Webb that the diaries both conceal and reveal, like one of those children's puzzles with a face in a tree. Sidney is described most elaborately in the introduction to *Our Partnership,* a tender and affectionate, if somewhat stiff tribute to "the Other One." But the portrait that emerges from the sum of diary entries about Sidney is rather different, and a good deal less attractive. He appears, in the end, as the opposite of Shaw, a man without a personality—a cheerful, unruffled, and single-minded bureaucrat who had never known insomnia or indigestion, or anger, or passion, or despair. One feels that his overwhelming efficiency was a failure of ordinary humanity, something that removed him from the company of common, feeling men. It can hardly have been a part of Mrs. Webb's intention to portray her husband in this inhuman way; on the contrary, she professed her continuing affection for him in terms that cannot be doubted. Still, the novelist in her created another character, who is credible but repellent. She did so principally by a large number of small strokes—a kind of literary pointillism, as for example in the two sentences at the end of this passage describing the muddle-headedness of trade union members:

> they enjoy the vicarious glory of the Labour Cabinet Minister being among the rulers of the earth—a man whom they address by his Christian name and who sits and smokes with them. They cannot see that their representative may be a mere tool in the hands of men who have been hardened oppressors of their class. "They are a hopeless lot," sighed Sidney as he turned with a contented smile to his morning's work. "We are in for some strange events this coming year—let us get on with our work while we can."

That preference for work over people was Sidney Webb's essential quality, but it's the contented smile that makes it so unpleasant. Beatrice notes it with detachment, as one datum in the range of her observation, but it seems nevertheless a kind of judgment, coming as it does from a woman who sometimes found research nauseating, and people fascinating.

Just as physical description is rarely a part of Beatrice Webb's "characters," so the description of places does not enter much into her narrative. Nature was a place to take exercise in, not a subject for careful observation, and though Mrs. Webb sometimes recorded the length of a walk, and the subjects of the walkers' conversation, she rarely noted what she had seen. One might say that she lacked a visual imagination, or one might argue that she had chosen a life in which physical experience could not play an important part, and that her avoidance of physical phenomena was deliberate. All accounts of the physical content of her life—the clothes she wore, the house she lived in, the meals she served—suggest extreme indifference, whether deliberate or not: "we sit in two lodging house rooms," Virginia Woolf noted with distaste "(the dining room had a brass bedstead behind a screen) eat hunks of red beef; and are offered whisky." Mrs. Webb is the only woman writer I can think of who pays no attention to other women's clothes or to the furnishings of their houses. Her world was composed of men's (and women's) minds and actions, not of appearances or of places.

The one important exception to this last point is in her descriptions of the lives of the poor. In her early accounts of life in the East End of London, and among her poor relations in Bacup, Lancashire, and in her later descriptions of Seaham, her husband's constituency in County Durham, she wrote with unusual and moving particularity. No doubt this is partly because description under these circumstances was an indictment of poverty, but the quality of the writing suggests more than this, suggests that there was a depth of feeling in Mrs. Webb that she did not find it easy to express, but that the lives of the poor brought it to consciousness.

Though she was not usually very good at visual scenes, she had an instinctive gift for the dramatic. Both her awareness of class and her concern for moral values led her to see men's relations to each other in dramatic, conflicting terms. (pp. 165-67)

As she grew older, Mrs. Webb's diaries lost some of their novelistic qualities. The later entries are longer and less frequent, and lack the sharp immediacy that the greatest diaries give us, the sense of present life. There are fewer scenes and dialogues, and an increasing inwardness, a turn to longer meditations that are often like informal essays; one could easily extract from the later diaries whole essays, and give them the sort of titles that Chesterton gave to his informal pieces: "On the Ethics of Friendship," and "Why Englishmen Hate Science." The intelligence is still there, and the fluent style, and occasionally a fine gossipy portrait emerges—of J. B. Priestley, Annie Besant, or Mrs. Webb's nephew-in-law, Malcolm Muggeridge; but the narrative is slacker and more trivial, begins to take note of the hot-water bottle and the nine o'clock news, and has an old woman's preoccupation with failing health, pain, and medicine. These diaries of old age are still good social history, but they sometimes read like letters that one might get from a very intelligent but elderly maiden aunt. Mrs. Webb was aware of this, and worried about it, not for stylistic reasons, but because she feared that she might be misusing her energies: "If I am to get on with the work," she wrote in 1934, "I must stop this drivelling in the diary at 3 o'clock in the morning. This scribbling has become what Benson termed 'logorrhea'—a symptom of senility?" Even at seventy-six, the conflict between "the history of a woman's life" and the chosen work went on.

If there is one dominant theme in the later diaries, it is Old Age. The subject turns up before one expects it, in entries written when Mrs. Webb was in her mid-fifties; as though she were hurrying towards old age, and out of life. She refers to Sidney and herself as "old people," "ancients," and thinks about how they should withdraw gracefully from the world. Reading *A Passage to India* in 1924, she was struck by the character of the old woman, Mrs. Moore, and especially by the passage (in chapter 23) in which Forster describes Mrs. Moore's feelings about the universe just before she dies.

> In this description of an old woman's mind [she wrote in the diary], what appeals to me are the phrases "the twilight of the double vision," "a spiritual muddledom is set up." Certainly with me there is a strange consciousness of standing on a bare and bleak watershed of thought and feeling—in itself a place without thoughts or feelings, but with countless thoughts and feelings streaming out of the past and into the future in directions so various and manifold that I can no longer estimate their relative value. And the concrete questions which I have investigated— trade unionism, local government, co-operation, political organization, no longer interest me. I dislike reading about them, thinking about them, talking or writing about them.

> In my present state of mind they seem stale and unprofitable. It is states of mind that interest me.

This mood was by no means constant in Mrs. Webb's last years, but there is a good deal of the Mrs. Moore state of mind in the diaries—the doubt about absolutes, the questioning of meaning and value, the sense of emotional exhaustion, and above all the desire to withdraw from the world's muddle. Like most old people, she thought of herself as belonging to a world that was past; she was an "aged Victorian," whose mind had been shaped by Victorian ideas, and she disliked and disapproved of much that she saw around her; the young Fabians were frightful, Bloomsbury was decadent, party leaders were weak and stupid. It was not a world that she belonged to; *her* world remained Victorian. "Looking back from the standpoint of today," she wrote in 1926,

> it seems to me that two outstanding tenets, some would say two idols of the mind, were united in this mid-Victorian trend of thought and feeling. There was the current belief in the scientific method, in that intellectual synthesis of observation and experiment, hypothesis and verification, by means of which alone all mundane problems were to be solved. And added to this belief in science was the consciousness

Beatrice and Sidney Webb at work.

of a new motive: the transference of the emotion of self-sacrificing service from God to man.

This is a just account of the motives that formed Beatrice Webb's life—the belief in science, and the belief in human obligation. It explains her work, her marriage, and the contents of her diary. (It also explains why, in her seventies, she became a devoted admirer of Soviet Russia, for in her terms Russia was the last Victorian society.)

Beatrice Webb was an artist who never wrote a work of art; for a diary is not really art, and can't be—it is too subject to accident, as life is, as history is. A diary is rather a kind of account rendered, the debits and credits of a self and a world. "I want to brood over the past and reflect on men and their affairs," Mrs. Webb wrote; "I want to summarise my life and see what it all amounts to." That is the true diarist's motive—to see what it all amounts to. In her case, the diary served two other functions: it allowed expression to the suppressed artist in herself, and it helped her to hold herself to the course that she had chosen, by re-defining her choice.

I am persuaded that if she had made the other choice, and had committed herself to art, she might have been a considerable novelist, a sort of latter-day George Eliot. But I see no reason to regret that she did not. It is surely only literary sentimentality to think that it is more worthy to be a novelist than to be a diarist, or a social researcher, and I am content that we have what we have, one George Eliot and one Beatrice Webb. (pp. 168-71)

Samuel Hynes, "The Art of Beatrice Webb," in his Edwardian Occasions: Essays on English Writing in the Early Twentieth Century, *Oxford University Press, 1972, pp. 153-72.*

GERTRUDE HIMMELFARB (essay date 1976)

[*Himmelfarb is a prominent American historian who specializes in studies of English Victorian society. In the following excerpt, she discusses the essential philosophical duality of the Webbs' Fabianism.*]

"Fabian 'Aberrances'" is the title of one of the chapters in Margaret Cole's history of Fabianism. The title refers to the favourable disposition of many Fabians—and the Webbs most notably—towards imperialism, protectionism, and a church-controlled system of education. One can well understand Mrs. Cole's use of that term. Indeed one might be inclined to extend it to a variety of other issues: Beatrice Webb's early opposition to women's suffrage (recanted only many years later); Sidney Webb's ill-concealed contempt for many trade union leaders; their "ambivalence," as Mrs. Cole put it, towards the Labour Party in its formative stage; their preference for the tactics of "permeation" rather than electoral activities—and their willingness, moreover, to permeate the Tory party as well as the Liberal; their indifference to the democratic political process ("no nonsense about democracy!" Beatrice confided to her diary in explaining her predilection for the Tories); the ruthlessness with which they pursued their plans for "social engineering" (Beatrice's term, used approvingly); and, most egregiously, their adulation of the Soviet Union, a sentiment that survived purges, trials, the Stalin-Hitler pact, and the other atrocities of the Stalinist era.

These "aberrances" are so plentiful that at some point one must consider the possibility that they are not aberrances at all but part of the very essence of the Webbs—and, to some extent,

of the socialist movement they helped shape. The aberration, one suspects, is less in them than in our image of them, our notion of what is befitting to progressive, enlightened, right-minded (which is to say left-thinking) intellectuals. (p. 789)

The most striking anomaly—if it is that—is the religious impulse that figured so prominently in Beatrice Webb's life and work. To anyone who has read Comte (as she did), it should come as no surprise to find an extreme rationality joined with an intense religiosity. Yet her acquaintances were as taken aback by her ardent professions of religious faith as later commentators have been. Her diary describes a memorable dinner-table conversation with the Haldanes (Haldane then being Lord Chancellor in the Liberal Government):

> The conversation drifted on to religious teaching in secondary schools, and I casually remarked that I liked a definitely religious atmosphere and the practice of prayer as part of the school life. "'Nonsense—Mrs. Webb,'" blurted out the usually calm Elizabeth, with a sort of insinuation in her voice that I was not sincere. I fired up and maintained my ground; and, in a moment of intimacy, asserted that prayer was a big part of my own life. Whereupon both the Haldanes turned round and openly scoffed at me, Haldane beginning a queer kind of cross-examination in law-court fashion as to what exactly I prayed to, or prayed about, and Elizabeth scornfully remarking that prayer was merely superstition. It was a strange outburst met by another vehement assertion on my part that the two big forces for good in the world were the scientific method applied to the process of life, and the use of prayer in directing the purpose of life.

"Process" and "purpose," science and religion—the duality was almost an obsession with Beatrice. It first makes its appearance in *My Apprenticeship* in the form of a "Controversy between the Ego that affirms and the Ego that denies": the affirmative Ego asserting the religious, spiritual, mystical, or moral (the words are used almost interchangeably) "purpose" or end of life, the negative Ego asserting the sufficiency of science for all the mediate "processes" that are the proper concerns of sociologists and social reformers. From the beginning, the controversy resolved itself, for Beatrice at any rate, in a stalemate, the two Egos presiding over their respective domains, each autonomous, self-sufficient, sovereign.

This is not the way it would have appeared to an outsider. To anyone knowing the Webbs through their writings or political activities, the "scientific" Ego, the Ego governing the "process" of life, must have seemed dominant to an unseemly degree. Even those familiar with Beatrice's protestations of belief, her daily prayers and private confessionals, might have been tempted to regard them as idiosyncrasies having no practical bearing on the "partnership" that was so extraordinarily productive. The "Webb firm," as it was known, succeeded in turning out scores of books, helped found a major university (the London School of Economics) and an influential journal (the *New Statesman*), played an important part in the leadership and activities of the Fabian Society, participated in affairs of government at both the local and national levels, lectured, pamphleteered, permeated, schemed, and otherwise exercised an incalculable influence on English intellectual and political life for half a century. There would seem to be little room here for religion of any sort, for any contemplation of ultimate "purpose," indeed for anything that was not purely utilitarian.

The Webbs themselves encouraged this impression by representing themselves, in all their public activities, as preeminently scientists, practitioners of the "science of society." This science was presumed to be both an intellectual and a political instrument, a method of analysis and a prescription for reform. It was thus a warrant of rationality in both senses: the rational understanding of social affairs and the rational ordering of those affairs. The conviction of the essential identity of these two activities, these two modes of rationality, was what sustained the Webbs through the arduous research that went into the ten volumes of the English Local Government series, to say nothing of their numerous other writings. Political to their marrow, they did not begrudge the time devoted to scholarship because they regarded that scholarship as essentially utilitarian: the scientific analysis of society was a necessary prelude to the scientific reorganization of society. Every now and then, in the privacy of her diary, Beatrice confessed that they were operating with a double standard, that they were less "honest" in their political and polemical activities than in their scholarly, "scientific" work. Sometimes she even confided the suspicion that their political commitments might induce some bias in their scholarship. But she quickly dismissed the latter possibility, and she did not overly trouble herself with the former.

Methods of Social Study was intended as a scientific manual, a summation of everything the Webbs had learnt in the course of their own research. It was predicated upon the assumption that whatever personal interest, beliefs, and prejudices the historian or sociologist might have—and the Webbs took it for granted that he had these in the same measure as all other people—he could be perfectly objective and scientific if only he utilized the correct methods. Critics have mocked the Webbs for their pride in some of these methods: the "art of note-taking," for example, which consisted of the "unit-fact" technique—the recording of each fact on a separate sheet of paper of uniform size and format. But the Webbs saw nothing trivial in that "art"; indeed they saw it as the very warrant of the scientific enterprise. Because those sheets of paper could be shuffled around, arranged and rearranged, they assumed that the facts recorded on those separate sheets had an independence and integrity of their own quite apart from the person of the researcher. Their other prescription for objectivity lay in the concept of the institution. Unlike the usual procedure, which starts with a question to which an answer is sought (the question itself predetermining the selection of facts and thus the answer), the Webbs recommended that the inquiry focus upon an entire institution and examine it without reference to questions or preconceptions. The social scientist would thus follow the example of the natural scientist, who sits down before a specimen and undertakes to discover every fact about it, every aspect of its constitution, activities, and relations.

But even the *Methods* book, for all its naive positivism, ended up by restating the familiar duality. The final chapter, "The Relation of Science to the Purpose of Life," affirmed the possibility of a science of society and its applicability to the practical affairs of society, but found that that science had "nothing to say of the purpose, either of our own life, or of the universe." Science could tell us how to cure and how to kill, but not whether we ought to cure or kill; the latter question could be answered only in terms of emotions, values, or religious creeds. The book concluded with two quotations, the first from Comte on the need for altruism as the foundation of any moral order,

and the second from Whitehead on the need for a religious creed, religion being "a vision of something which stands beyond, behind, and within the passing flux of immediate things . . . something which is the ultimate ideal, and the hopeless quest."

This side of the Webbs was not always apparent to contemporaries, not even to many of their friends, who saw their "partnership" as totally ordered and compulsively rational, without the usual distractions, complications, and confusions of life, lacking children (but this Beatrice regretted), undiverted by art, music, or literature, unrelieved by any playfulness or caprice. In *The New Machiavelli,* H. G. Wells parodied the couple who found trees "hopelessly irregular" and sea cliffs "a great mistake." And he found it difficult to credit the reports of Beatrice's "mysticism." "There is no more mysticism in Beatrice," he assured a friend, "than in a steam engine." But on this matter Wells was quite wrong, for it was precisely her sense of religion that provided the driving force for her engine.

Some of their friends, and most of their biographers, were prepared to grant Beatrice her religion while assuming Sidney to be quite innocent of that eccentricity. But this too may be an overstatement. Beatrice was, to be sure, the more overtly, conventionally religious of the two. But there is reason to accept her own assurance that Sidney shared her faith, although on a different level. The *Methods,* after all, was a joint work, and if the final chapter had all the earmarks of Beatrice's writing, Sidney seemed to have had no objection to issuing it under his name as well. In *Our Partnership* Beatrice spelt out their religious differences—and their essential similarity:

> By religion, I mean the communion of the soul with some righteousness *felt to be outside and above itself.* This may take the conscious form of prayer: or the unconscious form of ever-present and persisting aspirations—a faith, a hope and a devotion to a wholly disinterested purpose. It is this unconscious form of religion which lies at the base of all Sidney's activity. He does not pray, as I often do, because he has not acquired so self-conscious a habit. But there is a look in his eyes when he patiently plods on through his own and other people's work, when he unwittingly gives up what other people prize, or when he quietly ignores the spite or prejudice of opponents, that tells of a faith and a hope in the *eventual* meaning of human life— if not for us, then for those who come after us. He refuses to put his aspiration into words, because he would fear the untruth that might be expressed in those words—he has a dread of being even remotely irrational or superstitious. But for all that, he believes.

In the most minimal sense and in the most "unconscious" form, the Webbs shared a faith that was professedly altruistic and ascetic. Their altruism was the familiar kind that was directed to humanity at large rather than human beings in particular. And their asceticism was intended as much for others as for themselves. Their personal asceticism was all the more remarkable because it was achieved at such effort. Their policy of "permeation" required them to permeate incessantly, at dinner parties as well as committee meetings. But while they gave and attended numerous such parties, they were determined not to take pleasure in them—except perhaps as a means of furthering the cause. In her diaries Beatrice agonized over the rare purchase of a dinner dress and over the suspicion that she was enjoying the company of the great instead of merely using them, picking their brains and exploiting their positions. One of her few vices, as she thought it, was smoking, and she engaged in a constant battle with herself to reduce her daily consumption of cigarettes. Food presented less of a problem since she apparently required very little of it, although even here she was always trying to eliminate this or that from her already austere vegetarian diet. Nor was she more indulgent of others. Dinner parties at the Webbs' (a "political factory," Wells called it) were notoriously frugal and ruthlessly purposeful. Wine was not served, courses were reduced to a minimum, and the food was such as to earn the description "cold mutton." Guests were hurried through their pudding in order to get on with the conversation, and it was understood that no one was to waste time with such civilities as going to the lavatory. (Habitués devised ways of coping with their needs, discussing with each other the merits of different stratagems.)

It would take a George Orwell (who understood the ascetic impulse because he was himself prone to it) to do justice to this aspect of the Webbs, to relish the ludicrous details and at the same time appreciate their import. In one sense the Webbs were truly "new Machiavellians"—hard-headed ("hard-nosed," we would say today), pragmatic, manipulative, scheming. But this Machiavellianism was only a new form of utopianism, a utopianism, like any other, that required a rigid control of human beings, of the material, sexual, and natural passions that might interfere with the plans of the "social engineer." This was the basis of the Webbs' quarrel with Wells. In his espousal of "free love" Wells was not only advocating a degree of freedom that would play havoc with any planned society but also encouraging a "gross physical desire" that would subvert rationality itself.

It was not only the excesses of libertinism that provoked the Webbs. They were almost as impatient with the moderate passions and petty desires of the "average sensual man"—a term they used often and always invidiously. This is why they had no great interest in the extension of the suffrage, whether to men or to women. They were not against the suffrage. Indeed they were for it. But they were not much interested in the cause because it would not solve the problems they wanted to solve the way they wanted to solve them. "We have little faith in the 'average sensual man'," Beatrice wrote. "We do not believe that he can do much more than describe his grievances, we do not think that he can prescribe the remedies. . . . We wish to introduce into politics the professional expert—to extend the sphere of government by adding to its enormous advantages of wholesale compulsory management, the advantage of the most skilled entrepreneur."

Nor did they have much more respect for the parliamentary representative of the average man. Beatrice once described the typical member of Parliament as a "foolometer," a device by which the expert could take the measure of common opinion. Their *Constitution for the Socialist Commonwealth of Great Britain* . . . was largely designed to make the representative more of an expert. The main effect of the constitution would have been to create a new kind of bicameralism: a "political parliament" having jurisdiction over foreign and judicial affairs, and a "social parliament" charged with all social and economic matters. Ostensibly the two houses would be equal in status and distinguished only by their functions. "To use an old slogan of the Socialists," they wrote, "the government of men must be distinguished from the administration of things."

But that old slogan, as formulated by Saint Simon, actually was: "The government of men must be replaced by the administration of things." Replaced, not merely distinguished. There can be little doubt that the original slogan was closer to the Webbs' intention. The "social parliament" was to be the domain of the social administrator, the expert who dealt impersonally and objectively with things—institutions, arrangements, processes—rather than with men.

But even the new *Constitution* was inadequate to their aspirations. The ideal of impersonality, which was to be the basis of the new polity, was also to revolutionize human nature purged of selfishness, materiality and sensuality—of all those things that made up the "average sensual man." It is because of this ideal that one cannot explain the Webbs—neither of the Webbs—in purely secular terms, that one must invoke something like a religious faith. Beatrice's expression of that faith turns out to be suspiciously akin to Manicheism:

> Sometimes I try to discover what is the Ideal that moves me. It is not a conception of a rightly organized society; it is not a vision of a perfect man—a Saviour or a Superman. It is far nearer the thought of an abstract Being divested of all human appetite but combining the quality of an always working Intellect with an impersonal Love. And when I do think of the future man as I strive to make him in myself and in others, I forecast an Impersonality—if I may so express it—perpetually disentangling the material circumstances of the universe by intellectual processes, and, by his emotional will, casting out all other feelings, all other sensations other than that of an all-embracing beneficence. Physical appetites are to me the devil: they are signs of the disease that ends in death, the root of the hatred, malice and greed that make the life of man a futility.
>
>   . . .
>
> I cling to the thought that man will only evolve upwards by the subordination of his physical desires and appetites to the intellectual and spiritual side of his nature. Unless this evolution be the purpose of the race, I despair—and wish only for the extinction of human consciousness. Without this hope—without this faith—I could not struggle on. It is this purpose, and this purpose only, that gives a meaning to the constantly recurring battles of good and evil within one's own nature—and to one's persistent endeavour to find the ways and means of combating the evil habits of the mass of men. Oh! for a Church that would weld into one living force all who hold this faith, with the discipline and the consolations fitted to sustain their endeavour.

"Oh! for a Church." That was written in 1906. A quarter of a century later the Webbs found their church in the Communist Party of the Soviet Union. And they found it, not surprisingly, even before they visited the Soviet Union. Several months before that visit, in 1932, Beatrice explained what it was they expected to find there.

> What attracts us in Soviet Russia, and it is useless to deny that we are prejudiced in its

favour, is that its constitution, on the one hand, bears out our Constitution for a Socialist Commonwealth, and on the other, supplies a soul to that conception of government—which our paper-constitution lacked.

The Soviet constitution—the secular side of it—almost exactly corresponds to our Constitution—there is the same tripod of political democracy, vocational organization, and the consumers' cooperative movement. And the vocational or Trade Union side is placed in exactly the same position of subordination that we suggested. Also the position of the separately organized consumers' cooperative societies is similar to ours. There is no damned nonsense about Guild Socialism! But the spotlight of intriguing differences between the live creation of Soviet Russia and the dead body of the Webb constitution is the presence, as the dominant and decisive force, of a religious order: the Communist Party, with its strict disciplines, its vows of obedience and poverty. . . . It is the invention of the religious order, as the determining factor of a great nation, that is the magnet which attracts me to Russia. Practically, that religion is Comtism—the religion of Humanity.

The Soviet Union (or the Webbs' image of the Soviet Union) represented the culmination of their lives and thought, the long deferred resolution of the "controversy between the Ego that affirms and the Ego that denies." In the "new civilization" of Communism that duality was finally transcended. Process was imbued with Purpose; Science was enshrined in Religion. "Administrators in the Moscow Kremlin," they announced, "believe in their professed faith. And this professed faith is science." Since these administrators cum scientists were also members of the Communist Party, their faith had the quality of a religious order, with its "strict disciplines, its vows of obedience and poverty." The Webbs did not go so far as to invoke the vow of celibacy, but they did the next best thing in endowing the party with a puritanical ethic. They quoted, with apparent approval, a warning delivered by Stalin to an errant commissar: "I do not want to inquire into your private affairs, but if there is any more nonsense about women, you go to a place where there are no women." And they were pleased to find even among ordinary citizens a notable degree of propriety. "There is no spooning in the Parks of Recreation and Rest," Beatrice reported. Nor was there any vulgar quest for material goods. Unlike workers in the West, who measured success in terms of the quantity and quality of food, the amount of house-room, the availability of motorcars and wireless sets, workers in the Soviet Union, the Webbs were confident, appreciated the "moral uplift," the "intellectual advancement," and the "reformation of manners and morals" that were the unique benefits of Communism.

Bertrand Russell, impressed by Beatrice's consummate self-confidence, once asked her whether, even in her youth, she had ever had any feeling of shyness. "Oh, no," she replied, "If I ever felt inclined to be timid as I was going into a room full of people, I would say to myself, 'You're the cleverest member of one of the cleverest families in the cleverest class of the cleverest nation in the world, why should you be frightened?'" *Our Partnership*, and the numerous products of that partnership . . . , provide abundant evidence of that cleverness—and of something else as well, a soul-searching, self-conscious, high-minded sense of public dedication that is altogether fascinating. Fascinating but frightening. Too clever by half, the "average sensual man" might rightfully conclude. (pp. 789-90)

Gertrude Himmelfarb, "Process, Purpose and Ego," in The Times Literary Supplement, No. 3876, June 25, 1976, pp. 789-90.

HERB GREER (essay date 1984)

[*Greer is an American dramatist and critic. In the following excerpt, he examines the origins and implications of the Webbs' concept of the "housekeeping state."*]

For the brightest and the best of a hundred years ago in Britain, an individualist was by definition morally depraved. This judgment did not express a real sense of sin. It was a token of outrage at the bad (i.e., selfish) behavior of a relative few who possessed large amounts of money and property. These persons, it was felt, had to be rescued along with the rest of mankind from the bondage of their own selfishness—but not by individual conscience or grace or common sense. The only true redeemer was to be the state, with its ultimate sanction of coercive force.

Collectivism was the latest cry, and as Beatrice Webb put it in the first volume of her autobiography:

> . . . in the world of philanthropy as in the world of politics as I knew it in the eighties, there seemed to be one predominant question: Were we or were we not to assume the continuance of the capitalist system as it then existed; and if not, could we, by taking thought, mend or end it?

The aim of Mrs. Webb and her colleagues was to extirpate what they saw as a corrupt, anarchic individualism and replace it with a clean efficient "housekeeping state," in which everyone would be to some extent a public servant—not with the dirty motive of profit, but for the honorable rewards of praise and promotion.

Today this is a less respectable idea, because of what has happened where statism triumphed: the slaughter of millions upon millions of Russians (at a time when the Webbs were hailing the USSR as a "new civilization"); or the work of altruists like Heinrich Himmler, whose corps of efficient public servants included such stars as Adolf Eichmann. Our own generation has its examples of altruistic efficiency in more remote places like Vietnam and Cambodia, and of course in the Soviet system of psychiatric hospitals and the wide clean precincts of the Gulag.

The residue of nineteenth-century radical chic has been less dramatic in the free societies, but no less real. Its damage here is more subtle, mostly occurring in the minds of intelligent, honest, and genuinely compassionate people who still work unselfishly and long (as the Webbs did) for a dream which—as hard experience now shows—is a peculiarly horrible nightmare plausibly disguised. This paradox has puzzled many observers, not least some of the "liberals" themselves. Part of its origin can be explored in *The Diary of Beatrice Webb*. . . . These books, together with Beatrice Webb's autobiographies, do much to explain the bizarre politics of this complex and

Beatrice and Sidney Webb with Bernard Shaw. By kind permission of Lord Ponsonby.

fascinating woman; they cast a particularly cold light on why, as one of her family wrote, she crowned her life's work by commending "to her countrymen and the whole world a system of servitude more far-reaching and comprehensive than any hitherto known." (p. 30)

Disraeli's concept of "two nations" was no mere catchword in the last century. Until the cholera epidemics of the early 1800s, middle-class Britons had no accurate idea of how the poor lived or what they were really like. Poverty was supposed to be caused by defects of character such as laziness, or a supine acceptance of misfortune. When middle-class doctors went among the poor to fight cholera, they discovered a different reality: not a tribe of scroungers and malingerers but honest, hard-working folk trapped and suffering in what amounted to another world. Doctors were followed by researchers, by novelists like Dickens and Mrs. Gaskell, and finally by reformers intent on a rescue mission.

The well-to-do prided themselves on belonging to the greatest and richest empire in the history, served by the best scientists, engineers, and businessmen who had helped to make Britain the most successful and advanced country in the world. Now its prosperous burghers were told that many, indeed most, of their fellow-citizens were ill-housed, ill-paid, and, through no fault of their own, living "on the very verge of starvation." Evidently something was badly out of joint.

For us, to whom poverty is a kind of media cliché and a political football for pressure groups, it is not always easy to understand the impact of this new reality on Victorian society. There was a pervasive feeling of puzzled guilt among the middle classes and the well-to-do—what Beatrice Webb called a class consciousness of sin. It seemed obvious that if the poor were not at fault, then the villainy lay elsewhere, in the selfish individualism of the few who ruled in business and government. They made profits and enjoyed life while their workers made barely enough (and sometimes not enough) to live like human beings. This logic, leavened with a kind of perverted *richesse oblige*, led into a conspiracy theory, expressed by Mrs. Webb in these words:

> . . . the longer I studied the social organization in which I was born and bred, the stronger became my conviction that the distribution of power and wealth among my fellow-citizens was being controlled, and very deliberately controlled, in the interests of the propertied classes, to the detriment of the vast majority of the people . . .

This notional clearing-house for wealth and a species of power that (in Eric Hoffer's phrase) seemed to come in cans was not absurd to Victorians who were used to being ruled (and ruling) through an oligarchic elite. There was some talk of democratic action to set things right, but Mrs. Webb and her colleagues knew better than that. Instead of breaking up the system (her diary makes it clear that she knew this was neither possible nor desirable in Britain), she proposed to replace the plutocrats and their amateur political "artists" with a corps of experts professionally trained and indoctrinated with her ideas. This "housekeeping state" of (benevolent) despots would turn the system around and run it for the *benefit* of the vast majority.

Beatrice Webb is often portrayed as a kind of patron saint to the Welfare State. It is true that her Minority Report for the Royal Commission on the Poor Law outlined many of Britain's later "social" reforms. But the idea that she progressed from the "housekeeping state" to the Welfare State and then lurched into a strange uncritical admiration of the Soviet Union does not square either with her character or with her ideas as they appear in her diaries and autobiographies. The tyranny of the state is implicit in her earliest thinking about society. At the age of twenty-five she wrote with admiration, almost awe, of

> . . . the great central idea of Christianity, this
> sacrifice of the individual to the commu-
> nity. . . .

Four years later she carried it from religion into politics:

> . . . I maintain that *I* am the *true socialist*, through
> my willingness to sacrifice the individual to the
> community. . . .

Her "housekeeping state" was not to be run on an eighteenth-century system of values, with inalienable rights and all that. Mrs. Webb did not believe in unconditional rights of any kind. Her inspiration lay further back in time, in the feudal system with its tissue of mutual obligation between vassal and lord. That her "experts" would be lords and the rest vassals was beyond doubt, and she was not very concerned with what this would mean for the individual.

> "Experimenting in the lives of other people,
> how cold-blooded!" I hear the reader object.
> It is necessary to explain that "experimenting"
> cannot be avoided; that all administration . . .
> necessarily amounts to nothing less than "ex-
> perimenting in the lives of other people."

As she admitted, she came from a class of people who were accustomed to giving orders. This habit, together with a puritan temperament of extraordinary ferocity, guided her political and social ideas all her life, and with great consistency. She despised the common herd; one of her central concerns was to raise the moral tone of the lower classes—first by making them better off, then by compulsion if necessary. She meant to make sure that the elimination of poverty was answered by a proper expression of gratitude and obligation to the state.

British politicians, more concerned with the democratic business of getting votes, appalled her by their implementation of her ideas. Her "Welfare State" outline in the Poor Law Commission's Minority Report did not include the unconditional doling out of money. She hated Lloyd George's 1911 National Insurance Act because it entailed just that. Her conception included a quid pro quo for all state largesse. This meant real effort from the recipient to improve both his circumstances *and character,* and so contribute to the health of society. This contribution was to be the real motive behind welfare. For those who out of weakness or stubbornness failed to measure up, Mrs. Webb had a solution: They were to be shown the

error of their ways, i.e., sent to what we now call a re-education camp.

The ideas of the Webbs altered not only in the hands of Lloyd George, but (for all that Clement Attlee paid tribute to the Webbs) under the postwar Labour government which actually set up the Welfare State. If she had lived to see it, the sight would not have pleased her very much. Malcolm Muggeridge, who knew her well, wrote:

> . . . her severely practical side, inherited from
> her father, made her realize at once that handing
> out unconditional largesse to the citizenry of a
> universal suffrage democracy would have grave
> moral and social implications. . . .

During the postwar decades these implications have emerged with great force, not just among the poor but in the comfortable middle classes. The principal result has been and still is a pattern of expectation which centers on *government*, not just as the source of protection and guaranteed survival, but of general, almost godlike wisdom which confers a *constantly rising* standard of living. (pp. 31-2)

Even now political parties, especially Labour, make it their business to inflate Welfare-State expectations to an impossible degree, in particular exaggerating the control of government in economic matters. Consequent public dissatisfaction is then exploited in a zero-sum power game for control of revenue, administrative favor, and finally of Parliament with its unlimited sovereignty. It becomes the aim of the loser in this contest (Labour is by far the worst in this respect) not just to keep the ruling party honest in the normal way of a loyal opposition, but further to inflame and exploit popular discontent and expectations by fair means or foul, and to use these forces to destroy the current government. British democracy seems headed away from a ritual of electoral consent to govern, into a mutually destructive battle which actually impairs government.

This is happening today despite the fact that the poor are on the whole far more comfortable than they were in the time of Beatrice Webb, as is almost everybody else. It is a bitter comment on the Fabian belief that, if only people were better housed and clothed, they would *be* better or (which was the same thing to the reformers) behave better. Neither Mrs. Webb nor her Fabian friends, nor the postwar idealists in the Labour party realized the infinite nature of expectations. Their assumptions rested on a certain concept of human nature, much older even than Mrs. Webb's feudal model for society. This view appeared as a major influence in Europe on the cusp of the fourth and fifth centuries when another Briton, a monk called Pelagius, offered a famous heresy to the Western world, one which appealed (as Fabianism later did) to the sort of rough common sense which then held that the world was flat. Discounting the onerous myth of original sin, Pelagius held that salvation was a prize to be earned purely by human effort, without the complicating factor of God's grace. Fabian socialism was essentially a secular version of this belief. Like Nietzsche's ass-worshipers in *Also Sprach Zarathustra,* Mrs. Webb and her colleagues meant to achieve salvation (they called it socialism) not in the next world but in this one. Their anointed elite of experts were going to wipe out evil by getting rid of poverty and the inequalities of wealth; these good works, in true Pelagian fashion, would save society and mankind.

Of course Beatrice Webb did not consciously model herself on Pelagius. Neither in her diary nor in her autobiographies does she mention him. But her books stress again and again that the nature of her quest was religious—not just in her "Christian" faith in the sacrifice of the individual to the state, but in this summing up of her own true belief:

> I have staked all on the essential goodness of human nature, on that which maketh toward righteousness. If this be mere illusion, mere cant, then my own little life is a wretched failure, an absurd bubble pretending substance.

This might be an elegy for Beatrice Webb herself, or a lament for the mutually corrupting influence of her ideas and the democratic politics of Britain. It might also be an epitaph for those politics, if they were dead and gone. But they are not—yet. There is time enough still for this little confession to serve as a grim warning. (pp. 32-3)

> Herb Greer, "The Iron Lady of Collectivism," in The American Spectator, Vol. 17, No. 9, September, 1984, pp. 30-3.

LISANNE RADICE (essay date 1984)

[In the following excerpt from her biography of Beatrice and Sidney Webb, the only comprehensive work to date to cover the lives of both partners, Radice discusses their political philosophy and accomplishments.]

[The Webbs'] towering reputation rests partly on their writing. Here the achievements of the partnership are awe inspiring. Their *History of Trade Unionism* . . . and *Industrial Democracy* . . . remain standard works to this day, while the *Co-Operative Movement in Great Britain* . . . is still widely read. *A Constitution for the Socialist Commonwealth of Great Britain* . . . brilliantly sums up their ideas on the development of a democratic socialist state. They also produced innumerable pamphlets for the Fabian Society and the Labour Party which are a model of careful research and clear presentation.

However, their accomplishments were not merely intellectual. Above all they were practical reformers who helped to change the face of British society.

The Webbs' earliest successes were educational. Sidney was chairman of the prestigious Technical Education Board of the LCC for 16 years. As chairman, he set up the first scholarship scheme for bright working class children as well as establishing polytechnics and technical institutions which opened up opportunities for self improvement for poor London children. He also supported Haldane in setting up Imperial College, and, together with Beatrice, helped to promote the far-reaching educational reforms of 1902 and 1903 which, by placing education under the county councils, gave a logical structure to a system which was beginning to disintegrate.

The creation of the London School of Economics alone would have made the Webbs famous. According to Graham Wallas, the Webbs woke up one morning and decided to use part of the money which the Fabian Society had been left by a rich member to set up a School in London on the lines of the *Ecole Libre des Sciences Politiques* in Paris. Through their determination this vision of a centre of excellence devoted to the study of the social sciences (virtually ignored by the older universities) became a triumphant reality.

With Lloyd George and Beveridge, Beatrice and Sidney Webb can justly be said to be the founders of the modern welfare state. They were lifelong exponents of the concept of the National Minimum which they first discussed at length in *Indus-*

trial Democracy, as well as in innumerable Fabian tracts and pamphlets. They believed that it was the duty of the state to provide a safety net of basic welfare services, from education through to housing and health for all its citizens. They carried the argument further in their 1909 Minority Report to the Royal Commission on the Poor Law, of which Beatrice was a member. In it they laid down a blueprint for the development of welfare programmes to cater for the sick, the aged, and the unemployed. This and their subsequent Campaign for the Prevention of Destitution helped create a climate of opinion which made the demand for the establishment of a welfare state one of the main objectives of the Labour Party.

Educational reformers, propagandists for the welfare state, the Webbs also played a crucial role in the development of British socialism. Their name has been most closely associated with the Fabian Society. Sidney Webb and George Bernard Shaw moulded the early character of the Society, but it was due to the former that it changed from an idiosyncratic middle class debating society into the most influential research and policy discussion body of the Labour Party, whose members (Attlee, Gaitskell, Wilson, Crosland and Crossman) have been among the most famous within the labour movement. Sidney's approach became the Society's; ethical in character and evolutionary in practice, its socialism was firmly based on a systematic presentation of the facts—a novel and immensely powerful method of political argument and propaganda which still retains its persuasiveness.

They also founded the *New Statesman* in 1913, and encouraged the establishment of the *Political Quarterly* in 1930. The purpose of the *New Statesman* was to gain support for their ideas among a wider circle of radical opinion; the *Political Quarterly* was aimed at a more academic audience. Linking the two was their belief in the need for informed discussion of new political and social ideas.

Recent historians such as J. M. Winter and Ross McGibbin have rightly argued that Sidney's influence on the Labour Party's development was crucial. It was mainly due to his and Henderson's insistence that the Party became socialist in character and a genuine political alternative to the established parties. During the 1914-18 war Sidney was the most powerful member of the two most prestigious and influential committees of the labour movement—the War Emergency Committee and the policy sub-committee of the National Executive Committee. Out of these came the 1918 constitution and election manifesto *Labour and the New Social Order*.

Most historians accept that Sidney was the chief architect of the 1918 constitution by which the Labour Party opened its doors to individual members, accepted a new grass roots organisation and, through Clause 4 Part 4, established its socialist credentials. As to the manifesto, which Sidney wrote, it was not only a clear restatement of Webbian objectives—a national minimum, democratic control of industry, and increased municipalisation—but it also provided the Labour Party, for the first time, with a blue print for changing society. Although Sidney was a prominent Cabinet Minister in both the 1924 and 1929 governments, the Webbs' main contribution to the rise of labour was ideological. They captured the labour movement for their ideas, and helped prepare the Labour Party for power.

What links the Webbs' different achievements is a profound belief that society needed to be changed, and that its individualistic and selfish attributes could be transformed into a moral order. Their philosophy was also based on a belief in a meritocracy to be achieved through the provision of equal opportunities for all, while public service was seen as an intrinsic duty. Their approach was pragmatic, evolutionary, and collectivist and founded on a deep commitment to a democratic pluralist state.

However, Beatrice and Sidney have been called elitist. Is this a fair description? If by elitist is meant that some individuals are born natural leaders as of right, then neither of the Webbs can be accused of accepting the notion of a chosen few. They were, nevertheless, passionate believers in the rights of individuals to better themselves, and that opportunities had to be provided, as of right, for those who were disadvantaged. Sidney quite consciously hoped to replace the old aristocratic élite with a new meritocratic one based on talent, but his meritocracy was founded on a wide definition of equality of opportunity and environment. Later Socialist generations have developed the argument; Anthony Crosland in *The Future of Socialism* pointed out: "No one deserves either so generous a reward or so severe a penalty for a quality implanted from the outside and for which he can claim only a limited responsibility." . . .

The "spirit of public service" was also a crucial element in the Webbian concept of the future socialist state. It was certainly partly for this reason that the Webbs founded the LSE. Bright young men and women trained in the right principles would work with selfless dedication and devote themselves to the new democratic state. The creation of a new body of "Samurai"—public spirited guardians of a democratic society—had meritocratic overtones, but it was also very much tied to their belief that the "working of democratic institutions means . . . one long training in enlightened altruism" and that "we must reconstruct society, on a basis not of interest but of community of service . . . and of that willingness to subordinate oneself to the welfare of the whole." Perhaps it was misguided of them to believe that others could have the self same altruistic devotion to duty that they had. Occasionally they came across high ranking civil servants who proved their point; on the whole they set their fellow humans an impossible task. But their objective was an honourable one. What they wished to establish was a society where merit would be rewarded not by materialistic gain but by service to the community. (pp. 6-9)

The Webbs' socialism was evolutionary not revolutionary; a mixture of Positivism, Radicalism and collectivist socialism. In a phrase which later became famous—"the inevitability of gradualness"—Sidney explained to the 1923 Labour Party conference the nature of socialist aspirations. This has usually been thought to imply a reaffirmation of the old Webbian belief in the eventual triumph of Fabian permeation. Professor Norman Mackenzie, however, in *The First Fabians* argued that Sidney was merely putting forward the thesis that the Labour Party would inevitably come to power. There is a third interpretation which is more credible. Sidney believed it was essential for the Labour Party, particularly after 1917, to disassociate itself from all revolutionary, including Syndicalist, tendencies; to show itself both respectable and responsible. It had to assure the voters that any changes it made when once in power would be both democratic and parliamentary. Beatrice and Sidney were always passionately concerned with the manner in which democracy would evolve in a socialist state. Collectivists they might be, dedicated democrats they certainly were.

This brings me to the final element of their political philosophy; the Webbs' dedication to the pursuit of democratic socialism. This dedication provides a vital clue both to their written work and their political achievements and is a direct refutation of those, like Caute and Wright, who accuse them of totalitarian tendencies.

When discussing their *History of Trade Unionism,* Beatrice recorded in her diary that she and Sidney hoped to provide a framework for "a new democratic state." However, it was not until the last forty-three pages of *Industrial Democracy* (their second major book published some three years later) that the Webbs first examined this question in some detail. What they then aimed to solve was the seemingly intractible problem of combining administrative efficiency with popular control. As libertarians they were aware of the pitfalls of unrestrained power:

> not even the wisest of men can be trusted with that supreme authority which comes from the union of knowledge, capacity and opportunity with the power of untrammelled and ultimate decision. Democracy is an expedient . . . for preventing the concentration in any single individual or in any single class of what inevitably becomes, when so concentrated, a terrible engine of oppression.

And they went on to argue that only democracy was compatible with the freedom of all to develop.

The Webbs' earliest arguments for a democratic state were based on a belief that "the average sensual man" could only, given his lack of political education, play a passive role—though in time, the process of democracy would encourage participation. To compensate for this passivity, the Webbs argued for a new breed of professional representatives who would keep closely in touch with the electorate and act as pressure points against the state apparatus.

In 1912 the Webbs were forced into a new consideration of democracy by outside events. The years between 1909 and 1911 had been years of industrial unrest, growing unemployment and trade union expansion. One of the by-products of the unrest was the growth of the syndicalist movement whose main purpose—the overthrow of parliamentary government by the workers using the general strike as a political weapon, and its replacement by a government based on industrial unions—was anathema to the Webbs. Aware of the increasing power of syndicalism within the trade unions, and afraid of the consequences for democracy, the Webbs launched a vigorous counter attack in support of their type of democratic socialist state. They believed that, now the manual workers had the vote, "the ballot box has made obsolete the barricades." At the same time government by the Syndicalist National Unions would result in a new authoritarianism; as trade unions were now to become part of the structure of government they would no longer be able to represent employees. In addition, whole groups of citizens, such as women, professional people, pensioners and so on, who were not producers and therefore not in trade unions, would lose their political rights. In their view, Syndicalism was narrow, authoritarian, and based exclusively on producer rather than community interests.

However in an important article entitled **"A Stratified Democracy"** (published in 1919), influenced now by G. D. H. Cole and the Guild Socialists as much as by he Syndicalists, Sidney admitted that producers needed to have more power than they had previously allowed. But the Webbs' main quarrel with Cole remained unresolved: they believed that his form of industrial organisation was too narrow—there ought not to be one overriding authority, even if it were that of the producers. Otherwise, "presbyter is apt to be old priest writ large." So a diffusion of interests was necessary so "you do not have one sovereignty, you have a number of separate sources of authority and each authority has to restrict itself and be restricted by all the other authorities simultaneously."

"A Stratified Democracy" was followed a year later by the Webbs' only major book on democratic theory: *A Constitution for the Socialist Commonwealth of Great Britain*. This was both a critique of the British parliamentary system and an attempt to develop a blueprint for democratic change which took into account recent developments. Given the complexity of modern industrial society, there could be no "model constitution for a Utopian community" and therefore no single democratic solution. The Webbs based their new democratic theory on three major factors, man as producer, as consumer, and as citizen. What they hoped to achieve was a democracy in which no one stratum would hold the monopoly of power and where the individual enjoyed the maximum amount of liberty as was compatible with his place in a complex, interdependent society. At the same time democracy, they firmly warned,

> cannot afford to dispense with the complication in its administrative machinery because only by an extensive variety of parts in a deliberately adjusted relation between those parts, can there be any security for the personal freedom and independence and initiative in the great mass of individuals, whether as producers, consumers or as citizens.

The diffusion and variety which they advocated was reflected in their democratic model. Two Parliaments, political and social, were envisaged to reflect the two sides of man's interests. The organisation of industry in a socialist commonwealth was to be democratic, with worker participation at all levels. Consumer interests were to be safeguarded as well as "the permanent welfare of the community as a whole." The new democratic structure would be underpinned by the "disinterested professional expert," who would provide that "searchlight of published knowledge," which the Webbs regarded as the "cornerstone of successful Democracy." As to local government, they believed in extending its scope,

> the very differences among localities, with the different local administrations that they involve provide an increase in the scope of individual choice, a widening of personal freedom and a safeguard against the monotonous uniformity and centralised tyranny over the individual.

They therefore aimed for a complex and varied democratic pluralistic society in which liberty would be protected and individual rights and opportunities increased. The structure of the new socialist commonwealth was based on a system of countervailing checks and balances, a considerable dispersal of power and genuine participation—a model which is as relevant today as it was in the 1920s.

The myth, however, has persisted that the Webbs were bureaucratic collectivists at best and totalitarians at worst, a reputation which is mostly based on their last major work, *Soviet Communism—A New Civilisation?* The book, which was published in 1935, was the product of a visit Beatrice and Sidney made to the Soviet Union in 1932. Discouraged by the slump and other failures of Western capitalism, the Webbs went to Russia disposed to applaud: "without doubt we are on the side of Russia," Beatrice recorded in her diary before their voyage. And they were: they extolled the virtues of the Soviet regime,

laid stress on the virtues of the Communist Party and the Komsomols, and appeared to underwrite what was even then considered to be one of the most oppressive regimes in existence.

There are those like David Caute, in his *Fellow Travellers*, who put their approval of Soviet communism down not only to their pessimism and lack of understanding but, more important, to their own totalitarian tendencies. Confronted by the power of a strong collectivist state, they could no longer hide their anti-democratic views. Professor George Feaver, in an interesting article in *Encounter*, put forward a different and more persuasive hypothesis. He argued that the reason why Beatrice and Sidney were enthused by the Soviet system was not because they were undemocratic collectivists but because, as devout pilgrims, engaged in a hitherto barren voyage in search of a secular faith, they found in the apparent altruism and dedication of the Communist Party the faith which they had been seeking. Certainly Beatrice wrote enthusiastically, if inaccurately, that Russian communists had "voluntarily pledged themselves to two out of three of the characteristic obligations of the religious orders of Christianity, namely to poverty . . . and to obedience." . . .

However, my own conclusion is that their misrepresentation of Soviet society was more than the blindness of the religious convert. The Webbs genuinely believed that in the Soviet Union they were witnessing the birth of a democratic state in which all citizens were encouraged to participate at every level of society. Participation had been a crucial element of their own model in *Socialist Commonwealth;* their view of the Soviet system was that they had encountered "the personal participation in public affairs of an unprecedented proportion of the entire adult population." . . . Here is the clue to their embrace of the Soviet regime.

It is not difficult to criticise the Webbs for their eulogy of the Soviet Union. Never at their best abroad, they failed to see that Soviet grassroots democracy was only effective if the Communist leadership allowed it to be, and that the lack of competing political parties of independent sources of power, and of the checks and balances (so central to the *Socialist Commonwealth*) made a mockery of their argument in *Soviet Communism* that democracy could ever be equated solely with participation. Instead they mistakenly believed that the discussions which took place at all levels of Soviet society would provide an effective check on a centralised state and that the Communist Party was a selfless vanguard which would eventually produce an environment in which individual freedom would flourish. However, their espousal of the Communist regime should be seen not as a rejection of their life-long support for pluralist democracy, expressed most forcefully and convincingly in *Socialist Commonwealth*, but as the misjudgement of two disillusioned and tired septuagenarians, who characteristically saw in Russia only what they wanted to see. (pp. 10-14)

Lisanne Radice, in her Beatrice and Sidney Webb: Fabian Socialists, *Macmillan, 1984, 342 p.*

ADDITIONAL BIBLIOGRAPHY

Bentley, Eric. "Rescuing Beatrice Webb." *The New Republic* 114, No. 20 (20 May 1946): 736-37.
    Review of Margaret Cole's biography of Beatrice Webb which defends the validity of the primary Fabian tenets.

Braybrooke, Neville. "A New Kind of Woman." *Commonweal* CX, No. 18 (21 October 1983): 569-71.
    Review of Volume I of the *Diaries* in which Braybrooke concludes: "What is significant about this volume is the portrait it provides of a girl, who by her late teens had begun to feel that she had not the right to live unless she was fulfilling some duty towards humanity."

Caute, David. *The Fellow-Travellers*, pp. 78ff. New York: The Macmillan Company, 1973.
    Numerous references to the Webbs as moderate political leftists.

Cole, Margaret I. *Beatrice Webb*. New York: Harcourt, Brace and Company, 1946, 229 p.
    Biography which the author describes as "a portrait of Beatrice."

————, ed. *The Webbs and Their Work*. London: Frederick Muller Ltd., 1949, 304 p.
    Collection of essays by prominent Fabians, including Shaw, about various aspects of the Webbs' lives and work.

Feaver, George. "The Webbs as Pilgrims." *Encounter* L, No. 3 (March 1978): 23-32.
    Discussion of the Webbs' reactions to other cultures as recorded in their diaries.

Forster, E. M. "Webb and Webb." In his *Two Cheers for Democracy*, pp. 215-18. New York: Harcourt, Brace and Company, 1951.
    Some personal reminiscences of Forster's acquaintance with the Webbs.

Himmelfarb, Gertrude. "The Webbs: The Religion of Socialism." In her *Marriage and Morals among the Victorians*, pp. 192-209. New York: Alfred A. Knopf, 1986.
    Focuses on Beatrice Webb's ascetic nature, its implications, and its political ramifications.

Hobsbawm, E. J. "Labours of Love." *New Statesman* 95, No. 2461 (19 May 1978): 673-74.
    Review of published letters which discusses what they reveal about the Webbs' personalities.

Hynes, Samuel. "The Fabians: Mrs. Webb and Mr. Wells." In his *Edwardian Occasions*, pp. 87-131. Princeton: Princeton University Press, 1968.
    Discussion of the Fabians' ideas with emphasis on the ideological split between Beatrice Webb and H. G. Wells.

————. "A Marriage of Minds." *The New York Times Book Review* (30 July 1978): 7-8.
    Review of the published letters in which Hynes contends that "the only Webb books that might survive—and *should* survive on their literary merits—are those written by Beatrice alone."

Jones, Mervyn. "A Vocation of Leadership." *New Statesman* 109, No. 2808 (11 January 1985): 29-30.
    Discusses the Webbs' pattern of mistaken political judgments.

Kauffmann, Stanley. "A Fabian Abroad." *The New Republic* 148, No. 25 (22 June 1963): 28-30.
    Review of Beatrice Webb's *American Diary, 1898* which commends the writing despite its obvious "snobbism and chauvinism."

Laski, Harold J. "The History of Trade Unionism." *The New Republic* XXII, No. 284 (12 May 1920): 359-60.
    Praises the competency displayed in *The History of Trade Unionism* while taking exception to certain of its conclusions.

————. "The Cooperative Movement." *The New Republic* XXXI, No. 393 (14 June 1922): 80-1.
    Review of the Webbs' *The Cooperative Movement in Great Britain* in which Laski states: "the great virtue of their book is that,

while entirely admirable as a description of a very complex system of federal institutions, it has a most suggestive analysis of future possibilities."

Letwin, Shirley Robin. "Beatrice Webb: Science and the Apotheosis of Politics." In her *The Pursuit of Certainty*, pp. 321-78. Cambridge: Cambridge University Press, 1965.
    Places Beatrice Webb's political thought in the context of the Benthamite utilitarian tradition.

MacKenzie, Jeanne, and MacKenzie, Norman. *The Fabians*. New York: Simon and Schuster, 1977, 446 p.
    Comprehensive history of the Fabian Society.

Martin, Kingsley. "Books in General." *New Statesman and Nation* XXXV, No. 897 (15 May 1948): 397.
    Review of *Our Partnership* which focuses on the Webbs' political achievements.

Muggeridge, Kitty and Adam, Ruth. *Beatrice Webb: A Life*. London: Secker and Warburg, 1967, 272 p.
    Biography coauthored by a niece.

Nadel, Bruce Ira. "Beatrice Webb's Two Voices: *My Apprenticeship* and Victorian Autobiography." *English Studies in Canada* II, No. 1 (Spring 1976): 83-96.
    Analyzes *My Apprenticeship* as an example of the Victorian autobiographical tradition, contending that such works display a definite affinity with fiction.

————. "Beatrice Webb's Literary Success." *Studies in Short Fiction* XIII, No. 4 (Fall 1976): 441-46.
    Discusses the artistic quality of "Pages from a Work-Girl's Diary."

Nord, Deborah Epstein. *The Apprenticeship of Beatrice Webb*. Amherst: University of Massachusetts Press, 1985, 294 p.
    Study of Beatrice Webb's life in which Nord attempts, through analysis of the diaries and autobiographies, to formulate a modernized, objective assessment of her character.

Russell, Bertrand. "Sidney and Beatrice Webb." In his *Portraits from Memory*, pp. 105-10. New York: Simon and Schuster, 1956.
    Some biographical comments by a close friend.

Shaw, G. Bernard. "Beatrice Webb, Octogenarian." *The Spectator* No. 5717 (21 January 1938): 79.
    Shaw comments on Beatrice Webb's attributes in honor of her birthday.

Stigler, George J. "Bernard Shaw, Sidney Webb, and the Theory of Fabian Socialism." In his *Essays in the History of Economics*, pp. 268-86. Chicago: The University of Chicago Press, 1965.
    Refutes the economic theories of the Fabians.

Tawney, R. H. "Beatrice Webb, 1858-1943" and "The Webbs and Their Work." In his *The Attack and Other Papers*, pp. 101-28, pp. 129-46. London: George Allen & Unwin Ltd., 1953.
    A biographical essay about Beatrice and a discussion of the Webbs' achievements.

"A Partnership of Ideas." *The Times Literary Supplement* No. 3201 (5 July 1963): 485-86.
    Discusses the importance of the autobiographical writings in understanding the Webbs' work.

Vincent, J. R. "Marriage to Some Purpose." *The Times Literary Supplement* (19 May 1978): 551-52.
    Review of the letters which portrays Beatrice as the guiding force in the Webbs' partnership.

Wells, H. G. "Mrs. Webb's Birthday." *New Statesman* XV, No. 361 (22 January 1938): 110-11.
    Complimentary tribute written for Beatrice Webb's eightieth birthday.

(Maurice) Denton Welch

1915-1948

English novelist, short story writer, autobiographer, diarist, and poet.

Welch was the author of highly sensitive and impressionistic autobiographical novels and short stories which were published in the 1940s and formed a radical contrast to the predominantly realistic, war-conscious fiction being produced in England during that time. Recognized chiefly for their direct narrative style, sexual candor, and striking descriptive passages, Welch's works document his private, frequently aberrant, sensations and experiences. A semi-invalid due to injuries he received in a bicycling accident at age twenty, he often returned to the healthy days of his youth for his subjects. He is best remembered, however, for the posthumously published, unfinished novel *A Voice through a Cloud,* in which he related the trauma of his accident and the first agonizing months of his long recovery.

Welch was born in Shanghai, the youngest son of Arthur and Rosalind (Bassett) Welch. His mother was an American by birth and a fervent Christian Scientist; his father was a businessman whose profits in the rubber trade allowed the family to live comfortably and to travel often. Welch's childhood years were spent primarily in the company of his adoring but insecure mother, traveling with her between Shanghai and England, where his two older brothers were in school. He had made several crossings before he was finally, and to his "horror," enrolled in an English school at the age of nine. In March 1927, Welch's mother, in accordance with her religious beliefs, refused medical treatment and subsequently died of kidney failure. She had been dependent upon her youngest son for companionship and affection, and he was devoted to her; consequently, her death overshadowed and stained his impressions of prep-school life at St. Michael's in Uckfield, Sussex. Although the school catered to the sons of wealthy Christian Scientists, the comparative strangeness of its institutional atmosphere, after the cosmopolitan life he had led with his mother, caused him to feel increasingly confused and alienated. His anxiety escalated when he followed his brothers William and Paul to public school at Repton. He later wrote of this period: "Early adolescence was to me what I can only describe as a sordid and fearful time. I was frightened of everything and everything seemed sullied and 'slimed-over' with this fear." As Welch subsequently reported in his first novel, *Maiden Voyage,* he ran away after a school holiday rather than return to Repton. A young aesthete with a fascination for old curios and objets d'art, he toured cathedrals in Salisbury and Exeter before returning to London, where his relatives persuaded him to finish one more term at the school. Not long afterwards, his father wrote a letter inviting him to sail for Shanghai with Paul at the end of the term, and Welch gladly accepted the opportunity to escape the public school regimentation he detested. He remained in China for a year, returning to England in 1932 to attend Goldsmith's School of Art in New Cross. A student of only average ability, he was nevertheless much more content in the company of artists than he had been at Repton and joined his schoolmates in many of their social gatherings in London. He also found great enjoyment in solitary hiking or bicycling in the country. One afternoon in June, 1935, while still a

Self-portrait by Welch from his Maiden Voyage. L. B. Fischer, 1945. Reproduced by permission of David Higham Associates Limited.

student at Goldsmith's, Welch was cycling out of London to visit relatives in the nearby countryside when he was hit by a car. Hospitalized for many months, he never fully recovered from his injuries. His spine had been irreparably damaged, causing him pain and debilitation that culminated in his death thirteen years later.

In the years preceding his accident, Welch's ambitions had lain in painting; there is no evidence to suggest that he had ever considered a literary career. However, once he turned to writing (in 1940, according to his *Journals*), he wrote in a distinctive manner, relatively free from literary influences and associations. Critics have observed that he was never derivative as a prose writer, as he was as a painter and a poet. When Cyril Connolly, the editor of *Horizon,* published Welch's first article, a humorous account of a visit to the painter Walter Sickert, the magazine's audience was greatly pleased with the author's engaging self-portrait as well as his comic rendering of

Sickert. Welch received an immediate, personal response from Edith Sitwell, who called him "a born writer" and agreed to introduce him formally to the reading public by writing the foreword to *Maiden Voyage*. Essentially autobiographical, the picaresque novel treats the period of Welch's youth that begins with his flight from Repton and ends with his return from China. Some critics have noted that he set the tone of the novel by abruptly opening in medias res, and that by employing short sentences and simple constructions, Welch suggested the youthful inexperience of his narrator. This apparent artlessness is also implied by the extemporaneous quality of his metaphors and imagery, especially in his sometimes bizarre figures of speech involving food. Critics have praised *Maiden Voyage* for its frank and perceptive narrative and have noted with admiration the detachment with which Welch's literary persona relates sensitive autobiographical material. According to Philip Toynbee: "Without a hint of toughness, without the least false note of cynicism, there is a feline unsentimentality about Mr. Welch which is immensely stimulating."

A sense of detachment and isolation is central to much of Welch's work. Sometimes described as a solipsist, Welch is, at the very least, regarded as a highly personal writer. His vision was limited to himself, and he consistently chose his own life as the subject of his fiction. Generally, he portrayed that life as a series of disjointed, yet significant, events and situations filled with anxieties and disappointments. He used his own name for the narrator and central character of *Maiden Voyage,* which contributed to early confusion over the genre of that novel and caused some critics to view it strictly as a memoir. However, the fictional nature of Welch's second novel, *In Youth Is Pleasure,* has never engendered critical debate, even though the work is unmistakably based on his experiences as a fifteen-year-old schoolboy on holiday in Sussex with his father and brothers. Critics are less inclined to view *In Youth Is Pleasure* as an autobiography because it is written in the third person and its protagonist is not named Denton Welch, but Orvil Pym, whom Hamilton Basso has called "unquestionably the most desperately miserable English schoolboy who ever found his way into print." Some critics have commented that *In Youth Is Pleasure* in many ways repeats what Marguerite Young has called the "essential situation" of *Maiden Voyage.* According to Young, both narratives concern "an errant schoolboy's quest for self-knowledge in a more or less alien world, a world of mysteries, many of them engendered by the boy himself." In a novel described by Robert Phillips as "overtly Oedipal and homosexual," Pym becomes frustrated in his search for sexual identity; as a result, he manifests numerous deviant impulses, including masochism, sadism, necrophilia, and transvestism, among others. *In Youth Is Pleasure* is also notable for its concentration of sexual symbolism and imagery, resulting in a narrative that at times becomes surreal and obsessive. At one point, a peach melba dessert is described as the buttocks of a Kewpie doll, and at another, pastries are depicted as "phallic chocolate and coffee eclairs, oozing fat worms of cream." Considered his most mature and important work, Welch's third novel, *A Voice through a Cloud,* relates the story of his accident and long recuperative struggle. As critics have suggested, the metaphorical voyage is again present: in *A Voice through a Cloud,* Welch travels from sickness to relative fitness and from utter dependence to independence. In a plot development that parallels the events of *Maiden Voyage,* he moves from an institutional life that he dreads to new prospects in the world outside. *A Voice through a Cloud,* in which Welch returned to a first person narrative, is recognized chiefly for its characteristic attention to detail, its startling descriptive im-

agery, and its frank self-portrait of Welch in the months immediately following his accident. John Updike has commented that "the book is, especially in its first half, masterly; a fine intelligence, a brave candor, a voracious eye, and a sweet fresh sense of prose are exercised."

In his impressionistic short stories, as in the novels, Welch was candid in the rendering of his autobiographical material. Critics have commented that a homoerotic tension pervades many of Welch's short works, while in others the erotic intensity remains, although the protagonist has been recast as a woman. Frequently compared to the short fiction of D. H. Lawrence, Welch's stories often depict sexual encounters occurring across class boundaries; in many of these stories, the protagonist's longed-for union fails, resulting in bitter disappointment and anticlimax. Critics have agreed that when viewed with the insight afforded by the *Journals,* the frustration present in the short stories, sexual or otherwise, becomes central to Welch's unique and poignant vision.

The critical reception afforded Welch during his lifetime was enthusiastic, and his reputation was further enhanced by such posthumously published volumes as *A Voice through a Cloud,* the short story collection *Brave and Cruel,* and *The Denton Welch Journals.* Of the *Journals,* Cyril Connolly has remarked: "I have read every word of this long book with increasing delight, I have blotted out wind and rain, age and infirmity, anxiety and want in the recesses of his keen, bright, fresh, sensuous thought-stream and lived happily behind his mischievous observant eye." However, by the late 1960s most of Welch's works were out of print, and many admirers had only photocopies of his stories to pass along to friends. Thus he remained a cult figure until recently, when nearly all of his principal works were reissued, creating popular interest and inviting new critical assessments of his work. In 1982, John Lehmann offered an insight into Welch's continuing appeal: "[His] writing shows a fascinating mixture of naivety and sophistication: a purity of style, perfectly straightforward, without affectation of any kind, but with an astonishing command of words and their precise effect, and a sharp exactness of observation that does not spare the foibles and mannerisms of the people he is describing—himself included."

PRINCIPAL WORKS

Maiden Voyage (novel) 1943
In Youth Is Pleasure (novel) 1944
Brave and Cruel (short stories) 1948
A Voice through a Cloud (unfinished novel) 1950
A Last Sheaf (poetry, essays, and short stories) 1951
The Denton Welch Journals [abridged edition] (diaries) 1952, also published as *The Journals of Denton Welch* [unabridged edition], 1984
I Left My Grandfather's House: An Account of His First Walking Tour (autobiography and letters) 1958
Denton Welch: Extracts from His Published Works (novel excerpts, short stories, autobiography, diaries, and poetry) 1963
"Thirteen Texts by Denton Welch" (prose) 1972; published in journal *The Texas Quarterly*
Dumb Instrument: Poems and Fragments (poetry) 1976
The Stories of Denton Welch (short stories) 1985

EDITH SITWELL (essay date 1943)

[*An English poet, biographer, and critic, Sitwell was extremely cognizant of the value of sound and rhythmic structure in poetry and experimented widely in these areas in her verse. She first received public attention in 1916 as the editor of* Wheels *(1916-21), a series of anthologies of contemporary poetry that offered readers an alternative to the sentimental work of the popular poets of the era. Colored with idiosyncratic imagery and highly personal allusions, her own works reflect her belief that sound and rhythm should take precedence over meaning in poetry. Accordingly, she composed her poetry to be spoken aloud and often gave flamboyant recitals of her works. The author of many volumes of verse, she infused her later works with social commentary and a deep, religious emotion. Throughout her career, Sitwell also used her influence to draw attention to younger writers, including Wilfred Owen, Dylan Thomas, and Allen Ginsburg. In the following foreword to* Maiden Voyage, *Sitwell enthusiastically praises Welch's novel.*]

[*Maiden Voyage*] is a very moving and remarkable first book, and the author appears to be that very rare being, a born writer. I have not seen a first book that produces this impression more strongly—a single phrase (and a perfectly natural one, there is no affectation of writing), and one sees the central point of the person described. In the touching very youthful creature who is the central character, with his curious young wisdom and his occasional young silliness, his longing for affection and hatred of falsehood, his adventurousness, his enquiring nature, his courage, his fright, his shyness and agonies of mind, his youthful clumsiness, his warm kindness, and his pathos, we live again in our own youth. For we are inside that boy's heart and mind, and the whole book has a moving and youthful quality.

Mr. Welch uses words as only a born writer uses them. He never fumbles. In two episodes of the book, he produces, with absolute restraint, a feeling of overwhelming horror, for all that youthfulness. In another, the parting between this young being and his greatest friend, the writing is extraordinarily touching, real, and true. I feel that Mr. Welch may easily prove to be, not only a born writer, but a very considerable one.

> *Edith Sitwell, in a foreword to* Maiden Voyage *by Denton Welch, 1943. Reprint by L. B. Fischer, 1945, p. iii.*

PHILIP TOYNBEE (essay date 1943)

[*Toynbee was an English novelist and critic. The son of historian Arnold Toynbee, he gained a considerable reputation as the author of experimental novels such as* Tea with Mrs. Goodman *(1947) and* The Garden to the Sea *(1953).* Pantaloon *(1962-68), a series of four novels-in-verse, is generally considered by critics to be Toynbee's most important work. A contributor to several prominent English periodicals, he joined the editorial staff of the* Observer, London, *in 1950. In the following essay, Toynbee praises Welch's emotional restraint and stylistic control in handling the autobiographical subjects in* Maiden Voyage.]

To write an autobiography in one's early twenties is both a bold and a cautious decision. Bold because a whole army of irritable elders will be ready with their ridicule; cautious because this, after all, is the only material to which one can claim an absolute monopoly. Mr. Welch has written the boldest kind of autobiography, and his courage has been rewarded by a work of outstanding originality and merit. There is no self-consciousness in his self-absorption, and little reticence; better still, there is no disloyalty to his recent past. No attitude is commoner or more odious than the patronage of an adult towards his own adolescence, the complacent assurance of present superiority. Mr. Welch takes himself seriously, though humour is not lacking, and when he finds his actions discreditable he treats them with cold severity rather than whimsical disassociation.

The whole book is enclosed in the author's eventful seventeenth year. He runs away from Repton, but is later persuaded to return there for one term. That term ended, he goes out to his father in China, where he makes one journey into the interior and another to Pekin. The material is as rich as any young autobiographer could wish, but how easy it would have been to make the story either lifeless or pretentious. Mr. Welch avoids all the obvious pitfalls with bewildering assurance. The qualities which appear to give him this confidence are a rich sensibility and a merciless perception.

> She was between fifty and sixty and the ends of her silk scarves fluttered in the wind. Her head and neck were like the Roman symbol of an arc embedded in a bundle of sticks. The neck was all broken up into wrinkled skin and corded muscles, and the head jutted out at the top.

> I anxiously watched as the little plates were brought. Each one had some different cold and pickled vegetable piled on it. I began nervously to pick at them, tasting the delicate watery flavours on my tongue. It seemed a fresh, airy sort of meal but, being afraid of it, I hated every mouthful.

> ...the dried sediment in the empty decanters reminded me of scabs on sores.

There is nothing clamorous or sensational about such writing, but the impression is always precise, vivid and imaginative. And the descriptions of *objets d'art,* of people or of a human head rotting in the dust are all equally happy. Mr. Welch is a painter as well as a writer, and his illustrations suggest that his talent here, though less considerable, is an explanation of his dexterity in purely visual description.

Maiden Voyage will shock some people by its level relentless tone, by the author's instinctive hatred of illusion and pretence. Without a hint of toughness, without the least false note of cynicism, there is a feline unsentimentality about Mr. Welch which is immensely stimulating. I do not agree with Miss Edith Sitwell who speaks in her foreword of "a moving and youthful quality" [see excerpt dated 1943]. Youth is usually clouded, imitative and insecure, whereas Mr. Welch, even in his most defenceless moments, seems to be armoured by his alert and honest mind. But I agree with Miss Sitwell's conclusion that he "may easily prove to be not only a born writer but a very considerable one."

> *Philip Toynbee, "Repton to China," in* The New Statesman & Nation, *Vol. XXV, No. 642, June 12, 1943, p. 390.*

W. H. AUDEN (essay date 1945)

[*Often considered the poetic successor of W. B. Yeats and T. S. Eliot, Auden is also highly regarded for his literary criticism. As a member of a generation of British writers strongly influenced by the ideas of Karl Marx and Sigmund Freud, he considered social and psychological commentary important functions of lit-*

erary criticism. While he has been criticized for significant inconsistencies in his thought throughout his career, Auden is generally regarded as a fair and perceptive critic. In the following excerpt, he discusses the autobiographical perspective of Maiden Voyage.]

Every autobiography is a monologue which concerns two characters, the Ego and the Self, so that—excluding accounts of religious conversion which dogmatically presuppose a third character—there are two possible kinds of this theatre. In one (to which, for instance, Berlioz' autobiography and Isadora Duncan's *My Life* belong), the Self, as it were, occupies the stage and, like the Greek Messenger, narrates what the Ego, who is off-stage, is doing. In the other, of which **Maiden Voyage** is a distinguished example, their relative positions are reversed; it is now the Ego that has become the narrator, and the Self who is described without being allowed to answer back. Each method has its own principles of "approximate accuracy" and "essential omission," and if the same person were to be presented by both, it would be hard to recognize his common identity. . . .

The Self so lucidly described in **Maiden Voyage** is that of a 16-year-old English boy of the upper middle class. His mother is dead. His father, of whom he is rather afraid, is in business in Shanghai. He has an elder brother, with whom he is on good but distant terms, and a normal outfit of relatives. His interests are architecture, painting—some not very happy examples of his work are reproduced in the book—collecting *objets d'art* and eating. His sense modality is predominantly tactile. Emotionally, he is torn between a longing for affection, which leads him to make impulsive advances to total strangers, and a fear of being rebuffed.

The book is divided into three parts, set, respectively, in England, a London-Shanghai liner and China, and constructed around three journeys which are both explorations and escapes. . . . As he goes his way, he meets a hodge-podge of people, a hotel housekeeper, a nurse, boys, married women, unmarried girls, men, an invalid, Chinese and British soldiers, a Russian boxer, a drunken Dutchman, etc., but as they are all bound on voyages of their own, the meetings are accidental and brief.

The narrator of this expedition manages to give it all unity and significance by a kind of Hitchcock lighting under which both people and things stand out with startling and sinister sharpness. Not merely spectacular incidents, like finding a human head on a lonely road, seeing a man beaten up by the police, or coming upon a little group stoning a puppy to death, but also the best tea-table, are endowed with nightmare possibilities. A dressmaker's room "smells of skill and despair and overwork"; a schoolboy theft of candy sounds like a sex murder.

> I tore the shiny paper off the chocolate and threw it down so that it was swallowed up in the churning of the propellers; then I began to eat. It was like a communion feast. I was eating Mrs. Wright. Not from love but from hate. . . .
> I put large pieces in my mouth and savored them deliciously until the whole pound was finished.

It is this combination of scientific objectivity with subjective terror, I think, which makes **Maiden Voyage** a revealing comment on our historical situation. Are we not all, emotionally, what Mr. Welch is in fact—orphans, each traveling alone on

Title page designed by Welch for Maiden Voyage. *L. B. Fischer, 1945. Reproduced by permission of David Higham Associates Limited.*

a journey which, if it is headed in the direction of unknown dangers, at least is leading one away from the fears one knows? Are not our relations with others mostly of the pseudo-frank, casually desperate kind formed in dentists' waiting rooms and desert bus stops very late at night? Do we not all feel surrounded by immense, uncontrollable, irrational forces which might at any moment (on occasions they certainly do) appear suddenly from behind the solid pebble, the familiar old tree, the motherly features, in all their implacable fury? And is not the only weapon in which we put much faith, the one nerve tonic we swear by, the candid-camera eye, the ironic joke?

We may suffer and cause to suffer, but we can observe the pain with precision; life may lack meaning, but we can laugh at its absurdity. Our triumph, our consolation? . . . Well, sort of.

W. H. Auden, "Mr. Welch," in The New York Times Book Review, *March 18, 1945, p. 4.*

EDMUND WILSON   (essay date 1945)

[Wilson, considered America's foremost man of letters in the twentieth century, wrote widely on cultural, historical, and literary matters, authoring several seminal critical studies. He is often credited with bringing an international perspective to Amer-

ican letters through his widely read discussions of European literature. Wilson was allied to no critical school; however, several dominant concerns serve as guiding motifs throughout his work. He invariably examined the social and historical implications of a work of literature, particularly literature's significance as "an attempt to give meaning to our experience" and its value for the improvement of humanity. Although he was not a moralist, his criticism displays a deep concern with moral values. Another constant was his discussion of a work of literature as a revelation of its author's personality. Related to this is Wilson's theory, formulated in The Wound and the Bow *(1941), that artistic ability is a compensation for a psychological wound; thus, a literary work can only be fully understood if one undertakes an emotional profile of its author. Wilson utilized this approach in many essays, and it is the most-often attacked element of his thought. However, though Wilson examined the historical and psychological implications of a work of literature, he rarely did so at the expense of a discussion of its literary qualities. In the following excerpt from his review of* Maiden Voyage, *Wilson emphasizes its author's youth as an important factor in evaluating the work.*]

Maiden Voyage, *by Denton Welch . . . , is a book by a boy of nineteen about his experiences at sixteen. One of the curious and striking features of English writing since World War I has been the tendency of the younger men to go back over their schoolboy years, and in a spirit as different as possible from Kipling's* Stalky & Co. *Before the last war, the English upper-class public schools were more or less taken for granted. . . . You got such writing as Auden's early poetry and the school-day-haunting autobiographies of Christopher Isherwood and Cyril Connolly, works in which an irritated criticism of the ideals of the public schools was mingled with a certain complacency. You got the recklessly destructive burlesque of Evelyn Waugh's* Decline and Fall *as well as the cult of the schoolboy code that appears in his later books.*

Maiden Voyage *is the most recent installment in this series of memoirs of boyhood, and it represents a further stage, beyond that of those mentioned above, in that the reaction against the public school is even sharper and, apparently, final. Denton Welch ran away in his second year, and though he was persuaded to return and complete the term, he was afterward allowed to escape and visit his father in China. The first third of* Maiden Voyage *deals with his life at a school which seems to have had little to offer him—little, at least, of which the boy was aware—save brutality, homosexuality, and boredom, and with his rather touching attempt at flight; and the rest deals with his trip to China, where he was still to suffer extremely from his fastidiousness, shyness, and self-preoccupation.*

It is impossible to criticize a book written by a boy of nineteen as one would that of an adult author. The less attractive features of *Maiden Voyage* are perhaps mere symptoms of adolescence. The writer's talent may be later applied to different subjects and in a quite different way. The trait of the young visitor to China which is most likely to annoy the reader is his complete lack of sympathy with or interest in any other human being, whether school friend, member of his family, travelling companion, or exotic foreigner. He feels occasionally an admiration, which seems to be entirely physical, for the virility of some older man; he once nervously invites a soldier to tea, but he never gives the faintest evidence of any sort of personal warmth. He is not the type of sensitive young person who identifies himself imaginatively with others. He has, indeed, less imagination than taste, and the only element in his personality which can be said to approximate a passion is his appetite for fine antiques. He shrinks constantly from the people he encounters and almost anything sets his teeth on edge. "The

echoes in the passages were muffled by doubtful, unpleasant carpets. I hated it." "The maid who brought us tea revolted me a little. She was pale and pasty, like a blownup bladder." . . . The book is full of such infantile shudders and the narrator is always blushing. "'Why, I was painting when you were still being fed on your mother's breasts.' He smiled benignly at us and I found myself turning red." The adult reader may become impatient, but he should remember that all this is happening at a time when the narrator's voice has not changed yet, and one can discount the fear and antipathies, the awkwardnesses and shames of adolescence, for Denton Welch has some positive merits. I do not agree with Miss Edith Sitwell [see excerpt dated 1943] . . . that his book can be described as moving or that he makes himself sympathetic, but it is true, as she says, that his instinct for style is quite remarkable for a boy of his age. The writing runs rather too much to a succession of simple declarative sentences and so becomes a little monotonous, though it gets better as the book goes on, but, in Miss Sitwell's phrase, he never fumbles. He can usually hit off an apt simile and his sense of how to tell a story is remarkable, deft, and sure, so that, though nothing very dramatic happens, the reader is always carried on by a constantly renewed suspense. This skill at narrative and a literary sobriety which are admirable in themselves are sometimes applied to incidents amusingly and incongruously childish, as when, on the boat, he steals a whole box of chocolates from a lady he does not like. Yet, of course, to the adolescent, many inconsequential matters become serious, and what is unusual in Denton Welch and what commands respect is his scrupulousness in recording his experience. Uneasy though he shows himself so often in his actual personal contacts, he appears, for a beginner, as a writer amazingly unembarrassed and nonexhibitionistic. This may be partly the detachment of an immature boy who has never yet been stirred by emotion, but, for all that, it is rather impressive.

The book has also a certain interest as a picture of life in China—the hatred of the foreigner and native barbarity, the dullness and danger of the lives of the whites. Mr. Welch ran into a severed head on one of his walks in the country, made an arduous trip in a freight car, exposed to the harassments of the Chinese soldiery, and visited the house of a Canadian doctor whose predecessor had been massacred on his tennis court, but the young son of the British merchant is mostly concerned with porcelains and bronzes, and the main interest of the book for the reader is in its self-portrait, at once cool and quivering, of a young member of the British upper classes who has broken with the world of his school but is not yet at home in any other. (pp. 83-4)

Edmund Wilson, "'Maiden Voyage': Blushes and Shudders," in The New Yorker, *Vol. XXI, No. 10, April 21, 1945, pp. 83-4.*

ANNA KAVAN (essay date 1945)

[*Kavan was an English novelist, short story writer, and critic. Born Helen Woods, she published several novels under her married name, Helen Ferguson, before legally changing her name to "Anna Kavan," the protagonist of her novel* Let Me Alone *(1930). A heroin addict for thirty years who suffered from depression and emotional breakdowns, Kavan gained a reputation as a highly original, if mentally tortured, novelist whose works relentlessly demonstrate her vision of the world as a threatening place. Often compared to Anaïs Nin for her extreme subjectivity, Kavan used menacing surrealistic imagery to confuse reality and imagination in her fiction. In the following excerpt, published at the close of*

World War II, Kavan discusses In Youth Is Pleasure *in the context of the destructive impulse in human nature.*]

The western war ends messily in an enormous chaotic shambles, leaving us to contemplate the futile disintegration of an entire continent. That the contemplation does not cause deeper dismay is presumably due to man's long-standing intimacy with ruin. The world is closely acquainted with the triumph of the destructive force; disastrous conflicts; calamities; all forms of death: we know the pattern of destruction very well. We know the faces of the destroyers, the violent men lying in wait for blood; those who hunt, every one his brother with a net. Much less familiar is the causative factor underlying all this. (p. 63)

If, as the psychologists say, fourteen is the average mental age of rankers in all armies, it follows that the mental development of the vast majority of human beings ceases at puberty. In order, then, to understand the problem of the persistent destructive pattern—or any other human problem for that matter—one must first understand the personality of this adolescent in adult clothing who is the average citizen of our world. (p. 65)

Being highly gregarious, he derives intense satisfaction from identifying himself with a group of similar gregarious beings. He sinks his individuality in a sort of collective comradeship to which he adheres with blind loyalty; and this sense of union upholds him in dire situations, acting as a buffer between him and the horror without.

A leader of adolescents, if he is to maintain contact with his followers, must not himself develop too far from their mental level. He must remain sufficiently immature to participate wholeheartedly in the aggressive and destructive activities which are at once the main source of their enjoyment and of his power over them. . . . These boy-leaders, whose understanding cannot extend beyond the concrete, are bound to oppose cultural values which they perceive as a dangerous threat to their own vanity and self esteem. The intellectual ideals of peace; art, spiritual development, individual perfection, are to the adolescent leader only a cause for uneasiness, hatred, distrust, contempt. He feels inferior when confronted by these abstract valuations, and so is inevitably impelled to work for the downfall of the peaceful environment in which they flourish. He must work to establish the only situation which he is able to dominate and to understand; the havoc-chaos-death situation in which he feels most at home.

The work of every serious writer is a comment on some special aspect of the world these Dead-End dictators have prepared for him. Glenway Westcott's comment is direct, and expressed in an honest objective fashion. *Apartment in Athens* describes the sort of disaster which overtakes peaceable, simple, kindly people under the present-day brand of organized gangsterdom. (pp. 65-6)

Denton Welch and L. P. Hartley comment upon a hooligan-ridden world from more personal standpoints. Instead of describing situations resulting from a regime of violence, the work of these writers provides material which concerns the origin of such situations, and which is for that reason most relevant to considerations of emotional age. Both *In Youth Is Pleasure* and *The Shrimp and the Anemone* are above the general level as regards execution as well as interest.

In Denton Welch's case it is the style which is primarily striking. Mr. Welch writes with gaiety and verve and a vivid individual power of observation. His phrasing is highly imaginative; there are passages of poetic brilliance in his work; yet the charm of his writing is largely due to the fact that words like 'polished' and 'sparkling' are inapplicable to it. There is a feeling of real spontaneity throughout the book, which describes the summer holiday of a fifteen-year-old schoolboy, rather regrettably named Orvil Pym. Orvil belongs to the cultural minority. He is certainly not on the side of the destroyers, to whom he is none the less linked by the very over-sensitiveness which divides him from them. Orvil is afraid to grow up. The eternal fourteen-year-olds are, of course, unaware of their immaturity, while Orvil consciously clings to his boyhood, even to the extent of asking God to save him from the calamity of becoming adult. In an intelligent upper-class boy, naturally destined to some social responsibility, this is a dangerous attitude. Arising out of a sort of squeamishness, it is the basis of a deliberate self-blinding process that may lead him ultimately to tolerate, or even encourage, violent destructive elements to which his own repressed instincts are really opposed. In emotional development, Orvil is already ahead of the gangster boys; except for the persistence of some infantile sadism, as displayed in an incident which Mr. Welch describes terrifyingly well. (p. 66)

Anna Kavan, in a review of "In Youth Is Pleasure," in Horizon, *London, Vol. XXI, No. 67, July, 1945, pp. 63, 65-6.*

MARGUERITE YOUNG (essay date 1946)

[*An American poet, novelist, and critic, Young is chiefly known for* Miss MacIntosh, My Darling *(1965), a massive novel that has been compared in its thematic and stylistic ambitions to the masterpieces of James Joyce and Marcel Proust. According to Richard Ellmann, this novel treats "the residual questions in all fiction, including the validity of dreams, the deception of appearances, the confusion of identities, and the multiplicity of selves that cluster in each seemingly integral being." In the following excerpt, Young focusses on the poetic prose style of* In Youth Is Pleasure.]

[Denton Welch] is a subjective, impressionistic writer, aware of dualisms, paradoxes, and the truth which escapes any definition of it. His concern is largely with the wonderful, the deviate, the strange—not with the so-called "realism" which rejects the adventure of the dreamlike creation of language. Beauty goes hand in hand with terror, formal elegance with informal brutality, the archaic with the modern.

In Youth Is Pleasure has the distinction of style and vision which characterize *Maiden Voyage*—and it may be more complex in theme and symbol than the earlier volume. Welch's work shows, in both volumes, the influence of sensationalistic psychology and of other writers who have been influenced by it such as Joyce, Virginia Woolf, Alex Comfort. There is no escape into any general, vague statement. Every reality has to be broken down into smaller and smaller parts. For Welch, as for perhaps the best stylists in the tradition of the sensationalistic, reality is minute, made up of many diverse fragments, never wholly realizable.

No small detail misses Welch. We see the hand and then the cherry-colored fingernails—although we may never see the body. We always realize life only partially. Through a play with half-realized, unrelated details may come about a new understanding of our complex experience.

The impression given by *In Youth Is Pleasure* is thus one of considerable richness, even within a framework limited perhaps by the author's youth and perhaps by the youthfulness of his hero. *In Youth Is Pleasure* repeats, unfortunately, the situation of *Maiden Voyage*—an errant schoolboy's quest for self-knowledge in a more or less alien world, a world of mysteries, many of them engendered by the boy himself. Welch seems, in fact, the lyric, youthful poet celebrating youth—but while the poet can repeat himself, with slight variations, in poem after poem, prose narratives should not so nearly approximate each other as these do.

Marguerite Young, "Schoolboy," in The New York Times Book Review, *March 31, 1946, p. 6.*

HAMILTON BASSO   (essay date 1946)

[*An American novelist, biographer, and critic, Basso is best known for* Sun in Capricorn *(1942), whose characters include a ruthless politician reportedly based on Huey Long. Like much of his work, including* The View from Pompey's Head *(1954), this novel explores the social structure and cultural mores of the American South. In the following excerpt, Basso offers an unfavorable review of* In Youth Is Pleasure.]

[*In Youth Is Pleasure*] might have been more accurately called "The Sex-Conditioned Nightmare." Mr. Welch's story, like the one he told in *Maiden Voyage,* is simple. A fifteen-year-old English public-school boy, between terms, is taken by his rich father, who has vague business connections in the East, to one of those grand English hotels whose guests always fall into two categories, the Noel Cowards and the Colonel Blimps. He spends part of his holiday there with his father and two brothers, has several minor adventures, goes to visit an ex-schoolmate and his sister, returns to the hotel, has a few more minor adventures, and then returns to school. Mr. Welch's hero is named Orvil Pym and is unquestionably the most desperately miserable English schoolboy who ever found his way into print. The author, I presume, intended to present him as what is called a "sympathetic" person, too high-strung and sensitive to fit into a cruel and monstrous world, but I found him a rather cruel little monster. To me, Mr. Welch has made his hero enormously self-pitying (page 1 to the end of the book), just as dirty-minded (same pages), masochistic (pages 76-77), somewhat necrophilic (pages 90-91), satanic (page 95), sadistic (page 119), exhibitionistic (page 150), and, above all else, full of an almost ridiculous narcism.

Many of these qualities, judging by some of the writing now being produced by a few of the more advanced younger writers in England (let's not forget our own advanced, not-so-young Henry Miller, either), would seem to be essential to the makeup of the contemporary hero. I think that we can skip any such idiotic notion. No sensible person is likely to be taken in by these blown-glass imitations of Baudelaire's flowers of evil, and a very shrewd and intelligent friend of mine, in conversation, summed up the whole business when he said that we had come to the point where the ivory tower was giving way to the ivory gutter. It's much more difficult, however, to ignore how vastly overrated most of these performances are. W. H. Auden, for example, in an appreciative review of Mr. Welch's *Maiden Voyage* [see excerpt dated 1945], wrote that it was distinguished by a "kind of Hitchcock lighting under which both people and things stand out with startling and sinister sharpness," that "the best tea-table incidents are endowed with nightmare possibilities," and that it is Mr. Welch's "combination of scientific objectivity with subjective terror" which makes his writing a "revealing comment on our historical situation."

I felt, after I read *Maiden Voyage,* that Mr. Auden, despite his distinction as a poet, was talking nonsense. Now, with Mr. Welch's new novel behind me (no better and no worse a book than his first one), I feel it even more. What you get in Mr. Welch is the fuzziest kind of lighting, cast by the candles I have listed above (the exact opposite of the sort of light that Mr. Hitchcock uses in making his pictures), no scientific objectivity whatever (unless Mr. Auden is thinking of sentences like "The smell of the dead bird hovered like an evil threat"), absolutely no historical comment, and a subjective terror that I simply cannot believe in. It is doubtful, also, whether Mr. Welch believes in it himself.

There is a passage in the book that runs: "It was one of Orvil's fads that he only liked bread in the form of toast or crusty rolls, but he now quite willingly cut a large hunk of soft bread and spread it thickly with cherry jam. . . . How delicious was the plain bread, under the jam! It was a little like nuts, a little like earth, like blankets, like—Orvil's defining powers gave out. He knew really that it was only like bread." Mr. Welch elsewhere indicates that he sees horror in a suit of black clothes, and a girl's breasts as miniature volcanoes out of which pour milky-white smoke and thin, shivering tongues of fire, and hands whose plump fingers curl and wriggle like grubs. Yet I cannot rid myself of the suspicion that just as he knows that bread is bread, Mr. Welch also knows that a suit of black clothes is a suit of black clothes, that breasts are breasts, and that plump fingers are plump fingers—as plain, simple, and unhorrifying as that. Any man with the mind to can do a lot of things with mirrors. (pp. 106, 108)

Hamilton Basso, "Bread," in The New Yorker, *Vol. XXII, No. 8, April 6, 1946, pp. 106, 108-09.*

THE TIMES LITERARY SUPPLEMENT   (essay date 1950)

[*In the following excerpt, the critic observes in* A Voice through a Cloud *the culmination of themes and subjects introduced in Welch's earlier novels.*]

With the posthumous appearance of [Welch's] last, almost completed book, *A Voice through a Cloud,* the murmur of "genius" has already been raised. At times, reading these strange, dazzling pages, so full of pain and disgust and revolt, yet so lucidly detached in their self-inquiry, it is easy to understand why. Yet for all its wracked and searching brilliance, *A Voice through a Cloud* remains somehow incomplete in another way besides its physical lack of a concluding chapter. It is difficult to pin down the fugitive sensation of dissatisfaction, of unfulfilment, which the book leaves; does it come from too arbitrary an insistence on one point of view, or the premonition of an unresolved conflict which the writer painfully hints at but fails to reveal? Behind the alert eye and probing image the reader feels him to be constantly struggling with some horrible, baffling division of purpose; and then (it is soon after he has been knocked down on his bicycle and taken to hospital with a bad spinal injury) one comes upon this:

> As I looked at the green glow of the lamp, heard the hissingly quiet voices of the nurses, felt the drumming, thundering tingle in the legs which I could not move, it seemed to me that something had happened which I had expected all my life. The nurses appeared to take my situation quite calmly, to show no surprise at the terrible change in me. I began to believe that I ought not to feel bewildered and lost myself,

that I ought to accept the horror as something quite ordinary.

. . . something had happened which I had expected all my life. The undertone of the whole passage is of guilt, a guilt only emphasized by the writer's feeling that he should regard his condition as normal. The passage throws unexpected light on the whole of Denton Welch's work. Here, realized for the first time, is that uneasy sense of lurking doom implicit in his two earlier autobiographical volumes, *Maiden Voyage* and *In Youth Is Pleasure*. And with the recognition of guilt we are back with its original cause: the revolt of the lonely, sensitive, "difficult" child, who is nevertheless unable to carry his rebellion quite through to the end. . . .

A lonely childhood is often a great advantage to a writer. It refines and sharpens his vision (there is no one to be placated by kindly distortions); it is also a great breeder of images. Both tendencies may be seen in Denton Welch's first book, *Maiden Voyage,* which alternates between ruthless insights into the silly pretensions of the adult social comedy and highly involved private fantasies. The same pattern of acid observation interwoven with complex day-dream persists through almost everything he wrote. But there is a third characteristic which gives his writing its highly individual flavour. Feeling himself cut off from other people, the imaginative child inhabits a world of *things*. Each one of Denton Welch's books is full of objects, each one is a sort of cross between a Parnassian paradise of sculptured masterpieces and a shop full of discarded bric-à-brac.

But a mere mention of these three elements does not convey the essential quality of Denton Welch's writing: they are merely its outward adornments. It is an underlying tension which gives them life. That tension is the writer's constant struggle to relate himself to the outside world. Excluded, by cruelty or indifference, from the company of others who do not understand or do not want to understand him, the lonely child has his revenge. He becomes a small spy let loose in alien territory; he chooses his allies from the vegetable and mineral regions. But always a point is reached when the sense of his own loneliness overwhelms him again: and then he is all hunger for affection and care and solicitude. When he fails to find this among those near to him he turns elsewhere. At each stage in his autobiographical progress he seems to be searching for what is often crudely called a "father-substitute." The figure is perhaps only vaguely foreshadowed in *Maiden Voyage,* in the person of the amateur boxer, Ernst; in *In Youth Is Pleasure* it emerges much more clearly in the mission schoolmaster, with his rough kindliness, whom the hero meets on the river; and in *A Voice through a Cloud* it is more than ever substantial in the character of Dr. Farley. The ultimate horror is reached when the hero abruptly recoils from the images he has made of them. In a struggle Orvil actually kicks the schoolmaster of *In Youth Is Pleasure* in the face and draws blood. Towards the end of *A Voice through a Cloud* the hero already feels his growing estrangement from Dr. Farley. (The note of hysteria is always latent in these relationships, but nowhere does it leap to such shrill frenzy as in a curious **"Fragment of a Life Story,"** published in one of the last issues of *Horizon*.)

But in spite of this dark, tormented background of sinister ambiguities—or perhaps because of it—*A Voice through a Cloud* is an extraordinarily impressive achievement. Strange, original and disquieting images are threaded upon a style so compact and assured, the whole effect is so much one of effortless brilliance that it might be easy to overlook the remarkable nature of the achievement altogether were it not for the brief, moving foreword in which Mr. Eric Oliver, a friend of the writer, describes the circumstances in which most of the book was written. . . . "Towards the end he could only work for three or four minutes at a time and then he would get a raging headache and his eyes would more or less give out."

Yet pain only increased his fanatical concentration on his task, and with each fresh onset of pain he seemed determined to shed one more comforting illusion. The result is a picture of life as only the rare sufferer in hospital sees it—whittled down to the bare essentials. Yet, far from engendering poverty and a bleak surrender, this view paints everything with vivid newness. Here, for instance, is the writer's sensation on seeing the outer world again after more than a month in hospital:

> Everything was different. The sound of the car's engine was muted; it was no more than a soft purring. When a tram passed it did not clang and lurch as I had expected, it glided noiselessly like a skater on ice, or a swan on silky water. And the people inside—they had dark staring liquid eyes, like the eyes in portraits on the lids of late Egyptian mummy cases; their hair seemed dusty and still, unblown. They grasped their shopping bags unfeelingly, as children hold their dolls. With deep thoughtful faces they went about their almost sacred household tasks, keeping strict silence.

But perhaps the most remarkable achievement of all is the dispassionate manner in which he follows the course of his own illness, aware of every swiftly changing nuance in the obscure chemical wrestling match between mind and body, and prepared to struggle on with his lucid record at the lowest ebb of despair.

> His going drained me of everything. I was washed up on a desert beach where all was changed and made impossible. Writing in my notebook, drawing, reading, dreaming, were as unthinkable, as meaningless as playing Patience. All feeling for myself seemed dead, therefore I was evil, snapping down on every impulse to live, to work, demolishing every suggestion that might have helped to break the spell. . . .

This is a strikingly sad book. Yet its very existence is a conquest over that "feeling of universal damage and loss" of which Denton Welch speaks in its opening pages. To try to guess what such a writer might have produced had he lived is always a dangerous hazard, and never more so than in the case of Denton Welch, who embarked upon his first book fully armed with literary gifts, and whose succeeding books impress the reader not so much by any development of new potentialities, but by a patient, scrupulous refining of those he already possessed. No one who reads *A Voice through a Cloud* will fail to see in his early death a grievous loss to English literature.

"Brave and Cruel," in The Times Literary Supplement, *No. 2513, March 31, 1950, p. 197.*

MAURICE CRANSTON   (essay date 1950)

[*Cranston is an English biographer, educator, and critic whose numerous works reflect his long career as a professor of social philosophy and political science. In the following excerpt from an essay first published in the* Nineteenth Century *in October 1950, Cranston highlights prominent traits of Welch's major works and offers a brief assessment of his overall achievement.*]

Most of Denton Welch's work is sparkling with life. (p. 71)

Denton Welch's writings are hardly anywhere a sick man's work. It was his painting which had to serve towards the end as his catharsis, and the pictures reproduced in *A Last Sheaf* are distressing—half-heartedly meticulous, crowded, literary, almost psychotic. The little drawings are different and better. In graphic art his emphasis was always decorative and while the idioms—sea-shells, snakes, fish-bones, cats, fans, pointed arches and broken pediments—suggest the age of bogus ruin, they were all real to him.

Maiden Voyage is a magical book, not unconsciously naïve. It begins with an account of the author's running away from school. He takes a bus to a London station:

> When the conductor called out "Waterloo" I ran down the steps and stood for a moment in the road. A carthorse was pouring out a golden jet of water. I watched it bubbling and hissing into the gutter, then I began to climb the stone stairs between the fat statues. The trains inside the station were lying close together like big worms.

Denton Welch learned later to write a more sophisticated language, but he kept the trick of lighting up a passage of conventional narrative with one of his arresting child's images. Thus, from his second book, *In Youth Is Pleasure*, this paragraph:

> He walked slowly into the dark water and lay down flat. His exultation passed into a more sober delight. Water always soothed him. He felt calm and peaceful. As he floated, he felt the sun hot on his face and on the parts of his chest and arms which were still above water. The rest of his body was tingling with cold.
>
> "I'm like one of those Baked Alaskas," he thought, "one of those lovely puddings of ice cream and hot sponge."

In Youth Is Pleasure, for all the merits of its style, is Denton Welch's least good book. It is cast in the third-person form, and thus demanded an interest in the external world which Denton Welch could not sustain. He was a born solipsist, and it was nature which held the mirror up to him. *In Youth Is Pleasure* is not moving because it is artificial. Perhaps it is rightly called "precious."

To Denton Welch himself the thought that he was "precious" was never disagreeable. His tastes were for delicate, exotic things. His home was furnished with a remarkable collection of eighteenth-century pieces. He enjoyed the music of the harpsichord, candlelight, punch and fragrant snuff. In one of his poems he writes:

> In Total War I lead a life
> Epitomized by Chinese Chippendale.
> I still am Gothic on a painted bed,
> Rococo in a grotto underground,
> Baroque in cloisters pillaged from dead Spain,
> Enjoying what will never live again.

Clearly he was not the poet he wished to be. But he was a real artist and unusually complete as a personality. Only the su-

perficial eye would have been misled by the colourful accoutrements with which he fortified his spirits. He had no desire to *épater le bourgeois;* on the contrary he liked to be the perfect gentleman, and his manners were charming.

After *In Youth Is Pleasure* he worked slowly on his most important book *A Voice through a Cloud.* If only because its subject was his accident, the work at it was a great emotional strain. All the time, what is more, his health was worsening, and it was largely composed a few words at a time between the crises of his last great illness. Nevertheless he also wrote in those years between fifteen and twenty short stories. Several of them appeared in one volume with his *nouvelle* entitled *Brave and Cruel,* and there are several more less-finished ones in *A Last Sheaf.* The same book also carries an early draft of *A Voice through a Cloud,* and a most revealing piece called "A Fragment of a Life Story" which, if nothing else, should satisfy inquiring minds about events which followed those narrated in *A Voice through a Cloud.*

There is a sinister quality in much of Denton Welch's work. He suggests the plight of Adam immediately the forbidden fruit had been eaten: the eye still innocent, the heart filled with sudden shocked knowledge of iniquity. He was a visual writer with his own iconography of evil: lepers in a Chinese street, shabby shuffling perverts, ageing painted harpies and crumbling houses where the mad have lived. The very titles of his stories bear witness here: **"The Judas Tree," "Narcissus Bay," "The Coffin on the Hill."**

The most horrifying story he ever wrote is called **"A Diamond Badge"** and is about the visit of a lady to a young novelist whose domestic circumstances are precisely Denton Welch's own. She has never seen the young novelist before. He is ill, and must receive her in his bedroom. She is startled to discover that:

> He was terribly deformed, his hands all twisted and his body seemingly telescoped into itself, so that he was broad but perhaps only three feet tall. He had a smooth oval face with rather delicate features. His hair was red and a little silky fringe ran right round his jaw line, framing his face and making him look like a particularly well-groomed ill-disposed monkey.

As a picture of Denton Welch himself this is absurdly, monstrously false. But it suggests how he felt or feared others saw him. And as such it underlines his most conspicuous failing. He had no trust. This in turn connects with his greatest limitation as an artist. He built too many barricades and enclosed the range of his understanding. If he could have seen the wider human comedy with his miraculously penetrating eye, and described that world as he described his own, he would surely have been among the greater writers in our language. As it is he will survive as a minor genius, one of very few from an uncreative age. (pp. 72-4)

Maurice Cranston, "Denton Welch," in Spectator Harvest, *1952. Reprint by Books for Libraries Press, 1970; distributed by Arno Press, Inc., pp. 70-4.*

[VITA SACKVILLE-WEST] (essay date 1952)

[*An English poet, novelist, biographer, and critic, Sackville-West was closely associated with the "Bloomsbury Group," a circle of authors, artists, and intellectuals that included Virginia Woolf, Lytton Strachey, E. M. Forster, and John Maynard Keynes. Of her many works, she is best remembered for the novels* The Edwardians *(1930) and* All Passion Spent *(1931), the long poem* The Land *(1926), and the biography* Pepita *(1937). In the following excerpt, Sackville-West comments on Welch's journal writing.]*

Philosophers and priests have consistently remarked that it does not matter what happens to you: what matters is the way you take it. Denton Welch took what remained of his broken life very gallantly. There are very few complaints in the [*Journals*], which he kept in cheap exercise-books such as a schoolchild might use; but those few complaints slipping out now and again, as though it were against his brave will, allow us to look through a keyhole into the darker corners of his mind. . . .

Such passages are the more poignant for their rarity, and also for the relative frequency of their intrusion as the years go by and one sees the end approaching as the remaining pages of the book grow fewer to turn over, with all the implication of what that must mean. In the earlier part he has been so determined not to make an exhibition of his agony of mind and body; not to inflict his sufferings on his friends, even to pretend that nothing was irremediably wrong. Mr. Maurice Cranston has observed that if he had to keep to his bedroom for a day he would encourage his visitors to suspect him of hypochondriasis. . . .

Fastidious and sensitive, it is evident that his natural squeamishness sought defiance against the squalors of physical disability, and it is significant that he should refer to his misfortune as "that *obscene* accident." It is legitimate to infer that the fundamental purity and idealism of his spirit was driven by the imperfections of the flesh into the occasional coarseness some readers have deplored. The coin always has its reverse. Contrariwise, something of the same feeling inspired his admiration of physical vigour in others; the topic is recurrent; he would take a delight in meticulous description of muscular arms, sunburnt skin, almond-white teeth, shining gold hair, with a wealth of detail and an almost animal zest that at times recalls, though with no suggestion of imitation, certain passages from D. H. Lawrence. Mr. Brooke justly comments on Denton Welch's abnormally acute powers of observation [see entry dated 1952 in Additional Bibliography]; they served him well, whether he turned them to use in recording the "orange vomit" that might pour from his mouth, or to the delicacy of his appreciation of a ring he saw on the finger of a stranger, "a cloudy square ring, like blue soap, the most mysterious of all." His visual memory must indeed have been astonishing, and was probably responsible for the exaggerated relish he took in what Mr. Brooke calls *minutiae*, such as his own small treasures, which he rather touchingly alludes to as "my pretty things," and his expressed regret that writers in the past should not have gone into more detail about their houses, their meals, and their possessions. "I wish that people should mention the tiny things of their lives that give them pleasure or fear or wonder." In any final appraisement of Denton Welch as a writer, this peculiarity must be taken into account, for although it greatly contributed to the originality of his style it also affected the scope and scale of his vision. . . .

There is no possibility of suggesting that in these journals he was writing for his private delectation, small observations that he would have scorned to set down in his published work, for it is clear from internal evidence that he expected his diary, or note-books, call it what you will, to be given to the world when he would no longer be there to edit or suppress. Yet, when all this has been said, what a natural writer he was!

Utterly underivative, he was from the very first a master of the flashing phrase, with a power of sudden illumination which sprang from the sheer intensity of his own perception. Words were merely the clothes of his thought. He meets some soldiers on manoeuvre, with leaves and twigs stuck into the netting stretched over their tin hats. Instantly he grasps the essential character of their appearance: "The effect was wild and pastoral and fancy-dress." Or he goes to visit a Neolithic burial-ground on a lonely slope of the North Downs: "There were the fallen stones sunk into the ground like giant bullets in an ogre." No insistence; he has said what he wanted to say.

Perhaps the most impressive pages in the journal are those in which he describes the experience of being lost alone in a wood at night, for here is none of the somewhat finicky detail he too often indulged in: there is nothing but terror and a sense of the indifferent cruelty of the exterior world. These pages, though they may not compare in beauty with, say, the description of the young man bathing, are interesting in that they reflect a macabre element in the writer's mind, the element which comes out most clearly in his strange and frightening paintings, thick with the phantasmagoria of toadstools, distorted cats, sardonic cows and grotesque rabbits. Yet in those paintings there is also much delicate recording of beauty, sea-shells strewn about, a china hand holding a bunch of flowers, tiny insects lovingly observed.

Above all, his courage shines like a beacon; born to write, he struggled on to finish his last novel even when he had become physically unable to use his pen for more than a few minutes at a time. That novel, *A Voice through a Cloud,* which is in fact an autobiography, should be read in conjunction with the journals if the full measure of his valour and his suffering is properly to be understood.

[Vita Sackville-West], "*Voice through a Cloud,*" in *The Times Literary Supplement, No. 2651, November 21, 1952, p. 764.*

RUBY COHN (essay date 1958)

[An American critic and educator, Cohn has published numerous critical works on modern drama, including several studies of Samuel Beckett. In the following excerpt, she discusses techniques that lend artistic form to the autobiographical incidents in Maiden Voyage *and* A Voice through a Cloud.]*

In this day of documentary novels and fictionalized autobiography . . . , it would seem apparent that some liberalizing redefinition of each genre is necessary. Without attempting that, and simply accepting the once paradoxical term "autobiographical fiction" for most of Welch's work, I think that the very volumes which are most often dubbed autobiography, (*Maiden Voyage* and *A Voice through A Cloud*) are singularly instructive to students of the contemporary novel.

In Youth Is Pleasure is Welch's only complete book to wear the guise of a novel, by introducing a third-person hero and carrying him through a series of loosely connected adventures. But in neither construction, style, nor, it appears, separation from the facts of Welch's life, does it differ from *Maiden Voyage* or *A Voice through A Cloud.* Orvil Pym is replaced in the latter books by "I," but both personages possess a hypersensitive self-absorption which persists also in the Robert of the novel fragment Welch left when he died. From book to book only the name of the hero changes; his highly personal vision remains. Of motivation, character, and climax in traditional fictional usage, there is nothing.

Like many poets but few novelists, Denton Welch has only one large subject, himself—and yet he is able to be ruthlessly objective about that subject. Born and partially educated in China, more conversant with painterly than literary coteries, semi-invalided at eighteen by the accident which was to lead to his death, he was interested in neither the social nor literary events of his time. (pp. 153-54)

Welch's immersion in himself is often ascribed to his invalidism, but this explanation seems neither necessary nor sufficient. After all, the most celebrated invalid-writer of the century created not only Marcel but Swann, Odette, Gilberte, the Verdurins and the Guermantes; he created them as individuals *and* as composites of a social order. Nothing of the kind inhabits Welch's work, where a shadow-family hovers in the background while, from various vague milieux, friends of the moment play their scenes, and then vanish. Denton alone is always on stage—lucid, volatile, diabolically observant.

Although as a writer he may draw upon memory, neither as hero nor narrator does he seem to delve into the past. His fluency never falters; each incident is savored fully, with extraordinary immediacy—and then dismissed. "What was my life?" asks Welch in *A Voice through A Cloud,* "It was all a scraping together of little incidents, a sucking of them dry before I hurried on in search of one more drop of nectar." Of that nectar—a gourmet's selection among the plants in the field—he made his honey.

Since Welch has been classified as an autobiographer rather than novelist mainly because he seems to follow the vagaries of memory, it is important to realize that a striking aspect of Welch's artistry is precisely this pretense of scraping the incidents together, haphazardly as they occur. He even states:

> I found it best to stop picking and to look over the past with an animal indifference. Surely that was the way to look at things—to eat them up with your eyes for what they were, then to pass on, but never to chain them together in a silly pattern.
>
> *(A Voice through A Cloud)*

On the face of it, he yields to no obvious and "silly pattern" such as might be imposed by either novelistic plot or "spatial form," and yet his works are constructed; they have a unity beyond the ubiquitous "I" or the ramblings of memory. By choosing his events, especially those which begin and end his books; by plunging directly into the incidents of his short chapters and driving steadily to their understated, reflective conclusions; by consistently and deliberately juxtaposing the momentous and the trivial; by simply ignoring "incidentless" time; Welch orders his "scrapings" without seeming to chain them in place. Often, the title provides the key to unity—in both shorter and longer works.

Thus, *Maiden Voyage,* Welch's first book, has both a literal and broader meaning. The title suggests an initiation story, and it is evident that such was Welch's intention. The opening incident, a voyage to Salisbury, is also Welch's initial act of self-assertion, a process which is to dominate the book, and which is suggested in the very first sentence: "After I had run away from school, no one knew what to do with me."

The voyage to Salisbury is a voyage away from obedience-to-authority; Denton runs away from the fashionable public school he detests. Afterwards, although he consents to return until the end of the term, no one, indeed, knows what to do with him; nor does he know what to do with himself. He bounces from a school friendship to a vague relationship with his brother to a trip to China which, although summarized in some twenty pages after the book is one-third over, is usually taken to be the maiden voyage of the title. But Denton's discovery of China and his discoveries in China constitute more of the maiden voyage than the trip itself. Moreover, this was not in actual life Welch's first voyage to China, nor is it conceivable that memory alone could recreate the beautiful objects (mostly English) in his father's apartment, the Chinese antiques in "the interior," the dialogue in pidgin English, and the words of the people who brush by him. Far from random recollection, each of Denton's encounters is a "first"—an independent friendship in a soldier pickup, cruelty in the death of a puppy, horror in flies feasting on a dead man's head, fear on a dangerous horseback ride, friendship through shared love of "pretty things," and, finally, the necessity of assuming responsibility in the form of a return to England and enrollment in Art School. Each of these "firsts" is relatively independent of the others; if events were juggled to be recounted in a different order (but with the same muted self-discovery), the book would not suffer. Neither the chronology of traditional autobiography nor the character development of all novels except the picaresque, governs the narrative method. At the beginning of the book Denton runs away from school; at the end of the book, influenced by his best friend and his father, he agrees to go to Art School. And yet, for all the seeming circularity, there are direction markers.

One of them is stylistic; the radiant clarity of each incident, of each detail in each incident, is surely an effort to see and describe with "maiden" eyes; by contrast, the effects in *A Voice through A Cloud* are *presented* as pondered upon. And imposed upon Welch's fascination with all detail is a veritable obsession with clothes and names—particularly his own. The school uniform, a woman friend's clothes, sandals in the Country Club, formal attire, masquerade attire, his lost coat are as important as people in the book. Only slightly less does he dwell on what others call him—Welch, Denton, young master, Maurice, mate, Punky. By means of name and costume, Denton seeks, on this maiden voyage, his own identity. Nor is it neatly waiting for him at the end of the book, when, maiden voyage over, he embarks for England and responsibility. Instead, after waving good-bye to the woman he has only just recognized as his best friend, he sheds tears for that period when perceptions and imagination are at their all-time pinnacle, before they are eroded by commitments of maturity. (pp. 154-56)

In a sense, *A Voice through A Cloud,* Welch's last, almost completed book is also a voyage, a voyage of gradual recovery from a near-fatal accident; from the book itself, one could not know that the voyage ends in the death of the hero. Moreover, although every commentator has remarked upon his fantastic courage, writing on as he lay dying in anguish, Welch is scrupulous to portray a whining, complaining, self-centered invalid. Compressed into this recital of six months of illness is the querulous, hypochondriacal old age Welch was never to enjoy. Minute particulars are detailed of symptoms, surroundings, and pains; of nurse, patient, and doctor; visitors from the outer world flicker and disappear. There are terrible moments of triumph as fellow-patients die; there is a brief flirtation with Christian Science; there is the final bondage to the doctor he trusts.

In this book, too, Denton gives attention, after the first nightmare days when he is obsessed only with his physical torment, to what he is called and what he wears. The progression is poignant: from a bed number to Punky; from hospital pyjamas to his own pyjamas and robe and, finally, to "normal" clothes—old, new, and borrowed. Places and objects, given the invalid's circumscribed surroundings, take on more importance than in *Maiden Voyage,* and people, even apart from their professional functions, slowly come to mean more. Here again, the title is helpful in indicating Welch's rationale of selection.

When first regaining consciousness after the accident, he hears

> . . . a voice through a great cloud of agony and sickness. The voice was asking questions. It seemed to be opening and closing like a concertina. The words were loud, as the swelling notes of an organ, then they melted to the tiniest tinkle of water in a glass.

The voice, specifically, is that of the policeman who comes upon Denton Welch after the accident; it is also the voice of the outer world, forming unclear words, empty of meaning if rich in sound; through the cloud of his anguish, Denton Welch has attempted to answer its questions and register its sound.

In contrast to *Maiden Voyage* where the voyage theme is repeated at a literal level, the voice through a cloud *becomes* the book, without further explicit reference to it. There is, however, a curious passage on clouds which may relate to both meaning and title of *A Voice through A Cloud.* While he is out walking along the shore with Dr. Farley, even as he broods on their ultimate isolation from one another, Denton recognizes that Dr. Farley's firm help has saved him from the seduction of the sea "curling at me, pawing at me, wanting me to run back to float out on it and disappear." Then, in an unparalleled apostrophe, Denton invokes the elements of this seaside scene:

> Cold moment on the beach, curving stones under my feet, curling clouds sweeping down low, threatening my head with your sailing grey stomachs; nothing could make me forget you.

The mysterious menace of the sea has been transferred to the clouds, for both sea and clouds are rich in their suggestions of infinitude. This rhapsodic address shouts Denton's defiance at two levels: against the dissolution of that friendship evoked by the scene—a dissolution upon which the book ends; and against that death which was immanent in the accident—a death which actually ended the book. (pp. 156-57)

Though some reviewers have accused him of seeking too many details ("a maladif preoccupation with minutiae" Jocelyn Brooke calls it in his introduction to Welch's *Journals* [see entry dated 1952 in Additional Bibliography]), this preoccupation is rarely purple-patchy; descriptions are either integrated with dialogue and incident, or so brief and specific that the object is seized in its distinguishing features. Thus, on the very first page of *Maiden Voyage,* we find:

> The trains inside the station were lying close together like big worms. I saw that one was going to Salisbury. I thought, I'll go there. I had seen it once with my mother; we had been to look at the cathedral. She was dead now. I ran to buy my ticket.

Here the choppy, disconnected detail is functional. The juxtaposition of important and trivial—a dead mother and a train ticket—is essential and characteristic. The trains prepare both for the trip to Salisbury and the maiden voyage; the worms with their suggestion of graves prepare for the dead mother. In the rest of the chapter, mother, cathedral, and town of Salisbury all serve to emphasize Denton's loneliness—a major motif of the book, even though it is never baldly stated.

Usually, however, details are less stripped; frequently they are rich in emotional overtones. Thus, after the accident:

> . . . As I saw the sun glint on [the dahlia's] tongue petals, flashing them into scarlet spears, and on its smaller spoon petals, making them brim over as with molten sealing-wax, I was filled with an extraordinary upsurge of delight . . . For a moment my whole body was concentrated on the flower.
>
> *(A Voice through A Cloud)*

But more often, thing and image provide their own sensual excuse for being:

> . . . tiny vinaigrettes with pieces of aromatic sponge still imprisoned behind golden grills
>
> *(Maiden Voyage)*

> The room seemed like a brown casserole, a baked dish, warm and comforting and heavy.
>
> *(A Voice through A Cloud)*

From the daintiest to the densest, objects seem extraordinarily significant to Welch. The final quotation indicates best his astonishing response to the inanimate—a response that seemed to astonish even himself.

> I was thinking of that stained oak furniture and those dirty, cosy carpets and curtains, filling the house to the very attics. They watched and waited, watched and waited, preserving a suffocating calm. Each object held its breath, magnetizing the dust, charming every mote into settling; not even a tremor, a tickle, a wriggle of the skin through endless days and nights. I wondered again how furnishings were able to express this patient, silent, guardian quality.
>
> *(A Voice through A Cloud)*

Welch's readers wonder less, for both the object-in-itself and its emotional aura come to us through Welch's vivid descriptions. In both books, beneath an overall flatness of tone, there is a tension between the thingness of things and their evocative powers—a tension which I believe to be a major source of his literary strength.

Although these books lack both studied suspense and classical conflict, there is a structural substitute in the polarity between Welch's extreme self-awareness on the one hand, and his extreme thing-awareness on the other. And these awarenesses relate Welch to two separate strands in modern fiction: the self-preoccupation links to the English picaresque, and the thing-concentration to the French objective. Denton Welch, like many "Angry" authors, centers his work on a single character, bouncing through a series of non-sequential (and often non-consequential) adventures. But at the same time, like the French objectivists, Welch insists upon the valid and vivid immediacy of surrounding phenomena—to such an extent that he occasionally skirts the pathetic fallacy. Although his influence is improbable, working as he did in semi-isolation, Welch anticipated two of the major trends in the contemporary novel. (pp. 158-59)

Ruby Cohn, "A Few Novel Techniques of Denton Welch," in Perspective, Vol. 10, No. 3, Summer-Autumn, 1958, pp. 153-59.

JULIAN SYMONS (essay date 1963)

[*Symons has been highly praised for his contributions to the genres of biography and detective fiction. His popular biographies of Charles Dickens, Thomas Carlyle, and his brother A. J. A. Symons are considered excellent introductions to those writers. Symons is better known, however, for such crime novels as* The Immaterial Murder Case *(1945),* The Thirty-first of February *(1950), and* The Progress of a Crime *(1960). In the following excerpt, Symons attacks Welch and his writings.*]

What was Welch's reason for existence as a writer? The spring of it was a complete narcissistic self-absorption. It is not merely that all his work is autobiographical and most of it written in the first person, but that really he is not capable of seeing anything or person except in relation to himself. His descriptions of people are rarely sharply visual, his descriptions of places hardly ever take on the obsessional quality that may turn neurosis into art. His style avoids the preciosity of his drawings and the sub-Housmanic bathos of his verse ("O Roger I shall yet remember, In the winter's wet December"). There are a good many vivid images to be found in his work, but their effect is limited by the poverty of his subjects. These are his own youth, food—which is described at length in a way less adolescent than childish, with much emphasis on sweet cakes and toothsome delicacies—and sex, which is approached in a way both timid and disagreeable.

A Voice through a Cloud, in which he tells the story of the bicycling accident which he suffered at the age of twenty and from the effects of which he never fully recovered, is by a long chalk his best work. Here the description of the eighteenth-century house at Beckenham which he visited before the accident, with its colonnades, its splendid drawing-room, its tea-urn and advertisements for Schweppes and Player's, is brilliantly contrasted with the new and terrible world of pain which he enters after the accident. Yet even here Welch is the only figure with any reality: the doctors, nurses, friends, other patients, are shadows lacking individuality. The fragment of a novel included in *A Last Sheaf* but omitted from this selection begins excellently with an account of a grotesque female model at an art school, but it quickly collapses into homosexual fantasy.

The accounts of Welch's work had left me unprepared for the degree and extent of this fantasy. In a characteristic short story called **"When I Was Thirteen"** the narrator, who is on holiday in Switzerland with his elder brother, goes out for the day with an undergraduate named Archer. At the end of the day the two return to Archer's chalet. There the narrator massages his leg ("His calf was like a firm sponge ball. His thigh, swelling out, amazed me"), smells his foot "in its woolly, hairy, humid casing of sock," scrubs his back with a nailbrush ("Delicious tremors seemed to be passing through Archer"), bathes in his already used water, gets slightly drunk at dinner and is taken back to the chalet by Archer and put to bed. Technically their relationship has been innocent, but when on the following morning his brother learns what has happened he beats the boy, yelling at him in a hoarse, mad, religious voice, "Bastard, Devil, Harlot, Sod!"

Now, one can see that this anecdote might have been successful if it had been pointed to show the narrator's realisation of his own nature: but it is not told in that way at all. Here and throughout his writing Welch was unable to resist the luxury of titillating his own emotions by describing in detail the attraction of lovely young toughs. His narrators are forever taking off their shirts, letting their trousers drop to the ground, and comparing their own soft white bodies with the hardness of—say—that of the tramp in **"The Barn"** ("Through a rent in his trousers I could see his hard thigh") or the boys seen engaging in horseplay with a young man whose legs "glinted like silk" and were "like those of a wild animal." I do not think it is an overstatement to call the continual expression of these adolescent fantasies disagreeable and dreary. Frederick Rolfe, Baron Corvo, who was also a frustrated homosexual, was able in more than one book to make the imaginative effort needed to turn obsession into art. Welch never got further than writing about himself. [In his introduction to *Denton Welch: Extracts from His Published Works* (see excerpt dated 1963)], Mr. Brooke truly says that his work never developed, and the immaturity of adolescence was something to which his literary *persona* desperately clung. He almost always wrote about himself as a very young person, much younger than in fact he was. Dame Edith Sitwell, in her foreword to his first book [see excerpt dated 1943], *Maiden Voyage,* wrote of the "touching very youthful creature who is the central character," and it is difficult not to feel that the book has also been written by a very youthful creature. Welch was in fact twenty-eight years old when it was published.

There remains the question why such a high valuation was ever placed upon Denton Welch's work. The answer is interesting. The war period is thought of as a time when most writing was "over-solemn or boringly 'documentary' . . . hardly less drab and uninspiring than the 'utility' paper upon which it was printed," to quote Mr. Brooke. . . . It is perfectly true that the war period was like that, but most periods contain their opposites, and just as the aesthetic Nineties were also the time in which the talents of Wells and Kipling flowered, so an extreme and conscious aestheticism flourished in what is thought of as this "documentary" period. Welch's books filled the gap that was waiting for the appearance of a young "aesthetic" genius. Had they been published a decade later they would have caused much less critical excitement, and only one of them is now in print. He was a pathetic rather than a tragic figure. The pathetic thing about his career as a writer was not really the accident against the effects of which he struggled: it was the fact that when he had told the story of this accident he really had nothing more to say.

Julian Symons, "A Contrary Talent," in The Spectator, Vol. 210, No. 7040, May 31, 1963, p. 709.

JOCELYN BROOKE (essay date 1963)

[*Brooke was an English novelist and art critic whose works include book-length studies of Elizabeth Bowen, Ronald Firbank, and Aldous Huxley. He also edited Welch's journals for publication as well as a selection of Welch's prose and poetry. In the following excerpt from his introduction to the latter volume, Brooke discusses the stylistic traits and estimates the importance of Welch's works.*]

I first heard of Denton Welch in 1944, when a short story of his, **"The Barn,"** appeared in John Lehmann's miscellany *New Writing and Daylight*. The writer's name was unknown to me, but I was immediately impressed by the story which, slight as it was, struck me as being the product of a genuine and original talent. There was something direct, spontaneous, even a bit naïve, about it, and it seemed to have been written purely for the author's pleasure: all of which I found most refreshing, at a time when so much writing tended to be over-solemn or boringly "documentary," and hardly less drab and uninspiring than the "utility" paper upon which it was printed.

"The Barn," a brief reminiscence of childhood, seemed to belong to a different, a pre-war world. Who, I wondered, was Denton Welch? I myself was on active service in Italy at the time, and there was no means of satisfying my curiosity. One could, however, deduce a certain amount from internal evidence: **"The Barn"** was obviously the work of somebody fairly young, and one had the feeling, too (though this was the merest guess-work), that the author had somehow contrived to remain aloof—both morally and physically—from the war; plainly he felt an obsessional interest in his own past; and it could be inferred that he was homosexual.

Later, when I came to read his other work, and had made judicious inquiries about him, I found that these suppositions were mainly correct: a cruel accident at the age of twenty had left him a permanent invalid, totally unfitted for any form of war service, and very largely debarred from the pleasures and activities of ordinary life. It was hardly surprising that, in his writing, he should be chiefly preoccupied with the past, and that he should feel impelled, like Proust (another invalid), to reconstruct, with a wealth of nostalgic detail, the lost paradise of his childhood.

His total *oeuvre* forms, in fact, an extended though discontinuous autobiography. Nearly always he writes in the first person, and usually under his own name; occasionally he employs a pseudonymous, third-person narrative technique, as for instance in his second book, *In Youth Is Pleasure,* though here the leading character, Orvil Pym, is quite recognizably Denton Welch. Just how much he adapted or embroidered his own experiences for the purposes of Art is a matter of doubt; but it seems likely that very little, if any, of his work is pure fiction. Even in such a story as **"The Fire in the Wood,"** narrated from the point of view of a woman, it is evident that the writer himself has merely assumed, from prudential motives, a feminine disguise. (pp. vii-viii)

It has always seemed to me rather surprising that Denton Welch, preoccupied as he was with his own childhood, should have written so little about his schooldays: there is a flashback to Repton in *Maiden Voyage,* another in the *Journals,* and a few passing references elsewhere, but no continuous account of his experiences as a schoolboy. The reason for this omission is, I think, that Denton Welch really only enjoyed writing about what pleased or excited him, or about experiences which he felt to be of importance in his own development. No doubt the humdrum routine of school life seemed to him merely an intolerable bore, both at the time and in retrospect; passive suffering, said Yeats, is not a theme for poetry, nor (as he might have added, perhaps with greater truth) is sheer boredom, and if Denton Welch wrote mainly in prose, his whole approach to writing—and indeed to painting as well—was that of a poet. (p. ix)

"How tedious the little details seem, written down," he notes in his *Journals,* "yet it is always that littleness that seems to have banked up behind it, great walls of fight and resistance." In his writing he is fond of describing such "little details," and sometimes, indeed, he rather overdoes it, though he has

an extraordinary aptitude for communicating his own enthusiasm for his small treasures: it is as though a highly gifted and lively child were expatiating upon the attractions of a new toy.

It is this feminine, rather *chichi* side of him which is, I think, mainly reflected in his painting; what one misses, in his pictures, is the lyrical freshness of his response to the life around him which characterizes his writing. By contrast his painting seems *voulu,* over-contrived and lacking in force and liveliness. (pp. xii-xiii)

His writing has all the appearance of being dashed off spontaneously and at great speed, yet this impression is, as so often, deceptive: in fact, he usually wrote with great difficulty, and was constantly revising his work.

> The murderous part of writing, the trying to
> force thought into a form that can be shared by
> others, is something that one shrinks and turns
> away from in sick distaste. . . . But it will never
> stop gnawing. There is always the longing to
> put the thoughts into the crude mincing-machine.
> It is as if a madman were determined to make
> all the delicacies of a perfect music come through
> a brass trombone.
>
> *(Journals)*

For him, indeed, his writing was quite literally a "murderous"—or suicidal—process. During the last two years of his life, in spite of his rapidly worsening health, he was simultaneously engaged upon two books, besides sketching out other projects and, from time to time, making long entries in his journals, which for the most part are as carefully written as his other work, and which there is every reason to suppose he intended for eventual publication. For an invalid, the sheer bulk of his literary output—all produced in the years after his accident—is astonishing. (pp. xiii-xiv)

If his courage was extraordinary, so too was his almost total lack of self-pity. It is very seldom apparent in his writing, and from all accounts he remained outwardly stoical even during the worst phases of his illness. Every imaginative writer, of course—autobiographical or otherwise—projects into his work some kind of *persona,* a public image of himself which we are wont to refer to as his "literary personality," implying something distinct from his private character, to which it may or may not bear a recognizable relationship. I should say that in the case of Denton Welch these two "selves"—the man and the *persona*—were more nearly identical than is usually the case. Autobiographers, from Rousseau onwards, however honest by intention, have seldom resisted the temptation to exhibit themselves in the most favourable light, and to soft-pedal their own weaknesses, or—worse still—to make virtues out of their defects. About certain aspects of himself Denton Welch could not be quite frank: he could not, for instance, refer directly to his own homosexuality, though he makes it abundantly obvious by implication. It was not that he was ashamed of it, or thought it wrong; but publishers, even as lately as the nineteen-forties, were apt to shy at any open discussion of the subject. This apart, however, he reveals himself with a disarming naïveté: he makes no attempt, for instance, to disguise his vanity as an author, and his delight in his own small celebrity (as revealed in the *Journals*) would be embarrassing if it were not so ingenuous. After all, it *was* very exciting for an almost unknown writer to receive a letter of enthusiastic praise from Edith Sitwell, and who can blame him for saying so?

It is the same with his snobbishness: he was, without a doubt, easily impressed by social grandeur but, here again, his attitude is so naïve and childlike that one finds it easy to forgive him. (pp. xiv-xv)

One reviewer remarked of him that he had a "suburban mind" and the comment, if uncharitable, is perhaps not quite undeserved: his "culture," no doubt, was in part derivative, and based upon intellectual snobbery, but in the light of his achievement the fact seems of little importance. It is easy to point out his defects, both as a man and as a writer; but one has only to re-read *Maiden Voyage* or *A Voice through a Cloud* to realize how triumphantly he was enabled to transcend his limitations.

> When I read about William Blake, I know what I am for. I must never be afraid of my own foolishness, only of pretension. And whatever I have I must use, painting, poetry, prose—not proudly think it is not good enough and so lock it inside for fear of laughing, sneering. . . .
>
> *(Journals)*

This passage, I think, sums up admirably Denton Welch's intentions as an artist and his attitude towards his own work. He knew that his talent was primarily a lyrical one, and that he must give it free play; though himself an extremely self-conscious person, he realized to the full the dangers of self-consciousness, the "fear of laughing, sneering." He was well aware, too, of the limitations imposed by his egocentricity: he knew that he could only write really well about himself, or about other people in relation to himself, and seldom adopted an objective attitude which he knew himself unable to sustain.

During the last half-century English writing has, I believe, suffered more than it has gained from the growing sophistication of the reading public. There has been an increasing tendency, among serious writers, to conform to certain critical standards, and to adopt those moral or philosophical attitudes which happen to be fashionable at the moment. Above all, the writer has become—as Denton Welch recognized—excessively self-conscious, and liable to conceal or disguise the emotional sources of his inspiration, from a fear of being written off as naïve or exhibitionist. Denton Welch never succumbed to this temptation: though in some respects very sophisticated, he was basically, I think, a *naif;* and he was convinced—quite rightly—that he must have the courage of his own naïveté. It is this blend of subtlety and simplicity, of the worldly and the childlike, which gives his writing its peculiar and highly original flavour.

For Denton Welch, whether one admires him or not, was a true original: his work is remarkably free from obvious literary influences, and this might lead one to suppose that he was less well read than was in fact the case. His style is what Cyril Connolly would call "anti-mandarin," he never indulges in fine writing, nor uses a long word where a short one will do, and he makes free use of slang and colloquialisms. Though he cared greatly for literary values, he might almost be described as anti-literary, for to him Life was more important than Art; he had something to say, and the manner in which he said it was of secondary importance. His every utterance has an air of being entirely natural and spontaneous: one might, as one reads him, be listening to his own voice as he chats to a friend over the fire. This off-hand, colloquial manner occasionally reminds one of Christopher Isherwood, but the resemblance is only superficial: Denton Welch has none of Isherwood's glib, self-protective detachment, he makes no pretence of being a mere camera-eye. His observation of the world about him is exact and true, but heightened, nearly always, by a deeply imaginative perception of what lies beneath the surface. Thus, in describing a crowd seen from the top of a bus, he will write: "Along the pavement thronged the people, like bottles walking; their heads as inexpressive as round stoppers." That, in itself, is a vivid and effective description; but he goes on to say: "What if some god or giant should bend down and take several of the stoppers out? I thought. Inside there would only be black, churning depths like bile, or bitter medicine."

For all his apparent casualness, he has an extraordinary sureness of touch: as Dame Edith Sitwell remarked in her preface to *Maiden Voyage* [see excerpt dated 1943], he "uses words as only a born writer uses them. He never fumbles." Consider, for example, the description of the young man who befriends him in **"When I Was Thirteen"**:

> He had broad shoulders but was not tall. He had a look of strength and solidity which I admired and envied. He had rather a nice pug face with insignificant nose and broad cheeks. Sometimes, when he was animated, a tassel of fair, almost colourless, hair would fall across his forehead, half covering one eye. He had a thick beautiful neck, rather meaty barbarian hands, and a skin as smooth and evenly coloured as a pink fondant. . . .

With a minimum of fuss and in the simplest possible language Denton Welch hits off the young man's appearance exactly, so that we not only see him, but share the narrator's admiration for his physical charm. Notice, too, how his skin is compared to a "pink fondant": it is precisely the simile which might be expected to occur to a schoolboy of thirteen.

It is the same with descriptions of landscapes, interiors of houses or churches, and so forth: Denton Welch makes us feel the precise atmosphere, the "inscape" of the place he is describing, without ever resorting to a deliberately poetic or "evocative" diction. He achieves this, I think, chiefly by his selection and placing of significant or suggestive details. He was by nature unusually observant, and seems to have made a conscious effort to cultivate the faculty. In describing a riverside scene, for instance (in his journal), he remarks: "I watched carefully until I had remembered the sight," and the description itself has a haunting, almost *trompe l'oeil* vividness which suggests, not so much a photograph, as the lovingly painted foreground of some pre-Raphaelite picture.

Noteworthy, too, is his brisk and economical method of setting a scene: he wastes no time on "build-up," but plunges us at once *in medias res.* A good example is the opening passage of *A Voice through a Cloud;* in a short paragraph he gives us all the essential facts about the narrator, his background and his present situation. Most novelists would have taken several pages to do as much; Denton Welch says all that is necessary in less than a hundred words. This compact, almost telegraphic method of writing was partly dictated, no doubt, by the circumstances of his life: he was aware, always, of writing against time, and knew that what he had to say must be said briefly and succinctly or not at all.

All his writing is haunted by a sense of the transitoriness of life; the reasons for this are, of course, in his case obvious enough, yet many of his "epiphanies"—as Joyce would have called them—remain valid even for those of us who can expect to live out the normal term. A good example is the description (in the *Journals*) of a young man bathing. . . . This episode occurred some years before Denton's accident, and is related retrospectively, yet one feels that, if he had written it down at the time, his reactions would have been very similar. He is frankly thrilled by the young man ("He was all that I was not—stalwart, confident and settled into a 'manly' life"), and plainly finds him sexually attractive; yet when his new friend begins to talk of "being drunk and brawling," he thinks immediately—and not without a touch of priggishness—of how "the beer would decay his teeth or that they would be knocked out in the fights. This caused me the sort of pain one feels when some beautifully-made and intricate thing is threatened." There is a vague suggestion that they should go on a walking-tour together, but Denton is "too clear-sighted not to see the difficulties of money and also of temperament," and does not commit himself. Then, when the young man is gone, he feels "unbearably angry and frustrated. . . . I jerked my bicycle out of the hedge and pedalled viciously, cursing God and everybody, pouring scorn and pity in a deluge all over myself."

The theme of sexual frustration is a recurrent one in his work, and though this may be partly due to the disaster which made any erotic fulfilment impossible for him, it is fairly evident, I think, that even without what he refers to as his "obscene accident," he would have remained sexually timid and unenterprising. Though he greatly enjoyed the company of congenial people, he was by temperament a solitary, and—like a good many other artists—suffered from a fear of becoming emotionally involved.

I have said that the work of Denton Welch shows few literary influences, but if I were asked to name the writer with whom he has the closest affinity, I should without hesitation say D. H. Lawrence. I do not, of course, mean that Denton Welch is in the least *like* Lawrence, nor am I suggesting that he is a writer of comparable stature. The most *petit* of *petits maîtres* ["fop," "dandy"] (as one reviewer called him), he worked on a minuscule scale and had no particular axe to grind; yet his attitude to life and art is basically the same as Lawrence's, in that it implies an habitual affirmation of human values and a profound respect for the individual. As much as Lawrence, Denton Welch loathed the industrialized society in which he lived, and the increasing predominance of the intellect over the instinctive life of the body. I have suggested that he was "anti-literary," and he might fairly be called anti-intellectual as well. How often in his writing does he celebrate the joys of a purely physical existence, contrasting them, by implication, with the inhibited and devitalized pleasures of "civilized" life; and how vividly—like Lawrence before him—does he evoke the underlying vacuity and hopelessness of a society which, rejecting the traditions of its forebears, has evolved no stable or satisfying system of values to replace them. Describing the peace celebrations of 1946, he writes of the crowd round a bonfire: "The people stared, there was a great weight of emptiness. I felt that everybody was shamefaced and deadened—dumb, watching, waiting-for-death people. . . . I thought the whole night scene was a gaunt display of desperate failure. The people, for so short a time on the earth, watching their lives' hopelessness, as they stared into the flames. . . ."

It is almost certain that Denton Welch, like most young writers of his generation, was influenced by Lawrence's ideas, if not by his style. Yet one feels that, with or without Lawrence, his attitude would have been much the same, and that it can be largely attributed to the tragic circumstances of his own life. In other words, it was to a great extent a *compensatory* attitude,

enabling him to enjoy, vicariously and in imagination, the kind of life from which he was excluded. This can be seen at its most obvious in his innumerable descriptions of handsome young men—strangers, most of them, encountered casually in the fields or merely glimpsed in passing from his car or bicycle. It is these passages which, more than anything else in his work, remind one of Lawrence: one recalls, for instance, the chapter called "A Poem of Friendship" in *The White Peacock*, or the lyrical descriptions of the male body in *Women in Love;* nor, perhaps, is the parallel a purely literary one, for Lawrence, too, was a sick man, and—though loth to admit it—profoundly and predominantly homosexual.

Denton Welch was in love with life, passionately and disinterestedly, though it was a love which was doomed to be, as it were, unrequited, and he was capable, at times, of cursing "whatever brute or blackguard made the world." His most notable gift, perhaps, was for capturing and fixing the minor and more transient pleasures which came his way, and he is an adept at portraying what Cyril Connolly has called "the beauty of the moment, the gaiety and sadness, the fugitive distress of hedonism" (Mr Connolly's words refer to Ronald Firbank, with whom, again—though no two writers could be more dissimilar—Denton Welch has certain affinities). He had, above all, a faculty for making one see familiar things with a heightened vividness: a flower, a fragment of architecture or some other detail of the country scene is spotlighted, so to speak, by his imagination, and springs into sudden life, like a photograph seen through a stereoscopic lens.

This hypersensitive and passionate response to life may have resulted, as I have suggested, from the state of his health, yet it is not, for that reason, any the less commendable or attractive. Given his circumstances, many an imaginative man would have been tempted to retreat—like Lawrence's Sir Clifford Chatterley, who suffered from similar disabilities—into a sterile intellectualism, rejecting the life of the senses, and venting his bitterness upon others more fortunate than himself. Denton Welch did none of these things: he continued, up till the very end of his life, to respond with an almost undiminished vitality to the beauty of the visible world, and to the claims of friendship and affection.

I have said that his approach to his work was that of a poet, by which I mean that everything he wrote sprang directly from his imagination, even though it had to be forced through what he calls the "crude mincing-machine" of the conscious intellect. He will be remembered, of course, mainly for his prose, yet he did in fact write a great many poems, a few of which are reprinted in this volume. Verse was not his *métier,* and one imagines that he realized it: his poems are more or less on a par with his paintings—essays in a form which he found too demanding and too difficult. Yet his brief lyrics have an odd, freakish charm; they are amateurish and slipshod, for the most part, but at any rate they are vividly and abundantly *alive,* and the best of them, I think, recall Lawrence's *Pansies.*

It is often said that Denton Welch's early death was a serious loss to English letters. That he should have died so young was of course lamentable, but the tragedy, I think, was a personal rather than a literary one. It seems probable that, at the time of his death, he had said most of what he wanted to say; there might, if he had lived, have been other books—further fragments of autobiography, odd episodes and impressions which had not found a place in the previous works; yet there was already a danger of this particular vein becoming overworked, and one cannot easily envisage him launching out into an entirely different *kind* of writing. As it stands, his total output has a curious completeness and homogeneity: he cannot be said to have developed very much as a writer, for his latest work is hardly to be distinguished, in the matter of style or technique, from his earliest. There is a quality of rather gawky, coltish immaturity about all his writing, and one would be hard put to it, if one didn't know the dates of publication, to place his works in chronological order of composition; nor, for that matter—since three of his books were published posthumously—are these dates a very reliable guide.

I think myself that he is at his best in his shorter pieces, with the possible exception of *A Voice through a Cloud*. He had not much sense of form, and a book of novel-length was apt to put too great a strain upon his technical resources. He is such an exceedingly personal writer, he put so much of himself into his books, that it is hard to be objective about him, and any final assessment of his merits is therefore difficult. He is very much the sort of author whom one either immediately likes or immediately dislikes, depending upon whether or not one happens to be in sympathy with the kind of person he was. Without a doubt he was a very minor artist, yet he did, I think, achieve almost perfectly what he set out to do—in which, one is tempted to add, he was more successful than Lawrence, who, despite his enormous powers, too often failed to do justice to his conceptions, and (in his later works at any rate) lapsed with an increasing frequency into bathos and muddled thinking. The writing of Denton Welch, though he worked on a tiny scale, is all of a piece; he didn't aim very high, but his aim was sure, and he seldom missed his target.

His preoccupation with what, to many readers, will seem mere *trivia*, may well give an impression of triviality; and his obsession—more noticeable in the earlier than in the later books—with adolescent sexuality, will strike others as morbid or as just plain nasty. I myself have at times felt slightly irritated by his dolls'-houses, his cracked Nankin cups and so forth, and have found myself growing a trifle impatient, too, with the perpetual body-brooding. He might so easily, one feels, have been both trivial and nasty; yet somehow he isn't, his silliest and most unpleasant passages are just saved by some quality which is hard to define, but which can only, I think, be described as a touch of genius.

The word has been so loosely used that it requires definition. Lawrence, says Aldous Huxley, was possessed by a *daimon* which drove him onward relentlessly—and often against his will—to compose his novels and poems; and this, I think, is roughly what most of us mean by genius as opposed to mere talent. Genius implies some force or impulsion existing almost independently of the artist's normal personality, by which he is quite literally "possessed"; and it seems to me that Denton Welch, like Lawrence, was also possessed in this sense. Granted that his *daimon,* compared with that of Lawrence, was of a minor and inferior breed, I think that it was a real *daimon* nonetheless, and that the effect of its ministrations was to transmute what would have otherwise been an agreeable minor talent into something of greater and more permanent value. (pp. xvi-xxiv)

> *Jocelyn Brooke, in an introduction to* Denton Welch: Extracts from His Published Works *by Denton Welch, edited by Jocelyn Brooke, Chapman & Hall Ltd., 1963, pp. vii-xxvi.*

CYRIL CONNOLLY   (essay date 1963)

[*Connolly was an English novelist and critic who reviewed books for various prominent English periodicals from 1927 until his* *death in 1974. He was also the founding editor of the respected literary monthly* Horizon *(1939-50) and was considered a remarkably hard-to-please critic. In the following excerpt, Connolly expresses his admiration for* The Denton Welch Journals.]

The journal of a sedentary writer is an exercise in fascination. Confined in one place, condemned to a certain monotony, deprived of the resources of dialogue and plot, the writer pits his mind, his privacy, the whole quality of his imagination against the reading public. Will he lose them or hold them? One might see this as the supreme test of a contemporary writer, the mark of the professional rather than the amateur. Denton Welch passes it with flying colours. I have read every word of this long book [*The Denton Welch Journals*] with increasing delight, I have blotted out wind and rain, age and infirmity, anxiety and want in the recesses of his keen, bright, fresh, sensuous thought-stream and lived happily behind his mischievous observant eye.

A doomed and youthful poet, condemned to a horrible and lingering death by a twist of blind chance . . . , he yet manages to exude a quiet happiness as well as courage, intelligence and determination, while our foreknowledge of his death (a few weeks after the journal breaks off in 1948) illuminates many of the trivial entries with a lyrical underglaze as poignant as the becalmed sadness of the exquisite idling creatures in the dying Watteau's "Halt During the Chase." (p. 328)

Disease ever present, and the shadow of death, as if conscious of the meaningless cruelty to which they had condemned him, mitigated his fate by sharpening his gifts of clarity, intuition, an unfailing effortless liaison with the right words. One is never conscious of hard work and erasures: his style ripens like an October pear that measures every hour of sunshine against the inevitable frost. (pp. 328-29)

Denton Welch had some of the clairvoyance of genius and a little of the terrible malice of the sick, he glimpsed the appalling vulgarity inseparable from rude health except in the bodies of the Housmanesque farm labourers whom he could observe on his walks in their natural surroundings. Otherwise he was a very old-fashioned young man. Born in 1915, the younger son of a successful China merchant from Shanghai, utterly English in outlook and background, a felicitous misfit, he gave his work the atmosphere of the early 'twenties. Mr. Jocelyn Brooke, in his wise introduction, compares him to Firbank [see excerpt dated 1963]. I am also reminded of Barbellion, Katherine Mansfield, Mr. E. M. Forster.

He adored the eighteenth century and writes charmingly about period doll's houses, teapots and teaspoons, china, silver . . . the luxurious warmth and colour of the drawing room as it appears to those who see it from the nursery. Old houses he also loved and the old people who lived in them. Like many artists he was mildly snobbish and thus fortunately aware of the magical and sombre poetry of the Fall of the most haunted of all houses of Usher, the aristocratic civilisation built up by the English over two hundred years of plenty.

This is, however, but one aspect. It is a happy and absorbing book because the writer was happily absorbed by simple things. Mid-Kent, half suburban, half huge romantic park, is delineated in all weathers with careless affection; curious people come and go; we find ourselves in a bright microcosm of childhood as if we were inside a glass ball where it is snowing on red roofs and little painted people. I hope others will make their way inside and enjoy this picture of the happy, wholesome, dedicated monotony of the artistic life. (pp. 329-30)

Cyril Connolly, "Denton Welch," in his Previous Convictions, *Hamish Hamilton, 1963, pp. 328-30.*

JOHN UPDIKE (essay date 1966)

[*Considered a perceptive observer of the human condition and an extraordinary stylist, Updike is one of America's most distinguished men of letters. Best known for such novels as* Rabbit Run *(1960),* Rabbit Redux *(1971), and* Rabbit Is Rich *(1981), he is a chronicler of life in Protestant, middle-class America. Against this setting and in concurrence with his interpretation of the thought of Soren Kierkegaard and of Karl Barth, Updike presents people searching for meaning in their lives while facing the painful awareness of their mortality and basic powerlessness. A contributor of literary reviews to various periodicals, he has frequently written the "Books" column in the* New Yorker *since 1955. In the following excerpt, Updike praises the narrative artistry of* A Voice through a Cloud.]

"Promising" is a pale term of praise reviewers customarily employ to excuse themselves from reading closely the work at hand. But the term applies with some force to Denton Welch. . . . In his thirteen years of pain and invalidism, Welch composed three novels, of which the last, entitled *A Voice through a Cloud,* was left uncompleted at his death. While not quite a masterpiece (not only does it not end, it gives no sign of knowing how to end), the book is, especially in its first half, masterly: a fine intelligence, a brave candor, a voracious eye, and a sweet, fresh sense of prose are exercised. Possibly these gifts, liberated to wider use by a healthy life, would have proved equal to many subjects. It is also possible that Welch's gifts were best realized by the one subject he had—the effects of his absurd and savage accident—and that nothing else would have burnt away so much of his dilettantism or turned his somewhat sinister detachment to such good artistic account. Again, it could be argued that save for his accident he would have outgrown the distrustful and diffident brilliance of a schoolboy. But in the end a man is what happens to him plus what he does. In a world aswarm with might-have-beens, Welch took his shortened life, his remittances of pain and fever, and delivered a unique account of shattered flesh and refracted spirit.

This "novel," in which Welch rechristened himself Maurice and presumably used the convenience of fiction to change some names and fake a few details, begins with the hero, a London art student, setting out on his bicycle for his uncle's vicarage in Surrey. The landscape and a tea shoppe are rather adjectivally evoked; the hero resumes his pleasant ride; then

> I heard a voice through a great cloud of agony and sickness. The voice was asking questions. It seemed to be opening and closing like a concertina. The words were loud, as the swelling notes of an organ, then they melted to the tiniest wiry tinkle of water in a glass.
>
> I knew that I was lying on my back on the grass; I could feel the shiny blades on my neck. I was staring at the sky and I could not move. Everything about me seemed to be reeling and breaking up. My whole body was screaming with pain, filling my head with its roaring, and my eyes were swimming in a sort of gum mucilage. . . . Bright little points glittered all down the front of the liquid man kneeling beside me. I knew at once that he was a policeman, and I thought that, in his official capacity, he was

performing some ritual operation on me. There was a confusion in my mind between being brought to life—forceps, navel-cords, midwives—and being put to death—ropes, axes, and black masks; but whatever it was that was happening, I felt that all men came to this at last.

In spite of certain lazy, boyish locutions ("the tiniest," "screaming with pain," "swimming in a sort of"), a private apocalypse is rendered with icy exactness, and throughout the succeeding pages of hospital ordeal Welch does not funk his essential task—the portrayal of "the savage change from fair to dark." . . . (pp. 223-24)

It is strange to realize how incidentally narrative fiction treats the physical base of human existence; food is an occasion for conversation, sleep an interval of action, elimination a joke. Bodies are felt as mobile scaffoldings for conversing sensibilities, and pain, that sensation of ultimate priority, is almost never (Tolstoy and Samuel Beckett are exceptions) rendered solidly. In Welch's narrative, agony precedes psychology; introspection takes place only as pain's monopoly loosens. (pp. 224-25)

The action of this narrative is the narrator's recovery of the world, a recovery effected without much assistance from other people. Welch, though he can do a sketch of a doomed eccentric as well as the next literate hospital patient, is not a creator of characters. All the persons he meets are depicted flatly, on the inner walls of a neurasthenia that probably existed before his catastrophe. At the worst, other people outrage and torture him—most of the hospital attendants he met struck him as sadists—and at best they merely disappoint and irritate, like static obstructing a delicate tuning-in. Welch/Maurice seeks rapport not with any other person but with the world at large, and it is remarkable, considering that more than ten years had lapsed since his accident, how fully, how delicately he can conjure up the sense impressions that make this search credible. . . .

As he ventures into the outer world, everything is hungrily snapped up—"the leathery gray spread of the sea," "the faint gunpowdery smell of new stone," "the broad leaves in the gutter, splendid, decaying, rich, like some rare food." Returning from the verge of oblivion, he writes of familiar sights as might a visitor from another planet:

> I had not been in a night street scene for a long time. I watched the people's faces as they pushed through the theatre doors. The faces changed when they passed from the street into the building. Outside they were more hardened, more scoured and flinty, tragic too from all they had withstood. Inside they grew more cushiony and fluid; they lost the vagrant, haunted look. The look of anxiety melted into the sparkling monkey, or the soft bear look.

In an age quick to label any sufficiently bleak and sententious novel "existential," here is a work, by an author born again out of agony into the world, that seems to reconstitute human existence particle by particle.

Fiction captures and holds our interest with two kinds of suspense: circumstantial suspense—the lowly appetite, aroused by even comic strips, to know the outcome of any unresolved situation—and what might be called gnostic suspense, the expectation that at any moment an illumination will occur. Bald plot caters to the first; style, wit of expression, truth of observation, vivid painterliness, brooding musicality, and all the elegant rest pay court to the second. Gnostic suspense is not negligible—almost alone it moves us through those many volumes of Proust—but it stands to the other rather like charm to sex in a woman. We hope for both, and can even be more durably satisfied by charm than by sex (all animals are sad after coitus and after reading a detective story); but charm remains the ancillary and dispensable quality.

Toward the end of *A Voice through a Cloud,* the hero acquires some use of his legs, and the plane of concern shifts from the struggle with oblivion to a search for suitable housing. The writing, though more polished than before, begins to feel aimless. Detail becomes obsessive. Maurice walks up an ordinary road of two-family dwellings: "There was something monstrous about the long avenue of coupled pink brick boxes. I felt that I was climbing up between gigantic naked Siamese twins with eyes all over their bodies." Circumstantial suspense is deliberately generated; old characters reappear and are skillfully "used." The book, as the dying author wearies, begins to act like a conventional novel. Though Welch had the abilities of a novelist, misfortune made him a kind of prophet, and it is as a prophetic document, a proclamation of our terrible fragility, that his book possesses value. (p. 241)

John Updike, "A Short Life," in his Picked-Up Pieces, *Alfred A. Knopf, 1975, pp. 223-227.*

[PETER GREEN] (essay date 1973)

[In the following excerpt, Green considers the nature and value of Welch's work and the development of his reputation among readers and critics.]

During the latter part of his short lifetime . . . , and for several years thereafter (posthumous work, the all-important *Journals* included, went on appearing at intervals to keep public interest in him alive), Denton Welch enjoyed a quite remarkable literary *succès d'estime*. The nature, scope, value, and antecedent causes of this popularity deserve a more careful examination than they have had. It is interesting, for instance, that much of Welch's spell evaporated on the other side of the Atlantic. Despite the fan letters from American intellectuals, despite the championship of W. H. Auden (himself, after all, English by birth and temperament), despite the ultimate purchase of his manuscripts and copyright by the University of Texas, Welch never achieved quite the same impact in the United States as he did in England. Some American reviewers of *Maiden Voyage* (now reprinted) called him, as he himself noted, "a snip and a snob, effeminate and obnoxious, saying that I sit better with Miss Sitwell than I do with them." But in England he not only impressed the *literati*—his books sold, in very respectable quantities. He became something of a cult. When one looks back on the period of his fame, only one other contemporary work springs to mind which had, at the time, a comparable impact on the public, especially on the young: and that, significantly enough was Cyril Connolly's *The Unquiet Grave*.

These facts are at once suggestive. It is no accident that Welch's work appealed so strongly to Connolly himself, who bracketed its author with Barbellion, Katherine Mansfield, and E. M. Forster, and had, indeed, been the first major editor to publish an article by him. . . . Both writers were introspective analysts of the hedonistic and suffering ego. Welch may never have actually borrowed that expressive term *Angst* from *The Unquiet*

Grave—it became a melancholy watchword among students and conscripts in the middle 1940s—but all his work acknowledges its brooding presence. Both, too, were conditioned, perhaps even more than they realized, by the intricate mandarin hierarchy of the prewar English class system. Welch was always more of an open rebel than Connolly, running away from Repton, screaming like a steam whistle when assaulted (no stiff upper lip there), pressurizing his family into letting him attend an art school; while Connolly, as he recounts in *Enemies of Promise*, nimbly scrambled through the Eton *cursus honorum* to end in top-hatted splendour as a member of Pop, an apotheosis which apparently, on his own account, marked him for life.

But Welch was marked too: the gods of the English copybook headings would not let him escape so easily. The chauffeured Daimler, the comfortable bourgeois background, the "brass cans, swaddled in towels" that adorned the bedrooms in his grandfather's house, the all-pervading upper middle-class ethos exuded by aunts and uncles in England, the starchy expatriate ghetto world which awaited him in Shanghai among his father's business associates—all these produced a world, as Eliot wrote, "assured of certain certainties," in which a total lack of curiosity about finance or politics (we never learn what Denton's father *does;* and troubles in China are only glanced at) is matched by a passionately observant eye for unrelated minutiae. It was from his social background that the young Welch naturally acquired that double hallmark of naivety and sophistication which stamps all his work, and was, until very recently, the cross which almost every educated English intellectual had to bear.

Hence, of course, the irritation which his work provoked in the United States. There is a passage from his autobiographical novel, *In Youth Is Pleasure,* which illustrates this quality to perfection. Orvil, the fifteen-year-old protagonist, is about to be collected from boarding school for the holidays by his father, who appears from Shanghai once every three years, a benign *deus ex machina,* in his symbolic black Daimler. Orvil feasts his eyes on this welcome apparition: "'I did not need so large a car for my Escape,' he thought: 'but Magic would never niggle, never send a Baby Austin'." Catch any American boy of fifteen looking at the world like that—even while insisting on Mom and Pop showing up in a Lincoln Continental as the only acceptable status symbol. If Denton Welch had genius, then, it was essentially an English *genius loci,* of the same shy, oblique kind which infuses L. P. Hartley's *Eustace and Hilda* trilogy, or the work of a writer such as Julian Fane. Like some wines, this manifestation of the English spirit, with its undertones of snobbery, ultra-sensitivity and sexual ambivalence, tends to travel badly.

Yet in what, if anything, did Denton Welch's genius consist? As a painter and draughtsman he remained to the end not only precious but derivative, his amateur charm too often overlaid with mere sentimental kitsch. He had no more illusions (to give him due credit) over this than he did over his poetry. "I keep on wondering," he noted in his journal, "if I'm producing semi-demi A. E. Housman." He was. We are left with his creative prose; but even here an *oeuvre* that depends so heavily on its creator's own life and character, which is spun almost literally, like a spider's web, out of his own guts, becomes hard indeed to detach from external considerations. What, in such a case *is* external or irrelevant?

Here we touch upon one of the most potent, and seductive, factors in the whole Denton Welch case. His life as such forms an almost irresistible paradigm of what Mario Praz labelled the Romantic Agony: incipient genius cut short by a cruel fate, a desperate creative race against time. . . .

But is this in fact true? *Was* his cult of nostalgia (and, let's face it, chi-chi) due exclusively to the disability from which he suffered? Brooke did not believe so, and his judgment carries weight:

> Denton would hardly have found life easy in any circumstances, and might well have been tempted to retire into that *vert paradis* of childhood which, for so many European writers during the last half-century, has provided an easy escape from the contemporary predicament. It may seem a hard thing to say, but I suspect that his accident provided Denton with the perfect alibi. . . .

Fantasy could now take over from reality: the handicapped artist would always be relieved of that total responsibility for one's life which normal independence assumes. If art, as Brooke supposed, is always to some extent a substitute for living, then that calamitous accident "was quite possibly the means by which Denton Welch, the artist, was enabled to 'find himself' and to come to terms with the demon which possessed him" [see entry dated 1952 in Additional Bibliography]. Indeed, unless all Welch's descriptions of his childhood and adolescence are a retrospective falsification, this conclusion seems unavoidable; and there are in fact (though his editor did not cite them) two passages from *In Youth Is Pleasure* which specifically confirm such a verdict. In one, Orvil is trying not to think about going back to school: "'I may be dead before I have to go back,' he told himself. 'I may get chicken pox or measles; or I might be much luckier still and get awfully ill with consumption, *and then I wouldn't be interfered with again for the rest of my life*'" (Reviewer's italics). And at the very end, while shrieking hysterically in a railway carriage, he thinks: "'Now they'll never touch you again. You can be mad for the rest of your life, and they'll leave you alone.'" To that extent, Welch's accident surely gave him what he had always wanted.

So he joined the company of those artists who operate through, and perhaps are shaped by, their special physical disabilities: Keats, Pope, Byron, W. E. Henley, Richard Jeffries, Toulouse-Lautrec: perhaps above all Proust, whose interests, social instincts, and erotic proclivities were surprisingly akin to his own. Here, of course, is where comparisons made on a purely literary level operate very much to Welch's disadvantage. He had all the instincts of a creative genius, but neither the intellect nor the matter to sustain them. He may have shared Proust's taste for *chinoiserie*, childhood, elegant knick-knacks, and handsome, virile young men (preferably from outside his own social milieu); but he lacked Proust's enormous creative vitality, his superb prose style, his gift for characterization—all those impalpable but unmistakable qualities which distinguish the major artist from a minor, though genuine, talent. Not that Welch lacked serious dedication to his craft. "When I read about William Blake I know what I am for," he wrote in 1945. "I must never be afraid of my foolishness, only of pretension." His insights were sharp, his sensitivity acute. But somehow it was never quite enough. His most solid achievement, *A Voice through a Cloud,* the novel he left near completion at his death (and drove himself, despite blinding migraines and increasing exhaustion, to work on, if only for minutes at a time, till the very end), might perhaps have exorcised what he once called "the obscene accident" by describing it, and his subsequent

slow recovery, in the most minute detail. But by then it was too late.

What, then, are we left with? A group of autobiographical novels and stories, describing the author's early memories, his schooldays, his period in Shanghai (*Maiden Voyage* is particularly revealing here), and at last, just before the end, that culminating physical crucifixion. The emphasis (except, of course, in the *Journals*) is all on the period *before* his accident, almost as though time had stood still for him after it (though the end of *A Voice through a Cloud,* and some of the stories in *Brave and Cruel,* suggest that he was moving slowly towards the creative reshaping of his adult life as well as his childhood and adolescence). *In Youth Is Pleasure,* we may note, was dedicated to his mother, Rosalind Bassett, who died when he was eleven. All his fiction benefits from being studied in conjunction with the *Journals,* since almost invariably the material is adapted with remarkable fidelity from the latter to the former: indeed, a prolonged immersion in the corpus will often leave one uncertain where reportage ends and fiction begins. . . . How far, then, does this cumulative Portrait of the Artist as a Young Man succeed on its own terms, and how enduring are its qualities as art?

What we need to avoid, so far as this is possible, are purely personal reactions to Welch's character and personality, either pro or con. Here not only aesthetic, but also moral, even indeed political, preferences may begin to creep in. It is only too easy to see why Welch got taken up by people like Edith Sitwell and Herbert Read, but was studiously ignored by a critic such as George Orwell. To approve of Welch became the badge of a special sensitivity; it also (one can now see) implied a definite attitude towards the Second World War. One of the most crucial and least emphasized facts about Welch is that he was, primarily, a wartime writer. This to a large extent explains not only his ready acceptance by a certain sector of literary London, but his astonishing popularity, for a while, with the young—especially those in the armed services. Even a cursory glance through, say, Orwell's collected essays and journalism makes it abundantly clear how deep a vein of anti-war feeling ran through the English intelligentsia during the early 1940s while soldiers and airmen found peculiarly soothing comfort, a sense of proportion and sanity, in a writer so absorbed by old churches, antique bric-à-brac, dolls' houses, needle cushions, and his own comfortable but unhappy childhood that he forgot to mention the end of the war in his diary (though this last they never learnt till 1952). *The Unquiet Grave,* it seems clear, caught on for very similar reasons. Both books studiously ignored public attitudinizing or muscular heroics, and emphasized instead the still voice of the heart.

In one sense, of course, the war came as a boon to Welch, since it provided him, even at one remove—as it did so many other artists, whether they consciously admitted it or not—with a structured macrocosm of action against which his private world could operate (as we see from the *Journals*) with greater depth and perspective. It gave shape and drama to what might otherwise have been an over-anchoritic existence. There is a sharpness and excitement about the wartime diary entries which appear nowhere else in his published work. The actual fighting, to be sure, apart from an occasional doodle-bug or shower of flying shrapnel, takes place off-stage. Friends go missing, die, are decorated. Truckloads of bronzed troops roar past *en route* to what (judging from the date) must have been the Dieppe raid. Welch has a passion for watching soldiers or farmhands bathe in the river, and describes their bodies with a sensuous accuracy of detail that recalls D. H. Lawrence. Some of them made what were clearly sexual overtures to him, but of this element (unless his diary entries are disingenuous to a degree, which is unlikely) he seems oddly unconscious; there is an innocent streak about him behind the Beardsleyish attitudinizing.

While nearby ack-ack guns roar, he is busy exploring an eighteenth-century icehouse in Oxon Hoath Park. Italian POWs in "Pinkish chocolate battledress" drift dreamlike by. Churches bring out a kinky streak in him; he bestows erotic kisses on medieval brasses, surreptitiously swigs Communion wine. There is the fireman with a "froth of black hair on his chest"; the Normandy invasion of 1944 is carefully subordinated to a violent tiff between Welch and his devoted friend Eric Oliver. And Welch knows very well what he is about. A diary entry describing supper with Noel Adeney (like Keats and Jeffries, consumptives both, Welch dwells endlessly and lovingly on food), and the search through a trunkful of costumes afterwards, and the gift of a tin of Earl Grey tea, ends abruptly: "You see this is what goes on in nineteen forty-three, the year of the greatest war to stop all wars, if I have the quotation right." To a war-weary generation—as Herbert Read at once saw when he accepted **Maiden Voyage** for publication—such an attitude must have been infinitely seductive.

Now, a quarter of a century later, the immediate and epidemic appeal of Welch's work has been largely overtaken by history. The same, of course, is true of *The Unquiet Grave,* which nevertheless survives triumphantly as a minor literary masterpiece in its own right. How does Welch's work stand up by comparison? It has to be admitted that nothing he ever wrote conveys quite the same feeling of total creative achievement, the exhilarating sense that here one is in the presence of great art. That Welch was a true writer there can be no doubt, and had he lived it seems probable (to judge from **A Voice through a Cloud**) that he might in time have become a great one. The divine urge to recreate life in words he most certainly possessed, and described: ". . . it will never stop gnawing. There is always the longing to put the thoughts into the crude mincing machine. It is as if a madman were determined to make all the delicacies of a perfect music come through a brass trombone." Every fellow-practitioner will, instantly, recognize and sympathize with those symptoms. The trouble is that a total devotion to music does not guarantee mastery over the trombone or any other instrument. There must also be an adequate score to play. That is, and remains, the tragedy of every honest writer *manqué.*

Welch undoubtedly was something better than *manqué.* He had an extraordinary gift for coining vivid, suggestive metaphors ("pimento excitingly scarlet like dogs' tools" is one that sticks in the memory), and an imagination which obviously drew, more than has been recognized, on imagery borrowed from surrealism and the trendier poets of the New Apocalypse. This at times led him into odd, and rather self-indulgent, excesses. Orvil, of **In Youth Is Pleasure,** likens a peach melba to a "celluloid cupid doll's behind" which "has burst open and is pouring out lovely snow and great big clots of blood." Some of the dreams Welch records, both in his fiction and in the **Journals,** sound like borrowings from Dali's more exotic paintings. His style is simple yet disingenuously sharp, progressing in short, stabbing sentences, conveying, always, the private vision one associates with an immensely precocious child; at times it almost recalls Daisy Ashford's *The Young Visitors.* Sometimes (again like Daisy Ashford) he will knock off, in

seeming innocence, a shrewd and uncharitable thumbnail sketch of some wretched visiting intellectual; not operating through the analytic faculty himself, he was nervous of those who did, and had nothing but contempt for those who pretended to.

All artists need a measure of withdrawal if they are to survive; but Welch's congenital solitariness seems to have made it all but impossible for him to form genuine relationships except in the role of protegé, where safe guidelines were laid down for both parties; his friendship with Eric Oliver seems to have been the one outstanding exception to this general rule. For a literary lion he remained astonishingly isolated, and the isolation is reflected in his fiction, which suffers from a lack of genuine interplay and communication between characters: one is one and all alone and evermore shall be so—a severe handicap, one would have thought, to the practising novelist. This disability could, given time, have been overcome. More dangerous and damaging was the passion for camp domestic trivia, the cult of shy sensitivity, cosseted and flattered by a series of middle-aged or elderly ladies: that appalling physical and spiritual sweet tooth of his. "If people doted on their needlecushions more," he noted, "a great tree of civilization could grow out of them, instead of a wave of bad smells and famine." The imagery smacks of some Freudian nursery, the sentiment is pure mush—and in his heart of hearts Welch the artist must have known it. The trouble was that, through force of circumstance and temperament, he had no real material to work on but himself; and even the toughest, most dedicated artist must, in the last resort, find better grist for his mill than the self revealed at length in these **Journals.** Whether he would have done so had he lived is a question to which we will never know the answer. (pp. 1131-32)

[*Peter Green*], *"A Dream of Black Daimlers," in* The Times Literary Supplement, *No. 3734, September 28, 1973, pp. 1131-32.*

ROBERT PHILLIPS (essay date 1974)

[*An American poet, short story writer, critic, and editor, Phillips has been praised for the craftsmanship, wit, and inventiveness of his poetry. Among his critical studies are the volumes* The Confessional Poets *(1973),* Denton Welch *(1974), and* William Goyen *(1979). In the following excerpt, Phillips offers a survey of Welch's works.*]

Denton Welch was a very highly subjective writer, one whose artistic creed was in direct opposition to a Keats or to an Eliot—to name two writers who consciously strove to all but obliterate their own concrete personalities in their writing. Welch specifically aimed at self-portraiture, and his writings constitute an overt display of his personality. The hero of most of his books is even baldly named "Denton Welch," an authorial practice sometimes employed by such disparate writers as Marcel Proust, Somerset Maugham, Norman Mailer, and Christopher Isherwood.

But, because Welch used his own name and the outward events of his life to frame his books, we should not assume that Welch's fictions and poems were simple self-expression—factual reportage of his nights and days. We must recall Sir Herbert Read's admonition that "Selection is also creation." Although most events in Welch's "novels" have their sources in his life, and although a study of his **Journals** and unpublished letters confirms this fact, the use of an event, object, or motif in a work of art is quite different from that in a personal or autobiographical statement. For this reason, the same events recorded in Welch's *Journals* are infinitely more satisfying when recast in his novels. In reading his novels on even the most literal level, Welch's selection of details from his life—their order, arrangement, and embellishment—transforms the raw, experiential details so that they lose specifically personal meaning and begin to become universal human materials, elements of works of art. Moreover, the details he selects often assume outward symbolic value, as we shall see. (In his *Journals* he defined the art of writing as "making each tiny happening into a sign. . . .")

C. P. Snow places Welch as a son of Dorothy Richardson and James Joyce—as one who "set out to write of moment-by-moment experience, the moments of sight, sound, smell, which to such writers seemed the essential stuff of art." While none of Welch's novels is a so-called stream-of-consciousness novel, Sir Charles is correct in isolating Welch's preoccupation with the detail of the moment. In his *Journals,* as well as in his novels, Welch never makes broad generalities or vague statements; every moment has to be dissected into increasingly smaller elements. His method, then, literally is sensational; for, like Thomas Wolfe in *Look Homeward, Angel,* Welch feels compelled to record every sight, sound, smell and feeling.

For Denton Welch, then, all reality is composed of countless shards which we cannot begin fully to realize. But, through focussing upon the bits and pieces—the many half-realized and seemingly unrelated incidents and details—we eventually may come to some understanding of our fate. This vision of reality accounts for the loose structuring of Welch's novels and also explains why *Maiden Voyage* is largely episodic. An open-ended picaresque, the narrative is a parade of small moments followed by small moments, each to be enjoyed while it lasts. This vision also may account for Welch's fondness of the miniature, the delicate, and the antique. The ornate pet graveyard which "Orvil Pym" discovers early in *In Youth Is Pleasure* is, for example, precisely the kind of strange and differentiating detail which absorbed Welch's imagination. As one critic has mused, had Denton Welch never seen a pet cemetery, he surely would have invented one!

Maiden Voyage is not, therefore, an autobiography, although its events and elements are autobiographical. It is also not exactly a novel as we have come to understand one as "a fictitious prose tale of considerable length, in which characters and actions professing to represent those of real life are portrayed in a plot" (definition courtesy of Webster's *New Collegiate Dictionary*). For Welch's "novels" are neither fictitious, overly concerned with what passes for real life, or deeply plotted; more correctly, they are Romances as that genre was defined by Henry James—books in which one encounters "experience liberated . . . experience disengaged, disembroiled, disencumbered." Events and objects are not so important for what they are as for what they mean. In this sense, Welch's books are "poetic" or "poetic novels" as well as Romances, and the critic-biographer Max Wykes-Joyce rightly compares Welch's reverberating visual sense with that of Gerard Manley Hopkins.

Yet quite obviously, in another sense, the books are "symbolic"—and symbolism, by definition, is a granting to outward things an inner meaning, a practice Welch consistently exercised in his drawings and paintings. It is important to remember that, while Welch made his reputation as a fiction writer, Welch was trained as a painter and believed himself a poet; therefore, his was an education of the senses and emotions through art; and he was also very highly intuitive. By means of imagery

and symbols, Denton Welch communicated his day and his night dreams. A book which seems to exist outside of time in the eternal world of childhood, *Maiden Voyage* also evokes the fabulous and the mythical. It is no wonder critic Isabella Athey commented on the "amazing number of levels" of meaning to be found in *Maiden Voyage.* . . . (pp. 46-8)

Whether as poetic or symbolic novels, or as Romances, Welch's works must never be interpreted on less than two levels, the level of action and the other of meaning. Sometimes there are, intentionally or intuitively, more than one symbolic meaning, embracing deliberate and unconscious meanings. In the case of *Maiden Voyage,* we have a book which is even more than poetic or symbolic: it is also prefigurative—or, to use a term currently fashionable, it is "mythic." The world of Welch's imagination can reveal the mythic manner in which all of us reexperience life, the way we live on a variety of levels: thought and action, dream and reality, past and present, appearance and reality, personal and collective. Denton Welch saw, or intuited, how these levels can work together in harmony in a work of art.

Welch's use of myth in *Maiden Voyage* . . . was in all probability highly unconscious. He did not consciously employ the "mythical method" of Joyce and Thomas Mann, for nowhere did Welch appropriate a myth or a set of myths and deliberately weave a fictional tapestry about them. In Joyce and Mann, this method is usually successful; in certain recent novels, such as Frederick Buechner's *A Long Day's Dying* and John Updike's *The Centaur,* it is not. Those two novels calculatingly exploit myth and attempt to add depth or counterpoint to the literal, universal implication to the current secular reality through such mythic underpinnings. In both, the literal level and the prefigurative level become incompatible, for the myth and the reality are unsuccessfully interwoven.

On the other hand, Welch was one of those rare mythopoeic artists (like Franz Kafka) whose work unconsciously reflects archetypes from the collective unconscious—a novelist whose work exemplifies not mythology-consciousness (like Updike) but rather a mythic imagination. No better example can be found than *Maiden Voyage,* that poetic novel which successfully operates on a number of levels, the most important of which perhaps is the mythic. (pp. 48-9)

Maiden Voyage is Denton Welch's spiritual odyssey, a search for oneness, in which certain spontaneous symbols of the Self became indistinguishable from a God-image. "This is in exact agreement with the empirical findings of psychology, that there is an ever-present archetype of wholeness which may easily disappear from the purview of consciousness or may never [be] perceived at all until a consciousness illuminated by conversion recognizes it in the figure of Christ" [C. G. Jung, "Christ: A Symbol of the Self"]. Whether this archetype was consciously manufactured by Welch (he stated that he wished to create "biblical symbols") or subconsciously imposed, it is present and makes the book even more effective. Whichever interpretation the reader ultimately assigns to *Maiden Voyage,* we can say of that book what Henry James said of Whitman's Civil War letters to Peter Doyle: "The beauty of the natural is here, the overflow of the man's life in the deadly dry setting." This overflow of aspiration and hope characterizes Welch's writing from *Maiden Voyage* forward. (p. 71)

When Welch's second novel was published two years after *Maiden Voyage,* several disappointed American critics carped that the manuscript of *In Youth Is Pleasure* must have been resurrected from the bottom of Welch's trunk; and they called the craft and the vision inferior to those evident in the first book. A critical charge often heard in response to second novels, it is also one that neither biographical fact nor cool critical judgment can support in Welch's case. *In Youth Is Pleasure* is definitely a later product of Welch's imagination; his craft is a more mature one; the writing is tighter and harder, more incisive and sure; and the language is more sophisticated. However, as Maurice Cranston observes [see excerpt dated 1950], Welch "kept the trick of lighting up a passage of conventional narrative with one of his arresting child's images," as in the following description:

> He walked slowly into the dark water and lay down flat. His exultation passed into a more sober delight. Water always soothed him. He felt calm and peaceful. As he floated he felt the sun hot on his face, and on the parts of his chest and arms which were still above water. The rest of his body was tingling with cold.
>
> "I'm like one of those Baked Alaskas," he thought, "one of those lovely puddings of ice cream and hot sponge."

In passages such as this, in a book little over half the length of *Maiden Voyage*, Welch again gives a provocative examination of the secret life of a sensitive youth.

Hamilton Basso, the late American Southern novelist, considered this book's protagonist "the most desperately miserable English schoolboy who ever found his way into print" [see excerpt dated 1946], an accolade we might have thought would already have been retired by the protagonist of *Maiden Voyage*. This time, however, the hero is named Orvil Pym, not Denton Welch; but they are the same character, in background, and in spirit. Both are lonely searchers given to the wildest flights of fancy, and their situation is also the same: as in *Maiden Voyage*, we have the youthful errant scholar's quest for self-knowledge in an alien world which is at once thrilling and frightening. In the first novel, the hero conducted his quest, or voyage, in China; in *In Youth Is Pleasure*, the boy and his two older brothers vacation with their father in a grand hotel on the Thames. The novel's action is more limited; the time span, more condensed. But its greatest defect lies in the author's choice of the third-person point of view; it demanded an attitude to the external world which the solipsistic Welch could not sustain, as Maurice Cranston notes. Nevertheless, as rich in symbol and theme as Welch's first novel, the second lacks only the mythic implications to elevate it to the same level of complexity. In this work, mythic symbols have been displaced by consciously Gothic ones, and unconscious sexual ones.

In regard to my interpretation of the symbolism of this novel: some readers may think I overemphasize that old stock-in-trade of Freudian literary critics, the sexual symbol. To such readers I can only reply that, in *In Youth Is Pleasure*, Welch's quest for self-discovery is construed almost entirely in sexual terms. (Later, in *A Voice through a Cloud*, the sexual is displaced by the Existential, additional proof that Welch did grow from book to book, despite some critics' avowal that each new book was a rewriting of the last.) Symbolism, as we know, is one of the most important forms of expression of the unconscious; and Welch's sexual anxieties seem most certainly to have surfaced in the multitude of broken columns, threatening spears, snapped-off knives, and bottomless lakes and swimming pools which decorate the psychescape of all his novels, but especially that of *In Youth Is Pleasure*. His character, Orvil Pym, seems to possess a "one-track mind," and his sexual fears appear to reflect Welch's at the time of composition. The creative process, for all artists, begins with a relaxation of ego control. In this book Welch not only seems aware of the relaxation/regression but also seemingly willed it. Certainly, the framework given his symbols is consciously Gothic, as if the wild, uncivilized, and unrestrained conventions of Gothic literature gave point to his own wild sexuality.

The situation of the novel is overtly Oedipal and homosexual. Welch dedicated it "To Rosalind Bassett" without identifying her as his mother, without mention of the fact she had been dead nearly twenty years, and—interestingly enough—without appending her married name of Welch; but perhaps this is appropriate, because she was so alive in his mind, the bride of his imagination. The end papers which Welch drew especially to decorate the novel are also illuminating; for, executed in pen and ink in his somewhat *"art nouveau"* style, the designs are dominated by a broken spear crossing a totally devoured fish—that is, a broken male sex symbol crosses a broken female symbol. The drawing graphically announces that the novel concerns aborted sexuality. The facing end paper, which reinforces this theme, portrays a long snake (phallus) that is devouring an egg (yoni).

Orvil is every bit as high-strung and emotional as was the hero of *Maiden Voyage*. He is so sensitive that he twists or magnifies every event out of all reasonable proportion. He is also extremely lonely. His mother is dead and he barely knows his father, a self-centered man who drinks too much, who has taken opium on occasion, and who persists in calling the self-conscious boy alternately "Microbe" and "Maggot." The second name is especially unfortunate in view of Orvil's preoccupation with his mother's death and his persistent visions of her in a deathly state. His father will not even allow the boy's mother's name to be mentioned between them. Orvil's loneliness is exacerbated rather than assuaged by the presence of his two brothers during holidays since he simultaneously admires and resents the poise of one and the masculinity of the other. (The autobiographical parallels here are obvious.)

As a result of his familial alienation, Orvil wanders about and indulges in all manner of daydreams, the details of which could supply Kraft-Ebbing with another lifetime's work. Fifteen-year-old Orvil's imagination is far more erotic than was the protagonist's of *Maiden Voyage*, for the "Denton" of that book was fanciful, not libidinous. (pp. 72-5)

More so than in any other book by Denton Welch, the writing in *In Youth Is Pleasure* has an unreal quality; for the incidents seem part dream, part memory, part reality. (p. 76)

The prevailing mood, of course, is Gothic throughout. *In Youth Is Pleasure* literally drips with Gothic imagery and action. The romantic architecture of the hotel, the empty cottage, the dead bird on the hearth, the mysterious grotto, the torture instruments, and the flaunting of all taboos are part of the fictional landscaping of Gothic novels, just as the innocent voyage culminating in violence, lust, mutilation, and defeat which Orvil undergoes parallels the basic black Gothic plot. In this sense, Orvil Pym is a male version of the Gothic heroine, the maiden in distress who is pursued by vile villains. Like the Gothic heroine, Orvil saw the world as a maze from which he must somehow emerge whole.

The effect is somewhat shrill; at times, the pitch of the short novel rises toward hysteria. Welch most likely saw the appropriation of Gothic machinery as a means of giving an added dimension to his personal story which he had already told before in *Maiden Voyage*. . . . Welch may have been influenced by reading Matthew Lewis, Mrs. Radcliffe, or any number of Gothic writers; but Jane Austen's *Northanger Abbey* could have given him the notion of inflicting Gothic machinery upon his confessional novel. (We know from his *Journals* that he was a Jane Austenite.) Austen, however, used the Gothic trappings only to satirize them; Welch, on the other hand, drags them in in dead earnest, like so many of Marley's chains. The result is heavy-handed, especially in so short a novel. *In Youth Is Pleasure*, while displaying novelistic form and control and a concision far more admirably than that exhibited in *Maiden Voyage*, must ultimately be consigned to a place somewhat below that accorded Welch's first and third novels.

For some novelists the writing of short stories is purely a diversion, and the results are works which are of secondary importance. Such is not the case with Denton Welch, for his stories represent a significant portion of his work and the execution of them consumed a significant portion of his energies. Eric Oliver has related how Welch abandoned work on his unfinished masterpiece, *A Voice through a Cloud* for the expressed purpose of writing stories which eventually appeared in *Brave and Cruel* and which testify not so much to his economic need as to the seriousness with which he approached his shorter pieces. (pp. 85-6)

Welch personally had selected the contents from among all his stories written between 1943 and 1947, and the quality was consistently high. *A Last Sheaf*, the posthumous collection published in 1951 and edited by Eric Oliver, contains three stories Welch wrote in the last year of his life after *Brave and Cruel* had gone to press ("The Hateful Word," "The Diamond Badge," and "A Picture in the Snow"), plus eight others that Welch had chosen not to include in *Brave and Cruel*. His critical acumen concerning his own work appears correct; for, of the stories which remained unpublished at the time of his death, only "The Hateful Word" and perhaps "The Diamond Badge" are as successful as the best pieces in the first collection.

Several stories in *Brave and Cruel*—"The Fire in the Wood," "At Sea," "The Coffin on the Hill," and his best-known story, "When I Was Thirteen"—must be counted among Welch's most remarkable achievements. Though it is usually the novels *Maiden Voyage* and *A Voice Through a Cloud* for which Welch is remembered, when he is remembered at all, his stories are in some ways more satisfying and more artistically successful. Certainly "The Fire in the Wood" and "The Hateful Word" are much better examples of the short story than any of his novels is of the novel. "The Fire in the Wood," in fact, is a perfectly realized example of its genre which could not be said of any one of Welch's novels, however singularly interesting it may be. His exercise of greater control and selectivity when writing in the shorter form is a contributing factor to the power and economy of *In Youth Is Pleasure*, his shortest novel; and its technique bears testimony to his study of short-story craft. The most consciously formed of his novels, *In Youth Is Pleasure* is at least technically his best; and it is primarily the frankness of its subject matter which has caused the book to be overly denigrated by critics. Indeed, Jocelyn Brooke, who has written at length on two occasions about Welch's novels, has confessed that for him the book's "frequent descriptions of masturbation fantasies become slightly embarrassing" [see excerpt dated 1963].

The stories of *Brave and Cruel* are of widely varying kinds. Some, such as "Narcissus Bay" and "Leaves from a Young Person's Notebook," are mere sketches. Others—"The Trout Stream" and "The Fire in the Wood"—are well-structured stories approaching novella length. "Brave and Cruel," the title piece, is a short novel. The other five stories in the collection are of conventional length. For the most part, the themes of the stories are the concerns of all of Welch's writings: youth's vulnerability and growing awareness of mortality; the body's betrayal of the spirit; the impossibility of reciprocal love; alienation and instability; isolation and personal dissociation. The book bears evidence for the first time of Welch's existentialist thinking. His usual strong misogynistic feelings are scarcely evident, except in "The Barn" and in "The Fire in the Wood." In the latter story Welch employs what Stanley Edgar Hyman has called The Albertine Strategy; like Proust, Welch narrates the latter story from a woman's point of view. The feminine disguise may have been assumed for reasons of prudence, since the story recalls a love affair, but what is important is that Welch succeeds in projecting the persona, thereby making a breakthrough from his usual first-person singular confessional narratives.

Other currents running throughout the book include strong anti-American feelings expressed in several stories and a graphic statement in "The Trout Stream" about the sterility of materialism—an unusual development for a writer so personally preoccupied with collecting china, silver, antiques, and objets d'art. A number of the tales also are concerned with voyages, among them the opening story, "The Coffin on the Hill," which in reality is about one boy's voyage from childhood innocence to painful awareness of mortality. The story is told in highly symbolic terms and is worth examining in detail as a model for Welch's method in the shorter genre. (pp. 86-8)

"The Fire in the Wood" is the only story in the collection in which the sympathetic protagonist is a female and not a sensitive male. Whether or not the reader interprets Mary as another of Welch's personal personae, and the story one of homosexuality rather than heterosexuality, is ultimately beside the point. The story succeeds on both levels and is an impressive and somewhat inevitable conclusion to the collection. Inevitable because *Brave and Cruel* is a book which presents a chronological progression of protagonists who are the author's personae. From stories like "The Coffin on the Hill," "The Barn," and "At Sea"—in which Welch's fictional counterpart is a very young child—we move into adolescence with "When I Was Thirteen" and "The Judas Tree." Then "Leaves from a Young Person's Notebook" presents the artist as a young man. The narrator of "Brave and Cruel" is a young adult of some accomplishment. And, finally, "The Fire in the Wood" presents a mature individual quite set in a pattern of behavior who encounters for the first time an overwhelming emotion.

Whether the protagonist is called Robert, Dave, Denton, or even Mary, we are tracing the growth of the same sensibility. If we choose to read the volume as a kind of autobiography, it would serve as a parallel to Virginia Woolf's fictional homage to Vita Sackville-West, *Orlando*, in which the protagonist literally changes sex during the course of the action, a comment on the bisexuality present in us all. But to read *Brave and Cruel* only in such a manner ultimately would be to distort the author's intention. The parts were offered as individual stories, and as such several of them succeed as well as anything Denton Welch was to write. (pp. 106-07)

Welch's valedictory novel recounts yet another voyage, an odyssey from health to illness to partial recovery; and it explores along the way various stages in the liberation of a spirit tied to an infirm body. The novel's protagonist, who bears Welch's Christian name, Maurice, recalls Dante, who wrote of one who "awoke to find myself in a dark wood.... So bitter was it that death could be no worse," a soul who had to go through hell to reach purgatory and paradise. But Welch never lived to complete his novel, and the outcome of his character's torment is uncertain. During the course of his struggle, however, the protagonist did find human love, if not divine.

Maurice also recalls the figure of Job, whom God permitted the world, in the form of the Devil, to plague with boils in his very flesh. Like the Book of Job, Welch's *A Voice through a Cloud* demonstrates the experience of pain as teacher, as revealer of ultimate truth. The experience is especially difficult for Maurice, the artist, a sensitive person for whom the pain is most intense. When he looks into the mirror at his torn flesh, he sees the death of beauty, which for the artist is a spiritual death as well.

A Voice through a Cloud is in many ways unique, like the *Divine Comedy* and the Book of Job, which it resembles in subject and vision. Through the ages sickness has been an unlikely subject for art, especially for the novel, which partially explains the sensation at the time of its publication of Tolstoy's *The Death of Ivan Illych* and also of Dostoevski's *The Idiot*. In our own time we remember Samuel Beckett's trilogy in English, Thomas Mann's *The Magic Mountain*, perhaps Sylvia Plath's *The Bell Jar*, and only a few others. Since the rise of the novel, most novelists have concentrated on social rather than personal ills; and they have until recently, as in James Joyce, ignored the bodily functions as too crude or as too quotidian to warrant attention. In *A Voice through a Cloud,* as John Updike has observed, "agony precedes psychology; introspection takes place only as pain's monopoly loosens..." [see excerpt dated 1966]. Welch's last novel is basically an account of a man's crucifixion, ultimate suffering, pain, and death to the "ordinary" world of pretense, hypocrisy, and insincerity. Welch's "Maurice" is akin to Tolstoy's Ivan Illych in that both, in the primal experiences of pain and impending death, lose their "web of Maya," to borrow a phrase from Schopenhauer (who in turn borrowed it from Oriental philosophy). The phrase refers to the "solipsistic web which makes each individual secretly believe in his immortality and which prevents him from merging with his fellow humans in a mental flow of utter communion" [Charles Neider, *Short Novels of the Masters*].

Prior to an accident Maurice, like Ivan Illych, had spun around himself a web of deceit. A creature of vanity, he had deadened himself to humane values and had fooled himself into thinking he possessed a strong individuality. When he becomes one of many patients, all wearing identical gowns and suffering in identical beds, nature (or God) has its revenge. For, when Maurice needs help, sympathy, and understanding, he gets none—as when he wishes his classmate Mark would come see him. When Mark's absence causes Maurice to recall all the times he had abused Mark, Maurice finally realizes that he is subject to the same abuse and lies. At the novel's conclusion, as he ventures forth into the world, half cured and half ill, his broken Self has become an indistinguishable part of the universe. Instead of being splendidly independent, he must lean on his friends for what comfort there is. A new Maurice has been born through agony, and the course of events has caused him to lose his web.

In his search for identity, the novel's protagonist wears many guises. His dress changes from student clothes to a hospital gown to his own pajamas to an alderman's robe and finally to "normal" clothes. The shifts in his psyche are also accompanied by changes in his name: at different times he is known as Maurice, Sonny Boy, a bed number, Ted, and finally Punky.

His search for healing culminates in his meeting his ego ideal, Dr. Farley, who is a Christ figure, a healer of the soul as well as the body. The doctor is also an Apollo-Dionysus figure: Apollo, in his capacity as doctor, practicing a conscious, objective skill in medicine; Dionysus, in his spontaneous, charismatic, "human" actions (as when he throws the pineapple at Maurice). Maurice shares one perfect moment of communion with Dr. Farley during a walk on the beach—one suspended moment of idealized doctor-patient rapport—which later leads to disappointment and doubt. Dr. Farley ultimately is guilty of being human, not divine, as when he registers awkwardness and discomfort at entertaining the boy at tea in his new home. For Maurice, this realization is a beneficial one; the patient is suddenly free of dependence on the doctor, and he realizes for the first time he must plan for living on his own. (pp. 108-10)

[Despite] the fact that it is unfinished, [*A Voice through a Cloud*] seems remarkably whole.... It is not a perfect work of art—few novels ever are; but, toward the end, *A Voice through a Cloud* seems to ramble, as if Welch, fighting against time and fever in his fatal sickness, did not quite know how to terminate the book. And the last quarter becomes more obviously novelistic than all that preceded; for characters formerly introduced, such as Mark, somewhat gratuitously reappear.

But whatever its faults, *A Voice through a Cloud* is Denton Welch's most mature work. In its writing he found a spiritual rapport with his characters which was lacking in *Maiden Voyage* and *In Youth Is Pleasure,* books in which the protagonist, Welch, had been too much the dilettante—the precocious observer of life rather than the involved participant. Certainly the novel repudiates the charge leveled by both G. S. Fraser [see Additional Bibliography] and Edmund Wilson [see excerpt dated 1945] that Welch's work was flawed by an evasion of real problems and that it treated specialized aspects of life rather than life as a whole. In this book, life itself is now Welch's subject—life and the struggle to preserve it against awesome odds. (p. 116)

Many of Welch's characteristic topics and themes recur in *A Last Sheaf,* the second and posthumous collection of his shorter pieces. Among the book's concerns are the themes of isolation and alienation, the tension between the heterosexual and the homosexual principles, the relationship of characters to the past, the role of the artist in society, the disparity between appearance and reality, and the changing face of England as she approached the middle of the twentieth century. The effects of World War II are felt in this book more than in any other Welch wrote save the *Journals*. And, for the first time, there is an explicit expression of his belief in the supernatural. New sexual freedom and narrow human selfishness also pervade the book. To a much greater degree than in *Brave and Cruel,* the tone is one of pessimism: a recurring image in *A Last Sheaf* is that of humans as bottles full of bile, waiting to be uncorked. (p. 117)

Just as the majority of stories in *Brave and Cruel* concerned childhood or very early adolescence, so the second collection contains a majority about young artists. Welch had focused his inward vision to a later period in life. While the second collection may not be so consistently well-achieved technically as the first, it nevertheless rewards the reader.

The dichotomy between Welch's early and late work is well illustrated by the two novels-in-progress that he left at the time of his death. *I Left My Grandfather's House* was written as a rough draft, abandoned by the author in the spring of 1943, and not published until 1958 when the manuscript was discovered among his papers and was printed in its original form. *A Novel Fragment,* on the other hand, while begun in January, 1944, continued to absorb Welch at least until the summer of 1945 and quite possibly longer. Unlike *Grandfather's House,* it shows evidence of conscious craftsmanship and a concern for novelistic technique. In a letter to T. Murray Ragg, then managing editor of Routledge, Welch called it, ''The best I have done so far!'' (pp. 128-29)

In the earlier fiction, works like *Maiden Voyage,* ''The Barn,'' and *Grandfather's House,* the protagonist's quest for experience is conducted with singular innocence—an innocence almost total in its frankness and lack of inhibition. These works are written with what Walter Allen has called ''an astonishingly pure response to the sensual surface of things'' [see Additional Bibliography]. Throughout Welch's writing career his language maintained its freshness, but the vision informing the language changed, as a comparison between *Maiden Voyage* and *In Youth Is Pleasure* reveals. The world of childhood and promise of the earlier books is displaced by the world of illness and infirm adulthood in *A Voice through a Cloud.* And in that book, as well as in the stories in *A Last Sheaf* and in *A Novel Fragment,* the once total innocence is displaced by sketchily concealed eroticism. This eroticism is especially perceived in *In Youth Is Pleasure* and in those works that concern Welch's years at art school—the story ''A Party'' and the novel fragment. When read together, ''A Party'' seems an exercise in preparation for the writing of that incomplete novel.

As does *In Youth Is Pleasure,* both construe the experiential quest for self-discovery in sexual terms, as might be expected since the protagonist (named Ian in ''A Party'' and Robert in *A Novel Fragment*) is in late adolescence. As in the novels of Forrest Reid, adolescence and the act of attaining manhood in Welch's fiction rarely generate an expansion of the protagonist's sensibility; there is, instead, a sense of emotional constriction, something altogether the opposite of growth. Instead of the malleable and adventuresome Denton of *Maiden Voyage,* we are given the prim and inverted Robert of *A Novel Fragment*—and the difference is that between early and late Welch.

I Left My Grandfather's House is pure, early Welch. A straightforward and almost artless account of the author's first walking tour, this work is distinguished by uncluttered writing and by the total absence of symbols and sexual psychology. (p. 130)

That Denton Welch possessed a poetic eye there can be no doubt. His imagination was at times overburdened with its own inventiveness; when in great pain in the hospital, he asked himself, ''Would the images never stop forming?'' To him, the crests of roofs in the snow looked ''like the bones of big, rotting fishes, covered with salt.'' Carnations when carried bounced about ''like cocks shaking their combs.'' Caviar was black and glistening as ''oiled ball bearings.'' The sun sinking burned ''to the ground like a red poker sinking into wood.''

These are striking images, but they are not from Welch's poems. They were selected quite at random from the pages of *Maiden Voyage,* but other of Welch's prose works would have rewarded us with images just as poetic. This propensity makes it all the greater pity that Welch's poems—as poems—are so poor. In the total canon of sixty-seven poems collected in book form, there is only one image which I can compare with any of those just quoted; and it is found in **''A Night Poem''** in which Welch describes white orchids lying on a lady's hair as being ''like gasping sailors in sick-bay.'' We can see the supine, floppy, white bell-bottomed limbs.

Surely Welch possessed the proper sensibility and technique to have become a competent poet. But he himself recognized his failures in that genre. In an exchange of letters with the poet Henry Treece (1912-1966), one of the leaders of the self-styled Apocalyptic movement, Welch admitted:

> I agree with you in thinking that my poems are too narrowed down to one point. . . . And I also agree with you that they need attention. But here I must admit that however much I try, I still find it almost impossible to formulate to myself what I am *trying* to do when I write a poem. I just want to do it; and consequently what comes out of me will probably be rather shapeless, rather sexy and probably rather trite. My critical faculty, after the event, will tell me of these things, but it hasn't given me much help yet in remedying the faults.
>
> (pp. 138-39)

Remarks such as these indicate that Welch—always a fabulous original in his prose style, forging out *Maiden Voyage* as a very young man and under no real literary influence from anyone, for his Laurentian overtones came later—was at a loss when it came to poetic composition. For this reason I suggest he turned to another poet as model. . . . And it was not to the alliterative and curiously metrical poetry of Gerard Manley Hopkins, with whom Jocelyn Brooke seems to think Welch ''felt an especial and intimate kinship.'' Rather, it was a more austere model Welch chose: many of his poems seem to reveal an affinity for, and close reading of, A. E. Housman. And Welch acknowledges in his *Journals* the debt: ''I have got a poetry bout on, but I keep on wondering if I'm producing semi-demi A. E. Housman. I should hate this, although he is a lovely poet. . . .'' (p. 139)

The attraction of Housman is understandable, not from a stylistic point of view, but from a consideration of subject matter. Welch shared Housman's love of life, his celebration of the pleasures of youth, his unacknowledged homosexuality, and his ultimate pessimism. Both wrote from a profound sense of personal loss in youth: for Housman it was his crushing academic failure which made him somewhat of a recluse for years; for Welch, his invalidism. Both writers were possessed by an unappeasable sadness. The numerous young farmers Welch described in his *Journal,* all unaware of impending fate, could well be the healthy Shropshire lads of Housman. Both Housman and Welch perceived the skull beneath the skin; both seem driven by their sense of the imminence of death to an attitude of *carpe diem.* The shadow of inexorable death falls across even so placid a poem of Housman's as ''Loveliest of Trees.'' Rather than finding an objective correlative for death such as Housman's cherry trees, Welch was usually more direct: ''Death is dangling his bait / And Greedy-Guts can hardly wait.''

While Housman's subject matter and world view are compatible with Welch's, it is difficult to think that his unadorned and economic diction was. Housman's verse is a triumph of nouns and verbs; their powerful effect is achieved through the most sparing use of adverbs and adjectives. Welch's prose was heavily larded with both. In the first paragraph of *A Voice through a Cloud,* for instance, the comb is described as ivory, then must be further modified as being "creamy-white." The protagonist's black bag is not just black, but "shiny black." Welch was forever elaborating on appearances; and, from a technical point of view, Housman was an odd exemplar for him. While Denton Welch was always somewhat of a renegade in his stories and novels, chronicling the unspeakable and the shocking, Housman was not even a "modern" poet. His extreme Englishness, his simplicity, and his lucidity were quite out of vogue in the post-*Waste Land* era.

Nowhere did Denton Welch's poems approach the achievement of Housman's lapidary lines. But from the older poet Welch seems to have learned lessons in control and reserve; and Welch was content to stop with these as his gleanings. (pp. 139-40)

[Despite] readings of Housman and the droppings of bombs, Denton Welch's favorite subject remained Denton Welch. But his treatment of Self differs in the poems from the prose. His sexual conflict is not apparent from a reading of the sixty-seven poems reprinted in *A Last Sheaf.* Unlike his later novels and stories, in which the quest for experience and self-discovery was construed almost entirely in sexual terms, sex is subjugated in the poems to other passions. There is a tendency to intellectualize man, who in one poem is called "The jelly-fish, whose soul has spread, until it earns its daily bread." . . . Human sensuality is even found loathsome in "**Easter Midnight Mass,**" in which the poet does not wish to "drink from the cup / That so many other had lifted up." . . . The contrast between his poems and his prose is such that it almost seems that Denton Welch thought sexual love and lust improper subjects for poetry, that the genre demanded more elevated topics.

Because of these numerous limitations of technique and attitude, the poems of Denton Welch do not constitute an important part of his achievement. As works of art, they rank evenly with his paintings, which also were arresting personal statements which were nowhere as original and successful as the best of his prose. Indeed, the best of his poems recall his later paintings, which Dame Rose Macaulay once described as "precise yet ghostly, like an odd and beautiful and frightening dream." (p. 146)

Taken from the notebooks which Welch kept for a good many of his productive years, [*The Denton Welch Journals*] is a book which contains patches of some of his best writing. It also stands as a document of revelation and significance for anyone wishing to understand the man behind the books. Chronicling the life of the artist in close detail over a period of years, it is the kind of record of which far too few examples exist. Any journal represents years of reflection; but, as Cyril Connolly has observed [see excerpt dated 1963], the journal of a sedentary writer like Welch represents an even greater challenge: confined to one place, condemned to monotony, "the writer pits his mind, his privacy, the whole quality of his imagination against the reading public." (p. 147)

Taken as a whole, *The Denton Welch Journals* is one man's direct response to life. Like Gide, Welch used his journals for rapid writing, making no revisions, saving precious hours for revising what he considered his more important work. The result of such spontaneous creation is prose of an unusual purity and freshness, with no pretenses or personae assumed. The pages yield a vividness produced from enthusiasm. What unfolds is the life of a suffering young man which is tragic but never pathetic. Denton Welch made the most of what talent and time he had, and how many of us can say the same? (p. 156)

> *Robert Phillips, in his* Denton Welch, *Twayne Publishers, Inc., 1974, 189 p.*

ALAN HOLLINGHURST (essay date 1984)

[Hollinghurst is an English poet and critic. In the following excerpt, he discusses characteristic traits of Welch's works.]

In 1952, Jocelyn Brooke edited a selection from Denton Welch's journals. Restricted by both the danger of libel and the fear of boring or shocking his readers he included "a little over half" of the MS which Welch had compiled in school notebooks over the last six years of his short life. He also gave us only a little over half of the man. Some passages were sabotaged by discretion: "Just before we got out he said, 'I went to the — to see — —'s pictures, after I had read what — — said in the *New Statesman*'." And on the larger scale he suppressed much of Welch's imaginative concerns—with gossip, men, old buildings and *objets de vertu.* To Welch, himself sabotaged by the cycling accident which damaged his spine at the age of twenty and left him thereafter a permanent invalid, such concerns, and their record in the journal, were of heightened, emblematic significance. The *Journals* contain little that can readily be dispensed with, and Michael De-la-Noy's new complete edition, along with his biography of Welch [see Additional Bibliography], goes far to restitute the whole man.

Welch's was essentially an aesthetic sensibility. As a child and as an art student he felt constitutionally alone. The death of his mother and his accident were critical events which endorsed his isolation, his remoteness from ordinary human happiness, and the concentration of his feelings and ambitions on artistic objects, aesthetic ends. Though he observed people closely he was careless and exploitative of them, until his affair with Eric Oliver which surprised him in the last years of his life; the passions of the *Journals* are narcissistic and devoted to the exploration of himself and his sensibility. Physically damaged, lame, impotent, bedridden for weeks on end, Welch clung to the fragile endurance of old china and glass, the poignant dereliction of eighteenth-century grottoes and plaisaunces, the brief perfection of young men about to be "spoiled" by time or death (it was during the Second World War). "My thoughts are never on nature," he insists at the beginning of the *Journals;* they go out instead to "lovers lying on the banks, young men that are dead." So cruelly "spoiled" himself, his emotions recurrently focus in this Housmanesque nexus of voyeurism and the "torturing flood" of elegiac recall.

Welch's aestheticism helped him to arrest time, which promised him for thirteen years an early and painful death, and to master experience. It was a way of seeing which crystallized and distanced events into objects for plangent contemplation: "All still in the moonlight, stifled, spun into a glass picture," he writes after learning that the local squire is dead. That this airless, miniaturizing vision was a recourse from pain and distress is repeatedly made clear in *A Voice through a Cloud,* Welch's last, unfinished book, which deals with his accident and its aftermath. Lying in hospital, he dreams up and imaginatively inhabits houses and gardens which are like plates from books, or pictures on old china. When another patient goes for an appendectomy he sees the operation happening in his mind:

> There was something so arresting about this picture of the dreaming patient and the busy surgeon cutting and sewing with blood-stained fingers that I dwelt on it until it became bitingly clear and tiny, like the jewelled diminished picture reflected in a dewdrop.

Early in the journals, ill in bed, he escapes by bringing Zoffany conversation-pieces to life, in an animation that is both delicate and grotesque, and casts himself as a little boy wandering through an Elizabethan country house:

> I am alone by the great high feather-crested bed, rubbing my cheek on the darned and brittle silver-thread hangings, running my finger along the tortoise-shell and ebony cabinet which has cockled in the damp. I am by the withered oak of the window-sill where the rust of the latch seems to grow like an orange lichen. Out over the mist-drenched garden goes my breath in a plume as I push open the shaking, faintly smoky-purple panes.

It is a passage which typically combines an intense apprehension of physical objects with a nostalgic desire for sequestration. It makes one think of Knole (near which he lived)—and hence perhaps of *Orlando* and of the literary establishment towards which he aspired. It deploys its connoisseurship to enhance and inflect the writer's self-image.

Jocelyn Brooke's edition of the *Journals* has as its frontispiece a photograph of Welch sitting at an inlaid marble table, with candles burning in elaborate glass lustres and the corner of a baroque tapestry visible behind. It gives the impression of an altar or of the preparations for a séance (and Eric Oliver has recorded, though De-la-Noy does not, Welch's "strong, even fascinated, belief in the existence of ghosts"). Welch did the decorations for his own books, and the frontispiece to *Maiden Voyage* is evidently drawn directly from this photograph. A comparison of the two softly lit half-profiles illustrates how Welch enhanced his self-image, giving the face itself a haunted expression, and enlarging the eyes and mouth, while the details of the background tapestry are stylized into vermiculated or coralline forms. De-la-Noy detects self-disgust in the greater distortions of Welch's self-portrait in the National Portrait Gallery, painted a few years after his accident; but they can surely be read in another way. The attenuation of the features, the straightening out of the long, wavy nose and the hollowness of the orbits are balanced by the negroid plumpness of the lips. The image emphasizes spirituality as well as sensuality, and its mood, with half of the face cast into deep shadow, is charged ambiguously with both innocence and foreboding. Like Housman, Welch looked elegiacally upon the youth of others because that was how he looked upon his own. It is not surprising that the happiness of bathing boys made him think of Dorian Gray: these self-portraits only amplify the overriding concern of his writing to fix his youth for ever while he accelerates towards death. De-la-Noy's subtlest point, in the introduction to *I Left My Grandfather's House,* is that Welch was, in both senses, a ghost-writer, revisiting his past, and writing of it on behalf of his former self, with a child's mentality, unqualified by adult irony.

When not questing for antiques or ruined ice-houses, Welch searched out men. The *Journals* give an impression of a Kent almost unrecognizable today. Everywhere you went, apparently, working-class lads were stripping off their clothes and diving into rivers, and you could sit down and share your cheese and biscuits with them. Or dark young men would approach you and say significantly, "I'd do anything for a bob." The war being on, there were also soldiers—British and Commonwealth as well as American doughboys on exercises and getting drunk—and Italian and German prisoners grateful for any kindness. Drawings of some of these types, such as Eddy Link ("a half-naked baker and confectioner"), were included in the recent exhibition of Welch's pictures at Abbott and Holder; but their portraits in words are far more effective. Typically, Welch aestheticizes them, turning them into nacre or copper or bronze, or describing their café-au-lait backs, as if they were chairs. Antique-shopping in Sevenoaks he gaily mixes his two quests: "trying to find something worthy of being bought. I saw a Georgian milk-jug for £6. I saw a red-headed boy-man, dressed in red Harris tweed . . . like a toy."

Even so, confronting everything he most wants and most is not, his aesthetic control begins to crack. The obsession with jewelled or ceramic perfection has its underside in a passion for mud, dirt and wildness. . . . When he takes a light from a sailor he is magnetized by his difference: "His fingers were dirty, nicotined, something from another world." It is the familiar attraction of guilt-ridden middle-class homosexuals to a life that is dirtily, instinctually other. For Welch, though, such moments of exhilaration modulate, even as they are described, into occasions for regret.

There is a telling passage in *A Voice through a Cloud* where he recalls that on finding himself severely injured, "it seemed to me something had happened which I had expected all my life." The accident struck him as a retribution for guilt and also as a kind of fulfilment—the catalyst to his brilliant and successful career as an autobiographical writer. A comparable ambivalence can be found in all his work, in his love of the horrid, the "repellent-attractive" things he dwells on. (p. 1479)

There is an extraordinary passage (Welch's work is all extraordinary passages: he is an anthologist of his own life) in the journal for 1947, when his collected environment begins to rebel: "In all the illness I have had the horrible sensation that the tables, chairs, lamps and confusion of books near me were writhing into life and becoming extensions of myself, like new limbs, utterly unwanted, but insisting on living and doing my bidding." It is as if his reification of people has turned on him, and his possessions have taken on the autonomy he himself has lost. Many of his pictures occupy this world of paradoxical animation and petrifaction. His subjects often exist uncertainly on the margin of still life, living creatures are juxtaposed with china figures, a vase holding flowers takes the form of the human hand. (pp. 1479-80)

For all his aestheticism, Welch's writing is quite unlike the writing of the Nineties. It is agnostic, direct, pungently full of sensation and quite lacking in the camp or preciosity of many of the admirers it brought him. Forster deplored a "sham-innocence and cock-teasiness" in it, and it often fails to take responsibility for what it has deliberately suggested; but [Michael De-la-Noy's *Denton Welch: The Making of a Writer*] enables us to see in historical perspective the forthrightness, the "uncloaked" nature of Welch's effort by revealing the pressure of libel threats and bowdlerization on much that he did. It also elicits Welch's defence of what has been thought an amoral and inconsequential way of writing, as if any one experience were as valuable as another: it was to reflect life's tendency to anti-climax and fragmentation (and also, one suspects, a challenge to the heterosexual criteria of fiction). He is in many ways a narrow writer, and his style, though lucid, is short-winded and clinching. But seen in the embracing context of *Journals* and biography, his bright fragments find their place in his courageous attempt to salvage his life in perdurable words. (p. 1480)

Alan Hollinghurst, "Diminished Pictures," in The Times Literary Supplement, No. 4264, December 21, 1984, pp. 1479-80.

BRAD GOOCH (essay date 1985)

[*In the following excerpt, Gooch describes the characteristic themes and techniques of Welch's novels.*]

William Burroughs has written a new foreword to *In Youth Is Pleasure,* in which he says simply, "If any writer has been neglected it is Denton."

I'm not sure how to explain this neglect. I suspect, though, that Welch's literary posture is partly to blame. He behaved more like a poet than a novelist and persistently reminds the reader of the art involved in storytelling. Then, too, the people in his stories are as faraway and flat and exotic as the tea services or peach Melbas that flare up suddenly as details and then disappear. What's missing is the illusion of being dipped into the thoughts and feelings of his characters. Instead Welch's stories are sensual, private, playful and idiosyncratic. They read like heightened diary entries.

This autobiographical tack might at least be expected to keep the stories within a chalk circle of ordinary life, but it doesn't, because Denton is too extraordinary, too askew. He begins *Maiden Voyage* as an alien: "After I had run away from school, no one knew what to do with me." Like many outsiders, he feels that others are watching and discussing him. And like many outsiders, given to a voyeuristic approach to life, his impressions become increasingly surreal. Denton doesn't need to travel farther than his own backyard to be spooked: "The dried-up garden looked like a landscape on the moon." He treats strangers, too, as if they were homunculi under a laboratory glass. A man and a woman make love one evening in the snow, "like black shadows on a wall," while Denton runs off "with my face on fire." But the next morning he feels compelled fastidiously to retrace his steps, scouting telltale debris. A discarded cigarette butt triggers reverie: "I thought of it lighted and glowing, stuck between his teeth the night before."

Uncomfortable with either confession or empathy, Welch tries other ways to reveal people. For the most part he lets them act out. *In Youth Is Pleasure* features two boys who thrill to having *Jane Eyre* read aloud. Welch must have shared their enthusiasm, since his novel is filled with gestures as gothic as those described in Brontë's melodrama—but without their pathos. Orvil displays his masochistic longings by chaining himself to the shafts of a roller embedded in an abandoned field. And he signals his desire to get high by transvestism: "He absentmindedly rouged his nipples until they were like two squashed strawberries. He looked down at them vaguely and then began to rouge all the extremities of his body—the finger-tips, the toes, the earlobes. Next, he made gashes and spots all over his body until he seemed entirely dressed in crimson marks." Even in less heated moments, Welch tries to get at the inside by external clues. He is a miniaturist of expressions: "Her face

did not change, unless the same expression held in place can be called a change."

All of these masks and antics could be put down to a writer's precious timidity if Welch hadn't gone on to write *A Voice through a Cloud.* Here his smirk is relaxed, and his sadomasochistic fantasies are replaced by a stern delineation of human pain. The thrashings endured by English boys in public schools may be intriguing to watch, but the kind of unspecific pain that reminds people of their mortality is a subject of a different order. The beginning of Welch's sickness had, after all, also marked his beginnings as a writer. All his fiction was done in the years after the bicycle accident, so it makes even more sense that he heard a voice at that critical moment: "I heard a voice through a great cloud of agony and sickness. The voice was asking questions. It seemed to be opening and closing like a concertina." In describing his hospital awakening in *A Voice through a Cloud,* Welch continues to use the paraphernalia of torture crucial to his dormitory daydreams, but now they are more than fetishes—they are emblems of human life: "There was a confusion in my mind between being brought to life—forceps, navel-cords, midwives—and being put to death—ropes, axes and black masks; but whatever it was that was happening, I felt that all men came to this at last. I was caught and could never escape the terrible natural law."

Few other writers have been so early haunted by the fragility of life. The journal entries are filled with mortal twinges—but they're never simply lugubrious. Welch can even misbehave with Death, with whom he flirts brazenly, as when he records lying on top of a sculpted tomb and kissing the brass faces of the medieval man and woman. Yet these personal reveries seem to free rather than constrict him. They certainly account for a lot of the loveliness in his work. . . . (pp. 711-12)

You can't at last get at Denton Welch—the man or the work—if you ignore his habit of teasing. There's tease in the poetic language he uses to compare glowworms to "the stubs of the fattest most expensive cigars" or to record "the tea-time tinkle of all the surgical instruments on the trolley." There's tease when Denton tries to figure what's what in the world. Walking down a road in China, he fixes his eyes on a black speck which he first thinks is a cat crouching in the middle of the road, then a dark boulder, but which turns out to be a human skull. And there's certainly tease—E. M. Forster knocked him for "cock-teasiness"—in Denton's brief and repetitive meetings with uniformed sailors reeking of whiskey, or rustic farmers with stubbly cheeks.

There's fun in these teasing touches—serious fun. Welch can write novels like no one else's because he is satisfied to linger in special, often discontinuous, moments without feeling tugged at by the demands of character development or climactic plot. Shortly after *Maiden Voyage* was published, a friend of the author reported overhearing a shop assistant complain about the inconclusiveness of its story. Welch wrote back: "Why was the poor thing disappointed? I'm sorry. Was it because things led to a climax and then rather petered out? But isn't this what life usually does? You must remember that my book is supposed to be true, not fiction." Denton Welch hands us the things of this world—a plate of boiled chicken, some house keys—as carefully as if they were mementos. (pp. 712-13)

Brad Gooch, "Gossip, Lies and Wishes," in The Nation, Vol. 240, No. 22, June 8, 1985, pp. 711-13.

PAUL SKENAZY (essay date 1986)

[*In the following excerpt, Skenazy offers an appraisal of Welch's short stories.*]

Welch's personal story arouses one's sympathetic curiosity, but it also can deflect attention from the works to an admiration for the extraordinary discipline and passion required to create them. But as a writer, Welch is uneven at best. He is a phenomenon more than an accomplished artist, someone whose writings we savor as much for their frustrated promise as for their literary skill and polish. His best works, like his posthumous novel, *A Voice through a Cloud* and his *Journals,* are autobiography with poetic license, peculiar mixes of fact, self-pity, sentimentality and the brilliant rendering of the circumstantiality of everyday life.

Welch is not a fiction writer in the ordinary sense. There is little in the way of narrative structure or tension in his work. Instead, he concentrates on the texture of social rituals and the psychological weight of personal possessions. The stories amble rather than develop, moving from observation to observation, incident to incident. Welch relishes the minor encounters and objects of the world, but in consequence also abandons himself to extraneous asides and the unselective recording of conversations simply, it seems, because they occurred. He often seems indiscriminate: we learn in great detail of the taste of tea and scones, while the climaxes of the tales frequently seem truncated, as if there's a hidden story in Welch's mind which hasn't quite made it into the prose. You read him not for character revelation so much as to experience his sensibility.

In barely veiled form, the 26 stories in [*The Stories of Denton Welch*] report on Welch's years in China as a child, his brief art studies, his months of convalescence, and his semi-reclusive life in the English countryside after his accident. A large number of them come through the hypersensitive eyes of a boy finding his way among strange adults. Sometimes, as in **"In the Vast House"** and **"Constance, Lady Willet,"** it's not even clear what the boy is doing inside the story at all, since the dramatic energy is completely dissipated by his presence. But Welch seems willing to sacrifice everything to record his impressionable point of view.

The pastoral, if often pathetic, world Welch creates in these tales helps define a chapter in the history of English taste. We enter a leisured society of small villages and country roads. People bicycle where they need to go, and live surrounded by woodlands and fields and creeks perfect for picnics. The characters take their good clothes and good manners and good books for granted, and spend their days doing little else than nurturing their rather snobbish views. They often seem more passionately concerned about the quality of the sandwiches served at high tea than about the people they break bread with.

Almost all the stories concern a confused outsider seeking (frequently unsuccessfully) security and love. In fact, the basic pattern of the narratives is unappeased longing. The quiet life of the upper middle-class citizens of Welch's world is almost desperate, a long lonely misery broken into intermittently by startling incidents of passion. A few of the love affairs are consummated; most end in a teasing frustration.

Though some of the more overtly passionate stories are told by a woman, there is enough homoerotic tension in the others to suggest that the choice of a female protagonist is the result of pressures of convention more than the internal necessities of art. Lower-class workers and wandering vagabonds invade the landscape on occasion, but as characters from another realm. The women in the stories are often drawn to these ruffians as harsh lovers who might deliver them from their dull, sexless lethargy. In one tale, a woman artist convinces a woodsman

to pose for her; in another, a reclusive woman has a night of passion with a wanderer seeking shelter; in a third, a shy waif promises to marry a supposed lorry driver. In all these situations, we're at the edge of Lawrentian sexual exploitation of class difference for psychic resurrection. (pp. 3, 13)

Welch's writing remained wildly inconsistent throughout his life. He can write in clichés, of "tassels" of hair and people who leave their cottages with a "light heart." Then, a page or two later, you'll read a lovely line about a singing voice that is "sad and keen and sweet, like some fruit vinegar," or see Welch delicately describe a boy licking the brass trim of a porthole. In some instances, Welch's use of symbols is ludicrous (a frustrated woman who kisses a woodsman's axe); in others, such as a complex tale of an admirer's visit to a crippled artist, Welch is extraordinarily effective in drawing meaning from a diamond brooch.

Almost every tale is notable for its asides, the observations of bric-a-brac and costume, the sensuous pleasure in food. Few stories stand out, however, as finished performances. One, **"Narcissus Bay,"** is a haunting vision of childhood in China which combines the awkward jealousies involved in boyhood friendship with being an onlooker in a strange land to create a solemn, convincing portrait of youthful gloom and revelation. Another, **"Brave and Cruel,"** is a curious tale of class conflicts and cultural disruption that shows Welch more aware of the costs of snobbish civility than he usually appears to be. Five or six others are almost as good, or have sections that are moving and original.

In one of the strangest and most inconclusive of the stories, an invalid designs his own little world in his garden, complete with a trout stream stocked with fish. One feels Welch has done much the same thing in his fiction, turning each tale into a private world he can contemplate, a miniature kingdom which reflects the life remembered and the future lost to Welch through his accident. More memoir than fantasy, the *Stories* have that distracted, wandering feel of someone dusting his familiar household belongings one last time before they're gone for good. (p. 13)

Paul Skenazy, "The Sense and Sensuality of Denton Welch," in Book World—The Washington Post, *April 6, 1986, pp. 3, 13.*

ADDITIONAL BIBLIOGRAPHY

Allen, Walter. "War and Post War: British." In his *The Modern Novel in Britain and the United States,* pp. 242-92. New York: E. P. Dutton & Co., 1964.
> Includes a short discussion of Welch's novels. Allen states that the novels are "sensational in the literal meaning of the word. They have a lack of inhibition, a total frankness, which comes, one can only think, from a total innocence; and while I respond to them as psychological casebooks rather than as fiction, they are the casebooks of a writer who was touched with genius. They do not plead; they state; and the pity one reads into them oneself, if one wishes to."

Bolitho, Hector. "My Friendship with Denton Welch." *The Texas Quarterly* X, No. 4 (Winter 1967): 235-40.
> Sketches Bolitho's June 1945 visit to Denton Welch at his home in Kent.

Braybrooke, Neville. "Savage Wars: A Study of the Journals of W. N. P. Barbellion and Denton Welch." *Queen's Quarterly* LXXV, No. 4 (Winter 1968): 651-61.

Claims that the two English writers, although a generation apart, "shared to a remarkable degree a common determination to dispute death's triumph every inch of the way and to achieve immortality in their own works."

Brooke, Jocelyn. Introduction to *The Denton Welch Journals*, by Denton Welch, edited by Jocelyn Brooke, pp. v-xvi. London: Hamish Hamilton, 1952.

Discusses characteristics of Welch's journal writing and offers a short biography. According to Brooke: "His accident, in fact, disastrous as it was to Denton Welch as a man, was quite possibly the means by which Denton Welch, the artist, was enabled to 'find himself,' and to come to terms with the demon which possessed him. All art is to some extent a substitute for living; and this was more than usually—and more poignantly—true in the case of Denton Welch."

————. "The Dual Role: A Study of Denton Welch as Painter and Writer." *The Texas Quarterly* VII, No. 3 (Autumn 1964): 120-27.

Underscores the fundamental differences between Welch's painting and writing. Brooke observes: "In his pictures he is concerned with an artificial, an 'indoor' world of private symbols and obsessions; in his writing, he celebrates life itself, the sensuous world of the summer countryside and the transient beauty of the human body: an 'outdoor' world in which nature, for the most part, predominates over art."

Chevalier, Jean-Louis. Introduction to *Dumb Instrument: Poems and Fragments*, by Denton Welch, edited by Jean-Louis Chevalier, pp. vii-x. London: Enitharmon Press, 1976.

Defines significant themes and characteristics of Welch's poetry. According to Chevalier, Welch was "a temperamental, circumstantial, occasional poet too, endowed with hyper-sensitivity, whose poetry notebooks sometimes read like private journals in verse rather than the inspired, yet disciplined, pursuit of the word."

De-la-Noy, Michael. *Denton Welch: The Making of a Writer*. Harmondsworth, England: Viking, 1984, 302 p.

A detailed biography of Welch. De-la-Noy makes use of previously unpublished material, including Welch's letters and the personal recollections and documents of those who knew him.

Fraser, G. S. "The Novel." In his *The Modern Writer and His World*, pp. 53-137. London: Derek Verschoyle, 1953.

Briefly compares Welch's work with that of William Sansom. Fraser states that both novelists "seem taken up with expressions of the personal view, the special sensibility, life not so much as it is, or might be, in itself, but as it looks from a particular personal perspective, seen through one pair of eyes."

Gransden, K. W. "Denton Welch's *Maiden Voyage*." *The British Museum Quarterly* XXI, No. 2 (July 1957): 31-2.

Reports Sir Eric Miller's gift of Welch's original manuscript of *Maiden Voyage* to the Department of Manuscripts and attempts to date the manuscript using references drawn from Welch's journal entries.

Lehmann, John. Introduction to *In Youth Is Pleasure*, by Denton Welch, pp. v-ix. Oxford: Oxford University Press, 1982.

Offers biographical highlights and favorably compares *In Youth Is Pleasure* with Welch's other novels. Of Welch's writing, Lehmann says: "Sights, sounds, and smells leap from the page in vivid detail. It is obviously the work of a young man, but one who had taught himself his craft with the most rigorous care, perhaps helped by the fact that he had trained as an artist."

Mayne, Richard. "Chinese Chippendale." *New Statesman* LXV, No. 1679 (17 May 1963): 751-52.

Considers Welch in the context of literary trends in England during the 1940s and discusses strong points and shortcomings of Welch's writing. Mayne writes: "Spiteful, silly, snobbish, and sometimes modish, much of Denton Welch's writing annoys me considerably. I don't share his bird-bright vision. What makes him a considerable writer despite these reservations is not the genuine pathos of his situation, but the use he made of it in *A Voice through a Cloud*."

Pryce-Jones, Alan. "The Personal Story." In *The Craft of Letters in England*, edited by John Lehmann, pp. 26-43. Boston: Houghton Mifflin Co., 1957.

A paragraph noting the success of Welch's autobiographical technique. Pryce-Jones concludes by noting: "Had Welch lived to be 70, he could scarcely have added to the denseness and clarity which make him so memorable a writer."

Waldhorn, Arthur, and Waldhorn, Hilda K. Introduction to "When I Was Thirteen," by Denton Welch. In their *The Rite of Becoming: Stories and Studies of Adolescence*, pp. 197-98. Cleveland: World Publishing Co., 1966.

A brief, psychoanalytical foreword to the short story. According to the Waldhorns: "Never does the youth consciously understand (though he reports feelingly) the homoerotic nuances implicit in his rapport with Archer. Nor, the story implies, was there any reason that he should have tried to analyze or doubt Archer's motives. But because innocence rarely survives maturity, the narrator, in order to end as a man, must forego his pastoral idyll for domestic tragedy."

Appendix

The following is a listing of all sources used in Volume 22 of *Twentieth-Century Literary Criticism*. Included in this list are all copyright and reprint rights and acknowledgments for those essays for which permission was obtained. Every effort has been made to trace copyright, but if omissions have been made, please let us know.

THE EXCERPTS IN TCLC, VOLUME 22, WERE REPRINTED FROM THE FOLLOWING BOOKS:

Achard, Marcel. From "Appendix: Georges Feydeau," translated by Mary Douglas Dirks, in *Let's Get a Divorce! and Other Plays*. Edited by Eric Bentley. Hill and Wang, Inc., 1958. Copyright © 1958 by Eric Bentley.

Adcock, A. St. John. From *The Glory That Was Grub Street: Impressions of Contemporary Authors*. The Musson Book Company Limited, 1928.

Aldiss, Brian W. From *Trillion Year Spree*. Atheneum, 1986, Gollancz, 1986. Copyright © 1973, 1986 Brian W. Aldiss. Reprinted with the permission of Atheneum Publishers, Inc. In Canada by Victor Gollancz Ltd.

Allen, Walter. From *The Short Story in English*. Oxford University Press, Oxford, 1981. Copyright © 1981 by Walter Allen. Reprinted by permission of Oxford University Press.

Anwar, Chairil. From *The Complete Poetry and Prose of Chairil Anwar*. Edited and translated by Burton Raffel. State University of New York Press, 1970. © 1962, 1963, 1964, 1968, 1970 by The Research Foundation of State University of New York. All rights reserved. Reprinted by permission of the State University of New York Press.

Baker, Stuart E. From *Georges Feydeau and the Aesthetics of Farce*. UMI Research Press, 1981. Copyright © 1981, 1976 Stuart E. Baker. All rights reserved. Reprinted by permission of the publisher.

Béguin, Albert. From *Léon Bloy: A Study in Impatience*. Translated by Edith M. Riley. Sheed & Ward, 1947.

Bithell, Jethro. From *Contemporary Belgian Literature*. Frederick A. Stokes Company Publishers, 1915.

Borges, Jorge Luis. From "The Mirror of Enigmas," translated by James E. Irby, in *Labyrinths: Selected Stories & Other Writings*. Edited by Donald A. Yates and James E. Irby. Revised edition. New Directions, 1964. Copyright © 1962, 1964 by New Directions Publishing Corporation. All rights reserved. Reprinted by permission of New Directions Publishing Corporation.

Brady, Sister Mary Rosalie. From *Thought and Style in the Works of Léon Bloy*. The Catholic University of America Press, Inc., 1945.

Breton, André. From *Nadja*. Translated by Richard Howard. Grove Press, 1960. Copyright © 1960 by Grove Press, Inc. Reprinted by permission of Grove Press, Inc.

Breton, André. From "Leon Trotsky's 'Lenin'," translated by Stephen Schwartz, in *What Is Surrealism? Selected Writings*. By André Breton, edited by Franklin Rosemont. Monad Press, 1978. Copyright © 1978 by Franklin Rosemont. All rights reserved. Reprinted by permission.

Brooke, Jocelyn. From an introduction to *Denton Welch: Extracts from His Published Works*. By Denton Welch, edited by Jocelyn Brooke. Chapman & Hall Ltd., 1963. Introduction © 1963 Jocelyn Brooke. Reprinted by permission.

Burleson, Donald R. From *H. P. Lovecraft: A Critical Study*. Greenwood Press, 1983. Copyright © 1983 by Donald R. Burleson. All rights reserved. Reprinted by permission of Greenwood Press, Inc., Westport, CT.

Burness, Donald. From *Shaka, King of the Zulus, in African Literature*. Three Continents Press, 1976. Copyright © 1976 Three Continents Press. All rights reserved. Reprinted by permission.

Campbell, James L., Sr. From "Olaf Stapledon," in *Science Fiction Writers: Critical Studies of the Major Authors from the Early Nineteenth Century to the Present Day*. Edited by E. F. Bleiler. Charles Scribner's Sons, 1982. Copyright © 1982 Charles Scribner's Sons. Reprinted with the permission of Charles Scribner's Sons.

Carter, Angela. From "Lovecraft and Landscape," in *The Necronomicon*. Edited by George Hay. Spearman, 1978. © Neville Spearman (Jersey) Ltd. 1978. Reprinted by permission.

Caws, Mary Ann. From *The Surrealist Voice of Robert Desnos*. University of Massachusetts Press, 1977. Copyright © 1977 by The University of Massachusetts Press. All rights reserved. Reprinted by permission.

Chandler, Frank Wadleigh. From *The Contemporary Drama of France*. Little, Brown, 1920. Copyright, 1920, by Little, Brown, and Company. Renewed 1948 by Frank W. Chandler. All rights reserved. Reprinted by permission of Little, Brown and Company.

Chase, Mary Ellen. From *The Country of the Pointed Firs and Other Stories*. By Sarah Orne Jewett, edited by Mary Ellen Chase. Norton, 1968. Introduction copyright © 1968 by Mary Ellen Chase. All rights reserved. Used by permission of Grosset & Dunlap, Inc.

Phillips, Robert. From *Denton Welch*. Twayne, 1974. Copyright 1974 by Twayne Publishers. All rights reserved. Reprinted with the permission of Twayne Publishers, a division of G. K. Hall & Co., Boston.

Proffer, Carl R. From *From Karamzin to Bunin: An Anthology of Russian Short Stories*. Edited and translated by Carl R. Proffer. Indiana University Press, 1969. Copyright © 1969 by Indiana University Press. All rights reserved. Reprinted by permission.

Pronko, Leonard C. From *Georges Feydeau*. Frederick Ungar Publishing Co., 1975. Copyright © 1975 by The Ungar Publishing Company Inc. Reprinted by permission.

Radice, Lisanne. From *Beatrice and Sidney Webb: Fabian Socialists*. St. Martin's Press, 1984, Macmillan, 1984. © Lisanne Radice 1984. All rights reserved. Reprinted by permission of St. Martin's Press, Inc. In Canada by Macmillan, London and Basingstoke.

Raffel, Burton. From *The Development of Modern Indonesian Poetry*. State University of New York Press, 1967. Copyright © 1967 by The Research Foundation of The State University of New York. All rights reserved. Reprinted by permission of the State University of New York Press.

Reed, Henry. From an introduction to *Dialstone Lane*. By W. W. Jacobs. Eyre & Spottiswoode, 1947.

Reinhardt, Kurt F. From *The Theological Novel of Modern Europe: An Analysis of Masterpieces by Eight Authors*. Frederick Ungar Publishing Co., 1969. Copyright © 1969 by The Ungar Publishing Company Inc. Reprinted by permission.

Rowse, A. L. From *The End of an Epoch: Reflections on Contemporary History*. Macmillan & Co. Ltd., 1947.

St. Armand, Barton Levi. From *H. P. Lovecraft: New England Decadent*. Silver Scarab Press, 1979. © Barton Levi St. Armand 1979. Reprinted by permission of the author.

St. Armand, Barton Levi. From *The Roots of Horror in the Fiction of H. P. Lovecraft*. Dragon Press, 1977. © 1977, Barton Levi St. Armand. All rights reserved. Reprinted by permission.

Sessions, William A. From "Giovanni Papini; or, The Probabilities of Christian Egoism," in *The Vision Obscured: Perceptions of Some Twentieth-Century Catholic Novelists*. Edited by Melvin J. Friedman. Fordham University Press, 1970. Copyright © 1970 by Fordham University Press. Reprinted by permission of the publisher.

Sharp, William. From an introduction to *Dramatic Sonnets, Poems, and Ballads: Selections from the Poems of Eugene Lee-Hamilton*. By Eugene Lee-Hamilton. The Walter Scott Publishing Co., 1903.

Sheed, F. J. From *Sidelights on the Catholic Revival*. Sheed & Ward, 1940. Copyright, 1940 by Sheed & Ward. Renewed 1968 by F. J. Sheed. Reprinted with permission from Sheed & Ward, 115 E. Armour Blvd., Kansas City, MO 64141.

Siegel, Paul N. From an introduction to *Leon Trotsky on Literature and Art*. By Leon Trotsky, edited by Paul N. Siegel. Pathfinder Press, 1970. Copyright © 1970 by Pathfinder Press, Inc. All rights reserved. Reprinted by permission.

Sitwell, Edith. From a foreword to *Maiden Voyage*. By Denton Welch. Routledge, 1943.

Smith, Curtis C. From "Olaf Stapledon's Dispassionate Objectivity," in *Voices for the Future: Essays on Major Science Fiction Writers, Vol. I*. Edited by Thomas D. Clareson. Bowling Green University Popular Press, 1976. Copyright © 1976 by The Popular Press. Reprinted by permission.

Strachey, John. From *The Strangled Cry and Other Unparliamentary Papers*. William Sloane Associates, Inc., 1962. © John Strachey 1962. Abridged by permission of William Morrow & Company, Inc.

Symonds, John Addington. From "Eugene Lee-Hamilton," in *The Poets and the Poetry of the Nineteenth Century: Robert Bridges and Contemporary Poets*. Edited by Alfred H. Miles. George Routledge & Sons, Ltd., 1906.

Szabolcsi, Miklós. From *History of Hungarian Literature*. By Tibor Klaniczay, József Szauder, and Miklós Szabolcsi, edited by Miklós Szabolcsi, translated by József Hatvany and István Farkas. Collet's, 1964. © Tibor Klaniczay, József Szauder, and Miklós Szabolcsi, 1964. Reprinted by permission.

Tawney, R. H. From *The Webbs in Perspective*. The Athlone Press, 1953.

Taylor, G. R. S. From *Leaders of Socialism, Past and Present*. Duffield & Company, 1910.

Teeuw, A. From *Modern Indonesian Literature I*. Martinus Nijhoff, 1979. Reprinted by permission of the Royal Institute of Linguistics and Anthropology, Leiden, The Netherlands.

Thorp, Margaret Farrand. From *Sarah Orne Jewett*. American Writers Pamphlet No. 61. University of Minnesota Press, Minneapolis, 1966. © 1966, University of Minnesota. All rights reserved. Reprinted by permission.

Turquet-Milnes, G. From *Some Modern Belgian Writers: A Critical Study*. Robert M. McBride & Co., 1917.

Updike, John. From "A Short Life" in *Picked-Up Pieces*. Knopf, 1975. Copyright © 1966 by John Updike. All rights reserved. Reprinted by permission of Alfred A. Knopf, Inc.

Waliszewski, K. From *A History of Russian Literature*. D. Appleton and Company, 1900.

Ward, Alfred C. From *Aspects of the Modern Short Story: English and American*. University of London Press, Ltd., 1924.

Wauthier, Claude. From *The Literature and Thought of Modern Africa*. Translated by Shirley Kay. Pall Mall Press, 1966. © 1966 Pall Mall Press Ltd. Reprinted by permission.

Cumulative Index to Authors

This index lists all author entries in the Gale Literary Criticism Series and includes cross-references to other Gale sources. For the convenience of the reader, references to the *Yearbook* in the *Contemporary Literary Criticism* series include the page number (in parentheses) after the volume number. References in the index are identified as follows:

AITN: *Authors in the News,* Volumes 1-2
CAAS: *Contemporary Authors Autobiography Series,* Volumes 1-4
CA: *Contemporary Authors* (original series), Volumes 1-118
CANR: *Contemporary Authors New Revision Series,* Volumes 1-18
CAP: *Contemporary Authors Permanent Series,* Volumes 1-2
CA-R: *Contemporary Authors* (revised editions), Volumes 1-44
CLC: *Contemporary Literary Criticism,* Volumes 1-41
CLR: *Children's Literature Review,* Volumes 1-11
DLB: *Dictionary of Literary Biography,* Volumes 1-53
DLB-DS: *Dictionary of Literary Biography Documentary Series,* Volumes 1-4
DLB-Y: *Dictionary of Literary Biography Yearbook,* Volumes 1980-1985
LC: *Literature Criticism from 1400 to 1800,* Volumes 1-4
NCLC: *Nineteenth-Century Literature Criticism,* Volumes 1-13
SAAS: *Something about the Author Autobiography Series,* Volumes 1-2
SATA: *Something about the Author,* Volumes 1-44
TCLC: *Twentieth-Century Literary Criticism,* Volumes 1-22
YABC: *Yesterday's Authors of Books for Children,* Volumes 1-2

Beerbohm, (Sir Henry) Max(imilian)
    1872-1956................... TCLC 1
    See also CA 104
    See also DLB 34

Behan, Brendan
    1923-1964...........CLC 1, 8, 11, 15
    See also CA 73-76
    See also DLB 13

Behn, Aphra 1640?-1689 .... LC 1
    See also DLB 39

Behrman, S(amuel) N(athaniel)
    1893-1973...................CLC 40
    See also CAP 1
    See also CA 15-16
    See also obituary CA 45-48
    See also DLB 7, 44

Belasco, David 1853-1931........ TCLC 3
    See also CA 104
    See also DLB 7

Belcheva, Elisaveta 1893-
    See Bagryana, Elisaveta

Belinski, Vissarion Grigoryevich
    1811-1848................... NCLC 5

Belitt, Ben 1911- ....CLC 22
    See also CAAS 4
    See also CANR 7
    See also CA 13-16R
    See also DLB 5

Bell, Acton 1820-1849
    See Brontë, Anne

Bell, Currer 1816-1855
    See Brontë, Charlotte

Bell, Madison Smartt 1957-........CLC 41
    See also CA 111

Bell, Marvin 1937-............. CLC 8, 31
    See also CA 21-24R
    See also DLB 5

Bellamy, Edward 1850-1898 ...... NCLC 4
    See also DLB 12

Belloc, (Joseph) Hilaire (Pierre Sébastien Réné Swanton)
    1870-1953............... TCLC 7, 18
    See also CA 106
    See also YABC 1
    See also DLB 19

Bellow, Saul
    1915-.....CLC 1, 2, 3, 6, 8, 10, 13, 15,
                            25, 33, 34 (545)
    See also CA 5-8R
    See also DLB 2, 28
    See also DLB-Y 82
    See also DLB-DS 3
    See also AITN 2

Belser, Reimond Karel Maria de 1929-
    See Ruyslinck, Ward

Bely, Andrey 1880-1934......... TCLC 7
    See also CA 104

Benary-Isbert, Margot
    1889-1979...................CLC 12
    See also CANR 4
    See also CA 5-8R
    See also obituary CA 89-92
    See also SATA 2
    See also obituary SATA 21

Benavente (y Martinez), Jacinto
    1866-1954.................. TCLC 3
    See also CA 106

Benchley, Peter (Bradford)
    1940-.....................CLC 4, 8
    See also CANR 12
    See also CA 17-20R
    See also SATA 3
    See also AITN 2

Benchley, Robert 1889-1945 ...... TCLC 1
    See also CA 105
    See also DLB 11

Benedikt, Michael 1935-........ CLC 4, 14
    See also CANR 7
    See also CA 13-16R
    See also DLB 5

Benet, Juan 1927- ....CLC 28

Benét, Stephen Vincent
    1898-1943................... TCLC 7
    See also CA 104
    See also YABC 1
    See also DLB 4, 48

Benn, Gottfried 1886-1956....... TCLC 3
    See also CA 106

Bennett, (Enoch) Arnold
    1867-1931............... TCLC 5, 20
    See also CA 106
    See also DLB 10, 34

Bennett, George Harold 1930-
    See Bennett, Hal
    See also CA 97-100

Bennett, Hal 1930-.................CLC 5
    See also Bennett, George Harold
    See also DLB 33

Bennett, Jay 1912-................CLC 35
    See also CANR 11
    See also CA 69-72
    See also SATA 27

Bennett, Louise (Simone)
    1919-.....................CLC 28
    See also Bennett-Coverly, Louise Simone

Bennett-Coverly, Louise Simone 1919-
    See Bennett, Louise (Simone)
    See also CA 97-100

Benson, Jackson J.
    1930- .... CLC 34 (404)
    See also CA 25-28R

Benson, Sally 1900-1972...........CLC 17
    See also CAP 1
    See also CA 19-20
    See also obituary CA 37-40R
    See also SATA 1, 35
    See also obituary SATA 27

Benson, Stella 1892-1933 .... TCLC 17
    See also DLB 36

Bentley, E(dmund) C(lerihew)
    1875-1956................. TCLC 12
    See also CA 108

Bentley, Eric (Russell) 1916- ....CLC 24
    See also CANR 6
    See also CA 5-8R

Berger, John (Peter) 1926-...... CLC 2, 19
    See also CA 81-84
    See also DLB 14

Berger, Melvin (H.) 1927- ....CLC 12
    See also CANR 4
    See also CA 5-8R
    See also SAAS 2
    See also SATA 5

Berger, Thomas (Louis)
    1924-.......... CLC 3, 5, 8, 11, 18, 38
    See also CANR 5
    See also CA 1-4R
    See also DLB 2
    See also DLB-Y 80

Bergman, (Ernst) Ingmar
    1918-........................CLC 16
    See also CA 81-84

Bergstein, Eleanor 1938- ....CLC 4
    See also CANR 5
    See also CA 53-56

Bermant, Chaim 1929-............CLC 40
    See also CANR 6
    See also CA 57-60

Bernanos, (Paul Louis) Georges
    1888-1948................... TCLC 3
    See also CA 104

Bernhard, Thomas 1931- .... CLC 3, 32
    See also CA 85-88

Berrigan, Daniel J. 1921-...........CLC 4
    See also CAAS 1
    See also CANR 11
    See also CA 33-36R
    See also DLB 5

Berrigan, Edmund Joseph Michael, Jr.
    1934-1983
    See Berrigan, Ted
    See also CANR 14
    See also CA 61-64
    See also obituary CA 110

Berrigan, Ted 1934-1983 ....CLC 37
    See also Berrigan, Edmund Joseph
        Michael, Jr.
    See also DLB 5

Berry, Chuck 1926-...............CLC 17

Berry, Wendell (Erdman)
    1934-.................CLC 4, 6, 8, 27
    See also CA 73-76
    See also DLB 5, 6
    See also AITN 1

Berryman, John
    1914-1972..... CLC 1, 2, 3, 4, 6, 8, 10,
                                13, 25
    See also CAP 1
    See also CA 15-16
    See also obituary CA 33-36R
    See also DLB 48

Bertolucci, Bernardo 1940- ....CLC 16
    See also CA 106

Besant, Annie (Wood)
    1847-1933................... TCLC 9
    See also CA 105

Bessie, Alvah 1904-1985...........CLC 23
    See also CANR 2
    See also CA 5-8R
    See also obituary CA 116
    See also DLB 26

Beti, Mongo 1932-................CLC 27

Betjeman, John
    1906-1984...... CLC 2, 6, 10, 34 (305)
    See also CA 9-12R
    See also obituary CA 112
    See also DLB 20
    See also DLB-Y 84

Betti, Ugo 1892-1953.............TCLC 5
    See also CA 104

Burr, Anne 1937-...................CLC 6
See also CA 25-28R

Burroughs, Edgar Rice
1875-1950..................TCLC 2
See also CA 104
See also DLB 8
See also SATA 41

Burroughs, William S(eward)
1914-.............CLC 1, 2, 5, 15, 22
See also CA 9-12R
See also DLB 2, 8, 16
See also DLB-Y 81
See also AITN 2

Busch, Frederick 1941-......CLC 7, 10, 18
See also CAAS 1
See also CA 33-36R
See also DLB 6

Bush, Ronald 19??-..........CLC 34 (523)

Butler, Octavia E(stelle) 1947-......CLC 38
See also CANR 12
See also CA 73-76
See also DLB 33

Butler, Samuel 1835-1902 .... TCLC 1
See also CA 104
See also DLB 18

Butor, Michel (Marie François)
1926-.............CLC 1, 3, 8, 11, 15
See also CA 9-12R

Buzzati, Dino 1906-1972..........CLC 36
See also obituary CA 33-36R

Byars, Betsy 1928-................CLC 35
See also CLR 1
See also CANR 18
See also CA 33-36R
See also SAAS 1
See also SATA 4

Byatt, A(ntonia) S(usan Drabble)
1936-........................CLC 19
See also CANR 13
See also CA 13-16R
See also DLB 14

Byrne, David 1953?-..............CLC 26

Byrne, John Keyes 1926-
See Leonard, Hugh
See also CA 102

Byron, George Gordon (Noel), Lord Byron
1788-1824................NCLC 2, 12

Caballero, Fernán 1796-1877 .... NCLC 10

Cabell, James Branch
1879-1958..................TCLC 6
See also CA 105
See also DLB 9

Cable, George Washington
1844-1925..................TCLC 4
See also CA 104
See also DLB 12

Cabrera Infante, G(uillermo)
1929-.....................CLC 5, 25
See also CA 85-88

Cage, John (Milton, Jr.) 1912-.....CLC 41
See also CANR 9
See also CA 13-16R

Cain, G. 1929-
See Cabrera Infante, G(uillermo)

Cain, James M(allahan)
1892-1977..............CLC 3, 11, 28
See also CANR 8
See also CA 17-20R
See also obituary CA 73-76
See also AITN 1

Caldwell, Erskine 1903-......CLC 1, 8, 14
See also CAAS 1
See also CANR 2
See also CA 1-4R
See also DLB 9
See also AITN 1

Caldwell, (Janet Miriam) Taylor (Holland)
1900-1985........CLC 2, 28, 39 (301)
See also CANR 5
See also CA 5-8R
See also obituary CA 116

Calisher, Hortense
1911-...............CLC 2, 4, 8, 38
See also CANR 1
See also CA 1-4R
See also DLB 2

Callaghan, Morley (Edward)
1903-............... CLC 3, 14, 41
See also CA 9-12R

Calvino, Italo
1923-1985.......CLC 5, 8, 11, 22, 33,
39 (305)
See also CA 85-88
See also obituary CA 116

Campana, Dino 1885-1932...... TCLC 20
See also CA 117

Campbell, John W(ood), Jr.
1910-1971....................CLC 32
See also CAP 2
See also CA 21-22
See also obituary CA 29-32R
See also DLB 8

Campbell, (Ignatius) Roy (Dunnachie)
1901-1957....................TCLC 5
See also CA 104
See also DLB 20

Campbell, (William) Wilfred
1861-1918.................. TCLC 9
See also CA 106

Camus, Albert
1913-1960...... CLC 1, 2, 4, 9, 11, 14,
32
See also CA 89-92

Canby, Vincent 1924-.............CLC 13
See also CA 81-84

Canetti, Elias 1905-.........CLC 3, 14, 25
See also CA 21-24R

Cape, Judith 1916-
See Page, P(atricia) K(athleen)

Čapek, Karel 1890-1938......... TCLC 6
See also CA 104

Capote, Truman
1924-1984........CLC 1, 3, 8, 13, 19,
34 (320), 38
See also CANR 18
See also CA 5-8R
See also obituary CA 113
See also DLB 2
See also DLB-Y 80, 84

Capra, Frank 1897-..............CLC 16
See also CA 61-64

Caputo, Philip 1941-..............CLC 32
See also CA 73-76

Cardenal, Ernesto 1925-..........CLC 31
See also CANR 2
See also CA 49-52

Carey, Ernestine Gilbreth 1908-
See Gilbreth, Frank B(unker), Jr. and
Carey, Ernestine Gilbreth
See also CA 5-8R
See also SATA 2

Carey, Peter 1943-................CLC 40

Carleton, William 1794-1869..... NCLC 3

Carlisle, Henry (Coffin) 1926-......CLC 33
See also CANR 15
See also CA 13-16R

Carman, (William) Bliss
1861-1929.................. TCLC 7
See also CA 104

Carpenter, Don(ald Richard)
1931-........................CLC 41
See also CANR 1
See also CA 45-48

Carpentier (y Valmont), Alejo
1904-1980............CLC 8, 11, 38
See also CANR 11
See also CA 65-68
See also obituary CA 97-100

Carr, John Dickson 1906-1977 ......CLC 3
See also CANR 3
See also CA 49-52
See also obituary CA 69-72

Carr, Virginia Spencer
1929-................ CLC 34 (419)
See also CA 61-64

Carrier, Roch 1937- ....CLC 13
See also DLB 53

Carroll, James (P.) 1943-..........CLC 38
See also CA 81-84

Carroll, Jim 1951-................CLC 35
See also CA 45-48

Carroll, Lewis 1832-1898........ NCLC 2
See also Dodgson, Charles Lutwidge
See also CLR 2
See also DLB 18

Carroll, Paul Vincent
1900-1968....................CLC 10
See also CA 9-12R
See also obituary CA 25-28R
See also DLB 10

Carruth, Hayden
1921-................CLC 4, 7, 10, 18
See also CANR 4
See also CA 9-12R
See also DLB 5

Carter, Angela (Olive)
1940-.................... CLC 5, 41
See also CANR 12
See also CA 53-56
See also DLB 14

Carver, Raymond 1938-....... CLC 22, 36
See also CANR 17
See also CA 33-36R
See also DLB-Y 84

Cary, (Arthur) Joyce
1888-1957.................. TCLC 1
See also CA 104
See also DLB 15

Gelbart, Larry (Simon) 1923- ......CLC 21
　　See also CA 73-76

Gelber, Jack 1932- .... CLC 1, 6, 14
　　See also CANR 2
　　See also CA 1-4R
　　See also DLB 7

Gellhorn, Martha (Ellis) 1908- .....CLC 14
　　See also CA 77-80
　　See also DLB-Y 82

Genet, Jean 1910- ..... CLC 1, 2, 5, 10, 14
　　See also CA 13-16R

Gent, Peter 1942-.................CLC 29
　　See also CA 89-92
　　See also DLB-Y 82
　　See also AITN 1

George, Jean Craighead 1919- .....CLC 35
　　See also CLR 1
　　See also CA 5-8R
　　See also SATA 2

George, Stefan (Anton)
　　1868-1933................ TCLC 2, 14
　　See also CA 104

Gerhardi, William (Alexander) 1895-1977
　　See Gerhardie, William (Alexander)

Gerhardie, William (Alexander)
　　1895-1977....................CLC 5
　　See also CANR 18
　　See also CA 25-28R
　　See also obituary CA 73-76
　　See also DLB 36

Gertler, T(rudy) 1946?- ...... CLC 34 (49)
　　See also CA 116

Gessner, Friedrike Victoria 1910-1980
　　See Adamson, Joy(-Friederike Victoria)

Ghelderode, Michel de
　　1898-1962................. CLC 6, 11
　　See also CA 85-88

Ghiselin, Brewster 1903- ....CLC 23
　　See also CANR 13
　　See also CA 13-16R

Giacosa, Giuseppe 1847-1906 ..... TCLC 7
　　See also CA 104

Gibbon, Lewis Grassic
　　1901-1935.................. TCLC 4
　　See also Mitchell, James Leslie

Gibran, (Gibran) Kahlil
　　1883-1931................ TCLC 1, 9
　　See also CA 104

Gibson, William 1914- ....CLC 23
　　See also CANR 9
　　See also CA 9-12R
　　See also DLB 7

Gibson, William 1948- ...... CLC 39 (139)

Gide, André (Paul Guillaume)
　　1869-1951................ TCLC 5, 12
　　See also CA 104

Gifford, Barry (Colby)
　　1946-.................. CLC 34 (457)
　　See also CANR 9
　　See also CA 65-68

Gilbert, (Sir) W(illiam) S(chwenck)
　　1836-1911.................. TCLC 3
　　See also CA 104
　　See also SATA 36

Gilbreth, Ernestine 1908-
　　See Carey, Ernestine Gilbreth

Gilbreth, Frank B(unker), Jr. 1911-
　　See Gilbreth, Frank B(unker), Jr. and
　　　Carey, Ernestine Gilbreth
　　See also CA 9-12R
　　See also SATA 2

Gilbreth, Frank B(unker), Jr. 1911- and
　　Carey, Ernestine Gilbreth
　　1908-.....................CLC 17

Gilchrist, Ellen 1939- .... CLC 34 (164)
　　See also CA 113, 116

Giles, Molly 1942-........... CLC 39 (64)

Gilliam, Terry (Vance) 1940-
　　See Monty Python
　　See also CA 108, 113

Gilliatt, Penelope (Ann Douglass)
　　1932-.................. CLC 2, 10, 13
　　See also CA 13-16R
　　See also DLB 14
　　See also AITN 2

Gilman, Charlotte (Anna) Perkins (Stetson)
　　1860-1935................... TCLC 9
　　See also CA 106

Gilmour, David 1944-
　　See Pink Floyd

Gilroy, Frank D(aniel) 1925-........CLC 2
　　See also CA 81-84
　　See also DLB 7

Ginsberg, Allen
　　1926-.........CLC 1, 2, 3, 4, 6, 13, 36
　　See also CANR 2
　　See also CA 1-4R
　　See also DLB 5, 16
　　See also AITN 1

Ginzburg, Natalia 1916-........ CLC 5, 11
　　See also CA 85-88

Giono, Jean 1895-1970......... CLC 4, 11
　　See also CANR 2
　　See also CA 45-48
　　See also obituary CA 29-32R

Giovanni, Nikki 1943-........ CLC 2, 4, 19
　　See also CLR 6
　　See also CANR 18
　　See also CA 29-32R
　　See also SATA 24
　　See also DLB 5
　　See also AITN 1

Giovene, Andrea 1904-.............CLC 7
　　See also CA 85-88

Gippius, Zinaida (Nikolayevna) 1869-1945
　　See also Hippius, Zinaida
　　See also CA 106

Giraudoux, (Hippolyte) Jean
　　1882-1944................ TCLC 2, 7
　　See also CA 104

Gironella, José María 1917-........CLC 11
　　See also CA 101

Gissing, George (Robert)
　　1857-1903................... TCLC 3
　　See also CA 105
　　See also DLB 18

Glanville, Brian (Lester) 1931- ......CLC 6
　　See also CANR 3
　　See also CA 5-8R
　　See also DLB 15
　　See also SATA 42

Glasgow, Ellen (Anderson Gholson)
　　1873?-1945................ TCLC 2, 7
　　See also CA 104
　　See also DLB 9, 12

Glassco, John 1909-1981 ....CLC 9
　　See also CANR 15
　　See also CA 13-16R
　　See also obituary CA 102

Glasser, Ronald J. 1940?- ....CLC 37

Glissant, Edouard 1928-...........CLC 10

Gloag, Julian 1930-...............CLC 40
　　See also CANR 10
　　See also CA 65-68
　　See also AITN 1

Glück, Louise 1943- .... CLC 7, 22
　　See also CA 33-36R
　　See also DLB 5

Godard, Jean-Luc 1930-...........CLC 20
　　See also CA 93-96

Godwin, Gail 1937-....... CLC 5, 8, 22, 31
　　See also CANR 15
　　See also CA 29-32R
　　See also DLB 6

Goethe, Johann Wolfgang von
　　1749-1832.................. NCLC 4

Gogarty, Oliver St. John
　　1878-1957................. TCLC 15
　　See also CA 109
　　See also DLB 15, 19

Gogol, Nikolai (Vasilyevich)
　　1809-1852.................. NCLC 5

Gökçeli, Yasar Kemal 1923-
　　See Kemal, Yashar

Gold, Herbert 1924-......... CLC 4, 7, 14
　　See also CANR 17
　　See also CA 9-12R
　　See also DLB 2
　　See also DLB-Y 81

Goldbarth, Albert 1948-........ CLC 5, 38
　　See also CANR 6
　　See also CA 53-56

Goldberg, Anatol 19??-...... CLC 34 (433)

Golding, William (Gerald)
　　1911-........CLC 1, 2, 3, 8, 10, 17, 27
　　See also CANR 13
　　See also CA 5-8R
　　See also DLB 15

Goldman, Emma 1869-1940 ..... TCLC 13
　　See also CA 110

Goldman, William (W.) 1931-.......CLC 1
　　See also CA 9-12R
　　See also DLB 44

Goldmann, Lucien 1913-1970 ......CLC 24
　　See also CAP 2
　　See also CA 25-28

Goldoni, Carlo 1707-1793 ....LC 4

Goldsberry, Steven 1949-..... CLC 34 (54)

Goldsmith, Oliver 1728?-1774........LC 2
　　See also SATA 26
　　See also DLB 39

Gombrowicz, Witold
　　1904-1969.............. CLC 4, 7, 11
　　See also CAP 2
　　See also CA 19-20
　　See also obituary CA 25-28R

Leavitt, David 1961?- .... CLC 34 (77)
See also CA 116

Lebowitz, Fran(ces Ann)
1951?- .... CLC 11, 36
See also CANR 14
See also CA 81-84

Le Carré, John
1931- .... CLC 3, 5, 9, 15, 28
See also Cornwell, David (John Moore)

Le Clézio, J(ean) M(arie) G(ustave)
1940- .... CLC 31
See also CA 116

Leduc, Violette 1907-1972 .... CLC 22
See also CAP 1
See also CA 13-14
See also obituary CA 33-36R

Lee, Andrea 1953- .... CLC 36

Lee, Don L. 1942- .... CLC 2
See also Madhubuti, Haki R.
See also CA 73-76

Lee, (Nelle) Harper 1926- .... CLC 12
See also CA 13-16R
See also SATA 11
See also DLB 6

Lee, Lawrence 1903- .... CLC 34 (457)
See also CA 25-28R

Lee, Manfred B(ennington) 1905-1971
See Queen, Ellery
See also CANR 2
See also CA 1-4R
See also obituary CA 29-32R

Lee, Stan 1922- .... CLC 17
See also CA 108, 111

Lee, Vernon 1856-1935 .... TCLC 5
See also Paget, Violet

Lee-Hamilton, Eugene (Jacob)
1845-1907 .... TCLC 22

Leet, Judith 1935- .... CLC 11

Le Fanu, Joseph Sheridan
1814-1873 .... NCLC 9
See also DLB 21

Leffland, Ella 1931- .... CLC 19
See also CA 29-32R
See also DLB-Y 84

Léger, (Marie-Rene) Alexis Saint-Léger
1887-1975
See Perse, St.-John
See also CA 13-16R
See also obituary CA 61-64

Le Guin, Ursula K(roeber)
1929- .... CLC 8, 13, 22
See also CLR 3
See also CANR 9
See also CA 21-24R
See also SATA 4
See also DLB 8
See also AITN 1

Lehmann, Rosamond (Nina)
1901- .... CLC 5
See also CANR 8
See also CA 77-80
See also DLB 15

Leiber, Fritz (Reuter, Jr.)
1910- .... CLC 25
See also CANR 2
See also CA 45-48
See also DLB 8

Leithauser, Brad 1953- .... CLC 27
See also CA 107

Lelchuk, Alan 1938- .... CLC 5
See also CANR 1
See also CA 45-48

Lem, Stanislaw 1921- .... CLC 8, 15, 40
See also CAAS 1
See also CA 105

Lemann, Nancy 1956- .... CLC 39 (75)
See also CA 118

Lemonnier, (Antoine Louis) Camille
1844-1913 .... TCLC 22

L'Engle, Madeleine 1918- .... CLC 12
See also CLR 1
See also CANR 3
See also CA 1-4R
See also SATA 1, 27
See also AITN 2

Lengyel, Jozsef 1896-1975 .... CLC 7
See also CA 85-88
See also obituary CA 57-60

Lennon, John (Ono)
1940-1980 .... CLC 35
See also Lennon, John (Ono) and
McCartney, Paul
See also CA 102

Lennon, John (Ono) 1940-1980 and
McCartney, Paul 1942- .... CLC 12

Lennon, John Winston 1940-1980
See Lennon, John (Ono)

Lentricchia, Frank (Jr.)
1940- .... CLC 34 (571)
See also CA 25-28R

Lenz, Siegfried 1926- .... CLC 27
See also CA 89-92

Leonard, Elmore
1925- .... CLC 28, 34 (212)
See also CANR 12
See also CA 81-84
See also AITN 1

Leonard, Hugh 1926- .... CLC 19
See also Byrne, John Keyes
See also DLB 13

Lerman, Eleanor 1952- .... CLC 9
See also CA 85-88

Lermontov, Mikhail Yuryevich
1814-1841 .... NCLC 5

Lesage, Alain-René 1668-1747 .... LC 2

Lessing, Doris (May)
1919- .... CLC 1, 2, 3, 6, 10, 15, 22, 40
See also CA 9-12R
See also DLB 15
See also DLB-Y 85

Lester, Richard 1932- .... CLC 20

Leverson, Ada 1865-1936 .... TCLC 18

Levertov, Denise
1923- .... CLC 1, 2, 3, 5, 8, 15, 28
See also CANR 3
See also CA 1-4R
See also DLB 5

Levi, Peter (Chad Tiger) 1931- ..... CLC 41
See also CA 5-8R
See also DLB 40

Levi, Primo 1919- .... CLC 37
See also CANR 12
See also CA 13-16R

Levin, Ira 1929- .... CLC 3, 6
See also CANR 17
See also CA 21-24R

Levin, Meyer 1905-1981 .... CLC 7
See also CANR 15
See also CA 9-12R
See also obituary CA 104
See also SATA 21
See also obituary SATA 27
See also DLB 9, 28
See also DLB-Y 81
See also AITN 1

Levine, Philip
1928- .... CLC 2, 4, 5, 9, 14, 33
See also CANR 9
See also CA 9-12R
See also DLB 5

Lévi-Strauss, Claude 1908- .... CLC 38
See also CANR 6
See also CA 1-4R

Levitin, Sonia 1934- .... CLC 17
See also CA 29-32R
See also SAAS 2
See also SATA 4

Lewis, Alun 1915-1944 .... TCLC 3
See also CA 104
See also DLB 20

Lewis, C(ecil) Day 1904-1972
See Day Lewis, C(ecil)

Lewis, C(live) S(taples)
1898-1963 .... CLC 1, 3, 6, 14, 27
See also CLR 3
See also CA 81-84
See also SATA 13
See also DLB 15

Lewis, (Harry) Sinclair
1885-1951 .... TCLC 4, 13
See also CA 104
See also DLB 9
See also DLB-DS 1

Lewis (Winters), Janet 1899- .... CLC 41
See also Winters, Janet Lewis

Lewis, Matthew Gregory
1775-1818 .... NCLC 11
See also DLB 39

Lewis, (Percy) Wyndham
1882?-1957 .... TCLC 2, 9
See also CA 104
See also DLB 15

Lewisohn, Ludwig 1883-1955 .... TCLC 19
See also CA 107
See also DLB 4, 9, 28

Lezama Lima, José
1910-1976 .... CLC 4, 10
See also CA 77-80

Li Fei-kan 1904-
See Pa Chin
See also CA 105

Lie, Jonas (Lauritz Idemil)
1833-1908 .... TCLC 5

Lieber, Joel 1936-1971 .... CLC 6
See also CA 73-76
See also obituary CA 29-32R

McKay, Claude 1890-1948....... TCLC 7
See also CA 104
See also DLB 4, 45

McKuen, Rod 1933- .... CLC 1, 3
See also CA 41-44R
See also AITN 1

McLuhan, (Herbert) Marshall
1911-1980.................CLC 37
See also CANR 12
See also CA 9-12R
See also obituary CA 102

McManus, Declan Patrick 1955-
See Costello, Elvis

McMurtry, Larry (Jeff)
1936-............ CLC 2, 3, 7, 11, 27
See also CA 5-8R
See also DLB 2
See also DLB-Y 80
See also AITN 2

McNally, Terrence 1939- ..... CLC 4, 7, 41
See also CANR 2
See also CA 45-48
See also DLB 7

McPhee, John 1931- ....CLC 36
See also CA 65-68

McPherson, James Alan 1943- .....CLC 19
See also CA 25-28R
See also DLB 38

McPherson, William
1939-...................... CLC 34 (85)
See also CA 57-60

McSweeney, Kerry 19??- .... CLC 34 (579)

Mead, Margaret 1901-1978 ....CLC 37
See also CANR 4
See also CA 1-4R
See also obituary CA 81-84
See also SATA 20
See also AITN 1

Meaker, M. J. 1927-
See Kerr, M. E.
See Meaker, Marijane

Meaker, Marijane 1927-
See Kerr, M. E.
See also CA 107
See also SATA 20

Medoff, Mark (Howard)
1940-..................... CLC 6, 23
See also CANR 5
See also CA 53-56
See also DLB 7
See also AITN 1

Megged, Aharon 1920-.............CLC 9
See also CANR 1
See also CA 49-52

Mehta, Ved (Parkash) 1934- ....CLC 37
See also CANR 2
See also CA 1-4R

Mellor, John 1953?-
See The Clash

Meltzer, Milton 1915-.............CLC 26
See also CA 13-16R
See also SAAS 1
See also SATA 1

Melville, Herman
1819-1891...............NCLC 3, 12
See also DLB 3

Mencken, H(enry) L(ouis)
1880-1956.................. TCLC 13
See also CA 105
See also DLB 11, 29

Mercer, David 1928-1980..........CLC 5
See also CA 9-12R
See also obituary CA 102
See also DLB 13

Meredith, George 1828-1909 ..... TCLC 17
See also DLB 18, 35

Meredith, William (Morris)
1919-.................. CLC 4, 13, 22
See also CANR 6
See also CA 9-12R
See also DLB 5

Mérimée, Prosper 1803-1870...... NCLC 6

Merrill, James (Ingram)
1926-.......... CLC 2, 3, 6, 8, 13, 18,
34 (225)
See also CANR 10
See also CA 13-16R
See also DLB 5
See also DLB-Y 85

Merton, Thomas (James)
1915-1968...... CLC 1, 3, 11, 34 (460)
See also CA 5-8R
See also obituary CA 25-28R
See also DLB 48
See also DLB-Y 81

Merwin, W(illiam) S(tanley)
1927-.........CLC 1, 2, 3, 5, 8, 13, 18
See also CANR 15
See also CA 13-16R
See also DLB 5

Metcalf, John 1938-..............CLC 37
See also CA 113

Mew, Charlotte (Mary)
1870-1928.................. TCLC 8
See also CA 105
See also DLB 19

Mewshaw, Michael 1943-...........CLC 9
See also CANR 7
See also CA 53-56
See also DLB-Y 80

Meyer-Meyrink, Gustav 1868-1932
See Meyrink, Gustav
See also CA 117

Meyrink, Gustav 1868-1932..... TCLC 21
See also Meyer-Meyrink, Gustav

Meyers, Jeffrey 1939-....... CLC 39 (427)
See also CA 73-76

Meynell, Alice (Christiana Gertrude
Thompson) 1847-1922 .... TCLC 6
See also CA 104
See also DLB 19

Michaels, Leonard 1933- .... CLC 6, 25
See also CA 61-64

Michaux, Henri 1899-1984...... CLC 8, 19
See also CA 85-88
See also obituary CA 114

Michener, James A(lbert)
1907-...............CLC 1, 5, 11, 29
See also CA 5-8R
See also DLB 6
See also AITN 1

Mickiewicz, Adam 1798-1855 ..... NCLC 3

Middleton, Christopher 1926- ......CLC 13
See also CA 13-16R
See also DLB 40

Middleton, Stanley 1919- .... CLC 7, 38
See also CA 25-28R
See also DLB 14

Miguéis, José Rodrigues 1901- .....CLC 10

Miles, Josephine (Louise)
1911-1985......CLC 1, 2, 14, 34 (243),
39 (352)
See also CANR 2
See also CA 1-4R
See also obituary CA 116
See also DLB 48

Mill, John Stuart 1806-1873 ..... NCLC 11

Millar, Kenneth 1915-1983
See Macdonald, Ross
See also CANR 16
See also CA 9-12R
See also obituary CA 110
See also DLB 2
See also DLB-Y 83

Millay, Edna St. Vincent
1892-1950.................. TCLC 4
See also CA 104
See also DLB 45

Miller, Arthur
1915-.......... CLC 1, 2, 6, 10, 15, 26
See also CANR 2
See also CA 1-4R
See also DLB 7
See also AITN 1

Miller, Henry (Valentine)
1891-1980......... CLC 1, 2, 4, 9, 14
See also CA 9-12R
See also obituary CA 97-100
See also DLB 4, 9
See also DLB-Y 80

Miller, Jason 1939?-...............CLC 2
See also CA 73-76
See also DLB 7
See also AITN 1

Miller, Walter M(ichael), Jr.
1923-.................... CLC 4, 30
See also CA 85-88
See also DLB 8

Millhauser, Steven 1943- ....CLC 21
See also CA 108, 110, 111
See also DLB 2

Milne, A(lan) A(lexander)
1882-1956.................. TCLC 6
See also CLR 1
See also CA 104
See also YABC 1
See also DLB 10

Miłosz, Czesław
1911-...............CLC 5, 11, 22, 31
See also CA 81-84

Miner, Valerie (Jane) 1947-........CLC 40
See also CA 97-100

Minus, Ed 1938- .... CLC 39 (79)

Miró (Ferrer), Gabriel (Francisco Víctor)
1879-1930.................. TCLC 5
See also CA 104

Mishima, Yukio
1925-1970......... CLC 2, 4, 6, 9, 27
See also Hiraoka, Kimitake

Mistral, Gabriela 1889-1957 . . . . . . TCLC 2
  See also CA 104

Mitchell, James Leslie 1901-1935
  See Gibbon, Lewis Grassic
  See also CA 104
  See also DLB 15

Mitchell, Joni 1943- . . . . CLC 12
  See also CA 112

Mitchell (Marsh), Margaret (Munnerlyn)
  1900-1949 . . . . TCLC 11
  See also CA 109
  See also DLB 9

Mitchell, W(illiam) O(rmond)
  1914- . . . . CLC 25
  See also CANR 15
  See also CA 77-80

Mitford, Mary Russell
  1787-1855 . . . . NCLC 4

Modiano, Patrick (Jean) 1945- . . . . . CLC 18
  See also CANR 17
  See also CA 85-88

Mofolo, Thomas (Mokopu)
  1876-1948 . . . . TCLC 22

Mohr, Nicholasa 1935- . . . . CLC 12
  See also CANR 1
  See also CA 49-52
  See also SATA 8

Mojtabai, A(nn) G(race)
  1938- . . . . CLC 5, 9, 15, 29
  See also CA 85-88

Molnár, Ferenc 1878-1952 . . . . . . TCLC 20
  See also CA 109

Momaday, N(avarre) Scott
  1934- . . . . CLC 2, 19
  See also CANR 14
  See also CA 25-28R
  See also SATA 30

Monroe, Harriet 1860-1936 . . . . . . TCLC 12
  See also CA 109

Montagu, Elizabeth 1720-1800 . . . . NCLC 7

Montague, John (Patrick)
  1929- . . . . CLC 13
  See also CANR 9
  See also CA 9-12R
  See also DLB 40

Montale, Eugenio
  1896-1981 . . . . CLC 7, 9, 18
  See also CA 17-20R
  See also obituary CA 104

Montgomery, Marion (H., Jr.)
  1925- . . . . CLC 7
  See also CANR 3
  See also CA 1-4R
  See also DLB 6
  See also AITN 1

Montgomery, Robert Bruce 1921-1978
  See Crispin, Edmund
  See also CA 104

Montherlant, Henri (Milon) de
  1896-1972 . . . . CLC 8, 19
  See also CA 85-88
  See also obituary CA 37-40R

Monty Python . . . . CLC 21
  See also Cleese, John

Mooney, Ted 1951- . . . . CLC 25

Moorcock, Michael (John)
  1939- . . . . CLC 5, 27
  See also CANR 2, 17
  See also CA 45-48
  See also DLB 14

Moore, Brian
  1921- . . . . CLC 1, 3, 5, 7, 8, 19, 32
  See also CANR 1
  See also CA 1-4R

Moore, George (Augustus)
  1852-1933 . . . . TCLC 7
  See also CA 104
  See also DLB 10, 18

Moore, Lorrie 1957- . . . . CLC 39 (82)
  See also Moore, Marie Lorena

Moore, Marianne (Craig)
  1887-1972 . . . . . . CLC 1, 2, 4, 8, 10, 13,
                                19
  See also CANR 3
  See also CA 1-4R
  See also obituary CA 33-36R
  See also DLB 45
  See also SATA 20

Moore, Marie Lorena 1957-
  See Moore, Lorrie
  See also CA 116

Moore, Thomas 1779-1852 . . . . NCLC 6

Morand, Paul 1888-1976 . . . . CLC 41
  See also obituary CA 69-72

Morante, Elsa 1918- . . . . CLC 8
  See also CA 85-88

Moravia, Alberto
  1907- . . . . CLC 2, 7, 11, 18, 27
  See also Pincherle, Alberto

Moréas, Jean 1856-1910 . . . . TCLC 18

Morgan, Berry 1919- . . . . CLC 6
  See also CA 49-52
  See also DLB 6

Morgan, Edwin (George)
  1920- . . . . CLC 31
  See also CANR 3
  See also CA 7-8R
  See also DLB 27

Morgan, Frederick 1922- . . . . CLC 23
  See also CA 17-20R

Morgan, Janet 1945- . . . . CLC 39 (436)
  See also CA 65-68

Morgan, Robin 1941- . . . . CLC 2
  See also CA 69-72

Morgenstern, Christian (Otto Josef Wolfgang)
  1871-1914 . . . . TCLC 8
  See also CA 105

Mori Ōgai 1862-1922 . . . . TCLC 14
  See also Mori Rintaro

Mori Rintaro 1862-1922
  See Mori Ōgai
  See also CA 110

Mörike, Eduard (Friedrich)
  1804-1875 . . . . NCLC 10

Moritz, Karl Philipp 1756-1793 . . . . . . LC 2

Morris, Julian 1916-
  See West, Morris L.

Morris, Steveland Judkins 1950-
  See Wonder, Stevie
  See also CA 111

Morris, William 1834-1896 . . . . NCLC 4
  See also DLB 18, 35

Morris, Wright
  1910- . . . . CLC 1, 3, 7, 18, 37
  See also CA 9-12R
  See also DLB 2
  See also DLB-Y 81

Morrison, James Douglas 1943-1971
  See Morrison, Jim
  See also CA 73-76

Morrison, Jim 1943-1971 . . . . CLC 17
  See also Morrison, James Douglas

Morrison, Toni 1931- . . . . CLC 4, 10, 22
  See also CA 29-32R
  See also DLB 6, 33
  See also DLB-Y 81

Morrison, Van 1945- . . . . CLC 21
  See also CA 116

Mortimer, John (Clifford)
  1923- . . . . CLC 28
  See also CA 13-16R
  See also DLB 13

Mortimer, Penelope (Ruth)
  1918- . . . . CLC 5
  See also CA 57-60

Moss, Howard 1922- . . . . CLC 7, 14
  See also CANR 1
  See also CA 1-4R
  See also DLB 5

Motley, Willard (Francis)
  1912-1965 . . . . CLC 18
  See also obituary CA 106

Mott, Michael (Charles Alston)
  1930- . . . . CLC 15, 34 (460)
  See also CANR 7
  See also CA 5-8R

Mowat, Farley (McGill) 1921- . . . . . . CLC 26
  See also CANR 4
  See also CA 1-4R
  See also SATA 3

Mphahlele, Es'kia 1919-
  See Mphahlele, Ezekiel

Mphahlele, Ezekiel 1919- . . . . CLC 25
  See also CA 81-84

Mrożek, Sławomir 1930- . . . . CLC 3, 13
  See also CA 13-16R

Mueller, Lisel 1924- . . . . CLC 13
  See also CA 93-96

Muir, Edwin 1887-1959 . . . . TCLC 2
  See also CA 104
  See also DLB 20

Mujica Láinez, Manuel
  1910-1984 . . . . CLC 31
  See also CA 81-84
  See also obituary CA 112

Muldoon, Paul 1951- . . . . CLC 32
  See also CA 113
  See also DLB 40

Mull, Martin 1943- . . . . CLC 17
  See also CA 105

Munro, Alice 1931- . . . . CLC 6, 10, 19
  See also CA 33-36R
  See also SATA 29
  See also DLB 53
  See also AITN 2

Munro, H(ector) H(ugh) 1870-1916
See Saki
See also CA 104
See also DLB 34

Murdoch, (Jean) Iris
1919-......CLC 1, 2, 3, 4, 6, 8, 11, 15,
22, 31
See also CANR 8
See also CA 13-16R
See also DLB 14

Murphy, Richard 1927-...........CLC 41
See also CA 29-32R
See also DLB 40

Murphy, Sylvia 19??-........ CLC 34 (91)

Murray, Les(lie) A(llan) 1938-......CLC 40
See also CANR 11
See also CA 21-24R

Murry, John Middleton
1889-1957..................TCLC 16
See also CA 118

Musgrave, Susan 1951-............CLC 13
See also CA 69-72

Musil, Robert (Edler von)
1880-1942..................TCLC 12
See also CA 109

Musset, (Louis Charles) Alfred de
1810-1857...................NCLC 7

Myers, Walter Dean 1937-.........CLC 35
See also CLR 4
See also CA 33-36R
See also SAAS 2
See also SATA 27, 41
See also DLB 33

Nabokov, Vladimir (Vladimirovich)
1899-1977...... CLC 1, 2, 3, 6, 8, 11,
15, 23
See also CA 5-8R
See also obituary CA 69-72
See also DLB 2
See also DLB-Y 80
See also DLB-DS 3

Nagy, László 1925-1978............CLC 7
See also obituary CA 112

Naipaul, Shiva(dhar Srinivasa)
1945-1985.......... CLC 32, 39 (355)
See also CA 110, 112
See also obituary CA 116
See also DLB-Y 85

Naipaul, V(idiadhar) S(urajprasad)
1932-.......... CLC 4, 7, 9, 13, 18, 37
See also CANR 1
See also CA 1-4R
See also DLB-Y 85

Nakos, Ioulia 1899?-
See Nakos, Lilika

Nakos, Lilika 1899?-.............CLC 29

Nakou, Lilika 1899?-
See Nakos, Lilika

Narayan, R(asipuram) K(rishnaswami)
1906-.................... CLC 7, 28
See also CA 81-84

Nash, (Frediric) Ogden
1902-1971...................CLC 23
See also CAP 1
See also CA 13-14
See also obituary CA 29-32R
See also SATA 2
See also DLB 11

Nathan, George Jean
1882-1958.................. TCLC 18
See also CA 114

Natsume, Kinnosuke 1867-1916
See Natsume, Sōseki
See also CA 104

Natsume, Sōseki
1867-1916............... TCLC 2, 10
See also Natsume, Kinnosuke

Natti, (Mary) Lee 1919-
See Kingman, (Mary) Lee
See also CANR 2

Naylor, Gloria 1950-..............CLC 28
See also CA 107

Neihardt, John G(neisenau)
1881-1973...................CLC 32
See also CAP 1
See also CA 13-14
See also DLB 9

Nekrasov, Nikolai Alekseevich
1821-1878.................. NCLC 11

Nelligan, Émile 1879-1941...... TCLC 14
See also CA 114

Nelson, Willie 1933-..............CLC 17
See also CA 107

Nemerov, Howard
1920-..................CLC 2, 6, 9, 36
See also CANR 1
See also CA 1-4R
See also DLB 5, 6
See also DLB-Y 83

Neruda, Pablo
1904-1973....... CLC 1, 2, 5, 7, 9, 28
See also CAP 2
See also CA 19-20
See also obituary CA 45-48

Nerval, Gérard de 1808-1855..... NCLC 1

Nervo, (José) Amado (Ruiz de)
1870-1919.................. TCLC 11
See also CA 109

Neufeld, John (Arthur) 1938-......CLC 17
See also CANR 11
See also CA 25-28R
See also SATA 6

Neville, Emily Cheney 1919-.......CLC 12
See also CANR 3
See also CA 5-8R
See also SAAS 2
See also SATA 1

Newbound, Bernard Slade 1930-
See Slade, Bernard
See also CA 81-84

Newby, P(ercy) H(oward)
1918-.................... CLC 2, 13
See also CA 5-8R
See also DLB 15

Newlove, Donald 1928-.............CLC 6
See also CA 29-32R

Newlove, John (Herbert) 1938-.....CLC 14
See also CANR 9
See also CA 21-24R

Newman, Charles 1938-......... CLC 2, 8
See also CA 21-24R

Newman, Edwin (Harold)
1919-........................CLC 14
See also CANR 5
See also CA 69-72
See also AITN 1

Newton, Suzanne 1936-............CLC 35
See also CANR 14
See also CA 41-44R
See also SATA 5

Ngugi, James (Thiong'o)
1938-.................CLC 3, 7, 13, 36
See also Ngugi wa Thiong'o
See also Wa Thiong'o, Ngugi
See also CA 81-84

Ngugi wa Thiong'o
1938-.................CLC 3, 7, 13, 36
See also Ngugi, James (Thiong'o)
See also Wa Thiong'o, Ngugi

Nichol, B(arne) P(hillip) 1944-......CLC 18
See also CA 53-56
See also DLB 53

Nichols, John (Treadwell)
1940-........................CLC 38
See also CANR 6
See also CA 9-12R
See also DLB-Y 82

Nichols, Peter 1927-.......... CLC 5, 36
See also CA 104
See also DLB 13

Nicolas, F.R.E. 1927-
See Freeling, Nicolas

Niedecker, Lorine 1903-1970.......CLC 10
See also CAP 2
See also CA 25-28
See also DLB 48

Nietzsche, Friedrich (Wilhelm)
1844-1900............... TCLC 10, 18
See also CA 107

Nightingale, Anne Redmon 1943-
See Redmon (Nightingale), Anne
See also CA 103

Nin, Anaïs
1903-1977........ CLC 1, 4, 8, 11, 14
See also CA 13-16R
See also obituary CA 69-72
See also DLB 2, 4
See also AITN 2

Nissenson, Hugh 1933-.......... CLC 4, 9
See also CA 17-20R
See also DLB 28

Niven, Larry 1938-.................CLC 8
See also Niven, Laurence Van Cott
See also DLB 8

Niven, Laurence Van Cott 1938-
See Niven, Larry
See also CANR 14
See also CA 21-24R

Nixon, Agnes Eckhardt 1927-......CLC 21
See also CA 110

Norman, Marsha 1947-...........CLC 28
See also CA 105
See also DLB-Y 84

Norris, Leslie 1921-...............CLC 14
See also CANR 14
See also CAP 1
See also CA 11-12
See also DLB 27

North, Andrew 1912-
See Norton, Andre

North, Christopher 1785-1854
See Wilson, John

Norton, Alice Mary 1912-
See Norton, Andre
See also CANR 2
See also CA 1-4R
See also SATA 1, 43

Norton, Andre 1912-.............CLC 12
See also Norton, Mary Alice
See also DLB 8

Norway, Nevil Shute 1899-1960
See Shute (Norway), Nevil
See also CA 102
See also obituary CA 93-96

Nossack, Hans Erich 1901-1978 .....CLC 6
See also CA 93-96
See also obituary CA 85-88

Nova, Craig 1945-............. CLC 7, 31
See also CANR 2
See also CA 45-48

Novalis 1772-1801 .... NCLC 13

Nowlan, Alden (Albert) 1933- ......CLC 15
See also CANR 5
See also CA 9-12R
See also DLB 53

Noyes, Alfred 1880-1958 .... TCLC 7
See also CA 104
See also DLB 20

Nunn, Kem 19??-............ CLC 34 (94)

Nye, Robert 1939-................CLC 13
See also CA 33-36R
See also SATA 6
See also DLB 14

Nyro, Laura 1947-................CLC 17

Oates, Joyce Carol
1938-.....CLC 1, 2, 3, 6, 9, 11, 15, 19,
33
See also CA 5-8R
See also DLB 2, 5
See also DLB-Y 81
See also AITN 1

O'Brien, Darcy 1939-.............CLC 11
See also CANR 8
See also CA 21-24R

O'Brien, Edna
1932-............. CLC 3, 5, 8, 13, 36
See also CANR 6
See also CA 1-4R
See also DLB 14

O'Brien, Flann
1911-1966......... CLC 1, 4, 5, 7, 10
See also O Nuallain, Brian

O'Brien, Richard 19??-............CLC 17

O'Brien, (William) Tim(othy)
1946-.................. CLC 7, 19, 40
See also CA 85-88
See also DLB-Y 80

O'Casey, Sean
1880-1964........ CLC 1, 5, 9, 11, 15
See also CA 89-92
See also DLB 10

Ochs, Phil 1940-1976 ....CLC 17
See also obituary CA 65-68

O'Connor, Edwin (Greene)
1918-1968....................CLC 14
See also CA 93-96
See also obituary CA 25-28R

O'Connor, (Mary) Flannery
1925-1964...... CLC 1, 2, 3, 6, 10, 13,
15, 21
See also CANR 3
See also CA 1-4R
See also DLB 2
See also DLB-Y 80

O'Connor, Frank
1903-1966............... CLC 14, 23
See also O'Donovan, Michael (John)

O'Dell, Scott 1903-...............CLC 30
See also CLR 1
See also CANR 12
See also CA 61-64
See also SATA 12

Odets, Clifford 1906-1963 ...... CLC 2, 28
See also CA 85-88
See also DLB 7, 26

O'Donovan, Michael (John) 1903-1966
See O'Connor, Frank
See also CA 93-96

Ōe, Kenzaburō 1935- .... CLC 10, 36
See also CA 97-100

O'Faolain, Julia 1932- .... CLC 6, 19
See also CAAS 2
See also CANR 12
See also CA 81-84
See also DLB 14

O'Faoláin, Seán
1900-................CLC 1, 7, 14, 32
See also CANR 12
See also CA 61-64
See also DLB 15

O'Flaherty, Liam
1896-1984........... CLC 5, 34 (355)
See also CA 101
See also obituary CA 113
See also DLB 36
See also DLB-Y 84

O'Grady, Standish (James)
1846-1928................... TCLC 5
See also CA 104

O'Hara Family
See Banim, John and Banim, Michael

O'Hara, Frank
1926-1966...............CLC 2, 5, 13
See also CA 9-12R
See also obituary CA 25-28R
See also DLB 5, 16

O'Hara, John (Henry)
1905-1970......... CLC 1, 2, 3, 6, 11
See also CA 5-8R
See also obituary CA 25-28R
See also DLB 9
See also DLB-DS 2

O'Hehir, Diana 1922-.............CLC 41
See also CA 93-96

Okigbo, Christopher (Ifenayichukwu)
1932-1967...................CLC 25
See also CA 77-80

Olds, Sharon 1942-...... CLC 32, 39 (186)
See also CANR 18
See also CA 101

Olesha, Yuri (Karlovich)
1899-1960....................CLC 8
See also CA 85-88

Oliphant, Margaret (Oliphant Wilson)
1828-1897................. NCLC 11
See also DLB 18

Oliver, Mary 1935- ...... CLC 19, 34 (246)
See also CANR 9
See also CA 21-24R
See also DLB 5

Olivier, (Baron) Laurence (Kerr)
1907-.......................CLC 20
See also CA 111

Olsen, Tillie 1913-............. CLC 4, 13
See also CANR 1
See also CA 1-4R
See also DLB 28
See also DLB-Y 80

Olson, Charles (John)
1910-1970....... CLC 1, 2, 5, 6, 9, 11,
29
See also CAP 1
See also CA 15-16
See also obituary CA 25-28R
See also DLB 5, 16

Olson, Theodore 1937-
See Olson, Toby

Olson, Toby 1937-................CLC 28
See also CANR 9
See also CA 65-68

Ondaatje, (Philip) Michael
1943-................... CLC 14, 29
See also CA 77-80

Oneal, Elizabeth 1934-
See Oneal, Zibby
See also CA 106
See also SATA 30

Oneal, Zibby 1934-...............CLC 30
See also Oneal, Elizabeth

O'Neill, Eugene (Gladstone)
1888-1953................. TCLC 1, 6
See also CA 110
See also AITN 1
See also DLB 7

Onetti, Juan Carlos 1909- ...... CLC 7, 10
See also CA 85-88

O'Nolan, Brian 1911-1966
See O'Brien, Flann

O Nuallain, Brian 1911-1966
See O'Brien, Flann
See also CAP 2
See also CA 21-22
See also obituary CA 25-28R

Oppen, George
1908-1984........CLC 7, 13, 34 (358)
See also CANR 8
See also CA 13-16R
See also obituary CA 113
See also DLB 5

Orlovitz, Gil 1918-1973 ....CLC 22
See also CA 77-80
See also obituary CA 45-48
See also DLB 2, 5

Ortega y Gasset, José
1883-1955................... TCLC 9
See also CA 106

Orton, Joe 1933?-1967 . . . . CLC 4, 13
See also Orton, John Kingsley
See also DLB 13

Orton, John Kingsley 1933?-1967
See Orton, Joe
See also CA 85-88

Orwell, George
1903-1950 . . . . TCLC 2, 6, 15
See also Blair, Eric Arthur
See also DLB 15

Osborne, John (James)
1929- . . . . CLC 1, 2, 5, 11
See also CA 13-16R
See also DLB 13

Osceola 1885-1962
See Dinesen, Isak
See also Blixen, Karen (Christentze
Dinesen)

Oshima, Nagisa 1932- . . . . CLC 20
See also CA 116

Ossoli, Sarah Margaret (Fuller marchesa d')
1810-1850
See Fuller, (Sarah) Margaret
See also SATA 25

Otero, Blas de 1916- . . . . CLC 11
See also CA 89-92

Owen, Wilfred (Edward Salter)
1893-1918 . . . . TCLC 5
See also CA 104
See also DLB 20

Owens, Rochelle 1936- . . . . CLC 8
See also CAAS 2
See also CA 17-20R

Owl, Sebastian 1939-
See Thompson, Hunter S(tockton)

Oz, Amos 1939- . . . . . . CLC 5, 8, 11, 27, 33
See also CA 53-56

Ozick, Cynthia 1928- . . . . CLC 3, 7, 28
See also CA 17-20R
See also DLB 28
See also DLB-Y 82

Ozu, Yasujiro 1903-1963 . . . . CLC 16
See also CA 112

Pa Chin 1904- . . . . CLC 18
See also Li Fei-kan

Pack, Robert 1929- . . . . CLC 13
See also CANR 3
See also CA 1-4R
See also DLB 5

Padgett, Lewis 1915-1958
See Kuttner, Henry

Padilla, Heberto 1932- . . . . CLC 38
See also AITN 1

Page, Jimmy 1944-
See Page, Jimmy and Plant, Robert

Page, Jimmy 1944- and
Plant, Robert 1948- . . . . CLC 12

Page, Louise 1955- . . . . CLC 40

Page, P(atricia) K(athleen)
1916- . . . . CLC 7, 18
See also CANR 4
See also CA 53-56

Paget, Violet 1856-1935
See Lee, Vernon
See also CA 104

Palamas, Kostes 1859-1943 . . . . TCLC 5
See also CA 105

Palazzeschi, Aldo 1885-1974 . . . . . . CLC 11
See also CA 89-92
See also obituary CA 53-56

Paley, Grace 1922- . . . . CLC 4, 6, 37
See also CANR 13
See also CA 25-28R
See also DLB 28
See also AITN 1

Palin, Michael 1943-
See Monty Python
See also CA 107

Pancake, Breece Dexter 1952-1979
See Pancake, Breece D'J

Pancake, Breece D'J
1952-1979 . . . . CLC 29
See also obituary CA 109

Papini, Giovanni 1881-1956 . . . . . TCLC 22

Parker, Dorothy (Rothschild)
1893-1967 . . . . CLC 15
See also CAP 2
See also CA 19-20
See also obituary CA 25-28R
See also DLB 11, 45

Parker, Robert B(rown) 1932- . . . . . . CLC 27
See also CANR 1
See also CA 49-52

Parkman, Francis 1823-1893 . . . . . NCLC 12
See also DLB 1, 30

Parks, Gordon (Alexander Buchanan)
1912- . . . . CLC 1, 16
See also CA 41-44R
See also SATA 8
See also DLB 33
See also AITN 2

Parnell, Thomas 1679-1718 . . . . LC 3

Parra, Nicanor 1914- . . . . CLC 2
See also CA 85-88

Pasolini, Pier Paolo
1922-1975 . . . . CLC 20, 37
See also CA 93-96
See also obituary CA 61-64

Pastan, Linda (Olenik) 1932- . . . . . . CLC 27
See also CANR 18
See also CA 61-64
See also DLB 5

Pasternak, Boris
1890-1960 . . . . CLC 7, 10, 18
See also obituary CA 116

Patchen, Kenneth
1911-1972 . . . . CLC 1, 2, 18
See also CANR 3
See also CA 1-4R
See also obituary CA 33-36R
See also DLB 16, 48

Pater, Walter (Horatio)
1839-1894 . . . . NCLC 7

Paterson, Katherine (Womeldorf)
1932- . . . . CLC 12, 30
See also CLR 7
See also CA 21-24R
See also SATA 13

Patmore, Coventry Kersey Dighton
1823-1896 . . . . NCLC 9
See also DLB 35

Paton, Alan (Stewart)
1903- . . . . CLC 4, 10, 25
See also CAP 1
See also CA 15-16
See also SATA 11

Paulding, James Kirke
1778-1860 . . . . NCLC 2
See also DLB 3

Paulin, Tom 1949- . . . . CLC 37
See also DLB 40

Paustovsky, Konstantin (Georgievich)
1892-1968 . . . . CLC 40
See also CA 93-96
See also obituary CA 25-28R

Paustowsky, Konstantin (Georgievich)
1892-1968
See Paustovsky, Konstantin (Georgievich)

Pavese, Cesare 1908-1950 . . . . TCLC 3
See also CA 104

Payne, Alan 1932-
See Jakes, John (William)

Paz, Octavio 1914- . . . . . CLC 3, 4, 6, 10, 19
See also CA 73-76

Peake, Mervyn 1911-1968 . . . . CLC 7
See also CANR 3
See also CA 5-8R
See also obituary CA 25-28R
See also SATA 23
See also DLB 15

Pearce, (Ann) Philippa 1920- . . . . CLC 21
See also Christie, (Ann) Philippa
See also CA 5-8R
See also SATA 1

Pearl, Eric 1934-
See Elman, Richard

Pearson, T(homas) R(eid)
1956- . . . . CLC 39 (86)

Peck, John 1941- . . . . CLC 3
See also CANR 3
See also CA 49-52

Peck, Richard 1934- . . . . CLC 21
See also CA 85-88
See also SAAS 2
See also SATA 18

Peck, Robert Newton 1928- . . . . CLC 17
See also CA 81-84
See also SAAS 1
See also SATA 21

Peckinpah, (David) Sam(uel)
1925-1984 . . . . CLC 20
See also CA 109
See also obituary CA 114

Pedersen, Knut 1859-1952
See Hamsun, Knut
See also CA 104

Péguy, Charles (Pierre)
1873-1914 . . . . TCLC 10
See also CA 107

Percy, Walker
1916- . . . . CLC 2, 3, 6, 8, 14, 18
See also CANR 1
See also CA 1-4R
See also DLB 2
See also DLB-Y 80

Pereda, José María de
1833-1906 . . . . TCLC 16

Pownall, David 1938- ....CLC 10
See also CA 89-92
See also DLB 14

Powys, John Cowper
1872-1963...............CLC 7, 9, 15
See also CA 85-88
See also DLB 15

Powys, T(heodore) F(rancis)
1875-1953..................TCLC 9
See also CA 106
See also DLB 36

Pratt, E(dwin) J(ohn)
1883-1964....................CLC 19
See also obituary CA 93-96

Premchand 1880-1936.......... TCLC 21

Preussler, Otfried 1923-..........CLC 17
See also CA 77-80
See also SATA 24

Prévert, Jacques (Henri Marie)
1900-1977....................CLC 15
See also CA 77-80
See also obituary CA 69-72
See also obituary SATA 30

Prévost, Abbé (Antoine Francois)
1697-1763.....................LC 1

Price, (Edward) Reynolds
1933-....................CLC 3, 6, 13
See also CANR 1
See also CA 1-4R
See also DLB 2

Price, Richard 1949-...........CLC 6, 12
See also CANR 3
See also CA 49-52
See also DLB-Y 81

Priestley, J(ohn) B(oynton)
1894-1984....... CLC 2, 5, 9, 34 (360)
See also CA 9-12R
See also obituary CA 113
See also DLB 10, 34
See also DLB-Y 84

Prince (Rogers Nelson) 1958?-......CLC 35

Prince, F(rank) T(empleton)
1912-.....................CLC 22
See also CA 101
See also DLB 20

Prior, Matthew 1664-1721...........LC 4

Pritchard, William H(arrison)
1932-................. CLC 34 (468)
See also CA 65-68

Pritchett, V(ictor) S(awdon)
1900-..............CLC 5, 13, 15, 41
See also CA 61-64
See also DLB 15

Procaccino, Michael 1946-
See Cristofer, Michael

Prokosch, Frederic 1908-..........CLC 4
See also CA 73-76
See also DLB 48

Proust, Marcel 1871-1922.....TCLC 7, 13
See also CA 104

Pryor, Richard 1940- ....CLC 26

P'u Sung-ling 1640-1715.............LC 3

Puig, Manuel 1932-......CLC 3, 5, 10, 28
See also CANR 2
See also CA 45-48

Purdy, A(lfred) W(ellington)
1918-....................CLC 3, 6, 14
See also CA 81-84

Purdy, James (Amos)
1923-.................CLC 2, 4, 10, 28
See also CAAS 1
See also CA 33-36R
See also DLB 2

Pushkin, Alexander (Sergeyevich)
1799-1837...................NCLC 3

Puzo, Mario 1920-........CLC 1, 2, 6, 36
See also CANR 4
See also CA 65-68
See also DLB 6

Pym, Barbara (Mary Crampton)
1913-1980.............CLC 13, 19, 37
See also CANR 13
See also CAP 1
See also CA 13-14
See also obituary CA 97-100
See also DLB 14

Pynchon, Thomas (Ruggles, Jr.)
1937-.......CLC 2, 3, 6, 9, 11, 18, 33
See also CA 17-20R
See also DLB 2

Quasimodo, Salvatore
1901-1968....................CLC 10
See also CAP 1
See also CA 15-16
See also obituary CA 25-28R

Queen, Ellery 1905-1982....... CLC 3, 11
See also Dannay, Frederic
See also Lee, Manfred B(ennington)

Queneau, Raymond
1903-1976..............CLC 2, 5, 10
See also CA 77-80
See also obituary CA 69-72

Quin, Ann (Marie) 1936-1973.......CLC 6
See also CA 9-12R
See also obituary CA 45-48
See also DLB 14

Quinn, Simon 1942-
See Smith, Martin Cruz

Quiroga, Horatio (Sylvestre)
1878-1937................. TCLC 20
See also CA 117

Quoirez, Françoise 1935-
See Sagan, Françoise
See also CANR 6
See also CA 49-52

Rabe, David (William)
1940-...................CLC 4, 8, 33
See also CA 85-88
See also DLB 7

Rabinovitch, Sholem 1859-1916
See Aleichem, Sholom
See also CA 104

Radcliffe, Ann (Ward)
1764-1823...................NCLC 6
See also DLB 39

Radnóti, Miklós 1909-1944 ...... TCLC 16
See also CA 118

Rado, James 1939-
See Ragni, Gerome and
Rado, James
See also CA 105

Radomski, James 1932-
See Rado, James

Radvanyi, Netty Reiling 1900-1983
See Seghers, Anna
See also CA 85-88
See also obituary CA 110

Raeburn, John 1941-........ CLC 34 (477)
See also CA 57-60

Ragni, Gerome 1942-
See Ragni, Gerome and Rado, James
See also CA 105

Ragni, Gerome 1942- and
Rado, James 1939-...........CLC 17

Rahv, Philip 1908-1973 ....CLC 24
See also Greenberg, Ivan

Raine, Craig 1944- ....CLC 32
See also CA 108
See also DLB 40

Raine, Kathleen (Jessie) 1908-.......CLC 7
See also CA 85-88
See also DLB 20

Rand, Ayn 1905-1982.........CLC 3, 30
See also CA 13-16R
See also obituary CA 105

Randall, Dudley (Felker) 1914-......CLC 1
See also CA 25-28R
See also DLB 41

Ransom, John Crowe
1888-1974........ CLC 2, 4, 5, 11, 24
See also CANR 6
See also CA 5-8R
See also obituary CA 49-52
See also DLB 45

Rao, Raja 1909-...................CLC 25
See also CA 73-76

Raphael, Frederic (Michael)
1931-....................CLC 2, 14
See also CANR 1
See also CA 1-4R
See also DLB 14

Rathbone, Julian 1935-............CLC 41
See also CA 101

Rattigan, Terence (Mervyn)
1911-1977....................CLC 7
See also CA 85-88
See also obituary CA 73-76
See also DLB 13

Raven, Simon (Arthur Noel)
1927-.....................CLC 14
See also CA 81-84

Rawlings, Marjorie Kinnan
1896-1953................... TCLC 4
See also CA 104
See also YABC 1
See also DLB 9, 22

Ray, Satyajit 1921- ....CLC 16

Read, Herbert (Edward)
1893-1968....................CLC 4
See also CA 85-88
See also obituary CA 25-28R
See also DLB 20

Read, Piers Paul 1941-......CLC 4, 10, 25
See also CA 21-24R
See also SATA 21
See also DLB 14

Reade, Charles 1814-1884........ NCLC 2
See also DLB 21

Smith, Lee 1944-...............CLC 25
  See also CA 114
  See also DLB-Y 83

Smith, Martin Cruz 1942-........CLC 25
  See also CANR 6
  See also CA 85-88

Smith, Martin William 1942-
  See Smith, Martin Cruz

Smith, Mary-Ann Tirone
  1944-................. CLC 39 (97)
  See also CA 118

Smith, Patti 1946-...............CLC 12
  See also CA 93-96

Smith, Sara Mahala Redway 1900-1972
  See Benson, Sally

Smith, Stevie 1902-1971......CLC 3, 8, 25
  See also Smith, Florence Margaret
  See also DLB 20

Smith, Wilbur (Addison) 1933-.....CLC 33
  See also CANR 7
  See also CA 13-16R

Smith, William Jay 1918-..........CLC 6
  See also CA 5-8R
  See also SATA 2
  See also DLB 5

Smollett, Tobias (George)
  1721-1771.....................LC 2
  See also DLB 39

Snodgrass, W(illiam) D(e Witt)
  1926-.............CLC 2, 6, 10, 18
  See also CANR 6
  See also CA 1-4R
  See also DLB 5

Snow, C(harles) P(ercy)
  1905-1980......CLC 1, 4, 6, 9, 13, 19
  See also CA 5-8R
  See also obituary CA 101
  See also DLB 15

Snyder, Gary 1930-..... CLC 1, 2, 5, 9, 32
  See also CA 17-20R
  See also DLB 5, 16

Snyder, Zilpha Keatley 1927- ......CLC 17
  See also CA 9-12R
  See also SAAS 2
  See also SATA 1, 28

Sokolov, Raymond 1941-...........CLC 7
  See also CA 85-88

Sologub, Fyodor 1863-1927....... TCLC 9
  See also Teternikov, Fyodor Kuzmich

Solwoska, Mara 1929-
  See French, Marilyn

Solzhenitsyn, Aleksandr I(sayevich)
  1918-.....CLC 1, 2, 4, 7, 9, 10, 18, 26,
                    34 (480)
  See also CA 69-72
  See also AITN 1

Somers, Jane 1919-
  See Lessing, Doris (May)

Sommer, Scott 1951-..............CLC 25
  See also CA 106

Sondheim, Stephen (Joshua)
  1930-.............. CLC 30, 39 (172)
  See also CA 103

Sontag, Susan
  1933-............ CLC 1, 2, 10, 13, 31
  See also CA 17-20R
  See also DLB 2

Sorrentino, Gilbert
  1929-........... CLC 3, 7, 14, 22, 40
  See also CANR 14
  See also CA 77-80
  See also DLB 5
  See also DLB-Y 80

Soto, Gary 1952-................CLC 32

Souster, (Holmes) Raymond
  1921-.................... CLC 5, 14
  See also CANR 13
  See also CA 13-16R

Southern, Terry 1926-.............CLC 7
  See also CANR 1
  See also CA 1-4R
  See also DLB 2

Southey, Robert 1774-1843....... NCLC 8

Soyinka, Akin-wande Oluwole 1934-
  See Soyinka, Wole

Soyinka, Wole 1934-......CLC 3, 5, 14, 36
  See also CA 13-16R

Spacks, Barry 1931-..............CLC 14
  See also CA 29-32R

Spark, Muriel (Sarah)
  1918-........CLC 2, 3, 5, 8, 13, 18, 40
  See also CANR 12
  See also CA 5-8R
  See also DLB 15

Spencer, Elizabeth 1921- ....CLC 22
  See also CA 13-16R
  See also SATA 14
  See also DLB 6

Spencer, Scott 1945-..............CLC 30
  See also CA 113

Spender, Stephen (Harold)
  1909-............. CLC 1, 2, 5, 10, 41
  See also CA 9-12R
  See also DLB 20

Spicer, Jack 1925-1965........ CLC 8, 18
  See also CA 85-88
  See also DLB 5, 16

Spielberg, Peter 1929-.............CLC 6
  See also CANR 4
  See also CA 5-8R
  See also DLB-Y 81

Spielberg, Steven 1947-...........CLC 20
  See also CA 77-80
  See also SATA 32

Spillane, Frank Morrison 1918-
  See Spillane, Mickey
  See also CA 25-28R

Spillane, Mickey 1918- .... CLC 3, 13
  See also Spillane, Frank Morrison

Spitteler, Carl (Friedrich Georg)
  1845-1924.................. TCLC 12
  See also CA 109

Spivack, Kathleen (Romola Drucker)
  1938-........................CLC 6
  See also CA 49-52

Spoto, Donald 1941-........ CLC 39 (444)
  See also CANR 11
  See also CA 65-68

Springsteen, Bruce 1949-..........CLC 17
  See also CA 111

Spurling, Hilary 1940- ...... CLC 34 (494)
  See also CA 104

Staël-Holstein, Anne Louise Germaine
  Necker, Baronne de
  1766-1817................... NCLC 3

Stafford, Jean 1915-1979..... CLC 4, 7, 19
  See also CANR 3
  See also CA 1-4R
  See also obituary CA 85-88
  See also obituary SATA 22
  See also DLB 2

Stafford, William (Edgar)
  1914-.....................CLC 4, 7, 29
  See also CAAS 3
  See also CANR 5
  See also CA 5-8R
  See also DLB 5

Stanton, Maura 1946-..............CLC 9
  See also CANR 15
  See also CA 89-92

Stapledon, (William) Olaf
  1886-1950.................. TCLC 22
  See also CA 111
  See also DLB 15

Stark, Richard 1933-
  See Westlake, Donald E(dwin)

Stead, Christina (Ellen)
  1902-1983...........CLC 2, 5, 8, 32
  See also CA 13-16R
  See also obituary CA 109

Steffens, (Joseph) Lincoln
  1866-1936................. TCLC 20
  See also CA 117
  See also SAAS 1

Stegner, Wallace (Earle) 1909- ......CLC 9
  See also CANR 1
  See also CA 1-4R
  See also DLB 9
  See also AITN 1

Stein, Gertrude 1874-1946...... TCLC 1, 6
  See also CA 104
  See also DLB 4

Steinbeck, John (Ernst)
  1902-1968........CLC 1, 5, 9, 13, 21,
                    34 (404)
  See also CANR 1
  See also CA 1-4R
  See also obituary CA 25-28R
  See also SATA 9
  See also DLB 7, 9
  See also DLB-DS 2

Steiner, George 1929-.............CLC 24
  See also CA 73-76

Steiner, Rudolf(us Josephus Laurentius)
  1861-1925.................. TCLC 13
  See also CA 107

Stephens, James 1882?-1950 ...... TCLC 4
  See also CA 104
  See also DLB 19

Steptoe, Lydia 1892-1982
  See Barnes, Djuna

Sterling, George 1869-1926 ...... TCLC 20
  See also CA 117

Stern, Gerald 1925-..............CLC 40
  See also CA 81-84

Stern, Richard G(ustave)
  1928-................ CLC 4, 39 (234)
  See also CANR 1
  See also CA 1-4R

Vallejo, César (Abraham)
1892-1938................... TCLC 3
See also CA 105

Van Ash, Cay 1918- .... CLC 34 (118)

Vance, Jack 1916?-...............CLC 35
See also DLB 8

Vance, John Holbrook 1916?-
See Vance, Jack
See also CANR 17
See also CA 29-32R

Van Den Bogarde, Derek (Jules Gaspard Ulric) Niven 1921-
See Bogarde, Dirk
See also CA 77-80

Vanderhaeghe, Guy 1951- ....CLC 41
See also CA 113

Van der Post, Laurens (Jan)
1906-..........................CLC 5
See also CA 5-8R

Van Doren, Carl (Clinton)
1885-1950................. TCLC 18
See also CA 111

Van Doren, Mark
1894-1972................ CLC 6, 10
See also CANR 3
See also CA 1-4R
See also obituary CA 37-40R
See also DLB 45

Van Druten, John (William)
1901-1957.................. TCLC 2
See also CA 104
See also DLB 10

Van Duyn, Mona 1921- .... CLC 3, 7
See also CANR 7
See also CA 9-12R
See also DLB 5

Van Itallie, Jean-Claude 1936- ......CLC 3
See also CAAS 2
See also CANR 1
See also CA 45-48
See also DLB 7

Van Peebles, Melvin 1932-...... CLC 2, 20
See also CA 85-88

Van Vechten, Carl 1880-1964......CLC 33
See also obituary CA 89-92
See also DLB 4, 9

Van Vogt, A(lfred) E(lton)
1912-.........................CLC 1
See also CA 21-24R
See also SATA 14
See also DLB 8

Varda, Agnès 1928-...............CLC 16
See also CA 116

Vargas Llosa, (Jorge) Mario (Pedro)
1936-......... CLC 3, 6, 9, 10, 15, 31
See also CANR 18
See also CA 73-76

Vassilikos, Vassilis 1933- .... CLC 4, 8
See also CA 81-84

Verga, Giovanni 1840-1922...... TCLC 3
See also CA 104

Verhaeren, Émile (Adolphe Gustave)
1855-1916.................. TCLC 12
See also CA 109

Verlaine, Paul (Marie)
1844-1896.................. NCLC 2

Verne, Jules (Gabriel)
1828-1905................... TCLC 6
See also CA 110
See also SATA 21

Very, Jones 1813-1880........... NCLC 9
See also DLB 1

Vian, Boris 1920-1959 .... TCLC 9
See also CA 106

Viaud, (Louis Marie) Julien 1850-1923
See Loti, Pierre
See also CA 107

Vicker, Angus 1916-
See Felsen, Henry Gregor

Vidal, Eugene Luther, Jr. 1925-
See Vidal, Gore

Vidal, Gore
1925-........CLC 2, 4, 6, 8, 10, 22, 33
See also CANR 13
See also CA 5-8R
See also DLB 6
See also AITN 1

Viereck, Peter (Robert Edwin)
1916-.........................CLC 4
See also CANR 1
See also CA 1-4R
See also DLB 5

Vigny, Alfred (Victor) de
1797-1863.................. NCLC 7

Villiers de l'Isle Adam, Jean Marie Mathias Philippe Auguste, Comte de,
1838-1889.................. NCLC 3

Vinge, Joan (Carol) D(ennison)
1948-.........................CLC 30
See also CA 93-96
See also SATA 36

Visconti, Luchino 1906-1976.......CLC 16
See also CA 81-84
See also obituary CA 65-68

Vittorini, Elio 1908-1966 ..... CLC 6, 9, 14
See also obituary CA 25-28R

Vizinczey, Stephen 1933- ....CLC 40

Vliet, R(ussell) G. 1929-...........CLC 22
See also CANR 18
See also CA 37-40R

Voigt, Cynthia 1942-...............CLC 30
See also CANR 18
See also CA 106
See also SATA 33

Voinovich, Vladimir (Nikolaevich)
1932-.........................CLC 10
See also CA 81-84

Von Daeniken, Erich 1935-
See Von Däniken, Erich
See also CANR 17
See also CA 37-40R
See also AITN 1

Von Däniken, Erich 1935- ....CLC 30
See also Von Daeniken, Erich

Vonnegut, Kurt, Jr.
1922-......CLC 1, 2, 3, 4, 5, 8, 12, 22, 40
See also CANR 1
See also CA 1-4R
See also DLB 2, 8
See also DLB-Y 80
See also DLB-DS 3
See also AITN 1

Vorster, Gordon 1924- ...... CLC 34 (121)

Voznesensky, Andrei 1933- ..... CLC 1, 15
See also CA 89-92

Waddington, Miriam 1917-........CLC 28
See also CANR 12
See also CA 21-24R

Wagman, Fredrica 1937- ....CLC 7
See also CA 97-100

Wagner, Richard 1813-1883 ...... NCLC 9

Wagoner, David (Russell)
1926-...................CLC 3, 5, 15
See also CAAS 3
See also CANR 2
See also CA 1-4R
See also SATA 14
See also DLB 5

Wahlöö, Per 1926-1975 ....CLC 7
See also CA 61-64

Wahlöö, Peter 1926-1975
See Wahlöö, Per

Wain, John (Barrington)
1925-...................CLC 2, 11, 15
See also CAAS 4
See also CA 5-8R
See also DLB 15, 27

Wajda, Andrzej 1926-.............CLC 16
See also CA 102

Wakefield, Dan 1932-.............CLC 7
See also CA 21-24R

Wakoski, Diane
1937-...........CLC 2, 4, 7, 9, 11, 40
See also CAAS 1
See also CANR 9
See also CA 13-16R
See also DLB 5

Walcott, Derek (Alton)
1930-............ CLC 2, 4, 9, 14, 25
See also CA 89-92
See also DLB-Y 81

Waldman, Anne 1945-.............CLC 7
See also CA 37-40R
See also DLB 16

Waldo, Edward Hamilton 1918-
See Sturgeon, Theodore (Hamilton)

Walker, Alice
1944-............. CLC 5, 6, 9, 19, 27
See also CANR 9
See also CA 37-40R
See also SATA 31
See also DLB 6, 33

Walker, David Harry 1911-........CLC 14
See also CANR 1
See also CA 1-4R
See also SATA 8

Walker, Edward Joseph 1934-
See Walker, Ted
See also CA 21-24R

Walker, Joseph A. 1935- ....CLC 19
See also CA 89-92
See also DLB 38

Walker, Margaret (Abigail)
1915-......................CLC 1, 6
See also CA 73-76

Walker, Ted 1934-................CLC 13
See also Walker, Edward Joseph
See also DLB 40

Cumulative Index to Nationalities

Hippius, Zinaida 9
Ilf, Ilya 21
Khlebnikov, Velimir 20
Khodasevich, Vladislav 15
Korolenko, Vladimir 22
Kuprin, Aleksandr 5
Mandelstam, Osip 2, 6
Mayakovsky, Vladimir 4, 18
Petrov, Evgeny 21
Platonov, Andrei 14
Sologub, Fyodor 9
Tolstoy, Alexey
   Nikolayevich 18
Tolstoy, Leo 4, 11, 17
Trotsky, Leon 22
Tsvetaeva, Marina 7
Zamyatin, Yevgeny
   Ivanovich 8
Zhdanov, Andrei 18

Zoshchenko, Mikhail 15

SCOTTISH
Barrie, J. M. 2
Bridie, James 3
Gibbon, Lewis Grassic 4
Graham, R. B.
   Cunninghame 19
Lang, Andrew 16
MacDonald, George 9
Muir, Edwin 2
Tey, Josephine 14

SOUTH AFRICAN
Campbell, Roy 5
Schreiner, Olive 9

SPANISH
Barea, Arturo 14
Baroja, Pío 8

Benavente, Jacinto 3
Blasco Ibáñez, Vicente 12
Echegaray, José 4
García Lorca, Federico 1, 7
Jiménez, Juan Ramón 4
Machado, Antonio 3
Martínez Sierra, Gregorio 6
Miró, Gabriel 5
Ortega y Gasset, José 9
Pereda, José María de 16
Salinas, Pedro 17
Unamuno, Miguel de 2, 9
Valera, Juan 10
Valle-Inclán, Ramón del 5

SWEDISH
Dagerman, Stig 17
Heidenstam, Verner von 5
Lagerlöf, Selma 4

Strindberg, August 1, 8, 21

SWISS
Spitteler, Carl 12
Walser, Robert 18

URUGUAYAN
Quiroga, Horacio 20

WELSH
Davies, W. H. 5
Lewis, Alun 3
Machen, Arthur 4
Thomas, Dylan 1, 8

YIDDISH
Aleichem, Sholom 1
Asch, Sholem 3
Peretz, Isaac Leib 16

Cumulative Index to Critics

Bronner, Milton
Lionel Johnson **19**:234

Bronowski, Jacob
Pierre Teilhard de Chardin
9:488
A. E. Housman **10**:243

Brook, Stephen
Radclyffe Hall **12**:197

Brooke, Jocelyn
Denton Welch **22**:445

Brooks, Cleanth
Ivan Bunin **6**:47
F. Scott Fitzgerald **6**:163
O. Henry **19**:185
A. E. Housman **1**:355; **10**:249
Ring Lardner **14**:299
William Butler Yeats **1**:571;
11:517

Brooks, Van Wyck
Ambrose Bierce **1**:89
Randolph S. Bourne **16**:45
Willa Cather **1**:160
Kate Chopin **14**:58
F. Marion Crawford **10**:152
Havelock Ellis **14**:113
Emma Goldman **13**:219
Bret Harte **1**:342
O. Henry **1**:350
Henry James **11**:324
Vernon Lee **5**:311
Jack London **9**:262
Amy Lowell **8**:231
H. L. Mencken **13**:382
Constance Rourke **12**:317
Edgar Saltus **8**:351
Gertrude Stein **1**:430
Booth Tarkington **9**:462
Mark Twain **6**:461; **19**:362

Brophy, Brigid
Colette **1**:192
Ronald Firbank **1**:229
Thomas Hardy **10**:223
David Lindsay **15**:218
Francis Thompson **4**:441

Brosman, Catherine Savage
Alain-Fournier **6**:22

Brotherston, Gordon
Rubén Darío **4**:68

Broun, Heywood
Ring Lardner **14**:295
Damon Runyon **10**:422
Booth Tarkington **9**:454

Brouta, Julius
Jacinto Benavente **3**:93

Brower, Reuben Arthur
Virginia Woolf **20**:399
William Butler Yeats **18**:445

Brower, Robert H.
Masaoka Shiki **18**:220

Brown, Alec
Mikhail Zoshchenko **15**:497

Brown, Alice
Sarah Orne Jewett **22**:121

Brown, Clarence
Osip Mandelstam **2**:401; **6**:260,
262

Brown, Daniel R.
Sinclair Lewis **4**:261
Nathanael West **1**:491

Brown, E. K.
Bliss Carman **7**:144
Willa Cather **11**:99
Emile Nelligan **14**:390
Marjorie Pickthall **21**:255
Duncan Campbell Scott **6**:389
Thomas Wolfe **4**:514

Brown, Edward J.
Isaac Babel **13**:39
Velimir Khlebnikov **20**:141
Vladislav Khodasevich **15**:209
Vladimir Mayakovsky **18**:258
Andrei A. Zhdanov **18**:478
Mikhail Zoshchenko **15**:514

Brown, G. G.
Gabriel Miró **5**:339

Brown, Ivor
Lewis Grassic Gibbon **4**:122
Alfred Sutro **6**:422

Brown, J. F.
Aleister Crowley **7**:211

Brown, John L.
Valéry Larbaud **9**:205

Brown, John Mason
Philip Barry **11**:48
Anton Chekhov **10**:103
Ada Leverson **18**:191
Eugene O'Neill **1**:394
Bernard Shaw **9**:419; **21**:315
Robert E. Sherwood **3**:416
Josephine Tey **14**:449
John Van Druten **2**:573, 575
Alexander Woollcott **5**:525

Brown, Leonard
Harriet Monroe **12**:219

Brown, Malcolm
George Moore **7**:486

Brown, Morrison
Louis Bromfield **11**:81

Brown, Sterling
Charles Waddell Chesnutt
5:132
Paul Laurence Dunbar **12**:109,
110
Rudolph Fisher **11**:205
James Weldon Johnson **3**:241
Wallace Thurman **6**:447

Brown, Stuart Gerry
John Jay Chapman **7**:192

Browne, Douglas G.
R. Austin Freeman **21**:53

Brownell, William Crary
George Meredith **17**:262

Brownstein, Michael
Max Jacob **6**:203

Broyde, Steven
Osip Mandelstam **6**:267

Bruckner, D.J.R.
Charles Williams **11**:502

Bruehl, Charles P.
Georges Bernanos **3**:117

Bruffee, Kenneth A.
Joseph Conrad **13**:122

Bruford, W. H.
Anton Chekhov **10**:107

Brushwood, John S.
Amado Nervo **11**:403
Horacio Quiroga **20**:222
José Rubén Romero **14**:443

Brustein, Robert
Antonin Artaud **3**:50
Bertolt Brecht **1**:111
Henrik Ibsen **8**:149
Eugene O'Neill **1**:400
Luigi Pirandello **4**:345
Bernard Shaw **3**:404
August Strindberg **1**:451

Bryant, Joseph G.
Paul Laurence Dunbar **12**:104

Bryusov, Valery
Konstantin Dmitriyevich
Balmont **11**:29

Buber, Martin
Franz Kafka **2**:295

Bucco, Martin
Robert W. Service **15**:403

Buchan, A. M.
Sarah Orne Jewett **1**:363

Buchan, John
T. E. Lawrence **18**:131

Buchanan, Robert
Rudyard Kipling **8**:178
Algernon Charles Swinburne
8:423

Buck, Philo M., Jr.
Henrik Ibsen **2**:224
Jack London **9**:254
Eugene O'Neill **1**:388
Emile Zola **1**:588

Buckley, J. M.
Anthony Comstock **13**:87

Buckley, Jerome Hamilton
William Ernest Henley **8**:104

Buckley, Vincent
Henry Handel Richardson **4**:377

Budd, Louis J.
William Dean Howells **7**:380
Mark Twain **6**:473
Thomas Wolfe **4**:525

Büdel, Oscar
Luigi Pirandello **4**:351

Budyonny, Semyon
Isaac Babel **13**:14

Bufkin, E. C.
F. Scott Fitzgerald **14**:163

Bullock, Florence Haxton
James Hilton **21**:98

Bump, Jerome
D. H. Lawrence **9**:229

Bunche, Ralph J.
Walter White **15**:481

Bunin, Ivan
Ivan Bunin **6**:44
Aleksandr Kuprin **5**:298
Alexey Nikolayevich Tolstoy
18:364

Buning, M.
T. F. Powys **9**:375

Burbank, Rex
Sherwood Anderson **1**:55

Burch, Charles Eaton
Paul Laurence Dunbar **12**:105

Burdett, Osbert
John Gray **19**:142
Alice Meynell **6**:300

Burgess, Anthony
C. P. Cavafy **7**:162
John Galsworthy **1**:305
James Joyce **8**:164

Burgess, C. F.
Joseph Conrad **13**:121

Burgin, Diana L.
Mikhail Bulgakov **16**:91

Burke, Kenneth
Rémy de Gourmont **17**:151
Gertrude Stein **1**:425

Burkhard, Arthur
Stefan George **14**:194

Burkhart, Charles
Ada Leverson **18**:198, 200
George Moore **7**:493

Burleson, Donald R.
H. P. Lovecraft **22**:230

Burlyuk, David
Velimir Khlebnikov **20**:123

Burnam, Tom
F. Scott Fitzgerald **14**:153

Burne, Glenn S.
Rémy de Gourmont **17**:157

Burness, Donald
Thomas Mofolo **22**:259, 264

Burnshaw, Stanley
Rainer Maria Rilke **1**:418

Burpee, Lawrence J.
Wilfred Campbell **9**:29

Burroughs, John
Charles G. D. Roberts **8**:315

Burton, Katherine
Owen Wister **21**:380

Büscher, Gustav
Friedrich Nietzsche **10**:368

Bush, Douglas
Robert Bridges **1**:130

Bush, William
Georges Bernanos **3**:127

Butcher, Philip
George Washington Cable **4**:29

Butler, E. M.
Rainer Maria Rilke **6**:360;
19:303
Carl Spitteler **12**:342

Butler, John Davis
Jean Moréas **18**:285

Butor, Michel
Guillaume Apollinaire **3**:37

Buttel, Robert
Wallace Stevens **12**:384
William Butler Yeats **18**:463

Butter, Peter H.
Edwin Muir **2**:486
Francis Thompson **4**:439

Critic Index

Critic Index